Fitzhenry and Whiteside Book of

CANADIAN
FACTS *and* DATES

Fitzhenry & Whiteside

Fitzhenry & Whiteside Book of Canadian Facts & Dates

Third Edition
Copyright © 2005 Fitzhenry & Whiteside

Fitzhenry and Whiteside Limited
195 Allstate Parkway
Markham, Ontario L3R 4T8

In the United States:
311 Washington Street
Brighton, Massachusetts 02135

www.fitzhenry.ca   godwit@fitzhenry.ca

Fitzhenry & Whiteside acknowledges with thanks the Canada Council for the Arts, and the Ontario Arts Council for their support of our publishing program. We acknowledge the financial support of the Government of Canada through the Book Publishing Industry Development Program (BPIDP) for our publishing activities.

 Canada Council Conseil des Arts
for the Arts du Canada

 ONTARIO ARTS COUNCIL
CONSEIL DES ARTS DE L'ONTARIO

10 9 8 7 6 5 4 3 2

Library and Archives Canada Cataloguing in Publication
The Fitzhenry & Whiteside book of Canadian facts and dates / edited by Richard W. Pound. –
3rd ed., updated and enlarged.

Previous ed. published as: The Fitzhenry & Whiteside book of Canadian facts and dates / Jay Myers rev.
and updated / by Larry Hoffman, Fraser Sutherland.
Includes bibliographical references and index.

ISBN 1-55041-171-3

1. Canada – History – Chronology. 2. Canada – History – Miscellanea.
I. Pound, Richard W. II. Title. III. Title: Fitzhenry and Whiteside book of Canadian facts and dates.

FC24.F58 2005   971.002'02   C2003-903743-6

United States Cataloging-in-Publication Data
The Fitzhenry & Whiteside book of Canadian facts and dates / edited by Richard W. Pound.
3rd ed.
[1100] p.: cm.
Includes bibliographical references and index.
Summary : A single-volume chronology of Canada from its prehistoric beginning to the social, cultural, business and political happenings of the present age.

ISBN 1-55041-171-3

1. Canada – History. II. Canada – History – Study and teaching. I. Pound, Richard W. II. Title.
971 22   F1026.P88   2005

Interior layout and design: Darrell McCalla

Jacket design and cover image: David Drummond

Printed and bound in Canada

Fitzhenry and Whiteside Book of
CANADIAN FACTS and DATES

THIRD EDITION

Editorial Director
Richard W. Pound

Supervising Editor
Richard Dionne

Editors
Jay Myers
James Musson

Contributors

Elizabeth Ballantyne Larry Hoffman   Marie Peters
Anna Beaubien   Penny Hozy   David Phillips
Brian Brennan   Norman Inkster   Fraser Sutherland
Celine Cooper   Dale Jahnke   Peter Taylor
Nick Eyles   Evan Jones   Bill Waiser
Jim Ferrabee   Gare Joyce   Catherine Kobelka
Laura Garetson   Thomas P. Morley Caroline Walker
Richard Gokool   Peter Nasello   Susan Walker
Amy Hingston   Gregory Pearson

Fitzhenry & Whiteside

To Robert Irvine Fitzhenry,
born 1918,
for his vision and indomitable will.

PREFACE

On June 27, 1896, Louis Minier and Louis Pupier held the first commercial screening of a motion picture in Canada. The location Montreal, the screening device a Lumière Cinématographe, a wooden contraption with spindles and cranks and a host of other impossible gadgetry said to transform a strip of separate photographs into a moving, life-like panorama. Word spread quickly, with Montrealers lining up in droves to witness the inaugural event. They were not disappointed. With a click and a pop and a spin of a wheel, the Cinématographe whirred into motion; the machine took grip of the film and, as the images poured across the illuminated lens, a fascinating series of events unfolded, frame by frame …

We have, in this work, tried to create a panorama of the extraordinary history of Canada. This, too, is like a series of frames unfolding before the reader's eyes. It is a collection of Canadian facts, dates, people, places, events and lore, beginning with the geological formation of the land itself — when the many parts of Canada were pushed and pulled together through physical forces that continue to shape our landscape today.

Canada has some of the oldest rock on the planet, along with the continually evolving Rocky Mountains, barely into their geological puberty. Ice Ages have pulverized rock and created some of the most fertile land in the world. The ice has also scraped off much of the rock cover, providing access to natural wealth that has made Canada one of the most important producers of essential materials. We have one of the largest and most secure supplies of fresh water the world has ever known, abundant coastlines that provide access to fish and other resources, a system of lakes and rivers that made the opening of an entire continent possible.

440 Million Years Ago South America slammed into eastern North America, closing the Iapetus Ocean and adding Newfoundland and the Maritimes to the ever-growing land mass of what is now Canada. The collision created the Appalachian Mountains, the oldest on the continent…

The people of Canada — from the first to reach North America, to the early explorers, to the waves of European peoples seeking a better future — are all included. Thousands of their triumphs and tragedies have been recorded to capture the dynamics of a young country trying to tame the elements, or, more accurately, adapt to the forces of nature. A story emerges as the frames move through the projector's lens, and we see the nation forming in all its beauty, its passion, and its drama.

March 7, 1719 Michel-Philippe Isabeau (d 1724) was awarded the contract to build the King's Bastion and Château Saint-Louis at Louisbourg. Isabeau was responsible for the fortification's landward front, including the citadel barracks and the Royal and Island batteries. The director and designer of the fortifications was Jean-François de Verville (1680-1729), who 1st recommended the site in 1716. Referred to as the "Gibraltar of Canada," Louisbourg was designed to protect the St. Lawrence fisheries and the sea route to New France. The fortress took 25 years to complete. The end result was not only a fortress, but a complete French town, with governor's palace, barracks, houses, hospital, arsenals and warehouses.

This book does not present history grouped around a series of organized themes. It is not a common reference work designed to generate an endless list of footnotes, although it will provide an excellent base for further historical departure and, as important, a broader context within which specific subjects can be explored in depth. Many of the influences on particular events or trends can be discerned from a review of what else was going on in Canada, perhaps half a continent away. The extensive bibliography and comprehensive index of names, places and events do provide useful encyclopedic direction to assist those wishing to pursue more focused endeavours. Nuggets of information may serve as the precursors of new ideas, new inventions, new political initiatives, new social trends and a wealth of other features of our modern society. Above all, the *Fitzhenry & Whiteside Book of Canadian Facts & Dates* captures the variety, eclecticism and the richness of diversity that is Canadian history at any one point in time. It is varied, informative, and immensely browsable.

Also in 1969
• Calgary bartender Walter Chell (d 1997) developed the Bloody Caesar, a combination of tomato juice, vodka, celery, a lime wedge, pepper sauce, celery salt and ice all mixed in with his pièce de résistance, mashed clams. The Bloody Caesar became one of the most popular cocktails in Canada.

We have tried to identify basic facts without which it would be impossible to study or understand Canada. We have tried to include most of the major events in Canadian history, with brief entries that give the past both substance and flavour. The main actors and the roles they played are noted, but we have refrained from the exercise of too much editorial comment, letting the actions and events speak for themselves. Politics and social judgment are personal; we have left such conclusions to the reader. We have also tried not to be too "serious" and have made sure to include items that are whimsical, since odd turns and fanciful endeavours are also part of our historical quilt.

April 15, 1862 Twenty-three Bactrians — the first camels in Western Canada — were herded off ships at Esquimalt, BC, and driven to the Cariboo goldfields as pack animals. The beasts of burden, purchased in San Francisco for $300 a head by BC entrepreneur John Galbraith, could carry over 226 kg each, twice that of the traditional mule. Yet the Arabian animals of legend had one tragic drawback — mules and horses were terrified of them. The unexpected relationship caused stampedes, accidents, lost horses, mules and packs. The dilemma could not be solved; by Oct. all camels were either sold back into the US or left to fend for themselves. The last surviving Wild West camel died near Grand Prairie, Alb., in 1905.

We have tried to address a broad selection of themes. They include, of course, the major political and constitutional highlights, as well as significant business, cultural, legal, exploratory, artistic and military events and personalities. The arrangement by dates has been deliberate. The format allows for use by history buffs and scholars, reference librarians and those who relish Canadiana and want to use it as an occasional and enjoyable "read" to absorb a sense of what was going on in Canada at any particular time. *What happened in Canada the year you were born? When you finished school? When you got married? When your children were born? Who was Prime Minister in 1936? When did Canada get its flag? How close was the 1995 Quebec Referendum? Who was the 1st woman MP? How many Canadian soldiers were killed in WW I? What happened to the Avro Arrow? When was Treaty No. 10 signed? Who commanded the Canadian forces during World War I? When was the family allowance introduced? When was* Two Solitudes *published? When did Tom Thomson paint* Northern River? *Who 1st performed Tomson Highway's* Rez Sisters? There is almost no end to the fascinating details that are contained in this edition.

> **June 14, 1996** Bill C–47 (the Human Reproductive and Genetic Technologies Act) was introduced in the House of Commons in an attempt to prohibit genetic recombination that would lead to the creation of animal-human half-breeds. The bill was the outcome of geneticist Patricia Baird's Nov. 15, 1993, Royal Commission report *Handle with Care*. The bill stated, "No person shall knowingly cause the fertilization of a human ovum by sperm of an animal or the fertilization of an animal ovum by human sperm, for the purpose of producing a zygote that is capable of differentiation." The bill, which died in the House before the 1997 election call, also prohibited human cloning, the sale of sperm, and placed a prohibition against sex selection for the purpose of reproduction.

The format is much easier to read than in previous editions and the number of entries has been expanded, not only to reflect the additional history in the decade or so since the second edition, but also to add more material from earlier times. We have tried to ensure that we have material from across the entire country, to make the work as "Canadian" as possible. Selection for entries will, inevitably, be a combination of editorial judgment and the extent of the knowledge of the editors. There may, indeed, be entries that are "missing" and we hope that we have not missed too many. We welcome any suggestions and will undertake to give them serious consideration in future editions, so readers can help complete the picture by drawing them to our attention. We were forced, in the interests of completing this edition, to establish a cut-off date and selected December 2003 for that purpose.

Also in 1984

• Mingan Archipelago National Park was established off the north St. Lawrence shore between Havre-Saint-Pierre and Anticosti Is., Que. The unique archipelago comprises 40 islands and 800 islets, which include fantastic water-sculpted limestone formations, grottoes, arches, sea stack monoliths and 15-m cliffs. Common eiders, Atlantic puffins and kittiwakes are common, as are grey, harbour and harp seals. Nine types of whale feed off the archipelago, including minke, humpback, fin and the fabled blue whale.

I want, in particular, to thank the editors of both this and past editions and also the many contributors who so generously proffered their expertise and knowledge to this project. They have been immensely helpful through their research and their understanding of the usefulness of a work of this nature. Without them, it would have been all but impossible to produce such a comprehensive volume.

This is your book. It is your country. Learn more about Canada. It is a fabulous country and a fascinating epic.

Richard W. Pound
Editorial Director

Common Abbreviations Used In This Book

Alb.	Alberta	ka	kilo annum meaning thousand years ago
Approx.	approximately	kg	kilogram
Apr.	April	km	kilometre
Assn.	Association	km/h	kilometres per hour
Aug.	August	l	litres [litre]
b	born	L.	lake
BC	British Columbia	Lt-Gen.	Lieutenant-General
BCE	Before Common Era	Lt-Gov.	Lieutenant-Governor
BE	British Empire	Lt-Gov.-Gen.	Lt.-Governor-General
BNA	British North America	m	metre
bp	before present	Ma	Mega annum meaning million years ago
Brig-Gen.	Brigadier-General	Maj-Gen.	Major-General
Br.	Brother	Man.	Manitoba
°C	Celsius	Mar.	March
c	circa	mm	millimetre
CBC	Canadian Broadcast Commission	MLA	Member of Legislative Assembly
CCF	Co-operative Commonwealth Federation	MNA	Member of the National Assembly
CE	Common Era	MP	Member of Parliament
C-in-C	Commander in Chief	MPP	Member of the Provincial Parliament
cm	centimetre	MW	megawatt
CNR	Canadian National Railway	NATO	North Atlantic Treaty Organization
CPR	Canadian Pacific Railway	NB	New Brunswick
CRTC	Canadian Radio-television and Telecommunications Commission	NFB	National Film Board
		NDP	New Democratic Party
d	died	Nfld	Newfoundland
Dec.	December	NHL	National Hockey League
EU	European Union	Nov.	November
Feb.	February	NS	Nova Scotia
fl	era	NWC	North West Company
FLQ	Front de libération du Québec	NWMP	North West Mounted Police
Fr.	Jesuit Friar or Father	NWT	North West Territories
Ga	Giga annum meaning billion years ago	Oct.	October
Gen.	General	Ont.	Ontario
Gov.	Governor	OAS	Organization of American States
Gov-Gen.	Governor-General		
Gov-in-C	Governor-in-Chief	OPEC	Organization of Petroleum Exporting Countries
govt	government		
ha	hectare	PC	Progressive Conservative
HBC	Hudson's Bay Company	PEI	Prince Edward Island
HMS	Her (or His) Majesty's Ship (or Steamer)	PM	Prime Minister
		PQ	Parti Québécois
Jan.	January	pseud.	pseudonym

Que.	Quebec	Supt.	Superintendant
R.	River	U.	University
RCAF	Royal Canadian Air Force	UBC	University of British Columbia
RCMP	Royal Canadian Mounted Police	UN	United Nations
RCN	Royal Canadian Navy	UNESCO	United Nations Educational, Scientific and Cultural Organization
RNWMP	Royal North West Mounted Police		
Sask.	Saskatchewan	US	United States of America
Sept.	September	WTO	World Trade Organization
sq.	square	ya	years ago
Str.	Strait		

THE MAKING OF A PLANET

4.5 billion years ago (or Ga, meaning Giga annum) planet Earth began its evolution as a mixture of mini-planets, solar dust and gases all hovering about each other in a gigantic, circular mass. Over millions of years, gravitational forces pushed denser, heavier materials to the centre of the mass, while lighter, gaseous mixtures rose to the outer surface. Uranium-lead and rubidium-strontium age-dating show that the earth's moon and neighbouring planets were created around the same time as Earth.

As a result of gravitational processes, planet Earth is made up of 5 distinct layers. The first is a solid inner core of mostly nickel and iron (called *nife*) some 2,440 km in diameter at temperatures of 3,700°C. Surrounding this inner core is a liquid outer core containing iron, nickel and some silicon. This layer is about 2,000 km thick and is surrounded by a semi-molten layer called the mantle. This is about 3,000 km thick, and in a state of perpetual motion, being stirred by slow currents. The outermost layer is the earth's crust, which is as thin as 6 km under the oceans (called oceanic crust) and up to 70 km thick when measured from the highest mountain ranges on the continents (continental crust).

Seventy percent of the earth's surface is covered by oceans underlain by denser rocks made of basalt. Ocean basins occur simply because of the higher density of basaltic rock which is slowly sinking back into the mantle below. Continental crust, on the other hand, is made of lighter rocks such as granite, which explains why continents are above sea level.

Continents are continuously on the move, being part of large tectonic plates that make up the earth's surface. Continents are carried around by currents in the underlying mantle, a process known as *plate tectonics*. Evidence suggests that plate tectonic processes have operated pretty much since the planet was first formed.

The oldest crustal rock on planet Earth is the Acasta gneiss of the Northwest Territories, estimated to be almost 4 billion years old. Other old rocks occur in northwestern Ontario, such as those at Cedar Lake, estimated to be 3.18 billion years old.

Surrounding the crust is the atmosphere. Over the millennia it has changed from a volatile mixture of noxious gases into mixed layers comprising mostly nitrogen and oxygen.

3.46 Ga The first signs of life appeared in the form of cyanobacteria, fossils of which are found in present-day Australia.

2.5–1.9 Ga Ancestral Canada was located in the giant continent of Arctica, which included a landmass running in a line from what is now southern Alberta to northern Quebec, encompassing a predecessor to Hudson Bay and the early Arctic islands. Glaciers formed over northern Ontario in what is one of the oldest-known events on the planet. This early form of Canada did not include what is now BC, southern Ontario, southern Quebec, Labrador or the Maritimes. All these were to be added later during orogenic events when other landmasses collided with, and stuck to, Arctica.

About 2 Ga Arctica collided with 3 other landmasses to form Nena. Here, ancestral Canada fused with a large area that stretched down to Mexico and included what is now southwestern Ontario.

1.9 Ga A massive meteorite slammed into what is now the Sudbury area of Ontario, creating a wide crater and upwelling of nickel-rich volcanic rocks.

Between 1.5 and 1 Ga The continent of Nena collided with other landmasses during the Grenvillian Orogeny to form one of the largest supercontinents known — Rodinia. The collision fused southern Ontario, southern Quebec and Labrador to ancestral Canada. The flat, gently undulating Canadian Shield, which covers almost half the present country, was formed by slow erosion of Rodinia.

About 600 million years ago (or Ma, meaning Mega annum) The giant continent of Rodina broke up, and the newly formed Iapetus Ocean, separating eastern North America from Europe, flooded Ontario and the Canadian Shield with warm, shallow waters. Limestone reefs flourished throughout Ontario. A proto-Pacific Ocean was created along the west coast.

440 Ma South America slammed into eastern North America, closing the Iapetus Ocean and adding Newfoundland and the Maritimes to the ever-growing landmass of what is now Canada. The collision created the Appalachian Mountains, the oldest on the continent. The supercontinent of Pangea was formed as the continents, once dispersed after the break-up of Rodinia, came together one last time.

250 Ma Extensive coal swamps formed in the Maritime provinces. The coal deposits of Nova Scotia are of this age.

200 Ma Pangea began to break up, the North Atlantic Ocean began to widen, and North America started to drift westward at about 5 cm a year. Diamond-bearing pipes (called kimberlites) punched through to the earth's surface, waiting to be found by geologists working in such places as the Northwest Territories.

175 Ma What is now BC piled into the western-moving North America, creating the "modern" configuration of Canada. The collision resulted in the West Coast mountain ranges, including the Rockies. Dinosaurs roamed western Canada. The making of Canada was complete.

175–40 Ma A vast inland sea filled the region between the Canadian Shield and the Rocky Mountains, and from what is now the Arctic Ocean to the Gulf of Mexico. The swampy coasts of the Western Interior Seaway supported lush plant life, an important food source for dinosaurs. Sediment from decayed plant material and the remains of marine algae accumulated on the sea floor where they were buried to great depths by the continuous addition of new sediment on top. Slow subsidence resulted in heating and the formation of the oil, gas and coal wealth of current western Canada. The flat plains and prairies of central North America were born.

65 Ma Dinosaurs were extinguished by a massive meteorite that collided with the Yucatán Peninsula, creating the enormous 200-km-wide Chicxulub Crater. The meteorite vaporized on impact, throwing ash and dust into the atmosphere, drastically altering global climate.

30 Ma Temperate forests grew in the warm Canadian Arctic on Axel Heiberg Island.

25 Ma World climates began to cool. The Antarctic Ice Sheet began to form.

20 Ma Large mammals (giant beavers, mammoths, giant bears, giant sloths) first appeared in North America. Most are believed to have migrated to the western hemisphere from the Asian landmass, during periods when the Bering Sea was either dry or had low water levels. Animals such as mastodons and mammoths, the progenitors of modern elephants, horses, camels and giant sloths, moved into the Americas where they became part of the food supply for the continent's earliest human inhabitants, some 50,000 years ago.

2.5 Ma The North American climate entered a period of alternating glaciations (when large ice sheets formed) and interglaciations (such as the present day). Typically, each glaciation lasted about 90,000 years with brief 10,000-year-long interglacials. Most of North America was covered with ice during each glaciation. During the Wisconsian glaciation, the ice sheet expanded as far south as southern Ohio. The Laurentide ice sheet originated in the high uplands of Labrador-Ungava and Keewatin.

20,000 years ago (or ka, meaning kilo annum)
At the height of the Wisconsin glaciation, the Laurentide ice sheet was 3 km thick and had a volume of 34 million km^3. At the same time, the level of the world's oceans was lowered by approximately 150 m. The shallow Bering Strait and Chukchi Sea separating Alaska from Asia became dry land. This area, termed Beringia, formed a treeless plain that supported herds of migratory animals, such as mastodons and mammoths, ground sloths, camels and horses. It also probably provided the means of access to North America for the continent's first human inhabitants.

12 ka The last ice sheets retreated. Sea levels rose, cutting off Asia from North America. Huge lakes were dammed in the interior of Canada; the largest (Glacial Lake Agassiz) was nearly 2 million km^2 in extent, covering most of modern-day Manitoba and much of northern Ontario.

0 ka Much of Canada's modern landscape can be attributed to glaciation. Glacially scoured depressions are now filled with countless lakes, including the Great Lakes. A wide variety of landforms such as eskers, drumlins, moraines, glacial till and erratics dot the landscape, and extensive spreads of gravel left by melt rivers. The ice sheet also left Canada with rich soils.

FIRST PEOPLES

Creation Stories

Huron And Iroquois

In the beginning there was no land, only sky and a great sea inhabited by fish and beavers and loons and other aquatic animals. One day a divine woman — Sky Woman — fell from a hole in the sky above. She was tumbling toward a watery death below when 2 loons saw her and decided to help. Pushing their bodies together, the loons formed a soft bed and on this, Sky Woman landed safely. All the sea animals gathered to determine the plight of Sky Woman. Great Turtle decided she should live on his broad back, and told the other animals to dive deep into the sea and gather earth in their mouths on which Sky Woman could live. One after another the animals failed to find earth. Then Toad surfaced, half dead from exhaustion, yet in his mouth was a small bit of mud. Great Turtle took the mud and passed it to Sky Woman, who placed it around the edge of Great Turtle's shell, which grew larger and larger to form a great land on which trees and plants emerged. Then, Sky Woman gave birth.

Haida

In the beginning there was only sea and sky and a thin reef in the middle of the ocean on which all supernatural beings dwelt. The reef was a crowded place, and Raven had nowhere to live. Looking for a home of his own, Raven used his strong beak to poke a hole in the sky. In the sky world Raven found a village and large house of the village chief who had a new grandson. Raven disguised himself as the grandson and took the child's place. Raven lived well in the chief's house but after a while his deception was discovered and Raven was thrown out of the sky world and forced back to the water world below. There Raven heard a voice from the water and crawled down a carved post resembling kelp to find seagull man. This seagull man gave Raven two pebbles, which Raven used to create the Queen Charlotte Islands and the big continent beside them. Raven created the trees and rivers, the tides, moon and the stars, and divided night and day. One day when Raven was flying along the beach he discovered a clamshell full of human beings. The humans were afraid of the new world. Raven, always skilled in oratory, coaxed the people out of hiding and they wiggled free of their shell to begin life on earth.

Ojibway

In the beginning there was nothing but the sound of the shaker. In this great void the thoughts of the Great Spirit, Gitchie Manido, travelled forever and ever. But the Great Spirit required objects for these thoughts to strike and rebound

back to him. The Great Spirit created the Sun (Gisis) and the Morning Star (Wabun Anung). He tried his hand at land but his first attempt was covered with cloud, the next was very hot, and his third effort was laden with ice. On his 4th attempt the Great Spirit created Earth, where he sent his singers, birds, who spread the seeds of life. Mother Earth contained the Sun and Moon (Neebagisis); her blood was water. Earth was also given sacred directions — north, south, east and west. The Great Spirit took Earth's 4 elements — Fire, Water, Earth and Wind — and blew them with a sacred Megis Shell; and this is how he created people.

Cree

Maasu had a special relationship with the Creator. After the Kaachaamishikunich beings flooded the world, Maasu spied on them. He hid in a hollow tree in the water and watched the beings play, but they sensed an intruder and discovering the hollow tree, gave it a horrible shaking, surely killing whoever was inside. Maasu was not killed and decided to kill the Kaachaamishikunich. Maasu knew, however, that killing the Kaachaamishikunich would bring another disastrous flood, so he built a raft on which he placed 2 of every animal and all kinds of plants. Maasu returned to the place of the Kaachaamishikunich and killed them all. The disastrous floods came but all on the raft were safe. Soon the animals became hungry. Maasu knew he would have to create land. He tied a long string to each animal and turned them into the water to find the sand and reindeer moss needed to make earth. All the animals failed but Mink. Mink's drowned, lifeless body was pulled back to the raft by the string tied around her belly, and in her 2 paws was sand. Maasu breathed on Mink and she returned to life. Maasu then breathed on the sand, and Earth was created.

C. Vance Haynes and Paul S. Martin of the University of Arizona have argued that the first aboriginal American peoples had crossed Beringia over the land bridge from Asia to North America not long before 10,000 years ago. These Paleo-peoples were named after the distinctive Clovis stone tools, some embedded in bones of megafauna (mammoths, mastodon, and camel) now extinct. Critics of the theory point out that Clovis remains are found over too large an area and too far south to make such a short migration and adaptation scenario possible. Geologists have provided evidence that there was no ice-free corridor east of the Rocky Mountains at this time.

Recent genetic studies suggest many movements of peoples into the Americas, as long as 40,000 ya (years ago). After about 18,000 ya, other groups came. Most Native American lineages are from East Asia and Siberia, although one came via Europe from Eurasia. This research is very preliminary.

According to one theory, the mtDNA (Mitochondrial DNA, DNA received from the mother) separates into 4 haplogroups or lineages designated A, B, C and D. Of these, A, C and D are found 35–25,000 ya in both Siberia and America. B was present in East Asia at 30–24,000 ya and appeared in America about 15,000 ya. Thus, the main groups arrived in the Americas before the last glacial maximum.

A fifth haplogroup, linked to the rare European (or West Asian) haplogroup X has been identified among Native Americans, but not yet in East Asian or Siberian populations. It appears to be relatively recent, arriving 30–15,000 ya in the Americas.

A mutation within haplogroup A (16111T) marks the arrival, from the Amur Basin east of Lake Baikal, of the ancestors of the Koryaks, the Chukchi, the Inuit of Siberia and the Na-Dene Indians, including the Navajo and the Haida.

Today, scientists are working with numerous models.

Model 1a: Beringia mid-continental route. C. Vance Haynes Jr. argues that modern humans made their way across the Bering Strait from Siberia via a corridor of tundra 1,500 km wide during the Late Wisconsin glaciation. Arthur Dyke and Victor Prest argue that there was no ice-free corridor at the time. No archaeological sites dating to this period have as yet been found in the "corridor."

Model 1b: Coastal route. Ruth Gruhn and Knut Fladmark argue that deglaciation was sufficiently advanced that modern humans using watercraft made their way island hopping east and then south along the now-submerged continental shelf. There is evidence of sufficient food

Note on Dating: *Most dates are in standard BCE/CE format to be consistent with the rest of this book. Methods of absolute dating, beginning with C^{14} in the 1950s, are complex and are reported within a given range. They are constantly being improved and dates of sites are often revised. It is usual to report them as BP, before present, which is before 1950. Very old dates are reported as so many ya, "years ago." Thus all dates given below should be considered to be ranges and taken as indications only.*

resources, but few artifacts or human remains found to date are earlier than 10,500 ya.

Model 2: People made their way to the Americas by water or land over the past 50,000 years as conditions permitted.

Model 3: Dennis Stanford and Bruce Bradley argue that makers of Solutrean tools made their way from Europe (or from Africa) across the Atlantic to the Americas, island hopping along a northern route or from Africa to Brazil.

Model 4: Modern humans, who had already reached Australia by 50,000 ya, crossed the Pacific from Polynesia to South America. Monte Verde is a possible early site in Chile and Tiama-Tiama in Venezuela.

Pre-Clovis sites have been claimed in Chile, Brazil and in North America but they are controversial.

The Meadowcroft Rockshelter, in Pennsylvania, excavated by James Adovasio under exacting conditions, has yielded small laterally ground triangular points, knives, and a scraper dating to 12,500–12,000 BP. Lower strata are even earlier.

A. V. Jopling and others from the University of Toronto discovered bone shards in the Old Crow Basin, Yukon. 30,000 years ago it was a large plain, grazed by Pleistocene animals. A natural dam on the Porcupine River flooded it. As the lake was drained in recent times, numerous extinct animal bones have been recovered, in secondary contexts. A bone "flesher" was originally dated by C^{14} to 27,000 ya but has been dated again, to 1250 BP. The nearby Bluefish Caves I and II have layers of cultural debris, including microliths, a wedge-shaped core, flakes, and bones with butchering scars, interspersed with layers of loess. C^{14} tests, using bone collagen, date them to 15,000–12,000ya.

The late J. V. Wright, whose long and distinguished career at the National Museum of Canada and the Canadian Museum of Civilization culminated in the writing of a 3-volume series, *A History of the Native People of Canada,* suggested dividing Native history into five time periods.

Period I (to 8,000 BCE), Paleo-Indian and Paleo-Arctic Cultures at the End of the Ice Age

Period II (to 4000 BCE), Early Archaic Complexes, Ceremonialism and New Hunting Technologies

Period III (to 1000 BCE), Later Archaic Cultures, Mounds, Ceremonialism and Long Distance Trade

Period IV (to 500 CE), Woodland and Plains Cultures, Ceramics, Stratified Societies and Shamanism

Period V (to European Contact), Development of Historic Native Societies

Twelve thousand years ago, the glaciers that had covered the northern half of the continent began to melt, shorelines were drowned or emerged, icy lakes and cold dry tundra faced the small groups of human beings who lived in a hostile environment. It would be take five thousand years for our present-day climate with its familiar flora and fauna to develop.

The culture stages discussed below, the Paleo-Indian, Arctic, Archaic, and Woodland, describe in the most general ways social systems and subsistence strategies. They are generally applicable across Canada, although they manifest themselves at different times because of climate changes and local variations. In many instances they are related to cultural stages to the south, which in turn were influenced by Mexican and Central American cultures.

Period I:
Paleo-Indian and Paleo-Arctic Cultures

11,000 BCE Clovis Points, first recognized at the Blackwater Draw site near Clovis, NM, in the 1930s, have been found at kill-sites throughout the ice-free areas of North America. They were found in good stratigraphic context, below Folsom and Paleo-Indian remains. Clovis points are large and beautifully made of excellent materials. A flute or depression, made by removing long flakes, runs from point to base on both sides. A Clovis blade, a curved flake with a prismatic cross-section, is often found with these points. Slightly different points are found to the tip of South America. No Clovis antecedents have been found in Asia but some archaeologists cite similarities with European Solutrian points.

10,000 BCE *Clovis* and *Paleo-Indian Cultures*. Hearths have been found in caves and rockshelters as well as open-air campsites. Human remains include hair and perhaps fingerprints, but very few skeletons as there is no clear evidence of intentional burial. These people were probably broad-spectrum foragers, as large animals were not a numerous or reliable food source, and soon became extinct. Fish were very important to their diet. A small number of Clovis points have been found in Canada, from Alberta to the Atlantic, where the ice had receded.

The high-grade chert found on sites such as Parkhill, Ont., had only a few possible sources, indicating exchange. Lithic procurement was related to group homogeneity and solidarity.

10,000-8000 BCE *Clovis* and *Paleo-Indian* or *Plano Cultures* extended from the Southern Plateau of British Columbia to the Atlantic Coast and from the Northwest Territories to the Gulf of Mexico. Later Folsom points are generally smaller than Clovis points and are found associated with kills of an extinct bison. Bison, unlike mastodon, can be herded into kill sites, suggesting new hunting methods. Plano points are leaf-shaped but not fluted; they are less easily recognized, more variable than Clovis points. They are mostly found with modern animal species. There was a western Plano variant culture, on the West Coast and Prairies lasting to about 5000 BCE and an Eastern Plano or more commonly, Paleo-Indian Culture, in the forests of eastern Canada, giving way to the Eastern Archaic by 8000 BCE.

9250 BCE *Western Paleo-Indian Culture*. The delta of a glacial river was found at Wally's Beach, St. Mary R. Reservoir, southern Alberta, in 1997, by Shayne Tolman. There are tracks and bones of mammoth, camels, bison-like animals, extinct horses and other Pleistocene animals, as well as 3 Clovis points, a pair of antler flints, and 200 intact and 1000 partial stone projectile points, hide scrapers and drills. Some have been dated: C^{14} 11,350 BP, 11,330±70 BP (AMS YO-7696). The area was ice-free before 9300 BCE and had stabilized so that animals and people could inhabit it. As there were no ice-free areas north of the site, they must have come from the south. Contemporary sites include the Vermilion Lakes, Alb. (C^{14} 9990±50 BP); Charlie Lake Cave, BC, (C^{14} 10,553 BP); and Lake Minnewanka, Banff, Alb., which has yielded points ranging from Clovis points to the brass arrowheads mad during the fur trade with Europeans.

8250 BCE *Eastern Clovis* or *Paleo-Indian Cultures*. The Debert Site, Colchester County, NS, was excavated by the Robert S. Peabody Foundation (C^{14} 10,590 BP). No human remains have been found but the site was a settlement, not just a kill site, with artifacts clustered in 11 oval occupation areas, containing pits and hearths. Jim Tuck suggests that the people lived in skin-covered dwellings with wood or bone frames. The fluted spear points found there are called Debert points because, although similar to and contemporary with Clovis points, they have concave bases and long tangs. The 4,000 artifacts found include gravers, scrapers, awls and flakes. Although the ice had receded, most of the area was tundra and nearby snow fields suggest that the mean annual temperature was close to 0°C. Similar sites are Bull Brook, Massachusetts, and Vail, Maine.

Period II:
Early Archaic Complexes

8000-5000 BCE *Northwestern Plano Culture*. The first humans along the Pacific coast, about 10,000 ya faced a climate cooler and moister than today. The Namu Site in historic Bella Bella territory was continually occupied from 7000 BCE to European contact. In its earliest component, microblades were found, along with the bones of salmon, sea mammals, bear, deer and beaver. By 5000 BCE their toolkit was very similar to that of the Maritime Archaic.

8000-6000 BCE *Eastern Archaic Culture*. As the climate changed, a widely dispersed, highly mobile population hunted caribou and used river resources. Sites were small and of short duration. Plano tools persist in the Great Lakes Region. Non-stratified surface collections yield only chipped stone tools, of local materials lending themselves only to crude tools. Local traditions remain undefined, giving perhaps a false impression of uniformity. A few dart heads with fine ripple flaking, dated to about 7000 BCE, have been found in SW Ontario. Chert quarries on the north shore of L. Superior (Cummins site) and the Sheguiandah site on Manitoulin Island were mined by Plano peoples, making scrapers, dart heads, knives, hammerstones and burins. The Shequiandah site was used for 10,000 years.

7000-5000 BCE *Atlantic Maritime Archaic Tradition*. Small groups of hunter-gatherers were depended on the sea and its products, but also the caribou migration. Land submergence and erosion caused by a dramatic rise in sea levels has buried many sites. Submerged tree stumps can still be seen at very low tide in the Bay of Fundy. Gradually mixed forest covered the land that had been tundra.

6500 BCE *Western Plano Culture*. In 1996, Kennewick Man, a skull and post-cranial bones were discovered in the Columbia R. bank near Kennewick, WA. Anthropologist James Chatters found a Cascade point (a type of Plano point) in the pelvic bone, subsequently dated to C^{14} 6400 BP. Measurements of the skeleton indicated that it is different from those of Native Americans living in the area. The US army took possession of the specimens and Kennewick Man became a test case for the NAG-PRA (Native American Graves Protection and Repatriation Act) law. This discovery led to the re-examination of other skeletons in museum storage rooms. Few had been dated or otherwise studied. Several were found to be similar to Kennewick Man. Thus scientists were confronted with a new question: What did Paleo-Indians look like and were there several quite different peoples?

6500 BCE *Western Plano Culture*. In 1975, Morley Eldridge, found a skeleton missing its skull, below the Mazama ash layer at Gore Creek, BC, in the Thompson R. system upstream from the Kennewick find. These are currently the oldest human remains found in British Columbia. In 1979 Jerome Cybulski dated them to C^{14} 8340±150 BP. The skeleton differed slightly from later coastal finds, but was similar to Kennewick Man. The bones have since been reburied with other repatriated bones and no further testing can be done.

6500 BCE *Shield Archaic Culture.* The earliest skeletons to date in Central Canada were found in an Archaic Culture quarry north of Thunder Bay dated C^{14} 8480±390 BP. These few pieces were consumed in the dating process and so no further testing can be done. Bones found 600 km north of Thunder Bay were dated 7080-6300 BP but were reburied without being studied by modern methods. Bones found in Peel County, Ont., in 1977, were dated to 4000 BCE but are now missing from a University of Toronto laboratory. A skeleton at Coteau-du-Lac, QB, was dated to 6600 BP.

6000-3500 BCE *Middle* and *Late Archaic Cultures.* New technologies and developments of old technologies lay the foundation for the richness of the Late Archaic. There was a new settlement pattern: small family units gathered annually for ceremonies, marriages, and trade. River environments approached current conditions. Deep shell mounds and middens had rudimentary settlements nearby. Floodplain species such as wild cucurbit, chenopodium and goosefoot (starchy seeds), sumpweed and sunflower (oily seeds) thrived in areas disturbed by human activity. Dog burials suggest domestication.

6000-1000 BCE *Atlantic Maritime Archaic Culture.* A seasonal round with fishing in the summer, fall caribou hunting and sea bird harvesting in the winter, employed toggling harpoons, netsinkers, dugout canoes, inflated skin floats, and ground stone tools. As spruce forests thickened, woodworking technology developed. Large clam shell middens indicate the importance of shellfish as a food source. Collecting shellfish in many cultures is an important a social activity, for women and children. Shell also has ceremonial roles, with beads and shells as adornments, gifts, and offerings at death.

5600 BCE *Early Maritime Archaic Culture.* L'Anse Amour, LB, by far the earliest burial mound found in North America, was excavated by Jim Tuck in 1974. A low stone mound, 9 m in diametre and 0.6 m high, covered the burial chamber of a boy of 12. A large stone had been placed on his head,

perhaps in a ceremonial rite. Bird effigies and a human figurine were of carved bone and antler. Offerings included red ochre, a graphite paint stone, an antler pestle and toggling harpoon, chipped stone spear points, and a lance point. Seven needles were found in a caribou bone case. Stone axes, adzes and gouges were made for woodworking. The skeleton from L'Anse-Amour was not dated but a related piece of charcoal was dated C^{14} 7530±140 BP. No further analysis has been done on it. Another cemetery, but without elaborate burial chambers, was found at nearby Forteau Point with a cache of stone artifacts, dated C^{14} 5035±65 BP.

5000-1000 BCE The raised beaches of the Port au Choix site, on west coast of Newfoundland, were a sacred territory, used as a cemetery for over 700 years. Excavators, including Jim Tuck, have discovered a hundred skeletons and 3,000 artifacts. Weapons and ornaments were found: white quartz pebbles; red ochre; bone, stone and slate ground stone bayonets; antler combs; and ivory tools and toggling harpoons. They attest to the importance of burial ceremonialism, reverence for ancestors and group solidarity. According to the season, the people harvested sea and land resources. Several artifacts have been dated (C^{14} 3230±220, C^{14} 1788±48 BP). No occupation area has as yet been found.

5200-2500 BCE *Early British Columbia Interior Plateau Culture.* On the Columbia Plateau, cut by the Columbia, Fraser and Snake rivers, there was a generalized hunter-gatherer adaptation, with deer and bison the main food sources. Plano tools were gradually replaced by Archaic tools similar to those of the Eastern woodlands. At the Milliken site on the Fraser River, from about 5500 BCE, hunters used leaf-shaped points and pebble choppers.

5000 BCE-200 CE *Western Archaic Maritime Culture.* The faunal remains indicate that the people had sea-going canoes capable of fishing on the open ocean. At Namu, shellfish became an important food resource. Some tools were made of bone. The ancestors of the modern Tsimshian people settled in the Prince Rupert area. They speak a language that is so different from other native languages that it constitutes a separate linguistic family.

Period III:
Later Archaic Cultures

3700 BCE *Plains Late Archaic Culture.* The site known today as Head-Smashed-In Buffalo Jump, in Alberta, began to be used as a mass kill site. Buffalo were herded together and then driven to their deaths over a cliff to the processing sites below. Large bones were smashed and boiled in pits lined with hide and heated with hot rocks, to render the grease for making pemmican. A layer of loess covered the debris from each year's kill. Thousands of worn or broken bone and stone tools, including points, choppers and stone knives have been found.

3500 BCE–1000CE *The Shield Archaic "Old Copper Culture."* has been described, by Lewis Binford among others, as neither old nor a culture. Native (almost pure) copper was mined on the Keweenaw Peninsula and Isle Royale in the Lake Superior area of Michigan. Pits up to 15 m deep and 10 m in diameter were mined by fire setting and quenching. The fractured rock was broken with stone mauls and the copper removed with chisels and wedges. The area was the centre of a long distance copper trade network and, for several thousand years, magnificent copper artifacts were made by hammering and annealing. They were used primarily as grave offerings.

3500–1000 BCE *The Late Shield Archaic Tradition* developed in the Keewatin District and in Manitoba from remnants of the terminal Plano cultures. Caribou and fish were the main foods. Bands moved into the area from the US Midwest, following large game and bringing new dart heads, knives and scrapers, some of North Dakota flint. Only stone and copper tools have survived the acidic soils. A Lake Nipigon area grave included red ochre, copper socketed dart and lance heads, socketed knives, gaffs, awls, chisels, punches, bossed bracelets, disc pendants and hammered nodules of copper. A site near a caribou crossing at Aberdeen Lake had two shallow house floors and a range of chert tools.

3500–1000 BCE *The Laurentian Archaic Tradition* stretched from New England to the Great Lakes. The tools are similar to those of the Atlantic Maritime Archaic. A Picton, Ont., area cemetery has evidence of burial ceremonials for adult males. Grave goods include red ochre, green clay, shell pendants and conch-shell beads from the Gulf of Mexico, native copper celts and awls, and galena chunks, evidence of a long distance hand-to hand trade network.

3500–1000 BCE *Late Great Lakes Archaic.* Hunters from Ohio probably entered Ontario through the Windsor corridor. They followed a seasonal round, hunting large animals, fishing, and collecting shell-fish and wild plant foods. Typical tools were polished stone adzes, bayonets and gouges, atlatls or spear throwers, and chipped stone drills and darts, as well as native copper socketed spear points and darts.

3500–500 BCE *The Atlantic Late Maritime Archaic Culture* developed in northern Labrador. People moved north, to Saglek Bay and Black Island Cove (dates C^{14} 5740±100 BP, and C^{14} 4580±95 BP) as the climate ameliorated. Here they met early Inuit peoples, adopting their bows and arrows. Ramah Bay has deposits of a beautiful chert and a translucent grey silicate, so easy to flake that these materials brought about a refinement of stone tools, and a flourishing trade to the south. By 500 BCE the climate had cooled and fewer typical Indian remains are found as the Indian peoples moved back south following the receding tree line. Some may have moved inland, along the salty Lake Melville, on Hamilton Inlet, where William Fitzhugh has discovered campsites lacking ground stone tools.

3000–1500 BCE The Newfoundland coast continued to be submerged, rising sea levels have probably buried seaside sites. The Beaches Site, on Bonavista Bay, excavated by Paul Carignan, has been dated to C^{14} 4900±250 BP although acidic soil destroyed most organic remains. Points are similar to Ramah chert specimens from Labrador but are made from local chert. There are also end-scrapers, bifaces, stemmed projectile points, and true prismatic blades (narrow thin, parallel-sided flakes from prepared cores, common in early Inuit cultures). The site is contemporary with the later occupations of Port au Choix. The Curtis Site on Twillingate Is. (C^{14} 3770±80 BP) has chipped and ground stone tools similar to the Beaches Site.

3000–500 BCE *The Late Maritime Archaic* had a Pre-Ceramic period, described as "ceramic without the presence of ceramics!" New cultural traits brought change to the Atlantic region. Sites around the Bay of Fundy, dating to 2000 BC, feature elaborate burials, with cremated remains placed in ochre-lined pits with stone, bone and antler tools, broad-bladed knives and soapstone bowls. Such burials, more common in New England, suggest the arrival of small bands of Susquehanna Tradition peoples. They may be the ancestors of the historic period Malecites.

3000–500 BCE The continuing Maritime Archaic tradition was also influenced by the neighbouring Laurentian and Shield Archaic Cultures. Sites include McEvoy on Cape Breton, Rafter Lake and Tusket Falls, NS. Stephen Davis retrieved projectile points from the bottom of Rafter Lake at a time of low water. Some of these artifacts are similar to points found at the Turner Farm site in Maine (C^{14} 5290±95) and on sites near Penobscot Bay.

3000–1500 BCE *Pacific Coast Archaic Culture.* The Locarno Phase of the Georgia Strait Tradition introduced barbed harpoon heads, awls, ground slate lance points, earspools, and labrets. By the beginning of the Common Era people were living in large cedar plank houses. Their graves indicate social distinctions, with offerings of *Dentalium* shells, shell disc beads and copper.

3000–1500 BCE In the Prince Rupert area the first semi-permanent winter villages were built by the ancestors of the modern Tsinshian nation, establishing the traditional pattern of a row of houses facing the ocean. The houses were roughly the same size, with no evidence of rank differences in the artifacts. From 1966–1973, 10 of 50 sites around Prince Rupert and north to the Nass River were excavated. The "Boardwalk site" with hits huge shell midden, was excavated by George MacDonald and Richard Inglis. Over 400 artifacts of wood and basketry were retrieved and preserved for a display at the Museum of Civilization (C^{14} 3625±105 BP, 1675 BCE). Shellfish were important to their diet but from spring to fall small groups moved from place to place harvesting seasonally abundant resources.

2500 BCE *Middle Plains Culture.* The first circles of small stones on high hills, known as Medicine Wheel ceremonial sites, appear on the prairies from the south. People lived in conical hide tents with a hearth in the centre and a smoke flap at the point. A circle of stones held down the edge of the tipi. After 1000 BCE, long distance trade became important: stone from Oregon and North Dakota; copper from the Great Lakes region; and shell from the Pacific Ocean and the Gulf of Mexico.

2300–200 BCE *Late Archaic Poverty Point Culture.* The Poverty Point Site, Louisiana, is the best known of over a hundred sites, perhaps linked to Mexico or Central America, that are transitional to Early Woodland Culture. The dates of the concentric circles of cigar-shaped curved mounds at Poverty Point are still inconclusive but there are indications of plant domestication and ceramics. The cucurbit (gourd) was used as a container. There are stone hoes and ground stone plummets. The millions of fibre tempered pottery balls, thought to have been used for cooking in an area without stone, are thought to be the earliest ceramics in North America.

2000–1000 BCE *The Laurentian Tradition* of the upper St. Lawrence drainage, southern Quebec, New York State, eastern Ontario and Vermont, is characterized by distinctive ground and polished stone tools: slate spear points or knives, usually with a stem for hafting; semi-lunar knives or *ulus,* with a straight back and sharp semicircular cutting edge; stone celts or axes and adzes and polished stone gouges for woodworking. Chipped tools and weapons include spear points with notches for hafting, bifaces for knives and small scrapers, also with hafting notches. Laurentian people had adapted to living in hardwood and conifer forest and lived on fish, white-tailed deer, moose and small game. New Brunswick sites include Cow Point and Dead Man's Pool.

2000–1500 BCE *Early Paleo-Inuit Culture.* Small numbers of Paleo-Inuit people, part of the "Arctic Small Tool Tradition," who were physically, culturally and linguistically different from the Maritime Archaic Indians, arrived on the N. Labrador coast and stayed for about 500 years. They lived on maritime resources, hunting on the ice. Their sites have been found at Saglek Bay, Thalia Point, Okak, Napatok, Hopedale, and Hamilton Inlet.

2000 BCE–1000 CE *Paleo-Inuit Culture.* Jim Tuck found Paleo-Inuit remains at Upernavik in Labrador in 1969, near abundant evidence of Dorset occupations. There were tiny flakes of black, grey, green and banded cherts, and burins used for slotting or engraving organic materials. Stone tools included projectile points, harpoon end blades, celts, adzes, and knives. More than a dozen similar campsites were found, including Thalia Point, near Nain. They all lack organic remains. Nearby Dorset sites are richer, yielding bone tools, skeletons and house remains. The Dorset Inuit were probably the ancestors of modern Inuit but their settlements were abandoned by about 1000 CE.

2000–1000 BCE *Mound builders of the Ohio Valley.* A burial, discovered by W. J. Wintemberg in the 1930s in the Miramichi Valley, contained red ochre and chipped stone blades resembling Ohio blades. Early European residents of Dartmouth, NS, found distinctive fired-clay tubular smoking pipes made of Ohio Valley clay.

1500 BCE-500CE The population of Tsinshian in the Prince Rupert area increased. House sizes grew, with a very large "chief's house" in the centre of the house row. Differences in the distribution of artifacts also indicate the beginning of the ranked social structure of the historic period. There were more woodworking tools, increasingly sophisticated art, including zoomorphic art. The Lachane site, waterlogged by an ancient stream bed yielded hundreds of wooden bowls and boxes, digging sticks, arrow shafts, basketry and rope.

Period IV:
Woodland and Plains Cultures

1000 BCE–1750 CE *The Woodland Cultures* of Eastern and Central North America is often divided into early, middle and late eras, although Wright and others have suggested only two periods: Initial Woodland, 3000 BCE–1000 CE; and Terminal Woodland, 1000–1750 CE. Cultural innovations include pottery, burial mounds, and greater reliance on native cultigens. Larger seeds with thinner seed coats indicate plant domestication, beginning with casual tending of local plants, including tobacco. Although not yet a significant part of the diet, they were a dependable, storable, early spring resource.

Techniques for parching and milling seeds were developed. Ceramics and the greater availability of vegetative foods encouraged new cooking techniques, providing more palatable foods for the old and the young. Ceramics also offered new possibilities for decorative techniques, and marking social distinctions. There were advances in fishing tools, twining and textiles, basketry, and woodworking.

1000 BCE–100CE *The Adena Early Woodland Culture,* centred in Ohio, is known for its large incrementally-built earth mounds and enclosures and stone and copper gorgets and engraved tablets found in graves. One of the largest and most thoroughly excavated sites is the Robbins Mounds in Kentucky with 52 tombs in a number of earthen-walled enclosures. Most people lived on small, scattered farmsteads. While there is little evidence of corn horticulture; the sunflower, goosefoot, bottle gourd, squash and cucurbit were grown. The Adena Culture influenced the Ohio Hopewell and the other "eastern burial cults." Some Adena sites have been found in Canada: on Long Sault Island, in Ontario, on the upper St. Lawrence River and, especially, at the Augustine Mound Site in New Brunswick.

300 CE *Early Maritime Ceramic.* The Augustine Mound Site, on the Red Bank Indian Reserve at the forks of the Miramichi River, is unique in Canada. In 1972, Joseph Augustine reported to Christopher Turnbull a low man-made mound. Over a thousand copper beads, thousands of shell beads, reel-shaped gorgets, a banded rectangular slate gorget, and tubular smoking pipes characteristic of the Adena mortuary cult of the Ohio Valley were excavated. The copper preserved fabrics and cord mats, bags, baskets and clothing. Twenty skeletons and cremated and secondary burials were retrieved. The human remains were not dated, no studies have been published, and they have since been reburied. There were also chipped and polished celts and chipped bifaces. A very few similar but much less spectacular burials have been found in Ontario and Quebec. The appearance of a full-blown expression of Adena culture at the Augustine Mound is a mystery.

200 CE Serpent Mound, Rice Lake, Ont., discovered by Boyle in 1897, is unique in Canada and perhaps also linked to Adena Culture. Five low oval mounds, 7–14m in diameter, surround a sinuous earthen mound, 58 m long. William Adams and Richard Johnston further excavated them in the 1950s, finding skeletons in pits. Grave goods are not numerous: 3 of 13 burials had 41 shell discoid beads, fossilized coral, turtle shells, and copper beads (C^{14} 128±200 BP). The nearby Miller Mounds, East Sugar Island, Hastings and Cameron's Point Mounds also show Adena influence and resemble mounds in Adams County, Ohio.

1000–500 BCE *The Early Woodland Meadowood Culture* of New York and southern Ontario is contemporary with Adena Culture and influenced the later Saugeen-Point Peninsula, Princess Point Culture, and Laurel and Shield Cultures. Pottery is added to the cultural manifestations of the Archaic which persist. The beaker shaped, cord-impressed and plain pottery is known as Vinette 1. Graves, with only their red ochre remaining in acidic soils, are the most common and best-preserved sites. Burials are in sets of two, perhaps representing a social system with two clans, and perhaps defining territories. Diagnostic artifacts include the polished stone birdstones, ground slate gorgets, Ohio "pipe-stones," "boatstones," bar amulets, galena cubes and copper awls, beads and celts. There are some harvesting sites, probably used in the fall, and a few small campsites. Caches of stone tool blanks, sometimes in burials, suggest the beginnings of specialized production and exchange networks for chert. Meadowood sites include Liahn II, Ferris, Wyoming Rapids, Neeb, Welke-Tonkonoh, Bruce Boyd, Boyd Lakefront, Dawson Creek, Pointe-du-Buisson, Morrison's Island, See Mound, Long Sault Mound.

300 BCE-500 CE *Middle Woodland Hopewell Tradition* of Southern Ohio (at Scioto) and Illinois (at Havana). The Hopewell Interaction Sphere, a group of cultural traits and artistic expressions stemming from elaborate mortuary customs, influenced, to varying extents, many locally differentiated Middle Woodland Cultures, including Point Peninsula Culture in New York and Ontario. Monumental earthworks and earthen burial mounds were surrounded by raised walls and geometric low earthworks and topped by charnel houses. It was earlier thought that an elite priesthood presided over an elaborate religious cult but in fact evidence of the cult, beyond the artifacts, is sketchy. Its economy was built on extensive trade networks for marine shell, obsidian, copper, and

mica and a local horticultural but mainly hunting and gathering economy in the rich river "bottoms." Artifacts, usually grave goods, included copper and shell ear spools, headdresses, masks, bracelets, panpipes, chest ornaments, beads, pearl beads, beaded garments, stone and clay figurines and platform pipes with bird, animal and human effigies. They suggest a class of specialized craft workers.

700 BCE–1000CE *The Middle Woodland Point Peninsula Culture* slowly expanded, with each area developing regional differences. People with a matrilocal system seem to have migrated into the area now occupied by Iroquoians, bringing maize, and other cultural traits. The pottery on central Canadian sites shares attributes with pottery from Manitoba, northern Ontario and western Quebec. Semi-sedentary villages and campsites were used by successive generations. Burial sites are influenced by the Hopewell mortuary tradition. Le Vesconte Mound, Trent River, Ont., excavated by Ian Kenyon in 1962, found 15 burials in 8 clusters. Grave goods included bone daggers, worked antler, mica, whetstones, copper pins, gorgets and beads, a silver pan-pipe, horn coral, bone and stone implements (C^{14} 120±50 BP).

To 500 BCE *Late Atlantic Maritime Pre-ceramic Culture.* At Cow Point, Grand Lake, NB, David Sanger excavated sixty features in 1970. Each contained an oval stain of red ochre, and most had well-made stone artifacts. Engraved slate points and bayonets over 30 cm long were clearly meant for grave offerings. Acidic soils destroyed the human bone and other organic artifacts found elsewhere in similar graves. The small size of the features suggests flexed burials. The sophisticated sea-hunting technology included barbed and toggle-type harpoons for sword fish, and bone and ground slate lance points. Chipped stone spears and darts were used to hunt land mammals. Needles and awls were of bone. Woodworking tools include ground and polished axes, adzes and gouges. Charms and amulets represent sea creatures.

500 BCE–1500 CE *Atlantic Maritime Ceramic Culture.* The two groups of Algonquian-speakers in Atlantic Canada, the Mi'kmaq and the Malecite/Maliseet, are probably descended from makers of the early local ceramics. The Mi'kmaq language diverged earlier than Malecite from other Eastern Algonquian languages. Malecite is related more closely to New England groups. Malecite ceramic technology was imported from New England, while Mi'kmaq ceramics are more similar to those from the St. Lawrence Valley. Although pottery offered new ways to prepare and store food, pots were heavy, fragile and only marginally better than vessels of birch bark and wood. Clay vessels were abandoned when European kettles became available, if not before.

500 BCE–1500 CE Champlain and Lescarbot called the Malecite "Etchemins." Their sites are found on both sides of the Bay of Fundy: at Bear River, and Tusket Falls, Nova Scotia; and Teacher's Cove, Sand Point, and Fulton Island, in New Brunswick. Although some 17th C Europeans noted corn and pumpkins growing at Malecite settlements, the Little Ice Age may have discouraged horticulture when other foods were available. Around 1900, G. F. Matthew reported semi-subterranean oval "pit houses" near Bocabec, NB, containing Ceramic Period tools, and mounds of shellfish valves and bone. In the 1970s, David Sanger and Stephen Davis found similar remains on Passama-quoddy Bay, suggesting permanent coastal settlements. At the Sand Point site, house pits had tunnel-like entrances, were 3-4 m^2, and 50 cm deep. They were framed with poles or saplings held in place by a ring of stones, and covered with skins or sheets of bark. They had a central hearth and the floors were covered with successive layers of clean beach gravel. Housepits were also found at Teacher's Cove, NB.

300 BCE–1200 CE *The Middle Woodland Cultures* of southern Ontario developed more intensive horticultural economies. Like the Hopewellian cultural systems to the south, they came to rely more on plant resources, adding marsh elder, knotweed, and may grass to local cultigens, and processing them by hulling, parching, grinding or milling and boiling. Chert hoes and digging sticks were used, and there was some land clearing, land preparation, and weeding. Tobacco (*Nicotiana rustica*) reached the "American Bottom" in the St. Louis area by 500-600 CE and more northern points soon after. Farmstead settlements with 1–4 structures have

been found there. The timing and route of the entry of maize into the Eastern Woodlands is unknown. When it had been sufficiently adapted to northern climates to produce reliable and sufficient yields it quickly displaced local cultigens.

200 BCE–950 CE *Laurel Culture* may stretch back to the much earlier Poverty Point Culture. The type-sites of its Blackduck Variant are in Northern Minnesota. Distinctive grit-tempered ceramic pots have dentate stamping and pointed bottoms. There are chipped stone end scrapers, but no polished stone tools. A small amount of native copper is found in secondary burials, under mounds. The eleven almost circular Armstrong Mounds, on the Rainy River, Ont., are 20 m in diametre, built of heavy clay laid on a rectangular base of logs. Artifacts found in them include a sucking tube with a pair of frogs carved in relief. C^{14} 957 BP. The Pithers Point Mound was similarly constructed. The Oak Point Island Mound, near Rainy Lake, is 12 m in diametre, and 1.2 m high. Blackduck pottery and scattered bones were found in the original mound. An intrusive burial of a child, along with six adults, yielded many European trade goods dating to the 18th C: Copper kettles, iron hide-scrapers, a file, an axe, a hoe, a strike-a-light, conical copper bangles, wooden spoons, latten buttons, pewter ornaments, rings, thimbles, mirrors, gun flints, scissors, spiral beads, silver jewelry, and 3,599 glass beads.

100 BCE–500 CE *The Late Central Plains Culture* of Southern Alberta is linked by trade in obsidian, flint and grizzly bear teeth with North Dakota tribes and eastward to the mound builders of the Mississippi River. Despite this interaction, they do not seem to have adopted their cultures. Bands from North Dakota later introduced the bow and arrow into the Prairies.

200–700 CE *Middle Woodland.* A cooler period forced a reversion to earlier subsistence methods in marginal agricultural areas. There is evidence of a decline in trade, increased conflict, and an end to monument building.

200–750 CE *Beothuk.* Cape Freels, between Bonavista Bay and Hamilton Sound, is the largest site on Newfoundland. It is among shifting sand dunes, but near a fresh water lake. Europeans have long looted artifacts from the site. An undisturbed area excavated by Paul Carignan in 1973 found house rings, living floors, hearths and charcoal. Thin triangular bifaces, the earliest notched bifaces found in NF, and scrapers, but no goundstone tools or organic remains (C[14] 1200±80 BP). At Blanc Sablon, LB. Elmer Harp Jr. found similar remains (C[14] 1826±50 BP, 1260±46BP). No sites of this period have produced bone, antler or ivory artifacts, impoverishing our understanding of early Beothuk culture. A skeleton found in 1974 at Comfort Cove, Notre Dame Bay, confirms contemporary observations that Beothuks were tall. Looted burials indicate bodies wrapped in bark shrouds, covered with red ochre and provided with tools, weapons and ornaments. At Red Indian Lake, Helen Devereux excavated an interior caribou migration-hunting site. She found housepits, iron caribou spears, nails, trap parts. Beothuk artifacts included notched projectile points, scrapers and bifaces, similar to Cape Freels finds.

200–1750 CE A fully developed *West Coast Maritime Culture* included an elaborate hereditary system of rank and class based on marine resources, elaborate woodworking and tools and weapons of bone and stone. There were chiefs, nobles, commoners and slaves, with resources owned by matrilineal groups. Rank and prestige were gained and maintained by feasting (potlatches) and the gifting of goods assembled by a household or lineage. Seasonally, coastal villages packed up their possessions, including the planks of their houses, and moved inland. There the whole village harvested spawning fish, catching, cleaning, and drying or smoking the food surplus which was the basis for their astounding artistic achievements.

Period V:
Development of Historic Native Societies

500 CE–1000 CE *Plains Culture.* Pottery similar to that made in Saskatchewan and Manitoba by ancestors of the Cree was brought to Alberta. Athapaskan speakers moved south into Alberta by about 750 CE. The ancestors of the modern Blackfoot brought a more sophisticated pottery into the Prairies after

750 CE. Bison hunting intensified as did trade with the complex societies of the Mississippi Valley.

500–1000 CE *The Princess Point Culture* was centered around the Grand R. in Ontario. Semi-sedentary habitation sites, with round houses for 8–10 people, were arranged in a circle. Rare triangular points suggest use of the bow and arrow but stone tools are crude. The Grand Banks site has earliest corn remains yet identified in Ontario (1570±90 BP). Its relationship with historic-period cultures is not yet understood.

500–1500 CE The Mi'kmaq territory at Contact stretched from Cape Breton to the Gaspe, the Saint John River drainage north to PEI. The French called them "Souriquois." Some Mi'kmaq sites have discoid and long tubular shell beads, and bone slat armour. At Rustico Island shell middens spanning the last 2000 years, yielded stone and bone harpoons, needles, awls and scrapers. The Oxbow Site, near the Miramichi R., NB, excavated by Pat Allen, was seasonally occupied for 2500 years during peak anadromous fish runs. The Shubenacadie R. Site, near gaspereau runs, had pit-house depressions and a wide range of stone tools. Sites have also been found at Mahone Bay, Antigonish Harbour, and Pictou, NS; on Rustico Island, PEI; and Kouchibouguac, Tracadie, and Old Mission Point, NB.

900–1300 CE *Glen Mayer* and later *Pickering Cultures of Southern Ontario.* They were based on corn agriculture, supplemented by hunting and fishing, now living in long houses, suggesting matrilocality, in fortified villages. The "Migration Theory" holds that people with a more or less fully developed maize-oriented culture, and a matrilocal system migrated into the area now occupied by Iroquoian peoples. The "in place" theory argues that they developed from these local cultures and the Owasco Culture of New York State. The Iroquoian-speakers were surrounded by Algonquian-speaking peoples.

After 1000 CE Maize-centered horticulture, along with beans and squash, spread throughout southern Ontario. The earliest domesticated C[14] dates for beans are from the (Dick site 900 BP); for tobacco (Stratford Flats 945±165 BP); sunflower and squash (Dymock 900±80 BP). Maize agriculture seems to have entered Canada along with certain cultural traits: matrilocality, the "ownership" of hunting territories and trade routes, endemic warfare and a rapidly increasing population. On the other hand, the Nodwell Site, Bruce County, Ont., is a horticultural village, the result of long-term in situ development of indigenous hunter-gatherers.

1200–1600 CE *The Little Ice Age.* A decline in agricultural output decreased available surplus and forced those in marginal agricultural areas to shift to hunter-gatherer subsistence strategy. This continued to the time of European Contact, with especially cold winters in the early 1600s.

1300–1600 CE *Iroquoian Culture.* The ancestors of the historic Iroquoian-speaking Erie, Neutral, Huron and Petun began to move into the areas in which they were living when the Europeans arrived. Archaeologists do not yet understand why or by what stages this happened. The completely excavated Draper site, north of Toronto (1400–1450), covering 4 ha, had 35 longhouses, one 75 m long. It was surrounded by a palisade. Thousands of trees were cut to build the village, using only stone tools.

1500–1600 CE Tribal formations began to form confederacies, primarily defensive alliances between culturally similar tribes against mutual enemies. The St. Lawrence Iroquoians left the Lower St. Lawrence, perhaps because of declining crops, perhaps because of predation by rival Algonquians and Iroquois, or by European disease. Theories abound as to where the survivors went, based on finds of their pottery. Cartier found that Stadacona (Montreal Island) had been abandoned in 1541.

1650–1730 CE *Plains Culture.* Siouan-speaking peoples entered southern Alberta, bringing farming and horses which had much earlier escaped from the early Spanish in the southern United States. Horses brought increased mobility, changing hunting, trading and social patterns. A smallpox epidemic devastated the Sioux and they disappeared as a cultural force in Canada.

1500–1700 CE The arrival of European fishermen on the Atlantic coast after 1500 probably brought about an increase in burial ceremonialism, with

graves around 1600 yielding European and native goods. These graves have been found eroding out of cliffsides and many have been lost. The European copper articles in them preserved many pieces of fibre and basketry reed of cattail, cedar, basswood, birchbark, and leather goods. The Mi'kmaq made many rock carvings, including of European ships.

1580–1590 CE Pictou (Hopps) site, Northumberland Str., NS. In 1955, Kenneth Hopps, found the richest of many Mi'kmaq burials, 2 secondary burials, including axes, chisels, knives, scrapers, a basked and bulrush mats, red ochre, a piece of woolen blanket, glass beads, shell beads, iron caulkers, fishhooks, saw blades, harpoon heads and arrowheads, swords and daggers, remains of about 13 copper kettles.

700 BC-800 CE Port au Choix-2, Nfld., a Dorset site excavated by Elmer Harp in the 1970s, found 36 shallow oval depressions, lacking hearths, perhaps summer houses, and a rectangular winter house, with low earth or rock walls, a raised sleeping platform and a stone-lined hearth. These sites were base camps for a variety of activities. Harp seals were the major food source, along with migratory birds, other sea mammals, and fur bearing small mammals.

1450–1700 CE *Early Thule Tradition*, the ancestors of modern Inuit, were first identified in Greenland. Oval houses 5 x 4 m, with flagstone floors, a low sod-earthen walls were found at the Ikkusik site, LB. At the rear were raised sleeping platforms; near the door a cooking area. The roof was made with layers of baleen, covered with sods (C^{14} 1520±90 BP). Water and subsequent freezing preserved antler, ivory, bone, wood, basketry, baleen, hides and feathers. There were long "men's knives" of polished slate and *ulus,* or women's knives for butchering. Wooden snow goggles, small human effigies, soapstone lamps and bowls. At the end of this phase, a few European iron, brass, coins, and ceramics appear.

1500–1620 CE Excavations at the Fishing Station, Ferryland, on the Avalon Peninsula revealed Beothuk campfires near the remains left by 16th century Basque, Spanish, French and English fishermen.

1700–1850 CE *Thule "Communal House Phase."* The Tuglavina site, Labrador, had large, square "long houses" for many people; one was 15 x 9 m, with remaining sod walls 2 m above floor level. They had long entrance halls, some with storage chambers. The middens are rich with traditional artifacts, but European materials increase. Iron knife blades, pipe stems, ceramics, bottles, nails, files, copper and brass, gunflints. There is less baleen as Europeans and Americans hunted more and more whales.

1768 CE Exploits, Wigwam Brook, Raymond LeBlanc found 3 housepits and European manufactured goods, including "deer spears." These Beothuk seemingly lived here all year, no longer able to get to the coast, which was occupied by increasingly hostile Europeans.

?–1829 CE L'Anse au Diable, the Iceberg site may illustrate transition between Maritime Archaic and Beothuk cultures. (C^{14} 3055±75 BP, 2410±50 BP).

To present The Naskapi-Montagnais of Labrador speak Central Algonquian languages, but have no convincing archaeological roots or close relatives nearly today. William Fitzhugh suggests tracing Naskapi living today back a thousand years to Hamilton Inlet where people had a generalized coastal adaptation, living in small bands. The Naskapi, however, have an interior adaptation today. The decimation of the caribou herds in the 20th century forced the Naskapi to move near the trading post at Voisey Bay and to Davis Inlet. They have been slow to learn how to harvest coastal resources, as their values, skills, rituals and leadership are closely tied to their life as caribou hunters.

300 CE

• Celts and Picts from Ireland and Scotland made regular visits to Iceland.

500 CE

• Corn cultivation began in southern Ont., resulting in the emergence of agricultural societies.

• Hoei Shin, a Chinese Buddhist monk, described a visit to Fusant, a land resembling present-day British Columbia.

• The Irish began to sail to islands in the North Atlantic, and may possibly have reached Nfld. The discovery of Nfld. is often attributed to St. Brendan (c 521–c 597), although the claim remains unsubstantiated.

• Dorset habitation of Nfld. went into decline, until their extinction after 1000 CE. They were replaced by ancestors of the Beothuk, thought to be descendants of Maritime Archaic peoples who had been pushed into the interior by the Dorset.

750 CE

• Vikings began raiding the Outer Islands of the Faeroes and Shetlands, beginning their expansion into Ireland, Scotland and the islands of the western Atlantic Ocean.

874 CE

• The 1st Scandinavian settlement of Iceland was made by Ingolf and Hjorlief Vilgerdarsson.

875 CE

• Irish monks, fleeing Iceland, are believed to have landed at Brion Island (Magdalen Islands) in the Gulf of St. Lawrence and to have settled on Cape Breton Is. The settlement, called Huitramann land ("Country of the White Man"), was gradually taken over and the inhabitants absorbed into the native Mi'kmaq population.

900 CE

• The Algonquian moved into Labrador and along the north shore of the St. Lawrence, filling in areas abandoned by the Dorset.

900–1000 CE

• A new wave of nomadic people migrated into the Arctic from Alaska. They were the Thule Inuit, from which Canadian and Greenlandic Inuit of today are descended. The Thule were able to catch large whales with sophisticated harpoon technology. They also introduced the kayak. Their use of the dogsled facilitated their rapid expansion throughout the Arctic. By 1200, the Thule had completely displaced the Arctic Dorset.

• The Glen Mayer and Pickering peoples occupied southern Ont. They began to grow crops and smoke tobacco. They also lived in longhouses and large villages. Such traditions were characteristic of the Iroquois, who developed from these cultures about 400 years later.

981

• Eirik Thorvaldsson ("Eric the Red") (c 950), exiled from Iceland for killing 2 men in a quarrel, sailed west. For 3 years, Eirik explored the island he named Greenland, proving that it ran continuously from Angmagssalik, southward around Cape Farewell, and northward to Melville Bay.

985

• Eirik led the 1st group of Icelandic colonists to Greenland. Two colonies were established, the Western Settlement and the Eastern Settlement.

Aug. Bjarni Herjolfsson (c 950) sailed to Greenland from Iceland. Driven off course to the southwest, he sighted a wooded land with low-lying hills. Herjolfsson made 2 more sightings before arriving in Greenland. He had skirted Vinland ("Vine Land"), probably Nfld., Markland ("Forest Land"), probably southern Labrador, and Helluland ("Stone Land"), likely northern Labrador or Baffin Is.

c 995

• Leif Eiriksson (Eirik's son, "Leif the Lucky," c 971) set out to Vinland, the southernmost land sighted by Herjolfsson. With 35 men, he reached Nfld. 's Baccalieu Is. in the Baye de Verde Peninsula. He wintered in Trinity Bay. In spring, Leif returned to Greenland, his vessel laden with self-sown wheat, wild grapes and trees called "mosurr," most likely maple.

c 1004

• A colonizing expedition of 4 ships with 160 people and cattle sailed from Greenland for Vinland, led by Eirik's son Thorvald, Thorfinn Karlsefni, Snorri Thorbrandsson and Bjarni Grimolfsson.

• The expedition made first land at the Cumberland Peninsula of Baffin Is. From northern Labrador, they travelled southward, exploring Groswater Bay and Sandwich Bay. The party crossed the Str. of Belle Isle, which they named Straumfiord ("Fiord of the Strong Current"), to Belle Isle, which they named Straumey ("Island of the Strong Currents"). They landed at the northern tip of Nfld. , between Cape Bauld and Cape Norman, and made a winter camp in Epaves Bay, near the present L'Anse Aux Meadows.

• Late in the year, Thorfinn's wife, Gudrid, gave birth to a son named Snorri, the 1st North American child born of European parents.

c 1005

• Three separate expeditions set out from the base camp in Epaves Bay to explore the area.

• The 1st group, led by Thorfinn Karlsefni and Eirik's daughter Freydis, sailed down the west coast of Nfld. and established a camp in St. Paul's Bay. Here, they encountered Dorset Inuit, or Skraelings, as the Norsemen called them. At first they were met with open arms, but peace between the 2 cultures soon turned into hostilities. The Norse contingent abandoned the area and returned to Epaves Bay in spring.

• Thorvald Eiriksson led the 2nd expedition southwest along the north shore of the Gulf of St. Lawrence, returning to camp 3 months later.

• The 3rd expedition, led by Thorhall the Hunter, sailed north to Markland, but was blown out to sea and lost.

c 1006

• Thorvald Eiriksson, hoping to find Thorhall the Hunter, sailed to Groswater Bay, landing at Lake Melville. He and his men killed 8 Dorset. Thorvald was killed in the melee. His shipmates returned to Epaves Bay.

• Thorfinn Karlsefni made a final expedition from Epaves Bay, sailing down the east coast of Nfld. to the Hampden R. in White Bay. A meeting with Aboriginal inhabitants led to violence.

• Thorfinn and Gudrid returned to Greenland. Others remained at Epaves Bay for the winter, but returned to Greenland in the spring, disillusioned.

c 1025

• Gudleif Gudlaugsson was blown off course while sailing from Dublin to Iceland, landing on the coast of North America. One account suggests that Gudlaugsson was captured by Aboriginals and later freed by Bjorn Asbrunilsson, who, too, was blown off course toward North America. Another account suggests Gudlaugsson chose to remain in North America where he was raising a "mixed-blood" family.

c 1059

• Jon, a Celt or Saxon missionary, is believed to have undertaken a journey in search of Vinland, but was killed by Aboriginal inhabitants. Circumstances of his death are unknown.

c 1074

• Adam of Bremen, a German priest, mentioned the existence of Vinland in a history of the Arch bishopric of Hamburg.

c 1200

• Corn was grown for the 1st time at present-day Campbellville, Ont., and most likely squash and beans.

• Evidence shows that the Dakota occupied western Ont. and eastern Man., moving to the Red, Mississippi and Rainy R. drainage basins sometime before 1660.

1266
• An expedition was sent from Greenland's Eastern Settlement to Baffin Is. to determine the origin of the Skraelings who were migrating to northwestern Greenland.

1290
• Archaeological evidence shows that tobacco used in pipe ceremonies was prevalent in much of Southern Canada.

1360
• A Norwegian expedition under the command of Paul Knutsson was sent to Greenland to restore the Church of Rome. (Ivar Bardarson had visited the colony in 1350, found it abandoned, and said it was under the control of Skraelings.) The Knutsson expedition missed its mark, sailing through Hudson Strait, into Hudson and James Bays, landing near the mouth of the Albany R., and continued to a site near L. Nipigon.

1374
• A Norse expedition was sent from Greenland to lumber in Markland.

c 1398
• The Mohawk, Seneca, Cayuga, Oneida and Onondaga of upper New York and southwestern Canada joined to form the Iroquois League.

1398
June 30 Henry Sinclair, a Scot, is said to have landed in Guysborough Harbour, NS, and to have marched inland to the regions of Pictou and Stellarton.

1408-1409
• English merchants sent fishing vessels to trade in Iceland, later extending their activities to the west coast of Greenland.

c 1420
• Basque whalers from France and Spain began to hunt off the Greenland coast and in the Labrador Sea.

1476
• Danish king Christian I of Oldenburg and head of the Kalmar Union (Denmark, Sweden and Norway), sent an exploring expedition (Johannes Scolvus, Didrik Pining and Hans Pothorst) to discover a northwest passage to India. Scholars believe the expedition reached the coast of Greenland, and probably the north coast of Labrador where they interacted with Aboriginals.

1480
• Bristol merchant John Jay outfitted an expedition for "Brazil," a land in medieval tales said to lie off the west of Ireland. The expedition lost its way and returned without finding its goal.

1481
• The British "Merchants of Bristowe" claimed to have landed in Nfld. Little is known of their activities, as they kept their voyages secret for fear of competition from French, Spanish and Portuguese fishing merchants.

1490–1491
• According to Ayala (the Spanish representative in England), up to 4 ships a year left Bristol seeking the "Island of the Seven Cities," a mythical land where 7 bishops founded 7 cities.

1492
Aug. 3 Christopher Columbus set out from Palos, Spain, with 3 ships, the *Nina*, the *Pinta* and the *Santa Maria*.

Oct. 12 Columbus sighted land at San Salvador, "discovering" the New World for Europe. Columbus thought he had reached the East Indies.

1494

June 7 The Treaty of Tordesillas was completed between Portugal and Spain. Spain was given possession of all unclaimed land west of a line of demarcation running north and south through the Atlantic Ocean, about 480 km west of the Cape Verde Islands. Portugal was given all new lands east of this line. The treaty gave Spain North America, the Caribbean and the west half of South America; Portugal received the east half of South America. Although Nfld. fell into Spanish territory, Spain focused on her southern territory, paying little heed to the French and English who fished her northern waters.

1496

Mar. 3 Italian merchant and explorer Giovanni Caboto Montecatalunya (c 1450–c 1498), or John Cabot, received letters patent from Henry VII of England for a voyage of discovery. Although authorized to take 5 ships, Cabot sailed from Bristol with only one. He was forced to return the same year due to a combination of bad weather, shortages of food and disagreements with the crew.

1497

May 20 Cabot began his 2nd voyage of discovery. A crew of 20 sailed from Bristol in the *Matthew*, which flew the English flag.

June 24 Cabot sighted land, naming it *Prima Terra Vista* ("First Land Seen"). The exact course of his journey remains unknown, as his charts and logs have been lost, but it remains certain he sighted Labrador, Nfld. or Cape Breton Is. He called a large island St. John's Is. in honour of St. John the Baptist. The crew placed a cross in the middle of a clearing with the flag of England on one side and the winged-lion pennant of St. Mark of Venice on the other. These were the first European colours to be unfurled in North America. Cabot took formal possession of the land, in the name of King Henry VII. He then sailed south.

Aug. 10 Cabot arrived back in England. He had reached as far south as Nova Scotia or Maine. His 2nd voyage was published in his own mappemonde (atlas), and on the Juan de la Cosa map

of 1500. His reports of abundant fish and impressive forests encouraged Henry VII and the Bristol merchants to support further exploration.

1498

May Cabot began a 3rd voyage. Five ships sailed from Bristol. One vessel was damaged in a storm and landed in Ireland. The other 4 were lost. Cabot and his crew were not seen again. The English withdrew from exploration for some years. Bristol fishing merchants, however, were actively exploiting the newly found fisheries.

1499

Oct. 29 Portugal's King Manuel I granted Pedro Barcelos-Jao Fernandes and his partners the right to govern any westerly islands they should find.

• By the end of the 15th century, the St. Lawrence valley was home to 2 Aboriginal groups, known as the St. Lawrence Iroquoians. The large fortified village known today as Hochelaga on Montreal Is. was home to 1,500 people whose subsistence depended on horticulture, fishing and hunting.

• Downstream, between today's Portneuf and Cap Tourmente, were 7 smaller, unfortified villages with a total population of 3,000. Europeans called this area "Canada" after the local word for village. The main village at the site of Quebec City was called Stadacona. It owed a form of allegiance to Hochelaga.

• North of the St. Lawrence, from the Saguenay R. to the Strait of Belle Isle, lived bands of Montagnais hunter-gatherers who followed a seasonal round of summer and fall fishing and sea-mammal hunting, and caribou hunting in the interior in winter. These Aboriginals are believed to have been in contact with Europeans earlier than other First Nations on the continent.

1500

May 12 Gaspar Corte-Real (c 1450–c 1501) was also granted the right to any previous or future western lands he might find by the Portuguese Crown. He sailed north to Cape Farewell, Greenland, turning westward. It is believed he travelled as far south as Nfld.

Also in 1500

• Juan de la Cosa, a Spanish cartographer, published a map, with English flags, indicating discoveries from Nfld. to Florida.

1501

Mar. 19 Henry VII granted a patent to Jao Fernandez, Francisco Fernandes and Jao Gonsalves, merchants from the Azores, along with 3 Bristol merchants, a 10-year monopoly to explore, settle and import one shipload of goods duty-free each year. They made a voyage, but nothing is known of it, except that a Bristol man was rewarded in 1502 for his part in discovering an island.

Summer Corte-Real began his 2nd voyage. Sailing via Greenland and using Cape Farewell as a marker, he turned west and then south down the coast of Labrador and the east coast of Nfld., which he claimed for Portugal. Although the exact location is not known for sure, Corte-Real may have landed south of Cape Breton Is., meeting a group of Aboriginals, perhaps the Mi'kmaq, come to shore for summer fishing and sealing. The Mi'kmaq were nomadic hunter-gatherers who lived on the south shore of the St. Lawrence from Chaleur Bay south and eastward into Nova Scotia. They hunted in the interior in the winter. In the 16th century, their population might have been 300. Fifty of these Aboriginals were captured and shipped to Lisbon for sale as slaves. Corte-Real's ship was separated from the returning fleet and given up for lost.

1502

May Gaspar's brother Miguel Corte-Real (c 1450-1502) sailed with 2 vessels from Lisbon in search of Gaspar's lost vessel. He reached the shores of Labrador explored by Gaspar the previous year. Miguel's ship was lost, the other returned.

Dec. 8 Henry VII granted a new charter amalgamating the Gonsalves and the Cabot groups, calling it the Company of Adventurers into the Newfound Islands. It was to remain in operation from 1503 to 1505 or 1506. John Cabot's young son, Sebastian Cabot (c 1491–1557), became an active member.

Also in 1502

• The surviving partners of John Cabot revived their charter of 1496, buying the *Gabriel,* a French ship, and sending it on a fishing expedition. It brought back a profitable cargo of salted fish, marking the beginning of a vast European cod fishery in the Grand Banks that would last until the final decade of the 20th century.

1503

Sept. 20 Newfoundland, Canada's oldest-recorded place name of European origin, was first noted in an entry in the English *Daybooks of King's Payments.* The name Cape Race, Nfld., may be older, but was not cited on a map of 1504.

Also in 1503

• Vasco Annes Corte-Real, a 3rd brother, sailed with 2 ships provided by Portugal's King Manoel, to search for the lost Gaspar and Miguel, but returned in autumn with no further information.

• Customs duties were levied in Portugal on fish from *Terra Nova* (Nfld.).

1504

• St. John's, Nfld., was established as a shore station for the English fishery. Some fishermen may have remained there year-round. A priest went to the island during the year. Fishing vessels *Daniel* and *Jesus* returned with a profitable cargo of fish.

1505

• Huge Elyot, on the *Michell,* financed by William Clerk, brought back a large cargo of salt fish and cod livers, as well as parrots for King Henry, indicating British travel or trade south of Nfld.

1506

• Jean Denys (a captain from Honfleur, Normandy) explored the coast of North America, from the Strait of Belle Isle to Bonavista. He named one of the coves Le Havre de Jean Denys, now Renews, on the east coast of the Avalon Peninsula. This was the 1st recorded Norman fishing expedition to Nfld.

1507

• The 1st use of the name "America" to describe the New World appeared over South America in a map by German cartographer Martin Waldseemüller. The map was lost to scholarship soon after, and remained so for nearly 400 years. The only known surviving copy was re-discovered in 1901, in the Castle of Wolfegg, Württemberg Germany.

1508

• A world map by Johannes Ruysch showed John Cabot's discoveries in the new world as part of Asia. The peninsula representing Nfld. bore the name *Terra Nova*.

1509

• Thomas Aubert (fl 1508-9), a sailor from Dieppe, was one of the 1st French navigators to visit Canadian shores after Denys and the Breton fishermen. In command of the *Pensée*, intending to fish and explore, Aubert sailed up the St. Lawrence River (one of the 1st Europeans to do so), telling the Norman fishermen there about the fishing grounds off Bonavista, Nfld. He returned to France with 7 male Aboriginals, probably Mi'kmaq, perhaps the first to be brought to France.

• Although the circumstances are uncertain, Sebastian Cabot may have searched for a route to Asia north of Terra Nova between 1508-1509. According to this theory, Cabot discovered both Hudson Str. and Hudson Bay, which he thought was the Pacific Ocean. He may also have travelled as far south as Chesapeake Bay or Florida.

1510

• The French fishing vessel, the *Jacquette*, arrived in Rouen loaded with fish caught off Nfld.

1511

• England halted its voyages of exploration in the new world. At the request of Ferdinand of Aragon, Henry VIII sent Sebastian Cabot along with his knowledge of *Terra Nova* into the service of Spain.

1517

• At least 50 Spanish, French and Portuguese ships fished on the Grand Banks of Nfld.

• Thomas Moore's brother-in-law, John Rastell, organized a voyage to Nfld. to found a colony. The voyage was unsuccessful, as the crew mutinied after reaching Ireland. In 1536, John Rastell Jr. organized a voyage; however it ended in disaster, with the crew resorting to piracy, cannibalism, and dying of starvation.

1518

• Baron de Léry and his Portuguese associates attempted to establish a settlement on Sable Is. They landed the first horses and cattle there, and also on Canso, at the northeastern tip of NS. The settlement lasted perhaps until 1526, but ultimately failed.

1520

• Joao Alvarez Fagundes, with letters patent from King Manoel, undertook to found a Portuguese colony in Nfld. He is believed to have visited Nfld., NS, Cape Breton Is., and St. Pierre and Miquelon, and to have named Sable Is. Santa Cruz Is. King Manoel granted him complete rights over this land on his return.

1521

Mar. 13 Fagundes had a Lisbon notary record his discoveries of the previous year at Chedabucto Bay, between Cape Breton Is. and NS, and along the southern coast of Nfld., between Cape Race and Cape Ray. Fishermen from Portugal and the Azores began establishing fishing stations in Nfld.

1522

Sept. 7 Sebastian Elcano completed the Magellan-Elcano voyage around the world, proving there was a passage around South America to the Pacific.

1523–1524

• Giovanni Verrazzano (c 1485–c 1528), a Florentine navigator, sailed from Dieppe under a commission from Francis I of France. He was the 1st European recorded to have explored the coast of America from Florida to Nfld., claiming the area from Charleston to Maine for France. Of his observations, Verrazzano wrote: "We found…roses, violettes, lilies, and many sorts of herbes and sweete and odoriferous flowers, different from our own." During this voyage, on *La Dauphine,* he also explored the mouth of the Hudson R., Manhattan Is., Nova Scotia and Cape Breton Is., returning to France in July 1524, with an abducted Aboriginal boy. He met many Aboriginal groups along the coast, noted their copper ornaments and traded for maize and other foods. Verrazzano was one of the 1st Europeans to report that America was not joined to Asia, and that Canada was part of America. Francis I was taken prisoner and much of the French nobility slaughtered at Pavia, Feb. 26, 1525, by Emperor Charles V, a pivotal battle of the Italian Wars. Verrazzano's discoveries were therefore not exploited by the French.

Also in 1524

• Estevao Gomes explored the coast of North America from the Caribbean, north perhaps to Cape Race, trading bells, combs, scissors and cloth with inhabitants of the Penobscot area. He captured a large number of Penobscot; 58 survived the journey to Spain. They were meant for the slave trade but opinion in Spain was such that they were baptized and made into servants and interpreters.

1527

June 10 John Rut (fl 1512-28) left England in command of the *Mary Guildford* and the *Samson,* appointed by Henry VIII to find a passage to Asia around or through North America. In the *Mary Guildford* (the *Samson* disappeared at sea), Rut explored the Labrador coast, entering St. Lewis Inlet, and then returned via St. John's, Nfld., where he encountered 14 French and Portuguese fishing ships.

Aug. 31 Rut sent the 1st recorded letter from North America, from St. John's, describing conditions in Labrador and Nfld., to Henry VIII. He then continued as far south as Florida, and the Spanish West Indies, the 1st English sailor known to have travelled that way.

1529

• A map by Diego Ribeiro, a Portuguese cartographer, showed a section of the North American coastline between 30° and 45°N, an incorporation of Gomes' and Verrazzano's 1524 discoveries.

• By the end of the 1520s, ships from Brittany, Normandy, Portugal and England had informally divided up the best Nfld. fishing grounds.

1534

Apr. 20 Jacques Cartier (c 1491–1557), of St. Malo, on his 1st voyage, sailed with 2 ships and 60 men on the orders of King Francis I, to find a route to the Orient through North America.

May 10 Cartier sighted Cape Bonavista, Nfld., and was detained for 10 days by ice. He followed the eastern coast of Nfld. north to Château Bay. He then explored the south coast of Labrador, describing it as "the land God gave to Cain."

Also in May

• Jacques Cartier landed at Funk Island, north of what is now Musgrave Harbour, Nfld. to fill his ships' cupboards with meat from the Great Auk, a goose-sized flightless black-and-white bird once abundant in the Grand Banks. European explorers and fishermen had been eating the Great Auk since the early 16th century; it was easy to catch and provided much desired fresh meat and eggs to sailors who had been long at sea. The flesh was also preserved by salting for future consumption at sea. Often called Garefowl or penguin, the Great Auk was also used as bait and a source of feathers for mattresses. The last Great Auk is believed to have been seen, then killed, by an expedition on the Is. of Eldey, off Iceland, on June 3, 1844.

June 11 Cartier and his men celebrated the 1st Roman Catholic mass in Canada, at their camp of Brest, now Bonne Esperance, Labrador. They met a fishing vessel from La Rochelle, and Aboriginals willing to trade furs for metal goods.

June 15 Cartier steered farther south, through the Str. of Belle Isle, along the unexplored western coast of Nfld. to Cabot Str., where he turned west into the Gulf of St. Lawrence. He passed the Isles de la Madeleine, which abounded with birds, flowers and berries, reaching Cap Anguille on June 24.

June 29 Cartier sighted PEI, not realizing it was an island. He explored its northern and western shores, before entering the bay he named Baie de Chaleur, thinking it a passage to the Far East. Several hundred Aboriginals, probably Mi'kmaq, approached him in canoes, eager to trade. He sailed farther west to Gaspé Bay.

July 24 At the rocky headland of Gaspé known as Penouille Point, Cartier erected a 10-metre cross bearing the arms of France, and took possession of the land in the name of Francis I. Here he met Iroquois to whom he gave knives, hatchets, combs, rings and bells.

July 25 Cartier left Gaspé Bay with the newly named Taignoagny and Dom Agaya, 2 sons of the Iroquoian chief of Stadacona, Donnacona (c 1593), promising to return them the following year. He sailed west into the mouth of the St. Lawrence R. but, thinking it a bay, turned east, along the coast and around Île d' Anticosti.

Aug. 9 A storm forced Cartier and his men to shelter in a bay on the mainland, north of Île d'Anticosti. The next day, Cartier named it Baie Saint-Laurent (now Sainte-Geneviève), as it was the day of the Feast of St. Lawrence. The name "St. Lawrence" was later applied to both the gulf and the river. Cartier then set a course for home, having made the 1st circuit of the Gulf of St. Lawrence to be recorded by a European navigator. He was also the 1st European to map the Gulf of St. Lawrence. He arrived in St. Malo, Sept. 5.

1535

May 19 Cartier began his 2nd voyage, leaving St. Malo with 3 ships — *La Grande Hermine*, *La Petite Hermine*, the *L'Émérillon* — and 100 men, including Donnacona's 2 sons. After 50 days they reached the Gulf of St. Lawrence, sailed along the northern coast and erected a cross west of Natashquan, north of

Île d'Anticosti. Cartier and his men then sailed westward up the St. Lawrence R. to the mouth of the Saguenay R. His Iroquois returning passengers were familiar with the area and referred to their native village as Canada, the 1st time Cartier heard the name. The expedition reached the Île d'Orléans in Sept. where they again met Donnacona.

Sept. 14 Deciding to stay in Canada the winter, Cartier laid up 2 of his ships at the mouth of the St.-Croix R., now St.-Charles, across from Stadacona, Donnacona's village, now Quebec City. The smallest vessel, *L'Émérillon*, was anchored in the St. Lawrence to be used for further exploration.

Sept. 19 Cartier set out in *L'Émérillon* to visit the main Iroquoian village, Hochelaga, now Montreal. His expedition left the ship at a lake Cartier called Angoulême (now Lac St.-Pierre), and continued in longboats, arriving at Hochelaga, Oct. 2. Cartier was greeted by 1,000 Iroquois. He named Mont Royal and surveyed the St. Lawrence from its summit. Cartier left Hochelaga Oct. 3, arriving back at Lac St.-Pierre Oct. 4.

Oct. 11 Cartier returned to Stadacona for the winter. Crew members who had not travelled to Hochelaga, had built a fort in his absence. Twenty-five men died of scurvy that winter, although advice from First Nations in the area recommended an infusion of spruce buds (hemlock), which saved many other lives. Medical historians regard this as "The First Prescription in Canada."

1536

May 6 Cartier abandoned *La Petite Hermine* and left for France with his remaining ships and 10 captive Iroquois, including Donnacona, who had been lured aboard. Cartier arrived at St. Malo, July 16. He had little to show for the expedition but the kidnapped Iroquois. One by one, Cartier's captives died.

Also in 1536

• Richard Hore (1509–1569), on the *William*, combined a fishing trip and sightseeing tour of the Strait of Belle Isle. With the *William* unseaworthy, the group seized a French ship for the return trip.

1541

Jan. 15 By appointment of Francis I, Jean-François de La Rocque, Sieur de Roberval (c 1500–1560), became the 1st Viceroy of Nfld. and Labrador.

Mar. 9 Prevented by merchants in the French ports from recruiting colonists or crews, de Roberval obtained authorization to take a group of convicts to settle Canada.

May 23 Cartier began his 3rd voyage from St. Malo with 5 ships, including *La Grande Hermine* and *L'Émérillon*, and an army of 1,500 men to establish a colony and to capture the golden, mythical "Kingdom of Saguenay," thought to exist somewhere beyond Mont Royal.

Aug. 23 Cartier arrived at Stadacona, telling the Iroquois that Donnacona had died of natural causes, and the 9 other Natives he had taken to France had become wealthy and preferred to stay there. Cartier then established a settlement at Rivière du Cap-Rouge, 16 km upstream from Stadacona, complete with ovens and mills. Crops were planted. Nuggets of "gold" and "diamonds" were found. This 1st fort in Canada was named Charlesbourg Royal.

Sept. 17 Cartier set out to find the golden, mythical Kingdom of Saguenay, portaging around the Lachine Rapids, but was forced to turn back as winter arrived. He returned to Cap-Rouge to find increasing dissension amongst his men, who faced the anger of a local Iroquois population not completely satisfied with Cartier's story about Donaconna and the captives. The Iroquois eventually killed 35 of the colonists.

1542

Apr. 16 De Roberval, with 3 vessels and 200 convicts, sailed from La Rochelle with supplies for Cartier's settlement. The voyage was without incident, but de Roberval marooned his cousin Marguerite de la Roque and her lover on an island off Nfld. because of licentious behaviour on board his ship.

June 8 Cartier, having decided to return to France, met de Roberval at St. John's, Nfld. De Roberval ordered him back to the mainland, but Cartier refused. In France, his cargo of "gold and diamonds"

was proven to be nothing but iron pyrite (fool's gold) and quartz. The expression "false as a diamond of Canada" soon found currency throughout France.

July De Roberval reached Cartier's settlement at Cap-Rouge and renamed it France Royal.

• Michel Gaillon, one of de Roberval's crew, was hanged for theft at Cap-Rouge, the 1st instance of European-style capital punishment in Canada.

Sept. 19 In the oldest official Canadian document, de Roberval pardoned Aussillon de Sauveterre, who was convicted for murder.

Winter De Roberval wintered at Cap-Rouge. More than 50 of the 200 colonists died of scurvy. Several insubordinate colonists were hanged, others were imprisoned.

1543

June 6 After an unsuccessful trip to explore the Saguenay R., de Roberval and the surviving colonists returned to France. This marked the end of official French interest in Canada for the next 30 years. Subsequently, the St. Lawrence Iroquoian villages were abandoned and their inhabitants dispersed. Archaeological evidence and eye-witness accounts later given to Europeans indicate that the abandonment was the result of Mohawk and Huron attacks.

1545

• French Basques established whale and sea-mammal fisheries at Tadoussac, at the mouth of the Saguenay R., and on the St. Lawrence R. They also traded for furs.

• Inventories of Parisian furriers referred to beaver pelts for the 1st time.

1546

• One of the earliest printed views of Canada, the Desceliers Mappemonde, showed Aboriginal peoples, European explorers and native fauna, as well as the areas discovered by Europeans from Labrador to Florida. It incorporated information from all 3 of Cartier's voyages. The name "Canada" appeared on the north and south shores of the

Gulf of St. Lawrence. The rapids that prevented Cartier from going farther west in 1535 were called "La Chine."

• The discovery of silver at Potosi in present-day Bolivia disrupted European metal markets and its mining industry, setting off a race for riches in the Americas.

During the 1540s
• French and Spanish Basques established more than a dozen whaling stations along the north shore of the Gulf of St. Lawrence and north along the Labrador coast to Cape Charles. Labrador's Red Bay, *"Butus"* or *"Buteres,"* came to be the largest whale meat and oil processing centre in the contemporary world.

1555

• The Muscovy or Russia Company was incorporated by Queen Mary, to finance expeditions to locate a northeast passage and the northwest sea leading to the East Indies.

1556

• Venetian cartographer Giacomo Gastaldi depicted Nfld. as a group of independent islands.

• Guillaume Le Testu's map of eastern North America showed Canada as a land of turreted castles, pleasant meadows and forests. The St. Lawrence R. ran out of a tiny lake (L. Ontario) described by Cartier.

1557

• Jacques Cartier died in St. Malo.

1565

• The *San Juan,* a Basque whaler, sank in Red Bay Harbour with a full cargo of whale oil. The following year, the ship's outfitter Joanes de Portu salvaged most of the oil, which was stored in barrels. In 1978, the *San Juan* was found by Parks Canada divers, after Selma Barkham read about it in Basque "notarial" documents, and in 1979, the remains of the ship were disassembled for conservation and study. The ship's timbers (44 ceiling planks, 210 exterior planks, 230 futtocks, 50 floor timbers), other structural and

miscellaneous elements, as well as fragments of pottery have been retrieved and documented.

c 1566

• Engraver Paolo Forlani published one of the earliest maps to include only North America. Previously attributed to cartographer Bolognino Zaltieri, the map included "La Nova Franza" (New France), "Canada Pro" (Canada Province), "Stadacone" (Quebec City), "Ochelaga" (Montreal), "Terra Dellaborador," and "Larcadia."

1569

• Gerhardus Mercator published the Mercator Map, naming the Gulf of St. Lawrence. The Mercator Projection permitted navigators to indicate routes as straight lines. What appears to be Ungava Bay was represented, suggesting that Hudson Strait and Ungava Bay had already been discovered by Europeans, possibly Portuguese fishermen.

• Martin de Hoyarsabal, a Basque navigator, published sailing directions for whaling stations in Labrador. Whalers were forced to overwinter in Butu (Red Bay); an unknown number died. They were among the 140 burials unearthed at Red Bay in 1982.

1570

• The Five Nations Iroquois or Iroquois League — the Seneca, Oneida, Onondaga, Cayuga and the Mohawk — solidified into what was known as the Iroquois Confederacy.

1576

June 7 Martin Frobisher (c 1539–1594) sailed with the *Gabriel* and *Michael* from England to search for a northwest passage. The Muscovy Company granted Frobisher a licence with the support of Queen Elizabeth I and the London Merchants.

July 11 Frobisher sighted Greenland, but was prevented from landing by ice and fog. A storm caused the *Michael* to turn back, while Frobisher, aboard the *Gabriel*, continued westward.

July 20 Frobisher sighted Resolution Is. off the southeastern end of Baffin Is., naming it Queen Elizabeth's Foreland. Sailing north, he discovered a passage, that he thought divided Asia from America, and named it Frobisher's Str. It was actually the bay which now bears his name.

Aug. 19 Inuit traded meat and furs with Frobisher for trinkets and clothing. One Inuit piloted the *Gabriel* through the "strait," but he and 5 of Frobisher's men disappeared when put ashore. Before setting sail for England, on Oct. 9, Frobisher took possession of the Arctic land for England. A crew member found what was thought to be a lump of gold.

1577

Mar. 17 Frobisher began his 2nd voyage on a commission from the Cathay Company to search for gold.

June 22 Juan Martinez de Larrume dictated his will at Butes, Labrador, the oldest surviving legal document written in Canada.

July 19 Frobisher's expedition entered Frobisher Bay. The islands and both shores of the bay were explored for gold. Frobisher named Mount Warwick, traded with Inuit and searched unsuccessfully for sailors lost the previous year.

Aug. 23 With his ships' holds filled with 200 tonnes of ore, Frobisher set sail for England. He also had aboard 3 kidnapped Inuit, all of whom died within a month of landing in England Sept. 17.

Also in 1577
• First-known recorded use of the St. George's Cross in Canada, was in a watercolour painting of English explorers skirmishing with the Inuit. It is believed that the painting depicted Frobisher's expedition of the same year. (The St. George's Cross came into widespread use as a national emblem of England in 1274, although use of the cross predates that time.)

1578

Jan. 3 Henri III commissioned Troilus de La Roche de Mesgouez, Marquis de La Roche-Mesgouez (c 1540–1606), the 1st viceroy of New France, and authorized him to colonize the region.

May 31 Frobisher began his 3rd voyage with a fleet of 15 ships. He left Harwich to establish a settlement in Frobisher Bay, and to bring 2,000 tonnes of gold ore back to England.

June 30 Frobisher took possession of Greenland in the name of Elizabeth I and renamed it West England.

July 2 Frobisher's expedition sighted Baffin Is., then called *Meta Incognita*. Driven south by unfavourable winds, the fleet sailed up what Frobisher called the "Mistaken Strait," now called Hudson Str., his greatest discovery. For the rest of the month his fleet tried to reassemble, but without success. One ship was crushed by ice. The crew survived. Another ship deserted to England.

July 24 Eleven ships of Frobisher's fleet gathered within Frobisher Bay, which he named Countess of Warwick Sound.

July 30 Frobisher found the missing *Judith* and the *Michael*, behind Anne Warwick (Kodlunarn) Is. Chaplain Reverend Wolfal conducted what is believed to have been the 1st European Thanksgiving service in the Americas.

Aug. 1 Frobisher began mining operations on Anne Warwick Is., and other neighbouring locations. Approximately 1,200 tonnes of ore were mined, which eventually proved to be worthless iron pyrite. Remnants of Frobisher's activities are still visible on the island.

Aug. 31 Frobisher set out for England. The remaining 12 ships left on Sept. 2. All arrived in England safely by Oct. 1.

Nov. 19 Sir Humphrey Gilbert (c 1537–1583), who had been commissioned by Elizabeth I to discover new lands and found a colony in North America, left Plymouth with 10 ships and a crew comprising mainly pirates. Three of his ships deserted. The rest were forced to return to England. Gilbert was then forbidden to sail as planned in the new year.

c 1580

• Messamouet, Chief at La Heve, on the south shore of NS, visited France in the late 16th century, where he resided at the house of Philibert de Grandmont (1552–1580), Gov. of Bayonne.

• Sir Richard Whitbourne, at the age of 15, left Southhampton, in a vessel of 300 tonnes, for Nfld. The main purpose was hunting whales and the making of "trayne oyle," and trade with the Aboriginals, but the crew found fishing and hunting in the Trinity Harbour more lucrative. Whitbourne returned to Nfld. several more times, and served as Gov. of Renews from 1618 to 1620.

1581

• Merchants from St. Malo began to trade for furs up the St. Lawrence R.

• Spain and Portugal were united under one rule and stopped competing for American possessions.

1583

June 11 Gilbert's 2nd expedition sailed from Plymouth with 5 ships: *Delight, Raleigh, Golden Hind, Swallow,* and *Squirrel,* despite Queen Elizabeth I's attempts to keep him in England.

July 30 Gilbert reached Nfld. His fleet followed the coast southward and sighted Funk Is., which Gilbert called Penguin Is. after the Great Auks found there. They rounded Baccalieu Is. and Cape St. Francis.

Aug. 3 Gilbert arrived at St. John's, formally taking possession of Nfld. for Elizabeth I, Aug. 5, granting shore rights to 36 fishing vessels already in the region. He ordered the *Swallow* home to England with the sick, the wounded and the malcontents.

Aug. 20 Gilbert sailed to Cape Race to fish for cod and explore the mainland. Two more of his fleet returned to England.

Aug. 29 During a stormy night, the *Delight* ran aground, probably on Sable Is., and sank with the loss of all but 12 men.

Aug. 31 After returning to Cape Race, Gilbert's 2 remaining ships headed for England. The *Squirrel* was lost in mid-ocean, claiming the lives of all on board, including Gilbert.

Sept. 22 The *Golden Hind,* the last of Gilbert's fleet, landed in Dartmouth.

• Three ships from St. Malo traded as far west as the Lachine Rapids. A ship from Le Havre traded between Cape Breton and the Penobscot R.

Also in 1583

• The Russians lost Narva, their Baltic port, to the Swedes, thereby cutting off the traditional fur-supply route to Europe. Europeans now turned to North America for furs.

• Étienne Bellenger traded with Aboriginals along the coast of NS and Maine. He invested approximately 40 crowns for trinkets and returned to France with several varieties of fur and ore, said to contain silver. The cargo's value amounted to 400 crowns.

1584

• Five ships from St. Malo traded in the St. Lawrence.

• Richard Hakluyt (c 1553–1616) published *Discourse of Western Planting,* stating that 5 ships returned to St. Malo from Canada, loaded with furs, and that in 1585, 10 ships would be sent to Canada.

1585

June 7 The 1st voyage of John Davis (c 1543–1605) sailed from Dartmouth, with the *Sunneshine* and *Mooneshine,* bearing a royal patent to discover the Northwest Passage.

July 20 Davis sighted the east coast of Greenland, which he called the "Land of Desolation." He rounded Cape Farewell, skirting the Greenland coast, arriving at what had been the Norse Western Settlement, naming it Gilbert Sound. The 2 vessels crossed what was later named Davis Str. and landed on the east coast of Baffin Is., in Exeter Sound.

Aug. 8 Davis rounded the southern tip of the peninsula, which he named Cape of God's Mercy, now Cape Mercy. The ships then entered a deep sound, which was named Cumberland Sound and hoped to be the passage to the East. Two hundred and ninety km into Cumberland Sound, Davis found further progress blocked by land. He returned to England, arriving Sept. 30.

Also in 1585

• Sir Walter Raleigh (1552–1618), established a colony on Roanoke Is. The colony did not survive; Raleigh tried twice more to establish a settlement, both attempts unsuccessful. However, from the 1st attempt, Raleigh was able to introduce tobacco to England.

1586

May 7 Davis began his 2nd voyage with 4 ships: the *Sunneshine*, *Mooneshine*, *Mermayd* and *North Starre*.

June 7 The *Sunneshine* and *North Starre* separated to seek a passage between Iceland and Greenland, with no success.

Aug. 14 Fighting heavy ice, Davis, in the *Mooneshine*, reached Cumberland Sound on Baffin Is. from Davis Str.

Aug. 20 From a hilltop, Davis was unable to see a sea route through the islands at the head of Cumberland Sound. He sailed down the coast of Labrador, stopping at Davis Inlet and Hamilton Inlet.

Sept. 11 When contrary winds prevented exploration of Hamilton Inlet, Davis left for England, arriving Oct. 6.

Also in 1586

• Micheau de Hoyarsabal wintered with Aboriginals on the shore of the St. Lawrence R. Hoyarsabal had set sail from St. Jean De Luz, with a cargo which included 209 red copper kettles for trade.

1587

May 19 Davis began his 3rd voyage from Dartmouth with the *Sunneshine*, *Elizabeth* and *Ellen*.

June 16 Gilbert Sound was sighted. Davis continued north along Greenland's west coast to Upernavik, calling it Sanderson's Hope, in honour of his backer, William Sanderson, a wealthy merchant. Davis then travelled southward down the Baffin Is. coast, exploring Cumberland Sound and noting the

entrances to Lord Lumley's Inlet (Frobisher Bay) and Hudson Str.

Aug. 15 After sailing down the coast of Labrador and fishing in Château Bay, Davis returned to England, arriving Sept. 15. Davis made important descriptions and charts of Greenland, Baffin Is. and Labrador.

1588

• The Spanish Armada, including most of Spain's fishing boats, was destroyed, leaving Nfld.'s Avalon Peninsula open to England's fishing fleet. The production of dried salted cod, which became the mainstay of sailors' diets, led to a 3-way trade route between England, Nfld. and the Iberian Peninsula.

• Jacques Noel, Cartier's nephew, obtained a monopoly on trade from Francis III and permission to found a colony in Canada. Under pressure from French merchants, the monopoly was revoked.

1596

• Greek sailor Apostolos Valerianos, alias Juan de Fuca, sailed in the service of Spain. He claimed to have discovered the North Sea, a mythical waterway separating the Atlantic and Pacific Oceans.

1597

• Capt. Charles Leigh left London in the *Hopewell*, with a cargo of coats, knives, and trifles to trade in NS. Leigh also encountered hostile Basque fishermen.

1598

Jan. 12 Troilus de La Roche (d c 1600) received new letters patent from Henri IV appointing him Lt-Gen. of Canada, Hochelaga, Acadia, Nfld., Labrador and Norumbega, in what is now Maine. He was to build forts, grant lands, make laws and maintain a monopoly on all trade.

Apr. La Roche set sail with the *Catherine* and the *François* and 40 convicts. His party landed on Sable Is., NS, to build a semi-military colony. La Roche left the post under a commandant and continued on to the Nfld. fisheries. A storm forced him to return to France. The convicts were thus abandoned and forced to subsist on fish and wild cattle, left behind by the Portuguese who had failed in their attempts to colonize the island in the early decades of the century.

Nov. 18 Stephen Burkhall, aboard the 30-tonne *Grace*, returned from Nfld. with 15,000 fish, 1 tonne trayne oyle and 100 pelts, of which 60 were deer.

Also in 1598

• By the Edict of Nantes, Huguenots were granted equal civil status with Roman Catholics in France, and were thereby permitted to enter the North American trade.

1599

Nov. 22 François Gravé Du Pont (c 1554–1629), who had previously traded for furs up the St. Lawrence R., and Pierre Chauvin de Tonnetuit (d 1603), a Huguenot merchant from Honfleur, received a royal commission including a 10-year monopoly on the fur trade, and the obligation to fund the settlement of 500 colonists in Canada.

1600

- Du Pont and Chauvin left Honfleur with 4 ships and colonists to build the 1st permanent fortified trading post in Canada, at Tadoussac. Du Pont and Chauvin returned to France in the autumn with a cargo of furs, leaving 16 colonists at Tadoussac. The fort served as protection against Iroquois attack.

1601

- Only 5 Tadoussac colonists survived the winter. Chauvin sent the *Espérance* to rescue them in the spring. Tadoussac became a summer trading post.

1602

Feb. Aymar de Chaste (d 1603), Gov. of Dieppe, was named Lt-Gen. of New France, by King Henri IV. De Chaste also received a patent for a colony and a trading monopoly. He formed the de Chaste Trading Company.

Apr. Chauvin sailed to New France with 2 ships (but no colonists), for summer trading at Tadoussac.

May 2 Capt. George Waymouth (fl 1601–1612), an English mariner, sailed from Ratcliffe with the *Discovery* and the *Godspeed* to find a northwest passage for the East India Company.

June 28 Waymouth sighted land, but ice and fog prevented exploration. Sailing south, he entered Hudson Str. and travelled westward 480 km before turning back. Waymouth's two ships cleared Hudson Str. Aug. 5, arriving in England on Sept. 5.

1603

Mar. 15 Samuel de Champlain (c 1570–1635) boarded the *Bonne-Renommée* in Honfleur. He had accepted de Chaste's invitation to serve as cartographer and geographer on Gravé Du Pont's expedition to New France.

May 24 Two ships from Du Pont's expedition anchored at the mouth of the Saguenay R., near Tadoussac. Champlain witnessed the Montagnais "tabagies" or feasts, and met them at the fur trading post.

June 18 After exploring the Saguenay R. for 56 km, Champlain and Du Pont sailed up the St. Lawrence R. Only a few rotting palisades remained of Stadacona, the Iroquois village Cartier had visited in 1535.

June 29 Champlain reached Lac Saint-Pierre and entered the mouth of the Richelieu R. He journeyed up the river to the St. Ours Rapids, learning of other lakes farther upstream, which would later be named L. Champlain and L. George.

July 11 Champlain returned to Tadoussac, after investigating the Sault Saint Louis or Lachine Rapids, and the site of present-day Montreal, where only a few ruins remained of the Iroquois city of Hochelaga.

Sept. 20 After exploring the Gaspé, Champlain returned to France, and presented his map of the St. Lawrence to Henri IV. Champlain also learned that de Chaste had died on May 13.

Nov. 8 Pierre Du Gua, Sieur de Monts (c 1558–1628), was appointed the new Lt-Gen. of New France, and the Atlantic coast between 40°– 46°N latitude, including both sides of the Gulf of St. Lawrence. He received a royal commission to colonize Acadia. and a 10-year monopoly of the fur trade on the St. Lawrence.

Nov. 15 Champlain published an account of his trip to New France, *Des Sauvages: ou Voyage de Champlain de Brouage*.

Also in 1603

- Thomas Chefdostel (fl 1597–1603), a Norman captain, landed on Sable Is. to rescue 11 starving survivors of the colony established by La Roche. The convicts were presented to the king and pardoned of their crimes.

- The accession of James I to the throne of England brought peace with Spain and an increase in English interest in the colonization of North America.

1604

Feb. 8 The 1st chartered company in Canada, the de Monts Trading Company, was formed. Its members included de Monts, Du Pont and Champlain.

Mar. 7 The 1st ship of the de Monts Trading Company expedition left Havre-de-Grâce, France, with Du Pont on board.

Mar. 10 De Monts followed in the 2nd ship, arriving near Lunenburg, NS, May 8.

May 13 De Monts named Port-au-Mouton (Port Mouton, NS) when a sheep jumped overboard. He remained there while Champlain and Jean Ralluau (fl 1604–1615) explored the coast as far as the Bay of Fundy. The vessel was then taken to St. Mary's Bay at the entrance to the Bay of Fundy while de Monts and Champlain explored in a longboat. They were seeking a site for a settlement and for mineral deposits discovered the previous year by Jean Sarcelde du Prévert (d 1622). The explorers were encouraged by the wooded hills and fertile soil of the Annapolis Basin, and awed by the tidal action of the Bay of Fundy, the highest in the world.

June 24 Skirting the New Brunswick shore, Champlain and de Monts entered a river which they named Saint John, and continued westward along the coast until they reached a sandy island which de Monts named Île Ste-Croix. The location and good harbour, and the need to prepare for winter, convinced the French to settle there. They built a palisade, houses, and planted the 1st wheat in New France.

Sept. 5 Champlain set out to explore the coast of Norumbega, passing Grand Manan Is., Mount Desert Is. and Isle Haulte. He travelled as far as Georges Is. near the Kennebec R., arriving back at Île Ste-Croix, Oct. 2.

Oct. 6 The 1st snow of the winter fell. De Monts, Champlain and 77 men wintered on Île Ste-Croix, including the 1st Huguenots to settle in New France; 35 men died of scurvy.

Also in 1604

• The 1st Europeans to practise medicine in New France were Guillaume des Champs and Maître Étienne, at Île Ste-Croix.

• The 1st European iron ore discovery in North America was made at St. Mary's Bay, NS.

1605

June 18 De Monts and Champlain sailed south as far as Massachusetts Bay and Nauset Harbor, Massachusetts, seeking a better site for their colony. They chose Port Royal, in the sheltered Annapolis Basin. Buildings at Île Ste-Croix were dismantled and used to build a new habitation, and Port Royal became the 1st capital of Acadia.

Sept. De Monts returned to France to attend to the Company's finances, leaving Du Pont in charge of the settlement. Champlain undertook more explorations.

1606

Mar. 16 Champlain set out on an abortive exploratory expedition, reaching only as far as Port aux Coquilles on the Île Ste-Croix R.

May 13 De Monts dispatched the *Jonas* to Acadia, commanded by Jean de Biencourt, Sieur de Poutrincourt et de Saint-Just (1557–1615), a partner in the de Monts company. Among its passengers were Jean Ralluau (de Monts' secretary), Marc Lescarbot (c 1570–1642), the 1st historian of New France, Louis Hébert (c 1575–1627), the 1st officer of justice, Charles de Biencourt de Saint-Just (c 1591–1623), and de Poutrincourt's elder son. Also on board was Matthew Da Costa (d 1607), explorer, linguist and interpreter who spoke many languages, including English, French, Dutch and Mi'kmaq. Da Costa died at Port Royal, which he helped build, in 1607. He was the 1st-known black man in Canada.

July 27 The Poutrincourt expedition arrived at Port Royal. Grain and other foods were successfully grown.

Sept. 5 Poutrincourt and Champlain explored south as far as Martha's Vineyard, returning to Port Royal, Nov. 14.

Nov. 16 The 1st European drama in Canada, *Le Théâtre de Neptune*, written by Lescarbot, and staged on several small boats with a cast of 11, was performed at Port Royal.

Also in 1606

• The cultivation of apples from Normandy was begun at Port Royal.

• Port Royal established good relations with local First Nations, the Mi'kmaq and Abenaki. (Hunter-gatherer bands of northeastern North America, including the Mi'kmaq and Abenaki, are called Algonquian because they speak languages belonging to the Algonquian linguistic family.)

• The 1st highway in New France was built, between Port Royal and Cape Digby.

• Champlain organized *L'Ordre de Bon Temps* (Order of Good Cheer), the 1st social club in New France. Members took turns providing game for the table.

1607

May 24 The *Jonas* arrived at Port Royal with news that de Monts' trading monopoly had been cancelled, due, in part, to pressure from northern French merchants. Colonists were told to return to France.

Aug. 11 Champlain sailed from Port Royal for Canso, NS, drawing a map of the Atlantic coastline from Cape Breton to Cape Cod.

Also in 1607

• On his return to France, Lescarbot published his epic poem *Adieu aux François, La défaite des sauvages armouchiquois.*

• Poutrincourt built the 1st water-driven mill in North America on the Allains R. at Port Royal, after 6 men died from the exertion of grinding grain by hand.

1608

Jan. 7 De Monts persuaded the king to extend his trading monopoly for 1 year. De Monts promised to send 3 ships to the new colony: 1 to Port Royal to revive the settlement; 1 to the lower St. Lawrence; and 1 to establish a post at Que. under the direction of Champlain.

Apr. 13 Champlain left France aboard the *Don-de-Dieu*, arriving at Tadoussac June 3. Also on board was Étienne Brûlé (c 1592–1633), 1 of several French boys sent to live with the Algonquian in

1610 to learn their language and customs. In exchange, an Aboriginal youth, "Savignon," was sent to live with Champlain.

July 3 Champlain landed at the site of present-day Quebec City, and began to build a fortified trading post at the foot of the cliffs. Here the river narrowed enough to be controlled by canon. His *Habitation* stood on the site of present-day Place Royal.

Also in 1608

• One of the earliest printed views of Canada, *Habitation de Québec,* was drawn by Champlain.

• Champlain and 28 men spent the winter at Que.; 20 died of scurvy.

1609

Apr. 6 English navigator Henry Hudson (d c 1611) sailed in the *Half Moon* to find a northwest passage for the Dutch East India Company. The expedition took him up the Hudson R. as far as Albany, New York, his reports encouraged the Dutch to begin trading in the area.

Apr. 8 The 8 men who had survived the winter with Champlain at Que. witnessed spring's 1st thaw. For the 1st time, Huron visited the St. Lawrence settlement and contacted the French directly. (Huron, along with the closely related Petun and Neutral, lived south of the Canadian Shield in Ont. They spoke closely-related Iroquoian dialects. Shifting horticulturalists, growing corn, beans and squash, they lived in fortified villages that were moved every decade or so as the fertility of the land and firewood supply were exhausted. Their combined populations are estimated to have been 60,000, prior to European contact.)

June 28 Champlain set out to explore Iroquois country, with 11 Frenchmen and 60 Algonquin, Huron and Montagnais. He had decided to support Algonquin and Huron against their Mohawk and Oneida (Five Nations Iroquois) enemies, hoping to further French trade and exploration.

July 13 Champlain travelled up the Richelieu R. accompanied by 2 Frenchmen and his Aboriginal allies. They reached L. Champlain and L. George.

On July 29, the group met a large Mohawk war party near Ticonderoga, New York, and readied for battle.

July 30 Champlain and his allies defeated the Mohawk in the Battle of Ticonderoga, using firearms against the Mohawk for the 1st time.

Sept. 5 Champlain sailed from Tadoussac, arriving in France, Oct. 13.

Also in 1609
• Marc Lescarbot (1570–1629), who had visited Canada in 1606, wrote the *Histoire de la Nouvelle France, contenant les navigations, découvertes et habitations faites par les François és Indes Occidentales et Nouvelle-France*, etc. (A reprint of the original edition was published in 1866, at Paris, by *Edwin Tross*, 3 vols.)

• Unable to renew his monopoly with the king, de Monts was forced to form a partnership with Rouen merchants.

1610

Apr. 8 Champlain left on his 4th voyage to New France, arriving at Que., Apr. 28.

Apr. 17 Hudson sailed in the *Discovery* to search for a northwest passage. After entering Hudson Str. in June, he turned southward into Ungava Bay, believing he had reached the west side of North America.

May 2 King James I granted a charter to the Company of Adventurers and Planters of London and Bristol, to colonize Nfld.

June 14 Champlain led another expedition against the Iroquois with Algonquin and Huron allies. On June l9, near the mouth of the Richelieu R., his forces were successful in what was termed the Battle of Cap-de-la-Victoire. Champlain narrowly escaped death when an Iroquois arrow split his ear. The French harquebus, an early portable firearm, proved the deciding factor.

June 24 Jessé Fléché (d c 1611), a secular priest, became the 1st recorded Roman Catholic missionary in New France. He baptized Mi'kmaq Chief Membertou (d 1611) and 20 members of his family.

July 5 John Guy (d 1629), governor of the 1st English colony in Nfld., sailed with his brother, Phillip, and other colonists, from Bristol, arriving in Nfld. in Aug. Guy planned to settle Sea Forest Plantation, at Cuper's Cove, now Cupids, on Conception Bay. Archaeological evidence indicates that Europeans have occupied the area continuously ever since.

Aug. 3 Hudson entered Hudson Bay, and sailed along its east coast, possibly as far as James Bay, where he decided to winter. By Nov. his ship was frozen in.

Aug. 8 Champlain returned to France, leaving 16 men under the command of Jean de Godet du Parc (d 1627) at Que.

Dec. 27 In Paris, the 40-year-old Champlain, a devout Catholic, married Hélène Bouillé (1598–1654), the Protestant daughter of a wealthy secretary to Louis XIII. She was 12 years old and would not come to Que. until 1620.

1611

Jan. 26 Madame Jeanne de Poutrincourt, who would become the 1st-known aristocratic European female in Canada, left Dieppe for Port Royal. She was accompanied by Pierre Biard (c 1567–1622) and Enemond Massé (1575–1646), the 1st Jesuit missionaries to the Colony, and her son, Charles de Biencourt de Saint–Just.

May 21 Champlain arrived in Que. from France. Travelling as far as the Lachine Rapids, he chose Pointe Callières as the site of the future city of Montreal.

June 12 Hudson began his return voyage to England, but within a few days, the *Discovery* was again locked in the ice. His crew mutinied on June 24, setting Hudson, his son John and 7 others, adrift in a small boat. The mutineers sailed for England. Only 8 survived the voyage and they were not punished. Nothing more was ever heard of Hudson and his companions.

July 20 Champlain returned to France, with the 1st cargo of timber from New France.

1612

Jan. 26 A relief ship arrived at Port Royal with Gilbert Du Thet (c 1575–1613), a lay Jesuit, acting as administrator of missions.

Apr. 14 Welshman Thomas Button (d 1634) sailed with the *Discovery*, Hudson's old ship, and the *Resolution*, to locate a northwest passage, and, if possible, Hudson.

Aug. 15 Button reached Port Nelson, naming the island at the entrance to Hudson Str. after the *Resolution*. He discovered Coats Is. in Hudson Bay, and made winter camp in the estuary of the Nelson R. In June 1613, a cross was erected and the area named New Wales. Button explored the west coast of Hudson Bay and discovered the Churchill R. before returning to England in Aug. 1613.

Oct. 8 Following the collapse of de Monts' partnership, Louis XIII, deciding to continue the Canadian venture, named his nephew, Charles de Bourbon, Comte de Soissons, Lt-Gen. in New France. Champlain was named lieutenant.

Also in Oct.

• Gov. John Guy, of Nfld., accompanied by 18 men explored Trinity Bay to establish contact with the Beothuk.

Nov. 20 After the sudden death of Charles de Bourbon, the Lt-Gen. appointment was transferred to Henri de Bourbon, Prince de Condé. Champlain was not made gov.

Also in 1612

• De Monts organized a new company, continuing trade and exploration in New France until 1617.

• Antoinette de Pons, Marquise de Guercheville, agreed to finance the habitation at Port Royal, in return for Poutrincourt's permission to allow Jesuits to set up a mission there.

• Peter Easton used Harbour Grace, Nfld., as a base for his 10-vessel pirate fleet. He plundered 30 English ships in St. John's harbour and raided French and Portuguese ships at Ferryland, Nfld.

1613

Mar. 6 Champlain sailed from Honfleur with adventurer Nicholas de Vignau, to investigate de Vignau's story that he had seen a wrecked English ship in Hudson Bay, in 1612.

Mar. 12 René Le Coq de La Saussaye left Honfleur for Acadia, reaching Port Royal, May 16. He had been sent by the Marquise de Guercheville to quell the discord between Jesuits Frs. Biard and Massé, and the Poutrincourts. The Marquise subsequently withdrew her financial support of Port Royal.

May 21 After expelling Biard and Massé from Port Royal, Le Coq sailed to Frenchman's Bay in Maine, where he established the mission of St-Saveur, opposite Mount Desert Is.

May 27 Champlain, with Vignau, set out from the Lachine Rapids, travelling up the Ottawa R. At Allumette Is., Aboriginals contradicted Vignau's story that he had seen Hudson's ship. Vignau eventually confessed that he had lied in order to return to New France.

July 2 The English ship *Treasurer,* under the command of Samuel Argall (c 1572–c 1641), was sighted in Frenchman's Bay, Maine. Argall, appointed administrator of Virginia by the Virginia Company, led the 1st English expedition to contest French settlement in Acadia. On July 12, he attacked the mission of St.-Saveur, killing 2. Argall declared the survivors pirates and transported some of them to Virginia.

Aug. Champlain arrived at St. Malo, France, where he published an account of his journey, *Voyages du Sieur de Champlain,* and a map of New France.

Oct. Argall continued his attacks on French Acadia, sailing to Port Royal, where he found its inhabitants working the fields. He plundered and burned the habitation.

Nov. 13 Argall left Port Royal, having laid waste to all the French settlements in Acadia. He claimed the region for England. French Admiral Montmorency demanded the English release all French subjects and pay a cash compensation of 100,000 livres. The Council of Virginia replied by claiming all lands between 34°–45°N latitude.

1614

• The Estates General in Paris decided to establish a permanent missionary presence in New France, and chose 4 Récollet priests to accomplish the task. While in France, Champlain, together with merchants from Rouen and Saint-Malo, formed the Compagnie des Marchands de Rouen et de Saint-Malo. The company agreed to settle 6 families in Canada each year. Champlain also recruited the requisite 4 Récollet priests, including Denis Jamet (d 1625), the 1st Superior of the mission. Récollets arrived in Que. in 1615. One priest travelled to a mission at Tadoussac, another to Huronia.

• An English colony at Conception Bay, Nfld. was established with 60 residents.

• Fort Nassau was established by the United New Netherland Company, at the site of Albany on the Hudson R. to trade with the Mahican, an Algonquian First Nation. The fort was abandoned when the Company's monopoly expired in 1617.

1615

Mar. 15 William Baffin (c 1584–1622) sailed in the *Discovery*, exploring Hudson Str., the western end of Southampton Is., and Foxe Channel, until further travel was blocked by ice. Baffin returned to England in the fall.

Apr. 24 Champlain left Honfleur, arriving at Tadoussac on May 25, where he learned of renewed conflict with the Mohawk.

July 9 Champlain travelled to Huronia, accompanied by 10 Aboriginal allies and Étienne Brûlé, to lend his support to the Huron. The expedition paddled up the Ottawa R. to L. Nipissing, and down the French R. into L. Huron, arriving in Huronia, Aug. 1.

Aug. 3 Brûlé guided Champlain to the village of Carhagonha, about 16 km west of present-day Penetanguishene. There they met Récollet Fr. Joseph Le Caron (c 1586–1632), the 1st missionary to the Huron.

Aug. 12 Le Caron celebrated the 1st mass in Ont. Champlain and his party then left for the village of Cahiagué, (thought to be Warminster), near

L. Simcoe, to plan a campaign against the Onondaga of the Five Nations Iroquois.

Sept. 1 Champlain, 14 Frenchmen and 500 Huron left Cahiagué. Brûlé had gone ahead 2 days earlier to enlist the aid of the Iroquoian-speaking Susquehanna, who lived near present-day Washington, D.C. Champlain travelled down the Trent R. system into the Bay of Quinte, and across L. Ontario. Entering Iroquois country near present-day Stony Point, New York, the French and Huron expedition marched inland on foot toward a palisaded village near present-day Syracuse.

Oct. 10 Onondaga ambushed Champlain and the Huron. The battle lasted 3 hours. The Huron suffered heavy losses and withdrew the next day. Champlain would later publish a depiction of the scene, *The Battle of Onondaga Lake, 1615*.

Dec. 23 The defeated Huron arrived back in Cahiagué.

Also in 1615
• Dutch merchants joined a Mohawk raid against the Susquehannock, lending them military assistance. The merchants were captured by the Susquehannock and ransomed to Cornelis Hendricksen who was exploring the Delaware R. The Dutch were hoping to lure Montagnais and Algonquin traders south, away from the French. The Mohawk set out to control trade with the Dutch.

1616

Jan. 5 Champlain and Father Le Caron visited the Petun, whom Champlain called the Tobacco Nation. The Petun, who lived south of Nottawasage Bay were farming people closely related to the Huron. Historians believe the Petun acted as middle-agents in the fur trade between the Huron and the Ottawa and other Algonquian groups to the west and north.

Mar. 26 Baffin's 5th voyage, once more in the *Discovery*, passed Hope Sanderson on the Greenland coast and continued north for another 480 km. He discovered Ellesmere Is. and mapped Baffin Bay, including Smith, Jones and Lancaster Sounds.

May 22 Champlain left Huronia, arriving in Que. on July 11.

June 15 The 1st European conversion schools for Aboriginals in New France opened at Trois-Rivières and Tadoussac.

June 17 Nfld.'s Avalon Peninsula was purchased by William Vaughn (1575–1641), who founded a Welsh colony at Trepassey Bay.

July 20 Champlain sailed for France, arriving Sept. 10. In 1617, he presented a plan to the French Chamber of Commerce to send 300 families and 300 soldiers to Que., promising the king an annual income of 6 million livres from fish, fur, timber, minerals, grain and leather. Louis XIII and the French businessmen declined to support him.

Also in 1616
• Jesuit Pierre Biard (c 1567–1622) published *Relation de la Nouvelle-France*. Biard had arrived in Acadia in 1611, where he ministered to the Aboriginals, and was eventually taken captive by the English. On his return to France, he was accused of being in partnership with the English. *Relation de la Nouvelle-France* was his response to those accusations.

1617
June 14 Parisians Louis Hébert (c 1575–1627) and wife Marie Rollet (fl 1649) arrived at Tadoussac. They cleared 10 arpents (3.4 ha) of land near present-day Quebec City, planting grain, vegetables, and Normandy apples. Louis also acted as an apothecary, and Marie as a schoolteacher.

1618
Nov. 30 The 1st recorded sighting of a comet by Europeans in Canada.

1619
May 16 Danish sailor Jens Eriksen Munk (1579–1628) set out to find the northwest passage at the request of the king of Denmark.

May 24 Champlain spent the summer in New France, leaving for France, Aug. 28.

Aug. 8 Munk and his crew held a Lutheran church service, at Ice Cove on Hudson Str. Munk was forced to winter in the estuary of the Churchill R. By winter's end, only Munk and 2 of his crew of 64 had survived. Nevertheless, Munk managed to return to Copenhagen by Dec. 25, 1620.

1620
Feb. 25 Henri, Duc de Montmorency, became Viceroy of New France, with Champlain confirmed as his lieutenant.

May 8 Champlain, accompanied for the 1st time by his wife, Marie-Hélène Bouillé, set out on his 10th voyage to New France. He arrived at Que. on July 20, taking possession in the name of Montmorency. Champlain began construction of Fort Saint-Louis at Cap-aux-Diamants, the 1st fort built on the cliff at Que.

June 3 Récollets laid the cornerstone of the 1st stone church in Que., Notre Dame-des-Anges.

Nov. 8 Montmorency, who had bought the Prince de Condé's commercial interests, established the Compagnie de Montmorency pour la Nouvelle-France, which gave a trade monopoly to Guillaume de Caën (fl 1619–1643) and his cousin Émery de Caën (fl 1603–1633).

Also in 1620
• The European population of Que. was 60 persons.

1621
Jan. 3 Montmorency named de Caën head of the fleet of his new company, which gained an 11-year monopoly to trade in the St. Lawrence Valley, in return for maintaining 6 Récollet priests at Que., settling 6 families each year, and not trading arms with Aboriginals.

Sept. 10 King James I of Great Britain, disregarding French claims, granted the region from Cape Gaspé to the St. Croix R. to a friend, Scottish poet William Alexander (c 1577–1640), later the Earl of Stirling. Alexander persuaded James that the Scots needed a New Scotland comparable to New

France and New England. Alexander was made Lord Proprietor of the new territory, to be called Nova Scotia, although he was unable to settle any colonists during the next 6 years.

Also in 1621

• The Iroquois began to obtain firearms from the Dutch.

• Registration of births, deaths and marriages began in Que.

• Étienne Brûlé explored Georgian Bay.

• The Huron First Nation began its domination of trade between the French and groups west of the Lachine Rapids. Each summer, Huron trappers brought canoe-loads of furs east, usually along northern routes and down the Saguenay R. to avoid the Five Nations Iroquois on L. Ontario and the St. Lawrence.

1622

Mar. 20 Louis XIII amalgamated the Compagnie de Montmorency and the older Compagnie des Marchands de Rouen et de Saint-Malo, under the direction of de Caëns. The new entity became known as the Compagnie de Caën.

June William Alexander sent 32 colonists from Scotland to Nova Scotia. They wintered in St. John's, Nfld.

1623

Feb. 4 Montmorency, granted the fief of Sault-au-Matelot to Louis Hébert at Que. It was the 1st seigneury in Canada, and the beginning of New France's seigneurial system.

Apr. 7 George Calvert, 1st Baron Baltimore (c 1580–1632), obtained a royal charter for the "Province of Avalon," in Nfld., which he had acquired from William Vaughn. Calvert had already sent colonists to Ferryland in 1621 and 1622.

June 28 Récollet lay brothers Gabriel Sagard-Theodate and Nicolas Viel (1600–1625) arrived in Que. The 2 journeyed with Fr. Le Caron to the Huron, wintering in the Huron village of

Quieunonascaran. Theodate returned to France and published 2 books detailing his experience: *Le Grand Voyage du Pays des Hurons* in 1632, and *Histoire du Canada* in 1636. Theodate was also instrumental in producing the 1st dictionary of the Wendat language.

Nov. 17 A road was completed to the Upper Town at Que.

1624

May 6 Champlain laid the cornerstone for a new stone Habitation at Que., on the site of the original structure.

Aug. 15 Champlain and wife, Marie-Hélène Bouillé, left Que. for France, arriving at Dieppe, Oct. 1.

Oct. 18 King James I created the order of Knights Baronet of NS. Any man could become a baronet of NS if he lived on his land grant or paid a fee of £150.

Also in 1624

• A Mohawk initiative brought peace between the French, Algonquin, Huron and Mohawk. As a result, the Mohawk attacked the Mahican.

• The Dutch West India Company built Fort Orange near the old Fort Nassau on the Hudson River. The Company hoped to by-pass the Mohawk and trade directly with the Algonquian north of the St. Lawrence.

1625

Jan. Montmorency resigned in favour of his nephew, Henri de Lévis, Duc de Vantadour, who became viceroy. Champlain was again named lieutenant.

Apr. 1 NS was divided into 2 provinces, with counties, bishoprics and baronetcies.

Apr. 26 Jean de Brébeuf (1593–1649), Jesuit priest and founder of the Jesuit's Huron Mission, sailed from Dieppe with Charles Lalemant (1587–1674) and Énemond Massé (1575–1646), and 2 lay brothers, François Charton and Gilbert Burel. They arrived at Que., June 19, the 1st Jesuits to travel up the St. Lawrence R.

• Lalemant was the 1st superior of the Jesuit missions, and inaugurated the series *Relations* in Canada, an annual accounting of the missionary work conducted by the Jesuits. Frustrated by the lack of Que. support for his efforts to evangelize the Aboriginals, Lalemant returned to France to protest. Kirke captured the ship he was on and Lalemant was sent as a prisoner to England. It would be 1632 before Lalemant finally reached New France — after France regained control of Que. Lalemant became a friend and confessor of Champlain, who died in his arms.

June 25 The 1st martyr in Canada was Nicolas Viel, Récollet missionary to the Huron. He was deliberately drowned by the Huron in the Ottawa R. near Montreal. The rapids in which he died were named Sault au Récollet.

Also in 1625
• King Charles I granted NS its coat of arms. The shield featured the Cross of St. Andrew, with colours reversed, to differentiate NS's symbol from the Scottish coat of arms. A unique feature of the NS symbol was placement of the motto at the top, a common Scottish practice.

1626

Mar. 10 The seigneury of Notre-Dame-des-Anges, on the Saint Charles R. close to Que., was the 1st of a series of land grants given to the Jesuits.

Apr. 15 Champlain began his 11th voyage to New France, arriving at Que. on July 5. He completed an outpost at Cap Tourmente.

July Jesuits Brébeuf, Anne de Noue (1587–1646) and Daillon (d 1656) left Que. with Huron allies to re-establish a mission on Georgian Bay at present-day Penetanguishene.

Also in 1626
• Daillon left the Jesuit missionary, and travelled by foot to Neutral territory, where he was adopted by Tsouharrissen, the Grand Chief. Daillon spent 3 months with the Neutral, observing their culture. He also noted that they kept 3 large deer pens. Daillon returned to the Jesuit missionary, when he narrowly escaped death at the hands of the Neutral.

1627
Mar. England and France waged the Anglo–French War, 1627–1628, also known in France as the Third Bearnese Revolt.

Apr. 25 French king Louis XIII instructed Cardinal Armand-Jean de Plessis, Duc de Richelieu (1585–1642), to form the Compagnie des Cents-Associés, after the de Caën charter had been revoked.

Also in 1627
• Scot William Alexander seized Port Royal and its 20 impoverished inhabitants.

1628
Apr. 29 Guillaume Couillard-Lespinay (c 1591–1663), Louis Hébert's son-in-law, was the 1st recorded person in Canada to use a plough.

May 6 The Council of State of France gave the Compagnie des Cent-Associés full ownership of New France, a perpetual fur monopoly and a 15-year trade monopoly in the North American colonies. The company was to nominate a governor to be appointed by the king, and settle 4,000 colonists by 1643. A convoy of 400 settlers and supplies set out immediately for New France.

Also in May Taking advantage of the Anglo-French War, London merchants organized an expedition against Que. Their numbers included the Kirke (Kertk) brothers, Lewis, Thomas, John, James and David. The expedition organized under the command of David Kirke (d 1642) was authorized by Charles I to take possession of Canada.

July 10 The Kirkes captured Tadoussac, Miscou and Cap Tourmente, seized the 1st supply ship of the Compagnie des Cent-Associés as it arrived off Que., and demanded Champlain's surrender. Champlain refused, making a show of strength. The Kirkes withdrew.

July 18 On their return route to England, the Kirkes encountered the French convoy under the command of Claude Roquemont de Brison off Gaspé. The Kirkes captured all 4 ships, settlers and supplies. Claude de Saint-Étienne de La Tour (c 1570–1636) was taken to England as a prisoner.

• By 1628, the Mohawk had dispersed the Mahican living near Fort Orange, successfully blocking Dutch access to the Montagnais and Algonquian.

Also in 1628

• New France had a European population of 76. The settlers spent the winter.

• George Calvert moved his family, 40 settlers and 2 priests to live at Ferryland, a settlement he had started in 1621. Calvert had converted to Catholicism, in 1625, and planned to colonize Nfld. with English Catholics who were subjected to discrimination in England. After spending a winter in the settlement, and squirmishing with French privateers, Calvert moved his family south. He arrived in Jamestown, in Oct. 1629, but was forced to leave because he refused to take an Oath of Allegiance and Supremacy to the Crown. He returned to England, petitioning Charles I for a charter for present-day Maryland. Calvert died and the Charter was issued to his son.

1629

Feb. 4 The rival commercial interests of William Alexander and the Kirkes agreed to combine forces in the Company of Adventurers to Canada, with a monopoly over the St. Lawrence R. trade and authority to expel the French.

Apr. 24 The Treaty of Susa established peace between France and England, in addition to allowing for the restoration of captured land.

June 15 The Kirke brothers' 2nd expedition reached the Gaspé. Their attack fleet consisted of 9 ships.

July 1 James Stewart, 4th Lord Ochiltree (d 1659), who had been granted a barony by William Alexander, landed with 60 colonists at present-day Baleine, Cape Breton Is.

July 19 Lewis and Thomas Kirke captured a French relief ship sent by Champlain. The brothers then obtained Champlain's surrender at Que., because the settlement was close to starvation.

July 24 Champlain departed Que., a prisoner of the Kirkes. On Oct. 25, the English battled a ship commanded by Émery de Caën, who would also surrender.

Aug. 1 At Tadoussac, Champlain reprimanded Brûlé and Nicolas Marsolet de Saint-Aignan (c 1587–1677), who had gone over to the English. The Kirkes took Champlain to England, landing there on Oct. 29, only to discover that the Anglo-French War had ended with the Treaty of Susa, Apr. 24.

Sept. 8 French captain Charles Daniel (d 1661) attacked Lord Ochiltree's Cape Breton settlement, capturing the fort and colonists.

Nov. 30 Claude de La Tour, a prisoner in England since 1628, was enrolled as a baronet of NS, and transferred his allegiance to the English.

Also in 1629

• Approximately 117 persons wintered in Que., 90 of whom belonged to the Kirke party.

1630

Mar. 29 The Treaty of Saint-Germain-en-Laye was signed by England and France. The colonies of Que. and Acadia were returned to France over the next 2 years. Charles I had refused to restore the captured territories as set out in the Treaty of Susa, until this further treaty was made.

May 12 English ally Claude de La Tour enrolled his son, the Frenchman Charles de La Tour (1593–1666), as an English baronet. Charles knew nothing of his father's action until Claude appeared before Cape Sable, NS, where Charles commanded Fort Lomeron. Claude attempted to persuade Charles to surrender the fort to the English and, when this failed, father fought son until Claude and the English withdrew.

Also in 1630

• Champlain estimated that 13,607.8 kg of skins were exported to English merchants. The Huron became dissatisfied with the British and did not come to trade in 1631.

1631

Feb. 8 Louis XIII named Charles de La Tour Gov. and

Lt-Gen. of New France. La Tour later built Fort Sainte-Marie at the mouth of the Saint John R., the richest source of furs in Acadia.

• Charles I granted Cape Breton Is. to Robert Gordon of Lochinvar and his son, Robert.

Apr. 28 Luke Fox, or Foxe (1586–c 1635), set out from London in the *Charles* to find the northwest passage. After skirting the western shore of Hudson Bay, he found relics of Button's expedition of 1612.

July 10 Charles I instructed William Alexander to give Port Royal back to the French and to destroy the fort built by Alexander's son, also named William.

Aug. 29 Fox met Thomas James (c 1593–1635), an English explorer, near Cape Henrietta Maria. Fox sailed into Foxe Channel as far as Cape Dorchester, and determined that Hudson Bay did not offer a passage to the Far East.

Sept. 7 Thomas James explored the bay that now bears his name (James Bay) and wintered off Charlton Is.

1632

Mar. 27 Isaac de Launoy de Razilly (1587–1635) and Cardinal Richelieu agreed that Razilly would assume command of Port Royal.

• Cardinal Richelieu prohibited the return of the Récollets to New France, and turned over all missionary work to Jesuits, who were better organized and more generously financed.

Mar. 29 Emery de Caën was appointed provisional commander of New France for 1 year. He departed Honfleur with 40 men on Apr. 18, arriving in Que., July 5.

May 19 The Compagnie des Cent-Associés named Razilly Lt-Gen. of New France, and granted him a tract of land at Ste-Croix.

Aug. 28 Father Paul Le Jeune (1591–1664), Superior of the Jesuits in Que. from 1632–1639, sent the 1st report of the Jesuit *Relations* to the Provincial of his

order. The *Relations* would become annual accounts of the Order's missionary work and would supply regular descriptions of Aboriginal ways of life. An excellent example of early ethnography, they were sold as books to support missionary work.

Sept. 8 Razilly's expedition of 3 ships and 12 to15 families reached Acadia. Razilly built his settlement at La Hève, present-day Riverport, NS. The Capuchins opened the 1st boarding school in New France, used by both colonists and Aboriginals. Charles de La Tour returned to France after Razilly assumed control of La Hève, Port Royal and the Ste-Croix region. The Scottish settlers were sent home.

Nov. 27 An eclipse of the moon was visible in Que.

Also in 1632
• The long, narrow farms of the St. Lawrence Valley, running back from the St. Lawrence R., were 1st surveyed.

• One of the 1st references to lacrosse appeared in Gabriel Sagard's (fl 1614–1636) *Voyages au pays des Hurons*.

• Champlain's *Les Voyages de la Nouvelle-France* was published in Paris. It included his voyages from 1603 to 1629, and his famous map of 1632, which included all his knowledge of Canadian geography up to that time.

• The Shrine of St. Ann of the Mi'kmaq, the oldest place of Christian pilgrimage in Canada, was first founded on present-day Cape Breton Is. It was transferred to Restigouche, Que., in 1750.

1633

Mar. 1 Champlain was instructed by Richelieu to take command of New France. He arrived in Que., May 22, with Jesuits Brébeuf, Massé, Antoine Daniel (1601–1648), and Ambroise Davost (1586–1643).

May 14 Olivier Le Jeune (d 1654), a slave belonging to Guillaume Couillard de Lespinay (d 1663), was baptized at Que. He had been brought to Que. in 1628 from Madagascar by one of the Kirke brothers. His official status of "domestic servant" had been changed to "freeman" by the time of his death, May 10, 1654. Contrary to popular belief, Le Jeune was not the 1st black person to have lived in Canada. That honour belonged to Matthew Da Costa, the linguist and navigator who helped build Port Royal in 1606.

June Étienne Brûlé was killed and eaten by the Huron, probably near Penetanguishene, Ont.

Also in 1633

• To celebrate the return of Que. to France, the 1st parish church of New France, Notre-Dame-de-la-Recouvrance, was built by Champlain at Cap Diamant.

• Charles I established the infamous system of government by "Fishing Admirals." The title of governor was given to the captain of the 1st fishing vessel to reach Nfld. each year. The captain of the 2nd ship became vice-admiral, the 3rd became rear-admiral, and so on.

1634

Jan. 15 Robert Giffard de Moncel (1587–1668), master surgeon, received one of the 1st seigneuries from the Company of New France, at Beauport.

July 4 Trois-Rivières was founded by Laviolette (fl 1634–1636), a fur trader, and companion of Champlain.

Also in July

• Jean Nicollet de Belleborne (c 1598– 1642), interpreter and clerk of the Compagnie des Cent-Associés, travelled to Green Bay, on L. Mich-igan, to pacify the Puant and the Ounipigon, or Winnebago, and to investigate a rumoured route to the Pacific Ocean. His mission to achieve peace was a success. He also became the 1st European to explore the American West.

Aug. Champlain had the ruins of Que. rebuilt, enlarging its fortifications. He also built a fort at the mouth of the St-Maurice R.

Oct. 20 Brébeuf visited the Petun Nation, baptizing 3 dying children.

Also in 1634

• Brébeuf and 2 other Jesuits, Frs. Daniel and Davost, took over the Récollet mission to the Huron, establishing a permanent mission. The Aboriginals called them Black Robes. Disease brought by the Black Robes decimated the Huron population, as approximately 15,000 people died.

1635

Jan. 15 Charles de La Tour was granted land at the mouth of the St. John R., NB, where he built a trading post called Fort La Tour.

Apr. 22 William Alexander, now Earl of Stirling, was given new grants of land in Canada by Charles I.

May The French became involved in the Thirty Years War, declaring war on Spain and eventually taking control of Alsace and much of the Rhineland.

July 10 The 1st Huron canoes of the season arrived at Que. Champlain stated that French help depended on the safety of the priests and the adoption of Christianity. He encouraged the Huron to inter-marry with the French and learn to make the articles they were currently trading for from the French.

Dec. 25 Samuel de Champlain, "the Father of New France," who was stricken with a paralytic stroke in Oct., died in Que. on Christmas Day. His body is believed to be buried somewhere in the neighbourhood of present-day Château Frontenac. Champlain had crossed the Atlantic 22 times.

• Marc-Antoine Bras-de-fer de Chateaufort assumed the command of New France from Dec. 25 to June 11, 1636.

Also in 1635

• The population of Que. consisted of 150 settlers.

• The Jesuits' Petit École (elementary school) at Que. opened, giving instruction in French, Huron and Montagnais to 20 boys. Latin was added in 1636 and a senior school was opened in 1655.

• Jean Thomas, an illegal fur trader, incited a revolt by French and First Nations peoples allied at Fort Saint-François at Canso, NS. Lt-Gen. Razilly quelled the revolt and took Thomas prisoner.

1636

Jan. 15 Charles Huault de Montmagny (c 1583–1653), soldier and Knight of Malta, was appointed 1st titular gov. of New France before Champlain's death was known in France. Montmagny assumed office in Que. on June 11, serving until Aug. 19, 1648.

Mar. The Allumette requested the Huron, Algonquian and Nippissing who had all wintered together, to join in a retaliatory war against raiding Iroquois. The Allumette were turned down.

Also in 1636
• A resident of Que. was pilloried in the marketplace for the crime of blasphemy.

• Montmagny ordered the Château Saint-Louis at Que. rebuilt in brick and stone, and instructed engineer Jean Bourdon (c 1601–1668) to draw a plan for the town.

• Brébeuf witnessed a Feast of the Dead in Huronia, thought to be Ossossanë Ossuray, near his mission and the village of the same name (Mission of La Rochelle). The ceremony was held every 10 to 12 years.

1637

Jan. 16 The Compagnie des Cent-Associés received a grant to establish a nunnery, a Jesuit church and a seminary at Que.

May Pierre Pijart (1608–1676), a Jesuit priest, established the Mission of the Immaculate Conception at Ossossanë, the largest Huron village, near present-day Elmvale, Ont.

July The Jesuits founded a settlement of baptized Montagnais at Sillery, near Que.

Aug. 4 The Huron held a council to inquire into the cause of European-based diseases, such as smallpox and measles, which were ravaging the population. The deaths were blamed on Black Robe sorcery.

Aug. 16 The Duchesse d'Aiguillon, Cardinal Richelieu's niece, donated 22,400 livres to establish the Hôtel-Dieu at Que., the 1st hospital in North America north of Mexico.

Nov. 13 David Kirke was appointed co-proprietor of Nfld. with the Marquis of Hamilton and the Earls of Pembroke and Holland. The prior right of the late George Calvert was revoked. As gov., Kirke brought out 100 colonists and built forts at Ferryland, St. John's, and Bay de Verde. He later came into conflict with the Western Adventurers, who wanted to retain control of the Grand Banks fisheries by prohibiting settlement of the island.

Also in 1637
• King Charles I granted a coat of arms to Nfld. The symbol's design commemorated Cabot's discovery of the island.

1638

Feb. 10 Louis XIII made Charles de Menou d'Aulnay (c 1604–1650), a cousin of Razilly, Lt-Gen. of Acadia, with authority over Port Royal and La Hève and the command of Pentagouet, a trading post on the Penobscot R. La Tour was granted the rest of NS, and the command of Cap de Sable and Fort La Tour on the St. John R. This arrangement created ill feeling and hostility between the 2 men.

June 11 The 1st earthquake recorded by Europeans in Canada was felt near Trois-Rivières, and described in the *Jesuit Relations*.

June 25 Fr. Jérôme Lalemant (1593–1673) arrived in Que. Lalemant replaced Brébeuf as Superior of the Mission to the Huron. He arrived in Ihonatiria, Aug. 26. Brébeuf and several Jesuit Fathers moved to Teanaustaye. Lalemant implemented a policy of building a centralized mission house and bringing donnés (lay assistants) to Huronia.

Dec. 31 A lunar eclipse in Huron country caused panic among the inhabitants, who blamed the Jesuits.

Also in 1638
• David Kirke applied a 5% tax on fish taken from Nfld. in foreign ships.

1639

May 4 The *St. Joseph* sailed from Dieppe. On board were 3 Jesuits: Joseph Antoine Poncet de La Rivière (1610–1675), Pierre-Joseph-Marie Chaumonot (1611–1693) and Barthélemy Vimont (1594–1667), new Superior of the Jesuits in Canada. Also aboard were Marie-Madeleine de Chauvigny de La Peltrie (1603–1671): 3 Ursuline nuns, Marie Guyart, known as Marie de l'Incarnation (1599–1672), Marie de Savonnières de La Troche, Marie de Saint-Joseph (1616–1652) and Mother Cécile de Sainte Croix; and 3 Hospitallers, Mother Marie Guenet, Marie de Saint-Ignace (1610–1646); Anne le Cointre, Anne de Saint-Bernard; and Marie Forestier, Marie de Saint-Bonaventure (1615–1698).

Aug. 1 Soon after arriving at Que., Marie de La Peltrie and Marie de l'Incarnation founded the Ursuline convent.

Nov. 1 Jesuit Frs. Charles Arnier and Isaac Jogues attempted to visit Petun villages. The Petun were hostile, fearing further outbreaks of illness. The Jesuit priests were refused entry.

1639–1640 Lalemant founded Sainte-Marie-des-Hurons, near present-day Midland, Ont. It was the 1st important French outpost west of Que. The mission served 32 villages. Shortly thereafter, Charles Boivin, master builder, arrived with 14 workmen. By 1641, there were 20 workmen, donnés and lay brothers providing support.

• The Jesuits established the Mission of the Apostles to the Petun. Villages from south to north were named after 9 apostles.

Also in 1639

• Lalemant directed a census of the Huron Nation, noting the population had decreased almost 20,000 from Champlain's time: disease and famine were identified as the main causes, along with war.

• The Dutch West India Co. lost its monopoly on trade at Fort Orange on the site of present-day Albany, New York. Unauthorized Dutch and English traders freely sold muskets to the Mohawk.

• The epidemic of European-based diseases (1st noted in 1637), including measles and smallpox,

continued unabated, killing approximately half the Huron, Petun and Neutral populations. Huron Councils considered removing Jesuits from their territory.

• A Huron-Algonquian war party of 300 defeated the Oneida.

• The Oneronon (Wendat) took refuge with the Huron, an occurrence supported by the sudden appearance of Genoa frilled ceramics on sites near Ossossané.

• Coal was 1st mined in Canada (and possibly the 1st time in North America) at Grand L., near the Bay of Fundy (NB). The coal was shipped to Boston.

During the 1630s
• Onondaga raids into Huronia and Mohawk raids on the St. Lawrence from Trois-Rivières to the Ottawa R. continued. Nonetheless, the fur trade grew unabated.

1640

Aug. 7 Montreal Is. was purchased from the Compagnie des Cents-Associés by Jérôme Le Rouer, Sieur de La Dauversière, and Pierre Chevrier, Baron de Fancamp, who, with Fr. Jean-Jacques Olier, organized the Société-de-Notre-Dame de Montréal. The mission would provide a hospital, convent, seminary and fort for a proposed settlement, to be called Ville-Marie de Montréal.

Dec. 17 The Compagnie des Cents-Associés agreed to grant Montreal Is. to the Société-de-Notre-Dame, except for the mountain and an area to the southwest.

1640–1641 Frs. Garnier and Pijart travelled to the Petun for a 2nd winter. The Petun chiefs wanted them to leave, but there was less resistance from the villages. The Jesuits attempted to have a council with Petun chiefs but were unsuccessful. This was the last major attempt to conduct a mission in the area.

• The Allumette's power was weakened because of disease, Iroquois raids and the increased presence of the French. The Nipissing altered their trading patterns, to focus on the north, and only returned to Huronia in the winter.

Also in 1640

• An unofficial census of New France recorded 375 Europeans. The residential population was estimated at 240.

• Que. recorded 3 marriages, 21 births and 2 deaths during the year.

• Hostilities increased between the Five Nations Iroquois and the French, Algonquin and Huron.

• Gov. Montmagny punished Huron coming to Que. for violence against Jesuits, with fines and denial of right to trade.

1641

Feb. 13 As a result of pressure from Menou d'Aulnay, Lt-Gen. of Acadia, La Tour was asked to return to France. La Tour disobeyed and remained in Acadia. His commission was revoked 10 days later.

Also in Feb.

• Frs. Brébeuf and Chaumonot returned to Ste-Marie-des-Hurons from a visit to the Neutral, living between L. Ontario and L. Erie. The priests recorded the 1st European description of L. Erie.

May 9 Two ships bearing settlers for the new village of Montreal left France, including Jeanne Mance (1606–1673) and Paul de Chomedey de Maisonneuve (1612–1676), the new gov. of Montreal. Mance arrived in Que. Aug. 8; Maisonneuve, probably Sept. 20. It was too late in the season to continue to Montreal.

Oct. 14 Gov. Montmagny took formal possession of Montreal Is. for Maisonneuve.

c 1641 Brébeuf wrote the *Huron Carol* in the Huron language, to explain the birth of Jesus Christ. The song was translated into French sometime in the mid-1700s. In 1926, poet Jesse Edgar Middleton translated the song into English from the French version. It would be included in the Methodist Hymnal in 1971.

Also in 1641

• The residential European population of New France was 310.

• The Mohawk formally declared war against the French and attacked Trois-Rivières. Gov. Montmagny permitted the sale of muskets to baptized Aboriginal allies for the 1st time.

1642

Feb. 21 D'Aulnay was ordered by the govt of France to arrest Charles de La Tour for insubordination and perfidious conduct.

May 17 Maisonneuve, Jeanne Mance, Mme. de La Peltrie and the other colonists landed at Montreal Is. and founded the religious colony of Ville Marie to "bring about the glory of God and the salvation of the Indians."

Aug. 2 Jesuits Isaac Jogues (1607–1646), Guillaume Couture (d 1701) and René Goupil (1608–1642), travelling from Ste-Marie to Que., were captured by Iroquois near Trois-Rivières. Jogues, despite torture and mutilation, escaped and returned to France in Dec. 1643. He reported that the Mohawk goal was to unite the Iroquois into "one people and only one land," in efforts to thwart the ongoing European invasion.

Aug. 13 Montmagny, with 100 men, built Fort Richelieu at the mouth of the Richelieu R. to protect against the Iroquois.

Sept. 29 The Iroquois killed Jesuit captive René Goupil. Ehawae, a Petun village of 1,000 people near present-day Collingwood, was abandoned after a raid, likely by the Five Nations Iroquois.

Also in 1642

• The Ursuline convent was completed in Que. The Ursulines also opened a boarding and day school for young girls.

• Following the death of Cardinal Richelieu, Jules Cardinal Mazarin (1602–1661) became chief minister of France.

• War between the Esopus of the Hudson River and the Dutch led to the 1st formal treaty between the

Dutch and the Mohawk. Despite the treaty, the Mohawk complained the Dutch did little to defend them.

• The Dutch prohibited the sale of arms to the Mohawk, who responded by offering to make peace with the French in return for French muskets. The French refused.

• French settlers in Que. produced enough wheat, rye, barley, peas and other grain supplies to last 5 to 6 months.

• A hospice and chapel were built at Ste-Marie to accommodate visiting the Huron. The Jesuits baptised Atironta, a member of the Huron Arendahronon, who was in good health. Christmas was celebrated at Ste-Marie.

• Lalemant stated in his Register that the mission to the Petun could not be fully sustained, although, he noted, Frs. Garnier and Pijart continued to visit when possible.

1643

Jan. 6 Maisonneuve erected a wood cross on the top of Mont Royal. The colony had experienced severe flooding on Dec. 25, 1642. Maisonneuve made a vow to the Virgin Mary in writing and had it read publicly, that if the waters subsided, and no serious damage occurred, he would carry a wood cross through the brush to the top of the hill, which he did. In 1924, a 31.4-m-high illuminated cross was installed, and in 1992, the cross was converted to fibre-optic illumination. (Although Mont Royal cross has always been illuminated in white light, the system is capable of changing the colour to red, blue or purple — the latter being the colour used upon the death of a pope.)

Apr. Étienne de Mourron, commander of the warship *St. Clement*, left La Rochelle with 140 passengers heading for Port Royal. On reaching the Bay of Fundy, Mourron recognized enemy ships under d'Aulnay's command, and returned to the high seas. Under cover of darkness, Mourron sent 7 men to the fort, returning to the ship several nights later with La Tour. The ship then sailed for Boston.

Summer La Tour hired 4 ships to return with him to retake command of Fort La Tour, which they did in Aug. D'Aulnay returned to France and presented a memorandum to the court outlining La Tour's crimes for the past 20 years. La Tour was ordered by the king's council to appear and face charges. Madame La Tour sent an urgent warning to her husband, advising that they had been defeated in the courts.

Also in 1643
• Montreal expanded from 50 settlers to 70.

• Que. registered 1 marriage, 15 births and 5 deaths.

• Merchant ships entering the St. Lawrence R. had to carry a blue flag with a white cross, the former flag of the French Nation and the flag that Champlain used in 1603 when he first landed.

• The Iroquois captured 11 Huron canoes delivering letters and goods from Huronia. Fr. Issac Jogues was taken captive and almost all Huron cargo was lost, including a copy of the *Jesuit Relations* for 1641–1642.

• Christian Huron trading on the St. Lawrence R. were given better terms and treatment than non-Christian Aboriginals. This was particularly noticeable during times of famine, when Christian Aboriginals were given food, and non-Christian Aboriginals were not.

• By 1644 the Mohawk, estimated to have 400 muskets, successfully shut down the fur trade on the St. Lawrence.

1644

Mar. 30 Maisonneuve and 30 settlers defeated a large band of Iroquois intent on attacking Montreal.

Apr. 29 François-Joseph Bressani (1612–1672) was captured by Iroquois near Fort Richelieu. He survived torture and returned to France Nov. 15.

Sept. 23 The cornerstone of the church of Notre-Dame-de-la-Paix was laid at Que. by Fr. Lalemant and Gov. Montmagny.

Also in Sept. La Tour's wife, Françoise-Marie Jacquelin (1602–1645), escaped capture by d'Aulnay near Cape Sable. La Tour was in Boston requesting assistance to regain his former domain. The Boston council wrote a letter to d'Aulnay rehashing old grievances and claiming they had not participated in the raid on Port Royal. They enclosed an order forbidding attacks on French and Dutch settlements. La Tour could continue trade with Boston, but would not receive the help requested to continue battle with d'Aulnay.

Oct. 8 Hôtel Dieu at Montreal was opened by Jeanne Mance.

Also in 1644
• Fr. François Gendron wrote that there were 18 to 20 priests in Huronia.

• Frs. Brébeuf, Garneau and Chabanal, accompanied by 22 French soliders, arrived in Huronia.

1645
Mar. 6 The bankrupt Compagnie des Cent-Associés agreed to assign its fur trade monopoly to the Communauté des Habitants, which included all the inhabitants of New France, although members of the Compagnie retained their seigniorial rights.

Apr. After years of blockades and sporadic fighting, d'Aulnay attacked Charles de La Tour's stronghold of Fort Sainte-Marie, at St. John, NB, while La Tour was in Boston seeking help. La Tour's wife and his men held the fort for 3 days, but were forced to surrender, Apr. 13. Most of the survivors were hanged. Mme La Tour died soon afterward. D'Aulnay became undisputed master of Acadia. La Tour travelled to Que. in 1646, where he became a fur trader.

July 14 Peace was arranged between the Mohawk, led by Chief Kiotseaeton, and the French and their allies. The ceasefire was known as Montmagny's Peace. French protests forced the Dutch to ban the sale of muskets to the Mohawk. The fur trade revived in 1646.

Fall French soldiers returned to Trois-Rivières from Huronia with 60 Huron and canoes loaded with 181 kg of beaver pelts worth 30-40,000 francs. They had engaged in skirmishes with the Iroquois throughout the journey, capturing 2 prisoners.

Oct. 29 Total trade for the year, of 9,072 kg of beaver skins, was loaded in 5 vessels, and left New France for France.

Nov. Firewood was sold on the streets of Que. for the 1st time.

Also in 1645
• The European population of New France was 600 residents and approximately 200 indentured servants.

• Lalemant recorded that the Huron were considering cancelling their trade with the French because of the high cost of the ongoing war with the Iroquois.

1646
May 16 Fr. Jogues, acting as ambassador to the Iroquois, left Trois-Rivières on a successful peace mission to the Mohawk.

Aug. 16 The 1st of 80 canoes and 300 men arrived at Trois-Rivières with a large amount of furs for trade. Commerce was much better than in 1645, and some Huron returned home with their furs because there were not enough goods available to trade.

Sept. 24 Fr. Jogues and fellow Jesuit, Jean de La Lande, set out on another peace mission. Abandoned by their Huron guard at Fort Richelieu, the Jesuits were taken prisoner by the Iroquois, who blamed them for an outbreak of smallpox and famine.

Oct. 18 Fr. Jogues was executed by the Iroquois, who believed he was a sorcerer. Fr. La Lande was executed the next day. Montmagny's Peace was shattered.

1646–1650 Jérôme Lalemant authored the *Jesuit Relations*.

Also in 1646
• Jesuits presented the 1st play in Que., *Le Cid*, by Corneille.

• A religious procession consisting of various occupations filed through Que. Placement in the procession represented social standing. The clergy was 1st, followed in order by carpenters, masons, sailors, toolmakers, brewers and bakers.

1647

Feb. Acadia was granted to Menou d'Aulnay as a hereditary fief.

Mar. 27 The *Conseil de Québec* was created by royal decree. It comprised the Gov. of New France, the Jesuit Superior, and the Gov. of Montreal, and is considered by many to be Canada's 1st political constitution.

Apr. 13 A Huron delegation left to meet with the Susquehannock to discuss forming an alliance against the Mohawk. The Susquehannock were to make peace with 4 western First Nations and to attack the Mohawk if the Mohawk refused to join them. The Huron delegation returned Oct. 5, but could not agree among themselves to carry out the agreement.

June 12 The cornerstone of the Jesuit College at Que. was laid.

June 20 The 1st horses arrived at Que. from France.

July 8 A Native woman, Charite, was buried in a Que. cemetery next to her father, indicating that she was Métis.

July 16 Fr. Jean de Quen (c 1603–1659), founder of the Saguenay missions, was the 1st to discover Lac Saint-Jean and the route leading into the interior of the Saguenay.

Also in 1647
• The remaining Algonquian on the Ottawa were dispersed by the Mohawk.

• The Huron were unable to come to Que. to trade.

• An influenza epidemic killed many Aboriginals, English, French and Dutch settlers.

• The Jesuits distributed food to Huron refugees, but supply canoes were unable to reach Huronia because of the ongoing conflict with the Iroquois and Mohawk.

1648

Mar. 2 Louis d'Ailleboust de Coulonge et d'Argentenay (c 1612–1660) was appointed gov. of New France, serving from Aug. 20 to Oct. 20, 1651.

Apr. A Huron council sent 2 warriors to Ste-Marie with instructions to murder the 1st Frenchman they met. Jacques Douart, a worker at the mission, was killed. The Jesuits accepted a large payment in reparation.

July 4 When the Huron travelled to Que. to trade, the Iroquois broke a peace agreement and attacked Huron villages Saint-Joseph II and Saint-Michel (near present-day Hillsdale, Ont.). Fr. Antoine Daniel was killed and 700 captives were taken. The Iroquois invited non-Christian Huron to join them. It became clear to all that the French and Jesuits could not protect Huronia.

July 17 The 1st temperance gathering in North America took place at Que.

July 22 A Huron fleet of 60 canoes with 5 chiefs and 250 men arrived at Trois-Rivières as a united group. They had defeated an Iroquois war party en route. Total trade for all of New France during the year was 10,160.5 kg of furs.

Aug. 6 The Huron left Trois-Rivières accompanied by 26 Frenchmen, a heifer and a small cannon. The cannon now resides at Penetanguishine Military Establishment.

Sept. 19 Que.'s 1st tavern was opened by Jacques Boisdon.

Nov. 24 The 1st child born of European parents in Montreal was Barbe Meusnier.

Winter 1648–1649 The Huron planted no crops during the spring and summer because of ongoing hostilities. The result was famine.

1648–1650 Paul Ragueneau authored the *Huron Relations*, included in the *Jesuit Relations*.

Also in 1648
• The Dutch sold 400 muskets to the Mohawk on the understanding they would be used against French allies.

1649

Jan. 19 The 1st executioner in Canada, a pardoned criminal, performed his 1st assignment at Que., a 16-year-old girl found guilty of theft.

Mar. 16 More than 1,000 Iroquois armed with muskets attacked the Huron missions of Saint Ignace and Saint-Louis, where Brébeuf and Lalemant carried on their work. The Huron village of Ossassanë was destroyed Mar. 19. Brébeuf was tortured and killed.

Mar. 20 Brébeuf's bones were found and taken to Christian Is. and then to Que. His head was preserved in a silver urn at the Hôtel Dieu.

June 14 The Jesuits abandoned Sainte-Marie-des-Hurons and retreated with several hundred Huron to Île Saint-Joseph (Christian Is.) in Georgian Bay.

July 20 A few Huron arrived in Que. with the news that Huronia had ceased to exist.

Also in July Mme. Tessier of Montreal gave birth to the 1st twins in Canada. They died within 5 days.

Sept. 22 Fr. Bressani and a group of Huron and soldiers arrived at Trois-Rivières from Huronia.

Fall De Fosses, a French soldier, and his brother returned to Que. with 747 "litres" of beaver. They had spent 1 year among the Huron.

1650

June 10 The Jesuits abandoned Île Saint-Joseph, their last mission in Huronia. About 300 Huron fled with the Jesuits back to Que. A thousand Petun, Huron and Neutral refugees moved west, eventually becoming the present-day Wyandot of Kansas and Oklahoma.

Sept. 1 Fr. Gabriel Druillettes (1610–1681) left Que. for Boston as the gov.'s ambassador, to establish an alliance with New England against the Iroquois. He was the 1st official envoy from Canada. Another mission followed in 1651. Both were unsuccessful.

Dec. 30 The Ursuline convent at Que. was destroyed by fire.

Also in 1650
• The population of New France was 705.

1651

Jan. 17 Jean de Lauson (c 1584–1666) was appointed gov. of New France, serving from Oct 14,1651 to Sept.12, 1657.

Feb. 25 Charles de la Tour became Gov. of Acadia. La Tour's old rival, Menou d'Aulnay, had drowned in 1650.

1652

May 10 The Iroquois executed Fr. Jacques Buteux (1599–1652) north of Trois-Rivières.

Also in May
• A new Ursuline convent opened in Que.

Aug. 19 Guillaume Guillemot Duplessis-Kerbodot, gov. of Trois-Rivières, was ambushed by the Iroquois and killed, along with 22 Frenchmen.

Also in 1652
• Fur trade along the St. Lawrence declined drastically. Southern Ont. was almost deserted.

• New France comprised 6 major settlement areas: Tadoussac, located 480 km up the St. Lawrence R.; Que., some 195 km upriver from Tadoussac; Sillery, a few km southwest of Que.; Trois-Rivières, 145 km upriver from Sillery; Fort Richelieu, at the mouth of the Richelieu R.; and Montreal, 290 km upriver from Que.

1653

June 26 The Onondaga sent 18 chiefs to Montreal as a preliminary to peace negotiations.

Sept. 22 Marguerite Bourgeoys (1620–1700), founder of La Congrégation de Notre-Dame de Montréal, the 1st religious community to be founded in Canada, landed at Que. She opened a school. As there was only one school-age child in the community, she also cared for the sick and poor.

Nov. 3 The Iroquois Nation made a general peace with the French at Trois-Rivières, although the

Mohawk, Oneida and Onondaga continued to fight.

Dec. 3 Nicolas Denys (1598–1688) purchased the rights to the islands of the Gulf of St. Lawrence (from Cap Canso to Cap des Rosiers on the Gaspé) from the Company of New France.

Also in 1653
• Population of New France was about 2,000.

1654

Jan. 30 Denys was made gov. and lt-gov. of territories in the Gulf of St. Lawrence. He made his headquarters at Saint-Pierre on Cape Breton Is., present-day St. Peters, NS.

July 2 Fr. Simon Le Moyne (1604–1665), missionary to the Huron, journeyed to Iroquois country, promising to send missionaries the next year.

July 4 Robert Sedgwick (1611–1656), commander-in-chief of the New England coast, left Boston to retaliate for French attacks on English vessels. Attacking Acadia, he forced La Tour to surrender Fort Sainte-Marie on July 17; captured Port Royal on Aug. 16; and then Fort Pentagouet, on the Penobscot R., on Sept. 2. Sedgwick left for England later in the fall, with La Tour in captivity.

Aug. 6 One hundred and twenty Ottawa, Huron and Petun came to Que., re-igniting the fur trade. They returned west with Pierre Esprit Radisson (1640–1710) and his brother-in-law, Médart Chouart, Sieur des Groseilliers (1618-c 1696). It was the explorers' 1st westward journey. Their party is believed to have wintered at Green Bay, L. Michigan, and to have explored the Fox R. from May 1655 to June 1656.

Sept. 19 Marguerite Sedilot, the youngest bride in Canadian records (11 years, 5 months), married Jean Aubuchon of Trois-Rivières.

Also in 1654
• Gov. Lausson decreed that all coureurs de bois were required to obtain a licence before leaving settlements to hunt for furs. So many young men were engaged in the fur trade that few were left to defend the colony.

• Pierre Boucher (c 1627–1717) was appointed gov. of Trois-Rivières.

1655

Sept. 19 Frs. Chaumonot and Claude Dablon (1619–1697) left Que. to establish a mission in Onondaga territory.

Nov. 3 Acadia was restored to the French with the signing of the Treaty of Westminster between England and France.

1656

May 17 Zacharie Dupuy (c 1608–1676), commandant of Que., left Que. with a group of Frenchmen to establish a settlement among the Onondaga at Sainte-Marie-de-Gannantaha. On July 17, they began construction of a fortified mission, trading post and garrison on the site of Syracuse, New York. The settlement was abandoned in Mar. 1658.

Sept. 20 Thomas Temple (c 1614–1674) and William Crowne (1617–1682) acquired La Tour's rights to Acadia, in return for 5% of its products.

Also in 1656
• The Mohawk, Oneida and Onondaga put pressure on the French to force Huron refugees at Que. to join them. Most of the 400 Huron forced to leave Que. were killed by rival Iroquois bands. The remaining Huron became the Lorette Huron.

• Groseilliers and Radisson arrived back in Que. with furs, 50 canoes and 500 Aboriginals. They lobbied to open up the western Great Lakes to missions and to trading, thereby securing French control over the interior. French authorities rejected the idea.

1657

Jan. 26 Pierre de Voyer d'Argenson (1625–1709) was appointed Gov. of New France, serving from July 11, 1658 to Aug. 30, 1661.

Mar. 7 Louis XIV prohibited the sale of liquor to Aboriginals in New France.

May 17 Frs. Gabriel Thubières de Levy de Queylus (1612–1677), Vicar-Gen. of New France, Gabriel

Souart (1611–1691), Dominique Galinier and Antoine d'Allet (c 1634–1693) set sail from France, arriving in Que. July 29. They had been sent by the Société des Prêtres de Sainte-Sulpice to found a seminary in Montreal.

Sept. 12 Temple and Crowne agreed to divide Acadia. Temple received lands from Lunenburg, NS, to the St. George R., Maine.

Sept. 13 Louis d'Ailleboust de Coulonge (1612–1660) was appointed administrator of New France, serving from Sept. 13 to July 10, 1658.

Dec. 10 Emmanuel Le Borgne (1610–1675) was appointed Gov. of Acadia, although the territory was still occupied by the English.

1658

Feb. The Mohawk held a secret council and decided to renew hostilities with the French.

Mar. 13 Gov. d'Ailleboust and Abbé Vignal laid the corner stone of the Church of the Petit Cap, present-day Sainte-Anne-de-Beaupré. That day, Beaupré resident Louis Guimont was healed of rheumatism. The church has since become a famous place of healing and the oldest pilgrimage site in NA.

Mar. 20 Priests and workmen escaped from Sainte-Marie de Gannentaha in 2 flat-bottomed boats, secretly built in the attic of their fort, when they discovered an Iroquois plot to kill all Frenchmen and their allies. Young Pierre Radisson played a significant part in the escape. The escapees arrived safely at Que. on Apr. 13.

Mar. 24 Gov. d'Ailleboust received a delegation of Iroquois and admonished them severely for the attack at Gannentaha. The delegation then returned home with an invitation for their chiefs to renew peace talks with the French.

June 1 Radisson and Groseilliers began their 2nd expedition to the west. They explored L. Superior and visited with the Sioux.

June 11 Gov. d'Ailleboust turned over a small fort to the Huron and Algonquin, so they could take

refuge from the Iroquois under the protection of guns at Château Saint-Louis.

June 12 A band of Iroquois attacked Que.

Aug. 10 The newly renovated, 10–bed Hôtel-Dieu was completed in Quebec City.

Sept. 19 Fr. Chaumonot was recalled to Montreal by Gov. d'Argenson to conduct negotiations with the Onondaga.

Sept. 29 Marguerite Bourgeoys and Jeanne Mance left Montreal for France to recruit young girls for teaching positions in New France.

Also in 1658
- Father Le Moyne persuaded Onondaga chief Garakontie (d 1667/8) to return 2 French captives to Montreal.

- Louis XIV ruled that no inhabitant of New France could leave the colony without the Gov.'s permission.

1659

Mar. 27 In accordance with a papal appointment, June 3, 1653, Louis XIV ordered that François de Laval (1623–1708) be recognized as the 1st bishop of New France.

May 7–July 3 Fr. Le Moyne again travelled to Mohawk country as a peace ambassador.

May 13 The Company of New France in Paris convinced the Royal Council to pass a decree limiting the powers of Gov. d'Argenson, so the Company could assume greater political control over the colony.

June 16 Bishop Laval returned to Que., accompanied by 3 priests, including Fr. Jérôme Lalemant, who had spent the last 9 years in France. Lalemant resumed his position as superior of the Jesuit missions. Laval became a member of the Conseil de Québec.

July 22 Mohawk chief Teharahogen returned 8 Frenchmen, taken captive in an attack on Trois-Rivières, to d'Argenson, who in turn freed

3 Mohawk captives. D'Argenson invited the chief to a general peace and invited his people to settle among the French.

Aug.1659–Aug. 20, 1660 Groseilliers and Radisson made an expedition to the Great Lakes. They spent the winter with Huron and Ottawa refugees and became acquainted with the nearby Sioux.

Sept. 7 Marguerite Bourgeoys and Jeanne Mance arrived back in Montreal with 62 men and 47 women settlers. They established the congregation of Notre-Dame.

Oct. 18 Gov. d'Argenson decided to privatize the fur trade because the Communauteé des Habitants and the Conseil were unable to defray associated administrative costs.

Also in 1659
• The 1st organ was imported to Canada by Bishop Laval. Charles-Amador Martin (1648–1711) was the 1st organist.

1660

Feb. 3 In France, Toussaint Guenet and a group of Rouen merchants concluded an agreement, placing the beaver trade and the colonial import business under their exclusive control for 4 years. In return, the Communauteé des Habitants received an annual payment of 10,000 livres. The Communauteé des Habitants agreed to the privatization of the fur trade and colonial import business. The Conseil Royal ratified the decision.

Mar. 13 Henri de Bernières (d 1700) became the 1st priest ordained in Canada.

Apr. 15 Adam Dollard Des Ormeaux (1635–1660) borrowed money from Jean Aubuchon to arm an expedition of 16 Frenchmen to attack the Iroquois and abscond with their beaver furs. The group left Montreal for Long Sault, Apr. 19.

May 1 Dollard and his men arrived at Long Sault by canoe and took up positions in an abandoned fort previously built by the Algonquin. Dollard's force was joined by 40 Huron and 4 Algonquin.

May 2 Dollard and his men killed 13 Onondaga scouts, but 2 escaped to warn the main Onondaga force of the impending ambush.

May 3 Over 200 Iroquois attacked Dollard at Long Sault. The Iroquois were on their way to Richelieu Is. to rendezvous with the Mohawk and Oneida and to attack the French settlement there. 500 Mohawk and Oneida joined the Iroquois the next week. Dollard and his entire command were killed, as was Étienne Annaotaha, a Huron chief. The battle-scarred Iroquois, no longer in a position to mount a major attack on Ville-Marie returned to their homes.

May 5 Bishop Laval announced that he would excommunicate all New France residents who sold liquor to Aboriginals.

May 15 Que. authorities learned from an Iroquois prisoner, just before his death by torture, that an Iroquois army of 900 had launched a campaign against the French near Montreal.

May 19 Gov. d'Argenson ordered all nuns to vacate their convent every evening and to sleep behind the protective walls of the Jesuit college in case the Iroquois attacked.

May 31 Louis d'Ailleboust, former administrator of New France, died at Ville-Marie, at age 48.

June 5 Eight Huron, who had joined the Iroquois, kidnapped a woman and her 4 children from Ste. Anne du Petit-Cap. D'Argenson, commanding a group of Frenchmen and Montagnais, overtook the kidnappers and freed the captives. Three kidnappers were drowned and 5 captured, 3 of whom were burned at the stake.

Summer D'Argenson imprisoned 15 Iroquois who had come to parley.

July 21 The population of New France was 3,418.

Aug. 19 Radisson and Groseilliers reached Montreal with 200 Ottawa, a fleet of 60 canoes, and 90,719 kilos of beaver pelts. Gov. d'Argenson confiscated most of the furs as punishment for the coureurs de bois having gone west without his permission or permit. Groseilliers was jailed and both men were fined. Their urgent plea, that the French mount an expedition by sea to trade in Hudson Bay, went unheeded.

Aug. 28 Fr. René Menard (1605–c 1661) left Trois-Rivières with 8 Frenchmen and trade goods to establish Ste-Thérèsa on L. Superior. He was determined to take advantage of the opportunities described by Radisson and Groseilliers, and to rebuild the interior missions.

Sept. 7 Lawyer Jean Peronne Du Mesnil (c 1667), with his son Michel Peronne des Touches, arrived in Que. to inspect all fur-trading transactions carried out since 1645. Crown representatives did not recognize their authority.

Sept. 19 Jesuit Fr. Claude Allouez (1622–1689) became superior of the residence at Trois-Rivières.

Fall 600 Iroquois advanced on New France. A hunting accident on the way caused the death of their leader. Taking that as a bad omen, the war party dispersed.

Nov. 28 Bishop Laval removed Gov. d'Argenson as honorary churchwarden.

1660–1661 Iroquois raiding parties raided every settlement in New France, killing more than 100 settlers.

1661

Feb. 25 One hundred Iroquois kidnapped 13 unarmed Montrealers working in the fields.

Mar. 9 Cardinal Mazarin died. Jean-Baptiste Colbert (1619–1683), French Secretary of State, became chief administrator of New France. He promoted farming and safe settlements, over the fur trade, leaving the door open to the English, who would eventually take over the fur trade.

Mar. 24 An Iroquois war party killed 4 Frenchmen and captured 6 others.

Apr. 18 Bishop Laval excommunicated Pierre Aigron dit Lamothe (fl 1660-1685) for selling liquor to Aboriginals.

Also in Apr.
• The Onondaga captured 14 Frenchmen at Trois-Rivières.

June Thirty Algonquin and 2 Frenchmen, on their way to barter furs at L. Necouba, were attacked by 80 Mohawk. The French and most of the Algonquin were killed. The Mohawk lost 24 men in the 2–day battle.

• The Cayuga delivered 4 French captives to Montreal. They demanded, in return, the release of 8 Cayuga captives, and a missionary to serve the Onondaga. Father Le Moyne agreed.

July 2 Fr. Le Moyne left Que. with the Cayuga to serve as peace ambassador.

July 13 Fr. René Menard left Keweenaw Bay, L. Superior, to join Huron encamped near the mouth of the Black R. in the Wisconsin District. He became lost in the woods and was never seen again.

Aug. 28 or 29 Michel Du Mesnil was killed in a scuffle with Jean-Baptiste de Repentigny (1632–1709). Becancour, Denys and Baudran started the quarrel. Du Mesnil had been helping his father in a fraud investigation that might have implicated his attackers. A Sept. 13, complaint laid by Jean Du Mesnil against those implicated in his son's death was struck from the court record.

Aug. 28 Radisson and Groseilliers set off secretly to explore the region north of L. Superior. They may have reached James Bay. Thoroughly angered by their treatment in New France, they resolved to sell their new-found knowledge of the interior to the English.

Aug. 29 Iroquois Chief Orrayouati led 40 warriors in an attack on St. Gabriel farm, west of Montreal. Fr. Jacques Le Maître and a settler were killed.

Aug. 31 Gov. d'Argenson retired and left for France.

Sept. 17 The Conseil de Québec ruled that it would not recognize the Du Mesnil commission's investigation into fraud.

Oct. 5 Onondaga Chief Garakomtie (d 1677/8) returned a number of French prisoners to Montreal, insisting that the war must end and missions be opened among the Onondaga and the Seneca.

Oct. 11 Gov. Pierre Dubois d'Avaugour (appointed Aug. 31) ordered Frenchman Laviolette shot for selling liquor to Aboriginals. Another trader was whipped in the public square for the same offense.

Oct. 12 Fr. Paul Ragueneau (1608–1680) asked French General Louis II, the Grand Condé, to employ his influence and have troops sent to Canada to end the Iroquois threat.

Oct. 22 Pierre Boucher (d 1717) sailed for Paris as a representative of New France. He had been selected by the Gov. to present the colony's deplorable state of affairs to King Louis XIV.

Oct. 25 Thirty-five Mohawk attacked 12 Montrealers at Île-à-la-Pierre near present-day St. Helen's Is., capturing 4. The remaining settlers escaped in a boat. One of the captives, Fr. Guillaume Vignal (d 1661), died of wounds. He was then roasted and eaten. Grenadier Claude de Brigeac (d 1661) was tortured to death over a period of 2 days. Another captive was killed outright, yet another escaped.

Also in Oct.
• Two men were executed for selling liquor to Aboriginals.

Also in 1661
• One hundred fourteen births, 50 deaths, and 31 marriages were recorded in New France.

• Frs. Claude Dablon (d 1697) and Gabriel Druillettes (1610-1681) and 5 Frenchmen travelled up the Saguenay to Chicoutimi, continuing on to Lac Saint-Jean, to determine whether the Northern, Western and Southern Seas were linked. They reached Nekouba.

1662

Jan. A woman was imprisoned for selling brandy to Aboriginals. Fr. Lalemant asked Gov. d'Avaugour to forgive and release her. She was subsequently released and a new order allowing the sale of liquor to Aboriginals was issued. On Feb. 24. Bishop Laval, defying the new order, imposed excommuni-

cation on persons caught selling liquor to Aboriginals.

Feb. 6 The Mohawk attacked Montreal settlers working in the woods. Four men including Maj. Raphaël Lambert Closse were killed.

Mar. 10 A royal decree rescinded the fur trade monopoly granted to Toussaint Guenet in Feb. 1660. French merchants resumed trade with New France. Habitants resumed legal barter for furs with Aboriginals.

Spring Radisson and Groseilliers announced their intention to travel to Hudson Bay. Instead they sailed to Boston, and then to England, to find backers for a trading expedition to Hudson Bay.

June 2 Jesuit Fr. Chaumonot set off for Montreal to relieve the inhabitants suffering from an extreme shortage of supplies.

June 13 Bishop Laval formally opposed a royal tax on merchandise and provisions imported on behalf of the Sulpician priests of Montreal, who had previously been exempt by virtue of royal letters to Gov. d'Avaugour. The tax ordinance was overturned.

Also in June
• An expeditionary force set out from France in 2 ships, under the command of de Monts. It included 100 soldiers and 200 settlers. De Monts was ordered to report on the colony's needs. En route, he officially took possession of Plaisance (Placentia) Nfld., in the name of Louis XIV, leaving 30 soldiers and a priest at the site.

July 15 Pierre Boucher (d 1717) sailed from La Rochelle on the *Saint-Jean-Baptiste*, after the king promised that 2 ships, 100 soldiers, provisions and munitions would be sent to New France. Boucher himself recruited 100 working men for the crossing. Some 60 died at sea in fierce storms.

Aug. 12 Bishop Laval left for France to request that Louis XIV terminate the Company of New France.

Aug. 15 Gov. d'Avaugour's secretary, Louis Peronne de Maze, left for France to defend civil authority against the charges of Bishop Laval.

Aug. 31 Fr. Le Moyne returned to Montreal with 20 Onondaga and 9 Frenchmen who had been held prisoner by the Iroquois.

Oct. 1 The French established a small fishing village in Plaisance, Nfld.

Oct. 27 De Monts' expeditionary force reached Tadoussac. From there, soldiers and settlers travelled 195 km upriver to Que., in rowboats.

Nov. 6 Pierre Boucher arrived in Que. aboard the *Saint-Jean-Baptiste*.

Also in 1662
• There were 3,300 permanent French-Canadian residents in New France.

1663

Feb. 5 An earthquake rocked Que. so severely that great fissures opened in the snow, streams were diverted from their courses, and new waterfalls appeared. The quake extended from Gaspé to Lachine.

Feb. 24 The Company of New France's mandate ended and its assets in Canada were conveyed to the French Crown under Louis XIV, making New France a royal colony.

Mar. 21 Louis Robert (b c 1636) was appointed New France's first Intendant. He never made it to the colony.

• New France passed an ordinance stating that all lands not cleared within 3 months were to be returned to the Crown.

Mar. 26 Laval received a royal grant to found the Séminaire de Québec for the instruction and training of priests.

Apr. 2 Louis XIV issued an edict stating that New France would be governed by French laws as a royal province of France. A Conseil Souverain would succeed the Conseil de Québec formed by the Compagnie des Cent-Associeés. There were to be 5 Conseil members plus the Lt-Gov. the bishop and the intendant. The Conseil served as a source of judicial appeal and registered royal edicts.

May 1 Augustin de Saffray de Mézy (d 1665) was appointed 1st royal Gov. of New France, serving from Sept. 15, 1663 to May 5, 1665.

May 7 Louis XIV appointed Louis Guadais-Dupont commissioner with instructions to take possession of Canada in his name, and to examine Canada in all its aspects. He was also given the secret task of investigating the conduct and views of the previous gov., the present gov. and Bishop Laval.

July 5 Inhabitants of New France learned from Peronne de Mazé that Louis XIV had recalled Gov. d'Avaugour because of Bishop Laval's complaints.

July 21 Gov. d'Avaugour held his last meeting of the Conseil de Québec, to settle defenses and finances and appoint Lieutenant de la Tesserie, as Gov. *ad interim*.

• Laval named Fr. Claude Allouez (1622–1689) vicar-general of the Que. diocese, which extended through what is now Central US.

July 23 Gov. d'Avaugour made his final farewell to New France.

July 25 A flotilla of 35 canoes from the west, laden with furs and piloted by 150 Algonquin and 7 coureurs de bois, arrived in Montreal.

Aug. 18 The Sulpicians acquired the seignieury of Montreal.

Aug. 28 The Conseil Souverain issued an edict banning the sale of liquor to Aboriginals, directly or indirectly, on pain of heavy fines or banishment.

Oct. 7 Jean-Baptiste Legardeur de Repentigny (1632–1709) was appointed the 1st mayor of Que.

Oct. 21 Fur-trade investigator Jean Peronne Du Mesnil was forced to return to France at the point of a cannon. There he accused Que. settlers of misappropriating large amounts of money in the fur trade. His charges were never proven.

Nov. 19 Alexandre de Prouville de Tracy (c 1596–1670) was appointed lt-gen. of French territories in North and South America. He was given command of all French forces in the Americas, as well as ultimate judicial authority. Tracy's mandate was to restore order and French control, 1st in the West Indies, and then in Que. He had 4 companies of troops at his disposal.

Dec. 16 A law was passed to reduce profiteering on goods imported from France. Merchants were only allowed to mark up goods to a maximum of 65%, after paying a 10% duty.

1663–1673 Some 800 to 1,000 women, designated the King's daughters, "Filles du roi," were transported to New France to become wives of the men of the colony. The king provided each with a dowry of 11 crowns, 1 pig, 1 ox, 2 chickens, 1 cow and salted meat.

Also in 1663
- The population of Que. was approximately 800.

- The public debt in New France was approx. 200,000 livres.

- The Customs tariff was raised to 10% *ad valoremon* on all merchandise.

- New France's farmers were required to pay a tithe of 1/26, or about 4% of the total of the cereal grains produced from their land.

- Fr. Chaumonot and Fr. Marie-Barbe de Boullongue (c 1618–1685) founded the Confrérie de la Sainte-Famille (Holy Family Brotherhood) in Montreal.

- The 1st ship built at Que., the *Galiote*, was launched.

1664

Feb. 13 Gov. Mézy informed Bishop Laval of his intention to exclude 2 members of the Conseil Souverain on the grounds that they had formed a cabal against him, and were acting against the interests of the king. Mézy also declared that replacements would be chosen by a public assembly. Laval opposed the selection process.

Mar. 8 Chief administrator of New France, Jean-Baptiste Colbert, wrote to Bishop Laval advising him it was necessary to destroy the Iroquois.

Mar. 12 Charles II granted the territory between the St. Croix R. and Kennebec R. to James, Duke of York.

Apr. 21 The Conseil Souverain of New France passed the colony's 1st hygiene law, making it illegal to throw "straw, manure and everything else" on streets.

May 28 The French West India Company was given a royal grant of all French colonies in North America, with the power to grant lands in fief, build forts, appoint officials, legislate, declare war and make treaties.

June 18–19 Four companies of the Carignan-Salières infantry regiment arrived at Que. Their goal was to annihilate the Iroquois.

July 26 The Conseil Souverain fixed the price of commodities and stipulated that price tags be attached to goods.

Also in July
- After 2 unsuccessful attempts by Radisson and Groseilliers to sail to Hudson Bay, a representative of English King Charles II arrived in Boston and persuaded them to travel to London instead.

Aug. 19–20 Eight more companies of the Carignan-Salières Regiment arrived in Que. to destroy the Iroquois. More companies followed in mid-Sept.

Sept. Artist Abbé Hugues Pommier (c 1637–1686) arrived in Que. to teach in the Grand Séminaire, founded by Laval in 1663. During his 5 years at the Séminaire, Pommier is believed to have painted *Le Martyre des Pères Jésuites chez les Hurons*, *La Mère Marie-Catherine de Saint-Augustin*, and *La Mère Marie de L'Incarnation*.

Oct. Fr. Chaumonot established the Confréire de la Sainte-Famille in Que., the same congregation he established in Montreal.

1665

Jan. 29 At Laval's request, the seminary of Que. was affiliated with the Séminaire des Missions Ètrangeres in Paris, to maintain links of friendly collaboration.

Mar. 23 Daniel de Rémy, Sieur de Courcelle (1626–1698), was appointed Gov. of New France, serving from Sept. 12, 1665 to Sept. 12, 1672.

May 6–Sept. 12, 1665 Jacques Leneuf de La Potherie (1606–1685), Gov. of Trois-Rivières, served as temporary administrator of New France.

June 30 Tracy and the Carignan-Salières Regiment, which included 100 officers and 1,000 men under the command of Henri de Chastelard de Salières, arrived at Que. from the West Indies. Their first task was to build 5 forts for defence against the Iroquois.

July 23 Four companies of the Carignan-Salières Regiment left Que. for Sorel, about 112 km downstream from Montreal, to build Fort Sorel on the site of Fort Richelieu.

Aug.–Sept. Forts Richelieu, Saint-Louis, and Sainte-Thérèse were built to protect forward movement troops advancing on the Iroquois.

Aug. 1 Groseilliers and Radisson left New England for London aboard the *Charles*, commanded by Capt. Benjamin Gillam, to enlist support for the establishment of a trading company in Hudson Bay.

Aug. 8 Fr. Allouez named L. Superior "L. Tracy" in honour of the Marquis de Tracy. He and 6 Frenchmen had come to New France to continue Fr. René Menard's mission.

Aug. 16 Twelve mares and 2 stallions, which Aboriginals labelled "the moose from France," arrived in Que. from Louis XIV's Royal Stables.

Aug. 23–Oct. 22, 1668 Jean Talon (1625–1694) served as Intendant of New France in charge of justice, police, and finances. He had been appointed Mar. 23, arriving in New France Sept. 12. Talon had instructions to encourage the clearing and cultivation of land and to promote the establishment of local industries. He continued the policy of only trading for furs with Aboriginals who brought them all the way to Que. Montreal merchants undermined this policy, encouraging illegal trade with coureurs de bois. Talon returned to France at the end of his term.

Aug. 29 The 1st Canadian-born Catholic priest, Germain Morin (1642–1702), was ordained.

Sept. Tracy ordered Maisonneuve, who had founded Ville Marie in May, 1642, but was now at the end of his public career, to return to France on indefinite leave. Maisonneuve lived the rest of his life in seclusion in Paris, dying in 1676.

Dec. 13 The 4 western Iroquois tribes, weakened by warfare and disease, sent Chief Garakontie and a delegation to Que. to return prisoner, Fr. Le Moyne, and to renew peace with the French.

Also in Dec.
• Radisson and Groseilliers arrived in London.

Also in 1665
• The population of New France was approximately 3,215.

• Intendant Talon commissioned the building of a 120–ton ship at his own expense.

• The 1st highway was built between Montreal and Chambly.

• Dutch pirates attacked St. John's, Nfld.

1666

Jan. 9 Tracy ordered Courcelle and over 400 men, on snowshoes, to attack the Mohawk. Sixty soldiers died from the bitter cold. Courcelle and his troops pursued the Mohawk as far south as the Dutch settlement of Schenectady. Courcelle began the long march back to Que., Jan. 21. He was pursued by Mohawk war parties, and arrived in Que. Mar. 17, having made no significant impact against the Iroquois.

• Louis XIV declared war on England. The English, under Charles II, allied with the Dutch.

Jan. 20 René-Robert Cavelier de La Salle (1643–1687) settled in Montreal.

Jan. 21 The 1st Census in New France was taken. The population was 3,215, not including Aboriginal peoples and Royal troops. The figures included 2,034 men and 1,181 women. There were 528 married couples. The Census was supervised by Intendant Talon, who did much of the door-to-door canvassing himself.

May 25 A peace treaty was signed with the Seneca at Que.

July 12 Peace was reached with the Oneida.

July 24 Despite the peace, Tracy ordered Pierre de Saurel (1628–1682) to lead 300 men on a raid into Mohawk country. Tracy's nephew was killed and his cousins captured.

Sept. 1 Intendant Talon recommended that Tracy and Courcelle lead a punitive expedition into Mohawk country. Tracy and 1,500 forces marched out of Que., Sept. 14, in search of the northern New York Mohawk.

Sept. 20 Jesuit priest Fr. Jacques Marquette (1637–1675) arrived in Que. from La Rochelle, France.

Oct. 1 Four companies of soldiers left Que. for Trois-Rivières to shore up protection against future Iroquois attack.

Oct. 3 Tracy, supported by 300 boats and canoes, left Fort Ste. Anne at the northern end of L. Champlain. On Oct. 15, Tracy and the Carignan-Salières Regiment laid waste to 4 Mohawk villages including bean and corn supplies. Fields were also destroyed. Tracy then claimed the territory for France. The coldest winter in 30 years led to mass starvation amongst the Iroquois.

Oct. 25 Acting in response to advice from his cousin, Prince Rupert (1619-1682), King Charles II of England promised Radisson and Groseilliers ships for a Hudson Bay expedition. Other British noblemen and merchants would also invest in the venture.

Nov. 5 Tracy and Courcelle arrived back in Que. with Iroquois captives. One captive was hanged as a warning to others. A number of the prisoners were then released.

Dec. 16 The Conseil Souverain abolished the death penalty for those convicted of selling liquor to Aboriginals. Fines were introduced instead.

Also in Dec.
• The Sulpicians established a boys' elementary school in Montreal. It would expand to include a seminary for the education of priests.

1667

Feb. 4 The 1st Ceremonial ball was held in Que., by officers of the Carignan Regiment to celebrate victory over the Iroquois.

Feb. 5 Iron-ore mining began at Trois-Rivières.

Apr. 2 Louis XIV issued a civil code for New France and established a system of courts.

June 18 A coin counterfeiter was hanged in Que.

July 7 Tracy concluded the 1st genuine French-Iroquois peace treaty (in more than 5 decades) with 5 Iroquois nations, a peace that would last 20 years, paving the way for Jesuit missions. Representatives of the Oneida, Onondaga, Cayuga and Seneca signed the treaty with the French at Que. on Aug. 13, a result of the Tracy/Carignan-Salières Regiment expeditions of force.

Aug. 28 Tracy left for France.

Aug. 31 The Treaty of Breda ended the war between England and the Dutch, and France and its allies. The British ceded Acadia to the French, 15 years after the same stipulation was made in the Treaty of Westminster. No transfer would take place until all parties agreed to the transfer, on July 7, 1670.

Also in 1667
• The population of New France was 3,918.

• The Caughnawaga Reserve was established in Que.

• The Sulpicians granted a seigneury on Montreal Is. to La Salle.

1668

Apr. 8 Claude de Boutroue d'Aubigny (1620–1680) was appointed Intendant of New France, serving from Oct. 22, 1668 to Oct. 22, 1670.

Apr. 20 Fr. Marquette left Que. to join Fr. Claude

Dablon at Sainte-Marie-du-Sault (Sault Ste. Marie), a mission serving 2,000 Algonquin.

June 5 The *Nonsuch* and *Eaglet* sailed from London under Zachariah Gillam (1636–1682), to test the validity of Radisson and Groseilliers' scheme to by-pass the French and open a new fur trade route through Hudson Bay.

Aug. 5 The *Eaglet*, with Radisson aboard, was forced back to Plymouth because of severe storms.

Sept. 29 Groseilliers on the *Nonsuch* reached southern James Bay on the Rupert R. Groseilliers and his companions built Charles Fort and spent the winter trading with the Cree.

Oct. 9 Louis Jolliet (1645–1700) became a fur trader.

Also in 1668
• The population of New France was 6,282.

• Laval established the Petit Séminaire (Seminary of the Infant Jesus) at Que., the 1st institution of higher learning in Canada. Eight young Canadians and 6 Huron were the 1st students.

• A school at St. Joachim (near Que.) opened as a vocational school for boys, offering cabinetry, masonry, roofing, carving, shoemaking and tailoring. A model farm at Cap Tourmente provided instruction in agriculture.

• Intendant Jean Talon founded Canada's 1st brewery under Royal Charter of Louis XIV. Beer was produced from hops grown on Talon's seigneury. Talon assured a stable demand for his product by placing restrictions on the import of French wine and liquor.

1669

Mar. 8 Charles II ordered Sir Thomas Temple, Gov. of Acadia, to return the colony to France.

Apr. 5 Louis XIV established baby bonuses in New France, paying 300 livres to parents with 10 legitimate children and 400 to those with 12 or more.

Apr. 8 Louis XIV approved the building of a hospital in Montreal.

May 14 At the King's request, Jean Talon agreed to serve a 2nd term as Intendant of New France, arriving back in Que. in 1670.

June 14 The *Nonsuch* left the Rupert R. in James Bay for England, loaded with furs, supplied by the James Bay Cree, valued at £1,380. Before leaving, Comm. Zachariah Gillam negotiated a treaty with the Cree to purchase the Rupert R. area. The success of the expedition prompted King Charles II to consider granting a royal charter to the Company of Adventurers.

July 6 La Salle, and Sulpicians François Dollier de Casson (1636–1701) and René de Bréhant de Galinée (dc 1678), left Montreal for the Mississippi to convert the Potawatomi. La Salle dreamed of discovering a route to China via the "Southern Sea."

Aug. 10 La Salle's expedition met with the Seneca, and was brought to their village on the site of present-day Boughton Hill, New York. They remained as guests for a month.

Sept. 15 La Salle arrived at Niagara from Montreal, and would later meet fur trader Louis Jolliet (d 1700) near present-day Hamilton, Ont. Jolliet had been looking for copper in the L. Superior area. La Salle, suffering from poor health, left Frs. Dollier and Galinée at Hamilton on Oct. 1, and returned to Montreal. Casson and Galinée wintered at L. Erie, where they claimed the region for France. They returned to Montreal Oct. 23, 1670.

• Jolliet journeyed via Lakes Ontario, Erie and Huron to Sault Ste. Marie.

Also in Sept. Marquette travelled to the western extremity of L. Superior and established a mission at La Pointe du Saint-Esprit in Chequamegon Bay, among refugee Ottawa and Huron displaced from the shores of L. Huron and Georgian Bay.

Oct. 28 Sulpicians François de Salignac de La Mothe-Fénélon (1641–1679) and Claude Trouvé (d 1704) established a mission among the Cayuga near present-day Bay of Quinte, L. Ontario.

Dec. Charles Bayly (fl 1630-1680), a Quaker imprisoned in the Tower of London, petitioned the king for his liberty. It was granted on the condition that Bayly navigate and explore Hudson Bay.

Also in 1669

• Statistics recorded in New France included: 125 marriages, 288 births and 61 deaths.

• Wheat was declared legal tender by the Conseil Souverain; 3 bushels being equivalent to 4 francs.

• Fr. Claude Dablon (1619–1697) was named superior of the western missions based at Sault Ste. Marie.

• Louis XIV ordered all male citizens of New France between ages 16 and 60 into unpaid military service.

1670

Mar. 24 Louis XIV ordered 100,000 livres of silver and copper coins minted for use in New France.

Apr. 20 François-Marie Perrot (1644–1691) received a royal commission as Gov. of Montreal.

Apr. 27 Louis XIV granted a trading charter covering most of the Hudson Bay watershed to Jan Van Heemskerk, a Dutch mariner.

May 2 Charles II granted a royal charter to the Company of Adventurers of England Trading into the Hudson's Bay, better known as the Hudson's Bay Company (HBC). Prince Rupert (1619–1682) and 18 other investors (at £300 each) were its 1st shareholders. The HBC received perpetual title over the Hudson Bay watershed, the right to trade for furs, to rule the inhabitants, make laws, and if need be, declare war in the region. Prince Rupert served as the 1st Gov. of the region, known as Rupert's Land, which included all of northern Canada from Labrador to the Rocky Mountains.

May 31 Charles Bayly, the 1st Gov. of the HBC, together with Radisson and Groseilliers, left England for Hudson Bay on the *Wivenhoe*, captained by Robert Newland. It was the 1st voyage under the new royal charter to establish permanent posts on James Bay and the Nelson R.

June Gov. of New France Courcelle arrived at L. Ontario in a large flatboat with 56 volunteers.

He warned the Iroquois that if they did not discontinue hostilities against the Algonquian, he would return to destroy them.

July 5 Mme. Marie-Barbe d'Ailleboust Boullongue donated her remaining possessions to Hôtel-Dieu of Que. by notarial deed.

July 7 Hector d'Andigné de Grandfontaine (1627–1696), an officer of the Carignan-Salières Regiment, signed a treaty of restitution with Thomas Temple, the English Gov. of Acadia, at Boston. Temple would hand over Pentagouet, St. John or Jemseg located on the St. John R., Port Royal (Annapolis Royal) and Fort La Tour. Grandfontaine became the 1st French Gov. of Acadia (NS, NB, and Maine) since the English occupation in 1654.

July 18 Painter and missionary Frère Luc (1614–1685) travelled to Que. with 5 other Récollet to re-establish the monastery abandoned after the capture of the city by the Kirkes in 1629. With them was François-Marie Perrot (1644–1691), en route to assume his commission as Gov. of Montreal. Perrot arrived in New France later that year. He was not popular with the other leaders of New France, who eventually petitioned that he be removed from the colony.

July 27 Fort Jemseg on the St. John R. surrendered to Pierre de Joybert de Soulanges (d 1678).

July 31 HBC officers arrived at Fort Nelson to establish posts.

Sept. 2 In accordance with the Treaty of Breda, Port Royal was officially returned to France.

Sept. 3 Intendant Talon appointed Simon-François Daumont de Saint-Lusson (d 1677) deputy commissioner to undertake a systematic study of Canada in response to the growing involvement of the HBC. In Oct., Saint-Lusson and Nicolas Perrot (d 1717), his interpreter, left Montreal for Sault Ste. Marie to claim land and develop trade and military alliances for France.

Sept. 15 Because of a scarcity of hard currency, the Conseil Souverain issued a decree allowing colonists to pay their debts with beaver and moose hides.

Also in Sept. The *Wivenhoe* reached present-day Port Nelson in the Hudson Bay. Bayly went ashore and nailed His Majesty's arms "in Brasse" to a tree, formally laying claim to Rupert's Land for England. Bayly and Radisson then set out to join Capt. Gillam, in command of the *Prince Rupert,* at Fort Charles in James Bay, where they established HBC's 1st permanent trading post .

Oct. 23 Talon officially began his 2nd term as Intendant of New France. Still forbidden by Colbert to engage directly in internal trade, he ordered a series of expeditions to claim land for France. Talon returned to France in 1672.

Also in 1670

• Three hundred eleven births and 121 marriages were recorded among the settlers of New France.

• Fines were levied on the fathers of unmarried men 20 years old, and unmarried women 16 years old.

• The Conseil Souverain abolished a 10% duty on dry goods, imposing duties on liquor and tobacco instead.

• The Ottawa reoccupied their homeland on Manitoulin Is.

• The French built Fort Baie-des-Puants at Green Bay, Wisconsin. War had broken out along the frontier from Lake Superior to the Illinois River as refugees from Iroquois wars encroached on Winnebago and Dakota land.

1671

Spring Bayly and Radisson travellled to Moose R. where they traded for beaver skins which were taken to England in the *Wivenhoe* the following year.

Apr. 8 Marquette established a mission at Sault Ste. Marie, in Michigan.

Apr. 29 Marguerite Bourgeoys (canonized in 1982) received approval for the establishment of the Congrégation de Notre-Dame de Montréal. She also received royal letters patent which guaranteed the existence of the community of teachers she had previously established, with the authority to instruct on the Île de Montréal and in all other places in Canada that should require her services.

June 2 Courcelle set off from Montreal on a peace mission to L. Ontario, western Iroquois country. At his urging, the Iroquois agreed to a peace between the French and Algonquian.

June 4 At Sault Ste. Marie, Saint-Lusson called together 14 Aboriginal groups to lay general claim to Western America in the name of France. He erected a cross, which was later removed by the Ojibwa, who did not recognize his claim over their land. Saint-Lusson's actions marked the beginning of French explorations from James Bay south to the Gulf of Mexico and west to the Rocky Mountains.

June 22 Talon laid the cornerstone of the Chapel of the Hôpital-Général at Que. The chapel was designed by Frère Luc and still stands today.

Summer Talon sent Saint-Lusson to establish a means of communication between Que., Pentagouet and Port Royal, and to examine copper deposits in Acadia.

July 1 The 1st HBC expedition returned to England.

July 2 Marquette took final vows as a Jesuit at Sault Ste. Marie.

Aug. 6 Talon ordered Jesuit Fr. Charles Albanel (c 1613–1696) to Tadoussac on the first leg of a journey to Hudson Bay. Albanel met with Paul Denys de Saint-Simon (1649–1731) and Sebastien Provencher, and secured the services of Montagnais guides before continuing. His task was to divert Cree trade from the English, explore Hudson Bay, claim the area for France, and verify reports that Radisson and Groseilliers were working on behalf of the HBC. Albanel's 1st winter was spent on a lake near Chicoutimi.

• Fr. Marquette founded the Mission of Saint-Ignace on the north shore of the straits of Michilimackinac (present-day Mackinaw City, Michigan).

Oct. 21 Talon signed an ordinance that compelled bachelors to marry the *filles du roi* within 15 days of their arrival, or be prohibited from fishing, hunting and trading for furs.

Also in Oct.

• Laval celebrated the 1st mass in the new Chapel of the Hôpital-Général, Que.

1671–1680 Fr. Dablon returned to Que. to fill the position of superior of the Jesuit missions in New France.

Also in 1671

• The population of Acadia was 441.

• The population of Plaisance, Nfld., was 73 French-speaking persons.

• *L'Assomption*, a canvas by Frère Luc, was displayed in the new Hôpital-Général.

1672

Jan. Saint-Lusson arrived in Dieppe, France, with a 6-month-old moose, 1 fox and 12 large wild geese for the king.

Jan. 24 The 1st HBC fur sale was conducted at Garraway's Coffee House in England, led by Prince Rupert and his cousin, the Lord High Admiral Duke of York.

Mar. 12 Dollier de Casson laid out Notre-Dame, Montreal's main street, 2 parallel streets and 7 perpendicular routes, in the region of what is known today as Old Montreal.

Apr. 6 Louis de Buade de Frontenac et de Palluau, Count Frontenac (1622–1698) was appointed Gov. of New France, serving from Sept. 12, 1672 to Sept. 1682.

Apr. 15 A royal edict prohibited fur traders from forcing Aboriginals to trade their furs at established French settlements.

June 28 Fr. Albanel and his party reached the mouth of the Rupert R., where they found an English ship and 2 deserted houses. The English had gone on a hunting expedition. Albanel spent a few days exploring James Bay before entrusting one of the Cree with a note for Radisson. Albanel claimed the territory for France and proved that Hudson Bay was accessible by land. Fr. Albanel began his return trip from James Bay to Que., July 6, not having met any Englishmen or French deserters.

Nov. 3 Saint-Lusson was granted the Île aux Lièvres seigneury in the lower St. Lawrence region.

• Interpreter and distinguished Iroquois fighter Jacques Le Moyne de Sainte-Hélène (1659–1690), was given St. Helen's Is. in Montreal.

Dec. 8 Fr. Marquette met Louis Jolliet at Sault Ste. Marie. Jolliet was commissioned to lead an expedition to explore the northern Mississippi R. region. He had orders from Fr. Dablon for Marquette to accompany him. They left with 7 men and 2 canoes on May 17.

1672–1673 Charles Bayly built the second HBC post at Moose Factory on Hayes Is. on James Bay.

• Radisson wintered at Hudson Bay. Unhappy with his treatment by the HBC and disappointed in his hopes of riches in Canada, he travelled to France and joined the French Navy.

Also in 1672

• *Description géographique et historique des costes de l'Amérique septentrionale: avec l'histoire du país*, by Nicolas Denys, was published in France, in two volumes.

• Jean Talon returned to France.

• Colbert sent secret instructions to Gov. Frontenac not to allow settlers to visit France unless they were married, with children, and were well established in the colony.

1673

May 5 Jacques de Chambly (d 1687) was appointed Gov. of Acadia, replacing Andigne de Grand-fontaine.

May 29 A proclamation issued by Frontenac gave the Récollet title to land on the St. Charles R.

June 5 A royal decree prohibited coureurs de bois from entering the forest for more than a 24-hour period without permission. The annual number of permits issued was 25. Jean Talon had referred to the coureurs de bois as godless outlaws. The French approach to the coureurs caused the diversion of much trade to the English.

June 13 At Frontenac's request, La Salle established Fort Cataraqui (Kingston, Ont.).

Also in June

- Jolliet's expedition entered the Mississippi R. watershed in mid-June. Near the end of July, and fearful of entering Spanish territory, the expedition stopped 900 km short of the Mississippi R. mouth. However, Jolliet was to provide proof that the Mississippi flowed into the Gulf of Mexico, not the Pacific or the China Sea.

July 12 Frontenac, with 120 canoes, arrived at Cataraqui to construct a fortified base from which to control the western fur trade, for his own profit. Montreal merchants fought back by redoubling their illegal activities.

July 17 Dutch pirates attacked Ferryland, Nfld.

Also in 1673

- The Canadian population of New France was 6,705.

- The population of Plaisance, Nfld., was 63.

- Nicolas Bellanger (1633–1682) had a small house built in present-day Beauport, Que. One of the oldest houses to survive till present day, the Girardin House (named after its last owner) was re-built as a stone house between 1727–1735, and resembles the style of houses in Normandy, France. (The Girardin House has been designated a heritage site by Parks Canada.)

1674

Jan. 13 Fr. Albanel set out on his 2nd expedition to Hudson Bay. He wintered at Lac St-Jean, and arrived at Rupert R. Aug. 30, where he was arrested by the English and sent to England, but was later released.

Jan. 26 Frontenac arrested and imprisoned François-Marie Perrot, the Gov. of Montreal, for illegal involvement in the fur trade.

May 17 Frontenac renamed Fort Cataraqui, Fort Frontenac, establishing it as a fur-trading post, albeit without proper authorization.

July 16 Bayly sailed from Moose R. to the Shechittawam (Albany) R., entering into trade with local First Nations.

- Fr. Claude Dablon, superior-general of the missions of the Society of Jesus in New France, and rector of the Collège de Québec, laid the 1st chapel stone of Notre Dame-de-Lorette.

Aug. 10 Jurriaen Aernoutsz, a Dutch privateer and captain of the *Flying Horse*, attacked Pentagouet on the Penobscot R. He took Gov. Chambly of Acadia, and about 30 others, prisoner. After destroying Pentagouet, Aernoutsz proceeded to pillage all French posts along the west shore of the Bay of Fundy. Chambly and the other hostages were ransomed by Frontenac.

Aug. 31 The Conseil Souverain ordered beggars to leave Que. after 5 women were found begging in the streets.

Sept. 17 Two supply ships arrived at Rupert R. One carried William Lydall (d 1692), sent to replace Bayly, who was recalled to England.

Oct. 1 Laval was appointed the 1st Bishop of Que., a bishopric created by Pope Clement X.

Oct. 25 Fr. Marquette set out from the Saint-François-Xavier mission on the Fox R., Wisconsin, to visit the Illinois. On Dec. 4, he reached the Chicago R. and the site of present-day Chicago, Illinois. He suffered a severe attack of dysentery on Dec. 14, and was forced to winter there. On Apr. 8, 1675, Marquette reached Kaskaskia village on the Illinois R. where he established the 1st mission. He died Apr. 18 near present-day Luddington, Michigan, en route to his mission at Saint-Ignace (Strait of Mackimac).

Also in Oct.

- Radisson re-entered the service of the French king as a fur trader and explorer.

Nov. 4 Fr. Dablon blessed the completed chapel of Notre-Dame-de-Lorette, which became a place of pilgrimage.

Also in 1674

• Colbert awarded the Domaine de l'Occident the right to collect all taxes and duties in the colonies of the West Indies and New France for an annual payment to the Crown of 350,000 livres. The previous charter given to the French West India Company was revoked. The Domaine promptly sublet all rights to the Canadian beaver trade to François Aubert de la Chesnaye (d 1725) for an annual sum of 119,000 livres.

1675

Jan. 27 Charles II approved a new charter for Nfld., prohibiting settlers from cutting down any wood or inhabiting any area within 9 km of shore. These precautions were to keep settlers from competing in the fishing trade.

Jan. 13 La Salle was granted a patent of nobility and the seignieury of Fort Frontenac at Cataraqui.

Jan. 30 Jacques Duchesneau de La Doussinière et d'Ambault (d 1696) was appointed the 4th Intendant of New France.

June 5 Louis XIV increased the number of councillors on the Conseil Souverain to 7.

Also in 1675

• The population of New France was 7,833.

• Frère Luc painted *La France Apportant la Foi aux Hurons de la Nouvelle-France*.

• The Iroquois began attacks on New France's First Nation allies.

• François Jacquet dit Langevin commissioned Pierre Menage (1645–1715) to build him a 1-storey house of stone and crépi. In 1689 Menage's daughter, Marie-Anne, married architect François de Lajoue who eventually enlarged the structure. Today the Jacquet House is the only intact 17th century house in Quebec City. Located at 34 rue Saint-Louis in uptown Que., it is now a restaurant.

1676

Apr. 15 Trading of furs in Aboriginal villages was prohibited by royal ordinance, forcing First Nations peoples to trade their furs at French settlements.

May 11 Begging was prohibited in Montreal except for persons holding a certificate from a parish priest.

May 16 James Knight (d 1720) entered the employ of the HBC.

May 20 Jacques de Chambly was re-appointed Gov. of Acadia, serving until 1678. Nashwaak and Jemseg were granted to Pierre de Joybert de Soulanges et de Marson (d 1678).

July 22 Fr. Albanel arrived back in New France. He was appointed superior of the Sault Ste. Marie and Saint-François-Xavier missions.

Fall The French reoccupied Acadia.

Oct. 11 Public markets were established at Quebec, Trois-Rivières and Montreal. Public trade was elsewhere prohibited.

Oct. 27 Dutch Capt. Aernoutsz, with the help of Capt. John Rhoades of Boston, claimed Acadia. Aernoutsz had captured Acadia from the French in 1674. The Dutch West India Company appointed Cornelius Steenwijck Gov. of the newly acquired province.

1676–1759 Citizens of Quebec were prohibited from smoking on the street or from carrying tobacco.

Also in 1676.

• The population of New France was 7,832.

• Frère Luc completed 2 canvases, *Saint Joachim et la Vierge Enfant* and *La Vierge et l'Enfant Jésus*. They were later installed at Sainte-Anne-de-Beaupré.

• Montreal fur merchants established a base at the Straits of Mackinac for use by voyageurs who brought furs to Montreal. Frontenac opposed the development.

1677

May 9 Louis XIV established the Prévôt de Québec, a tribunal consisting of the Lt.-Gov., a King's Attorney and a clerk.

May 16 The Conseil Supérieur fixed fur prices.

June 7 Oliver Morel de La Durantaye (1640–1716) claimed the L. Huron and L. Erie regions for France.

Also in 1677
- The 2 largest towns in Nfld. were St. John's with 45 houses and Bonavista with 18 houses.

- An Ursuline convent was established at Trois-Rivières.

1678

May 12 Louis XIV granted La Salle permission to explore the area between New France, Florida and Mexico. He was to search for a water route to the Gulf of Mexico and build forts down the Mississippi. La Salle used the opportunity to ship furs illegally out of the Lake Michigan area.

Sept. 1 Daniel Greysolon Dulhut (c 1639–1710) secretly left Montreal, with 7 French followers and 3 Sioux slaves, to develop commercial relations between the French, Dakota, Ojibwa, Sioux and Chippewa. He feared the English were gaining a monopoly over the northwestern fur trade. The expedition lasted a year.

Sept. 15 La Salle's expedition arrived at Que. Dominique La Motte de Lucière (1636–1700), Henri de Tonty (c 1649–1704) and Récollet Fr. Louis Hennepin (1626–c 1705) were among its members.

Oct. 26 The informal Brandy Parliament with Frontenac, La Salle and important merchants met at the Château St. Louis, voting 15 to 5 in favour of legalizing the trade in liquor to Aboriginal peoples. The Conseil Supérieur lifted its ban on liquor Nov. 10, expecting increased returns from the fur trade.

Oct. 18 La Salle sent a party, which included Lucière and Fr. Hennepin, to Niagara to choose the site of Fort Conti along the Niagara R. The party entered the Niagara R. Dec. 6, arriving the next day at Niagara Falls, which Fr. Hennepin referred to as "the greatest falls in the world" and "the most terrifying waterfall in the universe." Then he sketched the falls. La Salle broke ground for Fort Conti at Niagara on Feb. 1, 1679.

1679

Jan. 26 Construction began on La Salle's 44-tonne *Griffon*, at the mouth of Cayuga Creek on L. Erie.

Mar. 10 Intendant Duchesneau granted Louis Jolliet and Jacques de Lalande joint ownership of the Mingan Islands and Islets.

Apr. 13 Louis Jolliet left Que. with 8 men, bound for James Bay. He came upon Rupert's Land Gov. Charles Bayly and some Englishmen trading in the Hudson Bay area, and was treated as an honoured guest before returning to Que.

May 24 Louis XIV published an ordinance forbidding trade in spirits outside the French settlements.

July 2 Dulhut, after whom Duluth is named, became the 1st known European to penetrate Minnesota. He planted the arms of France, claiming possession of the area around the Sioux village of Izatys, on L. Mille Lacs.

Aug. 7 After exploring the lower Great Lakes, La Salle launched the 39-tonne *Griffon* on L. Erie with a crew of 30 men and 7 cannons. The *Griffon* sailed from Saint-Ignace Mission, at Michilimackinac, to present-day Green Bay, Wisconsin. In spite of orders not to deal in furs, the *Griffon* loaded up with pelts and merchandise and headed back to Niagara. It was lost and never seen again. La Salle was not aboard, but continued south from Green Bay along the Wisconsin shore of L. Michigan with 14 men and 4 canoes.

Sept. 15 Dulhut met with First Nations of the area in a grand council. Peace was arranged between the Sioux, Assiniboine, Saulteaux and Cree. To strengthen the new bonds, Dulhut arranged for several marriages between Nations.

Oct. 16 The Conseil Supérieur voted against the transport of liquor to Aboriginal villages.

Nov. 1 La Salle met up with Tonty on the St. Joseph R., at the southeastern end of L. Michigan. They built Fort Miami.

Also in 1679
- The population of New France was 9,400.

• The population of Acadia was 515.

• Five to six hundred coureurs de bois were trading illegally in the interior.

• John Nixon (c 1623–1692) replaced Bayly as Gov. of the HBC. Bayly died Jan. 6, 1680, while awaiting trial on charges of mismanagement brought against him by the HBC.

1680

Jan. 5 La Salle arrived at the Illinois village of Pimitoui, on L. Peoria, and began building Fort Crèvecoeur, the 1st western fort. On Feb. 29, he sent Fr. Hennepin and 2 companions to scout the upper Mississippi R. On Mar. 1, La Salle left for Niagara.

Mar. Intendant Duchesneau granted Jolliet the Anticosti Is. Jolliet proposed to set up a fishing station.

Apr. 11 Sioux warriors, appearing in 33 canoes, captured Fr. Hennepin and his companions, and transported them to a Sioux village in the Thousand Lakes region.

Apr. 21 La Salle and his companions reached Niagara after great hardship. Fort Conti had been burned and 20,000 francs, worth of supplies were missing.

June Dulhut ascended the Bois Brûlé R. from L. Superior, then crossed to the St. Croix R., which he used to reach the Mississippi.

July 22 At Fort Frontenac, La Salle learned that his men had mutinied, destroying Fort Crèvecoeur, and causing a serious setback to the exploration of Illinois country. Moreover, the deserters planned to pillage all posts where La Salle kept supplies. They also wanted to hunt him down and kill him. La Salle left for Detroit, learning en route from the Potawatomi that the *Griffon* had sunk in L. Ontario, in a storm.

July 25 Dulhut and 5 Frenchmen rescued Fr. Hennepin and his companions. Hennepin returned to France and wrote a book, *Description de la Louisiane,* published in 1683. It was a great success, but was in many respects false and self-promotive.

Early Aug. La Salle ambushed and captured his

would-be assassins in the Baie de Cataraqui, near Fort Frontenac. He then undertook a 2nd expedition to Illinois territory.

Sept. 16 La Salle reached Sault Ste. Marie.

Also in 1680
• The population of New France was 9,719; in addition there were 960 Aboriginals living in surrounding villages.

1681

Jan. At Fort St. Joseph, on the Saint Joseph R. in present-day Michigan, La Salle encouraged the Miami and Illinois Nations to unite against the Iroquois to help promote French interests in the area.

May 22 La Salle set out for Michilimackinac, where he found Tonty.

Also in May
• In a change of policy, Colbert permitted Intendant Duchesneau to grant an amnesty to all coureurs de bois who had traded in the west without licences. The practice remained unlawful, however, subject to branding on the 1st offense and life in the galleys for the 2nd. The annual number of licences granted remained at 25.

Also in 1681
• The population of New France was 9,677.

1682

Jan. 8 James Knight was appointed chief factor for the HBC, at Fort Albany, in James Bay.

Also in Jan.
• La Salle, Tonty and army officer Jacques Bourdon d'Autray (1652–1688) set out to travel the Mississippi R., reaching it Feb. 6. The expedition was financed by La Salle.

Mar. 14 La Salle claimed what is now northern Arkansas for France.

Apr. 9 La Salle reached the mouth of the Mississippi R., and the Gulf of Mexico. He erected a cross and claimed possession of the land, which he named Louisiana, for France.

• Louis XIV recalled Gov. Frontenac.

Apr. 10 La Salle began his return journey to Michilimackinac.

May 1 Joseph-Antoine Le Febvre de La Barre (1622–1688) was appointed Gov. of New France, serving from Oct. 9, 1682 to Sept. 23, 1685.

• Jacques De Meulles (d 1703) was appointed Intendant of New France, replacing Duchesneau, and served from Oct. 9, 1682 to July 31, 1686.

May 11 James Knight became Deputy Gov. to John Nixon, retaining his position as chief factor at Albany.

June Capt. Zachariah Gillam (Williams), in the service of the HBC, set sail with 5 ships for Hudson Bay. Three ships proceeded to the southern part of the bay. The other 2 sailed to the Nelson and Hays Rivers to establish Port Nelson. Gillam had competition — 2 rival parties had already left for Hudson Bay: his son, Benjamin Gillam (c 1662–1706), who commanded the *Bachelor's Delight* from Boston; and also Radisson, Groseilliers and his son, Jean-Baptiste Chouart, who were now serving the French interests of financier Aubert de La Chesnaye (1669–1725) and Gov. La Barre of Que.

July 21 By special warrant, Prince Rupert granted the HBC the right to use the Red Ensign ("King's Jack") at its forts, and on all ships entering Hudson Str. No other private concern enjoyed the same privilege.

Aug. 18 Benjamin Gillam reached the Nelson R. and established a camp.

Aug. 20 Radisson and Groseilliers sailed into the Hayes R. They discovered Benjamin Gillam's camp, 6 days later, and took him captive.

Sept. 21 The *Prince Rupert* broke from its anchorage in a severe storm and sank. Capt. Zachariah Gillam, 9 men and all supplies were lost. John Bridgar, Gov. of Port Nelson, survived the disaster, but was taken captive by Radisson and Groseilliers. He was then taken to Que., with Benjamin Gillam. Groseilliers' son, Chouart, was left in charge of Port Nelson.

Nov. 29 Prince Rupert died of pleurisy.

Dec. 30 La Salle returned to the Illinois R. to build Fort Saint-Louis near the present-day town of La Salle. The fortification was completed, in May 1683.

1682–1712 The French fought a series of skirmishes against the British in the Hudson Bay and James Bay regions.

Also in 1682
• A charter and gov. sanction was granted to the Compagnie de la Baie d'Hudson under the direction of Charles Aubert de La Chesnaye (1652–1702). Also called the Compagnie du Nord, the association included Radisson, Groseilliers, La Salle, Jolliet and Charles Le Moyne de Longueuil et de Châteauguay (1626–1685). The concern intended to challenge English control of Hudson Bay trade.

1683

Jan.–Feb. 1685 James, Duke of York, served as Gov. of the HBC.

Spring Gov. La Barre sent Oliver Morel de La Durantaye (1640–1716) and Louis-Henri de Baugy (d 1720) to the Illinois country to stop unlicenced coureurs de bois from trading in furs, and to invite First Nations peoples to bring their furs to Montreal instead and meet the gov. The expedition was also told to look into the activities of La Salle.

May The Iroquois attacked Aboriginals allied with the French, and demanded that La Salle be expelled from Fort Saint-Louis.

July La Durantaye took command of Michilimackinac, where he would remain until 1690.

Aug. Baugy replaced Henri Tonty as commandant of Fort Saint-Louis by order of Gov. La Barre, who was concerned that La Salle's forts presented a threat to Montreal's fur business.

Sept. 2 La Salle returned to France on La Barre's orders.

Also in Sept.
• The ship *Diligence* arrived at James Bay, carrying the 1st three English women to arrive in the James

Bay area: the wife of the new HBC Gov. Henry Sergeant, her companion and a maidservant.

Nov. 21 Canada's 1st Native-born painter, Abbé Jean Guyon (1659–1687), was ordained in Que.; he would soon be appointed canon and secretary to Bishop Laval.

Also in Nov.
• La Mère Jeanne-Françoise Juchereau dite de Saint-Ignace (1650–1723) was elected superior of her convent, the 1st Canadian to hold the post.

• Claude Greysolon de La Tourette (c 1660–1716) built Fort Tourette at the mouth of the Ombabika R. on L. Nipigon.

Also in 1683
• The population of New France was 10,251.

1684

Mar. 15 Henry Kelsey (c 1667–1724) was apprenticed to the Hudson's Bay Company. On May 6, Kelsey sailed for Fort York, Hudson Bay, on the *Lucy*, captained by John Outlaw.

Mar. 21 Tonty and Baugy repulsed an Iroquois force at Fort St. Louis, Illinois, after a 6-day siege.

Apr. 10 An ordinance, prohibiting emigration from New France to the English colonies in the south, on pain of death, was issued.

• By order of Louis XIV, Fort Frontenac was restored to La Salle.

Apr. 14 La Salle received a commission to colonize the Mississippi Delta.

July 30 Gov. La Barre left Montreal, leading 700 French and 400 Aboriginal soldiers, to fight the Iroquois.

Aug. 29 La Barre's force caught up with the Iroquois at Famine Cove on L. Ontario, but could not fight because the men were inflicted with a severe bout of Spanish influenza.

Sept. 5 La Barre and the Iroquois negotiated a peace agreement, the Treaty of Famine Cove, wherein the

Iroquois agreed to make peace with the Miami but not with the Illinois.

Oct. 10 A French ship, commanded by Claude de Bermen de la Martinière (d 1719) arrived in Quebec City with a cargo of furs captured from a HBC boat.

c 1684 Abbé Jean Guyon completed the portrait of *La Mère Jeanne-Françoise Juchereau dite de Saint-Ignace*.

Also in 1684
• Radisson re-entered the service of the HBC, deserting the Compagnie du Nord. He was hired at £50 per year and issued £200 worth of HBC shares. Radisson returned to Hudson Bay and persuaded Chouart to surrender Port Nelson.

• The French set up a small trading post at L. Nipigon.

• The French appointed Perrot Gov. of Acadia. He arrived in Port Royal in 1685 to assume his post.

1685

Jan. 1 Jacques-René de Brisay de Denonville (1637–1710) was appointed Gov. of New France, serving from Aug. 1, 1685 to Aug. 12, 1689.

Jan. 6 The La Salle expedition sailed past the mouth of the Mississippi without recognizing it. They landed, probably at what is today Matagorda Bay, Texas, on Jan. 19. La Salle proceeded to lead a party overland in search of the Mississippi R. A 2nd party under Capt. de Beaujeu, conducted a search by water.

Feb. 20 La Salle's ship, the *Amiable*, was wrecked on a reef.

Apr. 1 John, Lord Churchill (later Duke of Marlborough) (1650–1722) accepted the post of Gov. of the HBC

June 8 Intendent Meulles issued the 1st paper currency to circulate in North America — playing cards. A value was written on the face of each card together with de Meulles' signature. Meulles issued an ordinance declaring that the cards would be redeemed when the annual supply of funds arrived from France. In the meantime, the cards were legal tender. They were withdrawn Sept. 5.

July A ship arrived in Que. with l'Abbé de Saint-Valliers, (who was to replace Bishop Laval), Denonville, the new Gov., and many officers and soldiers. Most were seriously ill.

• Colonists organized by La Salle occupied Fort Saint-Louis, probably built on the Garcitas R. near Lavaca Bay, Texas.

1685–1687 Radisson served as superintendent at Fort Nelson.

Also in 1685
• The population of New France was 12,263, including 1,538 Aboriginals living in surrounding villages.

• *Voyages of Pierre Esprit Radisson*, by Pierre Radisson, was published in Boston.

• The *Histoire naturelle des Indes occidentales*, by the Jesuit missionary Père Louis Nicolas, was published with pen-and-ink drawings (the *Codex canadensis*) of the flora, fauna and people of the New World.

• Gov. Denonville offered a reward of 50 pistoles to anyone who could bring Radisson to Que.

• When the relief ships from France bearing food-stuffs, soldiers and payroll moneys failed to arrive in New France by Aug., Meulles allowed members of the colony's militia to hire themselves out to local farmers for room and board, at not more than 12 livres a month for unskilled labour, and 15 sols a day for skilled labour.

1686

Feb. 9 Card money was issued for the 2nd time.

Feb. 13 Tonty arrived at the mouth of the Mississippi R. but was unable to find La Salle's fort.

Feb. 18 A convent was established at Lachine, Que.

Mar. 20 Pierre de Troyes (d 1688) led an expedition of about 100 men, out of Montreal to Hudson Bay to expel the English and capture unauthorized traders, particularly those working for Radisson.

Pierre Le Moyne d'Iberville (1661–1706) served as a member of the expedition, sponsored by the Compagnie du Nord.

Apr. 20 At the mouth of the Mississippi R., Tonty, La Salle's lieutenant, left a note with local Aboriginals. La Salle did not live to receive it. The missive was given to d'Iberville 12 years later.

Apr. 22–Oct. 17 La Salle searched for the Mississippi R.

Apr. 24–Fall 1702 Jean Bochart de Champigny (d 1720) served as Intendant of New France.

June 20 De Troyes and d'Iberville captured the English post of Fort Monsipi (Moose Factory) on James Bay. The fort was renamed Fort Saint-Louis.

July 3 De Troyes and d'Iberville captured the English post of Rupert House on James Bay. The fort was renamed Saint-Jacques.

July 26 De Troyes and d'Iberville captured the English post of Fort Albany on James Bay. The fort was renamed Fort Sainte-Anne.

Aug. 19 De Troyes left his James Bay conquests and returned to Que., leaving 40 men, and d'Iberville as regional Gov.

Sept. 23 Intendant Meulles was recalled to France after Denonville reported that he had been engaged in illegal enterprises, including the sale of fur-trading licences at 1,000 livres each.

Oct. 20 Fire destroyed the Ursuline convent in Que., founded in 1639.

Also in Oct.
• Card money was recalled.

Nov. 19 A Neutrality Pact, signed by Louis XIV of France and James II of England, settled the dispute in Hudson Bay and set the boundaries between New France and Rupert's Land. It also provided for the continuance of peace between the two countries in America, even in the event of war in Europe.

1686–1693 Fr. Dablon served a 2nd term as Superior of the Jesuit mission in New France.

Also in 1686
- The population of New France was 12,373.

- The population of Acadia was 885.

1687

Mar. 19 La Salle was murdered in ambush by one of his own men at Matagorda Bay, Texas. La Salle had been attempting to reach the Mississippi R. from the Gulf of Mexico.

Apr. Gov. François-Marie Perrot of Montreal was dismissed from his post for his long-time association in the illegal trading of furs.

June 13 Gov. Denonville's expedition, of 832 colonial regulars and 400 Aboriginal allies, departed Montreal to fight the Iroquois. Denonville ravaged Seneca villages on the south shore of L. Ontario and captured 200, who were sent to Montreal as hostages in case French forces were captured.

June 19 Intendant Champigny sent Iroquois captives to France, where they were made galley slaves.

July 31 Gov. Denonville rebuilt La Salle's Fort Niagara at the mouth of the Niagara R.

Aug. 13 Denonville and his forces returned to Montreal after an indecisive encounter with the Seneca. Seneca villages and their food supplies were destroyed. De Troys was left in command at Niagara.

Sept. 14 Henry Joutel, commanding the remainder of La Salle's expedition, arrived at Tonty's fort at Starved Rock on the Illinois R. Joutel concealed La Salle's death. The expedition wintered at Starved Rock, until Mar. 21, 1688, when it set out for Montreal.

Also in 1687
- The population of French-speaking colonists in Nfld. was 663.

- The 1st reported suicide in Canada took place at Beauport. The victim was Pierre Lefebvre.

1688

Jan. 24 Laval, who had been in spiritual retreat at the Séminaire de Québec since 1685, resigned as bishop of Que. because of ill health. Although his earlier (1684) resignation had been accepted, Laval agreed to remain in Que. until a successor was found. Abbé Jean Baptiste de La Croix de Chevrières de Saint Vallier (1653–1717) was consecrated bishop, on Jan. 25.

Jan. 25 Plague hit Fort Niagara, causing a substantial loss of life.

Apr. The HBC began construction of Fort Prince of Wales, at the mouth of the Churchill R.

- The Conseil Supérieur enacted the 1st public assistance program in New France. It authorized the establishment of civic departments responsible for the poor. Those who could work were found employment, those who could not were given enough aid to meet their needs. Begging was forbidden.

May 1 Construction started on the small Notre-Dame-des-Victoires Chapel, at Place Royal, Que. Designed by engineers Claude Baillif (c 1635–c 1698), Jacques Levasseur de Nere (dc 1723) and Chaussegros de Lery, it is the oldest full-sized church in Canada.

June 15 Chiefs of the Onondaga, Oneida and Cayuga signed a Declaration of Neutrality.

July 14 The remainder of La Salle's expedition arrived back in Montreal.

Aug. 1 or 2 Fort Prince of Wales, under construction at the mouth of the Churchill R. by the HBC, was consumed by fire before its completion.

Aug. 27 Louis-Armand de Lom d'Arce de Lahontan (c 1666–1716) destroyed Fort Frontenac, having insufficient supplies and ammunition to hold it. He set out for Michilimackinac, where he wintered.

Sept. 15 Denonville demolished and abandoned Fort Niagara at the demand of the Iroquois.

Sept. 24 Lahontan left Michilimackinac on a western expedition, claiming to have travelled partly down the Mississippi R. and then westward on what he called the Long R. He returned to Michilimackinac May 22, 1689.

Also in Sept.

• Leaving Fort Sainte-Anne, in a small vessel, d'Iberville encountered the crew of 2 armed English vessels attempting to re-establish Fort Albany. The English blockaded d'Iberville before he could escape the river, but their ships were eventually frozen in. Scurvy took the lives of 25 English and severely weakened the others, who were later captured by d'Iberville.

Also in 1688

• The population of New France was 11,572.

• Twenty-year-old fur trader Jacques de Noyon (d 1745), made the 1st reported trip by a European up the Kaministikwia R. along the Great Dog Portage and over the Height of Land to Rainy L. He was the 1st European to look upon L.-of-the-Woods. Along Rainy R. he met the Assiniboine.

• The French erected a small trading post on Rainy L.

• Radisson became a British subject.

1689

Jan. 28 A French force left Trois-Rivières to attack the New England frontier.

Apr. Frontenac was appointed to command a combined land and sea attack on New York that would cut off Iroquois supplies and bring them under French control. The plan never went into operation. Frontenac was then appointed to replace the exhausted Denonville as Gov. of New France.

May 1 Louis XIV granted the colonists of New France permission to import slaves from Africa to relieve the labour shortage. Several African slaves were brought to New France during the year.

May 7 Gov. Frontenac was ordered to expel the English from Hudson Bay and to attack New York.

May 17 Escalating hostilities between France and England led to the declaration of War of the Great Alliance (King William's War) in North America. New France was pitted against the English in New England and New York, and against their Iroquois allies.

• Henry Kelsey led an expedition for the HBC, sailing north from Churchill in search of Aboriginals willing to trade. In July, Kelsey and an Aboriginal boy walked 200 km northward in search of help after his ship was stopped by ice. Kelsey reported the 1st European sighting of muskox in North America.

May 27 French and their First Nations allies massacred the inhabitants of Cocheco (Dover, New Hampshire).

July 23 Fr. Sébastian Râle (1657–1724) arrived in Que., from France, and was sent to the Abenaki on the Kennebec R.

July D'Iberville captured an English vessel in James Bay, before setting out for Que.

Aug. 4 1,500 Iroquois attacked Lachine after hearing from New York authorities that England and France had gone to war. Twenty four settlers were killed. Forty two of 90 settlers were taken prisoner, never to be seen again.

Aug. 15 The Abenaki, led by the French, attacked the British Fort Pemequid near Kennebec, Maine.

Sept. 24 Denonville sent orders to Clement Du Vuault de Valrennes to blow up Fort Frontenac and return to Montreal with the surviving members of his garrison. The fort had been under constant surveillance by the Iroquois, rendering its inhabitants virtual prisoners.

Oct. 12–Nov. 28, 1698 Frontenac served as Gov. of New France for the 2nd time. He died in office.

Oct. 13 Fr. Râle was sent to a mission at the falls of the Chaudiere R. There he learned Abenaki and began writing the 1st Abenaki-French dictionary.

Oct. 16 Canadians under explorer-trader Daniel Dulhut took part in a raid, on a group of Seneca, at Lac des Deux-Montagnes.

Also in Oct.

• D'Iberville surrendered Fort New Severn, on Hudson Bay, but defended Fort Albany against English attack. He arrived back in Que. Oct. 28, laden with English prisoners, booty and prize furs from his campaign in James Bay.

Nov. 13 Residents of La Chesnaye, near present-day Terrebonne, were killed by the Iroquois.

1690

Jan. 11 Frontenac organized a three-pronged offensive against British settlements in New York, New Hampshire and Maine.

Jan. 22 At the village of Onondaga, the Iroquois concluded a peace treaty with the English and First Nations of the Great Lakes region.

Feb. 18 A French force of 114 Canadians and 96 Aboriginals under the joint command of Jacques Le Moyne de Sainte-Hélène and Nicolas d'Ailleboust de Manthet (1663–1709) attacked the sleeping inhabitants of Corlaer (Schenectady, New York), 2 hours before dawn. The entire settlement was pillaged and burned. Sixty inhabitants were killed, 25 were taken prisoner and some 50 were spared. The invading party returned to Montreal. The attack was a response to the Lachine massacre of the previous year.

Mar. 21 After engagements against the settlements of Penobscot and Passamaquoddy, an English force under Sir William Phips Provost-Marshall (c 1650–c 1695) of New England captured Port Royal, NS, and took 50 prisoners to Boston, including Gov. Louis-Alexandre Des Friches de Meneval.

Mar. 28 The French and their allies attacked Salmon Falls, Maine.

• A force of French and Aboriginals from NS, attacked Fort Loyal (Portland, Maine).

June 1 Jacques-François De Monbeton de Brouillan (1651–1705) was appointed Gov. of Placentia, Nfld.

June 12–Summer 1692 Henry Kelsey, guided by a group of Assiniboine, left York Factory and journeyed to northern Saskatchewan. Kelsey was the 1st reported European to see the prairies. His orders were to induce western First Nations to bring their furs to posts on Hudson Bay. Kelsey was also to look for minerals.

June 14 Joseph Robinau de Villebon (1655–1700) arrived in Acadia, as the official representative of the king in that colony.

July 10 Kelsey took possession of land believed to be present-day The Pas, Man., and named it Deering's Point after the deputy gov. of the HBC. He established a base camp on the site.

Also in July
• D'Iberville left Que., for Hudson Bay, with 3 small vessels carrying 30 guns and 80 men. The expedition arrived at Fort York in late Aug., but was forced to flee when faced with an English ship of 36 guns.

Sept. 4 An English and Iroquois force from Albany, New York, led by Sir William Phips, attacked a settlement south of Montreal, destroying farms and animals and killing more than 50 settlers. The attackers were on their way to take Que.

Also in Sept. D'Iberville attacked Fort Severn in Hudson Bay. The English occupants burned the post to prevent its capture and escaped overland to York Factory.

Oct. 16 Phips arrived at Que. with 32 ships and 2,200 men. He sent Frontenac, who had arrived with 3,000 men 2 days earlier, a summons to surrender. The reply was succinct: "I have no answer to give save from the mouths of my cannon and from my musketry." Following 3 days of skirmishes with Canadian militia, and cold temperatures, Phips decided to embark and sail for Bastonette. He agreed to a council of war and an exchange of prisoners.

Nov. 5 A chapel in Que.'s Lower Town was named Notre-Dame-de-Victoire, in honour of the French victory against the Phips expedition.

Also in 1690
• Frontenac announced he would conduct guerrilla warfare (*petit guerre*) against the English.

1691

Jan. 7 Card money was issued to pay garrison expenses at Que.

Mar. 15 The NS Abenaki attacked Haverhill, Massachusetts.

Apr. 7–July 5, 1700 Villebon, appointment by Louis XIV, served as commandant of the New France colony until his death.

June 7 François Le Moyne de Bienville (1666–1691), with 100 volunteers, attacked a group of Oneida hiding in a house in Repentigny. Fifteen Oneida were massacred and the rest were burned to death when the house was torched. Bienville and 8 volunteers were also killed.

Beginning of summer De Brouillan arrived at Placentia to assume his 1690 appointment as gov. He brought supplies and munitions, 23 soldiers and 25 fishers.

July 15 Kelsey commenced his westward exploration from Hudson Bay, claiming the Red R. area for Britain on Aug. 6.

July 20 Kelsey became the 1st European to record descriptions of buffalo and grizzly bear, and the 1st European to see present-day Sask. He participated in a buffalo hunt 3 days later.

Oct. 20 François-Marie Perrot died in Paris, probably the result of torture he suffered at the hands of English freebooters.

Nov. 26 Villebon arrived at Port Royal, taking possession of Acadia the next day. He did not change the provisional government, which was established by Phips and commanded by Chevalier Charles La Tourasse (d 1696), a sergeant in the French garrison at Port Royal. Instead, Villebon established his gov. at Fort Jemseg.

Also in 1691
• The population of French-speaking residents of Nfld. was 155.

• Capt. Denys de Bonaventure and Villebon, aboard the *Soleil d'Afrique*, captured a Boston vessel carrying Edward Tyng, named Gov. of NS, by New England authorities, and merchants John Nelson (1654–1734) and John Alden (d 1701). All were made prisoners. Tyng was sent to France, where he died.

1692

Feb. 5 Abenaki from NS attacked the British at York, Maine.

June 15 James Knight was made gov. and C-in-C of all forts, factories and territories in Hudson Bay and given orders to recover territory held by the French. Before the end of the month, he sailed for Hudson Bay with 4 ships and 213 men.

Aug. 31 The General Hospital of Ville-Marie was founded.

Sept. Five ships, under Commodore Francis Gillam (Williams), laid siege to Placentia. During a heavy exchange of fire, the British flagship was seriously damaged, causing the fleet to retire.

Oct. 22 Fourteen-year-old Marie-Madeleine Jarret De Verchères (1678–1747), with 2 soldiers, defended the fort of Verchères for 8 days, against an Iroquois attack. She was aided by her 2 younger brothers, an old servant and a few mothers with infants. Verchères escaped to the stockade where she fired a round from a cannon, warning neighbouring settlements, who then sent aid to the besieged group. This foiled the Iroquois who, nevertheless, captured 20 settlers.

Also in 1692
• Villebon constructed Fort Saint-Joseph on the St. John R.

• The HBC rebuilt Fort Nelson.

• Caterpillars destroyed most of the crops in New France.

1693

Jan. 25 Nicolas de Manthet, Zacharie Robutel de La Noue (1665–1733) and Augustin Le Gardeur de Courtemanche (1663–1717) left Montreal with a party of 625 men, including a force of Caughnawaga, on an expedition against the Mohawk in the region of Albany. About 3 weeks later, contact was made with the Mohawk. Villages were burned and 300 prisoners were taken, two-thirds of whom were women and children. An English force, commanded by Peter Schuyler (1657–1723), forced Manthet to retreat. He was not pursued. The raiders struggled back to Montreal. Captives were set free on the way.

Feb. 16 New France engaged the English and Aboriginals in battle near Albany, New York.

June 22 James Knight attacked Fort Albany and captured it back in the name of the HBC. The only defender was a French blacksmith chained inside a blockhouse cell. Five other Frenchmen escaped during the night.

Aug. 4 Two hundred canoes, laden with furs, arrived at Montreal, a signal that trade routes to the west had been reopened.

Aug. 23 Sir Francis Wheler, in command of a fleet of 24 ships, laid siege to Placentia. Gov. Brouillan of Placentia opened fire on Wheler's fleet the next day. A severe storm caused Wheler's fleet to withdraw.

Also in 1693

• The Abenaki signed a peace treaty with the Massachusetts colony.

• Pedro da Silva was paid 20 sous (about 10 cents) to carry letters between Montreal and Que., making him Canada's 1st-known professional mail carrier.

• Construction began on Récollet Church, designed by French Récollet architect Juconde Drue (1664–1739) to replace Notre-Dame-des-Anges. The church, built in dedication to Saint-Antoine, was destroyed by fire in 1796.

1694

Jan. 16 Sébastien de Billie and Louis-Pierre Thury (1663–1709) led 230 Abenaki in an attack on Oyster Bay, Maine, killing over 100 settlers.

June 9 Jolliet sailed for Labrador, systematically mapping and describing the coastline, as well as engaging in a little trading. He charted the unknown coastline from Pointe du Detour, and described the Inuit with whom he made contact. He made it to Zoar, Labrador, before turning back.

Summer D'Iberville was granted a monopoly of trade in Hudson Bay until July of 1697, in reward for his commitment to drive the English out of the area.

Aug. 10 D'Iberville, in command of the *Poli,* and his brother Joseph, Sieur de Serigny, commanding the *Salamandre,* left Que. for Hudson Bay.

Aug. 31 The English ship *William and Mary* defeated 7 French ships at Ferryland, Nfld.

Sept. 24 D'Iberville and his force arrived at the mouth of the Hayes R. and immediately landed a party to set up a winter siege of York Fort.

Oct. 3 D'Iberville invited the English occupying HBC's York Fort to surrender. Henry Kelsey (1667–1724) was sent to negotiate with the French on behalf of the HBC. Louis Le Moyne De Châteauguay, a brother of d'Iberville, was killed by a musket shot the next day.

Oct. 15 Thomas Walsh, in command of York Fort, surrendered to d'Iberville. In consequence, a large cargo of pelts was sent to France rather than England. The French and their prisoners wintered at the fort, which was renamed Fort Bourbon.

Also in Oct.

• Cartographer Jolliet completed the first maps of Labrador with 16 sketches and vivid descriptions, including those of the Inuit.

Also in 1694

• New France's military budget was increased to 200,000 livres (from 75,000 livres, in 1692).

• Frontenac appointed Antoine Laumet de Lamothe Cadillac (1658–1730) commandant of Michilimackinac, New France's most important military and trading station in the west.

• Jesuit Priest Sébastian Râle established a mission to the Abenaki at Norridgewock, Maine, on the Kennebec R.

1695

July 19 The 1st sawmill in New Brunswick was built at the mouth of the Nashwaak R.

Also in July

• Gov. Frontenac sent his right-hand man, Thomas Crisafy (d 1709), with 700 men, to restore Fort Frontenac. The group included 300 soldiers, 200 Aboriginals and 160 habitant.

Nov. 9 Louis Jolliet and his wife, Claire-Françoise Jolliet, and Charles-François Bissot formed a company to trade at Mingan, a large group of islands situated between Anticosti Is. and the Que. mainland.

1696

May 21 In an effort to reduce the flow of beaver pelts flooding the French market, Louis XIV issued edicts that abolished fur-trading licences, ordered the withdrawal of garrisons occupying principal western posts and restricted travel outside New France. Frontenac would not receive these orders until Sept.

July 4 Responding to attacks on French settlements, Frontenac left Montreal with 2,150 men, in a campaign to attack Iroquois villages. His force travelled up the St. Lawrence R. to Fort Frontenac, crossing L. Ontario to Onondaga land, only to find that their target village had already been destroyed. The attackers did destroy an Oneida village and crops, which resulted in some weakening of Iroquois resistance and a reduction in the harassment of New France.

July 14 D'Iberville and Simon-Pierre Denys de Bonaventure, a naval commander and Lt-Gov. of Acadia, captured the British ship *Newport* near St. John's, Nfld.

Aug. 15 D'Iberville captured Fort Pemaquid (Maine), commanded by Capt. Pascoe Chubb. The fort was destroyed and its garrison, of 92 men, sent to Boston.

Aug. 31 A British force, with 5 vessels and 400 men, commanded by William Allen, recaptured York Fort (Fort Bourbon) from the French, along with 136,000 livre's worth of furs. Fort Nelson was recaptured 3 days later.

Sept. 12 D'Iberville arrived at Placentia, Nfld., to begin his campaign to drive the English out of Nfld.

Nov. 1 D'Iberville left Placentia and began his advance across the Avalon Peninsula with the objective of taking St. John's. He destroyed an English settlement at Ferryland, Nfld., on Nov. 10. Its inhabitants fled to Bay Bulls and Petty Harbor.

Nov. 26 The French force killed 36 English settlers in a battle near Petty Harbor, Nfld.

• Pierre Le Moyne d'Iberville and Gov. Brouillon joined forces to besiege St. John's, Nfld., under Gov. Miners.

Nov. 28 Eighty-eight Englishmen tried unsuccessfully to stop d'Iberville's forces advancing on St. John's. Thirty-four were killed and the rest fell back to a crude fort near the town, where they were only able to hold out for 48 hours, before being forced to surrender.

Nov. 30–Mar., 1697 D'Iberville's force (400 French soldiers, Canadians, Aboriginals, members of the Placentia garrison and crews of several St. Malo privateers) committed to sea and land attacks on 36 English fishing outposts in Nfld. All settlements on the Avalon Peninsula, except Carbonear, were taken and destroyed. Settlers were taken prisoner; boats and winter supplies of fish were seized, and St. John's was torched.

1697

May 13 Thomas Lake (d 1743) bought his 1st significant shares of HBC stock during a drop in the market. He became a dominant shareholder.

May 19 Pierre Le Moyne d'Iberville was stationed at Placentia, when 5 ships of war from France commanded by d'Iberville's brother Joseph de Serigny (1668–1734) sailed into the harbour. King Louis XIV had ordered d'Iberville to abandon the Nfld. campaign and again drive the English from Hudson Bay.

June 31 An English force of 1,500 troops recaptured St. John's and established a garrison of 300 soldiers in the town, to enhance the security of Nfld. colonists. The 1st winter, 214 men died as a result of starvation and exposure. Construction of Fort William began in 1698, and was completed in 1700. The fort featured bombproof parapets, powder magazines and barracks.

Sept. 3 The British ship *Owner's Love* sank in Hudson Strait.

Sept. 20 The Treaty of Ryswick, reversed all conquests made by France and England during King William's War. Nfld. became English. Hudson Bay remained English, Acadia remained French.

Also in 1697
• Récollet Father Louis Hennepin published *Nouvelle Découverte d'un trés grand pays*.

• King William III of England granted Labrador to Joseph de La Penja, a Jewish merchant from Rotterdam.

1698

May 25 Kelsey was dispatched to the HBC post of Albany, after signing a new 3-year contract with the HBC.

July 1 Sister Bourgeoys founded La Congrégation de Notre-Dame de Montréal. She and her companions took the simple vows of the canonically constituted community.

Nov. 28 Frontenac died in Que.

Nov. 29 Louis-Hector de Callières (1648–1703) was appointed administrator of New France. He would serve until Sept. 16, 1699.

Also in 1698
• Récollet Fr. Louis Hennepin's book of adventure and discovery, *Nouvelle Voyage d'un Pais plus grand que l'Europe*, based upon his travels, was published.

• Construction began on Ferme Saint-Gabriel located in Pointe Saint-Charles, Montreal. The house was enlarged during 1726–1728, with the addition of a wing, at either end of the 15.9 x 6 m rectangular central portion. (It is the only 17th century farmhouse still in existence in Montreal. Now a museum, it was declared a monument of national interest by La Commsission des monuments historiques de la province Québec.)

1699

Jan. 22 Bishop St. Valier established an elementary school at Que., although it would not open until Oct.

Mar. 2 D'Iberville, with 4 vessels, entered the Birdfoot sub-delta of the Mississippi R. and proceeded northward to establish a French claim that encompassed the entire Mississippi basin from the Gulf of St. Lawrence to the Gulf of Mexico. Louis XIV's new expansionist policy called for containment of the English, east of the Appalachian Mountains.

Mar. 4 The Royal Academy of Sciences in Paris honoured New France's 1st great scientist, Surgeon-Major Michel Sarrazin (1659–1734), for his work in botany and zoology. Sarrazin catalogued more than 200 plants and their pharmacological properties, over a period of 30 years. The reknowned scientist died a pauper, of typhus, in Quebec City Sept. 8, 1734.

Mar. 25 An Anglo-French commission based in London, England, issued letters to the governors of Canada and New York with orders to end hostilities with the Iroquois and to disarm local First Nations.

Apr. 20 Louis-Hector de Callières was appointed gov. of New France, a position he would hold from Sept. 14 until May 26, 1703.

May 3 D'Iberville returned to France after building a temporary fort (Maurepas) on Biloxi Bay (present-day Ocean Springs, Mississippi). His brother, Jean-Baptiste Le Moyne de Bienville, and a garrison of 81 men, remained behind under the command of Ensign Sauvole (d 1701).

Oct. D'Iberville received instructions to lead another exploratory voyage to the mouth of the Mississippi and to contain, by covert means, any designs the English might have on the region.

1700

Jan. 12 Sister Bourgeoys died after contracting a high fever.

Jan. D'Iberville arrived back at Biloxi and began construction on a 2nd Louisiana fort (Mississippi), 64 km up the river. The fortification was built to discourage Spanish and English occupation of the lower Mississippi region.

Mar. 22 Jean-Baptiste Le Moyne de Bienville (1680–1767) explored the Red R.

July Two Onondaga and four Seneca chiefs announced their desire for peace, and invited Gov. Callières to send Frs. Bruyas, Chabert de Joncaire and Paul Le Moyne de Maricourt to their camps to negotiate a treaty. Callières agreed to send the Frs.

Aug.–Sept. 1701 D'Iberville returned to France to argue for a strong commitment to Louisiana so the French could resist English expansion west of the Appalachians. In 1701, Louis XIV advised Callières and Champigny that he intended to found a settlement at the mouth of the Mississippi R. to slow or prevent the English from advancing through the continent.

Sept. 8 Peace terms were agreed on, at Montreal, between Gov. Callières, most of the Iroquois (except the Mohawk), the mission natives, Abenaki, Huron and Ottawa. The 3 French peace ambassadors returned to Que. with 13 French prisoners who had been liberated by the Iroquois as a goodwill gesture.

Oct. 15 To offset falling beaver-pelt prices, Gov. Callières forced the Compagnie de la Colonie du Canada to sell goods to its Aboriginal allies at cut-rate prices to prevent them from trading with the English in Albany, New York.

Also in 1700

• The French population in Nfld. was approximately 15,000.

• Portrait of Marguerite Bourgeoys (oil on canvas), by Pierre Le Ber (1662–1714), was completed. It now hangs at the Congregation de Notre Dame in Montreal.

• St. Paul's Lodge, the 1st Masonic lodge in Canada, was established in Montreal.

• Properties fronting onto the St. Lawrence R. between Quebec and Montreal, were ceded by the crown opening nearly 200 seigneuriories for settlement — 75% of families living in New France were engaged in farming.

1701

June 4 Charles Juchereau de Saint-Denys (1655–1703) was granted the right to establish tanneries in the Mississippi Valley, at Michilimackinac, and on the lower Ohio R. near Cairo, Illinois. Within a year, Saint-Denys and his men had skinned more than 13,000 buffalo. The Cairo location was ultimately raided by Cherokee who seized the valuable collection of hides and killed most of the French workers.

June 5 Antoine Laumet (de Lamothe) Cadillac, in command of 100 soldiers and workmen in 25 canoes, left Que. to found a new settlement at Detroit, which was thought to be a more accessible fur-trading post. It was a more convenient location than Michilimackinac. The journey took 18 days. Upon arriving at Detroit, Cadillac and his force immediately began building Fort Ponchartrain, named in honour of the French Counts of Ponchartrain, Ministers for the Navy and the Colonies.

June 29 Jacques-François de Mombeton de Brouillan arrived in Acadia as commander and was appointed gov. in 1702. He served until his death Sept. 22, 1705, in Chedabouctou.

July 19 The Iroquois ceded territory north of L. Ontario and west of L. Michigan to England.

July–Aug. 4 One thousand, three hundred Aboriginals, representing over 30 First Nations, came together at Montreal to exchange prisoners and discuss peace with Gov. Callières. A treaty was drawn up, wherein signatories agreed to live at peace with each other, using the Gov. of New France to obtain redress when assaults were committed. The Iroquois also promised to remain neutral in the event of hostilities between the French and English.

Aug. Twenty-one-year-old Jean-Baptiste Le Moyne de Bienville succeeded as commandant of Louisiana upon Ensign Sauvole's death. De Bienville would be commissioned Gov. of the Territory on May 31, 1702.

Sept. 29 D'Iberville sailed out of La Rochelle (France) for Louisiana with crown authorization to found Mobile and to establish an active Aboriginal policy that would protect the Mississippi basin from English incursions.

Dec. 15 D'Iberville reached Louisiana and organized the removal of the colony to Massacre (Dauphin) Is., in preparation for a settlement on the Mobile R.

Also in 1701
• Under new French colonial policy, coureurs de bois and First Nations peoples were officially encouraged to move to Louisiana.

1702

Jan. 6 De Bienville left Biloxi to establish Fort Saint-Louis and new settlements on the west side of Mobile Bay, the 1st settlements in Alabama.

Apr. 1 François de Beautiarnois de La Chaussaye, Baron de Beauville (1665–1746), was appointed Intendant of New France. He would serve for 3 years before returning to France.

Also in Apr.
• Daniel d'Auger de Subercase (1661–1732) became Gov. of Placentia, although he would not arrive to take up his position until summer 1703.

May 15 England declared war on France, ushering in the War of the Spanish Succession (1702–1713), known in North America as Queen Anne's War.

1703

May 27 Phillippe de Rigaud de Vaudreuil (c 1643–1725) became the administrator of New France following the death of Callières.

Aug. 21 A detachment of Abenaki and French, under Alexandre Leneuf de La Vallière de Beau-Bassin (1667–1712), staged a surprise attack on the town of Wells (Maine), taking possession. The raiders laid waste to the surrounding country, killing and capturing more than 300 persons.

Oct. 17 Augustin Le Gardeur de Courte-Manche (1663–1717) received a 10-year trading and fishing licence from the French Crown for the northern shore of the Gulf of St. Lawrence and the coast of Labrador.

The period 1703–1713 was called the Warful Decade because of the seemingly endless series of raids, skirmishes and battles between the French, English and Aboriginal partners of each.

Also in 1703
• The Conseil Souverain (Sovereign Council), the governing body of New France, was renamed Conseil Supérieur, and the membership was increased to 12.

1704

Feb. 29 The French and their Aboriginal allies led by Jean-Baptiste Hertel de Rouville (1668–1722) and 4 of de Rouville's brothers, conducted a surprise attack on Deerfield, Massachusetts, destroying the settlement's 41 homes, killing 54 settlers and abducting 120 inhabitants who were taken to Canada. Reverend John Williams (1664–1729) survived the ordeal and later wrote a book entitled *The Redeemed Captive Returning to Zion*. The English labelled de Rouville the "Sacker of Deerfield."

May A fleet, commanded by Benjamin Church (1639–1717/18), sailed from Boston, Massachusetts to make retaliatory raids against Acadia. It captured Les Mines (Grand Pré), on June 20, before moving on to ravish Pigiguit, Cobequid (Truro, NS) and Beaubassin at the head of Chignecto Bay. Church and his ships returned to Boston without having attacked Port Royal. The Acadian colonies suffered from severe famine the following winter.

Oct. John Moody (c 1677–1736) was left in charge of the British forces in St. John's when Commodore Bridges returned to England.

Dec. 18–Oct. 28, 1706 Simon-Pierre Denys de Bonaventure (1659–1711) served as administrator of Acadia.

Winter 1704–1705 About 275 New England soldiers, under Winthrop Hilton, were sent to Norridgewock to destroy the village and capture Fr. Râle, in reprisal for the 1703 attack on Wells. Râle escaped, but his church was torched.

Also in 1704
• One hundred fifty French soldiers, under Jean Léger de La Grange (1663–1736), from Placentia, Nfld., attacked the English settlement of Bonavista, Nfld., burning 4 ships. New England skipper Michael Gill and his 24-man crew fought the larger French force for 6 hours, rallying the community to drive the French off.

1705

Jan. 1 Jacques Raudot (1638–1728) and his son, Antoine-Denis (1679–1737), were appointed joint Intendants of New France. Jacques, who received a salary, focused his efforts on justice and public order. Antoine-Denis, who was unsalaried, concentrated on financial affairs. The father/son duo served until 1711.

Jan. 8 Daniel d'Auger de Subercase, Gov. of Placentia, Nfld., set out with an expedition of 450 men, to fight the English. The French captured Bay Bulls and Petty Harbor. All settlements on Conception, Bonavista and Trinity Bays were destroyed. The town of St. John's was captured and burned, but the French were unable to take Fort William, although they besieged it for 5 weeks.

Aug. 1 Philippe de Rigaud de Vaudreuil (1640–1725) was appointed gov. of New France; he was inducted into office on Sept. 17, and held the position until 1725.

Sept. 24 The French govt established standardized circulation of card money.

1706

Apr. 10 De Subercase was appointed French Gov. of Acadia, following the death of Brovillan. De Subercase, the last French gov. of the colony, served until 1710.

June 22 An Order-in-Council required inhabitants of Montreal to repair roads and build sidewalks at street corners. Also, keeping pigs in the house was forbidden, incurring a fine of 3 sols for each pig.

July 9 D'Iberville died of yellow fever in Havana. He had been raiding the English colony of Nevis in the West Indies.

July 24 The Conseil Supérior granted the Compagnie de Canada a monopoly in the beaver trade.

Also in 1706
• The population of New France was 16,417.

• Philippe Pastour de Costebelle (1661–1717) was appointed gov. of Placentia. De Costebelle had plenty of experience. He had been acting gov. for those periods his 2 predecessors had been unable to take up office. De Costebelle was made a Knight of the Order of St. Louis in 1708.

1707

Mar. New England placed a bounty of £100 on Aboriginal scalps.

May 13 John March (1658–1712), a Massachusetts militia col. sailed from Boston with 1,526 men to attack Port Royal (June 6). He was repelled by de Subercase and Pierre Morpain (c 1686–1749), a Caribbean privateer, Intendant de Goutin and 300 soldiers.

Aug. 20 John March attacked Port Royal again. This foray was also repulsed by de Subercase, Morpain, and their associates.

Nov. French Prime Minister of Marine (Navy) Pontchartrain, called for an investigation into conditions in the west, especially concerning the activities of Cadillac, who was suspected of profiteering. François Clairambault d'Aigremont (1659–1728) headed the commission.

Also in 1707
• The painting on canvas, *Ex-voto de l'Ange-gardien*, by Michel Dessaillant de Richeterre, was completed and installed in the Hôtel-Dieu, Que. The painting was the artist's most spectacular work.

• Intendant Raudot issued an ordinance which

forbade young men living in Montreal from keeping their mistresses in the town.

1708

July 26 French and Aboriginals under De Rouville and Jean-Baptiste de Saint-Ours Deschaillons (1669–1747), a regular army officer, left Montreal to attack Haverhill, Massachusetts which they did on Aug. 29. Fifteen residents were killed; the raiders incurred losses of 10 dead and 19 wounded.

Nov. D'Aigremont's report revealed that Cadillac was interested only in profiteering and that his policy was a threat to French control of the interior. The report detailed tyrannical rule and the charge that Cadillac was hated by both Europeans and Aboriginals.

Dec. 14 A company of 170 men (soldiers, sailors, fishermen, privateers and settlers) commanded by de Costebelle and Saint-Ovide de Brouillan (1676–1755), left Placentia to attack St. John's.

Also in 1708

• A group of militia, formed at St. John's, marked the beginning of the Royal Newfoundland Regiment, the oldest in North America.

• Abbé Gervais Le Febvre was awarded the 1st doctorate in theology in Canada.

1709

Jan. 1 The French, under command of Saint-Ovide de Brouillan, took St. John's and 800 English prisoners. The French held the town only briefly. They had insufficient resources to maintain their position and de Costebelle ordered them to abandon it in Apr. The French took all guns and ammunition and St. John's forts were blown up.

Summer Hertel de Rouville launched another attack against Deerfield, Massachusetts, to forestall an attack against Montreal. Several settlers were killed. Two prisoners, John Arms and Joseph Closson, were condemned to run the gauntlet, a common form of torture for the Iroquois.

July Nicolas D'Ailleboust de Manthet was killed in an unsuccessful attack on Fort Albany.

Also in 1709

• Port Royal residents were stricken by a severe epidemic of purpura, a bleeding disease unchecked by normal blood clotting. Scurvy may have been responsible for the outbreak.

• Slavery became legal in New France.

1710

Mar. 18 Francis Nicholson (1655–1728) was commissioned C-in-C of an expedition to recover NS from the French.

Apr. Four sachems (civil chiefs) of the Five Nations Iroquois Confederacy travelled to London to request British military support against the French. Queen Anne commissioned Dutch artist Jan Verelst (c 1648–1734), to paint individual portraits of the 4 leaders — Tee-Yee-Neen-Ho-Ga-Row; Ho-Nee-Yeath-Taw-No-Row, Sa-Ga-Yeath-Qua-Pieth-Tow, and Etow-Oh-Koam. The result, known as the "Four Indian Kings," is now in the National Archives of Canada.

May 5 Cadillac was appointed gov. of Louisiana, the most dismal colony in the French empire.

June 12 The HBC awarded Pierre Radisson's widow £6 upon his death, as a charitable token.

July 7 Intendant Jacques Raudot issued a proclamation penalizing all unlicenced doctors from practising in the colony.

Sept. 29 Col. Francis Nicholson sailed from Boston with a 2,000-man force, attacking Port Royal on Oct. 5. The port was besieged by a combined fleet of 36 vessels. Gov. Subercase, greatly outnumbered, refused to yield and, with scarcely 300 men, attempted to defend his position. He was forced to surrender on Oct. 13 — marking the end of French rule at the port.

Oct. 10 The 1st Anglican service in Canada was held at Chebucto (Halifax).

Oct. 16 Gov. Subercase, was granted honourable surrender and his soldiers were allowed to return to France, as the British occupied Port Royal, renaming the town Annapolis Royal, and the fort, Fort Anne. Acadians were required to take an oath of allegiance to Queen Anne if they wished to remain in the area.

1711

Mar. Fort Condé was built on the Mobile R. near present-day Mobile, Alabama. The Louisiana colony was relocated to this new site.

July 6 Land owners of New France were told to cultivate their properties or face confiscation.

July 30 Sir Hovenden Walker (c 1656–1725) sailed from Nantucket with the objective of capturing New France. Walker planned a joint land and sea attack Aug. 23, with Nicholson's colonials and the Iroquois attacking Montreal, while Walker and Gen. Sir John Hill moved against Que. The operation was abandoned when 10 ships in Walker's fleet were wrecked on the north shore of the Gulf of St. Lawrence. Nearly 900 soldiers and sailors lost their lives. The incident became known as the "Magnificent Fiasco."

1711–Mar. 13, 1717 Thomas Caulfield served as lt-gov. of NS and Placentia.

1712

May 13 Jean-Baptiste Bissot de Vinsenne (1668–1719), agent of New France among the Miami, arrived at Detroit, which was besieged by the Outagami and Mascouten nations. The French, aided by their allies, forced the besiegers to surrender after a battle that lasted several days.

June Cadillac arrived in Louisiana to assume the position of gov. to which he had been appointed in 1710.

Aug. 19 The Treaty of Paris provided a 4-month truce between England and France.

Sept. Under Cadillac's influence, a company was formed to develop Louisiana. Antoine Crozat (1655–1738) contributed between 600,000 and 700,000 livres.

Oct. 20 Francis Nicholson (1655–1728) was appointed

gov. of NS and Placentia, but only remained in NS from Aug. 11 to Oct. 18, 1714.

Also in 1712
• Sir Bibye Lake (c 1684–1744) was appointed gov. of the HBC.

1713

Apr. 11 The Treaty of Utrecht ended the War of the Spanish Succession (Queen Anne's War). France gave Britain all forts and territories at Hudson Bay (giving the British undisputed control over the northern fur trade), Nfld. and Acadia, but retained St. Pierre Is., Miquelon Is., Île Royale (Cape Breton Is.) and Île St. Jean (PEI). The French were allowed to fish off Nfld., but not Acadia. The Iroquois were declared British subjects. The boundaries of Rupert's Land and Acadia were not clearly defined. Abenaki in Acadia refused to accept British sovereignty. The treaty was signed on Apr. 16, and Gov. Costebelle was ordered to evacuate the French from Nfld. to Île Royale, where the plan was to establish a fishing industry on the Grand Banks. Most French Newfoundlanders moved to Île Royale in the vicinity of where the new town of Louisbourg would arise. The majority of Acadian farmers opted to remain on their land, even under British rule, rather than begin again elsewhere.

June 23 Francis Nicholson received orders from Queen Anne to protect Acadians wishing to remain in their homes, as well as those wishing to leave. Acadians were given 1 year to take the oath of allegiance to the British Crown or vacate their lands.

July 11–13 As a result of the peace provided by the Treaty of Utrecht, Mog, Bomoseen, Moxus, Taxous and other Abenaki chiefs concluded a peace agreement with New England at Portsmouth, New Hampshire, pledging allegiance to Queen Anne and acknowledging the English right to land occupied before the war.

July 18 The Portsmouth, New Hampshire, peace agreement was taken to Casco Bay and read to some 30 chiefs in the presence of about 400 Abenaki. All expressed wonder when told that the French had surrendered their lands to the English.

Fr. Râle later convinced the Chiefs that the English were deceiving them.

Aug. Havre à l'Anglois or Louisbourg, founded on the east coast of Île Royale by the French, became the capital of New France. A fortress was planned to serve as the bastion of French power in the Gulf of St. Lawrence.

Also in 1713
• Jesuit Joseph-François Lafitau (c 1681–1746) travelled to Sault Saint Louis as a missionary to the Iroquois. He was the 1st Euorpean to discover ginseng in North America.

1714

Jan. 1 De Costebelle was appointed gov. of Île Royale.

Mar. 20 A French ordinance re-instituted a rule requiring vessels destined for Canada and the West Indies to take *engagés* (indentured workers) to relieve the labour shortage.

June 1 De Costebelle surrendered Placentia to the English under Capt. John Moody (c 1677–1736), as directed by the Treaty of Utrecht. Moody was promoted to lt-col. and appointed deputy-gov. of Placentia under Gov. Nicholson of NS.

July 10 A Royal decree by the king of France permitted 15 fur-trading licences to be issued for use exclusively in the areas of the Detroit, Michilimackinac and Illinois posts.

Aug. 23 A rioting mob threatened to storm Que. unless prices on goods were reduced.

Sept. 11 James Knight (1640–1719), administrator of HBC, and Henry Kelsey, received the formal surrender of all Hudson Bay territories from Nicolas Jérémie, the French commander, as provided by the Treaty of Utrecht.

1714–1718 Henry Kelsey served as deputy gov. of all HBC posts on Hudson Bay.

Also in 1714
• The 1st hospital in Canada to care for mental patients was established in Que., by Bishop Saint-Vallier. It treated female patients only.

1715

Jan. 20 Samuel Vetch (1668–1732) was appointed gov. of NS. He served until Aug. 17, 1717.

June 25 Acadians of Grand Pré and Beaubassin appeared before the Council of NS at Halifax and refused to take the oath of allegiance to the British Crown.

June 27 HBC administrator James Knight sent William Stewart (c 1678–1719) from York Factory on a mission to bring peace between the Cree and the Chipewyan, living north-west of the Churchill R. A truce was achieved and Stewart promised that the HBC would build a post at the mouth of the Churchill R. Thanadelthur (d 1717) a female Chipewyan captive slave, served as interpreter.

Aug. The Abenaki failed to prevent New Englanders, under John Gyles, from constructing a new post, Fort George (Brunswick, Maine), on the Androscoggin R.

Nov. 23 Joseph de Brouillan (1676–1747) was appointed administrator of Île Royal.

1716

Jan. 13 Acadians of Grand Pré and Beaubassin again refused to sign an oath of allegiance to the English Crown.

Mar. 3 Cadillac was removed as gov. of Louisiana because of his failure to get along with his colleagues, specifically Bienville.

May 7 William Stewart returned from his peace mission to Fort York accompanied by Thanadelthur and 10 Chipewyan. The journey was excessively rough, and they experienced bitter cold and starvation conditions.

Also in May
• The 1710 concession for Île St. Jean was revoked by France and the island became royal domain again.

Oct.–Mar. 1717 Bienville served as acting head of Louisiana while appointed Gov. Jean-Michel de

Lespinay (d 1721) was en route to assume the appointment.

Also in 1716

• The number of fur-trading licences allowed to be issued in the Detroit, Michilimackinac, Illinois territory was increased from 15 to 25.

• Louis de La Port de Louvigny (c 1662–1725) was placed in command of 400 coureurs de bois and a like number of Aboriginal volunteers in a march against the Fox at their stronghold of Baie des Puants (Green Bay, Wisconsin). De Louvigny's goal was to subjugate the Fox and bring about an end to their war against the French, because conflict was severely disrupting the fur trade. The Fox were forced to sue for peace, and tranquillity was restored to the west.

• William Stewart became the 1st person of European descent to travel in the Mackenzie watershed.

1717

Feb. 5 Thanadelthur died after enduring a severe 7-week-long illness.

May 11 Commercial exchange began in Montreal, when merchants were given permission to hold meetings.

May 25 Capt. John Doucette (d 1726) was appointed lt-gov. of the garrison of Annapolis Royal, succeeding Thomas Caulfield. Doucette held the position until 1726. He was also appointed administrator of NS (1717–1720), and reprised that position from 1722–1726.

June HBC administrator Knight dispatched William Stewart and an advance party to the mouth of the Churchill R. to establish Fort Prince of Wales (built 1719). The goal was to outflank the Cree who were preventing the Athabascan from visiting York Factory to trade.

July Zacharie Robutel de La Noue (1665–1733) was commissioned to discover access to the northern sea by an inland route through New France. He set out with 3 canoes and established the 1st post on

the Kanastigoya R. in the northern part of L. Superior. De La Noue remained exploring in the area until 1721.

Aug. 17 Richard Philipps (c 1661–1750) was commissioned gov. of Placentia, and capt.-gen. and gov.-in-chief of NS (Apr. 25, 1720–May 6, 1749).

Also in Aug.

• The French govt awarded The Compagnie d'Occident (Company of the West) a 25-year fur trade monopoly, a grant which exceeded any of those awarded to its predecessors. Beginning Jan. 1, 1718, all beaver skins had to be delivered to Company stores.

Sept. 20 Bienville was named a Knight of the Order of Saint-Louis.

Oct. 28 Capt. John Doucette arrived at Annapolis Royal to assume the duties of lt-gov. He attempted unsuccessfully in Nov. to make Acadians sign an oath of allegiance to the British Crown. Acadians refused to sign because they were not assured freedom of religion, their ancestors had never taken such an oath, and they feared retaliation raids from local Aboriginals.

Also in 1717

• A series of trading posts were erected as bases for exploration. These extended west from L. Superior, and came to be known as Postes de Nord. De La Noue, re-established the old French post on Rainy L. and commanded these operations from 1717–1720.

• The Illinois country was annexed to Louisiana.

• A lamp lit in the Ursuline Convent in Que. has remained burning ever since.

1718

Jan. The French govt issued an edict that made all debts incurred since 1714 payable with card money, which was reduced to 50% of its face value. Export duties on beaver and moose hides were cancelled and a long-standing 25% premium on French currency was eliminated. In addition, a new copper coin for exclusive use in New France was initiated. The use of card money was prohibited after 1720.

May 30 Henry Kelsey was appointed gov. of HBC settlements. He served in this post until 1722.

Sept. Thomas Smart, commanding a New England vessel, attacked French fishermen at Canso.

Dec. 13 Lt-Gov. Doucette urged Gov. Philipps to apply to the Lords of Trade for presents to give local First Nations of NS in an effort to win them over. This tactic did not succeed with the Abenaki.

1718–1722 Architect François de Lajoue built Ursuline Chapel, located at 2 rue du Parloir in Quebec City for the 1st centenary of the Ursulines' arrival. The chapel is now a tourist attraction and is open for public services.

Also in 1718
• New Englanders built Fort Richmond (Richmond, Maine), further aggravating the Abenaki nation.

1719

Mar. 7 Michel-Philippe Isabeau (d 1724) was awarded the contract to build the King's Bastion and Château Saint-Louis at Louisbourg. Isabeau was responsible for the fortification's landward front, including the citadel barracks and the Royal and Island batteries. The director and designer of the fortifications was Jean-François de Verville (1680–1729), who 1st recommended the site in 1716. Referred to as the "Gibraltar of Canada," Louisbourg was designed to protect the St. Lawrence fisheries and the sea route to New France. The fortress took 25 years to complete. The end result was not only a fortress, but a complete French town, with gov.'s palace, barracks, houses, hospital, arsenals and warehouses.

May 1 James Knight was commissioned by the HBC to undertake a voyage of discovery (with ships *Albany* and *Discovery*) north of the 64th parallel, to seek the Strait of Anian (and to discover the Northwest Passage), to enlarge and increase the company's trade, to discover gold and copper mines and to establish a whaling industry. His fleet left Gravesend, England, on June 4. The expedition vanished. Years later, Capt. John Scroggs, another

northern explorer, reported that both ships had been wrecked and all expedition members killed by Inuit. The report was later proved incorrect.

May 3 The Compagnie des Indies (Company of the Indies) was created with the amalgamation of The French East India Company, the China Company and the Company of the West.

June 19 HBC Gov. Kelsey left York Factory to sail north in the *Prosperous,* and the *Success,* to explore north of Marble Is. in search of the same copper mines sought by James Knight. Kelsey also hoped to trade 2 Aboriginal slaves for 2 Inuit whom he wished to train as interpreters. On Aug. 9, 1721, Inuit offered Kelsey objects belonging to the ill-fated James Knight expedition. Kelsey made no attempt to locate the lost explorers, although later evidence indicated that some of Knight's party may have still been alive at the time. On Aug. 22, 1722, Kelsey returned to York Factory after having explored the western shore of Hudson Bay. He and his men had found traces of James Knight's missing expedition at Marble Is. On Sept. 29, the HBC wrote off vessels *Albany* and *Discovery* along with all hands involved in the James Knight expedition.

Aug. Louis-Hyacinthe Castel, Comte de Saint-Pierre, was granted the Île Saint-Jean (PEI), Miscou, and nearby islands, by the Duc d'Orleans, Regent of Louis XV. Castel formed the Compagnie de l'Île Saint-Jean to colonize the island.

Oct. 25 William Stewart died at York Factory after several mental breakdowns.

Also in 1719
• Swan, a Cree leader, took the 1st sample of Athabaska tar sands to HBC Gov. Kelsey.

1720

Apr. 15 Castel sent 3 ships and 300 settlers from France to Île Saint-Jean (PEI) to establish the 1st European community on the island, and its capital, La Joie. The convoy arrived at La Joie on Aug. 23.

Apr. 25 His Majesty's Council of NS was established at Annapolis Royal by Gov. Philipps. The 1st meeting was held on May 6.

Spring Marquis Pierre de Rigaud de Vaudreuil, gov. of New France, ordered the building of 3 trading posts along L. Ontario, to prevent British expansion on the Great Lakes and along the western frontier. The central post overlooked the Niagara portage, used by all Aboriginal traders en route to Canada or New York. The other 2 posts were located at present-day Toronto and Quinte. All 3 posts were on Iroquois hunting grounds claimed by Britain under the Treaty of Utrecht. The French would gain an advantage in trading with First Nations peoples who would pass these forts on their way to New York.

June Pirate Black Bart's (Bartholomew Roberts) *Royal Rover* entered the port of Trepassey, Nfld., flying the Jolly Roger flag.

July The Massachusetts Council offered a reward of £100 for the arrest of Fr. Râle.

Aug. 8 Abenaki warriors raided a New England fishermen's camp at Canso, NS. Gov. Philipps sent Maj. Lawrence Armstrong (1664–1739) with a contingent of troops to help the fishermen build a small fort. Philipps himself moved to Canso the following year to establish a permanent settlement.

Nov. Abenaki chiefs Mog and Wowurna led a delegation to Georgetown protesting the spread of settlements to, what is now, Merrymeeting Bay, Maine. Instead of obtaining satisfaction, the chiefs were required to pledge payment of 200 skins, in addition to sending 4 hostages to Boston as security against any past and future raids by their constituents.

Dec. 28 British Lords of Trade proposed the removal of the Acadians from Acadia.

Also in 1720
• North America's 1st commercial coal mining operation was established at Morien, NS (Cow Bay, Cape Breton Is.) as French soldiers worked a mine to supply the fortress of Louisbourg.

1721

Jan. 27 Nicholas Lanouiller established a mail stagecoach service between Quebec City and Montreal, as the 1st regular postal service in Canada.

June 9 Nearly half of Montreal was destroyed by fire.

July 28 More than 250 Aboriginals, accompanied by Frs. La Chasse and Râle, appeared at a meeting at Georgetown to demand that the English leave their lands.

Also in 1721
• The population of New France included 24,951 European colonists.

1722

End of Jan. While Abenaki were away hunting, a party of 100 New Englanders, under Col. Westbrook, surrounded the village of Norridgewock and attempted to capture Fr. Râle, who escaped into the forest. The soldiers pillaged the church and seized Râle's dictionary of the Abenaki language.

Feb. 6 Intendant Michel Bégon introduced the death penalty for women who concealed pregnancy and then left their babies to die of exposure. Within months of the new law's enactment, 2 women were tried and executed.

Mar. 3 The Council of State divided New France into parishes: Quebec had 41; Trois-Rivières, 13; and Montreal, 28.

Mid June and July The Abenaki raided British settlements around Merrymeeting Bay near the mouth of the Kennebec R. in retaliation for the British attacks on the village of Norridgewock in Jan. The Abenaki also attacked shipping on the Bay of Fundy and along the eastern coast of NS, capturing some 36 vessels and boats. Gov. Vaudreuil of New France secretly encouraged these raids and supplied arms and ammunition. On July 25, Samuel Shute, gov. of Massachusetts, declared war on the French, as a result of the French encouraging Abenaki raids on his colony (Three Years War).

Sept. A party of some 400 Norridgewock, Abenaki, Lorette Huron and other First Nation warriors destroyed all English settlements on the lower Kennebec R. Raids continued from eastern Maine to the Connecticut valley.

Year
1722

Also in 1722

• The Tuscarora joined the Iroquois Confederacy, which became known as the League of Six Nations. The other members were the Mohawk, Oneida, Onondaga, Cayuga and Seneca.

1723

Mar. 22 The Company of the Indies was granted an exclusive tobacco trade monopoly.

• Presbyterian Rev. George Henry began preaching in Que., in a room provided by the Jesuit College.

Mar. Forces under Col. Westbrook again tried unsuccessfully to capture Fr. Râle.

Nov. 15 Étienne de Véniard de Bourgmond (c 1675–c 1730) commenced construction of Fort Orléans on the north bank of the Missouri R., about 480 km from its mouth.

1723–1726 Gov. of Montreal and gov.-gen. of New France, Marquis de Vaudreuil built *Château de Vaudreuil*, designed by architect Gaspard Joseph Chaussegros de Lery (1682–1756). The house, located on Rue Saint-Paul in Montreal, was destroyed by fire in 1803.

Also in 1723

• De Saint-Pierre's Compagnie de l'Île Saint-Jean went bankrupt; settlers dispersed by the end of the year. De Saint-Pierre's title to Île Saint-Jean was revoked June 1, 1730.

1724

Feb. 22 Edme-Nicholas Robert was appointed Intendant of New France, but died in a shipwreck off Île Royal, June 24, before assuming office.

Apr. 17 Pirate John Phillips was murdered by several prisoners and members of his own crew. His decapitated body was thrown into the sea off Nfld.'s shore.

May 13 A royal edict proposed a stone wall be built to defend Montreal.

Aug. 23 Fr. Râle was killed when a New England force under the joint command of Johnson Harmon and Jeremiah Moulton attacked the Abenaki settlement of Norridgewock. Chief Mog and his entire family were also killed. Their scalps were taken to Boston and the lot brought £505 in bounties.

Oct. The Council of First Nations, meeting at Fort d'Orléans, agreed to send 10 delegates to France because of the trust they had in Véniard de Bourgmond's assurances about the risks of the voyage. This group was later reduced to 3 chiefs, the daughter of 1 chief and her slave. The delegation, accompanied by Bourgmond, arrived in Paris where they had an audience with King Louis XV on Sept. 24, 1725.

Also in 1724

• Joseph François Lafitau's (1681–1746) *Moeurs des sauvages, américains comparées aux moeurs des premier temps* was published in Paris as a 4-volume work.

1725

Feb. 8 Lawrence Armstrong was commissioned lt-gov. of NS. He served until Nov. 19, 1729.

Aug. 11 Charles Le Moyne, Baron de Longueuil (1656–1729), was inducted into the office of administrator of New France. He served until Sept. 2, 1726.

Aug. 27 Michel Bégon de La Picardière (1667–1747) was appointed as interim Intendant of New France until a 2nd replacement for the late Edme-Nicholas Robert was found.

Oct. 10 Gov. Vaudreuil died in Que.

Nov. 23 Claude-Thomas Dupuy (1678–1738) was appointed Intendant of New France. He served from Aug. 28, 1726–Aug. 30, 1728.

Also in 1725

• All buildings built on land sold by religious communities in Que. were legislated to be no more than 1 storey high so that no structure could overlook the grounds of the convent.

• Mason Jean Mars built Maison du Calvet on Rue Saint-Paul, at Rue Bonsecours in Montreal. The 4-storey, 5-bay-window, gabled-roof house was commissioned by Huguenot merchant and fur trader Pierre du Calvet. In 1775, Benjamin Franklin stayed at the home when he visited Montreal, discussing the American Revolution with supporters, including Pierre du Calvet (1735–1786), son of the fur trader. The house is currently a hotel and restaurant, located in historic Old Montreal.

1726

Jan. 11 Charles de Beauharnois de La Boische was appointed gov. of New France. He served from Sept. 2, 1726–Sept. 18, 1747.

Apr. 28 Charles Le Moyne was appointed the 1st gov. of the French fort at Niagara, which had been rebuilt partly of stone. A permanent French garrison was also established.

June 4 War between the English and Abenaki in NS ended with the ratification of peace at Annapolis Royal.

June 27 Jacques d'Espiet de Pensens, ensign Alphonse Tonty and 26 men left France for Île Saint-Jean, to take possession of the island in the name of the king.

Aug. 5 Sauguaaram (fl 1724–1751), acting for the Penobscot, negotiated a peace treaty with Massachusetts, guaranteeing the maintenance of the Catholic religion and improved trade relations between First Nation Peoples and the English.

Aug. 25 Lt-Gov. Lawrence Armstrong of NS presented the Acadians with a British oath of allegiance. The Acadians did not sign, but instead requested an exemption from bearing arms.

Also in 1726
• The Society for the Propagation of the Gospel (S.P.G.) opened the "School for Poor People," at Bonavista, the 1st school in Nfld.

1727

May 5 The 1st justices of the peace were commissioned in NS. Francis Richards was appointed High Constable.

July After ratification by all Abenaki tribes,

Sauguaaram signed the treaty negotiated with Massachusetts the previous year.

Sept. 6 The Council of NS again demanded that Acadians sign an oath of allegiance to the British Crown. Once again the Acadians asked to be exempt.

Nov. 10 France excluded all foreign commerce from its colonies.

Dec. 26 Louis-François Duplessis de Mornay (1663–1741) was appointed bishop of Que. on the death of Saint-Vallier. De Mornay never made the journey across the Atlantic to Canada.

Also in 1727
• Fort Oswego was built by the British on the south shore of L. Ontario, at the mouth of the Oswego R.

1728

Apr. Anglican Richard Watts (1688–1739/40) became the 1st English schoolteacher in Acadia, when he opened his School for the Society for the Propagation of the Gospel in NS, at Annapolis Royal. Watts was assigned a former barrack room for both his church and school.

Aug. 12 Capt. Vitus Jonassen Bering (1681–1741), a Dane serving in the Russian Navy, sailed through the strait presently bearing his name, but without sighting Alaska. His expeditions proved that Asia and North America were only about 63 km apart.

1729

Jan. 3 Gov. Richard Philipps assured Acadians that his govt would take steps to confirm that they retained possession of their lands. As a result, 194 Annapolis Acadians signed an oath of allegiance to the British Crown.

Mar. 2 Louis XV authorized the issue of 400,000 livres of new card money for use in New France.

Apr. 30 The British govt decided to recognize future convoy commanders as the new gov.'s of Nfld. Capt. Henry Osborn (1694–1771) was appointed gov. of all of Nfld., beginning a series of naval rulers that lasted until 1841. The role of gov. was created to bring order to a fishing industry in which there was fierce competition between transient fishermen and those who actually lived on the island. Gov. Osborn divided Nfld. into 6 districts, each with constables and magistrates.

Sept. 1 The ship *Elephant,* carrying New France's new Intendant, Gilles Hocquart (1694–1733), and its new bishop, Pierre-Herman Dosquet (1694–1777), was wrecked on a shoalrock in the lower St. Lawrence. Both men survived. Hocquart would serve from Aug. 20, 1731 to Sept. 2, 1748.

Nov. 28 Approximately 242 French settlers were killed at Fort Rosalie, by the Natchez upon whose land the fort was built and for whom it was later renamed (Natchez, Mississippi).

Dec. 7 The Mississauga ceded 3,000,000 acres of land, consisting of present-day Norfolk, Haldimand and Wentworth Counties in Ont. to the British Crown.

1730

Mar. 25 Louis XV granted François Poulin de Francheville (1692–1733) a royal warrant to work iron-ore mines for a 20-year period in the area near Trois-Rivières, and also provided de Francheville with a generous loan.

May Richard Philipps received sworn allegiance to the British Crown from Acadians in the Minas and Chignecto areas.

Dec. France authorized the coining of silver money for its French American colonies.

c 1730 First Nations in what is now Alb. acquired horses.

1731

June 8 Pierre Gaultier de Verenneset de La Vérendrye (1685–1749), his 3 sons, Jean-Baptiste (1713–1736), Louis-Joseph (1717–1761), and François (1715–1794) and 50 adventurers left Montreal to explore the area west of Rainy L. with the intention of establishing new trading areas. Over a 3-year period (to 1734), the explorers established a chain of 8 fur-trading posts, extending from Fort St. Pierre on Rainy L., to the Red R. country, and ultimately to Sask. La Vérendrye's nephew, Christophe Dufrost de La Jemerais (1708–1736), built the 1st post, Fort St. Pierre, on Rainy L. by the end of 1731.

July 1 The Compagnie des Indies ceded Louisiana to the Crown of France. François-Marie Bissot de Vinsenne (1700–1736) began construction of a post located on the Ouabache and the Belle R.

July 17 Sieurs Claude Cottard, Joseph Du Boccage, Joseph-Philippe Narcis and Jean-Pierre Roma received a grant, signed by Louis XV, of lands on the eastern coast of Île Saint-Jean. These included all lands drained by the Brudenell, Montague and Cardigan Rivers. The 4 men formed the Compagnie de l'Est de l'Île Saint-Jean. They agreed to settle 80 persons in 1732, and 30 annually thereafter. This was the 2nd attempt by a chartered company to establish a settlement in Île St. Jean.

Aug. 26 The La Vérendrye expedition arrived at the Grand Portage at the western extremity of L. Superior.

Also in 1731
• The French built Fort Frederick at Crown Point on Lake Champlain.

1732

Feb. 19 Convents in New France were forbidden to harbour deserters and fugitives from justice.

Spring La Vérendrye opened up new fur trade areas with the establishment of Fort St. Charles at the "northwest angle" of the L.-of-the-Woods. This fort became his headquarters and was used to control the border country.

July Richard Watts applied to Lt-Gov. Armstrong and the council for old French church lands in the lower town of Annapolis Royal for use by the Church of England. He received the deed to these lands on Nov. 23. They were the 1st lands in Canada granted to a Protestant church. Today, the church remains as the parish of St. Luke's.

Also in 1732
• Crop harvest was affected by excessive summer heat, compromising the colony's commerce.

1733

Jan. 16 De Francheville founded Compagnie des Forges de Saint-Maurice to process mined iron ore in the Trois-Rivières region. De Francheville died later in the year, and his foundry went idle until Aug. 20, 1738.

May 29 Intendant Hocquart upheld the right of Canadians to buy, own and sell Aboriginal peoples as slaves.

Sept. 12 Pierre-Herman Dosquet (1691–1777) was appointed bishop of Que.

Also in 1733
• La Vérendrye sent Jean-Baptiste and La Jemerais to L. Ouinipigon (L. Winnipeg) to find a location for a new post. The 2 explorers were only able to travel as far as Barrière aux Esturgeons on the Winnipeg R.

1734

Apr. 1 The 1ˢᵗ lighthouse in Canada went into operation at Louisbourg. It was a fireproof tower of stone, some 20 m tall. The top wooden beacon chamber was illuminated by a fire fueled by coal from nearby mines. The tower was gutted by fire in 1736, rebuilt in 1738, and finally destroyed by the British in 1758. An octangular concrete tower with electric light and electronic foghorn now sits on the same point.

Apr. 10 Marie-Joseph-Angélique, a black slave owned by François Poulin de Francheville of Saint-Paul, Que., set fire to the Francheville house as a protest against slavery and to cover her escape to New England with her lover, Claude Thibault, a white man. The fire spread, and destroyed 46 homes, the Hôtel-Dieu, convent and church. Angélique was caught, tortured and hanged (June 21) in Montreal for her crime.

June La Vérendrye established Fort Maurepas, which was built by his son Jean-Baptiste on the west bank of the Red R., not far from its mouth at L. Winnipeg and about 10 km from present-day Selkirk, Man. Jean-Baptiste was placed in charge of the fort, until relieved by La Jemerais in 1735.

Also in 1734
• The total population of New France was 37,716.

• François Picquet, a Sulpician priest, arrived in Montreal.

• The 1ˢᵗ road between Montreal and Quebec, the Chemin de Roi, was completed.

• The 1ˢᵗ sailing ship appeared on L. Superior. Built by Louis Denys de La Ronde (1675–1741), it was used to locate copper deposits.

• Guillaume Gaillard of the Conseil Supérieur built the Manoir Mauvide-Genest on l'Île d'Orléans. The 9-bay-window-wide, 2-storey manor took its name from the young surgeon Jean Mauvide and his wife, Marie-Anne Genest, who lived there between 1752–1764. In 1926, the Pouliot family purchased and restored the house, which now contains a restaurant and small museum.

1735

May 18 La Vérendrye, Jean-Baptiste, La Jemerais and others formed a new partnership to finance their exploration farther west.

Also in 1735
• Bishop Dosquet ruled that wigs could not be worn by the clergy of the diocese of Que. without the approval of their superiors.

• François Pierre Olivier de Vézin (1716–1776) arrived in Que., sponsored by the French govt to verify if the Compagnie des Forges de Saint-Maurice could become a viable iron producer. Vézin confirmed that the forge could produce iron if a more efficient process was implemented.

1736

June 8 Jean-Baptiste de La Vérendrye and 20 men, including Father Jean-Pierre Aulneau (1705–1736), were killed on an island in Lake-of-the-Woods by members of the Sioux. The explorers had left

Fort Saint-Charles to collect provisions at Grand Portage.

Sept. 14 Louis-Joseph de La Vérendrye was sent by his father to re-establish Fort Maurepas, abandoned after La Jemerais's death.

Also in 1736

• *Memoirs of Odd Adventures,* by John Gyles (c 1680–1755) was published. It depicted the author's life as a boy captive of the Maliseet in the Saint John Valley between 1689 and 1698.

1737

May 28 Louis-Joseph Gaultier de La Vérendrye was forced to return to Fort Saint-Charles from an exploration trip to L. Winnipeg because of a smallpox epidemic among the Cree in that region.

May 30 After his efforts to bring peace among the First Nations in the area failed, Jacques Legardeur de Saint-Pierre (1701–1755), commandant of Fort Beauharnois (on L. Pepin), ordered the fort abandoned and burned for fear that the garrison would be killed by the Sioux.

July 4 Capt. James Napper, in command of an expedition to search for an ocean passage westward from Hudson Bay, set out in the sloop *Churchill,* accompanied by Robert Crow in the *Musquash.* The Napper expedition reached Whale Point at latitude 62 degrees 15 minutes north. On Aug. 7, Capt. Napper died.

Dec. 31 The Congregation of the Sisters of Charity of the Hospital General of Montreal (Grey Nuns) was founded by Marie-Marguerite Dufrost de Lajemmerais (Youville), who, with a few confederates, devoted herself to the service of the poor and took vows of poverty, chastity and obedience.

1738

June Erasmus James Phillips (1705–1760) founded the 1st Masonic Lodge in NS, at Annapolis Royal.

Aug. 20 De Vézin successfully blew the blast furnace at the Forges de Saint-Maurice, and production of iron was restarted. In 1739, Vézin added another forge. In the early years of production, the iron was used for shipbuilding by the French Royal Navy in Que. The company went bankrupt in 1741, and the Crown took over operation in 1743. The Treaty of Paris, 1763, transferred ownership to the British Crown. The complex was in use for almost 150 years.

Aug. 22 Abbé Jean-Louis Le Loutre (1709–1772) left Île-Royale to serve as a missionary to the Mi'kmaq at the Shubenacadie mission.

Sept. The 1st Jewish resident of Canada, 16-year-old Esther Brandeau (c 1718), came disguised as a man under the name of Jacques La Fargue. She was discovered and arrested, because Jews were denied entrance to Canada throughout the French regime. Brandeau was later deported to France in 1740, after refusing to convert to Catholicism.

Sept. 11 La Vérendrye left Lake-of-the-Woods to explore farther west. He arrived at the site Portage-la-Prairie Oct. 3, where he built Fort La Reine, on the Assiniboine R. Accompanied by his sons, Louis-Joseph and François, he reached the main Mandan village in North Dakota on Dec. 3. There he obtained information on routes to the west before returning to Fort La Reine.

1739

Mar. 22 François-Louis de Pourroy de Lauberivière (1711–1740) was appointed the 5th bishop of Que. He died Aug. 8, 1740, just 12 days after arriving in Que. to assume his position.

Apr. 1 Isaac-Louis de Forant (d 1740) was appointed gov. of Île Royale. He arrived at Louisbourg on Sept. 10.

Apr. 16 La Vérendrye's sons set out to find a river flowing westward from L. Winnipeg. At its northern end, they discovered a river (the Saskatchewan) flowing eastward into the lake. Paddling upstream to find its source, they came to the point where the river divides in two, near present-day The Pas, Man.

Dec. 7 John Adams (c 1672–1745) served as NS's administrator until Mar. 21, 1740.

Also in Dec. Lawrence Armstrong, gov. of NS, committed suicide.

Also in 1739

- The census of New France recorded a population of 42,701.

- La Vérendrye built Fort Bourbon, a fur-trading post on the Saskatchewan R. near its mouth.

- Fr. François Picquet (1708–1781) was assigned to the mission of Lake of Two Mountains at Oka, Que., where he trained Native peoples in military tactics.

- Canadian tobacco was exported to France for the 1st time.

- Beaver skins accounted for 70% of New France's exports.

1740

Mar. 22 Paul Mascarene (c 1684–1760) assumed office as president of the Council of NS, and was its administrator until July 12, 1749.

May 10–Nov. 2, 1740 François Le Coutre de Bourville (c 1670–1729) served as acting gov. of Île Royale.

Sept. 1 Jean-Baptiste-Louis Le Prévost Duquesnel (1685–1744) was appointed commandant of Île Royale, a post equivalent to that of gov.

Also in 1740

- The population of Louisbourg was 2,000.

1741

Apr. 7 Henri-Marie Dubreil de Pontbriand (1708–1760) was appointed bishop of Que., the last Frenchman to hold the post before the British Conquest.

June 5 Vitus Bering, on his 2nd expedition, sailed out of Petropavlovsk, Kamchatka, with the *St. Peter* and *St. Paul,* making the 1st recorded voyage from Asia to North America. Bering sighted the North American coast near Kayak Is. in the Gulf of Alaska on July 16. A landing party went ashore for several hours on July 31, before Bering and his ships returned to Kamchatka.

June 8 Christopher Middleton (d 1770) sailed out of the Nore with 2 vessels, *Furnace* and *Discovery*.

It was the 1st naval expedition to leave England in search of the Northwest Passage. William Moore commanded the *Discovery*.

Dec. 19 Danish explorer Vitus Bering died of scurvy, shipwrecked on one of the Commander's islands that now bear his name.

Winter 1741–1742 Middleton's expedition to find a Northwest Passage wintered at Churchill, the coldest of the HBC posts. Ten men died of scurvy. Many others suffered illness or had toes amputated because of frostbite.

Also in 1741

- La Vérendrye built the French fur-trading post Fort Dauphin, probably on the Waterhen R. where it entered the north-west corner of L. Manitoba.

- Exports from New France exceeded imports for the only time during the French regime.

1742

Feb. 27 France issued an additional 120,000 livre's worth of card money.

Apr. 20 A royal edict by France ordered all licences for western trade to be suspended and all trading posts auctioned to the highest bidder.

Apr. 29 Pierre de La Vérendrye sent his 2 sons, Louis-Joseph and François, from Port La Reine to follow the Souris R. to the Missouri R. watershed — in an attempt to find a viable trading route to the west. In 20 days they reached Mandan villages. After crossing the Missouri R. they travelled south-westerly across the prairies. Passing through the Bad-lands of N. Dakota, they came upon what their Mandan guides called the "Mountain of the Horse People" in Aug. The Mandan guides refused to continue. The La Vérendryes visited several First Nations settlements as they continued their journey toward the Rocky Mountains.

June 4 The *Canada,* the 1st warship built at Que., was launched and sailed for Rochefort, France.

Also in June

- Joseph La France (c 1707–c 1749) arrived at York Factory, with a large band of Aboriginals to trade furs to the English. He had been denied a trading licence in New France. La France explored and described Lakes Winnipeg, Manitoba and Winnipegosis and the lower Saskatchewan R.

July 1 Middleton's expedition set sail from Churchill to continue its search for the Northwest Passage. The men passed Scroggs' Whalebone Point, the most northerly point reached by any previous explorer, and came to unknown waters by July 12. They discovered Cape Dobbs, Wager Bay, Repulse Bay and the entrance to Frozen Strait.

1743

Jan. 12 The La Vérendryes reached the Rocky Mountains, probably the Big Horn range, in the company of a party of Bow.

Mar. 19 Louis-Joseph La Vérendrye and his expedition followed a clan of Pawnee–Arikara to their village at the junction of the Bad and Missouri Rivers, opposite present-day Pierre, South Dakota (now pronounced "Peer"). The explorers remained there for 2 weeks, before turning toward home. On Mar. 30, as the La Vérendrye party began its trek back east, Pierre La Vérendrye buried a lead plaque at Pierre, which read, "In the twenty-sixth year of the reign of Louis XV, the most illustrious Lord, the Lord Marquis of Beauharnois being Viceroy, 1741, Peter Gaultier De La Vérendrye placed this." The reverse side of the plaque contained names of other members of the expedition scratched in with a sharp instrument. La Vérendrye's plaque marked his claim of the country for France, but it was not discovered until 1913 when a group of South Dakotan schoolchildren stumbled upon it. The La Vérendrye party arrived back at Fort La Reine July 2.

May 16 The HBC opened Henley House, at the junction of the Albany and Kenogami Rivers. The settlement was founded by Orkneyman Joseph Isbister. William Isbister (fl 1739-1751) was appointed master of the post.

Nov. 25 An ordinance restrained religious communities from acquiring more land in New France without royal permission.

1744

Mar. 15 France declared war on Britain, beginning the War of the Austrian Succession, which was known as King William's War in British North America (1744–1748).

May 3 Duquesnel, commandant of Île Royale at Louisbourg, appointed Joseph Du Pont Duvivier (1707–1760) to lead 140 French troops on an expedition against the closest British settlement to Louisbourg, at Canseau (Canso, NS). Canso, commanded by Patrick Heron (fl 1709-1752), surrendered to the French at dawn on May 24.

July 12 Fr. Jean Louis Le Loutre incited his Mi'kmaq and Maliseet brethren to attack Annapolis Royal. On July 29, Duquesnel was able to dispatch 50 French colonial regulars and a number of Île Royale Mi'kmaq under Duvivier's command against the Annapolis Royal garrison.

Aug. 8 Duvivier and his forces landed at Baie Verte and tried unsuccessfully to rally Acadians against the English. Only a dozen Acadians responded.

Sept. 7 Duvivier was joined by 300 Mi'kmaq and Maliseet in a 4-week siege of Annapolis Royal under the command of British lt-gov. Paul Mascarene (1684–1760), who had no more than 75 able-bodied soldiers. The siege was unsuccessful, and on Oct. 2, Duvivier was ordered to withdraw to winter quarters at Minas, because expected naval support did not materialize. On Oct. 4, Duvivier's forces were forced to leave NS when Acadians refused to supply foodstuffs for the detachment.

Oct. 9–June 17, 1745 Following the death of Duquesnel, Louis Du Pont Duchambon (1713–c 1775) served as administrator of Île Royale.

Dec. 27 Poor conditions at Fort Louisbourg caused French soldiers and Swiss mercenaries to mutiny. There was anarchy at the fortress.

Also in 1744
• *Histoire et description générale de la Nouvelle-France* by Pierre-François-Xavier de Charlevoix (1682–1761) was published.

• La Vérendrye's fur-trading monopoly was canceled by the French govt.

1745

Mar. 24 William Pepperrell (1696–1759), commanding an expedition to attack Louisbourg, sailed from Boston. This force was joined on Apr. 4 at Canso by smaller groups from New Hampshire and Connecticut. A British naval squadron from the West Indies, commanded by Commodore Peter Warren (1703/04–1752), joined the force on Apr. 22, bringing the total number of British attackers to 4,300. Most of Pepperrell's men were untrained, and included Harvard students and Sam Moody, a 70-year-old Puritan preacher. The British left Canso on Apr. 29, arriving at Louisbourg the next day. The main body of the fleet anchored at Flat Point Cove in Gabarus Bay, off Louisbourg, with little opposition. The attack quickly settled down to a 7-week siege. Louisbourg was defended by 560 regular soldiers and 1,400 militiamen. There were also 2,000 townspeople.

May 19 British and French fleets engaged in battle off Louisbourg.

June 17 Gov. Louis Du Pont Duchambon surrendered Louisbourg to Pepperrell, marking the end of the French presence in the Maritimes. Duchambon and most civilians were sent to Rochefort, France. Warren was made the 1st British gov. of Île Royale on Sept. 6.

June 20 The Compagnie de l'Est de l'Île Saint-Jean, managed by Jean-Pierre Roma, ended when New England troops (sent from Louisbourg by Pepperrell), destroyed his establishment. Roma, his son, daughter and 5 servants escaped to Que.

June 21 Settlers harvested the 1st strawberry crop in New France.

Also in June
• A party of Penobscot attacked Fort St. George when Gov. Shirley of Massachusetts pressured them to join in the suppression of their Canadian Abenaki kin who, in alliance with the French, had begun open warfare against the English.

Oct. A New England scouting party attacked Sauguaaram and 3 Penobscot companions. Sauguaaram escaped, gathered the remaining Penobscot and fled to Canada, while 25 Penobscot warriors remained to take revenge on Massachusetts.

Nov. 8 Responding to repeated French and Aboriginal attacks, the Provincial Council of NS, under Lt-Gov. Paul Mascarene, requested that the Imperial govt transport "French Inhabitants (Acadians) ... out of the Province of NS and that they be replaced by good Protestant Subjects."

Also in Nov.
• The resident eastern elk herd in Que.'s St. John R. watershed was wiped out by the fur trade.

Dec. French lt. Legardeur led a contingent to provide relief at Fort Saint-Frédéric (Crown Point, New York), which was under threat from the British.

Also in 1745
• A mild winter and spring permitted settlers to sow the corn crop in late Apr. Harvesting thus occurred 3 weeks earlier, in late Aug.

• The French king published an ordinance requiring habitants to build houses on parcels of land larger than .6 ha.

1746

Mar. 14 Charles Knowles (1704–1777) was appointed gov. of Île Royale, serving from June 2, 1746–Nov. 30, 1747.

May William Moor (d 1765) sailed from England in search of the Northwest Passage, and the £20,000 reward offered for its discovery by the British Parliament in 1744. His voyage set in motion the expansion of British trade in North America and the Pacific. Moor had 2 vessels at his service, the *Dobbs Galley*, which he commanded, and the smaller *California,* captained by Francis Smith.

June 22 A fleet of 54 ships set sail from Rochelle, France, commanded by Jean Baptiste-Louis-Frédéric de La Rochefoucauld de Roye, Duc d'Anville (1709–1746), to recapture Louisbourg, take Annapolis Royal and attack Boston and the New England coast.

July 10 Seven hundred Canadians and Aboriginals under Jean-Baptiste-Nicolas-Roch de Ramezay (1708–1777) reached Baie-Verte, NB. The force then travelled to Beaubassin, near present-day Amherst, NS, where it planned to join with d'Anville's fleet.

Aug. 30 The fort at Crown Point, New York, was attacked by de Vaudreuil, with a force from Trois-Rivières.

Sept. 10 D'Anville anchored at Chebucto (Halifax), to find that the British West Indies squadron had sailed. D'Anville died of apoplexy on Sept. 27, as the rest of his fleet, which had been scattered by storms and fog, and wasted by famine and disease, reached Chebucto.

Sept. 30 Jacques-Pierre de Taffanel de La Jonquière (1685–1752) led remnants of the French fleet back to France. Some 2,400 sailors had died, none in action, and not one shot was fired in anger.

Dec. 5 Lt-Col. Arthur Noble (d 1746/47) set out with a detachment of New Englanders for Minas (Grand Pré, NS), to attack any French forces in the area and to winter among the Acadians. The expedition arrived at Minas on Jan. 1, 1747.

Also in 1746
- A French force from Que. under Paul Marin de La Malgue (1692–1753) staged a lightning raid against Saratoga, New York. In retaliation, Sir William Johnson (c 1715–1774) of New York, prompted the Iroquois to raid along the Richelieu R.

- John Bradstreet (1714–1774) was appointed to the newly created position of lt-gov. of St. John's, Nfld.

1747

Jan. 12 Capt. Nicolas-Antoine Coulon de Villiers (1710–1757), second-in-command of the French forces under de Ramezay, left Chignecto with 240 Canadians and 60 Aboriginals to attack 500 British, led by Arthur Noble, at Minas.

Feb. 9 A detachment of de Villiers' troops and their Aboriginal allies attacked Noble's New England forces in the early-morning hours during a raging snowstorm. Noble and some of his men were killed while still in their beds. De Villiers' left arm was shattered by a musket ball. The arm required amputation 3 years later, causing his death.

Feb. 12 Benjamin Goldthwait (1704–1761) surrendered the New England troops to Louis de La Corne (1703–1761), who had taken command when de Villiers was wounded.

May 1 La Galissonière became commandant general in New France (provisional gov.) in the absence of Marquis de La Jonquière.

May 10 Admiral La Jonquière, who was appointed gov-gen. of New France Mar. 19, sailed from France to New France, leading a French fleet to recapture Louisbourg. The French were defeated by a British fleet on May 14; French casualties — 800 men dead. La Jonquière and 6 French warships were captured and taken to England.

June 15 Louis La Corne was placed in command of a detachment, with orders to intercept a raiding party of Aboriginal peoples operating in the area of Montreal. Mohawk, Seneca and Oneida, along with some English and Dutch companions, were ambushed. Mohawk leader, Theyanoguin (d 1755), escaped.

June 24 The William Moor/Francis Smith (fl 1737-1747) Arctic expedition discovered Chesterfield Inlet in Hudson Bay, but failed to follow it to its end. Rankin Inlet proved to be a closed body of water. At the end of July, Moor and Smith discovered that Wager Bay was also a closed bay and provided no northwest passage.

Aug. 27 Marie-Marguerite d'Youville (1701-1771) was appointed temporary director of the bankrupt Hôpital Général of Montreal by its trustees. She had the building renovated so that large rooms were ready for the sick and poor of both sexes.

Sept. 19–Aug. 14, 1749 Roland-Michel Barrin de La Galissonière (1693–1756) served as temporary gov-gen. of New France.

Oct. 14 Admiral Edward Hawke (1705–1781) defeated a French fleet en route to Canada.

Also in 1747

• The painting, oil on canvas, *Ex-voto de l'Aimable Marthe,* attributed to Paul Beaucour (1700–1756), was completed. The painting is located in the Notre-Dames-des-Victoires Church in Quebec City.

• A French force under Rigaud de Vaudreuil destroyed Northfield, Massachusetts.

1748

Jan. 7 François Bigot (1703–1778), former financial manager of Île Royale, was appointed Intendant of New France, serving until 1760. His term of office saw a dramatic rise in govt spending, from 6 to 30 million livres per annum over the course of the Seven Years' War (1755–1759). Recalled to France in 1754 to defend himself against charges of corruption, Bigot was returned to his post in 1755. Joseph Cadet (1719–1781) was made commissaire-Général, a position that earned him sufficient wealth to become the Baron de la Touche D'Arrigny, with an estate in France.

Sept. Peregrine Thomas Hopson (d 1759) was appointed lt-gov. of Louisbourg for Britain.

Oct. 18 The Treaty of Aix-la-Chapelle ended King George's War and returned Louisbourg and Île Royale to the French in exchange for the port of Madras, in India.

1749

Mar. 7 Lord Halifax, British president of the Board of Trade, proposed that a town be established on Chebucto Bay, on the south shore of the NS peninsula.

Mar. 19 The Ohio Company, organized in 1747 by a group of Virginians (including George Washington) and a number of prominent Englishmen, secured a grant of 202,343 ha of Ohio valley land from the British govt for the purpose of settlement. The French, who also claimed title to the area, sent Pierre-Joseph Céloron de Blainville (1693–1759) to lead an expedition to the same region to maintain the French position in the west. De Blainville buried a number of lead plates, claiming the territory for France and attached a plaque with the royal arms to a tree. He discovered that the First Nations in the area were committed to an alliance with the English.

Apr. 18 The king of France authorized the issue of card money to be increased from 720,000 to 1 million livres, establishing the forerunner of Canadian paper money.

May 9 Edward Cornwallis (1712/13–1776) was appointed gov. of NS.

June 21 Cornwallis arrived at Chebucto Bay with 13 ships carrying 2,576 settlers. With £40,000 to cover the expenses, he was mandated to found a new capital — Halifax — to replace Annapolis Royal. British control over mainland NS was established.

June 29 Charles des Herbiers de La Ralière (c 1700–1752), appointed gov. of Île Royale, arrived at Louisbourg to repossess it for France.

July 3 The British evacuated Louisbourg, in accordance with the Treaty of Aix-la-Chapelle, and moved their base of operations to Halifax.

July 14 Cornwallis organized his govt in NS, swearing in his 1st council at Halifax.

Aug. 14–May 17, 1752 La Jonquière served as gov-gen. of New France.

Also in Aug.

• Mi'kmaq, encouraged by the French missionary Jean-Louis Le Loutre, began attacks on the British by seizing a vessel at Canso, attacking another at Chignecto and ambushing 4 men near Halifax.

Sept. 30 The Mi'kmaq killed settlers at the present site of Dartmouth, NS.

Also in Oct.

• The Penobscot ended their part in King George's War with the signing of a treaty at Falmouth (now, Portland, Maine).

• Marquis de La Galissonière, acting gov. of Canada, sent forces commanded by Charles Deschamps de Boishebert (1727–1797) and Louis La Corne to the Saint John R. and Chignecto Isthmus in an effort to limit British settlement. La Corne was also ordered to take oaths of allegiance from Acadian habitants coming to reside in French territory. The boundary between French territory and British territory ran through Beaubassin, where a large group of French Acadians lived, half on the French side of the border, half on the British side.

Nov. Louis La Corne arrived in French Acadia to strengthen fortifications in the Beauséjour area (near Sackville) while Jean-Louis Le Loutre tried to persuade French Acadians to move out of British territory and under La Corne's protection.

Dec. 5 La Vérendrye died in Montreal at age 64, one year after the French govt renewed his fur-trading monopoly for another 4 years. His estate consisted of used clothes, furniture and debt.

Also in 1749

• Several settlers from the area surrounding Que. migrated to the city to become carters, to do day work or to open taverns.

• The shipbuilding industry experienced a labour shortage — 150 carpenters were required.

1750

Jan. 2 An ordinance, according numerous advantages to Canadian families willing to settle at Detroit, was passed.

Apr. 16 Gov. Cornwallis sent a force of 400 men, under the command of Charles Lawrence (c 1709–1760) and John Rous (1700/10–1760), to Chignecto Isthmus to establish British authority. They were confronted by a French force, under La Corne, on the banks of the Missaguash R. La Corne ordered the torching of the village of Beaubassin to prevent it from falling into British hands. The order was carried out by Jean-Louis Le Loutre (1709– 1772) and his Mi'kmaq allies.

Apr. 17 Fort Rouillé (present-day Toronto) was established on the north shore of L. Ontario, to turn back British incursions into French fur-trading areas. Pierre Robinau de Portneuf (1708–1761) left Fort Frontenac May 20, for Toronto, with orders to build a small fortified post to attract First Nations

peoples in the region to trade with the French instead of the English at Fort Oswego. Fort Rouille was completed in Apr. 1751, and competed successfully with Oswego.

Apr. 19 Gov. Cornwallis of NS denied Acadian representatives permission to leave the country.

June 5 Capt. Jacques Legardeur de Saint-Pierre (1701–1755) left Montreal to continue his search for the western sea.

July 12 Intendant Bigot established a medical code for New France, with mandatory examinations for practicing doctors and a series of fines for physicians shown to be unqualified.

Also in July

• Legardeur left Michilimackinac for Fort La Reine (Portage la Prairie, Man.).

Aug. 16 Three hundred German settlers arrived at Lunenburg, NS, the 1st German immigration to Canada. Each settler was promised 20 ha of land, (tax free for 10 years), tools for fishing, building and farming, and free food for the 1st year.

Also in Aug.

• Lt-Col. Charles Lawrence returned to the Missaguash R. with a 2nd, larger, force. He routed a group of Aboriginals led by Abbé Jean-Louis Le Loutre (1709–1772).

Sept. 2 Reverend William Tutty (c 1715–1754) opened St. Paul's Church in Halifax. It remains today as the oldest Protestant church in Canada.

Sept. 23 A decree enacted at Halifax fixed labourers' wages at 18 pence per day and provisions; craftsmen at 2 shillings, with rum and beer occasionally added.

Also in Sept.

• Lt-Col. Charles Lawrence constructed Fort Lawrence on the Chignecto Isthmus in Acadia, near the mouth of the Missaguash R., opposite Fort Beauséjour, on the site of the French settlement of Beaubassin, which had been established in 1672.

• The French built Fort Gaspereau on Baie Verte.

Fall Capt. Legardeur arrived at Fort La Reine, his base of operations for the next 2 years. He would travel several times to the area of the Red R., Winnipeg R. and Lake-of-the-Woods.

Also in 1750

• The population of New France was 50,000; the Thirteen Colonies had a population of 1,200,000; Nfld.'s population was 7,000.

• Anthony Henday (c 1750–1762), a former smuggler, joined the HBC, volunteering to undertake an expedition to the west to secure trade with First Nations peoples of the west.

• Fort Paskoya was built by La Vérendrye, his sons and nephew, near present-day The Pas, Man., at the mouth of the Pasquia R., the 1st French trading post along the interior of the Saskatchewan R.

• The HBC built Fort Richmond, a small post intended to serve as a base for mineral exploration and the development of the fur trade.

• Que. weavers and spinners began to provide significant quantities of homespun woollen cloth to the settlers.

1751

Feb. 27 Pierre-Marie Raimbeau de Simblin established a fort at Lac de la Carpe to counter British influence south of Hudson Bay.

Mar. 1 Jean-Louis de Raymond, Comte de Raymond (c 1702–1771), was appointed gov. of Île Royale, serving from Aug. 3, 1751–Oct. 1753.

Apr. 12 La Jonquière asked all Acadians moving into French territory from British territory to take an oath of allegiance to France and to join the militia in order to avoid being considered rebels.

Aug. 3 Bartholomew Green Jr. (1699–1751) established the 1st printing business in Halifax, NS. His type and press came from Boston, where his family had been printers for several generations

Sept. 26 About 1,000 settlers from Wurtemberg, Germany, arrived at Halifax.

Also in 1751

• Joseph-Claude Boucher de Niverille (1715–1804) was ordered by Capt. Legardeur to establish Fort La Jonquière (in the Nipawin, Sask. area).

1752

Jan. 1 Ange Duquesne de Menneville, Marquis Duquesne (c 1700–1778), was appointed gov. of New France, serving from July 1, 1752–June 24, 1755.

Mar. 23 New Englander John Bushell (1715–1761) assumed control of the printing establishment begun by his former partner, Bartholomew Green, and began printing Canada's 1st newspaper, the *Halifax Gazette*. Appointed King's Printer, Bushell used his newspaper as a means of publicizing the proclamations and laws of NS govt.

Mar. 25 Charles Le Moyne de Longueuil (1687–1755), 2nd Baron de Longueuil, was appointed administrator of New France.

May 4 Peregrine Thomas Hopson (1685–1759) was appointed gov. of NS, serving from Aug. 3, 1752–Jan. 1756.

Nov. Gov. Hopson, Maj. Jean-Baptiste Cope and Mi'kmaq chief Sachem of Shubenacadia concluded a treaty halting hostilities between the Mi'kmaq and the English. The treaty promised annual gifts of blankets, tobacco, powder and shot, and "free liberty of hunting and fishing, as usual" to the Mi'kmaq.

Dec. 6 The *Halifax Gazette* published an 8-page pamphlet for the govt, the 1st book published in Canada.

Also in 1752

• The population of Louisbourg was 4,200, and the average annual fishing harvest of the town was 150,000 quintals, or 1,500 tonnes.

• Wealthy merchant Guillaume Estebe (1701–c 1779), along with builders Nicolas Dasilva dit Portugais, Pierre Delestre dit Beaujour and René Paquet built the historic Estebe House, located at 92 rue Saint-Pierre in Quebec City. The 2-storey structure with high attic, was designed upward to

compensate for the lack of building space in
Lower Town.

1753

June 3 The king of France recognized Montreal's
Hôpital Général as a legal entity and placed Mme
d'Youville and her companions in charge of its
administration. The previous rights and privileges
had been granted, in 1694, to the Frères
Hospitaliers.

• Appointed commandant of the Post de l'Ouest,
Louis de La Corne (1703–1761) headed west with
57 men. During his term, La Corne improved Fort
Paskoya and built Fort Saint-Louis (Fort-à-la-Corne,
Saskatchewan) near the forks of the Saskatchewan
R., thus completing a chain of forts controlling the
headwaters of the rivers flowing into Hudson Bay.
This occupation enabled the French to intercept
Aboriginal traders on their way to HBC posts. La
Corne also seeded several hectares of grain, the 1st
wheat planted in the west, in Sask.'s Carrot R. Valley,
and travelled farther west than his predecessors'.

Also in June
• Mohawk leader Theyanoguin and 17 Mohawk
warriors advised George Clinton (c 1686–1761),
gov. of New York, that the Mohawk treaty of friendship with the colony was ending because of
rumours indicating that the English planned the
destruction of the Mohawk Nation.

• Duquesne sent a military expedition, under Paul
Marin de La Malgue (1692–1753), to occupy the
Ohio Valley and build a line of forts linking L. Erie
and the Ohio R.

• Gov. Hopson of NS selected Charles Lawrence and
Patrick Sutherland (d c 1766) to direct the settlement of German Protestants at Lunenburg.

Sept. 3 Seneca leader Tanaghrisson (d 1754),
demanded that French commander La Malgue
withdraw his forces from the upper Ohio area. La
Malgue rejected the request.

Oct. 19 La Malgue died at Fort de la Rivière au Boeuf,
choosing to die on active service rather than return
home to convalesce. He was replaced by Legardeur.

Dec. 11 Maj. George Washington, commanding a
force from Virginia and accompanied by Chief
Tanaghrisson and 2 other chiefs, arrived in the Ohio
region to challenge the French occupation at Fort
de la Rivière au Boeuf. Legardeur stood firm, but
courteous in his refusal to vacate the fort. Washington withdrew, but claimed the Ohio Valley for
Virginia in opposition to the claims of Canada.

Dec. 18 Robert Monckton (1726–1782) volunteered to
lead a 200-man force to Lunenburg, where German
settlers were engaged in an armed confrontation
with the local garrison. He negotiated a return to
order, and remained to help settle the town.

1754

Feb. 1 Augustin de Boschenry de Drucour (1703
–1762) was appointed gov. of Île Royale, serving
from Aug. 15–Aug. 15, 1758 as the last French gov.

Apr. 17 A party of French and Aboriginals, commanded by Claude-Pierre Pecaudy de Contrecoeur
(1705–1775), attacked and captured British Fort Pitt
(Pittsburgh, Pennsylvania), during its construction
by Gov. Robert Dinwiddie (1693–1770) of Virginia,
at the junction of the Allegheny and Monongahela
Rivers. Contrecoeur completed the fort and
renamed it Fort Duquesne.

May 28 Washington, with his Virginia detachment
joined by Tanaghrisson, ambushed a French force
under Joseph Coulon de Villiers de Jumonville
(1710–1754), in Pennsylvania. De Villiers was killed
(reputedly by Tanaghrisson himself), along with 9
other Canadians; their scalped bodies were left
exposed to the elements. Washington withdrew
with 21 prisoners. England and France were not
at war.

Also in May
• The 1752 Peace Treaty between the English and
Mi'kmaq was violated when the Mi'kmaq killed the
crew of an English sloop sent to help them move
provisions provided by the English. The Mi'kmaq
burned their treaty after the massacre.

June 26 Anthony Henday left York Factory, with a
party of Cree, on a western expedition to encourage western Aboriginals to trade with the HBC.

This was a difficult assignment because of the great distance between York Factory and the traditional Aboriginal hunting grounds. He reached Paskoya (The Pas, Man.) on July 22. By Sept. 6, Henday had met up with a group of Assiniboine Eagles, who had never traded with Europeans. He convinced them to make an annual trading trek to York Factory.

• Louis Coulon de Villiers arrived at Fort Duquesne (Pittsburgh, Pennsylvania) in command of 600 French troops and some 100 First Nations allies.

Also in June
• Washington hastily established Fort Necessity at Great Meadows (near Farmington, Pennsylvania), south of Fort Duquesne. He surrendered the fort to the French force on July 4, after an engagement known as the Battle of the Great Meadows. This marked the beginning of the North American French and Indian War (1754–1763) waged between Britain and France.

Sept. 11 Henday became the 1st known European to enter present-day Alberta, near the present-day village of Chauvin. He reached a Blackfoot encampment (near Red Deer) on Oct. 14, and gathered furs while wintering there. His invitation to the Blackfoot to trade at York Factory was politely refused.

Sept. 21 Jonathan Belcher (1710–1776) was appointed the 1st chief justice of NS and Member of the Executive Council.

Also in Sept.
• Wappisis, chief of the Home Cree, and his 2 sons, murdered William Lamb, master of Henley House, and 4 other men, after the Cree were refused provisions which they had become accustomed to receiving from other masters. Wappisis and his 2 sons were hanged, June 21, 1755, at Albany Factory (Fort Albany, Ont.) for murder.

Also in 1754
• The population of New France was 55,000; the town of Que. counted 8,000 residents.

• The population of English colonies in North America was approximately 1.5 million.

• Charles Lawrence (1709–1760) was appointed lt-gov. of NS.

1755

Jan. Pierre de Rigaud de Vaudreuil de Cavagnial, Marquis de Vaudreuil (1698–1778) was appointed gov. of New France, serving from July 10, 1755–Sept. 8, 1760. He was the last French gov. of the colony, and supreme commander of its 16,000 troops and their Aboriginal allies.

Mar. 1 Jean-Armand Dieskau (1701–1767) was appointed commander of the French regular troops in Canada.

Mar. 5 Henday camped approximately 32 km downstream from present-day Edmonton, where the Sturgeon R. empties into the North Saskatchewan R. He paddled down the North Saskatchewan R. in Apr., to Fort Saint-Louis, 16 km below the forks of the Saskatchewan.

Also in Mar.
• Maj-Gen. Braddock (1695–1755), in command of 2 battalions with 800 men, sailed for North America under orders to attack Fort Duquesne, Fort Niagara and French forts on L. Champlain and the NS border. The French, learning of this plan, dispatched 6 battalions with 3,000 seasoned troops. The British, learning of the French force, ordered Admiral Edward Boscawen, with 21 ships, to intercept the French, but he could find only 3 ships.

Apr. Braddock appointed Sir William Johnson (1715–1774) to manage relations with the Six Nations and their dependent tribes. Johnson's 1st priority was to recruit the Iroquois to fight the French; he was also made maj-gen. of an expedition to take Fort Frederick, which ended in failure. Johnson was well liked by the Iroquois, who gave him the name Warraghiyagey.

May 1 NS Council discussed the Acadian problem. The suggestion for removal was brought forward.

May 19 Lt-Col. Robert Monckton, authorized to attack Fort Beauséjour, the principal French stronghold on the Chignecto Isthmus, sailed from Boston commanding a force of 31 transports and 3 warships, carrying nearly 2,000 New England provincial troops and 270 British regulars.

May 21 Henday and his Cree allies completed trading with the Blackfoot. On June 20, Henday arrived back at York Factory with 70 canoes carrying furs from his Rockies expedition. He had explored farther into the western interior than any European and his was the 1st-ever account of the Blackfoot.

June 4 Monckton's force landed at Fort Lawrence. Gov. Louis Du Pont Duchambon de Vergor of Beauséjour ordered his troops to set fire to all structures between Forts Lawrence and Beauséjour.

June 6 Soldiers from Fort Edward at Windsor, NS, arrived at Minas and confiscated guns belonging to the Acadians.

June 7 Two sailors burned down the Augustine Monastery, hospital and the Church of the Hôtel-Dieu in Que.

June 12 British forces, under Col. Robert Monckton, besieged Fort Beauséjour, capturing it on June 16, and renaming it Fort Cumberland.

June 17 Col. Monckton completed his conquest of Chignecto without firing a shot, by taking Fort Gaspereau on Baie Verte, commanded by Benjamin Rouer de Villeray (1701–1760). The French abandoned their garrison at the mouth of the Saint John R., on the same day. Thus, the last French forts in Acadia had fallen to the English.

June 25 The NS Council formally decided to expel all Acadians and to replace them with settlers from New England.

Also in June
• Edward Boscawen (1711–1761), commanding an English squadron, blockaded Louisbourg harbour and disrupted commerce.

July 8 Britain broke off diplomatic relations with France as hostilities in North America intensified between the 2 countries.

July 9 Maj-Gen. Braddock marched against Fort Duquesne with a force of about 1,500 British and colonial troops. They were routed by 750 French and Aboriginal troops in the Battle of Monongahela. Braddock was fatally wounded and died 4 days later. The French commander, Daniel-Hyacinthe-Marie Lienard de Beaujeu (1711–1755) was also killed. The British suffered nearly 1,000 casualties, while French losses were light.

July 18 Lt-Gov. Lawrence informed British authorities that he would expel some 10,000 Acadians from the colony if they persisted in their refusal to sign the oath of loyalty to Great Britain. Lawrence's letter did not reach England until The Expulsion was underway.

July 25 Fifteen Acadian delegates from Minas (Grand Pré region) appeared before the NS Council with several grievances. Lt-Gov. Lawrence took advantage of the occasion to enforce the oath of allegiance to Britain on them, but they once again declined and, as a result, were imprisoned.

July 28 Lt-Gov. Lawrence received the approval of the Council of NS to deport all Acadians who refused to take the oath of allegiance to the British Crown.

July 30 Jonathan Belcher accepted the advice of the NS Council of war and ordered all Acadian prisoners of war, who had earlier been concentrated in Halifax, deported to Boston, where the Massachusetts govt refused to receive them and sent them back.

Aug. 25 Mme d'Youville officially received the habit from the hands of the Sulpician Order and took the name of Sisters of Charity of the Hôpital Général, or Grey Nuns, for her Order.

Sept. 1 French troops under Dieskau camped at Ticonderoga, New York, while searching for a British expedition commanded by William Johnson (c 1715–1774). Johnson built Fort William Henry at the head of L. George, New York, 22 km north-west of his base at Fort Edward, on the Hudson R.

Sept. 4 Capt. Legardeur, with a force of Canadian militia and hundreds of Aboriginals, launched a major offensive against the British, in the vicinity of Lac Saint-Sacrament.

Sept. 5 At a church in Grand Pré, NS, Lt-Col. John Winslow (1703–1774), acting on orders from Lt-Gov. Lawrence to deport all Acadians refusing to sign an unconditional oath of allegiance to England, announced to 400 Acadian men and boys whom he had summoned, that all of their "Lands & Tenements, Cattle of all Kinds and Live Stock of all Sortes were Forfitted to the Crown with all other Effects Saving your Money and Household Goods and you your-selves to be removed from this Province." On Sept. 8, male Acadians of Grand Pré began to embark, unwillingly, onto the 5 transport ships Winslow had waiting offshore. Throughout the summer and fall, Acadians were deported from Annapolis Royal, Chignecto, Chepody, Memramcock and Petitcodiac to South Carolina, Virginia, Louisiana, Pennsylvania, Maryland, Connecticut, Massachusetts and New York. A total of 6,000 people were deported. About 4,000 others escaped to Que. and Île St. Jean.

Also in Sept.
• A 1,000-man British relief force under William Johnson, en route to Fort Edward at the head of L. George, defeated the French in the battle of L. George (Lac Saint-Sacrament) in the Crown Point campaign. No attempt was made to capture Crown Point. Jean-Hermann, Baron de Dieskau, commander of the French forces, was captured and taken to England as a prisoner. Capt. Legardeur was killed. William Johnson was wounded early in the attack.

Oct. 16 Massachusetts enacted a law empowering Justices of the Peace and Overseers of the Poor to serve as guardians of the welfare of expelled Acadians in the colony.

Dec. 9 Canada's 1st post office was opened in Halifax, NS.

Dec. 10 The ships, *Violet* and *Duke William,* sank in an Atlantic storm while transporting exiled Acadians. One thousand two hundred lives were lost.

Also in Dec.
• Robert Monckton was appointed lt-gov. of NS.

Also in 1755
• The population of NS was 11,200 before the Proscription (Expulsion) but dropped to 4,200 after the Proscription.

• The population of NB was 4,300 before the Proscription, and increased to 4,800 after.

• The population of Île St. Jean was 3,000 before the Proscription, and increased to 3,500 after.

• English cartographer John Mitchell (1690–1768) published his map of North America.

1756

Jan. 7 Charles Lawrence was appointed gov. of NS, serving from July 23, 1756–Sept. 24, 1761.

Mar. 11 Louis-Joseph de Montcalm, Marquis de Montcalm (1712–1759) was appointed commander in the field of French forces in New France and awarded the rank of maj-gen.

Mar. 27 Some 360 members of a French force under Gaspard-Joseph Chaussegros de Léry (1682–1756) attacked Fort Bull, a supply outpost south of L. Ontario, killing most of its 60 to 80 inhabitants.

Also in Mar. Robert Rogers (1731–1795) was commissioned to form a company of rangers for scouting and intelligence duties in the L. Champlain region.

May 8 Aboriginals attacked Mahone Bay, NS, as reprisal for the Acadian Expulsion.

May 13 Louis-Joseph de Montcalm (1731–1759) arrived in Que. to assume command over the army troops in New France.

May 17 The Seven Years' War began as Britain declared war against France. France declared war on Britain the next day. Lord John Loudoun was named C–in–C of the British forces in America.

May 29 Montcalm joined the 3,000 men at Fort Frontenac, commanded by François-Charles de Bourlamaque (1716–1764), and arranged to trans-port his army to Sackets Harbor, New York (Aug. 5).

June 14 After a 4-day siege, Montcalm captured and destroyed the British Fort Oswego, on the south shore of L. Ontario. The French killed 30, took 1,700 prisoners, several armed ships, a large number of cannon munitions and supplies of all types and gained control of L. Ontario and New York's western frontier.

c 1756 The portrait on canvas, *Le Père Emmanuel Crespel*, attributed to Père François (Jean-Melchior Brekenmacher), was completed.

Also in 1756

• Joseph Michael Cadet became Munitionnaire du Roi in charge of supplying French forces in Canada.

• Fort Richmond, built by the HBC in 1750, failed as a commercial enterprise and was closed. Its operations were moved to Little Whale R.

1757

Jan. 21 Montcalm's French-Canadian force defeated Roger's Rangers near Ticonderoga, New York.

Feb. 1 The play *The Old Man Duped*, written by a French soldier stationed at the House of Peace (Fort Niagara), was performed by members of the garrison at the fort. It was believed to be the 1st staged play performed in a frontier outpost.

Mar. 14 Former gov. of Nfld., John Byng, was executed before a firing squad on the *Monarch,* at Portsmouth, for failing to attack French ships off the British-held island of Minorca, and for failing to relieve the British Fort St. Phillip.

July 26 A British force under Col. Parker defeated the French under Montcalm and François de Lévis, Duc de Lévis (1719–1787), at Sabbath Day Point, L. George.

Aug. 3 Montcalm, with an army of 6,200 and 1,800 Aboriginal allies, besieged Fort William Henry on L. George, defended by 2,500 British under George Munro.

Aug. 9 Col. Munro surrendered Fort William Henry after being bombarded for 6 days. Montcalm promised the British safe passage to Fort Edward; 2,200 prisoners began the march, but only 1,400 reached Fort Edward. The others, men, women and children, were killed or taken prisoner by French allies.

Also in 1757

• Fort Lydius (Fort Edward, New York) was raided by a French force under Joseph Marin, and by Father Picquet, at the head of Iroquois warriors from his mission at Fort de La Présentation.

• Montcalm was promoted to lt-gen., and made C-in-C of all French forces in Canada with authority over Gov. Vaudreuil, with whom he had a long-standing feud.

• The 1st architect in English Canada, Henry Evans, worked in Halifax.

• The king of France outlawed all games of chance in New France.

1758

Feb. 7 The British Board of Trade ordered Gov. Lawrence to convene an elected assembly in NS. The gov. and Council complied by passing resolutions which organized the 1st legislature in Canada. Sixteen members were elected for the province at large, with 4 from Halifax and 2 from Louisbourg. The assembly's initial meeting was scheduled for Oct. 2.

Mar. 16 Maj-Gen. Jeffery Amherst (1717–1797) sailed for America to command the British forces in the Seven Years' War. In 1776, he became the 1st Baron Amherst.

Apr. 1 Bread rationing in Que. and Montreal allotted 57 grams per person per day. Women took to the streets in protest over continued food shortages caused by the war.

Apr. 28 A British expedition against Louisbourg sailed from Halifax. Edward Boscawen (1711–1761) commanded the naval forces while Maj-Gen. Amherst led the land forces. Amherst's brigade commanders were James Wolfe (1727–1759), Charles Lawrence and Edward Whitmore (c 1694 –1761). The British fleet, which numbered 27,000 men and 157 ships, anchored in Gabarus Bay, near Louisbourg, on June 2, to begin the seige. Louisbourg was commanded by Augustine Boschenry de Drucour. He controlled 3,500 soldiers and some 4,000 sailors and militia.

May Food supplies arrived in Que. and Montreal from France.

June 8 A British force, under the command of Gen. Wolfe, landed at Anse de la Cormorandière (Kenning-ton Cove), a few km west of Louisbourg, and defeated the French under Jean Mascle de Saint-Julien, who then withdrew into the fortress.

June 19 Wolfe's cannoneers opened fire on the Louisbourg fortress from Pointe à la Croix.

July 5 British Gen. James Abercromby (1732–1775) attacked Fort Carillon with 16,000 troops (6,000 regulars and 9,000 "colonial militia"). French defender Gen. Montcalm commanded a force of 3,600 men.

July 6 Brigadier George Augustus Howe, Gen. Abercromby's 2nd in command, was killed at the portage between L. Champlain and L. George.

July 8 Gen. Montcalm, entrenched at Fort Carillon, defeated Gen. Abercromby, inflicting 1,944 casualties and suffering only 377.

July 26 Hopelessly outnumbered, Louisbourg, under de Drucour, surrendered to the British forces under C-in-C Amherst, who credited Gen. Wolfe for the victory. The 66-day siege had the immediate impact of preventing the British from embarking on the 2nd military goal of their campaign — the capture of Que., which was postponed until the new year. On July 27, British forces occupied Louisbourg, and Wolfe's artillery systematically destroyed all of the fortress's defences.

Aug. 8 Rogers, with a force of 700, clashed with a French and Aboriginal force, under Joseph Marin de La Malgue, near Fort Ann, New York. Marin was forced to withdraw.

• Col. Andrew Rollo (1703–1765) was sent to Île St. Jean to arrange for French surrender of the island. Rollo built Fort Amherst at Port-La-Joie and deported 3,500 Acadian inhabitants to France. About 300 people remained in isolated parts of the island.

Aug. 25 British Col. John Bradstreet, with a force of 3,000, accepted the surrender of Fort Cataraqui (Kingston, Ont.) from Pierre-Jacques Payen de Noyan et de Chavoy (c 1700–1765). Bradstreet plundered, burned and demolished the fort before retreating to British territory.

Aug. 29 Wolfe left Louisbourg with 3 battalions convoyed by a squadron of 9 ships under Charles Hardy (c 1714–1780). He was on a campaign to destroy settlements along the lower St. Lawrence R., including Gaspé and Miramichi. On Sept. 4, Wolfe arrived at Gaspé Bay, and ordered destruction of the town (Sept. 10–11).

Sept. 11–Nov. 21 Col. Monckton was ordered to lead a force of nearly 2,300 men to destroy houses, cattle and crops for about 112 km up the Saint John R., and force any Acadians residing in British-held territory to retire to Que. by spring. On Sept. 20, Monckton landed his troops at the site of present-day Saint John, NB.

Sept. 14 An 800-man British force under James Grant was defeated by the French at Grant's Hill, near Fort Duquesne.

Also in Sept.
• Col. James Murray (1721/1722–1782), under Wolfe's orders, destroyed all the houses and a stone church in Miramichi.

Oct. 2 The 1st meeting of the NS Legislative Assembly was called to order, with 20 assemblymen present. All voted to serve without pay, in the 1st popularly elected parliament in Canada. Robert Saunderson was appointed 1st speaker of the NS legislature. One of the legislature's early acts was to enforce Sabbath observance, with fines for non-attendance at church and measures to prevent "looseness and brawling" on Sundays, a popular day of drink among workers.

Also in Oct.
• Gov. Lawrence began a drive to settle Acadian lands with a proclamation seeking proposals for settlement.

Nov. 9 Maj-Gen. Amherst received word that he was C-in-C in America, replacing Gen. Abercromby, who was recalled to England.

Nov. 25 Gen. John Forbes (1707–1759) took Fort Duquesne in a bloodless engagement renaming it Fort Pitt, later to become Pittsburgh. French rule in the Ohio Valley ended.

Also in Nov.
• Col. Rollo left Île Saint-Jean for Louisbourg.

Dec. The 1ˢᵗ Lunenburg representative entered the NS assembly.

1759

Jan. 12 Wolfe was promoted to maj-gen. and appointed C-in-C of the land forces for the expedition against Que.

Also in Jan.
• Gov. Lawrence issued a 2ⁿᵈ proclamation, directed primarily at New Englanders, informing them, as would-be settlers, that each grant of land would include cultivated and wild woodland to a maximum of 405 ha per family. Further grants would be available upon the completion of the terms of the first.

• Gen. Forbes returned as a hero to Philadelphia after securing the upper Ohio Valley to British control. He died in Mar. after a long illness.

Feb. 5 British PM William Pitt (elder Pitt) gave Maj-Gen. Wolfe secret orders to take Que.

Feb. 8 Montcalm sent aides to France to urge the govt to make an all-out effort to defend the colony from British attack.

Feb. 13 NS's House of Assembly adopted a resolution to employ the secret ballot in the election of its members. This was the 1ˢᵗ use of the secret ballot in any British territory.

Feb. 17 Wolfe sailed from Britain for Canada on the flagship *Neptune*, with 22 warships, frigates and sloops of war.

May 5 British Capt. Philip Durell (1707–1766) sailed from Halifax with a number of warships to block the St. Lawrence and prevent French reinforcements from getting through to Que.; the attempt was too late. French Admiral Louis-Antoine de Bougainville, Comte de Bougainville (1729–1811),

commanding a fleet of 23 French transports, had already sailed by.

May 22 Gen. Montcalm arrived at Que., expecting a British strike on the city. He made a military tour of the entire area, accompanied by Brigadier Lévis, and rearranged artillery batteries.

June 1 George Clark (d 1759) arrived at Henley House after being appointed master of a post that had been vacant since the murder of James Duffield, the former master.

June 21 Gen. Amherst arrived at the head of L. George with his army.

June 25 Wolfe's forces arrived off Que. His 8,500 men were carried in a fleet of 168 ships commanded by Charles Saunders (c 1715–1775). Two days later, Saunders landed troops on the south shore of the Île d'Orléans, opposite Que. Capt. James Cook (1728–1779) guided the ships with the help of captured French pilots who were forced to navigate the fleet upriver. The British secured the island with little resistance on June 29, despite a French attack with fire rafts. By July 3, Wolfe had established himself and his troops on Point Lévis, overlooking the defenses of Que.

July 9 Wolfe landed a brigade, under George Townshend, on the left bank of the Montmorency R., just east of the French defensive lines. Montcalm declined to oppose the brigade for fear of committing his forces in what might turn out to be a feint.

July 11 Montcalm ordered a night attack on Point Lévis against 3,000 British under Robert Monckton. The French, led by Jean-Daniel Dumas (1721–1794), included 1,400 volunteers with about 100 regulars and a detachment of schoolboys who had never seen action.

July 12 Wolfe ordered bombardment of Que. to begin from Point Lévis. A French counter-attack was repulsed. Both Upper and Lower Towns were soon in flames.

July 13 The British assault on Quebec City forced Augustine and Ursuline nuns, and wounded French soldiers, to take refuge in the Hôpital Général outside the city.

July 21 While Wolfe was attacking Que., Col. Guy Carleton (1724–1808) led an expedition about 35 km up the St. Lawrence R.

July 22 Amherst led his army via L. Champlain to join the invasion of New France, by besieging Fort Carillon.

July 24 William Johnson defeated a French force under François-Marie Le Marchand de Lignery (1703–1759) at La Belle Famille. De Lignery had been en route to aid Fort Niagara. He died July 28, of wounds received in battle.

July 25 Fort Niagara fell to the British under Brig-Gen. John Prideaux, effectively ending French competition for the western fur trade, as the British secured control of L. Ontario.

July 30 Wolfe attempted a frontal attack on the French at Montmorency Falls (Battle of Montmorency) but was turned back by Canadian militia under Montcalm, and by torrential rains, which soaked the men and ammunition and made the hill extremely slippery. British dead, missing and wounded totalled 443.

Also in July
• The British under Amherst retook Fort William Henry.

July–Aug. The French, under François-Charles Bourlamaque (1716–1764), retreated from Fort Carillon by water, but blew up the fort before abandoning it. The British captured Fort Carillon (July 26) and renamed it Fort Ticonderoga. The French fell back to Fort Saint-Frédéric, which the British captured July 31, and renamed Crown Point. The French retreated to Fort Île-aux-Noix in the Rivière Richelieu.

Aug. 9 Lower Town Que. was destroyed by British gunfire.

Aug. 17 The govt of NS divided the colony into 5 counties: Annapolis, Kings, Cumberland, Lunenburg, and Halifax.

Sept. 7 Part of the British fleet moved up the St. Lawrence to Cap-Rouge.

Sept. 9 Wolfe spotted a possible landing place, 3.2 km above Que., at a cove named l'Anse au Foulon.

Sept. 12–13 Under the cover of night, Wolfe landed 4,500 troops at l'Anse au Foulon (Wolfe's Cove), advanced on a path up cliffs west of Que., and stationed 4,000 men and field artillery on the Plains of Abraham, by morning. Montcalm was compelled to give battle. During the assault, Admiral Saunders bombarded Beauport as a cover for Wolfe's advance. The British were victorious after 10 minutes in a battle defined as the most decisive in Canadian history. Montcalm was wounded on the Plains of Abraham. Wolfe, having been shot 3 times, died of his wounds during the hour of victory, exclaiming, "Now, God be praised, I will die in peace."

Sept. 14 Montcalm died of wounds to the stomach and thigh, which he had received in battle the previous day.

• British forces celebrated Thanksgiving in Quebec City with an Anglican service in the Ursuline Chapel.

Sept. 15 Ramezay, in command of 2,200 men at Que. after the death of Montcalm, was urged by the city burghers to surrender the city to the British on honourable terms.

Sept. 17 George Clark was murdered by some 20 men, probably French and Aboriginal peoples, in an ambush outside of Henley House. Three other men at the post, John Spence, John Cromartie and James Inkster, put up a stout resistance and managed to escape after midnight. On Oct. 6, George Clark was buried at Albany. Two Aboriginals had recovered his body, and returned it to the HBC. Clark had been scalped.

• François de Lévis, Duc de Lévis (1719–1787) took command of the French troops at Point-aux-Trembles, and ordered a withdrawal to Montreal, at 3 p.m. the same day.

• The Commander of Quebec hoisted a white flag over the city and sent Maj. Armand de Joannes to discuss terms of capitulation and the surrender of the town. Ramezay signed the terms at 11 p.m. The next day (Sept. 18), Que. formally surrendered to the British under Gen. James Murray when Charles Saunders and George Townshend signed the capitulation. The formal capitulation would not occur until Sept. 19, when Ramezay officially handed Que. over to Townshend and the Que. garrison boarded British vessels as prisoners of war.

Sept. 21 Que. habitants, living within a 140 km radius of Quebec City, arrived in the city to take an oath of allegiance to Britain.

Sept. 22 Murray promised Quebec City's French inhabitants "mild and just government" and the right to remain Catholic.

Sept. 25 The ship *Tilbury of St. Esprit* was lost off Île Royale, taking 200 lives.

Oct. 1 Gov-Gen. Rigaud de Vaudreuil and the bishop of Que. arrived at Montreal (the gov.'s designated new headquarters) to prepare the city's defences against a British attack.

Oct. 4 Maj. Robert Rogers led a British force in an early-morning surprise attack against the sleeping Abenaki village of Odanak, destroying the village and killing about 30 people. Following the raid, Rogers retreated down the Connecticut R. pursued by the Abenaki. About 50 of Rogers's men died on the expedition, mostly from starvation.

Oct. 10 A royal decree invalidated paper money of the former govt of New France.

Oct. 12 Gen. James Murray was appointed gov. of the garrison of Que.

Oct. 18 Amherst halted his advance along L. Champlain after hearing about the fall of Que. Amherst feared the whole French army would be assembled at Montreal. His inaction delayed the conquest of New France.

Oct. 26 Gov. James Murray ordered Jesuit priests to leave the city for allegedly encouraging discontent among British troops occupying the city and trying to persuade British soldiers to desert their posts.

Nov. 12 Murray established English civil law in the conquered colony.

Nov. 24 French supply ships that had sheltered all summer in the Richelieu R. attempted to slip past Que. and return to France. Four ran aground and were destroyed.

Nov. 30 Murray ordered the disarming of French-Canadians living on the south side of the St. Lawrence R. because of frequent attacks against British soldiers and civilians.

1759–1760 The Sambro lighthouse was built on a granite island south of Halifax harbour. Commissioned by the NS legislature and paid for by taxes on alcohol and shipping, in addition to a lottery, Sambro Is. lighthouse is Canada's oldest serving lighthouse. Its 18 m tower was extended in 1907 to 24 m.

Also in 1759

• There were 3,604 slaves in New France; 1,132 were of African origin.

• James Cook carried out surveys in the St. Lawrence R.

• HBC's Little Whale R. post was closed and its operations moved to the Great Whale R.

1760

Jan. 9 The Mi'kmaq of NS made peace with the settlers.

Jan. 26 James Murray ordered about 300 British soldiers to burn the homes of French colonists on the south bank of the St. Lawrence R. between the Etchemin and Chaudière rivers. The colonists had broken their oaths of allegiance to King George.

Apr. 8 The French Superior Council met for the last time.

Apr. 17 François de Lévis left Montreal, with his 7,000-man army to try to retake Que. On Apr. 28 James Murray's 3,900 men engaged 7,000 French under de Lévis in the Battle of Sainte-Foy, one of the bloodiest encounters in Canadian history. Each side lost about 1,000 men. The British were defeated after a 2-hour battle, but were able to retreat to Que., which they still held.

Apr. 29 Col. Robert Monckton became commander of the British troops in the southern colonies.

May 9 The British frigate *Lowestoft* rounded the Island of Orléans, prompting Gen. Lévis to make a final assault on Gen. Murray's position in Que.

May 11 François de Lévis attacked Que. with a heavy artillery barrage.

May 14 A French fleet arrived from France, but retreated to the Bay of Chaleur when it learned of the fall of Que.

May 16 De Lévis lifted his siege of Que. and retreated to Montreal when a British fleet under Admiral Robert Swanton (d 1765) arrived with provisions and reinforcements. The British destroyed French frigates supporting the besieging army.

June 4 New England planters arrived at NS, on 22 ships, to replace expelled Acadians.

July 8 British ships commanded by John Byron defeated a French relief force under François-Gabriel d'Angeac (1708–1782) in the Battle of Restigouche at the mouth of the Restigouche R.

Aug. 10 Amherst embarked with 10,000 men on boats from Oswego, New York, and moved up the St. Lawrence R. towards Montreal.

Aug. 17 The last French ships on the Great Lakes, *Actaquaise* and *Iroquois*, were captured by 5 British rowing galleys at Point au Baril, near Brockville, Ont.

Aug. 22 Newly promoted Brig-Gen. Andrew Rollo attacked and destroyed Sorel, Que., in a raid that "laid waste the greatest part of the parish," many of whose inhabitants were still infants.

Aug. 25 Amherst battered Fort Lévis (east of Prescott, Ont.) into surrender, after a determined defence by a French force of less than 400 men under Capt. Pierre Pouchot (1712–1769).

Aug. 27 James Murray and his force of 4,000 men arrived at Montreal.

Aug. 28 A British force of 3,400, under William Haviland (1718–1784), marched up L. Champlain from Crown Point to capture Fort Île-aux-Noix on the Richelieu R., before turning toward Montreal.

Sept. 6 Amherst arrived at Montreal, which was defended by 2,000 French troops. The combined British army of over 17,000 men surrounded the city.

Sept. 7 The gov. of New France, de Vaudreuil, asked Amherst for terms of surrender. Amherst refused to grant the traditional honours of war. De Lévis ordered his regiments to burn their colours.

Sept. 8 De Vaudreuil ordered François de Lévis to surrender Montreal to the British under Amherst at the Place d'Armes without a shot being fired. Frederick Haldimand (1718–1791) took possession for the British, who marched into the city the next day.

Sept. 12 Amherst sent Major Rogers and his 200 Rangers from Montreal to take possession of Detroit.

Sept. 13 Leaders of the Maliseet, Mi'kmaq and Passamaquoddy met in Halifax to swear allegiance to King George, and thus acquire a source of much-needed supplies.

Sept. 16 All but a handful of the French army (6 captains, 3 lieutenants, 4 ensigns) were transported to France via Que., accompanied by the administrative officials of New France and several merchants.

Sept. 22 Amherst divided Canada into the military districts of Quebec, Montreal and Trois-Rivières. Thomas Gage (c 1719–1787) was appointed military gov. of Montreal; and Ralph Burton (1687–1753) of Trois-Rivières. All military governors reported to Maj-Gen. Amherst.

Sept. 30 Maj. Rogers and his Rangers took command of Fort Rouillé (Toronto).

• A proclamation by James Murray established military courts in Que.

Oct. 17 Sir William Pitt ordered Sappers under "Foulweather Jack" Byron (1723–1786), grandfather of poet Lord Byron, to destroy the fortifications at Louisbourg, NS, a task that took 2 years.

Oct. 19 Charles Lawrence, gov. of NS, died unexpectedly, of a chill.

Oct. 19–Sept. 25, 1763 Jonathan Belcher served as administrator of NS.

Oct. 27 Maj. Rogers, en route to Detroit, met Ottawa Chief Pontiac at the mouth of the Detroit R. on L. Erie near Cleveland. Pontiac demonstrated a peaceful attitude toward the British, his former enemies, in response to their promises of full and free trade. Pontiac promised allegiance.

Oct. 27–Aug. 1764 James Murray served as Military Gov. of the District of Que.

Oct. 29 The French garrison at Detroit surrendered to the British.

1760–1763 Britain governed New France by military rule under the British C-in-C, Gen. Jeffrey Amherst.

Also in 1760

• The population of New France was 64,041.

• At the time of the British Conquest, some 250 seigneuries existed in New France, each held by a seigneur who was responsible for clearing the land of forest and brush, operating a gristmill, holding a local court of law, subsidizing and building local roads, churches and bridges. In return, the king demanded all mineral rights, allegiance and a 20% land tax. Each seigneury was a rectangular property about 6 km wide by 50 km long, usually bounded by rivers with a manor house, church and mill in the centre. Local farms, leased from the seigneur by censitaires and contained within the seigneury, comprised an average of 30-35 ha. Censitaires paid their landlord a fee of 1/4 of each grain harvest, 1/11 of each fish harvest, 3 days per annum work and an annual tax/rent.

• The Grey Beard Club of English-speaking fur traders was established at Montreal.

1761

Feb. 14 The British occupied Michilimackinac.

Mar. 24 The 1st Lutheran church in Canada was established at Halifax.

June 25 The Mi'kmaq concluded a peace treaty with the British in an elaborate ceremony held in Halifax.

Sept. 24–Nov. 21, 1763 Henry Ellis, of Georgia, held the title of gov. of NS, but never set foot on Canadian soil to assume office. From late Nov. to Sept. 26, 1763 Jonathan Belcher served as acting gov. of NS in the absence of Ellis.

Fall In a letter to superintendent of northern First Nations peoples, Amherst forbade the custom of buying good conduct with presents.

Nov. 15 En route to France from Que., the French ship *Auguste* was wrecked during a gale, on the shores of Cape Breton Is. Louis-Joseph La Vérendrye was one of 113 passengers and crew who perished.

Dec. 12 British Secretary of State Lord Egremont urged that the French be treated humanely and kindly and be protected against insults and reviling from occupying forces.

1761–1762 James Cook surveyed Halifax Harbour.

1762

May 8 Charles-Henry-Louis d'Arsac de Ternay (1723–1780) sailed from Brest in command of an expedition to seize St. John's, Nfld., and "to cause as much harm as possible to the English."

May 16 About 200 English settlers from Massachusetts arrived at Maugerville to form the 1st British settlement in New Brunswick, establishing residences along the north side of the Saint John R.

June 27 French raiders under de Ternay took Fort Williams at St. John's, Nfld., in a surprise attack, after which most fishing stations of Nfld. were systematically destroyed and 460 ships, of all sizes, captured or sunk. Damage to the British was estimated at more than £1,000,000.

Sept. 7 Lt-Col. William Amherst, brother of Jeffrey Amherst, left Louisbourg in command of 1,500 British and American troops, to retake St. John's. He landed at Torbay, north of St. John's, Sept. 13, and drove the French forces back into Fort Henry.

Sept. 15–18 The last clash, in the Conquest of Canada between British and French troops, occurred at the Battle of Signal Hill. Under imminent attack by superior British forces, de Ternay left St. John's, hidden by night and fog, saving his entire squadron. He left behind the fusiliers under La Marine and all the grenadiers under Joseph-Louis-Bernard de Cléron d'Haussonville, to provide cover and to surrender honourably later. St. John's, Nfld., was recaptured by the British led by Lord Alexander Colville (1717–1770), C-in-C of the North American squadron.

1763

Feb. 10 The Treaty of Paris, ending the French and Indian War (Seven Years' War), confirmed the French in Canada as subjects of the British Crown. France withdrew from Canada. The British also received Île Royale; France was allowed to keep the islands St. Pierre and Miquelon and retained fishing rights in Nfld. and the Gulf of St. Lawrence. Those who did not wish to switch their allegiance to Britain were free to leave. Only 270 did.

• Quebec became the capital of the Province of Que.

Apr. 27 Ottawa Chief Pontiac called the 1st of a series of secret councils at Rivière à l'Écorce to raise western First Nations against the British. About 460 warriors joined him in what historian Francis Parkman termed "the Conspiracy of Pontiac." On May 10, Pontiac and his supporters commenced a series of raids on interior trading posts and besieged Fort Detroit for 5 months.

May 26 Forts Saint-Joseph and Miami (in present-day Indiana) fell into the hands of the Miami and Illinois.

May 27 The Delaware and Seneca occupied William Chapman's store and besieged Fort Pitt (formerly Fort Duquesne).

Also in May

• Lt. Abraham Cornelius Cuyler (1742–1810), in charge of transporting provisions to Detroit, was surprised by a party of Ottawa at Point Pelée. Forty-six English were taken prisoner and two boats captured.

June 1 The Wea, Kickapoo and Mascouten took Fort Ouiatanon (near Lafayette, Indiana).

June 2 The Ojibwa led by Madjeckewiss (c 1735–c 1805) and Minweweh (c 1710–1770) took Michilimackinac.

June 16 The Seneca burned Venango (Franklin, Pennsylvania).

June 19 or 20 The Seneca took possession of Fort de la Rivière au Boeuf (Waterford, Pennsylvania).

June 21 More than 200 Seneca, Ottawa, Huron and Ojibwa from Detroit seized Fort de la Presqui'le (Erie, Pennsylvania).

July 7 As a means of suppressing Pontiac's rebellion, Amherst suggested to Col. Henry Bouquet: "Could it not be contrived to send the small pox among the disaffected tribes of Indians? We must on this occasion use every stratagem in our power to reduce them." Such biological warfare may have been attempted with infected blankets and handkerchiefs.

July 14 The French govt appointed Baron de l'Espérance to take charge of the islands of St. Pierre and Miquelon off Nfld., which had been awarded to France as a fishing base by the Treaty of Paris. These islands were the last vestiges of the French Empire in North America, and welcomed displaced Acadians from the mainland.

Aug. 1 A contingent force of 247 men commanded by James Dalyell, sent to reinforce the English at Detroit under Gladwin, attacked Pontiac's besiegers and suffered bloody losses on a bridge across Parent's Creek (later called Bloody Run). The British retreated to the fort leaving many dead, including Dalyell.

Sept. 14 Seneca defeated the British at Devil's Hole.

Sept. 22 Capt. William Howard reoccupied Michilimackinac.

Sept. 25 Montagu Wilmot (d 1766) was appointed gov. of NS. He assumed office in May 1764, serving until his death.

Oct. 7 King George III issued a royal proclamation inviting his subjects to settle in Canada. He established the western boundary of Que. at a line running northwest from the point where the 45th parallel crossed the St. Lawrence R. to L. Nipissing. The Appalachian watershed became the western boundary of the Atlantic colonies, blocking British settlement of Aboriginal lands of the Ohio and Mississippi Valleys. Labrador, Anticosti Is. and the Magdalen Is. were given to Nfld. NS annexed all the area the French had known as Acadia.

Oct. 31 Pontiac lifted his siege on Fort Detroit because of desertions and exhaustion.

Nov. 7 Britain proclaimed the establishment of civil govt in Canada.

Nov. 21 Benjamin Franklin (1706–1790), Deputy Postmaster-Gen. for the American colonies, established post offices in Quebec, Montreal and Trois-Rivières. He also established a courier service between New York and Montreal.

c 1763 Using drawings prepared by an unknown military artist stationed in Halifax, Dominique Serres (1722–1793) completed 4 oil paintings, including *A View of Halifax, Nova Scotia: Part of the Town and Harbour Looking Down Prince Street to the Opposite Shore,* portraying the town in detail. All 4 works are in the Art Gallery of NS's permanent collection. Serres himself never visited North America.

Also in 1763

• Sir William Johnson estimated the number of First Nations warriors populating the St. Lawrence R. area from Quebec west at 11,980, with 2,230 of the Six Nation Confederacy, 630 allied with the Six Nations, 1,100 residents in the Ohio basin, 3,220 of the Ottawa Confederacy, 800 Miami or "Twightwee" and 4,000 Chippewa.

• Capt. James Cook received orders from the British Admiralty to survey and map the Nfld. and Labrador coastlines.

1764

Feb. 13 The Earl of Egremont devised a feudal scheme for the Island of St. John (PEI).

Feb. 17 William Gregory was appointed the 1st Chief Justice of Que.

Mar. 5 Gov. Murray ordered inhabitants of Que. to declare all French-Canadian money before Apr. 1.

Mar. 22 The 1st hard-bound book, a catechism, was printed in Canada.

May Joseph Frederick Wallet DesBarres began the survey of coasts and harbours of NS, which would be completed in 1773. The survey was approved by the British Admiralty on the recommendation of Commodore Richard Spry, commander of the Royal Navy in North America.

June 21 William Brown and Thomas Gilmore, both of Philadelphia, set up the 1st printing shop in Que., and published the city's 1st newspaper, *La Gazette de Québec* of Montreal, a bilingual weekly. It is the 2nd-oldest newspaper in Canada.

Aug. 10 The establishment of civil govt, as proclaimed in Britain, on Nov. 7, 1763, was inaugurated in Canada, and James Murray was formally confirmed as gov. of Que. He served from Aug. 13, 1764–Apr. 12, 1768.

Aug. 12 John Bradstreet (1714–1774) sent on an expedition against the Delaware and Shawnee, decided to conduct peace talks instead, at Fort Presqui'le. He then travelled to Detroit (Aug. 27) for more negotiations.

Sept. 17 Gov. Murray enacted an ordinance, implementing the English legal system in Que. Legal cases arising prior to Oct. 1 were allowed to be tried in the common courts in French using the French legal system.

Oct. 1 The 1763 proclamation, replacing military by civil rule, came into effect.

• HBC and other rival fur-trading groups were forced to set up food supply networks in order to support the increasing number of trading posts and communication between them. These networks relied heavily on the bison population of the Northwest.

Oct. 4 An ordinance regulated foreign currency.

1764–1767 Capt. Samuel Holland (1728–1801), acting on instructions of the British govt, surveyed Île St. Jean and divided most of the island into 67 townships of 8,094 ha each, plus the county towns of Georgetown, Charlottetown and Princetown.

1765

Jan. 7 French-speaking citizens sent an appeal to King George to change the legal system.

Mar. 8 The British Parliament passed the Stamp Act, requiring stamps on documents, pamphlets, newspapers, almanacs, playing cards and dice. American colonists opposed and ignored this tax, often placing the skull and crossbones where the stamp was required.

Mar. 17 St. Patrick's Day was celebrated for the 1st time in Canada, in Que.

Apr. 18 Saint-Ange and Lt. Alexander Fraser met Pontiac and convinced him to make peace with the British.

May 18 Fire destroyed one quarter of Montreal including the Hôpital Général, which was sheltering 18 sisters under Mme d'Youville, 17 ladies paying board and lodging, 63 poor persons and 16 illegitimate children. Rebuilding began almost immediately and, 7 months later, the poor were able to return to new lodgings.

May 21 The 1st Agricultural Fair in Canada was held at Windsor, NS.

June 4 Alexander Henry (1739–1824) was appointed captain of the western trading posts, with headquarters at Michilimackinac.

July George Croghan met with Pontiac at Ouiatanon and a preliminary peace agreement was signed. It was later ratified in Detroit by a gathering of Ottawa, Ojibwa, Huron and Potawatomi, all of

whom emphasized that they had never been conquered and had never sold their lands and, therefore, the French could not hand their territories over to the English.

Sept. 2 The British Board of Trade recommended that Roman Catholics be allowed to vote for members of a proposed assembly but not sit as members.

Nov. 15 By ordinance, French-speaking jurors were admitted to courts and lawyers were permitted to plead cases in French.

Also in 1765
• Brown and Gilmore published the 1st books in Que.: 300 copies of *Presentments to the Grand Jury* and 2,000 copies of *Le catéchisme du Diocèse de Sens* by Jean-Joseph Languet de Gergy.

• Moses Norton (c 1735–1773), Chief Factor of the HBC post at Churchill, reported that Cree would buy 1 ox from him for 1 beaver skin, carry it upstream and sell the same ox to the Chipewyan or Blackfoot for 10 beaver skins.

• Rev. George Henry established the 1st Presbyterian church in Que.

• The HBC built a whale fishery on Marble Is.

1766

Mar. 16 Pope Clement XIII appointed Jean-Olivier Briand (1715–1794) bishop of Que.

Mar. 18 Following the repeal of the Stamp Act, the Declaratory Act declared that the king, by and with consent of parliament, had authority to make laws binding in the colonies in all respects.

Mar. 21 Bishop Briand left Paris for London, where he received permission to return to Canada after taking the Oath of Loyalty to the king of England.

Apr. 7 Guy Carleton, was appointed to replace Gov. James Murray with the temporary rank of lt-gov. of Que., serving from Sept. 24–Oct. 26, 1766. Carleton was also given command of all the troops in the colony. Murray was ordered back to Britain to account for his behaviour in connection with hooliganism on the part of military personnel in Que. and complaints against him by merchants.

May 23–Aug. 22, 1766 Benjamin Green (1713–1772) served as administrator of NS.

June 30–Sept. 24, 1766 Aemilius Paulus Irving (1714–1796) served as administrator of Canada.

July 19 Briand took possession of his seat as 7th bishop of Que. in the chapel of the Séminaire de Québec.

July 24 Pontiac met with William Johnson at Fort Ontario (Oswego, New York), and agreed to peace terms.

Aug. 11 William Campbell (c 1730–1778) was appointed gov. of NS.

Aug. 15 The *NS Gazette* published its 1st issue.

Aug. 23–Nov. 26, 1766 Michael Francklin (1733–1782) served as administrator of NS.

1767

June 29 The Townshend Revenue Act imposed duties on American colonists for such items as paper, glass, lead and tea in order to pay the salaries of governors and judges in the colonies. The Act caused widespread anti-British sentiment throughout the American colonies and fueled the movement toward American Independence.

July 20 Some HBC sailors off the *Success* discovered the remains of the ill-fated James Knight expedition, including 288 bushels of good-burning coal and 3 large anchors.

July 23 St. John's Is. was assigned, by lottery, to 100 lords, military officers, politicians, high-ranking civil servants, wealthy merchants and business adventurers. The island's 8,000 ha townships were parcelled out to notable British subjects claiming patronage from the Crown. Selection was done randomly in the form of a lottery. No person received more than one parcel.

Dec. Robert Rogers (1727–c 1800) was charged with high treason for corresponding with a French officer,

on the strength of an affidavit signed by his secretary, Nathaniel Potter. Rogers was taken east, in irons, for court martial, tried in 1768, but escaped conviction and subsequently sailed for England.

Also in 1767
• Canada's 1st public library was established at Montreal College.

1768

Mar. 28–Feb. 16, 1776 Michael Francklin served as lt-gov. of NS, until the arrival of Lord William Campbell.

Aug. 12 An Order-in-Council confirmed the border between Canada and New York.

• A Beothuk woman and her toddler son were shot and killed by Nfld. fishermen who took another 4-year-old Beothuk boy prisoner. Named John August by his captors, the boy was put on exhibit in England before returning to Nfld. to captain a fishing boat. John August died in 1788.

Also in Aug. Nfld. gov. Hugh Palliser (1722/23–1796) commissioned Capt. John Cartwright to travel up the Exploits R. to contact and befriend the estimated 400 members of the Beothuk Nation. He found nothing but deserted camps.

Dec. 30 Montreal Jews formed Shearith Israel, the earliest Jewish congregation in Canada.

Also in 1768
• To accommodate those who favoured western expansion of settlements from the seaboard colonies, land south of the Ohio R. was removed from First Nations' territory.

1769

Apr. 20 Pontiac, Chief of the Ottawa, was murdered near the present site of St. Louis, Missouri, by a Peoria warrior, who was a nephew of Chief Maka-tachinga.

June 3 British astronomers William Wales and Joseph Dymond, representatives of the Royal Society of London, observed the transit of Venus at Churchill, Hudson's Bay Territory. Their objective was to ascertain the distance between the earth and the sun. Other observers took up positions at other points around the world.

June 28 An Order-in-Council made St. John's Is. a colony separate from NS, as a result of determined lobbying by the Island's proprietors. Walter Patterson (c 1735–1798) was appointed the 1st gov., on July 14. He would serve from Sept. 19, 1770–May 1784.

Nov. 6 Samuel Hearne (1745–1792), with 2 companions and a Cree guide, named Chawchinahaw, set out from Fort Prince of Wales to explore the interior of Canada and search for a fabled copper mine believed to be on the banks of the Coppermine R. Their expedition took 5 weeks.

Also in 1769

• Benjamin Frobisher (c 1742–1787) and his brothers, Joseph and Thomas, traders in the L. Michigan area, combined with the company of Isaac Todd and James McGill (1744–1813) of Montreal, to set up a trading post on the Red R. This was an early attempt at the consolidation of the fur trade by the fur traders themselves.

• Canada's 1st commerical still was established in Quebec City.

• *The History of Emily Montague* by Frances Moore Brooke (1724–1789), the 1st novel set in Canada, was published. It consisted of a collection of 228 fictional letters, blended into a tale of politics and romance in an English garrison in Que. Social customs and manners of French colonists were described. The book was dedicated to Guy Carleton.

1770

Feb. 1 Because the findings of a committee of inquiry confirmed that Justices of the Peace often exceeded their authority in expropriating lands and committing persons to prison, Gov. Carleton initiated an ordinance transferring jurisdiction over all cases involving private property, as well as disputes entailing sums of more than £12, from Justices of the Peace, to the Court of Common Pleas.

Feb. 23 Prompted by reports of mineral wealth, Moses Norton, at Fort Churchill, sent Samuel

Hearne on a 2nd expedition over the Barrens to try to discover the headwaters of the Coppermine R. Hearne reached Dubawnt L., in present-day NWT, about 640 km from the Coppermine, by Aug. 12. He was forced to turn back because of a broken quadrant. He was abandoned on the return journey by his Aboriginal guides and would have frozen to death, but was found, on Sept. 20, by Matonabbee (c 1737–1782), the great Chipewyan chief, who saved his life. The 2 became close friends.

Apr. 12 Continuing discontent between the North American Colonies and Britain, propelled the British parliament to repeal all Townshend duties except a small tax on tea, retained as a symbol to demonstrate the principle of parliamentary supremacy.

July 3 Bruin Romkes Comingo (1723–1820), although lacking in formal theological training, was ordained minister of the Dutch Calvinist church in Lunenburg at a ceremony held at St. Matthew's Church in Halifax, in the 1st Presbyterian ordination in Canada.

Aug. Francis Mugford led a Moravian missionary expedition to Labrador where the group encountered a large number of Inuit from whom they purchased land on which to found a mission.

Sept. The 1st legislative act of St. John's Is. regulated the sea cow (walrus) fishery in order to protect the species from depletion.

Nov. 25 Hearne arrived safely back at Fort Prince of Wales after travelling 500 km inland from Hudson Bay, the farthest subarctic penetration by a European at that time.

Dec. 7 Hearne, guided by Chief Matonabbee, his 6 wives, and a group of Chipewyan associates, left Fort Prince of Wales, on foot, for a 3rd expedition, searching for the copper mines reported to exist north of Churchill. Hearne planned to extend the Hudson's Bay trade with northern First Nations and Inuit, and to report on the navigability of the Coppermine R.

Also in 1770

• Artist Benjamin West (1738–1820) painted *The Death of Wolfe*, which now hangs in the National

Gallery in Ottawa. Believed by many critics to be one of Canada's most significant historical paintings, it was exhibited at the Royal Academy, in 1771. West was persuaded to make 3 copies (with some changes) of this work. One of these is in Canadian hands.

• Partners Richard Dobie and the Frobisher brothers engaged in an expedition that took them well beyond Fort Bourbon, at the mouth of the Saskatchewan R.

• Over 1,000 First Nations Peoples awaited arrival of HBC supply relief ships and food provisions at Churchill, Man.

1771

June 6 Hector Theophilus Cramahe was commissioned lt-gov. of Que., serving from Sept. 26–Apr. 3, 1782.

July 14 Hearne and his companions reached the Coppermine R., which they found useless for navigation. The Chipewyan massacred a band of Inuit at a place Hearne named Bloody Falls, near the mouth of the Coppermine R. (July 17). The next day, Hearne's expedition reached the mouth of the Coppermine R., at present-day Coronation Gulf, where it flows into the partially frozen Arctic Ocean. Hearne was the 1st European to reach the Arctic Ocean overland.

Also in July
• British authorities agreed with Gov. Carleton's recommendation that all new land grants in Que. be conferred in seigneurial tenure only, the collection of fees by officials and exercise of power by the Justices of the Peace.

Aug. 9 Moravian Brethren, led by Francis Mugford, arrived at Nain, Labrador to establish a mission for the Inuit. Building commenced immediately.

Also in Aug.
• Thomas Robinson led 1 of the HBC's most successful Arctic whaling expeditions, which killed 3 whales off Marble Is., before returning to Churchill.

Fall Extra foodstuffs, including 4,500 fish and 1,000 geese, were stored in Fort Albany to ensure that

Aboriginal Peoples who had come to trade during the winter were fed.

Dec. 23 Mme d'Youville died after a paralytic stroke.

Dec. 24 Samuel Hearne discovered Great Slave L., the 1st European to see and cross that body of water.

1772

June 27 Mathew Cocking (1743–1799) left York Factory on an expedition inland. Travelling up the Hayes, Fox and Minago Rivers, he reached the Saskatchewan R., and proceeded overland to the Eagle Hills (south of Battleford), where he wandered and hunted in the plains south of present-day Biggar, Sask., before returning to York Factory, June 18, 1773. Cocking wrote a rational account of the country, its people, the prairies, parklands, wildlife and vegetation, and he stressed the urgency of HBC's pushing their operations inland.

June 30 Hearne's expedition arrived back at Fort Prince of Wales, having been gone more than 18 months and travelling about 5,600 km on foot. Hearne was the 1st to describe Inuit life in the area. He concluded that there was no Northwest Passage, that the Coppermine R. would not accommodate ships, and that copper deposits seemed to be merely a myth.

1773

May HBC ordered Mathew Cocking and Samuel Hearne to establish Cumberland House, the HBC's 1st permanent western inland settlement.

July 3 St. John's Island's 1st Assembly met at the Crossed Keys Tavern in Charlottetown as no formal legislative chamber was available.

July 22 Francis Legge (c 1719–1783) was commissioned gov. of NS, serving from Oct. 8, 1773–July 29, 1782.

Sept. 15 After an 11-week Atlantic crossing, during which 18 children died, the brig *Hector* anchored off Pictou, NS, to disembark 178 Scottish immigrants who planned to farm land the British authorities had promised them.

Nov. 29 British citizens living in Que. petitioned for an Assembly.

Dec. 16 A group of Bostonians, in Mohawk dress, threw a cargo of British tea into Boston Harbor as an act of defiance against "taxation without representation." The incident became known as the Boston Tea Party.

1774

Mar. 25 The British parliament passed a bill to close the port of Boston until Boston's town meeting voted restitution to the East India Company for the lost tea.

• The British parliament passed a series of laws known as the "Intolerable Acts."

June 22 The British parliament passed the Quebec Act. It would become effective May 1, 1775. The Act superseded the Royal Proclamation of 1763. Roman Catholics were granted religious freedom and French civil law was established, along with the British system of public and criminal law, with trial by jury. The Quebec Act established govt by council appointed by the Crown, instead of an assembly as promised in the Proclamation of 1763. The boundaries of Que. were extended to Labrador and west to include the Great Lakes and Ohio country. This revision angered the 13 American colonies and helped to precipitate the American Revolution 2 years later.

July 4 Cocking set out from York Factory to help Samuel Hearne establish Cumberland House, near present-day Pine Island L., on the Saskatchewan R. He never got there. Instead, his guides took him to their own tribe up the Red Deer R., west of L. Winnipegosis, where he wintered at Witch L.

July 15 Juan Jose Perez Hernandez (c 1725–1775), commanding the frigate *Santiago,* sighted the Queen Charlotte Islands and made contact with the Haida. They traded cloth, beads, and pieces of copper for furs. This is believed to be the 1st contact between Europeans and Northwest Coast First Nations. Hernandez named the northwestern point of the islands Santa Margarita. It was the 1st BC location to be named by Europeans.

Aug. 8 Hernandez, sailing south along Vancouver Is., discovered an opening, which he named Surgidero de San Lorenzo (Nootka Sound). The next day, the crew of the *Santiago* traded with the Nootka, presenting them with California abalone shells.

Sept. 3 Hearne located HBC Cumberland House at Pine Is. (Cumberland L., Sask.) near L. Winnipeg, about 40 days from York Factory, 96 km above present-day The Pas.

Sept. 5 The 1st Continental Congress of American Colonies assembled at Philadelphia attended by all the American colonies except Georgia. The Declaration of Rights and Grievances was drawn up in protest against the Intolerable Acts, including the Quebec Act, which the American colonies referred to as a flagrant violation of human rights. On Oct. 21 the Congress passed "An Address to the People of Great Britain" criticizing the Quebec Act (referred to as the worst of laws). Prominent Americans including Franklin, Jefferson and Washington had speculated heavily in the Missouri, Mississippi and Ohio watersheds. The Quebec Act declared these areas to be under Que. jurisdiction. On Oct. 26, Congress invited the people of Canada to join their opposition to the Quebec Act and to send delegates to its next meeting in May. It also petitioned the Crown for a redress of grievances accumulated since 1773, and called for a boycott of all British goods.

Nov. 12 British citizens living in Que. protested against the Quebec Act, which restored French civil law.

Also in 1774
• *Acadius,* or, *Love in a Calm,* the 1st original Canadian play, was written in Halifax. Its author is unknown.

• *The Atlantic Neptune,* a collection of charts and views by Joseph Frederick Wallet DesBarres (1721–1824), was published on behalf of the British Admiralty.

1775

Apr. 19 Armed colonists and British redcoats clashed at Lexington and Concord, Massachusetts, opening the floodgates of the American Revolution.

May 10 The Second Continental Congress assembled at Philadelphia.

• American patriot Ethan Allen (1738–1789) and Benedict Arnold (1741–1801), joint commanders of an American force of about 100 men, captured Fort Ticonderoga on L. Champlain by walking into the fort when the garrison was sound asleep. Not a shot was fired. American forces under Seth Warner (1743–1784) captured Crown Point 2 days later. The victories at Ticonderoga and Crown Point opened the way for the invasion of Que. via the Richelieu R. Fort George (L. George, New York) was also taken.

May 18 Arnold and Massachusetts recruits raided Fort St. John (Saint-Jean-sur-Richelieu), Que.

May 20 Cocking set off down the Red Deer R. on his return journey to York Factory, after having spent the winter at Witch L. He arrived over a month later, on June 27.

May 22 Bishop Jean-Olivier Briand of Que. ordered his parishioners to be loyal to Britain and forbade Canadian women to marry American soldiers. The bishop warned that he would excommunicate any Catholic who collaborated with American revolutionaries.

June 9 Gov. Carleton declared martial law and suspended the administrative provisions of the Quebec Act, to facilitate the raising of a volunteer 6,000-man militia, to augment the 800 British troops stationed in Que.

June 15 Washington was appointed C-in-C of the Continental Army.

June 24 The NS House of Assembly promised the British govt that NS would remain loyal to Britain.

June 27 The 2nd Continental Congress of the 13 American colonies ordered Gen. Philip Schuyler to invade Que. He was to capture Île-aux-Noix on the Richelieu, Saint-Jean, and Montreal, and to defeat the British forces in Canada "if practicable and not disagreeable to the Canadians."

July 31 Fearing the loss of trained deep-water sailors to the colony, the British govt passed legislation (Palliser's Act — An Act for the encouragement of the fisheries carried on from Great Britain and for securing the return of the fishermen ... at the end of the season) to discourage settlement in Nfld. It allowed employers to pay out only half of a man's wages for the fishing season. The other half would be paid out upon return to England or Ireland.

Aug. 17–Sept. 7 The 1st Legislative Council met at Que.

Aug. 24 Bruno de Heceta led a Spanish expedition to the north Pacific coast in search of the Northwest Passage. He landed at Prince of Wales Is. and claimed the area for Spain.

Aug.–Sept. Peter Pond (c 1740–1807) crossed into Canada from the upper Mississippi to trade furs. Pond and Alexander Henry combined resources near a Cree village at the mouth of the Winnipeg R., to pursue the northwest fur trade via Grand Portage, near present-day Grand Portage. It was the beginning of what would become the North West Company (NWC).

Sept. 12 Gen. Washington appeared before the 2nd Continental Congress to argue in favour of a trained army, similar to the British army, rather than a citizens' army.

Sept. 16 Richard Montgomery (1736–1775) was appointed commander of the American expedition to invade Que. Two invasion routes were planned: one via L. Champlain and the Richelieu R., the other via Kennebec and Chaudière R. The latter force, commanded by Benedict Arnold, set out on Sept. 18 and arrived at Point-Lévis across from Que. on Nov. 9. The other army, commanded by Montgomery, captured Fort Chambly after a 2-day siege.

Sept. 24 Ethan Allen led his New Hampshire-based Green Mountain Boys on an unsuccessful guerrilla attack against Montreal. Allen and 80 of his men were captured by a force under Maj. Cardin, who was killed.

Oct. 1 Pond reached the mouth of the Saskatchewan R., ascending it to HBC Cumberland House, where he was greeted by Mathew Cocking.

Oct. 6 Cocking took command of Cumberland House from Samuel Hearne.

Oct. 30 Gov. Guy Carleton and 1,400 men attempted to cross the St. Lawrence from Montreal, but failed because of American gunfire.

Nov. 3 After a long siege at St.-Jean, Que., Maj. Charles Preston surrendered to Gen. Montgomery, removing the last British obstacle on the way to Montreal.

Nov. 11 Guy Carleton, with 130 regulars, evacuated Montreal and sailed for Que. Most of his men were captured, but Carleton escaped disguised as a habitant. On Nov. 19, he slipped through American lines in an open boat commanded by Capt. Jean-Baptiste Bouchette (1736–1804), and returned to Que. to discover many defections to the American cause and many enemies within the town. Carleton issued a proclamation ordering those who refused to perform their militia duties to "quit the Town in four Days."

Nov. 13 Montgomery's American force accepted the surrender of Montreal and occupied the town. Valentin Jautard (c 1738–1778) welcomed them on behalf of pro-American inhabitants.

• Benedict Arnold appeared on the Plains of Abraham with 500 men and invited the garrison at Que. to come out of their fortress town and do battle. He was unsuccessful in his attempt to force the city to surrender.

Nov. 17 Charlottetown was captured and pillaged by American privateers Broughton and Selman. Acting Gov. Phillips Callback (c 1744–1790) was taken prisoner. Gen. Washington was furious and immediately made arrangements to return the Canadian prisoners to Canada.

Nov. 19 Arnold retreated to Point-aux-Trembles to await reinforcements from Montgomery, who arrived Dec. 1. Montgomery assumed command of Arnold's men at Point-aux-Trembles, 32 km above Que., for a united force of some 2,000 men who then marched to Que. (Dec. 4) to begin the siege of Que. (Dec. 5).

Dec. 31 Siege warfare proving unsuccessful, Montgomery and Arnold made an unsuccessful attack on Que., which was commanded by Gov. Carleton. Montgomery was killed. Arnold was wounded, but reinstituted the American siege of the city.

Also in 1775

• Gov. Lord Dunmore of Virginia promised freedom to slaves whose owners joined loyalist forces.

• Samuel Hearne was appointed to command HBC's Fort Prince of Wales.

1776

Jan. 1 Gov. Carleton was made gen. of North America.

Jan. 10 The US Congress appointed Benedict Arnold, Brig-Gen., in recognition of his services during the assault on Que.

Jan. 26 Arnold appointed Eustache Chartier de Lotbinière (1716–c 1785), a Canadian priest, chaplain to those few Canadians who had joined the invading Americans. The US Congress ratified Lotbinière's appointment on Aug. 12, when be became the US army's 1st Chaplain.

Mar. 17 British forces left Boston for Halifax, following Gen. Washington's seizure of Dorchester Heights in a night attack. Halifax became temporary centre of British power in North America.

Mar. 18 Fleury Mesplet (1734–1794), bearing a printer's commission from the US Congress, left Philadelphia for Que., where he set up a printing and newspaper business in Montreal with his new partner, Charles Berger. The newspaper only survived for a year. The printing business, however, continued.

Also in Mar.

• John Burgoyne (1722–1792) sailed from England for Que. with reinforcements for Guy Carleton who was besieged by Arnold's forces.

Apr. 1 One thousand, one hundred and twenty-four United Empire Loyalists arrived in Halifax from New England.

• American Gen. Wooster succeeded Gen. Arnold at the siege of Que.

Apr. 12 Fur trader Thomas Frobisher (1744–1788) of Frobisher & Co. was sent to build a fort, which he named Île à La Crosse, on the Churchill R.

Apr. 20 Mariot Arbuthnot (1711–1794) was appointed lt-gov. of NS, and served from May 13, 1776 to Aug. 17, 1778.

Apr. 29 Benjamin Franklin, Charles Carroll and Samuel Chase, commissioned by the Continental Congress to pave the way for the American annexation of Canada, arrived in Montreal. They rapidly became discouraged and recommended abandonment of the country.

May 1 John Thomas, newly appointed commander of the American army in Canada, arrived at Que.

May 3 Americans attempted to set fire to ships at Que.

May 6 Sir Charles Douglas (d 1789) arrived at Que. with a relief force of 10,000 soldiers, including German mercenary troops under Friedrich Riedesel. Thomas abandoned his siege of the city, and died of smallpox (June 2), which was ravaging the American army. He was succeeded by John Sullivan (1740–1795).

May 20 Four hundred Americans surrendered to 40 British soldiers and 200 First Nations allies under Capt. George Forster, at Les Cèdres, some 64 km above Montreal.

June 8 Americans under Arthur St. Clair (1734–1818) appeared at Trois-Rivières, where they were defeated by British and Canadian forces under John Burgoyne, who took 200 prisoners.

June 14 American Brig-Gen. John Sullivan withdrew from Sorel, Que., to Crown Point on L. Champlain on the advice of Arnold. Arnold and Sullivan moved their armies back to Saint-Jean 4 days later.

June 25 Gov. Carleton prohibited the sale of liquor except by licence.

June 28 Three hundred Iroquois swore an oath of allegiance to Britain at a meeting held by Gov. Guy Carleton in Montreal.

Also in June
• Mohawk Chief Joseph Brant or Thayendanega (1742/43–1807) presented Mohawk land grievances to the British govt in London. While he was in England, Brant had his portrait painted by George Romney (1734–1802). The picture now hangs in the National Gallery of Canada.

July 4 The 2nd Continental Congress issued the American *Declaration of Independence,* drafted by Thomas Jefferson. This document formally broke ties between Britain and the Thirteen Colonies.

July 7 John Johnson (1741–1830), a Loyalist from Albany, New York, was granted permission to form the King's Royal Regiment of American Loyalists in Canada.

July 12 James Cook left Plymouth, England, in command of the ships *Resolution* and *Discovery*, seeking the Northwest Passage. He hoped to claim the £20,000 prize offered by Parliament in 1744.

July 23 Gov. Carleton issued a new commission appointing Justices of the Peace, thus implicitly re-establishing the Courts of Quarter Sessions of the Peace, which had been abolished by the passing of the Quebec Act.

Aug. 22 The British govt instructed Gov. Carleton to attend to civil duties, while placing Gen. Burgoyne in command of the Forces in Canada. After serving with distinction not only as Gov. but also as gen. in New York, Carleton considered the instruction a slight. This led to his resignation as gov. on June 26, 1777. He was ultimately persuaded to resume the position, and served from 1786–1795.

Sept. 23 Arnold's small fleet of vessels, which he had built on L. Champlain, took up a position off Valcour Is.

Oct. 12 During the battle of Valcour Is., Arnold lost his entire fleet (many ships he set ablaze himself) to a small British fleet commanded by Guy Carleton

at Split Rock Point (near Essex, New York) in
L. Champlain. Arnold escaped capture, but Carleton
recaptured the smouldering ruins of Crown Royal.
The British ships had been built on L. Champlain by
Sir Charles Douglas who demonstrated great
personal expertise.

Nov. 6 Americans from Machias, Maine, attacked
Fort Cumberland, NS, but were routed after a
3-week siege.

1776–1783 Quakers, Mennonites and other pacifist
groups settled in Upper Canada to escape persecution in the United States.

Also in 1776
• Fur merchant Simon McTavish traded fur pelts
worth £1,500 in the course of the season.

1777

Apr. 17 Pond entered into a partnership with trader
George McBeath (c 1740–1812), who in turn was
associated with Simon McTavish.

May 6 John Burgoyne returned to Que. as field commander of British forces. His task was to divide
the States along the line of L. Champlain and the
Hudson R. He was to march from Canada via
L. Champlain to Albany, New York, with a secondary
advance through the Mohawk Valley led by Barri-
more Matthew St. Leger (1733–1789). William Howe
was to advance up the Hudson from New York.

Also in May
• John Butler (1728–1796), a Loyalist from New York,
was commissioned by the British govt to collect as
large a force as possible among the Six Nations and
to join Lt-Col. St. Leger's expedition at Oswego for
an attack against Fort Stanwix (Rome, New York).

June 5 Walter Young led a British naval expedition
to complete a survey of Baffin Bay and to determine if the Bay connected to the Arctic Ocean.
The expedition turned back after reaching 72
degrees north.

June 17 A British force of 7,500 under Gen. John
Burgoyne moved down L. Champlain. By June 30,
Burgoyne's army, which had increased to about

8,000, reached Fort Ticonderoga, forcing the
Americans to evacuate. St. Leger besieged Oswego
and Fort Stanwix, and defeated the Americans,
on Aug. 6, at Oriskany.

Also in June
• A British naval force routed NS and American rebels
under John Allen (1747–1805), a NS citizen favouring
the American Revolution. Allen had planned to seize
the Saint John R. for the Americans.

Aug. 13–15 British forces under Burgoyne crossed
the Hudson R. at Saratoga (Schuylerville).

Aug. 16 American militiamen defeated the British at
the Battle of Bennington in Vermont. The British
lost about 900 men.

Aug. 18 Frederick Haldimand (1718–1791) was commissioned gov. of Que., following Carleton's resignation (June 26). Haldimand served from June 27,
1778 to Apr. 22, 1786.

Aug. 19 Burgoyne clashed with American forces
under Maj-Gen. Horatio Gates (c 1728–1806) near
Freeman's Farm. Burgoyne suffered heavy losses
but held the field.

Also in Aug.
• Mathew Cocking assumed his appointment as
Master of Severn House (Fort Severn, Ont.).

Sept. John Butler (1728–1796) was commissioned
to raise a corps of provincial rangers, known as
Butler's Rangers, from Loyalists who had fled to
Fort Niagara.

Oct. 7 Burgoyne again faced Gates, but this time
British forces were defeated and fell back on
Saratoga.

Oct. 15 John Graves Simcoe (1752–1806) was put in
command of the Queen's Rangers, a loyalist corps
consisting of loyalist refugees and American
deserters.

Oct. 17 Burgoyne surrendered at Saratoga, New
York, in the 1st great victory for the Americans.
Burgoyne blamed his defeat on Arnold who was
again wounded in the leg while capturing a British

redoubt. British losses numbered about 600 killed, wounded or missing out of a force of approximately 1,500 men. American losses were about 150.

Nov. The British completed the construction of Fort Howe, at the mouth of the Saint John R. as a defence against Americans and their Aboriginal allies.

Also in 1777

- Shearith Israel Congregation, Canada's 1st permanent Jewish Synagogue, opened on the corner of Nôtre Dame and St. James streets in Montreal.

1778

Mar. 29–Apr. 26 Capt. Cook moored in Resolution Cove, Nootka Sound, Vancouver Is. to trade with the Nootka. Cook charted the coast of BC, and along with George Vancouver (1757–1798) and members of his crew landed in BC. Cook received valuable sea otter pelts that he later sold at great profit in China, arriving there by way of the Bering Strait. The Nootka received Cook and his crew with such friendliness that he named the site "Friendly Cove."

Spring Pond left Cumberland House on an expedition into the Athabasca region, then known only to the Cree and Blackfoot.

Apr. 2 French-speaking merchants petitioned for the repeal of the Quebec Act.

Apr. 30 The HBC hired surveyor and mathematician Philip Turnor (c 1751–c 1799) on a 3-year contract to survey and map the entire company empire, including rivers and trading posts, and to keep geographical data.

Also in Apr. British Gen. Henry Clinton (1738–1795) replaced William Howe as C-in-C in NA because of George Washington's victory over Howe at Philadelphia.

- *Interior of a Communal House with Woman Weaving, Nootka* and *Interior of Habitation of Nootka Sound, Apr. 1778* were drawn by John Webber (1751–1793), a member of James Cook's crew during the exploration of the Pacific.

May An American privateer raided Placentia Bay, Nfld.

June 3 Fleury Mesplet published Montreal's 1st newspaper, the *Gazette du Commerce et Littéraire pour la Ville et District de Montréal,* out of his printing shop on Rue de la Capitale. The paper consisted of 4 pages of articles published in French. Mesplet was incarcerated after the 1st issue because the gov. found the paper radical. Publication was suspended until Mesplet's release, June 4, 1779.

July 4 George Rogers Clark (1752–1818), from Virginia, with a force of volunteers, accepted the surrender of Kaskaskia, the old French capital of the Illinois country.

Late Aug. Pond crossed the 19 km Methye Portage (Portage La Loche), separating the Hudson Bay and Arctic watersheds, in present-day northern Saskatchewan. Beyond lay the Mackenzie R. leading to the Arctic. Pond had opened up North America's richest fur-trapping area, and was the 1st European to see the Athabasca R. He built the 1st "Old Establishment" non-Native house in Poot, 48 km south of L. Athabaska, in Sept.

Also in Aug.

- Capt. James Cook's expedition in search of a Northwest Passage to Baffin Bay was halted by ice. Cook was forced to turn back after having sailed northeast from the Bering Strait. On his return journey, he followed the west coast of NA, still searching for the passage.

Sept. 24 Maliseet and Mi'kmaq leaders swore an oath of allegiance to Britain at Fort Howe, NS.

Oct. 14 Gov. Frederick Haldimand solicited help from the British govt for supplies and money to help resettle the flood of "loyalists in great distress" arriving in Que. from the Thirteen Colonies.

Also in Oct. Pond discovered a black flammable pitchlike substance by L. Athabasca and traded for furs with local First Nations peoples.

Nov. At Philadelphia, Gen. Washington vetoed plans to attack Canadian posts between Montreal and Detroit while engaging in naval action in the St. Lawrence. The strategy had been conceived by Marquis de Lafayette of France, who joined forces on the side of the American revolution.

Also in 1778

• Spain and France signed treaties of alliance with the American revolutionaries against Britain.

• Spaniards Bodega Quadra (1743–1794) and Juan Joseph Perez (c 1725–1775) explored the Queen Charlotte Islands.

• The 1st rabbi in Canada, Jacob Raphael Cohen (c 1738–1811), settled in Montreal.

1779

Apr. 24 The North West Company was formed: it was divided into 16 shares, held by separate partnership groups. Shareholders included Charles Patterson (d 1788), Isaac Todd, John McGill, Simon McTavish, George McBeath, John Ross (d 1787), Peter Pond, and Benjamin and Joseph Frobisher. The company was formed to compete with the HBC in the fur trade, although, unlike the HBC, the NWC held no royal charter granting fur-trading rights. NWC traders ventured deeper into the NA continent than their rivals.

June 2 Pond arrived at Cumberland House, near L. Winnipeg, with 3 canoes loaded with furs from the L. Athabasca area. He traded for about 8,400 beaver pelts, but was forced to leave many others behind for lack of space.

June 17 Lt-Col. Francis McLean (c 1717–1781) led a British expedition of 650 men to establish a fort at Castine, Maine, to provide refuge for loyalists and to defend NS against an attack from New England. From July 25–Aug. 14, McLean and his small force defended themselves against an American siege, until George Collier (1738–1795) came to the relief of the post by sea, routing the Americans and destroying their ships.

July 20 Mi'kmaq chief John Julian (c 1779–1805) signed a treaty with the British which awarded Julian's people "licence to occupy," but not own 8,000 ha of land along the northwest branch of the Miramichi R., in what is now New Brunswick.

Aug. 29 Butler's Rangers were defeated at Newtown (near Elmira, New York). The Americans followed up the victory by destroying First Nations villages in the Finger Lakes region.

Sept. 13 Gov. Haldimand asked dramatist Richard Cumberland to select books for a proposed public library at Que. which opened the same year. The annual membership fee was £5.

Also in 1779

• The impressment of men for the Royal Navy in Canadian ports was legalized.

1780

May 19 At 2 p.m. darkness fell over Canada and the New England States for reasons still not known today. The incident was called the "dark day."

Oct. 2 British officer John André was hanged for spying, in Tappan, New York, by Americans. He had been caught with documents furnished by turncoat Benedict Arnold, who escaped capture by fleeing to the British ship *Vulture*.

Oct. 25 Gov. of Que. Sir Frederick Haldimand protested against the laws favouring merchants rather than inhabitants.

Oct. 31–Nov. 1 *Ontario*, sloop-of-war ship, was shipwrecked near the mouth of the Niagara R. Built at the Carleton Is. shipyard in 1779-1780, *Ontario* measured 37.5 m in length, making her the largest ship on the Great Lakes. She was carrying 88 passengers, none of whom survived the wreckage.

Also in 1780

• *State of the Expedition from Canada* by John Burgoyne, a defence of his American campaign and conduct, was published in England.

• Caribou in the Fort Severn and Fort Albany areas were decimated by the fur trade.

• Loyalist poet Jonathan Odell (1737–1818), who fled New Jersey in 1776, pilloried American skills and American ambitions in his vitriolic heroic couplets of *The American Times*.

• HBC imported the 1st "point" blanket to its trading posts. The now classic blankets were made of 100% virgin wool and came in different colours. The most popular colour with Aboriginals was white with colour bands because it provided good camouflage. The 1st shipment of blankets was made by Thomas Empson of Witney, Oxfordshire. The "point" referred to the size of the finished blanket, and also the trade value of 1 "made" beaver pelt (good quality, from an average-size beaver). Blankets were available in a variety of "point" numbers from 1 to 6, including half-sizes. A point size measured 81 cm wide by 2 m, 44 cm long and weighed approximately 1.4 kg.

1781

Feb. 15 William Twiss (1745–1827) built North America's 1st lock canal at Côteau du Lac on the St. Lawrence R.

Mar. The Articles of Confederation became the 1st United States Constitution.

May 9 The British govt purchased a tract of land from the Mississauga for 300 suits of clothing. The parcel, 64 km wide and 40 km long, was on the west bank of the Niagara R., just opposite Fort Niagara. The purchase was made for several hundred Loyalist farmers with the expectation that they would supply provisions for the fort.

• An Iroquois party returned to Fort Niagara after a raid on Cherry Valley, a New York community in the Mohawk Valley. Sixteen American rebels were reported killed.

May 19 Britain purchased Michilmackinac Is. from the Chippewa for £5,000.

Aug. 28 American privateers raided Annapolis Royal.

Sept. 25 A public school lottery, passed by an act of the House of Assembly in Halifax, Oct. 1780, raised £750 of the £1,500 needed to build a school.

Oct. 19 Gen. Cornwallis surrendered at Yorktown, Virginia, ending the 1st British Empire in North America.

Nov. 13–15 Secret land sales were held in the home of Charlottetown tavern keeper John Clark. Owners in rent arrears had their land sold to officers of govt, the only purchasers: no money exchanged hands. Instead, the land was paid for by salary arrears. Gov. Patterson himself acquired the equivalent of 5 townships plus an additional 28,328 ha, in the names of 4 of his English acquaintances.

Dec. 24 Canada's 1st Christmas tree was erected in Sorel, north of Montreal, by Baron Frederick-Adolphus Riedesel (1738–1800) his wife and daughters.

Also in 1781
• Frances (Moore) Brooke (1724–1789) achieved theatrical success with her tragedy *The Siege of Sinope*.

1782

Mar. 2 Guy Carleton succeeded Sir Henry Clinton as British C-in-C in North America.

Mar. 21 Guy Carleton and Rear-Admiral Robert Digby were named joint commissioners of BNA "for restoring peace and granting pardon to the revolted provinces in America."

Also in Mar.
• Swiss-born fur trader Jean-Étienne Waddens was shot and killed in the Athabasca country. Peter Pond was tried and acquitted of the murder in the winter of 1784.

May–Nov. 1783 Guy Carleton, headquartered in New York, was in charge of the evacuation of 30,000 British troops and 27,000 refugees, including former slaves and Loyalists. Carleton, over the protests of George Washington, helped these people to emigrate to the Caribbean and to NS; 1,200 settled near Halifax.

June 11 The 1st Canadian Methodist minister, William Black (1760–1834), preached at Halifax.

June 24–Aug. 13, 1785 Henry Hamilton (c 1734–1796) served as lt-gov. of Canada.

July 1 American privateers attacked Lunenburg, NS. During the summer, Horatio Nelson (1758–1805) campaigned along the coast of NS against these raiders.

July 12 Through the influence of his patron, the Earl of Shelburne, Secretary of State for the Home

Department, John Parr (1725–1791) was commissioned gov. of NS, commencing his service Aug. 19, 1782.

Aug. 8 Fort Prince of Wales, under Samuel Hearne, was confronted by a French force under Jean-François de Galaup, Comte de La Pérouse (1741–1783). Overwhelmingly overmatched, Hearne surrendered without firing a shot. He was taken prisoner and sent to France. Hearne's Chipewyan friend Matonabbee hanged himself when he heard the news; Matonabbee's 6 wives and children starved to death that winter.

Aug. 25 York Factory surrendered to a French naval force of 3 warships under command of Comte de La Pérouse, who destroyed the post and fort.

Nov. 30 Britain and the US agreed to peace terms.

1783

Jan. 20 Britain and the US signed an armistice and hostilities officially ceased between the 2 countries, on Feb 4.

Mar. 14 John Johnson became superintendent-gen. of Indian Affairs in BNA.

May 4 Four hundred and seventy-one Loyalist families from New York landed at what would become Shelburne, NS.

May 18 The spring fleet of 10 ships provided by the British govt, carrying 1,707 Loyalist immigrants from New York, arrived at Parrtown, near the mouth of the Saint John R., NB.

May 26 Surveyor Samuel Johannes Holland was commissioned by Gov. Haldimand to inspect the land around Cataraqui (Kingston, Ont.) to ascertain its suitability for settlement by Loyalists, to whom the British govt promised land grants.

June 15 The June fleet, a 2nd convoy of 14 ships provided by the British govt, carried 2,000 Loyalist immigrants from New York to the Saint John R. area. Additional fleets would leave New York for the Saint John R. area in July, Aug., Oct. and late fall.

June 29 John Patterson, brother of the St. John's Is.

gov., convinced the island's London proprietors to give up 1/4 of their island land holdings to British Loyalists fleeing the US.

Summer Joseph Brant accused England of selling out its Aboriginal allies to the American Congress when Britain signed a treaty transferring all British-claimed land south of the Great Lakes, from the Appalachian Mountains to the Mississippi R., to the Americans without consultation. Most of the area transferred was Iroquois territory. During a First Nation Council at Lower Sandusky, Ohio (Sept. 7), Brant appealed to leaders of the Huron, Delaware, Shawnee, Cherokee, Mingo, Ottawa and Ojibwa, to unite in confederation and oppose American expansion into their territory. The British govt supported Brant's proposal.

July 16 Royal instructions created land grants to American Loyalists. Heads of families received 40.5 ha, members of families 20 ha each, single men 50 acres, and non-commissioned officers 81 ha. Families received a full year's supply of food for their 1st year of settlement, 2/3's the 2nd year and 1/3 year the 3rd year.

July 22 Gov. Parr of NS named the Loyalist settlement of Shelburne after his patron. The area was settled by about 10,000 United Empire Loyalists.

July 30 The 2nd Battalion, King's Royal Regiment arrived from New York to rebuild Fort Frontenac in preparation for Loyalist immigration.

Aug. Black Pioneers, soldiers from the all-black regiment that fought alongside the British in the War of Independence, arrived at Shelburne, NS, as new settlers.

Sept. 3 The Treaty of Paris, signed between Britain and the US ended the Revolutionary War. The boundary between British and American territories was drawn from the mouth of the St. Croix R. on the Bay of Fundy, north to the watershed between the St. Lawrence R., and the Atlantic, south to the headwaters of the Connecticut R.; thence the border ran through the middle of Lakes Ontario, Erie, Huron and Superior to the northwest corner of Lake-of-the-Woods. The US was given all lands between the Great Lakes and the Ohio R., fishing rights to Nfld. fisheries and the mouth of the St. Lawrence, and within the 3-mile limit of BNA waters, as well as the right to cure and dry fish on any unsettled shores. In turn, the US agreed to restore confiscated Loyalist properties. Navigation of the Mississippi R. would be open to both countries.

Sept. 23 Edmund Fanning (1739–1818) was sworn in as lt-gov. of NS.

Sept. 29 The crown assigned Lts. Jones and French to survey the area surrounding the Rideau R. and a chain of lakes for military purposes. Their report indicated that a canal was feasible.

Also in Sept.
• Hearne returned to Hudson Bay to build Fort Churchill.

Oct. The British govt purchased a tract of land, known as the Crawford purchase, from the Mississauga. This extended between the St. Lawrence and Grand (Ottawa) Rivers to the north. The land would be used to settle the influx of expected Loyalists. In return, the Mississauga received guns, clothing and ammunition.

• Charles III, king of Spain, agreed to pay transport from France to Louisiana (which was under Spanish rule) to all Acadians living in France who wished to join relatives and friends. More than 1,500 French Acadians accepted the resettlement offer.

Nov. 25 Britain retained the settlements of Detroit and Niagara as hostage for the guarantee that the agreed terms of peace would be carried out.

Nov. 27 Shipping service was restored between Halifax and New York.

Dec. 13 Penal laws against Roman Catholics were repealed in NS.

1783–1784 Approximately 44,000 Loyalists fled the American colonies and found refuge in Canada. NS received 35,000, Que., 9,000.

Also in 1783
• Gov. Parr wrote Lord Shelburne, reporting on his patron's namesake settlement: "...800 houses

already finished, 600 more in great forwardness, and several hundred lately begun upon..."

• Frances (Moore) Brooke's light pastoral operetta, *Rosina*, with music by William Shield (1748–1829), had its premiere in Que. Scottish poet, Robert Burns (1759–1796) wrote the words for *Auld Lang Syne* in 1783 and used the melody from *Rosina*.

1784

May 20 David Thompson (1770–1857) apprenticed to the HBC, set sail aboard HBC's *Prince Rupert* for HBC's Churchill Factory on Hudson Bay. He was 14 years old, a graduate of London's Grey Coat Charity school near Westminster Abbey, and would never see England again.

May 22 A large group of Mohawk, led by Chief Joseph Deseronto, arrived to settle on a British land grant at Tyendinaga, near the Bay of Quinte.

• A large number of United Empire Loyalist immigrants landed at the Bay of Quinte, to settle at present-day Kingston, Ont. Today, their arrival continues to be celebrated by Loyalist descendants through a worship service held on the nearest Sunday to this date — an overturned canoe is used as an altar.

• The Mississauga ceded vast land tracts along the Niagara peninsula and adjacent lands to the Crown for £900 worth of gifts. The land would be settled by several hundred Loyalist farmers and about 2,000 Iroquois. Land between Burlington Bay and the Credit R. was specifically excluded from the treaty, and became known as the Mississauga Tract.

May 23 Much of the site of present-day London, Ont., was obtained by treaty, from the Chippewa.

May 30 Sir Charles Douglas (d 1789), commander of the British fleet, which had ended the Americans' seige of Que. in 1776, arrived in Halifax to help the region adjust to the post-war situation. Douglas interpreted and applied treaty obligations with the US and provided transports for Gov. John Parr for the provisioning of Loyalist settlements.

June 16 United Empire Loyalists, under Major Peter van Alstine, established a settlement on the Bay of Quinte, in the community of Adolphustown, named after the 7th son of George III. This venture was sometimes referred to as the "Plymouth Rock" of Ont.

June 18 The large number of Loyalists immigrating into the Saint John Valley forced King George III to establish a new colony, New Brunswick, because communication between the Saint John area and Halifax, the capital of NS, was too difficult. George III partitioned NS at the Bay of Fundy and appointed Col. Thomas Carleton (1735–1817) gov.

Also in June
• Some 3,700 Loyalists, disbanded soldiers of the 1st Battalion, King's Royal Regiment of New York, and their families arrived at New Johnstown (Cornwall, Ont.) to settle.

July 7 Hugh Finlay (c 1730–1801) became the Deputy Postmaster Gen. for Canada.

Also in July
• Unemployed army veterans rioted in Birchtown, NS, destroying homes of black families who had secured employment in the area.

Aug. 16 The new colony of New Brunswick received representative govt.

Aug. 26 Cape Breton was separated from NS and remained so until 1820. Loyalists settling there established the town of Sydney, named in honour of Thomas Townsend, Lord of Sydney, then colonial secretary. Joseph Frederick Wallet DesBarres (c 1721–1824) was appointed the 1st lt-gov. of the new colony of Cape Breton Is. on Sept. 3, although he did not arrive in the colony until Jan. 1785. He would serve until Oct. 10, 1787.

Sept. 11 PEI was annexed to NS. Walter Coltersan served as lt-gen. until July 26, 1786.

Oct. 25 At Que., Gov. Haldimand formally turned over 700,000 acres of land, located on the peninsula between Lakes Ontario, Huron and Erie, to 1,800 refugee Iroquois under the leadership of Chief Joseph Brant. The land had been purchased from the Mississauga in May.

Also in Oct. One hundred and forty Loyalist settlers under the leadership of Abraham Cornelius Cuyler, from Que., arrived at Louisbourg and St. Peters, Cape Breton, to take up land.

Nov. 16–Nov. 2, 1785 Lt-Gov. Hamilton served as administrator of Canada during Haldimand's leave of absence in Britain.

Nov. 22 Parrtown became the capital of NB.

Nov. 29 Louis-Philippe Mariauchau d'Esgly (1710–1788) was appointed bishop of Que., the 1st Canadian-born bishop.

Also in Nov. The *Blenheim* landed at Spanish Bay (Sydney Harbour) with 129 settlers, mostly impoverished Englishmen and disbanded soldiers recruited by Joseph DesBarres to establish a settlement on Cape Breton Is. Some of Cuyler's settlers joined this group.

Dec. The 1st newspaper in New Brunswick, the *Royal St. John's Gazette*, was published at Parrtown, by William Lewis (d 1782) and John Ryan.

Also in 1784
• The census of Canada recorded 113,012 people.

• *Explorations of Capt. James Cook in the Pacific* by Capt. James Cook, an account of his travels in North America, was published posthumously.

• James Peachy painted *Encampment of the Loyalists at Johnstown, a New Settlement on the Banks of the St. Lawrence, in Canada,* a watercolour, now with the Public Archives of Canada.

• *Habeas Corpus* was established in Que. by ordinance issued by Gov. Haldimand.

• A 2nd North West Company agreement was drafted and ratified with 16 shares: Benjamin and Joseph Frobisher held a total of 3; Simon McTavish 3; George McBeath, Robert Grant, Nicholas Montour and Patrick Small 2 shares each, and Peter Pond and William Holmes 1 share each. William McGillivray (1764–1825), McTavish's nephew, joined the company as clerk.

• Acadians of the Saint John R. area were expelled from their lands to make way for United Empire Loyalists. Acadians founded new settlements in the Madawaska (NB) area.

1785

Jan. 7 Que. colonists petitioned the British parliament for govt by assembly.

Feb. 22 British law was established in Cape Breton, NS.

• By order of Thomas Carleton, Fredericks Town (Fredericton) was founded on the Saint John R. to serve as the capital of NB. The area had been known previously as St. Anne's Point. On Oct. 23, 1786, the govt of NB moved to the new location.

Also in Feb.
• The Beaver Club was founded in Montreal, by 19 partners of the NWC. Membership was restricted only to voyageurs who had wintered in the Northwest. Meetings were held every 2 weeks from Dec. to Apr., wherein members drank and dined magnificently, while swapping stories of their fur-trading exploits. Alexander Henry, Peter Pond, James McGill and Ben, Joseph and Thomas Frobisher were among the club's charter members. Maximum membership was restricted to 55, with an additional 19 honorary invitees.

Apr. 18 Canada banned imports from the US by sea.

Apr. 21 Trial by jury was established in Canada.

May 18 Parrtown, NB, became the 1st incorporated city in Canada and was renamed Saint John.

• Reverend Dr. John Stuart (1740/1741–1811) of the Church of England opened the 1st school in Upper Canada at Kingston. Initially, classes were held in his home, later in a govt building.

Aug. 25 Fleury Mesplet, previously jailed for his pro-American Revolution sympathies, established and published the 1st edition of the *Montreal Gazette/La Gazette de Montréal*, a bilingual newspaper with French in the left column and English in the right. Its style was Voltarian and anticlerical. It is the oldest newspaper still in existence in Canada.

Nov. 2–Oct. 23, 1786 Henry Hope (1746–1789) served as lt-gov. of Canada upon the resignation of Hamilton.

Dec. 13 NB Loyalists petitioned Gov. Carleton for the establishment of an Academy of Arts and Science which ultimately led to the creation of the University of NB.

Dec. 25 Christ Church was established at Sorel, Que. It remains the oldest Protestant church today in the province.

Also in 1785
• Reverend Jacob Bailey (d 1808) published his best-known poem, "The Adventurers of Jack Ramble, the Methodist Preacher."

1786

Jan. 9 The 1st legislature of NB opened in Saint John.

Jan. The Charitable Irish Society of Halifax was founded.

Mar. 24 A British government order-in-council prohibited the importation of US products into any port of Que.

Apr. 20 Former St. John Is. gov. Walter Patterson (c 1735–1798), reduced in rank to lt-gov., pushed a bill through the St. John Is. assembly, ratifying the 1781 land sales.

Apr. 22 Guy Carleton was re-appointed gov. of BNA and C-in-C of BNA as well as Nfld., serving from Oct. 23, 1786–Dec. 15, 1796.

May 20 St. John's Is. (PEI) separated from NS to become a province.

May 31 Lincolnshire immigrant John Molson (1763–1836) became sole owner of the Thomas Loid brewery in Montreal, which had a weekly capacity of 980 litres.

June 30 Lt-Gov. Patterson was ordered to England to answer charges of land fraud brought against him by those relieved of their holdings during the secret land sale of 1781.

July 26 Edmund Fanning was appointed lt-gov. of St. John Is. (PEI), replacing Patterson. Fanning arrived in Charlottetown on Nov. 4 to assume his duties, but Patterson refused to give up his job.

July 31 Capt. James Charles Stuart Strange (1753–1840) claimed Vancouver Is. for Britain. He also named Queen Charlotte Sound after the queen of England (Aug. 31).

Aug. 21 Guy Carleton received the title of Baron Dorchester.

Oct. 5 King George III's son, Prince William Henry (the future King Henry IV), capt. of the frigate *Pegasus*, arrived in Halifax where he and his crew had a royal night on the town. William was the 1st British royal to visit NS. He toured Que. in Aug. 1787 and Montreal in Sept. 1787.

Nov. Lord Sydney ordered Lt-Gov. Joseph DesBarres of Cape Breton to return to Britain and to hand over his office to William Macarmick (1742–1815). DesBarres was recalled because of his rigid military rule of civilians and his propensity to distribute supplies to his favourites.

Also in 1786
• The HBC appointed William Tomison (c 1739–1829) its 1st inland gov.

• David Thompson was dispatched inland to HBC's Manchester House (near present-day North Battleford, Sask). In Sept., Thompson, Mitchell Omam and 13 other men left Cumberland House (Sask.) to establish South Branch House (near Batoche) on the South Saskatchewan R.

• The 1st Methodist minister in what is now present-day Ont., George Neal, began preaching in the Niagara area.

• Jean François La Péruse (1741–1788), in command of 2 ships and sailing under the french flag, reached Alaska, and surveyed the northwest coastline from Alaska to Monterey. His expedition was lost in a storm at sea in 1789.

1787

Apr. 5 Walter Patterson was informed that "His Majesty has no further occasion for your services as lt-gov. of the Island of St. John." Patterson clung to his office until May when he finally relinquished the lt.-governorship of St. John Is. to Edward Fanning who would serve in that capacity until May 9, 1804.

• West Indian merchants and planters met in London, England, to propose that the 4 distilleries operating in Canada be closed and that duties on West Indian rum to Canada be eliminated.

Apr. 15 The English-speaking Loyalist population in Que. petitioned the British govt for the establishment of a British-style colony in the newly settled Upper St. Lawrence region.

Apr. 18 Guy Carleton ordered the free exportation of all Canadian products, except furs, to the US, and the free importation of American products such as lumber, naval stores and some foodstuffs into Que. via L. Champlain and William Henry (Sorel). Subsequent ordinances added other products.

May John Meares (c 1756–1809), a former British naval officer turned fur trader, was accosted by British Capts. Nathanial Portlock and George Dixon (fl 1776–1791), while trading off what is now the coastline of Alaska and BC. Portlock and Dixon accused Meares of illegally poaching on their tracking territory, and seized his ships. Meares was released only after he promised to abandon the area.

July 7 Frances Barkley, 17-year-old bride of British Capt. Charles Barkley of the *Imperial Beagle*, was the 1st European woman to arrive in BC.

July 25 George Dixon, commanding the *Queen Charlotte* and trading as a partner in the King George's Sound Company, discovered a large archipelago which he named the Queen Charlotte Is. He explored and purchased a large number of sea otter pelts from the Haida.

Aug. 12 Owing to the patronage of Guy Carleton, Charles Inglis (1734–1816), 1st Anglican bishop in the British Empire, was appointed to NS. His diocese included Nfld., St. John Is., Que., NS and Bermuda.

Sept. 17 The US Constitution was signed, sealed and approved at a convention in Philadelphia, presided over by George Washington.

Sept. 23 Guy Carleton purchased land from the Mississauga. This parcel occupied much of present-day Toronto, extending to L. Simcoe. The purchase had been encouraged by Montreal fur-traders. In return, the Mississauga were granted £2,000 and land between present-day Toronto and Hamilton, as well as other areas.

Dec. 18 Gregory, McLeod and Co. of Detroit and Montreal merged with the NWC. Twenty shares of stock were issued: Simon McTavish 4; Joseph Frobisher 3; 2 each to Patrick Small, Nicholas Montour and Robert Grant; and 1 each for John Gregory, Normond McLeod, Peter Pond, George McBeath, Peter Pangman and Alexander Mackenzie. The merger would last 5 years.

Winter Thompson and 5 HBC associates wintered with a band of Peigans camped on the Bow R. near present-day Calgary. For 4 months, Thompson boarded with a Plains Cree named Sarkamappee who taught him much about Cree customs.

1787–1814 A stone wall was constructed around Montreal.

Also in 1787

• Benedict Arnold, who had defected to the British in 1780, took up residence in Saint John, NB.

• Thomas Davies (c 1737–1812) painted the watercolour *View of Château Richer*.

• *Journal of the Operations of the Queen's Rangers* by John Graves Simcoe was published at Exeter.

• Alexander Mackenzie (1764–1820) was appointed second-in-command of the NWC Athabaska Department under Peter Pond and instructed to travel the 3,219 km to the territory immediately, with his cousin Roderick Mackenzie (1761–1844). They completed the trip in 52 days.

1788

Mar. 8 Estaban José Martinez (1742–1798) left San Blas, heading an expedition to determine whether or not the Russians were planning to expand their interests south to the Nootka area — an area the Spanish considered their sphere of influence, having built several trading posts along the coast. Martinez visited posts on Kodiak and Unalaska but found no threat to Spanish territory. He did learn of Russian plans to establish a post at Nootka.

May 13 Meares, in command of the *Felice Adventurer* and the *Iphigenia Nubiana*, and sailing under a Portuguese flag, landed at Nootka on the north-west coast accompanied by Chinese labourers, and began building a small trading post on land purchased from Chief Maquinna. On Sept. 29, the schooner *The North West America*, the 1st ship constructed on the BNA Pacific Coast, was completed by Capt. Meares at Nootka on Vancouver Is. Meares planned to use the vessel for trade.

July 24 Gov. Carleton divided (Upper) Canada into 4 judicial districts: Lunenburg, from the Ottawa R. to Gananoque; Mecklenburg, from Gananoque to Trent; Nassau, from Trent to Long Point; and Hesse, from Long Point to L. St. Clair. A judge and a sheriff were appointed to each. English law was put into effect and land was distributed among the Loyalists.

July The NB assembly held its 1st meeting in Fredericton.

Sept. Americans John Kendrick (c 1740–1794) and Robert Gray (1755–1806) arrived at Nootka Sound in the *Columbia Rediviva* and *Lady Washington*. Kendrick sailed to Marvinas Bay where he built Fort Washington.

Nov. 1 Under the direction of Bishop Charles Inglis, an academy was opened at Windsor, NS, by act of the NS legislature. This grammar school was the beginning of King's College, which was established on June 8, 1790.

Also in Nov.

• Angus Macdonell (d 1804) applied for a patent to protect his discovery of a new method of manufacturing pot and pearl ash. The patent was received, and granted, albeit later, and only as a result of an act passed by Que.

Dec. 5 Martinez's expedition arrived back at San Blas with the recommendation that Spain set up a post at Nootka no later than May 1789.

Dec. 23 Thompson fell and broke his leg while working out of Manchester House. The wound was serious, and he was moved to Cumberland House, where it was Aug. 1789 before he was able to sit in a chair, under the watchful eye of Malcolm Ross.

Also in 1788

• Frances (Moore) Brooke wrote the comic opera *Marian*, performed in Que.

• Church of England clergyman Roger Viets (1738–1811) published the poem "Annapolis-Royal," describing the area and the simple pleasures of life. This was the 1st poem to be published as a separate imprint in BNA.

• Fort Chipewyan, Alberta's 1st permanently settled community was established on the shores of L. Athabasca by Roderick Mackenzie.

• A regular sailing packet service was established between Britain and Halifax.

1789

Jan. 6 Gov. Carleton established an agricultural college at Que.

Mar. 26 Pictou Academy was established at Pictou, NS, by statute, influenced by Scottish Highlanders who settled the area in 1773. It became a famous educational centre that remains in existence today.

May 5 The Spanish warship *Princesa*, under Estaban José Martinez (1742–1798), arrived at Nootka to enforce Spanish claims to the Pacific Coast which originated from early Spanish explorations and the Treaty of Tortesillas (1494).

May 15 The final report on payments to United Empire Loyalists for losses resulting from the American Revolution was made.

June 3 Alexander Mackenzie left Fort Chipewyan on L. Athabasca with a crew of 7 including François Beaulieu, in a birchbark canoe, to find a route to transport furs to the West Coast. They travelled down the Slave R. to Great Slave L. where Mackenzie learned from the Yellowknife of a river flowing northward from the lake. Mackenzie entered the Mackenzie R. on June 29, and reached the Arctic Delta on July 10. His party struggled to within a short distance of the Arctic Ocean but was unable to reach it due to dwindling supplies and the oncoming winter.

Also in June The *NS Magazine and Comprehensive Review of Literature, Politics, and News* was established and published by Clergyman William Cochrane (c 1757–1833) in Halifax.

July 2 The British ship *Argonaut*, commanded by James Colnett (1753–1806), arrived at Nootka to find that the Spanish under Martinez had established a small battery with buildings and had planted gardens on the site of the Nootka village at Friendly Cove. A confrontation followed. Martinez placed Colnett under arrest and seized his ship for infringing on Spanish sovereignty. Shortly thereafter, Martinez captured a 2nd British ship, *Princess Royal*, and sent it with the *Argonaut* to San Blas, the royal Spanish seaport and supply base (in northwest Mexico). On July 14 Martinez seized the trading post owned by John Meares at Nootka Sound on the basis that the British were intruding on Spanish territory.

Aug. 5 The Protestant Episcopal Church held its 1st conference at Que.

Sept. 12 Alexander Mackenzie and his expedition arrived back at Fort Chipewyan. They had completed a round-trip journey of almost 4,800 km in just over 4 months.

Oct. Martinez returned to Mexico when he did not receive orders to set up a permanent base at Nootka.

Nov. 9 By Order-in-Council, every Loyalist son was to receive 81 ha, and every daughter, 81 ha when married, and the descendants of Loyalists would have their names distinguished with the letters U.E. (United Empire).

Also in Nov.

• Joseph Quesnel (1746–1809), with a group of friends, established a theatrical company in Montreal called the Théâtre de Société.

Dec. 27 Upper Canada's 1st stagecoach service was established between Queenston and Fort Erie, a distance of 42 km, at a fare of £100.

Also in 1789

• *A Voyage Round the World: but More Particularly to the North-West Coast of America performed in 1785, 1786, 1787, 1788,* by Captain Nathanial Portlock and George Dixon, was published in London in 1789.

• The Halifax garrison built the New Grand Theatre.

• The Quebec Turf Club, a horse-racing association, was established.

• Famine gripped Que. as a result of an unusually poor wheat harvest.

• Fur trader Peter Pond retired. Although semiliterate, Pond's knowledge and expertise in the field had led him to postulate the Mackenzie R. watershed and the existence of a polar sea to the north. Pond died in 1807 in Milford, Connecticut, his birthplace.

1790

Feb. 5 Chief Justice William T. Smith (1728–1793) suggested Confederation to Carleton.

Feb. 26 British Prime Minister William Pitt demanded restitution from Spain for British ships captured at Nootka, BC.

Apr. 10 Francisco de Eliza y Reventa (1759–1825), commanding the frigate *Concepcion,* and Salvador Fidalga in the *San Carlos,* retook possession of Nootka for Spain and established a fort. Martinez served as second-in-command on this expedition.

Apr. 17 England prohibited the export of wheat, oats, flour and meal from Canada in an attempt to reduce high-density prices.

Apr. 30 In a memorandum to King George III, Capt. Meares submitted his claims for redress for the loss of land suffered when the Spanish reclaimed his property to establish a fort. Meares' claim was a partial cause of the Nootka Sound Controversy, which brought Britain and Spain to the brink of war.

May 19 The Ottawa, Chippewa, Potawatomi and Huron ceded 809.371 ha of land–south of L. St. Clair and La Tranche (Thames R.) down to the northwestern shore of L. Erie in Ont.–to Britain for £1,200 and the right to hunt and plant through the area. They also received various goods including blankets, yard goods, hats, kettles, knives, firearms and ammunition, looking glasses and other sundries, smoking pipes, rum, tobacco, etc., and were given a reserve on which to live. The Chippewa, or Ojibwa (both words mean people whose moccasins have puckered seams), were the most populous nation in Canada and controlled all the northern shores of Lakes Huron and Superior from Georgian Bay to the edge of the prairies. They were made up of 4 distinct groups or tribes: Ojibwa, Mississauga, Ottawa and Potawatomi.

May–July Alferez Manuel Quimper in the *Prencesa Real* (formerly the *Princess Royal*) made a detailed exploration of the Straits of Juan de Fuca, 1st discovered by a Greek pilot named Apostolos Valerianos (1592) who had sailed in the service of Spain under the name of Juan de Fuca. His pilot, Gonzalo Lopez de Haro, charted the Straits as detailed in a map published by Quimper later that year. Quimper entered Esquimault Harbour and found Haro Str., but was unable to explore it.

June 9 David Thompson left Cumberland House to survey the Saskatchewan R. to Hudson Bay. He reached the Saskatchewan R. mouth on June 15.

July 24 Spain agreed to offer reparations for the seizure of British ships at Nootka Sound.

Oct. 28 The Nootka Sound Convention between Spain and Great Britain, signed at Madrid, Spain, abandoned its claims to the northwest of North America, occupied in 1789, and prepared to make reparation for British ships seized, and restitution to British subjects for property seized. Both parties agreed to rights of trade, navigation and settlement of unoccupied parts of the west coast of North America. The terms of the treaty effectively ended Spain's exclusive sovereignty in the area and marked the beginning of the Spanish empire's collapse.

Winter HBC's official surveyor, Philip Turnor, arrived at Cumberland House to begin planning a surveying trip through the fur-rich Athabasca country. Throughout the winter, Turnor tutored Thompson and Peter Fidler (1769–1822) in mathematics, astronomy, the use of the telescope, compass, thermometer, chronometer, sextant, the "Nautical Almanak" tables and the artificial horizon. Turnor instilled in Thompson his passion for surveying and geography, although Thompson did lose the sight of one eye during this period.

1790–1792 Peter Fidler undertook an extended expedition, on behalf of the HBC, to observe and report on the activities of the NWC and to find a short, direct route from Hudson Bay to the Athabasca and Great Slave Lakes.

Also in 1790

• Canada's 1st opera, *Colas et Callinette,* by Louis Quesnel, sea captain and poet, was 1st performed. Quesnal was an unlikely composer, having been an arms runner during the American Revolution. Captured and later freed by the British, he opened his own wine-importing business in Boucherville, Que.

• The 1st Protestant church in what is now Ont. was dedicated at Williamsburg. Reverend Samuel Schewerdfeger was pastor of the Lutheran congregation.

1791

Mar. 8 The British govt sent Capt. George Vancouver (1757–1798) to the Pacific Coast to work out details of an authoritative Pacific settlement with Spanish authorities, to make an accurate survey of the North Pacific coast, and to locate a water passage through North America from the Pacific to the Atlantic.

June 10 The British parliament passed the Canada Act or Constitutional Act, which officially recognized the name Canada for the 1st time. An Order-in-Council dated Aug. 24 divided what had formerly been Que. into 2 provinces at the Ottawa R.: Upper Canada with a capital at Newark (Niagara-

on-the-Lake, Ont.), and Lower Canada with its capital at Quebec City. Both Upper and Lower Canada and the provinces of NS and NB were subject to the rule of their gov. and his appointed council, who had control over revenues derived from Crown land reserves (1/7 of all grants reserved for Protestant clergy use, and 1/7 for use by the Crown). Each council was responsible solely to the Crown, and not to the local populace. Each province had its own lt-gov. and elected legislature. The Constitutional Act, dividing Canada into Upper and Lower Canada, was proclaimed on Nov. 18, and came into effect Dec. 26.

Summer Nfld. settlers captured a young Beothuk girl near Charles Brook. She was befriended by a Rev. Dr. Clinch (1748/1749–1819) who recorded several Beothuk words, transforming his notes into a small dictionary of the Beothuk language. The girl was ultimately taken to England, where she died.

July 15 The *Royal Gazette and Miscellany of the Island of Saint John* was founded at Charlottetown, PEI. The biweekly newspaper was commissioned by the Crown .

July 19 Philip Turnor, HBC surveyor, arrived at Great Slave L. from L. Athabasca.

July 31 A Court of Civil Jurisdiction was created in Nfld. to hear "all pleas of debt, account, contracts respecting personal property, and all trespasses committed against the person or goods and chattels." John Reeves (1752–1829) was appointed 1st chief justice of the Superior Court. He arrived in the colony to take up his post Sept. 10.

Also in July

• José Maria Narváez, commanding the schooner *Sontra Saturnina* (part of the 2nd Spanish exploratory expedition under de Eliza y Reventa searching for the Northwest Passage) sailed up the Gulf of Georgina, across the Georgian Strait, explored Nanaimo Harbour (which he named Bocas de Winthuysen), passed north of Gabriola Is. to chart the Flat Top Is., before rejoining the main body of the expedition. Narváez, an avid diarist, recorded both this journey and an earlier one (1790) to the Aleutian Is.

Aug. 11 Edward, Duke of Kent, 4th son of King George III, and father of Queen Victoria, arrived in Halifax to take command of the 7th Royal Fusiliers. He would be appointed C-in-C of BNA in 1799, holding the post until 1806.

Aug. 18 Gov. Carleton sailed for England where he was appointed Gov. of Canada on Sept. 12. His term lasted from Dec. 26,–Dec. 15, 1796.

Aug. 25–Sept. 24, 1793 Lt-Gov. Alured Clarke (c 1745–1832) served as administrator of Que. in Gov. Carleton's absence.

Nov. 25–May 14, 1792 Richard Bulkeley (1717–1800) assumed the administration of NS on the death of Gov. Parr.

Also in Nov.
• American Gen. Arthur St. Clair, gov. of the US Northwest Territories, led an army through the Ohio Valley to the Wabash R. against "some of the savage tribes whose depredations have become intolerable..." by order of President Washington. St. Clair and his men were ambushed by the Miami under Meshikinquah or Chief Little Turtle (c 1752–1812); 632 soldiers were killed and 232 were wounded. St. Clair, who survived, resigned his commission the next year.

Dec. 31 William Osgoode (1754–1824) was appointed 1st chief justice of Upper Canada. He would be assigned additional responsibilities in 1794 when he was also appointed chief justice of Que.

Winter 1791–1792 Peter Fidler wintered with the Chipewyan in the area of the Great Slave L., learning the Chipewyan language.

Also in 1791
• David Thompson's HBC apprenticeship ended. He was offered and accepted a job as HBC surveyor and trader at a salary of £15 (some $150) per annum.

• John Graves Simcoe was appointed Upper Canada's 1st lt-gov., serving until 1796. Simcoe, who was firmly rooted in British tradition, worked to remove all French and Aboriginal place names within his jurisdiction, substituting sobriquets that

had British connections. Elizabeth Simcoe, his wife, kept a diary of life in Upper Canada (Niagara and Toronto). It was published in 1965 as *Mrs. Simcoe's Diary*, ed. Mary Quayle Innis.

• The Montreal-Quebec post-road was extended eastward to NB and westward to Kingston, Upper Canada.

• Alexander Henry, the younger (1764–1814), joined the NWC, following in the footsteps of his uncle, Alexander Henry, the elder (1739–1824).

• Black Loyalist veteran Thomas Peters (c 1738-1792), who had been transported to NS from New York at the end of the American Revolution, was unable to secure a land grant from the British govt, in spite of the fact that Loyalists of European descent received sizable grants of up to 40 ha. Peters communicated with other black Loyalists of the area and, discovering they too were poorly compensated, agreed to petition the British govt on their behalf. Peter was aided by British abolitionist John Clarkson. Peters' plight and that of his fellow black Loyalists came to the attention of another British abolitionist, Granville Sharp, who urged the group to leave NS and accept land grants in Sierra Leone offered by the British-owned Sierra Leone Land Company.

1792

Jan. 15 One thousand one hundred and ninety black Loyalist settlers left Halifax in a fleet of 15 ships, headed for the British colony of Sierra Leone, where they had been promised land. On board were Thomas Peters and John Clarkson (who would become gov. of the new colony). Sixty-seven people died during the voyage, the rest arrived in Sierra Leone in Mar. and began clearing a site for a settlement they named Freetown. The promised land was not immediately forthcoming and many settlers lost heart. Peters and Clarkson disagreed as to how the new colony should be run. Peters was discredited and soon died.

Feb. 7 Lt-Gov. Simcoe issued a proclamation in Quebec City which established regulations for the granting of free crown land. Eligible applicants would receive grants of up to 405 ha, on condition that the lands be improved and that the applicant pledged allegiance to the king, and provincial parliament.

Mar. 8 Dionisio Alcala-Galiano (1762–1805) commanded an expedition of 39 men in the *Sutil* and the *Mexicana* to complete exploration of Juan de Fuca Strait, begun in 1790 by Francisco de Eliza y Reventa and Alferez Manuel Quimper. Spain hoped that the Strait would lead to the discovery of the much-sought Northwest Passage. Accompanying Alcala-Galiano was José Cardero, official artist.

Also in Mar.
• Citizens of Adolphustown, Ont., held a town meeting, setting a precedent for limited self-govt in Ont.

Apr. 29 George Vancouver (1757–1798), commanding the *Discovery*, and William Howard Broughton (1762–1821) in the *Chatham,* reached Juan de Fuca Strait while carrying out orders to chart the Pacific Coast of North America from 30 to 60 degrees north.

May 7 Lower Canada was divided into 27 electoral districts with 50 members in the legislature.

May 11 American Capt. Gray entered the Columbia R. in the ship *Columbia* (after which the river was named). Gray's voyage would later be cited by the US as claim of ownership for the region.

May 14–Apr. 12, 1808 John Wentworth (c 1768–1820) served as lt-gov. of NS.

June 4 Capt. Vancouver took possession of the North Pacific coast islands and straits from 39 degrees 20 minutes North to the entrance of the Strait of Juan de Fuca, plus those islands in the interior sea he called the Gulf of Georgia. Vancouver entered and named Burrard's Channel (Inlet) on June 12.

June 13 At Birch Bay, Alcala-Galiano in the *Sutil* and *Mexicana* encountered the *Discovery* and the *Chatham* under Broughton, second-in-command of the Vancouver expedition. Vancouver was away on a surveying trip. Alcala-Galiano, who spoke some English, established a strong rapport with the British expedition, and by the time Vancouver returned to the anchorage (after exploring Howe

Sound, Jervis Inlet and Vancouver harbour), both exploration parties were in a mood to share survey information. Vancouver learned that the Spanish explorers had preceded him in Juan de Fuca Strait and the Strait of Georgia. Alcala-Galiano heard about Burrard Inlet. Spanish and English explorers continued to work together charting the Northwest coast — although each nationality felt compelled to double-check the work of the other. The 2 expeditions parted company on July 13.

June 27 Prince Edward, Duke of Kent, halted a racial riot at Que.

June 29 William Osgoode was appointed 1st Speaker of the Legislative Council of Upper Canada.

July 16 Gov. Simcoe divided Upper Canada into districts and counties. The next day he presided over the 1st meeting of the Executive Council of Upper Canada wherein Newark (Niagara-on-the-Lake) was chosen as the site of the Upper Canadian capital.

Also in July
• HBC surveyor Philip Turnor returned to York Factory after a 2-year surveying expedition to the Athabasca country. He reported on NWC activity on L. Athabasca.

Aug. 9 George Vancouver reached Queen Charlotte Sound.

Aug.10 The Canada Banking Company issued the 1st bank notes in Canada, but Canadians were loath to use them, preferring hard currency. An example of the five shilling note, 1792, can be found in the Bank of Canada's National Currency collection in Ottawa.

Aug. 28 Vancouver arrived at Nootka Sound to work out a territorial arrangement with Spanish commander Bodega. The 2 were unable to concur on the required details for the property transfer specified in the Nootka Convention.

Also in Aug.
• André Michaux (1746–1802), French botanist, linguist, artist and explorer, became the 1st naturalist to explore the interior of the Quebec-Labrador peninsula. Michaux, a leading scholar of the day,

had previously explored the flora of the Middle East, including Persia (1782–1785), and also Virginia, the Carolinas, Florida, the Mississippi basin and the Bahamas. His proposal to seek out the source of the Missouri R. and other rivers draining into the Pacific Ocean became the basis for the Lewis and Clark expedition of 1804–1806. Shipwrecked upon his return to France in 1796, Michaux nevertheless managed to rescue most of his extensive plant collection. His works were *Principal Oaks of North America* (1801) and *Flora of North America* (1803). Michaux died of fever in Madagascar in 1802.

Fall David Thompson was ordered to the Athabasca country to survey waterways through the Muskrat country between the Nelson and Churchill Rivers, because the HBC needed to combat the aggressive presence of the NWC in the area. HBC officials hoped Thompson would also explore rivers flowing through the area in the hopes that a more direct route could be discovered to L. Athabasca via Reindeer L. He and his men built Seepaywisk House.

Oct. 10 Alexander Mackenzie left Fort Chipewyan and headed up the Peace R. on his 2nd expedition in search of the Pacific Ocean.

Oct. 15 Upper Canada's 1st legislature in Niagara passed legislation banning the sale of liquor in prisons on penalty of fines of £20.

Oct. 16 Upper Canada's 4 judicial districts, Hesse, Nassau, Mecklenburg and Lunenburg were changed to Western District, Home District, Midland District and Eastern District, respectively.

Oct. 21 Broughton in the *Chatham* navigated the Columbia R. upstream, claiming the area for Britain.

Dec. 17 The 1st Parliament of Lower Canada convened, with Jean-Antoine Panet (1751–1815) elected Speaker of the Legislative Assembly; Panet was elected president of the Lower Canada Parliament the next day.

Dec. 20 Regular mail service was established between Canada and the US.

Winter Peter Fidler undertook an expedition from Buckingham House (near Lindberg, Alb.) to the Rocky Mountains, mapping most of the area in the process. He observed and recorded various aspects of First Nations life on the plains and learned the Peigan language.

c 1792 The watercolour *West View of Château-Richer* by George Heriot (1759–1839) (probably Canada's 1st resident English-speaking artist) was completed.

Also in 1792

• The NWC reorganized to merge with the smaller firms of Todd McGill & Co., Forsythe Richardson & Co. and Grant Campion & Co. New partners included Roderick Mackenzie and William McGillivray (1764–1825). Alexander Mackenzie held 6 of the 46 shares. McTavish remained the dominant partner.

• Simon Fraser (1776–1862) entered the service of the NWC.

• Nfld. magistrate John Bland (Bonavista) investigated John Peyton Sr. (Twillingate) as instigator in the murder of several Beothuk, but laid no charges.

• José Cardero painted *Fiesta celebrada en Nutka por su Xefe Macuina a causa de haber dado su hija indicios de entrar en la pubertad,* an aquatint now held at Yale University.

1793

Feb. 12 Peter Fidler discovered coal in Alberta, on the Red Deer R. near the mouth of Three Hills Creek.

Apr. 18 Louis Roy (1771–1799) began publication of the 1st newspaper in Upper Canada, the *Upper Canada Gazette,* or *American Oracle,* a semi-official weekly appearing mostly in English.

Also in Apr.

• *History of the Government of the Island of Newfoundland* by John Reeves was completed for publication.

May 9 Alexander Mackenzie and a party of 9 left Fort Fork (Peace R. Landing, Alb.) near the junction of the Peace and Smoky Rivers, heading westward in search of a route to the Pacific Ocean. On May 17, Mackenzie's party sighted the Rocky Mountains.

On June 12, the Mackenzie expedition reached the Continental Divide at Portage L., portaging across the Divide to the Fraser R. By early July, the group was forced to abandon its canoes and the Blackwater R., and resorted to travel on foot. The expedition reached the Bella Coola R. on July 17 to be greeted by the local Aboriginals at a site Mackenzie named Friendly Village.

May 14 British Gen. James Ogilvie (c 1740–1813) raided the French Islands of St. Pierre-Miquelon and deported most of the resident Acadians to France via Halifax. Other Acadians escaped to Île Madeleine and Île Madame. By Sept. 1796, all Acadian residents of St. Pierre-Miquelon had been expelled.

May 31 The 2nd session of the 1st Parliament of Upper Canada met, until July 9. Items discussed included the destruction of wolves, which was heartily encouraged.

June 28 Bishop's sees for Upper and Lower Canada were established.

July 7 Jacob Mountain (1749–1825) was consecrated in the Chapel of Lambeth Palace as the 1st Anglican Bishop of Que. His diocese extended from the Gaspé Peninsula throughout Canada, west of Que.

July 9 Gov. Simcoe persuaded the legislature of Upper Canada to pass a law forbidding importation of slaves into the province and making freedom mandatory for slave children at the age of 25.

July 22 The Mackenzie expedition reached Dean Channel on the Pacific Ocean. There, on a large rock, Mackenzie wrote his famous inscription: "Alexander Mackenzie, from Canada, by land, the twenty-second of July, one thousand seven hundred and ninety-three." (There is now a monument at that location.) The expedition returned to Fort Chipewyan on Aug. 24.

Aug. 27 Gov. Simcoe named present-day Toronto the 1st permanent capital of Upper Canada. One month later he renamed the town York, in honour of the Duke of York, son of George III.

Sept. 4 The 1st Canadian Sunday School opened at Quebec City. It was a free school founded by Edward, Duke of Kent.

Oct. 5 Capt. Vancouver left Nootka and sailed north to explore Alaska.

Also in 1793
Montreal native François Beaucourt (1740–1794) painted *Marguerite Maihot*, oil on canvas, in the rococo style. The painting is now held in the Musée national des beaux-arts du Québec, Quebec City.

1794

Feb. 10 Lord Dorchester (Carleton) told Canadian First Nation leaders that British patience with the US was exhausted. He predicted war.

Spring–Summer Deputy Provincial Surveyor Augustus Jones was commissioned by Lt-Gov. Simcoe to establish an expected route for a military road extending north from York to L. Simcoe.

May 29 Bishop Jacob Mountain was given a seat in the legislature of Lower Canada and the title of Lord Bishop of Que.

May 31 The legislature of Upper Canada passed the Alien Act to guard against anti-British sentiment.

Also in May
• David Thompson (1770–1857) was appointed surveyor for the HBC, at a salary of £60 per year. Thompson and Malcom Ross built Reed Lake House (in what is now Grass R. Park, Man.).

June 2 The 3rd session of the 1st Parliament of Upper Canada met, until July 9. The Court of King's Bench was established, and an act was passed restraining cattle, sheep, horses and pigs from running at large.

June–Aug. William Berczy (1744/48–1813), German merchant, artist, architect and administrator (born Johann Albrecht Ulrich Moll), leading some 70 German families from Hamburg, and 250 head of cattle, settled on 25,900 ha in Markham, Upper Canada, on land granted to the new settlers by Lt-Gov. Simcoe, in return for their assistance in the construction of Yonge St. from York north to Georgian Bay. Simcoe originally ordered his Queen's

Rangers to build the military road, but they were seconded to military duty. Berczy was under pressure to complete the construction in 12 months or lose his remuneration (which also included four 81 ha properties along the new thoroughfare). Berczy and crew began their work with enthusiam, completing some 30 km of roadway from Eglinton to Bond L. during the winter months of 1794–1795, but that was it. The new settlers were not interested in a work project that offered little immediate benefit to their Markham community. Costs were high, supplies dwindling, and starvation a very real possibility. By winter 1795–1796, 1/3 of Berczy's Markham settlers had relocated to Niagara.

Aug. 19 Vancouver completed his survey of the Pacific Coast of North America from San Diego Bay to the Gulf of Alaska. He proved that a Northwest Passage from the West Coast to inland America did not exist.

Also in Aug.
• The battle of Fallen Timbers was fought near present-day Waterville, Ont., where, Tecumseh (Tikamthi, c 1768–1813) distinguished himself even as his Shawnee were defeated by the American Gen. Anthony Wayne.

Nov. 11 The 2nd session of the 1st Parliament of Lower Canada met, until May 31, 1795. Acts included the regulation of the militia and the division of the province into the districts of Quebec, Montreal and Trois-Rivières.

Nov. 19 Britain and the US concluded Jay's Treaty. Effective July 1, 1796, the British were to withdraw from interior posts, principally Detroit, Grand Portage and Michilimackinac, all of which became US property. Both parties were to have free use of the Great Lakes and the right to pass freely over the international boundary. A boundary commission was provided to determine the frontier west of Lake-of-the-Woods.

Also in 1794
• The NWC traded the following items for beaver pelts: long guns–14 pelts; 20 balls of shot–1 pelt; blanket–6 pelts; keg of liquor–30 pelts.

• The age limit for military service in Canada was raised to 60 years.

• Angus Shaw (d 1832) and Duncan McGillivray (d 1808) of the NWC built Fort Augustus on the North Saskatchewan R. about 32 km downstream from present-day Edmonton.

1795

Jan. 5 The 3rd session of the 1st Parliament of Lower Canada convened. Licences were imposed on peddlers, public houses and the retailers of wine and brandy. New taxes were placed on wines, sugar, coffee, salt and playing cards.

Mar. 23 Britain officially regained possession of Nootka from Spain, and the Spanish post at Nootka Sound surrendered to the British (Mar. 28).

July 6 The 4th session of the 1st Parliament of Upper Canada met, until Aug. 10. Business included the regulation of the medical profession and the registry of deeds and wills.

Aug. The Treaty of Greenville forced the Shawnee to give up most of present-day Ohio and smaller areas after their defeat in the Battle of Fallen Timbers.

Fall Peter Fidler built Carlton House (near Kamsack, Sask.).

Oct. 5 William Tomison, Inland Chief of the HBC, began building Edmonton House near the NWC's Fort Augustus.

Oct. 20 Vancouver arrived in England, officially completing his exploration of the Pacific Northwest Coast. His was the longest surveying expedition in history, lasting 4 1/2 years and covering 120,000 km.

Nov. 20–May 7, 1796 The 4th session of the 1st Parliament of Lower Canada met. Business included regulations for weights and measures.

Also in Nov.
• Discord between the wintering partners of the NWC and the Montreal members of McTavish Frobisher (its principal stockholder) was lessened at the annual Grand Portage meeting when the wintering partners were awarded an extra share each. Annual profits for the NWC averaged £72,000 between 1790–1795.

Dec. 23 Lt-Gov. Simcoe directed Augustus Jones, in charge of 30 Queen's Rangers, to complete the construction of Yonge St. as far as Fort Pine Landing, L. Simcoe. By Feb. 16, 1796, the crew had carved a pathway north to the Holland R. The 8.5-m wide highway was 55 km long, and, although little more than a cart path in places, opened up vast new areas for settlement. The new road was named after British Secretary of War, Sir George Yonge.

Dec. 27 Mrs. Simcoe, wife of the lt-gov. of Ont. recorded in her diary a "slight shock of an earthquake" in York; this is the earliest earthquake documented by Europeans in Ont.

Also in 1795
• *A Journey from Prince of Wales's Fort, in Hudson's Bay, to the northern ocean... in the years 1769, 1770, 1771 & 1772* by Samuel Hearne was published in London.

1796

Jan. 21 Gen. Robert Prescott (c 1726–1815) was commissioned lt-gov. of Lower Canada.

Feb. 1 The capital of Upper Canada was officially moved from Niagara-on-the-L. to York (Toronto).

May Lt-Gov. Simcoe issued a proclamation declaring forfeit of lands of all township proprietors who had failed to meet their settlement obligations. William Berczy's Markham lands were seized by the Crown.

June 1 In compliance with Jay's Treaty, Britain returned Detroit and other posts to the US. Britain complied with the treaty terms because it feared a war with France as well as one with the US.

June 21–Dec. 15 Robert Prescott served as lt-gov. of Lower Canada. From July 12–Apr. 27, 1797, he would serve as administrator of the Canadas, NB and NS as well as commander of the British forces in North America. In 1797, he would be promoted to Gov-in-C of Canada, serving until Aug. 29, 1807.

July 18 Peter Russell (1733–1808) was commissioned president of the Council of Upper Canada. He also served as administrator of Upper Canada from July 20–Aug. 17, 1799.

Late Summer David Thompson failed to find a navigable route from the Churchill R. to the fur-rich Athabaska country. He and Malcolm Ross, HBC's "Master to the Northland," and 15 men and women, were forced to spend the winter in the rapidly constructed Bedford House Post, where they existed primarily on fish.

Sept. 7 The Chippewa ceded about 89,000 ha in Upper Canada (in today's Middlesex, Oxford and Lambton Counties) to Britain, for £2000. They also received various goods including blankets, yard goods, hats, kettles, knives, firearms and ammunition, looking glasses and other sundries, smoking pipes, rum and tobacco.

Nov. 2 Chief Brant was authorized to sell land belonging to the Six Nations.

1796–1821 Peter Fidler served as chief surveyor and map-maker for the HBC.

Also in 1796
• John Askin, a Detroit merchant, contracted with the NWC to ship them 1,200 bushels of corn and 4,479 kg of flour per annum.

• John McIntosh (1777–1846) discovered the apple tree that now bears his name, when he accidentally came upon 20 trees in a previously cleared area on his farm near Dundas, Ont. He transplanted them. By 1830, all but 1 of the trees died, but, because his son Allan had learned the art of grafting, the family was able to produce apples on a large scale. The original McIntosh tree, although badly burned in 1893, continued to produce fruit until 1908.

1797

Jan. 24 The 1st session of the 2nd Parliament of Lower Canada met, until May 2. Business included agreements with Upper Canada on customs revenue.

May 2 The Lower Canada House of Assembly suspended the right of *habeas corpus* and ordered foreigners–especially Frenchmen–out of the colony for fear of sedition as a result of the French Revolution and the French declaration of war on Britain.

May 10 David McLane, a merchant from Rhode Island, was arrested for treason and for attempting to promote revolution in Canada. Found guilty, he was hanged, eviscerated and beheaded on July 21.

May 23 David Thompson quit the HBC after 13 years, and walked from Bedford House 120 km to Alexander Fraser's post on the Reindeer R., where he entered the service of the NWC. as surveyor and map-maker. His instructions were to survey the 49th parallel, locate the exact positions of all NWC posts and explore the upper Missouri R. valley. Thompson began his expedition in Aug. It would last 10 months, and take him as far as the Mandan villages of the Missouri.

May 24 In Fredericton, legislators John Coffin and James Glenie fought a duel over a constitutional dispute. Glenie was wounded.

July 3 The Law Society of Upper Canada was established by an Act of Legislative Assembly. Its initial membership was 15.

Aug. 23 The last slave transaction in Canada was made at Montreal, where Emanuel Allen was sold at public auction.

Nov. 4–Nov. 29, 1808 Robert Shore Milnes (c 1754–1837) served as lt-gov. of Lower Canada. He also served as administrator of Lower Canada from July 30, 1799–Aug. 12, 1805.

Nov. 28 The NWC began construction on the 1st Sault Ste. Marie Canal linking L. Huron and L. Superior. The canal, completed in 1801, was destroyed by the Americans in 1812.

Dec. 14 In response to a request from the Mississauga, the British administration of Upper Canada issued a proclamation protecting Native burial grounds and Mississauga fisheries.

Also in 1797

• J. MacKay published the poem "Quebec Hill" in English.

• The election of Lower Canada's 2nd Assembly resulted in a legislature dominated by French Canadians, a circumstance prompting

Gov. Prescott to advise the Colonial Office that English authority would only be maintained if English-speaking administrators and their associates dominated Lower Canada's executive branch — which was not subject to public election. This situation gave rise to the Château Clique, wherein a small circle of wealthy British families controlled the Lower Canada govt, and awarded themselves and their friends large land grants to entrench their positions.

1798

Feb. 26 David Thompson set out from the Mandan villages on the Missouri R. to return to Grand Portage. Along the route, he explored the headwaters of the Mississippi R. After journeying up the Red R., Thompson reached Turtle L., one of the Mississippi headwaters, on Apr. 27. He arrived at Sault Ste. Marie May 20, and back at Grand Portage on June 7, having completed some 6,500 km of travel and surveying. In July, Thompson travelled to L. Winnipeg, then up the Sask. R. to Cumberland House, where he wintered.

Feb. 22 The Chippewa ceded nearly 12,000 ha in present-day Simcoe County, Ont., for £101 Quebec currency and various goods including blankets, yard goods, hats, kettles, knives, firearms and ammunition, looking glasses, smoking pipes, rum, tobacco, etc. The ceded territory included present-day Penetanguishene Harbour and islands.

June 5 The 2nd session of the 2nd Parliament of Upper Canada met, until July 5, passing legislation providing for the establishment of the county system of administration and legislation that declared marriages performed by non-Anglican ministers valid.

June 12 Benedict Arnold was awarded a grant of 5,423 ha of land in Upper Canada.

June 30 The Chippewa traded St. Joseph Is., about 30 km southeast of present-day Sault Ste. Marie, Ont., for goods.

Sept. 6 Walter Patterson, former wealthy gov. of St. John Is., died in poverty at his lodgings in

Castle Street, Oxford Market, London, after suffering bankruptcy and imprisonment for debt.

Oct. 7 Forty-four French Revolution refugees were granted land in present-day Uxbridge, Gwillimbury and Whitchurch Townships, Upper Canada.

Oct. 25 A boundary commission made the St. Croix R. the southern border between New Brunswick and Maine.

Oct. 30 Nfld. Gov. William Waldegrave (1753–1825) reported much of the colony's population, close to 20,000 residents, was near starvation because the war in Europe caused rising prices and a loss of markets for their products.

Also in Oct.
• Several former partners of the NWC, fed up with the leadership of Simon McTavish, formed Richardson and Forsyth and Company (commonly called the XY Company, because of the "xy" insignia appearing on its kegs and bales of fur).

Nov. 29 The legislature of St. John's Is. voted to change its name to Prince Edward Island. The Act received Royal Assent on Feb. 2, 1799, and the official name change occurred on June 3, 1799. The new name was in honour of Edward, Duke of Kent.

Dec. 29 Royal Assent gave legal effect to an Upper Canada order of June 5, validating marriages celebrated by other than Church of England clergy. Previously only Anglican ministers were authorized to perform the service. The Royal Assent applied to Lutheran, Calvinist and Presbyterian ministers.

Also in 1798
• Coal was discovered in Pictou County, NS, by Dr. James McGregor. In 1807, the 13.7 m Foord Seam (Big Seam) was discovered near Stellarton. Seam after seam was subsequently discovered transforming the region into one of the continent's leading coal producers.

• Rev. Dr. John Clinch (1749–1819), doctor and Church of England clergyman, was probably the 1st person in the new world to administer vaccinations, the 1st of which was administered to his

nephew, Joseph Hart. Clinch learned the procedure from his old friend and former classmate, Edward Jenner. Later, he inoculated 700 persons of all ages for smallpox in Trinity, Nfld., beginning with his own children.

• The 1st circus to tour Canada was Rickett's of London, which gave its 1st performance in Quebec City.

1799

Jan. 7 The Quebec library was founded.

Mar. 8 David Thompson left Cumberland House for Fort Augustus, and explored the Pembina and Athabasca Rivers to Lesser Slave L. On June 10 David Thompson married Charlotte Small, the 13-year-old "mixed-blood" daughter of retired NWC partner, Patrick Small, at Île-à-La-Crosse. It would be a close and lifelong relationship.

Apr. 10 Peter Hunter (1746–1805) was commissioned lt-gov. of Upper Canada. He would serve from Aug. 17, 1799–Aug. 21, 1805.

Also in Apr.
• Gov. Prescott was recalled to England for consultations resulting from actions against land speculators, some of whom, like Chief Justice Osgoode and certain councillors, held high political offices.

June 12 The 3rd session of the 2nd Parliament met, until June 29, and passed legislation providing for the education and support of orphans.

June 21 Brig-Gen. John Murray arrived in Cape Breton to serve as its administrator.

July 26 Construction began, under the direction of Asa Danforth (1768–1821), on a new road that would run east from York (Toronto) toward Kingston. The Danforth Road was completed from York (Toronto) to Hope Township, about 96 km, on Dec. 31.

July 30–Aug. 12, 1805 Robert Shore Milnes served as administrator of Lower Canada.

Also in 1799

• Annual profits for the NWC averaged £98,000 between 1796–1799.

• John McDonald (1770–1866) of Garth established Rocky Mountain House trading post for the NWC on the North Saskatchewan R.

• John Molson built a distillery in Montreal that had an annual whisky production rate of 1,136,500 litres.

1800

Feb. 2 Philemon Wright (1760–1839) left Woburn, Massachusetts, where he had been a successful farmer, and moved to Ont. to take up free land with about 25 men, their wives and children. His group arrived near what is now Hull, Que., and began clearing land on Mar. 17.

Feb. 12 The College of NB was founded at Fredericton.

Mar. 5 The 4th session of the 2nd Parliament of Lower Canada convened until May 29. Legislation included penalties for harbouring runaway seamen.

Mar. 16 Following the death of Father Jean-Joseph Casot (1728–1800), the last Jesuit of the French regime, the Crown appropriated the remaining property held by the Jesuit Order in Canada and used it for education purposes.

Mar. 20 Simcoe granted 3,237 ha in York County, Upper Canada, to Timothy Rogers (1756–1828), a Vermont Quaker, who settled a Quaker community in King and Whitchurch Townships over the next several years. Settlers started to arrive in 1801.

Also in Mar.
• The 1st Baptist Association in Canada was organized at Granville, Lower Canada.

Spring David Thompson left Rocky Mountain House to begin a survey of the N. Sask. R.

June 2 The 4th session of the 2nd Parliament of Upper Canada met until July 4. Business included the introduction of British criminal law.

Aug. 18 Alexander Henry met a band of Ojibwa at the mouth of the Assiniboine R., and traded rum for dried buffalo meat.

Also in 1800
• Alexander Mackenzie joined the newly formed XY Fur Company, adding his prestige to the firm, which became commonly known as "Alexander Mackenzie & Co."

• St. Georges Church, Halifax, was built under sponsorship by the Duke of Kent for a German congregation and troops from the Halifax garrison. Its circular nave, outside cupola and internal gallery were designed by William Hughes.

1801

Jan. 8 The 1st session of the 3rd Parliament of Lower Canada met until Apr. 8. Business included ordering the demolition of the walls surrounding Montreal and the licencing of billiard tables.

May 28 The 1st session of the 3rd Parliament of Upper Canada met until July 9. Business included the regulation of the militia and the founding of a market at Kingston.

June 30 Simon Fraser became a partner in the NWC.

Also in June
• David Thompson, with 20 men and 13 horses, left Rocky Mountain House on an abortive expedition to cross the Rocky Mountains. The group explored the North Ram R. The 1st of Thompson's 15 children was born while he was on this expedition.

1801–1815 About 10,000 immigrants arrived in Canada from many parts of Scotland.

Also in 1801
• The Royal Institution for the Advancement of Learning was founded to foster public education in the colony.

• Alexander Mackenzie's journal of his 2 voyages, edited by W. Coombes under the title *Voyages from Montreal, on the River St. Lawrence, Through the Continent of North America, to the Frozen and Pacific Oceans, In the Years 1789 and 1793, With a Preliminary Account of the Rise, Progress, and Present State of the Fur Trade,* was published.

1802

Jan. 3 Three hundred Scottish Highlanders settled in Sydney, NS.

Jan. 11 The 2nd session of the 3rd Parliament of Lower Canada sat until Apr. 5. Legislation included police regulations.

Feb. 10 Alexander Mackenzie was knighted for his

contributions towards the exploration of western North America, and for becoming the 1st European to cross the North American continent.

May 12 Anglican King's College, Windsor, NS, received a Royal charter, granting university powers.

Also in May

• David Thompson explored and surveyed the Sask. R. from Rocky Mountain House to what is now Thunder Bay, Ont.

Oct. David Thompson explored from the mouth of the Lesser Slave R. and Lesser Slave L. to the forks of the Peace R.

Also in 1802

• Forts Augustus and Edmonton were moved to sites within the limits of the present city of Edmonton. The 2 forts would later merge and move to higher ground on the site of the present Parliament buildings.

• Deportation for life was instituted as a criminal punishment in Upper Canada.

• The 1st unofficial cavalry corps was formed in Montreal.

• The 1st issue of the *York Gazette* appeared.

1803

Jan. 24 The 3rd session of the 3rd Parliament of Upper Canada met until Mar. 5. Business included the regulation of property owned by married women, and incentives to destroy bears and wolves.

Mar. 12 Capt. John Salter, commanding the American trading ship *Boston*, cast anchor in Nootka Sound (Vancouver Is.).

Mar. 22 Maquinna, leading chief of the Nootka, attacked the *Boston* after being insulted by Captain Salter. Maquinna and his people killed the entire *Boston* crew with the exception of blacksmith John Rodgers Jewitt (1783–1821) and sailmaker John Thompson (c 1751–1822), both of whom were made slaves. On July 19, 1805, Jewitt and Thompson, were released through the efforts of Captain Samuel Hill of the brig *Lydia*. Hill had

captured Maquinna, bargaining the chief's freedom for the 2 slaves' release. Jewitt kept a journal while in captivity, which he later published in 1807 as *A Journal Kept at Nootka Sound*.

Apr. 30 French emperor Napoleon Bonaparte abandoned his plan to recapture Canada, and sold Louisiana to the United States. The Louisiana Purchase was negotiated on behalf of US President Thomas Jefferson for 77 million francs, or $15 million US. It included 800,000 sq. miles of land extending west from the Mississippi R. to the Rocky Mountains, thereby doubling the size of the United States.

May 21 William Osgoode, chief justice of Upper Canada, declared slavery inconsistent with the laws of Canada.

May 22 John Strachan (1778–1867) was ordained deacon by Bishop Jacob Mountain.

Summer The NWC completed construction of New Fort, at the delta of the Kaministiquia R. near what is now the junction of Minnesota and Ont. The new trading depot replaced the NWC headquarters at Grand Portage, in American territory. New Fort was renamed Fort William in 1807.

Aug. 2 The 4th session of the 3rd Parliament of Lower Canada met until Aug. 11. Business included the renewal of the 1794 Alien Act, a result of war between Britain and France.

Aug. 7 Eight hundred Highlanders from the Hebrides sailed for Orwell Bay, PEI, with Thomas Douglas Selkirk, 5th Earl of Selkirk (1771–1820), to settle Selkirk's 8,094 ha.

Aug. 11 British parliament passed the Canada Jurisdiction Act, aimed at regulating violent conflicts between the HBC and NWC. Offences committed on Aboriginal lands or other areas considered BNA were made subject to the laws of Upper or Lower Canada.

Nov. 5 A weekly public market was established at York.

Also in 1803

• William Berczy won the competition for the design of Christ Church, Montreal, which he fashioned in the Georgian style on a classic rectangular plan with a tall steeple and Doric portico.

• Cole Thomas Talbot (1771–1853), former secretary to Lt-Gov. Simcoe, obtained a British govt grant of 2,023 ha west of Kettle Creek in Upper Canada, in return for his military service to the Crown. Terms of the agreement allocated Talbot 81 ha of land for every family he settled, of which each family received 20 ha while Talbot retained the rest in return for services rendered. Talbot worked hard at settlement and by the end of his life had been awarded a total land grant of 202,350 ha.

• Architect Isaac Hildreth (1741–1807), with designs by royal engineer Captain William Fenwick, completed "Old" Town Clock (or Garrison Clock) located on Citadel Hill in Halifax, NS. The future father of Queen Victoria, Prince Edward ordered the large timepiece from royal clockmaster Vuillamy before leaving Halifax. The wooden multi-level structure contained three 57 kg weights and a 3.7 m pendulum, which hangs in the centre and can still be heard throughout the city.

1804

Jan. 10 The 5th session of the 3rd Parliament of Lower Canada met until Mar. 9. Business included confirmation of marriages performed by ministers of dissenting Protestant sects.

Feb. 29 Antoine Plamondon (1804–1895), French-Canadian portrait painter, was born in Ancienne–Lorette, Que. Trained in Europe, Plamondon would be named a founding vice-president of the Royal Canadian Academy of the Arts in 1880.

Mar. 5 David Thompson descended the Peace R. to L. Athabasca, which he reached on May 12, arriving at the mouth of the Clearwater R. on May 19, before heading back to Cumberland House.

May 9 Joseph DesBarres (1721–1815) was appointed lt-gov. of PEI at the age of 82, succeeding Edmund Fanning. DesBarres served from July 1805 to Aug. 4, 1812.

June 16 Alexander Mackenzie was elected to represent the County of Huntingdon in the House of Assembly of Lower Canada.

July 6 Simon McTavish, principal shareholder in the NWC, died of inflammation in Montreal at the age of 54. McTavish had come down with a cold in the early spring while supervising the construction of his home.

Also in July
• David Thompson became a partner in the NWC.

Aug. 28 The spacious stone Cathedral of the Holy Trinity was consecrated. Constructed in Que. at the site of the Récollet chapel, which burned down in 1796, its progress was overseen by Bishop Mountain. The architects were Capt. William Hall and Maj. William Robe.

Sept. One hundred Highland emigrants from the Isle of Mull in Scotland arrived in Upper Canada to settle the land Selkirk had acquired near L. St. Clair and start a colony called Baldoon. Their trek had taken over 4 months and many suffered from malarial fever. Forty-two of the original settlers died the 1st year.

Oct. 8 The govt schooner *Speedy* went down, with all passengers lost, in a storm on L. Ontario, off Presqu'ile Point, Brighton Township, after leaving York. Victims included Robert Gray, solicitor-gen. of Upper Canada; Thomas Cochrane, junior judge of the Court of King's Bench in Upper Canada; John Stegman, the provincial surveyor; and Angus Macdonnell, Member of Parliament in Upper Canada.

Nov. 5 The XY Company merged with the NWC. The result, called the NWC, issued 100 shares, 25 of which were allocated to XY partners.

Nov. 19 Montreal's 1st theatre was opened by a Scottish actor named Ormsby.

c 1804–1810 George Heriot (1759–1839), who was appointed Deputy Postmaster General of BNA in 1800, painted *The North West Part of the City of Quebec. Taken from the St. Charles River*, in oil.

Also in 1804
- The 1st Canadian Board of Trade in Canada was organized at Halifax.

1805

Jan. 5 Poet Thomas Cary (1751–1823) published the 1st issue of the weekly English-language newspaper, *Quebec Mercury*, which was strongly supportive of the British Constitution and the status quo. The Mercury continued until 1903.

Jan. 9 The 1st session of the 4th Parliament of Lower Canada met until Mar. 25. Business included a tax assessment to help pay for jails, legislation to provide a turnpike from Montreal to Lachine, and the prohibition of any sale of merchandise on Sunday.

June 21 The cornerstone of Christ Church, designed by William Berczy, was laid at Rue Notre-Dame in Montreal. The church was not completed until 1821.

Aug. 1 Mississauga Chiefs ceded more than 101,170 ha in York Country to the Crown for 10 shillings per chief. Fishing rights on the Etobicoke R. were reserved solely for the Mississauga. This agreement formalized a previous agreement made in 1787.

Aug. 2 The Mississauga ceded 28,650 ha from the Etobicoke R. to Burlington Bay, Upper Canada, for "£1,000 province currency." Much of the land became the property of Loyalist settlers. The Mississauga retained their lands under cultivation and sole fishing rights in rivers of the area including "one mile on each side" of the Credit R.

Aug. 14 Construction of the Union Hotel began in Que.; the luxurious establishment featured comfort, service and dining, a new concept for North American travellers.

Sept. 11 Alexander Grant (1734–1813), president of the Upper Canada Council, assumed office as administrator of Upper Canada until Aug. 25, 1806.

c 1805 William Berczy completed *Joseph Brant*, oil on canvas, which now hangs in National Gallery of Canada.

1805–1806 Archibald Norman McLeod built Fort Dunvegan for the NWC on the Peace R., 97 km upstream from Smoky Forks.

Also in 1805
- The Earl of Selkirk published *Observations on the present state of the Highlands of Scotland, with a view of the causes and probable consequences of emigration*, in London. Despite criticism from government agencies, the book was well received, and Selkirk became a celebrity; in 1806 he was appointed to the House of Lords in Great Britain.

1806

Jan. 22 Francis Gore (1769–1852) was commissioned lt-gov. of Upper Canada, serving from Aug. 25, 1806 to Jan. 1, 1818.

Jan. 27 Joseph Octave Plessis (1763–1825) was consecrated bishop of Que., serving until 1825.

Feb. 4 The 2nd session of the 4th Parliament of Upper Canada convened until Mar. 3. Business included provisions for sheriffs.

June 25 Ottawa settler and entrepreneur Philemon Wright founded a large lumber business which floated the 1st log rafts down the Ottawa R.

July 26 Simon Fraser and John Stuart (1779–1874) embarked on a journey up the Peace R. on behalf of the NWC. They established and built Fort St. James on the east end of Stuart L. and Fort Fraser at the east end of Fraser L. Fraser sent the 1st shipment of furs from west of the Rockies to Dunvegan, Alb. He named the new trapping area New Caledonia.

Sept. 6 The Mississauga ceded 34,400 ha in Peel and Halton Counties, Upper Canada, for "five shillings apiece (to the 10 chiefs) of lawful currency" and £1,000 to be received "at or before the ensealing and delivery" of the lands.

Sept. 27 Isaac Brock (1769–1812) assumed command of British forces in Upper Canada.

Oct. 11 William Weekes, representative of Durham, Simcoe and East York in the Upper Canada

Assembly, was killed in a duel with William Dickson (1769–1864), a member of the Legislative Council of Upper Canada, at Niagara. The duel was caused by Weekes's reference to the late Lt-Gov. Hunter as a "Gothic Barbarian," a remark to which Dickson took issue.

Also in 1806
• The NWC sent David Thompson, his wife and 3 children, Finan McDonald and 8 other men on an expedition to the Rocky Mountains and from there to the Columbia R. to determine if the Americans could use that waterway as a gateway to the NWC's trading area.

• Louis Dulongpré (1759–1843) completed a portrait of James McGill on canvas, now in the Musée du Québec.

1807

Jan. 6 Reine Lagimodière, the 1st child of European descent in Western Canada, was born at the Forks in the Red R. settlement to Jean-Baptist Lagimodière (1778–1855) and his wife, Marie-Anne Gaboury (1780–1875), who would become the grandparents of Louis Riel.

Jan. 21 The 3rd session of the 4th Parliament of Lower Canada convened until Apr. 16. Ezekiel Hart (1770–1843) was the Trois-Rivières representative — the 1st Jew elected to the legislature. He was declared ineligible to sit because his religion did not allow him to swear the customary oath "on the true faith of a Christian." Hart was expelled from the Legislative Assembly on Mar. 14. His constituents re-elected him early in 1808.

Jan. 22 Twenty Scottish Canadian curlers founded The Royal Montreal Curling Club, currently the oldest running sports club in North America still in continuous service.

Also in Jan.
• British Orders-in-Council, issued in retaliation against Napoleon's Continental System, instituted a blockade of all neutral commerce with Europe. A 2nd Order-in-Council was issued in Nov.

Feb. 2 The 3rd session of the 4th Parliament of Upper

Canada convened until Mar. 10. Business included provision for schools in every district.

Apr. 16 The Quebec Benevolent Society was incorporated.

June 1 Reverend Dr. George Okill Stuart (1776–1862) opened the Home District School, the 1st public school in York.

June 22 David Thompson, his wife and family reached Howse Pass while crossing the Rockies. They came to a small branch of the upper reaches of the Columbia R. known as Blaeberry R. Thompson was the 1st man of European descent to see the upper waters of the Columbia, which he named Kootenai R., a designation later given to the Columbia's main tributary. Thompson established Kootenai House, the 1st Columbia R. post, on June 25.

Also in June
• British frigate, *Leopard*, attacked the American warship *Chesapeake* off the coast of New England, killing and wounding its crew and impressing 5 men suspected of being deserters from the Royal Navy.

Summer New Fort, the NWC central depot at the western end of L. Superior, was officially renamed Fort William in support of the company leadership provided by William McGillivray.

July 24 At Niagara-on-the-Lake, Joseph Willcocks (1773–1814) began publishing the *Upper Canada Guardian* or *Freeman's Journal*, a small 4-page sheet, the 1st newspaper in Upper Canada opposing the govt.

Aug. 29 James Henry Craig (1748–1812) was appointed Gov-in-C of Upper and Lower Canada, succeeding Robert Shore Milnes. Craig served from Oct. 24, 1807 to Oct. 21, 1811.

Nov. 24 Joseph Brant (Thayendanegea), Iroquoian chief of the Six Nations, died at Burlington Bay, Upper Canada. He was born at Cuyahoga, near present-day Akron, Ohio, in Mar. 1742 or 1743.

Dec. 22 Thomas Jefferson persuaded the US Congress to pass the Embargo Act, stopping international trade at all American ports. He termed this action a "peaceful coercion" in response to Napoleon's Continental System and Britain's blockade of all neutral commerce with Europe.

Also in 1807

• The British parliament passed Orders-in-Council permitting British ships and Britain's allies to harass American vessels and, as necessary, to impress sailors of British background into the king's service.

• The Grammar School Act was passed.

• *The Royal Gazette* and *Newfoundland Advertiser* was 1st published.

• George Heriot published *Travels, Through the Canadas*, in London, a picturesque travel book in 2 volumes which contained much of Heriot's own artwork.

1808

Jan. 15 George Prevost (1767–1816) was commissioned lt-gov. of NS, succeeding Sir John Wentworth, and served from Apr. 13, 1808, to Aug. 25, 1811. He arrived in Halifax Apr. 7.

Jan. 29 The 4th session of the 4th Parliament of Lower Canada sat until Apr. 14. Business included provisions for funds to improve navigation on the St. Lawrence R.

Feb. 20 Joseph Willcocks, leader of the opposition in Upper Canada, was arrested for contempt in the House of Assembly, and imprisoned for making "false, slanderous, and highly derogatory" statements about Assembly members.

Apr. 20 David Thompson began a search to discover the route of the Columbia R. from British Columbia into the present state of Washington.

May 22 Simon Fraser arrived at Fort George, Prince George, BC, only to leave it 6 days later with John Stuart, Jules Maurice Quesnel (1786–1842), 19 voyageurs, 2 Aboriginal guides and 4 wooden dugout canoes to explore the river that now bears his name.

Also in May

• Portrait artist Robert Field (c 1769–1819) set up a studio in a bookshop on King Street in Halifax, NS, where he painted portraits of both Lt-Gov. Sir George Prevost and Sir John Wentworth, the New Hampshire Loyalist who had been the previous lt-gov.

July 2 Simon Fraser reached the village of Museum at the mouth of the Fraser, only a few km from the Pacific, and was forced to retreat up the Fraser R. when he encountered Cowichan warriors. Pursued by dozens of canoes, Fraser repelled each attack, arriving back at Fort George July 6. His 1,400 km exploration proved the entire length of the Fraser R. of no use as a travel route.

Nov. 29–Jan. 27, 1832 Francis Nathaniel Burton (1766–1832) served as lt-gov. of Lower Canada, content to be an absentee governor for most of his appointment, while collecting the requisite pay for 14 years. He did not arrive in Canada until 1822.

Also in 1808

• The 1st stagecoach, between Montreal and Kingston in Upper Canada, commenced operations.

• Toronto's 1st lighthouse, Gibraltar Point Lighthouse, located on Toronto Is. on L. Ontario, was opened. The lighthouse, which was originally 15.8 m tall, was raised to 24.9 m in 1832. It is now said to be haunted.

• Former US Vice-President Aaron Burr made a fleeting clandestine visit to Halifax in an effort to enlist Lt-Gov. Prevost's aid in establishing a new empire.

• Presbyterian minister and educator Thomas McCulloch (1776–1843) of Pictou, NS, published *Popery Condemned by Scripture and the Fathers*.

1809

Feb. 2 The 1st session of the 5th Parliament of Upper Canada met until Mar. 9. Business included the allocation of funds to build a bridge over the Grand R., and more encouragement for the killing of wolves.

Feb. 15 Thomas Talbot and Robert Nichol (c 1780–1824) received provincial commissions to determine the exact route of a proposed road that would link the Port Talbot settlement with the Niagara District. The completed road, known as the Talbot Road, was constructed by civilian rather than military labour under the direction of Mahlon Burwell (1783–1846).

Mar. 30 The Labrador Act established permanent courts of law in Nfld., and re-annexed Labrador to Nfld., so that Labrador settlers and fishermen would be protected by Nfld. warships.

Also in Mar.
• John Bruce began construction on the paddle-boat *Accommodation*. Ordered by John R. Molson for service on the St. Lawrence R., the Montreal-built boat carried a 21.6-m-long paddle. On Oct. 31, *Accommodation*, equipped with a Boulton & Watt engine, carried 10 passengers, including owner, John Molson, from Montreal to Que. on its maiden voyage. It arrived in Que. on Nov. 6. The *Accommodation* was retired from service in 1811.

May 15 Gov. James Henry Craig dissolved the Legislative Assembly of Lower Canada after Ezekiel Hart was expelled for the 2nd time because he was Jewish. The colonial secretary confirmed that a Jew could not sit in the legislature (Sept. 7) following Hart's expulsion. Nominated for the 3rd time by his constituents to sit in the Legislative Assembly, Ezekiel Hart declined because of his earlier expulsions. On June 5, 1832, the king gave Royal Assent to a bill passed by Lower Canada's legislature granting Jews the same political rights as Christians.

Nov. 2 King George III donated a communion plate to the Metropolitan Church Cathedral at Que.

c 1809 The Drury Lane Theatre opened in Saint John, NB. Experiencing financial difficulties, the building was sold in 1816. The new owners were not successful and the theatre was subsequently closed for good.

Also in 1809
• The 1st Canadian fire insurance company was founded in Halifax, appropriately named the Fire Insurance Association of Halifax.

• HBC paid out no shareholder dividends for the 1st

time in its history, because of declining fur prices and its struggle with the NWC.

• The 3rd oldest lighthouse in Canada still in its original form, the Île Verte (Green Is.) lighthouse, was completed on the seaward side of Île Verte, located opposite the village of L'Isle-Verte. It was the only light on the St. Lawrence R. for more than 20 years.

• Fur trader and merchant Alexander Henry (1739–1824) published *Travels and Adventures in Canada and the Indian Territories, between the Years 1760 and 1776*. This adventure classic was considered one of the best descriptions of First Nations life at the time.

• William Berczy painted *The Woolsey Family,* oil on canvas. Berczy charged £10 for each of the 8 family members in the painting but added the family dog for free. *The Woolsey Family* now hangs in the National Gallery of Canada.

1810

Feb. 1 The 2nd session of the 5th Parliament of Upper Canada convened until Mar. 12. Business included legislation against forgery, and a tax on billiard tables.

Mar. 17 Gov-in-C of Lower Canada, James Craig, ordered presses of the newspaper *Le Canadien* seized for treacherous remarks about the "govt's rabble." Many *Le Canadien* employees and associates were imprisoned on charges of treacherous practices.

Also in Mar.
• The 1st issue of the *Kingston Gazette* (now the *Whig-Standard*) was published.

July 22 Explorer David Thompson was ordered to complete his exploration of the Columbia R. to its mouth, forestalling American traders believed to be heading to the area. He set out on his trek Sept. 8.

Aug. 23 John Jacob Astor (1763–1848) purchased the 269-tonne ship *Tonquin* (built in New York), to allow his recently founded Pacific Fur Company (PFC) to compete against the NWC. On Sept. 6, Astor's ship, *Tonquin,* sailed from New York for the mouth of the

Columbia R., where the PFC intended to found a fur-trading post.

Also in Aug.

• Tecumseh met with William Henry Harrison (1773–1841), gov. of the newly created Indiana Territory, at Vincennes, Indiana, and conveyed to him the aims of his confederacy: unification of tribes and the establishment of the principle of common ownership of land by First Nations.

Sept. 3 Canadian artist Paul Kane (1810–1871) was born in Mallow, County Cork, Ireland, to Michael and Frances Loach Kane. Kane would become the most famous artist-explorer in Canada.

Nov. 6 The 1st steamboat in Canada, *Acachan*, made its maiden voyage from Montreal to Quebec carrying a total of 10 passengers. Built entirely of Canadian wood and iron, the vessel remained in service on the Montreal–Quebec route for slightly over 4 months.

Dec. 3 David Thompson reached the Athabasca R. where he rested briefly before continuing his journey on snowshoes in sub-zero weather towards the Rocky Mountains.

Dec. 12 The 1st session of the 7th Parliament of Lower Canada met until Mar. 21, 1811. Business included legislation against forgery.

1810–1883 Bad Head (Pakap-otokan), also known as Father of Many Children (Manistokos [d 1884]), kept a winter count of the Blackfoot First Nation. This record, painted on a tanned hide, is one of the few written historical records of Blackfoot activities and events of the period.

Also in 1810

• A subsidy of £43 was offered to farmers in Lower Canada for every tonne of hemp grown.

• Canadian-born Charles-Michel d'Irumberry De Salaberry (1778–1829), serving with distinction in the British army, was recalled to Canada, given the rank of lt. col., and assigned the task of recruiting and training a volunteer militia. On Apr. 15, 1812, the "Régiment de Voltigeurs Canadiens," a light infantry of French Canadians, was formed. De

Salaberry was a strict disciplinarian, and drilled his troops as if they were regular infantrymen. He subsidized the unit when govt funds were not forthcoming. His Voltigeurs proved themselves a crack regiment time and again during the War of 1812.

• John Strachan published *A Discourse on the Character of King George the Third* for the purpose of arousing patriotism and loyalty to the king.

• Presbyterian minister and educator Thomas McCulloch published *Popery Condemned Again*, a follow-up to his 1808 publication.

1811

Jan. 10 Thompson crossed the Rocky Mountains through the Athabasca Pass. On July 3, he set off down the Columbia R., and erected a British flag where the Snake R. joined the Columbia, near present-day Kennewick, Washington, claiming the country for Britain. He reached the Pacific Ocean at Cape Disappointment on July 15, the 1st European to follow the Columbia R. from its source to the Pacific. Thompson also called at the recently established American Fort Astoria, commanded by former Nor'Wester Duncan McDougall (d 1818) who represented Astor's PFC. On July 22 Thompson turned east from Fort Astoria, wintering in west Man.

Also in Jan.

• Nfld. Gov. Duckworth ordered naval officer David Buchan (1780–1830) to lead an expedition to contact the Beothuk. Buchan made contact with 75 Beothuk camped on Red Indian L., but the encounter went awry and Buchan returned to the Bay of Exploits, Nfld. (Jan. 30) after 2 of his mariners were killed.

• The South West Trading Company was formed by John Jacob Astor and principal shareholders of the NWC to delineate trading areas between the US and Canada.

Feb. 2 US President Madison demanded Britain rescind its policy of promoting British harassment of US ships.

Feb. 3 Alexander Henry the younger (d 1814) set out to find the source of the Sask. R.

May 3 Lord Selkirk, major HBC stockholder, bought 300,000 km^2 of settlement in Manitoba, Minnesota, and North Dakota from the HBC for 10 shillings. In return he agreed to establish an agricultural settlement, known as the Red R. colony, or Assiniboia. The deal was strongly opposed by the NWC on grounds that settlement would destroy the fur trade.

May 15 The British cargo ship *Fortune* sailed to Quebec City and announced its victory over a French privateer on Apr. 13. The privateer, with a crew of 120 men, had attacked the *Fortune*'s 19 passengers and crew, but a chance *Fortune* shot broke the French ship's fore-topmast, ending the battle.

• The PFC's ship *Tonquin,* while on a trading cruise, was attacked and seized by Nootka on Vancouver Is. Most on board were slain. The ship was blown up and sunk the next day with its captain, Jonathon Thorn, on board.

June 19–Sept.14 Thomas Dunn (1729–1818) served as administrator of Lower Canada.

July 4 George Prevost was promoted to Lt-Gen. and commander of British forces in North America.

July 26 The 1st shipload of Selkirk colonists, under Miles Macdonell (c 1767–1828), sailed from Scotland for Red R. They landed at York Factory, Hudson Bay, on Oct. 9, and remained there for the winter.

Sept. 14–July 15, 1812 George Prevost served as administrator of Lower Canada. His 1st task was to make a rapid tour of the Montreal region where he determined the colony was largely governed (if unofficially) by the clergy. Prevost sought clerical support for a new militia bill. He also needed the clergy as counterweight to nationalists and the democratically inclined Canadian party. On Oct. 21, Prevost was commissioned Gov-in-C of BNA, serving from July 15, 1812 to Apr. 4, 1814.

Oct. 9–Oct. 3, 1812 Maj-Gen. Isaac Brock (1769–1812) served as administrator and commander of the Upper Canadian forces.

Also in Oct.
• Moravian missionary Benjamin Gottlieb Kohlmeister (1756–1844) completed an expedition to Ungava Bay where he hoped to contact Inuit of the area and expand his missionary work in the North. His expedition was unsuccessful.

Nov. 7 An American force under Gov. William Henry Harrison attacked Tecumseh's Shawnee at Tippecanoe, Indiana, near the Shawnee village of Prophetstown. Tecumseh was not present; his brother Prophet was defeated. The Shawnee abandoned the town. Harrison was rebuked by US President Madison as to whether the attack was warranted, but went on to political success based on its result.

Also in Nov.
• Thomas Thomas (c 1766–1828), superintendent of the Southern department of the HBC, was appointed a justice of the peace for the area, holding the office until 1816.

• NS entrepreneur Enos Collins (1774–1871) purchased a captured Spanish schooner sold at an auction in Halifax for £420. He named the ship the *Liverpool Packet* and after utilizing it briefly as a transport for passengers and mail between Halifax and Liverpool, NS, commissioned it as a privateer during the war of 1812. The *Liverpool Packet* received its 1st letter of marque on Aug. 20, 1812 against the French and on enemies of the British Commonwealth. Over the next 2 years, under several captains, the *Packet* roamed up and down the northeastern Atlantic seaboard seeking prizes. Captured briefly by the Americans, recaptured by the British and auctioned once again to Enos Collins for another £420, the *Liverpool Packet* captured a total of 50 prizes — a record unequalled by any other ship — British or American.

1811–1812 Repeated Magnitude 8 earthquakes occurred near the community of New Madrid in what is now Missouri. Vibrations were felt as far north as Montreal.

Also in 1811
• Canada shipped 23,053 ships' masts, 24,469 loads of oak and 52,888 loads of pine to British shipyards.

• Johan Schiller planted a 20-acre (8-ha) vineyard in Ont. with lubrusca vines found along the Credit R., west of Toronto. It was the 1st recorded vineyard in the country.

1812

Feb. 3 The 4th session of the 5th Parliament of Upper Canada met until Mar. 6. Business included legislation to raise troops of volunteers.

Feb. 21 The 2nd session of the 7th Parliament of Lower Canada met until May 19. Business included a grant of money for the defence of Lower Canada.

Mar. 9 The letters of British spy John Henry (c 1776–1853), which helped precipitate the War of 1812, were read to the US Congress.

Mar. 13 David Thompson left Saleesh House for Montreal via Fort William on his last journey east. He arrived in Montreal on Aug. 24 whereupon he settled in Terrebone to produce his map. The NWC granted him a year's allowance to cover his supplies, and a 7-year pension once he had completed the work. The map was hung in the NWC's dining hall at Fort William.

Apr. 10 The US called out its militia forces in preparation for war against Canada.

Apr. 12 Alexander Mackenzie, 48, announced his marriage to 14-year-old Geddes MacKenzie. The couple then retired to an estate in Scotland.

Also in Apr.
• Gov-in-C Prevost obtained the new militia act he sought from the House of Assembly as well as funds for the defence of Canada.

May 28 Lower Canada passed a general order to employ 4 regiments of militia.

June 1 US President James Madison (1751–1836) sent a message to Congress that listed grievances against Britain and called for a declaration of war. Major grievances included: impressment of American seamen for service in the Royal Navy; violation of US neutrality rights and territorial waters, blockade of US ports; and the refusal of Britain to revoke the Orders-in-Council of 1807, which had instituted the blockade of Europe to prevent war supplies from reaching France. Britain was also

blamed for supporting First Nations peoples in the western US who opposed westward expansion. Other interests in the US wanted the lands of Upper Canada for American settlement. Although the New England states and many maritime and commercial groups opposed the war, the pro-war party (known as Hawks) from the southern and western areas secured a majority.

June 18 US Congress declared war on Britain with the objective of "liberating" Canada. Madison declared a state of war with Britain the next day. The War of 1812 would last 2 years.

June 22 The garrison at Halifax received warning from the British ambassador in Washington that there might be war between Britain and the US.

June 27 War between Britain and the US was confirmed when the British frigate *Belvidera* sailed into Halifax after suffering damage and 2 fatalities in an attack by 5 American ships.

June 30 Upper Canada gave American citizens 14 days to leave the province.

Also in June
• John Strachan, with his family, arrived in York as rector and chaplain of the garrison and Legislative Council.

July 3 Frederic Rolette (1785–1831) captured American Brig-Gen. William Hull's (1753–1825) hired schooner, *Cuyahoga,* destined for Detroit loaded with American sick, advance supplies and Hull's personal luggage containing detailed plans for his invasion of Canada. Hull was not aboard.

July 5 Brig-Gen. Hull, gov. of the Michigan Territory, arrived with 2,000 men at Detroit, the staging ground for his planned invasion of Canada.

July 12 About 2,500 Americans under Hull crossed the river from Detroit into Upper Canada, launching the 1st American invasion of the war. The Americans took peaceful possession of François Baby's farm near Sandwich (Windsor), and issued a proclamation stating that the US offered Peace, Liberty, and Security: the alternative was War, Slavery, and Destruction.

July 17 Captain Charles Roberts (c 1772–1816), supported by 600 British, Aboriginals and Canadians, captured Fort Michilimackinac in Michigan territory.

July 22 Gen. Isaac Brock issued a Canadian proclamation to counter that issued by American commander Gen. Hull.

July 27 The 5th session of the 6th Parliament of Upper Canada met until Aug. 5. Business included an act for the defence of the province.

July 28 Gen. Brock asked the legislature of Upper Canada to repeal *habeas corpus*, and to impose martial law. The legislature declined.

Aug. 2 Huron living near Detroit allied themselves with the British.

Aug. 5 Gen. Brock left Niagara for Detroit with the intention of capturing that outpost.

• First Nations, commanded by Shawnee chief Tecumseh (commissioned a brig-gen. by the British), slipped across the Detroit R. near Amherstburg into American territory, cutting Hull's supply line by ambushing one of the provision parties near Brownstown (by Trenton, Michigan).

Aug. 6 Gov. Prevost and US Gen. Dearborn signed an armistice ending the War of 1812, but the peace agreement was revoked by the US Congress on Aug. 29.

Aug. 8 Gen. Brock moved a small force of about 300 men, including 50 regulars, from Long Point to Amherstburg on the Detroit R., reaching his destination on Aug. 13. Tecumseh joined him with 600 troops the following day to begin the siege of Detroit and its 2,000 defenders.

Aug. 10 Gen. Prevost was advised not to expect immediate military help from Britain, because of that country's need for forces to engage Napoleon.

Aug. 11 Brig-Gen. Hull withdrew from Canada and fell back on Detroit, although his force outnumbered the British and its allies 2 to 1.

Aug. 15 The Potawatomi captured the garrison at Fort Dearborn (Chicago), securing new self-confidence. As a result, hundreds of First Nations peoples abandoned their neutrality and joined Tecumseh's confederacy, which swelled to about 1,000 troops. The British, having retaken François Baby's farm, commenced firing on the American fort at Detroit.

Aug. 16 A force of 1,300 regulars, militia and Aboriginals, under Gen. Brock, accepted the surrender of Detroit from Gen. Hull, who had not fired a shot. Thirty-five guns and other stores were captured. Hull and 300 prisoners were taken to Montreal. Hull was later court-martialled by the Americans for treason but acquitted.

Aug. 19 The US ship *Constitution*, commanded by Isaac Hull, defeated the British *Guerrière*, under Capt. Dacres, off NS. The *Constitution* earned its nickname "Old Ironsides" in this battle as British cannonballs seemed to career off its sides.

Aug. 30 Miles Macdonell, Selkirk's agent and HBC-appointed gov. of Assiniboia, reached the forks of the Red and Assiniboine Rivers, with the 1st wave of Selkirk settlers. They established Fort Douglas (Winnipeg) near the NWC post Fort Gibraltar. On Sept. 4, Macdonell invited his brother-in-law, Alexander Macdonell, commander of Fort Gibraltar, along with his employees, local Métis and First Nations peoples, to a ceremony during which Selkirk's title to the colony was proclaimed amid the firing of guns and loud cheers. Macdonell sought to cultivate good relations with the Nor'Westers because his party of 70 settlers was not skilled in the art of pioneer survival.

Also in Aug.
• Joseph DesBarres (c 1721–1824), lt-gov. of PEI, was recalled by Lord Bathurst, colonial secretary, who charged James Bardin Palmer (c 1771–1833), leading member of the Loyal Electors, with disloyalty. The Electors opposed govt "Old Party" members, and were also criticized as American sympathizers. Palmer was also stripped of his public office under the charges .

Sept. 1 Isaac Chauncey (1772–1840) was appointed

commander of the US naval forces on the Great Lakes. He made Sackets Harbor his headquarters.

Sept. 21 Americans raided and captured Gananoque, Ont.

Also in Sept.

• Some 6,300 US troops, ranged along the Niagara R., faced 1,500 Canadian and British soldiers, and 250 Aboriginals, commanded by Gen. Brock.

• First Nations allied with Britain attacked Pigeon Roast Creek, Tennessee, and Forts Harrison, Madison and Wayne.

Oct. 4 The British were repulsed at Ogdensburg.

Oct. 9 Two British ships, *Detroit* and *Caledonia,* laden with over $200,000 worth of furs, were captured on L. Erie by Jesse Elliott (1739–1814) in a surprise attack. The *Detroit* was ultimately abandoned, but the *Caledonia* became an important member of the US Great Lakes fleet.

Oct. 13 Under Stephen Van Rensselaer, 1,300 American troops crossed the Niagara R. from Lewiston, New York, in 13 boats. Brock, 11.2 km away at Fort George, hurried to Queenston with British, Canadian and Aboriginal troops, under command of Capt. John Brant, son of Joseph. The Americans were forced back across the river: 90 American lives were lost, 100 were wounded, and nearly 900 were taken prisoner. The British and Canadians lost 112, including Gen. Brock, who was shot by a sniper. Following the Battle of Queenston Heights, Roger Hale Sheaffe (1763–1851) was made C-in-C of British forces and administrator of Upper Canada (serving until June 19, 1813).

Oct. 23 The British were defeated at St. Régis, Que.

Oct. 27 A 2nd party of Selkirk settlers arrived at the Red R.

Nov. 9 As military commander of Upper Canada, Sheaffe appointed alien boards at Niagara, York and Kingston to examine all persons claiming to be American citizens. His purpose was to determine which persons were, in fact, exempt from military service.

Nov. 10 An American fleet bombarded, then blockaded Kingston, Upper Canada. The blockade lasted through the winter season.

Nov. 20 US Maj-Gen. Henry Dearborn (1751–1829) invaded Lower Canada from Champlain, New York, with 2,000 Americans. The US advance guard under Gen. Zebulon Montgomery Pike (1779–1813) attacked Lacolle Mills, Que. Lt-Col. De Salaberry and a force of Canadian Voltigeurs and 300 Caughnawaga drove the Americans back to Champlain, leaving 5 Americans dead and 5 wounded. Dearborn withdrew his force to Plattsburgh, New York, where he set up winter quarters.

Nov. 28 A 2nd American attempt to cross the Niagara R. was repulsed.

Dec. 12 The Loyal and Patriotic Society of Upper Canada was formed to care for the wounded, help destitute families and provide comfort for soldiers. John Strachan became president and later treasurer, of the society.

Dec. 29 The 4th session of the 7th Parliament of Lower Canada met until Feb. 15, 1813. Business included an increase in the circulation of army bills, and a grant of £25,000 for the war effort.

Dec. 30 The HMS *Java* surrendered to the US *Constitution.*

Also in 1812

• Richard Pierpoint (c 1744–c 1838), former slave and Butler's Rangers veteran, wrote Maj-Gen. Brock asking permission to assemble an infantry Corps of "Coloured Men" to serve in the War of 1812. Pierpoint's request was refused but a Coloured Corps of Canada was authorized, with the command going to Capt. Robert Runchey, a white man. Pierpoint enlisted as a private at the age of 68. The Coloured Corps fought at Queenston Heights, Stoney Creek, Fort George and other locations. It was disbanded in 1815 — but its black veterans did not receive the 6 months' severance pay awarded other soldiers, and individual land grants were half the amount awarded their white peers.

• Thomas Davies (c 1737–1812) completed the watercolour *Montreal.*

1813

Jan. 22 Maj-Gen. Henry Proctor (1787–1859), with 500 soldiers and 800 Aboriginal allies commanded by Tecumseh, defeated the Americans under James Winchester at Frenchtown on the Raisin R., Ohio.

Also in Jan.
• News of the War of 1812 reached Astoria (at the mouth of the Columbia R.) along with word that a British warship was on its way to capture the post. Astor's partners in the PFC worked to arrange a quick sale of the entire enterprise to the NWC for $58,000, because American control of the Pacific Coast was now unstable. The official transfer took place on Oct. 16. Duncan McDougall, an Astorian and former Nor'Westerner, negotiated the transaction.

Feb. 6 An American force under Maj. Forsyth from Ogdensburg, New York, raided Brockville, Ont., taking 52 Canadians back to Ogdensburg as hostages, plus all the livestock they could round up.

Feb. 19 James Yeo (1782–1818) was appointed commodore and C-in-C on the lakes of Canada.

Feb. 22 Lt-Col. George Richard John "Red George" Macdonnell (1780–1870) led 500 troops in a successful retaliatory attack against the American fort at Ogdensburg, New York, destroying the fort.

Feb. 25 The 2nd session of the 6th Parliament of Upper Canada convened until Mar. 14. Business included the legalization of Army Bills issued in Lower Canada and the prohibition of the export of grain.

Also in Feb.
• American naval officer Oliver Hazard Perry (1785–1819) was commissioned to build a US fleet on L. Erie with which to attack the English.

Mar. The Western Rangers — Caldwell's Rangers — promoted by Colonel William Caldwell (c 1750–1822), was formed. The British unit was fashioned after Butler's Rangers of the American Revolutionary War; as camouflage its members wore green coats instead of the customary red.

Apr. 12 Six companies, 549 men of the 104th NB Regiment of Foot, arrived at Kingston, Upper Canada, from Fredericton, after a 52-day trek covering about 1,100 km. Not a man was lost, although the journey was extremely difficult.

Apr. 25 One thousand, seven hundred Americans under Gen. Pike and Commodore Isaac Chauncey sailed from Sackets Harbor, New York, to attack the York garrison under Gen. Sheaffe.

Apr. 27 Gen. Pike made an amphibious assault against York. The defenders, under Sheaffe, numbered only about 600. Sheaffe decided to retreat to Kingston with his regulars, and ordered the ammunition dump at Fort York blown up. The explosion killed 38 Americans, including Pike, and wounded 222. The Americans, however, captured the fort.

May 1 American troops occupying York burned and looted govt buildings. They abandoned the town on May 8.

May 5 James Yeo, with 450 seamen, arrived at Que. where he was promoted to commodore of the Royal Navy.

• Twelve hundred Kentuckians attempted unsuccessfully to relieve the besieged Fort Meigs on the Maumee R. near the western end of L. Erie, losing about 400 men. British losses numbered 15.

May 8 American forces arrived at Fort Niagara from York.

May 9 Maj-Gen. Proctor attempted to take Fort Meigs but was repulsed by Maj-Gen. Harrison, although the Americans suffered tremendous losses. Proctor attempted to besiege the fort but was forced to abandon the field when large numbers of his army deserted the cause.

May 27 Americans Chauncey and Dearborn with 7,000 men took Fort George at Niagara. John Vincent (1765–1848) retreated toward Burlington, Ont., with the remainder of his 1,400 men.

May 29 The Battle of Sackets Harbor was won by the Americans, under Gen. Jacob Brown, defending their naval base on L. Ont. The British, under George Prevost, halted what seemed to be a successful attack for fear of insufficient artillery support from a fleet of ships commanded by Yeo.

June 1 British HMS *Shannon* under Capt. Philip Vere Broke engaged the American ship *Chesapeake* commanded by Capt. James Lawrence (1781–1813). The *Chesapeake* was defeated. Forty-eight Americans and 23 British were killed.

June 3 Comm. Yeo left Kingston, Ont., for the Niagara Peninsula laden with supplies and accompanied by 300 soldiers.

June 6 Seven hundred British and Canadian troops, under Col. John Harvey (1778–1852), and their First Nations allies, under Lt-Col. John Brant, won the Battle of Stoney Creek in a surprise night attack against 2,000 Americans. American Gen.'s John Chandler and William Winder were captured along with 123 soldiers. The remaining American forces retreated to Fort George.

June 13 HMS *Shannon* arrived in Halifax harbour with US warship *Chesapeake* in tow.

June 19 Francis, Baron de Rottenburg (1757–1832), assumed command of British forces in Upper Canada. Sheaffe was transferred to Montreal. De Rottenburg also served as president of the Council and administrator of Upper Canada until Dec. 13, 1813.

June 21 Charles Boerstler and 570 Americans, on their way to attack the British outpost at Beaver Dams, Ont. (commanded by James Fitzgibbon [1780–1863]), stopped at the farm of James Secord for the night. Laura Secord (1775–1868), James's wife, overheard the American attack plan, and walked more than 32 km, over parts of the Niagara escarpment, to warn the British of an impending attack at Queenston, Ont. US victory would give the Americans control of the escarpment. Shortly before reaching the British camp, Secord met a group of Mohawk who guided her directly to Fitzgibbon.

June 24 Fitzgibbon's 50 men and 400 Mohawk allies captured 462 Americans near Beaver Dams. The remainder of the American force retreated to the New York side of the Niagara R. as British and Canadian forces reoccupied Fort Erie.

June 28 British Commander de Rottenburg forbade the distilling of rye in order to save food because of the serious supply shortage.

July 20 Duncan McDougall married the daughter of Chinook chief Comcomly (d c 1830), cementing trade ties between the NWC and the Chinook.

Also in July
• Canadian journalist and politician Joseph Willcocks crossed the Niagara R. and offered his services to the Americans. He raised and commanded a unit of expatriate Upper Canadians known as the Company of Canadian Volunteers. Willcocks was killed in battle at Fort Erie in 1814, and, regarded as a traitor, posthumously stripped of his seat in the York legislature.

Aug. 2 Gen. Proctor failed to take Fort Stephenson (on the Sandusky R., Ohio), defended by Americans under Maj. George Croghan (1791–1849).

Sept. 10 American Lt. Oliver Hazard Perry (1785–1819) with 9 ships defeated Capt. Robert H. Barclay (1786–1837) with 6 ships in the Battle of L. Erie at Put-in-Bay, L. Erie. Here Perry uttered his famous words, "We have met the enemy and they are ours." Barclay's entire fleet was captured or destroyed. Perry lost his flagship.

Sept. 18 Americans under Gen. Harrison forced Gen. Proctor to evacuate Detroit and retreat to Canada for lack of naval support. Tecumseh had pleaded with Proctor to remain and fight, to no avail.

Oct. 5 The Americans captured 6 British schooners carrying reinforcements to Kingston.

• Gen. Harrison crossed into Ont. and won a victory at Moraviantown on the Thames R. against Proctor. The great Chief Tecumseh was killed in the battle. His body was never found.

Oct. 17 Harrison notified civil servants in the holding office in Upper Canada's Western District that they would keep their jobs as long as they took an oath of allegiance to the US.

Oct. 26 Lt-Col. Charles De Salaberry's 400 Voltigeurs repulsed 4,000 infantry and a squadron of calvary and 170 First Nations allies under Gen. Wade Hampton (1818–1902) at Chateauguay.

Nov. 1 US Gen. James Wilkinson (1757–1825) moved

his forces down the St. Lawrence R. from L. Ontario to attack Montreal.

Nov. 11 Eight hundred Canadian and British soldiers, under Lt. Col. Joseph W. Morrison (1783–1826), defeated 1,800 Americans, under Gen. Wilkinson, in the Battle of Crysler's Farm, halting the American advance and causing abandonment of the campaign against Montreal.

Nov. 12 John George McTavish (c 1778), fur trader and son of McTavish clan chief Alexander McTavish, took possession of Astoria for the NWC.

Nov. 30 The ship *Raccoon*, commanded by Capt. William Black, arrived at Fort Astoria to support British claims. John McDonald of Garth took charge of the fort.

Dec. 10 The American garrison at Fort George crossed the border to Fort Niagara, burning Newark (Niagara-on-the-Lake, Ont.) the next day, leaving 400 residents homeless.

Dec. 12 Capt. Black renamed Fort Astoria, Fort George, after the king of England, and with his associates, McTavish and McDonald, took possession of the surrounding lands for George III.

Dec. 13–Apr. 25, 1815 Gordon Drummond (1772–1854) served as President of the Council and administrator of Upper Canada.

Dec. 18–19 John Murray crossed the Niagara R. with 550 British-Canadian troops, taking and sacking Fort Niagara in a surprise night attack. Phineas Riall (1775–1850) entered New York with a party of Aboriginal soldiers and burned Lewiston, Manchester, Fort Schlosser, Black Rock and Buffalo in a campaign (lasting to Dec. 30) to avenge the American burning of Newark.

Dec. 19 Montreal merchant James McGill (1744–1813) died, leaving his 18.6-ha estate, Burnside Place, and £10,000 to the Royal Institution for the Advancement of Learning as an endowment for the establishment of McGill College.

Also in 1813
• The HBC moved Edmonton House to its permanent location within the present city limits.

• The whaling industry at Fort Churchill collapsed.

1814

Jan. 8 Assiniboia Gov. Miles Macdonell issued a proclamation prohibiting the export of provisions of any kind from within the limits of Assiniboia without a special licence from himself. The proclamation, known as the Pemmican Proclamation, was issued to help solve the colony's food problems and control trade, but Nor'Westers and Métis viewed it as a distinct infringement on their rights and an open declaration of war.

Jan. 13 The 5th session of the 7th Parliament of Lower Canada met until Mar. 17. Business included the extension of the Army Bill Act to allow the issue of £1.5 million in currency.

Feb. 15 The 3rd session of the 6th Parliament of Upper Canada convened until Mar. 14. Business included the Militia Bill, and the power to detain suspected traitors.

Also in Feb.
• An American force, from Detroit, raided Port Talbot, Ont.

• Gov. Macdonell dispatched Red R. Sheriff John Spencer to raid the Nor' Wester camp at Souris and to seize all pemmican (dried buffalo meat) there.

Mar.–May Commodore Yeo blockaded the American squadron at Sackets Harbor.

Mar. 4 One hundred and eighty American and 300 British troops engaged in the Battle of Longwoods between London and Thamesville, Ont., as the Americans attempted to capture the British posts of Talbot and Delaware. Although outnumbered, the Americans held the better position. The British, with 52 wounded, retreated after losing 14 men.

Mar. 30 Gen. Wilkinson crossed into Canada with 4,000 US troops, but was defeated by the British at Lacolle, Que., and forced to retreat to Plattsburg, New York.

Spring Gov. Macdonell confiscated pemmican from Métis at their Turtle R. Plains camp.

Apr. 15 The British warships *Prince Regent* and *Princess Charlotte* were launched at Kingston, Ont.

May 5 Yeo attacked Oswego, New York, with 1,100 British troops. When the town surrendered the next day, Yeo blockaded the Americans.

May 15 Five hundred American troops crossed L. Erie to loot and burn Port Dover and Long Point, Ont.

May 18 Robert McDouall reached Michilimackinac (Lake Michigan) with 24 seamen and a company of Nfld. regulars, to prevent American seizure of that post. McDouall also had access to a company of the Michigan Fencibles, a unit drawn from the Canadian population around L. Michigan and commanded by William McKay (1772–1832). McKay headed for the Mississippi with 150 Fencibles and a war party of Green Bay warriors. He appeared at Prairie-du-Chien (in what is now Iowa) on July 17 and forced the US gunboat *Governor Clark* to withdraw. The small American garrison surrendered the next day.

May 22 Colin Robertson (1783–1842) sailed from Liverpool for Canada in the employ of the HBC which had accepted his plan of expansion into NWC territory.

Also in May

• Alexander Henry the younger and Donald McTavish drowned near Astoria, Washington, when, after steering out of Fort George, their open boat capsized as it approached the *Isaac Todd*.

June 2 Nineteen Canadians were tried for treason by 3 judges at Ancaster, Upper Canada, in what is known as the "Bloody Assize." Fifteen were convicted and sentenced to hang. On July 20, Aaron Stevens, Dayton Lindsey, Noah Hopkins, George Peacock Jr., Isaiah Brink, Ben Simmons, Adam Crysler and John Durham were hanged at Burlington, Ont. The remaining five were sentenced to exile.

June 28 The HBC Selkirk colony and the NWC reached a temporary compromise regarding pemmican.

July–Sept. British and Canadian soldiers captured Eastport, Hampden and Bangor, and other areas in Maine.

July 3 Americans, with 5,000 men under Gen. Jacob Brown, took Fort Erie, commanded by Maj-Gen. Phineas Riall, who withdrew toward Fort George. Brown defeated Riall's 1,800 men at Chippewa or Street's Creek on July 5.

July 22 The Shawnee, Delaware, Seneca, Wyandot and Miami sided with the US in its war against Britain.

July 24-25 The Battle of Lundy's Lane began with 3,090 men, under the command of British Gen. Gordon Drummond, against 4,200 men under the command of American Gen. Jacob Brown, including 150 Canadian expatriate volunteers under the command of Joseph Willcocks. The battle proved indecisive. Americans withdrew to Fort Erie, but Canadians could not claim a victory. This was one of the most bitterly contested and bloodiest battles in the war, claiming 1,700 dead in the 5-hour clash.

Also in July

• A NWC trading post at what is now Sault Ste. Marie was burned by the Americans.

Aug. 4 Col. McDouall, with a garrison of less than 200 men, defeated an American attack on Michilimackinac, led by Maj. George Croghan commanding 750 men.

Aug. 8 Negotiations between the US and Britain to end the War of 1812 commenced in Ghent, Belgium.

Aug. 14–15 British troops under Gen. Drummond (1772–1854) carried out an abortive night attack on the American garrison at Fort Erie. The British were repulsed and suffered 900 casualties.

Aug. 15 American ships *Niagara*, *Tigress* and *Scorpion*, with 300 troops, attacked the British ship *Nancy* under Capt. Miller Worsley, at Wasaga Beach on Georgian Bay. The *Nancy* was carrying supplies to Michilimackinac. Worsley burned his ship to prevent capture.

Aug. 24 After landing in Chesapeake Bay, 4,000 British troops marched into Washington, D.C., setting fire to the Capitol, the White House and other govt buildings in retaliation for the American attacks on York and Newark.

Aug. 31 A British force led by John Sherbrooke, gov. of NS, attacked and captured Castine, Maine. On Sept. 10, Sherbrooke attacked Machias, Maine, bringing eastern Maine under British control.

Sept. 3–4 Worsley and 77 men boarded the American ship *Tigress* as it lay at anchor in False Detour Channel, about 88 km northeast of Mackinac Is. Worsley and his men had travelled from Georgian Bay by canoe after the loss of their ship *Nancy*. When the American ship *Scorpion* came into sight the next day, Worsley sailed the *Tigress*, still flying its American flag, out to meet it. As the ships came together, Worsley fired without warning and the *Scorpion* was quickly captured. Both ships sailed for Fort Michilimackinac.

Sept. 11 American Capt. Thomas Macdonough (1783–1825), commanding a squadron of 4 ships and 10 gunboats, defeated the British fleet, under Capt. George Downie, in the Battle of Plattsburg on L. Champlain. Capt. Downie was killed in the battle. Gen. George Prevost's British infantry, which had been reinforced with veterans in an attempt to launch a major British initiative down the Richelieu–Champlain corridor, was forced to retreat after the losses, leaving behind valuable supplies.

Sept. 14 The British broke off their 3-day attack on Baltimore and Fort McHenry. American lawyer Francis Scott Key (1779–1843) wrote "The Star Spangled Banner," the future American national anthem, while watching the bombardment.

Sept. 17 Americans, besieged at Fort Erie, left the fort to give battle to British forces under Gen. Drummond. Six hundred British soldiers were killed.

Sept. 21 Gen. Drummond lifted the siege of Fort Erie and retired to Chippawa in Upper Canada, ending the Niagara campaign.

Oct. 9 George Jehosaphat Mountain (1789–1863) preached the 1st service in the new Church of Christ in Montreal.

Oct. 10 The *St. Lawrence*, a 112-gun, 3-deck warship, the largest wooden ship ever built on fresh water, was launched at Kingston, Ont. Built under the command of Comm. Yeo, it was destined never to fire a shot in war.

• Traders at NWC Forts Dauphin, Gibraltar and Bas de la Rivière Winnipeg received notice from Gov. Macdonell to vacate their forts in 6 months, as these were declared property of Lord Selkirk.

Oct. 19 Following a brief battle at Cook's Mills, the Americans under Maj-Gen. George Izard blew up Fort Erie and retreated toward American territory.

Nov. 5 Gen. Drummond dispatched Captain James Fitzgibbon to Fort Erie. The fort was deserted.

Dec. 21 Maj-Gen. Proctor was tried by court martial at Montreal for his defeat at Moraviantown. Convicted, he was suspended for 6 months without pay.

Dec. 24 The Treaty of Ghent was signed by the US and Britain, officially ending the War of 1812. Britain gave up occupied territory at Fort Niagara, Michilimackinac, Prairie de Chien and part of Maine, while the US returned Sandwich and Fort Malden in Upper Canada. The boundaries of 1783 were restored.

Dec. 28 Gordon Drummond was appointed administrator of Lower Canada, serving from Apr. 4, 1815–May 21, 1816.

Also in 1814

• British warships transported close to 2,000 freed slaves from the US South to Canada, most of whom settled in the Halifax area.

• The Northern Department of Rupert's Land was divided into the districts of York Factory, Saskatchewan Inland, Churchill Inland, West Winnipeg, East Winnipeg and Rocky Mountain.

• Because all heavy artillery and ammunition needed in the war effort had to be transported by the St. Lawrence R., the Ordnance Department found its annual expenditures tripling over a 3-year period to £341,000 — as some 10,000 persons were required to move the supplies.

• Lt. George Macdonnell, a Canadian serving with the British army, proposed a series of canals connecting the Rideau interior to Kingston.

• Thompson revised his detailed map of the NWT *(Map of the Northwest Territories of the Province of Canada from actual survey during the years 1792–1812)*. The work measures almost 2 m x 3 m, and is currently housed at the Archives of Ont.

• *A Treatise on the Population, Wealth, and Resources of the British Empire* by Patrick Colquhoun (1745–1820) suggested that England's overpopulation and stagnation could be overcome by migration to the colonies, where colonists could consume British manufactured goods and provide raw materials for British factories.

1815

Jan. 10 Britain prohibited American citizens from settling in Canada.

Jan. 21 The 1st session of the 8th Parliament of Lower Canada met until Mar. 25. Business included grants to build the Lachine–Montreal Canal, to encourage vaccination, to publish maps of Canada and to establish a parliamentary library.

Mar. 1 The Lower Canada militia was disbanded.

Mar. 2 George Prevost was superseded as gov. and summoned to London to defend himself against charges concerning his conduct in the Plattsburgh campaign. These charges were laid by James Yeo, C-in-C on the Lakes of Canada. Prevost left for London in early Apr., applauded by Canadians but reviled by the British. In Aug., a naval court martial decided, in line with Yeo's evidence, that the Plattsburgh defeat was the result of both Prevost's urging the naval squadron into premature action and his failure to provide support with his forces. When Prevost arrived in England he obtained the Duke of York's permission to be retried in person. On Jan. 5, Prevost died of dropsy at age 48, one week before his hearing.

Mar. 9 The Treaty of Ghent was proclaimed at Que.

Apr. 11 Eighty-four Highlanders arrived at Fort Douglas, Assiniboia at Red R., via Hudson Bay, bringing the population of settlers to 270.

Apr. 12 Robert Semple (1777–1816) was appointed gov. of the HBC's territories.

Apr. 24 The Canadian Corps of Voltigeurs was disbanded.

Apr. 25–July 1 George Murray (1772–1846) served as provisional lt-gov. of Upper Canada.

Also in Apr.
• Eight hundred black loyalists arrived in NS from the US.

May 15 Many Selkirk settlers, uneasy with the developing violence and the increasing tension between Métis and settlers in the colony, took advantage of the NWC's offer of free transportation back to Upper Canada and left the Red R. They arrived at present-day Holland Landing, Ont., on Sept. 5.

May 18 Colin Robertson, representing the HBC, set out for the interior of the country with 16 canoes, 160 voyageurs and 3 former Nor'Westers (John Clark, François Decoying and Robert Loan). His mission: to compete actively with the Nor'Westers.

May 22 Fort Niagara was returned to the US.

May 25 Three hundred and seventy black loyalists from the US arrived in Saint John, NB.

• Métis leader Cuthbert Grant (c 1796–1854) attacked the fort at the Red R. settlement, causing its remaining settlers to evacuate the site 2 days later. The settlement was burned.

May 29 An Order-in-Council declared Canada open to US citizens for commerce.

June 11 Duncan Cameron (c 1764–1848) of the NWC arrested both Sheriff Spencer and Gov. Macdonell and sent them back to Upper Canada for their support of the Red River colony and its conflict with the Nor'Westers. Macdonell was transported to Montreal as a criminal.

July 1–Sept. 21 Frederick Robinson (1763–1852) served as provisional lt-gov. of Upper Canada.

July 18 Michilimackinac was restored to the Americans.

Sept. 15 Colin Robertson (c 1779–1842) and Robert Semple arrived at Red R. to restore the HBC settlement. A new group of colonists arrived at Red R. from Hudson Bay later in 1815.

Sept. 21–Jan. 6, 1818 Francis Gore served as lt-gov. of Upper Canada.

Also in Oct.

• John Clarke (1781–1852) led a force of nearly 100 men for the HBC and established Fort Wedderburn on Potato Is. in L. Athabasca across from the NWC's Fort Chipewyan (Alb.).

Nov. 3 Robert Semple was made Gov-in-C of Rupert's Land, and left Robertson in charge of the Red R. colony.

Nov. 15 John Wilson (1776–1833) was appointed administrator of Lower Canada. He served between May 21 and July 12, 1816.

Nov. 17–18 The Chippewa ceded 101,000 ha in Simcoe County, Upper Canada, for £4,000.

Nov. 23 The 1st street lamps in Canada were installed by private citizens on St. Paul Street west of the Old Market, in Montreal. They were fuelled by whale oil.

Dec. 16 John Molson purchased a private residence in Montreal. He added 2 wings the following year, and turned the structure into the Mansion House Hotel.

Also in 1815

• HBC paid out dividends to its shareholders — the 1st issued since 1808.

• Sancho and Peter Byers, 2 black residents of Charlottetown, PEI, were hanged for theft and larceny, respectively. Sancho Byers had stolen a loaf of bread and 454 g of butter, a value of 1 shilling. Peter Byers was convicted of stealing 5 shillings, property of James Gibson.

• Britain amended its Corn Laws to allow wheat to be imported duty-free when British wheat sold at over 80 shillings per quarter (1 quarter equalled 8 bushels). Colonial wheat could enter the country at a reduced rate when British wheat was over 67 shillings.

• Irish-born Attorney Gen. of NS, Richard John Uniacke (1753–1830), completed Uniacke House located 50 km west of Halifax. The 400-ha property was eventually extended by Uniacke to 4,720 ha and renamed Mount Uniacke. Uniacke's Georgian-style home is now one of the many historic buildings and properties owned and operated by the Nova Scotia Museum.

• David Thompson (1770–1857) and his family moved to Williamstown, Glengarry City, Upper Canada.

• William Smith (1769–1847) published his 2-volume *History of Canada*, the 1st English-language history of Canada.

• John Rodgers Jewitt, with the help of Richard Alsop, published *A Narrative of the Adventures and Sufferings of John R. Jewitt*, an expanded and improved version of the original, *A Journal Kept at Nootka Sound*.

1816

Feb. 6 The 5th session of the 6th Parliament of Upper Canada met until Apr. 1. Business included the establishment of common schools and appropriations for a parliamentary library.

Feb. 12 St. John's, Nfld., was almost completely destroyed by fire. On Nov. 21, 1817, fire again severely damaged the city, destroying about 300 homes and rendering 2,000 people homeless.

Feb. 14 The 1st coach between Halifax and Pictou (NS) carried 6 passengers, each of whom paid $6 for the journey.

Mar. 10 Jean-Baptiste Lagimodière arrived in Montreal after travelling almost 2,900 km from Red R. to bring Lord Selkirk news of the colony.

Mar. 17 Colin Robertson seized the NWC Fort Gibraltar and destroyed it. He arrested Duncan Cameron and sent him to England. It would be 17 months before Cameron returned to Canada.

May 21 The *General Smythe*, the 1st steamboat in the Maritimes, built by United Empire Loyalist John Ward, began operating on the Saint John R.

It carried 60 passengers and could reach a speed of 6 knots. Described as a floating palace, the vessel sailed between Saint John and Fredericton.

Also in May

• Peter Skene Ogden (c 1790–1854), clerk for the NWC, was involved in the murder at Green L. of an Aboriginal who persistently traded with the HBC.

June 1 Cuthbert Grant and his Métis captured HBC's Brandon House, hoping to facilitate passage of NWC supply boats down the Assiniboine R.

June 7 The Columbia district was divided into 2 parts. James Keith (1784–1851), a NWC partner, was in charge of Fort George and the coastal district. Donald Mckenzie (1783–1851) took charge of the inland district.

June 11 Colin Robertson left the Red R. settlement to return to England because of a conflict with the gov. of the colony, Robert Semple, over the supplying of pemmican to NWC brigades. Robertson was opposed to this policy.

June 19 The Battle of Seven Oakes occurred near Frog Plain in Assiniboia when Métis, led by Cuthbert Grant, attempting to transport supplies to the NWC, were challenged by Gov. Robert Semple. Semple and 20 of his men were killed. One Métis was also killed. Red R. colonists abandoned their settlement and took refuge at Norway House, an HBC post at the north end of L. Winnipeg on June 22. Métis poet and troubadour Pierre Falcon (1793–1876), who participated in the battle, wrote the Métis anthem *Chanson de la Grenouillère* in commemoration.

Aug. 12 Selkirk, with a private army of discharged veterans, seized the NWC's Fort William (Thunder Bay, Ont.) and arrested several Nor'Westers for treason, conspiracy, accessory to murder and complicity in the deaths of the Red R. colonists at Seven Oakes. Among those arrested were William McGillivray and 14 other NWC partners, all of whom were sent to Montreal for trial. The entire contents of the depot valued at £100,000 were seized. Selkirk sent Miles Macdonell and 140 men to recapture Fort Daer and Fort Douglas.

Sept. 7 The 51-m-long paddle steamer *Frontenac*, built on L. Ont. and launched into the Bay of Quinte at Bath, near Kingston, was the 1st steamship on the Great Lakes. The *Frontenac* ran between Prescott and York for a fare of $12, 1-way, including food.

Sept. 20 Stagecoach operations began between York and Niagara.

Sept. 28 John Caldwell and John Davidson formed a company with Montreal merchants Hiram Nicholas, François Languedoc, and John White, John Goudie of Que., and Pointe-Levy merchant Richard Lilliot to put a steamship into passenger and freight service between the 2 shores of the St. Lawrence R.

Oct. 24 George Ramsay (1770–1838), Earl of Dalhousie, arrived in Halifax to assume the duties of lt-gov. of NS.

Oct. 30 A Commission of Enquiry was established to mediate between Selkirk, the HBC and the NWC. William Coltman (d 1826) and John Fletcher (1784–1844) were appointed commissioners.

1816–1826 David Thompson accepted a position as astronomer and surveyor for a boundary commission created under the articles of the Treaty of Ghent to determine the precise location of the border with the US.

Also in 1816

• The legislature of Upper Canada supported by Lt-Gov. Francis Gore passed a Common School Act, which was largely drafted by John Strachan.

• Thomas Douglas, 5th Earl of Selkirk, published in London *A Sketch of the British Fur Trade in North America; with Observations Relative to the North-West Company of Montreal.*

1817

Jan. 1 The 1st agricultural society in NS was established at West R., Pictou County.

Jan. 4 Stagecoach service was inaugurated between Kingston and York, Ont., the fare being set at $18.

Jan. 10 Miles Macdonell and members of De Meuron's Regiment captured Fort Douglas on the Red R. from the NWC in an effort to resume control over the Selkirk colony.

Jan. 23 Archibald Norman McLeod, NWC partner and justice of the peace, imprisoned John Clarke, leader of the HBC expedition aimed at countering the NWC's trading activity in the Athabasca country.

Apr. 28-29 The Rush-Bagot Agreement was signed at Washington, D.C., by Charles Bagot (1781–1843) for Britain and Richard Rush (1780–1859) for the US. It restricted naval forces on the Great Lakes to 1 ship each on L. Champlain and L. Ontario and to 2 on the upper Great Lakes, all ships to be under 100 tonnes.

Also in Apr.
• Robert Nichol, a member of the Assembly at York (Toronto), moved to lift the ban on American settlement in Canada and also to list Crown reserves for sale. Lt-Gov. Francis Gore discontinued the Assembly, preventing the adoption of Nichol's resolutions.

May 1 A Royal proclamation was made against "open warfare in the Indian territories."

May 19 Articles of Association were adopted for the oldest Canadian chartered bank, the Bank of Montreal, which was officially founded on June 23 with capital of £250,000. On Nov. 3, the bank opened for business in a rented house in Montreal. The enterprise was spearheaded by John Richardson (1755–1831) and 8 Montreal merchants. In Jan. 1818, the bank initiated its 1st foreign-exchange deal by sending 130,000 Spanish dollars to Boston for the China trade.

June 10 Samuel Smith (1756–1826) was appointed administrator of Upper Canada, serving from Aug. 13 until 1818.

June 21 Selkirk arrived at Fort Douglas, followed by Commissioner Coltman with a proclamation requiring both to restore all goods seized during the dispute. Selkirk complied but the Nor'Westers refused and fled to avoid arrest. Selkirk appointed Alexander Macdonell gov. of the colony.

July 17 Construction of the Lachine Canal was begun, undertaken by a private consortium.

July 18 Selkirk negotiated the 1st treaty with western Cree and Ojibwa, on behalf of Britain. It involved land along the Red and Assiniboine Rivers, from the mouth of the Red R. as far south as Red Lake R., and along the Assiniboine R. beyond Portage la Prairie to Musk Rat Creek.

Nov. 24 A 3-member international commission established under the Treaty of Ghent awarded the islands of Passamaquoddy Bay (NB) to Britain, except Moose, Dudley, and Frederick Islands, which went to the US.

Also in 1817
• An investigation upheld the claim of Selkirk that settlement of his Red R. colony had been disrupted by the NWC.

• John Elliott Woolford (1778–1866) completed the watercolour *View on the Road from Windsor to Horton by Avon Bridge at Gaspreaux River.*

1818

Jan. 6 Peregrine Maitland (1877–1854) was commissioned lt-gov. of Upper Canada. He served from Aug. 13 to Aug. 28, 1828.

Feb. 5 The 2nd session of the 7th Parliament of Upper Canada convened until Apr. 1. Business included provision for the registration of wills and deeds.

Also in Feb.
• Reformer Robert Fleming Gourley (1778–1863) championed the cause of lifting the ban on American immigration to Upper Canada and accused the provincial govt of supporting "a system of paltry patronage and ruinous favoritism."

Mar. An indictment against Peter Skene Ogden of the NWC, for the 1816 murder of an Aboriginal at Green L., was drawn up in Lower Canada, Ogden charged that the man had been trading with rival HBC. The NWC quickly transferred Ogden to its Columbia Department (Fort George), to keep him outside the reach of the law.

Apr. 1 The legislature of Lower Canada passed an act incorporating the Company of Proprietors of the Chambly Canal, to build a canal on the Richelieu R. between Chambly and St. Jean, Que. Construction did not begin until 1833.

Apr. 13 Farmer and writer Robert Fleming Gourlay chaired the 1st official meeting of reformers in Upper Canada.

Apr. 18 The *Alexander* and the *Isabella*, under John Ross, left London on an expedition in search of the Northwest Passage. Another expedition, led by Cmdr. David Buchan, in the barque *Dorothea,* and John Franklin (1786–1847) commanding the brig *Trent*, headed for the North Pole ice pack. The Buchan-Franklin Arctic expedition was forced to return to England on June 30 when stopped by impenetrable ice.

May 8 Charles Lennox, Duke of Richmond (1764–1819), was appointed Gov-Gen. of Canada, serving from July 30, 1818–Aug. 28, 1819.

May 20 William Williams (d 1837) was appointed by the HBC as Gov-in-C of Rupert's Land.

May 27 Halifax, NS, and Saint John, NB, were declared custom-free zones or free ports.

June 9 The Bank of Que. was founded with capital of £75,000.

June 13 Richard Talbot (1772–1853) sailed for Canada with 200 Irish immigrants, many from North Tipperary, who settled in Carleton County, Ont. The British govt provided free passage, which cost a total of £1,270.

June 30 William Coltman (d 1826), a commissioner investigating the crisis between the HBC, the NWC, and Selkirk and his Red R. colony, submitted his report. He condemned all parties for the violence, which had culminated in the Battle of Seven Oaks.

July 15 Robert Gourlay was tried in Kingston for sedition and libel under the Alien Act of 1804, after challenging colonial authorities on the land grant system. He was acquitted. On July 31, Gourlay was again brought to trial, charged with sedition and libel, this time in Brockville, Ont. He was again acquitted but was ordered to leave Upper Canada.

July 16 Priests Joseph-Norbert Provencher (1787–1853) and Sévère Dumoulin arrived at Fort Douglas (Winnipeg) to establish a Catholic church at the Red R. colony. Shortly thereafter, the colony was decimated by a grasshopper plague.

July 19 During his expedition to find the Northwest Passage, John Ross named capes on either side of Smith Sound after the expedition's 2 ships: Cape Isabella on Ellesmere Is. and Cape Alexander on Greenland. Ross arrived off the inlet on July 30, and named Lancaster Sound. His ships entered the sound, found it free of ice, and proceeded westward until Ross reported seeing a range of mountains. Believing the sound closed to further navigation, he withdrew his ships.

Aug. William Williams arrived at York Factory aboard the *Prince of Wales*, and from there travelled to Cumberland House (Sask.) to take up his duties as Gov-in-C for HBC's Rupert's land.

Sept. 21 Selkirk went on trial for breaking into NWC headquarters at Fort William and arresting its partners. In addition, Duncan Cameron sued Lord Selkirk for false arrest. The action was successful and Cameron was awarded damages of £3,000.

Oct. 6 Fort Astoria was returned to the US by agreement, under the Treaty of Ghent.

Oct. 11 Colin Robertson of the HBC was kidnapped by Nor'Wester Samuel Black in Athabasca country and charged with attempted murder. Robertson was making his way to L. Athabasca in an effort to break the NWC's regional monopoly.

Oct. 12 The 3rd session of the 7th Parliament of Upper Canada met until Nov. 27. Assemblies held for seditious purposes were declared unlawful.

Oct. 17 The Chippewa ceded more than 600,000 ha of land to the Crown in Dufferin, Grey and Simcoe Counties, Ont., for £1,200 "yearly and every year for ever."

Oct. 20 Britain and the US signed the London Convention, which provisionally set the 49th parallel as the boundary between US and British territories from L.-of-the-Woods to the Rocky Mountains.

Oct. 28 The Mississauga ceded 263,000 ha to the Crown in Peel, Halton, Wellington and Dufferin Counties for "the yearly sum of five hundred and twenty-two pounds ten shillings [to be] paid yearly and every year [to the] Mississauga Nation."

Nov. 5 The Chippewa ceded another 768,000 ha to the Crown in Northumberland, and Durham, Ont., Haliburton and Hastings Counties, and the District of Muskoka for the yearly sum of £740 "paid yearly and every year for ever."

Nov. 18 Isaac Swayze (1751–1828) accused Robert Gourlay of violating the Sedition Act of 1804. It was the 1st time the act had been used against a British subject.

Nov. 24 Decisions by a joint commission provided for by the Treaty of Ghent gave the US the right to fish on the coasts of Nfld. and Labrador and to dry fish in unsettled bays from Cape Ray to the Ramea Is. off the coast of Labrador. (The west Nfld. shore had been designated solely for use by the French in 1783.) Territory west of the Rockies was to be jointly occupied for 10 years. All captured territory was returned and a commission to delimit the northeastern frontier was provided.

1818–1821 First Nations in interior Canada were decimated by smallpox, measles and whooping cough.

Also in 1818
• The non-sectarian Dalhousie University was established in Halifax by George Ramsay, Earl of Dalhousie, lt-gov. of NS.

• Province House, seat of the NS legislature, was opened in Halifax.

• St. Andrew's Presbyterian Church, located north of Cornwall in Glengary County in Williamstown, Ont., was completed. Quebec City mason François-Xavier Rocheleau (d 1812) built the walls of the church,

but died before completion and was succeeded by his foreman, John Kirby, under direction by Reverend John Bethune. The 20.7 m x 11 m French-and-English-style structure featured a steeple holding a bell donated by Sir Alexander Mackenzie.

1819

Jan. 4 Robert Gourlay refused to leave Upper Canada and was committed to the Niagara jail to await trial. On Aug. 20, Gourlay was tried and found guilty for disobeying a legal order to leave the province. He became the 1st Briton banished from Upper Canada.

Jan. 6 John Gilchrist received the 1st licence to practise medicine in Upper Canada from the newly established Medical Board of Upper Canada.

Jan. 12 St. Boniface College was founded by Bishop Provencher as a classical school for young men at the Red R. colony (Man.).

Jan. 16 William Edward Parry (1790–1855) was commissioned to command a 2nd expedition to investigate Lancaster Sound and determine whether it was blocked by mountains to the west as Ross believed. Parry set sail May 4 with 2 ships, the *Hecla* and the *Griper*.

Feb. 22 Spain abandoned all claims to the Pacific coast north of the 42nd parallel under the terms of the Treaty of Florida Blanca with Great Britain.

Feb. 23 John Franklin left Gravesend, England, on HBC supply ship, *Prince of Wales,* with orders to set out overland from Hudson Bay to explore and chart the north coast of the American continent eastward from the mouth of the Coppermine R., and to delineate the most direct route for a northwest passage. Also on the expedition were Robert Hood (d 1821), George Back (1795–1878) and Dr. John Richardson (1787–1865). The expedition wintered at Cumberland House (Sask.).

May 1 The 24-bed Montreal General Hospital opened. It was run on donations and geared for serving the city's poor.

June 7 The 4th session of the 7th Parliament of

Upper Canada met until July 12. Business included authorizing the lt-gov. to grant land to war veterans.

June 7 Writing from a Niagara jail, Robert Gourlay argued that the chief impediment to Upper Canadian growth was the existence of enormous amounts of idle land in public and speculative hands.

Also in June
• Acting on behalf of the HBC, William Williams, commanding a force of 30 men, captured a number of Nor'Westers at Grand Rapids as they were making their way to Fort William (Thunder Bay, Ont.). He served them with bench warrants secured from Montreal, on bills of indictment for murder, robbery and burglary. As magistrate of Rupert's Land, Williams also issued his own warrants for the arrest of John George McTavish, Angus Shaw and others for offences in Athabasca.

July 19 Selkirk settlers returned to their homes on the Red R.

July 28 Young Halifax lawyer Richard Uniacke Jr., was challenged to a duel by William Bowie, a prominent merchant. Uniacke killed his opponent and was brought to trial for murder. He was led into the courtroom by his father, Richard John Uniacke, the Attorney Gen. of NS. Uniacke was acquitted for respectably defending his honour.

Aug. 1–7 Lt. Edward Parry, commanding the *Hecla* and the *Griper*, entered Lancaster Sound and determined that no mountain barrier blocked its passage.

Aug. 28 The Gov-in-C of Canada, the Duke of Richmond, died of rabies. He had been bitten by a pet fox 2 months earlier.

Sept. 4 Parry's expedition crossed 110° West, off the south shore of Melville Is., earning the expedition £5,000 offered by the British Parliament for reaching this longitude. Parry was stopped by ice in McClure Str., and his expedition became the 1st to spend the winter with ships deliberately locked in the ice. This was also the 1st expedition to experiment with canned food.

Sept. 20–Mar. 17, 1820 James Monk (1745/46–1826) served as administrator of Lower Canada.

Fall James Kempt (c 1765–1854) was appointed lt-gov. of NS. He would not arrive in the colony until June 1, 1820.

Oct. 15 The HBC appointed John West (1778–1845) as its 1st Church of England chaplain in Rupert's Land.

Dec. 4 Jacob Mountain became principal of the Royal Institution and later prepared a plan for the establishment of McGill University.

1819–1820 One-third of the Blackfoot and Gross Ventre First Nations died in a measles epidemic.

Also in 1819
• The Allan Steamship Line, a Scottish-Canadian shipping line, was founded by Capt. Alexander Allan (1780–1854).

• Peregrine Maitland (1777–1854) lt-gov. (1818–1828) and administrator of Upper Canada, enacted the Assessment Act of 1819, authorizing the taxation of uncultivated land. It was hoped that this would encourage owners to either develop their holdings or sell out.

• The original National School in Quebec City opened its doors. It employed the Bell system of education, which utilized older children as monitors to teach younger students. These free schools were established through the influence of George Mountain and were sponsored by the British govt.

• St. Margaret's, the 1st English-speaking Catholic seminary in Canada, was established at Halifax.

• Presbyterian minister and educator Thomas McCulloch of Pictou, NS, published *The Nature and Uses of a Liberal Education*.

• John Ross published *A Voyage of Discovery,* in England.

1820

Jan. 18 John Franklin, George Black and John Hepburn set out from Cumberland House on snowshoes for Fort Chipewyan. They travelled as far as Winter L., between Great Slave L. and the Coppermine R., where they built Fort Enterprise, their 1820 winter quarters. Dr. John Richardson and Robert Ahood were ordered to remain at Cumberland House and to bring on supplies in the spring.

Jan. 26 George Simpson (1787–1860), from Scotland, entered the service of the HBC as associate gov. of Rupert's Land. He sailed for Canada on Mar. 4.

Jan. 28 The Mississauga ceded 809 ha of land in what is now Peel County, Ont., for £50.

Mar. 8–June 30 Samuel Smith served as administrator of Upper Canada.

Mar. 17–June 19 Peregrine Maitland served as temporary administrator of Lower Canada.

Mar. 25 The Bank of NB, the 1st established in the colony, was chartered in Saint John.

Apr. 8 Lord Selkirk died in Britain. His health and fortune had been ruined by lawsuits arising from the seizure of Fort William.

Apr. 12 The Earl of Dalhousie was commissioned Gov-in-C of Lower Canada. He served from June 19, 1820–Sept 8, 1828.

May 22 The cornerstone of Dalhousie University was laid in Halifax, NS, by George Dalhousie himself, with full Masonic and military honours.

May 28 At Fort William (Thunder Bay, Ont.), Simpson of the HBC addressed a meeting of NWC partners and called for an end to violence between the 2 companies.

July 20 The Mohawk ceded more that 13,500 ha in the Bay of Quinte region, Ont.

• The coronation of George IV was celebrated in Canada, 11 months before the actual event (July 10, 1821).

Sept. The Upper Canada Central School for boys and girls was opened under the direction of Joseph Spragg (1775–1848). The school, introduced in Upper Canada by Maitland, was fashioned after schools of the National Society in Britain. The major objective was to inculcate the love of God and king. Maitland hoped these schools would take the

place of non-denominational schools established in Upper Canada in 1816.

Sept. Nor'Westers Dr. John McLoughlin and Angus Bethune travelled to London with powers of attorney from 18 NWC winterers-hivernants (western all-season voyagers), to request that the HBC supply them.

Oct. 9 A proclamation announced the rejoining of Cape Breton Is. with NS, effective Oct. 16. The 2 had been separated since 1784.

Oct. 20 Parry's 2 expedition ships landed at Peterhead, Scotland, having proven that a passage to the west opened out of Lancaster Sound. Parry also demonstrated the possibility of wintering in relative safety above the Arctic Circle. He named some 20 islands including Somerset, Devon, Beechy, Cornwallis, Melville and Banks.

Also in Oct.
• John West, chaplain for the HBC, arrived at Red R. and opened a day school in a Kildonan (Winnipeg) log cabin for Red R. children. The curriculum involved "civilization" and Christianity. Domestic skills for girls and horticulture and cultivation skills for boys were also emphasized.

Nov. 12 Que. and Montreal Presbyterians petitioned the govt for a share of clergy reserves.

Winter Samuel Cunard (1787–1865), James Tobin and John Starr administered a soup house in Halifax. Three hundred and twenty people received 1 meal each day during a period of high unemployment and immigration. The NS legislature granted £33 the following year to continue the operation.

c 1820 Journalist Thomas Dalton, publisher of the pro-Tory, pro-Church of England *Kingston Patriot* weekly, is believed to have coined the term "Family Compact," used to describe the small group of wealthy Upper Canadians of English descent — members the executive council, who were largely responsible for policy-making and patronage in the province.

Also in 1820
• John Poad Drake (1794–1883) painted the oil

Shipping at Low Tide, now in the Art Gallery of Nova Scotia.

• The book, *A Visit to the Province of Upper Canada*, written by John Strachan but appearing under the name of his brother, James, was published in Aberdeen, Scotland.

1821

Jan. 21 Roman Catholic priest Jean-Jacques Lartigue (1777–1840) was consecrated bishop in Montreal's Church of Notre-Dame, and assumed responsibility for the largest Roman Catholic district in Lower Canada.

Jan. 31 The 1st session of the 8th Parliament of Upper Canada met until Feb. 14. Business included an act to preserve deer and salmon, and provision that tithes or ecclesiastical levies would never be applied in Upper Canada.

Mar. 16 John Molson's Mansion House Hotel, in Montreal, burned down. It would be rebuilt in 1824 and renamed the Masonic Hall Hotel.

• Agreement was reached to merge the NWC and HBC effective June 1, and to run the new company for 21 years in the name of the HBC. The actual agreement was signed May 28 by William (1764–1825) and Simon (c 1784–1840) McGillivray and Edward Ellice (1781–1863). The merger was necessitated by rifts within the NWC, American inroads into the fur trade, Selkirk's guerrilla warfare and the monopoly granted HBC on fur trading in selected regions of the continent. William Williams was appointed gov. of the Southern Department and senior executive officer of the new HBC, based at York Factory. George Simpson (1786–1860) was appointed gov. of the Northern Department, based at Moose Factory. The appointment of Williams disturbed NWC partners, and Nicholas Garry (c 1782–1856), sent to Canada to supervise the merger, made Simpson the HBC senior administrator.

Mar. 31 The Royal Institution for the Advancement of Learning received a Royal Charter for the University of McGill College, a legacy from Montreal merchant James McGill. McGill's heirs contested his will and

the estate was tied up for many years in litigation. George Jehoshaphat Mountain (1789–1863) was named McGill's 1st principal and also professor of divinity in 1824.

Apr. 21 The Bank of Upper Canada was incorporated at York. It would open for business in July 1822.

May 8 William Edward Parry, commanding the *Hecla* and *Fury*, sailed out of Deptford, England, to search for the Northwest Passage by continuing his 1819–1820 route.

June 6 The cornerstone of the Montreal General Hospital was laid. The building, which would contain 80 patient beds, opened May 1, 1822.

July 2 The Act for Regulation of the Fur Trade continued the monopoly enjoyed by the HBC.

July 10 NWC Montreal partners and winterers converged on Fort William to learn about the amalgamation with the HBC. NWC partners were offered positions as chief factors and chief traders in the new company, but were no longer partners. Former NWC chief William McGillivray would die in 1825, leaving his family impoverished.

July 17 John Richardson, a founder of the Bank of Montreal, director of the 1st Montreal Savings Bank, and city alderman, turned the 1st sod for the commencement of the building of the Lachine Canal, a project of the Lower Canada govt. When completed in 1825, the canal would run through 7 locks, over a distance of 14.5 km, and a water depth of 1.5 m, from the old port of Montreal to L. Saint-Louis. The project cost $440,000.

July 21 The Franklin expedition began its coastal voyage eastward from the Coppermine R., with 20 men including 5 Englishmen, 11 Canadians, 2 Aboriginal hunters and 2 Inuit, in 2 canoes. From July 21 to Aug. 18, the expedition charted 1,110 km of coastline, land never before seen by Europeans. Reaching Turnagain Point on Kent Peninsula, Franklin turned back to Fort Enterprise as supplies were nearly exhausted and the end of summer was imminent. In 1823, Franklin would publish *Journey to the Polar Sea,* which was devoured by a British readership hungry for stories of English exploits abroad.

Aug. HBC Gov. Simpson ordered John Lee Lewes and John Dugald Cameron (c 1777–1857) to conduct an inspection of old NWC posts west of the Rocky Mountains. Their subsequent report suggested elimination of excess personnel, although in the Columbia region, it was suggested that a presence be maintained as a buffer to keep American competitors out of the more profitable areas to the north.

Sept. 4 Tsar Alexander I declared the Pacific Coast from Alaska to north of Vancouver Is. (51°N) Russian territory and forbade the approach of non-Russian ships.

Oct. 8 Parry's 2 vessels put into winter quarters off the south shore of Winter Is., where they were frozen in for the next 9 months.

Also in Oct.
• HBC Gov. Simpson held a banquet at York Factory to introduce local HBC and NWC fur traders brought together under 1 company by the amalgamation of the 2 operations.

Dec. 11 The 2nd session of the 11th Parliament of Lower Canada convened until Feb. 18, 1822. Business included a resolution that the govt put its expenses to a vote every year.

Dec. 22–Mar. 1823 Thomas McCulloch published the humorous and satirical "Letters of Mephibosheth Stepsure" in serial form in the *Acadian Recorder* to induce his fellow Pictonians to improve their farming practices and style of life in general. McCullough would become the 1st principal of Dalhousie College in 1838.

Also in 1821
• The population of Lower Canada was 425,000, that of Upper Canada 150,000. Nfld. had a population of 50,000, NS 120,000 and NB 70,000.

• Swiss immigrant Peter Rindisbacher (1806–1834) painted the watercolour *A Labrador Eskimo in his Canoe*. Rindisbacher settled in the Red R. colony with his family. He was one of the 1st artists working west of the Great Lakes. Other works included *Sled Dogs Attacking Bison*, and *Hunting Buffalo*, both now held in the Hudson's Bay Collection at the Museum of Manitoba. Rindisbacher died of cholera at age 28.

1822

Jan. 4 Conservatives in the Upper Canada Assembly voted to expel Reform deputy Barnabas Bidwell (1763–1833) from the House on grounds that he had held public office in the US, where he had been charged with fraud.

Feb. 1 A group of Inuit wintered about 3 km from Parry's vessels, *Hecla* and *Fury*. They told Parry about a strait north of Winter Is., which provided access to open water to the west. Officers and men showed an interest in learning the Inuit language, culture and the way Inuit hunted, fished and found shelter.

Apr. 27 The St. Lawrence Steamboat Company was created. John Molson and Sons, with 26 of the 44 shares, assumed management.

May 1 John Caldwell (1775–1842), Receiver-Gen. of Lower Canada, was unable to meet the expenses of the civil list, and Gov. Lord Dalhousie was forced to take £30,000 out of military funds.

June 18 A Boundary Commission established the international border along the St. Lawrence R. and through the Great Lakes.

June 20 The Law Society of Upper Canada was incorporated.

July 2 The *Hecla* and *Fury* broke free from ice, allowing Parry to continue his expedition.

July 8 John Cameron was appointed chief factor of the HBC post at Fort George (Astoria).

• The Chippewa ceded 234,700 ha in Lambton, Middlesex, and Kent Counties, Ont., for "an annuity of two pounds and ten shillings to each member of the Chippewa people inhabiting this parcel of land. But the number of people receiving the annuity may not exceed 240."

July 10 William Williams arrived at Moose Factory to assume command of the Southern Department of the HBC.

July 12 Capt. Parry discovered Fury and Hecla Straits between Baffin Is. and Melville peninsula.

Aug. 5 The Imperial Trade Act regulated trade between Upper and Lower Canada. Lower Canada was forbidden to impose new duties without the approval of Upper Canada or the Crown.

Oct. 27 John Mcleod (1788–1849) began his journey through the Rocky Mountains and descent of the Fraser R. to the Str. of Georgia for the HBC.

Oct. 28 The Mississauga ceded 1,112,100 ha in Hastings, Addington, Frontenac, Lanark, Carleton and Renfrew Counties, Ont., for an annuity of 2 pounds 4 shillings payable to each person and their posterity forever, "provided the number of annuities at any time should not exceed 257."

Also in Oct

• Parry prepared to winter off Igloolik Is., Hooper Inlet, where the expedition passed its 2nd winter in the company of Inuit who were also using the island for winter settlement.

Also in 1822

• HBC sent out an abortive Bow R. expedition.

• The Executive Council of Upper Canada approved the appointment of a Gen. Board of Education with John Strachan as president. All members of the board belonged to the Church of England, with power to supervise school lands.

• The 1st map of soils in Canada, *Statistical Account of Upper Canada,* was created by Robert Gourlay and published as a guide for immigrants.

1823

Jan. 1 NS became the 1st province to issue coinage — penny and halfpenny tokens.

Jan. 10 The 3rd session of the 11th Parliament of Lower Canada met until Mar. 22. Business included the regulation of licences for public houses and the sale of liquor and wine.

Jan. 15 The 3rd session of the 8th Parliament of Upper Canada convened until Mar. 19. Business included the authorization of the Burlington Bay Canal, recommended by a select committee of the Upper Canadian Assembly. The canal would run from Burlington Bay to the Grand R.

• James Stuart (1780–1853) was sent to London as an agent for pro-unionists from Lower Canada to argue their case for the union of the provinces of Canada.

June 9 Parry's vessels were freed from their winter moorings and one last attempt was made to explore Fury and Hecla Straits, but ice barred the way. Parry was forced to return to England.

Aug. 20 Americans J.C. Beltrane and Maj. Long explored the area adjacent to the Red R. with the intention of acquiring it for the US.

Nov. 11 The 4th session of the 8th Parliament of Upper Canada sat until Jan. 19, 1824. Business included the incorporation of the Welland Canal Company on Jan. 19. William Hamilton Merritt (1793–1862) of St. Catharines, Ont., had formed the company to build the 1st Welland Canal to connect L. Erie to L. Ont., and thereby bypass Niagara Falls. Merritt had previously petitioned the govt for funds to complete an accurate survey of the route. Construction began of the 1st Welland Canal on Nov. 24, 1824. Merrit had obtained financial backing for the building of the canal from American investors. The completed canal (40 locks) would traverse the Niagara escarpment via Twelve-Mile Creek and the Chippewa R. to L. Erie.

Nov. 23 John Caldwell, Receiver-Gen. of Lower Canada, was removed from office by Gov. Lord Dalhousie for being £96,000 in arrears. The gov. established an investigative committee, chaired by Austin Cuvillier (1779–1849), which concluded that Caldwell lost more than £96,000 on speculations.

Nov. 25 The 4th session of the 11th Parliament of Lower Canada met until Mar. 9, 1824. Business included the repeal of the death penalty for theft.

Dec. 2 In a message to Congress, US President James Monroe (1758–1831) announced the Monroe Doctrine, which warned European countries that the US would view any expansion in the Americas as an unfriendly act.

Dec. 26 A chamber of commerce was established at St. John's, Nfld.

Also in Dec.

- Jews in Lower Canada petitioned the govt for permission to maintain their own registry of births, marriages and deaths. It was not until 1831 that Royal Assent was given to a law authorizing the keeping of such records.

Also in 1823

- John Rowand (c 1787–1854) was placed in charge of HBC's Sask. district with headquarters at Edmonton House.

- St. John's Church, the 1st Protestant church in the Red R. colony, was completed.

- Ferdinand von Wrangel (1796–1870), exploring for Russia, proved that North America and Asia were not connected by land.

- The HBC built Fort Assiniboine as a fur-trading post on the north bank of the Athabasca R., at the mouth of the Freeman R.

- William Morris (1786–1858) unsuccessfully attempted to have the Church of Scotland recognized as a national church in the Assembly of Upper Canada.

- Construction of fortifications at Quebec City was begun; the defences would not be completed until 1832.

- The Montreal Medical Institution was founded by 4 staff members of the Montreal General Hospital to offer lectures to medical students.

- Canada's oldest hardrock iron mine was established at Marmora, Ont.

- W.H. Keating, a geologist from Philadelphia, discovered the floor of an immense ancient lake that extended from the Rockies in the west to L. Superior in the east, and from South Dakota in the south to Hudson Bay, (more than 1 million km²). Warren Upham named it Glacial Lake Agassiz in 1895, after the famous Swiss discoverer of the ice ages. The lake arose as drainage of the Laurentide Ice Sheet was blocked.

- Peter Rindisbacher painted the watercolour *Captain Bulgar, Governor of Assinibois, and the Chiefs and Warriors of the Chippewa Tribe of Red Lake*.

- Lt. George Back drew the portrait *A Buffalo Pound*, which was later reworked as an engraving.

- Thomas Chandler Haliburton (1796–1865) published *A General Description of Nova Scotia*.

1824

Jan. 6 The Literary and Historical Society of Que. held its 1st meeting.

Jan. 17 Parry was again given the command of the *Hecla* and *Fury* with instructions to search for the Northwest Passage through Lancaster Sound, down Prince Regent Inlet, and then, if possible, along the north coast of North America. He sailed from England for the Arctic on May 19.

Feb. 21–Aug. 28 John Murray Bliss (1771–1834) served as administrator of NB.

Also in Feb.

- The legislature of NS under its new gov., the Earl of Dalhousie, voted in favour of carrying out a survey to determine the feasibility of constructing the Shubenacadie Canal connecting Dartmouth, NS, to the Bay of Fundy. Construction began 2 years later.

- Eighteen-year-old Patrick Bergen died on the gallows in Saint John, NB, after being convicted of stealing 25 cents.

Mar. 9 The Fabrique Act was passed in Lower Canada, empowering the priest in each parish to provide a school for every 100 families.

May 18 The 1st issue of the *Colonial Advocate*, founded and published by William Lyon Mackenzie (1795–1861), appeared with the avowed purpose of influencing an approaching election. Editor Mackenzie charged provincial authorities with corruption. Mackenzie moved his family and newspaper to York, Nov. 18, to be closer to the hub of Upper Canadian politics.

June 7–Sept. 16, 1825 Francis Burton (1766–1832) served as administrator of Lower Canada following Dalhousie's departure on leave to Britain.

June 8 The 1st patent in Canada was issued to Noah Cushing (b 1779) of Que. for his washing machine.

Aug. 1 Novelist John Galt (1779–1839) proposed the establishment of the Canada Land Company to colonize the L. Huron grant of land. The Canada Company, chartered in England, with Galt on its board of directors, was incorporated for settlement in Upper Canada in 1825.

Aug. 15 The London board of the HBC ordered Simpson and James McMillan (c 1783–1858) to travel to the Columbia District and institute measures for economy and efficiency in order to compete more aggressively with the Americans. This was Simpson's 1st transcontinental journey.

Sept. 1 The cornerstone of Nôtre-Dame Church in Montreal was laid at Place d'Armes. The structure took 6 years (1823–1829) to complete and was designed by James O'Donnell (1774–1830); it remained the largest church in North America for over 50 years.

Sept. 10 Parry entered Lancaster Sound, reaching Port Bowen, on the east coast of Prince Regent Inlet, on Oct. 1. There he established winter quarters.

Nov. 8 Simpson arrived at Fort George (Astoria, Oregon), 84 days after leaving York Factory.

Nov. 10 The Montreal Medical Institution began its 1st term with a student enrollment of 25.

Dec. 30 The parliament building of Upper Canada was destroyed by fire.

Also in 1824
• The Assessment Act of 1819 of Upper Canada was made permanent.

• HBC explorer John Finlay (1774–1833) crossed the Rockies through the Peace R. Pass, and explored the Finlay R. to its source.

• Edmonton became an important trade depot for the HBC when the 1st Alb. road was cleared from Edmonton to Fort Assiniboine.

• Windsor, Ont., experienced a smallpox epidemic.

• Irish-born designer Lloyd Johnston (1767–1842) completed St. John's Church, known locally as The Stone Church, located on a hill north of Union Street in Saint John, NB. The early Gothic Revival-style sanctuary survived the Saint John Great Fire of 1877, which destroyed more than half the city.

• Louis Hubert Triand painted the oil *La Procession de la Fête-Dieu à Québec*.

• Julia Catherine Beckwith (Hart) (1796–1867) of Fredericton, NB, wrote *St. Ursula's Convent*, the 1st English-language novel by a Canadian writer. It was published in Kingston.

• George Longmore (1793–1867) published the humorous poem *The Charivari*.

1825

Jan. 13 The 1st session of the 9th Parliament of Upper Canada convened until Apr. 13. The Reform Party held a majority.

Jan. 31 Colonial secretary Lord Bathurst appointed James Stuart to the post of Attorney Gen. of Lower Canada.

Feb. 16 John Franklin left England on his 2nd expedition to the Arctic with orders to explore the Mackenzie Delta, and the mainland coast east and west of the mouth of the Coppermine R. George Back, Dr. John Richardson and surveyor Edward Kendall (c 1800–1845) served under him. Reaching New York in Mar., they travelled overland north to the Mackenzie R. and Great Bear L., where the expedition wintered.

Also in Feb.
• Britain and Russia signed a treaty settling the inland boundaries of Russian Alaska at the 1st mountain range running parallel to the coast, and the 141st meridian.

Mar. 19 Fort Vancouver was established by Dr. John McLoughlin (1784–1857) of the HBC on the Columbia R. near Portland, Oregon. The site was selected by Simpson to serve as the new headquarters of the Columbia District.

Also in Mar.

• The Theatre Royal Company was formed to build and manage Montreal's 1st permanent theatre. The principal shareholder was John Molson. Construction of the lavish 1,000-seat structure was completed later in the year.

Apr. 16 Sir Thomas Cochrane (1789–1872) was appointed the 1st resident gov. of Nfld., ending over 100 years of naval administration. Cochrane would serve until 1834. His salary was £4,000 per annum. In keeping with his position, Cochrane commissioned Government House. This magnificent official residence in St. John's (which remains to this day), completed under the direction of Lt-Col. Lewis, Commanding Officer of the Royal Engineeers, and designed by Cochrane, cost £38,175 and was completed in 1829. The house is 2-stories tall and 5-bay windows wide. It was built with red sandstone and Portland-stone trim. The British govt was outraged at Cochrane's extravagance and reduced his salary to £3,000 per annum.

Apr. 26 Chief Joseph Wawanosh of the Chippewa signed a provisional treaty with the Crown ceding a massive tract of land in what is now Southwest Ont. to His Majesty George IV. The area required a survey to establish exact boundaries before a final treaty was signed on July 10, 1827.

May 14 Four hundred families (about 2,000 people) from Ireland, led by Peter Robinson (1785–1838), settled in Peterborough County, Ont. The British govt offered the settlers free passage and some assistance to help alleviate the problems of mounting poverty and social unrest in their homeland.

May 19 Frederick William Beechey (1796–1856), commanding the *Blossom*, sailed for Bering Str. via Cape Horn to aid Edward Parry and John Franklin, should they reach the strait in their separate attempts to discover the Northwest Passage. Beechey was also to conduct surveys of uncharted areas.

June 16 Jacob Mountain died at Que. and was buried under the chancel of the Cathedral of the Holy Trinity. His epitaph read "Founder of the Church of England in the Canadas."

June 22 Britain passed the Imperial Canadian Trade and Tenures Act, which abolished feudal and seigniorial rights.

July 9 Robert Logan (1773–1866) purchased Fort Douglas on the west bank of the Red R., just below the junction of the Assiniboine and Red Rivers, for £400.

July–June 1833 Donald Mckenzie served as gov. of Assinibois and HBC chief factor.

Also in July

• Lord Bathurst authorized Upper Canada Lt-Gov. Maitland to have legislation prepared by the Upper Canadian legislature to naturalize aliens and admit them to the same civil rights and privileges enjoyed by British subjects. This move was in response to the vast number of Americans who had entered Canada after the American Revolution.

• *Hecla* and *Fury* were released when the ice broke up at Port Bowen. Parry continued his expedition.

• In York, Francis Collins (c 1799–1834) established the *Canadian Freeman* newspaper in which he began attacking the administration of Sir Peregrine Maitland.

Aug. 31 Tea imported directly from East Indian ports was sold in Montreal for the 1st time; this helped reduce smuggling from the US.

Also in Aug.

• Parry's *Fury* was forced aground off the coast of Somerset Is. and badly damaged. Parry abandoned the ship. His crew boarded *Hecla* and returned immediately to England.

Sept. 3 The Halifax Banking Company, NS's 1st true bank, was founded by Enos Collins (1774–1871), the dominant partner, Henry H. Cogswell (Pres.) (1774–1874), William Pryor, James Tobin, Samuel Cunard, John Clark, Joseph Allison and Martin Gay Black. The enterprise would become known as Collins' Bank.

Oct. 5–7 The Miramichi Valley, about 15,600 km^2 in NB, was almost totally destroyed by one of the worst forest fires in Canadian history. The towns of

Newcastle, Douglastown, Moorfields and several other smaller settlements were destroyed. Over 160 people lost their lives; 15,000 were left homeless.

Also in Oct.

• William Parry's expedition in search of the Northwest Passage arrived back in London after having reached Lancaster Sound, wintered at Point Bowen, and made important scientific observations.

Nov. 7 The 2nd session of the 9th Parliament of Upper Canada met until Jan. 30, 1826. Business included the incorporation of the Desjardin Canal to join Burlington Bay and L. Ontario, and a reduction in the number of capital crimes.

Dec. 30 The Assembly of Upper Canada passed a resolution recognizing Americans whose fathers or grandfathers were born British subjects as British subjects.

1825–1826 George Back painted the watercolour *Winter View of Fort Franklin*.

Also in 1825

• The population of Lower Canada was 479,288, Upper Canada 157,923.

• Americans opened the Erie Canal, providing a direct waterway from the American Midwest to the Atlantic, bypassing the St. Lawrence R. Building costs were US$78 million.

• Black Loyalist Rose Fortune (c 1774–1864) became Canada's 1st policewoman in Annapolis Royal, NS. Fortune's parents arrived in the Annapolis Valley as slaves, but their daughter established her own business as a baggage handler ("baggagesmaster") at the Annapolis Wharf, around 1825. The business grew to include a wake-up-call service for travellers taking the boat out of Annapolis Royal. In 1841, Fortune named her business "The Lewis Transfer" when the firm began to use horse-drawn wagons. The Lewis Transfer would remain in business for 125 years.

• Fredericton-born author Julia Catherine Beckwith (Hart) published her 2nd novel, *Tonnewonte, or the adopted son of America*, portraying the simple virtues of family life on the American frontier.

1826

Jan. 2 The Supreme Court of Nfld. was established by Royal Charter.

Jan. 27 Upper Canada was made a separate diocese of the Catholic Church, with its seat in Kingston.

Also in Jan.

• Dr. Xavier Tessier (1799–1835) began publishing the *Quebec Medical Journal*, in both French and English. It was one of the earliest medical journals in the colony.

Feb. 26 William Williams, Gov-in-C of the Southern Department of Rupert's Land, was recalled by the London Committee. He left Canada Sept. 9. George Simpson (nicknamed "The Little Emperor") was made gov. of both the Northern and Southern Departments, serving in that capacity until Sept. 7, 1860.

May 26 Britain granted naturalized residents of Upper Canada the right to vote for, and stand for, election to the Assembly.

May 30 Col. John By (1779–1836) of the Royal Engineers arrived in Que. He was commissioned to build the Rideau Canal between the Ottawa R. and L. Ontario. By established his headquarters at the junction of the Ottawa and Rideau Rivers, naming the location Bytown in his honour. The British Parliament approved £5,000 for the canal's construction in 1826, the 1st in a series of annual, open-ended grants for that purpose. Working on cursory surveys and information, By and his associates budgeted the total cost of the canal at £169,000.

Also in May

• William Lyon Mackenzie fled to Lewiston, New York, to avoid being arrested in Upper Canada for debt.

June 8 A group of 15 well-connected Tories, members of the Family Compact, disguised as Aboriginals, raided Mackenzie's *Colonial Advocate* in broad daylight, smashing the presses and throwing type into Toronto's bay. This act of vandalism was known as the Type Riot. Mackenzie took the 8 major participants to court and was awarded £625 compensation, which amount enabled him to pay off his debts.

June 22 After wintering on Great Bear L., the Franklin Expedition set out for the Mackenzie delta. The group divided at Point Separation: Richardson and Kendall on the *Dolphin* and *Union* explored the coast eastward to the mouth of the Coppermine. Franklin and Back on the *Lion* and *Reliance* headed toward Bering Str., where they were harrassed by several hundred Inuit who were finally driven off at gun point.

July 19 The 1st regatta in Canada was held at Halifax.

Aug. 19 The British Crown sold 1 million ha of Upper Canadian land, originally purchased from the Ojibwa, to the Canada Land Company, for $295,000. Over half the land adjoined L. Huron.

Sept. 21 Franklin and Back, having explored 595 km of uncharted coast, arrived back at Fort Franklin, Great Bear L., 3 weeks after the return of Richardson and Kendall, who had completed their survey. Thick fog on Aug. 18 had prevented Franklin from reaching Point Barrow.

Sept. 26 An official ceremony designating the Rideau Canal was held at Rideau Falls, Upper Canada. Completed, the canal would run 200 km, 47 locks and 14 dams, from Ottawa to Kingston, servicing both military and commercial traffic. Lord Dalhousie turned the 1st sod.

Nov. 9 The newspaper *La Minerve*, founded and published by Augustin-Norbert Morin (1803–1865), was 1st published.

Also in 1826
• Scottish immigrant Peter McGregor (1794–1846), London, Ont.'s 1st settler, built McGregor's Tavern on the south side of King and Ridout Streets. He was the town's 1st entrepreneur and is credited with its founding.

• The Montreal Hunt Club was established, offering its members the opportunity to race horses or hunt foxes. First Master of the Hunt was John Forsythe (1762–1837).

• Construction began on the Union Bridge (finished 1828) across the Ottawa R. It was built by Royal Engineers to facilitate the movement of building

materials required for the Rideau Canal. The bridge connected Bytown and Wrightstown (Hull) over the Chaudière Falls in 7 stages.

• The 1st paid police force in Canada was established at Saint John, NB.

• The 1st Baptist church — Toronto's 1st black church — was founded by 12 escaped slaves who held regular prayer meetings on the Toronto lakeshore. Within a year, the congregation had increased enough to allow the leasing of St. George's Masonic Lodge for their meetings.

• Catherine Parr Traill (1802–1899) published *The Young Emigrants; or Pictures of Canada, Calculated to Amuse and Instruct the Minds of Youth*.

1827

Mar. 5 The NWC's Beaver Club, 1st established in Feb. 1785, was disbanded.

Mar. 15 John Strachan obtained a Royal Charter for King's College, an Anglican university, which would become the University of Toronto.

Also in Mar.
• Gov. John Ready (c 1777–1845) of PEI established a Central Agricultural Society to "extend the knowledge and practice of the best and most espoused modes of agriculture."

Apr. 4 Parry left England in the *Hecla*, on his last voyage to the Arctic, with James Clark Ross (1800–1862) as 2nd in command. They hoped to reach the North Pole by crossing the ice north of Spitsbergen.

Apr. 23 Construction began on the Shubenacadie Canal connecting Halifax with the Bay of Fundy.

Apr. 28 John Galt founded the town of Guelph, Ont., and moved quickly to develop it as a nucleus for settlement. In the same year, Galt and Dr. William "Tiger" Dunlop (1792–1848), surgeon, author, soldier and editor, founded the town of Goderich, Ont. Dunlop laid out the Goderich townsite and supervised its construction.

May 15 The HBC sent James Douglas (1803–1877)

to build Fort Connolly at the north end of Bear L. (which drains into the Skeena R.), in northern BC.

Also in May
- Royal Assent was given to a law passed in Upper Canada, allowing US immigrants living in the colony the right to vote and own land in Canada, provided they possessed a land grant from the govt, or held public office, or had sworn an oath of allegiance to the Crown before 1820. Other Americans could enjoy the same rights after living in Canada for 7 years.

June 22 The Parry expedition set out from Spitsbergen in an overland attempt to reach the North Pole. Instead of one unbroken plain of ice, Parry found small floes moving in a southerly direction.

July 10 The Chippewa ceded 890,000 ha in Lambton, Huron, Middlesex, Oxford, Perth, Wellington and Waterloo Counties, Ont., to the Crown for the annual sum of £1,100 forever, payable to Chief Joseph Wawanosh, 17 lesser chiefs, the 400 members of his band and their descendents.

July 26 The Parry expedition reached 82° 45′N, its most northerly point, before having to turn back.

July 30 The schooner *Cadboro*, commanded by Chief Factor James McMillan, arrived about 50 km upstream from the mouth of the Fraser R. There construction was begun on the HBC's Fort Langley, built to prevent American traders from coming up the Fraser, and to provide a site where farm produce could be cached for company posts west of the mountains.

Aug. 6 The convention of 1818, providing for joint US–Great Britain occupation of the Oregon country, was renewed indefinitely, with the provision that it might be terminated by either party upon a year's notice.

Dec. 3 Montreal Presbyterians requested a share of the clergy reserves.

Also in Dec.
- Joseph Howe (1804–1873) purchased the *Novascotian* from G.R. Young.

- Shades Mills, Ont., was renamed Galt.

- In a public meeting, Jesse Ketchum (1782–1867) was selected chairman of a public meeting called to protest clergyman Strachan's famous "Ecclesiastical Chart" and his efforts to secure the clergy reserves wholly for the Church of England. A petition containing 8,000 signatures was obtained challenging Strachan's position.

Also in 1827
- Lower Canada had 49 post offices, Upper Canada had 65.

- John Strachan published *An Appeal to the Friends of the Religion and Literature, on Behalf of the University of Upper Canada*, in London, creating great opposition to the University in Upper Canada because Strachan had unwisely described the university as a "missionary college" intended to train Church of England clergymen.

- Presbyterian minister and educator Thomas McCulloch and a group of supporters established the *Colonial Patriot*, a reform newspaper, in Pictou, NS, dedicated to progressive views, especially in the area of education.

- Joseph Bouchette (1774–1841) competed his watercolour landscape *Kilbourn's Mill, Stanstead, Lower Canada*. It hangs in the McCord Museum, McGill University, Montreal.

1828

Mar. 20 The Assembly of Upper Canada petitioned the king to divert clergy reserves to education and public welfare rather than to the support of the Church of England.

Spring Francis Collins, publisher of the *Canadian Freeman*, was indicted on 4 counts of libel. He would be sentenced to 1 year in prison.

Apr. 10 James Kempt was commissioned administrator of Lower Canada, serving Sept. 8, 1828–Oct. 20, 1830.

May 22 The Episcopal Methodist churches of Canada and the US separated.

Summer A meeting in York produced a petition that was sent to the Crown and the Colonial Office listing a series of Upper Canadian grievances, which included the composition of the Legislative Council, the "practical irresponsibility" of the Executive Council and the total ineptitude of military men for civil rule in Upper Canada.

July 12 Simpson and his "country wife," Margaret Taylor, left York Factory with HBC voyageurs for Fort Langley, on the Fraser R.

July 13 Seventeen-year-old Ann Harvey, her father, George, and a younger brother rescued 152 people when the brig *Dispatch,* en route to Que., was wrecked 5 km offshore from Isle aux Mort near Port aux Basque, Nfld. George Harvey was given £100 sterling and a gold medal by the gov. of Nfld. as a reward.

July 24–Oct. 9 "Western Rambles" by Joseph Howe appeared in his newspaper, the *Novascotian,* as a first-hand account of Howe's explorations of his native province.

Aug. 17 HBC Gov. Simpson arrived at St. James, New Caledonia, en route to Fort Langley on the Fraser R. He was greeted by James Douglas, who was in charge of the fort.

Aug. 23 John Colborne, Baron Seaton (1778–1863), was commissioned lt-gov. of Upper Canada to succeed Maitland. He would serve from Nov. 4 to Nov. 30, 1835.

Nov. 9 Construction on the Welland Canal was interrupted when excavation through a deep cut to the Welland R. collapsed. The cut went through sand, which could not support the weight of the high banks.

Nov. 21 The 2nd session of the 13th Parliament of Lower Canada met until Mar. 14, 1829. Business included an act of representation creating 44 counties and increasing membership in the Assembly from 50 to 84.

Also in 1828

• NA's oldest continuous sporting event, the St. John's Rowing Regatta, was 1st held in St. John's, Nfld.

• John Playter established a stagecoach service between York and Holland Landing. William Weller purchased Playter's line in 1832 and, due to the line's rapid expansion, became known as the stagecoach king of Ont.

• The Baptist Horton Academy was established in Wolfeville, NS. It would become Acadia University in 1891.

• The 1st experiment in communal living in Canada occurred at Sarnia, Ont., when Henry Jones (1776–1852) founded Toon O'Maxwell on a govt grant of 4,046 ha. His Scottish followers lived in a large community building with common kitchen and dining facilities. The experiment eventually failed and the colonists took up individual farming.

• "Tecumseh, or the Warrior of the West," a poem by John Richardson (1796–1852), depicted the warrior as the personification of goodness and humanity but transformed into a savage fiend by the Americans' murder of his (imaginary) son. The poem was published in London, England.

1829

Jan. 1 Gov. Howard Douglas (1776–1861) opened King's College, NB's 1st institution of higher learning. The school featured a classical curriculum. The college received its Royal Charter on Feb. 10.

Jan. 2 Scottish novelist John Galt, one of the founders of the Canada (Settlement) Company, which owned 97,125 km² of unsettled land in Upper Canada, was recalled from the top position in the company on the grounds of negligence. Galt was replaced by 2 commissioners, Thomas Mercer Jones and The Hon. William Allen, president of the Bank of Upper Canada.

Feb. 7 The Legislature of Lower Canada passed an act allowing a Jewish religious establishment to maintain civil registers and to hold property for religious purposes.

Mar. W.L. Mackenzie travelled to the US to study politics under the newly elected US President Andrew Jackson. Mackenzie was impressed with the simplicity and low cost of the US govt as well as the spoils system which could serve in Canada as a means of removing the Family Compact. Mackenzie also approved of Jackson's hard money, anti-bank ideas.

May 23 John Ross, financed by British distiller magnate Felix Booth, commanded the *Victory*, a small Liverpool steamer, out of London, on an expedition to search for the Northwest Passage and to prove the value of steamers in the Arctic. Ross was accompanied by his nephew James Clark Ross.

June 6 Nancy Shawnawdithit, the last living Beothuk, died of tuberculosis in St. John's, Nfld., at age 23. She had been the lone survivor of her nation since 1825.

June 7 Nôtre-Dame Church, in Montreal, commissioned by the congregation of St. Sulpice, was dedicated. It is the earliest surviving Gothic revival church in Canada.

June 9 The 1st public temperance meeting in Canada was held in Montreal, with 30 people "taking the pledge."

June 24 McGill University opened in Montreal.

June 28 The Montreal Medical Institute became the Faculty of Medicine at McGill University.

Aug. 11 John Ross sailed into Prince Regent Inlet.

Sept. Francis Collins received royal clemency and was released from serving a 1-year sentence for libel. He had served 45 weeks. Collins's fine and sureties were also remitted. He had continued to edit the *Freeman* while in jail.

Late Sept. John Ross was stopped by ice and forced to winter at Felix Harbour, near Thom Bay. His expedition spent 4 years in the Arctic because the *Victory* was frozen in and surrounded by ice. Ross and his men communicated regularly with local Inuit who helped the expedition explore west and north of their location.

Nov. 21 Adolphus Egerton Ryerson (1803–1882) published the 1st issue of the *Christian Guardian*, the official organ of the Methodist Church and forerunner of the *United Church Observer*.

Nov. 27 The final section of the 2.4-m-deep Welland Canal (18.3 m wide at top, 12.2 m wide at bottom), connecting Port Dalhousie with Port Robinson on Chippawa Channel, was opened. The American ship *R.B. Broughton* and the Canadian vessel *Anne and Jane*, both 85 tonnes, were the 1st to travel from L. Ontario to L. Erie.

Dec. 16–Aug. 4, 1831 "Eastern Rambles" by Joseph Howe was published in the *Novascotian*.

Dec. 23 Montreal merchants met to protest the possibility of Britain opening the West Indies to American trade, an action which would destroy Canada's privileged trade position.

1829–1833 John Ross completed the watercolour *Snow Cottages of the Boothians*.

1829–1834 Peter Rindisbacher completed the watercolour *Scene in Indian Tent*.

Also in 1829

• York General Hospital opened in York, Upper Canada, with the capacity to accommodate up to 100 patients. The hospital closed in 1854. Its replacement, Toronto General Hospital, located on Gerrard Street, opened in 1856.

• Sir John Colborne established Upper Canada College at York. The school opened its doors to 140 students on Jan. 4, 1830.

• The Methodist conference established the Methodist Press. Its literary department, known as the Methodist Book Room, would later publish Ralph Connor (1860–1937), Charles G.D. Roberts (1860–1943), Robert Service (1874–1958), Charles Mair (1838–1927) and Isabella Valancy Crawford (1850–1887), among others. In 1878, the Rev. William Briggs became, arguably, the 1st Canadian book publisher, as the Book Steward to the Book Room. In its peak year, 1897, the Methodist Book Room published 37 new titles.

• Thomas Chandler Haliburton published *An Historical and Statistical Account of Nova Scotia*. This work was the basis for the Longfellow poem, "Evangeline."

• British officer James Pattison Cockburn (1778/79–1747) completed the watercolour *Passenger Pigeon Net, St Anne's Lower Canada.*

1830

Jan. 1 Ogle Robert Gowan (1803–1876) founded the Canadian Grand Orange Lodge of BNA, a staunchly conservative pro-British, anti-Catholic brotherhood. Its 1st chapter was in Brockville, Ont. Gowan was chosen deputy grand master of the primarily Irish-Protestant members. The Orange Order was originally founded in Ireland in 1795.

Jan. 22 The 3rd session of the 13th Parliament of Lower Canada convened until Mar. 26. Business included the incorporation of the Que. exchange.

Jan. 30 Robert Baldwin (1804–1858), who formerly announced himself "a Whig in principle, and opposed to the present administration," took his seat in the Assembly of Upper Canada after defeating William Botsford Jarvis (1799–1864).

Apr. 13 Land was set aside in Upper Canada for a system of reserves under the newly appointed superintendent of Indian Affairs, James Givens (c 1759–1846), in a reorganized Indian Department.

Apr. 30 The Catholic Emancipation Act was adopted in PEI allowing Catholics the right to vote.

June 5 Jesse Ketchum established the Home District Savings Bank at York, Upper Canada. It sought to encourage thrift and industry among York's working class.

July 28 The Moravian church opened its 4th mission in BNA in Hebron, a small Inuit community on the coast of Labrador.

Aug. 13 Matthew Whitworth-Aylmer, Baron Aylmer (1775–1850) was commissioned administrator of Lower Canada. He served Oct. 20, 1830 to Feb. 4, 1831.

Sept. 22 Robert Campbell (1808–1894) arrived at the Red R. He had been hired by the HBC to aid his relative, Chief Factor James McMillan, in establishing an experimental farm.

Oct. 19 Samuel Hart was refused an appointment as justice of the peace in Lower Canada on the grounds that a Jew was ineligible for office.

Oct. 22 The 1st issue of the *Catholic*, a weekly newspaper established by Catholic priest William Peter MacDonald (1771–1847) and printed in Kingston by Thomas Dalton (d 1840), appeared as the 1st English Roman Catholic newspaper published in Canada.

Oct. 28 Josiah Henson (1789–1883), a US slave from Kentucky, reputed to be the character on whom Harriet Beecher Stowe fashioned Uncle Tom in her novel *Uncle Tom's Cabin*, escaped to Upper Canada and founded Dawn, a settlement for fugitive slaves, near Dresden, Upper Canada. He became pastor of a black church, and built a cabin out of tulipwood.

Nov. 24 Matthew Whitworth-Aylmer was appointed Gov-in-C of Lower Canada, serving Feb. 4, 1831 to Aug. 24, 1835.

Also in 1830
• The York Temperance Society was founded.

• Que. architect Thomas Baillairge (1791–1849) completed the Church of Saint-Charles Borromée in Charlesbourg, Que. The stone structure featured a twin tower façade and a Palladian window.

• John Galt published the novel *Lawrie Todd*.

• British officer James P. Cockburn completed the watercolour *Quebec Market*.

• Adam Kidd (c 1802–1831) published the poem *The Huron Chief*.

• John Richardson's novel *Écarté; or The Salons of Paris*, based on the author's experiences during the 3 years he lived in London and Paris, was published by Henry Colburn in London, England.

1831

Jan. 7 The 1st session of the 11th Parliament of Upper Canada met until Mar. 16. Business included the Marriage Act (passed Mar. 2, 1831), which legalized marriages by dissenting ministers.

Jan. 23 The 1st session of the 14th Parliament of Lower Canada met until Mar. 31. Business included an act conferring full civil rights on Jews.

Jan. 26 The Black and Campbell Co. of Que. completed construction of the 48.7-m steamship *Royal William*. The vessel was shipped to Montreal for the installation of its machinery and was launched at Cape Cove, Que. The ship was registered at the Port of Quebec to the Que. and Halifax Steam Navigation Company and equipped with sails and paddle wheels. J. P. Cockburn painted a commemorative watercolour, *The Launching of the Royal William*, Apr. 29, 1831.

Jan. 31 Quebec and Montreal were incorporated as cities.

May 31 James Clark Ross, second-in-command to the John Ross expedition, moving overland by dogsled, located the North Magnetic Pole at Cape Adelaide on the west coast of Boothia Peninsula (at 70°06.3N, 96°46W) and planted a British flag on the site.

Sept. 9 Matthew Whitworth-Aylmer suspended Attorney Gen. James Stuart, an outspoken opponent of the Patriote party, for malfeasance of office. Stuart challenged Aylmer to a duel, but Aylmer declined. The Colonial Office dismissed Attorney Gen. James Stuart in Nov.

Sept. 29 Sharon Temple, begun in 1825 at Sharon, Ont., was completed by John (1768–1852) and Ebenezer (1772–1866) Doan, following the designs of David Willson (d 1866), a leader of Children of Peace, a dissident Quaker sect. The building was 18.3 m² on 3 levels, with 40 windows, and exists to this day.

Oct. 31 Montreal-born James Kipp (1788–1865) established Fort Peigan at the junction of the Missouri and Marias Rivers (Montana).

Nov. 14 A group of Montreal businessmen came together to fund the Champlain and St. Lawrence Railroad, Canada's 1st railway, to run between La Prairie, Que., on the St. Lawrence R. and St.-Jean, Que., on the Richelieu. A bill to incorporate the railway was slated for Royal Assent Feb. 25, 1832.

Nov. 15 The 2nd session of the 14th Parliament of Lower Canada met until Feb. 15, 1832. Business included the 1st copyright law, and provision for boards of health.

Nov. 21 Britain's colonial secretary, Lord Goderich, broached a new "systematic colonization" policy for Upper Canada, which favoured the auctioning of land to wealthy settlers rather than granting it to poor settlers, who, it was suggested, would be burdened by colonial taxes and become destitute.

Nov. 30 St. Andrews College opened at St. Andrews, PEI as the 1st Catholic college in the Atlantic provinces.

Dec. 12 William Lyon Mackenzie was expelled from the Assembly of Upper Canada by a vote of 24 to 15 for referring to that body in his *Colonial Advocate* as a "sycophantic office." On the same day, a mob of several hundred entered the Assembly and demanded that Colborne dissolve Parliament.

Dec. 17 James Stephen, adviser to the Colonial Office, wrote a report supporting a Legislative Assembly for Nfld., thereby turning the scales in favour of the reformers and against Gov. Cochrane, who favoured the status quo.

Also in 1831

• Control of local revenues passed to the Canadian assemblies.

• A petition, drawn up by Jesse Ketchum and Egerton Ryerson and signed by "Friends of Religious Liberty," asked the imperial parliament to place all denominations in the province on an equal footing and appropriate clergy reserves for general education and public works.

• The HBC began construction of Lower Fort Garry, 32 km downstream of the fork of the Red and Assiniboine Rivers. Completed in 1833, the fort became a major business centre for the Red R. settlement. The bulk of its trade was farm produce. By the 1840s, the fort included a blacksmith shop, brewery and distillery, a gristmill, sawmill and lime kilns.

• Scottish-born architect John Ewart (1788–1856) completed London District (now Middlesex

County) Courthouse, located on the River Thames in the township of Westminster in London, Ont. The 30.5 x 15.2 x 15.2 m castlellated-style building contains county offices and jail cells on the 1st floor, with the courtroom and judges' chambers on the 2nd floor.

• Harbour Grace Courthouse, located in Harbour Grace, Nfld., was completed by one of Nfld.'s 1st professional designers and master builders, Patrick Keough (1786–1863) of St. John's. The rectangular 2-storey institution featured a courtroom on the upper level, reached from the street by wood staircases.

• Designer James Cooper and builders John Edward Clyde and Saxton Burr, completed St. Andrew's Presbyterian located in Niagara-on-the-Lake, Ont. The Georgian-neoclassical redbrick church was an essential part of the town's rebuilding. Niagara-on-the-Lake had been destroyed by the Americans during the War of 1812.

• John Galt published the novel *Bogle Corbet*.

• R.D. Chatterton established Canada's oldest weekly newspaper, *The Cobourg Star*, at Cobourg, Ont.

• British army officer James Pattison Cockburn, stationed in Que., published *Quebec and its Environs*, with illustrations by the author.

1832

Jan. 2 W.L. Mackenzie was re-elected in a by-election by 119 votes to 1, after having been expelled from the Upper Canada Assembly. He was expelled a 2nd time on Jan. 7.

Jan. 25 Lower Canada passed the Quarantine Act, setting up a quarantine station at Grosse Isle, 48 km below Quebec City, to monitor passengers on incoming ships for cholera.

Jan. 28 The Commercial Bank incorporated in Upper Canada.

Jan. 30 W.L. Mackenzie won another by-election and was returned to the Upper Canada Assembly. The British colonial secretary informed Gov. Colborne that the Assembly could not banish eligible members.

Feb. 25 A bill passed by the Legislative Assembly of Lower Canada (1831) to incorporate a railway between the St. Lawrence R. and L. Champlain received Royal Assent. Seventy-four Montreal merchants established the Champlain and St. Lawrence RR Company and issued stock to over 700 subscribers, including Peter McGill and John Molson, who became the principal stockholders. The railway opened July 21, 1836.

Mar. 30 The Bank of NS was incorporated by the NS Legislative Assembly to break the monopoly and autocratic policy of the Halifax Banking Company. William Lawson (1772–1848) was the 1st president.

Spring Ross and his crew abandoned the *Victory*, irreparably crushed in the ice after 4 years. Three members of the expedition had died during the interim, but the remaining men made their way on foot to the shore of Somerset Is., where they found the remains of Parry's *Fury*, which provided enough timber for the construction of a shelter.

May 5 Brockville, Ont., was incorporated as a town.

May 7 Passengers and crew of *Voyageur* and *Carrick* spread typhoid and cholera before being quarantined on Grosse Isle, Que. The resultant epidemics killed 3,800 persons in Quebec City, and 4,000 in Montreal by Sept.

May 21 British troops shot 3 French-speaking Canadians during a turbulent by-election in Montreal. A grand jury exonerated the military.

May 24-29 The Rideau Canal was officially opened. The steamer, *Pumper*, was the 1st vessel to pass through the canal's entirety from Kingston to Bytown (May 29).

May 25 Col. John By was accused of overspending in the construction of the Rideau Canal and summoned to England for questioning.

Also in May
• John Gilchrist (1792–1859), building committee chairman for Cobourg, laid the corner stone for his town's Upper Canada Academy. The building would not be completed until 1836.

June 5 The king gave Royal Assent to a bill passed by Lower Canada legislature granting Jews the same political rights as Christians.

July 8 The Chippewa ceded 234,718 ha of what is now part of Ont.'s Lambton, Kent and Middlesex Counties, to the Crown.

Also in July
- Author Susanna Moodie, née Strickland (1803–1885), her husband and child left England, emigrating to Canada largely for financial reasons. They arrived in Canada on Aug. 30.

Aug. 22 Gov. Cochrane of Nfld. was empowered to create a legislature with an executive council of 7 members and to divide the island into 9 districts from which a 15-member assembly was to be elected. Cochrane retained the power to adjourn, prorogue and dissolve the legislature.

Aug. 31 Lt-Col. By submitted the final cost of the Rideau Canal (£777,146) to the British Parliament.

Also in Aug.
- Articles in the *Quebec Gazette* attacked Irish immigration as the cause of a cholera epidemic.

Nov. 2 W.L. Mackenzie was expelled *in absentia* from the Assembly of Upper Canada for the 3rd time.

Nov. 8 A Red R. sheep-purchasing commission, under Robert Campbell, left Fort Garry for the US, to purchase sheep as a starter herd for the settlement.

Nov. 16 Fire destroyed Hamilton, Ont.'s business centre resulting in damages estimated at £13,000.

Also in Nov.
- W.L. Mackenzie was re-elected by acclamation to the Assembly of Upper Canada for the 4th time.

Also in 1832
- The HBC built Old Bow Fort, also known as Peigan Post, on the Bow R.

- William Gooderham (1790–1881) and James Worts (d 1834) opened their gristmill in York (Toronto). Their 1st distillery was built in 1837 at the same site.

- The Burlington Bay Canal, expansion was completed to give large, L. Ontario going ships access to Hamilton Harbour.

- The Chute à Blondeau Canal on the Ottawa R. was opened.

- *The Museum of Montreal Magazine* was founded as a women's journal.

- John Richardson's novel in 3 volumes, *Wacousta; or, The Prophecy, A Tale of the Canadas,* was published. It was the 1st Gothic novel in Canada, and was set during Chief Pontiac's uprising (the conspiracy of Pontiac) of 1763. This novel made Richardson famous. In 1840, the sequel, *The Canadian Brothers; or, The Prophecy Fulfilled,* was published in Montreal and designated "a Canadian national novel." The author called on personal experiences to describe border warfare in the War of 1812.

- William (Tiger) Dunlop published *Statistical Sketches of Upper Canada*, under the pseudonym "A Backwoodsman." The humourous book encouraged young people to come to Upper Canada.

1833

Jan. 1 Nfld.'s 1st representative Assembly met at St. John's.

Jan. 13 The Ont. legislature passed an act reducing the number of capital crimes from over 100 to 12. Those retained included high treason, murder, petit treason, rape, carnal knowledge of a girl under 10, sodomy with man or beast, robbery, robbing the mail, burglary, arson, being an accessory before the fact, and assisting a murderer to escape.

Feb. 13 The British American Assurance Company, the 1st assurance company in Ont., was incorporated in York.

Feb. 14 Joseph Signay (1778–1850) became the 3rd Roman Catholic archbishop of Que.

Feb. 17 George Back left Liverpool on a mission to find John Ross, who had disappeared in the Arctic in 1829 while searching for a northwest passage.

Also in Feb.

• Hamilton, Ont., was incorporated as a city.

Mar. 9 Halifax Harbour froze over.

May 24 William Leslie Logie of Montreal became Canada's 1st medical graduate, receiving the 1st Canadian university degree in medicine which was awarded by the Montreal Medical Institution at McGill University.

June 16 John Wilson (1809–1869) killed 19-year-old Robert Lyon at Perth, in what is believed to be the last duel in Upper Canada. Wilson was acquitted and later became a judge in the Ont. Supreme Court.

June 17 The *Royal William*, 1st Canadian steamer to enter an American harbour, docked at the port of Boston, Massachusetts, where it was inspected by US President Andrew Jackson.

Summer George Back located the Thleweechoh or Great Fish R. (now known as the Back R.) while searching for John Ross.

• John Rae (1813–1893) sailed to Moose Factory as a surgeon of the HBC ship *Prince of Wales*.

July–June 13, 1839 Alexander Christie (1792–1872), employed by the HBC, was placed in charge of Red R. and appointed gov. of Assiniboia.

Aug. 14 John Ross and the surviving members of his expedition set out in boats salvaged from the wrecked *Fury* after melting ice opened a navigable lane of water in Thom Bay.

Aug. 18–Sept. 6 The *Royal William* sailed from Pictou, NS, to Gravesend, England, becoming the 1st Canadian vessel to cross the Atlantic under steam power alone. It was also the 1st vessel in Samuel Cunard's great Cunard Steamship Company fleet.

Aug. 26 The whaler *Isabella* rescued Ross and survivors of his expedition and returned them to England.

Aug. 28 The British Parliament passed a law abolishing slavery in all BNA colonies. It would take effect Aug. 1, 1834.

Sept. 16 Robert Campbell's sheep-purchasing commission arrived back at the Red R. settlement with less than one-fifth of the original flock of 1,370 Kentucky sheep. Four-fifths had either died or were sold along the way.

Dec. 2 W.L. Mackenzie was expelled from the Assembly of Upper Canada for the 4th time. He was re-elected Dec. 17, unopposed, to the Assembly, but was unsuccessful in taking his seat. Colborne later ordered him sworn in.

Also in 1833

• The Grenville and Carillon Canals were opened. The Grenville Canal was an Ottawa R. canal that followed old fishing routes through the Kawartha Lakes.

• The final section of the Welland Canal was completed between Port Robinson (Chippewa R.) and Port Colborne (L. Erie). It was 45-km-long, rising 99.3 m between the 2 Great Lakes.

• Egerton Ryerson, travelling to England for the Methodist Church conference, presented the colonial secretary with a petition of 20,000 signatures requesting that Clergy Reserves be liquidated and the proceeds used for education.

• John Galt's autobiography was published.

• The 1st daily newspaper in Canada, *The Montreal Daily Advertiser,* was founded by Henry Samuel Chapman (1803–1881).

1834

Jan. 23 The old Château St. Louis, in Quebec City, was destroyed by fire. It had been constructed under the gaze of Samuel de Champlain in 1620, and had served as residence of the govt of Canada. The site now lies under the Château Frontenac.

Feb. 8 Chiefs of the Six Nations residing along the Grand R. ceded 20,320 ha along the Grande R. to Britain upon payment of 2 shillings to each chief and appropriate presents.

Feb. 17 The "Ninety-two Resolutions" were introduced into the Assembly of Lower Canada and adopted 56 to 32. Believed to have been drafted by

Augustin-Norbert Morin (1803–1865) and Louis-Joseph Papineau (1786–1871), it outlined grievances against the colonial administration. Resolutions presented involved the control of revenue by the legislature, the responsibility of the executive and the election of legislative councillors.

Mar. 6 York was incorporated as Upper Canada's 1st city and renamed Toronto, its original name, from the Mohawk word "tkaronto" meaning "where there are trees standing in the water" (another interpretation comes from the Huron word "toronton" meaning "place of meeting"). The city had a population of 9,000.

Mar. 22 The Central Bank of NB was chartered.

Mar. 27 W.L. Mackenzie was elected alderman in the 1st Toronto elections. When the Reformers obtained a majority on city council, Mackenzie was chosen Toronto's 1st mayor, defeating John Rolph (1793–1870). Mackenzie was sworn in on Apr. 3.

Apr. 28 George Back returned to Thleweechoh R. His descent took 1 month, after which he spent 3 weeks exploring Chantrey Inlet. Back arrived at Ogle Point on the Arctic coast, at the mouth of the Thleweechoh (Great Fish) R., with Dr. Richard King and 8 other men, in a 10-m open boat, on Aug. 16.

May 6 The London and Gore Railroad, the 1st railway in Upper Canada, was incorporated. It was re-incorporated as the Great Western Railway Company on Mar. 29, 1845. The railway would have stations at Niagara Falls, Hamilton, Toronto, Galt, Berlin, Guelph, London, and Windsor by 1871.

May 23 The 1st issue of the British newspaper *Whig* was published at Kingston, Ont. The paper was a weekly publication.

May 29 Journalist Francis Collins died after contracting cholera as a result of visiting Irish victims in the hospital during the epidemic of 1834. His wife and daughter also succumbed to the desease.

June 24 George Étienne Cartier (1814–1873) serenaded members of the Société Saint-Jean-Baptiste at a banquet in Montreal with his recently composed song "O Canada, mon pays, mes amours." The société, founded by journalist Ludger Duvernay (1799–1852), was created to inspire Que. nationalism and to defend French heritage.

July 31 Midnight Slavery was officially abolished in all British territories, including BNA.

Sept. The Canadian steamship *Royal William* was sold to the Spanish govt, which renamed it *Isabella Segunda*, gave it a battery of guns, and equipped the ship as a corvette to become the 1st steamer of the Spanish Navy in active war service.

Nov. 4 The last issue of W. L. Mackenzie's *Colonial Advocate* was published in Toronto.

Dec. 15 The Montreal Special Sanitary Committee released a report blaming ship owners and captains for the cholera epidemic, which had claimed the lives of over 6,000 people in Lower Canada. Filthy conditions aboard incoming ships were deemed a primary contributory factor.

Dec. 25 St. John's, Nfld., magistrates were forced to call out the militia to protect Henry David Winston (1793–1855), editor of the virulently anti-Catholic newspaper, *Public Ledger*. Five months later, Winston was seized and beaten by disguised assailants (believed to be local Catholics) who cut off one of his ears during the assault. Winston's arch rival was Robert J. Parsons, publisher of the *Newfoundland Patriot*, a paper sympathetic to Nfld.'s Irish Catholics.

Dec. 30 Fire destroyed the Parliament Building of Upper Canada at Toronto.

Also in Dec.
• The Canadian Alliance Society, one of the earliest political parties in BNA, sought to expand beyond its Toronto base by establishing regional branches so that its reform platform would gain wider public support.

c 1834 Ebenezer Birrell painted *The Good Friends* in oil.

Also in 1834
• The Marine Hospital opened at Quebec City.

• Nfld.'s oldest surviving lighthouse, located at Cape Spear, the most easterly point in North America, was commissioned by the British govt. The beacon took 2 years to build, and was officially opened Sept. 1, 1836. It would burn both whale and seal oil. The square 2-storey, wood lighthouse stood more than 70 m above sea level and was visible from 33 km away on clear nights. It is now restored and open to the public by Parks Canada.

• Canadian merchant Maj. Rains shipped 453,592 kg of maple sugar worth $75,000 from St. Joseph's Is., Upper Canada.

• Toronto began construction of its 1st sewer system

1835

Jan. 1 Joseph Howe published an editorial critical of the Magistrates of Halifax in his paper *Novascotian*. Although the editorial was signed "The People," Howe was tried for criminal libel.

Jan. 15 The 1st session of the 12th Parliament of Upper Canada met until Apr. 17. Sale of liquor to Aboriginals was prohibited after Jan. 5, 1836.

Also in Jan.
• The Huron Union Society, formed by Col. Anthony Van Egmond (1775–1838), protested against the Canada Company's land-speculation policies wherein settlers were forced off their land so it could be resold at higher prices. Van Egmond himself was never paid for his road-building activities done at the behest of the company in order to open up more land for settlement.

Feb. 16 The Upper Canada Assembly voted to expunge all official records of W.L. Mackenzie's repeated ejections from that house.

Mar. 3 Joseph Howe was acquitted of libel in Halifax by the Supreme Court of NS. Acting as his own defence attorney, Howe spoke for 6 hours, without notes, on freedom of the press.

Apr. 2 William Pitt Amherst, 1st Earl Amherst (1773–1857), was appointed Gov-in-C of Lower Canada by British PM Sir Robert Peel, but resigned in May when the Peel govt fell.

Apr. 10 In Toronto, the Committee on Grievances, with W.L. Mackenzie as chairman, presented its 7th Report to the Upper Canada House, charging exhorbitant Crown patronage expensed through salaries and pensions, extravagant postal charges and the lack of legislature accountability.

Apr. 16 The Erie and Ont. and Hamilton and Port Dover Railways were incorporated.

May 4 Mary Boyles Jarvis, wife of Sheriff William Botsford Jarvis, planted a sapling that grew into the famous Rosedale Elm in Toronto.

June 1 The Kingston Maximum Security Penitentiary (originally called Provincial Penitentiary of the Province of Upper Canada) officially opened at 555 King St. West in Kingston, Ont. Designed by American William Powers of Auburn, New York, it was the 1st large prison in BNA. For the 1st 99 years of KP's existence, it was the only waterfront penitentiary in the country. In 1840, it was designated to serve both Upper and Lower Canada by the Act of Union.

June 15 "Shiners," gangs of Irish hooligans in Upper Canada, encouraged by Irish timber baron Peter Aylen (1799–1868), forced Bytown's magistrate, George W. Baker, a leader in the fight against lawlessness, to resign his post in order to protect his family. Shiners' violence made the Bytown area unsafe for residents as subsequent beatings, rapes and knifings continued unchecked. Finally the army was called in to restore control.

July 1 Archibald Acheson, 2nd Earl of Gosford (1776–1849), was appointed Gov-in-C of BNA and placed in charge of a Royal Commission to look into the state of affairs in Lower Canada. He served from Aug. 25, 1836 to Nov. 1837, when he resigned. Gosford returned to England in Mar. 1838.

Sept. 10 British colonial secretary Charles Grant, Lord Glenelg (1778–1866), ordered Crown land in NB to be turned over to control of the NB legislature and out of the hands of Commissioner of the Crown lands and Surveyor Gen. Thomas Baillie (1796–1863). Baillie's dictatorial manner and lavish lifestyle outraged many settlers.

Oct. 5 Citizens at a public meeting held in St. Andrews, NB, supported a proposal to build a railway to Que. On Mar. 8, 1836, the NB and Canada Railway Company was chartered to build the line. A boundary dispute with the US delayed construction. On Aug. 27, 1836, King William IV awarded the Railway its 1st installment.

Oct. 27 The 2nd session of the 15th Parliament of Lower Canada met until Mar. 21, 1836. Legislation included provision to install gas lighting in Montreal, and the establishment of normal schools (teachers' colleges).

Dec. 28 Britain withdrew its assent to the NB–Maine border arbitration, awarded by the King of the Netherlands, after the US had previously rejected it.

Also in 1835

• Dundurn Castle, the largest Regency house in Upper Canada, was completed in Hamilton, for Allan Napier MacNab (1798–1862), lawyer, entrepreneur and politician. Architect of the structure was Robert Charles Wetherell.

• Sir Francis Bond Head (1793–1875) was appointed lt-gov. of Upper Canada. He would serve from Jan. 25, 1836 to Mar. 23, 1838, replacing Colborne.

• Robert Baldwin Sullivan (1802–1853), a Tory, was elected mayor of Toronto, defeating W. L. Mackenzie. Mackenzie, although popular, was a poor administrator; Sullivan, a lawyer, was more closely involved with municipal concerns.

• *The Clockmaker; or, The Sayings and Doings of Samuel Slick, of Slickville*, by Thomas Chandler Haliburton, began to appear in the *Novascotian*. It would run for 22 installments.

• "Avant tout je suis canadien," another patriotic song composed by George-Étienne Cartier, was 1st sung by him at a Montreal banquet.

1836

Jan. 1 Anglican priest John Strachan resigned from the Legislative Council at the request of the British colonial secretary who felt it inappropriate that a religious representative serve on the Executive Council.

Jan. 15 Gov-in-C Gosford of Lower Canada prohibited the formation and existence of privately armed groups, such as the British Rifle Corps.

Jan. 26 John Colborne became C-in-C of British forces in Canada.

Feb. 14 George Jehoshaphat Mountain was consecrated as suffrage bishop in the diocese of Que. under the title Bishop of Montreal.

Feb. 20 Lt-Gov. Francis Bond Head invited several reformers, including Robert Baldwin, to join the Upper Canada Council. Baldwin remained only briefly, quitting when he realized he had no real power.

Also in Feb.

• BNA's 1st institution for the mentally ill opened in Saint John, NB. Established by Dr. George Peters (1835–1848), the facility was located in the basement of a former cholera hospital and housed 14 patients.

Mar. 21 The College of Chambly was chartered in Lower Canada.

Apr. 10 The 30 m *Beaver*, 1st steamship to appear on the northwest coast of America, arrived at Fort Vancouver 225 days after leaving England, having sailed around Cape Horn and up the Pacific coast. Its arrival launched the era of steamboats on Canada's West Coast. The *Beaver* served as a supply boat for the HBC.

Apr. 11 Patriotes (French-Canadian Reformers) attended a public meeting in Deux-Montagnes County to compose resolutions urging Lower Canadians to boycott British goods and products. The idea of founding national factories to decrease the colony's dependence on imported goods was also discussed.

Apr. 18 In Toronto, the Assembly of Upper Canada voted 31 to 20 in favour of withholding funding and supplies from the govt of Upper Canada, in order to enforce demands for responsible govt.

Also in Apr.

• The City of Toronto and Lake Huron Railway Company was incorporated.

May 4 The HBC bought the Red R. colony from the 6th Earl of Selkirk (heir to the original Lord Selkirk who established the settlement) for £15,000 of HBC stock plus accrued interest. This worked out to a total purchase price of £84,111. Although the 5th Earl of Selkirk had originally paid only 10 shillings for the 300,000 km of land, Selkirk spent over £100,000 of his own money to colonize the settlement.

May 28 Lt-Gov. Francis Bond Head dissolved Parliament in Upper Canada in response to the Assembly's passage of a non-confidence motion, 32–18, tabled as a result of the govt's repeated refusal to recognize Reformers' demands for responsible govt.

June Arctic explorer George Back, commanding the 330-tonne *Terror*, set out with a crew of 60 men on an expedition to trace the coast from Repulse Bay or Wager R. to as far as Point Turnagain, the farthest point reached by Franklin on his 1st land expedition.

July 4 After having lost his seat as alderman of Toronto to Edward William Thomson (1794–1865), W.L. Mackenzie founded the newspaper *Constitution*, named to mark the 60th anniversary of the US Declaration of Independence.

July 16 The Constitutional Reform Society was organized in Upper Canada, replacing the Reform Alliance Society.

July 21 The Champlain and St. Lawrence, 1st Canadian passenger railway, opened with a gala celebration with 300 guests. It would be the only passenger railway in Canada until 1847. Backed by John Molson and other Montreal merchants, it ran 24 km from St. Jean-sur-Richelieu, on the Richelieu R. to La Prairie on the St. Lawrence R. Passengers then boarded a steam ferry to cross the St. Lawrence R. to Montreal. The initial locomotive for the train *(Dorchester)* proved temperamental, and during the 1st year of operation, the railway was horse drawn for most trips. *Dorchester*, or "Iron Kitten," was the 1st railway locomotive in Canada. Built in England by Robert Stephenson (1803–1859), son of railroad pioneer George Stephenson (1791–1848), it was delivered in

Montreal and assembled in Molson's machine shop. *Dorchester* cost £1,500, was slightly over 4 m long and weighed 5.5 tonnes.

Aug. 9 The Chippewa ceded 600,000 ha in Bruce, Grey, Huron, and Wellington Counties in Ont. to the Crown.

• Francis Bond Head, lt-gov. of Upper Canada, announced his belief that First Nations peoples were a dying race. He presented his new Aboriginal peoples policy to a gathering of Ottawa and Chippewa leaders, who, he said, for their own protection, should be removed to a huge reserve on Manitoulin Is., away from European settlers.

Aug. 27 King William IV awarded the St. Andrews and the Quebec Railway £2,000 as the 1st installment of a £10,000 grant.

Sept. 27 The *Terror*, under George Back, was beset by pack ice upon entering Frozen Str. and was forced to spend the winter drifting in the ice off northeast Southampton Is.

Oct. 3 The Assembly of Lower Canada refused to vote money for govt expenses.

Nov. Joseph Howe was elected to the NS assembly.

Also in 1836

• American geologist James Hall (1811–1898) named rocks of Niagara Escarpment. He also prepared the 1st scientific description of the rim of Niagara Falls to assess the erosion rate. Erosion surveys of the falls did not begin until 1842.

• Nineteen km of Yonge St., in Toronto, were paved with macadam, although with limited success.

• Central Academy, a non-denominational institute of higher learning, opened in PEI under a Royal Charter. The 1st headmaster was Charles Lloyd. Only males were allowed to attend.

• King William IV authorized a prize of 50 guineas to the winner of the King's Plate horse race held at Trois-Rivières.

Nov. 16 Gov-in-C Gosford issued warrants against 26 Patriote leaders including Wolfred Nelson, on charges of treason.

• The Patriotes at Saint-Denis, joined by Papineau and Edmond Bailey O'Callaghan (1797–1880), decided to resist arrest, obtain arms and ammunition for the people.

• Revolt began near Longueuil, Lower Canada, when some 150 Patriote rebels, under Bonaventure Viger (1804–1877) and Dr. Timothée Kimber (1797–1852) fired on govt troops, led by Constable Malo, who was en route to St. Jean-sur-Richelieu to arrest Patriote leaders.

• Shops in Montreal were 1st lit by gas.

Nov. 22 In an attempt to crush the rebels, C-in-C of BNA troops, John Colborne, dispatched 2,000 troops, reinforced with a large Upper Canada contingent, against Patriotes in the Richelieu area.

Nov. 24 Col. Charles Stephen Gore (1793–1869) with a large force and artillery attacked Saint-Denis, a rebel stronghold about 32 km east of Montreal. Dr. Wolfred Nelson led 800 Patriotes in the 7-hour encounter. The British suffered 6 dead and 11 wounded; the Patriotes 12 dead and 7 wounded. The British were forced to retreat. A Patriote victory at the Battle of Saint-Denis shocked Lower Canada and made a hero out of Nelson. Papineau fled the battlefield during the hostilities.

• As a result of a dispute with the British govt, Francis Bond Head, lt-gov. of Upper Canada, resigned his commission, although he would remain lt-gov. until his replacement arrived in 1838.

Nov. 25 Three hundred British troops, under George Augustus Wetherall (1788–1868), advanced north from Chambly to attack Patriotes, under Thomas Storrow Brown, at Saint-Charles, defeating them at the cost of 7 dead and 23 wounded. The Patriotes suffered 28 dead and 30 wounded in the 2-hour battle. Brown escaped to the US.

Nov. 27 W.L. Mackenzie published his *Handbill for Rebellion,* which called on Canadians to "revolt — not against 'lawful' but against 'unlawful authority.'"

Nov. 30 Wetherall entered Montreal in triumph with 30 Patriote prisoners.

Dec. 1 Gov-in-C Gosford declared Papineau a rebel and offered £1,000 for his capture. Papineau fled to the US.

Dec. 2 Col. Gore again moved against Dr. Wolfred Nelson at Saint-Denis and was successful in routing the Patriotes, who fled into the woods. Separated from his companions, Nelson wandered for 10 days without food before being captured. Gore's troops sacked and looted the village.

• W.L. Mackenzie composed a "Declaration of Independence."

Dec. 4 Eight hundred Upper Canada rebels gathered at Montgomery's Tavern, on Yonge St. north of Toronto, prepared to enter the city and attack Parliament on Dec. 7.

• Toronto Loyalist Col. Robert Moochie, discovering the rebels intent, attempted to warn authorities, but was shot and killed by the rebels.

Dec. 5 W.L. Mackenzie led his rebel force down Yonge St. to attack Toronto, 8 km away. The men were met at Gallow's Hill (south of today's St. Clair Ave.) by Dr. John Rolph (1793–1870) and Robert Baldwin who presented a verbal offer of amnesty from Gov. Bond Head if the rebels would disperse. No written confirmation of the offer was received, and the rebels continued to march until they were fired upon (south of present-day Maitland St.) by Sheriff William Jarvis (1799–1864) and a small group of Loyalists. One rebel was killed and 2 more mortally wounded. The rest fled north to Montgomery's Tavern. Rebels Samuel Lount (1791–1838) and David Gibson prevented Mackenzie from burning down Sheriff Jarvis's house.

• Gov-in-C Gosford declared Lower Canada to be in a state of marital law.

Dec. 6 W.L. Mackenzie seized a mail coach carrying Gov. Bond Head's plans for Toronto's defence.

• Eighty Patriotes attempting to return to Canada, having re-grouped and been re-supplied in the US, were ambushed by local military and retreated to the US.

• Rolph, who was a fomenter of Mackenzie's rebellion, fled to the US, where he stayed for the next 7 years.

Dec. 7 Gov. Bond Head dispatched 500 militia and 1,000 loyalist volunteers under Lt. James FitzGibbon (1780–1863) and Allan McNab to Montgomery's Tavern to put down the rebellion. The mission was successful, as 5 rebels were killed, 6 wounded and several captured, including Lount, Peter Mathews (1786–1838) and Anthony Van Egmond. Mackenzie's papers were captured and Montgomery's Tavern burned to the ground. Mackenzie escaped across the American border.

Dec. 11 Bishop Signay published a 2nd pastoral letter denouncing the Lower Canada insurrection.

Dec. 12–14 Dr. Charles Duncombe (1794–1867) preached rebellion in Upper Canada's London district and assembled a force in excess of 500 men. Duncombe led the group in a march toward Toronto, with more rebels joining in. MacNab and his troops skirmished with Duncombe and his rebels near Hamilton, Ont. The rebels were dispersed. MacNab took 500 suspected rebels captive, but released most of them. Duncombe escaped to the US.

Dec. 13 W.L. Mackenzie returned from the US and seized Navy Is. in the Niagara R., and proclaimed a provisional govt, the "Republic of Canada," with a new flag, bearing 2 stars: 1 for English Canada and the other for French. Mackenzie also proclaimed himself head of state.

• John Colborne left Montreal with a military expedition of 2 brigades with some 2,000 men, British and Canadian regulars and militia, to engage the Patriotes. Their goal was St.-Eustache, 31 km northwest of Montreal. Commanding the 2 brigades were Lt-Cols. John Maitland and Wetherall.

Dec. 14 Colborne attacked St.-Eustache where 400 rebels commanded by Amury Girod (c 1800–1837) and Dr. Jean Olivier Chenier (1806–1837) had taken over the church, presbytery and convent. The rebel

strongholds were torched and the Patriotes forced out of cover, into the open where they were slaughtered. Chenier and 70 of his men were killed, with another 118 taken prisoner. The British suffered 1 dead and 9 wounded, and followed their victory by going on a rampage, destroying 60 to 70 houses in addition to religious buildings.

Dec. 15 One hundred and fifty Patriotes at Saint-Benoît surrendered to John Colborne without a struggle, although the village was burned to the ground.

Dec. 22 George Arthur (1784–1854) was appointed lt-gov. of Upper Canada and served from Mar. 23, 1838 to Feb. 9, 1846. He was the last administrator to serve under the constitution of 1791.

Dec. 29 The American steamer *Caroline,* used for carrying supplies to Mackenzie's rebels on Navy Is., was cut adrift and burned by a Canadian force under the command of Andrew Drew (1792–1878). The attack was made on the US side of the border, and 1 American was killed. The incident almost caused a war between the US and Britain.

Also in 1837

• The Ont. town of Cobourg was incorporated.

• The collapse of English and American banks caused financial and commercial crises.

• Archdeacon George Jehoshaphat Mountain (son of the former bishop) became bishop of the diocese of Upper and Lower Canada. Strachan, in spite of his efforts to be named bishop of Upper Canada, was again passed over and the diocese remained undivided.

• Anne Langton (1804–1893) immigrated to Canada to join her brother at Sturgeon L., Upper Canada. She kept journals and letters depicting life in Upper Canada. These were compiled and published by her nephew in the book *A Gentlewoman in Upper Canada* (1950).

• Robert Davis (c 1800–1838) published *The Canadian Farmer's Travels in the United States of America,* in which remarks are made on the arbitrary colonial policy practised in Canada, and the free and equal rights and happy effects of the liberal insitutions.

• Thomas Roy (d 1842) presented a talk to the Geological Society of London, England, entitled *On the Ancient State of the North American Continent,* wherein he identified the raised shoreline left by Glacial L. Iroquois which appears around L. Ontario.

1838

Jan. 1 Thomas Jefferson Sutherland (d 1852) spoke in Cleveland, Ohio, before a large "Canada Meeting," which adopted resolutions sympathetic to the Patriotes of Canada. Sutherland offered 49 ha of land and $100 in silver to any who would join his army and attack Canada. One hundred men enlisted and left for Detroit under his command.

Jan. 2 Patriote leaders, who had succeeded in evading the British Army and made their way to the US, met at Middlebury, Vermont, to discuss the possibility of another insurrection. Among them were Dr. Robert Nelson (1794–1873), brother of Wolfred, Papineau, Edmund Bailey O'Callaghan (1797–1880), parish priest Étienne Chartier (1798–1853), Edouard-Étienne Rodier (1804–1840), Edouard-Elisée Malhiot (c 1810/1814–1875), Dr. Cyrille-Hector-Octave Côté (1809–1850), Thomas Bouthillier (1798–1853), Joseph-François Davignon and Julien Gagnon.

Jan. 5 US President Martin Van Buren issued a neutrality proclamation, which forbade Americans from taking sides in the Canadian revolt.

Jan. 8 Fort Madden at Amherstburg was fired upon by the vessel *Anne,* commanded by Edward Alexander Theller (1804–1859) while Thomas Sutherland occupied Bois Blac Is. Both men were members of secret societies of US sympathizers called Hunter's Lodges. Theller and all 20 of his associates aboard the *Anne,* which had run aground, were captured by Canadian militiamen under Col. Thomas Radcliffe (1794–1841).

Jan. 9–10 Sutherland issued proclamations from Bois Blanc Is., inviting Upper Canadians to join his Patriote forces in freeing Canada "from Tyranny." Learning of Theller's capture, Sutherland ordered a

retreat back to the US, an action for which he was accused of cowardice. Theller was arrested at Detroit (Jan. 13) for violating American neutrality laws but was later acquitted.

Also in Jan.
• W.L. Mackenzie and his rebels abandoned Navy Is. and retreated to Buffalo, New York, after being repeatedly shelled by British artillery fire. Once on US soil, they were arrested for violating American neutrality laws.

Feb. 10 An act of British Parliament suspended the constitution of Lower Canada until Nov. 1, 1840 and moved to appoint John George Lambton, Lord Durham (1792–1840), to replace Sir John Colborne as gov-gen. with orders to investigate Canadian grievances and arrive at a solution. In addition, a Special Council was established for Lower Canada to work alongside the Executive Council for settling matters.

Feb. 20 John Rolph was expelled, *in absentia,* from the Assembly of Upper Canada for having "combined, conspired and confederated, with the rebels."

Feb. 26 Van Rensselaer, commanding 500 US sympathizers of the Patriote cause, occupied Pelee Is. in L. Erie, only to be defeated by a combined Canadian force of regulars and militia on Mar. 3.

Feb. 28 Dr. Robert Nelson, and his chief lieutenant, Dr. Cyrille-Hector-Octave Côté, led 300 to 400 Patriotes and members of the Hunters' Lodge from Alburg, Vermont, on an expedition to invade Lower Canada. Upon reaching Canadian soil, the rebels distributed a declaration of independence and proclaimed a republic with Nelson as president. They were promptly attacked and pushed back into the US where they were immediately arrested for having violated American neutrality laws. A sympathetic jury acquitted them.

Mar. 4 Thomas Sutherland was captured at the mouth of the Detroit R. and taken to Toronto to be tried for treason. Fearing execution, he bungled an attempt at suicide, and was later released by Canadian authorities, ultimately returning to the US.

Mar. 5 The Bank of Upper Canada suspended payment until Nov. 1, 1839.

• The town of Kingston, Ont., was incorporated.

Mar. 30 John Lambton, Lord Durham, was commissioned Gov-in-C of Lower Canada, High Commissioner of Upper and Lower Canada and Gov-Gen. of BNA. He served from May 29, 1838 to Nov. 1, 1838.

Apr. 2 John Colborne appointed a Special Council of 22 members to govern Lower Canada. James Cuthbert (1769–1849) was elected chairman.

Apr. 6 *Le Canadien* published Pierre-Joseph-Oliver Chauveau's (1820–1890) 1st poem, "L'Insurrection," exalting the heroism of the Patriotes.

Apr. 10 Alexander Theller was convicted of treason in Toronto and sentenced to death. The punishment was later commuted to exile for life in New South Wales (Australia).

Apr. 12 Samuel Lount and Peter Mathews were publicly hanged at Toronto following their convictions for treason.

May 29 US pirate William Johnston (1782–1870) and a band of Patriotes seized, robbed and burned the Canadian steamer *Sir Robert Peel*, in the St. Lawrence R. in revenge for Canadians burning the *Caroline*. Johnston and crew made off with $175,000 in cash.

• The Bank of Montreal issued pennies, which were considered rare coins.

May 30 Queen Victoria allowed the HBC a 21-year extension of its NA trading monopoly initially granted in 1821 by George IV. In addition, the new royal grant expanded HBC territory to include lands west of the Rocky Mountains and the Columbia R. basin. Although HBC held royal charter to these rich fur-trading areas, its commerce was under constant attack from locally situated NWC members who did not recognize Britian's right to grant exclusive trading privileges.

June 1 Lord Durham dissolved the Special Council of Lower Canada appointed by Colborne and selected in its place his own Executive Council (June 2) which included Vice-Admiral Charles Paget (1778–1839), Col. Charles Grey, Col. George Couper, Buller, Turton Penn (c1795–1866), James Macdonell, Randolph Isham Routh (1787–1858) and Dominick Daly (1798–1868). The 1st sitting of Durham's council was June 28. Members of Colborne's council were excluded.

June 4 This 1st recorded baseball game in Canada was played in honour of King George IV's birthday in Beachville, Ont. Rules of the day allowed a total of 22 players between the 2 teams and 5 bases. All 11 players from each team would bat in an inning and all 11 would need to be retired to end an inning. The game pitted Beachville against the Zorras, and the ball was made of twisted wool yarn, covered with calfskin. Any wooden or crafted straight stick was used as a club (bat). All players in this game were inducted into the Canadian Baseball Hall of Fame in 1988.

June 11 James Morreau led a rebel raiding party across the Niagara R., advancing as far as Short Hills, Upper Canada (Pelham Township, Ont.), where they attempted to take the village but failed. Morreau was captured and hanged on July 30.

June 28 During the 1st meeting of his newly selected Special Council, Lord Durham banished 8 Patriotes, including Dr. Wolfred Nelson, to Bermuda, as an alternative to their death sentence for treason. He also prohibited 16 other Patriotes, including Papineau, from returning to Lower Canada on pain of death. All other prisoners except 2 were given amnesty. On Aug. 10 the British govt found these acts exceeded the responsibility of Lord Durham's role as gov-gen. because they were levied without proper jurisprudence.

Also in June
• The Dease expedition ascended the Dease R., reaching the mouth of the Coppermine R. July 1. They were stopped by ice at Cape Flinders on Aug. 9, 4.8 km south of Franklin's 1821 encampment at Point Turnagain. Thomas Simpson, with 5 HBC servants and 2 Aboriginal guides, continued on foot, exploring 161 km of coast, naming Victoria Land (Is.) and Cape Pelly and charting lands east of the Coppermine R. His group

reached the river mouth, but was halted by ice until July 7.

July 3 The 1st issue of reform newspaper *Toronto Examiner*, established by Francis Hincks (1807–1885), was published in Toronto with the motto "Responsible Government," to which the words "and the Voluntary Principle" were later added. Hincks held the positions of proprietor and editor.

Aug. HBC Gov. George Simpson travelled to St. Petersburg, and persuaded the Russian govt to sign a commercial pact with the HBC to supply Russian traders with grain, beef and manufactured goods which had formerly been supplied by Americans. In return, the Russian govt agreed to lease to the HBC fur-trading rights in the Alaska Panhandle. Simpson's negotiations were carried out with Baron von Wrangle, a director on the board of the Russian–American Company.

Sept. 16 Five Patriote prisoners, all members, of the Hunters' Lodges, led by Edward Theller, and aided by sympathizers, escaped from the Citadel of Que. Theller made his way back to the US where he was received as a hero. In 1841, Theller published *Canada 1837-8*, outlining his analysis of the causes of the late attempted rebellion and its failure.

Sept. 20 James Morris (1798–1865) was appointed commissioner to administer funds for the building of canals on the St. Lawrence R. to improve its navigation.

Nov. 1 Lord Durham left Que. for England on the *Inconstant* as large crowds watched. He had resigned his position as gov. of BNA because the British govt repudiated his decision to exile 8 rebels to Bermuda and ban others from returning to Canada.

Nov. 1–Jan. 17, 1839 John Colborne served as administrator of Lower Canada.

Nov. 3 Joseph-Narcisse Cardinal (1808–1838), brig-gen. of the Patriote army at Châteauguay, commanded a force that disarmed and arrested leading members of the English party in the parish.

• Some 800 Patriote rebels took the town of

Beauharnois, Lower Canada, including the seigniorial manor.

Nov. 4 Robert Nelson and Dr. Côté, joined by several hundred habitants, led a 2nd rebellion in Lower Canada. Nelson was declared president of the Canadian Republic upon his arrival at Napierville, Que. He commissioned Charles Hindenlang as commander of the military forces with the rank of brig-gen. and reissued his proclamation of independence, which had been proclaimed the previous Feb.

• Patriote leaders Joseph Cardinal, Joseph Duquet (1815–1838) and François-Maurice Lepailleur (1806–1891) entered a First Nations reserve at Caughnawaga to obtain weapons and ammunition for the rebellion. All members of the Patriote expedition were invited to join in negotiations, and once assembled, were surrounded by their hosts and taken to jail in Montreal.

• Gen. John Colborne proclaimed martial law in Lower Canada.

Nov. 5 Banks of Lower Canada suspended payment, until June 1839.

• Colborne appointed Jean Baptiste Toussaint Pothier (1771–1845) chairman of the Special Council of Lower Canada

Nov. 8 A proclamation by the govt of Lower Canada established emergency regulations suspending *habeas corpus*.

Nov. 9–10 Patriotes, under Robert Nelson and Dr. Côté, attacked militiamen, under Charles Taylor, at Odelltown. Patriotes suffered serious losses and retreated to the US. Nelson himself fled before the end of the fight.

Nov. 10 Govt militia drove Patriote rebels from their strongholds at Napierville and Beauharnois. Homes of all known rebels were torched.

Nov. 11 Hunters' Lodge members commanded by Nils von Schoultz (1807–1838), steamed out of Sackets Harbor, New York, aboard the *US Paul Pry* which towed 2 schooners full of men down the St. Lawrence. Their objective was to attack Prescott,

Upper Canada. The Hunters' Lodges were defeated by superior British forces in the battle of Windmill Pond, Nov. 16. On Nov. 28 Nils von Schoultz, Joseph-Narcisse Cardinal, Joseph Duquet, Charles Hindenlang and 8 companions were brought before a court martial set up by John Colborne, and tried for high treason. All 4 men and most of their companions were found guilty of high treason and hanged on Dec. 8 and Dec. 21. Two rebels were acquitted.

Nov. 12 William Johnston, US pirate and participant in the attack on Prescott, fled Canada when the battle turned against the rebels.

Nov. 21 President Martin Van Buren issued a 2nd proclamation, forbidding Americans from taking part in the Canadian rebellion.

Dec. 4 Canadian militia, under John Prince (1796–1870), repulsed a raid on Windsor, conducted by about 400 men under Gen. Bierce of the Detroit Brotherhood of Hunters. Four Hunters were summarily executed by Prince.

Dec. 10 The Second Rebellion in Lower Canada was quashed when some 400 Patriotes were defeated at the Village of Beauharnois, Que. A total of 850 prisoners were taken; 12 were executed on Dec. 12 and 58 sent to penal colonies in Australia.

Dec. 13 John Colborne was appointed Gov-in-C of Lower Canada. He served Jan. 17, 1837–Oct. 19, 1839.

Also in Dec.
• The magazine *Literary Garland*, founded by John Gibson, began publishing in Montreal and carried the distinctive honour of being the 1st Canadian literary journal to survive more than 3 years.

c 1838 Théophile Hamel (1817–1870) painted *Three Indian Chiefs Leading a Delegation to Quebec,* in oil.

• Philip J. Brainbrigge (1817–1881) painted the watercolour *Bush Farm Near Chatham*.

Also in 1838
• Thomas McKay (1792–1855), chief contractor of the Rideau Canal, built Rideau Hall, a large limestone house, which he designed in the style of a Scottish Regency villa.

• Smallpox killed two-thirds or more of the Assiniboine, Blackfoot and North Sask. Cree.

• The Canadian Post Office introduced perforation on Canadian stamps.

• Architects Francis Pickle and R.S. Stevens completed Myrtleville House, in Brantford, Ont. The 2-storey, 9-room house, originally owned by Allen and Eliza Good, was occupied for 4 consecutive generations by the Good family. The farmhouse, its contents and 2.2 ha, were donated by the Good family to Heritage Canada, which currently operates the building as the Myrtleville House Museum.

• The 1st issue of the *Saint John Morning News* was published as the 1st penny newspaper in the British Empire.

• *Winter Studies and Summer Rambles in Canada* by English gentlewoman Anna Brownwell Jameson, née Murphy (1794–1860), was published in London, England. Presented in the form of a journal to an absent friend, it recorded the risks of travel and the foibles of persons encountered by the author. It remains a classic among travel journals.

1839

Jan. 2 The govt shut down *La Fantasque*, the only newspaper in Lower Canada that had not ceased publication during the rebellion of 1837.

Jan. 21 Queen's College, founded by the NS Baptist Education Society as an extension of the Horton Academy, was opened at Wolfville, NS. It was later renamed Acadia College.

Also in Jan.
• William Lyon Mackenzie moved to Rochester, New York.

• St. James Cathedral in Toronto was destroyed by fire.

Feb. 4 Lord Durham submitted his *Report on the Affairs of BNA* (the Durham Report) to the British Colonial Office. It recommended systematic Anglicization of French Canadians in order to make them a minority in Canada. It also recommended responsible govt for a united Canada through legislative union of Upper and Lower Canada. Durham's report was presented to the House of Commons on Feb. 11. Durham described the Canadian situation as "two nations warring in the bosom of a single state."

Feb. 8 NB lumberjacks harvesting timber in Maine's Aroostook R. valley region (on the disputed border area between the US & Canada) seized Rufus McIntire, a land agent sent to remove them. Maine declared war on Canada and both Maine and NB called out their militias. No shots were fired, and a truce allowed both parties to seek arbitration. On Mar. 25, the Aroostook War (war of pork and beans) ended by negotiated compromise. Winfield Scott represented the US, Col. John Harvey represented NB. The exclusive claim of the British was surrendered and the Americans agreed to withdraw their forces.

• Papineau sailed from New York to Paris where he attempted to win French sympathy for the Lower Canadian cause, but produced no political result.

Feb. 11 The British Admiralty awarded Samuel Cunard a contract to provide steamships to carry the mails twice monthly between Liverpool, England, and Halifax and back, and to provide a branch service to Boston and another branch from Pictou to Quebec. This marked the beginning of the famed Cunard White Star Line. A 10-year subsidy of £55,000 per year was awarded Cunard, who did not own 1 steamship. However he set up the British and North American Royal Mail Steam Packet Company, and contracted with Scottish engineer Robert Napier to build 3 boats at £32,000 each.

Feb. 15 Six political prisoners were publicly hanged for their part in the rebellion of 1837–1838.

Feb. 27 The 2nd session of the 5th Parliament of Upper Canada met until May 11. Business included the adoption of resolutions favouring the union of Upper and Lower Canada.

Also in Feb.
• Meeting in Hamburg, Germany, officials of the HBC signed an agreement with the Russian govt to lease a strip of the Northern Pacific coast in Alaska from Russia for a period of 10 years, at an annual fee of 2,000 otter pelts and other benefits.

Mar. W.L. Mackenzie and John Montgomery (1788–1879) founded an association to organize Canadian exiles living in the US, in an effort to prevent rash military expeditions against Canada.

Apr. 12 Upper Canadian Reformer Francis Hincks wooed the support of his Lower Canadian counterpart, Reformer Louis-Hippolyte LaFontaine (1807–1864), for the unification of 2 Canadas, the goal of which would be responsible govt.

Apr. 22 In his report on the conditions of Aboriginal People in Upper Canada, James B. Macaulay, a judge of the Court of Queen's Bench, rejected the suggestion of Francis Bond Head that First Nations peoples be moved to a huge reserve on Manitoulin Is. in the belief that they were a dying race.

May 1 The last trial of leaders of the 1837 rebellions was held in Lower Canada.

May 11 The College of Physicians and Surgeons of Upper Canada was established.

May 18 Methodist minister James Evans (1801–1846) met George Simpson, gov. of the HBC, and convinced him that Methodist missionaries would not disrupt activities in the HBC territory. Simpson opened up the territory to the Methodists.

June 1 Banks in Lower Canada resumed payment.

June 20 Lord John Russell introduced a resolution in the British Parliament, based on the recommendations of the Durham report, calling for the union of the Canadas.

Also in June
• Having conducted his own defense, W.L. Mackenzie was found guilty of breaking the neutrality laws of the US and was given a $10 fine and 18 months in jail. He was pardoned in 1840 after having served less than a year.

Summer John Bell (c 1799–1868) explored the Peel R. from its junction with the Mackenzie for the HBC.

July 3 With the opening of the ice pack, Simpson and Dease set off to explore eastward.

July 4 The Council of Assiniboia increased the number of judges assigned to each of its districts to establish a more effective judicial system.

July 28 The Dease expedition doubled Cape Alexander, discovering Dease and Simpson Strait (now Simpson Strait) separating King William Is. from the mainland.

Aug. 4 John Strachan became the 1st Anglican bishop of Toronto. He accepted the position without stipend.

Aug. 7 Ludger Duvernay (1799–1852, founder of the St-Jean-Baptiste Society in 1834) , a Patriote exile living in the US, established the newspaper *Le Patriote Canadien* in Burlington, Vermont.

Aug. 16 Thomas Simpson and Peter Dease arrived at Montreal Is. in Chantrey Inlet and discovered a cache of pemmican, chocolate and gunpowder left by George Back. This find enabled Simpson to connect Franklin's explorations with those of Back. Simpson very nearly discovered the Northwest Passage.

• John Russell, head of Britain's colonial office, discontinued the practice of life appointments for public officials and introduced a new system of administration, wherein a public official would enjoy his office at the pleasure of the Crown and be removed when the Crown deemed the holder no longer useful.

Aug. 17 Members of the Dease expedition named Cape Britannia. Thomas Simpson made a run north 65 km to the northeast of Cape John Ross, naming the Castor and Pollux Rivers after the expedition's two boats. The expedition explored the south coast of King William Is.

Also in Aug.
• Back in the US, Edward Theller founded the newspaper *Spirit of '76*, which espoused the rebel cause in Canada and communicated almost daily with the rebels, including W.L. Mackenzie.

Sept. 6 Charles Poulett Thomson, Baron Sydenham (1799–1841), was appointed gov-gen. of Lower Canada. He arrived in Que. to take up his post Oct. 19, 1839, remaining in the position through Feb. 10, 1841. His mandate: to prepare the provinces of Upper and Lower Canada for union.

Sept. 11 The 1st Canadian track and field meet was held at Caer Howell grounds near Toronto.

Sept. 16 The Dease expedition arrived back at the Coppermine R., having completed the longest voyage on the polar sea in boats and having more than fulfilled the mandate issued them by the HBC.

Sept. 19 The 1st railway in the Maritimes and 2nd steam railway in Canada, the Albion Mines Railway, opened for the purpose of carrying coal from Albion Mines to the loading pier at Dunbar Point near Pictou, NS, about 95 km. It was the 1st railway in Canada to use a standard gage and split-switch movable rail.

Oct. 28 Augustin-Norbert Morin was arrested for high treason for his part in the rebellion of 1837–1838. He did not remain long in prison because the charge was ill founded.

Nov. 1 The Bank of Upper Canada resumed payments.

Nov. 11 Gov. Thomson convened the Special Council of Lower Canada to meet in Montreal. Because of snow, only 15 members arrived, 12 of whom voted in favour of the union of Upper and Lower Canada.

Nov. 22 Thomson, Baron Sydenham, assumed control of the govt of Upper Canada as Gov-in-C.

Dec. 3 The 5th session of the 13th Parliament of Upper Canada met, until Feb. 10, 1840. Business included the adoption of resolutions in favour of the union of the Canadas.

• The Erie and Ontario Railroad (a horse-drawn tramway) went into operation between Queenston and Chippewa, Ont.

Dec. 11 A public meeting held in Toronto proposed the establishment of a Presbyterian college at Kingston.

Dec. 13 Gov. Thomson's proposals for the union of the two Canadas were approved by the Legislative Council of Upper Canada by a vote of 14 to 8, over the strong opposition of Bishop John Strachan.

Also in 1839

• *Histoire de l'Insurrection du Canada*, by Louis Joseph Papineau, was published, in which he expressed his conviction that Canada was destined to become part of the US.

• Catholic priest Fr. Georges-Antoine Belcourt (1803–1874), a missionary to the Ojibwa and Saulteaux Nations, published his book, *Principles of the Saulteaux Indian Language*.

1840

Jan. 17 French Canadians met at Que. and adopted resolutions protesting the fact that the proposed union of Upper and Lower Canada was proceeding without consultation with Lower Canadians.

Jan. 23 Gov. Thomson submitted a draft bill to Britain's Secretary of State, Lord Russell, seeking to introduce the union of the two Canadas with "as little interference as possible" in existing institutions.

Feb. Robert Baldwin became solicitor-gen. of Upper Canada, but without a seat on council.

Mar. 14 Joseph Howe accepted a challenge to duel issued by John Halliburton, son of the chief justice of NS, Sir Brenton Halliburton (1775–1860). Halliburton (Jr.) objected to an editorial in Howe's *Novascotian*, which was sharply critical of his father. When Halliburton's shot missed the mark, Howe shot in the air.

Apr. 7 Methodist minister James Evans was apprised of his appointment as gen. superintendent, Northwest Indian Missions, and took up his new position at HBC's Norway House some 30 km north of L. Winnipeg, and 650 km north of Winnipeg. On Nov. 17, Evans, who had built his own printing press and invented the 9-character Cree and Inuit syllabic system of lettering, started printing hymns on birchbark. The alphabet is still in use.

Apr. 17 At Niagara Falls, Irish-Canadian Benjamin Lett, a Hunters' Lodges member, blew up the 19.8-m Tuscan column monument of Gen. Sir Isaac Brock (killed in battle on Oct. 13, 1812).

Also in Apr.

• James Douglas of the HBC was sent to Sitka to discuss arrangements for the takeover of the Stikine with the Russian authorities. This was done in accordance with the 1839 agreement reached with the Russian-American Company.

• The Catholic clergy, led by Bishop Signay, informed the British Parliament of their opposition to the union of Upper and Lower Canada.

June 14 Explorer Thomas Simpson, travelling east through Sioux country, was found dead of a shotgun wound. It is believed he took his own life after having shot and killed 2 of his Métis companions.

June 22 Henry Budd (c 1812–1875), an Aborignal orphan, set out for Cumberland House District to begin a new school and mission for First Nations peoples. He had been a protégé of John West. Budd later moved to W'passkwayaw (The Pas) and built a house wherein he taught and held services.

June 26 Lower Canada was divided into 4 districts.

Also in June

• W. Davies returned to Fort Smith after having explored up the Churchill (Hamilton) R. as far as Churchill (Grand) Falls in search of a supply route to Fort Nascopie for the HBC.

July 9 Gov. Thomson assumed control of the govt of NS and recommended remodelling its Executive Council to include leading members from both sides of the Assembly. Chief govt officials would be compelled to sit in that house.

July 17 The 1st scheduled Cunard Steamership, *Britannia*, 90 m long, with 2 paddlewheels, 3 furnaces and capacity for 115 passengers, plus cows, plus mail, arrived at Halifax from Liverpool at 2 a.m. with Cunard and his daughter Anne aboard. It carried 90 crewmen, 63 passengers, and took 12 days to cross the Atlantic. The *Britannia* left for Boston the next day, where joyous citizens presented Cunard with perhaps the largest silver cup in the world.

July 23 The Union Act, which had received Royal Assent in England on July 23, 1840, came into effect. It united the provinces of Upper and Lower Canada into one govt with one gov-gen. appointed by the Crown, aided by an appointed Executive Council, an appointed legislative council and a popularly elected assembly of 84 members, 42 from each province. Upper Canada became Canada West, and Lower Canada became Canada East. Kingston, Ont., was the 1st capital of this new Province of Canada. Gov. Thomson, 1st Baron Sydenham, became the 1st gov-gen. of the new province, of Canada.

July 27 Whaling Capt. William Penny (1809–1892), accompanied by Inuit guide Eenoolooapik (c 1820–1847), rediscovered an inlet on Baffin Is. visited by large numbers of whales each year. Penny named the inlet Hogarth's Sound (Cumberland Sound).

Also in July

• NS coal miners went out on strike. This was the 1st coal miners' strike in the colony.

Aug. 9 Royal Assent was given to the Clergy Reserves Act providing for the sale of certain clergy reserves (public lands set aside for the use of the Church) with 5/12 of the proceeds going to the Church of England.

Aug. 10 Louis Anselm Lauriat, from Boston, Massachusetts, took off from Barrack Square, Saint John, NB, in the 1st-known balloon flight in Canada. His airship was the *Star of the East*.

Aug. 18 Lower Canada received news of the passage of the Act of Union, causing the French-Canadian community to unite against the Act.

Aug. 28 Lower Canada Reformer, Louis-Hippolyte LaFontaine (1807–1864) published in *l'Aurore* urging unity in the struggle for responsible govt and denouncing the terms of union for the 2 Canadas as expressed in the Union Act.

Oct. 18 Robert Terrill Rundle (1811–1896), representing the Wesleyan Society of London, arrived at Fort Edmonton as the 1st Protestant missionary in the region (now Alb.) and the 1st to serve among the Blackfoot.

Oct. 19 The steamer *Ontario* was the 1st large vessel to navigate the upper St. Lawrence rapids.

Also in Oct.

• Joseph Howe entered the Executive Council in a coalition with Tory James William Johnston. During the coalition period, Howe became speaker of the Assembly.

Nov. 12 The British govt established a magnetic and meteorological observatory at Toronto. Situated in a log cabin on what is now the University of Toronto campus, the observatory was 1 of 4 established worldwide in conjunction with the Royal Society in London. Its sophisticated instruments allowed scientists to measure magnetic fields and their movement, chart weather patterns and measure astronomical time periods. A more permanent observatory was built in 1855.

• Alexander McLeod (1825–1841), deputy sheriff of the Niagara district, was arrested in Lewiston, New York, for alleged involvement in the *Caroline* affair and was indicted by the state grand jury for arson and murder. He was brought to trial in 1841 but acquitted when he produced a satisfactory alibi.

Dec. James Douglas of the HBC was sent to California to investigate trade prospects, the possibility of trapping expeditions, and to purchase cattle from the Mexicans. Also, on his advice, the HBC built the post of Yerba Buena at San Francisco.

c 1840 Que.-born Joseph Légaré (1795–1855) painted *Cascades de la Rivière Saint-Charles à Jeune-Lorette*, oil on canvas. Also in 1840, Légaré painted *Les Chutes de Saint-Ferréol,* oil on canvas, a beautiful landscape of the St. Anne R., near Quebec City. Both paintings are now in the Musée national des beaux-arts du Québec, Quebec City.

• Post office services were provided by approximately 400 country postmasters in Upper and Lower Canada.

Also in 1840

• The govt imposed a 2 pence per gallon tax on Canadian spirits and increased the still tax to £40 per still per annum. There were some 200 licenced distilleries in Upper and Lower Canada. Thomas

Carling (d 1875) opened his 1st commercial brewery in London, Upper Canada, and built Proof Line Road to facilitate transport of his stock to communities in the countryside.

• Robert Campbell of the HBC was the 1st European to discovered the Pelly R. and L. Finlayson.

• A Weller stagecoach travelled from Toronto to Montreal in 36 hours.

• Halifax received the queen's blessing for its Queen's Plate horse race, run by the Halifax Turf Club on a public race course constructed in 1826.

1841

Feb.13 The Draper-Ogden Ministry was formed, holding office until Sept. 1842. William Draper (1801–1877) became Attorney Gen. of Canada West, and Charles Ogden (1791–1866), Attorney Gen. for Canada East. Robert Baldwin accepted a seat on the Executive Council and became solicitor gen. of Canada West.

Mar. 29 St. Mary's College at Halifax was chartered.

Mar. 31 George Simpson, gov. of the HBC, began a trip around the world that took him 20 months.

Also in Mar.
• Canadians of Canada East and Canada West voted to select members to the 1st Canadian Assembly after passage of the Act of Union.

Apr. 10 Halifax was incorporated as a city.

Also in Apr.
• W.L. Mackenzie established the *Rochester Volunteer* in the US. The struggling paper devoted its energies toward whipping up war between Great Britain and the US.

May 17 Boulders from Cap Diamant fell on the Lower Town of Quebec City, demolishing 8 houses and killing 32 people.

June 9 Gov-Gen. Sydenham appointed a Legislative Council of 24 members, which held its 1st meeting at Kingston, Ont. The next day, Baldwin demanded Sydenham assign 4 cabinet posts to French

Canadians, and Baldwin warned that he would have to oppose the govt on a vote of confidence if this requirement was not met. This ultimatum was ignored and on June 14 Baldwin resigned from the Executive Council over the lack of French-Canadian and Reform (who held the Assembly majority) representation in the Executive and Legislative Councils.

Also in June
• The 1st session of the 1st Parliament of United Canada met at Kingston in a hospital: it sat until Sept. 18. Business included the District Council Act, organizing local govt in Canada West, a reduction in the number of capital crimes, abolition of the pillory, a unified banking system under the Banking Act, authorization of the govt to purchase the Welland Canal from a private company and grants for the construction of canals, roads, navigation of the St. Lawrence.

June–Aug. 1842 Author John Richardson published the *New Era*, or *Canadian Chronicle*, in Brockville, Ont., in an attempt to bring "polite literature" to Canadians.

July 20 The Natural History Society of Montreal and the Literary and Historical Society of Quebec petitioned the 1st united parliament of Upper and Lower Canada to allocate funds for carrying out a geological survey of Canada. William Edmond Logan (1798–1875) applied for and was awarded the survey job of the new Geological Survey of Canada agency.

July 27 Upper Canada Academy, established in 1836 as the country's leading Methodist academy, became Victoria College. In 1884, it became Victoria University, and in 1892 moved upriver to join the U. of Toronto.

Aug. James Douglas accompanied George Simpson to Sitka to negotiate once more with the Russians concerning the fur trade in Southeastern Alaska.

Sept. 3 The Canadian Parliament passed the "September Resolutions," in favour of responsible govt.

Sept. 18 Royal Assent was given to a bill introduced by Charles Day (1806–1884) for the establishment and maintenance of non-denominational elementary school education. It provided for an annual sum of $80,000 for schools in Canada West, and $120,000 for Canada East.

• Royal Assent was given to the Imperial Copyright Act, which went into effect in 1842. The Imperial Copyright Act ended the circulation of cheap, pirated copies of British authors' books in BNA. Thereafter, copyright agreements with America tended to lump Canada into the American market. France dominated the book market in Que.

Sept. 19 Gov-Gen. Sydenham died of lockjaw as a result of a riding accident.

Sept. 23 French-Canadian Reform leader LaFontaine, won a seat in the Canadian legislature in an English-speaking riding after Gov. Thomson prevented his running in a French-speaking riding. Robert Baldwin convinced his supporters to elect LaFontaine in his place. This action sealed the alliance between Reformers representing both languages in Canada.

Sept. 24 Richard Jackson (1777–1845), C-in-C of British forces in BNA, was appointed administrator of the province of Canada, serving until Jan. 12, 1842.

Also in Sept.
• Roman Catholic priest Modeste Demers (1809–1871), the 1st Christian missionary to reach the mainland of BC, visited Fort Langley in the Fraser Valley, where he baptized many First Nations Peoples.

Oct. 7 Charles Bagot was commissioned gov-gen. of Canada and served from Jan. 10, 1842–Mar. 29, 1843.

Oct. 13 James Sinclair (1811–1856), leading a party of 23 families, arrived at Fort Vancouver (Vancouver, Washington), hoping to strengthen Britain's claim to the Oregon country. Sinclair's brother-in-law, James Bird (1773–1856), and the Cree Maskepetoon (c 1807–1869), served as guides.

Oct. 16 The Presbyterian Queen's College in Kingston, Ont., received a Royal Charter from Queen Victoria.

The college would open Mar. 7, 1842 with 2 faculty and 10 students. The college was intended to prepare students for the ministry.

Dec. 1 The *Canadian Spelling Book* received the 1st copyright in Canada.

Dec. 17 A Catholic diocese, covering the western half of Upper Canada, was established with Michael Power (1804–1847) its 1st bishop. He chose Toronto as his seat.

Also in 1841
• A head tax of 5 shillings was imposed on each immigrant to Canada to provide a medical examination at the quarantine station at Grosse Île, Que., and to provide assistance to destitute immigrants.

• The population of Canada East was estimated at 625,000, and Canada West at 455,688.

• More than 2 million bushels of Canadian wheat and flour were exported to England.

• Toronto's Provincial Lunatic Asylum opened in a converted jail with 17 patients under the superintendency of William Reese (1801–1874).

• The city of Toronto, population 1,500, was served by 20 physicians. Medical consultations in the city cost 5 shillings by day and £1 at night.

• The eminent British geologist Sir Charles Lyell and the American geologist James Hall visited Niagara Falls to estimate the rate of recession. The Niagara Gorge had been cut after the last ice sheet left Ont.; their calculations suggested ice left 35,000 years ago. Geologists now estimate that the ice left about 13,000 years ago. At Niagara, Lyell discovered the buried St. David's Gorge.

• Dutch painter Cornelius Krieghoff (1815–1872) immigrated to Canada from the US, with his wife, settling 1st in Toronto then Montreal. He painted over 2,000 works depicting Que. habitant life, Aboriginal peoples and Canadian celebrations.

• Joseph Howe sold the *Novascotian* in order to devote all his energies to politics.

• Standish O'Grady (1793–1841) published the epic

"The Emigrant, a poem in four cantos," in Montreal, by John Lovell.

• Antoine Plamondon painted a portrait of *Soeur Saint-Alphonse*, oil on canvas, now at the National Gallery of Canada.

1842

Jan. 1 The Municipal Act went into force. It set forth city government guidelines wherein a board of control was assigned executive powers including nomination and dismissal of officials and employees.

Jan. 12 John Ings founded *The Islander* (PEI) newspaper.

Mar. 15 At a public meeting in Montreal, French Canadians drafted an open letter urging their fellow citizens to petition the British govt to repeal the Act of Union, on the grounds that it was designed to keep the French in the minority in the Assembly regardless of population.

Apr. 5 Abraham Gesner opened the Gesner Museum, the 1st public museum in Canada, in Saint John, NB. It featured rock and mineral samples, wildlife specimens and archaeological and ethnological artifacts Gesner had collected while a geologist with the geological survey in NB. The museum was a financial failure.

Apr. 11 The Bank of NS rescued the Cunard business empire from bankruptcy by approving a substantial loan, on the condition that all of Cunard's holdings be mortgaged to the bank.

Apr. 23 Gov-Gen. Sir Charles Bagot laid the cornerstone of King's College, Toronto.

Also in Apr.
• Bishop Strachan founded the Church Society, an establishment designed to provide a framework for clergy and laity to work together to advance the interests of the Church of England.

May 8 Michael Power was consecrated the 1st Roman Catholic bishop of Toronto, by Bishop Gaulin (c 1788–1857). William Peter MacDonald was appointed his vicar-gen.

June 19 Jean-Baptiste Thibault (1810–1879), a Roman Catholic Oblate priest from St. Boniface, arrived at Edmonton to establish a mission where he hoped to persuade the Métis to start farming. He also wanted to provide a place for the Cree to practice Christianity in safety.

June 23 HBC posts were ordered to expand their operations westward and to take control of the fur trade from Aboriginal middlemen.

Also in June
• Egerton Ryerson was inducted into the post of principal, Victoria College, in Upper Canada.

• Nelson Hackett, a fugitive slave who had escaped to Canada, was returned to servitude in Fayetteville, Arkansas, after his owner had travelled to Canada to charge Hackett with horse-stealing and other crimes, and hired influential politician John Prince as prosecutor.

Aug. 9 The Ashburton Treaty (Webster-Ashburton Treaty), signed by Daniel Webster for the US, and Alexander Ashburton (1774–1848) for Great Britain, awarded over half the territory claimed on NA's northeast frontier to the US. It established the boundary between Maine and the colony of Canada, and settled the US–Canada boundary from the headwaters of the Ste. Croix R. to the Lake-of-the-Woods. US citizens received the right to navigate the Richelieu R.

Aug. 31 The British govt imposed a new political structure on the Nfld. govt by amalgamating its 2 legislative houses (the Legislative Council and the Assembly) into one body with elected and appointed members. A simple majority decided each question. The change was prompted by constant conflict and chaos in the Nfld. legislature.

Also in Aug.
• HBC's Simpson assigned John Bell the task of finding a trade route to the west and First Nations who would trade directly. Bell was forced to end his expedition and return to Fort McPherson after his Kutchin guide abandoned him at the Richardson Mountains on the route to the Yukon R.

Sept. 8 The 2nd session of the 1st Parliament of

United Canada met, sitting until Oct. 12. Business included the enactment of a new election law, the imposition of duty on imported US wheat and a resolution declaring Kingston unsuitable for the seat of govt.

Sept. 10 Gov-Gen. Charles Bagot sent for Canadian Reform leader LaFontaine to discuss terms for his support in the Assembly. LaFontaine was also named Attorney Gen. of Canada East. He delivered his 1st speech to the united Assembly in French on Sept. 12.

Sept. 15 William Draper (1801–1877) resigned from the Executive Council and Assembly to allow the inclusion of French candidates in the govt, in the hope that there would be established a Conservative party embracing both French- and English-speaking interests.

Sept. 26 Baldwin and LaFontaine organized the Baldwin–LaFontaine Ministry, the 1st liberal Executive Council in Canada, representing victory for the Reform Party, responsible govt, and the rights of French Canadians. Two other Reformers, Augustin-Norbert Morin (1803–1865) and Thomas Aylwin (1806–1871), also joined the Council.

Oct. 5 Baldwin lost a by-election in his riding of Hastings County, Canada West, after being appointed as a cabinet minister.

Oct. 10 Gov-Gen. Charles Bagot appointed W. Rawson, William Hepburn and John Davidson to serve on a commission to report on the administration of the colony's Indian Department and to find out why the policy of assimilation was not working.

Also in Oct.
• Newly appointed Indian commissioner Joseph Howe, of NS, began a 5-week tour of Mi'kmaq reserves and encampments in northwestern NS. He found an impoverished and neglected people desperately in need of aid.

• The 1st Toronto synod was held by the Catholic Very Reverand William Peter MacDonald.

c 1842 Henry James Warre (1819–1898) painted the watercolours *Sleighing in the City of Montreal* and *Sleighing in the Country*.

Also in 1842
• Charles Dickens visited Montreal.

• Bishop John Strachan initiated the establishment of the Diocesan Theological Institution at Cobourg, Ont., in association with St. Peter's Church, for the training of clergymen for the Church of England. Alexander Neil Bethune (1800–1879) was appointed to head the institution.

• David Fife (1805–1877) discovered Red Fife, the 1st rust-resistant wheat in Canada. It yielded well on heavy clay soils, was a good thresher, and produced excellent flour. Use of Red Fife spread throughout the US and Canada.

• Construction of the 2nd Welland Canal was started. The success of the 1st Canal and the increased size of ships using it necessitated a new and improved waterway. The number of locks was reduced to 27, and the length and width of each lock was increased. The govt of Canada, having purchased the canal from the Welland Canal Company in 1841, supervised the construction.

• Robert Campbell established the Francis L. post, the 1st HBC post in what is now the Yukon Territory.

• Portrait artist William Valentine (1789–1849) introduced the daguerreotype in Halifax to satisfy his clients' demands for accurate, inexpensive portraits.

• John Fraser was the 1st North American to use a diving suit and helmet, at Pictou, NS. He had received a British patent for the equipment in 1835.

• Sir Charles Lyell, the eminent British geologist, visited Toronto to examine the raised shorelines left by Glacial Lake Iroquois, which were 1st identified by Thomas Roy in 1837. Lyell explained the shorelines were a result of submergence of the land under the sea, because he couldn't think of anything "capable of damming up the waters to such heights." That the St. Lawrence had been filled by glacier ice was only to be realized much later. To Lyell, and to many others, including Robert Bell as late as 1890, the ancient shorelines indicated progressive uplift of North America.

• The *Canadian Scenes* series of books written by Nathaniel Parker Willis (1806–1867) and illustrated by William Henry Bartlett (1809–1854) were published in London, England.

• Antoine Gérin-Lajoie (1824–1882) composed "Un canadien errant," one of the most famous of all Que. songs, which told of those exiled from Que. after the failure of the 1837 uprising.

• Roberts Art Gallery was established and remains Toronto's oldest private institution of its type.

1843

Jan. 19 Mount Allison Wesleyan Academy, named after Charles Frederick Allison for his gift of money and land, opened its doors at Sackville, NB.

Jan. 30 Robert Baldwin accepted a Lower Canadian seat in Parliament, for the riding of Rimouski, by acclamation, after he was defeated by Orange mobs in Hastings and Second York.

Jan.–July 1844 Author John Richardson published *The Canadian Loyalist and Spirit of 1812,* in Kingston, Ont. wherein he opposed Durham's union of the Canadas.

Feb. 16 James Douglas began construction of Fort Camosun (Fort Victoria) for the HBC, its 1st fort on Vancouver Is. It was renamed Fort Victoria in Dec.

Feb. 24 Charles Theophilus Metcalfe, Baron Metcalfe (1785–1846), was commissioned gov-gen. of Canada. He served from Mar. 30 to Nov. 26, 1845, succeeding Charles Bagot who was ill (and died of a heart condition within 3 months).

Apr. 13 John Henry Lefroy (1817–1890) left Toronto on an expedition, commissioned by the British govt, to conduct a magnetic survey of northern HBC territory.

Also in Apr.
• W.L. Mackenzie became a US citizen.

June 8 King's College (University of Toronto) was offi-

cially opened, 17 years after it was granted a charter. Bishop John Strachan became president.

June 11 Six strikers, working on the Beauharnois Canal (part of the St. Lawrence Seaway), were killed by govt troops called in to quell the strike. Workers were demanding a pay increase from 6 to 7 shillings daily.

June 19 The Canadian Baptist Union was founded at a convention in Paris, Canada West, to create a central voice for Baptist churches and associations in Canada.

Also in June
• Three canals opened: Cornwall, on the St. Lawrence R. system; Ste. Anne's Lock, on the Ottawa R. system; and Chambly, on the Richelieu and L. Champlain system. The latter, linking Chambly and St. Jean, Que., was not completed until Nov. 17.

July 9 *Prince Albert,* the 1st iron steamboat built in Canada, was launched at Montreal.

July 12 An Imperial Act (Canada Corn Act) allowed Canadian wheat and flour into Britain with only nominal duty, while classifying American grain milled in Canada as "naturalized" Canadian flour upon payment of a Canadian duty charge of 3 pence per quarter measure.

Aug. 18 George Brown (1818–1880) and his father, Peter, established the *Banner* at Toronto, a weekly newspaper holding Presbyterian and Reform principles.

Aug. 31 Two thousand people built Our Lady of Sorrow Chapel in Halifax, NS, in 1 day.

Also in Aug.
• John Rolph returned to Toronto after a grant of amnesty was issued to those who took part in the rebellion of 1837.

Sept. 28 The 3rd session of the 1st Parliament of United Canada met until Dec. 9. Business included the imposition of duty on American horses, cattle and grain, in answer to a US tariff.

Oct. 6 The Assembly voted to move Canada's capital to Montreal because Kingston was considered too small. The decision was sent to England for approval. On May 10, 1844, the capital of Canada was moved from Kingston to Montreal, where it would remain until Nov. 14, 1849. It would then alternate between Toronto and Quebec City approximately every 4 years until Ottawa was selected (1857) and became the permanent capital in 1859.

Nov. 8 An Orange mob burned effigies of Robert Baldwin and Francis Hincks outside Baldwin's home in Toronto for his part in attempting to control Orange Order violence by supporting passage of a bill suppressing all secret societies except Freemasons.

Nov. 24 The "Metcalfe Crisis" occurred when LaFontaine and his ministers demanded that Gov-Gen. Metcalf make no govt appointments without consulting them. On Nov. 27, LaFontaine and Baldwin and all the members of his ministry, with the exception of Provincial Secretary Dominick Daly (1798–1868), resigned en bloc after Gov. Metcalfe refused to confer with the ministers when making appointments, thus interfering with the accustomed patronage of the LaFontaine ministry.

Nov. 29 William R. Beaumont (1803–1875), physician and inventor of medical instruments, was appointed King's College's 1st professor of surgery at an annual salary of £200. Inaugural lectures for the King's College Medical School did not begin, however, until Jan. 1844.

Dec. 9 Royal Assent was granted for the establishment of Bishop's College in Lennoxville, Que., through George Mountain's influence. George Mountain's nephew became the 1st principal of this liberal arts institution.

Dec. 12 William Draper, Denis-Benjamin Viger (1774–1861) and Dominick Daly (the only member of the previous govt not to resign) formed the Draper–Viger Ministry.

Also in Dec.

• NS Lt-Gov. Lucius Bentinck Cary Falkland (1803–1884) weighted his ministry in favour of the Tories to demonstrate his preference for mixed rather than party govt. This resulted in the resignation of Joseph Howe and two other Reform councillors.

• Gov. Metcalfe announced British govt approval for the Canadian relocation of the capital from Kingston to Montreal.

Also in 1843

• The Archdiocese of Quebec counted 200,000 members, 145 churches or chapels and 4 orders of nuns.

• The Montreal School of Medicine and Surgery was founded.

• *The Banished Briton and Neptunian*, an autobiography by Robert Fleming Gourlay, was published in Boston as a 38-part serial.

• Thomas Chandler Haliburton published the 1st series of *The Attaché*, recounting Sam Slick's observations as a member of the American legation in London. Haliburton was influenced by Thomas McCulloch's "Letters of Mephibosheth Stepsure," published earlier, in 1821.

• The novel *Argimou: a Legend of the Micmac*, by Charlottetown-born writer Samuel Douglas Smith Huyghue (1816–1891), was published.

1844

Feb. Francis Hincks, with financial backing from LaFontaine, Baldwin, and Theodore Hart (1816–1887), a Montreal Reformer, established the newspaper *The Pilot* in Montreal as a voice for Reformers. The 1st issue was published Mar. 5.

Mar. 3 A non-confidence vote of 54 to 20 removed the Tory Draper–Viger govt from power. The Tory ministry resigned the next day.

Mar. 5 George Brown published the 1st edition of Toronto's *The Globe*, a liberal weekly for Reform politicians. (Brown and his father also continued to publish the *Banner*.) The new paper was 4 pages long; 300 copies were printed. *The Globe* was destined to become the most powerful newspaper in BNA. By Oct. 1, 1853, *The Globe* was issued daily with a circulation of approximately 6,000.

Mar. 15 Street processions were banned by the mayor of Saint John, NB, because of violence between Protestants and Catholics. The ban notwithstanding, violence broke out again between these 2 groups on Mar. 17.

Apr. 12 James K. Polk won the Democratic nomination for US president, on a platform calling for the annexation of Texas and Oregon. His slogan, referring to the Oregon country, was "fifty-four forty or fight." He served from Mar. 4, 1845 to Mar. 4, 1849 as the "manifest destiny" president.

Apr. 17 Reformer Lewis Thomas Drummond (1813–1882) defeated brewer William Molson — 1,383 to 463 — in a violently contested Montreal by-election. One man died and dozens others were wounded.

Apr. 22 William Harris founded the *Bytown Packet*, which is now the *Ottawa Citizen*.

May 25 British Army officer John Henry Lefroy completed a series of observations on magnetic activity at Fort Simpson, Rupert's Land, for the British govt. Such surveys sought to determine the exact location of the Magnetic North Pole.

Also in May

• The Vatican consented to the creation of the ecclesiastical province of Que.

May–Apr. 1846 Joseph Howe assumed the editorship of his old *Novascotian* and the *Morning Chronicle*, resigning his position in politics.

June 21 Russian explorer Lavrenty Alekseyevich Zagoskin (1807–1890) completed his survey of the Yukon interior.

June 27 The Banque du Peuple was incorporated in Montreal.

July 19 NB's 1st leper hospital opened on Sheldrake Is.

Sept. 3 The NB legislature passed a law permitting the sale of First Nations lands to Europeans, the proceeds of which would be used to establish a fund for Aboriginals.

Sept. 23 Gov. Metcalfe dissolved Parliament and called a general election.

Also in Sept.

• Canada defeated the US in the 1st international cricket match in North America.

• Egerton Ryerson was appointed assistant superintendent of schools in Canada West.

Oct. 14 John A. Macdonald (1815–1891) was elected to the Legislative Assembly of Canada from Kingston, Ont.

Oct. 26 In a letter published in the *Acadian Recorder*, Charles Fenerty announced he had discovered how to make paper from spruce wood pulp. Fenerty had been successful with his process earlier (1841), but had failed to announce it to the public. His delay cost him the patent on the production of paper from wood fibre.

Also in Oct.

• The national general election resulted in a Tory majority under William Henry Draper in Canada West, and a Reform majority (29 of 42 seats) under LaFontaine in Canada East, with an overall Tory majority. Draper continued in his position as leader of the govt. Viger, defeated in the election and without a seat until the following year, accepted an office from Gov. Metcalfe as president of the Executive Council.

Nov. 8 Knox College opened in Toronto.

Nov. 29 The 2nd session of the 2nd Parliament of United Canada met in Montreal, until Mar. 29. Business included the establishment of municipal govt in Canada East, new customs duties on almost all commercial imports and removal of restrictions on the official use of French.

Dec. 17 The govt of Upper Canada addressed the queen, unanimously requesting that she pardon all former rebels. An amnesty was granted 2 months later.

Winter 1844–1845 Dr. John Rae made a 1,931-km journey on snowshoes from Red R. to Sault Ste. Marie, carrying on the explorations begun by Thomas Simpson.

c 1844–1845 *A View of King Street, Toronto, Showing*

the Jail and Courthouse, oil, was painted by Toronto architect, Thomas Young (d 1860).

Also in 1844

• Several Hareskin people who had come to trade at Fort Good Hope starved to death.

• Institut Canadien, a literary and scientific society, was founded in Montreal by a group of young French Canadians. Its library became the largest free library in Montreal.

• The Toronto Typographical Union was founded.

• The population of the Red R. colony was 5,148.

• Architect Henry Bowyer Lane (1817–1878) designed and oversaw the construction of Toronto's 1st city hall, which cost $52,000 to build.

1845

Jan. 19 Thirty-nine Lower Canadian Patriote exiles were pardoned. They arrived back in Que. after 6 years of exile in Australia.

Feb. 17 The St. Lawrence and Atlantic Railroad Company was chartered to build a line from Montreal to the US border, where it would meet a railway built by a US promoter from Portland, Maine. The world's 1st international railway would provide year-round access to the Atlantic for Montreal.

Feb. 26 Reformer Thomas Cushing Aylwin challenged Dominick Daly to a duel. Shots were fired but neither party was injured.

Apr. 7 Construction began on St. Michael's Cathedral and the Bishop's Palace in Toronto, one of Bishop Power's important achievements. Both edifices were designed by William Thomas (1799–1860). The Bishop's Palace, a 3-storey building adjacent to the Cathedral, was to become the rectory. The Neo-Gothic cathedral was consecrated Sept. 29, 1848. Its 2-bell, 79-m bell tower was consecrated in 1866

Apr. 29 Toronto businessmen formed a board of trade to encourage sales and exports of local goods and services.

May 19 Sir John Franklin, at age 59, sailed from the R. Thames in command of 129 officers and men of the *Erebus* and *Terror* to continue the search for the mysterious Northwest Passage. This was his 3rd Arctic expedition and the best equipped to date. The ships were fitted with steam-driven screw-propellers for the 1st time. They also had ice-breaking bows and food for 3 years. This was the largest expedition ever sent in search of the Northwest Passage.

May 28 Fire destroyed most of Quebec City and the suburb of St-Roche, leaving about 5,000 residents homeless.

June 1 Explorer John Bell reached the Little Bell R. that led to the Porcupine R. He reached the mouth of the Porcupine R. (which flows into the Yukon R.), opening a route to the Pacific Ocean on June 16.

June 17 Painter Paul Kane left Toronto for the West Coast, alone with only his portfolio, sketching materials and gun. Influenced by artist George Catlin, Kane intended to sketch Canada's Aboriginal peoples before they were driven to extinction, as Catlin believed they would be.

June 28 A 2nd fire within a month devastated Quebec City, destroying 1,300 houses in the suburb of St. John and leaving about 700 families homeless.

Also in June

• Lt-Gen. Charles Cathcart, 2nd Earl of Cathcart (1783–1859), assumed command of the armed forces in BNA. The most probable reason for his appointment was the imminent threat of war with the US over the Oregon boundary. The British govt considered the situation to be serious.

• Robert Campbell descended the Pelly R. to the mouth of the Lewes R. where the 2 rivers joined to form the Yukon R.

July 20 Catholic Monsignor William Fraser (1779–1851) became bishop of Arichat, which included all of Cape Breton and what is now the counties of Antigonish and Guysborough. William Walsh (1804–1858) became bishop of Halifax, which included the rest of the province of NS and the Is. of Bermuda.

Aug. The 1st volume of François-Xavier Garneau's (1809–1866) *Histoire du Canada depuis sa découverte jusqu'à nos jours* was published in Que. Two more volumes would follow. Garneau was French Canada's 1st scientific historian.

Sept. 5 A Saulteaux was hanged from the wall of Fort Garry, in the Red R. Colony, after being tried and convicted of killing a Sioux and a fellow Saulteaux.

Oct. 9 Patriote leader Papineau returned from exile in the US, arriving in Montreal to a hero's welcome.

Oct. 16 The 1st issue of the weekly newspaper *Western Globe*, also known as the *London, Western and Huron District Advertiser*, was distributed in London, Canada West.

Also in Oct.
• Fire ravaged the leper hospital at Sheldrake Is., NB.

Nov. 24 Gov. Metcalfe appointed a commission to inquire into the losses suffered during the Lower Canada Rebellion of 1837-1838.

Nov. 26 Gov. Metcalfe returned to England for medical treatment of a terminal illness.

Nov. 26–Apr. 24, 1846 Charles Cathcart (1783–1859) served as colonial administrator of Canada.

Dec. 4 Point Prim, PEI's 1st lighthouse, became operational.

Dec. 15 The conservative govt only assigned 16 French-Canadian commissions in its reorganized militia of 118 commissions.

Dec. 23 William Ewart Gladstone (1809–1898) was appointed Secretary of State for the colonies.

Winter Paul Kane completed the paintings *Encampment among the Islands of L. Huron,* now in the Art Gallery of Ont., Toronto.

c 1845 *Canadian Wedding,* watercolour by James Duncan (1805–1881), was completed.

Also in 1845
• The Beauharnois Canal was completed between L. St. Francis and L. St. Louis, on the St. Lawrence R.

• Benjamin Franklin Tibbets (1813–1853) of Saint John, NB, invented the world's 1st practical compound marine steam engine, which revolutionized marine travel. Tibbets pioneered his new invention in the steamer *Reindeer.*

• Donald McLeod of New London, PEI, discovered a prehistoric bone known as Bathygnathus, or Canada's 1st dinosaur. It was not until 1905 that later research indicated the bone was from a pelycosaur. Today the specimen resides in the University of PEI collection.

• Robert C. Todd (1809–1866) completed his most famous painting, *The Ice Cone, Montmorency Falls,* oil on canvas, now in the National Gallery of Canada. The painting portrays the giant ice hill formed from the mists at the base of the falls, on which children are sliding.

• Joseph Legare painted *L'incendie du à Quartier Saint-Jean,* oil on canvas, now in the Art Gallery of Ont., Toronto.

• George Simpson published his *Narrative of a Journey round the World in 1841 and 1842 in 2 volumes,* edited by Adam Thom.

1846

Jan. 27 Britain's PM, Sir Robert Peel, announced the adoption of free trade. Also, timber imported from BNA would no longer enjoy preferential duty status.

Feb. 9 The US Congress ended joint occupancy of Oregon.

Mar. 16 Charles Cathcart was appointed gov-gen. of Canada. He served from Apr. 24, 1846 to Jan. 29, 1847.

Mar. 20 The 2nd session of the 2nd Parliament of United Canada met, until June 9. The rights of certain persons charged with treason in connection with the Rebellion were restored.

Spring The Ryerson School Act was passed, providing

for a Board of Education and making provision for the establishment of common schools in every parish in Canada East.

Apr. 24 Étienne-Paschal Taché (1795–1865) demanded that the Lower Canadian militia be reorganized, in light of strained relations between the US and Canada over the Oregon boundary issue.

Apr. 27 John A. Macdonald made his 1st speech in Parliament, advocating the repeal of usury laws.

Also in Apr.
• François-Xavier Garneau published the 2nd volume of his *Histoire du Canada depuis sa découverte jusqu'à nos jours.*

May 18 Kingston, Ont., received a city charter. John Counter (1799–1862) was the 1st mayor of the city.

May 26 Public meetings held at St. John's, Nfld., resulted in the adoption of resolutions favouring responsible govt.

June 9 An act of the British Parliament granted a civil list. Salaries of all govt employees, including that of the gov-gen., came under the control of the provincial administration of Canada. Royal Assent was given to the Act Aug. 16, 1847.

• Hamilton, Ont., received a city charter.

• Fire swept through much of St. John's, Nfld., destroying 2,000 homes.

• The Cobourg-Rice L., Plank Road and Ferry Company railway was incorporated.

June 15 The Oregon Boundary Treaty was signed by US President James Polk and later by Queen Victoria. It established the boundary between BNA and the US at 49° N latitude, from the crest of the Rockies to the middle of the channel between Vancouver Is. and the mainland. Britain received all of Vancouver Is. US Congress confirmed the Treaty July 15.

June 18 Following the resignation of Denis Benjamin Viger on June 17, Denis-Benjamin Papineau joined Draper to form the Draper–Papineau Ministry.

June 19 Abraham Gesner gave a lecture in Charlottetown and demonstrated caloric heat, in which a hydrocarbon lamp was fuelled by kerosene. Gesner had discovered the process of distilling kerosene from albertite, a bituminous material resembling asphaltum, which was found in Albert County, NB. This discovery marked the beginning of the petroleum industry. Gesner was unable to secure a patent in Canada, although he was ultimately successful in securing a patent in the US.

June 26 An Imperial Act terminated the Corn Laws and ended the preferential treatment of Canadian grain in Britain.

July 5–1847 Dr. John Rae, with a dozen hand-picked Orkneymen, sailed northward out of Churchill and crossed Melville Peninsula on his 1st voyage of discovery. He explored the vicinity of Committee Bay and proved Boothia to be a peninsula, not an island. Two 6-metre dinghies, the *Magnet* and *North Pole,* were used for the expedition.

July 8 Frs. Louis François Richer Laflèche (1818–1898) and Alexandre Antonin Taché (1823–1894) left St. Boniface, Hudson's Bay Territory, to convert First Nations Peoples in the Northwest.

July 13 The Franklin expedition was seen for the last time by Europeans in a brief rendezvous with the whaler *Prince of Wales,* at Melville Bay, just north of the 74th parallel. By Sept. 12, it sailed west through Barrow Str., and south through Peel Sound and Franklin Str., taking the expedition north of King Williams Is., only 160 km northeast of a charted coast and a waterway to the Pacific. Because of an error on Franklin's chart, the route did not appear navigable. Franklin's ships became trapped by ice flowing down McClintock Channel northwest of King Williams Is.

July 15 The 1st issue of the *Hamilton Spectator* was published.

July 29 The Comité Constitutionnel de la Réforme et du Progrès was set up under the chairmanship of René-Edouard Caron (1800–1876). It supported representation by population and responsible govt.

Aug. 28 The British Possessions Act gave Canada the power to enact tariffs and reduce or repeal duties.

Aug.–Jan. 1847 Author John Richardson published a political muckraking newspaper in Montreal, *The Weekly Expositor* or, *Reformer of Public Abuses and Railway and Mining Intelligencer.*

Sept. 10 Frs. Laflèche and Taché established the Roman Catholic mission of St. John Baptist at Ile-à-la-Crosse on the upper Churchill R.

Sept. 12 The 1st Ashkenazic congregation in Canada was established by English, German and Polish Jews in Montreal.

Sept. 29 James Cuthbertson asked the gov-gen. to grant him land near the mouth of the Thessalon R. to mine copper he discovered there.

Fall Five hundred men of the Royal Regiment of Foot, under Col. John Folliott Crofton (1801–1885), arrived at the Red R. Colony, presumably because of the now-resolved Oregon crisis. They would remain until Sept. 1848.

Oct. 1 James Bruce, Earl of Elgin (1811–1863), was commissioned gov-gen. of Canada. He served from Jan. 30, 1847 to Dec. 19, 1854.

Oct. 21 The 1st Provincial Manufacturers' and Traders' Exhibition was held in Toronto to display Canadian products.

Oct. 22 The 1st telegraph company in Canada, The Toronto, Hamilton, Niagara and St. Catharines Electro-Magnetic Telegraph Company, was established with Thomas Dennie Harris (1803–1873) its 1st president. The 1st line between Toronto and Hamilton opened Dec. 19.

Nov. 3 NS Lt-Gov. John Harvey was directed by the British colonial office to appoint a cabinet from the majority party in the Assembly and to act according to their will, thereby establishing responsible govt.

1846–1848 Paul Kane made an expedition from Toronto to Fort Victoria. He based his oil painting, *Medicine Mash Dance,* on sketches made during the trip.

c 1846 One of Toronto's 1st ice houses, owned by T.F. Carey and R.B. Richards, members of the black community, was started. Carey and Richards obtained their inventory from mill ponds north of present-day Bloor St. Business was profitable, and the partners expanded to 4 ice houses, a barbershop and bathhouse.

Also in 1846

• The Theatre Royal opened in Halifax.

• Rev. William King (1812–1895), from Louisiana, purchased 3,600 ha in southwestern Ont. (Kent Co.), which he subdivided into lots of 20 ha for settling several hundred escaped slaves and their families.

• Gov. Cathcart signed the Militia Act of 1846, the 1st of the United Province.

• Fredericton, NB's Christ Church Cathedral was built.

• Geologist William Logan reported oil on the Gaspé Peninsula.

• Silver was discovered near Thunder Bay.

• Swiss naturalist Louis Agassiz (1807–1873) made his first visit to Canada. Disembarking in Halifax, NS, he quickly found evidence of a former ice sheet in the form of "line engravings" (striations) made by ice.

• Vienna artist George Theodore Berthon (1806–1892) painted *The Three Robinson Sisters,* oil on canvas, while in Toronto. The painting, showing Mrs. Robinson's 3 daughters, was a gift from her 3 sons-in-laws. The painting is held in a private collection.

• *Charles Guérin, roman de moeurs canadiennes,* by Pierre-Joseph-Olivier Chauveau (1820–1890), was published in serial form.

• Alexander McLachlan's (1818–1896) 1st volume of poems, a 36-page booklet entitled *The Spirit of Love; and other Poems,* was printed in Toronto.

• A volume of verse entitled *Songs of the Wilderness,* by George Jehoshaphat Mountain (1789–1863), was published.

1847

Jan. 1 Toronto and St. Catharines, West Canada, were connected by telegraph.

Jan. 27 The govt of NS appointed a committee to study postal operations.

Feb. 23 Gov-Gen. Lord Elgin offered French Canadians more seats on the Executive Council in an effort to convince them that they were welcome in any regime formed under his rule.

Mar. 25 Paul Kane left Fort Vancouver to explore the lower Columbia R. On his trip, he sketched Mount St. Helens erupting probably at Goat Rocks dome, halfway up the north slope. That section of the volcano was completely blown-off during the massive 1980 eruption.

Mar. 28 In Fredericton, NB, Lt-Gov. William MacBean George Colebrooke (1787–1870) prorogued the legislature during a debate over the form responsible govt would take in the colony.

Spring Lord Elgin called a special conference to plan and implement uniformity of postal services in NS, NB and Canada.

Apr. 18 Dr. John Rae completed the survey of the West Coast from Fury and Helca Str. to Boothia Peninsula, for the HBC.

May 11 Henry Sherwood (1807–1855), Dominick Daly and William Draper formed a new administration. Sherwood became Attorney Gen. from Canada West and leader of the govt when William Draper retired May 29.

May 24 Graham Gore set out on foot from the ice-bound Franklin ships to seek the last link in the Northwest Passage. It is believed he crossed the ice as far as the southern end of King William Is., reaching a passage. On June 11, Franklin died, 14 of his men had predeceased him, and most of the rest had lead poisoning caused by lead-soldered canned food. On Apr. 22, 1848, the *Erebus* and *Terror* were abandoned by its 105 survivors. Most died between King William Is. and Ogle Point; the last probably died on Montreal Is., in Chantrey Inlet, on Apr. 26. The British govt and Lady Franklin posted rewards for evidence from the expedition. Altogether, 40 expeditions were dispatched for the purpose. No survivors were found. On May 6, 1859, Robert Hobson, located a cairn signed by the late Captains Fitzjames and Crozier, dated Apr. 25, 1845. This was the last log of the Franklin expedition and confirmed that Franklin was, indeed, dead.

June 1 The 52-m-long, steel-hulled paddle steamer *Passport* began its maiden voyage between Kingston, Ont., and Montreal, Que. On June 27, *Passport*, en route to Kingston, was grounded on a shoal, opposite Lancaster, Ont. The engineer immediately shut down the engine but forgot to shut off the intake valve. An increase in pressure caused a release of steam that spewed amid the passengers, drowning 2 and seriously scalding 44; 13 people died of burns.

June 2 John A. Macdonald was appointed receiver-gen. — his 1st cabinet post.

• The 3rd session of the 2nd Parliament of Canada met, until July 28. Lord Elgin announced that Britain was prepared to give control of the post office to the provincial legislature. Duties on American imports were lowered and those on British imports raised to a uniform 7.5%. Resolutions proposing reciprocity with the US were introduced, and a Board of Registration and Statistics was created.

June 11 Alexander Hunter Murray (1818–1874), of the HBC, left Lapierre House, on Bell R., to establish Fort Yukon. After descending the Bell R. to the Porcupine, Murray reached the Yukon R. on June 25 where he established Fort Yukon slightly north of the Arctic Circle.

June 28 Boundary Commission released its report on the boundaries of the St. Croix and St. Lawrence R.

Also in June

• Montreal's 1st Hebrew Philanthropic Society was founded to aid Jewish immigrants arriving in the city.

July 9 Joseph-Bruno Guigues (1805–1874) was appointed the 1st Roman Catholic bishop of Bytown (Ottawa).

July 12 Riotous Irish Catholics and Orangemen clashed in Saint John, NB, during celebrations of William of Orange's 1690 victory over Britain's last Catholic king. Two Irish Catholics died in the riot.

July 15 John Gaspard Le Marchant (1803–1874) arrived at St. John's, Nfld., to assume the duties of gov. He succeeded John Harvey.

July 22 An Imperial Act gave Canada control of taxation.

July 28 The St. Lawrence and Industry Railroad and the Canada, NS, and NB Railroad were incorporated.

• The Montreal Mining Company, BNA Company, and the British and Canadian Mining Company of Lake Superior were incorporated. The Montreal Mining Company sent surveyor Forest Shephard to explore mineral sites on L. Superior and the property of James Cuthbertson (Bruce Mines) on the north shore of L. Huron. The property was rich in copper, and Shephard recommended it for mining. Bruce Mines became the 1st commercial copper-mining operation in Canada in 1848.

Also in July
• Bytown (Ottawa) was incorporated as a town. In 1855, Bytown changed its name to Ottawa and its status was upgraded to city.

Aug. 3 A normal school opened at Fredericton, NB.

Aug. 12 The *Virginius* arrived at the immigrant quarantine base of Grosse Is., after a gruelling 63-day voyage from Liverpool, during which 158 out of 476 immigrants died.

Sept. 11 A hurricane off Nfld. took 300 lives.

Oct. 1 Bishop Power died of typhus contracted after he called upon several typhus victims.

Also in Oct.
• Ground was broken for the Great Western Railroad at London, Ont.

Nov. 1 The 1st normal school for the training of teachers opened in Toronto, with Thomas Jaffray Robertson (1805–1866) its headmaster.

Nov. 4 James Huston (1820–1854) was elected president of the Institut Canadien.

Nov. 18 A ban was placed on liquor brought into the Red R. colony from the US for trade with First Nations peoples.

Nov. 19 The 12 km Montreal and Lachine Railroad, built to bypass the Lachine Rapids, opened between Bonaventure Station in Montreal and the St. Lawrence R.

Nov. 30 Modeste Demers (1809–1871) was consecrated Bishop of Vancouver Is. and administrator of the diocese of Queen Charlotte Islands and New Caledonia.

Dec. 24 Peter Skene Ogden (1794–1854) successfully negotiated the release of 47 Americans taken prisoner in the Cayuse attack on the Waiilatpu mission (near Walla Walla, Washington), in which 14 people were killed.

c 1847 Cornelius Krieghoff completed the landscape painting *The Ice Bridge at Longueuil,* oil on canvas. It is currently at the National Gallery of Canada, Ottawa.

Also in 1847
• The 1st zoo in Canada was established at Halifax by Andrew Downs. It closed in 1868.

• The Irish potato famine forced 98,105 Irish emigrants to seek a new life in Canada, sailing in English disease-ridden "coffin ships:" 293 died at sea, 8,072 perished on Grosse Île, Que., and 7,000 more fell to disease on their way through Montreal, Kingston and Toronto.

• Hugh Allan (1810–1882) founded the Montreal Telegraph Company to link Canadian and American cities with an electric telegraph system. Telegraph service between Montreal and Toronto began Aug. 3; between Montreal and Que., Oct. 2; and between Montreal and Albany, New York, Oct. 23.

• William Henderson founded Canada Life Assurance Company in Hamilton, Upper Canada, with Gerald O'Reilly its 1st medical officer.

• The Montreal Gas Company was formed to supply and service the city's street lamps.

• The Canadian Geological report of 1847–1848 noted copper deposits in Que.'s Eastern Townships.

• The Toronto Society of Artists and the Montreal Society of Artists were founded to bring artists together with wealthy patrons.

• Paul Kane painted *The Fall on the Upper Pelouse River,* currently housed at the Stark Foundation, Orange, Texas. He also completed the oil painting *Return of the War Party.*

• *Eight Years in Canada*, by author John Richardson, was published. A sequel, *The Guards in Canada*; or *The Point of Honour,* was published the following year. These books were contemporary accounts of events under the administrations of Lord Durham, Lord Sydenham, Sir Charles Bagot and Sir Charles Theophilus Metcalfe.

• *New Brunswick, with Notes for Emigrants*, by Abraham Gesner, was published.

• Hugh Scobie (1811–1853), Toronto book dealer and journalist, began a new profession with the publication of the 1st edition of *The Canadian Almanac and Directory,* the 1st published annual in Canada. In 1869, two of Scobie's employees (William Copp and Henry Clark) bought his company and renamed it Copp Clark.

• Irish immigrant John Kinder Labatt (1803–1866) purchased London, Ont.'s, Simcoe Street Brewery with partner Samuel Eccles (d 1853). It was renamed John Labatt's Brewery when Labatt assumed full ownership in 1853. The savvy Labatt soon recognized the potential in expanding distribution using the Great Western Railway, which opened new markets in Toronto, Montreal and the Maritimes, and marked the beginning of one of Canada's largest and most successful companies.

1848

Jan. 1 The British govt extended its 10-year contract to Samuel Cunard, with a £145,000 subsidy to provide weekly mail service from Liverpool, alternating to Boston and New York.

Jan. 3 Louis-Joseph Papineau was elected by accla-

mation to the Assembly, in the riding of St. Maurice, Canada East.

Jan. 16 Bishop Ignace Bourget (1799–1885) consecrated a new religious order at Montreal, Eight Sisters of Mercy. Founded by Rosalie Cadron-Jetté (1794–1864), also known as Mother de la Nativité, it would care for unwed mothers.

Jan. 24 Reform candidates, led by Baldwin and LaFontaine in Canada East and West, won a large majority.

• Dr. Edward Dagge Worthington (1820–1895) of Sherbrook, Ont., was the 1st Canadian doctor to use chloroform. The operation involved examination of a fractured hip. Ether, another volatile liquid used to produce unconsciouness had been introduced in Canada only 1 year earlier.

Also in Jan.
• Construction of PEI's Province House, designed by architect Issac Smith in the neoclassical style, and begun in 1843, was completed, and opened as the seat of the PEI legislature. Province House (originally called Colonial Building) is the most elegant Georgian public building in the Maritimes, and was the site of the 1864 Charlottetown conference, which led to Confederation.

Feb. 2 NS elected its 1st liberal govt with James Boyle Uniacke as Attorney Gen. and nominal premier, and Joseph Howe, provincial secretary. NS was the 1st colony to achieve responsible govt. Howe boasted that this was done without "a blow struck or pane of glass broken."

Feb. 25 The 1st session of the 3rd Parliament of Canada met until Mar. 23. Business included legislation for the protection of immigrants, and the inspection of flour and other foods, and sanitary conditions.

Feb. 26 *Le Répertoire national*, a collection of French-Canadian literature by James Huston, appeared in its 1st installment edition. It would culminate in a 4-volume work completed in 1850.

Mar. 4 The Conservative Sherwood–Daly administration resigned following a non-confidence motion.

Gov. Elgin called on LaFontaine and Baldwin, as leaders of the Reform majority, to form the new executive council. The LaFontaine–Baldwin Ministry, known as the "Great Administration," was sworn in Mar. 11, the second administration headed by the two men. LaFontaine was Attorney Gen. in this all-Reform cabinet, thus becoming the 1st French Canadian to act as PM of the province.

Mar. 30 An ice jam at the mouth of the Niagara R. blocked the flow of water over Niagara Falls, and through Niagara Gorge for almost 24 hours. Sightseers found arms and armour thrown away after the War of 1812 along the riverbed.

Also in Mar.
• Dr. John Richardson and Dr. John Rae, chief factor of the HBC, left Liverpool to search for the Franklin expedition: their destination, the estuary of the Mackenzie R.

Apr. 5 The Institut Canadien, under the presidency of James Huston, established the Association des Établissements Canadiens des Townships to halt the steady stream of French-Canadian emigration to the US.

Apr. 15 The Toronto and Goderich Railroad was incorporated.

May 18 The Executive Council attacked the British Navigation Acts, which limited colonial trade to British ships.

May 21 At Saint-Aime, Canada East, Dr. Wolfred Nelson (1792–1863) publicly accused Papineau of cowardice for fleeing the rebel stronghold at St. Denis when British troops arrived in 1837.

May 31 NB asked permission of the British govt to be allowed to conduct free trade with the US.

June 30 Toronto City Council refused a request from Toronto School Board trustees for an increase in school funding of £1500 (from £500 to £2000). Trustees responded by closing down the public schools for 12 months, and dismissing all teachers — Toronto's public schools had been receiving public support since 1843. The Toronto School Board was established in 1894.

Also in June
• Fur trader Robert Campbell built HBC's Fort Selkirk near the junction of the Pelly and Lewes Rivers in Yukon Territory. It was the company's 1st installation in the Yukon, but was looted and burned by the Chilkat within a few months.

July 4 Robert Rundle, Methodist missionary in the future province of Alb., left Fort Edmonton to return to England because of failing health.

July 29 The Niagara Falls suspension bridge was completed. It spanned the Niagara R. between Niagara, Canada West and the US and was officially opened Aug. 9. The bridge collapsed during a windstorm Jan. 10, 1889.

July 30 Joseph-Bruno Guigues was consecrated bishop of the Bytown cathedral by Rémi Gaulin (1787–1857), bishop of Kingston.

Also in July
• The mass-produced lithograph *Indians and Squaws of Lower Canada,* by Cornelius Krieghoff, printed in New York, went on sale in Montreal.

Aug. 14 A clause in the Act of Union, making Canada's official language English, was repealed.

Aug. 29 St. Michael's Cathedral in Toronto was dedicated.

Also in Aug.
• Drs. John Richardson and John Rea reached the estuary of the Mackenzie R. in their search for Franklin. After travelling by boat as far as Cape Kendall on Coronation Gulf, they travelled overland to Fort Confidence on Great Bear L., to spend the winter. Rae continued the search in the spring but still found no trace of Franklin.

Sept. 10 A public library was established at Fort Garry (Winnipeg, Man.).

Sept. 26 The College of Bytown opened.

Nov. 9 Paul Kane held one of the 1st one-man art shows in Canada in the old city hall on Front St. in Toronto. The catalogue listed 240 sketches in oil and watercolour, as well as various Native Peoples' artifacts collected by Kane.

Also in Nov.

• A set of 4 lithographs by Cornelius Krieghoff, illustrating a habitant family, a Native Peoples settlement, Place D'Armes (the principal square in Montreal), and the sleigh of the gov., Lord Elgin, on the ice of the St. Lawrence R., went on sale.

Dec. 14 The Nfld. Assembly reopened. Liberals, including Roman Catholic Bishop Michael Anthony Fleming (1792–1850), demanded responsible govt similar to that enjoyed by mainland BNA.

Dec. 27 Fredericton, NB, was incorporated as the "celestial city."

Also in 1848

• A potato blight in NS threatened the economic security and health of Mi'kmaq farmers.

• Annual admissions to Kingston prison were 103. The total prison population was 454.

• Enoch Turner opened Toronto's 1st tuition-free school to serve Irish immigrants. Turner himself was an Irish Protestant immigrant.

• The Parti Démocratique, or Parti Rouge, was founded in Canada East. Formed by followers of Papineau, and members of the Institut Canadien, it favoured repeal of the Act of Union and annexation by the US.

• The Royal Lyceum Theatre opened in Toronto.

• Théophile Hamel painted oil portraits of *Robert Baldwin* and *Louis-Hippolyte LaFontaine*.

1849

Jan. 1 The NB Electric Telegraph began servicing the colony.

Jan. 13 The HBC accepted a 10-year royal grant for a monopoly of trade on Vancouver Is., at 7 shillings a year (about $175), to prevent American expansion northward. HBC agreed to set up a colony within 5 years.

Jan. 18 The 2nd session of the 3rd Parliament of Canada met until May 30. Both English and French were adopted as official languages. Commercial reciprocity was offered to the US for certain foodstuffs. In Canada East, imprisonment for debt was abolished, and members of the legal and medical professions were incorporated. The Municipal Corporations Act (Baldwin Act) established the municipal system in Canada West. Also passed were laws barring immigration to lunatics, idiots, the deaf and dumb, blind or infirm. Persons with such afflictions arriving at Canadian ports would be deported. Gov-Gen. Elgin recognized the legitimacy of Canada's 2 founding languages at the opening of Parliament by reading his speech from the throne in both French and English.

Feb. 1 The Canadian administration under Baldwin and LaFontaine passed the Amnesty Act, granting full immunity to those involved in the Rebellion of 1837. W.L. Mackenzie returned to Toronto from the US the same day.

Feb. 14 LaFontaine introduced in the Assembly the Rebellion Losses Bill, which provided compensation for Lower Canadians, loyalists or rebels, who had property destroyed during the 1837-1838 rebellion by persons under govt auspices. Tory supporters were outraged over the bill, believing that the rebels were being rewarded for treason. Pandemonium erupted in Parliament on Feb. 15.

Feb. 16 John A. Macdonald challenged William Hume Blake (1809–1870) to a duel because of Blake's assault on the Torys' resistance to the proposed Rebellion Losses Bill. The duel was prevented by quick action of the Speaker of the Assembly.

Mar. 22 Baldwin, Mackenzie and William Hume Blake were burned in effigy in a Toronto demonstration for their support of the Rebellion Losses Bill.

Spring John Richardson, failing to find any trace of Franklin, returned to England, leaving Rae in command in Canada. Rae's search also ended in failure.

Apr. 3 Baldwin introduced the University Bill of 1849, which stripped the Church of England's power over higher education and eliminated denominationalism at the universities. These institutions became secular, centralized, and under govt control.

Apr. 7 An early-morning fire, which started in a stable behind Corey's Inn at King St. and Jarvis, destroyed most of the agriculturally based city of Toronto. Lost in the blaze were bookstores, clothing stores, homes, business offices and the city hall. The cause of the fire is unknown, although some speculate it may have started from a cigar, a cow tipping over a lantern or even arson. The new city of Toronto was based around St. Lawrence Hall, which provided stores, offices and a new market, all of which remain standing today.

Apr. 14 Mount Allison University at Sackville, NB, was chartered.

Apr. 25 Gov-Gen. Elgin gave assent to the Rebellion Losses Act. As he left the House of Assembly in Montreal to go to Monklands (the gov-gen.'s residence), an angry English-speaking mob pelted his carriage with eggs and stones. Mobs burned the House of Assembly and attacked the residence of Francis Hincks and that of LaFontaine. Elgin was beset by the mob again on Apr. 30; violence continued throughout the spring and summer, forcing officials on Nov. 14 to declare Toronto the new capital of the province of Ontario.

May 17 Armed Métis, led by James Sinclair (1805–1856) and Louis Riel (Sr.) (1817–1864), intimidated the court at the Red R. Settlement during Guillaume Sayer's trial for unlicenced fur trading. Sayer was found guilty, but no sentencing took place and illegal trading continued.

May 25 An Act of Parliament provided for the engraving of postage stamps to prevent forgery.

May 29 David Anderson (1814–1885) was appointed the 1st Anglican bishop of Rupert's Land. He arrived in the Red R. Settlement on Oct. 3.

May 30 A series of bills introduced by William Hume Blake to reform the court system received Royal Assent. These included provisions for 2 common courts, the establishment of Queen's Bench and Common Pleas, each with 3 judges; the enlargement of the Chancery by the addition of 2 vice-chancellors; a Court of Error and Appeal consisting of the judges of all 3 courts and presided over by the chief justice. Restricted appeals to the queen in her privy council continued to be permitted.

Also in May
• King's College became the nonsectarian U. of Toronto. The King's College Faculty of Divinity was abolished. Official nondenominational status would not be conferred until Jan. 1, 1850.

• The construction of a ship canal from L. Champlain to the St. Lawrence R. to compete with the Erie Canal received govt authorization.

June 20 The Canadian Institute (now Royal Canadian Institute) was founded in Toronto to provide lectures, discussions and a library on science and the arts. It was incorporated by Royal Charter Nov. 4, 1851.

June 26 Britain repealed the British Navigation Acts and abolished restrictions on colonial shipping, which had favoured Canadian commercial interests. A financial panic followed. The repeal came into effect on Jan. 1, 1850, and allowed ships of all nations to use the St. Lawrence R.

Summer Father Charles-Paschal-Télesphore Chiniquy (1809–1899), leading temperance advocate and fiery orator, was honoured by a crowd of 9,000 in Canada East. Chiniquy made over 500 speeches for temperance during the course of his 12-year crusade in Lower Canada (1839-1851).

July 4 Four Montreal English newspapers supported the Annexation Association, a group of Tories proposing that Canada join the US.

July 12 Twelve people were killed in a riot between Orangemen and Catholics in Saint John, NB.

July 18 Tories and Canadiens brawled in Montreal, when Tories interrupted the singing of "La Marseillaise" with catcalls.

July 26 The Tory convention at Kingston, Ont., drew up a manifesto urging Canada's annexation to the US, in reaction to the Rebellion Losses Bill and Britain's repeal of the Nagivation Acts, which seriously affected Canada's financial future. John Joseph Caldwell Abbott (1821–1893), who later became the 3rd PM of Canada, signed the manifesto. The British American League stated their opposition to annexation.

Aug. 15 A Tory mob, infuriated over passage of the Rebellion Losses Bill, stormed the home of govt leader Louis-Hippolyte LaFontaine. LaFontaine and his friends fired on the approaching rioters, killing 1 and wounding 6 others.

Aug. 29 The Toronto, Sarnia and L. Huron Railroad was chartered.

Sept. 2 First-Lt. William John Samuel Pullen (1813–1887) of the *Plover,* commanded by Capt. Thomas Edward Laws Moore, reached the mouth of the Mackenzie R. with 2 officers and 22 men. They had been sent in search along the north coast of the continent for signs of Franklin. Pullen arrived at Fort McPherson (NWT) Sept. 6, where his men were dispersed to winter in various HBC posts in the area.

Sept. 3 Bishop Guigues of Bytown established a settlement society to supply useful information to new settlers, and to lobby the govt to open roads and survey land.

Sept. 10 *An Annexation Manifesto* was published by the Rouges, free-thinking French-Canadian liberals, and a group of wealthy, conservative English merchants favouring the annexation of Canada by the US. Many believed it manifest destiny that the US would occupy the entire continent of North America.

Oct. Construction began on the Great Western Railway linking Niagara Falls, Ont., with Windsor, Ont.

Nov. 12 The brig *Fanny* sailed from Charlottetown, PEI, for the California gold fields, with 40 islanders of the newly formed California Association aboard (each having paid the requisite £100 membership fee). These pioneers travelled not only in search of gold, but were well equipped with merchandise for resale at a large profit. They arrived in San Francisco on May 23.

Dec. 13 Newspaper publisher and editor George Brown, popularized the term "Clear Grit" in the *Toronto Globe* when he referred to a section of the

Reform Party, Canada West, which opposed the moderate policies of the Baldwin–LaFontaine Ministry. The phrase had been coined by Peter Perry (1793–1851), one of the party's founders.

1849–1855 Paul Kane painted *The Man That Always Rides*, oil on canvas, now at the Royal Ontario Museum in Toronto.

Also in 1849

• The Baldwin govt revoked the right of Upper Canadian women to vote, even when property qualifications were met.

• The Associated Press was established by 6 New York newspapers. European messages arrived at Halifax by ship and were carried by Pony Express to Digby, NS, then by steamship to Saint John, where they were telegraphed to the New York papers.

• The Province of Canada printed its 1st money notes.

• Vancouver Is. was created a Crown Colony under the management of the HBC. Fort Victoria became the western base of the HBC under the command of James Douglas (1803–1877).

• The act incorporating the town of Bytown was vetoed.

• NB adopted an anti-abortion law, which outlawed abortion at any time during the course of pregnancy.

• The Railroad Guarantee Act guaranteed 6% interest on up to 50% of bonds issued for any Canadian railway under construction wherein the proposed length was 125 km or more. Eligible railways had to have completed at least half of their proposed length.

• The Province of Canada legalized racial segregation by passing a law allowing municipalities to establish separate schools for African-Canadians.

• Joseph Légaré painted the oil *The Burning of Parliament.*

• Cornelius Krieghoff painted *A Winter Landscape,* which now hangs in the National Gallery of Canada.

• The 3rd volume of *Histoire du Canada* by François-Xavier Garneau was published.

• Thomas Chandler Haliburton published *The Old Judge.*

1850

Feb. 8 Britain's PM Lord Russell predicted Canada's independence.

Mar. 11 Richard Blanshard (1817–1894) arrived at Fort Victoria, aboard the *Driver*, to assume his non-salaried position of gov. of Vancouver Is. He had been appointed to the position July 16, 1849. After reading the proclamation establishing the new colony, Blanshard was forced to return to his ship because there was no suitable accommodation for him on shore. Blanshard's task called for enormous tact. The British govt expected him to administer a colony under 10-year lease to the HBC, wherein all European residents were employees of the HBC. Blanshard accepted the challenge in hopes of securing his own land grant.

Apr. 10 Bishop Strachan travelled to England with a petition containing 11,700 signatures, requesting an Anglican college for Toronto. (King's College became non-secular May 1849.) The trip resulted in establishment of the Anglican Trinity College in Toronto in 1852.

Apr. 19 Britain and the US signed the Clayton–Bulwer Treaty, providing for the construction of the Panama Canal as a joint venture, but the US later decided to build alone. The canal would serve as a boon for BC's development.

May 1 James Douglas, chief factor of the HBC, signed a series of treaties with local First Nations leaders, providing for the purchase of First Nations' lands in the vicinity of Fort Victoria for some £371 worth of blankets and a cap.

May 26 Armand-François-Marie de Charbonnel (1802–1891) was consecrated Roman Catholic bishop of Toronto.

Also in May

• The St. Lawrence and Industry Railroad opened. It extended 19 km from Lanoraie to the village of Industry, Joliette, Que.

June 12 Joseph Signay became the 1st Roman Catholic Metropolitan archbishop of Que.

June 25 Reverend Francis Fulford (1803–1868) was consecrated 1st Anglican bishop of Montreal, in Westminster Abbey, by Archbishop of Canterbury, John Bird Sumner.

Also in June

• The British govt announced its refusal to pay for the building of an Intercolonial Railway between the Atlantic Provinces and Canada.

• The Quebec and Richmond Railroad Company and the Bytown and Prescott Railway were incorporated.

• Canadian legislation regulating currency was passed at the encouragement of Francis Hincks. Canada would issue its own coins in pounds, shillings and pence.

• The Elgin Settlement was founded near Boxbon in Upper Canada, by Rev. William King, a former Louisian slave-owner, as a haven for ex-slaves. King received a 3,642-ha land grant in what is now Raleigh, Kent County, Ont.

Aug. 20 The colony of New Caledonia was renamed British Columbia, because of possible confusion with the French Is. of that name.

Also in Aug.

• Gov. Blanshard, gov. of Vancouver Is., established a provisional govt of 3 persons.

Sept. 7 Commissioner William Benjamin Robinson (1797–1873) negotiated the Robinson–Superior Treaty with the Ojibwa of L. Superior. The Ojibwa agreed to surrender land from Batchawana Bay to Pigeon R. in return for a cash payment of £2,000, an annuity of £600 per year, the setting-aside of reserves and the retention of hunting and fishing rights throughout the entire surrendered area. Mineral rights would be sold for the "sole use and benefit" of the Ojibwa.

Sept. 9 Commissioner Robinson negotiated a 2nd treaty, the Robinson–Huron Treaty, with the L. Huron Ojibwa, who also agreed to surrender the area between Batchawana Bay and Penetanguishene under the same conditions agreed to in the Robinson–Superior treaty.

Sept. 18 US President Fillmore signed into law the Fugitive Slave Bill, giving escaped slaves no refuge in the US. Canada became their nearest sanctuary.

Fall Edward Mulberry Hodder (1810–1878) and James Bovell (1817–1880) founded the Upper Canada School of Medicine in Toronto. On Nov. 7 the school became affiliated with the U. of Toronto as part of Trinity College, with a medical faculty of 6 doctors.

Nov. 1 Joseph Howe travelled to Britain to determine conditions on which NS might borrow money to build a railroad from Halifax to Windsor, NS. On Jan. 14, 1851, Howe delivered a speech at Southampton, England, which promoted a plan of vital public works for NS, through imperial credit, the preparation of Crown land for settlement, and the encouragement of migration to Canada, across the Atlantic by Britain's poor, who would take advantage of cheap transportation.

Also in Nov.
• Blanshard resigned his commission as gov. of Vancouver because of ill health.

Dec. 22 Henry Budd (c 1812–1875) was ordained as a deacon in St. Andrews Church, the 1st Aboriginal person in North America to be admitted to the ministry of the Church of England. In July 1852 Budd was ordained a priest.

During the 1850s Canadian sawmills replaced pitsaws (or straight saws), which had to be operated manually, with circular saws driven by water or steam power.

c 1850 Paul Kane painted *Métis Running, Buffalo,* oil on canvas; *Brigade of Boats,* oil on canvas, and *Big Snake, Chief of the Blackfoot, Recounting His War Exploits to Five Subordinate Chiefs,* oil on canvas.

• Toronto had 152 taverns and 206 beer shops to serve some 30,000 residents.

• William B. Berczy (1791–1873), completed the watercolour *Harvest Festival in Lower Canada.*

• James Duncan completed the watercolour *Montreal from St. Helen's Island,* which is now located in the McCord Museum, McGill University, Montreal.

c 1850/1851 Théophile Hamel painted the oil portrait of *Egerton Ryerson.*

Also in 1850
• Louis Agassiz visited L. Superior and identified ancient raised shorelines of former glacial lakes.

• HBC surgeon Dr. John Rae built a primitive 4.3 m by 9.1 m stone abode on Repulse Bay, which he called Fort Hope. Also this year, his *Narrative of an Expedition to the Shores of the Arctic Sea in 1846 and 1847* was published.

• The 1st archery tournament in Canada was held at the Yorkville Archery Club near Toronto.

• The School Act enlarged Roman Catholic rights to state-aided separate schools.

• Charlottetown-born writer Samuel Douglas Smith Huyghue published *Nomades of the West; or, Ellen Clayton,* a novel of Native Peoples' life in Canada.

• John Richardson published *The Monk Knight of St. John.*

1851

Jan. 1 The Canadian govt abolished the practice of primogeniture with regard to intestate estates. In its place, estates without a legal will were to be divided equally among all children.

• The 1st issue of the newspaper *The Voice of the Fugitive* was published in Windsor, Canada West, by founder Henry Walton Bibb (1815–1854), son of a white father and slave mother.

Jan. 28 Irish stonemason and architect James Purcell, along with builder Patrick Keough, completed the Colonial Building located in St. John's, Nfld. A 2-storey hipped-roof building with white Irish limestone, features 6 ionic columns, 9 m high, supporting a sculpture containing the Royal Coat of Arms. The cornerstone was laid May 24, 1847, and total cost of construction was £18,335. The Savings Bank was housed in the basement, and was robbed of £413 the night of Nov. 30, 1850. The building was the home of the legislature until July 28, 1959, and today houses the Provincial Archives.

Feb. 22 Queen Victoria approved the transfer of BNA's postal system from imperial control to control by NS, NB and the Province of Canada. James Morris was appointed 1st Canadian Postmaster-Gen. in the Baldwin–La Fontaine Ministry. The act officially came into effect Apr. 6, 1851. A uniform postal rate of 3d was established. The 1st Canadian stamp, a special issue, the 3-penny black, was made available on Apr. 7. One example survives.

• The *Bytown Packet* became the *Ottawa Citizen*.

Feb. 26 An Anti-Slavery Society was formed in Canada to support the abolitionist movement in the US, and to provide help to escaped slaves.

Mar. 28 NB passed an act to co-operate in the construction of the European and North American Railroad, to run between Moncton and Shediac, in 1857. The last spike was driven at Vanceboro, Maine, near the NB border, on Oct. 19, 1869.

Apr. 14 Britain disallowed Canadian currency regulations introduced by Francis Hincks. The British govt determined that currency was not a colonial responsibility and that the continued use of British currency facilitated trade with Britain.

Apr. 17 The *Marco Polo*, a 1,651-tonne sailing ship built in Canada to carry timber, was launched at Saint John, NB. She became the pioneer ship of the famous Black Ball Line and was known, for a time, as the fastest ship in the world. She arrived in Liverpool May 2, with a full load of timber, having completed her maiden voyage in only 15 days.

Apr. 23 Canada's 1st regular postage stamp, the 3-penny beaver, designed by Sir Sandford Fleming (1827–1915), was issued. It was the first pictorial stamp in the world that did not depict a monarch.

Apr. 25 George Coles (1810–1875), running on a platform of land reform, became the 1st premier of PEI, after the island received permission from the British govt to establish responsible govt. Coles, in

his position as Reform leader, had long been a strong proponent of responsible govt.

Apr. 30 The cornerstone of the University of Trinity College was laid. The independent university would receive its royal charter in Aug., and opened its doors to students on Jan 15, 1852.

Also in Apr.
• A telegraph line from Saint John to St. Andrews, NB, was established.

May 16 James Douglas was appointed gov. and vice-admiral of Vancouver Is. and its dependencies, succeeding Blanshard. He served from Sept. 1851–Sept. 1863.

May 20 The 4th session of the 3rd Parliament of United Canada met until Aug. 30. Business included provisions for a normal school in Canada East and medical schools in Montreal and Toronto.

June 30 Baldwin resigned from office as co-leader of the Reform govt, after a long disagreement over economic policy with fellow Reformer Francis Hincks. Baldwin subsequently retired from public life.

July 14 Several hundred Sioux attacked a band of 65 Métis in the Red R. colony. After a number of unsuccessful forays, the Sioux retreated, leaving behind one dead Métis. The skirmish became known as the Battle of Grand Coteau.

Also in July
• The Canadian legislature passed into law a requirement that all railroad companies receiving govt assistance under the 1849 Guarantee Act, use a 167.6-cm rail gauge, not the standard 143.5-cm used over much of the US.

Aug. 2 St. Mary's College, at Montreal, opened.

Aug. 8 All ships of the Austin, Penny, and Ross expedition were released from the ice to return to England.

Aug. 25 John Horden (1828–1893) arrived at Moose Factory, HBC Territory, from London, England, to serve as a missionary.

Aug. 26 Collinson's *Enterprise* entered Prince of Wales Str. just 20 days after McClure's *Investigator* had emerged from the ice.

Aug. 30 The Legislative Council of Vancouver Is. held its 1st session.

Also in Aug.
• Francis Hincks pushed a bill through the Canadian legislature authorizing Canada's participation with NB and NS in the joint financing of a railway from Halifax, to Windsor or Sarnia on Canada's western boundary.

• The Montreal and Champlain Railroad opened from St. Jean, Que., to Rouse's Point.

Sept. 22 The capital of Canada moved to Quebec City from Toronto.

Sept. 24–Oct. 1 George Mountain organized a conference of bishops in North America to draw up a plan for the erection of both diocesan and provincial synods for the archbishop of Canterbury.

Sept. 26 La Fontaine retired from govt to practice law in Montreal.

Sept. 28 John Black (1818–1882) performed the 1st Presbyterian service west of L. Superior at Red R. He would remain with the colony for 30 years.

Oct. 1 The 52-m paddle steamer *Ploughboy* commenced daily excursions on L. Erie between Chatham, Amherstburg and Detroit.

Oct. 4–6 A powerful ocean storm off the coast of Charlottetown, PEI, wrecked more than 80 fishing vessels, killing over 150 people. Many of the victims were American fishermen hunting mackerel off PEI's north shore.

Oct. 23 World-renowned soprano Jenny Lind (1820–1887), the Swedish nightingale, performed at Toronto's new St. Lawrence Hall.

Oct. 28 The Hincks–Morin Ministry assumed office with Francis Hincks as premier and inspector general for Canada West, and Augustin Norbert Morin (1803–1865) as provincial secretary for Canada East. Their program included secularization of clergy reserves, abolition of seigniorial tenure, an elective Legislative Council, increased representation in the assembly, extension of the franchise and the encouragement of railway construction.

Nov. 4 The Royal Canadian Institute for the advancement of science, founded in 1849 by Sir Sanford Fleming and other like-minded engineers, architects and surveyors, was granted a royal charter for the "encouragement and general advancements of the physical Sciences, the Arts and manufacturers…"

Nov. 11 Colin Francis MacKinnon (1810–1879) was appointed Catholic bishop of Arichat, the ecclesiastical centre of eastern NS.

Nov. 22 Frederick Newton Gisborne (1824–1892), former superintendent of Telegraphs in NS, founded the Newfoundland Electric Telegraph, which planned to buy the 1st submarine telegraph cable between NB and PEI. He was forced to declare bankruptcy in 1854. Unwilling to give up his dream, Gisborne travelled to New York City where he met and joined forces with Cyprus Field, a New York merchant of considerable means.

Nov. 25 A small group of young Christian males formed the 1st Young Men's Christian Association of NA, in Montreal, at St. Helen Baptist Church. Their group was fashioned after the original YMCA established in London, England, in 1844.

Dec. 14 George Brown was elected as an independent member to Parliament for the 1st time.

c 1851–1856 Paul Kane painted *Assiniboin Hunting Buffalo*, oil on canvas, portraying a buffalo in motion during a hunt. The work is now in the National Gallery of Canada.

Also in 1851
• The 1851 census calculated the population of Canada East at 890,261; Canada West, at 952,004. There were 1,631 mills worked by steam and water power producing 7.7 million board feet of lumber and 4.6 million planks per year.

• The Canadian census listed the following practicing craftsmen in the colony: Canada West 1,258 chairmakers, cabinetmakers and upholsters,

8,397 shipwrights, carpenters and joiners; Canada East 379 chairmakers, cabinetmakers and upholsterers, 8,923 shipwrights, carpenters and joiners.

• The Canadian govt passed an act regulating Canadian currency, proposing a decimal system with dollars and cents for the maintenance of public accounts.

• Examples of Canada's mineral wealth displayed at the Great Exhibition in London, England, created new interest in the country's resources. This underscored the need for systematic surveys of the country's geology and resources.

• Gold was discovered in the river gravels of the Fraser R. and in the Cariboo district of British Columbia starting a massive gold rush and a great influx of mostly American miners. Concern that the area would rapidly become part of the US accelerated formation of the province of British Columbia.

• Thomas Turnbull presented his "Andromonon Carriage" to the public at Saint John, NB. The carriage was a 3-wheeled vehicle drawn by a crank, operated by a lever on either side of the driver's seat.

• John Lovell's Montreal-based *The Literary Garland*, which serialized early Canadian works such as Thomas Chandler Haliburton's *The Clockmaker*, and was the 1st magazine to publish musical scores, was killed off by the success of Harper's *New Monthly Magazine*.

• Thomas Chandler Haliburton published *The English in America* in 2 volumes in London and in New York, as *Rule and Misrule of the English in America*.

• John Richardson's short novel, *Westbrook, the Outlaw*, made its 1st appearance in serialized form. The work was based on a real person, Andrew Westbrook, an Upper Canadian farmer who led American marauding parties into Canada during the War of 1812.

1852

Feb. William Kennedy, Joseph-René Bellot (1826–1853) and 12 crewmen left the *Prince Albert* locked in the ice at Batty Bay, and set out to explore the

Boothia Peninsula area. They reached Fury Beach in late Mar., and continued south.

• Tailors in Toronto went on strike against the Hutchinson Walker Company to protest the introduction of the 1st sewing machine in a Canada West factory. Hutchinson Walker agreed to remove the machine and the strike ended amicably. Sewing machines were installed in the factory 2 years later with the loss of several jobs.

Mar. 6 A telegraph line connecting St. John's and Carbonear, Nfld., went into operation.

Apr. 5 Kennedy's party reached Brentford Bay, whereupon 8 crew returned to the *Prince Albert*. Kennedy and his remaining crew continued southwest, where they discovered a new channel separating Somerset Is. from Boothia Peninsula on Apr. 7. This he named Bellot Str. Kennedy and the party arrived back at the *Prince Albert* on May 30, having completed a journey of about 1,803 km. They returned to England without losing a man.

Apr. 30 Francis Hincks, accompanied by delegates from Canada and the Atlantic Provinces, met with the British PM, Earl of Derby, for talks concerning construction and financing of railways in Canada.

May 4 William Walsh (1804–1858) was appointed the 1st Roman Catholic archbishop of Halifax.

Also in May
• Stonecutters in Kingston, Canada West, went on strike over the hiring of convict labour.

June Mary Ann Shadd Cary (1823–1893), born to a free black family in the slave state of Delaware, became the 1st black newspaperwoman in North America, as the editor and publisher of *The Provincial Freeman* in Toronto and later in Chatham, Ont. Shadd, a schoolteacher, also published *Notes of Canada West,* a pamphlet encouraging blacks to settle in Windsor. Her father was abolitionist Abraham Shadd (1801–1882).

July 8 More than 10,000 people were left homeless when the east side of Montreal went up in flames, destroying 1,100 houses.

• Fr. Albert Lacombe (1827–1916) arrived at Fort Edmonton with Chief Factor Rowand and a party of 80, in 10 York boats. Lacombe was assigned to Fort Edmonton by Bishop Joseph-Norbet Provencher to succeed Father Jean-Baptiste Thibault.

July 9 The British govt appointed Gov. James Douglas, lt-gov. of the Queen Charlotte Is., in addition to his role as gov. of Vancouver Is. The British govt did this to maintain British hegemony over the islands in the face of possible US infiltration as a result of the 1st gold rush in North America. Douglas was also HBC's chief factor for New Caledonia.

Aug. 5 The *Enterprise* was released from ice. Collinson explored Prince Albert Sound, and was able to prove that Victoria Is. was a single island. On Aug. 21, he rounded Point Barrow, where he met the crew of the *Plover,* for their 1st contact with Europeans in 3 years. On May 5, 1855, Collinson and the *Enterprise* arrived back in England.

Aug. 19 The 1st part of the 1st session of the 4th Parliament of Canada met until Nov. 10. Business included the authorization of a Bureau and Minister of Agriculture and an annual appropriation of £19,000 to establish a steamship line between Canada and Britain.

Aug. 24 Nanaimo, Vancouver Is. (Winthuysen Inlet, commonly called Nanymo) was established by Gov. Douglas, and the HBC took possession of coal deposits there. A 3-storey fort for protection of the miners would be built in 1853.

Also in Aug.

• The Royal Canadian Institute began publication of its monthly *Canadian Journal.*

• The Chilkat ransacked HBC Fort Selkirk at the fork of the Pelly and Lewes Rivers.

Sept. 18 The *Marco Polo,* belonging to the British Black Ball Line, arrived at Melbourne, Australia, 76 days after leaving Liverpool, England, with 930 passengers on board. Previous passages by earlier boats had taken at least 100 days. The return trip to Liverpool was also made in record time, earning her the honour of "Fastest Ship in the World," a title her owners' proudly painted on her side.

Sept. 29 NB contracted for the construction of a railroad from the NS boundary to the Maine boundary.

Fall Lt. George Frederick Mecham (1828–1858), officer on the *Intrepid* under Henry Kellett (1806–1871), led an exploring party to Winter Harbour (82 km west from where McClure's *Investigator* was locked in ice off Dealy Is.). There they found a record written by McClure stating that he had found the Northwest Passage and that his ship was presently icebound in the Bay of Mercy on the north shore of Banks Is.

Oct. 6 The Legislative Council of Vancouver Is. regulated the sale of alcohol by issuing licences.

Oct. 24 The Toronto Stock Exchange was established by 12 Toronto citizens hoping to attract new British capital. The 1st seats sold for $500.

Also in Oct.

• Sons of Allan Line founder, Capt. Alexander Allan, Hugh and Andrew Allan (1822–1901), with associates, established the Montreal Ocean Steamship Company, also known as the "Allan Line," for service between Canada and Britain. They were granted a govt contract to establish a line of screw propeller steamers.

Nov. 24 The Toronto Normal School celebrated the opening of its new location at St. James Square, bounded by Gerrard, Church, Yonge and Gould Streets. The new Gothic-Romanesque structure, designed by architects Thomas Rideot and Frederick Cumberland (1820–1881), would house the Ryerson Institute of Technology in 1948.

Dec. 8 Laval University, the oldest French-language university in North America, received a royal charter. The institution had been established as the Séminaire de Québec, a college of arts and theology, founded by Bishop Laval in 1663.

Also in 1852

• Following the passage of George Étienne Cartier's bill establishing the Grand Trunk Railway, the Grand Trunk Railway Company was incorporated and chartered to provide a main trunk line from Halifax to Windsor, with consent to amalgamate with 5 smaller, local railways. Financed by Baring Bros. Bank in London, construction of the Montreal-to-Toronto sector was contracted to

British contractors, Jackson, Brassey, Peto and Belts. Casmir Czowsky (1813–1898), chief engineer in charge of construction of the St. Lawrence and Atlantic RR, was awarded the remaining contract from Hamilton to Sarnia.

• St. Michael's College in Toronto was founded by Bishop Charbonnel.

• Gold was discovered at Mitchell Harbour in the Queen Charlotte Is.

• George Coles's govt passed the Free Education Act, making the PEI colony pay salaries of all schoolteachers. Enrollment in PEI schools doubled.

• The Diocesan Theological Institution at Cobourg was absorbed into Trinity College.

• Patients at the Tracadie Leper Hospital in NB set it ablaze in protest against the poor living conditions. The lazaretto burned to the ground.

• The Royal Canadian Yacht Club (RCYC) was founded as a recreational boating club and an unofficial auxilary to the Royal Navy. Originally called the Toronto Boat Club, it would occupy various locations along Toronto's waterfront before moving to the Toronto Islands in 1881.

• The final supplement (part 4) of *Histoire du Canada*, by François-Xavier Garneau, was published. It updated the work through 1840.

• Susanna Moodie (Strickland) published *Roughing It in the Bush*, a fictionalized account of her 1st 8 years in Canada as she and her husband settled near Cobourg, Ont.

• Catherine Parr Traill (1802–1899), sister of Susanna Moodie, published her children's book, *Canadian Crusoes*.

1853

Jan. 1 Sons of Temperance persuaded NB to bring in prohibition and to stop the importation of alcoholic beverages. The law was repealed in 1854.

Jan. 20 The 1st telegraph message between PEI and NB was transmitted by underwater cable.

Jan. 28 A charter was granted to Bishop's College, in Lennoxville, Que., designating it a university with right to grant degrees in divinity, law and medicine.

Feb. 14 The 2nd part of the 1st session of the 4th Parliament of Canada met until June 14. It was called the "railroad session" because 28 railroad laws were enacted (under the auspices of the standing committee regulating and granting charters to railways, chaired by Allan McNab). Customs duties were reduced on sugar, wine and molasses, and removed on salt. A decimal system of currency was adopted. The franchise was extended and provisions were made for registration of voters.

Mar. 31 At the request of HBC Vancouver Is. Chief Factor Douglas, the Company provided funding for Vancouver Is.'s 1st schools, a boys' school in Victoria and a girls' school at Colwood Farm.

Also in Mar.
• Bedford Pim (1826–1886) from Kellett's *Resolute* set out on a 262-km journey by dog sledge across Viscount Melville Sound to bring McClure word of the rescue ships.

• Lt-Gov. James Douglas proclaimed the Crown's ownership of gold on the Queen Charlotte Is. and set monthly fees for gold miners.

Apr. 4 King's College at Windsor, NS, was incorporated.

Apr. 6 Pim and his sledges arrived at Mercy Bay, Banks Is., to rescue McClure and his men. McClure refused to be rescued because the rescuer would share in the £10,000 prize offered for the Northwest Passage discovery. McClure ordered 24 starving and weakened members of his crew to leave with Pim for the *Resolute* (Apr. 15). He himself and the remainder of the crew would remain on board the *Investigator* until the ship broke free from the ice.

Apr. 10–July 15, 1853 Sherard Osborn (1822–1875), commander of the *Pioneer*, 1 of 4 ships belonging to Belcher's expedition in search of Franklin, and George Henry Richards, an officer on the *Assistance*, explored the north shore of Bathurst Is. and the northeast coast of Melville Is. Then, parting from Richards, Osborn explored the east coast of

Bathurst Is. In total, Osborn covered more than 1,475 km of unexplored area.

Apr. 22 The Hincks Act amended the charter of the University of Toronto to vest teaching powers in the new University College. Functions of the U of T. were limited to examination and degree granting only. The act was passed because of public anger over the non-denominational status of Toronto University. One immediate result was the closing of the U of T.'s medical school.

May 9 British Parliament approved Canada's right to dispose of clergy reserves.

May 10 The *Genova*, 1st Allan Line steamer to travel between Liverpool and Montreal, arrived in Montreal, offering 14-day service. The *Sarah Sands* and *Lady Eglinton* were scheduled on the route for the following year.

May 16 The Simcoe and Huron Railroad (Northern Railroad after 1858) was opened between Toronto and Aurora, Ont. The *Toronto*, the 1st locomotive built in Canada (by the Toronto Locomotive Works), was the 1st locomotive to serve the line. The railroad would be extended to Barrie by Oct. 11.

May 23 The Canadian Steam Navigation Company was incorporated and awarded an initial subsidy of £24,000 to offer transatlantic service between Montreal and Liverpool.

May 30 The 2nd Grinnell expedition sailed in the *Advance*, under Elisha Kent Kane (1820–1857), reaching Baffin Bay and pushing through Smith Sound to Kane Basin, a vital step in the attempt to reach the North Pole. Grinnell wintered at Rensselaer Bay, Greenland, where he was forced to abandon ship and struggle down the Greenland coast until rescued.

June 6 Anti-Catholic orator Alessandro Gavazzi visited Montreal, Que., and Canada East, on a speaking tour promoting Italian patriotism. His impassiond lectures denouncing the Catholic faith sparked violent riots wherever he appeared.

July 1 The Grand Trunk Railway amalgamated with The Grand Junction Railroad Company, the Grand Trunk Railway Company of Canada East, the Quebec and Richmond Railroad Company, the St. Lawrence and Atlantic Railway Company, and the Toronto and Guelph Railway Company, as specified in its charter.

July 11 George Étienne Cartier was appointed legal adviser, Canada East, for the Grand Trunk Railway Company.

July 16 Trinity College became Trinity University by royal charter.

July 18 The St. Lawrence and Atlantic Railway, built to provide Sherbrooke and other Que. towns with access to an ice-free Atlantic port, was opened.

July 20 Colin MacKinnon, bishop of Arichat, established Xavier College, at Arichat, Cape Breton, as a seminary for Roman Catholics.

July 27 The Grand Trunk Railway was completed from Sherbrooke, Que., to the US border at Portland, Maine.

Aug. 21 Joseph-René Bellot's *Breadalbane*, a 36.5 m 3-masted British barque sank in 91 m of water just off Beechey Is. in the Arctic. All 21 crew members were rescued by Inglefield in the *Phoenix*.

Aug. 23–June 10, 1854 William Rowan (1789–1879), C-in-C of British forces in North America, served as administrator of Canada during the absence of Lord Elgin.

Oct. 1 The *Toronto Globe* became a daily newspaper of 4 pages. Politically, it held Liberal orientation under editor and founder George Brown.

Oct. 7 The mail steamer *Fairy Queen* foundered off Pictou Is., NS. Seven of her 13 passengers died.

Oct. 13 The Saugeen and Newash band of Ojibwa signed Treaty No. 72, which surrendered the Saugeen (Bruce Peninsula, Ont.) to the British Crown, opening up the area to settlement. The Ojibwa retained land around the Saugeen R. to L. Huron on the west and north to Sauble Beach. The remaining land was to be sold by the govt with the interest on the principal sum arising from the sale paid to the Ojibwa at half-yearly periods as long as there were Ojibwa to receive the monies.

Dec. 2 Gov. Douglas of Vancouver Is. established a Supreme Court, naming David Cameron (1804–1872) its 1st chief justice.

c 1853 John O'Brien's (1828–1896) *Halifax Harbour, Sunset* was completed. It now hangs in the Halifax Board of Trade.

Also in 1853

• George Brown and the True Grits agitated for "rep by pop" — representation by population in the legislature — which would give more members to Canada West.

• Louis-Hippolyte LaFontaine was appointed chief justice in Canada East. He would be given the rank of baronet by Queen Victoria and that of papal knight by Pope Pius IX in 1854.

• The medical faculty of King's College and the Toronto School of Medicine were incorporated under the leadership of Dr. John Rolph.

• The PEI govt passed the Land Purchase Act of 1853, authorizing the purchase of lands from absentee British owners for resale to PEI residents — 185,047 ha were purchased under this program from 1853–1873.

• The Canadian govt established a Canadian currency of pounds, shillings and pence, and dollars, cents and mils for public accounts. Because minting of new coins remained the sovereign's prerogative, no coins were actually issued.

• British naval Lt. Sherard Osborn collected a number of fossil vertebrae while leading a party of sailors along the north coast of Bathurst Is. Scientists later identified the fossils as *Arctosaurus osborni* (Osborn's Arctic reptile), a Triassic carnivorous dinosaur, although more recent information suggests the bones may have belonged to a Triassic trilophosaur.

• Antoine Plamondon painted *La Chasse aux tourtes on canvas*, now at the Art Gallery of Ont., Toronto.

• Sainte-Foy artist Théophile Hamel painted *Madame Renaud and Her Daughters Wilhellmine and Emma,* oil on canvas.

• Robert Whale (1805–1887) completed his oil on canvas *General View of Hamilton,* now in the National Gallery of Canada.

• Thomas Chandler Haliburton published *Sam Slick's Wise Saws and Modern Instances.*

• Col. Samuel Strickland (1804–1867), brother of Susanna Moodie and Catherine Parr Traill published *Twenty-Seven Years in Canada West.*

• Susanna Moodie published *Life in the Clearings,* a sequel to *Roughing It in the Bush.*

• Designer Charles Baillairge (1826–1906) and builder Archibald Campbell, of a private association, completed Academy of Music (Music Hall) located on rue Saint-Louis in Quebec City. The neoclassical stone building is used for concerts, plays, banquets and balls.

1854

Jan. 5 Kildonan Presbyterian Church, the 1st Presbyterian church in the Red R. colony, serving the Scottish settlers in the area, built of limestone under direction of mason Duncan McRae from 1852–1854 (total cost of £1,050), opened for worship under Rev. John Black.

Jan. 27 The Great Western Railway was completed between Niagara Falls and Windsor, running through Hamilton and London. The Hamilton-Toronto spur was completed and opened Dec. 1895. Conceived as a connection line between Detroit and Buffalo, through Canada, the Great Western was funded by Canadian, American and British business interests and Canadian govt guarantees.

Feb. 1 Fire destroyed the Parliament buildings at Que.

• The NS railway opened the section from Truro to Pictou, NS. Construction continued through June to connect Halifax to Windsor Junction, then to Annapolis Royal and from Halifax to Truro.

Apr. 20 Cholera struck Saint John, NB.

Also in Apr.

• McClure was finally forced to abandon the

Investigator. He and the remainder of his crew set out by sledge to Beechey Is. where they boarded Belcher's *North Star, Phoenix* and *Talbot*, commanded by Englefield, on May 15, and sailed for England.

May 6 Cyrus West Field (1819–1892) founded the New York, Nfld., and London Telegraph Company.

June 5 Lord Elgin, representing Canada, and William Marcy, representing the US, signed the Elgin-Marcy Agreement, or Reciprocity Treaty, which effectively dismantled the protective tariff system by establishing mutual abolition or reduction of customs duties between the 2 countries, for a 10-year period (free trade). This treaty constituted Elgin's final act of personal diplomacy before he returned to Britain. The agreement would take effect Oct. 18, 1854.

June 6 A reciprocity treaty was signed by the US and NS wherein NS received import concessions in return for granting the US inshore-fishing rights.

June 13 Construction on the NS Railway began at Richmond, near Halifax. The line would extend from Halifax to Windsor Junction, then to Annapolis Royal and from Halifax to Truro.

June 27 Canadian chemist Abraham Gesner moved from Halifax to New York in 1853, where he obtained US patents for improvement on kerosene-burning fluids, including gasoline, kerosene and coal oil.

Also in June
• The NS govt transferred control of the unfinished Shubenacadie Canal to the Inland Navigation Company, whose mandate was completion of the 88-km project.

July 20 The 1st stone for the Victoria Railway Bridge, crossing the St. Lawrence R. at Montreal, was laid. When completed, the unique structure sited by Thomas Keefer (1821–1915) and designed by George Stephenson had 25 spans, each a tube of wrought-iron plates fashioned to become an enclosed box girder. The massive limestone piers were designed to hold firm against the crush of St. Lawrence winter ice.

Aug. 8 Lt-Gov. Douglas prohibited the sale of alcohol to Aboriginals living on Vancouver Is.

Aug. 11 The (Imperial) Union Amendment Act allowed the Legislative Council of Canada to be made elective.

Aug. 13 The Bank of PEI commenced operations as the Island's 1st locally owned bank.

Aug. 21 Collinson rounded Point Barrow in the *Enterprise* where he met the crew of the *Plover*, for their 1st contact with Europeans in 3 years.

Sept. 7 Work began on Cape Breton Is.'s St. Peter's Canal.

Sept. 8 The Hincks–Morin Ministry resigned when their minority govt was defeated after the 1st meeting of the 5th Parliament early in Sept. Hincks was accused of corruption in connection with Grand Trunk Railroad stock and in accepting a £10,000 bribe to throw his support behind the Northern Railway. The *Toronto Globe* printed a series of continuing articles exposing Hinck's activities.

Sept. 11 Augustin-Norbert Morin was elected unopposed in the united counties of Chicoutimi and Tadoussac. He and his Canada East colleagues agreed to join forces with Allan Napier MacNab from Canada West, resulting in the MacNab–Morin Ministry. MacNab served as president of the council and Minister of agriculture for Canada West; Morin, as commissioner of Crown Lands.

Sept. 16 The cornerstone of Canada's oldest railway tunnel was laid at Brockville, Ont. Officially opened on Dec. 31, 1860, the 535-m structure remained in use on the Brockville and Ottawa Railway Co. until 1954.

Sept. 20 Edmund Walker Head (1805–1868) was appointed gov-gen. of Canada. He served from Dec. 19–Oct. 25, 1861.

Sept. 21 London, Ont., received a city charter.

Sept. 27 Collins luxury liner *Arctic,* travelling from Liverpool to New York, collided with the French steamer *Vesta,* and sank within 2 hours off Cape Race; 370 people died.

Sept. 28 McClure arrived back in England. He, the officers and men of his ship were later awarded

£10,000 by Parliament for having discovered the Northwest Passage.

Oct. 17 John A. Macdonald introduced a bill to secularize clergy reserves.

Oct. 20 Lewis Drummond (1813–1882), Attorney Gen. for Canada East, introduced a bill for the abolition of seignorial tenure in Canada East. At that time, 160 seigneurs held land farmed by 72,000 tenants. Parliament abolished the seignorial system of Lower Canada on Nov. 23.

Oct. 27 A Great Western express train collided with a freight train at Baptiste Creek, Canada West, killing 52 people and injuring 48.

Nov. 14 Léon Antoine Lemière of Que. received the Canadian photographic patent for "a new polishing buff called the wheel or hand buff, for daguerreo-typic purposes." Daguerreotypes were common during the 1850s and prices per each ranged from 25 cents to $10.

Nov. 23 Liberals under Hinks and Morin aligned themselves with Tory-Conservative forces including John A. Macdonald to pass a bill secularizing Clergy Reserves and transferring proceeds of such reserves sales to cities and counties on the basis of population.

Nov. 27 The Grand Trunk Railway was completed from Richmond to Pointe Lévis, across the river from Que.

Dec. 1 The Money Order Branch of the Canada Post Office was authorized and commenced operation on Feb.1, 1855

Dec. 29 The Cobourg, Peterborough and Marmora Railway (incorporated 1852) was officially opened to Peterborough. Construction had taken 12 months and cost $1.1 million for 46.5 km. When completed, the line would run 76.6 km from Cobourg to Mar-mora. It would be abandoned in 1898.

Also in Dec.
• The Quebec and Saguenay Railroad was chartered.

Also in 1854
• Wolfred Nelson defeated Édouard-Raymond Fabre

(1799–1864), a Papineau supporter, to become the 1st popularly elected mayor of Montreal.

• L'Exposition Provinciale de Québec was founded.

• Ezra Butler Eddy (1827–1906) established the E.B. Eddy Company at Hull, Que., to manufacture matches.

• Sir John William Dawson (1820–1899), principal of McGill University until 1893, completed the manu-script of his monumental work *Acadian Geology*, published in Edinburgh and London the following year. It was a practical and authoritative guide to the geology and economic resources of NS, NB and PEI.

• Catherine Parr Traill published *The Female Emi-grant's Guide*. It advised pioneer housewives on all aspects of household maintenance — from gardening to making bread.

• Susanna Moodie published *Flora Lyndsay*.

• Que. poet Octave Crémaze (1827–1879) published *Premiers poèmes*.

1855

Jan. 1 Bytown, population 10,000, was incorporated as a city and renamed Ottawa.

Jan. 17 St. Dunstan's College, mandated to train young men for the Catholic clergy and as lay leaders, opened in PEI.

Jan. 26 Morin resigned from the govt due to ill health, causing the resignation of the entire cabi-net. Morin was appointed a judge of the Superior Court, but was forced to take respite from that position, again because of his health.

Jan. 27 The MacNab–Taché Ministry assumed office, with Étienne-Paschal Taché serving as receiver-gen.

Mar. 8 The Niagara Suspension Bridge spanning the Niagara R. was opened. Constructed from 1851–1855, and designed by John A. Roebling (1806–1869), it had "imposing gateways erected in the massive Egyptian style," cost $450,000 to build, and claimed the lives of 2 workers during its construction. The 1st Great Western Railway loco-motive crossed over the bridge the following day.

Mar. 11 Joseph Howe travelled to Georgetown, Virginia, on a secret, but unsuccessful mission to recruit Americans for the British Army serving in the Crimean War.

Mar. 16 The Militia Act constituted all males between the ages of 18 and 60 as the military force of Canada. All men under 40 were to be mustered once a year. The gov-gen. became the C-in-C.

Mar. 27 Through the efforts of Samuel Leonard Tilley (1818–1896), NB again prohibited the use of alco-holic beverages in a law that would take effect Jan. 1, 1856. The law was soon repealed.

Apr. 17 Charlottetown, PEI, was incorporated as a city.

May 5 Collinson and the *Enterprise* arrived back in England.

May 19 The Niagara District Bank and Molson's Bank in Montreal were chartered.

May 30 The Hamilton and South Western Railroad was chartered.

• The Upper Canada legislature passed the Supplementary School Act, allowing full establish-ment of Roman Catholic separate schools in Canada West. This was against strong opposition from George Brown and other Canada West Reformers.

Also in May

• Elisha Kent Kane abandoned the *Advance* at Peabody Bay (later renamed Kane Basin). The ship had been locked in the ice for two winters and faced the same fate for a third. Kane and his crew travelled 2,131 km on foot and by boat to Uper-navik, where they were taken aboard a Danish vessel. Only three members of the expedition were lost.

June 18 The rebuilt Sault Ste. Marie Canal was opened.

July 13 The French corvette *La Capricieuse*, captained by Henri de Belvéze, arrived at Quebec City, signify-ing the re-opening of trade between France and Canada East. The last time a French ship had sailed up the St. Lawrence R. was 1760.

Aug. 7 Charlottetown's 1st city council was elected with a £1,000 yearly budget.

Aug. 14 The Imperial Merchant Shipping Act provided for lighthouses.

Sept. 17 The Grand Trunk Railway opened service between Montreal and Brockville, the 1st phase of the line between Montreal and Toronto. Construction on the final section was not complet-ed until Nov. 23, when the track was opened between Lévis and St. Thomas, Que.

Fall James Buddington, an American whaling capt., found Kellet's *Resolute* drifting in Baffin Bay. Kellet had reluctantly abandoned the ship in the ice on June 15, 1854. Buddington sailed *Resolute* into New London, Connecticut, had it repaired, and presented it to Queen Victoria.

Oct. 20 Toronto became the new capital of Canada.

Also in Oct.

• St. Francis Xavier Academy moved into its new school at Antigonish, NS.

Also in 1855

• The govt of Lower Canada passed the Lower Canada Municipal and Road Act, which provided for the creation of municipalities corresponding to the church parishes and grouped them into county municipalities.

• John MacKinnon (1815–1866) built Earnscliffe, a large limestone house in Ottawa on the Ottawa R. This later became the home of PM John A. Macdonald.

• The Grey Nuns, a non-cloistered nursing order founded in Montreal, built a hospital in the Red R. Settlement.

• The Bank of Toronto was chartered. It opened for business July 8, 1856.

• Parliament abolished postage on newspapers published in Canada.

• The Grand Trunk Railway received a grant of £900,000 from the Canadian govt.

• The iron-hulled, 53.6-m-long steamer *Kingston* was built in Montreal for service on the Great Lakes.

• Kingstonian James Thomas Sutherland (1870–1955) claimed that the 1st hockey game ever contested was played at the frozen harbour in Kingston. The 2 teams were featured from the Royal Canadian Rifles, and totalled a number of 50 skaters per team.

• Jamaican-born Robert Sutherland (1830–1878), a graduate of Queen's University, Kingston, Ont., was admitted to the Bar, becoming Canada's 1st black lawyer.

• Toronto's Railway Festival inaugurated the opening of the Toronto and Hamilton Railway. Four thousand people crowded the workshop and warehouse of the Northern Railway (converted for one night into a ballroom complete with bunting, gas lights and a clock fountain) to dine, dance and party until 5 a.m. Toronto Mayor Allan was chairman of the dinner.

• *Geoffrey Moncton*, by Susanna Moodie, was published.

• *Nature and Human Nature*, by Thomas Chandler Haliburton, was published.

• John Mercier McMullen (1820–1907) of Brockville published a *History of Canada*.

• Amsterdam-born Cornelius Krieghoff painted *Self-portrait while returning to Quebec from Europe*. It is now at the National Gallery of Canada, in Ottawa.

• Théophile Hamel painted the portrait *L'Abbé Edouard Faucher,* oil on canvas. The picture now hangs at Église de Saint-Louis, Lotbinière.

1856

Jan. 1 NB attempted to enforce prohibition for the 2nd time, but the govt was defeated as a result. The new govt repealed the law.

Jan. 29 A Canadian officer, Lt. Alexander Roberts Dunn (1833–1868), was the 1st Canadian to win Britain's highest military decoration, the Victoria Cross, awarded for his courage in the charge of the Light Brigade at Balaclava in the Crimean War. Dunn saved the lives of others while placing himself in extreme jeopardy.

Also in Jan.
• Bishop Charbonnel of Canada East issued a pastoral letter, declaring that any Catholic in Upper Canada committed a mortal sin if he did not vote in favour of separate schools for Catholics.

Mar. 26 James Sinclair, Red R. independent fur trader and merchant, was killed in a raid by Native Peoples.

Mar. 30 The Treaty of Paris ended the Crimean War and secured the neutrality of the Black Sea.

Also in Mar.
• Parliament passed a bill allowing the Legislative Council of the Province of Canada (the 2nd chamber to the House of Assembly, and a forerunner to today's Senate) to retain current councillors in their seats until they died. Replacements would be elected.

Apr. 16 Gov. Douglas of Vancouver Is. announced the discovery of gold in New Caledonia (present-day BC). All gold found was declared the property of the Crown.

Apr. 30 The Montmorency (Que.) suspension bridge collapsed.

May 11 John Farrell (1820–1873) was consecrated 1st Roman Catholic bishop of Hamilton.

May 21 All Ministers, from Canada West, resigned forcing the resignation of Allan MacNab.

May 24 The Taché-Macdonald Ministry was formed, with John A. Macdonald the govt leader in Canada West. All members of the previous govt were returned to office, except Allan MacNab and Lewis Drummond.

June 4 The Legislative Council at Vancouver Is. convened to consider a British proposal for the establishment of an elected assembly.

Also in June

• *Le Progrès* was published in Ottawa, Ont.'s 1st French-language newspaper.

Aug. 12 The 1st Legislature of Vancouver Is. met at Victoria.

Also in Aug.

• Glaswegan William Notman (1826–1891) arrived in Montreal where he was initially employed in the wholesale–dry goods business of Ogilvy, Lewis and Co. Business was slow, however, and Notman decided to try photography. In Dec., William Notman opened his photographic studio on Bleury St. in Montreal.

Sept. 7 Toronto's 1st Jewish congregation, the Orthodox Sons of Israel Congregation, was founded. Located in rented rooms above Coombe's Drug Store, at Yonge and Richmond Streets, the name of the congregation changed to Holy Blossom in 1871.

Oct. 1 PEI officially opened its 1st Normal School to train and provide teachers for the 80% of school-age children who were not receiving an education because of the lack of trained teachers.

Oct. 27 The 1st passenger train travelled from Montreal to Toronto on the Grand Trunk line.

Nov. 10 The Nfld.–New York telegraph line opened.

Nov. 17 The Grand Trunk was completed from Guelph to Stratford, Ont. The last stretch from St. Mary's to Sarnia was finished on Nov. 21. The Grand Trunk had added 1,789 km of track to the 3,200 km already existing in Canada.

Dec. 4 The Buffalo and L. Huron Railroad began operations between Fort Erie and Stratford, Ont. The railway was later absorbed by the Grand Trunk.

• A Canadian Order-in-Council provided for free transit of goods by a bonding system through Canada from points in the US to other points in the US.

Dec. 18 Members of the Reform party called on the British govt to annex Rupert's Land for settlement, stopping the HBC's exploitation of Aboriginals.

c 1856 Artist-explorer Paul Kane painted *Mah-Min or "The Feather,"* oil on canvas. This painting can be found at the Montreal Museum of Fine Arts. He also painted *Assiniboin Hunting Buffalo*, oil on canvas, portraying a hunted buffalo in motion. It is now in the National Gallery of Canada.

Also in 1856

• The Toronto Rowing Club was founded.

• Nfld. introduced its 1st postage stamp.

• The Allan Line began bi-weekly transatlantic mail runs between Montreal and Liverpool (and back) after being awarded the mail contract between those 2 cities in 1855.

• English-born architect William Thomas completed the Second Brock Monument, located on the site of the Battle of Queenston Heights, in Queenston, Ont. The 57-m-high neo-classical-style monument raised on a high pedestal and supporting a statue of Sir Issac Brock, replaced the first Brock Monument that was damaged by explosives in 1840.

• One of the last Grand Trunk railway stations left in Canada, the Grand Trunk Station in Port Hope, Ont., was completed by an unknown designer. The station is a compact, symmetrical, thick walled, one-storey building. The fully-restored greystone station, now owned by CN, was designated a Heritage Railway Station by the Historic Sites and Monuments Board Canada in 1992.

• Fur trader Alexander Ross (1783–1856) published *The Red River Settlement*.

• *The St. Lawrence and the Saguenay and other poems*, by Charles Sangster (1822–1893), was published.

• Caralee Candidus published the *Female Consistory of Brockville*, one of Canada's 1st plays about a plot, formed by a group of women, to oust a local minister because of his hostile attitude towards the female sex.

• NS native John O'Brien completed *British Naval Squadron off Nova Scotia*, oil on canvas, a dismal yet striking portrayal of the sea during a storm. It is now in the National Gallery of Canada.

• Cornelius Krieghoff painted *Habitant Farm*, oil

on canvas, portraying one of Kreighoff's favourite themes, life in rural Que. It is now held in the National Gallery of Canada.

• *White Mud Portage,* oil on canvas, by Paul Kane was painted. It is now at the National Gallery of Canada, Ottawa.

1857

Jan. 19 The *Lord Ashburton* wrecked on Grand Manan Is. near Saint John, NB, at the entrance to the Bay of Fundy, taking 21 lives. Two men saved themselves by climbing an icy cliff.

Feb. 2 The 1st issue of a new daily newspaper, *Le Courrier du Canada*, was published to combat the liberal ideas of the Rouges. Joseph-Charles Taché (1820-1894) became head of the new enterprise.

Feb. 5 The British House of Commons appointed a committee to investigate the affairs and governing powers of the HBC.

Feb. 26 The 3rd session of the 5th Parliament of Canada met at Toronto, until June 10. It requested that Queen Victoria choose a site for the permanent Canadian capital.

Mar. 12 The steam engine *Oxford* derailed while crossing a bridge, plunging into the Desjardins Canal in Canada West; 59 people died.

Mar. 31 The British govt commissioned Capt. John Palliser to lead an expedition into the region bordered by the Red R., the Rocky Mountains, the North Sask. R. and the US border, crossing the Rockies, and, if possible, to ascertain the feasibility of a transcontinental railroad. Palliser was also expected to gain factual information about the physical features of the country: the nature of its soil; its agricultural potential; the quantity and quality of its timber; and whether coal or other minerals were there. Palliser left London May 15 with a contingent of scientists, including geologist James Hector (1834–1907), to explore the many facets of western Canada. The Royal Geographic Society sponsored the exhibition with a £5,000 Imperial grant.

Spring Placer gold was discovered at the intersection of BC's Fraser and Thompson Rivers.

May Attorney Gen. John A. Macdonald introduced a bill designed to ultimately eliminate First Nations reserves by allowing Aboriginals to apply for Canadian citizenship.

June 10 Canada passed legislation establishing the dollar as the sole unit of Canadian currency. All transactions were to take place in dollars and cents, the Canadian dollar was pegged at the same value as the US dollar and 1 British pound sterling was worth $4.862.

June 20–Nov. 2 William Eyre (1805–1859), C-in-C of the forces in Canada, served as administrator of Canada.

June 22 The Canadian Rifles Regiment travelled to Red R. to confront American influence in the area.

June 26 The *Montreal*, a 648 tonne paddle steamer carrying Scottish immigrants, burned and sank near Quebec with the loss of 157 lives. The sidewheeler *Napoleon* steamed to its rescue and took on board 119 survivors.

July 7 The Palliser expedition arrived at Lower Fort Garry via L. Superior.

Aug. 7–11 Initial attempts at laying a transatlantic telegraph cable from Ireland to Trinity Bay, Nfld., failed.

Also in Aug.
• Moravian missionary Mathias Warmow established winter quarters at Kekerten, Baffin Is., to minister to the Inuit.

Oct. 1 The Grand Trunk Railway amalgamated with London and Grand Trunk Junction Railway Company.

Oct. 8 The Palliser expedition reached Fort Carlton on the south branch of the N. Sask. R. near Duck L.

Nov. 2 John A. Macdonald invited Alexander Tilloch Galt (1817–1893) to leave the Rouge Party and join the Conservatives.

Nov. 25 Taché retired as joint premier but remained a member of the Legislative Council.

Nov. 26 George Étienne Cartier, Attorney Gen. for

Canada East, joined John A. Macdonald to form the Macdonald–Cartier Ministry.

Also in Nov.

• *Ungava; a Tale of Esquimaux-land*, by HBC fur trader Robert Michael Ballantyne (1825–1894), was published.

Dec. 28 An edict issued by New Caledonia (BC) Gov. Douglas provided that all gold found along the Fraser and Thompson Rivers belonged to the crown. Americans and others had begun to flock to the Columbia, Thompson and Fraser Rivers in the search for gold, and their numbers increased daily. Prospectors were required to take out licences.

Dec. 31 Queen Victoria chose Ottawa over Quebec, Montreal and Toronto as the new capital of Canada, on the advice of her colonial officials. Ottawa was farther away from the US border than its rival cities, and on a water route.

1857–1858 BNA suffered an economic depression.

Also in 1857

• George Étienne Cartier helped pass an act, "which provided for the codification of the laws of Lower Canada relative to civil matters and procedure."

• The Canadian govt employed Henry Youle Hind (1823–1908), chemistry professor of the U. of Toronto, as geologist and scientific observer on the 1st of 2 exploratory expeditions to the NWT (Assiniboine and Sask. regions) to determine the availability of land for cultivation and pasture.

• Alanson Harris (1816–1894) began manufacturing farm implements in Beamsville, Ont.

• Father Lacombe made contact with the Blackfoot.

• James Williams dug what is believed to be the 1st commercial oil well in North America at Oil Springs, Ont., near Sarnia.

• Coal was discovered on Manitoba's Souris R. by Sir James Hunter.

• Bill Phillips (d 1900), the 1st Canadian to play Major League Baseball, was born in Saint John, NB. The hefty 1st baseman appeared in more than 1,000 games, collecting over 1,000 hits. He was inducted into the Canadian Baseball Hall of Fame in 1988.

• NS was the 1st province to provide education for the deaf and the speech impaired when it opened the Halifax Institute for the Deaf and Dumb.

• European actress Lola Montez (1821–1861) performed to a packed house at the Royal Lyceum Theatre in Toronto.

• The 1st Normal Schools opened in Canada East.

• John A. Macdonald's wife, Isabella, died.

• John Sheridan Hogan (1815–1859), Irish immigrant, printer and journalist, was elected to Parliament for the Reform party. His 1855 essay, "Canada," was included in the Canadian display at the Paris Exhibition. Hogan was murdered in 1859.

• *Saul: a drama in three parts*, by poet and dramatist Charles Heavysege (1816–1876), was performed in Montreal. The work dealt with Saul's failure to carry out God's commands.

1858

Jan. 1 The dollar became the official monetary unit of the Province of Canada.

Jan. 14 Gov. Douglas fixed prices of land in New Caledonia (BC) at $250 per acre.

Jan. 25 The 1st session of the 6th Parliament of Canada met, until Aug. 16. An act calling for construction of an intercolonial railway between NS and NB with Montreal was passed.

Feb. Palliser visited Rocky Mountain House and met with Blackfoot chiefs whose land he hoped to explore the following summer.

• The HBC shipped 22 kg of gold from the goldfields of New Caledonia to the mint in San Francisco aboard the SS *Beaver*.

Mar. 3 Montreal bishop Ignace Bourget issued a pastoral letter charging the Institut Canadien, the young man's literary and public affairs club, with distributing "bad books, lying publications and irreligious discourses."

Spring Placer gold was discovered in the lower regions of present-day BC's Fraser Canyon — near Hope and Yale.

Apr. 3 A Pacific mail steamer docked at San Francisco with the news that there was a gold rush on the Thompson R.

Apr. 25 American sidewheeler, *Commodore*, landed at Ft. Victoria with 450 gold miners from California. This marked the beginning of the Fraser gold rush. Between May and July 1858, an estimated 31,000 gold-seekers panned the 225 km length of the Fraser R. The total yield of gold between 1858–1860 was 16.7 million ounces.

Also in Apr.
- Simon James Dawson (1820–1902) began to survey the country between L. Superior and the Red R. district of southern Man.

May 8 American abolitionist John Brown (1800– 1859) held a secret anti-slavery convention at Chatham, Ont., at the British Methodist Episcopal Church. Brown outlined his plan to attack the arsenal at Harper's Ferry, Virginia, in order to secure arms for his proposed revolution and overthrow the US govt.

May 30 The HBC's charter to present-day mainland BC was revoked.

Also in May
- HBC steamer *Otter* docked in San Francisco with 800 oz. of gold from the New Caledonia goldfields.

July 1 The 1st Canadian coins were minted in denominations of 1 cent (penny), 5 cent (nickel), 10 cent (dime), and 20 cents. They were introduced into public commerce on Sept. 1.

- Gov. Douglas issued 2,525 monthly mining licences for Vancouver Is. and the Fraser R. at $5 each. He also appointed several justices of the peace for the mainland.

July 6 Alexander Tilloch Galt, land and railroad speculator and son of John Galt, proposed the union of the BNA colonies.

July 7 Laying of the underwater telegraph cable, planned to link Ireland to Nfld., was begun under the direction of Frederick Gisborne. On Aug. 5, Gisborne completed the laying of the underwater telegraph cable from Ireland to Nfld., and on Aug. 16, the 1st message by underwater telegraph cable was sent from Nfld. to Ireland. The cable failed after 28 days' service because of an insulation problem.

July 28 The Macdonald–Cartier Ministry was defeated on a motion, introduced by Clear Grit leader George Brown, that Ottawa should not become the permanent capital of Canada. The ministry resigned the next day.

Aug. 2 An Imperial Act created a crown colony out of New Caledonia, later to be named British Columbia by personal choice of Queen Victoria.

- The Brown-Dorion Ministry, "Short Ministry," took office. This was a coalition of George Brown's True Grits and Antoine-Aimé Dorion's (1818–1891) Rouges party. Defeated in the House, the ministry was forced to resign on Aug. 4, when Gov-Gen. Head refused to dissolve the House and call elections.

Aug. 6 The Macdonald–Cartier Ministry resumed office. Taking advantage of a statutory provision by which a minister who changed his portfolio within a month of his appointment need not stand for re-election, the entire Macdonald-Cartier cabinet shuffled portfolios. They were then sworn into office.

Aug. 7 All ministers of the Macdonald-Cartier govt resumed their previous portfolios. Galt agreed to join the Conservatives on condition that Confederation of the 5 eastern provinces and acquisition of the Northwest be included in the party platform.

- George Étienne Cartier placed the confederation of the BNA colonies on the Conservative party platform for presentation to the British Colonial secretary.

Aug. 16 The Bank of Canada was chartered.

- An act abolishing imprisonment for debt received Royal Assent. It went into effect Sept. 1.

Aug. 23 Col. Richard Clement Moody (1813–1887), chief of the BC Detachment of Royal Engineers, was appointed chief commissioner of lands and works and lt-gov. of BC. He served from Jan. 4, 1859–1863.

Aug. 29 Sir James Hector, M.D. (1814–1907), a surgeon, naturalist and geologist with the Palliser expedition was injured when kicked in the chest by his own horse while attempting to coax and pull another pack horse from the river. The accident, which stalled the expedition for three days, prompted members of the group to name the accident's location on the BC-Alb. border Kicking Horse Pass.

Also in Aug.

• Gen. Joel Palmer arrived at the goldfields near Fort Kamloops with a herd of cattle and wagons he had driven up from Washington territory in a 3-month trail drive.

Sept. 9 Gov-Gen. Head requested the British Colonial Office authorize a meeting of colonial delegates to consider "the subject of Federative Union, and to report on which the same could be properly based."

Sept. 12 Gold was discovered at Tangier R., NS, by a Capt. Lestrange.

Also in Sept.

• The British colonial secretary rejected Cartier's party platform proposing confederation on the grounds that sufficient support of BNA colonies was lacking.

Oct. 4 James Douglas resigned his position as chief factor of HBC.

Oct. 30 Hamilton, Upper Canada, announced its plans to build a glass-walled crystal palace similar to, but smaller than, the one in London, England. Built on 9 ha of land in Victoria Park, King Street east to York Street, the palace was dedicated by the Prince of Wales (later Edward VII) in 1860. The architect was Robert Gordon and the building cost $20,964. It stood 2 stories high with windows covering 22.3 sq. dekametres. The dining area accommodated 100 guests. There were stables for 100 horses. The last event to be held in the building was a fair in 1890. The palace was condemned in 1891 and sold

for $450, after which it was dismantled for building materials.

Also in Oct.

• Amor De Cosmos (1825–1897), whose real name was William Smith, a photographer from NS, established the weekly newspaper *The British Colonist*, dedicated to winning responsible govt. The reform paper, critical of Gov. Douglas' colonial administration, published its 1st issue in Victoria on Dec. 11.

Nov. 4 Robert Simpson (1834–1897) opened his 1st store in Newmarket, Ont.

Nov. 19 James Douglas was sworn in as the 1st gov. of the new colony of BC. Sir Matthew Baillie Begbie (1819–1894), sent out from England as an appointed judge, took his oath of office as the 1st judge in BC just prior to administering the oath of gov.'s office to Douglas. Douglas served until 1864, simultaneously continuing in his role as gov. of Vancouver Is. The crown colony of BC was officially proclaimed at Fort Langley on Nov. 25.

Also in 1858

• The 1st Chinese immigrants arrived in BC (from San Francisco).

• Halifax Police Court presided over 1,288 cases between Oct. 1, 1857–Oct. 1, 1858: 458 were drunk and disorderly; 108 were larceny and 236 were assaults.

• Scottish immigrant and Detroit grain merchant Hiram Walker (1816–1899) purchased 190 ha (468 acres) of land along the Detroit R. at Walkerville, Ont., establishing Hiram Walker and Sons Limited. The firm would become the country's largest distillery by the 2nd quarter of the 20th century. The company's most famous brand was first called "Club Whisky," but was changed to "Canadian Club" when US customs dictated the place of import be identified on the label.

• Devonshire England–born architect Edward Horsey (1809–1869) completed the Frontenac County Courthouse located at 1 Court St. in Kingston, Ont., a mix between Greek Ionic, Greek Revival and Italianate-style stone structure.

• Mount Allison University in Sackville, NB, allowed women to attend classes.

• The NS Legislature passed an act transferring possession and control of all mineral rights and mines in the colony to the govt.

• Thomas Chesmer Weston (1832–1911) arrived from England to begin work with the Geological Survey of Canada, under Sir John W. Dawson. Weston immediately began searching for fossils in the Kootenay–Waterton Lakes area and was successful in finding numerous specimens, although these were lost when the ship *Glenfinlas* sank on L. Superior.

• James Edward (Tip) O'Neill (d 1915), Canadian baseball batting champion, was born in Woodstock, Ont. Beginning in 1883, his Major League career, which included the St. Louis Browns, New York Giants and the Cincinnati Reds, produced a lifetime batting average of .326 for 1,386 hits in 1,054 games. He was elected to the Canadian Baseball Hall of Fame in 1983.

• The world's 1st commercial oil well was dug at Oil Springs in southern Ont.

• Sir John W. Dawson identified the oldest fossil then known in Canada (*Eozoon canadense,* "the dawn animal of Canada") in Precambrian rocks; now known to be mineral, not organic.

• Cornelius Krieghoff completed *Indians in the Employ of the Hudson's Bay Company at a Portage,* oil on canvas, a classic example of Krieghoff's fascination with Native ways and the natural environment. It is now in a private collection.

• The novel *The New Priest in Conception Bay in 2 volumes*, by Church of England clergyman Robert Traill Spence Lowell (1816–1891), was published in Boston. The story drew upon Lowell's experiences as a missionary in Nfld.

• *Canadian Ballads and Occasional Verses*, by Thomas D'Arcy McGee (1825–1868), was published in Montreal.

• "Drapeau de Carillon," a poem by Octave Crémazie honouring the centenary of Montcalm's defense of Fort Carillon, was published.

1859

Jan. 7 Canada issued its 1st silver coinage.

Jan. 26 The Philharmonic Society, specializing in choral music, held its 1st meeting in Victoria, BC.

Jan. 29 The 2nd session of the 6th Parliament of Canada met until May 4, confirming the queen's selection of Ottawa as the new seat of govt. The office of Minister of Finance was created.

Also in Jan.
• Lt-Gov. Moody, instructed to search out a location for the new BC capital, selected Queensborough, a site that served the double function of capital city and seaport. He recommended the area to Gov. Douglas who immediately ordered it to be surveyed.

Feb. 13 A force of British marines from Hong Kong arrived at Esquimalt naval base in BC, in answer to a plea by Gov. Douglas for help in maintaining order during the height of the gold rush along the Fraser and Thompson Rivers. Thirty thousand people were searching for gold in the area.

Feb. 17 Gov. Douglas approved construction of a residence for the lt-gov., barracks, small church, offices and customs house at Queensborough.

Mar. 3 The British Colonial Office approved Douglas's appointment of William Alexander George Young (c 1827–1825) as colonial secretary for BC.

Mar. 13 American Abolitionist John Brown smuggled fugitive slaves from the US to Windsor, Ont., by the "underground railway."

Also in Mar.
• MacDonald's Bank was established at Victoria, by Alexander Davidson MacDonald, and was the 1st bank west of the Great Lakes.

Apr. 12 The PEI Assembly declined to discuss the subject of a union of the BNA colonies during its session: its unprecedented autonomy and the booming economy did not favour such a union.

Apr. 13 King's College at Fredericton, NB, was reconstituted as the University of NB.

May–June Royal Engineers surveyed and improved the 198-km Harrison-Lillooet trail which James Douglas had opened with volunteer labour during the winter of 1858–1859.

May 4 Parliament was prorogued and its offices moved from Toronto to Ottawa, in accordance with the Jan. 29 legislation. On Oct. 24, Ottawa became the capital of Canada.

• The Bank of Western Canada and La Banque Nationale were incorporated.

May 5 Queensborough, founded by Richard Moody, in Feb., was made the capital of BC and renamed New Westminster by Queen Victoria, on July 20.

June 8 Gov. Douglas established the Supreme Court of BC.

June 10 The *Anson Northrup*, 1st steamboat on the Red R., arrived at Fort Garry. The St. Paul, Minnesota Chamber of Commerce had offered $1,000 to the 1st person who could launch a steamboat on the Red R. to facilitate trade between Fort Garry and St. Paul. The offer was accepted by St. Paul contractor Anson Northrup (b 1817), who purchased the boat (originally called *North Star*) and brought it as far as Crow Wing R., Minnesota. There, he disassembled the steamer and dragged the pieces, including a 5,000-kg boiler, 241 km across land to LaFayette, Minnesota. After 6 weeks of reassembly, the steamboat was launched May 19, 1859, and started toward present-day Winnipeg.

June 19 Dr. Hector of the Palliser expedition received orders from the Colonial Office to explore "the remainder of as yet unknown country in the neighbourhood of the (US) boundary line." Permission was also granted to return to England via the Columbia R. and Vancouver Is. at the end of the season. Hector delivered these orders to Palliser.

Also in June
• W.L. Mackenzie resumed publication of the *Message*, after its earlier failure. The paper called for independence from Britain and postulated that Canada would soon be annexed by the US.

• The Welland Railway was completed in Ont.

between Port Dalhousie and Port Colborne largely because of William Hamilton Merritt's enthusiastic promotion. It supplemented, but did not compete with, the Welland Canal.

July 27 The US govt sent 60 of its soldiers to occupy the disputed San Juan Is., situated between Vancouver Is. and the US mainland.

July 28 The Palliser expedition reached Cypress Hills.

Also in July
• Gaslights went on in PEI streets for the 1st time.

Aug. 19 French tightrope walker Blondin made his 1st crossing of Niagara Falls — between the Canadian and American sides on a tightrope, with his manager, Harry Calcord, on his back.

Aug. 29 Sister Ste.-Thérèse (1835–1917), a member of the Sisters of Charity, or Grey Nuns, left St. Boniface, a Métis community near Fort Garry on the Red R. where her medical skills and sympathy had endeared her to the locals, to return to Ottawa. She was ambushed the next day by Métis, who wished her to stay in the community, and returned, safely, to St. Boniface.

Aug. 31 The BC Gold Fields Act, drafted by Judge Matthew Baille Begbie, went into effect. Begbie walked from New Westminster to Kamloops and back (550 km) in Sept. distributing copies of the act to BC miners.

Sept. 9 Downtown Halifax was destroyed by fire.

Oct. 8 Sgt. Adam Beame discovered gold on Rock Creek in southern BC.

Oct. 12–Feb. 22, 1861 William Williams served as administrator of Canada.

Oct. 28 William Hall (1829–1904), a black sailor from Horton, NS, was awarded the Victoria Cross for exceptional bravery at the Siege of Lucknow in North India (1857).

Nov. 9 The Reform party held its platform convention in Toronto. Representatives, including George Brown, favoured representation by population, and a united Canada.

Nov. 20 The 1st sod was turned for the construction of the Parliament Buildings at Ottawa.

Nov. 28 The 1st newspaper in the Red R. district, the *Nor'Wester*, was published at Fort Garry by 2 Englishmen, William Buckingham and William Caldwell.

1859–1860 David Roberts (1830–1907) was responsible for the construction of Gooderham and Worts' main distillery building located at Trinity St. in Toronto, Ont.

Also in 1859

• The inmate population at Kingston prison was 723.

• Black settlers from California arrived in Victoria, BC, where they hoped to find less persecution and/or prejudice.

• Alexander Galt introduced the "Galt Tariff" (which averaged 20%), and gave Canadian manufacturers a chance to compete in the market.

• The 1st teaching college in the U. of Toronto, University College was completed by architects Cumberland and Storm with commissions and help by Gov-Gen. Sir Edmund Walker Head. The High Victorian-style building was inspired by the University Museum at Oxford in England.

• The 1st steam foghorn, invented by Robert Foulis (1796–1866), was erected at Partridge Is., NB.

• The 1st street letter boxes were set out in Toronto. The boxes were affixed to post offices and used in off-hours.

• A pig owned by an HBC official on San Juan Is., near Vancouver, caused a dispute with the US when it strayed into a potato patch owned by an American. The American shot it, claiming the animal was on American territory. Because no one knew who really owned the island, Britain decided to send in occupying troops as a counterbalance to the US troops already present.

• Total gold production from the placer gold finds on the lower Fraser and Thompson Rivers was calculated at $1.7 million from 1857–1859 — with gold trading at $20.67/oz.

• Amelia Frances Howard-Gibbon (1826–1874) created an illustrated alphabet, believed to have been Canada's 1st English-language picture book. In 1971, the Canadian Library Association created The Amelia Frances Howard-Gibbon Medal to be awarded annually to the artist of the best-illustrated children's picture book published during the previous year.

• Simon J. Dawson published a report on his explorations of the country between L. Superior and the Sask. He paid particular attention to the possibility of settlement in the Northwest.

• *Wanderings of an Artist among the Indian Tribes of North America*, by Paul Kane, was published in London, England.

• Cornelius Krieghoff completed the paintings *Owl's Head, Lake Memphremagog*, oil on canvas, now at the National Gallery of Canada, Ottawa, and *Coming Storm at the Portage*, presently at Beaverbrook Art Gallery, Fredericton, NB.

• The poem "The U.E.: A Tale of Upper Canada," by William Kirby (1817–1906), portrayed U.E.L. Canada as an idyllic garden and opposed the doctrine of *laissez-faire*.

• The novel *The Manor House of De Villerai*, by Rosanna Eleanora Leprohon, née Mullins (1829–1879), appeared in installments in the *Family Herald* in Montreal.

1860

Feb. 19 The *Hungarian* was wrecked off Cape Sable, NS, with 205 lives lost.

Also in Feb.

• Hugh Nixon Shaw struck oil at Enniskillen, Ont causing the world's 1st oil gusher. The name of the community was changed to Petrolia.

Mar. 21 British marines landed on San Juan Is. between Vancouver Is. and the US mainland to take up joint occupation with US forces, until a dispute concerning ownership of the area was settled. Both nations occupied the island until 1873 when Kaiser Wilhelm of Germany, called in to arbitrate the dispute, decided in favour of the US.

determine how a 650-km road could best be built into the interior with only 20,000 people in BC to pay for it.

June 4 The steamer *Canadian*, contracted to carry mail, struck ice and foundered off Nfld.

July 15 The 52-m-long paddle steamer *Queen Victoria*, built in Hull, Quebec, by A. Cantin of Montreal, was delivered to the Ottawa Steamer Company for service on the Ottawa R. between Ottawa and Grenville, Que.

July 18 The PEI Land Commission issued its report on the land tenure problem. Its recommendations supported tenants in their struggle against absentee landlords.

Aug. 14 The St. Lawrence R. overflowed its banks, flooding 25% of Montreal.

Aug. 28 W.L. Mackenzie suffered a fatal apoplectic seizure.

Sept. 11 The 1st street railway line in Toronto opened. It used horse-drawn trams and ran from the Northern fringes of the city to its core via Yonge Street.

Oct. 2 Charles Stanley, 4th Viscount of Monck, (1819–1894) was commissioned gov-gen. of BNA. He served from Oct. 25, 1861–Nov. 28, 1867, replacing Sir Edmund Head.

• Victoria's 1st agricultural fair was held at the Victoria Market, on Fort St., in BC.

Oct. 16 Charles Hastings Doyle (1804–1883) arrived in Halifax to assume command of the British troops in the Atlantic area.

Oct. 21–24 Midget entertainer Tom Thumb gave 4 performances at St. Lawrence Hall, Toronto.

Also in Oct.
• The Upper Canada Historical Society was formed.

Nov. 5 The steamer *North Briton*, contracted to carry mail, sank on the Perroquet rocks, in the Gulf of St. Lawrence.

Nov. 8 Charles Wilkes (1798–1877), commanding the USS *San Jacinto*, stopped British steamer *Trent* in the Bahamas Channel, and seized 2 Confederate agents, James Mason and John Slidell, who were en route to England. Called the Trent Affair, this incident brought Britain and the US to the brink of war and suggested the vulnerability of BNA colonies to American attack.

Dec. 3 Britain dispatched 14,000 troops to Canada. The 1st contingent, the 62nd Wiltshire Regiment, arrived at St. Andrews, NB, on Dec. 30. The US govt released Mason and Slidell on the same day thus relieving some of the tension and threat of war between the Northern States and Britain.

1861–1872 Father Lacombe organized the Métis settlement at Saint-Albert, northwest of Edmonton.

Also in 1861
• Anderson Ruffin Abbott (1832–1913) became the 1st black man in Canada West to obtain a licence to practice medicine. By 1863, he had received a commission with the United States Army as a medical officer at a salary of $80 US per month, one of only 8 African-American surgeons in the Union Army. Abbott later became one of Canada's 1st African-Canadian coroners when he accepted that position for the County of Kent.

• Printer George Maclean Rose (1829–1898) and bookkeeper Robert Hunter (d 1877) founded Hunter Rose in Quebec City, later moving to Ottawa and finally settling in Toronto in 1871. Rose joined with Alexander Belford to sell pirated editions of American books such as *Tom Sawyer*. The 1891 Anglo-American Copyright Agreement ended the book-piracy business in Canada.

• The population of Canada East was 1,111,566, and that of Canada West 1,396,091.

• The average size of the Upper Canadian farm was 44.5 ha. The average area of cultivatable land per farm was 18.6 ha.

• The new Gooderham and Worts distillery, the largest in Canada, opened in Toronto. It was 5 stories high, employed 150 people and produced 21.2 million gallons per annum.

• William Notman was appointed photographer to the queen.

• William G.R. Hind (1833–1889), who moved to Toronto from England in 1851, completed a water-colour entitled *The Game of Bones*. This now hangs in the Montreal Museum of Fine Arts.

• *Légendes canadiennes*, by Abbé Henri-Raymond Casgrain (1831–1904), was published.

• *The Emigrant and other poems*, by Alexander McLachlan, was published in Toronto.

• *Trois légendes de mon pays*, by Joseph-Charles Taché, was published.

• *History of the Ojibway Indians: With Especial Reference to their Conversion to Christianity by Mississauga Methodist Missionary Sacred Feathers* (Peter Jones 1802–1856) was published posthumously by A.W. Bennett Publishers in London, England.

1862

Jan. 3 The Rifle Brigade of Britain (850 officers and men) landed at Saint John, NB, to defend BNA against feared attack from the Americans. British Grenadier Guards arrived at Halifax 6 days later for the same reason.

Mar. 20 The 1st session of the 7th Parliament of Canada met, until June 9. The Grand Trunk Railroad was authorized to issue $500,000 of bonds and allowed to postpone payment of govt loans, allowing the almost bankrupt company to continue operations.

Mar. 25 Reverend John Travers Lewis (1825–1901) was consecrated 1st Anglican bishop of Ont.

Apr. 3 The BC gov. contracted with Thomas Spence (1832–1900) to build a wagon road from Boston Bar to Lytton, a distance of 47 km, at a cost of £17,600. He began work on the Great North Road at Yale, BC, with 53 sappers in May. Royal Engineers blasted out another part of the road on the west side of the Fraser R. travelling north from Yale, and Joseph William Trutch (1826–1904) was awarded a road-building contract for south of Boston Bar.

Apr. 15 Twenty-three Bactrians — the 1st camels in Western Canada — were herded off ship at Esquimalt, BC, and driven to the Cariboo golfields as pack animals. The beasts of burden, purchased in San Francisco for $300 a head by BC entrepreneur John Galbraith, could carry over 226 kg each, twice that of the traditional mule. Yet the Arabian animals of legend had one tragic drawback — mules and horses were terrified of them. The unexpected relationship caused stampedes, accidents, lost horses, mules and packs. The dilemma could not be solved; by Oct. all camels were either sold back into the US or left to fend for themselves. The last surviving Wild West camel died near Grand Prairie, Alb., in 1905.

Apr. 17 PEI's Legislative Council became an elective assembly.

May 20 The Conservative govt of Cartier-Macdonald was defeated over an appropriation for conscription to strengthen the Canadian militia. French-Canadian Conservatives voted against the bill, which had been prompted by fear of war with the US.

• The paddle steamer *International* was launched on the Red R. at Georgetown, Minnesota. Its maiden voyage was to Fort Garry with a load of gold prospectors. The trip took 6 days.

May 24 John Sandfield Macdonald (1812–1872) and Louis-Victor Sicotte (1812–1889) formed a Liberal ministry.

May 28 Anglican missionary William Duncan (1832–1918) established the utopian Metlakatla missionary town to First Nations on BC's northwest shore. Its goal was to keep residents from the "temptation" and "evil" of the trading posts. The town would include the largest church north of San Francisco, a fish cannery, sawmill, hospital, homes and 50 residents. The town's 15 Rules included that Aboriginals give up "Indian deviltry," cease seeking the guidance of shamen, cease the tradition of gift-giving, and pay taxes. Duncan and the Anglican Church would clash in the early 1880s, and Duncan would move the 700 Tsimshian parishioners to Annette Is., Alaska, in 1887.

May 31 The Bank of BC, with headquarters in London, England, was established by royal charter with a secondary head office in Victoria, BC. The bank was founded in response to the BC gold rushes.

Also in May
• A smallpox epidemic struck First Nations tribes of BC, killing large numbers of people.

June 2 The 1st group of "Overlanders" (gold seekers), organized by Thomas (b 1829) and Robert McMicking (b 1843) plus a committee of 13, left Fort Garry with 97 carts, 110 animals and 136 people heading for Fort Edmonton. Their final destination was the Cariboo goldfields, which took them over 2 months to reach.

June 14 The Hamilton Powder Company, dealing in explosives, held its 1st directors' meeting in Hamilton, Canada West.

June 19 William Wentworth-Fitzwilliam, Viscount Milton (1839–1877) and Dr. Walter Butler Cheadle (1835–1910), members of the Royal Geographic Society, left England for a 2-year odyssey in the Cariboo goldfields of the Canadian West. Their subsequent memoir, *The North-West Passage by Land* (1865), described the country and people in detail and with considerable humour. The 2 men arrived in Quebec July 2, and promptly set out for Fort Garry.

July 6 The British govt approved in principle the union of BNA.

July 9 The Grand Trunk Arrangements Act was passed. This gave the Grand Trunk "permission to capitalize postal and militia subsidies" which gave the company a reserve fund of more than 1 million sterling.

July 19 As a result of the gold discoveries on the Stikine R., the Stikine territories were removed from HBC control and placed under the administration of BC Gov. Douglas.

Aug. 2 Victoria, BC, was incorporated as a city.

Aug. 12 An Order-in-Council established standards to be used by the Grand Trunk Railway travelling post offices. The railway increasingly displaced long distance mail delivery by steamer or horse. Postal officials sorted mail on board in specially designated cars while enroute.

Aug. 18 Simon Fraser, explorer and fur trader, died at St. Andrews, Canada West (Glengarry, Ont.). He was 86.

Aug. 21 William Barker, a Cornish sailor, struck gold on Williams Creek in BC's Cariboo region. He successfully drew gold from a 156-m shaft, recovering over 200,000 ounces, worth over $600,000. The town Barkerville, at the same site, was named after him.

Aug. 22 The sidewheeler steamer *Kaloolah*, attempting to rescue sailors from the foundering *Charles Napier* during a L. Huron storm, was driven onto a beach and broke in half.

Aug. 23 English explorers Wentworth-Fitzwilliam and Cheadle left Fort Garry, to search for the Northwest Passage by land. They wanted to explore a route through the Rockies on their way to the Cariboo.

Sept. 24 The Duke of Newcastle, the colonial secretary, demanded that Canada maintain a militia of 50,000 trained men. Premier John S. Macdonald replied in a state paper that such an expensive force would only be maintained during a state of war or imminent invasion.

Also in Sept.
• Alb.'s 1st school was established at Edmonton House. Brother Scollen became its 1st teacher on Father Lacombe's recommendation: his class, 20 students; their school, a log building.

• Delegates from Canada, NS and NB met at a conference in Que. and agreed on financing for the construction of an Intercolonial railway connecting the colonies. In 1863, Canada withdrew over financing, but a deal was eventually reached at the Quebec Conference (Oct. 10, 1864) and an act passed for the purpose in 1867.

Oct. 4 The 1st Overlanders arrived at the mouth of the Quesnel R. on rafts, after having traversed the many dangerous rapids and canyons of the Fraser R.

Oct. 6 William McDougall (1822–1905), commissioner of Crown lands in the Macdonald-Sicotte and Macdonald-Dorian administrations, signed Manitoulin Is. Treaty No. 94 with the Potawatomi. The treaty provided for the purchase of all of Manitoulin Is. from the Potawatomi except for the east portion of 42,492 ha, which became known as the unceded reserve. Each Potawatomi head of family residing on the island would receive clear title to 40.5 ha, and each single individual over 21 would receive 20 ha.

Oct. 14 The colonial secretary approved the proposed Intercolonial Railway connecting Canada, NS and NB.

c 1862 *Red River Cart Train*, oil on canvas, was painted by William G.R. Hind.

Also in 1862
- Oil was discovered at Wyoming, Ont., 22.5 km east of Sarnia.

- The Royal Highland Regiment (Black Watch of Canada) was organized in Montreal.

- The Saint John *Telegraph* was established.

- The US, responding to emergency conditions created by the Civil War, required reliable certification of all persons domiciled in Canada, prior to any entry into the US regardless of whether these persons were British subjects by birth or by naturalization. Accordingly, Gov-Gen. Viscount Monck set up a system for issuing passports.

- *Jean Rivard, le défricheur canadien*, by Antoine Gérin-Lajoie (1824–1882), was published in the journal *Les Soirées canadiennes*. The novel was a classic that extolled the prime importance of a rural destiny for French Canadians.

- *The Life and Times of Wm. Lyon Mackenzie*, by Mackenzie's son-in-law, Charles Lindsey (b 1820), was published.

- *Prehistoric Man: researches into the origin of civilization in the Old and the New World*, by Sir Daniel Wilson (1816–1892), professor of ethnology and literary criticism at University College, Toronto, was published in Cambridge, England, and in Edinburgh.

- Théophile Hamel painted the portrait *Sir Allan MacNab*, oil on canvas. This presently hangs in the Senate of Canada.

- Thomas McCulloch's *Letters of Mephibosheth Stepsure*, 1st published in serial form in 1823, was published as a book.

1863

Jan. 1 US President Abraham Lincoln signed the Emancipation Proclamation freeing slaves in the Confederate States.

Jan. 3 Canada's 1st covered skating rink opened in Halifax.

Also in Jan.
- Artist William G.R. Hind arrived in Victoria, BC, where he set up a studio to accept commissions and work his prairie and Cariboo sketches (gleaned from accompanying the Overlanders across the country) into finished watercolours and oils.

Apr. 14 PEI agreed to hear arguments and consider proposals from neighbouring colonies for the union of BNA.

Apr. 21 Under the leadership of former Red R. missionary, Fr. Georges Antoine Belcourt (1803–1874), the Farmer's Bank of Rustico was established at Rustico, PEI. This would remain the smallest bank ever chartered in BNA.

Apr. 27 The *Anglo Saxon* was wrecked off Cape Race, Nfld., with 237 lives lost.

Also in Apr.
- The novel *Les Anciens Canadiens*, by Philippe-Joseph Aubert de Gaspé (1786–1871), was published in *Le Foyer canadien,* in Quebec, as an immediate success.

May 5 Anglican bishop Dr. Benjamin Cronyn (1802–1871) founded Huron College at London, Ont., as a Low Church theological school. This was the founding college of the U. of Western Ont.

May 8 J.S. Macdonald and his coalition govt were defeated by a non-confidence motion moved by Conservative leader John A. Macdonald.

May 16 Antoine-Aimé Dorion replaced Louis-Victor Sicotte as Attorney Gen. for Canada East, to form the J.S.Macdonald–Dorion Ministry, and J.S. Macdonald assembled another coalition to retain his hold on power (June 22).

June 11 A legislative council was appointed for BC.

June 15 The International Financial Society, a syndicate of bankers headed by Robert Benson, bought up all the stock of HBC for £1.5 million when that institution went public.

July 28 The boundaries of BC were defined by Imperial Statute.

July 31 Colonial Secretary Duke of Newcastle directed Lt-Gov. Arthur Hamilton Gordon (1819–1812) of NB to support the union of the Maritime colonies. Gordon received a letter from the British govt on June 24, 1865, advising him to do everything in his power to urge the Maritime provinces into Confederation. Gordon was recalled to Britain, returning Oct. 28 under orders from the British govt to support Confederation.

Also in July
• Most of the Stikine territories were absorbed into the BC colony.

• Fire destroyed the community of Bruce Mines, Canada West, located on St. Joseph Is., at the northwestern tip of L. Huron. No loss of life was reported.

Aug. 8 Angus McAskill, the 7'9" Cape Breton giant, weighing 193 kg (425 lbs), died at age 38, reputedly of "brain fever." He had toured Lower Canada, West Indies, Cuba and the US demonstrating his great strength.

Aug. 13 The 1st session of the 8th Parliament of Canada met, until Oct. 15, establishing a new Militia Act, which included all male inhabitants between the ages of 18 and 60.

Aug. 13–Mar. 14, 1864 J.S. Macdonald served as PM of United Canada.

Aug. 29 Cheadle and Viscount Milton arrived at Kamloops on their journey to the Cariboo goldfields.

Fall An American named Linklater discovered gold at the foot of Fisher Mountain at Wild Horse Creek, northeast of Cranbrook, BC.

Nov. Architects Wright and Sanders completed the oldest standing synagogue in Canada: Temple Emanuel located in Victoria, BC. The Romanesque-style, 2-storey brick synagogue features stained-glass windows and a valuted ceiling with a skylight. Rev. Dr. Morris R. Cohen was the 1st rabbi of the congregation.

Dec. 8 The Allan (Steamship) Line won a new transatlantic mail contract from the Canadian govt.

Also in Dec.
• Five disguised Confederate sailors forcibly took possession of the US steamer *Chesapeake*, bound for Portland, Maine. They headed for Halifax, drawing Canada into an international dispute. Union govt soldiers recaptured the *Chesapeake* in NS waters on Dec. 12, taking it to the British Vice-Admiralty Court in Halifax. Judge Alexander Stewart ordered an immediate return of the vessel to its owners.

c 1863 William G.R. Hind, completed the watercolour *Self-Portrait*, one of the most memorable self-portraits in Canadian art. It is now with the Musée McCord in Montreal.

Also in 1863
• Architect Victor Roy (1837–1902), along with construction supervisor William Spier (1801–1878) and son completed Ravenscrag, located above Pine Avenue in Montreal for the Allan (Steamship) Line owner Sir Hugh Allan. Ravenscrag, the most luxurious Italian villa in Canada, built to exhibit Allan's wealth, was located on a large estate on a high slope of Mount Royal so that Allan could observe his ships in the harbour and so that his large house could be seen from most of Montreal.

• Engineer Andrew S. Hallidie (1836–1900) completed Alexandra Bridge for contractor and future Lt-gov. Joseph W. Trutch. The bridge, built over the Fraser Canyon at Spuzzum, BC, was the 1st suspension bridge in the West.

• Because of a problem with financial arrangements, Canada withdrew its agreement with NB and NS to build the Intercolonial Railway.

• There were 4,400 working gold miners in BC, of which some 4,000 were prospecting an 11-km stretch of Williams Creek. Total BC gold production for 1863 was $3,913,563 or an average of $889 per miner.

• The Montreal Board of Brokers, an unincorporated group of stock traders, began daily meetings in the old Montreal Board of Trade building.

• Palliser's report was published in the British parliamentary papers. It expressed a negative view concerning a railroad through the Canadian prairies. He considered much of the area arid and unfavourable for farming. This region became known as Palliser's Triangle.

• William Logan published his comprehensive *Geology of Canada*.

• *Forestiers et Voyageurs*, by Joseph-Charles Taché, was published.

• In Montreal, Jewish poet Isadore Gordon Ascher (1835–1914) published *Voices from the Hearth and Other Poems*.

• Photographer William Notman published his 1st book, *Photographic Selections*, which combined 44 photographs, many of which represented several famous Canadian artists, including Cornelius Krieghoff.

• The multi-volume *Eighty Years' Progress of British North America* was published in Toronto. Its editor, Henry Yule Hind, introduced the work with these words "...if in the next eighty years the provinces should prosper as they have in the eighty years that are past, which there seems no reason to doubt, a nation of forty millions will have arisen in the North."

1864

Jan. 11 Frederick Seymour (1820–1869) was appointed gov. of the united mainland BC, but would return to England in 1865. He would return to BC in 1866 when the colonies of BC and Vancouver Is. merged into one political unit.

Jan. 22 The 1st session of the Legislative Council of BC opened at Sapperton.

Mar. 21 The J.S. Macdonald–Dorion Ministry resigned because of its inability to maintain a coalition.

Mar. 28 The NS Legislature under Charles Tupper (1821–1915) passed a resolution appointing 5 delegates to a conference on Maritime Union, to be held at Charlottetown, PEI. NB passed a similar resolution 2 weeks later.

Mar. 30 The Conservative administration of Étienne-Paschal Taché and John A. Macdonald assumed office.

Also in Mar.
• John S. Fisher led a party of prospectors to Wild Horse Creek, in the East Kootenays, BC, after hearing reports that its gravel bottom held gold. The reports were true and by June, some 1,500 claims had been staked along the creek. The town of Fisherville, named after Fisher, developed as a result and, by 1865, had some 5,000 residents.

Spring Civil engineer Sanford Fleming was appointed by the provincial Canadian govt to survey potential routes of the proposed Intercolonial Railway. He submitted his report in Feb. 1865, recommending that the railway be built from Halifax to Quebec, following Chaleur Bay into the heart of NB and along the St. Lawrence, a route, for military and political purposes, that would keep the railway as far as possible from the US border.

Apr. 27 An Arctic storm in Nfld. waters caused the loss of 26 sealing vessels.

Apr. 30 A Chilcotin insurrection, led by Chief Tellot, resulted in the killing of a ferryman and members of a road crew employed by Alfred P. Waddington (1801–1872) to build a road from Bute Inlet to the Cariboo mines in BC. Eight Native Peoples were later captured and held for trial for their part in what became known as the "Chilcotin Massacre."

Also in Apr.
- After much heated debate the PEI Legislature authorized a delegation to attend the conference on Maritime Union.

May 2 The Merchants' Bank of Halifax opened. It would become officially incorporated in 1869. Merchants' was the precursor to the Royal Bank of Canada.

May 19 A motion in the Parliament by George Brown for the selection of a committee to inquire impartially into the sectional problems of Canada and to report on the best means of remedying those problems was passed. George Brown became the chairman of the select committee, which would deliver its report to Parliament June 14.

June 1 Harvey Farrington opened Canada's 1st commerical cheese factory at Norwich, in Oxford County, Canada West.

June 14 George Brown's select committee reported to Parliament "a strong feeling" in favour of "a federated system" and called for a vote on confederation in Parliament. This was defeated by 4 votes, 1 of which belonged to John A. Macdonald. The Conservative Taché-Macdonald govt went down to defeat in the house on the same day, as a vote of censure penalized it for not having given a previously promised loan to the city of Montreal. Brown approached the Conservatives, pledging his support if they in turn would support the findings of his committee.

June 17 John A. Macdonald, Galt and Cartier met with Brown to discuss the possibility of forming a coalition govt, with the federation of BNA as part of its program.

June 22 The "Great Coalition" was formed. George Brown, Oliver Mowat (1820–1903) and William McDougall joined the Conservative cabinet. Taché held the nominal post of PM, but effective power was wielded by John A. Macdonald and George Étienne Cartier.

June 29 A passenger train near St. Hilaire, Quebec, unable to stop for an open drawbridge on the Richelieu R., plunged through the gap onto passing barges, killing 99 people and injuring 100.

June 30 The Canada Temperance Act, also called the Dunkin Act after its sponsor, Christopher Dunkin (1812–1881), was passed. The act gave municipalities in Upper and Lower Canada an option on becoming either "wet" or "dry."

- Canada's Gov-Gen. Lord Monck asked the Maritime provinces to consider the union of all the BNA provinces.

Also in June
- The Canadian govt was granted permission to attend the Charlottetown Conference on Maritime Union.

July 13 Cabinet minister Thomas D'Arcy McGee, accompanied by 100 Canadians, travelled to NB and NS to lobby on behalf of Canadian Confederation.

Also in July
- Construction began on St. Peter's Canal, which would cross an almost 1-km isthmus on Cape Breton Is. between Peter's Bay and Bras d'Or Lakes.

- The HBC supply ship *Prince Arthur* sank off Mansel Is. in Hudson Bay. Another supply ship, *Prince of Wales*, ran aground on the island the same hour, but was refloated and made the journey to York Factory with the crew of the *Prince Arthur* aboard.

Sept. 1 The Charlottetown Conference was held to discuss the political union of NS, NB and PEI. Five representatives from each province attended. Representatives from Canada also attended but their mandate was to argue for the union of all provinces in BNA. John A. Macdonald and Cartier outlined arguments in favour of a BNA confederation on Sept. 2. Galt discussed the financial aspects of such a union on Sept. 3. On Sept. 5, George Brown presented the constitutional structure of Confederation. The Maritime provinces discussed a purely Maritime union on Sept. 7 and NB Premier Tilley argued that the Maritime provinces would obtain better terms under the proposed full-scale Confederation than under a Maritime union. The Charlottetown Conference concluded on Sept. 9.

Sept. 12 Maritime and Canadian delegates convened at Province House, Halifax, and agreed to meet at the Quebec Conference on Oct. 10 to work out final details of Confederation.

Sept. 19 Thirty-four Confederate soldiers, travelling *"incognito,"* boarded the sidewheeler steamer *Philo Parsons* at the port of Malden, Ont., near Kelly Is. The soldiers seized control of the steamer and at Middle Bass Is., captured the vessel *Island Queen*. They planned to attack the gunboat *Michigan* and liberate Confederate prisoners being held at Johnson's Is. near Sandusky, Ohio. The plan failed when soldiers backed out of the plot and mutinied.

Sept. 27 PEI's Executive Council appointed 7 delegates to the Quebec Conference to consider the Confederation of all BNA provinces.

Oct. 5 Anthony Musgrave (1828–1888) arrived in Nfld. to serve as the new gov. He had been appointed to the position in Sept.

Oct. 10 The Quebec Conference convened, until Oct. 28. Frederick Carter (1819–1900) and Ambrose Shea (1815–1905) represented Nfld. Four members were added to the Canadian delegation: James Cockburn (1819–1883), Oliver Mowat, Jean-Charles Chaplais (1811–1885) and Étienne-Paschal Taché. Peter Mitchell (1824–1899) and Charles Fisher (1808–1880) attended for NB, and Edward Whelan (1824–1867) and Thomas Haviland (1822–1895) joined the PEI delegation. The other delegates were the same as those at the Charlottetown Conference: from NB, Edward Chandler (1800–1880), John Hamilton Gray (1814–1889), John Johnson (1818–1868), William Steeves (1814–1873) and S.L. Tilley; from NS, Adams George Archibald (1814–1892), Robert Dickey (1811–1903), William Henry (1816–1888), Jonathan McCully (1809–1877) and Charles Tupper; from PEI, George Coles, John Hamilton Gray (1812–1887), Andrew Macdonald (1829–1912), Edward Palmer (1809–1889) and William Pope (1825–1879); from the Province of Canada, George Brown, Alexander Campbell (1822–1892), George Étienne Cartier, Alexander Galt, Hector-Louis Langevin (1826–1906), John A. Macdonald, William McDougall and Thomas D'Arcy McGee. Collectively, these men, plus William Pearce Howland (1811–1907), John William Ritchie (1808–1898) and R.D. Wilmot, are known as the Fathers of Confederation. Summation of the Conference proposals for Confederation were contained in the Quebec Resolutions, or Seventy-Two Resolutions, to be submitted to the provinces for examination and to the British govt for approval and authorization. J.A. Macdonald promised the Maritime provinces one-third of the seats in the Upper House to their concerns regarding under-representation (Oct. 13). NB Premier Tilley demanded a railway (the Intercolonial) be built between Canada and the Maritimes as a condition of Confederation (Oct. 15). The Seventy-Two Resolutions were formally adopted by Quebec Conference delegates on Oct. 28 and an official proposal for the BNA Union was made.

Oct. 19 Confederate soldiers, led by Bennett Young, crossed the Canadian border south of Montreal, raided 3 Vermont banks and killed a man. Arrested on their return to Canada, Young and his men were released on technical grounds because the presiding Canadian judge felt he had no jurisdiction in the case. Northern Americans were outraged.

Nov. 9 The 1st lumber exported from BC went to Australia, marking the beginning of BC's export trade.

Dec. 16 John Hamilton Gray, a strong supporter of Confederation, resigned as premier of PEI because of that province's overwhelming opposition to Confederation.

Dec. 17 For the 1st time, passports were required to enter the US from British North America.

Dec. 20 The Canadian militia was called to service on the border against possible attacks from US Fenians, members of an Irish-American secret society, who maintained plans to capture Canada and hold it for ransom in an attempt to free Ireland from British rule. The Fenians would make sporadic raids on Canada until 1871.

1864–1865 *La Revue canadienne* issued a new serialized edition of the novel *Une de perdue, deux de trouvées*, set in Lower Canada during the 1837

Rebellion. The novel was written by Georges Boucher de Boucherville (1814–1894).

Also in 1864

• Hugh Allan founded Merchant's Bank of Canada in Montreal with a capital of $6.78 million and a reserve fund of $6.8 million.

• James Douglas retired as gov. of BC. He died in Victoria — the city he had founded — on Aug. 2, 1877.

• S.P. Day's *English America* was published in London, England. Its 2 volumes, written after the author made an extensive visit to North America in the 1860s, extolled "the advantages of Canada over the United States as a future home for British emigrants."

• William Armstrong painted the pastel *Toronto Rolling Mills,* a vivid detail of work inside what was Canada's largest iron mill. The work is now held by the Toronto Public Library.

• *North American Scenery*, photographic reproductions of landscapes, by William Notman, was published.

• Rosanna Eleanora Leprohon's 2nd novel, *Antoinette de Mirecourt*, was published by John Lovell of Montreal.

• Arthur Buies (1840–1901) published *Lettres sur le Canada, Social Étude*, an intellectual lampoon-critique of the Canadian public spirit suffocated and made indolent by Conservative and church-dominated education.

1865

Jan. 11 Joseph Howe anonymously published the 1st of his "Botheration Letters," in the Halifax *Morning Chronicle*. The series, which vigorously attacked Confederation, continued until Mar. 2.

Jan. 17 A public meeting in Charlottetown, PEI, expressed overwhelming opposition to Confederation.

Jan. 19 The 3rd session of the 8th Parliament of Canada met until Mar. 18. A motion was passed to have the Imperial Parliament adopt measures for the union of BNA, based on the Quebec Resolutions. The speech from the throne called for measures to enforce Canadian neutrality in the US Civil War.

Jan. 26 In a speech before the Vancouver House of Assembly and Vancouver Is. Legislative Assembly members, Amor De Cosmos called for the union of the colonies of Vancouver Is. and the mainland of BC.

Feb. 6 The Canadian Parliament began its debate on Confederation, during which George Brown would make one of his most compelling speeches in support of Confederation. He based his arguments on 2 principles: that a united Canada could better defend itself against an American invasion; and a united British America would create new commercial outlets should the US annul its Reciprocity Treaty with Canada. "Mr. Speaker, I am in favour of a union of these provinces, because it will enable us to meet, without alarm the abrogation of the American Reciprocity Treaty … [S]hould this union of British American go on, a fresh outlet for our commerce will be opened up to us quite as advantageous as the American trade has ever been … Mr. Speaker, I am in favour of the union of the provinces, because, in the event of war, it will enable all the colonies to defend themselves better … The Americans are now a warlike people. They have large armies, a powerful navy, an unlimited supply of warlike munitions, and the carnage of war has to them been stript of its horrors … Unless we are willing to live at the mercy of our neighbours, we, too, must put our country in a state of efficient preparation."

Feb. 16 Étienne-Paschal Taché suffered an attack of paralysis. He died on July 30.

Feb. 18 Britain pressured PEI into accepting Confederation by announcing that funding for the lt-gov.'s salary would cease whether Confederation succeeded or not.

Feb. 20 The Legislative Council of Canada moved to support Confederation by a vote of 45 to 15.

Feb. 24 A telegraph line, planned to link BC to Russia,

was begun at New Westminister, BC, but it was never completed.

Mar. 4 Tilley's NB govt was defeated in an election called on the issue of Confederation. Albert Smith (1822–1883), former NB Attorney Gen. and hard-line anti-Confederationist, was a prime mover in the election. He became NB premier as his Reform party assumed power.

Mar. 6 The US revoked its Dec. 17, 1864 order requiring passports to enter the US from BNA.

Mar. 10 The Canadian Parliament formally requested that Britain unite its colonies in North America and approved the resolutions of Confederation by a vote of 91 to 33 (Mar. 13). Twenty-one of the dissenting votes came from French Canada. Antoine-Aimé Dorion, leader of the liberal-reform Rouge party, led the nays.

Mar. 17 The Canadian Parliament approved a defense budget of $1 million. This unprecedented amount was appropriated because of growing tension with the US, which simultaneously served notice of its intention to terminate the 1854 Reciprocity Treaty with BNA. The Reciprocity Treaty, unpopular in the US because it was believed to favour BNA, would become officially inoperative Mar. 17, 1866.

Mar. 22 PEI Lt-Gov. George Dundas (1819–1880) issued a proclamation notifying PEI farmers that organizations such as the Tenant League were illegal, and that membership in the Tenant League was a crime. Formed in Dec. 1863, the Tenant League was an organization of PEI farmers, mostly tenant farmers, who demanded that they be able to purchase land held by absentee landowners. Tactics in the cause included the withholding of rents. Despite Lt-Gov. Dundas's ban on the organization, the League persisted, and later in the year, clashes erupted between League members and authorities who were sent into rural areas to collect rents.

Mar. 23 The British Parliament voted £50,000 for the defense of Canada, as a result of the Alabama Incident. The *Alabama*, sunk in 1864 by the USS *Kearsarge*, was a British-built Confederate merchant raider that had aroused considerable anti-British feeling in the Northern states.

Apr. 3 A PEI legislative committee released its report opposing Confederation on the grounds that it would result in increased taxation, allow inadequate political representation, and would lead to the ruin of the Island's economy.

Apr. 10 Charles Bart Tupper, premier of NS, argued in favour of Maritime union rather than Confederation. His view was strongly opposed by the colony's population.

Also in Apr.
• Wesleyan Methodist Reverend Thomas Woolsey (1819–1894) baptized Cree Chief Maskepetoon (Broken Arm) under the name of Abraham and also, Maskepetoon's wife, under the name of Sarah.

• Edgar Dewdney (1835–1916) was commissioned to construct a trail from Fort Hope to Wild Horse in southern BC. When completed, the Dewdney Trail covered 721 km and served as a Canadian route to the goldfields.

May 1 Canadian ministers John A. Macdonald, Galt, Brown and Cartier arrived in London to present the British govt with the plan for Confederation, which was conceived at the Quebec Conference and approved by the Canadian legislature. They also solicited British financial support for a network of canals, railways, forts and munitions factories for defense against possible American aggression. Estimated cost: £8–10 million. On June 1, British officials told the Canadian representatives that North American colonies must "admit an obligation" to assume part of their own defense.

May 7 The Canadian Land and Immigration Company of London purchased 10 townships in Canada West, with which it later established the towns of Haliburton and Minden.

July 1 Quebec City became the capital of Canada East.

July 8 The BC govt commissioned Walter Moberly (1831–1915) to explore the Rocky Mountains in the vicinity of the Columbia and Kootenay Rivers to locate passes through which a railroad linking BC to the rest of Canada might be constructed.

July 15 Canada announced its decision to send ministers Galt and William P. Howland to Washington, D.C., to negotiate an extension of the Reciprocity Treaty, which had been in effect since 1854.

Also in July

• Scarlet fever, transmitted by HBC supply boat crews, rampaged through the Mackenzie and Yukon Valleys, killing hundreds of Native Peoples.

Aug. 7 Narcisse-Fortunat Belleau (1808–1894) joined John A. Macdonald in the Ministry as premier, succeeding Taché.

Aug. 15 The 1st public library in BC opened in New Westminster. The 1st books were donated by the recently disbanded Royal Engineers, who had cleared the site on which New Westminster stood.

Sept. The Confederate Trade Council met at Que. to consider the commercial future of BNA, as approaching termination of the Reciprocity Agreement with the US loomed.

Oct. 20 A proclamation fixed the permanent seat of govt at Ottawa.

Nov. 14 The Grand Trunk Railway bought Preston and Berlin Railway property.

• Cabinet minister George Brown toured Saint John and Halifax, seeking supporters for Confederation.

Nov. 30 A steam-powered mill at the Vancouver Is. Spar Lumber and Sawmill Company, in Burrard Inlet, BC, was opened by its owner, sea capt. Edward Stamp.

Dec. 19 George Brown resigned from the Cartier–Macdonald Ministry because of disagreements with Conservative members over Reciprocity Treaty negotiations with the US.

Also in 1865

• The 1st soda pulp mill to dissolve wood chips in a solution of caustic soda, was built at Windsor Mills, Que.

• The Cariboo Road, begun in 1862, was completed in central BC's Cariboo gold rush country, linking Yale to Barkerville. The road was 650 km long, 5.5 m wide, and cost some $2 million.

• The Star Acme Spring Skate — a removable blade that could be clamped to the bottom of any boot without the aid of leather straps — was developed by the Star Manufacturing Company of Dartmouth, NS. Sharp turns could now be performed without fear of losing a blade.

• Mitchell & Co.'s Classified Directory contained listings for over 360 photographers: including 16 in Quebec, 34 in Montreal and 17 in Toronto.

• *Jacques et Marie*, a heroic novel about Acadians, by Napoléon Bourassa (1827–1916), was serialized in the periodical *La Revue canadienne*.

• Charles Heavysege published the religious poem "Jeptha's Daughter."

• Ernest Gagnon (1834–1915) published the 1st part of *Chansons populaires du Canada*, a collection of French-Canadian music.

• James Griffiths (1825–1896) completed the watercolour *Flowers*, now in the National Gallery of Canada.

• German-born landscape painter Otto Jacobi (1812–1901) completed the canvas *Fall of Ste Anne, Quebec*, now in the Art Gallery of Ont., Toronto.

1866

Mar. 7 Ten thousand militiamen were placed under arms as a precaution against an anticipated Fenian attack on St. Patrick's Day, after Irish supporters held a mass meeting in New York and threatened to invade Canada.

Mar. 17 The American Reciprocity Treaty was cancelled by the US, and became inoperative. Opinion in NS and NB shifted in favour of Confederation. On Apr. 7, the NB Legislative Council requested the Crown include the NB province in Confederation. On Apr. 10, NS Premier Tupper moved the resolution for Confederation in the NS assembly. After a heated debate, the Assembly voted 31–19 in favour of a "scheme of union" with other Canadian provinces.

Also in Mar.

• The Nfld. Assembly passed a resolution postponing its decision on Confederation.

Apr. 10 A group of Fenians massed at Eastport, Maine, with the goal of invading Campobello Is., NB. They withdrew in the face of Canadian militia, British warships and American authorities.

Apr. 17 British troops were dispatched by ship from Halifax to meet a Fenian threat in the St. Croix estuary.

Also in Apr.

• NB Premier Smith was asked to resign the govt by Lt-Gov. Gordon because of his vacillation on Confederation. Pro-confederates, under Samuel Tilley, formed the new NB govt.

May 7 St. Francis Xavier University in Antigonish, NS, was granted full university status. The university had been established in Arichat in 1853, and moved to its present location in 1855.

• The PEI legislature resumed debate on Confederation.

May 14 The Windsor and Annapolis Railway, planned to link Halifax and Annapolis Royal, was chartered.

May 31 Six hundred-plus Fenians, under John O'Neill (1834–1878), crossed the Niagara R. into Canada from Buffalo, cut telegraph lines and the Buffalo and Lake Huron Railroads and occupied the village of Fort Erie. This was the 1st raid into Canada by Fenians whose objective was to "free Canadians from British tyranny." The Fenians would then move inland.

June 1 A majority of the Canadian militia was ordered into service; 20,000 had taken arms by June 3.

June 2 The Battle of Ridgeway pitted John O'Neill's Fenians against the Queen's Own Rifles of Toronto and the 13th Battalion of Hamilton, under Lt-Col. Alfred Booker (1824–1871). Canadians suffered 10 dead and 38 wounded. The Fenians withdrew to Fort Erie where they engaged in another battle with Canadian militiamen under John Stoughton Dennis (1820–1885). The Canadians were forced to retreat with a loss of 6 wounded and 54 prisoners taken.

June 3 The main body of the Canadian force, commanded by George Peacocke, entered Fort Erie, but O'Neill and his Fenians had already escaped back into the US, where they were received with a heroes' welcome. The Fenians were subsequently charged with breaking US neutrality laws, but charges were later dropped.

June 6 US President Andrew Johnson issued a proclamation condemning Fenian raids on Canada as illegal and declared that Fenians would not find safe refuge on US soil.

June 7 Some 1,000 Fenians, under "General" Spier, crossed the Canadian border and occupied Pigeon Hill, in Missisquoi County, Que. They plundered St-Armand and Frelighsburg, but retreated to the US when American authorities seized their supplies at St. Alban's, Vermont.

June 8 The 5th session of the 8th Parliament of Canada met at Ottawa, until Aug. 15. The writ of *habeas corpus* was suspended for 1 year for persons suspected of complicity in the Fenian invasions.

June 9 British and Canadian forces repulsed a 2nd Fenian raid at Pigeon Hill, and chased the invaders back across the border.

June 30 NB, under the pro-Confederation govt of Tilley, voted for Confederation and for the construction of the Intercolonial Railroad.

July 15 A large section of Charlottetown, PEI, was destroyed by fire.

July 26 James Nisbet (1823–1874), the 1st Presbyterian missionary to Native Peoples in the Northwest along with 10 settlers, founded Prince Albert, Sask., as a Presbyterian mission. Nisbet also established a school for Cree children.

July 27 The 2nd transatlantic cable (and the 1st functional) reached Heart's Content, Nfld., from Valentia, Ireland, facilitating communication between these points. Cyrus West Field was the driving force behind the project.

July–May, 1867 Joseph Howe led a NS delegation to England opposing passage of an act of union.

The group succeeded in stalling passage of the act for 10 months.

Aug. 1 Parliament approved the new Civil Code of Lower Canada, codified by Augustin-Norbert Morin, Charles Dewey Day and René-Edouard Caron. The Code was a systematic arrangement of all civil laws pertaining to Canada East. Influenced by the Code Napoléon and the Louisiana Civil Code, it contained provisions from the Custom of Paris and included books of law pertaining to Persons, Property and its Different Modifications, Acquisition and Exercise of Rights of Property, and Commercial Law. The Civil Code of Lower Canada was the product of the Commission of Codification, commissioned by the Parliament of Canada in 1857 to codify all civil statues pertaining to Lower Canada in a single bilingual collection.

Aug. 15 The College of Ottawa became the University of Ottawa.

• The Royal College of Physicians and Surgeons was chartered at Kingston, Ont.

Also in Aug.
• Dutchman Marcus Powell discovered gold on John Richardson's farm in Madoc Township, Ont. (Eldorado). It was the 1st discovery of gold in the Canadian Shield. The news spread rapidly and within months, thousands from around the world flocked to the region in what became known as the "Great Eldorado Gold Rush," the 1st gold rush in Ont. The rush was short-lived, although the Richardson mine is estimated to have produced 3,000 ounces of pure gold.

• The 1st railroad on Vancouver Is., the Esquimalt and Nanaimo Railroad, built by BC coal magnate Robert Dunsmuir (1825–1889) and his son James (1851–1920), opened for business.

Oct. 14 Fire in the St-Roch and St-Sauveur suburbs of Quebec City destroyed over 2,000 homes.

Nov. 19 The Act of Union joining BC and Vancouver Is. was proclaimed in BC. The Imperial Statute had been passed by British Parliament on Aug 6. Gov. Frederick Seymour remained gov. of the now-united British colony. New Westminster was proclaimed its capital.

Dec. 4 Sixteen Fathers of Confederation (from Canada, McDougall, Langeuin, MacDonald, Carter, Galt and William P. Howland; from NS, Archibald, Henry, McCully, John Ritchie and Tupper; and from NB, Fisher, Johnson, Mitchell, Tilley and R.D. Wilmot) held a series of meetings with representatives of the British govt in London, until Dec. 24. The group adopted the London Resolutions, which included a commitment to build an Intercolonial Railway, guarantees of Imperial aid and the rights of both Protestant and Catholic minorities to separate schools. Tilley suggested the name Dominion of Canada for the new country, replacing the original designation Kingdom of Canada.

Dec. 10–June 25, 1867 John Michel served as administrator of Canada. He was C-in-C of British forces in North America from 1865–1867.

Dec. 21 The Bytown and Prescott Railway, incorporated 1850, became the St. Lawrence and Ottawa Railway.

Also in 1866
• Blackfoot Chief Crowfoot (1830–1890) rescued Father Lacombe during a battle with the Cree.

• The Canadian Parliament Buildings were finished in Ottawa, with the completion of Centre Block. The East and West Blocks had been completed in 1865. Principal architects were Thomas Fuller (1823–1898) and Charles Baillairge. Samuel Keefer (1811–1890) directed the construction and arranged the 3 buildings in an open quadrangle. The library would not be finished until 1876. Together, the buildings cost over $3 million, nearly 6 times the original budget. The majestic structure was designed in the Gothic Revival style, complete with towers, flying buttresses, vaulted roofs and whimsical ornamentation, including stone carvings of flowers, plants, birds, unicorns, gargoyles and grotesques. The outer walls consisted of rough-hewn yellow sandstone from a local Nepean quarry. The buildings would be severely damaged by fire on the night of Feb. 3, 1916.

• Absentee landlords controlled 155,292 ha of land in PEI.

• Alexander Butin installed the 1st mechanical wood grinder in Canada at his paper mill in

Valleyfield, Que.; his was the 1st Canadian mill to use wood pulp for paper on a large scale.

• The Canadian govt purchased Rideau Hall (Ottawa) from builder Thomas McKay for $82,000.

• The Vin Villa winery was established on Pelee Is. in Ont., the 1st recorded winery in the country.

• Robert Dudley, an English illustrator working for *The London Illustrated News*, painted *Heart's Content, Newfoundland: Arrival of Transatlantic Cable, 1866*, a watercolour.

• Prussia-born artist William Raphael's (1833–1914) oil painting *Behind Bonsecours Market, Montreal* was 1st exhibited. It now hangs in the National Gallery of Canada.

1867

Jan. 7 At Quebec, Irishman Timothy O'Hea (1846–1874) of the Royle Brigade received the 1st Victoria Cross ever awarded for bravery that did not include the actual presence of an enemy. On June 9, 1866, O'Hea was 1 of 4 men guarding a munitions shipment attached to a Grand Trunk passenger train carrying 800 German immigrants. At Danville, Que., a fire broke out in the munitions car, which contained 95 boxes of gunpowder destined for troops fighting the Fenians at L. Erie. After the car was disconnected from the rest of the train, O'Hea entered it and fought the fire for nearly an hour before he single-handedly put it out.

Jan. 8 The sidewheeler steamship *Fawn* (55 m), built at Carleton, NB, was launched into service at the head of Grand L. for the Onion Steamship Line. It would serve Saint John, Fredericton and Chipman.

Feb. 12 The BNA Act received 1st reading in the British House of Lords. It provided for the union of the Provinces of Canada, NB and NS, and included all the fundamental machinery of the newly organized Canadian Confederation which had been hammered out at the Charlottetown Conference and the Quebec Conference.

Feb. 16 John A. Macdonald married Susan Agnes Bernard (1836–1920) (his 2nd wife) at St. George's

Church, Hanover Square, London, England. The bishop of Montreal conducted the service.

Mar. 8 The BNA Act was passed by the British House of Commons. The act would be signed by Queen Victoria on Mar. 29. British Colonial Secretary Lord Carnarvon (1831–1890) would remark of the momentous occasion: "We are laying the foundation of a great state, perhaps one which at a future day may even overshadow this country." The BNA was now ready to be proclaimed on July 1.

Mar. 11 A Western Union Telegraph Company expedition completed its survey for the construction of a telegraph line from Rupert's Land overland to Russia.

Mar. 18 Amor De Cosmos introduced a motion in BC's Legislative Council promoting union of BC with the Canadian federation. De Cosmos hoped to secure relief from the province's financial woes and avoid annexation by the US. The Legislative Council asked Gov. Seymour to work toward the admission of BC to the Dominion of Canada. An act enabling the province to enter Confederation was approved on Mar. 19.

Mar. 30 The US purchased Alaska from Russia for $7,200,000, following somewhat confused negotiations by Secretary of State William Seward, who mistakenly added an extra $200,000 to the $7-million deal already approved by Czar Alexander. The purchase of Alaska or "Seward's Folly," as American critics would call it, would lead to a boundary dispute with Canada that came to a head in 1903.

Apr. 3 The HBC relinquished all claims to Vancouver Is.

Apr. 12 The Imperial Canada Railway Loan Act was passed. It authorized an Imperial guarantee on a Canadian loan of £3 million for the construction of the Intercolonial Railway from Quebec to Halifax.

May 9 The cornerstone of Ottawa's St. Alban the Martyr Church was laid. Designed by Thomas Fuller and King Arnoldi (1843–1904), the Gothic Revival design would be completed in 1877.

May 10 The Bank of Canada (incorporated 1858) became the Canadian Bank of Commerce.

May 22 A Royal Proclamation declared that the Dominion of Canada would come into existence on July 1, 1867. A Senate of 72 life members was appointed, with 24 members each for Ontario (formerly Canada West) and Quebec (formerly Canada East), and 12 each for NB and NS.

June 1 Charles Stanley Monck, 4th Viscount, was appointed the Dominion of Canada's 1st gov-gen. He served from July 1, 1867 to Nov. 13, 1868.

June 10 The Great Association for the Protection of Canadian Workers, founded by Médéric Lanctot (1838–1877), organized a demonstration of 10,000 in support of Montreal bakers involved in a labour dispute.

June 28 Rules of Civil Procedure, those rules that affected the administration of Que.'s Civil Code, were given effect.

July 1 Twelve noon The BNA Act was proclaimed and the Dominion of Canada was born.

• John A. Macdonald was sworn in as Canada's 1st prime minister, serving until Nov. 5, 1873. Quebec City became the capital of the newly created province of Que., and Toronto the capital of the newly created province of Ont. Canada, though independent in most areas, continued to be ruled by Britain in the fields of foreign affairs, immigration and command of armed forces. The British Parliament relinquished its power to disallow Canadian parliamentary measures. There was no provision for a bill of rights. The *Halifax Chronicle* carried the following announcement: "Died! Last night at twelve o'clock, the freed and enlightened province of Nova Scotia."

• Macdonald, Cartier, Galt, Tilley, Tupper, McDougall and Howland received knighthoods.

• Adams George Archibald became 1st secretary of state for Canada. He had been a NS Assembly representative between 1851–1867.

July 8 *Le Moniteur Acadien*, the Maritime provinces' 1st French-language newspaper, was published at Shediac, NB.

July 18 Jefferson Davis (1808–1889), former president of the Confederate States during the American Civil War, arrived in Canada shortly after his release from Fortress Monroe, where he had been held as a war criminal for 2 years. His wife, Varina, their 2 children, and Varina's mother, Mrs. William Burr Howell, were living in Montreal.

Also in July
• The US Congress declared the new Canadian constitutional monarchy in possible contravention of the Monroe Doctrine.

Sept. 18 John A. Macdonald's Conservatives won the 1st federal election after Confederation, taking 101 seats against 80 for the Liberals under Edward Blake (1833–1912). Almost all Confederation supporters in NS were defeated in the provincial elections (of 19 seats in the House of Commons, 18 went to anti-confederates, 36 of 38 seats in the House of Assembly went likewise).

Also in Sept.
• The 1st Canadian-built automobile, a steam-powered car, was demonstrated at Stanstead, Que., by Henry Seth Taylor (1833–1887).

• Gov. Seymour travelled to the Aboriginal community of Metlakatla to visit Father William Duncan who had established a successful Church of England mission.

Oct. 9 William Jackman (1837–1877) saved 27 people from the ship *Sea Clipper* after it was wrecked off the coast of Spotted Is., Labrador.

Nov. 6 The 1st session of Canada's 1st Parliament opened. It sat until Dec. 21. Legislation was enacted to establish the departments of govt. A resolution was adopted for the admission of Rupert's Land and the NWT into the Dominion of Canada. An act authorizing the construction of the Intercolonial Railroad was passed. Joseph Howe addressed Parliament on Nov. 10 regarding NS's desire to be let out of Confederation. Nfld. Gov. Anthony Musgrave travelled to Ottawa to witness the opening of the 1st session of the new Dominion Parliament and to discuss with Gov-Gen. Lord Monck and John A. Macdonald the plausibility of admitting Nfld. into Confederation.

Nov. 19 The British govt rejected a request that BC be allowed to join Confederation.

Dec. 4 Conservative MP William McDougall (known as Wandering Willie because of his many shifts in political allegiance) moved a resolution in the House of Commons calling for the transfer of ownership of Rupert's Land from the HBC to Canada.

Dec. 17 The BC Legislature met for the 1st time in Victoria. The city would be proclaimed the new capital of BC May 25, 1868.

Dec. 21 Parliament passed an act establishing the Department of Public Works as responsible for all public works, including railways and canals. William McDougall was appointed Public Works Minister

Dec. 27 The Ont. and Que. Legislatures held their 1st meetings.

Also in 1867

• Canada's population was 3,463,000.

• Male teachers earned between $260–552 a year. Female teachers earned between $169–265 per year.

• Fourteen-year-old E.G. Lee found an astrolabe, reportedly lost by Champlain in 1613, on his father's farm near Pembroke, Ont. The boy sold the astrolobe to a Captain Cowley, who took the device (but never paid up), and sold it to R.W. Cassels of Toronto, who then sold it to New York collector Samuel Hoffman. The astrolobe was eventually willed to the New York Historical Society, where it was acquired for the Canadian Museum of Civilization in June 1989.

• Taxes on distilled spirits rose to 60 cents per gallon.

• The Canada Shipping Company was established by Montreal merchants to run cargo and passengers between Liverpool, England, Quebec and Montreal.

• Emily Howard Jennings Stowe (1831–1903) graduated from the New York Medical College and Hospital for Women, Homeopathic in New York City. She had been refused entry to the U. of Toronto because of her gender. Dr. Stowe moved to Toronto and set up practice, without a licence at 135 Church St., specializing in diseases of women and children. She had no hospital privileges. Her "foreign" degree meant she needed course credit from a Canadian medical facility in order to receive licence qualification, but no Canadian medical school would admit a female student.

• The Canadian rowing team took 1st place in the 4–oared event at the world rowing championships in Paris. The famous "Paris Crew" consisted of New Brunswickers George Price, Robert Fulton, Samuel Hutton and Elija Ross. Ross was a lighthouse keeper; the others, fishermen. The team returned home to a heroic welcome.

• Gorffwysfa house (Welsh for place of peace) was built by lumber baron Joseph Merrill Currier (d 1884) in Ottawa. The govt of Canada acquired the house in 1943, and from 1949–1951 remodelled its 34 rooms, approx. 12,000 sq ft. The house still stands today at 24 Sussex Drive, residence of the Canadian prime minister.

• The Blackfoot and Cree met at Wetaskiwin (the place where peace was made), Alb., and agreed to terms of peace.

• Kingston Prison had 907 inmates.

• Toronto General Hospital closed its doors for 10 months for lack of money.

• Dr. George Beers (1843–1900), of Montreal, helped organize the National Lacrosse Assn. He had previously set down the 1st set of codified rules for the sport in 1860.

• William Armstrong painted the watercolour *Thunder Cape, Lake Superior*, now in the National Archives of Canada.

• Toronto schoolteacher Alexander Muir (1830–1906) wrote *The Maple Leaf Forever*. His inspiration for the song came from a silver maple tree on Laing St., Toronto, which exists today. The song was pirated by a music publisher and became a bestseller. Muir received no royalty whatsoever.

• Graeme Mercer Adam (1839–1912) published the *Canadian Bookseller & Miscellany*, the 1st Canadian book trade journal. It would continue quarterly publication through 1872.

• The *New Dominion Weekly* magazine was founded by John Dougall in Montreal with an initial print run of 6,000 copies per issue. A general magazine, in strong support of temperance, it would last 12 years.

• The 1st scholarly guide to Canadian writers, *Bibliotheca Canadensis, or A Manual of Canadian Literature*, by Henry James Morgan (1842–1913), was published.

1868

Feb. 1 The BC Legislative Council in Victoria sent a written request to Gov-Gen. Lord Monck of Canada requesting immediate steps be taken to bring the colony into Confederation. The Canadian cabinet responded by passing an order-in-council advocating the admission of BC. On Mar. 8, Gov-Gen. Monck asked the colonial secretary to initiate proceedings to bring BC into Confederation.

Feb. 14 Joseph Howe, W.H. Smith and other citizens of NS travelled to London, England, to argue once more for the repeal of NS's entry into Confederation.

Feb. 19 Thomas Spence, from his retail store in Portage la Prairie, informed the British Colonial Office of the existence of a new govt, of which he had been elected president. The Republic of "Manitobah," soon more appropriately named Manitoba, stretched from L. Manitoba to the American border and from the District of Assiniboia to the 100th meridian. The Colonial Office refused to recognize the new republic and so informed Spence on May 30. Manitobah subsequently failed, and Spence would join Louis Riel's council at Fort Garry the following year.

Mar. 4 The Toronto Young Men's Christian Association (YMCA) was incorporated in Toronto.

Mar. 12 The 2nd part of the 1st session of the 1st Dominion Parliament met, until May 22. Provisions were made for free entry of raw materials from the US.

Apr. 1 An Act for the Regulation of the Postal Service became effective, establishing a uniform postal system throughout the new country. The Post Office would consist of the following departments: Deputy Postmaster General, Secretary's Branch, Accountant's Branch, Money Order Branch, and Cashier's Branch. This new legislation also created the Savings Branch department, which would function to make the Post Office available for small savings. The Post Office Act also reduced ordinary domestic postage from 5 cents to 3 cents; postage for periodicals under 1 ounce (28 grams) was charged 1/2 cent, transient newspapers 2 cents; parcels, 12 and 1/2 cents per 8 ounces (227 grams); and letters to the US lowered from 10 cents to 6 cents per 1/2 ounce (14 grams).

Apr. 7 Father of Confederation Thomas D'Arcy McGee was shot and killed while entering his home in Ottawa. This was Canada's 1st political assassination. Henry James Friel (1823–1869), mayor of Ottawa, immediately offered a $2,000 reward for the apprehension and conviction of the murderer. On Apr. 9, Patrick James Whelan (c 1840–1869), an Irish immigrant and Fenian sympathizer, was arrested for the murder of Thomas D'Arcy McGee. On Feb. 11, 1869, Whelan was hanged in Ottawa for his crime. Five thousand spectators witnessed the last public execution in Canada. Later evidence would cast some doubt as to Whelan's guilt.

Late Spring The nationalist movement Canada First was founded by George Taylor Denison (1839–1925), Henry James Morgan, Charles Mair, William Alexander Foster (1840–1888) and Robert Grant Haliburton (1831–1901). The elitist organization was created in the memory of Thomas D'Arcy McGee and sought to limit immigration to Canada from Britain only. The organization's pro-British, anti-Catholic, anti-Aboriginal leanings limited its appeal to Orange Ont.

May 14 The Institut Canadien's (Montreal) yearbook was placed on the index of banned literature by the Vatican because it promoted free thought.

May 22 The Dominion Militia Act was passed, retaining the theory of conscription but recognizing voluntary training as the backbone of the militia system. The act provided for a force of 40,000 infantry. The 1st active militia units were formed 3 years later.

May 25 Victoria was proclaimed the capital of BC, 1 day after the queen's birthday. New Westminster had served as the capital since the colonies of Vancouver Is. and BC merged in 1866.

May 26 The design of the Great Seal of Canada was approved by Royal Warrant. It depicted Queen Victoria seated beneath a Gothic canopy. Beneath her were the coats of arms of the 4 provinces.

Also in May
• Amor De Cosmos formed the Confederation League. Based in Victoria, BC, it agitated for admission to Canadian federation and responsible, representative govt.

June 4 The British govt formally informed the Canadian govt that it would not allow NS to withdraw from Confederation.

June 20 Gov-Gen. Lord Monck signed a proclamation for a celebration of the Dominion of Canada to be observed July 1. In 1879 a statute officially established July 1 as Dominion Day.

July 1 The Department of Marine and Fisheries was organized.

July 16 Barkerville, BC, the Cariboo gold-mining boom-town, was destroyed by fire, leaving thousands homeless.

July 31 The Rupert's Land Act passed, allowing the Crown to declare Rupert's Land and the North-Western Territory part of the Dominion of Canada. Canada would pay the HBC £300,000 for the territory, backed by Imperial guarantee, yielding to the HBC 1/20 of the fertile lands within. The Canadian govt and HBC shareholders both officially agreed to these terms in 1869. The 40,000 Aboriginal Peoples living in Rupert's Land were not consulted. On Nov. 19, 1869, the Deed of Surrender of Rupert's Land was authorized by the HBC, to

come into effect Dec. 1, 1869. The transfer of land would be postponed, however, in the face of a Métis uprising which originated from Ottawa's purchase of the territory without Métis consultation. Canada's purchase of the territory was driven in part by a desire to counter US expansionist aims.

Sept. Canadian Public Works Minister McDougall commissioned John A. Snow (1824–1888) to begin construction of the (800 km) Dawson Road, a land and water route linking Fort William to L.-of-the-Woods, then to St. Boniface in the Red River settlement. A survey of the route, which traversed a number of lakes and portages, had been completed by Simon J. Dawson in 1858. Snow assembled a work party in the Red R. settlement with poet Charles Mair as paymaster. No French-speaking members were included in the group. The road was completed in 1871.

Oct. 26 Joseph Howe began publishing a series of public letters in the *Morning Star* advocating that the federal govt and NS renegotiate the terms of Confederation.

Nov. 10 The Commercial Bank of NB suspended payment.

Nov. 14-Nov. 30 Charles Ash Windham (1810–1870) served as administrator of Canada. He succeeded Sir Charles Michel in command of British forces in NA. Windham was succeeded by John Young, Baron Lisgar (1807–1876), who served as administrator from Dec. 1 to Feb. 1, 1869. Young then served as gov-gen. of Canada from Feb. 2, 1869 to June 21, 1872.

Dec. 11 An Order-in-Council appointed 4 commissioners to oversee the construction of the Intercolonial Railway. Sanford Fleming was confirmed as chief engineer of the project. The 1st section of the railway would open between Truro and Amherst, NS, Nov. 9, 1872.

Also in 1868
• The Quebec Academy of Music was founded.

• Three divorces were granted throughout Canada.

• The 1st Canadian Insurance Law was passed.

• The Montreal Football Club was formed, playing a Canadian variety of rugby.

• The Montreal Mining Company sent a team of geologists to access its property at Kull Rock, a tiny islet in L. Superior near the Sibley peninsula. The group found a high-grade vein of silver. The resultant mine, renamed the Silver Islet Mine, would yield $3 million worth of silver from 1868–1884.

• Jersey cattle were 1st imported into Canada.

• The Department of Marine and Fisheries leased Samuel Wilmot's (1822–1899) fish hatchery in Newcastle, Ont.

• Books worth $479,000 were imported into Canada.

• James Anderson published *Sawney's Letters*, a book of poems.

• *Canadian Wildflowers*, a treatise on Canadian botany by Catherine Parr Traill, was published.

• The novel *Armand Durand*, by Rosanna Eleanora Leprohon, was published by John Lovell of Montreal.

• *Dreamland and Other Poems*, by Ont. poet Charles Mair, was published.

1869

Jan. 16 The *Montreal Star* published its 1st issue.

Jan. 30 Joseph Howe renounced repeal of union with Canada when his efforts failed in Britain. He entered the Macdonald govt as president of the Privy Council with hopes of gaining concessions for his home province of NS.

Also in Jan.
• Poet, Orangeman and inflammatory nationalist Charles Mair wrote a series of articles in Ont. newspapers critical of the Métis. Mair downplayed the starvation threatening the Red R. colony as a result of drought and plagues of insects. He suggested mass immigration to the Red R. as a way of overwhelming Métis culture. In Feb., Louis Riel (1844–1885) defended the Métis against Mair's

published criticisms in a strong reply "to the stupidities which a certain Mr. Mair had written." The defence was published in *Le Nouveau Monde* (Montreal).

Feb. 17 The Canadian Society for the Prevention of Cruelty to Animals was founded.

Mar. 13 PEI was reprimanded by the British Colonial Office for taking part in trade negotiations with the US. Under the BNA Act, Canadian foreign affairs were to be negotiated by the British govt in London, and would remain so until the Statute of Westminster, 1931.

Apr. 14 Colonial Secretary George Granville (1815–1891) informed Gov-Gen. Young that the policy of withdrawal of British garrisons from self-governing colonies would be applied in Canada. British garrisons would be maintained only in imperial fortresses. Garrisons in Que. and Ont. would be reduced to 4,000 immediately.

Apr. 15 The 2nd session of the 1st Dominion Parliament met until June 2. A temporary govt. was provided for Rupert's Land and the NWT.

Apr. Cree Chief Maskepetoon, who had devoted much of his energies to bringing about a lasting peace between the Blackfoot and the Cree, was murdered when he entered a Blackfoot camp near present-day Wetaskiwin, Alb., alone and unarmed to negotiate peace. His body was mutilated by Blackfoot Chief Big Swan (d 1872).

May 17 Gov. Seymour set forth from Esquimalt, BC, on the HMS *Sparrowhawk* to investigate a murderous quarrel between the Nass and Tsimshian. He picked up Fr. Duncan en route to act as interpreter. After a series of negotiations between the 2 First Nations, Gov. Seymour was able to reach a peace settlement.

June 2 Gov. Seymour started his return trip to Victoria, but took sick and died at Bella Coola, BC, on June 10, after a bout with dysentery.

June 17 Former gov. of Nfld., Anthony Musgrave, was appointed gov. of BC. He would arrive in BC Aug. 23 with a mandate to unite the colony with Canada.

June 11 Royal Assent was given to the Act for the Gradual Enfranchisement of Indians and the Better Management of Indian Affairs. Native women marrying non-Native men would lose their Native status, while Native men marrying non-Native women would not lose theirs.

July Bishop of Montreal Ignace Bourget, supported by Rome, placed the Institut Canadien under an interdict because it possessed a library containing many books prohibited by the Roman Catholic Index.

Aug. 12 American engineer Capt. Charles W. Raymond (1821-1901) advised HBC employees stationed at Fort Yukon that their fort was on US property and ordered them to leave. The employees left peacefully, moving their possessions up the Porcupine R. to Rampart House.

Aug. 20 A Canadian Survey crew, under the direction of John J. Dennis, arrived in the Red R. to survey the North West and notify the Métis that the govt had agreed to acquire Rupert's Land and the North-Western Territory from the HBC. The plan alarmed Métis farmers in the area, who feared the Canadian govt intended to strip them of their land.

Also in Aug.
• Speaking from the steps of St. Boniface Cathedral, Louis Riel declared the Red R. settlement survey a menace.

• Labourer Thomas Scott (c 1842–1870) led a strike against John A. Snow, superintendent of the Dawson Road project. Labourers, who were paid $20 a month, wanted $25. After the strike was settled Scott demanded strike pay. Snow refused but was forced to give in to Scott's demands when Scott dragged Snow down to the Seine R. and threatened to throw him in. Snow took the case to court. Scott was convicted of assault and fined £4.

Sept. 28 William McDougall was appointed the 1st lt-gov. of Rupert's Land and the NWT. He left immediately for Fort Garry.

Fall A smallpox epidemic devastated First Nations of the plains, killing thousands.

Oct. 6 Construction began on the Toronto, Grey and Bruce Railway at Weston, Ont., with the turning of the 1st sod by Queen Victoria's son, Prince Arthur (later Duke of Connaught).

Oct. 11 A survey party led by Adam Clark Webb attempted to survey a field belonging to Métis André Nault (1829–1924), at St. Vital, Man. About 20 Métis led by Louis Riel prevented the work and forced Webb to leave.

Oct. 16 Joseph Howe, Canadian Sec. of State for the Provinces, left Fort Garry to return to Ottawa after completing a tour of the territory slated to become Man. province. Howe was impressed with the Métis and wrote to Lt-Gov. McDougall warning him not to be influenced by anti-Métis factions.

Oct. 19 The National Committee of the Métis of Red R. was formed at St. Norbert, Man., a Metis' response to Canada's takeover of HBC territory (Rupert's Land). The committee's mandate: to insure that the transfer of Red R. land to the govt of Canada would not infringe on Métis' property rights. John Bruce became president and Riel secretary of the Committee.

Oct. 21 The National Committee of the Métis of Red R. ordered William McDougall, lt-gov. designate of the NWT, not to enter their settlement.

Oct. 25 Riel was summoned to appear before the Council of Assiniboia to explain his recent opposition to the work of Canadian survey crews in the Red R. settlement. Riel declared that the National Committee opposed the entry of any government into the Red R. settlement unless union with Canada was based on negotiations with the Métis and with the Red R. population in general. (Canadian survey authorities reached Métis territory several months in advance of Canada's acquisition of Rupert's land. The official date of transfer from the HBC was scheduled for Dec. 1, 1869.)

Oct. 29 Maria Susan Rye (1829–1903) left Liverpool, England, aboard the *Hibernia,* in charge of 68 abandoned and orphaned young girls. The girls would be shepherded to Niagara-on-the-Lake, Ont., before finding alternate homes or suitable work on Canadian farms and factories.

Oct. 30 Gov. William McDougall reached the border village of Pembina (North Dakota) where a US border guard handed him a note from Riel forbidding entrance into the NWT without special permission from the National Committee of Métis. McDougall waited at the border for an armed escort. His travelling companions, Charles and Eliza Mair, decided to travel on to Fort Garry. The pair were taken into custody by Métis at St. Norbert.

• The 1st issue of the *Canadian Illustrated News* was published at Montreal by Georges Edouard Desbarats (1838–1893). Half-tone photographic reproduction was used for the 1st time in Canada to embellish the publication's 16-folio depiction of H.R.H. Prince Arthur's visit to Montreal. Desbarats printed 6,000 sample copies and established maximum advertising rates.

Nov. 2 One hundred and twenty Métis, under Louis Riel, seized Upper Fort Garry, HBC headquarters at the forks of the Red and Assiniboine Rivers.

Nov. 3 A Métis patrol encountered Col. Dennis and Lt-Gov. McDougall travelling toward Fort Garry and turned them back to Pembina.

Nov. 16 The convention of English- and French-speaking Red R. settlers met at Fort Garry at Riel's invitation, and rejected a proposal to form a provisional govt.

• HBC Gov. William McTavish (1815–1870) of Red R. issued a proclamation requiring Métis to lay down their arms.

Nov. 19 Montreal typographer Joseph Guibord (1809–1869) died and was denied burial in consecrated ground by Bishop Ignace Bourget because of his refusal to renounce membership in the interdicted Institut Canadien. The case was taken to court. Appeals were taken to the Judicial Committee of the Privy Council in London, which decided in favour of the plaintiff. The parish of Nôtre Dame was ordered to perform the rites of a full Catholic burial for Guibord, with costs, and to pay $6,000 in legal fees. Therefore, on Jan. 16, 1875, Guibord's body was exhumed a 2nd time and taken to the Catholic cemetery. Public opposition to the burial required that the remains be escorted by 1,200 troops. Guibord was buried without incident. Two hours later Bishop Ignace Bourget declared the ground no longer consecrated, "under an interdict and separate from the rest of the cemetery."

Nov. 23 Riel, in answer to William McTavish's proclamation of Nov. 16, proposed the formation of a provisional govt to replace the Council of Assiniboia and to negotiate terms of union with Canada.

Nov. 26 PM Macdonald instructed John Rose, Canadian representative in London, not to pay the HBC for Rupert's Land until Lt-Gov. McDougall could guarantee peaceful possession of the colony. The official transfer of land from the HBC was scheduled for Dec. 1.

Nov. 30 Lt-Gov. McDougall slipped into the Red R. colony by night to read 2 proclamations: 1 announced the area's annexation to Canada and the other McDougall's entry into office.

Dec. 1 McDougall took formal possession of the NWT at Fort Dufferin, and commissioned Col. Dennis to raise a force to deal with the Métis.

• At Fort Garry, the Métis National Committee drew up a list of rights as a condition for annexation to Canada. These included the right of the Métis to elect their own legislature, the designation of both English and French as official languages, and that Métis customs be respected.

Dec. 6 Gov-Gen. John Young issued a proclamation for Métis rebels on the condition that they lay down their arms and disperse peacefully. The Canadian govt also appointed a 2-man goodwill mission consisting of Abbé Jean-Baptiste Thibault and Col. Charles-René-Léonidas d'Irumberry de Salaberry (1820–1882).

Dec. 7 The Métis captured a group of English-speaking Canadians, led by John Christian Schultz (1840–1896), who had attempted to seize supplies at Fort Garry. About 45 men were held in Fort Garry, including Orangemen and "Canada Firsters" Charles Mair and Thomas Scott.

Dec. 8 Riel issued the Declaration of the People of Rupert's Land and the North West, charging that the HBC's sale of the territory without their consent entitled the people of the Red R. district to establish their own govt. The National Committee was made the provisional govt of Assiniboia, retroactive to Nov. 24.

• Timothy Eaton (1834–1907) opened a dry-goods store in Toronto at the corner of Yonge and Queen Streets, with a staff of 4. He revolutionized the department store business by selling goods for cash at a fixed price. Eaton had operated dry-goods stores in Kirkton and St. Marys prior to his move to Toronto.

Dec. 10 The Macdonald govt appointed Donald Smith (1820–1914), special commissioner, to negotiate with the Métis at the Red R. settlement and to insure the inhabitants of a peaceful transfer of HBC lands to the Canadian govt. Smith was authorized to offer money and employment to any Métis leaders willing to cooperate. He arrived in the Red R. territory on Dec. 27.

• Riel, Ambroise-Dydime Lépine (1834–1923) and William B. O'Donoghue (1843–1878) hoisted the provisional-govt flag (a fleur-de-lis on a white background) in the centre square of Fort Garry.

Dec. 11 Col. Dennis fled the Red R. Colony.

Dec. 16 The Canadian govt offered PEI a yearly operating grant for its local legislature, a guarantee of "continuous stream communication" with the mainland, compensation for the Island's lack of Crown land and legislation enabling the local govt to buy out the remaining Island proprietors if PEI would join Confederation.

Dec. 18 Lt-Gov. McDougall was recalled to Ont. when the Canadian govt postponed the takeover of Rupert's Land until the HBC could guarantee a peaceful transfer.

Dec. 27 Riel assumed the presidency of the provisional govt, including hegemony over Rupert's Land and the North West, from John Bruce. Louis Schmidt became secretary.

• The *Ottawa Free Press* published its 1st issue.

Dec. 31 The *Toronto Globe* blamed the Canadian govt for the dispute with French-speaking Métis at Red R., accusing it of being insensitive to Métis interests.

Also in Dec.
• Charlottetown native Robert Harris (1849–1919) was commissioned by St. Peter's Cathedral in Charlottetown, PEI, to create scenes for its 1st Christmas celebration.

Also in 1869
• Canada revised its statute on capital punishment, reducing the number of capital crimes to 3: murder, rape, and treason.

• J.J. Healy and A.B. Hamilton of Fort Benton, Montana, built the notorious Fort Whoop-Up, a whiskey trading post, at the junction of the St. Mary and Oldman Rivers, near present-day Lethbridge, Alb. Healy and Hamilton were forbidden to trade liquor for Buffalo robes in Montana, so they moved their operations north. Fort Whoop-Up quickly became a symbol of Native misery and European exploitation. People living in the area around the fort were soon crippled with smallpox, chronic intoxication and starvation in the face of a quickly declining buffalo population. In 1870, carpenter William Gladstone, rebuilt Fort Whoop-Up, originally called Fort Hamilton, after the Blackfoot burned it down.

• Riel forced the closure of the *Nor'Wester*, the Red R. colony's only newspaper.

• Robert McLaughlin (1836–1921) established the McLaughlin Carriage Works in Oshawa, Ont. It would become the largest carriage works in the British empire.

• Gastown, Burrard Inlet, BC, named after the famous tavern keeper John "Gassy Jack" Deighton (1830–1875) (gassy because he rarely kept quiet) was incorporated as the town of Granville.

• German-born artist Adolph Vogt (1812–1871) completed *Niagara Falls,* oil on canvas, now in the National Gallery of Canada.

• Samuel Keefer designed the longest suspension bridge in the world — Clifton Bridge — which spanned the Niagara R. for 400 m, below the falls.

Keefer would win the Paris Exposition (1878) gold medal for this achievement, but the bridge collapsed in 1889 when a new roadway was added (without consulting Keefer).

• Toronto dentist J.W. Elliott patented the idea of a "compound revolving snow shovel" for use in clearing snow from railway tracks, but was unable to secure financing for manufacturing his new invention.

• James De Mille (1833–1880) published the novel *The Dodge Club,* its style anticipating *Innocents Abroad* by Mark Twain. The story caricatured a group of American travellers in Italy in 1859.

• Canadian soprano Emma (Lajeunesse) Albani (1847–1930) of Montreal made her debut in Messina, Italy.

• Canada's 1st geological map was published by Sir William E. Logan, the founding director of the Geological Survey of Canada. The highest mountain in the Yukon's St. Elias Mountains was named Mount Logan in 1891 in his honour.

1870

Jan. 5 The 1st issue of the newspaper *Le Courier* was published in Ottawa.

• Father Thibault and Col. de Salaberry met with Louis Riel and the Métis council to explain the govt's position on the acquisition of Rupert's Land. They were not received, and instead "politely imprisoned" at St. Boniface.

Jan. 7 The *New Nation* newspaper, under editor Henry M. Robinson (an American living in Winnipeg), commenced publication in Winnipeg.

• PEI again rejected Confederation, despite improved terms offered by the federal govt.

Jan. 8 An Order-in-Council eliminated the issuing of licences to American fishing vessels. The policy had been in operation since the end of Reciprocity in 1866. Police cruisers were ordered to patrol the waters and several US boats were seized. The conflict would be resolved with the Treaty of Washington, signed May 8, 1871.

Jan. 9 Mair and Scott escaped from Upper Fort Garry.

Jan. 19–20 More than 1,000 Métis and Scottish settlers assembled at the square at Fort Garry to hear Donald Smith's 5-hour oration on Canada's position regarding the transfer of Red R. territory.

Jan. 23 The American army attacked a Peigan band, 50 km south of the Canadian border, killing 173 men and capturing 140 women and children.

Jan 25–Feb. 10 Métis held a convention in Fort Garry to consider the proposals made by Smith. Louis Riel opened the meeting by nominating Judge John Black (1817–1879) as chairman. It was agreed that a new "List of Rights" be prepared.

Jan. 28 The Inmar cross-Atlantic steamer, *City of Boston,* sailed from Halifax with 191 passengers on board. The ship was out of Boston and destined for Liverpool — but vanished without a trace.

Also in Jan.
• Georges Edouard Desbarats published the 1st issue of *L'Opinion Publique,* the French-language counterpart to his *Canadian Illustrated News.*

• English-speaking businessman Andrew Graham Ballenden Bannatyne (1829–1889) agreed to be postmaster in Riel's provisional govt on the condition that union with Canada would be actively sought.

Feb. 3 Riel asked the convention of Métis and country-born residents to approve a list of rights to use in negotiations for union with Canada.

Feb. 7 Donald Smith invited at least 2 Métis to travel to Ottawa to present their list of rights to the govt.

Feb. 10 A committee appointed by the convention at Fort Garry proposed the establishment of 24 elected representatives for the 2nd provisional govt and the continuation of the General Quarterly Court of Assiniboia to administer the law. Riel was recommended for president. He, in turn, promised to release all prisoners held at Upper Fort Garry.

Feb. 12 Col. Dennis reported to the Minister of Public Works in Ottawa that the people of Red R. refused to allow surveyors to proceed with their work, for fear of the Métis.

Feb. 18 Fifty men from Portage la Prairie, led by Charles Arkoll Boulton (1841–1899) and including Thomas Scott, sought to overthrow the provisional govt but were captured instead. Boulton was sentenced to death, but Riel was persuaded to pardon him. Thomas Scott's insults and his intractability in captivity enraged his guards, who dragged him from his confinement and beat him.

Mar. 1 Finance Minister Francis Hincks introduced the 1st Canadian Bank Act in the House of Commons to standardize banking laws across the country. Among Hincks's proposals: that all banks post a minimum surety bond of $200,000 as a safeguard against default. The Banks and Banking Act was passed May 12.

Mar. 3 At the demand of the Métis, Thomas Scott was tried by "a council of war," presided over by Ambroise-Dydime Lépine, a chief Riel aide. The charge: taking up arms against Riel's provisional govt. Riel served as prosecutor and ignored pleas for clemency from Donald Smith, Rev. George Young and Father Lestanc. On Mar. 4 Scott was condemned by Riel's provisional govt, and shot by firing squad in the prison yard at Fort Garry.

Mar. 8 Alexandre-Antonin Taché (1823–1894), Catholic bishop of St. Boniface, arrived at St. Boniface to negotiate with Riel for an end to the rebellion. On Mar. 15, Taché spoke to the Métis Council at Fort Garry.

Mar. 9 The BC Legislature passed a resolution to send a delegation to Ottawa to negotiate for Confederation. On Mar. 11, the BC Legislative Council adopted terms for Confederation, including payment of BC's debt and the establishment of a transportation link with the rest of Canada. On June 3, the BC Confederation delegation arrived in Ottawa for negotiations.

Mar. 20 Bishop John Joseph Lynch (1816–1888) was consecreated the 1st Roman Catholic archbishop of Toronto.

Mar. 23 Father Joseph-Noël Ritchot (1825–1905) and Alfred Henry Scott (c 1840–1872) left Red R. for Ottawa to negotiate with the Canadian govt on behalf of Riel's provisional govt. Judge John Black

also took part in the negotiations on behalf of the provisional govt. After much prior negotiation, the representatives had what was referred to as a 4th "List of Rights," a list of requirements drafted by the provisional govt for the region's (Manitoba's) entry into Confederation. The demands included: Manitoba be admitted into Confederation as a full-status province with responsible govt; the lt-gov. be bilingual; those who participated in the establishment of the provisional govt be given full amnesty; the establishment of bilingual institutions and the creation of denomination schools; property rights for Aboriginal lands be guaranteed; and the organization of the provincial govt to mirror Quebec's, with an Upper House and Legislative Assembly.

Mar. 26 News of Thomas Scott's execution reached Ont., giving rise to a wave of anti-Métis, anti-Catholic and anti-French sentiment from much of the Protestant population.

Apr. 11 The 3 Red R. delegates, Father Ritchot, Alfred Scott and Judge John Black, were arrested in Ottawa on the charge of abetting the "murder" of Thomas Scott. They were released Apr. 23 after the Canadian govt ensured their defence.

Apr. 13 Donald Smith reported to the federal govt on negotiations with Riel at Fort Garry. He had left Fort Garry Mar. 18.

Apr. 15–May 2 Negotiations between the govt of Canada and Riel's Manitoba representatives were held. The federal govt refused to grant Riel and his followers official amnesty, although it did agree to most of the demands of Riel's govt, as presented by Ritchot, Scott and Black, for the entry of the territory into Confederation.

Also in Apr.
• Thomas Spence became the editor of the *New Nation*, print organ of Riel's provisional govt.

May 6 While at work in the Parliament Buildings, PM J.A. Macdonald suffered an attack of gallstones. His office was converted to a sickroom. His wife, Agnes, rushed to his side. Macdonald lay immobile on his office couch for a week, and for another 6 weeks remained within Parliament, recovering, before he finally went home.

May 7 The deed of surrender, transferring Rupert's Land to Canada, was sent to the British Colonial Office. On May 11, HBC received payment of £300,000 ($1.5 million) from Canada for Rupert's Land and the NWT.

• General Joseph Garnet Wolseley (1833–1913), commanding a military expedition, prepared to move to the Red R. from Toronto on an "errand of peace" to maintain Canadian rule. Some of the militia units were dominated by young Orangemen thirsting to avenge Thomas Scott's death. The Canadian steamship *Chicora* carrying Wolseley and his troops was refused passage through the American locks at Sault Ste. Marie. The federal govt ordered construction of new locks on the Canadian side of the border. These were completed in 1895.

May 12 The Manitoba Act was passed by Parliament, providing for the admission of Man. (formerly District of Assiniboia) into Confederation. English- and French-language rights, and Protestant and Catholic educational rights were safeguarded. Most of the Métis "List of Rights" was incorporated into the act, but the province did not have control over public lands or natural resources. On June 23, an Imperial Order-in-Council transferred Rupert's Land and the NWT to Canada and constituted Man. a province, all to take effect July 15.

• Parliament passed the Census Act, which established a new census every 10 years, beginning in 1871, to ensure accurate representation in the House of Commons by population.

May 15 The US Congress approved a bill granting land to aid in the construction of a railroad from Minnesota to Canada.

May 20–Dec. 1, 1872 Adams George Archibald, a Father of Confederation, served as the 1st lt-gov. of Man. and the NWT. He did not arrive in Winnipeg to assume office until Sept. 2, 1870.

May 24 Fire destroyed much of St. Roch, a suburb of Quebec City, leaving approximately 5,000 people homeless.

May 25 Irish Fenian John O'Neill and his American followers fought Canadians in the Battle of Eccles Hill, Que. They were routed by Canadian militia under Osborn Smith in a skirmish at Huntingdon, Que., on May 26. O'Neill was arrested by American authorities for again breaking US neutrality laws and was sentenced to 2 years in prison. In Oct., O'Neill and his followers were pardoned by President Ulysses S. Grant.

June 3 BC delegates Robert William Carrall (1837–1879), Joseph William Trutch and John Sebastian Helmcken (1824–1920) arrived in Ottawa to negotiate terms for BC to enter Confederation. These included provincial status with a fully elected legislative assembly and responsible govt, debt settlement, federal subsidies, the construction of a coach road between Fort Garry and BC, and commencement of construction on a railroad within 3 years. The Canadian govt accepted and exceeded their demands when it agreed to the "construction of a trans-Canada railway [to] commence, from both east and west within 2 years of the date of union, and be completed within 10 years of the union." BC joined Confederation July 20, 1871. On July 1, an Order-in-Council provided for the building of a railroad to the Pacific Coast on the condition that BC join Confederation.

June 7 The 1st General Assembly of the Presbyterian Church of Canada was held.

June 24 The Métis provisional govt formally and with unanimous approval accepted the Man. Act.

Summer The Twelve Apostles Society, founded by William A. Foster and George T. Denison (augmenting the Canada First movement with new members), established the North West Emigration Aid Society to offer advice to emigrants intending to settle in Man. A pamphlet was issued with information on climate, topography, agricultural potential, availability of land, travel arrangements and required gear. The society's purpose was to promote the settlement of Man. by anglophones who, society members hoped, would in time submerge the Métis population.

July 15 The Man. Act came into effect. All of BNA between Ont. and BC became part of the Dominion of Canada. Man. became the 5th province (25,900 km^2; population 15,000). English and French languages had equal status and 566,560 ha were set aside for Métis. The Man. legislature had 2 chambers, and a total of 6 Man. representatives would sit in Canadian Parliament.

July 16 The British Secretary of State for the Colonies authorized the Blue Ensign to be flown by Canadian govt vessels.

Also in July
• Archbishop Alexandre-Antonin Taché of St. Boniface informed Gov-Gen. John Young, in a letter, that the US had offered Riel and his govt $4 million plus weapons and men to back US annexation of Canadian territory, but Riel and his govt had remained loyal to Canada. Taché obtained a verbal promise, but no signed document, that Riel and the members of Red R.'s provisional govt would be given amnesty.

Aug. 9 The Imperial Loan Act for Canadian Defences guaranteed payment of loans for the construction of fortifications.

Aug. 24 Riel and other members of his govt fled to the US when Wolseley and his troops approached the Red R. settlement. Wolseley occupied Fort Garry without a fight, and the Red R. Rebellion ended.

Sept. 17 Riel returned secretly to St. Norbert, Man., to persuade Métis to reject support for a Fenian invasion.

Dec. 1 Man. held its 1st provincial election. Twenty-four members of the Legislative Assembly were elected in an open declaration of voters' preferences. Only property-owning men were eligble to vote. In 1888, Man. eliminated its property-owning voter requirements and began using the secret ballot.

Also in 1870
• Canada's population was 3,625,000.

• The federal govt issued its 1st paper money in the form of 25 cent notes, a temporary measure implemented while the country awaited a new issue of Canadian coins from Britain. The denomination would again be issued in 1900 and 1923; by 1929, over 5 million notes were in circulation. They were withdrawn from circulation by the Bank of Canada in 1935. Popularly known as "shinplasters" (a term

borrowed from American Revolutionary soldiers who used the near-useless Continental Congress currency to dress shin wounds), the paper note featured Britannia, the shield-bearing personification of Britain.

• Canada's 1st Young Women's Christian Association (YWCA) opened in Saint John, NB.

• Ont. established the Institute for the Deaf and Dumb in Belleville; it would have 100 students by 1871 and 280 by 1880.

• Hart Almerrin Massey (1823–1896), president of Massey Manufacturing Company, Newcastle, Ont., turned over his $100,000 farm implements firm to his son, Charles Albert Massey (1848–1884), who became vice president and superintendent.

• Timber baron J.R. Booth (1827–1925) owned what was at the time one of the largest commerical enterprises in the world operated by a single person. Booth's vast sawmill enterprise, centred in Ottawa, employed 2,000 millworkers and 4,000 men lumbering in the woods of Central Ont. and Que. Booth, who was born in Que.'s Eastern Townships, arrived in Ottawa in 1854 with $9 in his pocket. He began making shingles and was able to secure a lease on a sawmill in 1856. His 1st big break was landing the lumber contract for Canada's new Parliament Buildings. At his death in 1925, Booth had amassed a fortune in excess of $33 million.

• Landscape artist Allan Edson (1846–1888) painted *Mount Orford and the Owls Head from Lake Memphremagog,* oil on canvas, now in the National Gallery of Canada.

1871
Jan. 17 John Baker, Canada's last ex-slave, died. Baker was 93 years old and had lived in the Cornwall area all his life. Baker was freed in 1804.

Jan. 20 William Francis Butler (1838–1910) arrived back at Fort Garry after exploring western Canada as far as the Rocky Mountains. An intelligence officer, he was commissioned to report on conditions in the Sask. R. country, which he referred to as the "Great Lone Land" in the title of a book he published in 1872.

Feb. 15 The 4th session of the 1st Parliament met until Apr. 14. The Government Savings Bank was established.

Mar. 4 Sandford Fleming was appointed engineer-in-chief, in charge of the survey for the Canadian Pacific Railroad. The task would take him until 1878, costing the Canadian govt $3,734,000 and the lives of 40 people.

Mar. 15 The 1st Legislative Assembly of Man. opened. It was held in the home of Andrew Bannatyne because there was no other suitable meeting place large enough.

Mar. 19 Alexander Morris (1826–1889), minister of Inland Revenue, introduced a measure to legalize the metric system in Canada. The use of the metric system was made legal in 1873, but was little known outside the scientific community until the federal govt launched a program in 1970 to convert the country officially to metric measurements.

Apr. 2 The 1st census of the Dominion of Canada was taken. The total population was 3,689,257, including 2,110,502 of British origin and 1,082,940 of French descent. The population of Ont. was 1,620,851; Que. 1,191,516; NS 387,000; NB 285,594; and Man. 10,000. The population of PEI was 94,021 and that of BC was 36,247.

Apr. 14 The Uniform Currency Act, establishing the use of uniform decimal currency throughout Canada, was passed. It would take effect July 1.

Apr. 20 The Catholic hierarchy in Montreal ordered Catholics in Que. to vote for Conservatives.

Apr. 26 Eight land speculators from Ont. arrived at Fort Garry, Man., marking the beginning of a great influx of land-hungry settlers.

Also in Apr.
• Six Blackfoot were killed in a battle with the Cree directly across the river from Fort Edmonton.

May 3 The Man. legislature issued a charter to St. Boniface College, which had been established in 1818 by Bishop Provencher as a classical school for young men.

May 8 Britain and the US signed the Treaty of Washington, which became effective in 1873. The US was granted fishing rights in Canadian waters and the use of Canadian canals and the St. Lawrence R. Canadians were allowed to navigate L. Michigan, the St. Clair Flats Canal and Alaskan rivers. Damages by the Confederate ship *Alabama*, Fenian raids, territory claims to San Juan Is. and Nfld. fishery use all went to arbitration. By 1873, all issues were resolved. A decision made in Geneva ordered Britain to pay the US $15.5 million in gold for claims made against the *Alabama*; San Juan Is. was given to the US; the US was given 12 years' access to the inshore Atlantic fishery in return for $5.5 million and access to the US fish market; and Britain would later provide Canada with a $2.5-million loan guarantee as compensation for damages caused in the Fenian raids.

May 10 The Montreal Ladies' Educational Association (1871–1891) was established by Sir John W. Dawson, principal of McGill University, in consultation with Lucy Stanynought (Simpson), Anne Molson and others. The objective was to hold lectures for women on a variety of academic subjects and eventually to establish a women's college affiliated with McGill. The goal was finally realized Sept. 4, 1899 with the opening of Royal Victoria College.

May 16 An Imperial Order-in-Council admitted BC (948,596 km²) as a province to the Dominion of Canada, effective July 20, 1871.

May 17 A Common Schools Act established separate schools in NB.

Also in May
• The sternwheeler steamboat *Selkirk*, owned by James Jerome Hill (1838–1916) of St. Paul, Minnesota, arrived at Fort Garry becoming the 2nd steamboat to ply the Red R. It carried freight and passengers. The 1st was the *Anson Northrup* (later renamed the *Pioneer*) in 1859.

June 20 The *Polaris*, commanded by Charles Francis Hall (1821–1871), left Brooklyn, New York, to attempt to reach the North Pole by passage between Greenland and Ellesmere Is. The *Polaris* reached 82° 11' by the end of Aug., a new farthest north point before being blocked by ice in the

Lincoln Sea. The ship wintered off the coast of Greenland, where Hall mysteriously died on Nov. 8. The rest of the crew reached Nfld. in 1873.

June 29 The British Parliament amended the BNA Act, granting Canada the right to establish new provinces and change boundaries.

July 10 Canadian govt engineers arrived in Victoria, BC, to begin surveys for construction of the proposed transcontinental railway linking the West Coast province with central Canada.

July 20 BC joined the Dominion as Canada's 6th province. Confederation festivites at Victoria included a 21-gun salute fired from the flagship *Zealous*, stationed at the Port of Esquimalt.

July 25 Anthony Musgrave, BC's last colonial gov., left the new province.

Aug. 3 Treaty No. 1 (Stone Fort Treaty) was concluded with the Swampy Cree and Chippewa at Lower Fort Garry, Man. Lt-Gov. Archibald and Indian commissioner Wemyss Simpson (c 1824–1894) signed on behalf of the federal govt and Chiefs Red Eagle (Henry Prince), Bird Forever, Flying Down Bird, Centre of Bird's Tail, Flying Round, Whippoorwill and Yellow Quill signed on behalf of the Chippewa and Swampy Cree. Treaty No. 1 provided each Native person with a signing "present" of $3, an annuity of $15 per family of 5 or a proportional equivalent and reserve lands enough to provide for each family of 5 or a proportional equivalent. Each reserve would have a school. Hunting and fishing rights were not guaranteed, and no liquor would be allowed on reserves. The Swampy Cree and Chippewa ceded 43,253 km² from the international border to L. Winnipeg and Man. and east to Lake-of-the-Woods to the Crown. On Aug. 21, Treaty No. 2 (Man. Post Treaty) was concluded with the Saulteaux, Cree and Chippewa. It contained terms similar to Treaty No. 1, and ceded north and west Man. land that was contiguous to land ceded in Treaty No. 1. These were the 1st Aboriginal land treaties in post-Confederation Canada.

Aug. 16 Paddle steamer *Maude*, built by Charles H. Gildersleeve at Kingston, Ont., was launched for excursion service in the Kingston area.

Aug. 23 The "Paris Crew," of Saint John, NB's celebrated rowing squad, defeated the Renforth crew from England in a race at Saint John. British squad captain James Renforth suffered an attack during the race and died onshore. The town of Renforth, NB, was named in his honour.

Sept. 7 PEI awarded a contract to Sir Collingwood Schreiber (1831–1918) to build a railway from Alberton to Georgetown. Building of the PEI Railroad began Oct. 2. It opened May 12, 1875.

Oct. 4 The 1st fair held between the Red R. and the Rocky Mountains took place at Fort Garry (now Winnipeg).

Oct. 5 Fenians under William B. O'Donoghue crossed the border from the US and seized the HBC post at Pembina, Man. They were followed by US troops and arrested. Louis Riel secretly returned to Man. to assist the govt, and was publicly thanked by Lt-Gov. Archibald.

Oct. 6 The Merchants' Bank of PEI was founded during a favourable economic climate.

Nov. 11 The last British troops left Quebec City, ending the British occupation of Canada except for a small garrison at Halifax.

Nov. 28 Telegraph service was established between Winnipeg and Pembina, Man.

• The Canada Post Office issued its 1st postcards, unillustrated rectangular cards with a pre-printed stamp.

Dec. 8 The Ont. Liberal-Conservative govt of John Sandfield Macdonald was defeated on a vote of lack of confidence. It was replaced on Dec. 19, by a Liberal govt under Edward Blake. The Liberals remained in power until 1905.

Dec. 23 The legislature of Que. revised municipal laws and established municipal rules and regulations in its new Municipal Code.

c 1871 *Civilization and Barbarism, Winnipeg, Manitoba,* oil on canvas, was painted by William G.R. Hind.

Also in 1871

• Canada's infant mortality rate was 21 deaths for every 1,000 babies.

• The Toronto Trades Assembly was founded by 15 trades societies. John Hewitt (1843–1911), Toronto labour leader, was a major contributor to its establishment.

• The Halifax School for the Blind opened — the 1st school of its kind in Canada.

• The Ontario School Act was passed. Egerton Ryerson, pioneer in Canadian education, was the driving force behind the legislation. Attendance was made compulsory for 7–12-year-olds for a minimum of 4 months per year. Grammar schools were renamed high schools.

• Weather forecasting began in Canada with the formation of the National Meteorological Service.

• Frances Ann Hopkins (1838–1913) painted *Expedition to the Red River in 1870 under Sir Garnet Wolseley, Advance Guard Crossing a Portage,* oil on canvas.

• Cornelius Krieghoff completed one of his last paintings, *The Blacksmith Shop,* now in the Art Gallery of Ontario, Toronto.

• Watercolour artist Daniel Fowler (1810–1894) painted *The Wheelbarrow,* now in the Art Gallery of Ontario, Toronto.

• *Le Canada sous l'Union, 1841–1867,* by Louis-Philippe Turcotte (1842–1878), was published. Successive installments appeared in 1872.

• Historian Alexander Begg (1839–1897) published *The Creation of Manitoba.*

1872

Jan. The Ont. legislature offered a $5,000 reward for the capture of Louis Riel, wanted in Ont. for the Mar. 4, 1870, execution of Thomas Scott.

• The 1st issue of *Canadian Monthly & National Review Magazine* appeared, edited by Graeme M. Adam. A general-interest magazine, its chief editorial policy was "to deal with Canadian questions and call forth Canadian talent." Publication would last 6 years; 54 issues were published.

Feb. 15 The BC legislature met for the 1st time since Confederation.

Mar. 25 The Toronto Typographical Union went on strike, against George Brown's *Toronto Globe,* for a 9-hour workday, part of a growing labour movement in North America and Britain toward a shorter workweek. Strike action was considered illegal, and unions, under law, considered conspiracies against trade. Twenty-four union members were subsequently arrested for conspiracy.

Mar. 30 The *Toronto Mail* was 1st published. Its editorial stance was conservative and supported the policies of John A. Macdonald.

Also in Mar.

• *Le Journal d'Athabaska,* a newspaper, was established with Ernest Pacaud (1850–1904) as proprietor and Wilfrid Laurier (1841–1919) as contributing editor.

Spring Parliament established the Canadian Archives in Ottawa. Douglas Brymner (1823–1902) was appointed Canada's 1st Dominion Archivist.

Apr. 11 The 5th session of the 1st Parliament met until June 14. The Dominion Lands Office was established. Designed to attract settlers to the West, it would also help the govt administer natural resources in Man. and the NWT. Lands were laid out in quadrilateral townships of 36 sections, each 2.6 km² (1 mile sq.) with road allowances. Land reserved for the HBC was defined, as well as land for educational uses. Homesteaders were allowed to acquire 65 ha for a fee of $10. Specific improvements to the land in a specified time were required before clear title would be transferred. Mineral rights remained under control of the govt of Canada.

Apr. 15 The world's 1st Labour Day parade was organized by the Toronto Trades Assembly to protest the recent imprisonment of 24 Toronto Typographical Union members, and to demand that the federal govt repeal its law against unions. Ten thousand

Torontonians turned out to the landmark labour parade, which involved 4 marching bands and 27 unions.

Also in Apr.

• Sandford Fleming selected Yellowhead Pass, the most northerly pass through the Rocky Mountains, as the most appropriate route for the CPR.

May 7 George-Étienne Cartier introduced the Canadian Pacific Railway Bill in the House of Commons. It stipulated that a railway line be completed from the Pacific to a point near L. Nipissing within 10 years. Legislation authorizing construction of the transcontinental railway by the private sector was passed in June.

May 15 Fifteen hundred Hamilton, Ont., workers from different trades put down their tools and took to the streets as part of the "Nine Hours Movement" to reduce the workday of labour (the average Hamilton worker laboured from 11–12 hours a day). Employers did not recognize the movement and failed to recognize workers' demands. Strikers would filter back to work over the coming week.

May 22 Frederick Temple Hamilton Blackwood, Earl of Dufferin (1826–1902), was commissioned Gov-Gen. of Canada. He served from June 25, 1872 to Nov. 14, 1878.

May 30 Portage la Prairie settlers organized the Marquette Agricultural Society and elected Kenneth McKenzie (1811–1874) its president.

June 11 The iron-hulled steamer *Kingston* was destroyed by fire, 30 km out of Brockville, Ont. Two women drowned. The steamer *Bavarian* was later constructed out of materials salvaged from the *Kingston*.

June 14 The Parliament of Canada passed the Trade Union Act, which had been introduced by John A. Macdonald. It declared that unions were legal and not associations in restraint of trade. The right to strike was recognized, but picketing remained a criminal offense. Passing of the act was prompted by the Toronto Typographical Union printers' (TTU) strike. Prior to the act, striking was illegal and considered a conspiracy against trade.

Also in June

• The Grand Trunk Railway purchased the Montreal and Champlain Railway.

• NB exported some 675 kgs of fresh salmon meat to the US.

• Louis Riel returned to Man. from the US in spite of the $1,000 given him by Man. Gov. Archibald to remain in voluntary exile in the US. Ambroise Lépine had also accepted $1,000, but had returned to Man. in May.

July 1 John Sanderson arrived at Fort Garry to take up a homestead in the Northwest. He filed on N.E. 35–12–7, a 65-ha plot, the 1st homestead claim in Western Canada.

Also in July

• The Trades Assembly in Toronto joined the Hamilton, Ont.-inspired movement toward a 9-hour workday.

Aug. 28 James Butler "Wild Bill" Hickock (1837–1876) performed in the world's 1st Wild West Show at Niagara Falls, Ont.

Aug. Louis Riel was nominated as the candidate for Provencher in a federal election.

Sept. 1 John A. Macdonald and his Conservatives were returned to office with a majority of 103 seats in the national election. The Liberals took 97.

Sept. 3 A parade organized by 7 unions, stretching over 1 km, filed through Ottawa. Led by an artillery band and flanked by local firemen, it passed the house of PM Macdonald to protest the recent imprisonment of 24 Toronto Typographic Union members. Macdonald was then carried in a carriage by torchlight procession to City Hall, where he pledged that his govt would further address anti-labour legislation and "sweep away all such barbarious laws from the statute books." Macdonald had already begun the process with the Trade Union Act of June 14.

Sept. 14 George-Étienne Cartier was elected *in absentia* by acclamation in the riding of Provencher in Man. after Riel agreed to withdraw his candidature on condition that Cartier defend Métis rights.

Sept. 25 David Lewis Macpherson (1818–1896) formed the Inter-Oceanic Railway Company in the hope of obtaining the contract to build the CPR. Inter-Oceanic Railway received a federal charter, but not the CPR contract, which went to Hugh Allan's (1810–1882) CPR Company on Feb. 5, 1873.

Oct. 15 The Canadian Pacific Railway Company was formed with 13 directors, many of whom were American and some of whom also represented CPR rival the Inter-Oceanic Railway. Hugh Allan was elected president. The company was given a federal charter on Feb. 5, 1873, a subsidy of $30 million and 20,234,000 ha of land. It was later revealed (Apr. 1, 1873) that Hugh Allan had secured the contract to build the railway by giving John A. Macdonald, George-Étienne Cartier and Hector Langevin $360,000 in campaign funds for the Sept. election. The funds, it was also learned, had been requested by the politicians.

• Edward Blake resigned as Liberal premier of Ont. to pursue a career in federal politics. He was succeeded as premier by Oliver Mowat who championed provincial rights over federal rights. Mowat would remain premier through 1896.

Nov. 9 The 1st section of the Intercolonial Railway between Truro and Amherst, NS, opened. On Nov. 11, the part linking Halifax and Saint John, NB, was completed.

• The initial issue of the *Manitoba Free Press*, owned by William Fisher Luxton (b 1844), was published in Winnipeg.

Nov. 16 PEI Lt-Gov. William Robinson wrote Gov-Gen. Lord Dufferin to inquire about the terms PEI might expect should it enter Confederation.

Dec. 2 In a message to Congress, US President Grant recommended the appointment of a commission to determine and mark the location of the boundary between Alaska and Canada. The govt of Canada had made a formal request to the British Foreign Office regarding the nature and extent of the boundary on June 11.

Dec. 15 *Mary Celeste* (the mystery ship), built in Spencer's Is., NS, and launched in 1860 was found midway between the Azores and Cape Roca on the Portuguese coast. The ship had left New York City, Nov. 7 for Italy with a cargo of 1,700 barrels of alcohol. The crew consisted of Capt. Briggs, his wife and daughter and a crew of 8. When boarded, the ship's sails were set on a starboard tack, cargo and ships supplies were untouched — but no crew was aboard, and there were no signs of struggle. The incident was made famous in Conan Doyle's short story *J. Habakuk Jephson's Statement* (1883).

• John Horden (1828–1893) was appointed the 1st Anglican bishop of Moosonee, Ont.

Dec. 23 BC Lt-Gov. Joseph William Trutch (1826–1904) called on Amor De Cosmos to become premier of BC and form a new govt, following the defeat of BC's 1st premier, John Foster McCreight (1827–1913). De Cosmos formed the 1st of a series of govts composed of men, usually born and raised in North America, who had supported Confederation and fought for reform.

• 1872–1877 Alexander Morris served as lt-gov. of Man. and the NWT.

Also in 1872
• Nick Sheran established a coal mine at Coalbanks, later to become Lethbridge, Alb.

• The govt of Canada dispatched Col. Patrick Robertson-Ross to report on the effects of American whiskey traders on western First Nations. Robertson-Ross would note in his travel diaries that the Blackfoot numbered 2,523 men, 3,384 women and 4,245 children. On his return to Ottawa, he would recommend that a police force be immediately established in the West.

• The Ont. Society of Artists was organized.

• Robert Simpson moved his Newmarket, Ont., dry-goods store to Toronto. In 1881 he established his landmark Simpson's Department Store on Queen St., west of Yonge.

1873

Feb. 12 In response to a Canadian appeal that steps be taken to establish a boundary between Canada and Alaska, US Secretary Fish expressed doubt that the US Congress would be willing to spend the money needed. Canada agreed to share the costs equally.

Feb. 15 PEI Premier Robert Poore Haythorne (1815–1937) led a delegation to Ottawa to negotiate a deal with John A. Macdonald for joining Confederation. After a series of meetings with a sub-committee of the Privy Council, including Macdonald, the 2 groups reached accord on the terms of PEI's entrance into the Dominion of Canada. On May 21, Parliament approved the entry of PEI into Confederation. On June 26, an Imperial Order-in-Council admitted PEI into Canada as the 7th province, effective July 1. Canada assumed responsibility for PEI's debts and the province was given a debt allowance of $45 per person. (In the event that PEI's debt was less per capita, it would be paid interest at the rate of 5% per annum on the difference.) PEI received a total of 10 seats in the federal legislature and Canada assumed all expenses involved in fisheries protection, lighthouses and marine hospitals.

Mar. 5 The 1st session of the 2nd Parliament met until Aug. 13. The Secretary of State for Provinces was abolished, and the Department of the Interior Ministry was established.

Mar. 8 The NWT council prohibited the sale of liquor.

Mar. 29 The School of Practical Science for Mining and Mechanical Engineering was established at the U. of Toronto.

Apr. 1 White Star liner *Atlantic*, on its voyage from Liverpool to New York, sank on a reef after striking Meagher's Rock, outside Halifax Harbour, at 3:15 a.m. Five hundred and forty-six people died.

Apr. 2 Liberal MP Lucius Seth Huntington (1827–1886) charged that Hugh Allan and G.W. McMullen had contributed campaign funds to the Macdonald govt in return for the charter to build the CPR. A non-confidence motion was defeated 107–76, but the charge of corruption would set in motion the "Pacific Scandal," leading to the forced resignation of Macdonald's govt on Nov. 5.

Apr. 21 Parliament passed the Oaths Act, giving its select committee examining the Pacific Scandal power to question witnesses under oath. The act was declared unconstitutional in July, after receiving Royal Assent May 3.

May 4 Fifteen American wolf hunters ("wolfers") from Fort Benton, Montana, ambushed Assiniboine, under Chief Little Soldier. Thirty Assiniboine and one American were killed in the resulting Cypress Hills Massacre. The wolfers, who had been drinking heavily, believed the Assiniboine had stolen some of their horses. No convictions were ever made.

May 7 Joseph Howe was appointed lt-gov. of NS. He would serve from May to June, 1873, when he died of exhaustion.

May 13 An explosion ripped through a Westville, NS, coal mine in Pictou County, killing 60 miners. Two years would pass before the bodies were recovered.

May 18 St. Vincent de Paul Penitentiary opened near Montreal.

May 20 George-Étienne Cartier died in London, England, of Bright's Disease. In Oct, Louis Riel ran unopposed in a by-election left vacant by Cartier in the riding of Provencher. He did not, however, enter Ottawa, for fear of assassination or arrest.

May 23 In the wake of the Cypress Hills massacre, and based on the recommendations of Robertson-Ross and officials in the Northwest, especially Alexander Morris, creation of the North West Mounted Police was authorized by an Act of Parliament (the Administration of Justice, NWT Act). The creation of the North West Mounted Police (later named the Royal Canadian Mounted Police) was based on reasons that included safeguarding the proposed transcontinental railroad, stifling the whiskey trade, establishing law and order, establishing a Canadian presence against US incursions and expansion and encouraging Native Peoples to sign treaties with the govt of Canada. The force was fashioned after the Royal Irish Constabulary.

May 24 Torontonian John Wilson Bengough (1851–1923) established the 4-page satirical weekly publication *Grip*, which became famous for cartoons about John A. Macdonald. *Grip* would ultimately comprise 14 pages, including cover, and would remain popular with Canadians for 21 years.

June 4 The *Montreal Herald* and *Toronto Globe* published incriminating letters from PM Macdonald to Hugh Allan, which, for the 1st time, directly implicated the PM in the Pacific Scandal.

June 25 The BC govt protested the federal govt's failure to fulfill the terms of Confederation by not yet completing the transcontinental railroad.

June 29 Two hundred and eighty-five Icelanders reached Canada, landing at Que., and travelled to L. Winnipeg, where they founded a new settlement, Gimli (which means "paradise" in Icelandic), on Oct. 4.

Also in June
• George Barnes founded Canada's oldest winery, Barnes Wines Ltd., in St. Catharines, Ont., on the Niagara Peninsula. The winery is still in existence.

July 1 PEI joined Confederation as the nation's 7th province. At 5,660 km², it was the nation's smallest province. Its motto would be *Parva Sub Ingenti,* or "The small under the protection of the great."

Aug. 14 A Royal Commission was appointed to hear evidence based on Lucius Huntington's charges of corruption concerning PM Macdonald and the CPR contract.

Aug. 23 The Great NS Cyclone struck Cape Breton Is. with gale-force winds, heavy rainfall and severe thunderstorms. One thousand two hundred ships were lost, 500 people died and 900 buildings were destroyed. Damage was estimated at $3.5 million. Halifax and Truro also suffered from the storm, which was unexpected because telegraph communications between Toronto (which received the transmitted storm warnings from Washington, D.C.) and Halifax malfunctioned.

Aug. 28 Henry Thibert and Angus McCulloch discovered gold in the Cassiar region of BC. A wild gold rush ensued, lasting 5 years.

Aug. 30 Joseph Whitehead received a contract from

the federal govt to build the Pembina Branch railway from St. Boniface, Man., to the international boundary at Emerson, as part of the plan for construction of the Canadian Pacific Railway. The line was completed in Nov. 1878. It would link-up to the St. Paul and Pacific Railway and begin regular north-south service.

Sept. 23 Organized labour convened in Toronto to form the Canadian Labour Union, which represented 31 unions.

• Ambroise Dydime Lépine, who had presided over the court martial that condemned Thomas Scott to death in 1870, was arrested after John Harrison O'Donnell (1844–1912), a member of the Man. Legislative Council, signed an arrest warrant for both Louis Riel and Lépine in relation to the case. On Dec. 22, Lépine was released on bail while awaiting trial for the murder. Andrew Bannatyne put up one-fourth of the $8,000 bail, the Métis put up the remainder. On Nov. 4, 1874, Lépine was sentenced to death for his part in the court martial and death of Thomas Scott. Lord Dufferin commuted the sentence to 2 years' imprisonment with the permanent forfeiture of Lépine's political rights.

Sept. 25 Recruitment and appointment began for the NWMP. The govt sought 150 policemen to patrol all 603,375 km² of the Northwest.

Oct. 3 Treaty No. 3 (The North-West Angle Treaty) was signed with the Ojibwa–Saulteaux ceding 142,540 km² in Ont. and Man. from the L. Superior watershed to the northwest angle of the L.-of-the-Woods. Lt-Gov. Alexander Morris, interim commissioner of Indian Affairs, Provencher, and Simon J. Dawson represented Canada during the negotiations. Each Saulteaux family of 5 received a reserve of 259 ha, a lump sum payment of $12 and a $5 annuity per person. Chiefs received $25 per year and a new suit of clothes every 3 years, plus a flag and metal. Hunting and fishing rights were to continue with an annual payment for ammunition. Agricultural tools were also given.

Oct. 22 Methodist missionaries John and David McDougall left Edmonton with 25 Métis to establish a mission and ranch among the Stoney in the southern Alb. foothills.

Oct. 27 Liberal leader Alexander Mackenzie moved a vote of extreme censure against Macdonald's Conservative govt over the Pacific Scandal.

Oct. 31 The International Bridge, designed and built by Casimir Stanislaus Gzowski (1813–1898), linking Fort Erie and Buffalo, New York, over the Niagara R., was completed and opened to traffic. Its official opening was Nov. 5.

Also in Oct.
• The 1st of 3 detachments of NWMP recruits set out from Collingwood, Ont., for Fort Garry, Man., where they planned to winter. George Arthur French (1841–1921) was named 1st commissioner. His assistant was Col. James Farquharson Macleod (1836–1894). Samuel "Sam" Benfield Steele (1849–1919) also joined the NWMP as Sergeant-Major A-troop and Rough-Riding Sergeant-Major for all troops. All 3 detachments (troops A, B & C — 150 men in total) would arrive in Fort Garry by Nov. NWMP constables were paid $1 per day and granted 65 ha of prairie land after 3 years' satisfactory service. Subconstables received 75 cents a day.

Nov. 3 In a dramatic and compelling 5-hour speech before a packed House of Commons, PM Macdonald pleaded with his parliamentary supporters not to abandon his govt.

Nov. 4 Conservative MP Donald Smith withheld his support of Macdonald's Conservative govt: "For the honour of the country, no government should exist that has a shadow of suspicion resting on it, and for that reason I cannot give it my support."

Nov. 5 Macdonald's govt was forced to resign over evidence that members of the govt had accepted campaign funds from Hugh Allan in return for the CPR contract. Gov.-Gen. Lord Dufferin called on the leader of the opposition, Alexander Mackenzie, to form the new govt.

Nov. 6 The steamer *Bavarian* burned near Oshawa, Ont., taking the lives of 14, including Capt. Charles Carmichael of Toronto. The burned-out iron hull was salvaged and used in the building of the *Algerian*.

Nov. 7, 1873–Oct. 16, 1878 Liberal leader Alexander Mackenzie, a Sarnia newspaperman and protégé of George Brown, served as PM and as his own minister of Public Works, in the absence of other suitable Liberal personnel. Richard John Cartwright (1835–1912), free trade supporter, was minister of Finance.

Nov. 8 The fur station known as the Forks and a part of the Red R. colony was incorporated as the new city of Winnipeg. Winnipeg, a Cree word meaning "murky water," became the 1st city in the new province of Man.

Dec. 6 A new political party, Canadian National Association (CNA), was founded in Toronto as an offshoot of the Canada First association.

Dec. 10 Gabriel Dumont (1837–1906) was elected president of the Sask. Valley Métis.

Also in 1873
• The federal govt established the Miramichi Fish Hatchery for Atlantic salmon.

• The Royal Montreal Golf Club was established. It remains the oldest golf club in North America.

• The Canada-US boundary commission was established to survey and mark 1,450 km of border between Lake-of-the-Woods and the Rocky Mountains at the 49th parallel.

• The federal govt guaranteed Mennonites wishing to settle in Canada, military exemption and separate schools.

• NS prohibited the employment of boys under 10 in and about mines, and limited the workweek of boys under 13 to 60 hours, or 10 hours a day.

• *A Shot in the Dawn, Lake Scugog,* oil on canvas, by John A. Fraser (1838–1898), was exhibited in the 1st Ontario Society of Arts exhibition in Toronto. The painting is now in the National Gallery of Canada. Fraser helped found the Society of Canadian Artists, Montreal, 1867, the Ontario Society of Artists, Toronto, 1872, and the Royal Canadian Academy of Arts, Ottawa, 1880.

• Frederick Arthur Verner (1836–1928) painted *Indian Encampment at Sunset,* oil on canvas, now in the Winnipeg Art Gallery.

• George Monro Grant (1835–1902) published *Ocean to Ocean,* an account of his 1872 survey journey with Sanford Fleming.

• James and Gilbert Ganong established Ganong Brothers chocolatiers in St. Stephen, NB. The nation's oldest candy company was 1st in North America to produce the 5-cent chocolate bar (1910) and 1st in Canada to produce heart-shaped boxes of valentine candies (1932).

1874

Jan. 5 Winnipeg held its 1st civic election. Although only 308 names appeared on the voters' list, some 331 votes were cast.

Jan. 16 The federal govt repeated its request to the American State Department to take steps to define the Alaskan-Canadian boundary.

Jan. 22 Liberals under the leadership of Alexander Mackenzie were re-elected, with 138 seats in a house of 206. Louis Riel was elected from Provencher, Man. Macdonald's Conservatives held 67 seats.

Feb. 7 Eight hundred BC residents held a meeting in the provincial Parliament Buildings, protesting delay of the railroad connection between the East and BC, promised as an incentive for joining Confederation. Some angry protestors advocated union with the US. The route from the East had yet to be determined.

Feb. 13 Edward Blake, former Ont. premier and one of the most respected ministers in the Liberal cabinet, resigned from the party to sit as a private member in Parliament. Blake felt that he, not Mackenzie, should have been Liberal leader, and thus prime minister.

Also in Feb.
• The 1st Canadian branch meeting of the US farmer's association, the Grange, was held in London, Ont. The organization would work to eliminate the middleman from farm commerce, and would lobby federal and provincial govts for legislation favourable to agriculture interests.

• Two hundred new NWMP recruits, with 16 officers and 244 horses, set out for the Northwest by train to Fargo, N. Dakota, then by foot 1,666 km across the prairies, to meet up with NWMP troops A, B and C in Dufferin, Man. The new recruits, NWMP troops D, E and F, arrived at Fort Dufferin June 19, to rendezvous with troops A, B and C. Each troop had horses of a specific colour: A–dark bay; B–brown; C–chestnut; D–dark gray or buckskin; E–black; and F–light bay.

Mar. 5 The legislature of PEI held its 1st post-Confederation session.

Mar. 30 Louis Riel, wanted in connection to the 1870 execution of Thomas Scott, entered Ottawa, and presented himself before an astonished clerk to sign the roll as a member of the House of Commons. He then walked out and disappeared, in the direction of Montreal.

Also in Mar.
• James Walker (1848–1936) was appointed superintendent and sub-inspector in the NWMP.

Spring Fifty members of the NWMP had deserted the force since its creation in 1873.

Apr. 9 Riel, who had not sat in Parliament, was expelled from the House of Commons and his seat declared vacant.

Apr. 16 The Ontario School of Agriculture was established at Guelph, Ont. It opened June 1, with William Johnston (1848–1885) as principal.

May 3 Reverend William Carpenter Bompas (1834–1906) was consecrated as the 1st Anglican bishop of Athabaska including all the NWT. He would serve in that position until 1891.

May 26 The federal govt passed the Dominion Elections Act, introducing vote by secret ballot, ensuring that all ridings vote in the general election on the same day, abolition of property qualifications for MPs, closing of all bars on election day and the itemization of all politicians' election expenses within 60 days after the vote.

June 1 Central Prison for Men opened in Toronto as 147 convicted criminals were transferred from smaller jails in the province. As part of a rehabilitation experiment, convicts helped build railway cars in the Canada Car and Manufacturing Company, and were paid 50 cents a day for their labour.

July 4 Robert Hodgson (1798–1880) became PEI's 1st native-born lt-gov.

July 7 The 53-m-long steel-hulled paddle steamer *Corinthian* hit Split Rock while shooting the Cascade Rapids in the St. Lawrence R. Its 250 passengers were taken to shore in lifeboats. Damage was not serious and the ship was put back in service after minor repairs.

July 8 Lt-Gov. Morris called on Marc-Amable Girard (1822–1892) to accept the premiership of Man. Girard thereby became the province's 1st premier. The previous position of power had been held by the office of the chief administrator.

• To establish a presence in the West, 318 NWMP troops commenced the Great March westward from Fort Dufferin, Man., to the southwest tip of the NWT. The troops reached the junction of the Bow and South Sask. Rivers on Sept. 10. They recrossed the prairies to arrive at the Swan R. barracks at Pelly, Sask. on Oct. 21, while others continued to Winnipeg.

July 31 The 1st group of Russian Mennonites arrived at Que. on the steamer *International* on their way to settle in Man.

Also in July
• The *Manitoba Free Press* began daily publication, becoming Canada's 1st daily west of Toronto. The farm paper, the *Manitoba Weekly Free Press,* also began publishing.

Aug. 1 "A" Division of the NWMP, under Inspector W.D. Jarvis, Sub-Inspector Gagnon and Sergeant-Major Steele set out for Edmonton with supplies and stores. Their mission: to set up a new post called Sturgeon Creek Post and later Fort Sask.

Aug. 24 Alexander Graham Bell (1847–1922), by his own admission, 1st conceived the idea of the telephone in Tutelo Heights, Brantford, Ont. He would continue to work on the idea before inventing and patenting his invention in the US in 1876.

• The P.T. Barnum Circus staged a parade in Halifax that attracted viewers from all over the city, includ-

ing all the clerks from the Bank of NS, who discovered $22,000 had been stolen from the bank in their absence. The crime was never solved.

Aug. 27 The 6.3-ha Victoria Park in London, Ont., was officially dedicated. It was built and designed by William Miller for "passive" recreation and amusement.

Sept. 15 Treaty No. 4 was signed with the Cree and Chippewa at Fort Qu'Appelle, Sask., ceding parts of Man., Assiniboia and Sask. districts. Each band member would receive immediate payment of $5 and an annuity of $12; each chief $25, a coat and a Queen's silver medal. The govt of Canada would provide agricultural implements for farming, a flag and $750 worth of powder, shot and twine. Hunting and fishing rights remained Aboriginal prerogatives. Man. Lt-Gov. Morris was chief negotiator.

Sept. Louis Riel was again elected in the riding of Provencher. He did not take his seat and was expelled from the House of Commons for the 2nd time.

Oct. 1 Free letter-carrier delivery service was introduced in Montreal.

Oct. 9 NWMP, under Col. Macleod and guided by Métis Jerry Potts (Ky-yo-kosi or Bear Child [1840–1896]), arrived at the coulees above the notorious whiskey trading post Fort Whoop-Up in southern Alb. They found the fort empty and built their own post, Fort Macleod, on an island in the Oldman R. The 1st arrest was made soon after when 2 wagon-loads of whiskey, 5 men, rifles and buffalo robes were seized.

Oct. 15 A Man. court issued a warrant outlawing Louis Riel.

Oct. 27 The *William D. Lawrence,* named after its owner, was launched in Maitland, NS, as the largest wooden sailing vessel ever built in the Atlantic provinces.

Nov. 13 Canada's 1st train robbery occurred between Toronto and Port Credit as bandits dressed as Klu Klux Klan members robbed a Great Western Railway train of some $45,000.

Nov. 17 Colonial Secretary Lord Carnarvon decided that Canada would begin building the CPR from Esquimalt to Nanaimo on Vancouver Is., in addition to initiating surveys on the mainland. Proposed expenditure for the BC section of the line was at least $2 million per year.

Nov. 30 Lucy Maud Montgomery (d 1942) was born in Clifton, PEI, to Hugh John and Clara Woolner Montgomery.

Also in Nov.
• Quebec newspapers demanded amnesty for Lépine and Riel.

Dec. 1 Frederick Bowker Terrington Carter (1819–1900) became premier of Nfld. after his party defeated Premier Charles Fox Bennett (1793–1883), who had previously won support by opposing Confederation with Canada

1874–1880 Father Lacombe served as curé of Sainte-Marie, Winnipeg, where he worked to increase the number of French-speaking settlers from Quebec and New England. He also compiled the landmark grammar and dictionary of the Cree language.

1874–1881 Canada was stricken by a severe economic depression, which affected all sections of the economy, leading to widespread unemployment and a sharp rise in the number of bankruptcies.

Also in 1874
• The St. Catharines (Ont.) General Hospital opened, and included the 1st Canadian training school for nurses.

• Liberals raised tariffs, hoping to stimulate domestic production.

• The excise tax on Canadian spirits rose to 74 cents a gallon.

• The Anticosti Is. Company was formed by members of the Forsyth family of Que. to colonize the island with settlers from Nfld. The enterprise failed.

• The Montreal Stock Exchange was established. There were 63 issues including 21 banks, 3 mining companies, 4 railways, 9 government/municipal issues and 10 industrials. Average daily turnover was 800 shares.

• The 1st modern football game was played in Boston between McGill U. and Harvard U. McGill lost.

• Twenty pairs of English sparrows arrived in New Glasgow, NS.

• The Church of St. Paul's was officially opened in Metlakatla, BC. The 1,200-seat church was designed by William Duncan of the Church Missionary Society.

• Civil engineer Thomas Keefer completed the Ottawa Water Works.

• Letitia Youmans, née Creighton (1827–1896), inspired by the women's temperance movement in the US, organized the Women's Christian Temperance Union in Owen Sound, Ont.

• Books worth $959,000 were imported into Canada.

• The independent Ontario Ladies College, run by the Methodist Conference, opened in Trafalgar Castle in Whitby, Ont. The castle was the largest private residence in the country until the completion of Casa Loma, Toronto, in 1914.

• *The Emigrant and Other Poems*, by Alexander McLachlan, was published.

1875

Jan. 14 The 1st issue of the *Halifax Herald* was published.

• Riots persisted for 2 weeks in Caraquet, NB, over plans to cut funding to French-language schools. The militia was called in to restore order.

Also in Jan.
• A total of 19 Liberals under Oliver Mowat were returned to power in Ont.'s provincial election. Liberals took 51 seats to the Conservatives 33.

• BC became the 1st province to grant women the right to vote in selected municipal elections.

Feb. 4 The 2nd session of the 3rd Parliament met, until Apr. 8. Louis Riel was re-elected for Provencher and again expelled *in absentia*.

Feb. 12 Parliament voted to grant amnesty to Riel, Ambroise Lépine and provisional govt leaders, for the execution of Thomas Scott, on the condition that Riel and Lépine serve a 5-year exile.

Mar. 1 The Hospital for Sick Children opened in Toronto to treat children 12 years of age and under. Its founder was Elizabeth McMaster.

Mar. 3 James Creighton (1850–1930), along with other students at McGill University, participated in the 1st indoor hockey game at Victoria Skating Rink in Montreal. The game used "Halifax Rules" written by Creighton, and consisted of 9 skaters per team. The game was played on a confined area, called a rink (61.5 m x 25.9 m); the game was pre-announced to the general public and played between two identified and uniformed teams, under a prewritten set of rules, with a recorded score; and the game was played with a wooden puck, the 1st time such was used instead of a lacrosse ball.

Apr. 3 The federal govt awarded a contract to Sifton, Cochrane, Ward and Co. to construct a 72-km railway from Prince Arthurs Landing, Ont., to L. Shebandowan, Ont., in the Thunder Bay region. This was part of PM Mackenzie's plan to produce mainline for the Pacific Railway. Construction began at the Kaministiqua R. near Thunder Bay on June 1, when the 1st sod was turned.

Apr. 8 The Parliament of Canada, under the *Constitution Act of 1867*, passed a bill establishing a federal appeals court, known today as the Supreme Court of Canada. William Buell Richards (1815–1889) served as the 1st chief from Oct. 8–Jan. 9, 1879. The court initially consisted of 6 justices, and was an appeals court whose decisions could be overturned by the then highest appeals court in Canada, the Canadian Judicial Committee of the Privy Council. In 1949, the Privy Council's superior appellate jurisdiction ended as the Supreme Court became Canada's highest appellate court with its present 9 members: 1 chief justice and 8 puisne judges: 3 mandated from Que., 3 typically appoint-ed from Ont., 2 from the West and 1 from Canada's Atlantic provinces. Along with functioning as Canada's highest court, the Supreme Court also serves today as a referential body that considers important questions of law and renders opinions on matters of constitutional importance and federal or provincial interpretation of legislation or division of power. Justices of the Supreme Court are appointed by the Governor in Council and serve a life term until age 75. Supreme Court hearings are open to the public at the court's home in Ottawa.

Apr. 10 RCMP Inspector Éphrem Brisebois (1850–1890) established a fort in present-day Alb. where the Bow and Elbow Rivers meet. He named it Fort Brisebois and ordered all fort documents be headed the same. Briseboise was not popular enough to maintain the self-granted designation, and in 1876, RCMP Commissioner Macleod changed the name to Fort Calgary (Calgary meaning "Cove Bay" in Gaelic, and the name itself inspired by Calgary Bay, Isle of Mull, Scotland).

May 12 The PEI Railway, one of the world's most serpentine roadbeds with a full third of its line forming curves, opened. At 236 km in total length, the railway was longer than PEI (224 km).

• Dr. Jenny Kidd Trout (1841–1921) became the 1st licenced woman doctor in Ont. A former associate of Dr. Emily Stowe, Dr. Trout soon became a rival.

May 24 On Victoria Day, NWMP at the Swan R. post staged a snake-killing competition which claimed 1,100 snakes.

May 25 Grace Annie Lockhart (1855–1916) received a B.Sc. and literature degree from Mount Allison College in Sackville, NB, becoming the 1st woman in the British empire to receive a bachelor's degree.

May 29 A British polar expedition under George Strong Nares (1831–1915), commanding the British navy vessel *Alert*, left Portsmouth, England, with hopes of reaching the North Pole, via the channel between Greenland and Ellesmere Is. The expedition lasted 1 year and climaxed with Albert Hasting Markham's sled traverse to 83° 20' 26" N, the northernmost penetration to date.

Also in May

• John Wilson Murray (1840–1906) was appointed govt detective for the province of Ont. at an annual salary of $1,500. Murray pioneered the use of forensic science in detection in Canada, and would remain with the govt until his death.

June 4 The steamer *Manitoba* sank when the steamer *International* collided with it near the junction of the Stikine and Red Rivers. These were the only 2 steamers travelling the entire Red R. Both vessels returned to service within weeks.

June 13 The 1st B'nai B'rith Lodge in Canada was established in Toronto.

June 15 The Canadian Church of Scotland united with free and secessionist Presbyterian churches of central Canada and the Atlantic provinces to form the Presbyterian Church of Canada.

Also in June

• Construction began on the western section of the CPR telegraph, extending from Fort Pelly to a point just south of Fort Edmonton (near present-day Leduc). Richard Fuller was awarded the contract.

July 19 The Parliament of Canada Act was passed, defining the powers and privileges of members of Parliament.

July 22 The *Northcote* was the 1st steamboat to arrive at Edmonton.

Aug. 4 Treaty No. 5 (the Winnipeg Treaty) was concluded at L. Winnipeg with the Swampy Cree and Chippewa ceding land around Lakes Winnipeg and Winnipegosis, west into Sask. and then north. The land area was approximately 26,000 ha. The govt of Canada based the acquisition of the treaty land on the need for farmland and pasture, and river access to L. Winnipeg. The minister of the Interior stated "that it was essential that the Indian title to all the territory in the vicinity of the lake should be extinguished so that settlers and traders might have undisturbed access to its waters, shores, islands, inlets, and tributary streams." Treaty terms mirrored previous post-Confederation NWT treaty terms.

Nov. 9 The *Liberal Quebec Daily Telegraph* was founded by James Carrel.

Dec. 7 Joseph Edouard Cauchon (1816–1885) was sworn in as president of the Privy Council.

Dec. 21 Protestant Defense Association was founded in Montreal.

Dec. 24 Sherbrooke, Que., received a city charter.

c 1875 Allan Edson painted *Trout Stream in the Forest,* now in the National Gallery of Canada.

Also in 1875

• Alexander Graham Bell patented his harmonic telegraph, which permitted simultaneous transmission of 30–40 messages. Bell sold the invention to Western Union. A sidelight invention, the automatic telegraph, also patented, was a precursor of the modern-day fax machine.

• Gov-Gen. Dufferin addressed Quebec City, urging the city to retain its fortification walls as a potential tourist site.

• The federal govt passed PEI's Compulsory Land Purchase Act, which established a maximum holding of 202 ha for each landowner in the province.

• Canada abandoned the use of the ball and chain within its penal system.

• Robert Whale painted *The Canada Southern Railway at Niagara,* oil on canvas. It is now in the National Gallery of Canada.

1876

Jan. 10 The BC legislature rejected Ottawa's financial offer of compensation for delays in building the CPR, and petitioned Queen Victoria about grievances concerning Confederation.

Also in Jan.

• The Catholic Order of Christian Brothers opened the Christian Brothers Schools in St. John's, Nfld.

Feb. 4 Man. abolished its legislative council.

Feb. 10 The Ontario Crooks Act transferred the power

of granting tavern licences from municipalities to a provincial board.

Also in Feb.

• Egerton Ryerson retired as Ont.'s superintendent of education, a post he had filled for 22 years.

Mar. 6 Louis Riel was admitted to the mental asylum at Longue-Pointe (Hospital Louis-H. La Fontaine, Montreal) under the name of Louis R. David. Riel had had a nervous breakdown and would develop an obsession that he was part of a religious quest. Riel would be transferred to the asylum at Beauport, near Quebec City, and discharged Jan. 23, 1878. The same year, he moved to Montana, finding work as an interpreter and trader. He became a US citizen and married Marguerita Monet.

Mar. 25 Sub-Inspector Edmond Fréchette of the NWMP arrived at Battleford, NWT, to choose a site for a police post.

Apr. 6 A telegraph line between Battleford and Winnipeg was completed and the 1st successful message sent.

Apr. 12 The Beaver Steamship Line introduced iron screw steamers *Lake Champlain*, *Lake Nipigon* and *Lake Megantic*.

Also in Apr.

• By Act of Parliament, the District of Keewatin ("north wind" in Cree), comprising northern Man. and western Ont., was created, to be removed from the jurisdiction of the Northwest Council of the NWT, and administered by the lt-gov. of Man. The seat of govt was designated as Fort Livingston in Swan R. The 1st legislative session was held May 8.

May 1 St. Catharines, Ont., was incorporated as a city.

May 19 The legislature of BC passed the School Act, providing for the establishment of public schools, supported by a $3 per year tax on all male residents.

May 24 Mount Royal Park (200 ha) was officially opened in Montreal.

May 30 Fire in Montreal destroyed 411 homes.

June 1 The Royal Military College of Canada, at Kingston, opened as Canada's 1st military college. Its 1st class consisted of 18 cadets. The college was established by an Act of Parliament in 1874 "for the purpose of providing a complete education in all branches of military tactics, fortification, engineering, and general scientific knowledge."

June 5 The Supreme Court of Canada held its 1st session in Ottawa with Chief Justice W.B. Richards and 5 puisne judges.

June 25 Lt-Col. George Armstrong Custer and the American 7th Cavalry were defeated and killed in the Battle of the Little Big Horn, Montana, by Sioux warriors led by Chief Sitting Bull (Ta-tanka I-yotank) (1834–1890). On May 6, 1877, Sitting Bull arrived at Wood Mountain (now Cypress Hills Provincial Park on the Sask.–Alb. border) with 1,500 Sioux and 3,500 horses to join others of his band. The Sioux would live a 5-year unwelcome exile in Canada until July 19, 1881, when Sitting Bull, accompanied by local trader Jean-Louis Légaré, led 1,064 destitute followers out of Canada to surrender to American authorities at Fort Buford, North Dakota. Sitting Bull and the Sioux had been denied a reservation by Canada, and were forced under threat of starvation to accept the terms of an American treaty and settle at Standing Rock Reserve, North Dakota.

Also in June

• The final section of the 1,000-km Intercolonial Railway was completed between Mont-Joli, Que., and Campbellton, NB. In line with requirements of the BNA Act, a railroad ran from Halifax to Montreal; total cost was $34 million. The Intercolonial was absorbed by the Canadian National Railway (CNR), in 1919.

July 22 James Macleod was appointed commissioner of the NWMP. He served until 1880.

Aug. 3 The 1st telephone call from one building to another took place between Alexander Graham Bell at Mount Pleasant, Ont., and his uncle David Bell at Brantford, Ont. Bell used the Shakespearean line "to be or not to be" in the 1st long-distance call (Aug. 10) from Brantford, Ont., to Paris, Ont., a distance of 128 km, when Dominion Telegraph let him use their line for the test.

Aug. 16–Sept. 19 Gov-Gen. Dufferin visited BC, touring Victoria, Nanaimo, Burrard Inlet and the interior. During a speech in Victoria, Dufferin asked that BC be patient with construction of the promised railway link to eastern Canada.

Aug. 23 Treaty No. 6 was concluded with the Plains and Wood Cree at Fort Carlton, Sask. The Cree gave up 313,390 km^2, roughly the area encircled by a line running through the modern towns of The Pas, Man., west to Athabasca, Alb., Jasper, L. Louise, east to Stettler to Empress and Swift Current and Hudson Bay Junction returning to The Pas. Treaty No. 6 included a "medicine chest" provision — later interpreted to mean free health care for Native Peoples — and a system of relief in case of famine. The treaty was signed on Sept. 9. Cree Chief Big Bear (Mistahimaskwa) (c 1825–1888) refused to sign because he felt valuable hunting grounds were sacrificed for very little gain from the federal govt.

Sept. 3 Fire destroyed 500 homes in St. Hyacinthe, Que.

Sept. 7 Reverend Edmund James Peck (1850–1924) arrived at Moose Factory, NWT, from London, England, to do missionary work among the Inuit.

Oct. 7 The NWT Act was proclaimed creating the separate political division of the NWT and a Northwest Council having legislative and executive powers. David Laird (1833–1914) was made the 1st lt-gov. of the NWT. Laird was sworn in on Nov. 26, but did not arrive at the NWT capital, Battleford, until Aug. 1877.

Oct. 21 The 1st western Canadian wheat, 857 bushels of Red Fife grown in Kildonan, Springfield, and Rockwood, Man., was shipped to Ont. by Higgins and Young. It arrived in Toronto 6 days later.

Also in Oct.

• The Ontario School of Art opened in Toronto. Founded by the Ontario Society of Artists, its purpose was to provide professional training in art.

• The Montreal Northern Colonization Railway (of which Sir Hugh Allan was chairman) opened the 1st stretch of its P'tit Train du Nord 40 km north of Montreal at St. Jerome. The project, a vision of

Curé Antoine Labelle (1833–1891) would facilitate commerce and tourism in the Laurentian countryside (las Pays d'en Haut). The full line was not completed until 1904, when tracks reached Mont Laurier, 240 km north of Montreal.

1876–1877 John A. Macdonald and his Conservatives toured the country pushing for higher tariffs. They held numerous political picnics during the summer months arguing for protection of Canadian farming and industry amongst a rising tide of Canadian nationalism.

Also in 1876

• David Laird, superintendent gen. of Indian Affairs, drafted the Indian Act, which was passed into law by the federal govt. The Act consolidated all earlier laws regarding Native Peoples and placed Aboriginal peoples in a separate legal category based on race. The act focused on Native Status and membership, land ownership and local govt. Indian agents became intermediaries between Aboriginals and the govt of Canada; the superintendent gen. was given administrative powers over Native Affairs. The Indian Act influenced the lives of all Native Peoples; it had been constructed and proclaimed without Native participation or approval.

• Dr. Emily Stowe established the Toronto Women's Literary Social and Science Club to "service a free interchange of thought and feeling upon every subject that pertains to woman's higher education, including her moral and physical welfare."

• There were 6 operational glass works in the country employing 309 males at total annual wages of $104,800. Raw material utilized was valued at $102,275, resulting in the production of goods valued at $293,130.

• Montreal architect William T. Thomas, completed one of Montreal's largest mansions, the Shaughnessy House, located at 1923 Dorchester St. W. in Montreal, Que. The stone house received its name from Lord Shaughnessy who eventually took over the entire estate when he became the president of the Canadian Pacific Railway in 1899.

• Edward Blake, former premier of Ont., became chancellor of the University of Toronto.

• The headquarters of the NWMP was moved to Fort Macleod, Alb., from Fort Dufferin, Man.

• *The Countess of Dufferin*, Canada's 1st entrant in the America's Cup yachting race, lost to the US yacht *Madelaine*.

• Toronto's Granite Curling and Skating Club was established with 80 members, including John A. Macdonald.

• The 1st post office for the NWT was established at Battleford, Sask.

• Designer Father Emile Petitot (1838–1917) and carpenter Father Jean Sequin with assistance by Br. Joseph Patrick Kearney, completed Our Lady of Good Hope Church, located at Fort Good Hope in NWT, the most northerly of Oblate Missions. Father Petitot's designs gave the 14-m-long and 6-m-wide church a Gothic Revival appearance. The church was finally completed in 1885, after numerous additions.

• A seat on the Montreal Stock Exchange cost $2,500.

• Stony Mountain Penitentiary in Man. was built.

• Samuel Wilmot was appointed superintendent of Fish Culture by the Department of Marine and Fisheries. He would remain in that position until 1895, establishing 15 fish hatcheries across Canada.

• The YMCA named Barrie, Ont., the wickedest community in Canada. Winnipeg was rated 2nd.

• John Ross Robertson (1841–1918) founded the *Evening Telegram* newspaper in Toronto.

1877

Jan. 6 McLean's flour mill, the 1st in Man., began operations.

Feb. 8 The 4th session of the 3rd Parliament met until Apr. 28. The Geological Survey of Canada became a branch of the Department of Interior.

Feb. 28 The U. of Man., founded by Alexander Morris, received a charter. The U. of Man. became the 1st

institution of higher learning to be established in western Canada. It officially opened June 20.

Spring Work began on Que.'s Hôtel du Parliament, designed by Eugene-Étienne Taché (1836–1912), who had the phrase "Je me souviens" engraved over the main entrance. A second-Empire-style quadrangle building with 3 towers — Cartier, Champlain and Maisonneuve, and an interior courtyard — the Hôtel du Parliament was completed in 1887.

May 31 Brantford, Ont., was incorporated as a city.

June 5 Construction started on the PEI Hospital for the Insane. Similar institutions had been established in NB (1847) and NS (1857).

June 15 Sulpician priests accused Chief Joseph Onasakenrat and his Iroquois followers of setting fire to the Roman Catholic church located at L. of Two Mountains, Que., about 50 km west of Montreal.

June 20 Saint John, NB, was ravaged by fire caused by sparks from a lumber mill. Eighteen people died, 1,600 buildings were destroyed. Damage was estimated in excess of $27 million. Two-fifths of the city was destroyed and 13,000 people left homeless. The federal govt sent $20,000 as relief aid. The city of Chicago (which had also been devastated by fire in 1871) sent $25,000.

July 12 Orangemen and Roman Catholics clashed in Montreal.

Also in July
• The Athabaska Landing Trail was officially established by the HBC from Fort Edmonton to the Athabasca R.

Sept. 10 The 1st North America Icelandic newspaper, *Framfari* (Progress), was published by Sigtryggur Jonasson (1852–1942) in a log cabin near Lundi (now River-ton), Man.

Sept. 22 Crowfoot, chief of the Blackfoot, signed Treaty No. 7 at Blackfoot Crossing, about 10 km east of Calgary. Chief Red Crow, representing the Blood, also signed. The federal govt was represented by Commissioners Macleod and Lt-Gov. Laird. This was the last major post-Confederation-era treaty between First Nations and the federal govt. With its execution, all lands between the Rockies and the Cypress Hills were ceded to the federal govt, thereby paving the way for construction of the railroad to BC. Provisions for the First Nations were similar to those in Treaty No. 6, plus a $1,000 grant to any Native person who took up farming, or alternatively, a supply of cattle for ranching. The federal govt also agreed to supply the Blackfoot with $2,000 worth of ammunition annually.

Sept. 29 In a speech given in Winnipeg as part of his cross-country tour, Gov-Gen. Lord Dufferin referred to Man. as the "keystone of the mighty arch of sister provinces which span the continent from the Atlantic to the Pacific."

Oct. 8 Henri Charles Wilfrid Laurier (1841–1919) was sworn in as a member of Parliament from Drummond-Arthabaska, Que.

Oct. 9 The 1st locomotive on the prairies, *Countess of Dufferin*, arrived at Winnipeg. It had been transported down the Red R. from Moorhead, Minnesota, on a barge tied to railroad magnate J.J. Hill's steamer, *Selkirk*. Accompanied by 6 floaters and a conductor's van, the *Countess* had been purchased secondhand from the Northern Pacific Railway for $5,600. It would be used on the Pembina branch line.

Oct. 11 A general pastoral letter to the clergy of Que. declared that strictures of the Holy See against Catholic Liberalism were not to be applied to Canadian political parties. Priests were forbidden to teach that it was a sin to vote for any particular candidate or party.

Nov. 20 Edmonton, Alb., opened its 1st telegraph service.

Dec. 29 Grand Trunk Railroad employees went on strike in support of members of the Brotherhood of Locomotive Engineers who had been fired. The strike was broken with the aid of militia.

Also in 1877

• The Montreal Harbour Commission became the 1st in Canada to use electricity for lighting its waterfront.

• The Northwest Council passed an Ordinance for the Protection of the Bison, which made the slaughter of bison for "amusement or wanton destruction" subject to a fine. It also provided a closed season for female bison between Nov. 15 and Aug. 14. The Northwest Council also outlawed the use of buffalo jumps as part of its efforts to preserve the bison population. The law, however, did not have the required effect of stabilizing the dwindling bison population. By 1885, the free-roaming prairie bison had become virtually extinct, and by the turn of the century, there were only an estimated 250 wood bison left in the country.

• British Columbia made the employment of boys under 12 years of age illegal.

• Wheat replaced fur as Man.'s main product.

• *The Golden Dog*, an historical novel set in Quebec in 1748, by William Kirby (1817–1906), was published.

• Painter Homer Ransford Watson (1855–1936) completed one of his earliest canvases, *The Death of Elaine,* probably at Doon, Ont. The painting is now at the Art Gallery of Ont., Toronto.

• Louis-Honoré Fréchette (1839–1908) published his 2nd collection of verse, *Pêle-mêle.*

• Geologist G.J. Hinde published the seminal report "Glacial and interglacial strata of Scarboro Heights and other localities near Toronto, Ontario," in the *Canadian Journal of Science, Literature and History.* He wrote: "Among all the North American localities of interglacial deposits, Scarboro's presents questions of the greatest interest and importance in their relation to the changes of climate... attending the ice age."

1878

Jan. 1 Belleville, Ont., received a city charter.

Jan. 15 "The National Policy" was introduced at the Conservative party convention in Toronto and became the cornerstone of the party's platform. The NP favoured protectionism in the form of high tariffs and low custom duties on necessary raw materials and semi-processed products, "to benefit the agricultural, the mining, the manufacturing and other interests of the Dominion."

Jan. 22 Canada was given the right to be included in British treaties.

Feb. 7 The 5th session of the 3rd Parliament met until May 10. The Canada Temperance Act, or Scott Act, provided local options on liquor licencing.

Also in Feb.
• Montreal's luxurious Windsor Hotel opened.

Mar. 1 The town of Edmonton opened its 1st official post office.

Mar. 2 Conservative Premier of Que., Charles-Eugène Boucher de Boucherville (1822–1915), was dismissed from office by the Liberal Lt-Gov. Luc Letellier de St. Just (1820–1881), over secret financial dealings. A Liberal govt under Henri Gustave Joly de Lotbinière (1829–1908) was installed after de St. Just dismissed his cabinet on Mar. 24. This drastic measure led to de St. Just's dismissal by Gov-Gen. Lorne, on the advice of the Macdonald govt, July 26, 1879. On that date, Théodore Robitaille (1834–1897) succeeded de St. Just as lt-gov. of Que.

Mar. 7 The U. of Western Ont. (London) was founded by Anglican Bishop Isaac Hellmuth (1817–1901). Classes began in 1881 with a roster of 15 students. The first 4 facilities were Arts, Divinity, Law, and Medicine. The 1st students graduated in 1883.

• J.J. Hill, George Stephen (1829–1921), John S. Kennedy, Donald Smith and Norman Kitson, the Associates, purchased the St. Paul and Pacific Railroad charter between St. Paul, Minnesota and Emerson, Man. (with a potential land grant from Minnesota of 1,011,714 ha should the line be completed on time) for a cash outlay of $280,000.

May 10 Donald Smith denied charges laid by John A. Macdonald in the House of Commons that he supported a bill giving an American railway, the St. Paul and Pacific Railroad, rights to run into Winni-peg because he owned shares in it.

Also in May
• George Anthony Walkem (1834-1908) was elected

premier of BC on a platform calling for secession from Canada because of the federal govt's delay in providing a transcontinental railway link as promised. On Aug. 9, the BC legislature voted to secede from Canada if construction of the CPR did not begin by May 1879.

June 10 Victoria, BC, was fortified in anticipation of a possible attack from Russia.

June 12 Construction workers employed in the building of Quebec's Hôtel du Parliament went on strike. Two were killed when the govt brought in armed forces.

June 24 The earliest recorded tennis tournament in Canada was held at the Montreal Lacrosse Club.

July 1 Canada was admitted as a member of the Universal Postal Union, established in 1874 to provide co-operation between member countries. By 2003, the Union had 190 members and was 2nd to the International Telecommunications Union as the oldest international organization in the world.

July 12 Mackenzie's Liberal govt chose the Fraser R.–Burrard Inlet route for the BC section of the CPR.

July 15 The 1st telephone exchange in the British empire was opened at Hamilton by the Hamilton District Telegraph Company. The company had obtained a 5-year Canadian licence on Alexander Graham Bell's telephone patent from Bell's father, A.M. Bell, who had obtained majority interest in the Canadian patent from his son in 1877.

Aug. 2 John Lorne McDougall (1838–1909) was appointed Canada's 1st auditor-gen., a position he held until his retirement in 1905.

• An Ordinance Respecting the Marking of Livestock was passed at the 2nd session of the Council of the NWT at Battleford. This represented the 1st effort to institute brand recording on the prairies.

Aug. 11 Patrick Laurie (1833–1903) founded the *Saskatchewan Herald* in Battleford. It was the NWT's 1st newspaper.

Aug. 28 The Sherbrooke, Que., *Examiner* was 1st published.

Sept. 17 John A. Macdonald's Conservatives swept to power with 142 seats, defeating Alexander Mackenzie and his Liberals who took 64 seats. Protective tariffs and Macdonald's National Policy were the major issues. Macdonald was personally defeated in his Kingston riding. Secret ballots were used for the 1st time in a national election.

Oct. 16 John Norquay (1841–1889) was elected premier of Man., succeeding Robert Atkinson Davis.

Oct. 17–June 6, 1891 John A. Macdonald served as PM until his death in office of a stroke.

Nov. The Winnipeg-Pembina railway line was completed. It ran from St. Boniface to the Man. border, providing a link with the St. Paul and Pacific Railroad, which began service between Minnesota and Man. on Nov. 11, when the 1st train arrived at Emerson, Man.

Dec. 2 John Douglas Sutherland Campbell, the Marquess of Lorne (1845–1914), and his wife, Louise, daughter of Queen Victoria, arrived in Ottawa. Campbell had been appointed Gov-Gen. of Canada Oct. 5, and served to Oct. 21, 1883.

Dec. 19 Marguerite Bourgeoys, founder of the Congrégation de Nôtre-Dame, passed the 1st stage of canonization and was declared venerable by Pope Leo XIII, 178 years after her death.

Winter Seven thousand starving Blackfoot were fed at Fort Macleod. Their plight was a result of the nearly eradicated prairie bison which had been a primary food source.

Also in 1878

• The BC Penitentiary was built in Westminster.

• L'Universite Laval opened a branch in Montreal, which gained independence, becoming the Université de Montréal in 1920.

• Guernsey cattle were 1st imported into Canada.

• The Department of Public Works and supervising architect Robert Gage completed the Mackenzie Building, named after Prime Minister Alexander Mackenzie, at the Royal Military College in Kingston, Ont. The stone building's purpose was to house the administrative and educational services of Canada's 1st military college.

• Irish-born designer W.H. Lynn (1829–1915) completed St. Louis Gate, and then Kent Gate the following year. The 2-turreted Victorian gates are located at Quebec Citadel in Quebec City.

• Architects Henri-Maurice Perrault (1828–1903) and Alexander C. Hutchison (1838–1922) completed Hôtel de Ville, located in Montreal, Que. The 2nd Empire-style building was modelled from the design of the Hôtel de Ville in Paris, France.

• Sgt-Maj. Sam Steele was appointed commander of Fort Qu'Appelle, NWT.

• The Montreal Bicycle Club was formed.

• Edward Hanlan (1855–1908) of Toronto defeated Eph Morris for the US singles rowing championship on the Allegheny R.

• The *Canadian Horticulturalist* monthly magazine was founded by the Ontario Fruit Growers Assn., with Delos W. Beadle as editor.

• Homer Watson painted *Landscape with River,* now in the Art Gallery of Ont., Toronto.

• Honoré Beaugrand (1849–1906) published the novel *Jeanne-la-Fileuse* (Jeanne the Ropemaking Machine), the story of a French-Canadian worker's migration to the US.

1879

Jan. 4 The Winnipeg Board of Trade was registered.

Jan. 8 The 1st issue of *La Gazette d'Ottawa* was published.

Jan. 23 The 1st issue of *La Patrie* was published in Montreal.

Feb. 6 Francis Hincks, president of the Consolidated Bank of Canada, was indicted for making a false and deceptive return after the failure of the bank. He was acquitted.

Feb. 8 Sandford Fleming lectured at the Canadian Institute in Toronto, proposing to divide the world into 24 equal time zones, with a standard time within each zone. Fleming's idea was adopted by 25 countries at a conference in 1884, and standard time went into effect on Jan. 1, 1885.

Feb. 9 The North Shore Railroad between Montreal and Quebec City was completed.

Feb. 13 The 1st session of the 4th Parliament met until May 15. The govt was authorized to grant land to the Métis.

Also in Feb.
• Lucius Richard O'Brien (1832–1899), vice-president of the Ontario Society of Artists, solicited Gov-Gen. Lorne and his wife, Louise, to become patrons of the society. Lorne accepted.

Mar. 1 Henry Birks (1840–1928) opened a jewelry store in Montreal. Goods were only sold for cash and all prices were predetermined.

Mar. 11 An Act to Incorporate the Industrial Exhibition Association of Toronto was passed by the Ont. legislature. On Sept. 3, the 1st Toronto Industrial Exhibition opened for a 3-week run, on 8 ha of L. Ont. waterfront property. This exhibition was the forerunner of the CNE (Canadian National Exhibition).

Mar. 14 PM Macdonald's National Policy regarding the "judicious readjustment of the Tariff" came into effect. Known as Tilley's Tariff, after Minister of Finance Samuel Tilley, the protection measure averaged 25% on goods coming from the US. Unlike previous tariffs imposed to raise revenue, Tilley's Tariff was designed to protect Canada's developing secondary industries.

Apr. 23 Guelph, Ont., was incorporated as a city.

May 10 Charles Tupper, Conservative minister of Public Works, outlined the govt's railway policy in the House of Commons and rejected the Burrard Fraser R. Inlet route for the BC section of the CPR, as established in 1878 under the Liberals. Tupper announced that 200 km of railroad would be built immediately in BC, in cooperation with the British Imperial govt. Furthermore, 40,468,564 ha of Canadian land were to be appropriated, and money from land sales used to pay for the railway.

May 20 The Department of Railways and Canals was organized by Tupper, its 1st director.

June The 1st known official meeting of North American accountants was held at Mechanic's Hall in Montreal to establish a society to promote the profession and restrict the use of the term "chartered accountant." The meeting led to the establishment of North America's 1st accountant's society, established July 24, 1880, with Scotsman Philip Ross its 1st president.

• The 1st telephone directory in Canada was printed and distributed in Toronto, Ont.

July 31 Richard Cowan, Charles Grimely and Charles Page made the 1st Canadian hydrogen balloon flight at Montreal.

Aug. 6 Buctouche, NB, was hit by a vicious tornado. Seven people died, 10 were injured, 25 families were left homeless and property damage was in excess of $100,000.

Sept. 1 The 1st trade union to be legalized in the Canadian coal mines was the Provincial Workman's Association (PMA), organized at Springhill, NS, in a successful walkout aimed at regaining a wage cut. The PMA would be incorporated by an act of the NS legislature in 1880. Membership began to decline in 1909 as workers began opting to join the United Mine Worker's Union.

Sept. 19 The Credit Valley Railway opened from Toronto to Milton, Ont. A full one-way trip took approximately 1 hour.

Sept. 22–27 The Dominion Exhibition was held in Ottawa at present-day Lansdowne Park.

Fall Crowfoot led his starving band of Blackfoot to Montana in search of the ever-scarce buffalo. They would return to the Old Man R. reserve in July, 1881, after a long and exhausting trek on foot from the Musselshell R. in Montana.

Oct. 14 A federal govt order-in-council set the route

of the CPR through Edmonton and then westward via the Yellowhead Pass, then along the Fraser R. to the Pacific at Burrard Inlet.

Oct. 23 PEI's 1st hospital, the Charlottetown Hospital, founded by Roman Catholic Bishop Peter McIntyre (1818–1891), opened and welcomed all denominations.

Nov. 4 The Supreme Court ruled that only the queen or gov-gen. had the right to appoint Queen's Counsel.

Nov. 22 The 41 m-long sidewheeler steamer *Waubuno* left Collingwood, Ont., for Parry Sound and disappeared in Georgian Bay during a terrible storm. The capsized hull of the steamer was found in a shallow channel near Moose Point on Mar. 25, 1880. There had been 24 passengers on the steamer but not one body was ever found. The steamer's anchor was located by scuba divers in 1962 and now rests in Parry Sound's Waubuno Park.

Also in 1879
• Canadian exports declined to $71,000; imports were $82,000,000.

• Edgar Dewdney, Conservative MP from BC, was appointed the 1st Indian commissioner of the NWT.

• The 1st grain elevator in western Canada was built by William Hespeler (1830–1921) in Niverville, Man. The rectangular wooden structure, which towered over the prairies, was used to store grain for transport.

• The headquarters of the NWMP was moved to Fort Walsh (Sask.), from Fort Macleod (Alb.).

• Halifax architect Henry F. Busch completed the Provincial Normal School, located at 748 Prince St. in Truro, NS, constructed by the provincial Department of Education as a teachers' training centre.

• The Gore Bay Lighthouse (officially, Janet Head Light Station) was completed, on Manitoulin Is. between Julia Bay and Gore Bay in the North Channel of L. Huron.

• The Cleveland Blues, with Bill Phillips of Saint

John, NB, at 1st base, were admitted into Major League Baseball's National League. Phillips played in 81 of 82 games, batting .271 with 29 RBI and 58 runs. He concluded his Major League career, with Cleveland, in 1884.

• Architect and civil engineer Hermann Otto Tiedemann (1861–1891) painted the watercolour *Bluff above Murderers' Bar Homathko River, Bute Inlet Route,* the name of the bluff a reference to the "Chilcotin Massacre" of 1864.

• Homer Ransford Watson completed the painting, *Coming Storm in the Adirondacks,* now in the Montreal Museum of Fine Arts.

• Montreal-born artist Henry Sandham (1842–1910) painted *Beacon Light, Saint John,* now in the National Gallery of Canada.

• *Ten Years in Winnipeg*, by Alexander Begg, was published. The book recounted the growth of Winnipeg in the years after Man.'s entry into Confederation.

1880

Feb. 1 The keel was laid at Burrard Inlet, BC, for the sternwheeler *William Irving*. The 45-m steamer was part of the growing fleet of the Canadian Pacific Navigation Co. (later taken over by the CPR). This largest and most powerful sternwheeler on the Fraser R. was launched on Mar. 19. Cabin fare to Yale, BC, was $3. Outside fare was $1. The *William Irving* was wrecked in 1894.

Feb. 4 Thirty-one men, most armed with clubs, murdered James Donnelly, his wife and 3 children. The Donnelly clan, known as the "Black Donnellys," had terrorized Lucan, Ont., and Biddulph Township's farming area by beating victims, burning barns and homes, and poisoning cattle as part of a retaliatory long-standing feud with neighbours that originated in Tipperary County, Ireland. On Feb. 2, 1881, James Carroll, leader of the Black Donnellys massacre, was acquitted of murder and set free. Charges against 5 others were dropped and the case was closed.

Feb. 12 The 2nd session of the 4th Parliament met until May 7. The Department of Indian Affairs was formed, and the office of Canadian High Commissioner created to provide representation and promote Canadian interests in England.

Also in Feb.
• Fire destroyed the Parliament Buildings at Fredericton, NB.

Mar. 6 Gov-Gen. the Marquess of Lorne established the Royal Canadian Academy of Arts in Ottawa. Lucius O'Brien became its 1st president.

Mar. 25 George Brown was shot in the thigh in his *Globe* office by George Bennett, a disgruntled and intoxicated former employee. Bennett was quickly disarmed and arrested. Although Brown's wound did not seem serious, it got progressively worse, resulting in his death on May 9. Brown was 61. Bennett was hanged for the murder.

Apr. 8 The Grand Trunk Railway put its 1st passenger train into service between Port Huron, Ont., and Chicago, Illinois.

Apr. 26 A Liberal caucus meeting was held without PM Mackenzie, and it passed a resolution asking Mackenzie to reconsider his leadership role. The next day Alexander Mackenzie resigned as leader of the Liberal party, and on Apr. 28 Edward Blake became leader of the opposition Liberal party. He would serve in that position until 1887.

Apr. 29 The Bell Telephone Company of Canada was incorporated by a federal charter, establishing the Hamilton District Telegraphy Co. as a branch plant.

May 11 Alexander Galt was appointed Canada's 1st Canadian high commissioner in England.

May 14 Andrew Onderdonk (c 1849–1905), a New York contractor, began construction of the CPR line in BC from Port Moody to Savona's Ferry, Kamloops L.; 6,000 Chinese labourers worked the line.

May 22 The Conservative govt terminated Sanford Fleming's position as engineer-in-chief of the CPR project with a severance payment of $30,000. Collingwood Schreiber, who had extensive experience with the Intercolonial Railway and the Northern Railway, was appointed engineer-in-chief in his place.

June 24 "O Canada," the music composed by Calixa Lavallée (1842–1891), was performed for the 1st time at a banquet attended by the Marquess of Lorne. The song's 1st lyrics were in French, written by Adolphe-Basile Routhier (1839–1920).

June 30 Net earnings for the St. Paul and Pacific Railroad, renamed the St. Paul and Man. Railroad, were $1 million. As one of the most profitable lines in North America, it attracted the interest of the Canadian govt, which was seeking a partner for the CPR.

July 16 Emily Stowe received her licence to practice medicine from the Council of the College of Physicians and Surgeons of Ontario. She had been practising medicine without a licence since 1867.

July 31 All British possessions in North America, including the Arctic archipelago, but excluding Nfld., were annexed to Canada by Imperial Order-in-Council.

Also in July
• Wilfrid Laurier and a group of Que. associates established the newspaper *L'Electeur,* with Ernest Pacaud editor.

Aug. 5 Louis-Honoré Fréchette, a lawyer, politician, poet and playwright from Lévis, Que., was awarded the Prix Montyon for poetry by the French Academy for his work *Les Fleurs Boreales* and *Oiseaux de Neige.* Fréchette was the 1st Canadian to be so honoured, and one of the 1st Canadian men of letters to receive international acclaim. In recognition of this honour, he was appointed clerk of the Quebec legislature.

Sept. The Imperial Oil Company was founded in London, Ont.

Oct. 21 The federal govt signed a contract with CPR Company, a private consortium that included George Stephen, John S. Kennedy, James J. Hill (1838–1916), R. B. Angus, (1831–1922) and Donald Smith, to complete the approximately 3,115 km of the CPR from L. Nipissing via the Yellowhead Pass to Port Moody on the Burrard Inlet. The govt granted the enterprise $25 million and 10,117,141 ha of land, plus 1,127 km of track already laid worth

$75 million, exemption of import duties on materials, delayed taxes on land-grant property, free additional land for stations and other purposes with no taxes in perpetuity and a 20-year monopoly on railway construction on all lands south of the CPR line. The federal govt and the CPR signed the final agreement on Nov. 20. The CPR Company was incorporated Feb. 16, 1881.

Nov. 2 Father Albert Lacombe arrived at Rat Portage, Lake-of-the-Woods, to become the 1st chaplain to 2,000 men working on the CPR. Lacombe was instrumental in dealing with the Blackfoot who, as a nation, were outraged by the intrusion of the railroad through their territory.

Nov. 12 Fifty coal miners were killed in an explosion at Stellarton, NS.

Nov. 15 World rowing champion Ned Hanlan of Toronto defeated Australian Edward Trickett in "the race of the century" in London, England.

Dec. 6 The *Edmonton Bulletin* was founded by Frank Oliver (1853–1937) using press and type purchased for $21. It was the 1st newspaper published in what would become the province of Alb.

1880–1890 Que. migrants represented nearly half the textile labour force in the Merrimack Valley mills, north of Boston.

Also in 1880

• Canada's population was 4,255,000.

• The National Gallery of Canada was founded by Gov-Gen. the Marquess of Lorne.

• Dorchester Penitentiary opened in NB.

• Hunting and widespread extermination efforts led to the extinction of the wolf in NB. The wolf would become extinct in NS by 1900, and in Nfld. by 1913.

• Canadian mill owner Orange Jull (from Orangeville, Ont.), drawing on the earlier work of J.W. Elliott, pioneered the Jull-Elliott rotary snowplow, and promptly assigned manufacturing rights to 2 mechanically minded brothers named Leslie, who assembled and tested the device at CPR's

Parkdale, Ont. shop. In 1888, CPR adopted the Jull-Elliott plow for use in clearing snow from its tracks.

• Thomas Mower Martin (1838–1934) painted *Encampment of Woodland Indians* and *Summer Time,* oils on canvas, now in the National Gallery of Canada.

• John A. Fraser painted *Laurentian Splendour,* oil on canvas. *Laurentian Splendour* portrays Mount Orford, and was submitted by Fraser as his diploma piece at the Royal Canadian Academy. It is now in the National Gallery of Canada.

• *The Treaties of Canada with the Indians of Manitoba and the NWT including Negotiations on which they were based,* by Alexander Morris, was published. It was a comprehensive history and discussion of Aboriginal treaties in the Northwest from 1871 to 1876. A reprint was issued in 1991.

• Painter Robert Harris completed *The Chorister,* in Toronto, Ont., shortly after returning from Paris, where he had studied at the studio of Leon Bonnat, considered one of the great painters of biblical and historical subjects. *The Chorister* is now in the National Gallery of Canada.

• *Orion, and other Poems,* by school principal Sir Charles G.D. Roberts of Fredericton, NB, was published in Philadelphia.

• Homer Watson's *The Pioneer Mill*, purchased for Queen Victoria by the Marquess of Lorne at an exhibition of the Royal Canadian Academy in Toronto, became famous overnight. The painting remains in Britain's Royal collection.

• Geologist Sir John W. Dawson, principal of McGill University, published *Fossil Men and Their Modern Representatives.*

1881

Feb. 1 Maj. James Walker, superintendent and sub-inspector of the NWMP, resigned his position to manage the Cochrane Ranch Company. Located about 35 km northwest of present-day Calgary, the ranch was incorporated the same year, with Senator Matthew Henry Cochrane (1823–1903) holding the majority of the shares. The arrival of Cochrane's large herd of shorthorns marked the beginning of the western Canadian cattle business, particularly because Cochrane was able to lease grazing rights on 144,000 ha along the Bow R. from the federal govt.

• After 6 weeks of maneuvring and debate, the Pacific Railway Bill was passed by the House of Commons, 128 votes to 49, and given Royal Assent on Feb. 15.

Feb. 16 The CPR Company was incorporated when its sponsors deposited the $1 million required as a performance security bond. Less than 20% of the stock was controlled by Canadians, most of that by George Stephen (president of the CPR until 1888), Richard Bladworth Angus, Duncan McIntyre and Donald A. Smith. The group, which also included James J. Hill and John S. Kennedy, were known as the CPR Syndicate. George Stephen called the incorporated CPR Company's 1st board meeting on Feb. 18.

Mar. 4 St. Thomas, Ont., received a city charter.

Mar. 21 Man.'s boundaries were extended to its present boundary with Sask. and north to 52° 50′, by an Act of Parliament, effective July 1.

Also in Mar.
• George Stephen purchased the Canada Central Railway from Duncan McIntyre, giving the CPR the beginning of a through line from Brockville on the St. Lawrence through Ottawa and on to Montreal.

Apr. The CPR commissioned the veteran American railway surveyor and engineer Maj. Albert Bowman Rogers (1829–1889) to locate a pass through the Rocky Mountains. He set out with his nephew, and 10 Native Peoples. They headed up the Illecillewaet R. in search of a pass through the Selkirk Mountains on May 15. On July 24, 1882, Rogers discovered a pass through the Selkirk Mountains south of Kicking Horse Pass. It was named Rogers Pass in his honour. In Aug. of that year, CPR officials confirmed Rogers Pass as the route through the Rockies, which the CPR would follow to the West Coast. In May the Yellowhead Pass route, surveyed by Engineer-in-Chief Fleming at the cost of millions of dollars and 40 lives was abandoned.

May 1 The federal govt transferred 383 km of completed, operating railroad track in the areas of

Thunder Bay, Pembina, and from St. Boniface to Portage La Prairie, to the CPR. The CPR began construction of its own prairie section of track at Portage La Prairie, Man., on May 2.

May 24 The overloaded paddle steamer *Victoria* capsized and sunk on the Thames R. near London, Ont.; 182 people died, many of them children.

May 28 Britain awarded the US £15,000 as reparation for an 1878 mob attack on American fishermen in Fortune Bay, Nfld.

Also in May
• The Royal Society of Canada, a national organization of distinguished scholars in the arts and sciences, was founded under the auspices of the Gov-Gen. the Marquess of Lorne. Its initial membership was 80.

June 8 A Montreal fire destroyed 642 homes.

July 9 The CPR assumed control of the Canada Central rail system in Ont., from Anprior to Mattawa.

July 21 The 1st national congress of the National Society of Acadians was founded and met in Memramcook, NB. Some 5,000 people attended.

Aug. 2 The 47-m-long sidewheeler *Princess* was launched in Winnipeg, Man., for service on the Saskatchewan R. It carried 600 passengers and a $5,000 piano.

Aug. 15 The Rat Portage War began when James C. Aikens (1823–1929), lt-gov. of Man., signed a proclamation extending provincial jurisdiction eastward to include Rat Portage, or what is now Kenora, Ont. Man. would then incorporate Rat Portage on July 22, 1882, touching off a heated boundary dispute with Ont. By 1883, both provinces had sent constables and magistrates to Rat Portage to officiate over "their" jurisdiction. Man. passed an official proclamation calling for an election Sept. 28, 1883, to fill the Rat Portage seat in its legislature; Ont. began plans for building a jail and started issuing business and liquor licences to residents. Man. authorities arrested those operating with Ont. licences; and Ont. authorities did likewise with those with Man. licences. The war was eventually concluded when the Privy Council awarded the area to Ont. on Aug. 11, 1884.

Aug. 16 The 1st sod was turned on the 1st railway in Nfld. A narrow-gauge line (3′6″ or 1.06 m), it would run from St. John's to Hall Bay, with branch line to Harbour Grace. Known as the Harbour Grace Railway Southern Division, the last spike would be driven Oct. 11, 1884. The Harbour Grace Railway was the 1st track in what would later be known as the Newfoundland Railway, or "The Newfie Bullet," a 882-km (with branch lines, 1,458 km) narrow-gauge railway from St. John's to Port-aux-Basque. The final link to Port-aux-Basque was laid in June 1898. The jocular nickname was given because the trains were rather slow.

Sept. 10 Gov-Gen. the Marquess of Lorne attended a powwow at Blackfoot Crossing, Alb., where Chief Crowfoot pleaded for rations to save and support his starving people. Food, which the federal govt had agreed to supply, was being improperly distributed.

1881–1884 Geologists George Mercer Dawson (1849–1901) and R.G. McConnell of the Canadian Geological Survey identified the basic structure of the Rocky Mountains where old rocks had been thrust eastward over much younger strata. Dawson and McConnell explored the Oldman R. area in Alb., where they found evidence of dinosaur remains. McConnell would collect several fossilized bones from the Scabby Bette area (north of Fort Macleod) the following year.

1881–1885 Over 15,000 Chinese workers arrived in Canada to work on the CPR, of which approximately 7,000 worked the rails at any given time. They were paid $1 a day — half the rate given to white workers. One thousand five hundred Chinese workers died during the construction of Canada's 1st transcontinental railroad.

Also in 1881

• The population of Canada was 4,324,810; 2,548,514 persons were of English descent and 1,298,929 of French descent.

• The population of Ont. was 1,926,922; Que.,

1,359,027; NS, 440,572; NB, 321,233; PEI, 108,891; Man., 62,260; BC, 49,459; and the NWT, 56,446.

• A census report indicated that the area that is now Sask. had a population of 1,000 settlers, 15,000 Native Peoples and 3,000 of mixed Native and European descent.

• The population of Fort Calgary, now Calgary, Alb., was 75.

• The Ogilvie Milling Company introduced the 1st angular grain elevator at Gretna, Man. which was stronger and easier to build than the 1879 Hespeler structure. The new elevator had a short and wide design with a storage capacity of 25,000 bushels.

• Evon Williams, a Welsh slate miner, discovered asbestos on the property of Charles Webb in the Thetford Mines area of Que. Williams persuaded W.H. Jeffrey to open an asbestos mine, paying Webb $10/ton in summer and $5/ton in winter. The Jeffrey mine currently produces 600,000 tons of chrysotile asbestos a year.

• Indian Head lighthouse, located in Central Bedeque, PEI, was completed. The isolated lighthouse, which originally used oil lamps, is accessible by walking along the ocean floor during low tide in the summer.

• The Bank of PEI collapsed after one of its cashiers fled the country with over $1 million in unauthorized advances.

• *The Last Forty Years: The Union of 1841 to Confederation*, by Canadian historian John Charles Dent (1841–1888), was published.

• Canadian Quakers separated into 2 factions — Conservative and Progressive.

• Toronto inventor J.J. Wright exhibited the world's 1st electrical appliance: a coffee grinder.

• Holstein-Freisen cattle were 1st imported into Canada.

• Edgar Dewdney (1835–1916) was appointed lt-gov. of the NWT, serving until 1888.

• By year's end, the CPR railhead was just short of Flat Creek (Oak Lake), 259 km west of Winnipeg.

• The Ont. govt passed the Rivers and Streams Bill, providing for the protection of public rights on provincial waterways. The federal govt disallowed the bill 3 times, contesting that it interfered with federal jurisdiction. Ont. took the matter to the British Privy Council, which awarded the decision to the province.

• Paul Peel (1860–1892) painted *Devotion*, oil on canvas, now in the National Gallery of Canada.

• Homer Watson completed his canvas, *The Stone Road*, now in the National Gallery of Canada.

1882

Jan. 1 American William Cornelius Van Horne (1843–1915), former superintendent of the Chicago, Milwaukee and St. Paul Railway, became the 1st general manager of the CPR.

Jan. 19 The 1st edition of the Brandon (Man.) *Sun* was published by Will White (b c 1851).

Feb. 9 The 4th session of the 4th Parliament met, until May 17. The Dominion Redistribution Act adjusted representation in the House on the basis of population, as determined by the census.

Mar. 1 The CPR signed a contract with Langdon, Shepard & Company of Minnesota for construction of 805 km of main line across the prairies.

Spring The CPR purchased the Montreal, Ottawa and Occidental Railway.

Apr. 15 The Bank of NS opened a branch in Winnipeg.

Apr. 21 The Canadian House of Commons passed the Costigan Irish resolution, requesting that the British govt grant Ireland home rule. The resolution was submitted by NB MP John Costigan (1835–1916).

Also in Apr.
• Canadian-born artist Paul Peel enrolled in the École des Beaux-Arts in Paris.

May 2 The Civil Service Act was passed by the House of Commons, providing for the assessment and screening of potential civil servants.

May 7 The Manitoba Bank was chartered.

May 8 The NWT was divided into 4 provisional districts by an Order-in-Council: Athabasca, Assiniboia, Alberta and Saskatchewan. The capital seat, located in Battleford, would be moved to Regina (Wascana) in 1883, so it would be situated along the CPR main line.

May 12 The Qu'Appelle Valley Farming Company was incorporated to subdivide 233 km along the CPR east of Qu'Appelle, NWT, and settle about 300 families. Land was purchased at $1.25 per acre and was sold to the settlers in 213-acre (86-ha) farms.

May 17 Queen's College in Kingston, Ont., was given university status.

Also in May
• Irish poet and dramatist Oscar Wilde visited Toronto on a tour of North America.

• Two hundred and forty-seven Russian-Jewish immigrants arrived in Canada to take up free homesteads in Man., promised to them by the Canadian govt.

• Harry Piper's Zoo in Toronto featured the 1st alligator to be exhibited in Canada.

June 1 Winnipeg received gas lighting.

June 20 Macdonald's Conservatives won the general election, taking 139 seats, to Edward Blake's Liberals 72. Voter turnout was 70.1%

June 22 The Judicial Committee of the Privy Council upheld the Canada Temperance Act of 1878 (*Russell v. Regina*) as legislation meant "to apply a remedy to an evil which is assumed to exist throughout the Dominion." Temperance was ruled a national concern that did not fall under provincial jurisdiction.

Summer The CPR sold 5 million acres (2,023,428 ha) of land in Sask. to the Canada North-West Land Company, controlled by Donald Smith, for $13.5 million, or $2.70 an acre.

July 15 Maj. Thomas Moore established the 1st official Canadian Salvation Army corps in Toronto, on British founder William Booth's philosophy of "soup and salvation." Organized on military lines, the Army had 11 "corps" in Canada by 1882. The church and social service agency expanded cross-country and gained legal recognition by Parliament in 1909. Early salvationist contributions included the 1890 Prison Gate Home for ex-convicts (the 1st halfway house in Toronto) and the 1st Maternity home in Saint John, NB, in 1898. In 1908, the Army took on a recycling program in Toronto, which led to the proliferation of its thrift stores cross-country.

Also in July

• C.E.D. Wood, former member of the NWMP, began publishing the *Macleod Gazette*, Alb.'s 2nd newspaper.

Aug. 1 The 1st International Polar Year commenced this date. Scientists were posted at 12 stations scattered throughout the Arctic to make magnetic and meteorological observations.

Aug. 12 The Grand Trunk Railway and Great Western Railway amalgamated as the Grand Trunk Railway Company.

Aug. 16 The Peter Redpath Museum of Botany and Geology opened at McGill U.

Aug. 18 Methodist minister John Lake of the Temperance Colonization Company of Toronto selected and named Saskatoon on the east side of the Sask. R. for the site of his new colony, which would be "free forever from the threat of distilled damnation." The 1st settlers arrived in 1883.

Aug. 20 The 1st CPR train arrived at Wascana, Sask.

Aug. 23 Wascana, Cree for "pile of bones," so called for the once-abundant buffalo bones found in the area, was renamed Regina (Latin for "queen").

Sept. 25 The 61-m-long sternwheeler *Marquis* made its maiden voyage on L. Winnipeg. Later it would travel up the Sask. R. as far as Prince Albert.

Oct. 3 Hector Fabré (1834–1910) was appointed agent gen. for the Canadian govt in Paris.

Oct. 20 Winnipeg's 1st horse-drawn streetcar went into operation.

Dec. 8 Starvation forced Cree chief Big Bear and his band to accept and sign Treaty No. 6 in order to become eligible for govt rations. Chief Big Bear had refused to sign the treaty in 1876.

1882–1884 *Picturesque Canada* (2 volumes), edited by artist and president of the Royal Canadian Academy of Arts Lucius O'Brien, was published.

Also in 1882

• The North-Western Coal and Navigation Co. began mining coal in Coalbanks, Alb.

• E.D. Smith founded E.D. Smith & Sons Ltd. in Winona, Ont. The family-owned fruit and vegetable firm developed its Garden Cocktail juice in 1969, and its Tomato Clam (Zesty) Cocktail in 1978. Both of these products were sold to Motts, a subsidiary of Britain's Cadbury Schweppes in 1989, so that E.D. Smith could concentrate its future efforts on marketing jams and jellies. In 2001, E.D. Smith was recognized as one of Canada's 50 best-managed private companies by a consortium including Queen's U. School of Business, the CIBC and the *National Post*.

• Ottawa published its 1st telephone book, listing 200 subscribers.

• The Canadian Rugby Union was formed.

• Canada's 1st steel ingots were produced by the NS Steel Company.

• Women were admitted to Dalhousie U. for the 1st time.

• Canada adopted its 1st codification of criminal laws.

• Ont. enacted legislation allowing unmarried women to vote in municipal elections, provided they met property qualifications.

• Dominion botanist John Macoun (1832–1920) published *Manitoba and the Great North-West*.

• The Ontario Medical Act allowed Ont. municipalities to appoint medical health officers and provided for the establishment of a provincial board of health.

• The CPR assumed control of the Dominion Express Company, a parcels-forwarding service.

• Félicité Angers (Laure Conan) (1845–1924), Que.'s 1st female novelist, published the daring novel *Angéline de Montbrun* in serial form in *La Revue canadienne.*

• The *Daily Patriot* began publishing in Charlottetown, PEI.

• Artist Lucius O'Brien completed *Kakabeka Falls, Kamanistiquia R.,* which is now in the National Gallery of Canada.

• Frederick Arthur Verner painted *The Upper Ottawa,* now in the National Gallery of Canada.

1883

Jan. 23 The 1st ice palace carnival was held in Montreal.

Jan. 31 John A. Macdonald purchased Earnscliff (Eagles Nest) for $10,040. The private residence in Ottawa would be Macdonald's home until his death in 1891. Earnscliffe would become the residence of the United Kingdom high commissioner in 1930.

Also in Jan.
• Work on the CPR main line through the prairies halted at Maple Creek, Sask., due to winter conditions; 673 km of track had been laid since Apr. 1882.

Feb. 8 The 1st session of the 5th Parliament met, until May 25. A subsidy on Canadian-manufactured iron was passed.

Feb. 9 Ont.'s 1st public library opened in Guelph.

Feb. 27 Ont. Premier Oliver Mowat's Liberals were returned to power with a 12-seat majority.

Also in Feb.
• Immigration sheds were built at Qu'Appelle, Sask., to shelter throngs of settlers.

Mar. 12 The steamship *Duke of Abercorn* landed the 1st steel at Port Moody, BC, for construction of the Pacific section of the CPR.

Apr. 6 Canada Cotton Mill's new weave shed in Cornwall, Ont., became the 1st plant in Canada to use electric lighting.

Apr. 19 Fire destroyed the Parliament Buildings at Quebec City.

May 10 Dr. Abraham Groves (1847–1935) performed the 1st appendectomy in North America, on a 12-year-old boy in a farmhouse near Fergus, Ont.

May 30 Charles Tupper, a Father of Confederation and minister of Railways and Canals, was appointed Canadian high commissioner in England. He resigned his cabinet position in 1884 to assume his new post.

June 10 A special locomotive, carrying American railroad dignitaries, travelled from Winnipeg to Medicine Hat, a town consisting entirely of tents, in the 1st traverse of the CPR's new prairie main line.

July 25 The ship *Marco Polo,* once known as the fastest ship in the world, ran aground during stormy weather near the village of Cavendish, on the north coast of PEI. The entire crew was saved by local residents. The event was witnessed by 8-year-old Lucy Maud Montgomery, who published an account of the incident in the *Montreal Witness* in Feb. 1891. It was her 1st newspaper article.

Also in July
• The sternwheeler *Baroness* was launched at Coal Banks (Lethbridge), Alb., and floated down to Medicine Hat. Constructed by the North-Western Coal Company, it would transport coal from the rich bituminous seams in the Lethbridge region to the CPR at Medicine Hat.

• The newspaper *Le Temps* was founded by Honoré Mercier (1840–1894) and Félix-Gabriel Marchand (1832–1900) in Montreal. Toussaint-Antoine-Rodolphe Laflamme (1827–1893) became its editor. The paper would close after 2 1/2 months.

Aug. 11 The CPR reached the tiny tent town of Calgary on its journey westward toward the Pacific.

For the 1st few years after the NWMP built Fort Calgary, the settlement was little more than a way station along the stagecoach trail that connected Fort Edmonton with Fort Benton, Montana. The only permanent structures in the community were the barracks of the police fort and the cabins of the Hudson's Bay and the I.G. Baker trading companies. However, when the CPR decided to build its line along the southern route across the Rocky Mountains through the Kicking Horse Pass, entrepreneurs and speculators moved in and pitched their tents around Fort Calgary. As the only existing settlement along the CPR route, it was widely anticipated that Calgary would become the centre of the supply industry.

Aug. 18 Henry Charles Keith Petty-Fitzmaurice, Marquess of Lansdowne (1845–1927) was appointed gov-gen. of Canada, and served from Oct. 23 to May 30, 1888. PM Macdonald would call him "the ablest chief" he had ever served.

Aug. 31 The weekly newspaper the *Calgary Herald Mining and Ranch Advocate and General Advertiser* published its 1st issue from a wooden-floored tent. It was printed on the 1st printing press to reach Alb. by train. R.B. Bradon, in association with A.M. Armour, set up the press. The enterprise employed 1 newsboy.

Sept. 1 The CPR built its 1st wheat elevator at Port Arthur, Ont.

Sept. 5 Methodist churches of Canada, Methodist Episcopal Church, Primitive Methodist Church and Bible Christian Church merged to form the Methodist Church.

Oct. 1 The 1st medical school exclusively for women, Toronto Women's Medical College, opened in Toronto, as an affiliate of the U. of Toronto and Trinity College, under the presidency of Dr. Michael Barrett (1816–1887).

Dec. 15 Henry Beatty (1834–1914), commissioned by the CPR to organize a Great Lakes shipping service, arranged for the building of steamships *Alberta* and *Athabaska* in Scotland.

Dec. 31 "A" Company of the Infantry School Corps, the 1st unit of the Canadian Permanent Force, was

based at Fredericton, NB. It would later become the Royal Canadian Regiment.

1883–1902 Dominion Botanist John Macoun's exhaustive, systematic *Catalogue of Canadian Plants* was released in 7 parts. Research for the landmark work required Canada's 1st great botanist to travel cross-country studying and collecting botanical species. The work took him over 40 years. Macoun's collection of more than 100,000 Canadian plant species formed the basis of the Dominion Herbarium, which he founded in Ottawa.

Also in 1883

• Internationally acclaimed British-American stage actress Lillie Langtry performed at the Grand Opera House in Toronto to a sold-out house.

• Emily Stowe founded the Toronto Women's Suffrage Association.

• Emily Stowe's daughter, 26-year-old Augusta Stowe-Cullen (1847–1943), became the 1st female doctor to graduate from a Canadian medical school, the Toronto Women's Medical College.

• Nicholas Flood Davin (1843–1901) established the *Regina Leader*, the 1st newspaper in Assiniboia.

• Henry Pellat (1859–1939) founded the Toronto Electric Light Company.

• Natural gas was 1st struck at Alderson, Alb. by CPR workers probing for water.

• Chief Crowfoot was rewarded by the CPR with a pension for keeping the peace when CPR survey crews crossed his southern Alb. reserve.

• The Alb. Railway and Irrigation Company established the 1st substantial Alb. irrigation project in the Lethbridge district.

• Women's Medical College at Queen's U. was founded in Kingston, with an initial class of 3. Boarding charges were $2.50 per week and the *Gray's Anatomy* text cost $6.50.

• Nickel and copper were 1st discovered by European-Canadians during the construction of the CPR across the Sudbury Basin in northern Ont.

• James Grand and Samuel Toy opened their 1st retail "office outfitters" outlet in Toronto. Today, Grand & Toy has more than 70 locations across the country.

• *The Iroquois Book of Rites*, by philologist and ethnologist Horatio Emmons Hale (1817–1896), was published.

• The govt of Canada commissioned Robert Harris to paint *The Fathers of Confederation* for a fee of $4,000. Initially, the commission was to feature the Charlottetown Meeting, but the govt revised its decision and stipulated Quebec as the scene of the picture. Harris painted all 34 participants of the Conference in a hall of his imagination (because the Quebec Parliament Buildings had burned down). The painting was finished in 1884, launching Harris as one of Canada's most fashionable portraitists. The painting was destroyed by fire in 1916.

1884

Jan. 2 Two trains collided in a whiteout, opposite Grenadier Pond, High Park, Toronto. One train was carrying an estimated 40 workers from the Swansea Bolt Works. Thirty-one lives were lost. No memorial has been placed to mark Toronto's worst train disaster.

Jan. 4 The CPR leased the Ontario and Quebec Railway (with 604 km of track completed and over 323 more under construction), thus expanding its operations eastward from Toronto to Ottawa, north from Toronto to Owen Sound, and west from Toronto to St. Thomas, Woodstock and to London. The lease covered 99 years.

Also in Jan.
• CPR President George Stephen asked the Macdonald govt for a loan of $22.5 million, on the security of a 1st mortgage on the property of the CPR. The CPR Relief Bill was introduced in Parliament Feb. 6, providing for a govt loan of $22.5 million to rescue the half-built railway from bankruptcy. The bill passed in the House of Commons Feb. 28. On Mar. 6 the CPR Relief Bill became law. The CPR received an immediate cash loan of $7.5 million and an additional $15 million to be paid in installments.

Feb.14 Que. Premier Joseph-Alfred Mousseau (1838–1886) and his entire provincial cabinet, supported by an almost solid block of 48 Que. federal Conservatives, demanded from PM Macdonald a retroactive subsidy to compensate the province for the building of the North Shore Railway. Mousseau threatened that no money for the North Shore meant no money for the CPR. Que. was granted $2,394,000 "in consideration of their having constructed the railway from Quebec to Ottawa."

Feb. 18 Calgary's 1st school opened with 12 children in attendance.

Mar. 5 The Ont. legislature approved a motion that provision be made for the admission of women to University College, Toronto. The motion was carried Oct. 6. Six women attended that year; 68 were enrolled in 1889.

Mar. 6 The Toronto Public Library was established with 18,400 books in a building that formerly housed the Mechanics Institute.

Mar. 25 Victoria College in Toronto became Victoria U.

Mar. 28 The Settlement Act provided a solution to the BC/federal govt railway dispute. The federal govt contributed $750,000 toward the building of the Esquimalt-Nanaimo Railroad, and the BC govt turned over provincial railway lands to the federal govt.

Apr. 19 The federal govt outlawed the BC Native potlatch under pressure from missionaries. The potlatch ceremony included feasting and gift-giving and was a process that solidified bonds, established and reinforced relationships, redistributed wealth, and ensured the continuation of community. The ban was ruthlessly enforced. Authorities often seized essential ceremonial regalia, such as the masks and robes of potlach participants. West Coast Native Peoples were forced to move the potlach underground, until an amendment to the Indian Act revoked the legislation in 1951.

Apr. 25 In hopes of securing a stable, duty-free sugar market in Canada, Barbados Gov. Francis Hincks sent a letter to PM Macdonald asking, "Would the Dominion of Canada favourably entertain an application from Barbados to be admitted a member of their Confederation." Canada declined to make Barbados its southernmost territory.

May 24 Royal Assent was given to a private member's bill introduced into the Ont. legislature authorizing the Supreme Court of Canada to allow Delos Rogest Davis (1846–1915) to practise law upon the successful completion of the final exam prepared by the Law Society of Upper Canada. Although Davis, a young black paralegal from Amherstburg, Ont. had had many years' experience, no legal firm of his acquaintance would give him the articling experience required to becoming a full-fledged lawyer.

June 4 Gabriel Dumont, Michel Dumas, Moise Ouellette and James Isbister arrived in the small Montana settlement where Louis Riel was teaching school. They invited him to return to the Northwest to lead a 2nd protest against the govt of Canada. Riel left his teaching position in Montana on June 10.

June 9 Explorer Joseph Burr Tyrrell (1858–1957) discovered a rich deposit of dinosaur bones along the Red River near what is now Drumheller, Alb. Tyrrell was on a coal expedition with the Geological Survey of Canada. Twenty species of dinosaur have since been uncovered in what has become a world-famous prehistoric graveyard.

June 16 The United Empire Loyalist settlement celebrated its centennial at Adolphustown, Ont.

June 21 Seven starving survivors of a 26-member American scientific expedition into the Arctic were rescued from their camp in Smith Sound at the top of Baffin Bay. They had hoped to carry out experiments as part of the 1st International Polar Year, begun Aug. 1882.

July 4 A Royal Commission was appointed to examine Chinese immigration into Canada.

July 8 Louis Riel arrived at Duck L., NWT, in the North Sask. Valley. On July 19, he spoke to a crowd of 500 people in Prince Albert, NWT, calling for responsible govt and the creation of provinces in the northwest.

Aug. 6 A public school system, including separate schools, was established for the NWT.

Aug. 22 The Calgary Agricultural Society was organized, to promote the agriculture industry and provide opportunity for producers to display and sell animals and other commodities. The group would help initiate the 1st Calgary Exhibition on Oct. 19–20, 1886, which was a precursor to the 1st Calgary Stampede (established Sept. 2, 1912).

Also in Aug.
• Cree chiefs, under Big Bear, met at Duck L. to voice opposition to the federal govt's Indian-reserve policy. They adjourned, agreeing to hold a larger council the next summer.

Sept. 7 German anthropologist Franz Boas (1858–1942) arrived in Saint John, NB, after a year-long expedition studying the Inuit of Cumberland Sound and Baffin Is.

Sept. 15 The Nile Voyageurs sailed for Egypt to rescue Gen. C.G. Gordon, besieged in Khartoum, Sudan, by the revolutionary leader, the Mahdi. The force of 386 lumbermen, Caughnawaga and Ottawa boatmen serving under command of Frederick Charles Denison (1846–1896) did not reach Khartoum until Jan. 28, 1885, by which time the city had fallen and Gordon was dead. Sixteen Canadians lost their lives, and the survivors arrived back in Que. on May 25, 1885.

Sept. 24 Vital Grandin (1829–1902), bishop of St. Albert, authorized July 24 as a Métis national holiday, with St. Joseph the patron saint. Grandin also allowed a special inaugural celebration on this date at St. Antoine Padua Church in Batoche. Following the religious service, Louis Riel gave a 3-hour speech to the crowd of several hundred.

Also in Sept.
• Louis Riel, representing English and French Métis, and William Jackson, representing the Settlers Union, drafted a petition to be sent to the federal govt demanding responsible govt, rights of an individual to own land, squatters' rights, the

issuance of script, abolition of the protective tariff, local control of natural resources, a railroad to Hudson Bay, provincial status for Sask. and the right to send delegates to Ottawa with a bill of rights.

Oct. 15 The 1st issue of *La Presse*, Montreal, was published.

Nov. 5 The BC portion of the CPR reached Golden.

Nov. 17 Calgary, population 500, was incorporated as a town.

Nov. 18 The International Prime Meridian Conference, held in Washington, adopted Sanford Fleming's system of international standard time measurement; 25 countries voted to implement the scheme.

Dec. 16 The Riel/Jackson petition was sent to Ottawa. It was in English and was not signed by Riel, who had failed to get clauses regarding Aboriginal title to the Northwest included in the document. The federal govt acknowledged receipt of the petition on Jan. 5, 1885, and the Macdonald cabinet discussed it in depth on Jan. 9. The Macdonald govt subsequently appointed a 3-man commission to investigate Métis land claims on Mar. 30, 1885.

Dec. 20 The Man. and Northwest Farmers' Union was established. One of its 1st items of business was to draft a list of grievances against the federal govt. These involved a protest against the CPR monopoly and a request for the building of a Hudson Bay railway alternative.

Dec. 23 Riel met with NWT Council representative D.H. MacDowell to demand the $100,000 he believed was due him from the govt.

Also in 1884

• Widows and spinsters were given the right to vote in Ont. municipal elections.

• The Imperial Federation League was formed between British empire countries to strengthen traditional ties and work out empirical trade and tariffs.

• The 1st Eaton's Mail Order Catalogue was published and distributed, from Toronto to the nation's sprawling populace. Its 32 pages expanded to 400 by the 20th century to include a seemingly endless variety of needs — from hockey equipment to barns, from boots to birthing supplies. It was given such nick names as the "Wish Book" and "Homesteaders Bible." Eaton's catalogue was discontinued in 1976.

• An HBC expedition was initiated by Albert Peter Low (1861–1942) for the Geological Survey of Canada.

• The CPR completed track for 649 km of the required 1,057 km of its L. Superior section.

• George M. Dawson and A.R.C. Selwyn published *A Descriptive Sketch of the Physical Geography and Geology of the Dominion of Canada.*

• Montreal artist William Brymner (1855–1925), who studied at the Académie Julian in Paris, completed his masterpiece, the canvas *A Wreath of Flowers*, which is now in the National Gallery of Canada.

• Isabella Valancy Crawford published in Toronto, at her own expense, a book of poetry entitled *Old Spookses' Pass: "Malcolm's Katie" and Other Poems*. Fifty copies were sold.

1885

Jan. 1 Canada adopted standard time, conceived by Sanford Fleming, which divided the country into 7 time zones — Nfld., Atlantic, Eastern, Central, Rockies, Pacific and Yukon. Total time difference between the extreme zones was 5 1/2 hours.

Jan. 24 The CPR telegraph was completed from the Atlantic to the Pacific.

Jan. 29 The 3rd session of the 5th Parliament met, until July 20. The Chinese Immigration Act imposed a $50 head tax on every Chinese immigrant.

Also in Jan.

• A statue of Father of Confederation George-Étienne Cartier was unveiled in Ottawa.

Feb. 9 George Stephen informed PM Macdonald, by letter, of the CPR's dire need for more funds. Stephen wrote that he and Donald Smith had personally endorsed a 5-month note for $1 million to keep the railroad afloat.

Mar. 5 Riel, Dumont and 9 other militant Métis signed a revolutionary oath.

Mar. 8 The Que. Assembly passed the Manufacturers Act, placing limits on hours of work and providing measures for safety in the workplace.

Mar. 11 Leif Newry Fitzroy Crozier (1847–1901), superintendent of the NWMP at Fort Carlton (32 km north of Batoche), issued a warning that a Métis rebellion in Sask. was imminent.

Mar. 13 BC passed the Chinese Restriction Act, refusing entry to Chinese immigrants. On Mar. 31, the federal govt disallowed the legislation.

Mar. 19 Armed men under Riel seized the Batoche parish church and formed a provisional govt of the Northwest. Gabriel Dumont was appointed adjutant-general with 12 other councillors. This act constituted rebellion. Riel issued a proclamation on Mar. 21, demanding surrender of Fort Carlton by the NWMP.

Mar. 22 Frederick Dobson Middleton (1826–1898), commanding the Canadian militia, was ordered to place a force of 8,000 troops on alert for action.

Mar. 23 The Council of the Métis provisional govt dispatched runners from Batoche, requesting military support from Native Peoples in the area.

Mar. 25 Dumont and 16 men travelled to Duck L., 96 km west of Batoche, to seize a store owned by Hillyard Mitchell, thought by Dumont to be a spy for the NWMP.

• Winnipeg's 90th Battalion and field battery left Winnipeg for Sask. in anticipation of a clash with the Métis.

Mar. 26 NWMP Supt. Crozier, with 98 NWMP officers and volunteers, was ambushed by Métis under Dumont at Duck L., Sask. Crozier's force retreated to Fort Carlton after having lost 12 men. The Métis lost 5 men. Métis dead were taken to the St. Laurent mission, 10 km north of Batoche, where they were buried by Fr. Fourmond. Riel carried a crucifix during battle, but no weapon.

Mar. 28 Acheson Gosford Irvine (1837–1916), arriving with 90 men after a gruelling 7-day 484-km march from Regina in freezing temperatures, reinforced the NWMP force and withdrew it from Fort Carlton to Prince Albert, Sask.

• "A" and "B" Batteries, on their way from Montreal to Sask. with 228 men under Lt-Col. C.E. Montizambert, arrived at the eastern railhead of the CPR's L. Superior section, having left Montreal 2 days earlier. They would require another 5 days to reach Winnipeg by foot, horse and rail. A similar military journey during the 1st Northwest Rebellion had taken 90 days.

• Ont. Premier Oliver Mowat introduced the Niagara Falls Park Act for "the preservation of the natural scenery about Niagara Falls." It was passed the same year and led to the creation of Queen Victoria Park, opened on May 24, 1888, as the country's 1st provincial park. The bill also led to what would become the Niagara Parks Commission.

Also in Mar.
• Chiefs Poundmaker (1826–1886) and Little Pine (Minahikosis) led a force of 200 Cree in an attack on settlers at Battleford, Sask., forcing the latter to take refuge in the NWMP barracks for 30 days.

Apr. 2 A party of Cree, led by Wandering Spirit (Kapapamahchakwew, [c 1845–1885]), shot 9 people in the Frog L. Massacre, including Frog L. Indian agent Thomas T. Quinn and two Roman Catholic priests. Two women and a Hudson's Bay agent survived.

Apr. 6 Maj-Gen. Frederick D. Middleton led 800 militiamen from Fort Qu'Appelle toward Batoche.

Apr. 13 Colonel William Dillon Otter (1843–1929) marched with 550 men from Swift Current, Sask., toward Battleford.

Apr. 15 NWMP Inspector Francis Jeffrey Dickens (1844–1886) withdrew his detachment from Fort

Pitt, located on the N. Sask. R. east of the Alb.-Sask. border. The fort was threatened by Big Bear and Cree troops. Dickens reached Battleford on Apr. 22.

Apr. 17 Gen. Frederick D. Middleton arrived at Clarke's Crossing, 90 km from Batoche.

Apr. 20 Thomas Bland Strange (1831–1925), commanding the Alberta Field Force, moved toward Edmonton from Calgary with 600 men.

Apr. 24 Gen. Middleton and his force were ambushed in Sask. by Dumont's Métis, in the Battle of Fish Creek. The battle ended in a draw, but 6 militiamen were killed and nearly 50 wounded out of a force of about 400. The Métis suffered 5 dead and a small number of wounded. Dumont withdrew his forces to Batoche.

Apr. 29 Colonel Otter and his forces relieved the town of Battleford, which had been harassed by marauding Cree and Assiniboine of Poundmaker and the Yellow Grass reserves.

Also in Apr.
• Federal reinforcement troops arrived at Qu'Appelle station by rail.

May 1 Ottawa installed electric lighting.

• Lt. Col. Otter left Battleford with 325 men including 75 members of the NWMP, in pursuit of Poundmaker, hoping to prevent him from joining Big Bear and relieving Riel. Otter attempted a surprise attack on Poundmaker's village May 2, but the troops were expected and the resultant 7-hour Battle of Cut Knife Hill ended in victory for the Stoney and Cree warriors commanded by Fine Day (1850– c 1930s). Otter's force suffered 8 dead and 15 wounded, and retreated to Battleford.

• Thomas Strange and his troops relieved Edmonton.

May 8 Govt forces occupied Dumont's farm, setting his buildings on fire.

• The steamers *Marquis* and *Northcote* were hired to take part in the attack on the Métis capital of Batoche. The *Marquis* was later used as a floating headquarters by Gen. Middleton.

May 9 Middleton's force engaged Métis in the Battle of Batoche and charged trenches defended by Riel and Dumont's men. After 3 days of fierce fighting, Métis supplies were exhausted. Colonels Arthur Williams (1837–1885) and H.J. Grasett led a final charge, resulting in a rout of the rebels on May 12. Dumont evaded capture and fled to the US.

May 11 The 1st through CPR train between Montreal and Winnipeg departed Montreal with 299 soldiers, to arrive in Winnipeg May 20.

May 14 Poundmaker's Cree captured an army supply train and 22 prisoners near Battleford.

May 15 Louis Riel surrendered to the NWMP.

May 17 Riel boarded the riverboat *Northcote* under guard and was taken to Regina by special train where he was immediately confined in the guardroom of the NWMP barracks to await trial. He was formally charged with acts of treason on July 6.

May 18 CPR's Col. Oswald drove the last spike of the L. Superior section at mile 718. Henry Abbott (d 1915), construction manager of the CPR eastern section, and William Van Horne were in attendance. The CPR had completed continuous track between Montreal, Winnipeg and the Rocky Mountains.

May 24 Poundmaker dispatched one of his prisoners to Gen. Middleton requesting surrender terms in writing, to avoid any possible misunderstanding.

• The largest cattle roundup in the history of the Canadian West began at Fort Macleod: 100 cowboys, 16 chuckwagons and 500 saddle horses were employed in collecting over 60,000 cattle.

May 26 Poundmaker, his followers and 150 Métis surrendered unconditionally to Gen. Middleton at Battleford.

May 28 Gen. Strange attacked the Cree under Big Bear in the Battle of Frenchman's Butte. Results were indecisive. Both sides withdrew, each thinking the other side victorious. One Cree was mortally wounded.

Also in May
• The CPR transported a total of 2,750 troops from

East to West over finished and unfinished rail lines to help put down the 2nd Northwest Rebellion.

June 3 Samuel B. Steele, commanding a NWMP force, engaged the Cree under Big Bear at Steele Narrows, Sask., in the last military engagement of the Northwest Rebellion. Five Cree were killed, including Woods Cree chief Cut Arm, a leading pacifist who had prevented the Plains Cree from killing white prisoners. Big Bear escaped.

June 23 Hockey wonder Fred "Cyclone" Taylor (1885–1979) was born in Tora, Ont. Playing roving centre, Taylor was with the Ottawa Senators in 1908–1909 (winning the Stanley Cup), before moving to the Renfrew Creamery Kings (1909–1911). He finished his career with the Vancouver Millionaires, winning the Stanley Cup with the team in 1915, and was elected to the Hockey Hall of Fame in 1947. Widely considered the nation's 1st hockey superstar, Taylor played 189 professional regular season games, gathering an incredible 205 goals and 108 assists.

July 1 Fishery clauses in the Treaty of Washington were terminated by the US, when the mackerel population shifted to American waters. The US had been assessed an annual payment of $458,333 for its fishing privileges in Canada. Americans were, however, allowed to fish under treaty terms until the end of the season.

July 2 Big Bear, his son and a Cree named All-and-a-half surrendered to Sergeant Smart of the NWMP at Fort Carlton. This marked the end of the Northwest Rebellion.

July 11 Parliament passed the CPR Aid Bill (introduced June 16) which called for the issuance of $35 million worth of 5%, 1st-mortgage bonds, secured by CPR assets and guaranteed by the federal govt. Baring's of London subscribed half the CPR bonds and optioned the remainder.

July 17 Big Bear arrived at Regina to await trial for his part in the Northwest Rebellion.

July 20 Louis Riel appeared in court to face the charge of treason. His trial began in Regina July 28. He was defended by 3 lawyers appointed by the Quebec-based Riel Defence Committee. Council

recommended a plea of guilty with insanity. Riel rejected that advice and pleaded not guilty.

• The sidewheeler *Enterprise* collided with the *R.P. Rithet* off the coast of BC. Two people and 24 cattle drowned.

• Parliament passed the Electoral Franchise Act after bitter Liberal opposition. It established criteria for voting and disenfranchising widows, spinsters and Native Peoples in Eastern Canada.

July 29 Contractor Andrew Onderdonk completed the western section of the CPR line from Port Moody, BC, to Savona's Ferry at Kamloops L. The BC branch of the CPR was completed between Savona's Ferry and Eagle Pass, BC, on Sept. 30.

Also in July
• Métis and Native rebels took refuge in Montana following the Northwest Rebellion.

Aug. 1 Louis Riel was convicted of treason by a jury without French-Canadian or Métis representation. Deliberation lasted 1 hour before a verdict was reached. The jury consisted of 6 white Anglophone Protestants. Although mercy was strongly recommended, Justice Hugh Richardson (1826–1913) negated the recommendation and pronounced the death sentence. Riel was scheduled to hang by the neck, Nov. 16.

Aug. 24 The 1st census of the NWT set the population of Assiniboia as 22,083, Sask., 10,746, and Alb., 15,533, for a total of 48,362.

Also in Aug.
• Chief Sitting Bull visited Toronto as part of Buffalo Bill's Wild West Show.

Sept. 7 Alb. ranchers formed the North West Stock Association, hoping to work together against increasing incidents of horse theft and rustling.

Sept. 15 Jumbo, P.T. Barnum's elephant, purchased in England, was killed in St. James, Ont., when he was struck by a freight engine while heading toward a railway car about to be loaded.

• Henry Jackson, a follower of Riel, was acquitted of treason.

Sept. 24 The CPR opened its branch line connecting Dunsmore, Alb., on the main line, to Coal Banks, Alb., which was renamed Lethbridge.

Sept. 28 Mobs protesting mandatory smallpox vaccinations attacked Montreal's city hall and St. Catherine St. businesses. The militia was called out. The subsequent smallpox epidemic killed 1,391 Montrealers, 1,286 of which were French-Canadian.

Oct. 12–15 Three hundred people died when the Great Labrador Gale swept the coast of Labrador, sinking an estimated 89 ships and causing extensive land damage.

Oct. 22 Riel's appeal to the Judicial Committee of the Privy Council was heard but his guilty verdict was upheld.

Nov. 2 The 1st scheduled CPR passenger train left Montreal for Winnipeg.

Nov. 7 The last spike of the CPR was driven by Donald Smith at Craigellachie, BC. The official spike, made of gold, bent and had to be replaced by one of iron. The completed railway was 4,653 km long, stretching from Montreal to Port Moody, BC. "The work was done well in every way," said William Van Horne, president of the CPR.

Nov. 11 The federal cabinet declined to intercede in the Riel sentence. It ruled Riel should hang as scheduled in spite of thousands of petitions to the contrary.

Nov. 16 Louis Riel was hanged for high treason in Regina, Sask., and pronounced dead at 8:22 a.m. Flags flew at half mast in Que., and patriots wore mourning bands. Bleus and Rouges joined together spontaneously in a political movement aimed at bringing down the Macdonald govt.

Nov. 27 Cree chief Wandering Spirit, warriors Napaise, Apischikoos, Miserable Man, Paypamakeesik and 3 others were hanged at Fort Battleford for their part in the Frog L. Massacre.

Dec. 12 The 1st load of Man. wheat to be carried on a CPR freight train left Portage La Prairie for Montreal.

Dec. 21 Charlottetown, PEI, installed electric streetlights.

Also in 1885

• The 30.5-m-long sternwheeler *Alberta*, built in Medicine Hat in 1884, was transformed into a hospital ship during the Métis uprising, to take wounded from Prince Albert.

• The *Wrigley* was the 1st steam vessel to cross the Arctic Circle when it travelled to the mouth of the Mackenzie R. to service communities along the river.

• Army surgeon George Sterling Ryerson (b 1848) was the 1st to fly the Red Cross. The flag was flown from a horse-drawn ambulance to ensure the safe transport of wounded soldiers from Northwest Rebellion battlefields.

• Father Lacombe acted as an emissary during the Northwest Rebellion and throughout the building of the CPR. He was instrumental in soothing potentially abrasive relations between Métis, Native Peoples and those of European descent.

• Crowfoot's Cree remained neutral during the Northwest Rebellion despite heavy pressure brought to bear on the chief by his adopted son, Poundmaker.

• Lawrence Morris Lambe (1863–1919), a graduate of Kingston's RMC, joined the Geological Survey. By 1898, he was working in the Red Deer Valley identifying fossil specimens and describing new species — including trachodon, triceratops, laetops and Nodosaurus.

• Several Canadian horsemen established the 1st stud book for the Canadian Horse, a registered breed, with the National Livestock records. They also gained legal sanctions against export of the breed from Canada.

• The federal govt established Canada's 1st national park, a 26-km² section of land named Banff Hot Springs Reserve, located around the sulphur hot springs at the foot of Sulphur Mountain in the Rocky Mountains. The area was brought to general attention after 3 CPR workers stumbled upon the region in 1883. The park changed to Rocky Mountain Park in 1887 and was renamed Banff National Park in 1911. The 6,640-km² park has since become one of the world's most visited areas. Banff forms part of a chain of Rocky Mountain parks that includes Jasper and Yoho National Parks and also a number of provincial and wilderness reserves that together constitute over 2 million ha of protected land.

• Two million dollars' worth of placer gold was taken from the sands of the Chaudiere R. in Que. between 1875–1885. Production continued to 1912.

• Coal mining began at Anthracite near Banff, Alb., spurred by demand from the CPR.

• The federal govt banned the Sun Dance, a complex 3-day Plain Aboriginal celebration during which a sun spirit and young warriors danced in voluntary self-torture around a sacred pole in gratitude for the protection and continued good health of an endangered family member.

• Robert Harris painted his portrait of *Sir Hugh Allan*, oil on canvas.

• *Studies of Plant Life in Canada,* by Catherine Parr Traill was published.

• Félix-Gabriel Marchand produced the comic opera *Les Faux Brillants*.

1886

Jan. 6 American Samuel J. Ritchie (1838–1908) established the Canadian Copper Company and purchased the Frood, Stobie and Coppercliff claims outside of Sudbury, Ont. Mining began in May 1886. The ore found in quantity was not copper, but nickel, and the selling price was $1 per pound.

Feb. 6 William Des Voeux (1834–1909) was appointed gov. of Nfld. in place of Ambrose Shea, a popular, but Catholic, candidate.

Feb. 18 Roman Catholic Archbishop Taché baptized Poundmaker and 28 of his warriors at the Stony Mountain Penitentiary where they were imprisoned.

Feb. 25 The 4th session of the 5th Parliament met, until June 2. The Supreme Court of the NWT was constituted, and a Fisheries Act required licences from foreign vessels.

Also in Feb.
• The CPR presented Crowfoot with an unlimited pass to ride the entire route of its western division.

Mar. 12 Riots broke out during the Toronto street railway workers' strike in Toronto as replacement workers attempted to move streetcars into duty. The Toronto police used horses for the 1st time in city history to quell a riot. The workers had been fired and replaced when they joined the Knights of Labour in an attempt to lower the number of hours worked from 14 hours a day, 6 days a week.

Mar. 18 Robert Gillespie Reid (1842–1908) began construction of the CPR Lachine Bridge across the St. Lawrence R. at Montreal. Local Mohawk day labourers were hired to work the heights, which they did with such skill and daring that the Akwesasne and Kahnawake residents quickly became the most sought-after high-rise steelworkers on the continent. Knowledge and tool belts were passed from father to son, so by the late twentieth century, Canadian and American Mohawk workers had contributed to the upward growth of every major city in North America. Unparalleled Mohawk skills and utter fearlessness at great heights made possible the completion of such landmarks as the CN Tower, the World Trade Center, the Golden Gate Bridge and the George Washington Bridge in New York City.

Mar. 25 Canada's 1st Workman's Compensation for Injuries Act was passed in Ont.

Apr. 2 Mount Allison Wesleyan Academy at Sackville, NB, received a college charter.

Apr. 6 Vancouver was incorporated as a city. The population exceeded 2,000 and included 800 businesses.

May 14 NWT was represented in Parliament by an Act of Parliament.

Also in May
• Archbishop of Que. Elzéar-Alexandre Taschereau (1820–1898) decreed to priests throughout Que.

that any Catholic associating with the Knights of Labour organization would be excommunicated. He also proclaimed that priests should announce the policy at Sunday masses. On June 7, Taschereau was made Canada's 1st Roman Catholic cardinal by Pope Leo XIII.

June 2 Dominion Experimental Farm, the federal agricultural research agency, was established in Ottawa to conduct experiments for the improvement of crops and agricultural production in Canada. William Saunders (1836–1914) was its 1st director.

June 8 Edouard Charles Fabre (1827–1896) was ordained 1st Roman Catholic archbishop of Montreal.

June 13 Fire destroyed all but 4 houses in Vancouver and claimed the lives of 50 people. The conflagration was caused by workmen burning brush along the waterfront for a Stikine camping area.

June 15 Ex-journalist William Stevens Fielding (1848–1929) led the NS Liberals to victory, winning 29 seats to the Tories' 8, on the platform of removing NS from Confederation.

June 28 The 1st westbound CPR transcontinental passenger train and mail car (Pacific Express No. 1) left Montreal for Port Moody, BC, arriving at the western terminus 7 days later on July 4. The 1st eastbound CPR transcontinental passenger train and mail car left Port Moody, BC, for Montreal 2 days later on July 6. This marked the beginning of a national mail service of world repute.

July 1 The CPR redeemed all its outstanding loans from the federal govt with a $19 million cash payment and the transfer of 6,000,000+ acres (2,428,114 ha) of CPR land grants at $1.50 per acre.

July 9 A general amnesty was granted to those involved in the Northwest Rebellion of 1885, excepting convicted murderers.

July 11 PM John A. Macdonald and wife (Susan, née Bernard) began a journey across Canada to the West Coast on the CPR. This would be their 1st trip West (although Macdonald had been a member of Parliament for Victoria since 1878, after being defeated in his local constituency of Kingston, Ont.).

• Carlisle D. Graham of Philadelphia, Pennsylvania, was the 1st person to navigate Niagara Falls' Whirlpool Rapids in a barrel. He survived but banged his head during the stunt. He vowed to keep his head outside the barrel for his next plunge, which he did on Aug. 19. He survived but suffered permanent hearing impairment.

July 17 The 1st mail-stage robbery in Sask. took place when a lone desperado held up the Prince Albert stage.

July 22 Métis leader Gabriel Dumont, touring the US with Buffalo Bill's Wild West Show, refused to accept the govt of Canada's offer of amnesty.

July 29 Joseph Thomas Duhamel (1841–1909) became the 1st Roman Catholic archbishop of Ottawa.

July 30 The 1st tea train left Vancouver for Montreal carrying a cargo of 17,430 half chests of tea from the US barque *W.B. Flint*, which had arrived at Port Moody from Yokohama.

Aug. 13 John A. Macdonald drove the last spike of the Esquimalt and Nanaimo Railroad near Shawnigan L., BC.

Sept. 13 The Montreal-based CPR opened the Canadian Pacific Telegraphs system, a commerical enterprise that would send 567,840 telegraphs during its 1st year of operation.

Sept. 14 A Toronto trade unionists meeting established a new national umbrella group representing all unions in Canada. It would be known as the Trades and Labour Congress of Canada.

Oct. 24 Charles Ora Card (1839–1906), member of the Church of Jesus Christ of Latter-Day Saints, Utah, selected land between the Belly and St. Mary Rivers in present-day Alb., to establish a settlement for 40 Mormons he planned to bring to Canada. Cardston, Alb., would be founded in 1887.

Nov. 7 Fire destroyed 14 businesses in Calgary.

Nov. 15 Delos Rogest Davis of Colchester, Ont. was admitted to the bar by the Law Society of Upper Canada, becoming the 1st Canadian-born black lawyer. On Nov. 10, 1910, the govt of Ont. appointed him a King's Counsel, the 1st such appointment given to a black person in the British empire.

Nov. 16 An Ordinance to Incorporate Agricultural Societies was passed by the Territorial Council at Regina. Its objectives were to encourage improvement in agriculture by using quality seeds and the awarding of prizes for excellence in the agriculture profession, the creation and publication of essays on agriculture and the development of systems for protection against prairie fires.

Dec. 14 Yoho National Park (1,310 km²) was established as a reserve to protect the peaks and valleys created by the Kicking Horse R. Thirty of the park's mountains exceed 3,000 m. Yoho, which means "wonderment" in Cree, is located along the Rocky Mountains in BC, and is linked by Banff and Kootenay National Parks. It contains some of the country's most spectacular montane, subalpine and alpine ecosystems, and is home to an abundance of wildlife, including mountain goats, grizzly bear, black bear, wolves, cougar, lynx, mountain bluebirds and the golden eagle. The park also includes the 254-m Takakkaw Falls, and the world-famous Burgess Shale, which contains 120 fossilized species, some as old as 515 million years. The reserve gained National Park status in 1911 under the Dominion Forest Reserves and Parks Act.

Also in 1886

• The Ontario Factory Act was passed, making it unlawful for boys under 13 and girls under 14 to work. The workweek was limited to a maximum of 60 hours.

• The newly formed Amateur Hockey Association of Canada declared the 3" x 1" rubber disc its official puck, replacing the popular wooden puck.

• Glacier House, one of three hotels or "dining stations" built along the CPR railway in the mountains of BC was completed by architect Thomas Sorby. The purpose of these dining stations was to attract travellers and to serve as restaurants in substitution for dining carts on trains, because the latter were too heavy to haul up steep cliffs. Glacier House was the most visited of the three early CPR dining stations because of its location within sight and walk-ing distance of the Illecillewaet Glacier. It was demolished after the railway was rerouted in 1929.

• The Canadian govt estalished a 76 km² reserve of mountainous terrain in eastern BC surrounding Rogers Pass and Mount McDonald. By 1930, this area had grown to 1,349 km² and was known as Glacier National Park. Glacier, which was accessible only by railroad was, and is, the site of more than 400 glaciers (including Asulkan and Illecillewaet), which comprise more than 12% of the park's total area. Glacier achieved National Park status under the 1911 Dominion Forest Reserves and Parks Act.

• Paul Oscar Esterhazy (1831–1912) led 35 families from the mining towns of Pennsylvania to Sask. where they founded New Hungary (Esterhazy).

• John A. Fraser painted *At The Rogers Pass Summit of the Selkirk Range, BC,* oil on canvas, now in the National Gallery of Canada. Fraser also painted *Mount Baker from Stave River, at the Confluence with the Fraser on Line of CPR,* oil on canvas, as a result of free train passage offered him by William Van Horne, president of the CPR. The painting is now at the Glenbow Museum, Calgary.

• Robert Harris painted *A Meeting of the School Trustees,* oil on canvas, an early feminist theme showing Pine Creek School (PEI) teacher Kate Henderson standing her ground against a board of trustees. The painting is now in the National Gallery of Canada.

• Daniel Fowler painted the watercolour *Fallen Birch,* which is now in the National Gallery of Canada.

• Poet Charles Mair published the long poem "Tecumseh."

• Isabella Valancy Crawford's novel *A Little Bacchante* was serialized in the *Evening Globe.*

• Joseph Edmund Collins (1855–1892) published the novel *Annette, the Métis Spy,* one of the earliest pieces of Western Canadian fiction.

• Susie Francis Harrison, née Riley (1859–1935), produced the short-story collection *Crowded Out and Other Sketches.*

1887

Jan. 6 The 1st union in Alb. was formed at Medicine Hat, when Cascade Lodge No. 342 of the Brotherhood of Locomotive Firemen was established.

Jan. 29 Que. provincial Liberal leader Honoré Mercier, became premier, following the resignation of the Conservative Louis-Olivier Taillon administration. Mercier, a founder of the Parti National, was one of the 1st Que. premiers to embrace Que. nationalism.

Feb. 22 John A. Macdonald's Conservatives won 123 seats, to Wilfrid Laurier's Liberals' 92, in the general election. Louis Riel's hanging was an important election issue.

Feb. 24 Vancouver's city charter was suspended by the BC govt as a result of citywide riots against Chinese immigration.

Also in Feb.
• The Canadian Society of Civil Engineers was founded as a not-for-profit organization to advocate for engineer interests and provide network, education and exchange opportunities cross-country. The society elected its 1st woman president — Cathy Lynn Borbely — in 2004.

Mar. 3 The US Fisheries Retaliation Act provided for the exclusion of Canadian vessels in US waters and prohibited the importation of Canadian goods. This law, which was not used, was enacted following the July 1, 1885, cessation of fishery clauses in the Treaty of Washington, and also after Canada barred port privileges to US deep-sea fishing vessels in 1886.

Mar. 4 Big Bear was released from the Stony Mountain Penitentiary after serving 2 years for treason, a felony related to the 1885 Northwest Rebellion.

Mar. 14 Federal Liberal Richard J. Cartwright introduced a parliamentary motion for "the largest possible freedom of commercial intercourse" between Canada and the US.

Also in Mar.
• Homer Watson completed *Before the Storm*, oil on canvas, now in the Art Gallery of Windsor, Ont.

Spring The Man. Parliament, under Premier John Norquay, passed the Red River Valley Railway Act, providing for the construction of a railroad from Winnipeg to West Lynne, Man., connecting to the Northern Pacific Railway at Pembina. Man. was bitterly opposed to the CPR monopoly in the province. On July 16, the federal govt ordered Man.'s lt-gov. to disallow the act. The Man. govt ignored this disavowal and proceeded with construction. However, when funds promised for the project under federal land-grant policies failed to materialize, Norquay's govt was forced to resign. It was replaced by the nonpartisan govt of David H. Harrison (1843–1905) on Dec. 26, 1887.

Apr. 2 The US seized Canadian sealing ships in North Pacific open waters. A declining seal population forced sealers farther afield. The US and Canada sparred over sealing limits, and subsequent Canadian ships were seized on Apr. 9, 12 and 17, and also the *Anna Bick* in the Bering Sea on July 2. On Feb. 19, 1892, Britain and the US submitted their Bering Sea fishing dispute to arbitration. On Mar. 23, 1893, the Bering Sea international tribunal met in Paris to determine whether Canadians had the right to hunt seals in open waters near the American-owned Pribilof Islands. The tribunal upheld Canadian rights, with some restrictions, denying the US the right to prohibit fishing beyond its 3-mile (4.8-km) limit.

Apr. 4 Canada sent Alexander Campbell and Sandford Fleming to the 1st Imperial Conference in London as official representatives.

Apr. 13 The 1st session of the 6th Parliament met until June 23. The Department of Trade and Commerce was established. Employees of incorporated companies were allowed to establish pension fund societies.

Apr. 23 McMaster University was founded on Bloor St. in Toronto by the union of Woodstock College and the Toronto Baptist College. The institution moved to its present location in Hamilton in 1930.

Apr. 27 The NS legislature passed a motion postponing withdrawal from Confederation.

May 3 A coal-mine explosion at Nanaimo, BC, killed 150.

May 26 Britain gave Canada power to negotiate its own commercial treaties with foreign powers.

June 1 Sir Alexander Campbell was appointed lt-gov. of Ont.

June 2 Edward Blake resigned as Liberal leader of the opposition in Parliament, to be succeeded by Wilfrid Laurier.

• Last Lake Bird Sanctuary (10 km^2) was established in the NWT (Sask.) as the 1st bird sanctuary in NA.

June 14 The 3,063-tonne CPR steamer *Abyssinia* arrived in Vancouver from Yokohama, Japan, with first-class passengers, tea, silk and mail, inaugurating direct trade between Vancouver, Yokohama, Shanghai and Hong Kong.

June 23 Federal charters were issued to the Halifax and West India Steamship Company and the Canada Atlantic Steamship Company.

July 18 Col. Sam Steele, commanding the NWMP, left Golden, BC, for Wild Horse, near Cranbrook, to settle conflict between the Kootenai and new settlers. He reached Wild Horse on July 30 where he proceeded to establish Fort Steele.

July 20 The province of BC officially opened its dry-dock facility of Esquimalt. The facility was part of an 1885 agreement making Esquimalt the Pacific headquarters of Britain's Royal Navy.

Sept. 23 John Bayne MacLean (1862–1950) resigned his editorial position with Toronto's *The Mail* to launch the *Canadian Grocer*, with upfront capital of $2,000. The 1st issue was 16 pages, and subsequent issues appeared weekly.

Also in Sept. The Toronto Conservatory of Music, now the Royal Conservatory of Music, opened in Toronto. It was incorporated Nov. 20, 1886. The Conservatory offered programs in music history, composition, orchestra and ensemble playing. The 1st student body numbered 600 and was taught by a faculty of 50.

Oct. 2 A sturgeon measuring 3.58 m was caught at Ladner's Landing, BC. It weighed 374 kg.

Oct. 20 An Interprovincial Conference of Premiers headed by Oliver Mowat was held at Quebec. PM Macdonald asked Conservative premiers to boycott the meeting, which, with the exception of Premier Norquay from Man., they did. Twenty-one resolutions were adopted, including a free trade resolution with the US. Also included on the conference agenda was a discussion of grievances against the federal govt. Que. Premier Mercier threatened separation and the formation of an independent "Laurentian State" in an attempt to force the federal govt to provide Que. with increased powers over administrative and fiscal matters.

Dec. 3 *Saturday Night Magazine* published its inaugural issue with Edmund Ernest Sheppard (1855–1924) as editor. It was a weekly publication in newspaper format, priced at 5 cents. The entire print run of 9,500 copies sold out. Sheppard's editorial critiques published in future issues under the "Don" signature became a magazine highlight.

Also in 1887
The population of Vancouver was 5,000.

• The Langevin Block on Wellington St. in Ottawa was built to accommodate the federal govt civil service.

• Montreal's Royal Victoria Hospital was founded by Donald Smith and George Stephen.

• Victoria School, Sask.'s 1st school and oldest public building was established. Classes were held until 1905. The old stone school is now situated on the U. of Sask. campus.

• The CPR opened the Hotel Vancouver. Critics argued that the original 4-storey, 60 room wooden structure at Georgia and Granville Streets was located too far from the downtown core. The hotel has since become an award-winning Fairmont Hotel.

• Four hundred American fishing vessels were seized by Canadian patrols for violations of Canadian fishing regulations.

• George M. Dawson and R.G. McConnell explored

northern BC and the headwaters of the Yukon River.

• There were 135 brokers and individuals engaged in the Toronto real estate business, according to the Toronto Directory. Also this year, the Toronto Real Estate Exchange held its 1st property auction.

• Quebec artist Ozias Leduc (1864–1955) painted *Les Trois Pommes*, oil on canvas, now in a private collection.

• Graeme Mercer Adam and Agnes Ethelwyn Wetherald (1857–1940) co-authored the romance novel *An Algonquin Maiden*.

• Sarah Anne Curzon's (1833–1898) 1876 blank-verse drama in 3 acts, *Laura Secord: the Heroine of 1812*, was published.

• Socialist, labour radical and influential spokesman for the Knights of Labour, Thomas Phillips Thompson (1843–1933) published *Politics of Labor*.

1888

Jan. 9 A bascule railway drawbridge linking the CPR to US railroads was completed at Sault Ste. Marie, Ont.

Jan. 23 Natural gas was discovered at Kingsville, Ont., and the country's 1st gas well drilled there in 1889.

Feb. 15 The Chamberlain-Bayard Treaty, signed by Britain and the US, gave US ships access to Canadian harbours. The treaty was rejected by the US Senate, but Canada allowed American fishermen to take out Canadian fishing licences, as per treaty terms, at a flat fee of $1.50 per ton.

Feb. 23 The 2nd session of the 6th Parliament met until May 22, and decreed that the average rate of duty on imports be set at 22%.

Feb. 24 The Grand Trunk Railway amalgamated with The Hamilton and North-Western Railway Company and the Northern Railway Company of Canada.

Mar. 1 Parcel post between Canada and the US was established.

Mar. 14 The Vancouver Real Estate Board, the 1st of its kind in Canada, was established to provide a uniform system of sales commissions, accurate and rapid communication between land owners and real estate agents, and to conduct business in a suitable central office.

May 1 Frederick Arthur Stanley, Lord Stanley of Preston (1841–1908), was commissioned gov-gen. of Canada, succeeding the Marquess of Lansdowne. He served from June 11 to Sept. 6, 1893.

May 24 Queen Victoria Park, at Niagara Falls, was opened to save the area from hucksters and speculators. It was the 1st Canadian provincial park.

June 1 The CPR opened the log-framed Banff Springs Hotel in the Bow Valley outside Banff National Park, as part of CPR general manager William Van Horne's scheme to get more tourists onto the railroad. "If we can't export the mountains," he said, "then we shall have to import the tourists." Plans for the hotel had to be quickly revised after construction started and Van Horne discovered, to his horror, that the kitchens would overlook the scenic Bow Valley and the guest rooms would face the foot of Sulphur Mountain. The revised plans included a viewing pavilion for guests, and the finished hotel opened on schedule.

June 19 Que. Premier Mercier instituted factory regulations, putting into effect an 1885 law on child labour and minimum factory sanitary conditions. He also appointed the province's 1st factory inspectors to insure the law was enforced.

July 26 The *Beaver*, the 1st steamer to ply West Coast waters, was wrecked just outside Vancouver Harbour.

Also in July

• The Que. legislature passed the Jesuits Estate Act authorizing payment of $400,000 for property confiscated from the Jesuit Order in 1773. On Jan. 10, 1889, Pope Leo XIII, appointed as arbitrator by the Que. legislature, divided the funds: to the Jesuits, $160,000; the Université de Laval, $100,000; the Montreal branch of the Université de Laval, $40,000; the prefecture apostolic of the Gulf of St. Lawrence, $20,000; and to each diocese, $10,000.

Aug. 7 George Stephen officially announced his resignation as president of the CPR. William Van Horne, his successor, would remain the CPR president until June 12, 1899.

• Fort Steele established under NWMP direction in 1887 was abandoned as relations between the Kootenai and settlers improved under Sam Steele's administration.

Aug. 16 A tornado hit Que., travelling between St. Estique and Valleyfield. Nine people died, 14 were injured and damage to property was extensive.

Sept. 26 Printer Alphonse-Télesphore Lépine, a member of the Knights of Labor, became the 1st labour MP elected in Que.

Sept. 27 Vancouver city fathers under the leadership of Mayor David Oppenheimer (1834–1897) dedicated Stanley Park, with 11.6 km of seafront walkways, to people "of all creeds and colours."

Also in 1888

• The Canada Copper Company began smelting operations in Sudbury, Ont.

• Constable Alfred Symonds of the NWMP detachment of Stand Off was accused of murdering a Blood woman named Mrs. Only Kill by giving her a fatal dose of iodine. In Aug. 1888, Symonds appeared before Judge James F. Macleod, former commissioner of the NWMP. The crown prosecutor made application for "nolle Prosequi," which was granted and Symonds was released.

• BC increased its timber-licencing fees from 1 to 10 cents an acre with royalties of 20 to 25 cents per 1,000 feet rental, and to 5 cents an acre rental with royalities 50 cents per 1,000 feet. Future leases were limited to a 30-year term.

• The federal govt cancelled the monopoly clause in its contract with the CPR.

• CPR engineers designed 6 rotary snowplows based on the designs of Orange Jull, to keep rail lines clear of snow

• John R. Barber generated Canada's 1st hydroelectric power at his Georgetown, Ont., paper mill.

• Archibald Lampman (1861–1899) published *Among the Millet and Other Poems.*

• Hamilton, Ont., native William Blair Bruce (1859–1906) completed *The Phantom Hunter,* oil on canvas, inspired by C.D. Shanly's poem "The Walker of the Snow." It is now in the Art Gallery of Hamilton, Ont.

• Marmaduke Matthews (1837–1913) completed the painting *Hermit Range, Rocky Mountains,* now in the Art Gallery of Ont., Toronto.

• James De Mille's anti-Utopian novel, *A Strange Manuscript Found in a Copper Cylinder,* was published.

• *De Roberval,* an historical drama based on the life of Jean-François de La Rocque de Roberval, by John Hunter-Duvar (1830–1899), was published in Saint John, NB.

1889

Jan. 31 The 3rd session of the 6th Parliament met, until May 2. The average rate of customs duties was increased to 31.9%, and a $200,000 per annum mail subsidy was granted to the Canadian Pacific Steamship Company for bi-monthly service to the Far East.

Feb. 11 The Montreal L. and Lac La Ronge Woodland Cree signed an extension to Treaty No. 6, adding 28,490 km² of land between the North Sask. and Churchill Rivers, north of Prince Albert, to the original Treaty signed in 1876.

Feb. 14 Weavers at Cornwall, Ont., walked out on a 5-day strike.

Feb. 19 The govt of Canada issued a pardon to Gabriel Dumont for his involvement in the Northwest Rebellion.

Mar. 6 Toronto customs authorities seized and destroyed copies of the novels of Emile Zola.

Mar. 21 Sorel, Que., received a city charter.

Mar. 28 Parliament defeated a motion to disallow the Que. Jesuits' Estate Act on the basis that public funds were being given to religious organizations.

May 2 The federal govt passed An Act for the Prevention and Suppression of Combinations in Restraint of Trade, to prevent price fixing, restraint of trade, or restraint of output. Corporations found guilty of this act could be fined between $1,000 and $10,000; individuals between $200 and $4,000. Canada was one of the 1st nations in the world to pass competition legislation.

May 22 The Allan Line steamer *Polynesian* collided with the Donaldson Line steamer *Cynthia* in the St. Lawrence. Eight lives were lost.

May 24 Colonist, a 3-year-old brown gelding owned by Joseph Duggan, groundkeeper of Woodbine Racetrack in Ont., and his partner J.D. Matheson, a druggist, won the Queen's Plate in a record 2:16, with jockey Richard O'Leary aboard. Duggan and Matheson had bought the horse only 2 months previously for $400.

June 2 The Short Line Railroad, built by the CPR through Maine to connect Montreal and Saint John, was opened.

June 7 Political adversaries Conservative PM Macdonald and Liberal Premier of Ont. Oliver Mowat both received honorary LL.D. degrees from the U. of Toronto.

June 11 The Equal Rights Association, an anti-Catholic and anti-French organization, headed by D'Alton McCarthy (1836–1898), was formed in Toronto to ensure that Catholicism did not receive preferential treatment from the govt. The organization was formed in response to the Jesuits' Estate Act, passed in Que. in July 1888.

June 17–30 Thomas Weston discovered the rich dinosaur fossil deposits in Alb.'s Red Deer R. valley, which he described as the most important field in Canada, so far as the bones of extinct animals were concerned.

June 23–25 The Que. govt staged a rally, in Quebec City for the Feast of Saint-Jean Baptiste, Patron of French Canadians. The Saint-Jean Baptiste Society unveiled a monument to Jesuit martyr Jean de Brébeuf and Jacques Cartier. Premier Honoré Mercier and federal Liberal leader Wilfrid Laurier both spoke in defence of French Canadians.

July 15 The British postmaster awarded the CPR a contract to transport mail by CP trains and ships from Halifax or Quebec to Hong Kong.

Also in July

• Future reformer and women's rights activist Nellie McClung, née Mooney (1873–1951), passed her exams in Brandon, Man., making her eligible to train as a teacher, which she did at the Normal School in Winnipeg.

Aug. 12 The Privy Council resolution of the boundary dispute between Ont. and Man. was legislated into law by the British Parliament; 58,291 ha (144,000 acres) between Port Arthur and L. of the Woods (including Rat Portage) were transferred to Ont., and Man. became a landlocked province.

Aug. 15 The Murray Bay Canal connecting the Bay of Quinte to L. Ont. opened.

Aug. 17 The Canadian College of Music opened in Ottawa.

Sept. 19 A landslide at Quebec City killed 45 people.

Oct. 9 The Soulanges Canal opened, completing a waterway from Que. to L. Superior.

Nov. Kathleen "Kit" Blake Watkins (1856–1915) began her "Fashion Notes and Fancies for the Fair Sex" column in the *Toronto Mail* under the pen name Kit Coleman. Her salary was $35 per week. The column would continue as a popular part of the paper for 22 years.

Dec. 4 Lt. William Grant Stairs (1863–1892), of the Canadian Royal Engineers, entered Bagamoyo, on the east coast of Africa, commanding the surviving members of Henry Morton Stanley's cross-Africa expedition. Stanley had preceded his men. The largest African expedition ever assembled included 600 porters. It began at the mouth of the Congo on the other side of the continent in 1887. Expedition members battled malaria, starvation, even insanity, in their quest to locate and relieve former British Lt. Emin Pasha, believed to be stockpiling ivory in the depths of central Africa. Emin was finally located, brought to Bagamoyo, but refused to leave Africa. He was eventually murdered by Arab slave traders in 1892. Stanley was feted as a hero on his return to Europe; Lt. Stairs died somewhere along the Congo in 1892. The expedition was the inspiration for Joseph Conrad's *Heart of Darkness*.

Dec. 18 The CPR Telegraph was connected with the Atlantic cable at Canso, NS.

Also in Dec.
• The municipal govt at Port Arthur, Ont., confiscated a CPR train, holding it until the company paid $15,000 in back taxes.

Also in 1889
• Toronto's Board of Trade Building was completed. Located on the corner of Front and Yonge Streets, the 6-storey structure was Toronto's 1st steel-framed building.

• The U. of Ottawa received a pontifical charter to grant degrees in philosophy, theology, and canon law.

• Springhill, NS, was incorporated.

• BC fisheries packed 9,054,957 kg of salmon.

• Ukrainian Germans settled near Medicine Hat.

• *Lake Lyrics and Other Poems*, by William Wilfred Campbell (1858–1918), was published at Saint John, NB.

• Paul Peel painted *A Venetian Bather*, which appeared in a one-man auction show in Toronto in 1890, as the 1st nude to be publicly exhibited in the city. Peel also completed *After the Bath* in 1890, for which he won a bronze medal at the Salon in Paris. This, his most famous picture, is now in the Art Gallery of Ont., Toronto.

• George Reid (1860–1947) painted *Forbidden Fruit*, oil on canvas, now in the Art Gallery of Hamilton.

• George Frederick Cameron's (1854–1885) libretto for the military opera *Leo, the Royal Cadet,* was published posthumously by brother Charles John Cameron and appeared over the joint names of George and the composer Oscar F. Telgmann (1855–1946). The work was a lighthearted piece about love and war, somewhat similar to the works

of Gilbert and Sullivan. It was performed in Kingston and several other Ont. cities.

c 1880s Frank McGee (d 1916), one-eyed hockey centre and rover for the Ottawa Silver Seven was born. McGee's career lasted 4 seasons (1903–1906) during which the Ottawa team won 3 Stanley Cups. During 1 game in the 1905 playoffs, McGee scored 8 consecutive goals in less than 8 minutes. McGee was killed fighting in France in WW I, and was elected to the Hockey Hall of Fame in 1945.

1890

Feb. 1 James Wilson Robertson (1857–1930) was appointed the 1st Dominion Dairy Commissioner and agriculturalist on the staff of the Central Experimental Farm in Ottawa.

Feb. 14 The main building of the U. of Toronto was partially destroyed by fire, with $500,000 in damage.

Also in Feb.
• Canada Atlantic Railway opened a bridge spanning the St. Lawrence R. at the village of Coteau, Que.

Mar. 19 The 38.4-m paddle steamer *Dagmar*, built for the Ottawa River Navigation Company to carry passengers to ports along the Ottawa R. and Montreal, was destroyed by fire at the wharf at Como, Que.

Mar. 31 The Man. Parliament passed the Man. School Act abolishing separate schools for Catholics and Protestants. As of May 1, the newly created Man. Department of Education assumed control over a non-sectarian system of public education, and full authority over curriculum, textbooks, examinations, qualifications of teachers, and the limited religious exercises authorized in the now non-sectarian schools. English became the official language of instruction.

Apr. 7 The Ont. govt granted its municipalities the option of whether or not to allow the sale of liquor.

Apr. 25 Blackfoot chief Crowfoot died of tuberculosis.

May 6 The asylum for the insane at Longue Point, Que., was destroyed by fire. Seventy people died.

May 12 NWMP Lt-Gen. Middletown was convicted by Parliament of misappropriating furs during his command of the Northwest Rebellion. He resigned from his post under censure, but went on to become keeper of the Crown Jewels in London, England.

June 27 Halifax boxer George Dixon (1870–1909) won the world bantamweight boxing crown in London, England. He was the 1st black man to win a world title, and became the 1st boxer to hold 3 world titles: paperweight, bantamweight and featherweight.

July 1 Cable communications between Canada and Bermuda were established.

July 21 Eugene Sayre Topping (1844–1917), writer, sailor and miner, purchased Le Roi gold mine in BC for $1,250. Le Roi would become one of the richest mines in the world.

Aug. 15 The Toronto Railway Company launched its 1st high-speed electric trams for travel in the city.

Also in Aug.
• A Church of England conference at Winnipeg established the union of all synods.

Sept. 14 Petroleum was discovered in Alb. along the Athabasca R.

Oct. 1 The US McKinley Tariff Act went into effect, raising American tariff protection to its highest level in history. Canada's few export specialties to the US, especially the lucrative trade in barley, were seriously affected.

Oct. 22 A CPR branch line, linking Prince Albert with the main CPR line through Regina was completed.

Nov. 21 Ont. and Que. First Nations petitioned to elect their own chiefs, while still subject to the Queen.

Nov. 24 The Cape Breton Railway from Point Tupper to Sydney, Cape Breton, via Bras d'Or Lakes, was added as part of the Intercolonial Railway.

Dec. 15 Law enforcement officers shot and killed Chief Sitting Bull in North Dakota while attempting to arrest him on orders of the US Army.

Dec. 29 One hundred and fifty-three Sioux women and children were massacred by US Cavalry at Wounded Knee Creek in South Dakota.

c 1890 The National Archives holds the earliest-known photograph of women playing hockey, taken at Rideau Hall, Ottawa, circa 1890. The action shot shows 7 women in skate-length skirts chasing down Lord Stanley's daughter, Isobel, the only participant dressed in white. By the early 1900s, women had organized teams throughout the country, even in Dawson City, where teams battled it out on an indoor rink at the height of the gold rush.

Also in 1890
• Canada's population was 4,779,000.

• There were 75,964 factories in Canada, employing 369,595 people.

• The federal govt prohibited the killing of wildlife at Rocky Mountain Park at Banff Hot Springs except on the authorization of the park superintendent.

• Bishop's U. in Lennoxville, Que., admitted women to its faculty of medicine.

• The CPR opened Chateau Lake Louise, a 1-storey log cabin with a central eating area, office and bar, a kitchen, 2 small bedrooms and a veranda ("a hotel for the outdoor adventurer and alpinist," in the words of CPR President Cornelius Van Horne). The cabin sat on the foot of Lake Louise, a bright turquois lake surrounded by towering mountaintops and glacial snowfields. Fifty guests stayed at the chalet during its 1st year of operation; by 1912, the number had risen to over 50,000. When CPR worker Thomas Wilson was led to the area by Stoney Aboriginals in 1882, he exclaimed, "As God is my judge, I never in all my explorations saw such a matchless scene." The remodelled Chateau is now part of Banff National Park and is one of the world's foremost destination spots.

• Craigdarroch Castle, located on an 11-ha site at the highest point on Victoria Is., BC, was completed for coal baron Robert Dunsmuir by architect Warren H. Williams (1844–1888) in association with Arthur Smith. Dunsmuir died a year before his castle was finished and it became residence to his widowed wife, Joan, and their three unmarried daughters until her death in 1908. The castle was then occupied by various institutions including, Victoria College and the Victoria Conservatory of Music. Today the castle is a historic-house museum owned by the city of Victoria.

• John J. McLaughlin (1865–1914), Toronto chemist, 1st produced his McLaughlin Belfast Style Ginger Ale, the predecessor to his Canada Dry Pale Dry Ginger Ale, which he patented in 1907.

• There were 41 commercial wineries in Canada, of which 35 were in Ont.

• German-American Emile Berliner (1851–1929), inventor of the gramophone disc recording (making records producible from a master recording) opened the Berliner Gram-O-Phone Company in Montreal, which produced, manufactured and sold gramophone discs in both French and English. Also in 1900, Berliner trademarked the famous "Nipper" logo (a dog listening to the gramophone) which 1st appeared on the Montreal-produced record "Hello My Baby" by Frank Banta. By the end of 1901, Berliner had sold more than 2 million gramophone records.

• Louis Rubenstein (1861–1931) won the world's 1st unofficial figure-skating championships in Russia. He had been Canadian figure-skating champion from 1883–1889.

• Sara Jeannette Duncan (1861–1922) published her 1st novel, *A Social Departure,* based on experiences drawn from her 1888 round-the-world tour.

• *A Short History of Newfoundland: England's Oldest Colony,* by Presbyterian clergyman and essayist Moses Harvey (1820–1901), was published.

• George Reid , who studied under Robert Harris at Central Ontario School of Art in Toronto and also in Paris, completed *Mortgaging the Homestead,* oil on canvas, now in the National Gallery of Canada.

• The adventure novel for boys, *Up Among the Ice Floes,* by James Macdonald Oxley (1855–1907), was published.

1891

Jan. 21 A coal mine explosion in Springhill, NS, killed 125 men.

Mar. 5 Working under the slogan, "the old man, the old flag, the old policy," the Conservatives under John A. Macdonald won 123 seats in the general election against 92 for the Liberals under Wilfrid Laurier. Support of protective tariffs were key factors in the campaign.

Spring A group of French-Canadian colonists from Eastern Canada under Abbé Jean-Baptiste Morin (1852–1911) established a settlement 30 km north of Edmonton. On Oct. 15, the 1st chapel was established and in 1892 the settlement was named Morinville.

Apr. 20 The Edison Electric Plant (Canadian General Electric) in Peterborough, Ont., celebrated its grand opening.

Apr. 21 Liberal leader Frederick Peters (1852–1919) became premier of PEI following a series of Conservative by-election defeats.

Apr. 28 The *Empress of India*, 1st of 3 liners the CPR ordered from Great Britain in Oct. 1889, docked in Vancouver after crossing from Yokohama in record time. The remaining 2 ships, *Empress of Japan* and *Empress of China*, would arrive shortly after. The CPR advertised all 3 with the slogan "Round the World in 80 days — $600" and their white hulls and yellow funnels became a welcome sight in BC waters.

Apr. 29 The 1st session of the 7th Parliament met, until Sept. 30. This was known as the "scandal session" because of the numerous charges of poor administration directed at various Macdonald govt departments.

May 4 The Bureau of Mines of Ont. was established.

May 23 Victorious, Joseph Seagram's (1841–1919) 3-year-old bay gelding won the Queen's Plate in record time (2:14:5), with jockey Michael Gorman aboard.

June 6 PM John A. Macdonald, a Father of Confederation and the country's 1st PM, died in his Ottawa home, Earnscliffe, after suffering a stroke. In a speech given 6 years before he 1st became PM on July 1, 1867, Macdonald summed up a belief in nationhood that would carry him through the rest of his political career: "Whatever you do, adhere to the Union — we are a great country, and shall become one of the greatest in the universe if we preserve it; we shall sink into insignificance and adversity if we suffer it to be broken."

June 16–Nov. 24, 1892 Conservative John Joseph Caldwell Abbott of Que. served as Canada's 3rd PM. He had previously been solicitor-gen. and mayor of Montreal.

July 28 The 1st annual Harvest Excursion train left from points east for the prairies, carrying 1,300 temporary workers to help grain farmers bring in their crops.

Aug. 11 The CPR branch line between Calgary and Strathcona (Edmonton) was completed.

Also in Aug.

• Sir Hector Langevin, minister of labour, resigned his position following charges of corruption levied against him and the Labour Department. Although acquitted of malfeasance, he was found guilty of negligence in office.

Sept. 19 The nearly 2 km-long underwater St. Clair Tunnel linking Sarnia and Port Huron, Michigan, the world's 1st international sub-marine tunnel, was completed for use by the Grand Trunk Railroad. The tunnel would be enlarged to accommodate triple-deck cars and monster cargo carriers and reopened Dec. 8, 1994.

Oct. 28 The Supreme Court declared the Man. School Act unconstitutional. The act, which abolished separate schools in the province, was passed in the Man. Parliament Mar. 31, 1890. However, on July 30, 1892, the Imperial Privy Council upheld Man.'s right to abolish separate schools. The Supreme Court of Canada would deny Catholic Manitobans the right

to appeal the province's School Act, ruling on Feb. 20, 1894 that legislation concerning schools was outside federal jurisdiction.

Dec. 8 Canada set a duty on fish from Nfld. in retaliation for Nfld.'s law restricting bait for Canadian fishermen.

Dec. 15 Que. Premier Mercier was dismissed from office by Lt-Gov. Auguste Réal Angers (1838–1919) because of allegations that he had accepted contributions to the Liberal party in return for public contracts (Baie des Chaleurs Scandal).

Dec. 21 Before more than 10,000 witness at Sohmer Park in Montreal, Louis Cyr (1863–1912) of St. Cyprien de Napierville, Que., lived up to his billing as the "Strongest Man on Earth" by standing his ground and not being budged by 4 massive draught horses. The following year, 1892, Cyr won the world weightlifting championship and would eventually go on to lift 1,967 kg at one time.

Dec. 28 James Naismith (1861–1939) of Almonte, Ont., introduced the game of basketball at the YMCA International Training School in Springfield, Mass. Bushel baskets were used as hoops during this, the 1st basketball game ever played.

Dec. 31 British-born writer Goldwin Smith (1823-1910) published *Canada and the Canadian Question*, arguing for a continental union between Canada and the US as the best means to facilitate and further natural trade routes running north and south.

Also in 1891

• The population of Canada was 4,833,239: Ont., 2,114,321; Que., 1,488,535; NS, 450,396; NB, 321,263; Man., 152,506; PEI, 109,078; BC, 98,173; and the NWT, 98,967.

• The Granby Copper Mine was established in Phoenix, BC.

• John B. MacLean's magazine empire included, in addition to the *Canadian Grocer, Bookseller and Stationer, Hardware Merchandising*, and *Dry Goods Review*. He would add *Canadian Printer and Publisher* in May 1892 and *Art Weekly* in 1893.

• The *Toronto Star* was 1st published.

• The Royal Montreal Golf Club became the 1st in North America to allow women members.

• Vasyl Eleniak (1859–1956) and Ivan Pylpypiw (1859–1936) were the 1st Ukrainian immigrants to arrive in Canada.

• Lady Hariot Dufferin's (née Hamilton, 1866–1918) weekly letters home to her mother were published as *My Canadian Journal*.

• *An American Girl in London*, by Sara Jeannette Duncan (1861–1922), was published.

• Lily Dougall's (1858–1923) novel *Beggers All* was published as the 1st in a series of 10.

1892

Jan. 9 Edmonton was incorporated as a town and Matthew McCauley (1850–1930) became the 1st mayor.

Also in Jan.
• The sidewheeler *Acadia* (originally named *Fawn*) burned in Saint John Harbour.

Feb. 10–15 Reciprocity discussions in Washington between Canadian and US representatives failed; no decision was reached.

Feb. 19 Mohawk poet Emily Pauline Johnson (Tekahismwake) (1861–1913) made her stage debut at Association Hall in Toronto, reading original poems to a sold-out audience.

Feb. 25 The 2nd session of the 7th Parliament met, until July 9. The Criminal Code was enacted as a consolidated codification of all criminal offences in Canada, with definitions regarding procedure and sentencing.

Apr. 1 The NA Canal Company was contracted to deepen the St. Lawrence R. and build canals from L. Erie to L. Ontario and from L. Francis to L. Champlain and on to the Hudson R.

Apr. 14 Windsor, Ont., received a city charter.

Apr. 20 Attorney Gen. Thomas Chase Casgrain (1852–1916) charged former Que. Premier Honoré Mercier of defrauding the public treasury of $60,000 by awarding a contract to bookseller Joseph-Alfred Langlais (d 1928). Mercier was acquitted of the charge on Nov. 4.

Apr. 30 The Université Sainte-Anne at Church Point, NS, was given university status. Founded by Eudist priests on Sept. 1, 1890, the Université remains the only French-language university in the province.

May 10 The Grand Trunk Railway amalgamated with the Northern and Pacific Junction Railway Company.

Also in May
• Forty-seven Jewish families took up farming homesteads at Hirsch, NWT (Sask.), sponsored by the Young Men's Hebrew Benevolent Society of Montreal and Baron Maurice de Hirsch (1831–1896).

July 6–9 A fire, set by arson, destroyed two-thirds of St. John's, Nfld.; 12,000-plus people were left homeless, and 2 people were killed. Investigating Justice Daniel Woodley Prowse (1834–1914) blamed the extent of the fire on the fire department's gross negligence.

July 23 Man. voted in favour of prohibition, although the legislation was not put into effect.

July 30 Thomas Ahearn (1855–1938), electrical entrepreneur, invented an electric cooking stove that he had installed in Montreal's Windsor Hotel and upon which he cooked a full meal for Windsor guests on this date. It was the 1st meal cooked entirely with electricity and a marvellous publicity boon for Ahearn and his Ottawa Electric Company.

Sept. 20 The paddle steamer *Corinthian* caught fire while passing the St. Lawrence R. Coteau Rapids and burned to the water's edge. It was beached and all passengers escaped.

Sept. 28 NB abolished its Legislative Council.

Nov. 10 The 1st National championship Canadian football game was held at Rosedale Field, Toronto, between the Montreal Foot-Ball Club and the

Osgoode Hall Rugby Club, Toronto. Two-thousand fans set aside their Thanksgiving lunches to witness Osgoode shellac Montreal 45 to 5. A total of 5 rouges were recorded.

Nov. 24 PM Abbott resigned due to ill health. He was succeeded by John Sparrow David Thompson (1844–1894), who served as Conservative PM from Nov. 25, 1892 to Dec. 12, 1894.

Dec. 3 Mackenzie Bowell (1823–1917) became Canada's 1st minister of trade and commerce. A newspaper man and Orangeman, Bowell held the North Hastings (Ont.) riding.

Also in 1892

• Massey Hall opened to the public. Its inaugural concert featured Handel's *Messiah*. Designed by C.R. Badgely and built on Shuter St. in Toronto at a cost of $150,000, Toronto's 1st major concert hall was given to the city by Hart A. Massey, the farm implement manufacturer. Massey Hall had 4,000 seats and was ranked 1 of the 6 best acoustic halls in the world by a Professor Winckel of Berlin U.

• Abortion and the sale of all forms of birth control were made illegal by Section 179 of the Canadian Criminal Code. Offenders were subject to 2 years in jail. This law would not change until 1969.

• Thomas "Carbide" Wilson (1860–1915) discovered carbide, the basis of batteries, by mixing lime and coal tar. Wilson would receive over 70 patents for his wide range of discoveries and inventions, including the production of acetylene gas in commercial quantities.

• Businessman Jeffry Hall Brock opened the Great-West Life Assurance Company in Winnipeg. By the mid-1970s, Great-West would cover over 2 million people in both Canada and the United States.

• *Ericsson,* a 9.15-m sidewheeler barque (built in 1853 by Swedish-born inventor John Ericsson) sank in Barkley Sound, BC. The boat had been equipped with an experimental caloric hot-air engine, which made it cumbersome to navigate.

• The Columbia and Kootenay Railroad connecting Nelson, BC, to the Columbia R. was built.

• *Calgary Herald* printers went on strike for pay. Times were tough and general manager J.A. Ried neglected to pay his staff their weekly $16–18 wage for a 54-hour workweek.

• The Continental Union League was created in New York, espousing the union of the US and Canada. Its members included John Jacob Astor, Theodore Roosevelt, Andrew Carnegie, Charles L. Tiffany, William C. Whitney, Elihu Root and others. Like-minded Canadians formed the affliated Continental Union Association with Goldwin Smith as honorary president.

• Canadian physician William Osler (1849–1919), specialist in diseases of the heart, lungs and blood, published the textbook *The Principles and Practice of Medicine* while serving as professor of medicine at Johns Hopkins U. in Baltimore, Maryland.

• Ozias Leduc painted *L'Enfant au pain*, oil on canvas, now in the National Gallery of Canada.

• George Robert Parkin (1846–1922), who referred to himself as the "wandering evangelist of Empire," published *Imperial Federation*, a response to Goldwin Smith's call for a North American union in his book *Canada and the Canadian Question* (1891).

1893

Jan. 22 The Que. Assembly voted beer of not more than 4% alcohol a "temperance drink."

Jan. 26 The 3rd session of the 7th Parliament met until Apr. 1, granting a subsidy for steamship service between BC and Australia and New Zealand.

Feb. 6 A commercial treaty between Canada and France allowing the French importation at low rates of duty was signed, effective Oct. 14, 1895.

Feb. 23 The 1st Stanley Cup was awarded to the Montreal Amateur Athletic Association (Montreal AAA) hockey club. The cup was named in honour of Fredrick Arthur Lord Stanley, who purchased the 15.9-kg, 19-cm-high by 29-cm-wide, gold-lined silver bowl for 10 guineas (about $48). The original cup was retired in 1969 because it had become too brittle with age. It is now displayed in the Hockey

Hall of Fame in Toronto. The Stanley Cup is the oldest trophy awarded to professional athletes in North America.

Mar. 23 A petition signed by 10,000 supporters of the radical English Protestant Orange Order demanded that Acadian Catholics not be allowed to fund a religious convent school using public-school funds.

Mar. 25 A Toronto cab driver was fined $2 or 10 days in jail for driving on Sunday.

Spring The Christian Emigration Society, based in the Netherlands, sent 102 immigrants to Winnipeg and Yorkton (Sask.) as the 1st wave of organized Dutch immigration to Canada.

Apr. 1 The Grand Trunk Railway amalgamated with the Beauharnois Junction Railway Company; the Brantford, Norfolk and Port Burwell Railway Company; the Cobourg, Blairton and Marmora Railway and Mining Company; the Galt and Guelph Railway Company; Georgian Bay and L. Erie Railway Company; the Jacques Cartier Union Railway Company; the L. Simcoe Junction Railway Company; the London, Huron and Bruce Railway Company; the Midland Railway of Canada; the Montreal and Champlain Junction Railway Company; the North Simcoe Railway Company; the Peterborough and Chemong L. Railway Company; Waterloo Junction Railway Company; and Wellington, Grey and Bruce Railway Company.

• Ont. Premier Oliver Mowat officially opened the new Ontario Parliament Buildings (Queen's Park). Designed by Englishman R.A. Waite (1848–1911), the structure cost $1.5 million, and took 6 years to build. Originally, the govt had conducted an international competition for the commission, but rejected the winning designs as too expensive and awarded Waite — one of the jurists competing — the job.

Apr. 20 The Legislative Council of PEI amalgamated with the PEI Assembly.

May 1 Joseph Burr Tyrrell, of the Geological Survey of Canada, left Ottawa on an expedition to explore

from L. Athabasca through the Barren Lands to Chesterfield Inlet. His brother, James Williams Tyrrell (1863–1945), accompanied him in the capacity of typographer and Inuit interpreter. They covered about 5,150 km in less than 1 year, mapping many lakes and rivers, and assigned the name Barren Lands to an area of the subarctic between Hudson Bay on the east and Great Slave L. and Great Bear L. on the west and extending from about latitude 59° to the shores of the Arctic Ocean. They would complete their survey and return to Winnipeg in Jan. 1894.

May 22 John Campbell Hamilton Gordon, Earl of Aberdeen (1847–1934), was appointed gov-gen. of Canada, serving from Sept. 18, 1893 to Nov. 12, 1898.

May 24 The Nfld. legislature passed an act forbidding the killing of seals on Sundays.

• Martello, Joseph Seagram's 4-year-old bay gelding, won the Queen's Plate in 2:14, a record time with jockey Harry Blaylock aboard.

May 27 Algonquin Provincial Park was established in central Ont. as a wildlife sanctuary. Its wind-swept pines, rolling hills and abundant lakes provided endless inspiration to the Group of Seven. Its 2,100 km of canoe routes has made it one of the world's most popular wilderness camping destinations.

Also in May

• The Ont. legislature passed An Act for the Prevention of Cruelty to, and Better Protection of, Children, with provisions to remove a child from any home that violated this act.

June 8 The *Miowera*, 1st steamer of the Canadian Australian Line, organized by Australian James Huddart, arrived at Victoria from Sydney, Australia.

June 19 Wilfrid Laurier's Liberal party held the 1st national Liberal political party convention in Canada, with the goal of unifying the party.

• The Liberal Reform Club of Ottawa opened. Laurier was the keynote speaker.

Also in June

• HMS *Royal Albert* arrived at Esquimalt, BC, from Portsmouth, England, after a passage of 84 days, the fastest passage to date.

Sept. 6 Future scholar, minister of labour and Liberal PM, William Lyon Mackenzie King made the 1st entry in what he called his "real companion and friend" — a prodigious diary he kept daily until his death in 1950. The work, considered by many scholars as one of the greatest literary achievements in Canadian history, spanned 30,000 pages and included 7.5 million words. It would gradually be made public between 1960 and 1980, and be fully digitized by the National Archives, May 2003.

Sept. 16 Calgary was incorporated as the 1st city in Alb. The word "Onward" graced its new coat of arms.

Oct. 27 The National Council of Women was formed in Toronto at a meeting of about 1,500. Lady Aberdeen (1857–1939) was elected president. Prominent organizers were Lady Gzowski, Dr. Emily Stowe and Adelaide Hoodless (1857–1910).

Oct. 31 Redpath Library at McGill U., Montreal, opened. It was built in the Richardsoniam Romansque style by Andrew Taylor, and donated by Peter Redpath of Redpath Sugar. All 3 floors of the innovative building were made of heavy glass to allow light to diffuse throughout the stacks.

Nov. 1 A statue of John A. Macdonald was unveiled at Hamilton, Ont.

Nov. 20 A US Supreme Court decision held that the Great Lakes and connecting waters constituted the "high seas."

Dec. 5 The 1st electric car in Canada built by Dickson Carriage Works of Toronto for F.B. Featherston-haugh made its 1st appearance. Maximum speed was 24 km/h and the car could travel 26 km before needing to be recharged.

Dec. 13 PEI voted for prohibition.

Dec. 17 The Canadian Bankers' Association was organized as a voluntary association at Montreal.

Dec. 18 Robert Machray (1831–1904) was elected 1st Anglican primate of all Canada.

Also in 1893

• The Château Frontenac Hotel opened in Quebec City, with 170 rooms, 5 wings in a U-shaped plan with a central courtyard and 2 towers. Described by its architect, Bruce Price (1846–1903), as an "early French château adopted to modern requirements," each room was filled with 16th-century furniture reproductions. The hotel, situated in the centre of the city on the cliffs, overlooking Lowertown and the St. Lawrence, was immediately one of the most recognizable landmarks in the country.

• Geologist professor A.P. Coleman (1852–1939) discovered ancient warm climate beds older than the last glaciation at Don Valley Brickyard, Toronto.

• Moraine Lake and Valley of the Ten Peaks in the Canadian Rockies (Banff National Park) were 1st seen by a European explorer — Walter Wilcox (1869–1949).

• Five farmers from Zorra, in Ont.'s Oxford County, became the world tug-of-war champions at the Chicago World's Fair. The fair also featured a 9,979.2-kg cheese made at Perth, Ont.

• The *Canadian Magazine of Politics, Science, Art and Literature* was published by the Ontario Publishing Company, whose president was lt-gov. of Man. James Colebrooke Patterson (1839–1929). The business manager was Thomas Henry Best. Issues were 150 pages or more and the magazine was priced at 15 cents a copy.

• Wilfred Thomason Grenfell (1865–1940), medical missionary, master mariner and writer established a mission and hospital for Labrador fishermen at Battle Harbour on the eastern tip of Labrador.

• René Emile Quenyin painted *Sir Alexander Mackenzie,* oil on canvas.

• Anglican bishop of the NWT, William Bompas (1834–1906), published *Northern Lights on the Bible.*

• *Low Tide on Grand Pré*, Bliss Carman's (1861–1929) 1st collection of poems, was published in New York.

Educated at the U. of New Brunswick, Fredericton-born Carman moved to New York as an editor and writer for such publications as the *Independent*, *Atlantic Monthly*, the *Cosmopolitan* and the *Chap Book*. He is also remembered for his anthology and editing work on the 10-volume *The World's Best Poetry* (1904).

• Homer Watson painted *Log-Cutting in the Woods*, which won 1st prize at the Art Association of Montreal Spring Show. The painting was immediately purchased by Lord Strathcona, and is now in the Montreal Museum of Fine Arts.

• *Stories from Canadian History*, by Thomas Guthrie Marquis (1864–1936), was published.

• Duncan Campbell Scott (1862–1947) published his 1st volume of poems, *The Magic House and Other Poems*.

• *Stories from Indian Wigwams and Northern Campfires*, by Egerton Ryerson Young (1840–1909), was published.

1894

Jan. 1 Ont. voted in favour of prohibition.

Jan. 8 The Que. legislature passed the Industrial Establishments Act, replacing its 1885 Manufacturers Act, which provided limits on hours of work and measurers for increased safety in the workplace. The new act incorporated the principle of employer civil responsibility to labour legislation and applied to all industrial establishments within provincial jurisdiction, except mines and family workshops.

Feb. 12 The NS legislature voted to conduct a plebiscite on prohibition, and voted yes to prohibition on Mar. 15.

Mar. 15 The 4th session of the 7th Parliament met, until July 23. Young offenders were to be separated from older criminals in prisons, and tea imported from England was made duty free.

Mar. 22 The Montreal Victorias won the Stanley Cup, the 1st of 4 consecutive seasons in which they would do so, beating the Ottawa Generals 3–1.

The Victorias were the 1st professional hockey team to win the trophy, which would henceforth be awarded only to professionals.

May 15 The PEI govt imposed a 1% income tax on all residents earning more than $350 a year.

Also in May
• The Great Fraser R. Valley flood ruined farms, drowned livestock and washed away railroad track, suspending CPR service for 41 days.

June 28 The Intercolonial Trade Conference opened at Ottawa (to July 10), attended by representatives of Britain and its colonies in Australia, South Africa and New Zealand, all of whom sought to develop commercial ties among themselves.

June 29 The *Montreal Witness*, a popular paper known for crusading on behalf of temperance and Protestantism, was bombed in the middle of the night. The blast caused serious damage to the building but not to the press.

June 30 The sternwheeler *William Irving* was wrecked at New Westminster, BC.

July 6 Moravians from Volhynia, in the western Ukraine, arrived at Edmonton to inspect land offered them by the federal govt.

July 23 The federal govt passed the Unorganized Territories Game Preservation Act, creating closed seasons that forbade the hunting of selected birds and mammals and forbade outright the hunting of buffalo or bison for 6 years. The act was created in response to dramatically decreasing animal populations in the NWT. Sask., Alb. and Assiniboine regions were exempted from the Act.

Sept. 3 Parliament designated Labour Day an official Canadian holiday, although labour's contribution to Canada had been celebrated unofficially since 1872. Canadian Alexander Whyte Wright (1845–1919) was a prime proponent of the official designation. Labour Day was designated as the 1st Monday of every Sept.

Nov. 3 The 1st issue of *Le Temps* was published in Ottawa.

Dec. 10 Nfld.'s Union Bank and Commercial Bank suspended business.

Dec. 12 PM John Sparrow Thompson (b 1844) died one hour after being sworn in by Queen Victoria as a member of the Imperial Privy Council, at Windsor Castle.

Dec. 21 to Apr. 27, 1896 Mackenzie Bowell, former owner and editor of the *Belleville Intelligencer* newspaper, served as PM, succeeding John Thompson.

1894–1895 The 3-volume *History of the North-West*, by journalist and historian Alexander Begg, was published in Toronto.

Also in 1894
• Rondeau Provincial Park (33 km^2) was established on a peninsula in L. Erie to protect the area's plant, animal, and bird life (with well over 300 species recorded). Rondeau became Ont.'s 3rd provincial park, after Niagara Falls and Algonquin Parks respectively.

• Que.'s 1st provincial park, Mount Tremblant (1,248 km^2), was established in the Laurentian Mountains north of Montreal. With over 100 lakes, 6 rivers, and a seemingly endless vista of rolling mountains, the park quickly became one the province's most popular destinations for campers, canoeists, hikers, skiers and mountain climbers.

• The Montreal Symphony Orchestra was founded by Belgian violinist J.J. Goulet with 40 other musicians. It would remain in existence for 20 years.

• Ozias Leduc painted *Le Petit Liseur*, oil on canvas, a striking image of his younger brother in high-school cap and uniform copying an illustration from a textbook. The painting is now held in the National Gallery of Canada.

• *Lights of a City*, oil on canvas, by Frederick Marlett Bell-Smith (1846–1923) was completed.

• *Beautiful Joe: An Autobiography of a Dog*, by Margaret Marshall Saunders (1861–1947), was published in Philadelphia; it became the 1st Canadian-authored book to sell 1 million copies.

• Six Nations minister and author Oronhyatekha (Peter Martin) (1841–1907) published *History of the Independent Order of Foresters*.

1895

Jan. 31 The Bank of NS, Royal Bank of Canada and Bank of Montreal established branches in Nfld. following the collapse of Nfld.'s Commercial and Union banks, which had suspended operations Dec. 10, 1894.

Feb. 15 U. of Toronto student William Lyon Mackenzie King (1874–1950), called "Billy" by his classmates, and other U. of Toronto students, led a boycott of classes in response to administration attempts to suppress publication of the student-run *Varsity* newspaper and the dismissal of popular Latin professor William Dale.

Mar. 21 A federal govt Order-in-Council ordered the Man. govt to restore the full rights of its Catholic minority, taxing them only for those schools which their children attended. Denominational schools were to be reopened and would share in provincial education moneys under the threat of federal govt remedial action. The Order was issued in the wake of a controversy fuelled by the Mar. 2, 1894, Man. Act to Amend the Public Schools Act of 1890, which ensured that Catholic schools were not deemed public schools, and therefore would be denied access to legislative school grants. In May, 1894, the entire Roman Catholic episcopacy signed a petition demanding that the federal govt disallow the new ammendents. However, on July 26, 1895, following the Man. govt's June 13 defiance of the Order-in-Council, PM Bowell announced that there would be no federal remedial bill during the Parliamentary session. A cabinet crisis erupted in Ottawa the next day.

Mar. 29 A federal Royal Commission, appointed Mar. 14, 1892, to examine the sale of liquor, concluded that restrictive laws did not curtail sales.

Apr. 4–16 The Nfld. Confederation Conference held at Ottawa failed to bring Nfld. into Confederation. Delegates representing Nfld. were Edward Patrick Morris (1859–1935), George Emerson, Robert Bond

(1856–1927) and William Horwood. A 2nd round of talks held in Nfld. also yielded no positive result.

Apr. 16 Chatham, Ont., was incorporated as a city.

Apr. 18 The 5th session of the 8th Parliament met, until July 22 and decided against Dominion-wide prohibition, because of its Royal Commission findings of Mar. 29.

Also in Apr.
• A monument to patriote Dr. Jean-Olivier Chenier was erected in Square Viger in Montreal.

June 5 Nicholas Flood Davin introduced a motion in the House of Commons to give women the vote. The motion was defeated.

July 2 Joshua Slocum (1844–1909), 51, began his solo voyage around the world from Yarmouth, NS, in the 11-m sloop, *Spray*. On Aug. 4, the *Spray* reached Gibralter, after an Atlantic crossing faster than all except the big steamers. On July 16, 1896, the *Spray* cast anchor in Samoa where Slocum met Robert Louis Stevenson's widow, who presented him with Stevenson's 4 volumes of sailing directories for the Mediterranean and a 5th for the Indian Ocean. And finally, on June 26, 1898, Slocum reached Newport, Rhode Is. and the end of his journey around the world, thereby becoming the 1st man to sail around the world alone.

July 15 The Banque du Peuple incorporated in Montreal on July 27, 1844, failed. Depositors received only 25% of their money.

July 24 NWMP Inspector Charles Constantine (1849–1912) arrived at the junction of Forty-mile Creek and the Yukon R., with a force of 20 men and proceeded to build Fort Constantine. The Inspector was appointed Gold Commissioner, Magistrate Land Agent and Collector of Customs for the area.

July 29 The Territorial Exhibition opened in Regina.

Aug. 5 The 79.2 m steamship *Prince Rupert*, built in Scotland, arrived in the Bay of Fundy and was described as one of the fastest boats in North America waters. A floating palace, it was capable of accommodating 850 passengers.

Sept. 9 The rebuilt Sault Ste. Marie Canal was opened, with locks on the Canadian side of the border.

Oct. 2 An Order-in Council enlarged Athabasca District eastward, and established the Provisional Districts of Yukon, Ungava, Mackenzie and Franklin.

Also in Oct.
• Almighty Voice, or Kah-kee-say-mane-too-Wayo (Voice of the Great Spirit) (1874–1897), a Cree, was jailed for illegally butchering a cow. He escaped, killing Sergeant Colin Colebrook of the NWMP. A 19-month manhunt followed. On May 30, 1897, Almighty Voice was killed along with 2 companions in a 2-day shoot-out with 1,000 NWMP and civilian volunteers near Batoche, Sask. Also killed were Corporal C.H.S. Hockin, Constable J.R. Kerr and Ernest Grundy, Duck L. postmaster.

Dec. 16 Violence broke out between workers of the CPR and workers of the Kaslo and Slocan Railway when the latter wrecked a CPR depot in the mining town of Sandon, BC.

c 1895 David Hysop (an insurance claims adjuster) in Man. and N. Stewart Dunlap (a tax and insurance commisioner) in Montreal, working separately, developed the CPR garden plan, which ultimately provided for stroll gardens at every CPR station.

c 1895–1901 George M. Dawson served as director of the Canadian Geological Survey.

Also in 1895
• Henri Menier, French millionaire chocolate manufacturer, purchased Anticosti Is. to develop as a private sports preserve.

• Clara Brett Martin (1874–1923) became the 1st woman law graduate in Canada, receiving a Bachelor of Civil Law from Trinity College, U. of Toronto. When the law society refused to call her to the Bar of Ont., she brought her case to the Ont. legislature. The legislative body took action, and in 1897, Martin became Canada's 1st female lawyer and the 1st woman to practice law in the entire British Empire.

• Northern Electric Manufacturing Company,

originally a branch of the Bell Telephone Company, was incorporated.

• The 1st Forest Reserve Act was passed. Que.'s Laurentides National Reserve (8,000 km²) was established.

• One hundred and forty km² in southern Alb., adjacent to the American border, was set aside as Kootenay Lakes Forest Reserve. In 1911, the area was renamed Waterton Lakes National Park, and the protected domain increased to 525 km². Seventy-one-year-old soldier, hunter, prospector and conservationist John George "Kootenai" Brown (1839–1916) was the park's 1st superintendent. In 1932, Waterton Lakes National Park combined with American Glacier National Park to form the world's 1st international peace park, which UNESCO honoured as a world heritage site in 1995.

• The Canada Cup was established as the trophy for a perpetual series of challenge races between Canadian and American yacht clubs on the Great Lakes.

• Canada's Arctic sovereignty, as set out in a British Order-in-Council, was confirmed by British statute.

• The US and Canada agreed to a joint survey to determine the exact boundary location between Alaska and Canada.

• The Toronto newspapers *Mail* (founded 1872) and *Empire* (founded 1887) merged to become the *Mail and Empire*.

• Judge D.W. Prowse published *A History of Newfoundland*.

• The periodical *Le Passe Temps*, covering the music scene in Canada, was established.

• Bliss Carman (1861–1929), with Richard Hovey (1864–1900), published the poem "Songs from Vagabondia."

• The novel *Pour la Patrie*, by Jules-Paul Tardivel (1851–1905), an advocate for French-Canadian independence, was published.

• *Barbara Heck, A Tale of Early Methodism in America,* by William Henry Withrow (1839–1908), was published.

• Ukrainian Dr. Joseph Oleskiw published his pamphlet *On Emigration and About Free Lands*, detailing the advantages of settlement on the Canadian prairies. It became widely read in western Ukraine.

• Emily Pauline Johnson published the collection of poetry *White Wampum* and became the 1st Native poet published in Canada. The daughter of a Mohawk father and an english mother, Johnson would assume her great-grandfather's Mohawk name "Tekahionwake," meaning "double life." After the success of *White Wampum*, she went on to establish a successful career as a poet, novelist, comedienne and entertainer. Johnson is best remembered for her poem "The Song My Paddle Sings."

1896

Jan. 7 Seven ministers in the Mackenzie Bowell cabinet, Foster, Haggart, Montague, Tupper, Dickey, Ives and Wood (Bowell's "nest of traitors") resigned en masse, protesting federal govt support of separate schools in Man.

Feb. 11 The Manitoba Remedial School Bill, which would force Manitoba to restore separate schools (which it had refused to do June 13, 1895, despite an Order-in-Council), was introduced in the Canadian House of Commons. Compromise was not reached on the hotly debated topic, and the bill was withdrawn Apr. 21, after no decision was made.

Apr. 23 Parliament was dissolved. A general election was called, and held June 23.

Apr. 24 Donald Smith (Lord Strathcona) was appointed Canadian high commissioner in Britain.

Apr. 27 Mackenzie Bowell resigned as PM. Charles Tupper, former Canadian high commissioner, was called on to form the new govt, which he completed May 1. Tupper served as Conservative PM until July 8, when his govt resigned following its defeat in the general election, June 23.

May 1 The Public Printing Bureau adopted an 8-hour day.

May 10 The Imperial Privy Council upheld the right of Ont. to enforce local prohibition, but denied its right to stop the manufacture of liquor or its importation into the province.

May 26 The Imperial Privy Council gave the federal govt rights over fisheries.

Also in May
• During celebrations for Queen Victoria's birthday, a span along the Point Ellice Bridge in Victoria, BC, fell away, killing 55 persons riding a streetcar that plunged into the harbour. It was the worst streetcar accident in North American history.

June 23 Liberals under Wilfrid Laurier defeated the Conservatives under Tupper in the national election, 123 seats to 88. It was the 1st Liberal victory since 1874. Of significance was the overwhelming Liberal majority in Que. — 49 seats to 16. Wilfrid Laurier served as Liberal PM of Canada from July 11 to Oct. 6, 1911, the 1st French-Canadian PM since Confederation. Laurier's cabinet, appointed July 14, was widely experienced, with Oliver Mowat (former premier of Ont.) in Justice; William S. Fielding (former premier of NS) in Finance; Andrew George Blair (1844–1907, former premier of NB) as Railways and Canals minister; Clifford Sifton (1865–1929) as Interior minister and supt. gen. of Indian Affairs; and Joseph-Israel Tarte (1848–1907) in Public Works.

June 27 In Montréal, Louis Minier and Louis Pupier screened the 1st motion picture for a paying audience in Canada using a Cinématographe, invented by the Lumière brothers (Louis and Auguste) of France, who had been inspired to invent the moving-picture viewing machine following a demonstration in Paris of Thomas Edison's Kinetoscope, a peephole machine that allowed 1 individual at a time to view moving pictures.

July 6 By Order-in-Council, Que. boundaries were enlarged to the shores of Hudson Bay, adding 306,765 km² to the province.

Also in July
• Roman Catholic missionary Father Joseph Adeodat Therien established the agricultural mission of St. Paul des Métis on 4 townships outside today's St. Paul, Alb. Conceived as a haven for Métis, the mission was underfunded and failed to plant crops in its 1st year. Nevertheless it remained in operation until 1909.

• The *Glencairn*, a Canadian yacht owned by capitalist and engineer James Ross (1848–1913) and sponsored by Fr. Lacombe won the Seawanhaka-Corinthian race in American waters.

Aug. 11 Twenty-seven Ukrainian families established the 1st Ukrainian settlement in southern Man.

Aug. 16 Acting on earlier advice from prospector Robert Henderson (1857–1933), who had staked a claim on Goldbottom Creek in the Klondike, George Washington Carmack (1850–1922), his wife, Kate (d 1920), and 2 Native Peoples, Skookum Jim (1856–1916) and Tagish (Dawson) Charlie, discovered gold at Rabbit Creek, a tributary of the Klondike R. On Aug. 17, Carmack staked 2 claims (the "Discovery" and "No. 1 below"); Skookum Jim staked "#1 above," and the "No. 2 below" was staked for Tagish Charlie. After the claims were registered at Forty Mile, the Klondike Gold Rush began. Rabbit Creek, renamed Bonanza, was staked out, as was a small rich tributary called the Eldorado. Each claim was 152.4 m with a maximum of 2 claims per miner. Henderson, considered by many the real discoverer of the Klondike, subsequently staked a potentially rich claim along Hunter's Creek but was forced to sell up his rights when he was injured. He received $3,000 and, later, a pension from the federal govt.

Also in Aug.
• Joseph Ladue (1855–1948), who had been in charge of the trading post at Ogilvie, Yukon, established the town of Dawson City on the east bank of the Yukon R. at the mouth of the Klondike R., with a sawmill and saloon.

Sept. 12 Thomas George Shaughnessy (1853–1923), assistant general manager of the CPR, proposed a railway be built from Lethbridge/Fort Macleod through the Crowsnest Pass and Kootenay Valley as far as Nelson, BC, to serve gold, copper and coal mines of the area before the Americans. The proposal led to the Crow's Nest Pass Agreement of June 10, 1897.

Sept. 21 The Central Exposition opened in Ottawa.

Sept. 27 CPR telegraph operators and dispatchers went on strike for shorter hours and higher wages, until Oct. 7.

Nov. 8–9 Joseph-Israel Tarte, with Henri Bourassa (1868–1952), negotiated a settlement (Laurier-Greenway compromise) to the Man. Schools Question, which recognized the right to Catholic teaching and to teaching in the French language. In each school of 40 pupils and in each village school of 25, there could be one qualified Catholic teacher. Religious instruction could be given during the last half hour of the school day, from which children of other faiths could be excused. This would also hold true for other cultures where numbers warranted; separate schools, however, were not restored. The Laurier-Greenway compromise would be passed by the Man. legislature Mar. 30, 1897.

Nov. 20 NWMP Insp. Constantine listed trading of liquor to Native Peoples as the number one problem in Yukon Territory.

Nov. 27 Minister of the Interior Clifford Sifton announced plans to encourage immigration, particularly from the farming sectors of Eastern Europe, to fill the prairies with experienced settlers used to farming in a similar physical environment. Sifton's program was particularly successful in attracting Ukrainians.

Dec. 22 Donald Mann (1853–1934) and William Mackenzie, 2 former CPR contractors, purchased the Lake Manitoba Railway and Canal Co. which had been chartered by the Man. govt in 1889, and had a land grant from the federal govt for 6,000 acres (2,428 ha) per mile for 125 miles. They announced plans for the construction of a railway between Gladstone, Man., and L. Winnipegosis, in the 1st stage of what would ultimately be called the Canadian Northern Railway.

Also in 1896
• The Dominion Women's Enfranchisement Association organized a mock parliament that comically debated and defeated a motion to permit men the right to vote. Doctors Emily and Augusta Stowe were participants at this event.

• Bookseller C.J. Musson founded the Musson Book Company in Toronto. It would later become a key element in the Stoddart family book empire known as General Publishing.

• Klondike gold production was $300,000.

• The 1st Canadian skiing championships were held at Rossland, BC.

• Increased farming efficiencies reduced the cost of harvesting 1 acre (.4 ha) of wheat to 3 man-hours and 72 cents, from 64 man hours and $3.74 in 1830.

• A covered bridge across the Saint John R. was built at Heartland, NB; the structure was 391 m long, comprised 7 spans and took 4 years to complete. Built as a toll bridge, it is the longest covered bridge in the world and exists to this day.

• Mosson Boyd (b 1855) of Bobcaygeon, Ont., began to breed hybrid buffalo with some success. He continued for 19 years, then shipped his herd to the National Bison Range in Wainright, Alb.

• *In the Days of the Canada Company*, a history by Robina Lizars (d 1918) and Kathleen M. Lizars (d 1931), was published.

• Nfld.-born artist Maurice Galbraith Cullen (1866–1934) painted *Logging in Winter, Beaupré,* oil on canvas, now in the Art Gallery of Hamilton, Ont.

• Ernest Thompson Seton (1860–1946) published his 1st book, *Art Anatomy of Animals.*

• Ont.-born artist Edmund Morris (1871–1913) exhibited his painting, *Girls in a Poppy Field,* in the Royal Canadian Academy of Arts and the Ont. Society of Arts. It was purchased by the famous local collector Byron Walker (later Sir Edmund, 1848–1924), and is now owned by the Art Gallery of Ont., Toronto.

• *The Seats of the Mighty*, Sir Horatio Gilbert Parker's (1862–1932) most popular romance novel, was published. The book focused on an English spy whose intrigues led to the fall of Que. in 1759.

• *Earth's Enigmas*, by Charles G.D. Roberts, was published. The work was an example of the author's most noteworthy contribution to literature, the animal story.

• Hegelian philosopher John Watson (1847–1939), professor of logic, metaphysics and ethics at Queen's U., published *Christianity and Idealism*.

1897

Jan. 29 Isabel Maria Gordon, Lady Aberdeen (1857–1939), wife of the 7th gov-gen., established the Victorian Order of Nurses in celebration of the year of Queen Victoria's Diamond Jubilee. The Order's primary objective was to provide bedside nursing care to the sick in their own homes, under the direction of a family physician.

Jan. 30 The boundary between the Yukon and BC was established.

Also in Jan.
• The pamphlet *Le Clergé canadien*, by Laurent Oliver David (1840–1926), suffered condemnation by the Catholic Church: the work was placed on the Index for criticizing its political activities. The Quebec City newspaper *L'Électeur*, edited by Ernest Pacaud, was also declared forbidden reading by the Church for having published excerpts from David's pamphlet.

Feb. 4 The federal govt agreed to build a bridge across the North Sask. R. at Edmonton, provided the city put up $25,000 towards its cost. Ratepayers endorsed the plan and assumed the liability. The bridge was completed in 5 years.

Feb. 11 Part of the Western Department Building, a wing of the Parliament Buildings at Ottawa, was destroyed by fire.

Feb. 19 Adelaide Sophia Hoodless established the 1st Federated Women's Institute of Canada in the village of Stoney Creek, Ont., so that women would have their own organization to study homemaking. The organization later spread throughout Canada and Britain.

Feb. 22 After a failed attempt to establish a settlement in Brazil, 43 Canadians returned home to Que. They had experienced an inhospitable environment and great hardships.

Mar. 16 At 8:08 a.m., Charcoal, alias Bad Young Man, from the Blood reserve, was hanged for the murders of Medicine Pipe Stem, killed Oct. 11, 1896, over suspected indiscretions with Pretty Wolverine Woman (Charcoal's wife), and Sgt. W.B. Wilde, killed Nov. 10, 1896 while in pursuit of the suspect. The execution took place at the Common Gaol at Fort Macleod.

May 15 Toronto voted to allow the operation of streetcars on Sundays.

May 22 *Ferdinand*, Joseph Seagram's 3-year-old chestnut colt, won the Queen's Plate in a record 2:13 time with jockey Harry Lewis aboard. Popular favourite of the day, chestnut colt *Wicker*, entered by the 1st female owner in the history of the race, Miss Elsie Wicker, placed 3rd.

Also in May
• Que. Liberal leader Félix-Gabriel Marchand became premier of Que., defeating the Conservative govt of Edmund James Flynn (1847–1927).

June 1 Gold was discovered near L. Wawa (an Ojibwa word meaning "wild goose"), Ont.

June 10 The Crow's Nest Pass Agreement was reached by the federal govt and the CPR to build a southern railway through the Crowsnest Pass from Lethbridge, Alb., to the silver-lead and zinc mines near Nelson, BC. The CPR received a $3.3 million cash subsidy (or $11,000 per mile) and agreed in return to reduce freight rates on eastbound flour and grain and westbound freight rates on settlers' effects. Building of the new Crowsnest Pass Railway commenced July 14 in Lethbridge, although the actual agreement was not signed by both parties until Sept. 6.

June 19 The Allan Steamship Company was formed in Montreal to secure needed capital to rebuild the Allan Line's declining fleet.

June 20 Queen Victoria celebrated her Diamond Jubilee, the 60th year of her reign, with a grand imperial pageant attended by dignitaries from around the world. PM Laurier and his wife, Zoë (1841–1921), in England for the 1st time, were in attendance. Laurier was knighted the next day.

June 24 Frederick William Haultain (1857–1942) became premier at Regina as responsible govt was obtained for the NWT.

July 3 Albert Lancaster from California staked the 1st bench claim (a hillside claim, as opposed to a creek claim) on the Klondike. His little 100-foot (30.5-m) property at Eldorado Creek eventually produced $200,000 for him on the hill which would later be known as Gold Hill.

July 17 The steamer *Portland* docked at Seattle, carrying miners who had struck it rich in the Klondike.

July 24 The US Dingley Tariff Act, designed to increase protection rather than earn revenue, went into effect, making reciprocity with Canada impossible.

July 28 The federal govt placed a royalty of 2% on minerals from Canadian mines, including Klondike gold.

Aug. 1 The Laurier govt enacted the Imperial preferential tariff, to allow goods entering Canada from Britain and its colonies a duty reduction of 25% from the regular import tax assessed on non-British imports. The tariff aimed at once to protect Canadian producers and to stimulate trade with Britain. German and Belgian objections to the new tariffs would be denounced.

Aug. 12 British naval authorities gave permission to the US to dry-dock the battleship *Indiana* at Halifax.

Aug. 16 The Yukon Judicial District was created by Order-in-Council. Law and order was administered by a commission of 6 known as the Yukon Administration. James Morro Walt (1843–1905) of the NWMP was appointed commissioner of the Yukon.

Aug. 27 The Lower Arch Bridge (Whirlpool Rapids Bridge), a steel railway bridge known as a 2-hinged spanded-braced arch, was completed over the Niagara R. Construction had begun Apr. 9, 1896.

Sept. 5 The Alaska Commercial Company's steamer *Alice* arrived at the Klondike loaded with men from Forty Mile, Alb.

Sept. 8 Frederick Knapp (b 1854) launched his 38-m-long Knapp Roller Boat in Toronto. It was built from 2 cylindrical tubes, one within the other, and was ultimately unmanageable in water. The boat is believed to be buried in the mud, deep under the Gardiner Expressway in Toronto.

Sept. 17 The 58.2-m-long sidewheeler *Victoria*, with a 995-passenger capacity, reached a speed of 28 km/h on its 1st trip on the Saint John R. It was the most luxurious boat ever to travel on the river.

Also in Sept.

• Minister of the Interior Clifford Sifton, and a sizable party, left Ottawa for the Klondike on a fact-finding mission. Sifton was convinced that the development of an all-Canadian railway in the territory was necessary if Canada was to maintain federal control of the region against American encroachments.

Fall Some 5,000 Yukon gold seekers attempted to travel 72 km through the White Pass to the goldfields, a treacherous route which would claim many lives.

Oct. 24 R.J. Bowen conducted the 1st service at St. Paul's Church at Dawson, in the Yukon.

Dec. 18 Pope Leo XIII's encyclical *Affari Vos*, dealing with the Man. School Question, was issued in Rome, criticizing the Laurier-Greenway settlement as "defective, unsuitable, insufficient." It encouraged bishops to "protect and defend what was most sacred," and further advised that until Catholics could obtain full rights, they should not accept partial satisfaction.

Dec. 22 The Bering Sea Claims Commission in Ottawa ruled that the US should pay Canadian sealers $463,454 as compensation for the 1887 seizure of their vessels.

Also in 1897

• Four women graduated from St. Francis Xavier University (Antigonish, NS), making it the 1st Catholic university on the continent to grant degrees to women.

• Entrepreneurs took advantage of an amendment to the Post Act, allowing private companies to produce their own postcards. Postcards carrying images of Ottawa, Niagara Falls, patriotic symbols and cartoons flooded the market.

• Sacré-Coeur Hospital opened in Montreal to service cancer patients and the disabled. The hospital was founded by Georgiana and Léontine Généreux and Agalée Laberge.

• The Winnipeg Grain Exchange, the largest in NA, was opened. It served as a cash market for western farmers and merchants. Its name would change to the Winnipeg Commodity Exchange in 1972, and today it remains the only agricultural commodity-exchange market in Canada.

• England-born architect Francis Mawson Rattenbury (1867-1935) completed the British Columbia Legislative Buildings, located at the south end of the inner harbour in downtown Victoria, BC.

• Robert Bond became the leader of the Nfld. Liberal party.

• Canada's 1st gasoline-driven car was built by bicycle repairman George Foote Foss (1876-1968), of Sherbrooke, Que. The engine contained 1 cylinder and could travel 50 miles (80 km) on 1 gallon (4.5 L) of gas.

• Jack K. McCulloch (1872–1918) won the world speed skating title in Montreal.

• Montreal businessman and civic reformer Herbert Brown Ames (1863–1954) published *The City Below the Hill*, a thoughtful analysis of life in the working-class districts of Montreal.

• *The Habitant and other French-Canadian Poems*, a best-seller, by Dr. William Henry Drummond (1854–1907), was published.

1898

Jan. 29 Superintendent Sam Steele received orders to take command of the NWMP post in the Yukon. He would remain there through Sept. 1899.

Apr. 2 The 1st gasoline car imported from the United States, a 1-cylinder Winton, was purchased by Col. John Moodie (b 1859) of Hamilton, Ont.

May 6 The Yukon Field Force, consisting of 203 volunteers drawn from the Canadian militia, left Vancouver for Dawson to assist in maintaining order during the gold rush. The detachment reached the goldfields on Oct. 1, accompanied by 4 members of the Victorian Order of Nurses who were to set up a hospital.

May 27 Gene Allen arrived at Dawson by dogsled to establish the *Klondike Nugget*, the town's 1st newspaper. The initial issue would be published at Dawson in June. The *Yukon Midnight Sun* and the *Klondike Miner* would also appear in June.

June 13 The Yukon Territory was established and joined Confederation with the purple fireweed as its floral emblem. Dawson became its 1st capital. Local administration was entrusted to a commissioner, who was advised by a legislative council of 6 members appointed by the federal govt. William Ogilvie (1846–1912) became the Territory's commissioner.

Also in June

• William Henry left Calgary for Dawson, Yukon, with 22 saddle and pack horses carrying dressed meat and hides, and arrived in Dawson Sept. 30, after rafting the provisions down the Pelly R. The meat was purchased at P. Burns and Co. of Calgary, Alb. (later Burns Meats Ltd.), owned by "cattle king" Pat Burns (1856–1937), who was the main meat provisioner to Dawson prospectors. Burns had made his 1st fortune in the 1880s selling meat to railway crews, and in 1928 would be the 1st to introduce canned meat to the Canadian market.

July 3 Canadians were kept on alert as the Spanish-American War entered Cuban waters at Santiago Bay. Hostilities ceased Aug. 12, and a formal peace signed in Paris, Dec. 10, 1898. Americans gained control of both Cuba and Puerto Rico in the aftermath, fuelling fears about further US expansionism.

July 27 The 1st locomotive operated on the White Pass and Yukon Railway. Construction of the narrow-gauge railway had begun in May, from Skagway, Alaska, under the direction of Michael J. Heney. The terminal point of the railway was Whitehorse, in the Yukon. Construction reached the summit of White Pass Feb. 18, 1899. The last spike was driven July 29, 1900. Of the 35,000 men working on the project, 35 lost their lives.

Aug. 1 Clauses pertaining to Canada in the treaty of 1865 between Britain and Germany were terminated, a result of the Imperial preferential tariff enacted Aug. 1, 1897. German goods would now enter Canada under a general instead of a preferential tariff.

Aug. 23–Oct. 10 The Joint High Commission comprising 6 delegates representing Canada and the US met in Que. to consider all questions at issue concerning the Alaska boundary dispute, especially the Lynn Canal, the upper end of which was claimed by Canada under the British-Russia treaty of 1825. The commission would meet in Washington in 1899 to no avail.

Sept. 11 The business section of New Westminster, BC, was destroyed by fire.

Sept. 29 A national prohibition plebiscite showed 278,380 in favour of prohibition and 264,693 against. No action was taken by Parliament because of the close results. Every province except Que. voted dry. Que. voted overwhelmingly wet.

Nov. 12–Nov. 18, 1904 Gilbert John Elliot (1845–1914), Earl of Minto, served as gov-gen. of Canada, succeeding Aberdeen.

Dec. 7 The 49.4-m steamer SS *Moyie* began passenger service on the Nelson–Kootenay Landing route, connecting the BC Southern Railway which ran from Alb. through the Crowsnest Pass to the Kootenay L. region. The SS *Kuskanook* replaced *Moyie* on the Nelson–Kootenay Landing route in 1906, relegating *Moyie* to service Kootenay L., including Nelson, Proctor and Kaslo. The *Moyie* was retired on Apr. 27, 1957, having been the last working passenger steamwheeler in the country. The steamer was preserved by the Kootenay Lake Historical Society at Kaslo, BC.

• Canada Post introduced the world's 1st Christmas stamp, a 2 cent Imperial penny postage with a black, lavender and carmine map of the British Empire over the motto, "We hold a vaster empire than has ever been."

Also in 1898

• Reginald Saunders began SJ Reginald Saunders Publishing, which would later publish humorist Greg Clark (1892–1977). The company was absorbed by Thomas Allen in 1955.

• Ben Boyer and Jim Sayers staked claim on what would become the Helen Iron Mine, north of Wawa L., Ont. The mine, renamed the Macleod, remains in operation.

• The 1st Europeans to see the Columbia Icefield in the Canadian Rockies were explorers Hermann Woolley, John Norman Collie and Hugh Stutfield. Located between Mount Columbia and Mount Athabasca at the Alb.–BC border, the icefield comprises 30 separate glaciers which feed the N. Saskatchewan, Columbia and Athabasca Rivers.

• Emma Casgrain graduated from the Quebec College of Dentists as Canada's 1st woman dentist.

• Olaus Jeldness (1855–1925) of Rossland, BC, won Canada's 1st championship ski-jump contest.

• Dr. Maud Elizabeth Seymour Abbott (1869–1940) was appointed assistant curator of the Medical Museum of McGill U., where she would pioneer the use of museum facilities in pathology instruction. She would be promoted to curator in 1901 and gain worldwide acclaim throughout her career at McGill.

• The novel *The Forest of Bourg-Marie*, by Susie Francis Harrison, née Riley (pseud. Seranus), was published.

• *Wild Animals I Have Known*, by artist-naturalist Ernest Thompson Seton, was published.

• Montreal artist William Brymner, who studied at the Académie Julian in Paris, completed the canvas *Two Girls Reading*, which is currently housed in the National Gallery of Canada.

1899

Jan. 1 The 2 cent Imperial postage providing for letter delivery anywhere in the British Empire took effect.

Feb. 2 Joseph-Israel Tarte was appointed head of the Paris Exposition Commission for Canada, to organize Canada's display at the 1900 World's Fair in Paris.

Feb. 23 Imperial Oil assumed control of the Sarnia refinery in Sarnia, Ont., and all of Standard Oil's other Canadian resources, after Imperial Oil, incorporated in Toronto in 1880, sold its controlling interest to John D. Rockefeller's Standard Oil in 1898.

Also in Feb
• W.C. Ditmars of Vancouver bought a Stanley automobile powered by gas and steam. It was the 1st automobile in BC.

Mar. 16 The 4th session of the 8th Parliament met, until Aug. 11. The Pacific Cable Act, proposed by Sanford Fleming, provided for the construction of an underwater telegraph cable from Canada to Australia and New Zealand. The cable link between Vancouver and Brisbane, Australia, was completed Oct. 31, 1902. Sandford Fleming sent the 1st message.

Also in Mar.
• The Dominion Iron and Steel Company was incorporated in Halifax, NS.

June 12 William Cornelius Van Horne resigned as president of the CPR but retained his position as chairman of the board. Thomas Shaughnessy (1853–1923) replaced Van Horne as president, serving until 1918.

June 21 In return for being assured hunting and fishing privileges and annuities, Native Peoples of Lesser Slave L. accepted Treaty No. 8, involving a huge land area (840,000 km²) in the northern regions of BC, Alb., Sask. and a southern section of the NWT.

July 8–9 Troops were called in to stop rioting streetcar workers on strike in London, Ont.

July 21 A new suspension bridge over the Niagara R. between Queenston, Ont., and Lewiston, New York, was opened.

Aug. 7 The steamer *North West* sank in the North Sask. R. after breaking from its moorings and striking ground. The elegant sternwheeler had been built in 1881 and was 61 m long and 11.5 m wide. During the Northwest Rebellion of 1885, the *North West* transported troops and equipment along the Saskatchewan R. system to Prince Albert and Batoche. The steamer was sold for scrap in Edmonton in 1903.

Sept. 4 Royal Victoria College for Women was opened at Montreal's McGill U. where it had been established with a gift of some $1 million from Donald Smith, Lord Strathcona.

Sept. 18 Col. Sam Hughes (1853–1921), a militia member, invited applications from all those willing to fight in the 2nd Boer War (1899–1902) in South Africa. He placed ads in a number of Canadian newspapers and received an estimated 1,200 applications.

• Toronto's 3rd city hall was opened by Mayor John Shaw, (the 1st was located at King and Jarvis [1834–1845], the 2nd at South St. Lawrence Market [1845–1899]). Designed by architect Edward James Lennox (1855–1933) in the Romansque Revival style, the $2.5 million Credit Valley stone structure included a clock tower rising 103.6 m above Queen St. (the 1st bells rung Dec. 31, 1900), and an elegant 2-storey entrance once called "Toronto's grandest indoor space." The classic example of late-nineteenth-century urban architecture was turned into a courthouse when Toronto's current city hall opened in 1965.

Sept. 19 A massive rock slide from the cliffs over Quebec City's Lower Town destroyed most of Champlain St., killing 45 people.

Sept. 28 A telegraph line connected Dawson, Yukon, to BC.

Oct. 1 Diomede Falconio (1842–1917) arrived in Que. from the Vatican as the 1st permanent Apostolic delegate to Canada.

Oct. 11 Great Britain officially declared war against the Boers, and Gen. Redvers Buller sailed out of Southampton, England, on Oct. 14, in command of the largest army in the history of the British Empire.

Oct. 18 Minister of Finance William S. Fielding announced Canada's decision to send a contingent of 1,000 troops to aid Britain in the Boer War. Canada paid for recruitment, transportation and equipment, but cost of supplies, pay for troops and pensions were Britain's responsibility. The 1st Canadian troops, consisting of the 2nd Battalion, Royal Canadian Regiment, would set sail from Que. for South Africa Oct. 30 under veteran commander William Otter. There were 57 officers and 1,224 men. Their voyage to Cape Town, South Africa, would take 1 month.

• Henri Bourassa resigned his seat in Parliament to protest Canada's involvement in Britain's war against Dutch settlers in South Africa.

Dec. 1 Montreal's Victoria Bridge spanning the St. Lawrence, completed in 1859, was rebuilt to accommodate vehicles, trains and pedestrians.

Dec. 7 Man. Conservative leader Hugh John Macdonald (1850–1929), son of John A. Macdonald, was elected premier.

Dec. 12 W.C. Smith and Co., the fishing company based in Lunenberg, NS, was incorporated.

Also in 1899

• The 135-m Capilano Suspension Bridge was built in BC. The famous pedestrian bridge, which creaks and sways to the winds some 70 m above the Capilano River, now attracts over 850,000 visitors a year.

• Harry Gibson became the 1st Canadian to win a world cycling title.

• The Port Arthur, Duluth and Western Railway was purchased by the Canadian Northern Railway.

• Frontier College, Canada's oldest adult-literacy organization, was founded by Alfred Fitzpatrick, who was appalled by the conditions he saw in isolated logging camps while searching for his long-lost brother. Fitzpatrick convinced university students to volunteer as labourer-teachers to work in the camps during the day and teach reading and writing at night. The labourer-teacher program of bringing education to the people has since expanded to include urban and rural communities, prisons, factories and street corners.

• More than 7,400 Doukhobors were granted 16,187 ha near Yorkton, Sask., the result of negotiations between Count Tolstoy and Professor James Mavor (1854–1925), of the U. of Toronto, aided by British and American Quakers.

• Joshua Slocum published, in 9 installments, the account of his solo journey around the world in the sloop *Spray* in the *Century Illustrated Monthly*. It was later published as a book entitled *Sailing Alone Around the World*, and translated into six languages.

• Horatio Walker (1850–1938) painted *Oxen Drinking*, now at the National Gallery of Canada.

• *The Sky Pilots*, a western novel by Ralph Connoer (Charles Gordon) (1860–1937), was published.

• Ozias Leduc painted *Mon portrait*, now in the National Gallery of Canada.

• William Brymner painted *Early Moonrise in September*, oil on canvas, now at the National Gallery of Canada.

• *Christmas in French Canada,* by Louis-Honoré Fréchette, was published.

1900

Jan. 18 Ont.-born painter Horatio Walker's work was featured at the Art Association of Montreal, now the Montreal Museum of Fine Arts. Walker became the best-paid painter of his day.

Jan. 21 A segment of the 2nd contingent of Canadian troops (2 battalions of Mounted Rifles and a brigade of artillery — 1,281 men in all) sailed from Halifax for South Africa. The rest of the contingent left Jan. 27 and Feb. 21.

Feb. 1 The head tax on Chinese immigrants was raised to $100.

Feb. 13 The 1st chapter of the Imperial Order of the Daughters of the Empire, a woman's patriotic and philanthropic organization, was established at Fredericton, NB, by Margaret Polson Murray (1884–1927); its motto "One flag, one throne, one Empire."

Feb. 18–27 During the South African Battle of Paardeberg, 2 Canadian Maritime companies ignored an order to retreat during an Afrikaner counter attack, resulting in the capture of 4,000 exhausted Afrikaners under the command of Gen. Piet Arnoldus Cronje. Canadians suffered 123 wounded and 31 killed.

Feb. 27 BC Premier Charles Augustus Semlin (1836–1927) was dismissed from office by Lt-Gov. Thomas Robert McInnes (1840–1904), even though Semlin had enlisted support among the opposition to form a coalition govt. All but one member left the legislature when the lt-gov. arrived to prorogue. On June 18, the BC legislature passed a resolution forcing McInnes's resignation.

Mar. 1 There were 3 days of street rioting in Montreal, as McGill students, celebrating recent British successes in the South African War, clashed with anti-war students from Laval.

Mar. 7 Canadians participated in artillery fire against the Boers at Poplar Grove in South Africa.

Mar. 13 James Williams Tyrrell began a 2,782-km journey to survey the area from Great Slave L. to Chesterfield Inlet for Dominion Lands.

Mar. 16 Lord Strathcona's Horse, a regiment comprising over 500 mounted riflemen, recruited from Man., BC and NWT, sailed for South Africa. Commanded by the legendary Sam Steele (1849–1919), it arrived on Apr. 10.

Mar. 19 Union leaders, led by Dominion Trades Congress vice-president John Flett, demanded Laurier reduce labour competition by excluding illiterate immigrants from Canada and increasing the head tax on Chinese.

Apr. 19 Canadians Jim Caffery, Bill Sherring (1877–1964) and Frank Hughson completed the Boston Marathon, finishing 1st, 2nd and 3rd, respectively. Jim Caffery would win the event again in 1901.

Apr. 20 Amund Ringnes Is., in the Arctic archipelago, was discovered by Norwegian Gunerius Isachsen, a member of the 1898–1902 Norwegian Sverdrup expedition. Canada obtained ownership of the island in 1931, ending a lengthy sovereignty dispute with Norway.

Apr. 25 Canadians engaged in the Battle of Israel's Port, South Africa.

Apr. 26 What began as a simple chimney fire in Hull was fanned by high winds, so the flames engulfed much of that town and spread across the river into Ottawa. Three lives were lost and 15,000 people left homeless. Two-thirds of Hull was destroyed. Property damage was estimated at $1 million.

June 9 PEI adopted prohibition. The province would run "dry" until 1948, when the sale of liquor in stores was allowed. Only in 1964 was public drinking allowed on the Island.

June 15 Man. Catholics presented a resolution to the federal govt, seeking relief from the Man. law abolishing separate schools.

July 23 A proclamation prohibited the immigration of criminals or "paupers" to Canada.

July 29 The last spike of the 177-km, $10 million White Pass and Yukon Railway was driven at Carcross, Yukon. Construction of the narrow-gauge railway had begun in May 1898, under the direction of Michael J. Heney (1864–1910). The railway connected Skagway, Alaska, to Whitehorse, Yukon.

Also in July

• The Man. Grain Act was passed by Parliament. Created in response to western growers' dissatisfaction with the local storage and transport of goods, the act provided for govt inspection of the weighing, grading and storage of grain, and the appointment of commissioners to investigate and make provisions for complaints.

Aug. 3 Workers in CPR shops went on strike when opportunities to meet and discuss issues with management, as specified by contract, were not upheld.

Nov. 7 Several hundred Boer horsemen surrounded 90 Royal Canadian Dragoons who were covering the retreat of the British infantry near Leliefontein. Three Canadians were killed. The British retreated safely.

• Liberals under Laurier retained power in the general election, winning 128 seats to the Conservatives' 78. Independent candidates won 8 seats. Voter turnout was 77.4%.

Nov. 10 The 70.7-m sidewheeler *City of Monticello* foundered off Cranberry Head, Yarmouth, NS, killing 37 persons; 4 made it safely to shore.

Dec. 6 Alphonse Desjardins (1854–1920) founded the 1st co-operative savings-and-loan society in Canada — the Caisse Populaire — at Lévis, Que.

Dec. 23 The 1st Canadian contingent arrived at Halifax from South Africa, having completed its term of service.

• Canadian inventor Reginald Aubrey Fessenden (1866–1932) made the 1st radio broadcast from Cobb Is. in the Potonac R. His words, heard by his assistant Thiesson over 1 km away, were "One-two-three-four, is it snowing?"

Also in 1900

• Canada's population was 5,301,000.

• The population of Saskatoon, Sask., was 113.

• The average Canadian factory worker made $500 a year.

• Katherine Ryan, aka "Klondike Kate" (1870–1932), became the 1st woman member of the North West Mounted Police. In 1898, the nearly 6-ft tall New Brunswicker made her way along the Klondike employing her nursing skills to make a living. Famous for her generosity and for being one of the 1st European women to walk into the North over the rugged Stikine Trail, Ryan inspired many contemporaries including the infamous prostitute Kitty Rockwell, aka "Klondike Kate," with whom she is often confused.

• Robert Bond became prime minister of Nfld., serving until 1908.

• William Lyon Mackenzie King became editor of the *Labour Gazette*, published to provide statistical information on labour and labour issues.

• The Department of Labour was established to "aid in the prevention and settlement of trade disputes."

• An amendment to the Copyright Act of 1875 (supported by the new Society of Canadian Authors) gave Canadians the right to negotiate agreements with foreign publishers. The agency system was born. William Copp was the 1st branch plant to set up in Canada.

• 201 private banks operated in Canada.

• The 1st Montessori school in Canada was established at Baddeck, NS.

• Ont. had 1,100 cheese factories in operation.

• PEI had 227 lobster canneries.

• The Art Museum of Toronto (later to be renamed the Art Gallery of Ontario) was incorporated.

• The 1st "commercial" was made in Canada — a promotional movie sponsored by the CPR to encourage immigration.

• Three Americans were arrested after trying to blow up the Welland Canal, at Thorold, Ont.

• The 1st Coloured Hockey League of the Maritimes was formed, which included teams from Dartmouth, Truro, Amherst, Summerside, Charlottetown, Halifax, Hammond's Plains, and Africville. Admission to games was 25 cents. The league ran until 1920.

• Klondike gold production equalled $22,275,000.

• Que.-born artist Charles Huot (1855–1930) completed the historical painting *La Bataille des Plaines d'Abraham*.

• Homer Watson completed *The Flood Gate*, a painting he considered his masterpiece, which now hangs in the National Gallery of Canada.

• Horatio Walker completed *Ploughing – The First Gleam at Dawn*, now at the Musée du Québec.

• Honoré Beaugrand published *La Chasse-Galérie: Légendes canadiennes*.

• The romance novel *The Heart of the Ancient Wood*, by Sir Charles G. D. Roberts, was published.

• The National Council of Women of Canada published *Women of Canada: Their Life and Work*. It represented the 1st national portrait of Canadian women.

• *The Poems of Archibald Lampman*, edited by Duncan Campbell Scott, was published.

1901

Jan. 3 Winston Churchill spoke at Massey Hall in Toronto on the South African war during a lecture tour of Canada.

• Striking Pictou coal miners returned to work after management agreed to a 12% pay hike.

Jan. 7 The Ont. govt established the Temagami Forest Reserve — nearly 5,800 km² of pristine wilderness around L. Temagami.

Jan. 15 The Northern Pacific Railroad (NPR) obtained a 999-year lease on a railway line in Man. The lease would be transferred to the Canadian Northern Railway within 30 days.

Jan. 18 Glace Bay, NS, was incorporated, as a town. It's population was 6,945.

Jan. 22 The Victorian Era ended with the death of the 82-year-old British queen. Edward VII of England was proclaimed king the next day.

Also in Jan.
• The CPR purchased the aging fleet of the Canadian Pacific Navigation Company, a freight and passenger railway operating in BC since 1883.

Feb. 3 The 1st of 4 new blast furnaces opened at the Dominion Iron and Steel Company at Sydney, NS.

Feb. 4 Quebec City revived its Winter Carnival as a permanent annual event. The week-long pre-Lenten carnival began in 1894. Today it still features opening and closing parades that meander through downtown streets, ice-sculpting contests, canoe racing across a partially frozen St. Lawrence R., and lots of Caribou — a fortified wine consumed by revellers from hollow walking canes. The festivities are presided over by Bonhomme, a snowman-like mascot who is the symbol of the event.

Feb. 6 Robert Laird Bordeon (1854–1937) became leader of the federal Conservative party, succeeding Charles Tupper.

• The 1st session of the 9th Parliament met until May 23. A Canadian branch of the Royal Mint was established at Ottawa. Laurier designated May 24 as Victoria Day, a public holiday in honour of the late monarch. The Fruit Marking and Inspection Act provided for the grading and inspection of fruit.

Feb. 11 The 1st annual report of the Ont. Bureau of Labour noted that many of the province's children under the age of 12 worked in deplorable conditions and received low wages.

Mar. 6 A Que. bill to allow a crematorium in Montreal was opposed on the grounds that cremation was a "relic of heathenism" and would contribute to insurance fraud.

Mar. 8 Lord Strathcona's Horse arrived in Halifax from South Africa.

Mar. 9 Naturalized Japanese won the right to vote after a successful appeal of the BC Elections Act.

Mar. 20 Canadian General Electric began construction on a large factory in Toronto.

Mar. 30 In the Delpit marriage case, marriages of Roman Catholics by Protestant clergy were deemed valid by a court.

Also in Apr.
• The 1st sale organized by the Territorial Pure Bred Cattle Breeders' Association was held in Frontier Stables at Calgary, where 64 bulls were listed.

• NS adopted the Trailing Arbutus (*Epigaea Repens*) — also called the Mayflower or ground laurel — as its provincial flower.

May 20 Captain John C. Voss (1858–1922) and Norman Luxton (1876–1962) set out from Victoria, BC, in a tricked-out 100-year-old red cedar Nootkan canoe named *Tilikum*, to circumnavigate the globe. Luxton was injured on coral and left in Suva, Fiji. Voss carried on alone, to Australia, through the Indian Ocean, around South Africa, ultimately to England on Sept. 2, 1904. The *Tilikum,* purchased by Voss in 1901 for $80, is on display at the Maritime Museum in Victoria, BC.

June 3 Ottawa carpenters went on strike for higher wages and union recognition.

June 14 Clarence Henry "Hap" Day was born in Owen Sound, Ont. After playing professional hockey from 1924–1938, he went on to coach the Toronto Maple Leafs to 4 Stanley Cups between 1942–1949.

July 2 Cardston, Alb., was incorporated as a town. Charles Ora Card, son-in-law of US Mormon leader Brigham Young, became the 1st mayor.

July 3 Motoring enthusiast W.F. (Billy) Cochrane introduced the automobile to Calgary; a steam-powered Locomobile steered by a tiller rather than a wheel. It was fully equipped with a wicker basket for umbrellas in case of inclement weather. It would be another 5 years before the Alb. govt required vehicles to be registered.

Aug. 18 CP Navigation Co.'s steamer *Islander* struck an iceberg on its way from Skagway to Victoria and sank within 15 minutes. More than 90 passengers and crew were lost.

Aug. 30 Five thousand striking CPR railway workers from across the country returned to work after an 11-week stoppage, when their employer officially recognized the Trainmen's Brotherhood union. Workers' wage grievances, however, went unheard.

Also in Aug.
• The Union of Canadian Municipalities was formed in Toronto to eliminate parties from municipal politics and to extend the principle of municipal ownership and control of public utilities.

Sept. 16 The Duke and Duchess of Cornwall, later to become King George V and Queen Mary, visited Canada until Oct. 21.

Oct. 3 At Canada's request, Japan banned emigration of its citizens to Canada.

Oct. 24 Sixty-three-year-old Michigan schoolteacher Annie Taylor was the 1st to survive a plunge over Canada's Niagara Falls in a barrel. When pulled to safety on the Canadian side, she exclaimed, "No one ought ever do that again!"

Oct. 26 The Michigan–Lake Superior Power Company's hydroelectric canal was completed at Sault St. Marie, Ont., running 4 km long, 61 m wide, and 4.6 m deep.

Nov. 5–7 NWMP officers inspected a flock of 41,565 sheep being imported from Utah into Canada by Jesse Knight. The Knight family became Canada's largest sheep ranchers.

Winter Typhus and starvation annihilated the entire Sadlermiut Inuit population of Southampton Is. in the Hudson Bay.

Dec. 12 Italian inventor Guglielmo Marconi (1874–1937) received a wireless (radio) message at Signal Hill, St. John's, Nfld., from Poldhu, Cornwall, England. This was the 1st cross-Atlantic radio broadcast.

Dec. 16 Dawson City, Yukon, was incorporated.

Dec. 18 At a meeting at Indian Head, Sask., angry farmers organized the Territorial Grain Growers' Association (forerunner of the Saskatchewan Grain Growers' Association and the Alberta Farmers' Association) because of dissatisfaction over handling of the 1901 bumper crop. Homesteader William Richard Motherwell (1860–1943) was elected provisional president.

Also in Dec.
• The 1st settlers of a socialist Finnish colony arrived on Malcolm Is. off the coast of BC, under the leadership of famous Finnish writer Matti Kurikka (1863–1915). The island was renamed Sointula, meaning Harmony. The colony was established to promote and sustain socialist principles and Finnish culture.

c 1901 Montreal-born James Wilson Morrice (1865–1924) painted *Return from School*, based on sketches made at Beaupré, Que., with Maurice Cullen. The picture is now with the Art Gallery of Ont.

1901–1944 Liberal reformer John Wesley Dafoe (1866–1944) served as editor of the *Winnipeg Free Press*.

1901–1911 Canada's rural population increased by 17.16%, its urban population by 62.25%.

Also in 1901
• The Ont. govt passed the Highway Improvement Act (1901), which provided a yearly subsidy of $1 million to improve roads built to provincial standards.

• The population of Canada was 5,371,315, with 3,063,195 of English and 1,649,371 of French descent. The population of Ont. was 2,182,947; Que., 1,648,898; NS, 459,574; NB, 331,120; Man., 255,211; BC, 178,657; PEI, 103,259; the territories of Sask. and Alb., 91,279 and 73,022 respectively; Yukon, 27,219; and NWT, 20,129.

• Seventy-five percent of Albertans lived in rural areas.

• There were 53 paper mills in Canada producing an annual value of $8.6 million.

• E. Cora Hind (1861–1942) was appointed agricultural editor of the *Winnipeg Free Press* — a position for which she had 1st applied in 1882. Hind was awarded the job of covering prairie agricultural news, and travelled widely investigating sources. The accuracy of Hind's annual wheat-yield predictions made her an international reputation in addition to impacting wheat prices worldwide. E. Cora Hind was inducted into the Canadian News Hall of Fame in 1972, the 1st female to be so honoured.

• Fortune seekers flooded the Yukon Territory in search of gold, raising the population to 27,219. Two years later, 4,157 remained in the Territory.

• The Territorial Administration Building (48.8 m x 13.1 m) was completed in Dawson, Yukon. It would house documentation for all territorial mining claims, as well as the city council.

• The Royal Bank of Canada was founded in Halifax, NS.

• University of Toronto Press was established.

• American book salesman George McLeod formed a partnership with Thomas Allen in Toronto to market American bestsellers.

• Canada had 10,948,905 ha of improved farmland, all but 2,189,781 ha in the 5 eastern provinces.

• The Montreal Stock Exchange had 45 members: a seat cost $12,000.

• Psychiatrist Richard Maurice Bucke (1837–1902) published *Cosmic Consciousness*, a book about his metaphysical experiences. Bucke was Walt Whitman's literary executor and assisted in editing the completed works of the great poet. Bucke also founded U. of Western Ont.'s. medical school.

• There were 49 BC salmon canneries in operation during the year, which had the largest recorded run of Fraser R. sockeye. The canneries packed 1,200,000 cases of salmon for worldwide distribution during the season.

• *The Man from Glengarry*, a novel by Ralph Connor (1860–1937, pseud. Charles Gordon), was published.

• Businessman George A. Cox (1840–1914) founded Dominion Securities.

1902

Jan. 14 The Canadian Mounted Rifles sailed from Halifax for South Africa aboard the *Manhattan*.

Feb. 13 The 2nd session of the 9th Parliament met until May 23. The Immigration Act was amended to prohibit the immigration of diseased persons.

Feb. 18 The 1st steel was poured from the furnace of US businessman Francis Hector Clergue's (1856–1939) Algoma Steel Corporation Ltd., of Sault Ste. Marie, Ont. Algoma, which incorporated a Bessmer iron-to-steel converter, 1st made rails for Canada's transcontinental railways.

Mar. 4 Humorist Bob Edwards (1864–1922) launched the satirical newspaper the *Eye Opener*, in High River, Alb. His motto was, "Because no one can refuse taking one." Edwards moved the paper to Calgary in 1904, by which time it had gained a national reputation for originality and wit.

May 12 Construction began on the Temiskaming and Northern Ont. Railway, which would cover a distance of 409 km between North Bay, Ont., and Cochrane. The line was financed by the Ont. govt to bring settlers into the sparsely settled north.

May 22 One hundred and twenty-eight miners lost their lives in a mine explosion at Coal Creek Mine, near Fernie, BC.

May 31 The Treaty of Vereeniging ended the Boer War. Canada had spent almost $3 million on the war effort; 7,368 Canadians served, 224 died, most from disease.

June 21-24 A settlement mediated by the Toronto Board of Trade forced Toronto Street Railway employees back to work in the wake of a violent, 3-day strike.

July 19 Sir James Outram and his guide, Christian Kaufmann, became the 1st climbers to reach the top of Mount Columbia, the highest peak in Alb. and the 2nd highest in the Canadian Rockies after Mount Robson.

Aug. 21 Doukhobors living on the prairies turned their horses, cattle and sheep loose, "giving them to the lord." Govt officials rounded the animals up to save them from freezing or being destroyed by wild animals.

Aug. 25 Fire destroyed the 38-m-long sidewheeler *Star* at Indiantown near St. John, NB. The same fire also destroyed a neighbouring coal shed and warehouse.

Sept. 6 Oil started flowing from a well drilled by the Rocky Mountain Development Company in what is now Waterton Lakes National Park in Alb. The flow dwindled to a trickle within 2 years and in 1906 the well was closed. Although short-lived, Rocky Mountain Development No. 1 was western Canada's 1st producing oil well.

Oct. 18 PM Laurier demanded the resignation of Minister of Public Works Joseph Israel Tarte for attempting a leadership coup.

• An agreement was reached between Nfld. and the US on free trade. The arrangement allowed Nfld. saltfish to be exported to the US duty free, while also allowing American fisheries to purchase Nfld. bait duty free.

Nov. 6 The town of Medicine Hat, Alb., activated Canada's 1st municipally owned natural gas system. Gas had 1st been discovered in the region in 1883 by a CPR drilling crew looking for water reserves. In 1901, natural gas was found again, this time during an unsuccessful search for CPR coal reserves. In 1901, the town council claimed the rights to all natural gas sitting directly under Medicine Hat (21 billion cubic m), and created the town's own distribution system to supply gas to residents for heating, lighting, manufacturing and electrical power.

Nov. 21 Henri-Elzéar Tashereau (1836–1911) was appointed chief justice of the Supreme Court of Canada.

Nov. 25 Hockey great Edward W. (Eddie) Shore (d 1985) was born in St. Qu'Appelle-Cupar, Sask. Shore played defence for the Boston Bruins (1926-1940), winning the Hart Trophy 4 times. Shore also made the All Star Team's 1st team 4 times.

Dec. 1 Doukhobor spiritual leader Peter Verigin (d 1924) arrived in Sask. Shortly thereafter, Doukhobors paraded nude through the Yorkton, Sask., area, protesting a law requiring their children to attend school.

Dec. 5 Guglielmo Marconi (1874–1937) successfully sent and received radio signals between Glace Bay, NS, and Britain. In Feb. 1902, Parliament had granted him $80,000 to build the Glace Bay Wireless Station. On Oct. 8, 1907 the transatlantic wireless service would be opened to the public, transmitting between Glace Bay and Ireland.

Dec. 15 Canada's Gov-Gen., the Earl of Minto (1845–1914), sent greetings to King Edward VII by way of Marconi's radio system.

Also in 1902

• McGill's MacDonald Professor of Physics, Ernest Rutherford (1871–1937), working in conjunction with Professor Frederick Seddy (1877–1956), developed the disintegration theory of the atom.

• The Trades and Labour Congress of Canada amended its constitution to allow only 1 union to represent 1 craft or trade. Overlapping unions were expelled, thereby weakening the representation of the Congress.

• The International Nickel Company was incorporated in New Jersey with the amalgamation of the Canadian Copper, the Orford Copper Company and Société Minier Caledonienne. The new firm, the predecessor of Inco (est. 1916), would become a major exploiter of nickel in the Sudbury area.

• Orchestre symphonique de Québec, the 1st symphony orchestra in Canada, was founded.

• A smallpox epidemic hit Galt, Ont.

• John A. Schuberg opened the Edison Electric Theatre in Vancouver, the 1st permanent movie theatre in the country.

• Isaac Coffin, third-generation descendant of Sir Isaac Coffin (1759–1839), sold the 12 islands that make up the Îles de la Madeleine (affectionately known as the "Maggies") to the province of Quebec for $100,000. Sir Isaac was given the islands in 1798 by a grateful British govt in reward for his services during the American Revolution.

• Lawrence Morris Lambe (1863–1919) published *On Vertebrata of the Mid-Cretaceous of the Northwest Territory*, with an introduction by Henry Fairfield Osborn (1857–1935). Lampe was the 1st Canadian scientist to compile dinosaur fossils in Alb., and to record those findings in annual reports, that outlined new genera and species.

• The Indian Head Federal Tree Nursery was established in Indian Head, Sask., as a source of shelterbelt protection for prairie farmers.

• Lands and mountains surrounding L. Louise were incorporated into Rocky Mountains Park.

• Marc-Aurèle de Foy Suzor-Côté (1869–1937) painted the historical composition *La Mort de Montcalm*, now in the Musée du Québec.

• Sara Jeanette Duncan published *Those Delightful Americans*.

• Ralph Connor (pseud. Charles Gordon) published the novel *Glengarry School Days*.

• Charles G.D. Roberts (1860–1943) published the animal story, *The Kindred of the Wild*.

• The Canadian Pacific Railway commissioned British producer Charles Urban to shoot a series of films called *Living Canada* to attract immigrants to western Canada. Urban formed Canada's 1st film production company, the Bioscope Company, recruited cameramen and technicians and, using a flatcar pulled by a CPR engine, set out to film every part of the country that could be reached by rail. The only provision from the CPR: no snow scenes.

1903

Jan. 27 US industrialist Andrew Carnegie (1835–1919) offered a $350,000 grant for a central public library and 2 branch libraries in Toronto. It was accepted Feb. 23. Carnegie, and later his Carnegie Corporation of New York, founded in 1911, would provide gifts for libraries and church organs in Canada throughout much of the 20th century.

Feb. 11–July 4 Members of the Western Federation of Miners went on strike at Dominion Coal Mines in Ladysmith, BC, resulting in a loss of 88,200 person days.

Mar. 1 La Ligue Nationaliste was founded in Montreal by a group of journalists and lawyers. The group pushed for an autonomous Canada composed of autonomous provinces, goals illustrated in its weekly, *Le Nationaliste*.

Mar. 4 Grain growers formed the Man. Grain Growers' Association at a meeting in Brandon, Man. J. W. Scallion was elected the association's 1st president.

Mar. 12 The 3rd session of the 9th Parliament met until Oct. 24. The head tax on Chinese immigrants was raised to $500.

Apr. 10 Immigrants from England under Rev. Isaac M. Barr arrived at Saint John aboard the dilapidated *Manitoba*. They proceeded cross-country to what is today Lloydminster, Sask./Alb., and established a settlement. Barr, however, was deposed. Rev. George Exton Lloyd (1861–1940) was elected new settlement leader.

Apr. 16 Canada raised the tariff on goods imported from Germany in response to a similar German tariff on Canadian goods.

Apr. 23 The SS *Montrose* became the 1st CPR ship to sail the Atlantic.

Apr. 29 A landslide from Turtle Mountain dumped 82 million tonnes of rock on the town of Frank, Alb., located in the Crowsnest Pass. Over 70 people were killed. Approximately 1 km² of the valley was covered by 14 m of rock slide. Surveys and studies later showed the mountain was unstable and critically weakened by natural forces such as erosion, earthquakes and also by a local coal mine, a major local employer. Despite the tragedy, the mine was quickly reopened and remained in operation for a further 10 years.

May 7 Dock workers in Montreal went on strike until May 10.

Also in May.

• CPR president Shaughnessy met with a committee to negotiate building of a CPR hotel in Victoria, BC. The CPR, having received generous concessions from the city, built the famous chateau-style Empress Hotel, designed by Francis Mawson Rattenbury (1867–1935). Construction began in 1905; the hotel opened Jan. 20, 1908. With pitched roofs, prominent dormers, polygonal turrets and skyline proportions, the Empress is reminiscent of Quebec City's Château Frontenac.

June 1 Conservative party leader Richard McBride (1870–1917) formed the 1st BC administration based on party lines.

June 12 Ont. established a 7 mph (11.5 km/h) speed limit for cars.

June 19 Regina, NWT, was incorporated as a city.

Also in June

• The 1st youth conference of the newly organized Association Catholique de la Jeunesse Canadienne-Française was held in Montreal. The organization's main objective was to promote both the study of religion and national and social issues.

July 13 Minister of Railways and Canals George Andrew Blair (1844–1907) resigned his portfolio because of a Grand Trunk Railway policy dispute with PM Laurier.

July 30 PM Laurier announced a bill representing his own National Dream, the Grand Trunk Pacific, a railway that would reach uncharted territory north of the CPR, and move wheat and mineral resources more quickly than that older line. On Oct. 20, the Grand Trunk Pacific Railroad was chartered as a 2nd transcontinental railroad running from Moncton, NB, to Prince Rupert, BC. The eastern part of the line from Moncton was to be built by the federal govt, the western line from Winnipeg by the Grand Trunk Pacific. The line was to be completed by Dec. 1, 1911. It reached Prince Rupert Apr. 9, 1914. The National Transcontinental Railway (NTR) Bill was also passed by Parliament to provide a 3rd transcontinental railway (the National Transcontinental Railway), linking Moncton to Winnipeg through Que. and Ont.

Construction began in 1905; the railway was completed in 1913.

Aug. 7 NWMP Sergeant Francis Joseph Fitzgerald (1869–1911) and Constable F.D. Southerland arrived at Herschel Is., NWT, to establish a police post and an official Canadian presence. They were concerned that the US had designs on the region. Another post would be established by the NWMP at Cape Fullerton on the Hudson Bay near Chesterfield Inlet in 1904.

Aug. 22 The *Neptune* sailed from Halifax. With Captain Robert Abram Bartlett (1875–1946) as captain, and commanded by A.P. Low of the Geological Survey, it was to patrol, explore and establish the authority of Canada in the waters and islands of Hudson Bay and the North.

Sept. 15 Local folklore tells of a railway blacksmith, one Fred Larose at Long L. (now Cobalt), Ont. throwing his hammer at a mischievous fox, missing, and, while retrieving his hammer, stumbling upon fragments of what he thought was copper ore. Fred, and his boss, Duncan McMartin, both staked a claim on the property immediately. Examined by a provincial govt geologist later in the month, the fragments were recognized to be smaltite, niccolite and native silver. Fred eventually sold his stake for $30,000, returning to his native Hull, Que. The property produced 17.5 million ounces of silver and 90 tonnes of cobalt. This find and another in Kirkland L. triggered a series of mineral discoveries in northern Ont.

Oct. 10 The Ford Motor Company of Canada (incorporated Aug. 7) began production at Walkerville, Ont. The company produced 117 cars in its 1st year.

Oct. 20 A tribunal of 6 — 3 Americans, 2 Canadians and 1 Briton — voted 4–2 in favour of US claims, ending the Alaska boundary dispute. Americans received a continuous strip of the mainland from 25–50 km wide, from the entrance of Portland Canal to Mount St. Elias, thereby eliminating Canadian seaports in northern BC or the Yukon. British representative Lord Alverston had the deciding vote, putting British-American friendship ahead of Canadian interests. Anti-British sentiment swept the country. PM Laurier had agreed to the makeup of the tribunal in Oct. 1902.

Nov. 11 The *Edmonton Journal* was founded as the *Evening Journal* by John Macpherson, John W. Cunningham and Arthur Moore, all of Portage La Prairie.

Dec. 2 The central building of the U. of Ottawa, was completely destroyed by fire: including the library and 300,00 volumes.

Also in 1903

• The Winnipeg Real Estate Exchange was founded. Membership was limited to 60, and a seat on the exchange cost $100.

• The Canadian Motor Vehicles Act established a maximum automotive speed of 16 km/h in the city and 22 km/h in the country. These figures would be amended in 1919 to 30 km/h in the city and 40 km/h in the country.

• Ontario required all automobile drivers to obtain licences for the operation of their vehicles. Any applicant who could prove that he/she had driven 800 km without incident, and who had no physical or mental impairments was entitled to a licence upon payment of a $1 fee.

• Canada's men's curling teams in Halifax, Quebec, Montreal, Ottawa, Toronto, and Winnipeg beat a touring Scottish team to win the 1st Strathcona Cup.

• Klondike gold production was $96 million.

• The Royal Vancouver Yacht Club was founded.

• The Trades and Labour Congress of Canada established close relations with the American Federation of Labour (AFL), becoming a Canadian branch of the AFL.

• Stephen Leacock (1869–1944) published *Elements of Political Science*, which became the standard political science text in North America. Translated into 18 languages, it was Leacock's best-selling book during his lifetime.

• Montreal-born artist Clarence Gagnon (1881–1942) painted *Oxen Ploughing*, which so impressed wealthy collector James Morgan, he sent Gagnon to the Académie Julian in Paris for further study. *Oxen Ploughing* is held at the Montreal Museum of Fine Arts.

• Syndicated columnist and poet Bliss Carman published *The Kinship of Nature*, a volume of reprinted essays.

• Norman Duncan (1871–1916) published *The Way of the Sea*, a set of sketches of Nfld. outpost life.

• Ernest Thompson Seton (1860–1946) published *Two Little Savages*, a children's work.

• Louis Dantin published a collection of poems written by Émile Nelligan (1879–1941) under the title *Émile Nelligan et son Oeuvre*.

• Louvigny Testard de Montigny's (1876–1955) satiric play *Boules de Neige* appeared at Le Monument National in Montreal.

1904

Jan. 18 Speaking at the Canadian Club of Ottawa, PM Laurier explained "The 19th century was the century of the United States. I think we can claim that it is Canada that shall fill the 20th century." It was from this speech that Laurier would later wrongly be credited as having said, "The 20th century belongs to Canada."

Jan. 20 The federal govt disallowed a BC act restricting Chinese immigration. On Mar. 25, BC legislation restricting Japanese access to the job market was also disallowed.

Feb. 1 The Dominion Railway Commission was established, with power to fix rates, regulate operations and settle disputes.

Mar. 10 The 4th session of the 9th Parliament met until Aug. 10. Provisions were made for the subsidy of crude oil from Canadian wells.

Apr. 8 The Lansdowne-Cambon Convention was signed in London, England, to effect a settlement to the "French Shore" question. France surrendered the right granted in the 1713 Treaty of Utrecht to land and dry fish on certain coasts of Nfld., in return for cash and territorial concessions in Africa.

Apr. 11 Sydney, NS, was incorporated as a city.

Apr. 19 Fire broke out in Toronto's mercantile district causing over $10 million in damage to 139 businesses. It took 230 firefighters 9 hours to control the blaze.

May 14 Montreal policeman Etienne Desmarteau (1877–1905) became the 1st Canadian gold medallist in the 56-lb hammer throw at the St. Louis Olympics. (George Orton [1873–1958] won gold in the steeplechase at the 2nd Olympic Games in Paris in 1900, but as a member of the American team.) Golfer George S. Lyon, the only Canadian, and the only non-American in the field, won the 1st and last Olympic golf competition. Other golds were awarded to the Galt Football Club (soccer) and Winnipeg Shamrocks (lacrosse). Also of note was a bronze by the Mohawk Athletic Club from the Six Nations Reserve, Ont. The team included Black Hawk in net, Black Eagle at point, Almighty Voice at counter point, Flat Iron and Spotted Tail on defence, with home positions held by Snake Eater, Red Jacket, Night Hawk, Rain In Face, and Man Afraid Soap. The men were the 1st Aboriginals to receive Olympic medals.

June 7 Douglas Mackinnon Baillie Hamilton, Earl of Dundonald (1852–1935), was dismissed as C-in-C. of military forces in Canada for criticizing the minister of militia for political interference. This ended the practice of having imperial officers command the forces in Canada. Canadian forces have been controlled by the Canadian govt ever since.

June 24 The designation "Royal" was extended to the NWMP.

Aug. 28 Randall Davidson, the archbishop of Canterbury, arrived in Que. for a Canadian visit.

Oct. 8 Edmonton was incorporated as a city. K.W. MacKenzie (1862–1929) became its 1st mayor.

Nov. 3 PM Laurier and the Liberals maintained power in the general election, taking a majority with 64 seats. Federal Conservative leader Robert Borden lost his riding of Halifax. Voter turnout was 71.6%.

Dec. 10–Oct. 21, 1911 Earl Grey (1851–1917) served as gov-gen. of Canada.

Also in 1904

• More than 130,000 immigrants entered the country.

• Charles Saunders (1867–1937) developed Marquis wheat at the Dominion Experimental Farm in Ottawa, which had been established by his father, William, in 1888. Marquis, a hardy disease-resistant variety suited to the Canadian climate, was a cross between Red Fife and Red Calcutta. It became the standard ingredient in bread.

• The 1st Canadian Open Golf Championship was played on the Royal Montreal Golf Club. John H. Oke shot 156 over 36 holes to take the $170 purse. The Canadian Open was the 3rd oldest national championship in the world, behind the British Open (1860) and the US Open (1895).

• John Ross Robertson (1841–1918), executive director of the Ontario Hockey League (OHA) (and founder of the *Toronto Evening Telegram*), concluded, "We must call a halt to slashing and slugging, and insist upon clean hockey… before we have to call in a coroner to visit our rinks." Robertson would be inducted into the Hockey Hall of Fame in 1947 for his support of amateur hockey.

• Male members of the Montreal Bookbinders Union led a strike to force women employees from the bookbinding industry.

• Frank Wise opened a Canadian branch of the US publishing firm Macmillan's, in Toronto.

• Brother André (1845–1937), known as the miracle worker of Mount Royal, built St. Joseph, a small chapel on the present site of St. Joseph Oratoire, on the slopes of Mont Royal.

• Sara Jeanette Duncan published the novel *The Imperialist*.

• Rudolphe Girard published his satirical novel *Marie Calumet*, which dared to place clerics into a humorous context. The book was denounced by the archbishop of Montreal.

• Léon Pamphile Lemay (1837–1918) published his collection of sonnets entitled *Les Gouttelettes*, generally considered to include his finest works.

• Butchart Gardens in Victoria was begun by Jennie and Robert Butchart (1856–1943) in a limestone quarry they owned, exhausted, then began to fill with topsoil and concept gardens. By the 1920s, the site attracted some 50,000 visitors a year. By the turn of the century, Butchart Gardens sported nearly 1 million plants and 700 varieties, with annual blooming cycles covering Mar. through Oct.

• Brownsville, Ont., farmers produced the 1st milk powder in Canada.

1905

Jan. 16 Dawson City made its only appearance in the Stanley Cup final. The visitors from the Territories were humbled 23–2 in game 2 by the Ottawa Silver Seven with the 1-eyed Frank McGee scoring 14 goals.

Jan. 25 Ont. Conservative leader James Pliny Whitney (1834–1914) defeated the Liberal govt of George William Ross (1841–1914) and assumed premiership Feb. 8. The Conservatives had not held power in Ont. since 1871.

Jan. 26 Clifford Sifton resigned from the federal govt, protesting the Laurier-supported educational provisions in the Alb. and Sask. Autonomy Bill. The provisions gave minorities the right to establish schools, teach in their own language and share in public funds to maintain these schools. After Sifton's departure, Laurier modified the terms to continue the system established by a NWT ordinance of 1901, allowing for a minority of ratepayers in any district, whether Protestant or Catholic, to establish a separate school and earmark their taxes for that school.

May 25 Peterborough, Ont., was incorporated as a city.

June 4 The CPR began offering daily service from eastern Canada to Vancouver.

June 15 Nfld. prohibited the sale of bait and the granting of licences to foreign fishing vessels, a reaction to the US cancellation of a Nfld.–US trade agreement.

July 12 Treaty No. 9, also known as the James Bay Treaty, was signed between Cree and Ojibwa First Nations and the provincial govt. The treaty marked the 1st time a provincial govt took an active role in treaty negotiations. As a result, the first Nations relinquished 336,698 km² of land running from Que. to Man., from north of the watershed line midway through northern Ont. in exchange for annual payments of $4 per year per individual, reserves totaling 1,331 km², govt-funded schools, and hunting, trapping and fishing rights throughout the area (subject to govt regulations).

July 25 The Northwest Territories Act established new boundaries for the NWT to accommodate Alb. and Sask., made provinces Sept. 1. It also provided the appointment of a commissioner and a council of 4.

Aug. 13 During the Russo-Japanese War, the Canadian ship *Antiope* out of Victoria was seized by the Japanese as a carrier of contraband.

Sept. 1 Alb. and Sask. became Canada's 8th and 9th provinces under the Alb. and Sask. Acts. The northern boundary of the 2 provinces was the 60th parallel, the same as BC, and the boundary between the 2 was the 110th meridian. George Hedley Vicars Bulyea (1859–1928) became the 1st lt-gov. of Alb.; and Amédée Emmanuel Forget (1847–1923), the 1st lt-gov. of Sask. On Sept. 4, Sask. held inaugural ceremonies. Prime Minister Laurier and Gov-Gen. Earl Grey were in attendance at the ceremonies.

Sept. 11 Construction began on the L. Superior branch of the Grand Trunk Pacific Railroad, at Fort William, Ont. (Thunder Bay).

Sept. 29 The Carnegie Library opened in Guelph, Ont., funded by the Carnegie Foundation of New York.

Oct. 10 A fire ravaged Summerside, PEI, destroying over 100 homes.

Nov. 9 The 1st provincial election in Alb. was held. Liberals under Alexander Cameron Rutherford (1857–1941) took 22 of 25 seats, and Rutherford became the 1st premier.

Nov. 24 The CNR was completed to Edmonton. Lt-Gov. G.H.V. Bulyea hammered home the silver spike, marking the completion of the railway line to the city. The 1st passenger train, composed of 2 special cars carrying dignitaries, including promoters William McKenzie and Daniel Mann, made the trip to Edmonton from Winnipeg in 27 hours.

Dec. 13 The 1st provincial election in Sask. was held. The Liberals took 16 seats. Walter Scott (1867–1938) became the 1st premier of Sask. The Provincial Rights Party under Frederick W. Haultain (1857–1942) received the remaining 9 Assembly seats.

c 1905 Edmund Montague Morris (1871–1913) painted *Cove Fields, Quebec*, oil on canvas, now in the National Gallery of Canada.

• Maurice Cullen (1866–1934) completed the canvas *Winter Evening, Quebec*, now in the National Gallery of Canada.

1905–1914 An average of 21 new Canadian novels appeared annually.

Also in 1905
• Canada's 1st Buddhist temple opened at the Ishikawa Hotel on Powell Street, Vancouver.

• The 1st Polish immigrants arrived in Man.

• G.W. Balcom and Reuben Balcom from NS opened the land-based Pacific Whaling Co. processing station near Ucluelet, BC.

• The federal govt assumed control of the fortifications at Esquimalt, BC, from Britain. It became the base of the Canadian navy on the Pacific Coast.

• John Bayne Maclean purchased the *Busy Man's Magazine,* the predecessor to *Maclean's Magazine.*

• Frederick Philip Grove (Felix Paul Greve) (1979–1948) published *Fanny Essler.* The work was reminiscent of Dreiser's *Sister Carrie* in its account of the social constraints on a woman's life.

1906

Jan. 16 The British garrison at Halifax was transferred to the Canadian federal govt. On May 22, the last British forces in Canada were withdrawn from Esquimalt, BC. By June 18, all military property in the country was formally transferred to the federal govt by Britain.

Jan. 23 Tommy Burns (born Noah Brusso [1881–1955] in Hanover, Ont.) won the world heavyweight boxing title from Marvin Hart in a 20-round bout in Los Angeles. At 162 pounds (73.482 kg), Burns was the smallest world heavyweight champ ever.

Jan. 24 The US Steamer *Valencia* sank after hitting a reef off Vancouver Is., 126 people died.

Jan. 31 Britain and Japan signed a trade agreement opening up Japanese trade with Canada.

Mar. 4 Motorist H.W. White completed the 1st automobile trip from Edmonton to Calgary. Driving a 29-horsepower Ford, White and his passengers left Edmonton on Saturday morning, travelled at speeds of up to 40 mph, overnighted in Red Deer (approximately the halfway point) and drove into Calgary on Sunday evening.

Mar. 9 Coal miners at Lethbridge, Alb., went on strike until Dec. 2.

Mar. 15 Amid much pomp and ceremony, Lt-Gov. G.H.V. Bulyea formally opened the inaugural session of Alb.'s 1st provincial legislature, held in Edmonton's Thistle Curling Rink (which was decorated with flags and banners for the occasion). The ice was taken out and church pews from local churches were brought in to provide seating for the thousands of spectators.

Mar. 19 The 49.4-m-long paddle steamer *Sovereign* burned right down to the waterline at Lachine, Que. The magnificent steamer was built in 1889 in Montreal for the Ottawa River Navigation Company, to run between Montreal and Carillon.

Mar. 29–30 Striking Winnipeg Electric Railway employees rioted in Winnipeg. Soldiers were called to maintain order. Workers returned to work after a settlement awarded wage increases and a 10-hour day.

Also in Mar.
• Toronto's 1st movie house, the *Theatorium*, opened.

Apr. 6 After 15 years with the Methodist Book and Publishing House (later Ryerson Press), John McClelland (1877–1968), opened his own publishing house in Toronto in partnership with Frederick Goodchild (1883–1925). Signalling what would eventually become the company's commitment to Canadian authors, McClelland & Goodchild published *The Watchman and Other Poems* by Lucy Maud Montgomery. In 1919, after the departure of Goodchild and the arrival of George Stewart (1876–1955), the company changed its name to McClelland & Stewart and continued its tradition of publishing Canadian authors.

Apr. 23 In response to the growing number of cars in Alb., J.R. Boyle, member of the provincial legislature for Sturgeon, introduced a motion to "regulate the speed and operation of motor vehicles on highways." The speed limit was established at 20 mph in the country and 10 mph in the city. If a horse was on the road and appeared startled, the vehicle had to come to an immediate and complete stop until the horse moved on. Despite complaints that the regulations were only a means for the province to raise revenue, all vehicles had to be registered and the owners had to take out permits.

May 1 The Carnegie Public Library opened at Ottawa.

• Billy Sherring (1877–1964) of Hamilton, Ont., won the Olympic marathon in Athens, Greece. On the last lap, the 51-kg Sherring was paced by Crown Prince Constantine. Sherring had placed 2nd in his 1st running of the Boston Marathon in 1900.

May 8 The University of Alb. at Edmonton was founded.

• American desperado train robber Bill Miner and 2 accomplices robbed a CPR passenger train near Kamloops, BC, of $15. The bandits were captured by the RNWMP several days later. It was Canada's 1st recorded train robbery.

May 9 The Alb. legislature passed acts incorporating the cities of Medicine Hat, Lethbridge and Wetaskiwin.

May 14 The Ontario Hydro-Electric Power Commission was created, with Adam Beck (1857–1925) chairman. It was the 1st publicly owned electric utility in the world.

June 4 Charles Fitzpatrick (1853–1942) was appointed chief justice of the Supreme Court of Canada.

July 6 After much bitter debate, Parliament passed the Lord's Day Act, forbidding stores and other businesses from staying open on Sundays, Sunday transportation (with certain exceptions), and Sunday entertainments for which a fee was charged.

July 20 Reginald Aubrey Fessenden (1866–1932) formed the Fessenden Wireless Telegraph Company of Canada. On Dec. 25, Fessenden transmitted the 1st radio program. United Fruit Company ships in the Atlantic and Caribbean heard the sound of Fessenden singing Christmas carols, reading from the Bible and playing the violin.

• In Saskatchewan, Treaty No.10 between the Chipewyan of English R., the Cree of Canoe L. and the govt of Canada was signed. Aboriginals surrendered 220,149 km^2 of northern Sask. land in return for 2.58 km^2 (maximim) of reserve land for every family of 5; $32 for every chief; $22 for every headman; and $12 to all others. The govt would also pay every year, $25 to each chief; $15 to each headman and $5 to all others.

Aug. 13 Norwegian explorer Roald Amundsen (1874–1928) reached Nome, Alaska, in the *Gjoa* after the 1st east-to-west navigation of the Northwest Passage. Amundsen began his voyage on June 17, 1903.

Sept. 5 The co-operative Grain Growers' Grain Company opened in Sask. Established by farmers in 1905 to handle grain interests, it was the 1st farm-owned grain company to trade on the Winnipeg Grain Exchange.

Sept. 22 Miners at Fernie and Michel, BC, went on strike until Nov. 13.

Nov. 16 A delegation from the Man. Grain Growers Association in Ottawa asked that the protective principle of tariffs be wholly eliminated.

Nov. 22 The 3rd session of the 10th Parliament met until Apr. 27. An act provided for the inspection of meats, canned goods and cold-storage warehouses. The Department of Mines was formed. The Industrial Disputes Investigation (Lemieux) Act prevented strikes and lockouts until the dispute had been sent to a govt arbitration board.

Dec. 7 Striking Hamilton Street Railway workers returned to their jobs. Violence and riots had punctuated the strike as the Hamilton Street Railway Co. tried to introduce replacement workers.

Also in 1906
• The Consolidated Mining and Smelting Company (COMINCO) was formed

• Travelling salesman Peter L. Robertson (1879–1951) applied for a Canadian patent on a socket-head screw. Robertson, born in Caledonia, Ont., was an inveterate tinkerer and inventor, creator of such well-known tools as Robertson's 20th century wrench, Robertson's cufflinks, Robertson's mousetrap, and even Robertson's corkscrew. It was his square-headed screwdriver, however, that would make him famous.

• William Andrew White was the 1st African-Canadian to graduate from Acadia University, NS.

• Man. adopted the pasque flower (prairie crocus–*Anemone Patens.*) as its provincial flower.

• Ozias Leduc completed *Erato (Muse in the Forest)*, oil on canvas.

• *Poésies*, by Alfred Garneau (1836–1904), was published.

• The novel *Set in Authority*, by Sara Jeanette Duncan, was 1st published in the weekly edition of the *London Times*.

• Missionary doctor, Sir Wilfred Thomason Grenfell (1865–1940), published the novel, *Off the Rocks*.

1907

Jan. 28 Nationalist politician Armand Lavergne (1880–1935) was expelled from the Liberal party for attacks made on PM Laurier and the federal

Liberal Party. On Feb. 25, Lavergne unsuccessfully moved for the adoption of bilingual currency and bilingual postage stamps. On May 25, 1908, Lavergne resigned his federal seat to campaign with Henri Bourassa (1868–1952) in the provincial elections.

Also in Jan.

• Toronto telephone employees went on strike.

Mar. 8 The Supreme Court of Sask. was established.

Mar. 14 Technical schools were established at Montreal and Quebec City.

Mar. 15 Strathcona, across the Sask. R. from Edmonton, was incorporated as a city. Its population was 3,500.

Mar. 18 The Railroad Commission ordered the Canadian Pacific and the Grand Trunk Railroads to reduce passenger fare to 3 cents per mile.

Apr. 1 PM Laurier forced the resignation of Henry Robert Emmerson (1853–1914), minister of railways and canals, on invalidated charges that he had been in a Montreal hotel with a woman of ill repute.

Apr. 3 A provincial charter was granted to the U. of Sask., at Saskatoon.

Apr. 15 Over 3,000 coal miners in Alb. and eastern BC went on strike until May 6. As a result, the Industrial Disputes Investigation Act, drawn up by Mackenzie King, was passed. It provided mandatory govt intervention of industrial disputes on application of either party involved, and a 3-party board to review grievances and recommend solutions.

Apr. 19 Onondaga Thomas Charles Longboat (1887–1949) won the Boston Marathon in record time to become the champion long-distance runner in America.

Apr. 20 Port Arthur and Fort William (now Thunder Bay, Ont.) were incorporated as cities.

May 7 The Vancouver Stock Exchange was established.

May 15 Toronto plumbers went on strike until Sept.

June 22 Four died when the sidewheeler *Crystal Stream* was destroyed by fire at Coles Is. in the Washademoak R., 98 km from Saint John.

Also in June

• 101,200 ha were taken away from the Doukhobors for violating the Dominion Land Act, which required all settlers to take up quarter parcels individually and swear allegiance to the British monarch. According to Doukhobor belief, land was to be held in common and allegiance was to be given only to God. As a result, many Doukhobors from areas around Prince Albert and Yorkton, Sask., moved to the Kootenay region of BC.

• The 1st school dental inspection in Canada was inaugurated at Halifax.

July 31 A plant designed to generate electrical power from coal was established at Maccan, NS. Among its founders was Thomas Alva Edison (1847–1931).

Also in July

• Thomas Alexander Crerar (1876–1975) became president of the Grain Growers' Grain Company.

Aug. 1 Coal miners at Springhill, NS, went on strike until Oct. 31.

Aug. 8 Train robber Bill Miner escaped from the New Westminster Penitentiary, where he was serving time for a train robbery. He fled to the US and resumed his familiar ways.

Aug. 10 John Underwood became the 1st man in Canada to be lifted off the ground in a heavier-than-air craft: he spent 15 minutes on a homemade kite tethered 3.1 m above the ground.

Aug. 29 The south arm of the Quebec Bridge collapsed while under construction, killing 82 people. An inquiry indicated engineers' miscalculations caused the accident. The bridge was completed in 1917, the longest trussed span bridge in the world.

Aug. 31 The world's largest cinema, the opulent, 1,200-seat air-conditioned Ouimetoscope was opened in Montreal by L.E. Ouimet (1877–1972).

Sept. 8–9 The recently formed Asiatic Exclusion League, 7,000 men who opposed Asiatic migration, stormed Vancouver's "Chinatown," starting a riot. Shocked residents mounted a defence, and expelled the League with knives, bottles and sticks. On Oct. 12, the federal govt agreed to pay damages caused by the Vancouver mobs. W.L. Mackenzie King (1874–1950) was appointed to hold hearings on the losses.

Sept. 19 Canada signed a commercial treaty with France. Ratified on Feb. 1, 1910, the agreement allowed Canada minimum rates on many agricultural products, agricultural implements, lumber and pulp, furniture, boots and shoes, and asbestos products.

Sept. 23 The RNWMP completed a route from Edmonton, Alb., to Dawson, establishing access to the Yukon town entirely through Canadian territory.

Sept. 30 A.G. Bell, in partnership with John Alexander Douglas McCurdy (1886–1961), Frederick Walker "Casey" Baldwin (1882–1948) and other engineers established the Aerial Experimental Association at Baddeck, NS, to experiment with flying machines.

Oct. 13 Author Rudyard Kipling stopped in Medicine Hat, Alb., during a trip across Canada. He noted that the city had a plentiful supply of natural gas directly below it, telling reporters that Medicine Hat had — among other virtues — "all hell for a basement."

Nov. 20 Fourteen miners were killed in a gas explosion at No. 1 tunnel, Crow's Nest Pass Coal collieries, at Carbonado, near the town of Morrissey, BC.

Also in Nov.

• Likely the 1st dial telephones in Canada came into use at Sydney Mines, NS.

Dec. 1 In Montreal, Archbishop Louis Joseph Paul Napoléon Bruchési (1855–1939) issued an edict banning his parishioners from attending movie theatres on Sundays.

Dec. 6 The 1st recorded flight in Canada of a heavier-than-air machine took place at Baddeck, NS, when Thomas Selfridge was lifted in a tetrahedral kite, the *Cygnet*, designed by A.G. Bell. Selfridge later became the 1st person in history to die in a powered air crash when, in 1908 the plane he was flying with Orville Wright lost control and plummeted to the ground.

1907–1909 The CPR began construction on its 1.6-km-long, 100-m-tall, High Level Bridge in Lethbridge, Alb. The bridge was completed in Oct. 1908 at a cost of $1.3 million.

Also in 1907

• The Canadian govt established Jasper National Park (10,878 km^2) in northern Alb., as the largest of the Rocky Mountain parks. Land for the park was expropriated from local First Nations and Métis peoples, although one determined couple (Lewis and Suzette Swift) held out until 1962, when the govt was finally able to purchase their ranch for $227,850. Jasper National Park, named after Jasper Hawes, manager of a NWC trading post in the area (whose sobriquet was also given to the townsite), features the Athabaska R. and glacier, subalpine forest, the spectacular Maligne Canyon, and a wide variety of flora and fauna, including a population of 2,000 bighorn sheep. The park is accessible by CN Rail and by the Columbia Icefields Parkway.

• John J. McLaughlin (1865–1914) patented Canada Dry ginger ale.

• Richard Common Purdy established R.C. Purdy Chocolates in Vancouver. The store would become Purdy's by the 1960s and in the 20th century the largest chocolate retailer in western Canada, with 44 stores throughout BC and Alb., and 3 in Toronto, Ont.

• Dr. Andrew Macphail (1864–1938) was appointed McGill U.'s 1st professor of the history of medicine, a post he would hold for 30 years. However, Macphail is best known for his fictional, semi-autobiographical work set in PEI, *The Master's Wife*, which was published posthumously in 1939.

• Sobeys grocery stores was begun in NS as a meat-delivery service by William Sobey. By 2002, Sobeys Inc. would include IGA, Price Chopper, Bonichoix, Foodland and Needs, with more then 1,300 outlets.

• The Kenora Thistles beat the Montreal Wanderers 2 games to 1, to win the Stanley Cup. A rematch 2 months later returned the cup to the Montreal team.

• Geologist A.P. Coleman (1852–1939) discovered evidence of the world's oldest glaciation in northern Ontario (the Gowganda Formation, now known to be 2,300 million years old). In the same year, Coleman published his account of nickel-cooper deposits in the Sudbury area, a most important contribution to the development of Ont.'s mining industry.

• The Western Associated Press was founded by a group of Winnipeg publishers.

• There were 47 brothels operating on Dupont St. in Vancouver.

• There were 1,550 people living in 575 tents in Edmonton, not uncommon arrangements for early nineteenth-century western workers and recent immigrants.

• Artist Homer Watson became the 1st president of the Canadian Art Club.

• Ont.-born artist Albert Curtis Williamson (1867–1944) painted *Fish Sheds, Newfoundland*, now in the National Gallery of Canada.

• William Brymner completed the canvas *Evening*, now in the National Gallery of Canada.

• W.H. Clapp, born in Montreal of American parents, painted *Morning in Spain*, oil on canvas, in a decorative, pointillist style.

• *The Measure of the Rule*, by Robert Barr (1850–1912), was published. The work provided an autobiographical account of Toronto Normal School in the 1870s.

• The volume of poems, *L'Âme Solitaire*, by Albert Lozeau (1878–1924), was published in Paris through the generosity of PM Laurier.

• Poet Robert Service (1874–1958) published *The Spell of the Yukon and Other Verses*, which included "The Heart of the Sourdough," "The Shooting of Dan McGrew" and "The Cremation of Sam McGee." Service had emigrated to Canada from England in 1894 before serving as a war correspondent for *The Toronto Star* during the Balkan War of 1912–1913 and WW I.

• The Royal Alexandra Theatre in Toronto, designed by John MacIntosh Lyle (1872–1945), was completed.

• *An Acadian Elopement* was the 1st US film made about Canada.

1908

Jan. 1 A group of Doukhobors from the radical extremist sect the Sons of Freedom, who had begun a pilgrimage from Yorkton, Sask., in July 1907, reached Fort William, Ont. (Thunder Bay), where they paraded naked through the streets, a symbolic act repudiating materialism. The Ont. govt then returned them to their homes by train.

Jan. 2 The Royal Mint opened at Ottawa. The mint's 1st coin, a gold sovereign, was struck by Gov-Gen. Lord Grey.

Jan. 16 The Man. govt assumed responsibility for telephone service in the province.

Jan. 21 The Japanese govt agreed to limit the immigration of railway workers to Canada to 400 a year. This quota was revised in 1928 to restrict annual Japanese immigration to 150.

Feb. 13 Federal authorities ordered *habeas corpus* writs be issued by BC authorities to release any immigrants held under the province's new Natal Act, designed to exclude Asian immigrants.

Feb. 19 American explorer Frederick Albert Cook set out in the *John R. Bradley* to reach the North Pole. His land trek on foot across the ice began Mar. 18. Cook claimed to have reached the North Pole on Apr. 21, where he said he remained for 2 days, the 1st man to do so. His claim was rejected in 1909.

Mar. 7 The U. of BC was founded as a branch of McGill U. It became an independent university in 1915.

Mar. 12 Frederick Walker (Casey Baldwin) (1882–1948) became the 1st Canadian to fly an airplane, the *Red Wing*, at Hammondsport, New York. Baldwin worked under A.G. Bell in the Aerial Experiment Association at Baddeck, NS.

Mar. 17 The National Battlefields Commission (NBC) was created to establish the Battlefield Park, incorporating the Plains of Abraham, site of the battle conquest of 1759, and Des Braves Park, created to honour the combatants.

Apr. 5 Edmonton, Alb., installed one of the 1st dial telephone systems in NA.

Apr. 25 The Montreal residential area of Westmount was incorporated as a city.

May 1–June 1912 Vilhjalmur Stefansson and Rudolph Martin Anderson (1876–1961) undertook a scientific expedition, backed by the American Museum of Natural History, to study the Inuit and make zoological surveys in the Arctic, east of the Mackenzie R.

May 1 Tenor Enrico Caruso gave a concert at Massey Hall. Top ticket prices were $4.

May 6 The 36.6-m-long sternwheeler *City of Medicine Hat* struck a concrete bridge pier on the South Sask. R. in Saskatoon, and sank. All on board survived.

May 16 The 42.7-m-long steamer *Aberdeen* caught fire while docked at Cody's Wharf on Coles Is., NB. It was towed away from the wharf, where it sank near the wreck of the *Crystal Stream*.

May 23 Fire ravaged the city of Trois-Rivières, Que., destroying the Ursuline monastery, the Tonnancour Manor and almost all buildings established during the French regime.

June The 1st Canadian automobile service station appeared at the corner of Smith and Cambie Streets in Vancouver.

July 6 American explorer Admiral Robert Edwin Peary (1856–1920) sailed from New York in the *Roosevelt* on an expedition to reach the North Pole. The expedition reached the Arctic Ocean on Sept. 5, and Peary set out from his ship on the journey to the Pole Feb. 22, 1909. After establishing supply caches, Peary was left with 4 Inuit, 40 dogs and assistant Matthew Alexander Henson, veteran African-American explorer, for the final stretch of the journey. On Apr. 2, 1909, they passed to the 89th parallel and arrived on Apr. 6 at what they identified as the North Pole. Peary was unable to send a message of their achievement until Sept. 6.

• Canada Post issued 8 new stamps commemorating the 300th anniversary of Champlain's founding of Quebec.

Also in July
• Vilhjalmur Stefansson and Rudolph Martin Anderson arrived on the east bank of the Peel R. at Fort McPherson, NWT.

Aug. 1–3 The coal-mining town of Fernie, BC, was destroyed by a fire that spread 12.9 km to the outskirts of Hosmer. The Kootenay Valley Fire killed 70 people and caused $5 million in damage.

Aug. 5 CPR machinists and carmen went on strike until Oct. 5.

Aug. 26 Notre-Dame de la Salette, Que., was partly destroyed by a landslide; 37 lives were lost.

Sept. 23 Forty-five students attended the 1st English, mathematics and modern languages classes of the U. of Alb. Because the university had no campus, classes were held on the top floor of Strathcona's Queen Alexandra Elementary School. The 1st director was Dr. Henry Marshall Tory (1864–1947).

Oct. 10 The 1st free rural mail delivery began between Hamilton and Ancaster, Ont.

Oct. 26 Wilfrid Laurier led the Liberals to a 3rd victory in the national election, winning 133 seats. Borden's Conservatives took 85 seats. Independents received 3 seats. Voter turnout was 70.3%.

Dec. Ernest Rutherford received the Nobel Prize in Chemistry for his work in radioactivity and atomic fission (disintegration theory of the atom), conducted at the Macdonald Physics Laboratory, McGill U., between 1898 and 1907.

c 1908 Emily Carr (1871–1945) completed the watercolour *War Canoes,* now in a private collection.

Also in 1908
• Robert Stanley Weir (1856–1926), Montreal-based lawyer and author, wrote English lyrics to the original 1880 French version of "O Canada," melody by Calixa LaVallée (1842–1891), French lyrics had been written by Adolph-Basile Routhier (1839–1920).

• Robert Samuel McLaughlin (1871–1972), of McLaughlin Carriage Works, began building Buick car bodies for William C. Durant, founder of General Motors. McLaughlin produced 200 bodies within a year. This arrangement led to the mass production of McLaughlin-Buicks in Oshawa, Ont.

• The Dominion Lands Act came into effect to liquidate the remaining railway land grants; 12,141,000 ha were released for sale, with the revenue used to build the Hudson Bay Railway.

• Driving an automobile in PEI was limited to Mondays, Wednesdays and Thursdays. Further, any community could and, some did, keep a total ban on cars. This resulted in owners, if delayed, having to wait until the next permissible driving day to return their car home. Often, it resulted in the driver pulling his car across a town that did not allow driving at all.

• The 1st Alberta music festival was held in Edmonton.

• E.A. Pelletier led a 9-month-long RNWMP expedition to explore the barren lands east of Great Slave L.

• Scoutmaster Will Gloves formed the 1st Boy Scout troop in NA at Port Morien, NS.

• William E. Atkinson (1862–1926) painted *Willows Evening*, an exemplary "tonalist" Dutch-influenced work, now in the National Gallery of Canada.

• Clarence Gagnon painted *Les deux plages: Parame et Saint Malo*, now in the Beaverbrook Art Gallery, Fredericton, NB.

• *Anne of Green Gables*, by Lucy Maud Montgomery, was published by L.C. Page Company of Boston.

• A novel about West Coast logging camps, *Woodmen of the West*, by Martin Allerdale Grainger (1874–1941), was published.

• The novel, *Sowing Seeds in Danny*, by Nellie McClung, was published. It sold 100,000 copies.

• William Wilfred Campbell published 4 verse plays in *Poetical Tragedies*.

1909

Jan. 11 The Boundary Waters Treaty, signed by the US and Canada, established the International Joint Commission to fix and apply the rules of boundary water resource use. Both countries also fixed an agreement to protect the beauty of Niagara Falls from industrial exploitation.

Jan. 20 The 1st session of the 11th Parliament met until May 19. A Commission of Conservation of Natural Resources was authorized.

Jan. 27 An agreement was signed by the US and Britain to submit fisheries disputes between Canada and the US to the Permanent Court of Arbitration at The Hague, Netherlands.

Also in Jan.
• The Alb. Farmers' Association and a local branch of the American Society of Equity joined forces at a convention held in Edmonton, establishing the United Farmers of Alb. James Bower was elected president of the 5,000-member organization.

Feb. 23 John Alexander Douglas McCurdy flew the A.G. Bell–designed aircraft *Silver Dart* in a test flight at Bras d' Or Lakes, Baddeck, NS, the 1st powered flight in Canada (and the BE).

Mar. 13 Lord Strathcona (Donald Smith) established the Strathcona Trust, the 1st national physical education and military drill program in elementary and secondary Canadian schools. Strathcona contributed $500,000 for its implementation.

Apr. 1 Over 2,000 coal miners in Alb. went on strike until June 30.

Apr. 7 The board of governors chose Saskatoon as the site for the U. of Sask. The 1st building opened its doors for student admission Oct. 12, 1912.

June 1 PM Laurier created the Department of External Affairs under civil servant Joseph Pope (1854–1926). The department served as an archive, a liaison with the British Colonial Office and issuer of passports for Canadians travelling abroad. Charles Murphy (1863–1935), of Ottawa, was appointed secretary of state for the new department.

June 3 Mackenzie King (1847–1950) became the 1st minister of labour in the newly formed Department of Labour.

June 17 Calgary's ratepayers, in a public vote, narrowly approved the purchase of the 1st motorized firefighting wagon in Canada.

July 1 Joseph-Elzéar Bernier (1852–1934), captain of the Canadian steamship *Arctic*, unveiled a plaque on Melville Is. which officially claimed the Arctic Islands, extending from 60°W to 141°W up to latitude 90°N, for Canada. In salute, Bernier fired 19 shots in the air, and then gave the rifle to his Inuit companion and told him to fire the 20th, since he was now a Canadian.

July 5 The Calgary Municipal Railway made its inaugural run between downtown Calgary and the exhibition grounds at Victoria Park, 4.8 km away. An estimated 9,000 passengers were aboard.

July 6 Coal miners at Glace Bay, NS, went on strike.

July 13 Prospectors George Bannerman and Tom Geddes discovered gold in the Cochrane district of northern Ont.

July 17 The Juvenile Delinquent Act of 1908, the 1st federal legislation dealing with juvenile delinquents, went into effect. The act established the state as a sympathetic guardian, treating each juvenile as a misguided child. Judges were given a great deal of leeway in dealing with individual cases.

Also in July
• The CPR purchased the controlling interest in the Allan Line, the former Montreal Ocean Steamship Company founded by Hugh Allan in 1854, for £1,609,000. The purchase was kept secret until 1915.

Aug. 15 The Celtic Cross Monument on Grosse Île, Que., built in honour of the thousands of Irish immigrants who died on the island of ship fever (typhus) between 1847–1848, was unveiled before a solemn crowd of 9,000. The monument was cut from grey Stanstead granite and stands on Telegraph Hill, 43 m above the St. Lawrence River.

Aug. 18 Vilhjalmur Stefansson (1879–1962) reached Herschel Is. aboard the schooner *Challenge*

where he studied the language and customs of the Inuit.

Aug. 25 The 79th meeting of the British Association for the Advancement of Science was held in Winnipeg. The meeting was referred to as the "Parliament of Science."

Aug. 27 The 59.4-m paddle steamer *Bohemian*, renamed the *Prescott* in 1905, was destroyed by fire in Montreal harbour.

Also in Aug.
• The Spiral Tunnels were completed on the CPR line between Hector and Field, BC, to avoid "Big Hill," where trains often became runaways on the steep inclines of Kicking Horse Pass.

Sept. 7 For 35 minutes, carpenter Reginald Hunt flew a balloon shaped like an airship over Edmonton, Alb.

Oct. 4 Gov-Gen. Earl Grey laid the cornerstone of the Legislature Building in Regina. The $1.8 million structure was officially opened in 1912.

Oct. 9 The Grand Falls paper mill opened in Nfld.

Oct. 19 Calgary Power Company Ltd. was established by Richard Bedford Bennett (1870–1947) to provide hydroelectric power for the city.

Oct. 21 The Royal Edward Institute for tuberculosis opened in Montreal. It quickly became one of Canada's foremost hospitals specializing solely in the care and prevention of tuberculosis. It became a McGill U.–affiliated teaching hospital in the early 1930s.

Nov. 11 The 2nd session of the 11th Parliament met until May 4, 1910. The Department of Naval Service was established. The Currency Act provided for the issue of gold coins and a silver dollar. The importation of insects and pests harmful to the Canadian environment was prohibited. The Combines' Investigation Act was passed, providing for the investigation of monopolies, trusts and mergers.

Dec. 3 The Regina Symphony Orchestra, founded by conductor Franklin Laubach (1857–1923), performed its 1st concert.

Dec. 4 U. of Toronto defeated Parkdale Canoe Club 26–6 to win the 1st Grey Cup, a new trophy donated by Gov-Gen. Lord Grey to be awarded to the country's best amateur football team. Since 1954, the Grey Cup has been awarded annually to CFL champs.

c 1909 James Wilson Morrice (1865–1924) painted *The Ferry, Québec,* oil on canvas, showing Quebec City from Levis, across the St. Lawrence R. It is now in the National Gallery of Canada.

Also in 1909

• Jack Miner (1865–1944) devised a system of tagging birds at his bird sanctuary near Kingston, Ont. to study their migration routes. Miner would go on to band as many as 50,000 wild ducks in his lifetime.

• Botanist John Macoun published the 1st *Catalogue of Canadian Birds,* with his son Jed Macoun, for the Canadian Geological Survey.

• The Criminal Code was amended to criminalize the abduction of women. Prior to this amendment, the abduction of any woman over 16 was legal, except if she was an heiress. At the time, the maximum penalty for stealing a cow was significantly higher than that for kidnapping an heiress.

• American geologist Charles Doolittle Walcott discovered exquisitely preserved fossils in the Burgess Shale of BC's Yoho National Park, one of the most important geological sites in the world, as it records the 1st explosion of multicellular life. The diversity of invertebrate organisms found in the slate exceeds the entire spectrum of invertebrate life in today's oceans. At the time it was thought that the Burgess fossils were simply primitive ancestors of today's arthropods, but scientists have discovered that many of the types cannot be placed in any modern group.

• The Porcupine goldrush began in northern Ont., leading to the development of the "Big Three" mines around Porcupine L. in Timmins, Ont.: the Placer Dome Mine, discovered by Jack Wilson; the Hollinger Mine, discovered by Benjamin Hollinger and Alex Gillies; and the McIntyre Mine, discovered by Alexander Olifant (aka Sidney McIntyre).

• 5-pin bowling was pioneered by Thomas F. Ryan (d 1961) in Toronto, Ont. Bill Bromfield bowled the 1st 450 perfect game in 1921. In 1922, the 1st intercity match was played between Toronto and Montreal via telephone connection. The 1st official rule book for the game would not be printed until 1928.

• There were approximately 124 breweries in Canada.

• The 1st flying exhibition for paying spectators in NA took place at Scarborough Beach, near Toronto.

• Winnipeg's Assiniboine Park (121 ha) was officially opened. Designed in the English-landscape style by George Champion, it had taken 5 years to develop. By 1914, it would contain 9,261 trees, 18,257 shrubs, 2,970 perennials and 2,000 annuals.

• 1909 Hamilton, Ont., native Florence "Baby Flo the Child Wonder Whistler" Lawrence (1886–1938) appeared in 72 of her lifetime total of 270 films. Also known as the "Biograph Girl," the star of D.W. Griffith's Biograph films, Lawrence was the 1st actor to be identified on film by name, and is considered by critics the world's 1st movie star.

• Marc-Aurèle de Foy Suzor-Côté painted the impressionist-influenced landscape *Settlement on the Hillside*, oil on canvas. This painting is held by the National Gallery of Canada.

• Methodist minister James Shaver Woodsworth (1874–1942) of Winnipeg published *Strangers Within Our Gates*, a critical account of Canada's immigration policy, with the recommendation that only immigrants who could be assimilated into Canadian society be allowed entrance.

• *Ballads of a Cheechako*, by Robert Service, was published.

• Ernest Thompson Seton published *Life Histories of Northern Animals*, a 2-volume book on Man. fauna.

• 6 volumes of poetry entitled *Andvökur* (Wakeful Nights), by Stephan Gudmundsson Stephansson (1853–1927), an Alb. farmer and emigrant from Iceland, were published.

1910

Jan. 10 *Le Devoir*, a daily newspaper, was 1st published in Montreal by Henri Bourassa.

Jan. 12 PM Laurier introduced the Naval Service Bill. It included the establishment of a naval college, a naval board and a recruited force that would be under control of the federal govt. The construction of 5 cruisers and 6 destroyers was planned, and $3 million a year was allocated to maintain the navy. The bill specifically excluded compulsory service, but provided that the naval service might fall under the command of the British admiralty in an emergency. The bill was passed Apr. 20, despite widespread Conservative and French-Canadian opposition. The Royal Canadian Navy was established Mar. 4.

Jan. 16 The National Hockey Association (NHA), the forerunner to the NHL, launched its 1st season at Jubilee Arena in Montreal. The NHA included teams from Ont. and Que., including the Quebec Bulldogs, Montreal Canadiens, Ottawa Senators and Toronto Shamrocks.

Also in Jan.
• About 1,000 delegates of the Association Canadienne-Française d'Éducation d'Ontario, an organization dedicated to the protection and extension of the French language and religious privileges in education, met in Ottawa to discuss French-language education in Ont., and to make recommendations for improvements.

• Mary Malcolmson organized the 1st Canadian Girl Guides troop in St. Catherines, Ont. Other troops in Toronto, Moose Jaw and Winnipeg were organized within the year.

Feb. 15 Canada agreed to remove the surtax from German imports. Germany in turn agreed to allow minimum rates of duty on many Canadian imports.

Feb. 19 Johnny Coulon (1889–1973) knocked out Jim Kendrick of England to win the world bantamweight boxing championship. He held the title for 4 years. Nicknamed "The Cherry Picker from Logan Square," the 5′, 102 lb (46.2664 kg) Coulon was born in Toronto and raised in Chicago. He was elected to the Boxing Hall of Fame in 1965.

Mar. 4 Que. established a Public Utilities Commission.

Mar. 5 Sixty-two men were killed in a snow slide at Bear Creek while working in the Rogers Pass, Rocky Mountains. Only 1 man survived.

Mar. 10 Prince Rupert, BC, was incorporated as a city. It had been founded by the Grand Trunk Pacific Railroad in 1906.

Mar. 20 Finance Minister William Stevens Fielding, met secretly with US President William Howard Taft at Albany, New York, to discuss the possibility of reciprocity between the 2 countries.

Apr. 21 Vilhjalmur Stefansson and his Inuit companions Natkusiak, Pannigabluk and Tannaumirk, began their journey eastward for Victoria Is. in search of reported Inuit with blond hair.

May 1 Que. prohibited the export of wood pulp.

May 4 The Canadian Northern Alberta Railway Company was chartered and granted govt aid.

May 8 An explosion at a powder works in Hull, Que., killed 10 people.

May 13 Vilhjalmur Stefansson encountered Inuit near Dolphin and Union Strait who told him of "Copper Eskimos" to the north on Victoria Is. On May 17, Stefansson entered a village on Victoria Is. where he found the "Copper Eskimos." They displayed a striking resemblance to Europeans and many were blond. Stefansson thought they might be descendants of Greenland Vikings from the Middle Ages.

May 20 Briton John French, inspector-gen. of the Imperial Army, landed at Que. to inspect Canadian military forces.

May 21 The Passamaquoddy Bay Boundary Treaty gave Pope's Folly Is. to the US, while the fishing grounds south of Lubec, Maine, were given to Canada.

May 26 Alexander Rutherford resigned as premier of Alb. after it was discovered that American speculators had profited from trading govt bonds extended to the Alb. and Great Waterways Railway. Liberal Arthur Lewis Sifton (1858–1921) served as premier May 26–Oct. 30, 1917.

June 6 Canada and Italy agreed to a reciprocal tariffs reduction.

June 8 The Steel Company of Canada (Stelco) was formed by financier William Maxwell Aitken (1879–1964), who merged Hamilton Steel and Iron Co. with Montreal Rolling Mills. Through mergers and acquisitions, Stelco Inc. would become the largest steel producer in the country.

June 15 The *Trillium*, owned by the Toronto Ferry Company, was launched for service to Toronto Island. It would remain in duty 46 years.

June 18 The Blackfoot surrendered 46,500 ha (115,000 acres) of reserve in Alb., at an average price of $14 per acre.

July 9 PM Laurier began the greatest of all his tours across Canada at the feuding twin cities of Fort William and Port Arthur. He urged them to remain together and pool their strength: "We will help you. For every step you take we will take two; for every dollar you spend we will spend two." Laurier reached Medicine Hat, Alb., Sept. 2, where he started homeward.

July 11 A fire at Campbellton, NB, took 3 lives and left 4,000 homeless

July 18–Aug. 2 Train and yard employees at the Grand Trunk Railroad went on a strike that ended with a 15% wage increase. Minister of Labour Mackenzie King mediated between Charles Hays (1856–1912), the heavy-handed president of the Grand Trunk Railway, and his striking employees. Laurier, who had carefully planned his tour through Canada on the railway, was forced to shift to the CPR.

July 27 Joseph Elzéar Bernier set out on a voyage of exploration aboard the *Arctic* in an unsuccessful attempt to sail the Northwest Passage. The *Arctic* would return to Que. on Sept. 25, 1911.

Also in July
• Emily Carr and her sister, Alice, left Vancouver for Paris where Emily hoped to add more force to her art. She was 39 years old.

Aug. 27 On a flight over New York, John A. McCurdy sent the 1st air-to-ground telegraph message ever recorded.

Aug. 28 The Queen's Own Rifles arrived at Aldershot, England, for manoeuvres.

Sept. 7 The Hague Tribunal determined that Great Britain had sovereign right to regulate fisheries for 3 nautical miles in and off the coast of Nfld., thereby ending a 125-year territorial dispute with the US.

Sept. 8 William Wallace Gibson (1876–1965), of Victoria, BC, made a short 64 m test flight in an aircraft powered with a 50 horsepower engine of his own design. It was the 1st Canadian aircraft engine ever tested. His flight ended when the aircraft crashed into an oak tree.

Sept. 9 The 20th Eucharistic Congress was held in Montreal, Que., the 1st ever to be held in NA.

Oct. 11 The 1st Ontario Hydro-Electric Power Commission transmission line brought Niagara Falls–generated electricity to Berlin, Ont. (Kitchener).

Oct. 17 The cruiser *Niobe*, the 1st ship in the Royal Canadian Navy, arrived at Halifax. It had been purchased from Britian's Royal Navy. The *Rainbow*, also bought from the Royal Navy, arrived at Esquimault, BC, on Nov. 7.

Nov. 17 The 3rd session of the 11th Parliament met until July 29, 1911. A grant was approved to build the Northern Ontario Railroad as part of the 3rd National Transcontinental line.

Dec. 16 A group of 800 farmers marched on Ottawa to demand increased preference for British goods and reciprocity with the US.

Dec. 21 A RNWMP patrol set out from Fort McPherson, NWT, for Dawson, Yukon, a distance of

765 km. What was known as the "lost patrol" became confused on the trail and attempted to return to Fort McPherson, but the last of its 4 men died on Feb. 5, 1911, only 40 km from the post. W.J.D. Dempster, of the RNWMP, commanded a rescue patrol that set out from Dawson on Feb. 28, 1911. On Mar. 22, the bodies of 2 men, Francis J. Fitzgerald and Sam Carter, were found.

Dec. 28 Canada and the US agreed to form an international railroad commission to regulate rates.

c 1910 St. John's, Nfld. native Maurice Cullen (1866–1934) painted *Cape Diamond*, oil on canvas, showing Wolfe's Cove, Que., in the glow of sunset with snow-covered cliffs and rooftops. Cullen used 20 different colours to create the look of "white" snow. The work is in the Art Gallery of Hamilton, Ont.

Also in 1910

• Canada's population was 6,988,000.

• The value of all agricultural production in Canada was $760.3 million. The value of manufactured goods was $1.17 billion.

• The Farmers' Bank collapsed. A Royal Commission concluded that its demise was caused by a management "characterized by gross extravagance, recklessness, incompetence, dishonesty, and fraud."

• Scotsman William Kimmer laid out the 6,700-yard Riverside Golf Course in Saskatoon, Sask., one of the finest in Canada, despite the fact that Kimmer was neither a golf course architect nor golf professional.

• Legislation in Quebec was introduced to reduce the workweek of women textile workers from 60 to 58 hours.

• The Eastern Press Association was founded by a group of Atlantic newspapers publishers.

• Ont.-born painter Lawren Stewart Harris (1885–1970) painted *Old Houses, Wellington Street*, the 1st important work of his to survive. It hangs in a private collection.

• Toronto-born artist John William Beatty (1869–1941) painted *Evening Cloud of the Northland*, now in the National Gallery of Canada.

• *Literary Lapses*, Stephen Leacock's 1st comic miscellany, was published.

• Emily Murphy published *Janey Canuck in the West*.

• By the end of the decade, carpenters made between $1.75–$4.05 a day, bricklayers made between $2.50–$5 a day and coal miners anywhere from $3–$5 a day, depending on where they worked. Ironworkers, boilermakers, machinists, blacksmiths and sheet-metal workers made between $1.50–$5, depending on location.

• At the end of the decade, it cost anywhere from $20–$150 for a phonograph; $21.50–$35.50 for a wood stove and 55 cents–$2 for a teakettle. Butter cost 26 cents a pound; milk was 8 cents a quart; and eggs were 30 cents a dozen. Sirloin steak cost 19 cents, pork roast 9 cents a pound, and a pound of bacon was 24 cents. A loaf of bread cost about 6–8 cents. Tea and coffee cost anywhere from 14–40 cents a pound. Oranges were a luxury item, costing about 30 cents a dozen.

• Canadian-born Florence Nightingale Graham (1884–1966), aka Elizabeth Arden, opened a beauty salon on New York City's Fifth Avenue. (Arden was born and raised on the current site of Black Creek Pioneer Village, Toronto.) With a brilliant bright-red door advertising beauty products and treatments to the city's most refined element, by 1920, the Elizabeth Arden Company was selling over 100 products — more than any other company in the world. As her business expanded, Ms. Arden maintained her company's prestigious image by making her products available at only the most exclusive stores around the world. An industry leader, she was 1st to develop "beauty cream" and maintain a staff of "Beauty Ambassadoresses" to visit women's homes. Elizabeth Arden is now a publicly traded corporation headquartered in Miami Lakes, Florida.

1911

Jan. 1 Cadet training in high schools was made compulsory.

Jan. 21 A commercial reciprocity agreement was reached between Canada and the US. The agreement was ratified by the US Senate in July, but never received approval from Parliament.

Also in Jan.
• Inspired by the social Catholicism of Pope Leo XIII, Jesuit priest Joseph-Papin Archambault (1880–1966) helped found the École Sociale Populaire to promote the social teachings of the Catholic Church.

Mar. 21 Arthur William Patrick Albert, Duke of Connaught and Strathearn (1850–1942), was appointed gov-gen. of Canada, serving until Oct. 11, 1916.

• Shell Company of Canada was established with a working capital of $50,000 and began marketing gasoline in Montreal.

Also in Mar.
• *Busy Man's Magazine*, the 1st consumer magazine to be published in Canada, was officially renamed *Maclean's*. It had been purchased by John Bayne Maclean in 1905.

• The Saskatchewan Co-operative Elevator Company was created within a competitive market of privately owned and operated grain handlers.

Apr. 28 Thousands of people gathered at the exhibition grounds in Edmonton to watch Hugh Robinson make the 1st airplane flight in Alb. The Curtiss biplane executed turns and circles less than 100 m in the air.

May 1 Philippe Ray was appointed Canadian commissioner to France.

May 21 Calgary Power Company Ltd. began producing power after damming the Bow R. at the Horseshoe Falls, 74 km west of Calgary.

May 27 Springhill, NS, coal miners were unable to win union recognition or wage increases and returned to work, ending a strike that began in Aug. 10, 1909.

May 30 The 48.1-m-long *Filgate*, built in 1879 at Montreal to carry passengers to ports along the St. Lawrence and Ottawa Rivers, was destroyed by fire at Valleyfield, Que.

July 4 William Christopher Macdonald (1831–1917) donated 10 ha, known as Macdonald Park, to McGill U. for the construction of an athletic stadium.

July 11 A forest fire in the Porcupine district of Ont. took 70 lives.

July 21 Olivier-Elzéar Mathieu (1853–1929) was appointed the 1st Roman Catholic bishop of Regina.

July 29 The CNR. was completed between Montreal and Port Arthur, Ont. (Thunder Bay).

Sept. 21 Laurier's Liberals were defeated by the Conservatives under Robert Borden. The Conservatives took 132 seats to the Liberals' 86. The proposed trade reciprocity agreement with the US, together with the Naval Service Act of 1910, effectively ruined Laurier's chances. Many Canadians feared that US trade reciprocity would diminish ties with Britain, kill east-west trade and pave the way for American continentalism. French Canadians were still stinging from Laurier's naval bill, believing the provision to hand over the navy to Britain in cases of emergency was tantamount to treason. Some imperialists, on the other hand, thought it did not go far enough. Voter turnout was 70.2%.

Oct. 6 The Laurier ministry resigned.

Oct. 10–July 10, 1920 Sir Robert Borden served as Conservative PM.

Oct. 16 Winnipeg received its 1st electric power.

Also in Oct.
• Borden appointed Col. Sam Hughes (1853–1921) as Minister of Militia and National defence.

Nov. 2 Montreal citizens donated $1.5 million to McGill U.

Also in Nov.

• Artist Lawren Harris met James Edward Hervey MacDonald (1873–1932), who brought him into contact with a group of artists that would become the Group of Seven. The group included Frank Carmichael (1890–1945), Franz Johnston (1888–1949), Arthur Lismer (1885–1969), Alexander Young Jackson (1882–1974), and Fredrick H. Varley (1881–1969). Tom J. Thomson (1877–1917) was also among the friends, but he died in 1917 before the group organized in 1920.

• Since 1900, 680,000 immigrants arrived from the British Isles; 620,000 came from the US.

Also in 1911

• Jennie Smillie Robertson (1878–1981), Canada's 1st female surgeon, cofounded Women's College Hospital in Toronto, to bring serious medical attention to neglected women's health concerns. Robertson graduated from the U. of Toronto medical school in 1909, but was forced to intern in Philadelphia, as no Canadian hospital was accepting women interns.

• The Canadian Mint issued its King George V silver dollar. The coin, originally conceived as part of a collection set (with $2.50, $5, $10 and $20 gold coins) was discontinued after the minting of only 2 specimens — one of which is now in the Bank of Canada Currency Museum, the other of which recently sold at auction for $690,000 US.

• The population of Canada was 7,216,742: 3,896,985 were of English and 2,054,890 of French descent. The population of Ont. was 2,527,292; Que., 2,005,776; Sask., 492,432; NS, 492,338; Man., 461,000; BC, 392,480; Alb., 374,295; NB, 351,889; PEI, 93,728; Yukon, 8,512; and NWT, 17,000.

• Sixteen-year-old Lithuanian immigrant Max Wolfe (1893–1987) began a grocery business in Newmarket, Ont., with a horse, wagon and an investment of apples. Start-up costs were $85. By 1914, the fledgling enterprise had evolved into the Ontario Produce Co., to supply food for the war effort. Later the business would become the Oshawa Group Ltd. which, by 2003, included Food City, Dutch Boy, Towers department stores, Drug City and IGA.

• The number of immigrants entering Canada totalled 350,374, including 144,076 from the UK and 131,114 from the US.

• 27,568 Chinese people lived in Canada.

• Construction began on Casa Loma on Davenport Hill overlooking central Toronto. The $2 million, 50-room mansion was designed by E.J. Lennox and commissioned by owner Sir Henry Mill Pellatt (1860–1939). Construction lasted 3 years.

• Sask. wheat farmer Seager Wheeler (1869–1961) won the 1st of 5 world wheat championships for his hard spring wheat. Among the varieties he developed were Early Triumph, Red Bobs, Supreme and Kitchener. Wheeler was also successful in developing hardy fruits.

• There were 104 strikes, involving 28,918 employees.

• The Ontario School of Art reorganized as the Ontario College of Art.

• The provincial Anti-Tuberculosis League was formed in Sask. It would later become the Lung Association.

• The Fingerprint Bureau of the Dominion Police, a small federal force of about 200 men, was established.

• BC processing plants harvested over 1,000 whales.

• The Dominion Forest Reserves and Parks Act placed federal parks under one federal administration.

• Forest fires gutted 1,600 km^2 of Ontario's northland.

• A.Y. Jackson exhibited *The Edge of the Maple Wood* in the Ontario Society of Arts show in Toronto. The painting is with the National Gallery of Canada.

• Edmund Morris painted *Indian Encampment on Prairie*, now in the Art Gallery of Ont., Toronto.

• J.E.H. MacDonald painted *By the River, Early Spring,* oil on canvas.

• *Legends of Vancouver*, prose tales by Pauline Johnson (1861–1913), inspired by Squamish legends, was published.

• The novel *Maria Chapdelaine* by Louis Hémon (1880–1913) was published.

• *Nonsense Novels* by Stephen Leacock was published.

• James Shaver Woodsworth published *My Neighbour*, a chilling description of urban poverty.

1912

Mar. 17 The Political Equality League was founded in Winnipeg under the promotion of Lillian Beynon (1874–1951). The league pushed for prohibition and universal suffrage.

Mar. 18 PM Borden announced the suspension of the Naval Service Act, without providing a permanent policy to replace it. On the same day, Winston Churchill, 1st Lord of the Admiralty, announced that Britain was proceeding with a crash program of dreadnought construction in the face of German naval threats.

Mar. 29 Representatives of the West Indies attended a trade conference at Ottawa.

Also in Mar.
• 7,000 members of the union of International Workers of the World went on strike to protest working conditions at the CNR.

Apr. 14–15 The *Titanic* sank off Nfld., a few days out of Southampton, England, on its maiden voyage. Of the 2,224 passengers and crew, only 711 survived. The ship struck an iceberg after Capt. E.J. Smith ignored radio warnings of ice and maintained full speed.

Also in Apr.
• The Ont. govt established a policy known as Department of Education Instruction 17, or, more popularly, "Regulation 17," providing that public

funds be made available only to those schools employing teachers fully capable of teaching in English. English instruction was to begin on school entrance, with French as a language of communication only where existing conditions demanded it, and in no case beyond the first 2 elementary years.

May 15 By Act of Parliament, the Ungava Peninsula was added to Que. under the name New Quebec, and the remainder of the NWT south of 60°N. latitude was divided between Ont. and Man.

May 24 The 1st parachute jump in Canada was made by Charles Saunders at Vancouver.

Also in May
• The first $5 and $10 Canadian gold pieces were minted.

June 2 The National Council of YMCAs of Canada was formed at a convention in Winnipeg.

June 12 Architects Ross and MacFarlane of Montreal, Que., commissioned by the gen. manager of the Grand Trunk Pacific Railway, American-born Charles Melville Hays, completed the Château Laurier located next to the Parliament buildings in Ottawa. The French Renaissance-style hotel was named after the 1st person to sign the guest register, former PM Sir Wilfrid Laurier.

June 24 During the celebrations of Saint-Jean Baptiste, Archbishop Louis Philippe Abélard Langevin (1855–1915) proposed that the 3 million French in NA should form a great union for the protection of common rights and religion.

June 26 As Europe drifted toward war, a party of Canadian officials left for England to discuss the naval crisis and what Canada's role might be in helping the British admiralty.

June 30 A rare prairie tornado struck Regina, Sask., killing 65 people, injuring 300 and leaving hundreds homeless. It turned over freight cars and destroyed entire blocks of houses. The devastation occurred over a span of 20 minutes.

July 6 Fred G. Wells piloted the 1st seaplane flight in Canada, at Hanlan's Point, in Toronto Harbour.

July 12–15 Montreal transport workers were on strike.

July 24 The Canadian Western Natural Gas, Light, Heat and Power Company completed construction of Alb.'s 1st natural gas pipeline to carry gas from the "Old Glory" well in Bow Is., west of Medicine Hat, to consumers in Calgary, 275 km away.

July 29 The Imperial Privy Council upheld the authority of provincial legislatures to make marriage laws.

Aug. 17 Thomas Wilby set out from Halifax in a Reo Special. He arrived in Victoria 52 days later, becoming the 1st person to drive across Canada.

Aug. 20 Dock workers at Fort William, Ont. (Thunder Bay) went on strike.

Sept. 2 The 1st Calgary Stampede celebration, organized and managed by American cowboy-showman Guy Weadick (1855–1953), began with a parade through downtown Calgary; 75,000 spectators lined the streets.

Sept. 3 The Alb. Legislature Building was officially opened by Gov-Gen., the Duke of Connaught.

Oct. 12 French-speaking students at Garneau, Ont., walked out of class to protest instruction given by their anglophone teacher.

Nov. 18 *The Duke of Connaught*, a floating steel dry dock, was dedicated in Montreal.

Nov. 21 The 2nd session of the 12th Parliament met until June 6, 1913. The Banking Act was revised to provide better inspection of banks and security for depositors.

Dec. 4 Abitibi Pulp and Paper Company was formed in Que.

Dec. 5 Borden's Navy Aid Bill was introduced and forced through the House of Commons, despite a Liberal filibuster. The Bill authorized the expenditure of $35 million for the "construction and equipment of battleships and armoured cruisers of the most modern and powerful type" to be used by "His Majesty for the common defence of the Empire." The bill was defeated by the Liberal-dominated Senate, May 30, 1913.

Dec. 12 The Sask. legislature made it illegal for European-Canadian women to work for businesses owned by Chinese people.

Also in 1912

- Edmonton and Strathcona amalgamated.

- The Board of Grain Commissioners was established with passage of the Canada Grain Act. The commission was the official inspector and weigher of Canadian-produced grain, and also regulated the grain trade.

- The dinosaur *Monoclonius cutleri* was named in honour of William Edmund Cutler (b 1878). Cutler, who found the fossils on an exploration of the Alb. badlands, decided to trade them with Barnum Brown (1873–1963) in exchange for fossil-collecting techniques and information, and a promise that one specimen would be named in his honour.

- U. of Toronto entomologist E.M. Walker discovered the ice-worm, a pale yellow wingless insect with a cricket-like ovipositor and legs similar to those of a cockroach. The famous insect, found on Sulphur Mountain, Banff, gained the immediate attention of entomologists worldwide. Because it was so unique, a new family had to be created for its classification, the *Grylloblattidac*.

- Gold was discovered at Kirkland L., Ont.

- Man. boundaries were extended to include the southern part of the district of Keewatin.

- The 1st geologic map of Toronto (the so-called "Willet Miller" map, named after the provincial geologist at the time) was published by Ont. Department of Mines and completed by renowned geologist A.P. Coleman.

- A stained-glass window built in England during the English Civil War (1642–1648) was installed in the west wall of All Saints Anglican Church, Watrous, Sask. The 7-paneled, multi-hued glass was a gift to the church's 1st vicar, Rev. F.L. King, and shipped to Canada in 2,000 pieces.

- The 1st commercially produced hockey goalie pads cost $3.50.

• Lawren Harris and J.E.H. MacDonald entered their 1st large canvases at an exhibition held by the Ont. Society of Arts. Harris's most acclaimed contribution was of log drivers, entitled *The Drive*, now in the National Gallery of Canada; MacDonald's was his now-famous *Tracks and Traffic*, held by the Art Gallery of Ont., Toronto.

• Emily Carr visited a number of Native villages along the east coast of Vancouver Is., the Upper Skeena R. and Queen Charlotte Is. One of the paintings inspired by the tour was *Potlatch Figure*, oil on canvas, now in a private collection.

• David Milne painted *Billboard*, now in the National Gallery of Canada.

• *A Prairie Trail*, oil on canvas, by Charles William Jefferys (1869–1951), was completed.

• *Sunshine Sketches of a Little Town* by Stephen Leacock, his 3rd major work of fiction, was published. The fictitious town of Mariposa bore a striking resemblance to Orillia, Ontario.

• *Flint and Feather*, a collection of poems by Pauline Johnson (Tekahionwake [1861–1913]) was published.

• *Propos Canadiens*, by literary critic Camille Roy (1870–1943), was published.

• The volume of verse, *Le Coeur en Exil*, by nature poet Joseph Fabien René Chopin (1885–1953), was published.

• *Corporal Cameron of the North West Mounted Police*, one of the earliest and most popular Mountie films, was made by Canadian film entrepreneur Ernest Shipman. Born in Hull, Que., in 1871, Shipman made several films about pioneer life in northern Canada. His most notable production was the 1919 silent film classic *Back To God's Country*, starring his second wife, Vancouver-born Nell Shipman (1892– 1970), a talented actress, writer and director. The film relied heavily on Nell's brief nude scene and made a 300% profit on its initial investment of $67,000.

• George Hodgson (1893–1983) won 2 gold medals in freestyle swimming (400 m and 1,500 m) at the Summer Olympic Games in Stockholm, Sweden.

Canada's 3rd gold was won by George Goulding (1884–1966) in the 10,000-m walk. Altogether, Canada won 7 medals.

1913

Jan. 2 A million-dollar blaze destroyed the Calgary meat-packing plant of cattle rancher Pat Burns, leading to fears of food shortages across southern Alb.

Jan. 5 Ian Hamilton, inspector-gen. of the Imperial forces, arrived in Que. to inspect Canadian troops.

Mar. Jesuit priest Archambault helped found the Ligue des droits du français, followed by the Ligue d'action française in 1917, as instruments to promote and protect the French language in Canada.

Apr. Emily Carr exhibited a collection of paintings depicting Native carvings, completed after her 1912 tour of West Coast villages. The show was a failure; not one work sold.

May 22 The Collingwood Shipbuilding Company's 165-m-long steamship *James Carruthers,* one of the largest of its time, was built and launched in Collingwood, Ont.

Also in May
• The 8-storey, Edwardian-style Sylvia Hotel was opened on Beach Road, overlooking English Bay, Vancouver. It was declared a heritage building in 1975.

June 2 A trade agreement with the British West Indies came into effect. About 50 Canadian exports received a 20% tariff reduction.

July 5 Vilhjalmur Stefansson left Seattle, Washington, in the *Karluk*, on a 3-year Arctic expedition sponsored by the federal govt. He would undertake a comprehensive study of the central Arctic coast that would embrace the topography, geology, zoology, botany, oceanography and ethnography of the region, including the exploration of yet undiscovered territory.

July 31 Alys Bryant became the 1st woman in Canada to make a solo flight, as she took wing from a Vancouver racetrack.

Aug. 13 Canadian troops were called out at Nanaimo, BC, to stop rioting coal-mine strikers who had taken over the town and looted and burned the houses of strikebreakers and Western Fuel Co. executives.

Oct. 3 The US Congress passed the Underwood Tariff Act, eliminating the import duty on Canadian newsprint.

Also in Oct.
• PM Borden named poet and editor Duncan Campbell Scott (1862–1947) superintendent-gen. of Indian affairs.

Nov. 7–10 A raging storm with winds approaching hurricane force caused more than $100 million in damage and took the lives of 251 seamen on Lakes Superior and Michigan, where 26 ships were lost within 48 hours. On Lakes Huron and Erie, 41 ships were sunk, with a loss of 194 lives.

Nov. 17 The eastern division of the Grand Trunk Pacific Railroad was completed in Que. near the Ont. boundary.

Nov. 30 Canada's Chief Justice Hunter ruled that Ottawa's Order-in-Council barring Hindus from entering BC was illegal.

Dec. 8 An Order-in-Council prohibited the landing of skilled or unskilled labourers at BC ports because of unemployment and labour strife in the province.

Also in 1913
• Frank P. O'Connor founded Laura Secord chocolates in a single shop on Yonge St., Toronto, with candy made in a kitchen above the store. The fledgling enterprise was named in honour of the War of 1812 heroine, who 100 years earlier (June 21, 1813) warned the British of a planned American attack at Queenston, Ont. The popularity of the chocolate led to expansion and by 1950 there were 96 Laura Secord shops coast to coast, with total sales of $4.5 million. By 1972, 70% of all outlets carried ice cream. Despite many mergers and acquisitions since the candymaker acquired the Montreal outlets of Mary Lee Candy in 1962, Laura Secord remained Canada's largest chocolatier through the turn of the century.

• Canadian Steamship Lines (CSL) was founded as a result of a merger between Companies du Richelieu, a water-transport operation on the St. Laurence R., and 11 other companies. The new company was headed up by Walter Grant Morden.

• Winnipeg hosted the National Association of Real Estate Exchanges' annual convention. It was an international event, attracting some 1,000 brokers from 79 (mostly American) cities. Meetings were held in the convention hall of the Industrial Bureau on Main and Water Streets.

• A record number of immigrants — 400,870 — arrived in Canada.

• Ont. established municipally guaranteed bonds for public-housing projects.

• The Home and Domestic Employees Union was formed in Vancouver. Member Helena Gutteridge (1879–1960) would ensure that equal pay was written into the Vancouver Trades and Labour Council constitution in 1915. Her work to bring together women's groups and labour activism resulted in BC's 1st minimum wage act in 1918.

• The Alb. Farmers' Co-operative Elevator Company was incorporated.

• Organization of the Women's Section of the Sask. Grain Growers' Association began.

• Alice Wilson became the 1st female geologist hired by the Geological Survey of Canada.

• The federal govt established Elk Island National Park (194 km²) in Alb.'s Beaver Hills, the only national park to be totally fenced in, and one of the 1st large-hoofed mammal sanctuaries in Canada. It is now refuge to some 3,000 ungulates, including wood buffalo, elk and plains bison. The park began as a 41 km² elk preserve in 1906; in 1907, the Canadian govt purchased 400 head of endangered plains bison from a Montana rancher at $200 (US) an animal, and initiated expansion plans. In 1987, the park initiated a successful reintroduction and breeding program for the trumpeter swan.

• The 1st ascent of the 3,954-meter Mount Robson, BC, was completed by W.M. Foster, A.H. McCarthy

(1876–1955) and Conrad Kain. Robson is the highest peak in the Canadian Rockies

• Publishers J.M. Dent & Sons and Thomas Nelson & Sons were formed.

• The Bank of NB merged with the Bank of NS.

• The federal govt paid British and European booking agents $5 for each domestic servant they sent to Canada. Advertisements issued to prospective maids told of Canadian wages in excess of $10 a month.

• A breeding pair of silver foxes was sold in PEI for $35,000.

• The Winnipeg School of Art was founded.

• Que.-born artist Charles Huot completed *Le Premier parlement de Québec* for the Salle de l'Assemblée Législative du Québec.

• Marc-Aurèle de Foy Suzor-Côté completed the impressionist painting *La Jeunesse en plein soleil,* oil on canvas, now in the National Gallery of Canada.

• Ozias Leduc completed the canvas *Fin de journée,* now in the Montreal Museum of Fine Arts.

• A.Y. Jackson painted *Terre Sauvage,* oil on canvas, while a guest at Dr. MacCallum's summer home at Georgian Bay. The painting is held by the National Gallery of Canada. (MacCallum would become a significant supporter of the Group of Seven.)

• Claremont, Ont., native Tom Thomson exhibited his 1st large canvas, *Northern Lake,* at a show sponsored by the Ontario Society of Arts. The painting, based on sketches done in the summer of 1912 in Algonquin Park, was purchased by the Ont. govt for $250. It is now in the Art Gallery of Ont., Toronto.

• Painter David Milne (1882–1953) was invited to exhibit his work in the famous Armory Show in New York City. The only other Canadian included was Arthur Crisp (1881–1974) of Hamilton, Ont.

• *My Life with the Eskimos*, by Vilhjalmur Stefansson, was published.

• The novel *The Shagganappi*, by Pauline Johnson, was published posthumously.

1914

Jan. 1 The Canadian Northern's transcontinental service opened.

Jan. 11 The whaling ship *Karluk*, commanded by Robert Abram Bartlett (1875–1946), sank in the Arctic Ocean. Vilhjalmur Stefansson had already left the ship. Twenty-two men, 1 woman, 2 children, 16 dogs and 1 cat, trapped on an ice floe, watched the *Karluk* sink. The survivors named their new abode "Shipwreck Camp." On Mar. 12, survivors, after an exhausting 128-km trek from Shipwreck Camp, arrived on the desolate, snow-covered shore of Wrangle Is. They were rescued by the trade scourer *Kins and Winge*, Sept. 7, 1914. Eleven had died.

Jan. 15 The 3rd session of the 12th Parliament met until June 12. Representation in the House of Commons was expanded to 234 members.

Jan. 28 Nellie Letitia McClung (1873–1951) and other suffragettes held a mock parliament in Winnipeg to agitate for women's suffrage.

Also in Jan.
• A.Y. Jackson and Tom Thomson agreed to share a studio in Toronto.

Feb. 23 In *Quong-Wing vs Regina*, the Supreme Court upheld a Sask. law that prohibited Chinese businesses from hiring European-Canadian women.

Mar. 22 Stefansson left Martin Point, Alaska, for Cape Kellet.

Mar. 31 The strength of the Canadian Armed Forces was 3,000 officers and men in the permanent force, and 5,615 officers and 68,991 men in the militia.

Apr. 1 A severe and unpredicted winter blizzard lowered temperatures to below -23C, trapping 77 sealers on an ice floe off the southeast coast of Labrador. There were no survivors. The same storm claimed the lives of 173 men and caused the loss of 17,000 seals aboard the SS *Southern Cross*, which did not return to its home port of St. John's, Nfld.

• The Ont. govt passed the Workmen's Compensation Act.

Apr. 9 The 1st Grand Trunk Pacific train arrived at Prince Rupert, from Winnipeg.

Apr. 25 CPR president Sir Thomas Shaughnessy formally opened the sluice gates of the Bassano Dam, in Alb., that was built to irrigate arid land along the railway's right-of-way, and make it attractive to settlers. *Scientific American* magazine called the dam "America's Greatest Irrigation Project." The earthen embankment and its associated works provided the water for the Eastern Irrigation District, an area of almost 600,000 ha.

Apr. 29 The Supreme Court of Ont. prohibited the employment of teachers who were not legally qualified.

May 14 Alb.'s oil industry took root when, in the Turner Valley, Calgary Petroleum Products Company "Dingman 1" struck oil at just over 822 m. A wild speculative spree followed.

May 23 The *Komagata Maru* arrived at Vancouver with 376 Sikh migrants. They were not allowed to land, under Canadian immigration laws, and most did not have the required $200 entry fee. They sat aboard the ship in harbour for 2 months. Eventually the ship was forced out of Vancouver on July 23. Only 24 passengers were allowed entry into Canada.

May 24 The paddle steamer *Berthier,* of the Richelieu and Ontario Navigation Company, burned and sank at its moorings alongside Victoria Pier in Montreal.

May 25 Que. Archbishop Louis-Nazaire Bégan (1840–925) became a cardinal.

May 29 The CP steamer *Empress of Ireland* collided with the Norwegian ship *Storstad* in the Gulf of St. Lawrence and sank, claiming 1,012 lives. Only 464 passengers from the *Empress of Ireland* survived. It was the worst marine disaster in Canadian history. On July 11, a commission found the Norwegian coal steamer *Storstad* responsible for the collision.

Also in May
• Tom Thomson painted *Parry Sound Harbour*, on board, now in the National Gallery of Canada.

June 11 The House of Commons unanimously approved Borden's measures to increase the number of western senators. The next day the Liberal-dominated Senate refused to pass the resolution.

June 19 A methane gas explosion at the Hillcrest coal mine No. 1 tunnel in the Crowsnest Pass, Alb., killed 189 men; 130 women were widowed. It was the worst mining accident in Canadian history.

June 20 The Borden cabinet authorized the purchase of land for a huge military training camp at Valcartier, a few km northwest of Quebec City.

June 28 Archduke Franz Ferdinand of Austria, heir to the Austro-Hungarian Empire, was assassinated at Sarejevo, Serbia, while on a state visit. On July 28, Austria-Hungary declared war on Serbia.

• Montreal and Toronto Stock Exchanges were closed for 3 months, for fear of war.

July 29 The Grand Trunk Railway amalgamated with Canada Atlantic Railway Company.

July 30 The Militia Council, chaired by Minister of Militia Col. Sam Hughes, announced plans to mobilize 25,000 troops from across Canada should Britain should become involved in war.

July 31 Borden cut short his summer vacation and returned to Ottawa for an emergency cabinet meeting concerning the looming war in Europe.

Aug. 1 Germany declared war on Russia.

• The gov-gen. offered the services of Canadian troops to Britain. The offer was accepted Aug. 6.

Aug. 3 Germany declared war on France, attacking through Belgium the same day.

• Coined money payments were suspended to conserve the gold supply. Banks were authorized to make payments in their own notes instead of gold.

Aug. 3–4 BC Premier Richard McBride, an ardent imperialist, supported the idea of a Canadian contribution to the Imperial navy, and on his own initiative had the province purchase 2 submarines from a Seattle shipyard to protect its coastal waters. The deal was made quickly to beat an expected US neutrality ban on military equipment. McBride later sold the vessels to the federal govt, which ordered them to Halifax June 21, 1917. They were scrapped in 1920.

Aug. 4 Canada and Nfld. entered WW I as Britain declared war on Germany and Austro-Hungary.

- The 90th Winnipeg Rifles was mobilized under Colonel J.W. O'Grady.

Aug. 5 The federal govt granted German merchant ships 10 days to leave the port of Halifax.

Aug. 6 The Borden cabinet authorized mobilization of the militia units of officers and men who were willing to volunteer for overseas service.

- The export of food, military and naval stores, and coal was prohibited except to Britain, Japan, France, Russia and the US.

Aug. 7 An Imperial Act allowed the issue of naturalization certificates to aliens with proof of 5 years' residence, thus making them British subjects.

Aug. 11 Recruiting began for a new Canadian regiment, the Princess Patricia's Canadian Light Infantry. The unit was named after the daughter of the Gov-Gen., the Duke of Connaught, and was commanded by Lt-Col. F.D. Farquhar, and raised by Andrew Hamilton Gault (1882–1958). On Aug. 19, 1,098 men had been selected out of 3,000 applicants. Most had already fought somewhere under the Union Jack. They would land in France Dec. 21, 1914, and would be the 1st Canadian Infantry Regiment in the theatre.

Aug. 18–22 A special war session of Parliament, the 4th session of the 12th Parliament, met until Aug. 22. The War Measures Act gave emergency powers to the gov-gen.-in-council (Cabinet); $50 million was allotted for military and naval purposes.

Aug. 19 Canada made a statement of war on Germany and Austria-Hungary.

Also in Aug.
- The Canadian Patriotic Fund was incorporated by Parliament to provide financial assistance to the

families of soldiers overseas. A soldier's family could receive $30 per month in eastern Canada and $40 in western Canada.

Sept. 5 George Herman "Babe" Ruth pounded his 1st professional home run against the Toronto Maple Leafs at Hanlan's Point Stadium on the Toronto Islands. Ruth also pitched in the game, surrendering one hit to beat Toronto 9–0.

Sept. 9 The Grand Trunk Railway began operating between Winnipeg and Prince Rupert.

Sept. 14 French-Canadian nationalist Henri Bourassa spoke out against Canada's participation in the war in Europe.

Sept. 16 Sam Hughes formed the 1st Canadian military air service, the Canadian Aviation Corps.

Sept. 21 During a visit to Valcartier training camp near Quebec City, PM Borden decided that all 31,200 volunteers should be sent to England, instead of just the 25,000-person divisional force, as originally planned.

Oct. 3 The 1st Canadian Contingent sailed from Que. for England, a total of 33,000 men, 7,000 horses and 144 pieces of artillery. Transported in 32 ships and escorted by 10 British warships, it was the largest armed force to cross the ocean to date.

Oct. 5 Lt-Col. F.M. Gaudet was given the command of the 22nd Battalion, a special French-Canadian unit. The Royal 22nd, one of the finest and most respected regiments in the European theatre, was the 1st and last French-Canadian battalion established in the Canadian Corps. Their emblem included a crown and large stylized beaver, with the motto "Je me souviens." The regiment is nicknamed the "Vandoos," a mispronunciation of vingt-deux (22).

Oct. 28 An Order-in-Council required registration of all enemy aliens.

Nov. 11 The 1st Canadian Stationary Hospital (Unit No. 2) arrived in France.

Also in Nov.
- A.Y. Jackson completed *The Red Maple* from

sketches made in Oct. in Algonquin Park. The painting is now in the National Gallery of Canada.

Dec. In Halifax, PM Borden pledged that "there has not been, there will not be, compulsion or conscription" for overseas duty.

1914–1915 Tom Thomson painted *Northern River,* oil on canvas, now in the National Gallery of Canada.

Also in 1914

• The Royal Ontario Museum was completed in Toronto with the mandate to "inspire, wonder and build understanding of human cultures and the natural world." By the end of its 1st century, the museum had more than 5 million objects in its possession.

• The Viking gas field was discovered near Viking, Alb.

• The St. Lawrence Islands National Park, the 1st national park founded east of the Rockies, was established to protect 21 islands stretching some 80 km between Kingston and Brockville, Ont. The total landmass of the park is 9 km². The islands are remnants of the Frontenac Axis, an ancient granite bridge that once linked the Canadian Shield to the Adirondack Mountains in New York State. Part of the historic Thousand Islands chain, the park is home to Canada's largest snake, the endangered black rat snake, which can grow to 2.5 m long.

• The Canadian govt established Mount Revelstoke National Park, a 260-km² sanctuary on British Columbia's southeastern border, home to stands of 1,000-year-old western red cedar, mountain goats and bighorn sheep, pikas, hoary marmots, grizzly and black bears, wolverines and many other species of note, including the long-eared bat.

• PM Borden was knighted.

• The Royal Bank had 22 branches in Cuba.

• The CNR was nationalized, fearing its failure might bring about a collapse of national credit.

• The Exhibits and Publicity Bureau, a film division of the Department of Trade and Commerce, was established. It was the world's 1st govt film production agency.

• The charter of the 4-year-old Vancouver Bank was suspended after it became insolvent.

• The International Ice Observation Patrol was organized in the North Atlantic by 14 countries, including Canada. It was based at Halifax.

• *Interior with Paintings,* by David B. Milne, oil on canvas, was completed

• William Brymner painted *The Coast of Louisbourg,* now in the National Gallery of Canada.

• A.Y. Jackson completed *Frozen L., Early Spring, Algonquin Park,* oil on canvas, now in the National Gallery of Canada.

• J.E.H. MacDonald began work on a large canvas based on sketches made when visiting Georgian Bay. The finished work was *Fine Weather, Georgian Bay,* presently in a private collection.

• Tom Thomson painted *Moonlight, Early Evening,* oil on canvas, directly under A.Y. Jackson's tutelage at their new studio in Toronto. The painting is now at the National Gallery of Canada.

• Arthur Lismer produced his 1st ambitious impressionist canvas, *Guide's Home, Algonquin,* while visiting Algonquin Park with Jackson, Thomson, and Varley. The painting is now in the National Gallery of Canada.

• The 1st 12 of 32 volumes of *The Chronicles of Canada,* a series of monographs edited by George MacKinnon Wrong (1860–1948) and Hugh Hornby Langton (1862–1953) was published.

• *The Land of the Open Doors,* by Canon John Burgon Bickersteth, was published.

• *Arcadian Adventures with the Idle Rich,* by Stephen Leacock, was published.

• *Chez Nous,* by Adjutor Rivard (1868–1945), was published. The book of sketches challenged linguistic conventions.

• Flora Macdonald Denison, née Merrill (1867– 1921), president of the Canadian Suffrage Association, published her book *War and Women,* in which she contended that "war was a crime committed by men," and would no longer happen when women "were allowed to say what they think of war."

• *Evangeline*, a dramatization of Henry Wadsworth Longfellow's poem, was the subject of Canada's 1st feature film, produced by the Canadian Bioscope Company.

• Architects A. Frank Wickson (1861–1936) and Alfred H. Gregg (1868–1945), commissioned by Flora McCrae Eaton (widow of Sir John Craig Eaton — son of department-store tycoon) completed Timothy Eaton Memorial Church, located on St. Clair Ave. West in north Toronto. The gothic-inspired group of buildings, built for a Methodist congregation (and now ruled by the United Church of Canada), features a square 30-m tower that contains a set of 21 bells.

• Ozias Leduc worked on the canvas *Pommes vertes,* entering it in the Art Association of Montreal Spring Show. A.Y. Jackson singled it out as the best painting in the 1915 Spring Show. The work is now in the National Gallery of Canada.

1915

Jan. 6 The Princess Patricia's Canadian Light Infantry, formed primarily from former British soldiers settled in Canada, went into action in France.

Jan. 15 The Canadian Northern Railroad between Que. and Vancouver was completed at Basque, BC. The last spike was officially driven on Jan. 23.

Feb. 4 The 5th session of the 12th Parliament met until Apr. 15. A Special War Revenue Act imposed new taxes on railroad and steamship tickets, parlour car seats, sleeping car berths, telegrams, bank cheques and notes. A stamp tax was placed on money orders, postal notes, patent medicines, perfumes, spirits and wines.

Feb. 14 The 1st Canadian Division, commanded by Gen. Alderson, arrived in France and proceeded to Belgium.

Feb. 20 Vilhjalmur Stefansson travelled along the coast of Banks Is. to Alfred Point. He then landed on Prince Patrick Is. in May.

• British Field Marshal John French inspected the 1st Canadian Division on the western front.

Feb. 24 Canadians took over a 6.5-km section of trench line near Armentières, France.

Feb. 26 Author and suffragist Nellie McClung led a large delegation to the Alb. legislature to present a petition demanding women receive the provincial franchise.

Mar. 10 Canadians fought in the Battle of Neuve Chapelle.

Mar. 16 The 2nd Canadian Division began arriving in England.

Apr. 8 The Ont. Liquor Licence Act created a board of commissioners to regulate the sale of liquor.

Apr. 17 Alb. women were given the right to vote in municipal elections.

Apr. 22 The Canadian 1st Contingent faced the 1st German chlorine-gas attack at the 2nd Battle of Ypres in Belgium. The 1st Canadian Division held the line; the German advance was halted. Canadians suffered 6,000 casualties in the week-long engagement.

May 2 Germans again attacked the Canadians with gas at Ypres, 10 days after the 1st assault.

May 3 Dr. John McCrae (1872–1918), of Guelph, Ont., wrote the poem "In Flanders Fields." It was composed in 20 minutes while McCrae was at Ypres. His poem was 1st published in Dec. 1915, in the English magazine *Punch*.

May 7 The Cunard liner *Lusitania* was torpedoed by a German submarine off the coast of Queenstown, Ireland, causing the death of about 1,200 passengers and crew, including many Canadians. Survivors numbered 764. It was the 1st and only Cunard vessel lost at sea.

• The War Purchasing Board was appointed after PM Borden declared Messrs Garland and DeWitt Foster *persona non grata* for corrupt dealings in the acquisition of drugs and horses for the military.

• The Princess Patricia's Canadian Light Infantry halted a German offensive near Frezenberg Ridge; 392 out of 546 men were wounded.

May 9 The 1st Canadian Division saw action at Festubert, France.

May 13 Liberals under Tobias Crawford Norris (1861–1936) formed the new govt of Man. after Conservative Premier Rodmond Roblin (1853–1937) resigned under charges of corruption. A report of the Mathers Commission would later implicate Roblin of defrauding the provincial treasury.

May 19 The BNA Act, 1915, received Assent, increasing the numbers of senators from 72 to 96: Ont., 21; Que., 24; Maritimes, 24 (NS,10; NB,10; 4-PEI); western provinces 24, (Man., 6; Sask., 6; Alb., 6; BC-6).

Also in May
• Dr. Cluny Macpherson (1879–1966) was decorated for inventing the gas helmet to provide protection against airborne poison, the 1st such device used by Allied troops in WW I.

June 15 Stefansson found a cairn left by McClintock in 1853 on Prince Patrick Is.

• Canadian troops saw action at Givenchy, France.

June 18 Storker Storkerson, a member of the Canadian Arctic Exploration under Stefansson, discovered a new island, which was named Brock Is. Ole Andreasen was the 1st to set foot on the landmass which Stefansson claimed for the empire in the name of King George V on behalf of the Dominion of Canada. A larger island, recognized by Stefansson as being separate from Brock Is., was named Borden Is., after the PM. Stefansson then set off for Melville Is., where muskox were killed to replenish his food supply.

June 30 A hospital commission was established to provide treatment for wounded veterans. Its name was changed to the Military Hospitals Commission in Oct.

Also in June
• Artist A.Y. Jackson joined the Canadian army.

July 12 Harvest furloughs were permitted to men of the Canadian Expeditionary Force who were still in training camps in Canada.

July 14 The Curtiss JN-3 training prop biplane, the 1st Canadian-produced aircraft, was test-flown near Toronto. It was built by Canadian Airplanes Ltd.

• Borden became the 1st Canadian PM to attend a British cabinet meeting.

July 20 Stefansson and his party left Mercy Bay on Banks Is. (the site where McClure abandoned the *Investigator* in 1851) and headed across the island for Cape Kellett.

Aug. 3 The 53-m-long paddle steamer *Alexandria*, built in Montreal in 1883 and owned by the Richelieu and Ontario Navigation Company, was wrecked during a bad storm on L. Ont. The vessel was beached; all aboard were saved. Captain W. M. Bloomfield was the last to leave the sinking ship.

Aug. 4 The Ottawa School Board was replaced by a 3-member commission when it refused to insist that teachers be qualified to speak English.

Also in Aug.
• The federal govt floated its 1st loan in New York for $45 million. A 2nd loan for $75 million would be floated in 1916.

Sept. The 1st and 2nd Canadian Divisions were formed into the Canadian Corps, commanded by British officer Edward A. H. Alderson, with divisional commanders Arthur William Currie (1875–1933) and Richard Turner.

Oct. 15 The last surviving Father of Confederation, Charles Tupper, died in Britain.

Nov. 20 The cornerstone of the Montreal Free Municipal Library was laid.

• Canada declared war on Bulgaria and Turkey.

Nov. 22 The 1st domestic Canadian war loan was issued. It was raised from $50 million to $100 million on Nov. 30. The domestic war loan was 1st issued under the name "Victory Loan" on Nov. 12, 1917.

Nov. 27 Private Albert Mountain Horse, the only member of the Blood Nation to serve at the front during WW I, was buried with full military honours in Fort Macleod, Alb.

Dec. 15 After more than 12 years as BC Premier, Richard McBride resigned to become BC's agent-gen. in London, England, where he hoped to get treatment for Bright's disease, which ultimately took his life.

Dec. 23 Man. suffragists presented a petition containing about 45,000 names in support of universal suffrage to Premier Tobias C. Norris.

Winter The Great Famine of 1915, caused by an abrupt decline in caribou and muskox populations, devastated the Caribou Inuit of the southern portion of what is now Nunavut. The Haumiqturmiot society was hardest hit. More than half its population died during the winter. The famine lasted 10 more years. By 1925, only 500 Caribou Inuit remained.

c 1915 Clarence Gagnon completed the impressionist painting *La Croix du Chemin, l'automne*, oil on canvas, now in the National Gallery of Canada.

Also in 1915
• Ontario veterinarian Charles Saunders pioneered a procedure for spaying dogs.

• The Chevrolet Motor Co. of Canada was formed in Oshawa, Ont., when the McLaughlin family acquired the rights to build the Chevrolet car.

• Canyon Antelope Reserve (140 km^2) was established on federal grassland, along the South Sask. R. in Alb.'s Kootenay region, as a refuge for the dwindling pronghorn antelope population. Designated Wawaskesy National Park in 1922, the land was shared by ranchers, 1,200 cattle and 300 horses. In 1938, with the antelope population stabilized, the park was abolished and the land transferred to the Alb. govt. In return, new lands were given to the federal govt to expand Elk Island National Park near Edmonton.

• George Reid, influenced by the work of French impressionist Claude Monet, completed the canvas *Vacant Lots,* now at the National Gallery of Canada.

• Tom Thomson painted Algonquin Park's *Tea Lake Dam,* oil on panel, now in the McMichael Canadian Art Collection.

• Nellie McClung published *In Times Like These,* a forceful feminist credo.

• *In Pastures Green*, by Peter McArthur (1866–1924), was published.

• *The True Makers of Canada: The Narrative of Gordon Sellar, Who Emigrated to Canada in 1825*, by Robert Watson Sellar, was published.

• The novel *Prairie Wife*, by Arthur John Arbuthnott Stringer (1874–1950), was published. It told the story of a fashionable New England woman who moved West with her Canadian husband. The marriage failed and she devoted herself to an independent life with her son.

• Arthur Stanley Bourinot (1893–1969) published his 1st book of verse, *Laurentian Lyrics*.

• Aristide Beaugrand-Champagne (1876–1950), professor of architecture at Montreal's École Polytechnique and École des beaux-arts, completed the Roman-Byzantine-inspired Église Saint-Michel-Archange, located on rue Saint Urbain in Montreal, Que.

1916

Jan. 1 Edmonton reformer, suffrage-activist Emily Murphy (1868–1933) became the 1st woman magistrate in the Commonwealth. Her initial jurisdiction of Edmonton was later extended throughout Alb.

Jan. 4 PM Borden protested in a letter sent to Sir George Perley, Canadian high commissioner in London, that despite its significant contributions to the war effort, Canada's role in the decision-making process was minimal.

Jan. 12 An Order-in-Council authorized an increase in Canadian troops to 500,000.

• The 6th session of the 12th Parliament met until May 18. The Business War Profits Tax imposed a 25% tax on war profits.

• A train crash in Brandon, Man., killed 19 people when a locomotive, making its way through a thick, freak icefog, rammed into the rear of another train crowded with snow-removal workers in the rail yards.

Jan. 27 Man. women were the 1st in Canada to be granted the provincial franchise, as the Enfranchisement of Women Bill was passed unanimously in the Man. legislature.

Feb. 3 The sidewheeler *Victoria* was destroyed by fire at the wharf at Indiantown, NB.

• French-speaking teachers in Ottawa went on strike. They had not been paid since their refusal to accept requirements defined in Regulation 17, designed to stamp out French instruction in Ont. The strike led to the closing of 17 bilingual schools in Ottawa.

Feb. 3–4 The original Centre Block of the Parliament Buildings burned to the ground, including the Peace Tower, House of Commons, Senate, all chambers, innumerable files, the mace and historic pictures. Seven died in the blaze. Only the library survived because the fire doors were closed. A temporary parliament was established at the Victoria Museum, now the Museum of Nature, Ottawa.

Feb. 8 PM Borden introduced the BNA Act, 1916, extending the life of the 12th Parliament for 1 year as a wartime measure. It was passed unanimously by the House of Commons, and received Assent in June.

Mar. 14 Women in Sask. won the right to vote in provincial elections.

Also in Mar.
• J.E.H. MacDonald exhibited *The Tangled Garden* at the Ontario Society of Arts, now in the National Gallery of Canada.

Apr. 3–20 Over 1,000 members of the 2nd Canadian Division were killed, wounded or taken prisoner in the Battle of St. Eloi, also known as the Battle of the Craters.

Apr. 17 German military attaché to the US, Captain Franz Baron Von Papen was indicted by a New York grand jury for conspiracy to blow up the Welland Canal.

Apr. 19 Women in Alb. won the right to vote in provincial elections.

May 9 Julian Hedworth George (Bungo) Byng (1862–1935) was appointed commander of the Canadian Expeditionary Force in Europe, succeeding Gen. Alderson on May 28.

• In answer to Ont.'s Regulation 17, opposition leader Laurier drafted, and Ernest Lapointe (1876–1941) introduced in the House, a resolution calling for children of French parentage in Ont. to be allowed the right to be taught in their mother tongue. The resolution failed.

May 28 Field Marshal Douglas Haig confirmed Gen. Alderson's criticism of the Canadian Ross rifle (championed by Sam Hughes). Haig advised the govt to abandon the weapon "without delay." His recommendation was accepted, and Ross rifles were replaced by Lee-Enfields July 18. The Ross was 1st developed in 1903, but worked poorly in wet, muddy conditions.

• An Order-in-Council established a sub-committee of the Privy Council to take charge of all measures to foster the scientific development of Canadian industries and to extend Canadian trade abroad.

June 2–13 Canadians engaged battle at Mount Sorrel, which ended in a Canadian victory. The 4th Canadian Mounted Rifles and Princess Patricia's Canadian Light Infantry suffered a total of 8,430 casualties.

June 3 The Board of Pension Commissioners was established to administer naval and military pensions.

June 14 Vilhjalmur Stefansson, Charlie Anderson and Harold Noice discovered an Arctic island, which they named Meighen Is.

June 28 Local residents of Berlin, Ont. voted to rename the town Kitchener.

July 1 The 1st Newfoundland Regiment was devastated on the 1st day of the Battle of the Somme.

Casualties were more than 700, one-third fatal. Only 68 soldiers escaped serious injury. Every officer involved was either killed or wounded. After being reinforced by 130 recruits, the 150 members capable of carrying on were transferred to Ypres Salient.

July 13 By Order-in-Council, a Royal Commission was appointed to consider Canada's transportation systems, especially the 3 existing transcontinental railway systems, including "the reorganization of any of the said railway systems, or the acquisition by the State." Alfred H. Smith, president of the New York Central Railroad, was named chairman of the commission. The commission report favoured public ownership.

July 25 The International Nickel Co. of Canada Limited (INCO) was incorporated, assuming all control of mining, smelting and refining of the International Nickel Company of New Jersey. With mines in Sudbury, it would become the world's largest nickel producer.

July 29 A forest fire killed an estimated 228 people and destroyed the towns of Cochrane and Matheson in northern Ont.

Aug. 19 Victor Christian William Cavendish, Duke of Devonshire (1868–1938), was appointed gov-gen. of Canada, serving from Nov. 11, 1916–July 19, 1921.

Also in Aug.
• In Alb., the Western Coal Operators' Association and the United Mine Workers of America signed a supplementary agreement, increasing miners' wages and protecting workers against Japanese labour competition.

Sept. 4 The Canadian Corps took over a section of the Somme line in France, directly in front of the village of Courcelette, from the valiant but mangled ANZACs (Australian and New Zealand Army Corps).

Sept. 11 Thirteen men were killed when the centre span of the Que. bridge collapsed while it was under construction. This was the 2nd such collapse since 1907.

Sept. 15 The British offensive began again on the Somme front. The 22nd Battalion from Que., the

25th from NS and the 26th from NB captured Courcelette, taking more than 1,000 prisoners.

Sept. 21 Wilfrid Laurier, speaking in Que., appealed to francophone Canadians to enlist in the armed forces, if not to fight for England then "for the liberation of French territory," and if not for that then for themselves.

Oct. 8 James Richardson (1895–1916) received the Victoria Cross for marching in front of the enemy at the Somme, playing the bagpipes and inspiring the men of the 16th Battalion to capture the German position.

Oct. 25 The Canadian 4th Division attacked on the Somme, and again on Nov. 18. The 3 other Canadian divisions were transferred to Artois in mid-Oct.

Oct. 28 George Halsey Perley (1857–1938), high commissioner in London, was appointed minister of the overseas military forces for Canada in Britain.

Nov. 10 An Order-in-Council established price controls.

• Sam Hughes resigned as minister of militia and defence at PM Borden's request. On Nov. 23, Albert Edward Kemp (1858–1929) was appointed as Hughes's replacement.

Nov. 18 The Battle of the Somme ended. Allies conquered 125 miles (201 km) of territory and advanced 7 miles (11 km). Some 1 million soldiers died — 600,000 on the Allied side and between 400,000 and 500,000 on the German side. Canadians and Newfoundlanders lost 24,713 men. On this last day, the Canadian Corps won a trench called Desire, just beyond Courcelette.

Nov. 29 An Order-in-Council was passed cancelling services of the RNWMP in the provinces after Mar. 1, 1917.

• The National Research Council of Canada was established at Ottawa, to further scientific planning and development.

Nov. 30 The United Farmers of Alb., Alb. Farmers' Co-operative Elevator Company and the Man.

Grain Growers' Association amalgamated with the Grain Growers Grain Company at a meeting in Winnipeg, forming United Grain Growers Ltd.

Dec. 4 The Asquith govt in England was brought down, and David Lloyd George formed a coalition govt.

Dec. 11 The Sask. legislature abolished liquor stores after Sask. voters approved prohibition in a plebiscite. On Dec. 31, Sask. was proclaimed officially "dry." The prohibition legislation would not be repealed until 1925.

Dec. 12 Fr. Albert Lacombe died in Calgary, Alb., at the home for Aboriginal children, which he founded.

Dec. 16 The CPR opened its 8.082-km-long Connaught Tunnel under Rogers Pass in the Selkirk Mountains of BC. The tunnel, which took 3 years to construct, was 6.1 m wide, and eliminated a series of dangerous curves through the mountains, in addition to chopping 7.28 km from CPR's transcontinental route.

1916–1917 *The Jack Pine,* oil on canvas, by Tom Thomson, was completed.

1916–1931 Henry Wise Wood (1860- 1941) served as president of the United Farmers of Alb.

Also in 1916

• Alb., Man., Ont. and NS entered the era of prohibition. Man. would run completely "dry" until the sale of liquor in stores was allowed in 1923 and public drinking allowed in 1928. Alb. would allow public drinking and bottle sales in 1924; NS, bottle sales in 1930 and public drinking in 1948; and Ont., bottle sales in 1927 and public drinking in 1934.

• Despite the war, 65,836 immigrants entered Canada, including 8,596 from Britain and 51,701 from the US.

• The Man. Pension Act was established, providing basic allowances to widowed, divorced or deserted wives with children.

• Production of zinc began at Cominco Mines plant in Trail, BC.

• The Canada–US Migratory Birds Conservation Act was created, establishing hunting quotas on specified migratory birds and providing total protection for others.

• Tom Thomson painted *Autumn Foliage,* oil on panel, and *Petawawa Gorges,* oil on canvas. Both are in the National Gallery of Canada.

• David Milne painted *The Boulder,* oil on canvas, now in the Winnipeg Art Gallery.

• *Further Foolishness*, by Stephen Leacock, was published.

• The long-unpublished *David Thompson's Narrative,* covering his explorations in western Canada, was edited for the Champlain Society by Joseph Burr Tyrrell, and published.

• *The Last Voyage of the* Karluk: *Flagship of Vilhjalmur Stefansson as told by Robert Abram Bartlett, Captain of the lost Karluk, to Ralph Hale* was published in Boston by Small Maynard.

1917

Jan. 1 Sask. Provincial Police assumed routine policing duties from the RNWMP. The force was replaced by the RCMP in 1928.

Jan. 18 The 7th session of the 12th Parliament met until Sept. 20. The Soldier Settlement Act was passed to help men returning to Canada settle on the land. The Soldier Settlement Board was established.

Mar. 1 The Alb. Provincial Police was created to replace the RNWMP. The 96-man force patrolled public buildings, including theatres, restaurants and pool halls, helped fight forest fires, inspected mines, enforced school attendance, collected hospital fees and, most unpopular of all, enforced prohibition regulations. John Daniel Nicholson was the 1st deputy chief. The force remained active in Alb. until 1932, when the RCMP agreed to assume policing services within the province.

Mar. 20 PM Borden and other Dominion PMs attended the 1st meetings of the Imperial War Cabinet in London to discuss the war. The cabinet was created by British PM George to bring together Allied policy making.

Also in Mar.

- A 3rd war loan of $150 million was issued by the federal govt.

Apr. 5 An act to amend the Provincial Election Act gave women in BC the right to vote in provincial elections.

Apr. 6 The US entered the war against Germany and its allies.

Apr. 7 A Royal Commission was appointed to investigate the high cost of living.

Apr. 9 Easter Monday: 4 divisions of Canadian troops, under Commander Julian Byng (1862–1935), stormed the ridge at Vimy, France, and captured what was considered an impregnable German position; 10,602 Canadians were killed or wounded over the 5-day battle.

Apr. 15 Thirty-four miners were killed in a coal-dust explosion in No. 3 East Mine at Michael, Coal Creek, Fernie, BC.

Apr. 16 PM Borden moved for, and New Zealand PM William Massey seconded, Resolution IX of the Imperial War Conference, requiring a special Imperial Conference to be summoned after the cessation of hostilities to readjust constitutional relations between component parts of the empire. These relations would be based on full recognition of the Dominions as autonomous nations in the Imperial Commonwealth.

- By federal Order-in-Council, wheat flour and semolina were made duty free.

Apr. 17 The Ontario Franchise Act granted women in Ont. the right to vote in provincial elections.

Also in Apr.

- Public pressure forced the federal govt to impose a business-profits tax to support the war effort. An "anti-loafing" law provided for the incarceration of any man not gainfully employed.

- The Great War Veterans' Association (GWVA), the most important of the WW I veterans' associations, was founded to secure benefits for its members.

May 1 Schoolchildren were let out of school in Sask. on an organized gopher hunt — marking the province's 1st annual Gopher Day.

May 3 Lt. Robert G. Combe from Sask. died in the line of duty south of Acheville, France. He became the 1st Sask. soldier to be awarded the Victoria Cross.

May 18 PM Borden announced before the House of Commons that there was a need for conscription. On May 24, anti-conscriptionists in Montreal rioted in protest.

June 2 William Avery "Billy" Bishop (1894–1956) was awarded the Victoria Cross. He was the most successful Canadian airman in the history of the Royal Flying Corps, with an estimated 72 enemy aircraft shot down.

June 7 Temperance activist Louise McKinney (1863–1935) became the 1st woman in Canada to win a seat in a provincial legislature, taking the riding of Claresholm in the Alb. provincial election, as member of the Non-Partisan League.

June 9 Gen. Arthur William Currie (1875–1933) assumed command of the Canadian Expeditionary Force (troops raised in Canada for overseas service in WW I). He was the 1st Canadian to hold the position. On June 19, Currie succeeded Julian Byng as commander of the Canadian Corps in France.

- PM Borden introduced the Military Service Bill (Conscription Act) provoking the Conscription Crisis between Que. and English Canada. It passed the House by 102 to 44 on June 24 and became law Sept. 26. The bill made all British subjects between 20 and 45 years of age, with certain exceptions, eligible for military service. Five thousand Montrealers demonstrated against the legislation.

June 21 Charles Alexander Magrath (1860–1949) was appointed fuel controller with authority over the price of coal, wood and gas, and the production, distribution, sale, delivery, consumption and use of these commodities. The controller position had been created by a federal Order-in-Council on June 8.

July 2 The 1st Chautauqua tent show to tour Canada stopped in Gleichen, Alb., for 6 days of "oratory, music, lectures, entertainment, and cartooning."

July 8 Painter Thomas John "Tom" Thomson drowned mysteriously in Canoe L., Algonquin Park, Ont. His body was found July 15. Among the paintings he completed before his death were *The Jack Pine* (now with the National Gallery of Canada) and *The West Wind* (at the AGO). Following the tragedy, fellow painters J.W. Beatty and J.E.H. MacDonald erected a cairn beside Canoe L. in memory to the great artist.

July 25 The Income Tax War Bill was introduced as a temporary wartime measure by Finance Minister Thomas White (1866–1955) to fund the war effort. It imposed the 1st national tax on personal incomes, and it passed Parliament Aug. 20.

Also in July
• The federal govt floated a loan in New York of $100 million.

Aug. 9 The home of Hugh Graham (Lord Atholstan), Montreal's leading conscriptionist, was bombed.

Aug. 13 Minister of Justice Charles Joseph Doherty (1855–1931) introduced the Military Voters' Bill, giving the vote to all servicemen who were British subjects, whatever their age or origin, and adding a provision that would enable the govt to apply all floating votes to constituencies where they were most needed. It passed Sept. 20.

Aug. 15 Canadian troops gained a victory at Hill 70 near Lens, France; 1,056 Canadians were killed and 2,432 wounded.

Aug. 25 Two Inuit from the Coppermine region of the NWT were convicted in a Calgary courtroom of the 1913 murder of 2 Oblate missionaries. An Edmonton court had previously acquitted them.

Aug. 30 Anti-conscription riots broke out in Montreal.

Also in Aug.
• Artist A.Y. Jackson became an official war artist.

• Finance Minister White presented legislation to authorize the takeover of the insolvent CNR. The govt already held 40% of its stock.

Sept. 1 The Canadian Press Company was founded, in part to act as a co-operative news agency exchanging news among various newspapers.

• To date, 331,578 men had been sent overseas to the Canadian Expeditionary Force. In training in Canada were an additional 831 officers and 20,179 men.

Sept. 6 Minister of Justice Arthur Meighen introduced the War Times Election Act, giving the federal vote to sisters, widows, wives and adult daughters of servicemen, and disenfranchising naturalized subjects of alien enemy birth and conscientious objectors. The bill was passed Sept. 20.

Sept. 13 The *Polar Bear*, on which Stefansson was returning from the Canadian Arctic Expedition, was grounded in a storm at the east end of Barter Is., and became icebound for the winter.

Sept. 15 The final section of the Quebec Bridge, the largest cantilever bridge in the world, was lifted into place. The bridge was completed 5 days later, and opened to traffic Dec. 3. Its construction had cost the lives of 93 workers.

Oct. 6 Parliament was dissolved and a coalition cabinet was formed due to a Liberal party split over conscription, which Laurier opposed. On May 25, Borden had approved Laurier to form a coalition govt, an idea Laurier rejected.

Oct. 12–July 10, 1920 Borden served as PM of the newly formed Unionist govt, which consisted half of Conservatives and half of Liberals in favour of conscription. The Unionist govt's goals were to fight the war, re-organize the railways and eliminate political patronage.

Oct. 24 The Alexander Graham Bell Memorial was unveiled in Brantford, Ont. Bell stated he 1st conceived of the telephone in Brantford in 1874, although he built it in Boston in 1876.

Oct. 26 The Canadian Corps, under Lt-Gen. Currie, engaged in the Passchendaele offensive in

Belgium, until Nov. 30. Allies took control of 5.2 km² of German-held territories, but the battle was a complete bloodbath. A total of 500,000 soldiers died, including 16,000 Canadians. Canadians fought heroically. Six men were awarded the highest British military honour, the Victoria Cross: Major George Randolph Pearkes, of Victoria, BC; Private Cecil John Kinross, of Alb.; Capt. Christopher Patrick John O'Kelly, of Man.; Lt. Robert Shankland, of Man.; Corp. Colin Fraser Barron, of Ont.; and Private Thomas William Holmes, also of Ont.

Oct. 30 The Montreal and Toronto stock markets established a minimum-price system.

Oct. 30–Aug. 13, 1921 Liberal Charles Stewart (1868–1946) served as premier of Alb.

Nov. 5 The use of grain to manufacture liquor was prohibited for the rest of the war as a way to preserve food.

• The Russian Revolution ended with the Bolsheviks (Communists) taking power under leadership of Vladimir Lenin in Petrograd. Russia withdrew from WW I.

Nov. 7 Canadians took the village of Passchendaele, Belgium, a few miles from Ypres.

Nov. 12 The 1st Victory Loan of $150 million was floated, and yielded $400 million.

Nov. 22 The National Hockey League (NHL) was founded, with Frank Calder (1877–1943) the 1st president. The original league included 5 teams: Montreal Canadiens, Montreal Wanderers, Ottawa Senators and Toronto Arenas; Quebec City had a franchise but did not play that season. Clubs played a 22-game schedule. The Toronto Arenas won the inaugural NHL season and went on to beat the Vancouver Millionaires of the Pacific Coast League to win the Stanley Cup.

Nov. 26 Former US President, Theodore (Teddy) Roosevelt visited Hamilton, Ont., to take part in a Victory Bond rally to raise money for the war effort. His slogan: "Stand behind the men behind the guns."

Dec. 6 The worst disaster in Canadian history occurred in Halifax Harbour, when the *Mont Blanc*, a French munitions ship carrying over 1,816 tonnes of picric acid, benzol, gun cotton and TNT, collided with the Belgian relief ship *Imo*, in the narrows where the harbour is only 1.2 km wide. The resulting explosion killed 1,800 people and seriously injured 4,000 others. Much of the city was destroyed, leaving 6,000 homeless, and causing property damage estimated at $50 million.

Dec. 8 The 1st special relief train with doctors, nurses and supplies arrived in Halifax from New England to assist victims of the disaster.

Dec. 17 Robert Borden's Unionist govt was returned to power in the general election, taking 153 seats to the Liberals' 82. The Unionists won only 3 seats in Que., due in wide measure to conscription. The Liberals won 62 Que. seats. Voter turnout was 75%.

Dec. 24 The federal govt prohibited the manufacture, importation and transportation of any beverage containing more than 25% alcohol.

Also in 1917
• BC, Sask., NB and Nfld. entered the era of prohibition. Store sales of liquor would be allowed in BC in 1921; in Sask., 1925; Nfld., 1925 and NB, 1927. Public drinking would resume in BC in 1925; Nfld., 1925; Sask., 1935; and NB, in 1961.

• The federal govt took over the failing Mackenzie and Mann network (Canadian Northern Railway). It would fall under the Canadian National Railways umbrella Dec. 20, 1919.

• The Alb. govt passed the Dower Act, which protected a woman's right to a 1/3-share of her husband's property.

• *L'Action Française* was 1st published by members of the Ligue droits du français, to help protect and promote the French language. It was headed by Abbé Lionel-Adolphe Groulx (1878–1967).

• BC's 1st female judge, Helen Emma MacGill (1864–1947), was appointed to the bench of the juvenile court in Vancouver.

• The average price of a man's haircut in Toronto rose to 35 cents from 5 cents.

• NB native William Maxwell Aitken (1879–1964) was made a peer and took the title of Lord Beaverbrook. He also acquired his 1st English newspaper, the *London Daily Express*.

• *Canadian Troops at the Front*, oil on canvas, by James Wilson Morrice, was completed.

• The 1st permanent film studio in Canada was built in Trenton, Ont. Local citizens lent financial support and worked as technicians, actors and extras. The Ontario Motion Picture Bureau, a government film agency, purchased the Trenton Film Plant in 1923. In 1927, the British filmed *Carry on Sergeant* in Trenton and it was billed as Canada's 1st "epic" production. A silent film, it was released at the same time as the 1st "talkie," Al Jolson's *The Jazz Singer*, and failed to achieve financial success. The studio closed in 1934.

• Designer Alex Horkoff completed the Doukhobor Prayer House in Veregin, Sask., a 2-storey 15.3 x 15.9-m house with double verandas on all 4 sides.

1918

Jan. Almost 100 lives were lost in a mine explosion in the Allen shaft in Pictou County, NS.

Feb. 6 The War Trade Board was established under the chairmanship of George Eulas Foster (1847–1931).

Feb. 7 The War Purchasing Board was established by Order-in-Council, with authority to make all purchases for the govt.

Feb. 11 A Food Board controlled by the Ministry of Agriculture was established, replacing the Food Controller.

Feb. 21–July 1920 James Alexander Lougheed (1854–1925) served as Minister of Soldiers' Civil Re-establishment, responsible for relocation, hospital care and pensions of returning soldiers and war workers.

Feb. 25 The Carnegie Corporation donated $1 million to McGill U.

Also in Feb.
• Artist Fred Varley travelled overseas as a war artist.

Mar. 2 Joe Malone of the Montreal Canadiens scored his 44th goal, beating Harry Holmes of Toronto and setting a single-season NHL scoring record that would stand for more than 25 years.

Mar. 4 The federal govt ordered troops to patrol the Canada-US border at Niagara to prevent would-be draft dodgers from fleeing to the US.

Mar. 16 By Order-in-Council, the NWT was divided into the Districts of Keewatin, Mackenzie and Franklin, and brought into the Dominion of Canada, effective Jan. 1, 1920.

Mar. 18 The 1st session of the 13th Parliament met until May 24. A luxury tax of 10% was placed on cars, gramophones, records, player pianos and jewelry.

Mar. 28 The offices of commissioner and administrator were abolished in the Yukon, their powers shifted to the office of the gold commissioner.

Mar. 28–Apr. 1 In Quebec City, crowds of rioters destroyed offices of administrators of the Military Service Act. Buildings were burned, equipment smashed, and files and official documents were dumped into the streets. Eight hundred troops were called out to quell the disturbance; 4 civilians were killed and 6 soldiers were wounded in a shootout. On Apr. 4, the Habeas Corpus Act was suspended in Que., and the city was all but under martial law.

Mar. 30 Edwin Albert Baker (1893–1968), who lost the sight of both eyes in the 1915 battle at Mount Kennel, France, founded the Canadian National Institute for the Blind (CNIB) in Toronto.

Also in Mar.
• The Dominion of Canada prohibited the shipment of liquor from one province to another. Liquor traffic became clandestine.

Spring Parliament introduced daylight saving time, which would begin on the 1st Sunday in Apr. and end on the last Sunday in Oct.

• An Order-in-Council stipulated that every male between 16 and 60 be gainfully employed.

Apr. 17 For the 1st time, the House of Commons held a secret session. Its members were told what the public was not — that the Allied armies in Europe faced possible defeat. German submarines had nearly cut off British supplies, Russia was in disarray, and the French infantry was in a state of near revolt.

Apr. 20 Men from the ages of 20 and 22 were called to military service. By war's end, 124,588 soldiers, out of 401,882 registrants, had been added to Canada's armed forces; 24,132 of the call-ups made it to the European theatre.

Apr. 21 Captain Arthur Roy Brown (1893–1944) was credited with shooting down the German flying ace Baron Manfred von Richtofen, better known as the Red Baron.

Apr. 26 The Franchise Act gave women in NS the right to vote in provincial elections.

May 2 Ninety employees from Winnipeg's light and power department went on strike for better wages.

May 6 The Dominion Astrophysical Observatory opened for operations in Victoria, BC. Its 1.8-m Plaskett Telescope was the largest in the world. The observatory was renamed the Herzberg Institute of Astrophysics in 1995.

May 7 Winnipeg's teamsters went on strike.

May 13 Liberal opposition leader Wilfrid Laurier and his wife, Zoe, celebrated their golden wedding anniversary, receiving a magnificent golden salver from House and Senate Liberals.

May 14 Five thousand angry members of the United Farmers of Ont. crowded into Ottawa's Russell Theatre to protest the Apr. 19 cancellation of draft exemptions for farmers' sons. PM Borden told them that the war effort was paramount.

May 16 Winnipeg's telephone operators went on strike.

May 21 Winnipeg's 4,000 railway workers went on a sympathy strike in support of other striking trades. During the war years, inflation almost doubled and the cost of living skyrocketed 50%. (Industrial war contracts did not include fair-wage clauses.)

May 24 The Act to confer the Electoral Franchise upon Women granted Canadian women (except women from many Asian groups, Inuit and Status Indian women) the right to vote in federal elections, effective Jan. 1, 1919.

June 3 An airmail service was inaugurated between Montreal, Quebec City, Boston and New York City.

June 19 Canadian ace Billy Bishop shot down 5 enemy aircraft.

June 22 A 2nd national registration was held, with compulsory registration of men and women over the age of 16, except for cloistered nuns, persons on active service, and inmates of asylums, prisons and penitentiaries.

June 24 Capt. Brian Peck flew the 1st official Canadian airmail from Montreal to Toronto. Also aboard were so many caseloads of liquor (Que. was "wet," Ont. "dry") that the Curtis JN-4 could not fly higher than 12 m.

Also in June
• Two hundred people in Winnipeg attended the opening of William Ivens's Labour Church, pledging their determination "to support an independent and creedless Church based on the Fatherhood of God and the Brotherhood of Man."

July 9 American Kathleen Stinson (1891–1977) flew the 1st air mail flight in Western Canada, from Calgary to Edmonton in 2 hours, 5 minutes.

Aug. 8 Canadian and Australian troops broke through German trenches at Amiens, France, using airplanes, tanks, artillery and cavalry. The event became known as "the black day of the German Army," and the beginning of the "100 Days of the Canadian Army." Between Aug. 8 and Nov. 11, over 100,000 Canadians advanced 130 km, taking 31,537 prisoners, 2,842 machine guns and 336 mortars. Canadian casualties totalled 45,830.

Sept. 12 The Department of Public Instruction was established, with the public to provide information on the war effort.

Sept. 16 Vilhjalmur Stefansson returned to Vancouver from a 5-year govt-sponsored Arctic Expedition.

He was one of the last Europeans to 1st sight major world landmasses — Lougheed, Meighen, Borden and Brock Islands. This Arctic expedition, which had begun in 1913, was his last of three. Altogether, Stefansson travelled some 32,000 km² of Arctic territory.

Sept. 19 The Khaki University of Canada was established by the Canadian YMCA in England, to provide vocational academic training to Canadian soldiers. Dr. Henry Marshall Tory of the U. of Alb. served as its 1st president.

• The Privy Council authorized the creation of the Canadian Air Force (CAF) in England. It was dismantled after the war.

Sept. 27-30 Canadian forces, supported by tanks and a rolling artillery barrage, overwhelmed the Germans at the Canal du Nord, breaking through the last section of the Hindenburg Line.

Sept. 28 Fourteen organizations, including the International Workers of the World and the Social Democratic party, were branded as subversive and excluded from Canada. Also banned were meetings in enemy languages (German, Ukrainian and Czech).

Also in Sept.
• The federal govt established the Exhibits and Publicity Bureau to promote trade and commerce through the filming of travelogues. This marked the beginning of the longest record of govt presence in film production in the democratic world. The 1st series produced under govt auspices was *Seeing Canada*, 10- to 20-minute short films extolling the virtues of Canada's wilderness, including such titles as *Where the Moose Run Loose*, *Nimrods in Duckland* and *Rushing Waters*.

Oct. 1 The Borden govt announced the banning of books, newspapers and other materials printed in enemy languages, unless published under licence from the secretary of state.

Oct. 2–17 The 10th General Conference of the Methodist Church called for the social reconstruction of Canada through an economic system based on co-operation and public ownership instead of capitalism.

Oct. 9 Canadian forces, 100,000 strong, captured Cambrai, France.

Oct. 10 Edward Wentworth Beatty (1877–1943) became president of the CPR.

Oct. 11 An Order-in-Council established regulations for wartime labour and prohibited strikes and lock-outs.

Oct. 21 The 5-km Mount Royal tunnel in Montreal was opened for service. It was built by the Canadian Northern Railroad for $5 million.

Oct. 23 The CPR steamer *Princess Sophia*, bound from Skagway, Alaska, to Vancouver, hit a submerged rock and was stranded on Vanderbilt Reef, Lynn Canal. Rescue vessels arrived but the *Sophia's* captain refused to transfer his passengers. Weather conditions worsened, and the *Sophia* sank before another rescue could be attempted. All 268 passengers and 75 crew drowned.

Oct. 27 A brigade of approximately 4,000 Canadians arrived at Vladivostok, Siberia, to support anti-Bolshevik forces.

• The great flying ace William George "Billy" Barker (1894–1930) of Dauphin, Man., began one of the most celebrated aerial dogfights in the annals of war. Setting off for England from France in a Sopwith Snipe, Barker single-handedly engaged 60 German Fokker D. VII's, Albatross biplanes and Rumpler C's in 5 separate battles — all in the same flight. Taking several hits that mangled both arms and a leg, Barker fired his way out of each dogfight, taking down 4 German aircraft. He crash-landed behind British lines in France after German Spandau guns took out his gas tank. The Scottish infantry, who witnessed the epic battles above, dragged him to safety, where he lay in hospital unconscious for 2 weeks. Barker was awarded the Victoria Cross for his heroics.

Oct. 28 British Prime Minister Lloyd George sent a message to PM Borden informing him that Germany's surrender was imminent and advised Borden to come to Europe for the peace negotiations.

• The 2nd Victory Loan, issued for $300 million, raised $660 million.

Nov. 7 The Canadian Trade Mission was established in London, England.

Nov. 11 An armistice ending WW I was signed in a railway car at Compiègne, France on the 11th hour of the 11th day of the 11th month. At that moment, Canadians under Lt-Gen. Arthur Currie were engaged in heavy fighting at Mons. The war claimed more than 10 million lives. A total of 628,462 Canadians served in the armed forces, including 424,589 who went overseas; 61,356 Canadians were killed (Canada's population was 8 million) and many more were permanently injured.

Nov. 29 A meeting of the Canadian Council of Agriculture (Farmers' Party) in Winnipeg adopted a "New National Policy" program, supporting free trade with Britain, reciprocity with the US, nationalization (particularly of railways) and direct democracy. The council also supported land taxes, a graduated income tax, and a corporation and business tax. The Progressive Party, established in 1920, was born out of this organization.

Also in Nov.
• The Marconi Wireless Telegraph Company of Canada began broadcasting experiments in Montreal. Its 1st radio transmission of music took place between Montreal and the Château Laurier Hotel in Ottawa in Dec.

Nov.–Dec. "Col. Sam" McLaughlin, Canada's automotive pioneer and owner of McLaughlin Carriage Co., sold out to General Motors, and the McLaughlin companies were reorganized into General Motors of Canada, Ltd.

Dec. 10 The issue of $5 War Savings Stamps totalling $50 million was authorized by the federal govt.

Dec. 11 The federal govt appointed Hoyes Lloyd supervisor of wildlife protection. He became the 1st ornithologist to be employed by the Dominion Parks and Forest Reserves.

Dec. 31 At a meeting of the Imperial War Cabinet in London, England, PM Borden demanded a greater role at the peace talks for Britain's dominions, suggesting Canada should be treated as an independent allied power.

Also in 1918
• The federal govt established the Civil Service Commission. Its 3 appointed members were responsible for recruiting and classifying civil servants, determining their rate of remuneration, requirements and levels of promotion, and the procedures for personal transfer.

• The Yukon went "dry" under prohibition. Bottle sales would resume in 1921 and public drinking made legal again in 1925.

• Canadians completed their 1st T-1 income tax forms: 31,130 individuals were required to pay income tax.

• Canada was the world's largest exporter of paper.

• Adanac Military Cemetery (the name was created by reversing "Canada") was established after the Armistice by the concentration of graves from the Canadian battlefields near Courcelette, where the Canadian Corps fought from Sept. to Nov. 1916, suffering 24,000 casualties. In the 1920s, Adanac was transformed into a concentration cemetery and Canadian bodies from the 1916 Somme offensive were relocated to the area. Adanac houses more than 3,000 graves on this site, over 50% of which remain unidentified.

• Approximately 10,000 Ukrainian-born immigrants enlisted in the Canadian military for service during WW I.

• Census takers concluded that a typical family of 5 needed $20 a week to secure the basic necessities of life, including food, lighting and housing.

• US Hutterites settled 10 colonies in Calgary and Lethbridge and in Man. west of Winnipeg. The conscientious objectors had experienced widespread harassment during the American draft call-ups.

• Point Pelee National Park (20 km^2) on the northern shores of L. Erie, the smallest of Canada's national parks, was established. The park represents the most southern point in Canada, touching the 42nd parallel, the same line that runs through Rome, Italy, and northern California, and is one of the world's great birdwatching sanctuaries. Its Carolinian forest has 70 tree species, 27 reptile species and 20 kinds of amphibian.

• The citizens of Halifax donated their 1st annual Christmas tree to the people of Boston as a special thank-you for the generous donations of food, clothing, building materials, medical aid and money received following the Explosion of 1917. Boston's official Christmas tree is now donated each year by the Nova Scotia Department of Natural Resources. The tree is lit in Boston Commons at 4:00 p.m. on the 1st Saturday of every Dec.

• American novelist William Faulkner enlisted in the CAF after being declared too short by the US military.

• *In the Ward,* oil on canvas, by Lawren Harris, was completed.

• Winnipeg artist Lionel LeMoine FitzGerald (1890–1956) painted *Late Fall, Manitoba,* which is held by the National Gallery of Canada.

• Albert Laberge (1871–1960) published *La Scouine* (translated into English as *Bitter Bread*) in extracts in *Le Terroir, La Presse* and other papers. The work was widely condemned as anti-clerical and immoral, but established Laberge as one of Que.'s 1st naturalist writers.

• Wilson Pugsley MacDonald (1880–1967), Cheapside, Ont., salesman, magician and poet, published *Song of the Prairie Land,* a book of verse.

• McClelland & Stewart published *Canadian Poems of the Great War,* edited by John Garvin.

1919

Jan. 4 PM Borden opened an exhibit, in London, England, of 400 war paintings by British and Canadian artists.

Jan. 12 The Preliminary Peace Conference began at Paris. A proposal for distinct representation for British dominions met with US objection, but US delegates conceded the issue at the subsequent meeting and the proposal was carried.

Jan. 19 King George V presented the Victoria Cross to Private Thomas Ricketts, 17, the youngest soldier ever to receive the honour. Ricketts had enlisted in the Royal Newfoundland Regiment when he was 15. In 1918, fighting near Ledeghem-Drie-Masten, Ricketts drove the Germans back under heavy fire, enabling his platoon to advance. After the war, Ricketts returned to Canada and opened a pharmacy in St. John's, Nfld.

Feb. 1 The Grand Trunk Pacific Railroad, a subsidiary of the Grand Trunk Railroad, defaulted on one of its debenture payments. The govt placed it in receivership under the War Measures Act and eventually took it over along with its parent GTR on Oct. 10. The GTR fell under Canadian National Railways (CNR) management in 1923.

Feb. 17 Sir Wilfrid Laurier died in Ottawa of a stroke. He was 78. Fifty thousand mourners filed past his coffin as he lay in state in Ottawa. The great statesman's funeral was one of the 1st Canadian public events to be captured on film.

Feb. 26 The 2nd session of the 13th Parliament met, until July 7. The Department of Health and the Board of Commerce were established. The Soldiers' Settlement Act was revised to provide financial aid to soldiers settling on govt land. An amended Immigration Act (June) excluded "anarchists," "enemy aliens" and illiterates over 15 years old.

Mar. 5 Canadian soldiers, suffering long transportation delays home from England, rioted in Kinmel Park, North Wales. Five were killed and 27 injured.

Mar. 29 The Industrial Conditions Act of Man. was established to settle industrial disputes between workers and employers.

Apr. 9 A Royal Commission on industrial relations was appointed to examine the social consequences of the high cost of living.

Apr. 17 Women in NB were granted the right to vote in municipal and provincial elections.

Also in Apr.
• Quebecers voted in a referendum to continue the sale of beer and light wines throughout the province.

• A brigade of 4,000 Canadians, sent to Siberia in Oct. 1918 to support anti-Communist forces, was withdrawn. Another group of 500 in northern Russia remained until June.

May 1 Two thousand workers in the Winnipeg metal trades walked off their jobs at Vulcan Iron Works, Man. Bridge and Iron, and Dominion Bridge and Iron. They demanded a 44-hour workweek and an 85 cent per hour wage.

May 8 Workers in Ottawa's building trades ended a strike after a settlement awarded them a 20% wage increase and an 8-hour workday.

May 13 Members of the Winnipeg Trades and Labour Council voted 11,000 to 500 in favour of conducting a general strike in support of the demands of striking building and metal trades workers. On May 15, as negotiations between striking metal trade workers and management broke down, a general strike was called. Thirty thousand Winnipeg workers represented by 53 unions walked off their jobs. Govt and civic employees were also included. The Winnipeg General Strike began. It was a period of high unemployment and high inflation. Workers, many just home from war, wanted better wages, collective bargaining and better working conditions. Some, inspired by socialist successes in Russia, wanted to re-organize the economic system.

May 16 Winnipeg strikers shut down the city's 3 major newspapers, including the *Manitoba Free Press* (now the *Winnipeg Free Press*), which opposed the strike.

May 17 The Winnipeg Citizen's Committee of One Thousand, made up of influential manufacturers, bankers and politicians, was organized. The committee declared the general strike the result of a revolutionary conspiracy organized by "alien scum." On May 25, at the request of Winnipeg Mayor Charles F. Gray, federal authorities sent the North West Mounted Police to Winnipeg for security.

May 22 The House of Commons passed the Nickle Resolution, requesting that English monarchs refrain from conferring titles to any Canadian subject. Although not a law, it made Canada the only Commonwealth nation to have such a policy.

Also in May

• Sympathetic strikes in support of Winnipeg workers erupted, from Victoria, BC, to Amherst, NS.

• An Order-in-Council was passed to curb the flow of American Hutterites into Canada. It prohibited the entry of immigrants "deemed undesirable owing to their particular customs, habits, modes of living and methods of holding property and because of their probable inability to become readily assimilated or to assume duties and responsibilities of Canadian citizenship within a reasonable time." The Order-in-Council was rescinded in 1922.

June 3 A general strike of about 12,000 workers was called in Vancouver.

June 5 Winnipeg Mayor Gray forbade all parades in the city, fearing they might result in violence.

June 6 Thomas Alexander Crerar resigned as minister of agriculture in the Borden cabinet. He would become leader of the new Progressive Party in 1920.

• The Borden govt approved amendments to the Criminal Code, providing penalties for "seditious conspiracy," a law that would later be used to detain and incarcerate labour organizers. The amendments also provided for the deportation of aliens, if convicted of seditious offences.

June 9 All but 15 members of the Winnipeg Police Force were fired after the police commissioner failed to obtain a retraction of the force's vote in support of the general strike. The regular force was replaced by a volunteer force the next day.

June 14 British pilots John William Alcock (1892–1919) and Arthur Whitten Brown (1886–1948) made the 1st non-stop flight across the Atlantic, travelling 3,154 km from St. John's, Nfld. to Galway, Ireland.

June 16–17 In the middle of the night, 8 leaders of the Winnipeg General Strike, including Robert Boyd "Bob" Russell (1888–1964), were rounded up and charged with conspiring to overthrow the govt. They were sent to Stony Mountain Federal Penitentiary. On Dec. 24, Russell received the longest sentence among the 8 charged — 2 years for seditious conspiracy.

June 21 Five thousand strike sympathizers rioted in downtown Winnipeg, knocking a streetcar off its tracks. Mayor Gray read the Riot Act, demanding that all disperse within 30 minutes. Before the allotted time, a Mountie shot into the swelling crowd, intensifying the frenzy. By day's end, 2 lay dead, 20 were injured, on a day that became known as "Bloody Saturday." On Monday morning, June 23, Winnipeggers returned to work in the shadow of .30-calibre machine guns mounted on trucks, ready to silence any further protest. On the 25th, the Trades and Labour Council announced an end to the Winnipeg General Strike.

June 23 Fred Dixon, editor of the *Western Labour News*, published his editorial "Kaiserism in Canada," deploring the "murderous assault which was committed" against the Winnipeg strikers.

June 28 WW I officially ended with the signing of the Treaty of Versailles in Paris.

June 30 James Shaver Woodsworth was charged with sedition for editorials published during the Winnipeg General Strike. Charges were dropped Feb. 14, 1920.

Also in June
• The House passed amendments to the Immigration Act, barring immigration to persons deemed likely to become public charges, or who showed symptoms of mental or physical inferiority, chronic alcoholism, physical defects, or those deemed sympathetic to the violent overthrow of the Canadian system of govt. Immigration would also be denied those involved with prostitution. These amendments were made amidst widespread beliefs that the Winnipeg General Strike was the product of foreign radicals.

• Official war artist David Milne produced 107 works by war's end. All are in the National Gallery of Canada.

July 7 Section 98 of the Criminal Code was passed by Parliament in the wake of the Winnipeg General Strike, outlawing any organization whose professed purpose was to bring about "governmental, industrial or economic change" by force. Police could now act on mere suspicion of sedition. Materials judged to be seditious were subject to censorship, and property belonging to those suspected of sedition was subject to confiscation. The new legislation received Assent June 17.

July 29 Liberal Sarah Ramsland (1882–1964) was elected as the 1st woman to sit in the Sask. Legislative Assembly.

July 31 The 1st Canadian Wheat Board (CWB) replaced the Board of Grain Supervisors, which was established during WW I to regulate prices and control trade for the 1917–1918 and 1918–1919 seasons. The CWB mandate was to market Canadian domestic and exported wheat at world prices. The CWB was disbanded in 1920, but returned permanently on July 5, 1935.

Aug. 5–7 The Liberals called Canada's 1st leadership convention. Mackenzie King was selected over William Stevens Fielding on a platform supporting lower tariffs and the Reciprocity Treaty with the US (which the US Congress approved in 1911).

Aug. 12 The Prince of Wales (the future Edward VIII) arrived in Nfld. on an official visit. He would also tour Canada, arriving in Quebec City Aug. 21. On Sept. 1, Edward laid the cornerstone of the new Peace Tower on Parliament Hill, then journeyed to Calgary for a 5-day visit. In Alb. he toured George Lane's Bar U Ranch near High River, and later purchased the nearby property that would become EP Ranch.

Sept. 1 The 3rd session of the 13th Parliament met until Nov. 10. An amendment to the Criminal Code prohibited aliens from possessing weapons or firearms without a permit.

Sept. 9 The *Hydrodome–4*, a hydrofoil boat built by Casey Baldwin and Alexander Graham Bell, set a world water speed record of 114 km/h at Baddeck, NS.

Sept. 20 The Conservative govt of William Howard Hearst (1864–1941) was defeated by the United Farmers of Ont. in the Ont. general provincial election. Ernest Charles Drury (1878–1968) led the party, winning the riding of Halton in Feb. 1920. He was able to form a coalition govt with labour and independent members.

Sept. 31 Werner Horn (1888–1931) was sentenced in Fredericton, NB, to 10 years in prison for trying to blow up the St. Croix R. bridge in 1915, a plan organized by a German spy ring operating in the US.

Oct. A 3rd Victory Loan was issued for $300 million.

Dec. 2 Torontonian Ambrose Small (1867–c 1919) sold his chain of theatres for $1.7 million to Trans-Canada Theatres. After receiving a $1 million installment payment, he disappeared, never to be heard from again.

Dec. 3 The govt appropriated $25 million for a program to help tenants buy homes.

Dec. 20 Based on recommendations of a Royal Commission established July 13, 1916, an Order-in-Council created the govt-owned Canadian National Railways Co. (CNR), which had been incorporated June 6, 1919. By 1923 the CNR would unite the Intercolonial, Canadian Northern, Grand Trunk, and Grand Trunk Pacific and smaller lines into 1 unit. The CNR operated through a board of management appointed by the govt and responsible to Parliament. It became one of the biggest railways in the world, with 108,000 employees and 35,000 km of track.

• The War-Time Restrictions Act was rescinded, lifting the ban on horse racing and the manufacture of liquor. A general amnesty was offered to those who illegally evaded conscription.

Also in Dec.

• Under the Radio-Telegraph Act of 1913, the minister of marine and fisheries issued the 1st radio broadcasting licence for $100 to XWA, an experimental station in Montreal operated by Marconi Wireless. On May 20, 1920, XWA broadcast the 1st regular radio program in the world from the Montreal Marconi Plant. XWA became CFCF Nov. 4, 1922, and is considered the oldest radio station in the world.

1919–1920 A.Y. Jackson painted *First Snow, Algoma*, now in the McMichael Canadian Collection, Kleinburg, Ont.

c 1919 James Wilson Morrice painted *Village Street, West Indies*, oil on canvas, while visiting the Caribbean. It is now with the Montreal Museum of Fine Arts.

Also in 1919

• Que. banned public drinking until 1921.

• There were 428 strikes, involving 149,309 people, causing 3,942,189 working days lost.

• The Canada Highway Act was passed, providing $20 million toward the cost of improving and building roads over 5 years.

• The Methodist Book Room, a publisher founded in Toronto in 1829, was renamed Ryerson Press, after educator Egerton Ryerson. In 1920, Lorne Pierce was appointed its literary editor. He would publish Bliss Carman, Charles G.D. Roberts and E.J. Pratt.

• Cap de Rabast lighthouse was completed on Cap de Rabast on the north side of Anticosti Is., featuring an octagonal tower, keepers' houses and service buildings.

• Montreal Canadiens defenceman and forward Edouard "Newsy" Lalonde (1888–1970) of Cornwall, Ont., was awarded his 1st of 2 Art Ross scoring title (most points) trophies. Lalonde played 17 games over the 1918–1919 season, scoring 23 goals, with 10 assists. He was awarded his 2nd Art Ross for the 1920–1921 season, in which he played 24 games, with 32 goals and 11 assists. Lalonde played with the Canadiens from 1910–1922, and coached the team between 1926–1934. He was elected to the Hockey Hall of Fame in 1950. The cross-over player would also be voted the best Canadian lacrosse star of the half-century in 1950.

• Stuart Graham (1896–1976) was the 1st to fly air patrols for fire protection when he flew an HS-2L flying boat in the service of Que. forestry companies. Graham also became one of Canada's 1st bush pilots.

• Lawren S. Harris painted *Shacks*, a fine early example of the Group of Seven style. The work is now in the National Gallery of Canada.

• Jessie Georgina Sime (1868–1958) published *Sister Woman*, a collection of short stories portraying the impact of war on art and life and the female realities of poverty, single parenthood, stillbirth and divorce.

• America's Canadian-born sweetheart, Mary Pickford (1892–1979), cofounded United Artists Motion Picture Studio with her husband, Douglas Fairbanks, director D.W. Griffith and Charlie Chaplin. Pickford was born Gladys Smith at 211 University Ave. in Toronto. She was the star of many Hollywood films and plays, including *Warrens of Virginia* written by William deMille. Pickford was rumoured to have refused a job offer from Famous Players impresario Adolph Zukor with the words "No, I really cannot afford to work for only $10,000 a week."

1920

Jan. 1 Approximately 10 of Vancouver's hardiest celebrated the city's 1st polar bear swim in English Bay, one of the world's oldest such events. The annual New Year's Day cure-all would be celebrated by over 2,000 people at century's end.

Jan. 10 The League of Nations was formed, with Canada a founding nation. Its goal was "to promote international co-operation and to achieve international peace and security." Its headquarters were in Geneva, Switzerland. The League dissolved Apr. 18, 1946 and was replaced by the United Nations.

Also in Jan.
• One hundred delegates from 4 provinces attended a special conference of the Canadian Council of Agriculture at Winnipeg, establishing the National Progressive Party. The party's 1st leader was ex-Liberal and ex-Unionist Thomas Alexander Crerar.

Feb. 1 The RNWMP and the Dominion Police (the Eastern Federal Police Force) officially became the RCMP, with federal jurisdiction from coast to coast. The size of the force was set at 2,500 men. RNWMP headquarters were moved from Regina to the new

RCMP headquarters in Ottawa. The act to create the new force (the RNWMP Act) received Assent Nov. 10, 1919. The force's training centre remained in Regina.

Feb. 5 King's College at Windsor, NS, was destroyed by fire.

Feb. 14 The Université de Montréal was incorporated.

Feb. 18 The Privy Council authorized the re-establishment of the Canadian Air Force.

Feb. 26 The 4th session of the 13th Parliament met until July 1. A federal sales tax of 1% was imposed.

• The new 6-storey, 30,500 m² Centre Block of the Parliament Buildings in Ottawa opened. Its exterior was fashioned with Nepean sandstone with Ohio sandstone trim. It and the new Peace Tower, completed in 1917, were designed by John Pearson (1867–1940) of Toronto and J.O. Marchand (1972–1936) of Montreal.

Mar. 4 In his 1st major speech in the House of Commons as leader of the newly formed Progressive Party, Thomas Crerar declared, "Implements and tools of production should be free and the necessities of life should be made as free as possible." The Progressive Party then asked "for a substantial all-round reduction in the customs tariff."

Also in Mar.
• British Empire Steel and Coal Corporation (BESCO) was formed by Montreal financier Roy Wolvin, who merged NS Steel and Coal and Dominion Iron and Steel.

May 7 The Art Gallery of Toronto held the 1st Group of Seven exhibition — members included Franklin Carmichael, Lawren Stewart Harris, Alexander Young Jackson, Franz Johnston, Arthur Lismer, J.E.H. MacDonald and Frederick Horsman Varley, all of whom refused to focus on canals and cow pastures of Europe, and instead, uncovered the wonders of home, especially the North.

May 10 An announcement was made in Ottawa and London, England, that Canada would henceforth appoint a diplomatic minister in Washington. The British imperial government, however, continued to exert all foreign policy powers.

May 14 Frank Hawkins Underhill (1889–1971), Charles Bruce Sissons (1879–1965), Barker Fairley (b 1887) and other writers founded *Canadian Forum* magazine.

July 1 An amendment to the Indian Act took effect, providing for the enfranchisement of all Native Canadians (as defined in the statute) and the eventual transformation of the Department of Indian Affairs created in 1880. In 1936, the Department of Indian Affairs was made a branch of the Department of Mines and Resources; in 1950, transferred to the Department of Citizenship and Immigration; and in 1966 it was reborn as the Department of Indian Affairs and Northern Development.

July 10 Robert Borden resigned as PM because of ill health. He was succeeded by 9th PM Arthur Meighen (1874–1960), who served as head of the Unionist govt until Dec. 29, 1921.

Aug. 28 The 3,626-seat Pantages Theatre in downtown Toronto, designed by Thomas W. Lamb (1871–1942), opened to the public.

Oct. 7–17 The 1st trans-Canada flight began at Halifax. It arrived in Winnipeg Oct. 11, then in Vancouver Oct 17. Total flying time: 49 hours, 7 minutes. Total number of pilots: 5. Total distance flown: 5,488 km.

Also in Oct.
• Vilhjalmur Stefansson advised Arthur Meighen that the govt should support extensive exploration of the North, establish police posts on Baffin Is. and in other strategic locations, and put in service a patrol boat organization to exert sovereignty over the North. He also advised Canada to proclaim its sovereignty over Wrangel and Ellesmere Islands. In summer 1921, the federal govt decided to send a permanent patrol vessel to the Arctic and to establish police posts on Baffin Is. and elsewhere throughout the Arctic, as proposed.

Nov. 15 The 1st meeting of the League of Nations was held at Geneva, until Dec. 18. George Foster,

Charles Joseph Doherty (1855–1931) and Newton Wesley Rowell (1867–1941) represented Canada.

Nov. 20 McGill U. raised more than $4 million from alumni and citizens of Montreal, in addition to grants of $1 million from the Que. govt and the Rockefeller Foundation.

Dec. 1 An Order-in-Council provided that no immigrant could enter Canada with less than $250, plus $125 for each family member over 18, and $50 for each child between 5 and 18.

1920–1921 Arthur Lismer painted *A September Gale, Georgian Bay,* and Frederick Varley painted *Stormy Weather, Georgian Bay*, while on a sketching trip to Dr. MacCallum's island in Georgian Bay. The works were the artists' 1st major canvases. Both paintings are in the National Gallery of Canada.

Also in 1920
• Canada's population was 8,556,000.

• British-born Isabella Preston (1881-1965) joined the Horticultural Divison of Ottawa's Central Experimental Farm. She was the nation's 1st professional woman plant hybridizer. Specializing in lilacs, Preston developed the hardy, and now ubiquitous, *Syringa x prestoniae*, the "Canadian Lilac." The plant is similar to the common lilac, but blossoms later, has more tubular-shaped blooms, and thrives in cooler temperatures. Preston remained with the experimental farm and developed as many as 200 new plant hybrids over her career.

• The Winnipeg Falcons won the gold medal in ice hockey at the (summer) Olympic Games in Antwerp, Belgium. The other 2 golds were awarded to boxer Bert Schneider (1897–1986), in the welterweight division, and Earl Thomson (1895–1971), in 110-m hurdles.

• Kootenay National Park was established along the Continental Divide in southwestern BC on lands traditionally hunted by the Kootenay and Shuswap First Nations. The 1,406 km^2 park encompasses a rich diversity of landscape, including snowcapped peaks, grasslands, mountain canyons and arid stretches complete with cacti. The park is home to Radium Hot Springs, the largest hot-spring pool in the world, and the majestic grey-limestone Marble Canyon. Kootenay, together with Banff, Jasper and Yoho National Parks, and the BC provincial parks Hamber, Mount Assiniboine and Mount Robson form the Canadian Rocky Mountain Parks World Heritage Site.

• The Ontario Mothers Allowance Act was introduced.

• There were 459 strikes involving 76,624 workers.

• *Maclean's* magazine went from a monthly to a bi-weekly publication.

• J.E.H. MacDonald painted *Falls, Montreal River*, now in the Art Gallery of Ont., Toronto.

• Franklin Carmichael completed *Autumn Hillside*, now in the Art Gallery of Ont., Toronto.

• Frederick Varley completed the portrait, *Vincent Massey*, now at Hart House, U. of Toronto.

• Jean-Aubert Loranger's (1896–1942) *Poèmes,* an experiment in haiku, was published.

• James Sinclair Ross (1908–1996) published the classic novel *Main Street*.

• *A History of English Canadian Literature to the Confederation*, by Ray Palmer Baker, was published.

1921

Feb. 14 The 5th session of the 13th Parliament met until June 4. A tax was placed on playing cards and wine.

Also in Feb.

• A.Y. Jackson returned to Que. after an absence of 8 years to sketch in the region of Cacouna, on the south shore of the St. Lawrence. *Winter Road, Quebec* was the most famous painting to emerge from the trip. It is now in a private collection.

Mar. 12 The Canadian Authors Association was founded in Montreal to promote Canadian literature and to fight for greater writers' control of copyright privilege. More than 100 writers, including novelist Frank Packard, humorist Stephen Leacock and poet Bliss Carman elected John Murray Gibbon (1875–1952) the CAA's 1st president. The organization initiated Canada Book Week, and in 1936, founded the Governor-General's Literary Awards.

Mar. 26 The *Bluenose*, Canada's most celebrated sailing ship, was launched at Lunenburg, NS. The 40-m schooner was designed for both fishing and racing. On Oct. 24, the *Bluenose*, under the command of Angus Walters (1882–1968), won its 1st of many International Fisherman's Trophies in a contest against the *Elsie* of Gloucester, Massachusetts. It finished a full 15 minutes ahead of its opponent. The schooner took its 2nd and consecutive trophy in 1922.

May 10 A preferential tariff agreement between Canada and the British West Indies came into effect.

May 26 The House of Commons debated a Criminal Code amendment that would make it an offence for any white man to have an "illicit connection" with an Aboriginal woman. The provision was not passed.

July 1 Assent was given to the Dominion Elections Act, 1920, providing for virtual universal franchise at the age of 21 and the right of women to sit as members in the House of Commons.

July 15 The US cancelled wartime legislation permitting Canadian vessels free access to American ports.

July 18 The United Farmers of Alb. Party, under Herbert Greenfield (1865–1949), won the provincial election, taking 39 seats. The Liberals took 14, Labour 4, Independents 3 and Conservatives 1. They assumed office Aug. 13 to Nov. 23, 1926. Nellie McClung, elected the Liberal MLA for Edmonton, campaigned on issues relevant to women such as old age pensions, mothers' allowances, legal protection for widows, better factory conditions, minimum wage and birth control.

July 30 A tornado hit Regina, Sask., killing 65 people.

Aug. 2 Julian Byng, Viscount Byng was appointed gov-gen. of Canada, serving from Aug. 11 to Sept. 29, 1926.

Also in Aug.

• Deskaheh, or Levi General (1873–1925), a Cayuga chief and Speaker of the Six Nations Hereditary Council of Brantford, Ont., travelled to London, England, to petition that the Six Nations were, in fact, an independent people comprising a sovereign nation. British Secretary of State Winston Churchill ruled the subject an internal Canadian matter, to be dealt with by Ottawa.

Sept. 9 Members of the Stefansson Arctic Exploration and Development Company Ltd. (a group of 5 colonists with 6 months' worth of supplies), left Nome, Alaska, on the *Silver Wave* for Wrangel Is., to claim it for Canada. Colonists arrived on Wrangel Is. Sept. 15, but the venture proved a disaster as all lost their lives with the exception of 1 Inuit woman named Ada Blackjack (1898–1983), who was rescued Aug. 19, 1923.

Also in Sept.

• Franz Johnston assumed the directorship of the Winnipeg Art Gallery and became principal of the Winnipeg School of Art. LeMoine FitzGerald held his 1st one-man exhibition at the Winnipeg Art Gallery, consisting mostly of sketches but including such larger canvases as the impressionist painting *Summer Afternoon*, now in the gallery's permanent collection.

Nov. 12–Feb. 6, 1922 The US-initiated Washington Conference on Naval Disarmament convened. Former PM Robert Borden represented Canada. On Feb. 6, the US, British empire, France, Italy and Japan signed the Conference on the Limitation of Armament, to limit their respective naval armament.

Nov. 21 King George V of England declared red and white Canada's official colours.

Dec. 6 The Liberals under Mackenzie King defeated the Meighen govt in the general election. The Liberals won 116 seats to the Progressives' 65 and the Conservatives' 50, with 2 Independents and 2 others. Mackenzie King took office Dec. 29, serving as Liberal PM until June 28, 1926. King was Canada's 10th PM. The election marked the nation's 1st of 9 federal minority govts over the 20th century. Voter turnout was 67.7%.

• Agnes Campbell MacPhail (1890–1954) became the 1st woman elected to the House of Commons. She ran as a Progressive for the rural Ont. riding of Grey South East. The 1921 election was the 1st federal election in which women had the vote.

• James Shaver Woodsworth, Methodist minister and social worker from the Independent Labour Party, was the 1st socialist elected to the House of Commons.

Also in Dec.

• The 1,123 megawatt (MW) Sir Adam Beck No. 1 Generating Station was opened at Niagara Falls, the world's largest at the time.

• In BC, dozens of Kwakiutl were arrested and their possessions confiscated for participating in Daniel Cranmer's potlatch. The potlatch, a traditional West Coast Native ceremony, had been banned by the federal govt in 1884. This ban would not be repealed until 1951.

Also in 1921

• The population of Canada was 8,788,483. The population of Ont., was 2,933,662; Que., 2,361,199; Sask., 757,510; Man., 610,118; Alb., 588,454; BC, 524,582; NS, 523,837; NB, 387,876; PEI, 88,615; NWT, 7,988 and Yukon, 4,157.

• The *Dalhousie Review* was established at Dalhousie U. by philosophy professor Herbert L. Stewart.

• BC passed Canada's 1st maternity leave legislation.

• E.L. Bruce pioneered the use of float planes to map Canada's North, thereby relieving geologists of vast amounts of footwork.

• Canadian publishing pioneer Hugh Eayrs became president of Macmillan Canada at age 26.

• The forward pass became a legal option in Canadian football.

• J.E.H. MacDonald painted *The Solemn Land* on canvas, now in the National Gallery of Canada.

• Paisley, Ont., native David Milne (1882–1953) completed *Across The Lake*, watercolour over graphite, on paper, a scene of Darts L. in the New York

Adirondacks, a site where Milne spent several summers working. The piece is now in the National Gallery of Canada.

• Lawren Harris painted *Elevator Court, Halifax,* a depiction of the Halifax slums. It is now at the Art Gallery of Ont., Toronto.

• Randolph Stanley Hewton (1888–1960) completed *Portrait of Audrey Buller*, now in the National Gallery of Canada.

• Edward Sapir (1884–1939) published *Language*, a treatise on the connection between language and cultural psychology.

• *The Friendly Arctic*, by Vilhjalmur Stefansson, was published in New York by Macmillan.

1922

Jan. 1 BC drivers changed from driving on the left-hand side of the road to the right-hand side.

Jan. 3 The Royal Mint in Ottawa produced Canada's 1st 5-cent pieces made entirely of nickel.

Also in Jan.
• BESCO slashed the wages of its workers in the mines and mills of Cape Breton Is.

Feb. 10 Peter Charles Larkin (1856–1930) was appointed high commissioner for Canada in Britain.

• Winifred Blair of Saint John, NB, was crowned the 1st Miss Canada. Paid an allowance of $500 — the equivalent of a year's salary at her previous job as a stenographer — Blair was kept busy attending teas, luncheons and garden parties.

Feb. 11 The discovery of insulin, an effective treatment of diabetes, was announced in Toronto by the U. of Toronto research team composed of Frederick Grant Banting (1891–1941), Charles Herbert Best (1899–1978), James Bertram Collip (1892–1965) and James Joseph Richard Macleod (1876–1935).

Mar. 22 Twelve thousand coal miners in BC and Alb. went on strike until Aug. 24, 1923.

Apr. About 10,000 Ukrainian Canadians paraded in Winnipeg to demand that the Mackenzie King govt support the creation of an independent Ukraine, which had been taken over by the Soviet Union in 1920.

May 1 Alb.'s 1st radio station, CJSA Edmonton, went on the air, followed by CQCA Calgary, on May 2. CQCA became CFAC in Aug.

May 3 Women over the age of 21 were granted the right to vote in PEI municipal and provincial elections and were given the right to hold political office in the province.

May 12 The Royal Canadian Navy was reduced to 3 small ships on each coast.

May 16 A general railway strike began in Nfld.

June 11 *Nanook of the North*, the world's 1st feature-length documentary film, premiered in New York City. It was produced by explorer, geologist and filmmaker Robert J. Flaherty in the Ungava Peninsula, and portrayed the life of Nanook, an Inuit hunter in northern Que., and his family.

Jun 27 Jock Palmer left Lethbridge, Alb., to attempt the 1st sanctioned airmail flight from western Canada to Ottawa. He failed.

June 28 The National Defence Act, 1922, was passed (later redesignated the Department of National Defence Act). It established the Department of National Defence, placing all Canadian defence forces under a single minister for the 1st time. The act came into effect Jan. 1, 1923.

July 3 The Anglo-Soviet Trade Agreement of 1921 was extended to include Canada.

July 5 Canadian staff officers, led by James Sutherland Brown (1881–1951), toured New York State by car, gathering information for Defence Scheme No. 1 — a secret plan to invade the US in the event of an Anglo-American war. The plan was officially cancelled in May 1931.

July 13 PM Mackenzie King travelled to the US on his 1st venture in diplomacy to revise the Rush-Bagot agreement of 1817, which limited naval armament on the Great Lakes. No changes to the original agreement were made.

July 18 A federal govt Arctic expedition left Quebec City. On Aug. 28 it established the most northerly post to date, at Craig Harbour (76° 10′N), Ellesmere Is.

July 19 CKCK Regina, Sask.'s 1st commercial radio station, broadcast for the 1st time.

Also in July
• The Zionist Federation of Canada met in Ottawa to lobby for increased trade with Palestine to help build a Jewish state.

Aug. 1 John Bracken (1883–1969), leader of the United Farmers Party, became premier of Man., replacing Tobias C. Norris.

Aug. 4 Scottish-born inventor Alexander Graham Bell was buried at Beinn Bhreagh, NS, his summer home.

Aug. 26 In defiance of the Treaty of Sevres, Turkish troops invaded the Ionian coast, confronting British forces occupying a position of the Dardanelles known as Chanak. Without notifying PM King, British Secretary of State Winston Churchill warned the Turks of Mustapha Kemal that a war with Britain was a war with every member of the British empire. On Sept. 15, the British govt appealed to Canada for assistance for its soldiers who were pinned down. PM Mackenzie King responded on Sept. 18 that such a commitment to Britain must 1st be approved by Canadian Parliament, making it clear that a British war was no longer automatically a Canadian war. King's response created a stir known as the Chanak Affair.

Also in Aug.
• Twenty-two thousand coal miners were on strike across Canada.

Sept. 15 John W. and Alfred J. Billes bought Hamilton Tire and Garage Ltd. in Toronto. The name would change to Canadian Tire in 1927.

Sept. 19 The US Congress passed the Fordney-McCumber Tariff Act, which called for the highest tariff rates in US history. Canadian exports were adversely effected.

Sept. 22 Arthur Meighen, in a speech to the Conservative Business Men's Association of Toronto, took a stance on the Chanak Affair stating: "Let there be no dispute where I stand. When Britain's message came then Canada should have said: 'Ready, aye ready; we stand by you.'"

Oct. 4 A forest fire at Haileybury, Ont., killed 41 people.

Oct. 20 New Brunswicker Andrew Bonar Law (1858–1932) became the 1st person not born in Britain to become PM of Great Britain. He served for 209 days.

Oct. 31 The steamer *Marion* burned at Whycocomagh, NS.

Nov. 26 Art critic James Colerick purchased Paul Peel's painting *After the Bath* from the Hungarian National Art Gallery, Budapest, returning it to London, Ont., Peel's hometown. It is now with the Art Gallery of Ont., Toronto.

c 1922 *Above Lake Superior*, oil by Lawren Harris, was completed. It is now with the Art Gallery of Ont., Toronto.

Also in 1922
• Wood Buffalo National Park (44,807 km^2), overlapping the Alb. and the NWT border, was established to protect a declining herd of 1,500 wood buffalo. The park's buffalo population reached 10,832 in 1971 but dwindled to 4,000 in 2002 due to disease (bovine tuberculosis and brucellosis) and natural factors such as predation. Nevertheless, the park remains refuge to what remains the world's largest herd of wild buffalo, and also the last wild flock of whooping cranes. Wood Buffalo is the largest national park in the country and was declared a World Heritage Site by UNESCO in 1983.

• Wallace Rupert Turnbull (1870–1954) invented the variable-pitch propeller, which made aircraft more efficient and allowed more cargo to be carried. In 1902, the mechanical engineer and aviation pioneer had designed and constructed the 1st wind tunnel in Canada at Rothesay, NB. It allowed him to test aviation theories. Turnbull's career in early aviation included 17 patents.

• There were 39 commercial radio stations in Canada.

• Joseph-Armand Bombardier (1884–1951) produced the 1st snowmobile in his workshop in Valcourt, Que. On June 29, 1937, Bombardier patented a 7-passenger snow machine, and in 1942 founded his now-renowned company in Valcourt, Que. to manufacture the world's 1st commercially produced snowmobile — a massive multi-purpose, multi-window 2-track cabin machine called the B–12. The company would go on to revolutionize Canadian winters with the Ski-Doo, 1st produced in 1959.

• Toronto held its 1st Royal Winter Agricultural Fair, which evolved into the world's largest annual indoor agricultural exhibition. The fair includes renowned equestrian competition, agricultural, horticultural, canine and various other "country" exhibits and entertainment.

• J.E.H. MacDonald painted *Autumn in Algoma*, oil on canvas, now in the National Gallery of Canada.

• *L'Appel de la Race*, a novel by Abbé Lionel Groulx (using the pseud. "Alonié de Lestres") was published. It was later translated into English under the title *The Iron Wedge*.

• *Over Prairie Trails*, by Philip Grove, was published.

• *Poèmes de Cendre et d'Or*, by Paul Morin (1889–1963), was published.

• *The Woodcarver's Wife and Later Poems*, by Marjorie Lowry Christie Pickthall (1883–1922), was published.

1923

Jan. 4 Canada and Italy signed a trade agreement.

Jan. 24 NS Liberal premier George Henry Murray (1861–1929) retired after 27 years in office. He was succeeded by Liberal Ernest Howard Armstrong (1864–1946).

Jan. 31 The 2nd session of the 14th Parliament met until June 30. Nonprescription use of opium was prohibited.

Feb. 11 Ex-slave Susan Maxwell, who came to Canada via the underground railroad, died at 117 years of age. She was Canada's oldest citizen, and had lived in the country for more than 70 years.

Mar. 2 The "Halibut Treaty," covering fishing rights in the North Pacific, was signed by Ernest Lapointe (1876–1941) on behalf of Canada, and Charles Evans Hughes on behalf of the US. It was the 1st time a Canadian representative signed a treaty with a foreign state without British intermediation.

Mar. 22 Foster Hewitt (1904–1985), known as the "voice of hockey," announced his 1st hockey game, over the *Toronto Star*'s radio station CFCA. His broadcast was carried through a telephone. Hewitt would go on to coin that most Canadian exclamation "He shoots! He scores!" which has since been repeated in every street and pond hockey game since. Hewitt was inducted into the Hockey Hall of Fame in 1965.

Also in Mar.

• The US govt requested that Canada decline clearance papers to vessels carrying liquor to US ports unless a US permit authorizing entry was 1st presented. (Prohibition was in effect in the US from 1929 to 1933.)

Apr. 1 The 1894 British embargo on Canadian cattle was removed, creating a new export market. The embargo was initiated on the pretext of keeping British cattle isolated from foreign diseases.

Apr. 23 Under conductor Luigi von Kunits, the New Symphony Orchestra (to be renamed the Toronto Symphony Orchestra in 1926) performed its 1st concert at Massey Hall.

June 13 The Combines Investigation Act, 1923, formed the basis of modern legislation designed to control mergers, trusts and monopolies that limited or eliminated competition.

June 25 Conservative George Howard Ferguson (1870–1946) became premier of Ont., beating out Premier Ernest Drury and his United Farmers of Ont.

July 1 The King govt passed the 1923 Exclusion Act, making Chinese people the only group ever excluded from Canada specifically on the basis of race. Chinese Canadians referred to this day as "Humiliation Day." Between the time the act was repealed in 1947, fewer than 50 Chinese people were admitted into the country. Between 1881 and 1884, 15,000 Chinese people immigrated to Canada; an estimated 6,500 worked on the CPR.

July 5 Miners and steel workers at Sydney, NS, went on strike for higher wages and union recognition. A govt investigatory commission accepted their demands.

July 9 Chuckwagon races made their debut at the Calgary Stampede. Promoter Guy Weadick persuaded 6 local ranchers to risk their wagons and horses in what became known as "the half mile of hell."

July 23 Liberal Nfld. PM Richard Anderson Squires (1880–1940) resigned, and was succeeded by William Robertson Warren (1879–1927).

July 26 The Conservatives returned to power in the PEI elections, led by James David Stewart (1874–1933).

• US President Warren Harding visited Vancouver, the 1st US president to visit Canada while in office.

Aug. 17 The Federal Pension Appeal Board was appointed.

• The Home Bank of Montreal failed, the 1st chartered bank to do so since the Farmers' Bank in 1911. Many top bank executives were charged with signing and approving false statements. The collapse led to a revision of the Bank Act and the establishment of the Office of Inspector Gen. of Banks, responsible to the minister of finance.

Sept. 10 Notorious bank robber Norman "Red" Ryan (1895–1936), also known as Canada's Jesse James, escaped from Kingston Penitentiary.

Oct. 22 During talks at the Imperial Conference in London, England, PM Mackenzie King insisted on Canadian autonomy and on Canada's determination to decide its own foreign policy.

Oct. 25 The Nobel Prize for Medicine was jointly awarded to Drs. F.G. Banting and J.J.R. Macleod, for their discovery of insulin. Dr. Banting declared he would share his portion of the award with Charles H. Best. Macleod shared his with J.B. Collip.

Oct. 29 The Alb. Wheat Pool, formed by the United Farmers of Alb., officially opened its office in Calgary. It was formed to regulate the prairie grain trade in the absence of the Canadian Wheat Board, which had been disbanded in 1920. By year's end, all 3 prairie provinces had wheat pools.

Dec. 27 Canada concluded an agreement with the US concerning the reciprocal application of copyright regulations.

Also in 1923

• Ornithologist, naturalist and conservationist Jack Miner published his 1st book, *Jack Miner and the Birds, and Some Things I Know about Nature*.

• The Edmonton Grads women's basketball team (1915–1940) won their 1st Canadian championship. They also beat the US to win the inaugural Underwood Trophy, which they won continuously until 1940, when the trophy was retired and given to the Grads for keeps. The team was founded in Edmonton in 1915 and coached by Percy Page. During their 25 years of play, the Grads compiled an astounding record of 502 wins against only 20 losses — all in a uniform consisting of long woollen stockings and billowing bloomers. From 1924 to 1936, the Grads proudly wore the red maple leaf to 4 consecutive Olympic Games — and won all 27 of their matches. Each Canadian was denied a gold medal, however, as the women's sport was not considered an official Olympic event until the 1976 Montreal Olympics.

• The Redistribution Bill increased seats in the House of Commons from 235 to 245. Eastern provinces lost 2 seats; western provinces gained 12.

• The CNR established a 2-station radio network connected by telephone to enable passengers to listen to music and news.

• Toronto lawyer James Murdoch (1890–1962) incorporated Noranda Mines Ltd. With head offices in Toronto, the firm began acquiring mining interests throughout Ont. and Que., and internationally in the 2nd half of the century. By the mid-1980s it had nearly 10,000 employees; and its annual profits soared in the billions.

• The internationally renowned Hart House String Quartet was formed with its home base in Hart House, U. of Toronto. Founding members were Harry Adaskin (1901–1984), Boris Hambourg (1884–1954), Milton Blackstone and Géza de Kresz. The quartet disbanded in 1945.

• Lavoie Automotive Devices of Montreal produced a 5-passenger sedan, which retailed for $1,800. The car, designed and produced by Joseph Lavoie (1876–1941), had a 4-cylinder engine and could achieve a maximum speed of 56 km/h. Built for Quebec's winter climate, the vehicle did not attract the public and Lavoie was forced to abandon production.

• J.E.H. MacDonald painted *Sea Shore, Nova Scotia*, oil on canvas, based on a sketch done in 1922. The painting is now in the National Gallery of Canada.

• Lawren Harris (1885–1970) painted *Clouds, Lake Superior,* oil on canvas, now in the Winnipeg Art Gallery.

• A.J.M. Smith (1902–1980) and F.R. Scott (1899–1985) founded the *McGill Fortnightly Review*.

• *The Chaste Diana,* a novel by Lily Adams Beck, née Moresby, using the pseud. E. Barrington, was published.

• The novel *The Magpie,* set during the Winnipeg General Strike, was published by Douglas Leader Durkin (1884–1967).

• *Roundabout Rhymes*, by Thomas Robert Edward McInnes (1867–1951), was published.

• *Emily of New Moon,* by Lucy Maud Montgomery, was published.

• The western *Justice of the Peace,* by BC native Frederick John Niven (1878–1944), was published.

• *The Witching of Elspie*, a collection of short stories about Native Peoples and traders, by Duncan Campbell Scott, was published.

• *Newfoundland Verse,* by E.J. "Ned" Pratt (1883–1964), was published.

• Robert Laroque de Roquebrune published the historical novel *Les Habits Rouges*.

• *The Viking Heart,* a 1st novel by Laura Goodman Salverson (1890–1970) was published. The work explores Icelandic culture in Man.

• Musician, teacher and organist Rudolphe Mathieu (1890–1962) received the 1st financial grant ever awarded by the Que. govt to a composer. In 1929, he founded the Canadian Institute of Music.

1924

Jan. 1 Ernest Hemingway quit his post with the *Toronto Star*, where he had been on the payroll since 1920. On Jan. 12, he left his apartment at Cedarvale Mansions at 1599 Bathurst St. and moved to Paris, where he began *The Sun Also Rises*.

Jan. 17 Members of the United Farmers of Alb. overwhelmingly defeated a motion at their annual meeting that would have approved BC, Alb., Sask. and Man.'s secession from Canada.

Jan. 25–Feb. 5, 1924 Canada won 1 medal — a gold at the 1st winter Olympics, held in Chamonix, France. The recipient was the Toronto Granite Club men's hockey team, which romped to victory in the round robin with such scores as 22–0, 30–0, and 33–0. Figure skater Cecile Smith became the 1st Canadian female athlete to compete in the winter Olympic Games. She was 15.

Jan. 26 The Canadian Red Ensign was approved as the official flag for govt buildings at home and abroad.

Feb. 28 The 3rd session of the 14th Parliament met until July 19. The census became the basis of determining representation in the House of Commons. The income tax exemption allowed for each child was raised from $300 to $500.

Apr. 1 The Royal Canadian Air Force (RCAF) was formed. Highest rank was air chief marshal (*maréchal et chef de l'air*).

Apr. 22 An inquiry into corruption of Nfld. premier Richard Squires resulted in his arrest.

May 23 Laurentide Airforce Ltd. began the 1st Canadian scheduled air service, linking Angliers, L. Fortune and Rouyn, Que.

June 6 Minister of Justice Ernest Lapointe (1876–1941) signed the Convention to Suppress Smuggling with the US.

June 19–29 Postal workers went on the nation's 1st postal strike.

June 27 Parliament passed an amendment approving the formation of the United Church of Canada, an amalgamation of the Union of Methodist, Presbyterian and Congregational Churches, effective June 10, 1925. First services were held in Toronto.

July 3 Canada and Belgium signed a trade agreement.

July 11 Canada signed a trade agreement with the Netherlands.

Sept. The 1st regular Canadian airmail service began between Haileybury, Ont., and Rouyn, Que.

Oct. 14 After digging below the Dingman Well in Alb.'s Turner Valley, Royalite Well No. 4 struck gas in the Paleozoic limestone at 1,233 m below the surface. The well took 2 weeks to contain and would produce 20 million cubic ft (0.6 million m^3) of wet gas per day. The discovery paved the way for Alb. to surpass Ont. as the largest producer of natural gas in the country.

Oct. 24 Peter Verigin (1859–1924), a Doukhobor leader, died when his rail coach blew up near Grand Forks, BC. The cause of the accident was unknown.

Nov. 29 Margaret Is. Burgess became the 1st woman lawyer in Sask. to open her own office.

Dec. 17 The BC legislature adopted a resolution opposing the continued immigration of East Asian people into Canada.

c 1924 Marc-Aurèle Fortin (1888–1870) painted *Landscape at Ahuntsic*, now in the National Gallery of Canada.

• Jack Bush (1909–1977) completed *Orange Center*, acrylic on canvas, an attempt to make the image appear as flat as the canvas itself. The work is now in the Edmonton Art Gallery.

Also in 1924

• Industrial capitalist and future multibillionaire Kenneth Colin (K.C.) Irving (1899–1992) founded Irving Oil in NB as a regional processor, transporter and marketer of gasoline, diesel and home-energy products. It marked the beginning of what would become a vast NB empire, which included, hundreds of service stations, Canada's biggest oil refinery, a shipyard, lumber company and railroad, radio and television stations, and in the 1970s, all 5 of NB's English-language news-papers.

• Dodge Brothers Canada Inc. began manufacturing cars at Walkerville, Ont.

• A new Canadian Copyright Act took effect, protecting the book-agency business. It would remain in place, unchanged, until the 1980s.

• Frank Nighbor (1893–1966), of the Ottawa Senators, was the 1st recipient of the Hart Trophy, presented yearly to the most valuable NHL player. The trophy was named after Cecil Hart (1883–1940), former Montreal Canadiens coach. Winners are selected in a poll of members of the Professional Hockey Writers' Association.

• Construction began on the basilica of St. Joseph's Oratory in Montreal. It would not be completed until 1967.

• Works by the Group of Seven dominated the prestigious Wembley exhibition in England.

• Lawren Harris painted the inspired *Maligne L., Jasper Park*, oil on canvas, now in the National Gallery of Canada, Ottawa; and *Lake Superior*, oil on canvas, now in the Art Gallery of Ont., Toronto.

• David Milne painted *Carnival Dress, Dominion Square, Montreal*, which was purchased by the Agnes Etherington Art Centre, Queen's U., Kingston, Ont.

• The novel *Nipsya*, by western francophone writer George-Charles-Jules Bugnet (pseud. Henri Doutremont, 1879–1981), was published.

1925

Jan. 19 Alb. automobile dealers petitioned the provincial govt to improve roads, which would permit year-round driving. The petition noted that over 80% of the approximately 45,000 cars in the province went into storage at the 1st sign of snow, and were not taken out of the garage until spring.

Feb. 5 The 4th session of the 14th Parliament met until June 27. Post office employees were brought under civil service regulations.

Feb. 24 Canada signed a boundary treaty with the US, providing for an International L. of the Woods Control Board.

Mar. 4 Que. rejected Nfld.'s offer to sell Labrador for $30 million.

Mar. 6 Twelve thousand coal miners in NS went on strike until Aug. 6.

Apr. 13 Women in Nfld. aged 25 and older were awarded the right to vote in provincial elections.

Apr. 18 Power Corporation of Canada, a major investment and management company, was incorporated in Montreal, to acquire interests in power generating plants coast-to-coast. Its portfolio would include Dominion Power, Winnipeg Electric Company, East Kootenay Power and the Manitoba Hydro-Electric Commission. The company would diversify in 1968 to include interests in such areas as publishing, pulp and paper and life assurance.

May 25 Twenty-four high-powered electric lamps illuminated Niagara Falls for the 1st time.

June 1 At a convention of Alb. mining delegates, the Mine Workers' Union of Canada was formally inaugurated. It was formed out of growing dissatisfaction with British-based United Mine Workers.

June 2 In a Sask. provincial election, the Liberals under Charles Avery Dunning (1885–1958) were returned to power.

June 25 Conservatives under Edgar Nelson Rhodes (1877–1942) won 61% of the popular vote and 40 out of 43 constituencies in the NS election, ending 43 consecutive years of Liberal rule.

July 6 A new Canada–British West Indies trade agreement was signed at Ottawa.

July 23 The HBC steamer *Bayeskimo* sank in Ungava Bay.

Aug. 10 The Conservatives won the NB provincial election, with John Babington Macaulay Baxter (1868–1946) serving as premier until 1931.

Sept. 7 Canadian Senator Raoul Dandurand (1861–1942) was elected president of the Assembly of the League of Nations in Geneva.

Sept. 12 Famed western jumping horse, Burra, set a world record, clearing a bar set at 2.476 m at the Exhibition Grounds, New Westminster, BC. Burra later died due to internal injuries caused by the jump.

Oct. 29 The federal general election resulted in 116 seats for the Conservatives, 101 for the Liberals, 24 for the Progressives and 4 Independents. King remained PM, forming a minority govt with the support of the Progressives, even though he lost his own North York seat. Voter turnout was 66.4%.

Nov. 10 Canada experienced the largest wheat yield (423 million bushels) to date.

Nov. 23–July 10, 1934 John Edward Brownlee (1884–1961) served as premier of Alb. as a member of the United Farmers of Alb. party.

Nov. 28 Montreal Canadiens' goaltender Georges "the Chicoutimi Cucumber" Vézina (1887–1926) collapsed in net during a game against the Pittsburgh Pirates. He would die of tuberculosis the following year. The Vézina Trophy, established in his honour in 1926, has been awarded each year to the NHL's best goalkeeper.

Dec. 15 Canada and Britain signed an agreement, that reduced transportation rates for immigrants to Canada.

Also in 1925

• The Canadian govt signed the Railway Agreement, allowing the CNR and the CPR to recruit agricultural immigrants in Europe and transport them to Canada without passing through normal channels of the Department of Immigration and Colonization. The agreement would facilitate the post-war growth of the West.

• The Marriage and Divorce Act of 1925 permitted wives to sue for divorce from their husbands on the same grounds that a man could divorce his wife — simple adultery. Before this, a wife had to prove adultery in conjunction with other acts such as sodomy, bestiality, rape, bigamy and desertion.

• The Northern Aluminium Company (originally incorporated in 1902) changed its name to the Aluminium Company of Canada (Alcan).

• BC became the 1st province to legislate a minimum wage for male workers, passing the Men's Minimum Wage Act. Man. and Sask. followed in 1934; Alb. in 1936; and Ont. and Que. in 1937. By 1960, all East Coast provinces had implemented a men's minimum wage. The equal-pay principle would eliminate minimum-wage gender disparities throughout Canada by 1974.

• Evangelist William "Bible Bill" Aberhart (1878–1943) made his 1st radio broadcast from the Palace Theatre in Calgary.

• A group led by A.H. MacCarthy was first to reach the peak of Mount Logan. The 5,959-m mountain, located in the Saint Elias Range in the Yukon, is the highest in Canada, and 2nd highest in North America to Mount McKinley (6,194 m), also called Denali, in the Alaska Range. A.H. MacCarthy was first to climb Mount Robson in 1913.

• A modern, 7-room house on Calgary's 17th Ave. SW could be rented for $50 a month.

• Electric cars accounted for 38% of the North American automobile market.

• The Association of Canadian Bookmen was formed. It printed 100,000 copies of the 1st edition of *Books for Everybody*, a consumer catalogue.

• 20,115 relatives of deceased soldiers qualified for military pensions.

• Toronto speedskating sensation Leila Brooks (1908–1991) broke 6 world records.

• A one-piece, yellow birch hockey stick fashioned by Mi'kmaq master carver Isaac Paul of Newville, NS, cost 25 cents.

• English-language radio dramas began in Canada when the CNR began broadcasting plays.

• Chrysler Corporation of Canada was incorporated and began production at Windsor, Ont.

• NS boasted 12 steam trawlers.

• Charles Comfort (1900–1994) painted *Prairie Road*, now in Hart House, U. of Toronto.

• John Lyman (1886–1967) painted *Reading*, on canvas, now in a private collection.

• Plains Cree Edward Ahenakew (1885–1961) published *Cree Trickster Tales*, a collection of Cree legends and stories.

• *Candid Chronicles*, by Hector Charlesworth (1872–1945), was published.

• A book of verse, *À Travers les Vents*, by Robert Choquette (1905–1991), was published.

• *Settlers of the Marsh*, by Frederick Philip Grove, was published.

• *Songs of the Copper Eskimo*, by New Zealand-born anthropologist Diamond Jenness and Helen Roberts, was published.

• *Lyrics of the Earth*, by Archibald Lampman, was published.

• *Winnowed Wisdom*, by Stephen Leacock, was published.

• Jean-Aubert Loranger's *Le Village* was published.

• The novel *Wild Geese*, depicting pioneer life in Man., by Martha Ostenso (1900–1963) with Douglas Leader Durkin, was published.

• *The Witches' Brew* and *Titans* (poetry) by E.J. Pratt, were published.

• *When Sparrows Fall,* by Laura Goodman Salverson, was published.

• *La Bourrasque*, by Maurice Constantin-Weyer, was published.

• A book of verse, *The Lost Shipmate*, by Theodore Goodridge Roberts (1877–1953), was published.

• *The Poems of Duncan Campbell Scott*, by Duncan Campbell Scott, was published.

• The novel *Grain*, a realistic study of prairie life by Robert James Campbell Stead (1880–1959), was published.

• *Appraisals of Canadian Literature*, by Lionel Stevenson, was published.

1926

Jan. 14 Fire caused $2 million in damage to the Château Frontenac in Quebec City.

Feb. 2 Henry Herbert Stevens (1878–1973) charged in the House of Commons that customs officials were accepting bribes. A special investigations committee tabled its report in June, having uncovered serious examples of corruption. The report led to the resignation of the King govt June 28.

Feb. 10 Eldorado Gold Mines Ltd. was incorporated in Ont.

• Tom Thomson's painting *West Wind* was donated to the Art Gallery of Ont., Toronto, by the Canadian Club of Toronto.

May 9 Richard Evelyn Byrd (1888–1957) and Floyd Bennett (1890–1928) made the 1st airplane flight over the North Pole in a 3-engine Fokker monoplane starting from Spitsbergen Is., Norway.

June 16 Blatchford Field (Hagmann Estate), Edmonton, became the 1st licenced airport in Canada.

June 22 Three Native chiefs from Kamloops, BC, arrived in London, England, to present Native land rights grievances to the king.

June 28 Amidst the ongoing customs scandal, PM Mackenzie King advised Gov-Gen. Byng to dissolve the House of Commons, but Byng refused, a move critics denounced as an act of imperial interference. The minority Liberal govt then resigned, leaving the country with neither a PM nor a cabinet.

June 29 Arthur Meighen became Conservative PM.

July 1 Canada was restored to the gold standard, until 1931.

July 2 A motion in the House of Commons by James Alexander Robb (1859–1929) challenged the Conservatives' right to hold office. It passed by a majority of 1, resulting in the Meighen ministry being the shortest-lived govt in Canadian history and the 1st to be defeated by a vote in the House of Commons.

Aug. 19 Viscount Willingdon of Ratton (1866–1941) was appointed gov-gen. of Canada (succeeding the retiring Byng). He served from Oct. 2 to Jan. 1931.

Sept. 14 Mackenzie King's Liberals defeated the Conservatives in the federal general election, 116 seats to 91, with 38 seats spread among smaller parties. Voter turnout was 67.7%.

Sept. 25–Aug. 6, 1930 Mackenzie King served as Liberal PM, with his 1st majority govt.

Also in Sept.
• Group of Seven artist Frederick Varley arrived in Vancouver, BC, where he became head of drawing, painting and composition at the Vancouver School of Decorative and Applied Arts.

Oct. 28 Queen Marie of Romania visited Ottawa.

Nov. 18 The Balfour Report was adopted at the Imperial Conference in London, declaring Britain and the Dominions of Canada, South Africa, Australia, New Zealand and the Irish Free State as "autonomous Communities within the British Empire, equal in status, in no way subordinate one to another in any aspect of their domestic or external affairs, though united by a common allegiance to the Crown, and freely associated as members of the British Commonwealth of Nations."

Nov. 26 Charles Vincent Massey (1887–1967) was appointed Canadian Minister to Washington, marking the 1st internationally recognized diplomatic appointment made by Canada.

Dec. 1 Voters in Ont. re-elected Tory Premier George Howard Ferguson with a mandate to repeal prohibition and establish provincial control over the sale of liquor.

Dec. 9 The 1st session of the 16th Parliament met until Apr. 17, 1927. The Department of National Revenue was formed.

Dec. 20 Canada signed a trade agreement with Czechoslovakia.

c 1926 Clarence Gagnon completed the celebrated *Village dans les Laurentides,* now at the National Gallery of Canada.

1926–1930 Influenza was the 2nd leading cause of death after cardiovascular disease, killing more Canadians than cancer or tuberculosis.

Also in 1926

• There were 838,673 new automobiles in Canada.

• The US replaced Great Britain as the largest foreign investor in Canada.

• There were 6,460 vacant and abandoned farms in Palliser's Triangle, the southern prairie grasslands stretching from Sask. through Alb.

• *Canadian Plays from Hart House Theatre*, in 2 volumes, edited by Vincent Massey, was published.

• Alfred Joseph Casson (1898–1992) accepted an invitation to join the Group of Seven, replacing Franz Johnston, who resigned.

1927

Jan. 9 The Laurier Palace Theatre in Montreal caught fire, killing 77 children. The theatre doors opened inward, thereby preventing a mass escape. Subsequent fire-code regulations would require theatre doors to open outward.

Jan. 16 Seventeen-year old George Young (1910–1972) of Toronto beat 102 of the world's best

swimmers in the $25,000 Wrigley Marathon, a 32-km race between Santa Catalina Is. and the California mainland. It took Young 15 hours and 45 minutes, and he was the only swimmer to complete the race.

Also in Jan.

• The King govt agreed to complete the Hudson Bay Railway (opened Apr. 3, 1929). It also agreed to send an expedition to Hudson Strait under the direction of the Department of Marine and Fisheries. The expedition was directed to obtain, by air photography and reconnaissance, information regarding ice conditions and requirements to ensure safe navigation. The expedition was completed Aug. 3, 1928, after 227 air patrols and 2,285 photographs.

• Man. artist Bertram Richard Brooker (1888–1955) was the 1st Canadian to exhibit abstract paintings at the Arts and Letters Club, Toronto.

Mar. 1 In a long-standing dispute between Que. and Nfld., Britain's Privy Council awarded Labrador to Nfld.

• The 1st Brier was held at Toronto's Granite Club to determine the nation's best curling team. Halifax skip Murray Macneill led his team to victory, winning 6 of 7 matches. Each member was awarded a silver tea set.

Also in Mar.

• Mine workers joined 15 independent Canadian unions in Montreal to form the All-Canadian Congress of Labour. Aaron Ronald Mosher (1881–1959) became the 1st president.

• Edward Samuels Rogers (1900–1939) received a patent for the AC batteryless radio, the 1st that could operate on normal household current.

Apr. 1 The US Department of Labor placed an immigration quota on Canadians looking for work in the US. Canada officially protested the quota June 8.

Apr. 9 A special joint committee of the Senate and the House of Commons rejected a claim by the Allied Indian Tribes of BC claiming title to most land in the province.

May 9 Prince Albert National Park (3,874 km²), located north of Prince Albert, Sask., was established as a recreation area and boreal forest reserve. It officially opened Aug. 10, 1928. The park preserves rare sweeps of rough fescue, and is home to 195 species of bird. It also has the 2nd largest breeding colony of white pelicans in the country. Prince Albert was home to Grey Owl (aka Archie Belaney) between 1931 and 1938.

May 21 *Two Sketches for Strings*, by renowned composer and conductor Ernest MacMillan (1893–1973), was 1st performed by the Hart House String Quartet in Quebec City.

May 25 Canada ended trade relations with the Soviet Union. They would be resumed Dec. 20, 1929.

May 28 The House of Commons approved the Old Age Pension Plan. It would provide pensions for British subjects who resided in Canada at least 20 years and were 70 years of age or older. The maximum pension was $270 per year, to be paid to those with demonstrable need, in co-operation with those provinces that wished to join. It was the federal govt's 1st major venture into public welfare.

June 1 William Phillips, the 1st US minister to Canada, arrived in Ottawa.

June 6 The largest Klu Klux Klan rally in Canada was held in Moose Jaw, Sask.

June 12 The Imperial Privy Council dismissed an appeal by Roman Catholics for separate schools in Ont.

June 25 Liberals under Albert Charles Saunders defeated the Conservatives in the PEI provincial election.

July 1 Canada celebrated the Diamond Jubilee of Confederation, as PM King connected the country coast to coast with a national radio broadcast.

• Direct communication between the govts of Canada and Britain, without mediation of the gov-gen., was begun.

July 16 Canada refused to join the US in developing a St. Lawrence waterway from the Great Lakes to the Atlantic. The 2 countries had formed a Deep Waterways Commission in 1895 and an International Joint Commission in 1909 to study the matter.

Aug. 7 Mackenzie King, US Vice-President Charles G. Dawes, Edward, Prince of Wales and British PM Stanley Baldwin opened the Peace Bridge between Fort Erie, Ont., and Buffalo, New York. The 1,770-m highway bridge commemorated 100 years of friendship between the countries and made Buffalo the chief US entry point into Canada. By the turn of the century, the bridge was travelled by over 8 million vehicles annually.

Aug. 31 The federal govt placed the responsibility of Inuit welfare in the hands of the commissioner of the NWT.

Also in Aug.
• Artist Frederick Varley went on a camping trip to Garibaldi Park, BC, where he conceived the canvas *The Cloud, Red Mountain*, painted immediately on his return to Vancouver. The painting is now in the Art Gallery of Ont., Toronto.

Sept. 14 In an attempt to combat the spread of infantile paralysis (polio), Alb.'s provincial board of health passed a temporary order forbidding children under 18 to leave their place of residence.

Sept. 15 Canada served on the Council of the League of Nations until 1930.

Oct. 3 Transatlantic telephone service between Britain and Canada was inaugurated.

Oct. 10–12 Richard Bedford Bennett (1870–1947) succeeded Arthur Meighen as Conservative party leader at the Conservative National Convention in Winnipeg, on a platform of preferential tariffs, Asian exclusion, the granting of natural resources to western provinces free from restrictions, federal responsibility for old age pensions and the maintenance of the CNR as a publicly owned and operated utility. Meighen had resigned Sept. 26, 1926.

Nov. 21 With a 500-watt signal, CKUA Radio went on the air as the voice of the U. of Alb., becoming Canada's 1st public broadcaster.

Also in 1927

• Over 9,000 km of new roads were constructed in the country; 4,043 km of these routes were dirt roads, 4,481 km were gravel roads, 388 km were asphalt roads, and 240 km were concrete roads.

• Postage stamps became bilingual.

• Toronto's Union Station was completed and opened by the Prince of Wales.

• Canada produced 440 million bushels of wheat. This amount had dropped to 219.2 million by 1936.

• Raymond-Marie Rouleau (1866–1931) was the 3rd Canadian to be elected a cardinal.

• Southern Ont. produced over 2.7 million kg of Virginia bright leaf tobacco.

• Homogenized milk was marketed for the 1st time in North America, in Ottawa, Ont.

• The Liquor Control Board of Ontario (LCBO) was established following the repeal of prohibition. At the time, the province had 57 licenced wineries, and the LCBO immediately instituted a moratorium on the issuing of new licences. The moratorium would remain in effect for 47 years. By 1974, as a result of consolidation and purchase, the number of licenced wineries in Ont. had been reduced to 6. Govt stores in the province also began to sell liquor to adults in possession of permits costing $2 each.

• LeMoine FitzGerald painted *Williamson's Garage*, now in the National Gallery of Canada.

• The biography *The Four Jameses*, by William Arthur Deacon (1890–1977), was published. The work was a seriocomic account of the careers of four very minor poets, all named James.

• The novel *A Search for America*, by Frederick Philip Grove, was published.

• The novel *The Spreading Dawn*, by Basil King (1859–1928), was published.

• Mazo de la Roche (1879–1961) won the $10,000 *Atlantic Monthly* competition and an international reputation for her novel *Jalna*, an account of Ont.'s country gentry. The book would go on to sell 85,000 copies within its 1st few weeks of publication, working through 143 English-language editions and 41 Braille editions. It was the 1st in a series of 16 *Jalna* books, which would have over 9 million copies in print.

1928

Feb. English-born Winnipeg resident Bertram Brooker (1888–1955) exhibited, with the Group of Seven, his abstract canvas *Sounds Assembling*, now in the Winnipeg Art Gallery.

Mar. 2 Samuel Bronfman's (1889–1971) Distillers Corporation Ltd. merged with Joseph Seagram and Sons Ltd, marking the start of the largest distilling company in the world.

Mar. 13 Although not the 1st Canadian woman in flight, Eileen Vollick (1899–1972) became the 1st Canadian woman to receive a pilot's licence. (Alys Bryant was the 1st woman to fly in Canada, July 31, 1913.)

Mar. 21 Alb. passed the Sexual Sterilization Act, which provided for the forced sterilization of inmates in mental hospitals. Sterilization of the "feeble-minded" was supported by leading suffragist women such as Nellie McClung and Emily Murphy.

Mar. 31 Hockey legend Gordie Howe was born in Floral, Sask.

Apr. 5 De Havilland Aircraft of Canada Ltd. was incorporated in Toronto.

Apr. 14 Ottawa's Russell House Hotel was destroyed by fire.

• The 18-gun sloop *Acorn* sank near Halifax, taking 115 lives.

Apr. 15 A Canadian aircraft discovered and rescued the crew of the German airship *Bremen*, which had been forced down on Greenley Is. in the Strait of Belle Isle.

Apr. 23 William H. Clark was appointed the 1st British high commissioner to Canada, taking office Sept. 22.

Apr. 24 The Supreme Court of Canada unanimously decided that "persons" referred to in the BNA Act, 1867, did not apply to women. Women could therefore not become members of the Senate.

Also in Apr.
• A Man. school trustee named Maczewski appealed his job termination, which had occurred when a school inspector determined he could not read or write English. The County Court judge in Selkirk, Man. granted the appeal, noting that although the words "able to read and write" were accurate qualifications for the position of school trustee, there was no inherent assumption that the words "in the English language" should be appended to the requirements. Mr. Maczewski was able to demonstrate his competency in the Polish language.

May 28 The Post Office began a systematic airmail delivery system, signing 5 contracts for regular service between Ottawa, Toronto and Montreal.

May 31 The Legislative Council of NS was abolished, leaving Que. the only province with a bicameral legislature.

June 1 The RCMP absorbed the provincial police of Sask.

June 18 Explorer Roald Amundsen was lost with 4 companions in an attempt to rescue Umberto Nobile, whose dirigible *Italia* crashed on an Arctic expedition.

• The Conservatives won the BC provincial election. Simon Fraser Tolmie (1867–1937) became premier.

July 20 Japan opened a legation in Ottawa.

Aug. 25 A Ford Trimotor airplane crashed into Puget Sound during bad weather, causing the death of 7 people. It was Canada's 1st major air disaster.

Sept. 1 The Old Age Pension Act came into effect in Man.

Sept. 8 RCAF squadron leader A. Earle Godfrey landed at Vancouver after completing the 1st direct mail flight across Canada, from Ottawa.

Sept. 21 Canada introduced airmail stamps.

Oct. 29 Richard A. Squires was returned to power as Liberal PM of Nfld. after winning the general election.

Nov. 9 The Imperial Privy Council determined that gold and silver on HBC lands belonged to the Canadian govt.

Nov. 16 The 1st French ambassador to Canada, Georges-Jean Knight, officially presented his credentials in Ottawa.

Dec. 25 Penny postage was restored after its discontinuance in 1914.

• James Rafferty, a striking coal miner, was bludgeoned to death by a company watchman near Wayne, Alb.

Also in 1928
• Sask. farmers produced 8.75 million tonnes of wheat or 1.6 tonnes per ha. By 1937, this production had dropped to 920,000 tonnes or .2 tonnes per ha.

• Canadian diplomatic representatives to Japan and France were appointed.

• Canadians consumed over 31 million tonnes of coal to heat their homes.

• Anna Dexter became Canada's 1st woman radio broadcaster.

• One of Canada's 1st literary presses, Louis Carrier, was established in Montreal.

• Trapping, hunting and poisoning caused the extirpation of the swift fox from its Canadian range (Man., Sask., Alb.). The swift fox was reintroduced to Alb. from Colorado in 1983, and although considered endangered, is making a comeback: many 3rd- and 4th-generation wild swift foxes currently roam southern Alb. and Sask.

• Work on the Detroit–Windsor tunnel under the Detroit R., linking Windsor, Ont., to Detroit, Michigan, commenced. It would be completed in 1930 and opened to vehicular traffic by US President Herbert Hoover, as the 1st international vehicular tunnel in the world.

• Henry Marshall Tory, president of the National Research Council from 1923–1935, established a national laboratory in Ottawa.

• At the Olympics in Amsterdam, Russian-born Fanny "Bobbie" Rosenfeld (1905–1969) anchored the Canadian team to Olympic gold in the women's 400-m relay, the 1st year women were officially recognized at the Olympic Games. Percy Williams (1908–1982) of Vancouver won Olympic gold medals in the 100-m and 200-m dashes, earning the title "the world's fastest human," and Ethel Catherwood (1908–1987) of Saskatoon cleared the bar at 5'2" and 9/16" to win the women's high jump.

• Canada won 1 medal at the Winter Olympics in St. Moritz, Switzerland, a gold by the U. of Toronto Grads men's hockey team.

• No.1 Northern wheat sold for $1.63 a bushel; 545 million bushels were produced during the year.

• The women's magazine *Chatelaine* was launched by Maclean Hunter Ltd.

• The popular song "Sweethearts on Parade" was composed by London, Ont., native, Guy Lombardo (1902–1977) and his brother Carmen.

• *The People of the Twilight*, by Diamond Jenness, was published.

• *Strange Fugitive*, by Morley Edward Callaghan (1903–1990), was published.

• Ernest Thompson Seton published the last of his 4-volume *Lives of Game Animals* (vol. 1 appeared in 1925). The work had taken over 8 years to prepare and contained 1,500 illustrations. It won the John Burroughs Medal for excellence.

• *Un homme se penche sur son passé*, by Maurice Constantin-Weyer (1881–1964), was published.

• *Rockbound*, by Frank Parker Day (1881–1950), was published.

• The novel *Our Daily Bread*, by Frederick Philip Grove, was published.

• *Canadian Short Stories*, by Raymond Knister (1899–1932), was published.

• *The Green Pitcher*, a collection of poetry by Dorothy Kathleen Livesay (1909–1996), was published.

1929

Jan. 1 The city of Vancouver absorbed neighbouring suburbs, south Vancouver and Point Grey to become Canada's 3rd largest urban centre.

Jan. 2 Canada and the US signed an agreement to preserve Niagara Falls and further convert water from the Niagara R. into hydroelectricity.

Jan. 6 The 740-seat Duke Hall, commissioned by businessman Franklin Duke and designed by T.H. Pentkin, opened in Regina, becoming home to the Regina Conservatory of Music.

Feb. 7 The 3rd session of the 16th Parliament met until June 14. The illicit selling and distribution of narcotics became a criminal offence.

Also in Feb.
• The Sask. Power Corporation began operations.

Mar. 22 The Canadian schooner *I'm Alone* was sunk by the US Coast Guard. Although it was carrying 2,800 cases of liquor, the ship was 322 km (200 mi) off the coast of Louisiana. Captain John Thomas Randell (1878–1939) and the crew were taken to New Orleans as prisoners. On Apr. 9, in Washington, D.C., Canadian Ambassador Vincent Massey (1887–1967) protested the sinking of the schooner. The Canadian crew was released and the case referred to arbitration. The US govt apologized to Canada July 21, 1935, and paid $50,000 in compensation.

Apr. 3 The Hudson Bay Railway Line, stretching 819 km between The Pas, Man., to Churchill, Man., on Hudson Bay, went into service.

June 18 Though its labels are a nod to the original owners, boasting "Homemade Tradition Since 1918" it was on this date that a Montreal soup maker, Dominion Preserving Company, applied for trademark protection of the brand Habitant and later, on May 28, 1932, introduced a line of Habitant soups. The brand has changed hands many times, having been purchased and resold over the years by Catelli Ltd., Ogilvy Flour Mills and John Labatt

Limited. In 1989, the Habitant brand was taken over by the Campbell Soup Company.

July 1 The great bush pilot and aviation pioneer Clennel Haggerston "Punch" Dickins (1899–1995) was the 1st to reach Canada's western Arctic coast on a postal flight, arriving at Aklavik in his Fokker Super Universal. He handed out oranges to local Inuit and took others on their 1st plane ride. (Alexander Mackenzie 1st arrived in the region, by foot, on July 10, 1789. The round trip from Fort Chipewyan took him over 4 months.) Dickins's one-way trip from Edmonton, including stops in Fort McMurray, Chipewyan, and Forts Fitzgerald, Smith and Resolution, took 2 days.

Aug. 7 The CNR acquired Kent Northern Railway Co.; Inverness Railway and Coal Co.; Quebec, Montreal and Southern Railway Co.; Quebec Oriental Railway; Atlantic, Quebec and Western Railway; and Saint John and Quebec Railway.

• Immigrants were prohibited to enter Canada under labour contracts, except for farm and domestic service workers.

Also in Aug.
• LeMoine FitzGerald became principal of the Winnipeg Art School, succeeding Franz Johnston of the Group of Seven.

Sept. 4 Lignite, a soft brown carbonaceous fuel intermediate between peat and coal, was discovered at Abitibi R. in Ont.

• Toronto Jews attended a meeting at Massey Hall to hold a memorial service for several hundred Jews killed in Palestine.

Sept. 6 The Sask. Liberal party under James Garfield Gardiner (1883–1962) went down to defeat on a vote of want of confidence. On Sept. 9, Dr. James T. Anderson (1878–1946), leader of the provincial Conservative party, was called on to form a new govt, bringing together a coalition of Conservative, Progressive and Independent members to form the Co-operative Government.

Sept. 11 The Royal Commission on Radio Broadcasting (Report of the Aird Commission), under the chairmanship of John Aird (1855–1938), president of the Canadian Bank of Commerce, unanimously advised that a public body should regulate broadcasts as well as broadcast its own materials. The Canadian Radio Broadcasting Commission (CRBC), forerunner to the Canadian Broadcasting Corporation (CBC), was established in 1932 as a result.

Also in Sept.
• Lady Victorine, the world-famous hen owned by the U. of Sask., finished laying 358 eggs in a record 365 days.

Oct. 18 The Judicial Committee of the Privy Council overturned a Canadian Supreme Court decision of 1928 on the "Persons Case," granting women the status of "persons" as stated in the BNA Act, and making women eligible for membership in the Senate. Their Lordships ruled that political exclusion based on gender "was a relic of days more barbarous than ours," and that women were, in fact, "persons." The struggle for inclusion was brought forth by Emily Murphy (1868–1933), Henrietta Muir Edwards (1849–1941), Louise McKinney (1868–1931), Irene Parlby (1868–1965) and Nellie McClung, together known as the "Famous Five."

Oct. 24 The New York Stock Market collapsed ("Black Thursday"), marking the beginning of the Great Depression. On Oct. 29, Canada's economy collapsed. More than 850,000 shares were dumped on the Montreal and Toronto Stock Exchanges on this "Black Tuesday." Ten years of economic hardship followed. Canadian workers and companies were severely affected as unemployment hit a record 27% in 1933. Canadian corporate profits of $396 million in 1929 became corporate losses of $98 million in 1933, the gross national product (GNP) dropped by 43%, and Canadian exports shrank by 50%. Canadian regions that suffered most were those that depended on primary industries such as mining, logging and farming, with net farm income of $417 million in 1929 dropping to $109 million in 1933. Tens of thousands of people depended on govt relief, charity and food handouts for daily survival. Canadian death rates rose, while birth rates dropped from 13.1 live births per 100 in 1930 to 9.7 in 1937. The number of immigrants to Canada dropped from 169,000 in 1929 to less than 12,000 in 1935; almost 30,000 immigrants were forced to return to their home country due to illness and unemployment, and the number of deportations rose from fewer then 2,000 in 1929 to more than 7,600 within 3 years. While the economy began to recover slowly after 1933, the Depression lasted into WW II.

Nov. 13 A 2nd stock market crash hit Canada.

Nov. 18 An earthquake and subsequent tidal wave killed 27 people on the Burin Peninsula, Nfld.

Also in Nov.
• Viljo Rosvall and John Voutilainen, 2 Finnish organizers of the Lumber Workers' Industrial Union, mysteriously disappeared near Onion L., Ont. Their badly mutilated bodies would be found in the spring ice melt. The funerals on Apr. 28, 1930, were the largest held in Port Arthur. Ceremonies were darkened by a solar eclipse.

Dec. 14 After years of negotiation, Alb. premier John Brownlee (1883–1961) signed an agreement with the federal govt awarding Alb. control of its own natural resources. Control of natural resources in Man. and Sask. was also given to the respective provincial govts. Alb., Man. and Sask. had not been given control of their resources on joining Confederation.

Also in Dec.
• Airmail service between Fort McMurray and Aklavik linked the NWT with the Canadian postal system. The route covered 2,697 km in total, and came to within 482 km of the Arctic Circle.

1929–1937 Drought caused the abandonment of 13,900 farms.

Also in 1929
• Dr. Archibald Huntsman, a scientist at the Halifax Biological Board, pioneered the idea of fresh frozen fish for human consumption when his ice fillet packages were 1st offered for sale in Hamilton, Ont.

• The Ambassador Bridge, spanning the Detroit R. between Windsor and Detroit, was completed, at a cost of $20 million. It was the longest suspension bridge in the world.

• Georgian Bay Islands National Park in Ont. was established to protect a group of 59 freshwater islands along the southern end of the L. Huron bay. The islands are reminiscent of paintings by the Group of Seven and, especially, Tom Thomson — glaciated Canadian Shield granite with gnarled cedar and windswept white pines set against blue-green waters and rolling, distant hills. The park is home to 35 species of reptiles and amphibians, including the massasauga rattlesnake, the cobalt-blue ringed-neck snake, fox snake, spotted turtle and Canada's only lizard — the five-line skink. Birds include osprey, turkey vultures and palliated wood-peckers.

• Riding Mountain National Park was created, south of Dauphin, Man. Its 2,978 km2 features highland plateau and black spruce muskeg ecosystems situated on the 475-m high Man. escarpment. The park is known for its black bear, bison and beaver populations. (In 1931, park officials hired Grey Owl, aka Archie Belaney, to re-establish the beaver colony, which today numbers 18,000 animals). During the 1930s, Riding Mountain supported a work camp, whose residents built many of the park's official buildings. In 1991, land expropriated from the Keeseekoowenin First Nation for the founding of the park was returned.

• The 1st ski tow in Canada was erected on the Big Hill in Shawbridge, Que., by Alec Ross. It was a rope tow powered by a Dodge engine.

• The price of raw paper pulp was $29.57 per ton in 1929. It would drop to $19.65 per ton by 1932.

• Vancouver's 1st traffic light was installed at Hastings St. W. and Carrall St.

• Canadian automobile plants employed 13,000 workers, producing 188,721 vehicles.

• Bush pilot Stanley Ransom McMillan (1904–1991) was one of the 1st pilots to explore the Canadian Arctic Barren Lands for Dominion Explorers. When a geological expedition he was transporting was forced down, McMillan led the group on an arduous journey across the frozen Arctic Ocean to sanctuary at Cambridge Bay. McMillan would later fly commercial flights for Canadian Airways Ltd.,

Mackenzie Air Services and Alaska Airlines, before returning to his real love, surveying the Arctic.

• The price of raw copper was $19.75 in 1929, and would drop to $7.02 by 1932.

• Charles Comfort completed the dramatic portrait *The Dreamer*, now in the Art Gallery of Hamilton, Ont.

• *A Native Argosy*, by Morley Callaghan, was published.

• Alfred DesRochers (1901–1978) published his poetic works *À l'ombre de l'Orford*, praising the immensity of the country.

• Raymond Knister published his 1st novel, *White Narcissus*, set in rural Ont.

• Ernest Thompson Seton published *Krag, the Kootenay Ram and Other Stories*.

• Real estate supersalesman Albert Edward LePage of A.E. LePage (founded 1913) sold 2 Toronto residences for $1 million each — on the same weekend.

1930

Jan. 14 Canada signed an agreement with Germany pertaining to the settlement of German property seized in Canada during the WW I.

Feb. 20 Four months after the ruling in the "Person's Case," PM King appointed Cairine Wilson (1885–1962) Canada's 1st woman senator.

Mar. 12 Col. William Barker, the Canadian ace who brought down 52 German planes during WW I, was killed while test flying a 2-seater Fairchild at Rockliffe Aerodome, near Ottawa.

May 2 The Dunning Tariff became effective, giving imports from Great Britain preferential treatment. The Dunning Tariff was created in response to the US Smoot-Hawley Tariff, signed by US President Herbert Hoover on July 17 over the protests of more than 1,000 trained economists. The US Tariff virtually eliminated Canada's exports of cattle and dairy products to the US.

May 16 Prospector and cofounder of Eldorado Gold Mines (1926), Gilbert LaBine (1890–1977), discovered pitchblende, a source of radium and uranium, at Great Bear L., NWT. The mining town of Port Radium was founded shortly thereafter.

May 30 The Fair Wages and Eight Hour Day Act was enacted to include all govt employees.

June 19 The United Farmers, under John Edward Brownlee, was re-elected in the Alb. general election.

June 28 The Winisk band of Crees in Ont. turned their land over to the federal govt, marking the last land "adhesion" to Treaty No. 9 (July 12, 1905).

June 29 Eight Jesuit martyrs killed by the Hurons in the 1600s — Jean de Brébeuf, Noël Chabanel, Antoine Daniel, Charles Garnier, René Goupil, Isaac Jogues, Jean de La Lande and Gabriel Lalemant — were canonized as the 1st North American saints.

July 28 Conservatives under R.B. Bennett (1870–1947) defeated the Liberals in the federal election, taking 137 seats. The Liberals took 88, with 20 seats going to Independents and small parties. Bennett was sworn in as Canada's 11th PM on Aug. 7, and would serve until Oct. 23, 1935. Voter turn out was 73.5%.

Aug. 1 The British dirigible *R–100* made its 1st transatlantic flight to Canada, arriving at St-Hubert Airport, Montreal, in 78 hours and 51 minutes. Plans were to use the dirigible to provide an airship service throughout the British Commonwealth. The ship returned to England Aug. 13.

Aug. 23 Percy Williams of Vancouver set a new world record in the 100-yd sprint at the 1st British Empire (now Commonwealth) Games, in Hamilton, Ont., completing the race in the remarkable time of 9.9 seconds.

Sept. 8 The 1st session of the 17th Parliament met until Sept. 22. Emergency tax and unemployment-relief measures were enacted, including a $20 million grant for public works and an increase in duties on 130 articles.

Sept. 22 The Unemployment Relief Act was passed by the House of Commons, the 1st in a series of public works projects designed to offset the effects of the Great Depression.

• The Bennett govt passed an Amendment of the Customs Tariff, authorizing large increases to tariff rates on a considerable range of commodities.

Fall Severe drought hit prairie farmers.

Oct. 1 PM Bennett attended an imperial conference in London, England.

Nov. 12 Norway recognized Canadian sovereignty over the Sverdrup Islands in the Arctic.

c 1930 Edwin Holgate (1892–1977) painted *Ludovine*, oil on canvas, now in the National Gallery of Canada.

Also in 1930
• Canadian govts, at all levels, spent $18 million on domestic relief.

• Canada's population was 10,208,000.

• William H. Clarke and J.C.W. Irwin partnered to form Clarke Irwin. The firm would agent for 6 British educational publishers.

• *The Viking*, a tale of 2 seal hunters lost in a blizzard, was filmed by the Nfld.–Labrador Film Co. Produced by Varrick Frissell, it was the 1st sound film made on location.

• The 21-storey Marine Building, designed by J. F. McCarter (1886–1981) and George C. Nainme (1884–1953), was completed. Located on the corner of Hastings and Burrard, it is Vancouver's only art deco skyscraper, and remains one of the finest examples of that genre on the continent. Construction costs were $2.3 million.

• Lawren Harris completed *Mount Lefroy*, oil on canvas, now in the McMichael Canadian Collection, Kleinburg, Ont.

• David Milne completed *Painting Place No. 3*, oil on canvas, of Big Moose L. in the Adirondacks. Milne studied art in New York in 1904, then became a war artist in 1918. The painting is now in the National Gallery of Canada.

• Emily Carr exhibited with the Group of Seven in Toronto.

• Montreal artist Edwin Holgate (1892–1977) accepted an invitation to join the Group of Seven, becoming the 8th member.

• Edwin Holgate painted *Nude*, oil on canvas, now in the Art Gallery of Ont., Toronto.

• Frederick Varley completed his masterpiece *Vera*, which was exhibited across the country 6 times before being purchased by Vincent Massey. It is now in the National Gallery of Canada.

• James ("Jock") Williamson Galloway Macdonald (1897–1960), under the tutelage of Frederick Varley, painted *Lytton Church, British Columbia,* now in the National Gallery of Canada.

• *The Fur Trade in Canada: An Introduction to Canadian Economic History*, by Harold Adams Innis (1894–1952), was published. Innis introduced his Staple Theory, arguing that the fur trade was instrumental in determining Canada's political boundaries.

• *La Ferme des Pins*, by Harry Bernard, was published. The novel was set against a fictional "colonization" of Que.'s Eastern Townships.

• *Les bois qui chantent*, a collection of poetic songs and legends by Gonzalve Desaulniers (1863–1934), was published.

• *The Heart of Lunenburg*, by Thomas Gill (pseud. "Sabattis"), was published.

• Montreal architects Harold Lawson (1885–1969) and Harold Little (1887–1948), with Finnish-Canadian master builder Victor Nymark, completed the Seigniory Club (now known as Château Montebello), Canada's largest log structure. The 186-bedroom private fishing lodge, located in Montebello, Que., where the Laurentian Mountains meet the Ottawa R., was constructed from 10,000 western red cedar logs, and is now owned by Fairmont Hotels.

• The name of Rocky Mountains National Park in Alb. was officially changed to Banff National Park in commemoration of Banffshire, Scotland, birthplace of Lord Strathcona and George Stephen, both directors of the CPR.

• Rio Vista, located on Vancouver's luxurious south-west Marine Drive, was completed for the son of pioneer brewer and distiller Harry F. Reifel by British-born architect Bernard C. Palmer (1875–1936). The house is Spanish colonial revival with stucco walls, round arches, wrought-iron ornaments, set off with a red tile roof.

1931

Jan. 22 The 1st episode of the early Canadian history drama *The Romance of Canada*, produced by William Tyrone Guthrie (1900–1971), was broadcast on radio by CRBC from Montreal.

Feb. 9 Vere Brabazan Ponsonby, Earl of Bessborough (1880–1956), was appointed gov-gen. of Canada, serving from Apr. 4, 1931 to Sept. 29, 1935. He was fol-lowed by Lord Tweedsmuir, who served until 1940.

Also in Feb.
• At a United Farmers of Canada (Sask. Section) conference, a resolution was passed calling for the organization to form a political party. Also passed was a Charter of Liberty, nationalization of the CPR, socialization of currency and credit and national-ization of all land and resources.

Mar. 15 American film director Varrick Frissell and his crew of 26 were killed in an explosion on board the SS *Viking* while filming additional footage for *The Viking*, the 1st Canadian feature film shot with synchronous sound. Shot during the Nfld. seal hunt, it was the story of 2 lost men's love for the same woman. The film's dramatic documentary footage of the seal hunt showed men climbing onto ice floes in the North Atlantic.

May 1 Five thousand Communists rallied at May Day festivities in Vancouver's Stanley Park.

June 18 The Tariff of 1930 was revised as a protec-tion against foreign competition affecting an estimated 2/3 of the goods previously imported from the US. On Aug. 3, Parliament passed the Tariff Board Act, establishing a board to provide expert advice and to meet criticism of the Bennett govt's measures.

July 1 The Vancouver Parks Board opened the largest saltwater pool in North America at Kitsilano Beach.

Also in July
• Skeletal remains from Sir John Franklin's ill-fated 1845 Arctic expedition were found on the southern shore of King William Is. by William Gibson of the HBC.

Aug. 6 The Conservatives under James David Stewart (1874–1933) won the provincial election in PEI.

Aug. 11 RCMP and members of the Toronto and Ont. police forces received a special assignment to strike a death blow at the Canadian Communist Party, founded in 1921. Tim Buck (1891–1973) and 8 other Communist Party of Canada leaders were arrested and charged under Section 98 of the Criminal Code as members of an "unlawful association."

Aug. 25 The Rural Relief Commission was set up in Sask. by the Anderson govt.

Sept. 21 Britain went off the gold standard, as did 25 other countries. PM Bennett refused to follow, but his objections were overcome within the year.

Sept. 29 Striking Bienfait and Estevan, Sask., coal miners marched through the streets of Estevan, protesting recent wage reductions and the lack of union recognition. Estevan Mayor D. Bannatyne called on the RCMP and local police to stifle the demonstration. Instead, a wild mêlée ensued, ending in the deaths of 3 strikers, the injury of more than 20 and 14 arrests. The 3 dead strikers were Nick Nargan, Julian Gryshko and Peter Markunas. All were unarmed. The strike began Sept. 8 and ended with a signed agreement Oct. 22. Labour activist Annie Buller (1895–1973) was charged Feb. 23, 1932, and sentenced to 1 year in prison for her role in organizing the strike. During the strike, Oct. 3, Sask. Premier J.T.M. Anderson addressed the local branch of the legion in Bienfait, and urged veterans to guard the community against revolutionary elements.

Oct. The *University of Toronto Quarterly* began publication, with philosopher George Sydney Brett (1879–1944) its 1st editor.

• The *Bluenose* beat the schooner *Gertrude L. Thebaud* to win the International Fisherman's Trophy. The schooner would again see *Thebaud* in an Oct. 1938 rematch, also the *Bluenose's* last race.

Nov. 12 Maple Leaf Gardens opened in Toronto. The hometown Leafs lost to the Chicago Blackhawks 2–1 before a capacity crowd of 13,233. Tickets ranged from 95 cents to $2.75.

Nov. 18 The highest hourly windspeed ever recorded in Canada was 201.1 km/h at Cape Hopes Advance (Quaqtaq), Que.

Also in Nov.

• Que.-born artists Marc-Aurèle Fortin (1888–1970) and André Biéler (1896–1989) helped establish the Atelier Art School, in connection with the McGill U. Department of Extra-Mural Relations.

Dec. 1 Administration of the Royal Mint in Ottawa, a branch of the Royal Mint in London, was taken over by the Canadian govt.

Dec. 11 British Parliament passed the Statute of Westminster, giving Canada control over its foreign and domestic policy. The gov-gen. became a representative of the Crown, and Canadian independence from Britain was finalized. Amendments to the BNA Act, however, would be by redress to the Parliament of the United Kingdom only after the full consent of all provinces.

Also in Dec.

• The 8th and final joint exhibition of the Group of Seven was held in Toronto. Included in the show were 24 invited contributors as well as each of the remaining original Group of Seven members, J.E.H MacDonald, Arthur Lismer, Fredrick Varley, A.J. Casson and Franklin Carmichael. The signal for the end of the group came the following year, with the death of founding member J.E.H MacDonald, who died at his home in Toronto on Nov. 26, 1932 after suffering a stroke 4 days earlier.

1931–1932 The Beauharnois Scandal broke when the Beauharnois Power Company of Que. was discovered to have paid the ruling Liberal party (under the leadership of Mackenzie King at the time) approximately $700,000 to dam the Beauharnois R. for electricity.

1931–1937 Drought spread through the Canadian prairies, and hot, dry summer winds evaporated moisture and carried away rich topsoil.

Also in 1931

• The population of Canada was 10,376,786. The population of Ont. ,was 3,431,683; Que., 2,874,622; Sask., 921,785; Alb., 731,605; Man., 700,139; BC, 694,263; NS, 512,846; NB, 408,219; PEI, 88,038; NWT, 9,316; and Yukon 4,230.

• Canadian govts at all levels spent $97 million on domestic relief.

• Toronto Drs. Frederick Tisdall, Alan Brown and T.G.H. Drake developed Pablum, the 1st scientifically engineered baby food. The new formula consisted of wheat meal, oatmeal, cornmeal, wheat germ, brewer's yeast, bone meal and alfalfa.

• The Vancouver Art Gallery was founded.

• There were 728, 623 farms in Canada, which were home to 31% of the country's population. For the 1st time in Canadian history, more people lived in urban areas than in rural areas.

• A.Y. Jackson painted *Laurentian Hills, Early Spring*, on canvas, now in the Art Gallery of Ont., Toronto.

• LeMoine FitzGerald painted *Doc Synder's House*, on canvas, now in the National Gallery of Canada.

• English-born nature writer Archibald Stansfeld Belaney (1888–1938), writing under the pseud. Grey Owl, published his 1st book, *The Men of the Last Frontier*.

• Emily Carr painted *Big Raven*, oil on canvas, now at the Vancouver School of Art.

• Toronto-born artist Yvonne McKague Housser (1898–1996) painted *Cobalt*, now in the National Gallery of Canada.

• Saint John, NB, native Jack Weldon Humphrey (1901–1967) completed the self-portrait on panel, *Draped Head*, now at Hart House, U. of Toronto.

• The novel *La chair décevante*, by Saint-Fabien, Que. native Jovette-Alice Bernier (1900–1981), was published.

• Que. writer Léo-Paul Desrosiers (1896–1967) published *Nord-Sud*, an historical novel about Quebecers in the 1849 California Gold Rush.

• Ont. writer Agnes Ethelwyn Wetherald (1859–1940) published *Lyrics and Sonnets*.

• The Chief Architect's Branch of the Department of Public Works under supervision by architect Thomas Dunlop Rankin (1886–1965) completed Confederation Building, located west of the Parliament Buildings in Ottawa. The so-called Canadian-style, L-shaped, 8-storey government structure features exterior decoration with carved bear heads representing various occupations, Canadian wildlife, and the maple leaf, fleur-de-lis, rose, thistle and shamrock — symbols of Canada and its founding peoples.

1932

Jan. The League for Social Reconstruction was founded in Montreal and Toronto. Its manifesto of 1932 called for the reorganization of the Canadian economy based on "the common good rather than private profit." League members included historian F.H. Underhill (1889–1971) and law professor Francis Reginald Scott (1899–1985).

Feb. 17 Albert Johnson, known as the Mad Trapper, was killed by the RCMP in a shootout on the Rat R., Yukon. He was the object of a 48-day manhunt after killing a Mountie and, allegedly, prospectors for their gold teeth.

Mar. 2 The Senate rejected a bill to legalize sweepstakes.

Apr. 1 The RCMP absorbed the provincial police forces in Alb. and Man. NS also came under the protection of the RCMP during the year. The RCMP also replaced the provincial police force of NB this day, and the PEI police force May 1.

Apr. 5 Rioting broke out in St John's, Nfld., outside the legislature because of unemployment and accusations of govt misconduct.

May 26 The Canadian Radio Broadcasting Act was passed, incorporating many of the recommendations set forth in the 1928 Aird report. The act

established a commission with powers to regulate and control all radio broadcasting in Canada. It also established publicly owned radio network broadcasting in French and English. The Canadian Radio Broadcasting Commission (CRBC) began transmitting in both languages in May, 1933. It would become the Canadian Broadcasting Corporation (CBC) Nov. 2, 1936.

June 2 The legendary Canadian radio station that helped define American rock'n'roll in the '60s and '70s began operations out of Windsor, Ont., as CKOK, AM 540. The call letters were switched to CKLW ("L" for London and "W" for Windsor) in 1933, and its spot on the dial moved to 800khz ("The Big 8") in 1941. In 1949, CKLW's power was boosted to an incredible 50,000 watts so on a clear night, the station reached over 62 million people in 4 provinces and 28 states. With an ear for great rock-'n'roll, much of it selected by CKLW former staffer Rosalie Trombley, and presented in a Top 40 rotation, CKLW broke hit after hit, introducing much of North America to the sounds of Motown, the British Invasion and the counterculture of the late '60s and '70s; it also ranked as Detroit's No.1 rock'n'roll station during this period. CKLW lost much of its edge when the CRTC introduced 30% Canadian-content requirements in 1972, and later with competition from stations on the FM band. In 1993, CKLW was purchased by CHUM Radio and placed on an all-news and talk format.

July 18 Canada and the US signed the Great Lakes–St. Lawrence Deep Waterway Treaty to build the St. Lawrence Seaway and improve transportation of grain and other commodities across the continent. The St. Lawrence Seaway project would not begin until Aug. 10, 1954.

July 21–Aug. 21 The Imperial Economic Conference was held in Ottawa, hosted by PM Bennett. Britain gave Canadian raw material exports a 10% competitive advantage and removed restrictions on the import of Canadian cattle.

July 25 The Sask. Independent Labour Party held its 2nd convention in Regina. Maj. James William Coldwell (1888–1974) was re-elected president. The next day, the United Farmers of Canada (Sask. Section) met with Tommy Douglas's (1904–1986)

Independent Labour Party and merged into the Sask. Farmer-Labour Party. Maj. James Coldwell was elected its 1st president.

Aug. 1 The Co-operative Commonwealth Federation (CCF), the forerunner of the New Democrats, was founded in Calgary as a political voice of labour and farm leaders, trade unionists and left-leaning intellectuals. Its aim was the development of a political party controlled and directed by popular policy. J.S. Woodsworth was elected president. The CCF became Canada's 1st national socialist party.

Aug. 6 The 4th Welland Canal between Port Weller on L. Ontario and Port Colborne on L. Erie was opened. Bypassing Niagara Falls, the 43.5-km long, 7.62-m deep canal included 8 locks that raised and lowered ships a total of 99.36 m. Less extensive predecessors linking L. Ontario and L. Erie were established in 1829, 1845 and 1887.

Aug. 20 The Ottawa Trade Agreement providing mutual but limited tariff reductions between the UK, Canada and other dominions was signed.

Also in Aug.
• The 1st annual Couchiching Conference was held at Geneva Park on L. Couchiching, near Orillia, Ont. It was organized by the YMCA National Council to discuss Depression era social and economic reform.

Sept. 17 Ross "Sandy" Somerville (1903–1991) of London, Ont., became the 1st Canadian to win the US Amateur Golf Championship, considered a major tournament at the time. Somerville defeated Johnny Goodman 2–and–1 in the final. Somerville was inducted into Canada's Sports Hall of Fame in 1955.

Oct. 8 An unemployment relief program was begun under the Department of National Defence, providing relief camps to single, homeless men. In return for work on national projects such as airports, roads and planting trees, the men received housing, food, clothing, and medical care. They also received 20 cents a day — thereby acquiring the nickname the "Royal Twenty Centers." One hundred and forty-four work projects were established across the country, except in PEI. Up to 20,000 men lived in these camps by year-end.

Oct. 20 Kingston Penitentiary was swept by riots. Communist Party of Canada leader Tim Buck, who had been sentenced in 1931 under Section 98 of the Criminal Code, was suspected as one of the instigators. Two prison guards, 1 with a shotgun, the other with a pistol, fired 5 shots into Buck's cell. By some miracle, Buck was not killed and was paroled 2 years later.

Nov. 1 The nationalist youth movement Les Jeunes-Canada, was founded in Montreal. Included in its membership was journalist and politician Joseph-Edmond-André Laurendeau (1912–1968).

Also in Nov.
• The 1st Co-operative Commonwealth Federation (CCF) rally was held in Toronto, attracting 3,500 people and 1,000 new members.

c 1932 Emily Carr painted the haunting *Forest, BC*, oil on canvas, now in the Vancouver Art Gallery.

• David Milne completed the canvas *Ollie Matson's House in Snow*, now in the National Gallery of Canada.

Also in 1932
• Canadian govts at all levels spent $95 million on domestic relief.

• The Trans-Canada Telephone System opened to integrate national telephone service.

• Dr. Elizabeth Bagshaw (1881–1982) and Dr. Rowena Hume (d 1966) opened and staffed Canada's 1st family planning clinic in Hamilton, Ont. Dr. Bagshaw would remain medical director of the Hamilton Birth Control Clinic for 31 years.

• Duncan McNaughton (1910–1997) of BC won the high-jump gold at the Los Angeles Olympics with a leap of 6' 5.5". In 1930, McNaughton was the 1st Canadian jumper to use the newfangled western roll, not the scissor-jump, in competition. Canada's only other gold was won by Horace Gwynne (b 1912) in boxing, Bantam Division.

• Canada won 7 medals at the Winter Olympic Games at L. Placid, New York, including 1 gold, awarded to the men's Winnipeg Hockey Club.

• The Canadian Writers' Foundation was founded to provide financial aid to needy, Depression-era authors.

• Ont. horticulturalist Henry Moore established the International Peace Garden, which covered 586 ha in southern Man. and 360 ha in North Dakota. The park, dedicated to international peace, boasts 120,000 fragrant annuals and a vast collection of purple clematis and orange and yellow Asian lilies.

• No.1 Northern wheat sold for 38 cents a bushel.

• Torontonian Don Munro patented the 1st table-hockey game, a board with 4 wooden player-figures per side and a steel ball for a puck.

• Charles Comfort completed the watercolour *Young Canadian*, now in Hart House, U. of Toronto.

• Frederick Varley completed the *Dhârana*, now in the Art Gallery of Ont., Toronto.

• *The Indians of Canada*, by Diamond Jenness (1886–1969), was published.

• Merrill Denison (1893–1975) published *The Unheroic North*, a collection of 4 comedies.

• Clarence Malcolm Lowry (1909–1957) published the novel *Ultramarine*.

• E.J. Pratt published *Many Moods and The Fable of the Goats and Other Poems*.

• Arthur John Arbuthnott Stringer (1874–1950) published the sentimental novel *The Mud Lark*.

1933

Jan. Communists won the municipal election in Blairmore, Alb., and renamed the main street "Tim Buck Boulevard."

Feb. 14 MP J. S. Woodsworth, representing Winnipeg North Centre, moved to repeal Section 98 of the Criminal Code, which made membership in the Communist Party illegal. His motion was defeated.

Feb. 17 A British Royal Commission was appointed to examine the economic and political status of Nfld. The commission recommended that Nfld. be temporarily governed by a commission responsible to the UK, which it was Dec. 2.

Apr. 12 The Visiting Forces (British Commonwealth) Act, 1933, was passed, forming the legal basis for military co-operation between Canadian and other Commonwealth forces, but not naval forces.

Also in Apr.
• The annual Dominion Drama Festival's 1st competition of amateur and semi-professional theatre groups took place in Ottawa. The festival was founded in Ottawa Oct. 29, 1932.

May 12 A trade agreement with France provided for reciprocal tariff preferences on 1,148 items. It went into effect June 10.

May 23 The Canadian National-Canadian Pacific Act was passed by Parliament, directing the 2 competing rail companies to co-operate in affecting economies and reduce duplication. One result was the co-operative "pool trains" in central Canada, jointly operated by the 2 systems.

May 29 Vancouverite Jimmy "Babyface" McLarnin (b 1907) won the undisputed world welterweight boxing championship with a 1 round KO over Young Corbett III at Wrigley Field, Los Angeles.

Also in May
• Artist David Milne built a tarpaper painting shack in the wilderness at Six Mile L. on the Severn R., just north of Orillia, Ont.

June 5 La Ligue d'Action Nationale addressed a letter to acting PM George Perley (1857–1938), advising that Jewish immigrants wanting to enter Canada from Germany "could not be a useful element for Canada" because it was probable that they held to Communist views.

July 19–21 The CCF, under J.S. Woodsworth, held its 1st annual convention in Regina, Sask., with more than 150 delegates in attendance. The *Regina Manifesto* was adopted, setting out the party principles in 14 points, which included the replacement of capitalism with a new social order.

July 24 Canada Post issued a 20-cent stamp commemorating the 1933 World Grain Exhibition & Conference held in Regina, Sask., which showcased exhibits from over 40 countries.

Aug. 7 The Banff Centre for the Arts began as a 2-week summer drama school for rural schoolteachers, sponsored by the U. of Alb. and the Alb. Department of Education.

Aug. 22 Liberals under Angus Lewis Macdonald (1890–1954) won the NS general election.

Aug. 25 Canada, the US, Argentina, Australia and the Soviet Union joined in a wheat agreement. A maximum amount of exports for the years 1933-1934 was agreed upon, followed by a 15% reduction in acreage or exports.

Sept. 14 Furniture workers and meat packers went on strike in Stratford, Ont. Troops and armoured vehicles moved into town on Sept. 27. The strike was settled Nov. 4 without violence.

Nov. 2 BC Liberal leader Thomas Dufferin Pattullo (1873–1956), an advocate of "socialized capitalism," won the provincial election under the banner "Work and Wages" for every BC resident. Pattullo called for massive public investment to put Canadians back to work. The CCF formed the opposition.

Dec. 2 Facing bankruptcy, Nfld.'s Dominion status was removed under the Newfoundland Act of 1933. Its constitution was suspended, and Nfld. reverted to a Crown colony. On Feb. 16, 1934, Nfld. was governed by a commission appointed by Britain. David Murray Anderson (1874–1936) presided over the commission, composed of the gov. and 6 commissioners, 3 from Nfld. and 3 from Britain, as recommended by the Amultree Report of 1933.

Dec. 9 The Toronto Argonauts defeated the Sarnia Imperials 4–3 in the lowest-scoring Grey Cup in history.

c 1933 Lilias Newton, née Torrance (1896–1980),

completed *Portrait of Eric Brown*, now in the National Gallery of Canada.

Also in 1933

• Canadian govts at all levels spent $98 million on domestic relief.

• There were 1,517,531 Canadians on some form of public relief. The unemployment rate was approximately 23%, compared to 3% in 1926.

• Jean-Marie-Rodrigue Villeneuve (1883–1947) was elected Canada's 4th cardinal.

• Alb.-born actress Fay Wray (1907–2004) starred in the Hollywood film *King Kong*.

• 5,578 wooden grain elevators stood in the West. By 1997, only 327 of these "prairie skyscrapers" remained.

• The Canadian Group of Painters, an outgrowth of the Group of Seven, was formed to encompass the modern movement in Canadian painting. Founding members included Lawren Harris, A.J. Casson, Arthur Lismer, A.Y. Jackson and Franklin Carmichael. The 1st exhibition was held during the summer in Atlantic City, New Jersey.

• Ont.-born painter Gordon Webber (1909–1965), a member of the Art Students' League, completed *Skating in the Park*, now in the Art Gallery of Ont., Toronto.

• Russian-born painter Paraskeva Clark, née Plistik (1898–1986), painted *Myself, a Self-Portrait,* now in the National Gallery of Canada.

• *Village of Souls*, Philip Albert Child's (1898–1978) 1st novel, was published. The work was a romance set in 17th-century New France.

• *Dominantes*, by nature poet Joseph Fabien René Chopin (1900–1953), was published.

• *Poésies nouvelles*, by Robert Guy Choquette, was published.

• Alain Grandbois (1900–1975) published *Né à Québec,* a historical novel on the life of explorer, fur trader and seigneur Louis Jolliet.

• *Un homme et son péché* was published, establishing Claude-Henri Grignon (1894–1976) as one of the country's premier novelists.

• *Fruits of the Earth*, by Frederick Philip Grove, was published. This landmark work of fiction captured the pioneering spirit of the prairies.

• Poet and critic John Leo Kennedy (b 1907) published *The Shrouding*, a volume of verse.

• Oscar Ryan and the Theatre of Action Collective produced a narrated pantomime "worker's play" entitled *Eight Men Speak*.

• The novel *Mon Jacques*, by Éva Sénécal (1905–1988), was published. The public library of Sherbrooke, Que., was named in her honour.

• The semi-autobiographical novel *The Yellow Briar*, by Patrick Slater (pseud. John Mitchell) (1882–1951), was published.

• British-born designer brothers Robert Percival Twizzell (1877–1964) and George Sterling Twizzell (1885–1957) completed St. Andrew's–Wesley United Church in Vancouver, BC. The reinforced-concrete church covered with ornate granite features beautiful stained-glass windows. It also includes a tall corner tower and a protruding facade.

1934

Jan. 6 Alb. cowboy singer and NS native Wilf Carter (1904–1996) released his 1st record on 78 rpm vinyl. Recorded in a small studio in Montreal, the record included the songs "My Swiss Moonlight Lullaby" and "The Capture of Albert Johnson." The record became a 1934 bestseller, making Carter an international star.

Feb. 2 Catholic Archbishop of Regina James Charles McGuigan (1894–1974) declared all forms of socialism contrary to tenets of the faith.

• The House of Commons passed a resolution appointing a select special committee of the House to inquire into manufacturer price-fixing. The committee was known as the Price Spreads Commission. It was chaired by Henry Herbert Stevens (1878–1973), the minister of trade. Stevens would make damning charges against big-business abuses on Oct. 4. Stevens resigned from cabinet Oct. 27. In 1935, he formed the small-business-friendly Reconstruction Party.

Also in Feb.

• Adrien Arcand (1899–1967) founded the Nazi-inspired National Social Christian Party, in Montreal. In Oct., it merged with the Prairie-based Canadian Nationalist Party, and in 1938 with Ont. and Que. Fascists to form the National Unity Party/Parti unité national. Also called the "Blue Shirts," the Unity Party was banned with other Fascist and Communist groups June 5, 1940.

Mar. 9 Women were granted the right to run for provincial office in NB.

Mar. 19 Thousands of people in central Alb. were startled by a huge fireball that streaked across the night sky and then exploded "like a star bomb." Shock waves were felt in a number of communities. Within days, people reported finding small fragments of the "great Alberta meteor."

Apr. 14 The United Farmers of Alb. govt voted to abolish the office of lt-gov. and convert Government House in Edmonton into a sanitarium for the treatment of tuberculosis. Although the motion was later rescinded, Government House was permanently closed in 1938, then sold and variously used as a residence, a convalescent hospital, and a veterans' home. The provincial govt reacquired it in 1967.

May 28 The Dionne Quintuplets — Annette, Cécile, Émilie (d 1954), Marie (d 1970) and Yvonne (d 2001) — were born in Callandar, Ont., to Oliva and Elzire Dionne. Delivered by Dr. Allan Roy Dafoe (1883–1943), they were the 1st-known surviving quintuplets. The Ont. govt would remove them from the custody of their parents and showcase them in North Bay, Ont., as a profit-generating tourist attraction. It was estimated the Quints generated over $500 million for the province over the 9 1/2 years they were on display. In 1998, the 3 surviving Quints accepted a $4 million compensation package by the Ont. govt.

June 3 Nobel Prize winner Dr. Frederick Banting was knighted in England.

June 11–July 14 Metal miners, members of the Communist-led Workers' Unity League, went on strike against Hudson Bay Mining and Smelting in Flin Flon, Man.

June 19 Liberals under James Garfield Gardiner (1883–1962) won the Sask. general election.

• Mitchell Frederick Hepburn (1896–1953) led the Liberal party to victory in the Ont. general election.

June 30 John Edward Brownlee resigned as premier of Alb. after a jury found him guilty in the seduction suit of Vivian MacMillan, a 19-year-old govt stenographer. Richard Gavin Reid (1879–1980), of the United Farmers of Alb. party, replaced Brownlee, serving from July 10 to Aug. 22, 1935.

July 3 The Bank Act of Canada, 1934, was passed by the Bennett govt, creating for the 1st time a national central bank (Mar. 11, 1935) to serve as an agency for national monetary policy. Its stock would be privately held.

• The Natural Products Marketing Act was passed, providing for the creation of a federal marketing board with powers to form local boards and to co-operate with marketing boards created by the provinces.

Aug. 8–9 J. R. Ayling and L. Reid made the 1st non-stop transatlantic airplane flight from Canada to England in *The Trail of the Caribou*, a twin-engine bi-plane. The *Caribou* started on the sands of Wasaga Beach, Ont., and touched down in London, England, 30 hours and 55 minutes later. The pilots had originally intended to fly to Baghdad, but icing problems forced them to land in England.

Aug. 14 John Sackville Labatt (1880–1952), president of the John Labatt Brewery, was kidnapped in London, Ont., and held for ransom. He was released unharmed at Toronto's Royal York Hotel 3 days later. The ransom was never paid.

Aug. 16 A special 2 cent stamp was issued to commemorate the 150th anniversary of the founding of NB as a separate colony.

Aug. 27 Neurosurgeon Wilder Graves Penfield (1891–1976) established the Montreal Neurological Institute at McGill U., where he undertook the 1st systematic mapping of the human brain.

Oct. 1 The federal Companies Act went into force, repealing the Companies Act of 1927 and establishing stringent regulations safeguarding the security of investors, shareholders and creditors.

Nov. 16 The Montreal Symphony Orchestra, now the Orchestre symphonique de Montréal, was founded. Wilfrid Pelletier (1896–1982) was its 1st artistic director.

Also in Nov.

• Communist leader Tim Buck was paroled from Kingston Penitentiary, after serving slightly more than half his 5-year, 9-month term. The Communist-inspired Canadian Labour Defence League claimed to have had a petition signed by 200,000, demanding Buck's release.

Dec. 12 The RCMP issued a warrant charging 61 Canadians, including 4 Bronfman brothers, with conspiracy to evade more than $5 million in custom duties on smuggled liquor.

Also in 1934

• Canadian govts at all levels spent $159 million on domestic relief.

• Lawyer Helen Kinnear (1894–1970) became the 1st woman appointed to the King's Counsel. In 1935, she became the 1st woman to argue a case before the Supreme Court of Canada. In 1943, she became the 1st woman county court judge in Canada — and the British Commonwealth.

• Gold was found in Yellowknife. The NWT's 1st gold rush was on.

• The TSE merged with the Standard Stock and Mining Exchange. The 2 had been major competitors.

• Macmillan Canada published 34 new titles on its fall list and 24 on its spring list.

• The Schomberg River Valley in Ont., known as the Holland Marsh, was settled, and improved by

15 Dutch farming families. It has since become one of the most productive agricultural areas in the nation.

• The Sask. Teacher's Federation was formed.

• Herman "Jackrabbit" Smith Johannsen (1875–1987), believed to be the father of cross-country skiing in North America, designed and helped clear Mount Tremblant's Kandahar and Tachereau ski runs, in addition to plotting additional runs at the resorts of Ste. Agathe, Ste. Marguerite, St. Sauveur and Shawbridge in Que.'s Laurentian Mountains. Earlier, 1929, he had designed and laid out the course for the 1st Dominion slalom race at Shawbridge. He was also responsible for creating the Maple Leaf Trail, 128 km of skiing to Shawbridge from Labelle, Que. Johannsen was awarded the Order of Canada in 1972.

• Vancouver painter William Percy Weston (1897–1967) completed *Whytecliffe*, oil on canvas.

• Ont.-born Carl Fellman Schaefer (b 1903) painted *Ontario Farmhouse*, presently held by the National Gallery of Canada.

• Bertram Brooker painted the portrait of his daughter Phyllis, *Piano! Piano!,* now in the Art Gallery of Ont., Toronto.

• Jock Macdonald painted his 1st abstract or "automatic" work, *Formative Colour Activity*, now in the National Gallery of Canada.

• Jean-Charles Harvey (1891–1967) published the explosive novel *Les demi-civilisés* (translated as *Fear's Folly* in 1982), which satirized Que.'s bourgeois and religious elite.

• Frederick John Niven published the novel *Triumph*.

• Frederick George Scott (1861–1944) published *Collected Poems*.

• Morley Callaghan published *Such Was My Beloved*, a story about a priest's friendship with 2 prostitutes.

1935

Jan. 11 PM Bennett delivered the last in a series of 5 radio broadcasts outlining his "New Deal," a state-controlled program of social and economic reform to deal with the Depression. Bennett's New Deal would encompass the Trade and Industry Commission Act; the Minimum Wages Act; the Limitation of Hours of Work Act; the Weekly Rest in Industrial Undertakings Act; the Natural Products Marketing Act; the Employment and Social Insurance Act; and the Farmers Creditor's Arrangement Act. All acts but the Farmers Creditor's Arrangement Act and an Amendment to the Criminal Code on unfair practices were invalidated by the Supreme Court June 17, 1936.

Mar. 11 The Bank of Canada opened for business, charged with issuing currency and regulating the money supply, as agent and banker for the federal govt.

Apr. 7 The David Dunlap Observatory at Richmond Hill, Ont., was completed. The 188-cm reflector telescope, donated by Mrs. David Dunlap, was the 2nd largest in the world. The 1st observations took place on June 9.

Apr. 9 The Price Spreads Commission recommended that a Federal Trade and Industry Commission be established with powers to regulate commerce and industry.

Apr. 15 Canada was selected a member of the Committee of Thirteen, created by the League Council of the League of Nations, to examine how economic sanctions could be used against violators of peace in Europe.

Apr. 17 The Prairie Farm Rehabilitation Act, 1935, was passed by the Bennett govt to deal with prairie drought and soil-drifting problems.

Also in Apr.

• The Relief Camp Workers Union led 7,000 BC camp members out on strike; 1,800 men converged on Vancouver, refusing to return to the camps until promised "work and wages." Workers held parades and ceremonies, and were supported through the assistance of local citizens and Vancouver unions.

June 3–4 One thousand two hundred striking relief-camp workers in Vancouver launched the "On to Ottawa Trek" by climbing on to the roofs of CP freightcars on their way to Ottawa. Hundreds of BC citizens cheered them on. The trekkers' numbers would swell to 3,000 by the time they reached Regina, on June 14, where their leaders continued to Ottawa for an unsuccessful meeting with PM Bennett on June 22. On July 1, the Dominion Day Riot occurred when RCMP and city constables clashed with the 3,000 plus trekkers and sympathizers who had remained in Regina. One policeman was killed, 80 trekkers and sympathizers were injured, and approximately 100 men were arrested. Much of downtown Regina lay in ruins.

June 27 Liberals under A. Allison Dysart (1887–1957) won the NB provincial election.

June 28 Assent was given to the Employment and Social Insurance Act but it was struck down by the Supreme Court of Canada and the British Privy Council as an infringement on provincial jurisdiction.

July 5 The Canadian Wheat Board Act became law, providing for the establishment of a new Canadian Wheat Board (CWB) to purchase wheat at a fixed minimum price and resell it at a profit. Profits were given to producers whose commodities were marketed through the CWB, while the CWB (the federal govt) incurred associated losses. Grain-farmer association with the CWB was voluntary until 1943, at which time all deliveries of Canadian wheat had to be made through the CWB. The Canadian Wheat Board Act was amended in 1949 to cover the marketing of oats and barley.

• The Dominion Trade and Industry Commission was empowered to administer the Combines Investigation Act, prohibiting monopolies from operating to the detriment of the public.

July 23 PEI Conservatives under William Joseph Parnell MacMillan (1881–1957) swept every seat in the province, defeating the Liberals under Walter Maxfield Lea (1874–1936).

Aug. 14 Parliament was dissolved and a general election was called (Oct. 14).

Aug. 22 Albertans elected the 1st Social Credit govt in Canada, giving new premier William Aberhart (1878–1943) 56 out of the 63 seats. The incumbent United Farmers of Alb. failed to capture a single seat. The Liberals won 5 and the Conservatives 2.

Oct. 14 Liberals won a landslide majority in the federal general election, winning 171 seats to the Conservatives' 39. Social Credit candidates won 17 seats, the CCF 7 and the Reconstruction Party 1. Various other parties and Independents won 10 seats. Mackenzie King took office as PM on Oct. 23, serving until Nov. 15, 1948. Voter turnout was 74.2%.

Oct. 29 Newly elected PM Mackenzie King issued a statement endorsing economic sanctions against Mussolini's Italy for its Oct. 3 invasion of Abyssinia (Ethiopia). On Nov. 31, the federal govt put in force an embargo on the export of arms and munitions to Italy and devised voluntary measures to ensure the prohibition of loans and credit.

Nov. 2 Dr. Walter Alexander Riddell (1881–1963), Canada's acting delegate to the League of Nations, proposed that League members cut off all coal, oil, iron and steel exports to Italy. Riddell was later reprimanded for his initiative, and his proposal was withdrawn.

Nov. 15 PM Mackenzie King and US President Franklin D. Roosevelt signed a reciprocal trade agreement in Washington, D.C. Canada was granted lower rates or other concessions on 2/3 of its exports by volume to the US, and the US received concessions on 3/4 of its dutiable exports to Canada.

Also in Nov.
• The 1st specially designed bush plane, the *Norseman*, built in Montreal by Robert (Bob) Noorduyn, made its 1st flight. Nine hundred of the single-engine aircraft were built.

Dec. 5 Police broke up a protest involving approximately 200 people at the Royal York Hotel, Toronto, where officials of Hitler's Germany were meeting with Canadian officials to boost Canadian interest in the forthcoming Olympic Games, scheduled for Berlin in 1936.

c 1935 Emily Carr painted *Sky*, oil on paper, now in the National Gallery of Canada.

• Que.-born artist Alfred Pellan (1906–1988) painted *Jeune Comédien*, oil on canvas, now in the National Gallery of Canada.

Also in 1935

• Canadian govts at all levels spent $173 million on domestic relief.

• Martha Louise Black (1866–1957) was elected to the Canadian Parliament, representing the Yukon.

• Toronto native Arthur J. "Jack" Dempster (1886–1950), professor at the U. of Chicago, discovered uranium–235, which was later used in the development of the 1st atomic bomb.

• The monthly magazine of the Canadian book trade *Quill & Quire* was launched by Wallace Seccombe's Current Publications as an office supplies and stationery periodical.

• Dr. Henry Norman Bethune (1890–1939) visited the Soviet Union, where he became a dedicated Communist.

• A.Y. Jackson painted *Algoma, November*, oil on canvas, now in the National Gallery of Canada.

• A. J. Casson painted *Golden October*, now in Hart House, U. of Toronto.

• Ont. painter Isabel McLaughlin (1903-2002), a member of the Art Students' League, completed *Trees*.

• Charles Comfort painted the landscape *Tadoussac*, now in the National Gallery of Canada.

• Montreal native Efa Prudence Heward (1896–1947) painted the nude *Dark Girl*, now at Hart House, U. of Toronto.

• Kitchener businessman A.R. Kaufman founded the Parents Information Bureau to provide families with health facts and family planning advice. In Sept. 1936, one of his nurses, Dorothea Palmer, working in Ottawa, was arrested and charged with disseminating information about birth control. She was brought to trial and acquitted on Mar. 17,

1937, after a 6-month court case. Her acquittal set precedent for legal distribution of birth control information.

• The nature stories *Pilgrims of the Wild* and *The Adventures of Sajo and Her Beaver People*, by Archibald Belaney, under the pseud. Grey Owl, were published.

• George-Charles Bugnet published the novel *La Forêt*. The English translation, *The Forest,* was published in 1976.

• Morley Callaghan published the novel *They Shall Inherit the Earth*.

• Jean Charbonneau (1875–1960) published *L'École Littéraire de Montréal,* tracing the history of the literary school he founded.

• Watson Kirkconnell (1895–1977) published the anthology *Canadian Overtones*, an anthology of Canadian poetry in 5 foreign languages.

• Taxonomist Frère Marie-Victorin (1885–1944) responsible for developing much of Que.'s botanical vocabulary, published the monumental *Flore Laurentienne.*

• Frederick John Niven published the novel *The Flying Years*, the 1st in a trilogy of historical western fiction.

• Poet E.J. Pratt published *The Titanic*.

• Geologist Francis P. Shepherd proved that the Great Lakes basins were created by erosion.

1936

Feb. Socialist artist Fritz Brandtner (1896–1969) held his 1st Montreal one-man art exhibition at Morgan's department store (later acquired by the HBC) in support of the Canadian League Against War and Fascism.

Mar. 24–25 The visiting Detroit Red Wings beat the Montreal Maroons 1–0 in the longest NHL game to date. The game entered its 6th overtime before Detroit's Modere "Mud" Bruneteau scored the game's only goal — after 176 minutes, 30 seconds.

Also in Mar.

• Artist and critic John Goodwin Lyman (1886–1967) began an art column in the *Montrealer* that would run for 4 years.

Apr. 12 An explosion trapped 3 men in NS's Moose River mine. A CRBC broadcast team headed by J. Frank Willis (1909–1969) began a series of 99 consecutive telephone reports on the incident, totalling 69 hours, before 2 survivors were brought to the surface Apr. 22. The broadcasts were picked up by 650 US and 58 Canadian radio stations.

May 24 Notorious bank robber Norman "Red" Ryan was killed in a shootout with police while attempting to rob a liquor store in Sarnia, Ont. A police officer was killed in the gunfight.

June 16 Turner Valley Royalties Company Well No. 1 struck a major oil resource, marking the beginning of the Turner Valley golden era that would see 70 wells dug in the region by 1939. Royalties was founded by Que. engineer R.A. (Bob) Brown in the 1930s and began drilling in the Turner Valley in 1934.

June 18 CCF leader J.S. Woodsworth argued in the House that the nation's foreign policy should conform to 3 principles: Canada should remain neutral in the event of war; Canadians should not be permitted to profit from the sale of war supplies; and the federal govt should try to root out the causes of international friction and social injustice.

June 26 The Vimy Memorial in France, designed by sculptor Walter S. Allward (1875–1955), was unveiled by British King Edward VIII. The twin towers sit on a 15,000-tonne bed of concrete and are graced by 20 sculptured figures. The $1.5 million memorial, begun in 1925, is a tribute to the valiant Canadian soldiers who sacrificed their lives to take the ridge in Apr. 1917. Over 7,000 Canadian soldiers are buried within a 16-km radius of the monument.

July 17 Civil war erupted in Spain. Fighting against Franco's Fascists were approximately 1,600 Canadian volunteers, called the Mackenzie-Papineau Battalion, the "Mac-Paps," named in memory of the 1837 Rebellion leaders. They joined the 15th English-Speaking International Brigade in Albacete, Spain, taking part in the Sept. 13th assault on Fuentes de Ebro, and the 1938 defence of Teruel. The battalion was led by Toronto labour journalist Edward Cecil Smith, and Saul Wellman, a New York union organizer. On Feb. 4, 1939, the battalion returned to Union Station, Toronto, where they were welcomed by a crowd of thousands. The soldiers were not given an official welcome, however, because they had violated a non-interventionist policy set against Canadian involvement in the war. On Oct. 20, 2001 the Canadian govt unveiled a monument in Toronto dedicated to the soldiers, more than half of whom did not survive the war.

Also in July

• One of the worst heat waves in Canada was recorded during a 7-day stretch in southern Ont. Temperatures ranged from 33.3°C (92°F) to 40.6°C (105°F), causing the deaths of an estimated 230 people. Thirty-six bare-breasted men were arrested for indecent exposure in Toronto's Sunnyside Park during the heat.

Aug. 17 The Union Nationale, under leader Maurice Duplessis (1890–1959), won 76 of Que.'s 90 seats, ending 39 years of Liberal rule.

Sept. 5 The Joint Staff Committee of the Department of National Defence recommended a 5-year re-armament plan costing $260 million. The federal govt ultimately decided to spend half that amount.

Oct. 15 Mary Teresa Sullivan (1902–1973) was sworn in as a member of the Halifax City Council, the 1st woman alderman in Canada.

Nov. 2 The Canadian Broadcasting Corporation (CBC) was established with powers to regulate private stations and support and promote Canadian culture. It replaced the Canadian Radio Broadcasting Commission (CRBC), which had been established in 1932. The CBC became the largest broadcasting system in the world.

Nov. 18 The *Toronto Globe* (founded 1844) purchased the *Mail and Empire* (founded 1895) newspaper to form the *Globe and Mail*.

Dec. 4 The Townley and Matheson architectural firm, along with builders Carter-Halls-Aldinger Company, completed the $1 million Vancouver City Hall, located at 453 West 12th Avenue.

Dec. 9 Canada was informed that British King Edward VIII planned to abdicate so he could marry American divorcée Mrs. Wallis Simpson. Edward VIII left the throne to his brother, George VI, the next day.

c 1936 John Lyman painted the portrait of Mrs. Leonard Marsh, *Woman With a White Collar*, now in the National Gallery of Canada.

Also in 1936

• Canadian govts on all levels spent $159 million on domestic relief.

• Banknotes became bilingual.

• The average Sask. farmer was in debt to the tune of $9,771.00

• Rev. Lydia Emelie Gruchy of Sask. became the 1st woman to be ordained as a minister by the United Church. In 1953, Rev. Gruchy became the 1st Canadian woman to receive an honorary Doctor of Divinity.

• Dr. Norman Bethune put into operation the 1st mobile blood transfusion service, which he organized for the Republican forces in the Spanish Civil War.

• At the Olympic Games in Berlin, Germany, Frank Amyot (1904–1962) won a gold medal in canoeing and Canada took silver in men's basketball — the only Canadian basketball medal of the 20th century — after losing 19–8 to the US in the final (the game was played outdoors in the rain). The Olympics were completed under the gaze of German leader Adolph Hitler.

• 3,706 farms were abandoned in Alb. between Hanna and the Red Deer R.

• The 1st commercial production of mustard began with 40 ha planted in southern Alb. Sask. has since become one of the top 5 producers in the world, and accounts for 89% of Canadian production.

• Antigonish miners created the town of Tompkinsville, NS, which consisted entirely of co-operative

housing. The town was named after priest and educator Fr. Jimmy Tompkins (1870–1953).

• Morley Callaghan published *Now that April's Here*.

• *The White Savannahs*, a modern study of 9 Canadian poets, established William Edwin Collin (1893–1984) as a major Canadian critic.

• Louis Dantin (1865–1945) (pseud. Eugène Seers) published *Contes de Noël*.

• Nellie McClung published her autobiography, *Clearing in the West: My Own Story*.

• Poet Jean Narrache (1893–1970) (pseud. Émile Coderre) published *Quand J' Parl'tout Seul*.

• Sir Charles G. D. Roberts published *Selected Poems*.

• The anthology *New Provinces*, by A.J.M. Smith and F.R. Scott, was published.

• Charles Comfort completed the painting *Smelter Stacks, Copper Cliff*.

• Pegi Nicol MacLeod's (1904–1949) painting *Torso and Plants* was 1st exhibited. It is now in the Robert McLaughlin Gallery, Oshawa, Ont.

• Lawren Harris completed *Poise*, now in a private collection.

• Alfred Pellan completed the abstract canvas *La Fenêtre ouverte*, now at Hart House, U. of Toronto.

• Influential pre–WW II playwright, Herman Arthur Voaden (1903–1991) produced the drama *Murder Pattern*.

• Legendary NS country singer Hank Snow (1914–1999) recorded the songs "Lonesome Blue Yodel" and the "Prisoned Cowboy."

1937

Jan. 28 The Judicial Committee of the Privy Council in London, England, upheld the June 17, 1936, Supreme Court of Canada decision to strike down the Bennett govts "New Deal" legislation.

Feb. 9 A patent for the zipper was issued to the Lightning Fastener Company of St. Catharines, Ont.

Apr. 8–23 Auto workers conducted a sit-down strike at the General Motors plant in Oshawa, Ont. Workers wanted an 8-hour day, 40-hour week, a standard grievance committee, seniority rights and union recognition. The federal govt declared the work action illegal. Premier Mitch Hepburn recruited a special police force of 300, known to strikers as "Hepburn Hussars" and "Son's of Mitches." The force was never used. An agreement was eventually reached Apr. 23 between GM and the striking men and women (500 women worked in the upholstery shop alone), providing better wages and recognition of union representatives, but not the UAW.

Also in Apr.
• Under the banner of the Congress Industrial Workers (CIO), 5,000 Montreal garment workers went on strike for better working conditions and recognition of the International Ladies Garment Workers Union (ILGWU). The strike ended with the establishment of Local 262 of the ILGWU, the largest in Canada.

Mar. 24 In Que., the Padlock Act (Act Respecting Communistic Propaganda), proposed by the Union Nationale govt of Premier Duplessis, was passed. Its provisions empowered the attorney general to close, for 1 year, any building used for the propagation of Communism or Bolshevism. A judge could order the lock removed only if the owner could prove that the building was not so used during the preceding year. Printed material could be confiscated and destroyed, and anyone printing subversive material could be imprisoned for up to 1 year. The Supreme Court of Canada declared the act unconstitutional in 1957.

June 10 Former PM Robert Borden died of heart failure in Ottawa.

June 14 *The Happy Gang*, one of CBC's most popular radio programs, was 1st broadcast. Created by Bert Pearl (1913–1986), it included jokes, talk and upbeat music. The show wound up in 1959.

June 30 PM Mackenzie King met with German leader Adolph Hitler in Berlin, later describing him as "a

simple sort of peasant" presenting no serious danger to the world. On July 1, King stopped in Paris to open the Canadian Pavilion at the International Exposition.

July 5 The temperature hit 45°C at Midale and Yellow Grass, Sask., the highest ever recorded in Canada.

July 6 The *Caledonia*, from Foynes, Ireland, an Imperial Airways water plane commanded by Captain A.S. Wilcockson, landed at Botwood, Nfld., inaugurating transatlantic service.

July 7 Construction began on the Lions Gate Bridge, a Vancouver landmark. The project was initiated when the Guinness family (of Guinness Breweries) purchased property on the North Shore with a plan to build a bridge over the First Narrows and encourage settlement there. The final cost of construction was $5,873,837.17. The bridge opened to traffic on Nov. 12, 1938. It was the largest suspension bridge in the country.

July 30 Clarence Decatur Howe (1886–1960), minister of transport, and Herbert James Symington (1881–1965), director of the newly formed Trans-Canada Airlines (TCA), flew to Vancouver in the "Dawn to Dusk Across Canada" flight to publicize the new service. TCA was chartered as a Crown corporation to operate intercity, transcontinental and international flights. It was established by the Trans-Canada Airlines Act Apr. 10, 1937. TCA would become Air Canada in 1965.

Aug. 2–16 Ten thousand members of the Canadian Catholic Confederation of Labour went on strike at 9 Que. Dominion Textile plants. Strikers returned to work with better working conditions and union recognition.

Aug. 15 PM Mackenzie King appointed the Royal Commission on Dominion Provincial Relations to examine the BNA and the relationship between the federal and provincial govts. Known as the Rowell-Sirois Commission, the group was chaired by Newton Wesley Rowell (1867–1941), and from 1938, by Joseph Sirois (1881–1941). The commission made its report in May 1940.

Also in Aug.

- The 1st chartered credit union was formed in Regina, Sask., to help farmers pool their dwindling Depression-era resources.

Sept. 1 Scheduled operations of the TCA began; the 1st regular flight was between Vancouver and Seattle, Washington.

Fall Two-thirds of rural Sask.'s population was on relief. Sask. relief expenditures (food, clothing, medical supplies, heat and agricultural aid) were $5.5 million for fiscal year 1937–1938.

1937–38 Emily Carr painted *Forest Landscape II*, oil on paper, now in the National Gallery of Canada.

Also in 1937

- The Western black-footed ferret was last seen in Canada in Sask. It is now considered extirpated.

- Canadian govts on all levels spent $165 million on domestic relief.

- Canada produced 4.3 million tons of paper products, 85% of which was newsprint.

- The Sask. Métis Society (SMS) was incorporated.

- The Canadian Mint placed a likeness of the schooner *Bluenose* on the dime.

- The Association of Canadian Bookmen, formed in 1925, held its 1st book fair and exhibition. Participants included bookseller Roy Britnell (1900–1983), Toronto Public Library chief librarian Charles Sanderson, Canadian Authors Association president Pelham Edgar (1871–1948), children's librarian Lillian Smith (1887–1983), publishers John McClelland and Thomas Allen, and *Globe & Mail* literary critic William Arthur Deacon.

- Prince Edward Island National Park was established to protect a narrow 40-km stretch of classic PEI beach and dune (37% of the park) and Acadian mixed forest (39%). The park includes estuaries, shallow sun-warmed waters, red sandstone cliffs, 200 kinds of bird, and perhaps its greatest attraction, the original Anne of Green Gables house, made famous by native-born PEI author Lucy Maud Montgomery.

- A.Y. Jackson painted *Alberta Foothills*, now in the McMichael Canadian Collection, Kleinburg, Ont.

- Carl Fellman Schaefer (1903–1995) painted *Storm Over the Fields*, oil on canvas, now in the Art Gallery of Ont., Toronto.

- David Milne painted *Young Poplars among Driftwood*, in one sitting. It is now in the National Gallery of Canada.

- Russian-born Paraskeva Clark completed the landscape painting *The Pink Cloud*, now in the National Gallery of Canada.

- Charles Comfort completed the landscape *Lake Superior Village*, now in the Art Gallery of Ont., Toronto.

- Bertram Brooker painted the nude *Torso*, now in the National Gallery of Canada.

- *Modern Times,* watercolour by Nathan Petroff (b 1916) was completed. His depiction of an exhausted woman in a dirty dress, head in hands, poring over the employment news, captured a spirit of the late-Depression period.

- Morley Callaghan published the novel *More Joy in Heaven*, a story about a reformed bank robber who returns to his hometown.

- Chicoutimi priest and writer Félix-Antoine Savard (1896–1982) published *Menaud, maître-draveur,* later translated under the titles *Boss of the River* (1947), and *Master of the River* (1976). The main character, a lumberjack, is driven to the brink as he witnesses his land and people exploited by foreign companies.

- The Governor-General's Literary Awards were presented for the 1st time (to winners of 1936 publications). Bertram Brooker won in the fiction category for his novel *Think of the Earth*, and T.B. Robertson won in the non-fiction category for *T.B.R.-newspaper pieces.*

- Historian Donald Grant Creighton (1902–1979) published *The Commercial Empire of the St. Lawrence.*

• Que.'s Hector de Saint-Denys Garneau (1912–1943) published the collection of verse *Regards et jeux dans l'espace.*

• Poet Floris Clark McLaren (b 1904) published *Frozen Fire.*

• John William Coulter (1888–1980) wrote the play *The House in the Quiet Glen.*

• Architects George and Moorhouse, with S. H. Maw (1881–1952) as associate architect, completed the Toronto Stock Exchange on Bay St. The art deco building was constructed out of granite and limestone, and had a 12-m trading floor located 1 storey aboveground. The 2nd-floor exterior frieze was designed by Charles Comfort. The Toronto Stock Exchange moved to First Canadian Place in 1983.

• Architect Adrian Gilbert Scott (1882–1963), of London, England, with associate architects Sharp and Thompson, completed St. James's Anglican Church in Vancouver.

1938

Jan. 18 The 1st Canada–US military staff talks were held in Washington, D.C.

• The 256-m Honeymoon Bridge, crossing the Niagara R. at Niagara Falls, collapsed after its foundations were crushed by ice. It had been built in 1898.

Mar. 4 The Supreme Court of Canada invalidated the Alb. Press Act (passed by the Aberhart Social Credit govt, Oct. 5, 1937), that forced Alb. newspapers to disclose news sources to a govt board and also publish govt rebuttals to any newspaper-published govt criticism. Alb. newspapers — led by John Imrie (1885–1942) of the *Edmonton Journal* — fought strenuously against the act. As a result, the *Journal* was awarded a special Pulitzer Prize for its efforts on behalf of the freedom of the press, becoming the 1st newspaper outside the US ever to receive the prestigious award.

Apr. 13 Writer Archibald Belaney (Grey Owl) died of pneumonia in Prince Albert National Park, Sask. A fury erupted when the public later learned that

Grey Owl was not a Mexican-born Apache but a British immigrant.

Also in Apr.
• The 1st electron microscope was completed at the U. of Toronto, where it was invented by Eli Franklin Burton (1879–1948), Charles Edward Hall, James Hillier and Albert Prebus.

May 20 A long-range nationwide program combining conservation and development designed to stimulate employment was unveiled by Minister of Labour Norman McLeod Rogers (1894–1940). It included federal public works with highway construction to open up areas to mining and tourism, forest and fisheries conservation projects, the development of historic sites, a federal program for youth job training and other economic stimulants.

• Unemployed members of the Relief Project Worker's Union in Vancouver occupied the Hotel Georgia, the Vancouver Art Gallery and the central post office and began sit-down strikes. The 500 men in the Hotel Georgia were soon paid $500 to leave, but 500 remained in the art gallery and 1,000 in the post office until June 19. On that date, later termed "Bloody Sunday," RCMP and city police used tear gas and clubs to forcibly remove the strikers.

June Action Comics released the 1st *Superman* comic book, created by *Toronto Star* artist Joe Shuster (1914–1992) and American Jerry Siegel. The 13-page comic sold for 10 cents.

July 1 The King Liberal govt passed the Bank of Canada Act Amendment Act, 1938, making the Bank of Canada a publicly owned institution.

• PM Mackenzie King announced that his govt would oppose any military establishment on Canadian soil that was not controlled by Canada, except as required in the case of war.

Aug. 18 US President Franklin D. Roosevelt was presented with an honorary degree from Queen's U. in Kingston, Ont. In his acceptance speech, Roosevelt stated, "I give you the assurance that the people of the US will not stand idly by if domination of Canadian soil was threatened by any other empire."

Sept. 18-24 At Madison Square Garden in New York City, Torchy Peden (1906–1980) of BC won one of the last, 6-day indoor bicycle marathons. Peden, at 6'3" 220 lbs, was the best and most feared of the era's marathon pedallers. The 6-day bike race was a sports craze that faded after 1938.

Oct. 23 Canadian singers and orchestras participated in *A Musical Portrait of Canada*, the 1st major Canadian production broadcast around the world.

Oct. 26 The famed *Bluenose* defended its title for the International Fisherman's Trophy for the last time by beating the *Gertrude L. Thebaud* of the Gloucester fleet. It would never race again. In 1942, Captain Walters sold the historic schooner to the West Indian Traders Company, which used it to freight commodities between Caribbean Islands. On Jan. 28, 1946 *Bluenose* hit a reef off Haiti during the night and sank the next day. The pride of Lunenburg was not recovered.

Nov. 17 Canada and the US signed a trade agreement at Washington, D.C.

Nov. 19 The RCAF achieved equal status with the Royal Canadian Navy (RCN) and the Canadian army.

Dec. 1 A recommendation that 10,000 European Jews be accepted into Canada, made by Thomas Crerar, Liberal mines and resources minister responsible for immigration, was met with overwhelming opposition. Between 1938–1939, Canada accepted only approximately 2,500 European Jews fleeing the growing horror of Nazi persecution.

Dec. 10 Future chief referee in the NHL, Red Storey (b 1918), came off the Toronto Argonaut bench to score 3 touchdowns in the 4th quarter as Toronto beat Winnipeg in the Grey Cup 30–7.

Also in 1938
• The Queen Elizabeth Way (QEW) opened in Ont., from Toronto to Hamilton, as the 1st four-lane, limited-access highway in North America.

• A new law in Ont. mandated the replacement of Grade 3 and 4 readers with Canadian-written and published books.

• Thomas Carrol developed the self-propelled combine for the Massey-Harris Company.

• Malton Airport opened near Toronto on 170 ha of farmland. It would be Toronto's only major airport until Terminal 1 of the new Toronto International Airport opened in Feb. 1964.

• The Gaelic College at St. Ann's Bay, NS (population 64), was established to preserve the Gaelic language and traditions in Canada; it remains the only Gaelic college in North America. It offers six-week summer courses in Gaelic, and singing, bagpipe playing, Highland dancing, arts and crafts.

• The Winnipeg Ballet was founded by Gweneth Lloyd (1901–1993) and Betty Hall Farrally (d.1989) as the Winnipeg Ballet Club. The company would 1st perform in 1939, and receive its royal title in 1953. Lloyd would go on to create over 30 original ballets for the RWB.

• Russian-born dancer and choreographer Boris Volkoff (1900–1974) founded the Volkoff Canadian Ballet in Toronto.

• LeMoine FitzGerald painted *The Jar,* oil on canvas, one of his most acclaimed still lifes, now at the Winnipeg Art Gallery.

• Charles Comfort completed the landscape *Pioneer Survival*, now in the Art Gallery of Ont., Toronto.

• Léo-Paul Desrosiers published the novel *Les Engagés du Grand Portage.* Set in the years of the fur trade it is generally regarded as his masterpiece.

• The novel *Trente Arpents* (translated as *Thirty Acres*), by Philippe Panneton (1895–1960), pseud. Ringuet, was published.

• Journalist and novelist Frederick John Niven (1878–1944) published his autobiography *Coloured Spectacles.*

• F.R. (Budge) Crawley (1911–1987) and his wife, Judith (1927–1999), founded Crawley Films. They made training and recruiting films during WW II, and became the largest independent-film production company in Canada during the 1950s, winning close to 300 national and international awards. The Crawleys were honoured by the Canadian Film Awards in 1957 for their unique contribution to Canada's filmmaking art and industry.

1939

Jan. The Contemporary Arts Society was founded in Montreal to promote and support modern art. Founding members included Prudence Heward Paule-Émile Borduas (1905–1960) and Stanley Cosgrove (1911-2002)

Mar. 1 TCA began transcontinental airmail service.

Mar. 30 Federal party leaders agreed on a basis of unity should Canada become involved in war: no neutrality, fight alongside Britain, and no conscription for overseas service.

Apr. 5 The Supreme Court of Canada ruled in a dispute between the federal govt and Que. that the term "Indian" in the BNA Act referred to all original inhabitants of Canada, including the Inuit.

Also in Apr.
• Parliament voted for a $60 million military expenditure, the most ever allocated during peacetime.

May 21 The National War Memorial at Ottawa was unveiled by King George VI , who was in Canada on a state visit. Originally designed to commemorate the over 60,000 Canadians who died during WW I, the majestic arched monument in Confederation Square was rededicated in May 1982, to also commemorate all those who died in WW II (1939–1945) and the Korean War (1950–1953).

June 7 The Mackenzie King govt refused to allow the Hamburg-American liner *St. Louis*, carrying 907 German-Jewish refugees, to dock. The passengers had previously been refused sanctuary in all South American countries, the Caribbean, the US and now Canada. They were forced to return to the looming spectre of Nazi occupation in Europe, where many of them ended up in concentration camps.

Sept. 1 Nazi Germany, allied with the Soviet Union, invaded Poland. The War Measures Act was proclaimed. The Canadian militia was called to active service.

Sept. 3 Great Britain and France declared war on Germany.

• Defence of Canada regulations, giving the federal govt sweeping authority to protect the country against subversion and to control dissent, was proclaimed in force under the War Measures Act.

• The Wartime Prices and Trade Board, responsible to the minister of labour, was established to prevent hoarding and profiteering and to conserve civilian supplies. The board would be given power to control the prices and distribution of necessary goods and services.

Sept. 3–10 During this brief stretch, the US exported military aircraft to Canada, which could not be shipped to either Britain or France due to a US neutrality law. Exports would stop with the Canadian declaration of war Sept. 10.

Sept. 6 James Layton Ralston (1881–1948) was sworn in as minister of finance and at once began preparing a war budget.

Sept. 8 PM Mackenzie King formally repeated his promise that his govt would not introduce conscription for overseas service.

Sept. 9 Communist leader Tim Buck wired PM Mackenzie King, pledging his party's full support of Poland. Canadians would not learn until Sept. 17 that the Soviets had affiliated with Germany in the invasion plan.

Sept. 10 Canada declared war on Germany. Canadian forces on this date included an army of 4,500 regulars and 60,000 militia reservists, the RCAF of about 4,500, and the RCN with 1,800 men and 13 ships.

Sept. 15 Loring Cheney Christie (1885–1941) was appointed Canadian minister to the US.

Sept. 16 The 1st transatlantic convoy departed from Halifax, escorted by the RCN's *Saguenay* and *St. Laurent* destroyers.

• The Foreign Exchange Control Board was established to conserve Canada's supply of US dollars. It immediately devalued the Canadian dollar by 10% and imposed restrictions on the purchase of US funds for any but essential war purposes.

Sept. 19 The Emergency Council announced a program to establish an expeditionary force of 1 army division and intensive air training in Canada at a total cost of $250 million.

Sept. 27 Warsaw, Poland, fell to the Germans.

Also in Sept.
• Defence Industries Ltd. was established by the federal govt to produce explosives and ammunition for the war effort.

Oct. 5 The 1st Canadian Infantry Division came under the command of Gen. Andrew G.L. McNaughton (1887–1966).

Oct. 25 PM King made the 1st of 2 public radio broadcasts, about Canada's involvement in the second world war of the century. This 1st broadcast was called "The Issue." The 2nd, made Oct. 31, was called, "The Organization of Canada's War Effort."

Oct. 26 Que. Union Nationale Premier Maurice Duplessis was defeated by the Liberals under the leadership of Joseph-Adélard Godbout (1892–1956). The Liberals won 70 seats against the Union's 15. Duplessis had called a snap election Sept. 24 to gauge Que.'s response to the recent implications of federal war measures. Before the election, Federal Minister of Justice Earnest Lapointe and 3 other federal Que. ministers threatened to resign if the Duplessis govt was re-elected.

Nov. 12 Dr. Norman Bethune, medical member of Mao Zedong's Chinese Communist Army, died in a peasant hut in the village of Huangshikuo, North China. He had contracted septicemia after cutting his finger during an operation at the battle front. Bethune's dedication to Communism and his sacrifice helping China repel the Japanese made him a symbol of internationalism and selflessness. On May Day, 1940, Bethune's tomb, set in spacious grounds, with a statue of the man, was dedicated in Zhucheng, Tang Xion.

Nov. 13 Canadian military headquarters were established in London, England, by Henry Duncan Graham Crerar (1888–1965).

Dec. 5 The Cabinet War Committee was formed to deal with logistics of the war effort.

Dec. 10 The Canadian 1st Division sailed out of Halifax for Great Britain on the liners *Aquitania*, *Empress of Britain*, *Empress of Australia*, *Duchess of Bedford* and *Monarch of Bermuda*. All were escorted by the battleship *Resolution*. They began arriving in Britain Dec. 17.

Dec. 17 The Air Training Agreement was signed at Ottawa by representatives of Australia, Britain, Canada and New Zealand. Under the plan, aircrew for the 4 countries would be trained in Canada by the RCAF. The British Commonwealth Air Training Plan began in Apr. 1940. By the time it was terminated Mar. 31, 1945, 131,553 airmen had been trained in the program.

c 1939 *Trees in the Sky*, oil on canvas, by Emily Carr, was completed.

Also in 1939
• The National Film Board of Canada (NFB) was established out of the National Film Act of 1939 to be "the eyes of Canada." Dr. John Grierson (1898–1972) was named Canadian film commissioner in 1939 and became the 1st head of the NFB. During WW II, the NFB produced patriotic films serving the war effort, including the series *Canada Carries On*. The NFB has won more than 4,000 international film awards and citations. In 1989, it received a Special Achievement Award from the Academy of Canadian Cinema and an honorary Oscar in recognition of its 50th anniversary.

• About 530,000 people, or 11% of the labour force, were unemployed.

• The federal govt passed the Prairie Farm Assistance Act, which provided an insurance plan against crop failure in specified areas.

• Isabel McLaughlin became the 1st woman president of the Canadian Group of Painters.

• William Goodridge Roberts (1904–1974), influenced by John Lyman and Henri Mattisse, painted *Nude on a Red Cloth*, on board, now in a private collection.

• Montreal-born artist Stanley Morel Cosgrove completed the painting *Madeleine*, now in a private collection.

• Irene Baird (1901–1981) published the novel *Waste Heritage*, set in Depression-era Vancouver.

• Franklin Davy McDowell published *The Champlain Road*, a Canadian historical romance.

• Poet Joyce Anne Marriott (b 1913) published *The Wind Our Enemy*.

• Howard O'Hagan (1902–1982) published *Tay John*, a novel of the Rocky Mountains.

• Laura Salverson, née Goodman (1890–1970), published *Confessions of an Immigrant Daughter*, a novel set in an Icelandic settlement in Man.

• Montreal architect Ernest Cormier (1885–1980) completed the Supreme Court of Canada building in Ottawa. The modern classic, château-style structure features the 12 x 6-m courtroom reserved for the use of the Supreme Court. A statue of former Prime Minister Louis St Laurent (1949–1957), by sculptor Erek Imredy, was erected on the front lawn in 1976.

1940

Jan. 1 The 1st municipal govt in the NWT was inaugurated in Yellowknife.

Jan. 25 The 6th session of the 18th Parliament met. PM Mackenzie King dissolved it immediately and called an election (Mar. 26).

Feb. 6 Gov-Gen. Lord Tweedsmuir suffered a stroke from which he did not recover. He died on Feb. 11. On Apr. 3, Alexander Augustus Frederick William Alfred George Cambridge, Earl of Athlone (1874–1957), was appointed gov-gen. of Canada. He served June 21, to 1946.

Also in Feb.
• Twenty-three thousand new Canadian recruits landed in Britain.

Mar. 13 John Babbitt McNair (1889–1938) succeeded A.A. Dysart as Liberal premier of NB.

Mar. 21 The Social Credit Party was re-elected in Alb. under William Aberhart.

Mar. 26 The Liberal party under Mackenzie King won a decisive victory over Dr. Robert James Manion's (1981–1943) Conservatives in the general election. The Liberals won 178 seats, Conservatives 39, Social Credit 10, CCF 8. Ten seats went to Independents and other parties. Voter turnout was 69.9%.

Apr. 25 Que. women were granted the right to vote and run for office in provincial elections.

Also in Apr.
• C.D. Howe was named minister of the new Department of Munitions and Supply, created to run Canada's war production program.

May 13 Richard Burpee Hanson (1879–1948) of Fredericton was chosen Conservative leader of the NB opposition.

May 19 US President Franklin D. Roosevelt agreed to allow American citizens to enlist in the Canadian forces, provided they took an Oath of Obedience rather than the Oath of Allegiance.

May 23 Charles "Chubby" Gavin Power (1888–1968) became minister of national defence for air.

• The British govt appealed to PM Mackenzie King to send all available Canadian destroyers across the Atlantic to help guard Britain's shores. The Canadian War Committee sent 4 Canadian vessels — HMCS *Restigouche*, *Fraser*, *Ottawa* and *St. Laurent*.

Also in May
• The Rowell-Sirois Report was published, recommending a transfer of functions and a shifting of taxation power to the federal govt and the creation of federal grants to the provinces to equalize provincial tax revenues. It also recommended that the federal govt assume responsibility for unemployment insurance and contributory pensions, and take full responsibility for provincial debts. On Jan. 14 and 15, 1941, a Royal Commission on dominion-provincial relations convened to address the report. No agreement between Ottawa and the provinces was made, and the Rowell–Sirois Report was officially shelved.

June 5 Nazi, Fascist and Communist groups were declared illegal in Canada and their leaders were jailed under Defence of Canada regulations. Tim Buck spent the War years underground.

June 10 Benito Mussolini allied Italy with Germany. Canada and its allies declared war on Italy.

• Minister of National Defence Norman Rogers was killed in an air crash near Newcastle, Ont. On June 11, Charles Power (1888–1968) became acting minister, until July when J.L. Ralston (WW I hero and 1920s defence minister) assumed the position.

• Netherlands Princess Juliana arrived in Canada to live in exile while her country was occupied by Germany.

June 13–14 The 1st Canadian Division landed at Brest, France, and proceeded to Laval and Le Mans. With the surrender of Paris and the fall of France to the invading Germans, the Canadians managed to recross the channel to England, with only 6 men missing.

June 14 PM Mackenzie King addressed an appeal to French Premier Paul Reynaud, urging the French govt to continue its resistance against the Germans.

June 21 The National Resources Mobilization Act was passed, providing for a policy of conscription for home defence only. From Apr. 1941, men called up for military service were required to spend the entire war on home-defence duties. Critics referred to them as "Zombies" because they had not volunteered for overseas service.

June 24 France signed an armistice with Germany and Italy.

Also in June
• Two fully equipped RCAF squadrons flew to England for service against the Axis powers.

July 4 Jehovah's Witnesses, conscientious objectors to war who refused to swear allegiance to any nation, were outlawed under the War Measures Act.

July 6 Canada suffered its 1st casualties of WW II when a lone German bomber machine-gunned and then bombed Canadian soldiers digging air-raid shelters in Aldershut, England. Three Canadians were killed.

July 10–Oct. 31 No. 1 (Fighter) Squadron, RCAF, flew its Hawker Hurricanes in the Battle of Britain. Three crew members were killed, 10 were wounded. The battle was fought against the German Luftwaffe, which unsuccessfully attempted both to destroy the Allied air force in Britain and assume complete control over British airspace.

July 14 Canadian Gen. Andrew McNaughton (1887–1966) was placed in command of the British 7th Army Corps, which included British and New Zealand troops, as well as the Canadian Overseas Contingent.

July 29 The British Admiralty sent a telegram warning that the German cruisers *Nürnberg* and *Leipzig* might be operating off the coast of Vancouver.

• The 75-piece Montreal Women's Symphony Orchestra, Canada's 1st women's symphony, performed its inaugural concert at Plateau Hall, Montreal. On Oct. 22, 1947, it became the 1st Canadian orchestra to perform at Carnegie Hall in New York City.

Aug. 5 Minister of Justice Ernest Lapointe signed a warrant for the arrest of Montreal Mayor Camillien Houde (1889–1958) for sedition. The mayor had openly argued that Que. men should defy the compulsory military-service registration. Houde was arrested at city hall by the RCMP and spent 4 years of internment in Ont.

Aug. 7 The Unemployment Insurance Act was passed, creating the Unemployment Insurance Fund made up of contributions from the federal govt, employees and employers. It was the 1st compulsory unemployment insurance plan in the country. It became effective July 1, 1941.

Aug. 17–18 PM Mackenzie King met with US President Franklin D. Roosevelt at Ogdensburg, New York, in the president's private railway car. Roosevelt proposed the establishment of a Canada–US Permanent Joint Board on Defence. King accepted the proposal. The Ogdensburg Agreement, signed Aug. 18, was Canada's 1st military pact with a country other than Britain. The agreement formed the highest-ranking bilateral defence forum on North American security.

Aug. 23 German and Italian Canadians, who had become Canadian citizens after Sept. 1, 1922, were termed alien enemies and lost their citizenship.

Sept. 1 German prisoners of war arrived at Quebec City, the 1st POWs to be transferred from Britain to Canada. They were placed in internment camps throughout Canada. By war's end, 35,000 POWs had been interned on Canadian shores. Many stayed in Canada.

Sept. 26 Thomas Pattullo, Liberal premier of BC, advised PM Mackenzie King not to call up Japanese and Chinese Canadians for compulsory military training. PM King, in turn, told the War Committee that he felt it unwise to arm Japanese Canadians "at a moment when war with Japan was possible."

Sept. 27 German Foreign Minister Joachim von Ribbentrop announced that an agreement between Germany, Italy and Japan (Triple Axis) had been arranged. It stated that if any country not at present engaged in hostilities entered the war against any one of the 3, the others would come to its assistance.

Oct. 26 The CPR's *Empress of Britain II* was set on fire by German bombers off the coast of Ireland. Under tow to Britain, it was twice torpedoed by German U-boats and sunk Oct. 28. It was the largest liner to be sunk during WW II; 45 crew members died.

Nov. 5 Democrat Franklin D. Roosevelt was re-elected president of the US.

Nov. 10 The Trans-Atlantic Ferry Service began transporting planes, men and supplies from Canada, via Goose Bay and Gander, Nfld., to Britain.

Also in 1940

• Canada's population was 11,381,000.

• Ownership of 50 older Town Class American destroyers was transferred to the Royal Navy at Halifax, in return for military basing rights in the UK.

• Carl and Jack Cole, creators of the ubiquitous students' study aid *Coles Notes*, opened the 1st Coles bookstore in Toronto. Start-up capital was $35. In 1980, the brothers opened The World's Biggest Bookstore, a 6,224.5-m² megastore in downtown Toronto. Coles and Smithbooks (established in Toronto in 1950 as a division of British-based W.H. Smith) would come under the ownership of Southam Inc., who then sold it to Pathfinder Capital in 1994. Coles and Smithbooks merged with Chapters in Aug. 1995.

• An unemployment insurance scheme was added to the Old Age Pension Plan of 1927.

• Man. scientist and Royal Navy Lt.-Comm. Charles Goodeve (1904–1980), invented a method of degaussing ships (counter-acting the magnetic disturbance created by ships) to render them immune to magnetic mines.

• The Big Bend Highway opened through the mountains between Golden and Revelstoke, BC, and connected the 2 areas by road for the 1st time. Construction on Big Bend started in 1929.

• William Samuel Stephenson (1896–1989), known as the "Quiet Canadian," was appointed Britain's chief espionage agent in North America, operating under the code name Intrepid.

• A vast program to construct naval and merchant vessels was begun at Montreal, Lauzon, Sorel and Quebec City on the St. Lawrence; at Collingwood, Kingston, Toronto and Port Arthur (Thunder Bay) on the Great Lakes; and at Esquimalt, Victoria and North Vancouver on the West Coast.

• The federal govt passed legislation to guarantee recognition of membership in a union.

• Landscape artist Carl Schaefer (1903–1995) became the 1st Canadian to be awarded a Guggenheim Fellowship.

• Goodridge Roberts painted the landscape *Hills and Rivers, Laurentians*, now in the Art Gallery of Ont., Toronto.

• Abstract artist Marian Mildred Dale Scott (1906–1993) completed the mural *Endocrinology*, for the McGill U. medical building.

• Calgary-born artist Philip Surrey (1910–1990) completed *The Crocodile*, oil on canvas, now in the Art Gallery of Ont., Toronto.

• Jewish-Canadian poet A.M. Klein (1909–1972) published *Hath Not a Jew*.

• Poet E.J. Pratt published *Brébeuf and His Brethren*.

1941

Jan. 1 The CBC introduced its national radio news service with Lorne Greene (1915–1987) its 1st announcer.

Jan. 28 Agreement was reached at a meeting of the War Committee on the extension of compulsory military training from 1 month to 4, with arrangements made to avoid interference with harvesting and seeding time required by farmers' sons.

Also in Jan.
• The sale of tires and inner tubes to civilians was halted.

Feb. 9 PM Mackenzie King rejected a request from the British govt to stop some Russian vessels carrying cargo of California vegetable oil. Britain feared the oil would be sent to Germany.

Feb. 18 Sir Frederick Banting died in a plane crash in Nfld., while en route to England.

Mar. 11 The US Congress passed the Lend-Lease Act, permitting the US to provide Allied countries with necessary defence articles, not to exceed $1.3 billion total. The act effectively voided US neutrality.

Mar. 14 PM Mackenzie King's cabinet received a delegation of the Trades and Labour Congress, which argued that the govt was failing labour by not carrying out its labour policies.

Apr. 20 PM Mackenzie King and US President Franklin D. Roosevelt signed the Hyde Park Declaration, establishing cooperation in the production and purchasing of defence equipment. Canada would be able to buy needed supplies from the US.

Apr. 23 Minister of National Defence James Ralston, speaking to the War Committee on the difficulties of recruiting for the war, spoke for the 1st time about the possibility of conscription for overseas service.

May 7 Australian PM Robert Menzies arrived in Ottawa where he spoke to the War Committee on the need for a conference of PMs, to hold support for Dominion interests when differing from those of Britain.

Also in May
• The 1st group of new corvettes, the 1st products of Canada's wartime shipbuilding industry, set sail to join Canadian destroyers at the naval base at St. John's, Nfld. The corvettes — the *Agassiz, Alberni, Chambly, Cobalt, Collingwood, Orillia* and *Wetaskiwin* — were each named after a Canadian town. These small but highly manoeuvrable submarine killers were modelled after whaling ships, whose prey surfaced, dove and turned in much the same way as submarines. Corvettes and destroyers formed the Nfld. Escort Force, to protect merchant vessels cross the Atlantic

June 27 On a speaking tour of the West to promote his wartime policies, PM Mackenzie King was confronted in Calgary by a pro-conscription demonstration.

• The federal govt announced that women had the right to enlist in the Canadian army.

Also in June
• The National Film Board's documentary *Churchill's Island* won an Academy Award.

July 1 Cape Breton Highlands National Park (950 km^2), located at the northern most end of Cape Breton Is., opened. The park is bordered by both the Gulf of St. Lawrence and the Atlantic Ocean and includes precipitous cliffs and the world-famous Cabot Trail.

July 13 Canada approved the Anglo-Soviet Treaty made in the wake of Germany's invasion of the USSR. Canada and the Soviet Union were now allied.

July 26 The Japanese foreign minister called on PM King to protest the freezing of Japanese assets by Canada, in retaliation for the Japanese intervention in French Indo-China.

• Approximately 400 workers seized the Aluminium Company of Canada plant at Arvida, Que. Troops were sent in to evict the strikers, but workers had evacuated the plant before any action was taken. During the dispute, the aluminum hardened in the pots causing several million dollars' damage. Workers later won a slight wage increase through conciliation.

July 29 An Order-in-Council gave the minister of munitions and supply authority to call out troops to assist police in the event of war production-plant sabotage.

Aug. 14 At Placentia Bay, Nfld., Winston Churchill and F.D. Roosevelt signed the Atlantic Charter. Although the US was not officially at war, it pledged support for British war aims and agreed to help protect British shipping in the western Atlantic from attacks by German submarines.

Aug. 19 PM Mackenzie King made his 1st wartime trip to England. He visited with the king and queen at Balmoral Castle, Aug. 30-31, before seeing Canadian troops at Digby, Sept. 6.

Sept. 19 The British govt cabled Ottawa, requesting 1 or 2 Canadian battalions to reinforce the garrison of Hong Kong against the invading Japanese. Lt. Gen. Harry Crerar agreed to the request Oct. 2. On Oct. 27, two Canadian infantry battalions, the Winnipeg Grenadiers and the Royal Rifles, consisting of 1,975 men, sailed from Vancouver for Hong Kong to help defend the colony. The soldiers, not yet prepared for heavy combat, landed on the island Nov. 16. Fifty thousand combat-hardened Japanese troops were already stationed within 50 km of Hong Kong. The tragedy began Dec. 18.

Oct. 18 PM Mackenzie King broadcast his "Price Ceiling" speech on radio. The Wartime Prices and Trade Board imposed a general price ceiling on all goods, wages and services under the authority of the War Measures Act to combat wartime inflation.

Oct. 21 PM Mackenzie King met with a delegation from the Canadian Legion who argued for a "total war effort" that included conscription for overseas duty.

• After the BC provincial election, a coalition Liberal-Conservative govt took office, with John Hart (1879–1957) as premier.

Also in Oct.

• Vilhjalmur Stefansson was commissioned by the US govt to serve as consultant to Gen. Simon Bolivar Buckner, head of the Alaska Defence Command, on all aspects relating to military construction in the Arctic. The Canol project, a 1,000-km oil pipeline connecting NWT Norman Wells to refineries at Whitehorse, Yukon, was a result of Stefansson's involvement. The strategically located Canol Pipeline was built by the US army inland along difficult territory — away from potential sabotage by the Japanese. It was created to provide Canadian oil to the US war effort and ceased operations in Mar. 1945, after only 13 months' operation.

Nov. 7 Portia White (1911–1968), the great African-Canadian contralto from Truro, NS, sang at the Eaton Auditorium in Toronto after performing only 3 recitals before this date.

Nov.–Jan. 1942 Gold miners belonging to the International Union of Mine, Mill and Smelter Workers were on strike against 8 gold mines in the Kirkland L. region. Organized labour throughout Canada sympathized with the strikers, accusing PM King of ignoring the interests of labour during wartime.

Dec. 6 The federal govt passed the War Exchange Conservation Act, banning the importation of certain non-essential items from non-sterling countries.

• Camp X, the 1st WW II "Secret Agent Training School" in North America, was established along the shores of L. Ontario between Oshawa and Whitby. The camp was designed to connect Britain with the United States by developing and training all agents in every condition of silent killing, sabotage, partisan work, recruitment methods, demolition, map reading, weaponry and Morse code. William Stephenson, "the man named Intrepid," was an instructor. The camp was officially known by many different names: S25-1-1 by the RCMP, Project-J by the Canadian Military and STS-103 (Special Training School 103) by the SOE (Special Operations Executive.)

Dec. 7 Japan attacked the US naval base at Pearl Harbor. Nineteen ships were sunk or disabled, and

188 planes destroyed; 2,403 Americans were killed and 1,178 wounded. Shortly after, the Canadian govt ordered the confiscation of all Japanese-Canadian-owned fishing vessels, approximately 1,200.

• Japan also bombed the British colony of Hong Kong, as well as Singapore, Malaya, Thailand, the Philippines and several South Pacific islands.

• PM Mackenzie King completed formalities concerning Canada's declaration of war against Finland, Hungary and Romania.

• At 9:15 p.m., PM Mackenzie King signed an Order-in-Council recommending that King George VI declare Canada at war with Japan.

Dec. 8 Canada declared war on Japan.

Dec. 10 Louis Stephen St. Laurent (1882–1973) attended his 1st cabinet meeting. He was sworn in as minister of justice on Dec. 11. On Feb. 9, 1942, St. Laurent defeated Paul Bouchard by 4,000 votes in a by-election in the riding of Quebec East, Ernest Lapointe's former constituency. PM Mackenzie King had appointed Laurent to the cabinet after Lapointe's death in Nov. 1941, even before Laurent had won a seat in the House of Commons.

Dec. 15 Humphrey Mitchell (1894–1950), labour leader and politician, was sworn in as minister of labour after the Kirkland L. strike intensified union criticism of the federal govt.

Dec. 17 The Man. legislature unanimously passed a resolution calling on the federal govt to introduce conscription for overseas service.

Dec. 18 After a week of heavy bombardment, the Japanese landed on Hong Kong and then on the 19th overran Canadian headquarters, killing Brigadier J.K. Lawson. The ill-prepared and under-supplied Canadians fought valiantly, but were eventually overmatched by the highly under-estimated Japanese. On Dec. 22, the Winnipeg Grenadiers were driven out of Wong Nei Chong Gap. By Christmas Day, the Canadians were forced to sur-render: 290 Canadians were killed, 500 wounded; 264 would later die of abuse, disease and malnourish-ment in Japanese prison camps. Others would be forced into slave labour in Tokyo shipyards.

Dec. 24 Admiral Muselier of the Free French naval force engaged in convoy work in the western Atlantic, taking possession of St. Pierre and Miquelon from Vichy France. The islands lay only 20 km from the Burin Peninsula, Nfld.

Dec. 30 In the House of Commons in Ottawa, British PM Winston Churchill gave his famous "some chicken, some neck" speech, in response to German estimations that in 3 weeks, "England will have its neck wrung like a chicken." One of the best-known photographs of Churchill was later taken by Yousuf Karsh (1908–2002) and used on a Canadian postage stamp after the great statesman's death.

Also in Dec.
• Henry Crerar was appointed General Officer Commanding, I Canadian Corps, in the UK.

1941–2001 The number of farms in Canada dropped from 732,800 to 246,923. During the same period, the number of pigs increased from 6 million to 14 million, and the number of cattle from 8.4 million to 15.6 million.

Also in 1941
• The population of Canada was 11,506,655. The population of Ont. was 3,787,000; Que., 3,332,000; Sask., 895,000; BC, 817,000; Alb., 796,000; Man., 729,000; NS, 577,000; NB, 457,000; PEI, 95,000; and the Yukon and NWT, 16,000.

• The Canadian Women's Army Corps (CWAC) and a women's division of the RCAF were established to bring women into the armed forces in non-combat support functions. In 1942, the Women's Royal Canadian Naval Service was authorized for recruit-ment. Altogether, nearly 50,000 Canadian women volunteered for military service through these divisions by war's end in 1945.

• Corporate and personal income taxes fluctuated under federal authority to help finance the war effort. The govt also introduced an excess-profits tax and succession duties.

• A small British-Canadian force sailed to Spits-bergen Is., north of the Arctic Circle, to destroy radio and meteorological stations and coal supplies to prevent their falling into German hands.

• Hugh MacLennan (1907–1990) published *Barometer Rising*, based on the explosion of the *Mont Blanc* munitions ship in Halifax Harbour on Dec. 6, 1917.

• Lawren Harris completed the abstract canvas *Composition No. I*, now at the Vancouver Art Gallery.

• Montreal-born artist Louise Gadbois (1896–1988) completed the portrait *Le Père Marie-Alain Couturier*, now in the Musée du Québec, Quebec City.

• Que.-born artist Jean-Paul Lemieux (1904– 1990) completed the allegorical painting *Lazarus*, now in the Art Gallery of Ont., Toronto.

• Emily Carr published her 1st book, *Klee Wyck*, which won a Gov-Gen.'s Award for non-fiction. Much like her painting, her writings provided a highly visual interpretation of West Coast life.

• Robert Charbonneau (1911–1967) published *Ils Posséderont la Terre*, a psychological novel about the quest for self.

• Sinclair Ross published his 1st novel, *As For Me and My House*, a classic portrayal of life in a small prairie town during the droughts of 1930.

• Alan Sullivan (Sinclair Murray) (1868–1947) published the historical novel *Three Came to Ville Marie*.

• Poet E.J. Pratt published *Dunkirk*.

1942

Jan. 1 Canada was one of 26 nations to sign "The Declaration by United Nations" in Washington, D. C., pledging support to the Atlantic Charter and committing to the full use of resources against the Axis Powers (Germany, Italy, Japan). The Atlantic Charter was the 1st to officially use the term "United Nations." The term would later be used loosely throughout the war until the UN was officially established June 26, 1945.

Jan. 13 "Operation Drumbeat" (Paukenschlag), Germany's 1st strategic offensive against North America, began. The operation resulted in the sinking of over 300 Allied vessels by U-boats along North American coast.

Jan. 22 The 3rd session of the 19th Parliament met until Jan. 27, 1943. The Speech from the Throne announced that a plebiscite would be held Apr. 27 to determine whether the Canadian people would release the govt from its pledge not to introduce conscription for overseas duty.

Feb. 26 Under the War Measures Act, Minister of Justice Louis St. Laurent ordered the confiscation of Japanese-Canadian property and the removal of 22,000 Japanese-Canadians living within 160 km of the West Coast to inland concentration camps. The removal was complete Sept. 31.

Mar. 24 Canadian Pacific Airlines Ltd. was established through the amalgamation of 10 Northern bush-plane operators. The Vancouver airline began regular transcontinental flights in 1958.

Apr. 1 Gasoline rationing came into effect.

Apr. 6 Nearly 170,000 men were organized into 2 corps as the 1st Canadian Army, falling under the command of Gen. Andrew McNaughton.

Apr. 27 A national plebiscite asking the public to release the federal govt from "any past commitments restricting the methods of raising men for military service" was supported by 64% in English Canada, and opposed by 72% in Que.

May 11 The Battle of the St. Lawrence began when a German submarine *U-553* torpedoed the British Steamer *Nicoya* and the Dutch freighter *Leto* in the St. Lawrence R., near Anticosti Is.

May 12 Clarence Decatur Howe became acting minister of transport upon the resignation of Pierre Joseph Arthur Cardin (1879–1946) over the cabinet's agreement to introduce Bill 80, which would repeal Section 3 of the National Resources Mobilization Act, and allow conscription for overseas service.

May 13 PM Mackenzie King invited Louis St. Laurent into the War Committee.

May 28 The Dominion-Provincial Taxation Agreement Act, 1942, was passed as a war measure.

June 3–4 The Japanese attacked Dutch Harbor in Alaska's Aleutian Islands.

June 5 Chief Justice Lyman Duff's (1865–1955) Report to Parliament on the Hong Kong incident exonerated the federal govt of any error in judgment in sending the ill-prepared Royal Rifles and Winnipeg Grenadiers to unsuccessfully defend the British colony in 1941 (Dec. 19). The 1-man Royal Commission was referred to as the Duff Commission. It would be criticized July 13 by George Drew (1894–1973) for improper use of evidence to exonerate the govt of blame in the tragedy.

June 10 PM King opened debate in the House on the amendment of the National Resources Mobilization Act, exclaiming, "Conscription if necessary, but not necessarily conscription."

June 15 PM King 1st learned about research into the atomic bomb (the Manhattan Project) during an interview with British Commissioner Malcolm MacDonald and 2 scientists from England, Professor G.P. Thompson and Michael Perrin, who inquired about "the acquisition of some property in Canada, so as to prevent competition in price on the mineral much needed in connection with the manufacture of explosives…a military weapon of immense destructive force."

June 20 A Japanese submarine, *I-26*, shelled Estevan Point on Vancouver Is., hurling approximately 30, 55-in shells at a wireless station and lighthouse, but causing no damage or casualties.

June 25 PM King arrived in Washington to join President Franklin D. Roosevelt and PM Winston Churchill at a meeting of the Pacific Council.

July 3 The Canada-US joint military, naval and air staff was formed at Washington, D.C.

July 20 The Veterans' Land Act was passed, enabling ex-servicemen to purchase land with a small down payment and a govt loan. Additional funds were made available for livestock and equipment.

July 23 Bill 80, an amendment to the National Resources Mobilization Act, which allowed the govt to conscript Canadians for overseas service, passed 3rd reading by a large majority.

July 24 The Canadian warship *Ste. Croix* sank the German submarine *U-90* in the mid-Atlantic.

Aug. 5–10 Eleven ships in the protection of a Canadian convoy were sunk by German U-boats in the Atlantic.

Aug. 19 Canadian troops from 7 regiments of the 2nd Division, under the command of Maj.-Gen. J.H. Roberts (1891–1963), raided the German-fortified French port of Dieppe. Canadians formed about 5,000 of the 6,000 attacking force; the others were British, American and Free French commandos. The attack was ill prepared and ill supported: 907 Canadians were killed, 1,946 were taken prisoner. Of the 582 members of the Royal Hamilton Light Infantry who took part in the battle, 197 were killed and 175 were taken prisoner. Two Canadians won the Victoria Cross for valour that day: Capt. John Weir Foote (1904–1988) of the Canadian Chaplain's Service, who spent 8 hours dragging wounded men from the line of fire, then allowed himself to be taken prisoner so he could aid his fellow POWs; and Lt-Col Charles Cecil Merritt (1913–1990), who despite being wounded, led 4 parties across a bridge that was heavily covered by enemy machine-gun fire, toward successful attacks on the deadly German pillboxes.

Sept. 5–7 A group of Conservatives met at Port Hope, Ont., to draw up a future party program called the "Report of the Round Table on Canadian Policy," which included a liberal code for labour, a long-range, low-cost housing plan and an extensive social security program. The party would become the Progressive Conservative Party.

Sept. 9 The Canadian War Cabinet closed the St. Lawrence to all Allied shipping.

Sept. 14 The Canadian destroyer *Ottawa* was lost in the North Atlantic after it was torpedoed while on convoy duty.

Also in Sept.

• The Bloc Populaire Canadien, a federal and Que. provincial political movement, was formed in reaction to the National Resources Mobilization Amendment Act (Bill 80), which removed a ban on conscription for overseas military service.

• Because of German submarine activity in the Gulf of St. Lawrence, the National Defence Headquarters raised a reserve army to serve in the Gaspé Peninsula under the command of Brig. Gen. Georges-Philéas Vanier (1888–1967).

Oct. 11 The RCMP patrol vessel *St. Roch*, commanded by Sergeant Henry Larsen, arrived at Sydney, NS, with a crew of 8, after completing the 1st crossing of the Northwest Passage from west to east. The *St. Roch* had left Vancouver in June 1940. It is now on display at the Vancouver Marine Museum.

Oct. 14 A German U-boat sank the ferry SS *Caribou* in Cabot Str., taking 137 lives.

Oct. 21 Gordon Daniel Conant (1885–1953) succeeded Mitchell Frederick Hepburn (1896–1953) as Liberal premier of Ont.

Oct. 23 Commonwealth forces, under Gen. Bernard Montgomery, opened a counter offensive at El Alamein, 120 km west of Alexandria in North Africa, against Field Marshal Erwin Rommel (the Desert Fox).

Oct. 30 German U-boats destroyed 15 ships in a convoy under Canadian protection in the Gulf of St. Lawrence.

Nov. 6 German secret agent Werner Janowski was landed at the Gaspé town of New Carlisle, Que., by the German submarine *U-518*. He was captured Nov. 9 by the RCMP and charged with spying. Janowski later became an RCMP double agent.

Nov. 9 Canada severed diplomatic relations with Vichy France.

Nov. 20 The $148 million (US) Alaska Highway (dubbed the Alaska-Canada Military Highway, or Alcan) was opened. It stretched 2,451 km from Dawson Creek, BC, to Fairbanks, Alaska, over 1,900 km of which were in Canadian territory. The road was built and maintained by the US military as a land route connecting Alaska to the lower mainland states in the event of a Japanese invasion of North America. It would become a permanent year-round road in 1943.

Nov. 30 CCF candidate Stanley Howard Knowles (1908–1997) won the Winnipeg constituency in a federal by-election.

Dec. 9 Arthur Meighen resigned the leadership of the Conservative party and retired from politics.

Dec. 9–11 The Progressive Conservative Party, modelling its platform on the Sept. 5–7 Port Hope "Round Table" report, was launched at its Winnipeg convention under the leadership of John Bracken (1883–1969), progressive premier of Man. The platform supported Compulsory National Selective Service, full employment through individual initiative and enterprise, free of bureaucratic controls, and a social security program that included unemployment and retirement insurance, low-cost housing and slum clearance. Bracken was elected new leader on the 2nd ballot, 3rd was Prince Albert, Sask., lawyer John George Diefenbaker (1895–1979).

Dec. 10 The shackling of war prisoners in Canada was officially stopped.

Dec. 12 A fire killed 99 people at a Knights of Columbus hostel barn-dance celebration in St. John's, Nfld.

Dec. 15 An Order-in-Council prohibited the advertising of liquor throughout the duration of the war and restricted its sale to 8 hours a day. On Feb. 19, 1943, an Order-in-Council prohibiting liquor advertising was amended to permit public relations advertising by brewers and distillers.

Dec. 21 Butter rationing was introduced.

Dec. 26–30 A huge pack of U-boats attacked a convoy of 44 merchantmen and their Canadian escorts, destroying 16 ships in Canadian waters.

Also in 1942

• The US govt's Manhattan Project, designed to produce an atomic bomb for the war effort before either Germany or Japan, spurred growth of the uranium industry in Canada. As a result, Canadian-based Eldorado Gold Mines re-opened uranium mines near Great Bear L.

• The Canadian govt began to issue ration books with coupons for fixed amounts of butter, meat, tea, coffee and other commodities. Every family received 1 ration book per month. Over 11 million ration books were distributed over the war.

• Dunn's Pavilion, now known as the Kee to Bala, opened at Bala, in the heart of Ont.'s Muskoka country. One of North America's premier summer dance halls, the Pavilion attracted hundreds each night who arrived by train, canoe and cedar-strip motorboat to dance to bands such as the Dorsey Brothers, Les Elgart, Duke Ellington, Count Basie, Guy Lombardo, Les Brown, the Glenn Miller Orchestra and Woody Herman. When Louis Armstrong played the Pavilion in 1962, an estimated 1,000 who could not get in listened from boats on Bala Bay.

• The number of immigrant arrivals was 7,576 — the lowest since 1860.

• D'Alton Corey Coleman (1879–1956) became president of the CPR.

• The 1st unemployment cheques were issued. Singles could receive up to $14.40 per week; those with dependents could receive up to $18.30 per week.

• The Beauharnois Hydroelectric Station on the St. Lawrence became operative.

• Ten squadrons were added to the RCAF, and a Canadian bomber group was established.

• The Polymer Corp. was formed as a Crown corporation, producing synthetic rubber from oil to compensate for an acute, wartime shortage of natural rubber. Polymer would produce its 1st artificial rubber in Sarnia, Ont., in 1943.

• Japanese-Canadian Rokosoke Maeda (1889–1970), renowned wood-duck carver known for his cedar-hewn mallards and pintails, was interned. His possessions were confiscated and sold, including a classic string of 50 hand-carved birds.

• Montrealer George "Buzz" Beurling (1921–1948) shot down 15 enemy aircraft while serving with the RAF in Malta. By war's end, the flying ace shot down 32 enemy aircraft while flying for both the RAF and RCAF.

• Emily Carr painted *Cedar*, now at the Vancouver Art Gallery. She also published *The Book of Small*, about her childhood.

• LeMoine FitzGerald painted *Green Self-portrait*, on canvas, now in the Winnipeg Art Gallery.

• Alfred Pellan completed the abstract painting *Le Couteau à pain*, now in a private collection.

• Jack Nichols (b 1921) painted *Sick Boy with Glass*, now in the Art Gallery of Ont., Toronto.

• Stephen Leacock published *My Remarkable Uncle*.

• William Bruce Hutchinson published *The Unknown Country: Canada and Her People*, which won the Gov-Gen.'s Award.

• Alfred Earle Birney (1904–1995) published *David and Other Poems*, which won the Gov-Gen.'s Award.

• Poet Anne Hébert (1916-2000) published her 1st collection of poetry, *Les Songes en équilibre*, which was awarded the Prix David.

• The Dairy Farmers Association of Canada was founded.

1943

Jan. 1 An RCAF bomber group based in England went into operation.

Jan. 8 Stewart Sinclair Garson (1898–1977) succeeded John Bracken as premier of Man.

Jan. 19 Princess Juliana of the Netherlands, who had arrived in Canada after fleeing the Nazi occupation, gave birth to her third child, Margriet, in Ottawa's Civic Hospital. The birth room was temporarily — and officially — ruled Dutch soil so the child would remain a true Dutch heiress. In June 1946, Queen Juliana sent 20,000 tulips to Canada as a gift of appreciation for receiving her in exile during the war. The gift became an annual tradition.

Jan. 28 The 4th session of the 19th Parliament met until Jan. 26, 1944. The Speech from the Throne announced "a charter of social security for the whole of Canada."

Feb. 22 The corvette *Weyburn* sunk after hitting a mine off Gibralter.

Also in Feb.

• Child prodigy André Mathieu (1929–1968), dubbed the "Quebec Mozart," completed his *Concerto de Quebec (Symphonie romantique pour piano et orchestra)*, at the age of 13. Born in Montreal to musical parents, Mathieu composed his 1st works at age 4. He debuted on CBC radio in 1936, when he played his *Concertino No. 1* to a national audience. His symphonic poem *Mistassini* was written in 1954. Mathieu's adult life was deeply troubled. He became an alcoholic, abandoned his career as a performer and died in poverty at age 39, having left a legacy of over 200 compositions.

Mar. 2 Income tax was put on a pay-as-you-earn basis, with the imposition of the 1st deductions-at-source.

Also in Mar.

• The Atlantic Convoy Conference met at Washington, D.C., and established the Canadian North-West Command, giving the RCN responsibility for convoys in the western Atlantic north of New York.

• The *Report on Social Security for Canadians*, prepared by Leonard Charles Marsh (1906–1982) for the Committee of Reconstruction, was published. It called for a comprehensive national social security system guaranteeing provisions in old age, sickness, maternity and disability.

• Hutterites and enemy aliens could no longer buy or lease land under a new amendment to Alb.'s Land Sales Prohibition Act.

Apr. 1 The federal govt began to pay the full cost of maintaining the RCAF overseas.

Apr. 30 Rear Admiral Leonard Warren Murray (1896–1971) took over as C-in-C of the Canadian Northwest Atlantic, with headquarters in Halifax.

May 17–18 International delegates, including Lester Bowles Pearson (1897–1972) representing Canada, left Washington, D.C., for the 1st formal United Nations conference held in West Virginia. On the 18th, a continuing interim commission was set up to carry on the work and to draw up detailed plans for a permanent international body. The UN would not be officially established until 1945.

May 18 PM King arrived in Washington for a meeting of the Pacific Council. British PM Winston Churchill was also in Washington for the Conference. On the 19th, Lord Cherwell briefed PM King on atomic energy experiments.

May 23 Alb. Social Credit premier William Aberhart died in Vancouver, BC. He was succeeded by Ernest Charles Manning (1908–1996), who served from May 31 to Dec. 12, 1968.

May 26 A Que. law was passed stipulating free and compulsory education.

June 5 Johnny Longden (1907-2003) rode Count Fleet to a Belmont Stakes triumph, becoming the 1st Canadian to win American horse racing's Triple Crown (Belmont, Preakness and Kentucky Derby). Over his career, Longden had 32,413 mounts and 6,032 winners. He was also the only person to win the Kentucky Derby as both a jockey and a trainer.

June 18 At a War Committee meeting, PM Mackenzie King opposed a Canadian navy policy refusing acceptance of French-speaking recruits who could not speak English, and ordered that "the minutes record the fact that any practice of the kind was opposite to the policy of the govt, and should not be countenanced for a moment longer."

Also in June

• Soong Mei-ling, wife of Chinese general Chiang Kai-shek, addressed both Houses of Parliament in Ottawa to enlist support for China against Japan.

July 3 Mohawk-Algonquin Kateri Tekakwitha (1656–1680) became the 1st Native person declared venerable by the Roman Catholic church. Tekakwitha was beatified by Pope John Paul II on June 22, 1980. She is buried near La Prairie, Que.

July 10 The Canadian Infantry Division and the 1st Canadian Army Tank Brigade landed on Sicily as part of the main invasion armada of 3,000 ships. Three Canadian bomber squadrons and No. 417 Squadron, RCAF, supported the ground troops in Sicily and in the subsequent Italian campaign.

After landing at Pachino, the Canadians took 5 towns before going into reserve Aug. 6. The conquest of Sicily was completed with the capture of Messina, Aug. 17.

July 22 The BNA Act, 1943, provided for representation in the House of Commons to remain unadjusted until war's end even though western provinces suffered a population reduction during the war and, accordingly, their representation should have been reduced.

July 24 The Italian govt of Benito Mussolini was deposed.

Aug. 4 The Conservatives under George Drew (1894–1973) won the Ont. provincial election. The CCF became the official opposition. Rae Luckock (1893–1972) and Agnes MacPhail became the 1st women elected to the Ont. legislature.

Aug. 9 Labour Progressive (Communist) Party member Fred Rose (1907–1983) was elected MP in a by-election for the Montreal riding of Cartier.

Aug. 10–24 Churchill, Roosevelt and Mackenzie King attended the 6th Anglo-American War Conference (1st Que. Conference) in Quebec City. They reaffirmed the principle of nuclear collaboration.

Aug. 15 Fifty-three hundred Canadians of the 13th Canadian Infantry Brigade and the 1st Special Service Force landed on Kiska Is., in the Aleutians, to discover that Japanese occupiers had slipped away.

Aug. 16 A strike that began Aug. 3 between members of the International Association of Machinists (IAM) and Fairfield Aircraft, in Montreal, was settled as the employer met workers' wage demands.

Aug. 25 US President Franklin Roosevelt visited Ottawa, the 1st US president to visit Canada's capital.

Sept. 3 Allied forces crossed the Straits of Messina to mainland Italy. After pushing to Potenza, the 1st Canadian Brigade occupied Campobassa on Oct. 14, while the 2nd Brigade took Vinchiatro on Oct. 15. Canadian tanks supported British units in the attack on Termoli on the Adriatic coast. From the Moro R., the Canadians pushed through San Leonardo toward Ortona.

Sept. 8 Italy surrendered to the Allies. German and Fascist supporters continued to fight.

Sept. 20 The Canadian destroyer *Ste. Croix* was sunk by enemy U-boats in the North Atlantic: 148 died in the attacks, including PM Mackenzie King's nephew. Eighty-one *Ste. Croix* crew members were rescued by the destroyer HMS *Itchen*, which was also carrying crew from the torpedoed corvette *Polymanthus*. The *Itchen* was then torpedoed Sept. 23, and sank in minutes. In all, there were only 3 survivors, one from each of the three lost Canadian ships.

Sept. 27 Private trading in wheat was suspended to curb rising prices and speculation on the Winnipeg Grain Exchange. The Canadian Wheat Board became the sole agent of Canadian wheat.

Oct. 14 The Canada Medal was approved by King George VI and the Canadian cabinet. It was the 1st distinctly Canadian decoration, although it was never awarded.

Oct. 19 An RCAF Liberator bomber crashed near St-Donat, Que., killing 24. The wreckage was not found until June 1946.

Oct. 22–23 A German submarine crew from *U-537* landed an automatic weather station at Martin Bay, Labrador, which transmitted data to the Germans for an estimated 3 months.

Nov. 9 Canada signed the United Nations Relief and Rehabilitation Agreement, known as UNRRA.

Dec. 20 Canadians arrived at the outskirts of Ortona, Italy. The Battle for Ortona began the next day, as Canadian troops engaged German troops in close-quarter street fighting. The Canadians entered Ortona on Dec. 27: 1,372 men of the 1st Division lost their lives in the battle.

Also in 1943
• *Bomb Aimer, C. Charlie Battle of the Ruhr,* watercolour by RCAF war artist Carl Fellman Schaefer (1903–1995) was completed. The work is a

haunting depiction of war as seen through the nose of an RCAF Halifax Mk. III.

• Edwin Holgate (1892–1977) completed *Stephen Leacock*, in oil.

• Goodridge Roberts painted *Nude*, now in the National Gallery of Canada.

• Marian Scott (1906–1993) completed the acclaimed abstract, *Atom, Bone and Embryo*, now at the Art Gallery of Ont., Toronto.

• Robert "Scottie" Wilson (1890–1972) completed the painting *The Bird Head-Dress*, now in the National Gallery of Canada.

• *At the Long Sault and Other New Poems*, by Archibald Lampman (1861–1899), with a foreword by his friend Duncan Campbell Scott, was posthumously published.

• *Adagio*, a collection of stories by Félix Leclerc (1914–1988), was published.

• Edward Killoran Brown (1905–1951) published his influential study *On Canadian Poetry*.

• *News of the Phoenix and Other Poems*, by Arthur James Marshall Smith (1902–1980), was published. It was his 1st collection, and received the Gov-Gen.'s Award for poetry. He also published *A Book of Canadian Poetry*.

• John Sutherland (1919–1956) started *First Statement*, the 1st literary journal to publish Montreal poets.

1944

Jan. 2 Canadian Army Routine Order, 1944, required that the Canadian Red Ensign be flown at all units of the Canadian army serving with the forces of other nations.

Jan. 5 Senior puisne justice of the Supreme Court, Thibaudeau Rinfret (1879–1962), was appointed chief justice, succeeding Sir Lyman Duff.

Jan. 11 The King cabinet agreed to the establishment of 3 new departments: Reconstruction, Veterans Affairs, and National Health and Welfare. Ministerial appointments for the departments were made Oct. 13.

Jan. 12 The Hon. Leighton Goldie McCarthy (1869–1952) became Canada's 1st ambassador to the United States.

Jan. 15 The 1st issue of the Canadian army newspaper the *Maple Leaf* was distributed to Canadian troops in Italy. The paper would include cartoon character "Herbie" (created by William G. "Bing" Coughlin), which was so identified with the typical Canadian private that Canadian soldiers came to be known as "Herbies."

Feb. 10 The Mackenzie King govt announced its policy of removing Canadian air squadrons from mixed squadrons, making it known that Canada planned to control its own air force and decide for itself what contribution it would make toward the Japanese war.

Feb. 17 Wartime Order-in-Council P.C. 1003 was passed, establishing the National War Labour Relations Board and collective-bargaining measures to ensure labour conflict would not hamper the war effort.

Mar. 19 Contralto Portia White made her New York City debut at Town Hall to great acclaim. The performance led to a contract with Columbia Concerts Inc. of New York, the largest entertainment agency in North America.

Mar. 20 Lt-Gen. Henry Duncan Graham Crerar's (1888–1965) appointment to C-in-C of the 1st Canadian Army became effective. He replaced Gen. Andrew McNaughton. The 1st Canadian Army was the largest field formation ever formed in Canada, and included British, Dutch, Belgian and Polish units.

Mar. 28 Humorist Stephen Leacock died of cancer in Toronto. The Stephen Leacock Memorial Medal for Humour has been awarded each year since 1947 in his honour. Leacock was also a well-respected political economist, who once wrote, that "socialism won't work except in Heaven where they don't need it and in Hell where they already have it."

Apr. 14 The Crown corporation Quebec Hydro-Electric Commission, now Hydro-Quebec, was created as the Que. govt expropriated Montreal Light, Heat and Power Consolidated and its subsidiary, Beauharnois Light, Heat and Power Company. Ownership and administration of the 2 companies was transferred to Quebec Hydro-Electric Commission.

Apr. 29 The Royal Canadian Tribal Class Destroyer *Athabaskan* was destroyed by enemy U-boats just days after it, and destroyers *Huron* and *Haida*, sank the German destroyer *T-29,* off the coast of Brittany. The Captain and 128 men perished, 83 were taken prisoner by the Germans.

May 1 The meeting of Commonwealth PMs opened at 10 Downing St., London, with PMs Churchill, Mackenzie King, John Curtin of Australia, Peter Fraser of New Zealand, and J.C. Smuts of South Africa in attendance.

May 11 A UAW strike against Ford Motor Company of Windsor, Ont., was settled after the National War Labour Relations Board vowed to clarify grievance procedures. The strike began Apr. 20 and was fought over diverging grievance-procedure interpretations.

• In a speech delivered to the British Parliament, PM Mackenzie King advocated for a decentralized, laissez-faire empire, not a centralized organization as envisaged by Lord Halifax, British ambassador to Washington, in his speech in Toronto, Jan. 24.

May 23–31 The 1st Canadian Corps broke through the Hitler Line across the Liri Valley, near Casino.

June 6 The Allied forces landed on the Normandy beaches in *Operation Overlord*. A Canadian parachute battalion was part of the advance landing. The 3rd Canadian Infantry Division, 2nd Canadian Armoured Brigade and 1st Canadian Parachute Battalion landed on the beaches at Courselles, St. Aubin and Bernières-sur-Mer, between British and American forces. The 1st objective of the Canadians and British was the town of Caen, which was taken on July 9.

June 15 The CCF won the Sask. provincial election. Thomas Clement Douglas (1904–1986) became premier. The Sask. CCF was the 1st socialist provincial govt in Canada.

June 23 Canadian nurses of Number 10 Canadian Gen. Hospital Royal Canadian Army Medical Corps landed at Arromanches, France.

• In Normandy, Canadian forces began to fight as a separate army.

June 25 Montreal's Canadian Black Watch regiment battled Germans at Verrieres Ridge, France. The regiment was virtually destroyed. At battle's end, only 15 members of the regiment survived.

June 28–29 No. 6 (RCAF) Bomber Group made night attacks on Hamburg, Germany.

June 30 Canada attended the United Nations Monetary and Financial Conference at Bretton Woods, New Hampshire. The result was the establishment of the International Monetary Fund (IMF) in 1945, an international body organized to fix international exchange rates and prevent financial collapse such as that in 1929, which led to the Depression and eventually world war.

June 31 Germans were driven from Normandy by Allied forces.

Summer–Fall André Breton (1896–1966), founder of the Surrealist movement in France, lived for 3 months in a cabin in Sainte-Agathe, Que., at the tip of Gaspé near Percé Rock. There, he wrote the brilliant *Arcane 17*.

July 24 Soviet soldiers were the 1st Allies to witness a Nazi concentration camp — Majdanek — as they moved into Lublin, Poland.

Aug. 1 The Family Allowance Act was passed, providing monthly payments to parents and guardians of children under the age of 16. It was Canada's 1st universal welfare program, and began July 1, 1945.

Aug. 8 The Union Nationale under Maurice Duplessis returned to power in the Que. provincial election.

Aug. 17 The 1st Canadian Army took Falaise, completing a pincer movement of the Allied forces that caught the Germans in the Falaise Gap.

The battle for Normandy was won, at a cost of 5,000 Canadian lives.

Aug. 18 Former Montreal mayor Camillien Houde was released from 4 years of confinement for his opposition to conscription, and welcomed home by a throng of 50,000 Montrealers.

Aug. 21 The Dumbarton Oaks talks officially began in Washington, D.C., and extended to Sept. 27. The talks focused on the establishment of the UN as a permanent international organization.

Aug. 23–24 Paris was liberated by Allied forces. On Sept. 16, Canada recognized the provisional govt of the French Republic.

Aug. 30–Sept. 3 Canadian soldiers played a leading role in breaking through the German Gothic Line, north of Florence, along Italy's Foglia R. Canadians entered the Po Valley, as the Allies fought the Germans up the boot of Italy.

Sept. 1 The 1st Canadian Army liberated Dieppe.

Sept. 11–16 Allied leaders (Churchill, King and Roosevelt) met at the Château Frontenac for the 2nd Que. Conference, to discuss war strategy in Europe and Japan, and the future of Germany.

Sept. 18 In Toronto, sports entrepreneur and WW I veteran Conn Smyth (1985–1980) suggested that the Zombies — troops conscripted for home defence under the National Resource Mobilization Act (1940) — be sent overseas and put into combat. Canadians had suffered heavy losses during the Normandy invasion (Aug. 17).

• Coffee and tea rationing ended.

Also in Sept.
• A riot occured in Moose Jaw between airmen and local youth.

Oct. 1–Nov. 8 Canadians fought in the Battle of the Scheldt to destroy German defences along the Scheldt R. estuary in Holland and Belgium and open the port of Antwerp for Allied shipping. As part of the liberation of the Netherlands, the 3rd Canadian Infantry Division cleared the South Bank of the Scheldt, while the 2nd Canadian Infantry Division cleared the north bank. There were 6,367 total Canadian casualties during the battle. It was the last major campaign before the ground assault on the Rhineland. On Nov. 8, Canadian and British troops overcame German strongholds at Beveland Isthmus and Walcheren in Holland, ending the Battle of the Scheldt.

Oct. 7 Canadians took part in the largest-single air raid of the war, bombing the German industrial city of Dortmund.

Oct. 13 Brian Brooke Claxton (1898–1960) was sworn into office as Canada's 1st minister of National Health and Welfare; Ian Mackenzie (1890–1949) was appointed to the new portfolio of Veteran's Affairs; and C.D. Howe accepted the post of minister of Reconstruction.

Oct. 16 The RCMP vessel *St. Roch*, under the command of Sgt. Randy Larsen, arrived at Vancouver after crossing the Northwest Passage for the 2nd time, this time from Halifax. The crossing took 86 days.

Oct. 19 Minister of Defence James Ralston met in cabinet and announced that the war would not come to an end in 1944 and that an additional 15,000 well-trained infantrymen would be needed within 2 months. Ralston argued that conscripts for home service must be sent to the European theatre. The announcement touched off the conscription crisis of 1944.

Nov. 2 James Ralston resigned as minister of national defence over the issue of conscription for overseas service. He was replaced by Gen. Andrew McNaughton.

Nov. 8 PM Mackenzie King, in a radio address to the nation, appealed to conscripted soldiers, Canada's home-defence forces, to volunteer for overseas duty.

Nov. 20 Finance Minister James L. Ilsley, Defence Minister for Naval Services Angus L. Macdonald, and Minister of Mines and Resources Thomas A. Crerar threatened to resign if conscription for overseas duty was not introduced.

Nov. 21 Crerar was promoted to full general. He commanded the field army throughout the Northwest Europe campaign.

Nov. 22 PM Mackenzie King, under pressure of pro-conscriptionist ministers, announced that conscripts would be sent overseas for duty. On Nov. 23, an Order-in-Council was tabled, authorizing the dispatch of 16,000 conscripts to Europe.

Nov. 25 Maj-Gen. George Randolph Pearkes (1888–1984) reported to Ottawa that 1,600 NRMA men in Terrace, BC, had seized control of their training camp because of the decision to send conscripts overseas.

Nov. 28 The Port of Antwerp was secured and opened to Allied use.

Also in Nov.

• Gen. Charles Foulkes (1903–1969) assumed command of the 1st Canadian Corps in Italy, and Northwest Europe in 1945.

Dec. 6 Justice Minister Louis St. Laurent, in a speech to Parliament, gave support to overseas conscription despite volatile opposition in Que.

Dec. 9 The Académie canadienne-française was founded by a group of writers led by Victor Barbeau (1896–1994) to support French language and culture in Canada.

Dec. 11 Camillien Houde was re-elected mayor of Montreal for the 5th time.

Also in 1944

• Conscription was extended to Chinese-Canadians.

• The RCAF Squadron commanded by Russell Bannock (b 1919) shot down 82 German V–1 flying "buzz bombs" over England and the English Channel.

• The book publisher's division of the Toronto Board of Trade released *Report on Canada Book Trade*, the 1st of several surveys on the problems in Canadian publishing.

• Canadians were prohibited by law from moving to certain overpopulated cities, including Victoria, Vancouver, New Westminster, Hamilton, Toronto, Ottawa, and Hull, without prior permission.

• Some 342 million board ft of sitka spruce were shipped out of BC mills for the war effort, much of it used by De Havilland and other aircraft manufacturers.

• Halifax-born immunologist Oswald Avery (1877–1955), with colleagues Colin McLeod and Maclyn McCarty at the Rockefeller Institute in Manhattan, 1st recognized that DNA, not protein, was the controlling molecule of life. Avery's conclusions revolutionized 20th-century science and led to the birth of a new field of study, molecular biology.

• Lawren P. Harris, the son of Group of Seven founder, Lawren Harris, painted *Tank Advance in Italy*, oil on canvas, while serving in the Canadian Forces as an official war artist. The painting is now in the Canadian War Museum, Ottawa.

• Hugh Garner (1913–1979) published *Storm Below*, a novel set over 6 days on a Canadian corvette.

• Gwethalyn Graham (1913–1965) published the novel *Earth and High Heaven*, about family life and anti-semitism in wartime Montreal.

• Frederick Philip Grove published the novel *The Master of the Mill*, a story about workers and industrial capitalism.

• Roger Lemelin (1919–1992) published his satirical account of working-class Quebec City life *Au pied de la pente douce*, translated as *The Town Below*.

• Poet Dorothy Livesay (1909–1996) published *Day and Night*, for which she received the Gov-Gen.'s Award. She would win again for poetry with *Poems of the People,* in 1947.

• Patricia Kathleen Page (b 1916) published her 1st novel, the romantic *The Sun and the Moon*, written under the pseud. Judith Cape.

• Yves Thériault (1915–1983) published his 1st book, *Contes pour un homme seul.*

• *Allegro*, a collection of fables by Félix Leclerc was published.

• Ronald Hambleton (b 1917) edited the poetry anthology *Unit of Five*.

• A.M. Klein published *Poems and The Hitleriad*.

• Poet Alain Grandbois published *Îles de la nuit*.

1945

Jan. The federal govt agreed to furnish about 18,000 troops and 13 air squadrons to the British occupation zone in Germany, but declined to extend their stay beyond the 1st period of occupation.

Feb. 8 The 1st Canadian Army under Gen. Crerar attacked German positions in the Reichwald as part of *Operation Veritable*. On Feb. 21, Canadians reached Goch, cracking the Seigfried Line, the main German defence line. On Mar. 10, they reached the Rhine opposite Wesel, having lost 5,304 soldiers. On Mar. 24, Allied forces, including Canadians, crossed the Rhine R.

Mar. 3 Victoria, BC, painter and writer Emily Carr, who was given her 1st solo exhibition at age 67, and began writing at age 70, died in a Victoria nursing home. She was 74.

Mar. 18 The Montreal Canadiens' Maurice Richard became the 1st NHL player to score 50 goals in 50 games.

Apr. 2 The Canadian army was united in Holland.

Apr. 25 Representatives from Canada and 50 other nations met in San Francisco for the United Nations Conference on International Organization. A 111-article UN Charter was drawn, and unanimously adopted June 26.

Apr. 28 A truce was arranged between Canadian and German forces in Holland.

Apr. 29 Hitler shot himself in a Berlin bunker as Russian troops entered the city.

May 2 Fighting ended in Italy.

May 4 The 1st Canadian Parachute Battalion met Russian troops at Wiemar, Germany.

May 5 German forces surrendered in the Canadian sector near Wilhelmshaven, Aurich, and Emden.

May 7 Germany surrendered to the Allies. Alfred Jodl, German C-in-C, signed the terms of unconditional surrender in a French school house at Rheims, France.

• Riots broke out in Halifax. About 10,000 servicemen looted and vandalized the city's downtown.

May 8 Victory in Europe Day (V-E Day).

May 18 PM Mackenzie King announced in Edmonton, Alb. that 43,500 Canadian soldiers would begin operations against Japan.

May 22 Japanese incendiary "balloon bombs" were found in western Canada.

June 4 Ont. premier George Alexander Drew (1894–1973) led the Tories to victory in the provincial election, winning 66 of 90 seats.

• A photo of Regina's Mary Baker (1919-2003) in a familiar catcher's stance was featured in *Life* magazine. Baker was a star infielder for the South Bend (Indiana) Blue Sox, and the most identifiable player in the All-American Girls Professional Baseball League (A-AGPBL, 1943–1954). Actor Geena Davis played a fictionalized version of Baker in the Hollywood film, *A League of their Own*. In all, 64 of the 600 women who played in the A-AGPBL were Canadian, half of whom came from Sask.

June 11 Mackenzie King's Liberals won the federal election taking 125 seats. The Conservatives took 67, the CCF 28, Social Credit 13, and independents and other parties 12. Voter turnout was 75.3%.

June 26 Canada became a founding member of the United Nations (UN) as PM Mackenzie King and Minister of Justice Louis St. Laurent, along with delegates from 50 other nations, signed the UN Charter in Herbst Theatre, San Francisco. The charter was officially ratified Oct. 24, and the League of Nations replaced by the United Nations.

July 4 Canadian troops, drawn from the Loyal Edmonton Regiment, Les Fusiliers Mont-Royal, and the Argyll and Southerland Highlanders of Canada, entered Berlin to serve with the other occupying forces.

July 5 Harold Pringle of Flinton, Ont., was tied to a post in southern Italy and shot by a military firing squad — the only Canadian soldier to be executed during WW II. Pringle, a deserter, had joined a criminal gang in Rome and was involved in the shooting of a gang member. He was captured and court-martialled for murder, with no proof he had actually fired the fatal shot.

Also in July

• Meat rationing was reintroduced, limiting the amount of meat a Canadian could buy to between 1 and 3 lb per week, depending on the type of meat.

• An ammunition dump in Halifax caught fire. Explosions continued for 24 hours causing $4 million in damage. There were no casualties.

Aug. 6 The *Enola Gay*, an American B-29 bomber, dropped a single atomic bomb on Hiroshima, Japan.

Aug. 6–10 A federal-provincial conference was held in Ottawa to discuss economic reconstruction.

Aug. 9 *Bockscar*, an American B-29 bomber, dropped a single atomic bomb on Nagasaki, Japan.

• Lt R.H. Gray was posthumously awarded the Victoria Cross for sinking a Japanese destroyer at Onagawa Bay, Japan.

Aug. 14 Japan surrendered unconditionally to the Allies.

Aug. 15 Victory Day in Japan (V-J Day).

Sept. 2 The Japanese formally surrendered on the USS *Missouri* in Tokyo Bay, ending WW II. Almost 80,000 Canadians had volunteered to go to the Pacific to fight the Japanese but had not yet left when the war ended. Altogether in WW II, 1,086,771 Canadians, including 49,252 women, served in the armed forces (army, 730,625; air force, 249,624; navy, 106,522). Total fatal casualties were 41,992 (army, 22,964; air force, 17,047; navy, 1,981); over

55,000 were wounded. The total monetary cost of the war to Canada was $11,344,437,766.

Sept. 5 Armed with documents containing details of a Soviet spy ring in Canada, Igor Gouzenko (1919–1982), a KGB officer posing as a cipher clerk in the Russian embassy in Ottawa, quit his post and defected to Canadian authorities. On Feb. 5 a Royal Commission was established to examine Gouzenko's allegations. PM King announced the existence of spying activities to the nation on Feb. 15, and special measures were invoked to investigate and detain suspects. Eventually, 22 local agents and 15 Soviets were charged under the Official Secrets Act; 11 were convicted. Gouzenko, whose novel *The Fall of Titan* won the Gov-Gen's. Award for fiction in 1954, died in Ont. where he lived out his life under an assumed name.

• An Order-in-Council authorized the Canadian Red Ensign to fly over federal govt buildings within, as well as without, Canada, and wherever place or occasion dictated.

• The 1st atomic fission in Canada — and the 1st controlled atomic reaction outside the US — was sustained at 3:45 p.m. within the ZEEP (Zero Energy Experimental Pile) research reactor at Chalk River Laboratories at Chalk R., Ont. ZEEP was followed by another experimental Chalk R. reactor, the heavy-water moderated NRX (National Research Experimental) which began operation July 22, 1947. The 3rd and largest experimental reactor, the heavy-water moleculated NRU (National Research Universal), went operational at Chalk R. on Nov. 3, 1957. The NRU would become the world's leading supplier of medical isotopes used in the treatment of diseases such as cancer. All 3 experimental reactors fell under the administration of the National Research Council (later Atomic Energy of Canada Limited [AECL]) and were designed for study of fission for pure science and commercial purposes.

Sept. 8 Angus L. Macdonald became Liberal premier of NS for a 2nd time.

Sept. 12–Dec. 13 Seventeen thousand striking members of the UAW and Ford Motor Company agreed to binding arbitration under Justice Ivan Rand (1884–1969) of the Supreme Court of Canada.

While arbitrating the strike, Justice Rand handed down the Rand Formula, establishing a form of union security where an employer would deduct a portion of the salaries of all employees whether they belonged to the union or not, and pay it to the union as union dues.

Sept. 24 Argus Corporation, Canada's largest holding company, was incorporated in Toronto. Founded by Edward Plunket (E.P.) Taylor (1901–1989), Argus was a closed-end investment fund that controlled some of the country's most notable companies, including Domtar Paper, Dominion Stores, Hollinger Mines, Massey-Harris and BC Forest Products.

Oct. 16-Nov. 1 The United Nations' Food and Agriculture Organization Conference was held at Quebec City to draft its constitution.

Dec. 1 Britain's Hawker Siddeley Aircraft formed A.V. Roe (later Avro Canada Ltd.) from the purchase of Crown-owned Victory Aircraft of Malton, Ont. The storied, cutting-edge designer and manufacturer produced the nation's 1st jet engine (tested Mar. 17, 1948), NA's 1st jetliner (tested Aug. 10, 1949), the 1st Canadian-designed and built jetfighter (tested Jan. 19, 1950), and the fabled but star-crossed Avro Arrow CF–105 (tested Mar. 25, 1958). The company also produced flying-saucer prototypes — the 5.5-m in diameter, 1.47-m thick, 2,563-kg Avrocar VZ–9A. The fighter-bomber saucer was designed to carry a crew at up to 500 km/h and reach an altitude of 3,000 m. The federal govt funded the Avrocar project in 1952 but abandoned it in 1954, when it was picked up by the US govt. The 1st untethered test commenced Nov. 12, 1959, but the units proved slow and unstable. The US govt cancelled the project in 1961. One Avrocar is held by NASA at Ames, California; the other is with the Smithsonian National Air and Space Museum, Washington, D.C.

Dec. 8 Montreal opera soprano Pierrette Alarie (b 1921) made her Metropolitan Opera debut as Oscar in Giuseppe Verdi's *Un Ballo in Mashera.*

Also in Dec.
• PM Mackenzie King notified Britain's PM Attlee that the Canadian occupation force in Germany would be progressively reduced and entirely repatriated to Canada by the summer of 1946.

1945–1951 Radio announcer and actor Lorne Greene founded the Academy of Radio Arts in Toronto as a training school for aspiring actors and announcers. Among its featured courses were production, sound effects, singing and speech. In 1950, the academy introduced courses related to television.

Also in 1945
• During an off-the-record discussion with journalists, an anonymous senior govt official was asked how many Jews would be allowed into Canada after the war. His response, "None is too many," has since become a touchstone in discussions regarding how Canada closed its doors to thousands of persecuted Jewish refugees during the Holocaust. During the lead-up to war in Europe, the US accepted 150,000 Jewish immigrants, the UK 35,000, Argentina, Colombia and Mexico 20,000 each; and Canada 4,000.

• Approximately 17,000 Jewish-Canadian men and women fought in the Canadian military during WW II.

• Vancouver-born Osgoode Hall graduate Kew Dock Yip (1906–2001) became the 1st Asian-Canadian lawyer in Canada, and the 1st Chinese-speaking lawyer in Toronto's Chinatown. Yip played a pivotal role in getting the 1923 Chinese Exclusion Act repealed in 1947, and was honoured for his efforts by the Canadian Chinese National Congress, who gave special tribute to Yip on the 50th anniversary (1997) of the act's repeal. A towering figure in Chinese-Canadian communities coast to coast, Yip became a Law Society of Upper Canada Medal recipient in 1998.

• Czech refugee Lotta Hitschmanova (1910–1990) established the Unitarian Service Committee in Ottawa to aid refugees from wartorn Europe. The Unitarian Service would later expand its services worldwide.

• Canada's GNP was $12 billion, up from $5 billion in 1939.

• Alfred Pellan painted the canvas *La Magie de la chaussure*, commissioned by shoe manufacturer Maurice Corbeil of Montreal. He also painted *Quatre Femmes*, now in the Musée d' art contemporain, Montreal.

• Montreal artist Prudence Heward painted *Farmer's Daughter*, on canvas, now at the National Gallery of Canada.

• Lawren Harris completed the landscape painting, *Mountain Spirit*, now at U. of BC, Vancouver.

• William Richard Bird (1891–1984) published the novel *Here Stays Good Yorkshire*.

• Canadian author Thomas B. Costain's (1885–1965) *Black Rose*, published in the US, sold 1.1 million copies.

• Hugh MacLennan's *Two Solitudes* sold 50,000 copies in Canada, and also won the Gov-Gen.'s Award.

• Gabrielle Roy (1909–1983) published the novel *Bonheur d'Occasion*, later translated into *The Tin Flute*. The book won the Prix Fémina in Paris, making Roy the 1st Canadian to win a major French literary award.

• Philip Child published *Day of Wrath*. Considered his most important work, the novel tells the story of a man of goodwill striving to maintain his integrity in Nazi Germany.

• Germaine Guèvremont's (née Grignon) (1893–1968) 1st in a fictional trilogy, *Le Survenant*, was published in both Canada and France. It won the Prix Duvernay, Prix David and Prix Sully-Olivier de Serres.

• The 1st book of poems by Irving Peter Layton (b 1912), *Here and Now*, was published.

• Miriam Waddington's (née Dworkin) (b 1917) 1st book of poetry, *Green World*, was published.

• Poet Frank R. Scott (1899–1985) published *Events & Signals*.

• Elizabeth Smart (1913–1986) published her 1st and only major work, *By Grand Central Station I Sat Down and Wept*, a masterpiece of poetic prose. For various reasons including family opposition it was not released in Canada until more than 30 years later.

• Poet Earle Birney published *Now was Time*.

• *Fiddlehead* magazine, one of Canada's preeminent poetry magazines, was founded at the U. of New Brunswick in Fredericton.

1946

Jan. 10 The 1st General Assembly of the UN was held in London, England, until Feb. 15. Canada was represented on the Atomic Energy Commission, the Economic and Social Council and the International Court of Justice.

Also in Jan.
• The federal govt declared the Canada Mortgage and Housing Corp. (CMHC) a Crown corporation by an act of Parliament.

Mar. 2 Alb. residents were outraged when PM Mackenzie King unilaterally decided to rename Castle Mountain, in Banff National Park, Mount Eisenhower. The name was changed to honour General Dwight D. Eisenhower, Supreme Commander of the Allied Forces in Europe during WW II. The decision remained controversial for the next 33 years. Local efforts were finally rewarded in 1979, when the name was officially changed back to Castle Mountain.

Mar. 16 Children playing in woods near Hamilton, Ont., discovered the headless, armless and legless torso of railway worker John Dick. Within days police had charged Evelyn Dick (b 1920) as an accomplice to the murder of her estranged husband. During the investigation, police also discovered the body of their infant boy in a suitcase in the attic of Mrs. Dick's home. She was sentenced to hang for murder but Mrs. Dick's guilty verdict was overturned when statements she had given police at the time of her arrest were ruled inadmissible. She was found guilty of manslaughter and sentenced to life in prison. She was released from prison in 1958, given a new identity, and disappeared from public view. The Dick case was one of the nation's most sensational true-crime stories of the era.

Also in Mar.
• The Union of Saskatchewan Indians (now the Federation of Saskatchewan Indian Nations) was formed with John Tootoosis (1899–1989) as president and John Gambler as vice-president.

Apr. 3 Canada purchased the 1,954-km Canadian portion of the Alaska Highway, from Dawson Creek to the Alaska border, from the US for $108 million.

Apr. 12–Jan. 28, 1952 Field Marshal Harold Rupert Leofric George Alexander, Alexander of Tunis (1891–1969), served as gov-gen. of Canada, succeeding Earl of Athlone.

Apr. 18 Jackie Robinson broke Major League baseball's colour barrier making his debut with the Montreal Royals, the triple-A affiliate of the Brooklyn Dodgers. The African-American 2nd baseman had 3 singles, a 3-run homer, 2 stolen bases and 4 runs scored to beat hometown Jersey City 14-1. Robinson was called to the big team in 1947.

Apr. 20–29 Six Montreal Surrealist artists, brought together by Paul-Émile Borduas, held an exhibition on Amherst St. in Montreal. They would be known as Les Automatistes. Between June 20 and July 13, 1947, the group exhibited at the Galerie du Luxembourg in Paris.

Apr. 25 The last session of the Dominion-Provincial Conference on Reconstruction met.

June 20 Montreal MP Fred Rose was sentenced to 6 years in prison for communicating official national secrets to the Soviet Union. Igor Gouzenko testified against him as a chief witness.

June 21 Gordon Macdonald (1894–1962) took office as Nfld.'s last gov-gen., serving until 1949.

July 10 Canada's 1st drive-in movie theatre opened in Hamilton, Ont.

July 14 About 2,700 employees went on strike against Stelco in Hamilton, Ont. Their demands included a 40-hour workweek. The strike was punctuated by violence July 26 as Stelco tried to employ strikebreakers.

Also in July
• The Canadian dollar was revalued at parity with the US dollar.

Aug. 3 The Anglo-Canadian Wheat Agreement provided for large British purchases of Canadian wheat at prices considerably below world-market values, thereby creating a guaranteed wheat export market.

Sept. 5 Louis St. Laurent was sworn in as secretary of state for external affairs. Lester B. Pearson was recalled from Washington to become St. Laurent's under-secretary. Norman Robertson (1904–1968) was appointed high commissioner in London.

Also in Sept.
• Lawren P. Harris, son of Lawren Harris, assumed the directorship of the Mount Allison University School of Art in Sackville, NB.

Oct. 16 Gordie Howe (b 1928), wearing number 17 for the Detroit Red Wings, scored his 1st NHL goal. It came against the Toronto Maple Leafs. Howe would switch to number 9 on Oct. 29.

Oct. 29 In a speech before the UN Gen. Assembly, Louis St. Laurent supported the establishment of an international peace force and reiterated Canada's readiness to be a part of a "world force behind world law."

Nov. 1 The 1st Basketball Association of America (later the NBA) game was played at Maple Leaf Gardens, where the New York Knickerbockers knocked off the Toronto Huskies. The Huskies folded after 1 season.

• Viola Desmond, a Halifax businesswoman, sat in a "Whites-Only" section of the racially segregated Roseland Theatre in New Glasgow, NS. She was arrested, given a $20 fine and sentenced to 30 days in jail. The Nova Scotia Association for the Advancement of Coloured People (NSAACP) raised enough money to pay the fine and brought the incident to national attention.

Dec. 1 Restrictions on the right to strike in the war industries and the freezing of prices and wages were lifted to allow for readjustment of industries to civil production.

Also in 1946
• The govt 1st introduced Canada Savings Bonds, at 2.75%.

• The Atomic Energy Control Board was established through the Atomic Energy Control Act, to regulate the production and use of atomic energy.

• Carrie Best (1903-2001), an African-Canadian woman from New Glasgow, NS, began publication of *The Clarion*, a local newspaper later called *The Negro Citizen*. The paper examined racism and the treatment of African-Canadians in NS.

• Constance Beresford Howe (b 1922) published her 1st novel, *The Unreasoning Heart*, while an undergraduate at McGill U.

• The nonprofit New Play Society was founded in Toronto by Dora Mavor Moore (1888–1979). The society flourished for 10 years, producing 72 plays.

• The Lakehead Technical Institute was established at Thunder Bay, Ont.; in 1957, the Lakehead College of Arts, Science & Technology was added.

• The literary journals *Preview* (founded in Montreal by F.R. Scott and others) and *First Statement* merged to form *Northern Review*.

• Phyllis Gotlieb's novel *Sunburst*, a seminal work of Canadian science fiction, was published.

• Montreal poet Louis Dudek (1918-2001) celebrated the publication of his 1st collection, *East of the City*. Dudek, in conjunction with fellow literati Irving Layton and Raymond Souster (b 1921), would later found Contact Press in 1952, dedicated to publishing Canadian poets. During the 1950s, Dudek, a McGill professor, would establish the McGill Poetry series, which was instrumental in bringing many younger Canadian poets, including Leonard Cohen, to public attention.

• Montreal labour organizer Madeleine Parent (b 1918) succeeded in organizing 6,000 Que. textile workers in a union. She was arrested in 1946 and 1947 by Que. authorities for leading textile workers in strikes at Valleyfield and Lachute.

• David Milne completed the watercolor *White Poppy*, now in the National Gallery of Canada.

• Paul-Émile Borduas completed the abstract

canvas *946,* or *L'Écossais redécouvrant l'Amérique,* now in the Musée d'art contemporain, Montreal.

• Fernand Leduc (b 1916) completed the abstract *Dernière Campagne de Napoléon,* on board, now in a private collection.

• Marcel Barbeau (b 1925) completed the abstract canvas *Le Tumulte à la mâchoire crispée*, which was severely criticized by Paul-Émile Borduas. The painting is now in the Musée d'art contemporain, Montreal.

• Artist Jock Macdonald completed *Russian Fantasy,* in watercolour and ink, now in the Art Gallery of Ont., Toronto.

• John "Jack" Hamilton Bush (1909–1977) completed the painting *Village Procession*, now in the Art Gallery of Ont., Toronto.

• Alexander Colville (b 1920) completed *Infantry Near Nijmegen, Holland,* after serving in the Canadian Armed Forces as an official war artist. The work is now in the Canadian War Museum, Ottawa.

• *Growing Pains*, an autobiography of Emily Carr, was published posthumously.

• The fictionalized autobiography *In Search of Myself*, by Frederick Philip Grove, was published and received a Gov-Gen.'s Award.

• Roderick Haig-Brown's (1908–1976) novel *Starbuck Valley Winter* was published.

• Poet Gilles Hénault (b 1920–1996) published *Théâtre en plein air.*

• Stephen Leacock's *The Boy I Left Behind Me* was posthumously published .

• Historian Arthur Reginald Marsden Lower (1889–1998) published *Colony to Nation*, a search for a common thread between English- and French-speaking Canadians.

• Robert Finch (1900-1995) published *Poems*, which received the Gov-Gen.'s Award for Poetry.

1947

Jan. 1 The Canadian Citizenship Act was proclaimed. Canadians became Canadian citizens rather than British subjects.

• Canadian women no longer automatically lost their citizenship when they married non-Canadians.

• Sask. became the 1st province to provide universal, public hospital insurance when its Hospital Insurance Act, passed in 1946 under the CCF govt of Tommy C. Douglas became effective.

Jan. 14 Canada was elected to the Economic and Social Council of the UN. It would become a member of the UN Security Council Jan. 1, 1948. On Jan. 8, 1948, Andrew McNaughton was appointed permanent delegate from Canada to the UN and Canada's representative to the Security Council.

Jan. 30 The 3rd session of the 20th Parliament met until July 17. The House of Commons expelled convicted spy Fred Rose from his seat in Parliament.

Feb. 3 The lowest temperature in NA was recorded at Snag, Yukon, at -64°C.

Feb. 13 After drilling 133 wells, Vern "Dry Hole" Hunter struck oil for Imperial Oil Company near Leduc, Alb. The well was known as Leduc Oil Well No. 1 and began producing 155 cubic meters of oil a day.

Feb. 19 The 1st discovery of potash in Canada was made near Radville, Sask.

Also in Feb.
• William Merton Neal (1886–1961) became chairman of the board and president of the CPR, taking over from D.C. Coleman.

Apr. 3 The Defence Research Board was created as a military think tank.

Also in May
• Ont. Premier George Drew initiated the Drew Plan, an effort to "restock the population with Britons." Some 10,000 British immigrants arrived in Toronto during the summer under the program.

• The play *Bienêtre*, by Claude Gauvreau (1925–1971), was performed in Que.

• The Canadian Association for Adult Education (CAAE) created an awards program to support and promote Canadian film and radio, and intended to be comparable in stature to the Gov-Gen.'s Award for literature. After much discussion and debate, it was decided the awards would be called the Canadian Film Awards and the Canadian Radio Awards.

June 1 Telephone service in Sask. was made a public utility called Saskatchewan Government Telephones, or Sastel for short.

June 10–12 US President Harry S. Truman visited Ottawa.

June 17 PM Mackenzie King decided to retire after talking with C.D. Howe about Louis St. Laurent succeeding him.

June 26 A heart attack claimed the life of 77-year-old former PM R.B. Bennett.

Also in June
• Louis St. Laurent introduced the Visiting Forces Agreement, granting American armed service courts jurisdiction over the discipline and administration of their own forces in Canada.

July 1 A bill making blind Canadians 21 years of age or older eligible for a pension became effective.

July 22 The heavy water-cooled NRX (National Research Experimental) reactor began production at Chalk R., Ont.

Aug. 12 Canadian aviation pioneer John Alexander Douglas McCurdy, was appointed lt-gov. of NS.

Aug. 15 India and Pakistan, having achieved independence from Britain, were admitted to the Commonwealth with Dominion status.

Aug. 16 The De Havilland DHC-2 Beaver prototype airplane was test-flown at Downsview, Ont. The STOL (short takeoff and landing) aircraft was capable of operating on wheels, skis or floats. Regarded by many experts as one of the most manoeuvrable utility airplanes ever built, the Beaver's specifications were based on a survey undertaken by aviation pioneer Punch Dickins. The DCH-2 had a maximum range of 1,300 km, and could carry 9 people (including crew) plus cargo weight of over 680 kg. By 1965, there were more than 1,650 De Havilland Beaver DCH-2's operating in 63 countries around the world.

Oct. 30 Canada and 22 other nations signed the General Agreement on Tariffs and Trade (GATT) in Geneva, Switzerland. Effective date was Jan. 1, 1948. The agreement provided a basic framework for trade between the nations with an aim to reducing tariffs and other financial barriers to the international flow of goods. Seven major GATT Conferences of trade and tariffs would follow: Annecy 1949; Torquay 1951; Geneva 1956 and 1962; Geneva "Kennedy Round" 1967; Geneva "Tokyo Round" 1973–1979; and Geneva "Uruguay Round" 1986–1993. The GATT was replaced by the creation of the World Trade Organization (WTO), Dec. 15, 1993.

• PM King left for Britain to attend the royal wedding of Princess Elizabeth and Philip Mountbatten. Louis St. Laurent became acting PM.

Nov. 2 Wartime food rationing ended.

Nov. 7 Canada accepted terms for bringing Nfld. into Confederation; the projected cost was estimated to be as high as $180 million over a 10-year period.

Nov. 20 Joseph (Joey) Roberts Smallwood (1900–1991) began to explain and defend the terms of Canadian Confederation to a National Convention, appointed to consider Nfld.'s constitutional future.

Dec. 12 The federal govt passed the Gold Mining Assistance Act, providing subsidies to gold mining companies.

Also in 1947

• The Canadian House of Commons voted unanimously to establish the National Wildlife Week Act, in honour of conservationist Jack Miner. National Wildlife Week centres around Apr. 10th, Miner's birthday.

• Canada and the US established 2 of 5 Joint Arctic Weather Stations (JAWS) in Eureka, Alaska and Resolute Bay (now Nunavut). The other stations were located in Isachsen (now Nunavut) and Mould Bay, NWT, both built in 1948; the last was built in Alert (now Nunavut) in 1950.

• Canada persuaded Britain and Australia to accept the inclusion of republics as members of the Commonwealth.

• LeMoine FitzGerald painted *The Little Plant*, on canvas, now in the McMichael Canadian Collection, Kleinburg, Ont.

• Montreal Automatiste painter Pierre Gauvreau (b 1922) completed the painting *Sans Titre*, now in the Musée d'art contemporain, Montreal.

• Automatiste painter Jean-Paul Riopelle (1923–2002) completed the painting *Abstraction*, now in a private collection.

• Artist Lawren P. Harris completed the geometric abstraction *Project*, now in a private collection.

• Alfred Pellan completed *Citrons Ultra-Violets,* oil on canvas, incorporating a wide range of connections between atoms, cells, eyes, snakes, insects and sexual imagery. It is now held at the Musée national des beaux-arts du Québec, Quebec City.

• Hand-carved wooden duck decoys by Ont. fruit farmer William Ellis (1865–1963) sold for $3 apiece. Each head took more than 5 hours to complete and many bodies required the application of more than 30 different colours. Ellis's decoys have since fetched more than $300 each.

• William Ormond Mitchell (1914–1998) published his 1st and most popular book, *Who Has Seen the Wind*. The $14,000 royalties allowed the Weyburn, Sask. native to pursue writing full-time. His body of work would include such classics as *Jake and The Kid*, broadcast as a series on CBC Radio between 1950–1956, and the novels *The Kite* (1962), *The Vanishing Point* (1973) and *How I Spent My Summer Holidays* (1981).

• William Robertson Davies (1913–1995) published

The Diary of Samuel Marchbanks, a collection of humorous essays.

• Literary critic Northrop Frye (1912–1991) published *Fearful Symmetry*.

• Clarence Malcolm Lowry (1909–1957) published *Under the Volcano*.

• U. of Man. Professor Paul Hiebert (1892–1987) published the comic novel, *Sarah Binks*.

• The novel *Music at the Close*, by Edward Alexander McCourt (1907–1972), was published.

• Jean Simard (b 1916) published the semi-autobiographical novel *Félix, livre d'enfant pour adultes*.

• Ethel Davis Wilson's (née Bryant) (1888–1980) 1st novel, *Hetty Dorval*, was published.

• Raymond Holmes Souster (b 1921) published his 2nd collection of poems, *Go to Sleep, World*.

• Confederation poet Duncan Campbell Scott (1862–1947) published *The Circle of Affection*, a collection of short stories about Native Peoples and traders.

• Poet E.J. Pratt published *Behind the Log*.

• Soprano Lois Marshall (b 1924) made her professional debut with Ernest MacMillan and the Toronto Symphony Orchestra in a performance of J.S. Bach's *St. Matthew Passion*.

• Historian A.R.M. Lower (1890–1988) published his best-known work, *From Colony to Nation*.

1948

Jan. 20 Mackenzie King announced his retirement. King held the office of PM longer than anyone in the history of the British Commonwealth, having served 21 years, 5 months and 1 day. In all, he had won 6 gen. elections.

Feb. 2 Canada's 1st provincial arts board, the Sask. Arts Board, was created.

Feb. 6 Barbara Ann Scott (b 1928) of Ottawa won Canada's 1st Olympic gold in figure skating at St. Moritz, Switzerland. Canada's other gold was awarded to the RCAF Flyers, a ragtag group of little-known amateur players sporting the blue-circle-with-red-maple-leaf RCAF rondel on their sweaters. Their manager was RCAF squadron leader and Medical Officer Sandy Watson.

Mar. 17 The Avro *Chinook*, Canada's 1st jet engine, was tested at the Avro site at Malton, Ont.

Apr. 1 The longest-running annual Canadian revue, the musical *Spring Thaw*, was 1st performed at Museum Theatre in Toronto. It ran until 1973. The 1st performance included Donald "Don" Harron (b 1924).

Apr. 19 Gérard Côte (1913–1993) of St. Hyacinthe, Que., won his 4th and final Boston Marathon. He had also won in 1940, 1943 and 1944.

Apr. 26 Floods caused millions of dollars' damage in Man., leaving 2,500 homeless.

Apr. 29 In the House of Commons, Louis St. Laurent suggested the creation of a "collective-security league." St. Laurent would become an architect and significant sponsor of NATO, which was formed Apr. 4, 1949.

June 3 A Nfld. referendum resulted in 69,000 votes for self-govt, 64,000 for union with Canada and 22,000 for no change in political status. Another vote was called for July 22.

June 7 The Ont. Conservative govt, under Premier George Drew, was re-elected.

June 24 Women teachers in Toronto were given wage parity with their male counterparts.

June 30 The Industrial Relations and Disputes Investigation Act, repealing wartime measures entrenching workers' rights to collective bargaining, was passed.

• PM Mackenzie King made his last speech in the House of Commons.

July 1 Canada became the 1st country to introduce domestic "all-up" service — all 1st class mail was carried by air at regular postage rates.

July 6 Delegates from Belgium, Canada, France, Luxembourg, the Netherlands, the UK and the US met at Washington, D.C., to begin discussions which led to the North Atlantic Security Pact.

July 22 A 2nd Nfld. referendum was held. Voters decided 78,408 to 71,464 to enter Confederation.

Also in July
• John Bracken resigned as leader of the Progressive Conservative Party after 3 years.

Aug. 7 Louis St. Laurent was elected leader of the Liberal party at the Ottawa Coliseum on the 1st ballot with 838 votes, more than twice as many as his closest rival, James (Jimmy) Garfield Gardiner (1883–1962).

Aug. 8 Four hundred copies of the 1st edition of *Refus global* went on sale in Montreal. The manifesto, inspired and carried out by Automatiste artist Paul-Émile Borduas (1905–1960), denounced established values in Que. and proclaimed the need for total freedom of expression. Borduas contributed the title essay and others. On Sept. 2, Borduas was removed from his teaching position at the École du Meuble by the minister of social welfare and youth of the province, Paul Sauve, "because of the writings and manifestos he published, as well as his general attitude…"

Aug. 18 A blue, 4-door Deluxe Champion rolled off the Studebaker of Canada assembly line in Hamilton, Ont. It was the 1st of 179,325 cars and trucks built in Hamilton until the plant — and Studebaker — ceased making cars in 1966. The Hamilton plant had been the last Studebaker plant in North America between Dec. 1963 and 1966.

Sept. 10-June 17 1957 Lester B. Pearson served as Canada's secretary of state for external affairs, succeeding Louis St. Laurent.

Oct. 2 George Drew became national leader of the Progressive Conservative Party.

Oct. 6–27 Representatives of Canada and Nfld. met in Ottawa to discuss final arrangements for Nfld.'s entry into Confederation. An agreement was signed on Dec. 11. Nfld. became the 10th province Mar. 31, 1949.

Oct. 19 Thomas Laird Kennedy (1878–1959) succeeded George Drew as Conservative premier of Ont.

Also in Oct.
• The 1st peacetime civil defence co-ordinator was appointed to supervise planning for public air-raid shelters, emergency food and medical supplies, and the evacuation of likely target areas throughout the country.

Nov. 7 Douglas Lloyd Campbell (1895–1970) became Liberal premier of Man.

Nov. 15 Mackenzie King resigned as PM. Louis St. Laurent served as Liberal PM until June 21, 1957. He was the nation's 12th prime minister.

Nov. 27 Three hundred Calgarians, most wearing white cowboy hats, travelled by train to Toronto to witness the Calgary Stampeders defeat the Ottawa Rough Riders 12-7 to win Calgary's 1st Grey Cup.

Dec. 10 The UN General Assembly adopted the Universal Declaration of Human Rights. Canada was an early signatory.

Dec. 14 The Supreme Court of Canada ruled against a ban on margarine. The ban had been established by an act of Parliament in 1886 after dairy farmers contested its introduction into Canada. The ban was repealed for a period between 1917–1923 due to a postwar shortage of butter.

1948–1998 Seven thousand nine hundred Canadian Jews emigrated to the new State of Israel.

Also in 1948
• Heavy flooding in the Fraser River Valley south of Vancouver, BC, caused nearly $20 million in damage, and forced the evacuation of 16,000 from their homes.

• Artist, author and filmmaker James Houston (b 1921) moved to the Arctic where he became civil administrator of West Baffin Island. Houston popularized Inuit art in the south, and in 1959 helped establish the West Baffin Eskimo Co-operative (WBEC) in Cape Dorset, now Nunavut. WEBC was the 1st Inuit co-operative established with federal start-up capital. It regulated the sale of Inuit sculpture and other works to southern communities, and also provided regular employment and stable incomes to Northern artists. Members of WBEC have included some of the nation's most celebrated and revered artists, including Kenojuak Ashevak (b 1927), Pitaloosie Saila (b 1942) and Kananginak Pootoogook.

• Canada sent military observers to Kashmir after the 1st India-Pakistan War.

• *Magnificent*, the 212-m aircraft carrier launched in 1944, was commanded into the Royal Canadian Navy as the 1st Canadian-owned vessel of its type. It would serve for 9 years as a training vessel before being decommissioned in 1957.

• Japanese-Canadians were given the right to vote in federal elections.

• Civil marriages were legalized in BC.

• Bay of Fundy National Park was established in NB to preserve 12 km of Bay of Fundy coastline and 206 km² of interior Acadian forest. The famous Fundy tides drop 9 m twice daily within park territory (the biggest drop is 16 m at Cape Hopewell), exposing expansive saltwater mudflats and rugged, highly contoured eroded shorelines.

• The Mackenzie Highway was opened from Hay R., NWT, to Grimshaw, Alb.

• Edwin Mirvish (b 1914) opened Honest Ed's discount store in Toronto. The store, a $212 investment, was built on the site of a small ladies' sportswear shop, and grossed $100 on its 1st day. Honest Ed's now covers an entire block, and grosses upward of $65 million a year.

• Fishing guide Don Gapen of Nipigon, Ont., created the Muddler Minnow fly pattern during the Northern Ont. brook trout season. It proved so successful it was detailed in *Field & Stream* the following year,

transforming the local sculpin imitation into one of North America's most popular fly patterns.

• Montreal Automatiste painter Jean-Paul-Armand Mousseau (b 1927) completed the picture *Bataille moyenâgeuse*, now in the Musée d'art contemporain, Montréal.

• Marcel Barbeau, the most experimental of the Montreal painters, completed *Forêt vierge*, now in a private collection.

• Bertram Charles Binning (1909–1976) completed one of his 1st abstract oils, *Ships in Classical Calm*, now in the National Gallery of Canada.

• Historian Jean Bruchési (1901–1979) published *Canada, Réalités d'hier et d'aujourd'hui*, translated in 1950 as *A History of Canada*.

• Gratien Gélinas's (1909–1999) highly successful, full-length play *Tit-Coq*, a tale of a woebegone illegitimate orphan, premiered in Montreal.

• U. of BC professor Roy Daniells (1902–1979) published the book of poems *Deeper Into the Forest*, demonstrating a mastery of the sonnet form.

• Roger Lemelin published the novel *Les Plouffe*, which was later turned into a popular CBC 1950s television drama, *La Famille Plouffe*.

• Françoise Loranger (1913–1995) published the novel *Mathieu*, a story set in Duplessis-era Que.

• Igor Gouzenko, Soviet spy and defector, published his memoir, *This Was My Choice*.

• A.M. Klein published *The Rocking Chair and Other Poems*.

• Austrian-born novelist Henry Kreisel (1922–1992) published *The Rich Man*, the story of a successful Austrian immigrant in Toronto returning to his native land.

• Paul-Marie Lapointe (b 1929) published *Le Vierge incendié*, a violently surreal collection of poetry.

• Poet Douglas Valentine Le Pan (1914–1998) published *The Wounded Prince*.

1949

Jan. 1 The Income War Tax Act, introduced in 1917 as a temporary measure to finance the war effort, was officially renamed the Income Tax Act.

Jan. 26 The 5th session of the 20th Parliament met until Apr. 30. It was Louis St. Laurent's 1st session as PM. For the 1st time, movie cameras were allowed to photograph the initial proceedings in the Commons chamber.

Feb. 11 PM St. Laurent flew to Washington, D.C., for a meeting with President Truman, chiefly to discuss the St. Lawrence Seaway and power project and to inform the president that if American delaying tactics did not end, Canada would be forced to go it alone. The PM flew again to Washington on Sept. 28, 1951, for the same purpose. American commitment to the seaway came with passage of the Wiley-Dondero Bill on May 13, 1954. Ground breaking ceremonies commenced Aug. 10, 1954.

Feb. 14 The Que. Asbestos Strike began, involving 5,000 workers from Johns-Manville, Asbestos Corp., Johnson's Company, and Flintkote, located in Thetford, Asbestos, Que., and elsewhere. On May 5, workers seized the town of Asbestos after learning that the employers intended to hire replacement workers. Strikers took several provincial police captive. The insurrection was eventually crushed by a force of 400 heavily armed police; 180 strikers were arrested. The illegal 4-month strike was settled July 1, with the intervention of the archbishop of Que.

Feb. 19 Robertson Davies' play, *Fortune My Foe,* won 1st prize at the Eastern Ont. Drama Festival.

Mar. 23 Assent was given to the North America Bill, passed by the British Parliament, for the union of Nfld. and Canada.

Mar. 28 The North Atlantic Treaty was submitted to the Canadian House of Commons and approved in a single day. Two Independents from Que. were the only members who opposed it.

Mar. 31 Nfld. entered Confederation as the 10th province. England's oldest colony became Canada's youngest province. On Apr. 1 Albert Joseph Walsh (1900–1958) was appointed the 1st lt-gov. of Nfld.

Apr. 4 External Affairs Minister Lester Pearson signed the North Atlantic Pact in Washington, D.C. Canada thereby became 1 of the 12 original members of the North Atlantic Treaty Organization (NATO), which included the US, Britain, France, Italy, Belgium, the Netherlands, Luxembourg, Denmark, Norway, Iceland and Portugal. Other countries that later joined were Greece (1952), Turkey (1952), West Germany (1955) and Spain (1982). All members pledged to defend each other in the event of Soviet aggression, and later, attack by other countries or groups. NATO headquarters is in Brussels, Belgium.

Apr. 8 The appointment of Vincent Massey as chairman of the Royal Commission on the National Development in the Arts, Letters and Sciences (Massey Commission) was announced. The commission's task was to assess the state of Canadian cultural affairs and advise on govt policy regarding radio and television broadcasting, the National Film Board, the National Gallery, the National Museum, the Public Archives and the planned National Library. The report was tabled June 1, 1951.

Apr. 27 At a PM's conference in London, England, the Commonwealth of Nations replaced the British Commonwealth to accommodate those countries that had gained independence from Britain but still wanted to maintain an association with former empire members.

• The 1st Canadian Film Awards presentation was held in Ottawa at the Little Elgin Theatre to honour the best productions of 1948. Twenty-nine films were entered in the competition, including 28 short subjects and 1 full-length feature film, *Un Homme et son Péché* (A Man and His Sin), which was given a special award for making a "definite advance in Canadian film history." *The Loon's Necklace*, produced by Crawley Films Ltd. of Ottawa, was declared film of the year.

May 4 Leslie Miscampbell Frost (1895–1973) succeeded T.L. Kennedy as Progressive Conservative premier of Ont.

May 17 The federal govt granted full recognition to the State of Israel, which had been formed May 14, 1948.

May 27 Joey Smallwood was elected premier with a Liberal majority in Nfld.'s 1st provincial election. He had been appointed premier Apr. 1.

June 27 Federal elections resulted in 190 seats for St. Laurent's Liberals, and 41 seats for the Progressive Conservatives, under George Drew. The CCF took 13 seats, Social Credit 10, and independents 8. Voter turnout was 73.8%.

July 13 The 1st provincial Legislature of Nfld. opened at St. John's.

Also in July
• Artist Paul-Émile Borduas published *Projections libérantes,* describing how he was treated by the Que. establishment after he published *Refus global.*

Aug. 10 The Jetliner *Avro C–102,* the world's 2nd jet transport and the 1st commercial jet transport in North America, was test-flown at Malton, Ont. The experimental Avro Canada Limited aircraft was built for TransCanada Airlines (TCA) and carried 4 Rolls Royce Derwent engines. Only 1 jetliner was built. The jet reached 805 km/h during the test flight. The plane carried the 1st jet-transported air-mail in a run from Toronto to New York in Apr. 1950 and was later leased to eccentric American tycoon Howard Hughes. It was scrapped in 1957.

Sept. 9 A DC–3 Canadian Pacific Airlines plane exploded north of Quebec City, killing 23 passengers. The explosion was the result of a bomb placed on board by Que. jeweler J. Albert Guay in a plot to rid himself of his wife, who was aboard the plane, and collect the insurance money. Guay and 2 accomplices were later convicted and hanged.

Sept. 15 The 1st session of the 21st Parliament met until Dec. 10. The Supreme Court Bill was passed, making the Supreme Court of Canada the final court of Canadian appeal.

Sept. 17 The largest Canadian passenger ship on the Great Lakes, the *Noronic,* of the Canadian Steamship Lines Ltd., was destroyed by fire at its pier in Toronto harbour; 118 lost their lives.

• External Affairs Minister Lester B. Pearson represented Canada at the 1st NATO meeting in Washington, D.C.

Sept. 19 The Canadian dollar was devalued by 10% following the devaluation of the British pound.

Dec. 10 The Trans-Canada Highway Act came into effect, authorizing the construction of a 2-lane roadway across Canada via the shortest route. Specified by law to be 22 to 24 ft wide (6.7 x 7.3 m), the Trans-Canada was scheduled for completion by 1956. It would be officially opened Sept. 3, 1962. Determination of its specific route was left to the provinces, who were responsible for 50% of the construction costs. The federal govt assumed responsibility for the remaining 50% and 100% of any section that passed through national parkland.

Dec. 12 Nancy (Austin) Hodges (1888–1969) was named speaker of the Legislature of BC, the 1st woman in the British Commonwealth to hold such a position.

1949–1952 Plymouth Deluxe automobiles were offered in a variety of new colours, including Edmonton beige, Kitchener green, New Brunswick blue and Yukon grey.

1949–1955 Hockey greats Ted Lindsay (b 1925), Sid Abel (1918-2000) and Gordie Howe led the Detroit Red Wings to 7 straight Prince of Wales Trophies.

Also in 1949
• Canada Post instituted a First Day Cover service wherein the slogan "First Day of Issue" appeared on the envelope. This service was made bilingual in 1951, and in Apr. 1971 Canada Post began to issue Official First Day Covers.

• Ont.-born Mohawk Harold J. Smith, aka Jay Silverheels (1919–1980), was cast to play the faithful companion Tonto on the television series *The Lone Ranger.*

• The least amount of annual precipitation to fall on any region of Canada was 12.7 mm, recorded in Arctic Bay, NWT (now Nunavut).

• Full citizenship was extended to all Asian Canadians.

• The Iron Ore Company was founded to exploit iron from the Schefferville region. Between 1951 and 1954, the 576-km Quebec North Shore and

Labrador Railway between Sept–Iles on the St. Lawrence and Schefferville, located in the heart of the Que.–Labrador peninsula was established to facilitate transport. Two hydroelectric plants were also built to supply power to Schefferville mines and a receiving terminal at Sept–Iles. By 1955, the Iron Ore Company was the nation's largest producer of iron ore.

• Hamilton, Ont.'s 2 CFL teams, the Tigers and the Wildcats, merged to form the storied Hamilton Tiger Cats. Also this year, the CFL introduced new rules making the wearing of helmets mandatory.

• The Toronto Maple Leafs beat the Detroit Red Wings to become the 1st NHL team to win 3 consecutive Stanley Cups.

• Man. skip Ken Watson won his 3rd curling Brier, the 1st skip ever to do so.

• The House passed the Canada Forestry Act, allowing Ottawa to enter into provincial forestry agreements covering forest protection and use.

• CP began to convert its locomotive engines from coal to diesel.

• The 1st small indoor community shopping centre in Canada, Norgate Shopping Centre, in the Montreal suburb Ville de Sainte-Laurent, was completed by architect, Maxwell M. Kalman (b 1906). The rectangular L-shaped structure was part of a large residential apartment project inspired by models of suburban New York.

• The 1,300 km Crowsnest Highway, or Southern Inter-Provincial Highway 3, was opened through the Rocky Mountains by BC Premier Byron Johnson (1890–1964). The road stretched from Medicine Hat Alb. to Hope, BC. The distinctive highway marker sports a striking black crow with the number 3 in the foreground.

• Hay R., on Great Slave L., NWT, was connected to Peace R., Alb., by an all-weather road (Highway 1), thereby becoming the 1st NWT community connected year-round by road south to the provinces.

• There were over 1,000 producing oil wells in Alb.

• The 7,424-seat Stampede Corral was completed in Calgary as the home to the Calgary Stampeders of the Western Hockey League (WHL). The $1.25 million structure was the largest hockey rink west of Maple Leaf Gardens, Toronto. The Corral would become home to the World Hockey Association (WHA) Calgary Cowboys between 1975–1977 and the NHL Calgary Flames between 1980 and 1983. It has hosted a vast array of entertainers, from Bill Haley and His Comets to the Vienna Boys Choir. The Corral remains an essential agricultural exhibit hall for the annual Calgary Stampede.

• There were a total 90,509 dwelling starts cross country, up from 16,400 in the 1st year of the 20th century.

• Canada became a member of the International Criminal Police Organization (ICPO), often refereed to as Interpol, the world police force that focuses and coordinates efforts on crime with international implications. By 2004, 182 countries were members of the organization, whose headquarters are located in Lyon, France.

• Canadian consumption of coal exceeded 40 million tons for the year; 8.4 million tons were consumed in 1900.

• Jeunesses musicales du Canada was established in St-Hyacinthe, Que., as a non-profit organization to support and promote the careers of promising Canadian musicians.

• Don Johnson and George Taylor formed country music label Rodeo Records in Montreal. Its 1st recording was Earl Mitton's *York County Hornpipe*, a 78-rpm disc. The firm would go on to produce such country notables as Graham Townsend (1942–1998), Mary Osburne, and Winston "Scotty" Fitzgerald (1914–1987).

• Jack DeLorme of the *Calgary Herald* was awarded the 1st National Newspaper Award for Spot News Photo, for his dramatic photograph of a fireman rushing from a burning house, cradling a child.

• Winnipeg printer, and former HBC fur trader Richard Bonnycastle (1903–1968), began publishing romance novels under the Harlequin imprint.

The "nice little [paperback] books with happy endings" were priced at 25 cents each. By the year 2000, Harlequin Books was selling more than 160 million volumes a year.

• E.J. Hughes (b 1913) completed *Farm Near Courtenay, BC,* in oil, now located at the Vancouver Art Gallery.

• LeMoine FitzGerald painted *From an Upstairs Window, Winter,* on canvas, now in the National Gallery of Canada.

• Norman Mailer's novel *The Naked and the Dead* was banned in Canada after it had been on the nation's best-seller list for 10 months.

• Earle Birney published the novel *Turvey,* for which he received the Stephen Leacock Medal for Humour.

• *Poésies complètes,* a posthumous work of poems by Saint-Denys Garneau, was published.

• Poet James Crerar Reaney (b 1926) published his 1st book, *The Red Heart,* for which he won the 1st of his 3 Governor-General's Awards.

1950

Jan. 9–14 External Affairs Minister Lester B. Pearson attended the 1st Conference of Commonwealth Foreign Ministers held at Colombo, Ceylon (now Sri Lanka), the 1st meeting of its kind held on Asian soil. The Colombo Plan, an Asian economic development program geared toward the reduction of poverty in South and Southeast Asia, developed from the meeting. On Mar. 10, the Canadian cabinet formally ratified the Colombo Plan, agreeing to full membership on its committee. In Feb. 1951, Canada gave $25 million toward the 1st year of the Colombo aid scheme.

Jan. 10–12 A federal-provincial conference was held in Ottawa to discuss constitutional amendment issues.

Jan. 19 A prototype long-range, all-weather Avro Canada *CF-100 Canuck* jet fighter was test flown at Malton, Ont. It was the 1st Canadian-designed and manufactured jet fighter. Avro would produce 692 *CF-100* fighters between 1950 and 1958. On Dec. 18, 1952, an Avro *CF-100* became the 1st straight-winged aircraft to exceed Mach 2 without rocket power.

Jan. 29 External Affairs Minister Lester B. Pearson visited Tokyo for talks with Gen. Douglas MacArthur, Supreme Commander of Allied Forces in the Pacific.

Feb. 27 Canada and the US signed the Niagara Diversion Treaty, diverting the flow of Niagara R. water to power plants equally between the countries and ensuring a steady flow over Niagara Falls. On Mar. 27, the federal govt transferred water rights on the Niagara R. to the province of Ont.

Apr. 11 Twelve thousand Ford workers in Windsor, Ont., voted to accept a new contract. Provisions included a plan giving retired employees as much as $55 a month. The company retirement plan was the 1st of its kind in Canada.

Apr. 24 A flood of the Red R. killed 1 person, forced approximately 100,000 inhabitants to flee their homes, and caused $100 million in damage.

May 6 A fire at Rimouski, Que., caused $10 million in damage.

May 29 The RCMP ship *St. Roch* reached Halifax after passing through the Panama Canal from Vancouver. It was the 1st ship to circumnavigate North America.

June 15 The 1st issue of the left-leaning periodical *Cité Libre* was published under the joint editorship of labour journalist Gérard Pelletier (1919–1997) and labour lawyer Pierre Elliott Trudeau (1919–2000). The magazine provided readers with liberal interpretations of contemporary Que. politics, religion and social structure.

June 25 The Korean War broke out. Canada supported the UN decision to support the South. The next day, External Affairs Minister Lester B. Pearson, speaking in the House of Commons, stated that North Korea was guilty of "an action of unprovoked aggression," and urged support of a UN Security Council resolution condemning North Korea and demanding its immediate withdrawal from South Korea. On July 7, the UN Security Council, with the Soviet representative absent, voted in favour of a multilateral force to aid South Korea.

June 28 The Des Joachims hydroelectric power generating plant in Ont. was officially opened. Located 21 km southeast of Deep R., Ont., it was the largest hydro plant on the Ottawa R.

June 30 Canadian Inuit received the right to vote.

• PM St. Laurent announced that Canada would make a military contribution to the Korean action, and on July 5, Canadian destroyers *Cayuga*, *Athabaskan (II)*, and *Sioux* left Esquimalt, BC, for Pearl Harbor as part of that contribution. The destroyers came under UN command in Pearl Harbor on July 12 and were later used to support the Inchon landings and the UN evacuation of Chinnampo. On July 20, an RCAF transport squadron became operational to assist the UN airlift in Korea.

July 15 The 18,160-tonne ocean liner *Franconia* ran aground off Île d'Orléans, in the St. Lawrence R., after leaving Quebec City for Liverpool, England.

July 22 Former PM Mackenzie King died at 76, of pneumonia, at his Kingsmere estate in the Gatineau Hills, near Ottawa.

Year
1950

Also in July
• Brig-Gen. H.H. Angle, the chief military observer of the UN Military Observation Group in India and Pakistan, was killed in an air crash, the 1st Canadian to die on a UN peacekeeping mission.

• Diamond prospectors Frederick W. Chubb, Ken McTaggart and Victor Ben Meen discovered the Ungava Meteorite Crater in northwest Quebec. Measuring over 3.21 km in diameter and over 414.5 m deep, the crater is also called the Cratère du Nouveau-Quebec, or colloquially, the Chubb Crater.

Aug. 1 The RCMP absorbed the Nfld. Rangers and assumed policing of Nfld. and Labrador.

Aug. 7 Members of a special cabinet meeting agreed to create a distinct Canadian armed force to serve with the UN in Korea. PM Laurent announced on nationwide radio that the force would be raised for service "under the United Nations charter or the North Atlantic pact." John Meredith Rockingham (b 1911) was appointed commander of the Canadian brigade on Aug. 9. By Sept. 6, there were 8,691 enlistment's in the new Canadian Army Special Force (CASF), created for combat in Korea.

Aug. 15 The Canada Steamship Lines cruise ship *Quebec* burned down to its freight deck near Tadoussac, Que. Seven passengers died. All others escaped serious injury.

• The RCMP absorbed the BC Provincial Police.

• Canada and New Zealand signed an agreement to provide direct air service between the 2 countries.

Aug. 22 At 6 a.m., a nationwide rail strike of approximately 125,000 members of the Canadian Brotherhood of Railway and Steamship Clerks began, causing the worst transport crisis in Canadian history. On Aug. 26, PM St. Laurent, Labour Minister Milton Fowler Gregg (1892–1978) and Transport Minister Lionel Chevrier (1903–1987) met labour leaders and management, and appealed to each group to reach a compromise in the national interest. At the PM's insistence, talks were resumed, but were unsuccessful. Rail service resumed Aug. 30 when strikers were legislated back to work. An

arbitrator was provided for this and future rail strikes. On Dec. 18, railway workers were awarded a 3 cent per hour raise and a 40-hour workweek.

Sept. 19 Lester B. Pearson was chairman of the Canadian delegation at the 5th regular session of the UN General Assembly, at Flushing Meadows, New York, until Dec. 15.

Also in Sept.
• The Essential Materials Act, giving the govt increased and extensive control over defensive industries, was adopted.

Oct. 2 The Canadian exchange rate was freed from the US dollar, and allowed to float.

Oct. 4 The 1,770-km, $95-million Interprovincial Oil Pipeline from the Leduc oil fields around Edmonton, to Superior, Wisconsin, at the northeast corner of L. Superior, went into full operation. Oil reached Superior on Dec. 5. The Interprovincial was extended to Sarnia, Ont., in 1953, and Montreal in 1976.

Oct. 9 US Gen. Douglas MacArthur ordered UN troops north over the 38th parallel in Korea.

Oct. 26 Canada signed an agreement with the US outlining 6 economic principles for joint defence production; these were designed to eliminate all barriers to the free flow of arms and equipment between the 2 countries.

Oct. 28 Gov-Gen. Alexander's term of office was extended for 1 year.

Nov. 10 A US Air Force B-50 bomber accidentally dropped a Mark IV nuclear bomb carrying a 2,200-kg chemical detonating charge near St-Alexandre-de-Kamouraska, Que. The explosion rocked houses for 40 km. The Mark IV was not loaded with nuclear material. The bomber was returning from Goose Bay, Labrador. The accident was not made public until the 1990s. The US Air Force had stored its Mark IV atomic bombs in Goose Bay since 1950.

Nov. 21 A troop train collided with a CNR passenger train at Canoe R., BC, killing 21 and injuring 53.

Dec. 9 Canadian export permits for Korea, China, Hong Kong and Macao were suspended.

Dec. 11 British PM Attlee and PM St. Laurent met in Ottawa and expressed mutual concern about the US crossing of the 38th parallel in Korea.

Dec. 18 The 1st Canadian troops, the 2nd Battalion Princess Patricia's Canadian Light Infantry, arrived in Korea, at Pusan.

Dec. 31 Canadian sportswriters declared Lionel Conacher (1900–1954) the greatest athlete of the half century. Conacher was multitalented. He won the 1916 lightweight wrestling championship of Ont., and became the Canadian light heavyweight boxing champion. In 1921, he scored 15 points to lead the Toronto Argonauts to a Grey Cup victory. In 1922, he helped Toronto capture the Ont. lacrosse championship. In the 1934–1935 season, Conacher was selected to the NHL All Star team and then led the Chicago Blackhawks to the Stanley Cup.

Also in 1950

• Canada's population was 13,712,000.

• The hamlet of Port Brabant (NWT), east of the Mackenzie R. delta on the Beaufort Sea, officially became known as Tuktoyaktuk, meaning "place where there are caribou." The change marked the 1st historic French or English place name to be restored to traditional Inuit usage or preference.

• Alert, a joint Canada-US weather station, was established at the northern tip of Ellesmere Is., only 800 km from the North Pole. It was the northern-most permanent habitation in the world.

• Bobbie Rosenfeld (1904–1969), ferocious track, basketball, ice hockey and softball competitor, was named the Outstanding Canadian Woman Athlete of Half the Century. The Canadian Press Female Athlete of the Year Award was named in her honour.

• Broadcaster Danny Gallivan (1917–1993) began his broadcasting career with the Montreal Canadiens. The NB native broadcast over 1,800 games between 1950–1984 with a flair that made even the dullest contest exciting. His unmatched phraseology — which included "Savardian spin-orama," "scintillating blast," "cannonading drive," "skates with alacrity" and "enormous save" —

transformed the hockey lexicon and helped make Gallivan one of the most beloved sportscasters of all time.

• Calgary-based Dome Exploration (Western) Ltd., the forerunner to the multibillion-dollar Dome Petroleum Limited, was incorporated by founder Jack Gallagher (1916–1998).

• John Hopps (b 1920) produced the 1st heart pace-maker prototype. It was not until 1958, however, that a revised edition of the device would be 1st implanted into a human patient. Hopps received the Order of Canada in 1986.

• W.H. Smith opened its 1st bookstore in Canada at 224 Yonge St., in Toronto.

• Alex Colville painted *Nude and Dummy*, now in the New Brunswick Museum, Saint John.

• In Vancouver, Lawren Harris completed the abstract landscape *Nature Rhythm*, now in the National Gallery of Canada.

• Gabrielle Roy published her second novel, *La Petit Poule d'Eau*, which would be translated into English by Harry Binsse, and published as *Where Nests the Water Hen* in 1951. Many critics regard this book as Roy's finest work.

• Political economist Harold Adams Innis (1894–1952) published *Empire and Communications*.

• Catherine Anthony Clark (1892–1977) published *The Golden Pine Cone*, a children's fantasy.

• NB Acadian writer Donat Coste (1912–1957) raised the issue of racism in the novel *L'enfant noir*.

• Robert Élie published the novel *La Fin des songes*.

• Anne Hébert published her 1st book of short stories, *Le Torrent*.

• Dorothy Livesay published the prose *Call My People Home*.

• Thomas Head Raddall (1903–1994) published the historical novel *The Nymph and the Lamp*, set on Sable Is. during WW I.

• The play *Riel*, by John William Coulter (1999–1980), was staged in Toronto.

• Robertson Davies' *At My Heart's Core*, a full-length play based on the lives of the Strickland sisters, Susanna Moodie and Catherine Parr Traill, was staged.

• Canada's 1st film festival dedicated to documentary films, the Yorkton International Documentary Film Festival, was held in Sask. The Festival introduced the Golden Sheaf Award in 1958; the 1st award went to a Czechoslovakian film called *Inspiration*. The international competition was dropped in 1977 when entries were limited to Canadian short films. In 1981, the festival added a video category and has since been known as the Yorkton Short Film & Video Festival.

1951

Jan. 4–12 PM St. Laurent attended a meeting of Commonwealth PMs in London, England, to discuss Commonwealth defence policy.

Jan. 22 The Canadian destroyer *Huron* was placed under UN command.

Feb. 1 Canada approved a resolution, sponsored by the US at the UN, which named China as an aggressor in the Korean conflict.

Feb. 5 Canada announced rearmament plans, which included the expenditure of $5 million over 3 years and an increase in the number of military personnel from 90,000 to 148,000.

Feb. 23 The Princess Pats joined with the 27th British Commonwealth Infantry Brigade, and made their 1st contact with the enemy in Korea. Canada suffered its 1st casualties of the war. On Mar. 2, the 1st Canadian casualty list from Korea reported 6 Canadian soldiers killed.

Mar. 9 The govt approved incorporation of Trans-Canada PipeLines, a company created to build a 3,700-km natural gas pipeline running from western to central Canada. TransCanada was incorporated Mar. 21. A federal scandal over funding erupted in 1956, which disrupted completion of the line.

Mar. 27 Canada and the US ratified an agreement for the establishment of civil defence along the Canada–US border.

Apr. 1 The Department of Defence Production was established, with C.D. Howe as minister.

Apr. 5 Ont. introduced the Fair Employment Practices Act, which prohibited discrimination in the workplace based on race or religion.

Apr. 5–8 Vincent Auriol, president of France, visited Ottawa and addressed the Senate and House of Commons.

Apr. 10 US President Harry Truman fired Gen. Douglas MacArthur for publicly declaring his desire to expand the Korean War into China. Gen. Matthew Ridgeway was assigned MacArthur's command the next day.

Apr. 21 In overtime against the Montreal Canadiens, Bill Barilko (1927–1951) took a pass from Howie Meeker and scored the Stanley Cup winning goal for the Toronto Maple Leafs. Weeks later Barilko went missing on a flight in northern Ont. and was presumed dead. His remains would not be found until June 7, 1962 — not long after the Leafs won their 1st cup since Barilko's disappearance.

Apr. 24–25 Canadian troops defended the Kapyong Valley in Korea against a Chinese attack, at the cost of 10 dead and 23 wounded. "B" company of the Princess Patricia's Canadian Light Infantry was awarded a US presidential citation for this action, the 1st time such an honour was awarded to a Canadian unit.

June 1 The report of the Massey Commission on culture was tabled in the House of Commons. It recommended that a Canada Council for the Encouragement of the Arts, Letters, Humanities and Social Sciences be established. It also supported federal spending on universities, CBC control of the new television media, a national library, a national endowment fund to support writers, artists, theatres and orchestras, and the development of a domestically owned publishing industry. The Canada Council would subsequently be established Mar. 28, 1957.

June 15 The Northwest Territories Act was amended to provide for a partially elected council. The 1st election for the NWT Council was held Sept. 17.

Also in June
- All members of the Canadian Army Special Force, redesignated the 25th Canadian Brigade, went into action in Korea.

- The Indian Act of 1876 was revised, ending a ban on traditional ceremonies, including the potlatch, prohibited in 1884. The revisions gave Native Peoples the right to raise money for political purposes and to consume liquor in public.

July 10 Peace talks began at Panmunjom, Korea, but were suspended after 6 months because of an impasse concerning the repatriation of prisoners.

- Canada formally ended its state of war with Germany.

July 31 A Canadian Pacific DC-4 flight between Vancouver and Alaska crashed, killing 36.

Aug. 16 Winnie Roach Leuszler (1926–2004) became the 1st Canadian to swim the English Channel. The feat took her 13 hours, 25 minutes. Leuszler, competing in a race sponsored by Britain's *Daily Mail*, was swept off course during the event and finished 7th.

Also in Aug.
- Le Théâtre du Nouveau Monde was founded in Montreal.

Sept. 8 External Affairs Minister Pearson signed the Japanese Peace Treaty for Canada in San Francisco.

Sept. 10 Canada and Pakistan signed a technical assistance pact, with Canada providing $10 million in aid for the 1st year of a 6-year Pakistan development plan.

Sept. 15–20 The Council of NATO met at Ottawa, marking the 1st time the council convened in Canada. The Parliament was used for meetings, and for the 1st time, the House of Commons was used for a news conference. The Ottawa meetings were preceded by a visit from NATO Supreme Commander Gen. Dwight Eisenhower, on Jan. 26.

Sept. 28 The International Monetary Fund lifted restrictions on the sale of gold.

Oct. 8 Princess Elizabeth of England and the Duke of Edinburgh toured Canada until Nov. 12.

Oct. 18 The federal govt announced Canada would maintain 12,000 army and air force personnel in Europe as part of its NATO commitment. On Nov. 15, the 1st units of the 27th Canadian Infantry Brigade (27 CIB) arrived in Hanover, Germany, for NATO service. The group was commanded by Brig-Gen. Geoffrey Walsh.

Oct. 27 The world's 1st cobalt radiotherapy unit, the cobalt "bomb" developed by Dr. Harold Elford Johns (1915–1988) to treat cancer patients, was put to clinical use in London, Ont.

Nov. 12 The National Ballet of Canada, founded this year by Celia Franca (b 1921) gave its 1st performance. Principal dancers Franca, Irene Apiné, Lois Smith (b 1929), David Adams (b 1928) and Jury Gotshalks performed Fredric Chopin's *Les Sylphides* and Alexander Borodin's *Polovtsian Dances from "Prince Igor,"* at the Eaton Auditorium in Toronto.

Dec. 14 The federal govt abolished all foreign-exchange controls.

Also in Dec.
- William Andrew Cecil "Wacky" Bennett (1900–1979) joined the BC Social Credit League.

Also in 1951
- The population of Canada was 14,009,429. The population of Ont. was 4,597,542; Que., 4,055,681; BC, 1,165,210; Alb., 939,501; Sask., 831,728; Man., 776,541; NS, 642,584; NB, 515,697; Nfld., 361,416; PEI, 98,429; NWT, 16,004; and Yukon 9,096.

- Triggered by the Fred Rose spy case of 1946, the Citizenship Act was amended to allow the stripping of citizenship from naturalized Canadians convicted of offences involving "disaffection or disloyalty" to the crown.

- After nearly dying of a head injury in the playoffs the season before, Gordie Howe returned to the ice to lead the NHL in goals, assists and points, a feat not accomplished since Howie Morenz in 1928.

• The Aluminum Company of Canada (ALCAN) began construction of a hydroelectric plant and aluminum smelter at Kitimat, BC. The project was completed in 1954.

• The Tom Longboat Awards, given annually to an outstanding male and female Aboriginal athlete in Canada, were established in honour of the great runner from the Onondaga Nation. The awards were 1st given by the Department of Indian and Northern Development.

• Fort Battleford National Historic Park was established northeast of Saskatoon, Sask., to preserve the battle site of the 1885 Northwest Rebellion.

• Peesee Oshuitoq (Oshaweetok-A) (1913–1979) carved *Mother and Child,* a 20.3 x 9.0 cm soapstone sculpture. Oshuitoq lived on the south coast of Baffin Is. near Cape Dorset and was 1st encouraged to carve by James Houston in the early 1950s. *Mother and Child* is held at the Metropolitan Museum of Art in New York City.

• Que. poet and singer-songwriter Félix Leclerc (1914–1988) won Le Prix du disque in Paris for his song "Moi et mes souliers."

• Historian Harold Innis published *The Bias of Communication.*

• Morley Callaghan's novel, *The Loved and the Lost,* for which he received the Gov-Gen.'s Award for fiction, was published.

• Eugène Seers (pseud. Louis Dantin) (1865–1945) published *Les Enfances de Fanny*, a posthumous semi-autobiographical novel.

• Robertson Davies published the satirical novel *Tempest-Tost,* the 1st of the Salterton trilogy, which included *Leaven of Malice* (1954) and *A Mixture of Frailties* (1958).

• A.M. Klein published the novel *The Second Scroll,* in which Jews return to the promised land after WW II.

• André Langevin (b 1927) published the novel *Évadé de la nuit.*

• Hugh MacLennan published *Each Man's Son*, set in a NS mining town.

• Robert de Roquebrune (1889–1976) published his autobiography, *Testament de mon enfance.*

• Roger Viau (1906–1986) published the novel *Au milieu, la montagne.*

• Marshall McLuhan (1911–1980) published his 1st book, *The Mechanical Bride: Folklore of Industrial Man.*

• L.J. Chapman and D.F. Putnam published the classic *Physiography of Southern Ontario*, the 1st systematic account and mapping of the region's glacial legacy.

• Poet Anne Wilkinson, née Gibbons (1910–1961), published her 1st book, *Counterpoint to Sleep.*

• Elizabeth Winifred Brewster (b 1922) published her 1st book of poetry, *East Coast.*

• Poet Charles Tory Bruce (1906–1971) published *The Mulgrave Road*, for which he received the Gov-Gen.'s Award.

1952

Jan. 1 A new Old Age Security Act came into effect, providing universal pensions to those 70 and over. The Old Age Assistance Act provided pensions to needy people 65 to 69.

Jan. 11–15 British PM Winston Churchill, who had again become prime minister Oct. 1951, visited Ottawa.

Jan. 21 Canada and the US signed an agreement to use radio on the Great Lakes as a safety measure.

Jan. 24 Vincent Massey was appointed the 1st Canadian-born gov-gen., serving Feb. 28 to Sept. 15, 1959.

May 14 The 17-store Sunnybrook Shopping Centre opened in northern Toronto, followed by Lawrence Plaza, North York, in 1953. Sunnybrook and Lawrence Plaza are the oldest planned shopping centres in Ont.

June 12 BC's Social Credit Party formed a minority govt after the BC provincial election, with William Bennett (1900–1979) as premier. Bennett assumed office Aug. 1.

June 30 Canada applied to the International Joint Commission for approval to build power developments in international rapids on the St. Lawrence R. The commission approved the project on Oct. 29.

Also in June

• The Redistribution Bill, a measure re-allocating the seats in the Canadian House of Commons, was passed in accordance with the population changes revealed by the census of 1951.

July 4 The CNR Capital Revision Act became law, wiping out 50% of the CNR's debt ($736 million) and easing interest payments for 10 years.

July 11 In Que., Maurice Duplessis' Union Nationale govt was returned to office with 68 of 92 seats.

July 23–Aug. 9 The International Red Cross held its 18th international conference in Toronto. Delegates from more than 150 nations revised and reaffirmed the fundamental Red Cross principles: impartiality, independence, equality and universality.

Aug. 4 The Parliamentary Library in Ottawa was badly damaged by fire. Restoration was undertaken between 1953 and 1956 by contractor Angus Robertson at a cost of $2.4 million. The library was officially reopened June 19, 1956.

Aug. 13 The govt announced that it would provide Britain with a Mutual Aid Gift worth $150 million.

Sept. 6 Canada's 1st television station, CBFT in Montreal (part of the CBC French network), began transmitting. Canada's 1st English-language television station, CBLT, operated by the CBC, began broadcasting in Toronto Sept. 8.

Sept. 8 The Boyd Gang (Edwin Alonzo Boyd, William Russell Jackson and Leonard Jackson) escaped from Toronto's Don Jail. They had been charged with murder and armed robbery. On Sept. 17, after the biggest manhunt in Canadian history, the gang was apprehended following a gun battle in a North York, Ont., barn.

Sept. 22 The Conservatives won the NB election, with Hugh John Flemming (1899–1982) becoming premier.

Oct. 11 "La Soirée du hockey" was 1st broadcast from Montreal between the Canadiens and the Detroit Red Wings. "Hockey Night in Canada" would first broadcast a Leafs game from Maple Leaf Gardens on Nov. 1. The French-language "La Soirée du hockey" would cease broadcasting Montreal games after the 2003–2004 season.

Oct. 14 Minister of External Affairs Lester B. Pearson was elected president of the UN General Assembly at the opening of its 7th session in New York.

Oct. 17–23 Canadian troops fought to capture Hill 355 in the battle of Little Gibraltar Hill, in Korea. There were 183 Canadian casualties.

• The federal govt replaced the cost of living index with the new consumer price index.

Oct. 30 The 3rd Battalion of the Princess Pats Infantry arrived in Korea to replace the 1st Battalion.

Nov. 2–3 The Chinese launched offensives against the Royal Canadian Regiment in Korea, against the Princess Pats on Nov. 4 and against Le Royal 22 Régiment on Nov. 23–25.

Nov. 8 Ten years to the day after his 1st NHL game, Maurice Richard, of the Montreal Canadiens, scored his 325th career goal to become the league's all-time leading scorer, passing Nels Stewart (1902–1957).

Nov. 27 PM St. Laurent attended the Commonwealth Conference in London, England, until Dec. 11.

Dec. 1 A federal-provincial agricultural conference opened at Ottawa.

Dec. 15 Montreal accountant George Currie's report on illegal activity at the Petawawa, Ont., military base was tabled in the House of Commons. It revealed a breakdown of administration, accounting and discipline, leading to profiteering and criminal activities. Currie made 44 recommendations. The investigation led to the arrest and conviction of 4 military personnel and 8 civilians.

1952–1959 656 American-built Lockheed T-33 Silver Star MK 3 aircraft were acquired by the RCAF.

Also in 1952

• Canada won 3 medals at the Summer Olympic Games in Helsinki, Finland, including 1 gold, by George Genereux (1935–1989) in the clay pigeon shooting event.

• Fortuitously, Vancouver's Dave Broadfoot (b 1925) arrived in Toronto on the very day that CBC TV went on the air in that city. Shortly thereafter, a chance meeting with Canadian theatre's Mavor Moore (b 1919) led to a 10-year engagment with the annual satirical review "Spring Thaw," a guest spot on the *Ed Sullivan Show* and, in 1959, a Comedian of the Year award as voted by Canadian television critics. In 1973, Broadfoot joined CBC TV's *Royal Canadian Air Farce*, where his comedic personalities Cpl. Renfrew of the RCMP and the cornball Member for Kicking Horse Pass kept Canadians laughing for 15 years.

• The Edmonton Mercurys men's hockey team won Canada's only gold at the Winter Olympics in Oslo, Norway. Gordon Audley (b 1928) won the nation's only other medal, a bronze in the 500-m speed-skating event.

• Women in Man. were 1st to serve on juries.

• Simpson's department store chain partnered with the US-based Sears chain to form Simpson-Sears.

• The Canadian Retail Booksellers Association had its founding convention, establishing the standard trade practice of providing booksellers with a 40% discount on books, along with a returns policy.

• Atomic Energy of Canada Ltd. (AECL) was established by the federal govt as a Crown corporation to investigate the production of nuclear energy for peaceful purposes.

• 150,000 Canadians owned television sets.

• The 1st widespread use of the helicopter to map Canadian geology began; between 1952 and 1958, more than half as much of Canada was mapped as had previously been completed over the preceding 110 years.

• A body of work depicting significant events in Canadian history by sketch artist Charles Jefferys was bought by Rockefeller's Imperial Oil (Canada). All reproductions thereafter were imprinted with the name of the oil producer.

• Jack Bush exhibited his painting *The Old Tree*, using forms derived from cubism, in a one-man show at the Roberts Gallery, Toronto. The painting is now in the Art Gallery of Ont., Toronto.

• Historian Harold Innis published *Changing Concepts of Time*.

• Farley Mowat (b 1921) published *People of the Deer*, a beautiful chronicle of the Ihalmuit peoples of Canada's barren lands.

• Ted Allen and Sydney Gordon published *The Scalpel and the Sword*, the 1st biography of Dr. Norman Bethune.

• Historian Donald Creighton (1902–1979) published *John A. Macdonald: The Young Politician*.

• Ernest Buckler (1908–1984) published the novel *The Mountain and the Valley*, about a gifted boy's problematic attachment to life in rural NS.

• Roger Lemelin published the novel *Pierre le magnifique* (translated in 1955 as *Quest of Splendour*).

• Norman Levine (b 1923) published the novel *The Angled Road*.

• Poet E.J. Pratt published *Towards the Last Spike*.

• George Woodcock (1912–1995) published *Ravens and Prophets*.

• Earle Birney published his verse drama *Trial of a City*, originally called *Damnation of Vancouver*.

• Alex Colville painted *Child and Dog* and *Woman, Man and Boat*; both paintings are now in the National Gallery of Canada.

• Fred Cogswell (1917–2004) was appointed editor of *Fiddlehead* magazine, a position he would pursue with passion until 1966, when he left to establish Fiddlehead Poetry Books.

1953

Jan. 5 The federal govt Goodwill Trade Mission visited 9 Latin American countries, until Feb. 10.

Jan. 9 Margaret Petri was the last woman in Canada to be hanged. She had abetted Albert Guay in the Sept. 9, 1949 bombing of a Canadian Pacific passenger plane that killed 23.

Mar. 1 The US removed an embargo on Canadian livestock 1st imposed in 1952 after an outbreak of foot-and-mouth disease.

Mar. 19 Norman McLaren (1914–1987) won an Academy Award for his National Film Board production *Neighbours.*

Mar. 27 The 7 main doors of the new UN Building in New York City were formally presented to the UN by External Affairs Minister Lester B. Pearson as a gift from Canada. The $75,000 nickel-silver doors had been installed in Oct. 1952, when the UN Building was completed.

May 7 PM St. Laurent paid his 1st visit to US President Eisenhower in Washington to establish the best possible communication with the new administration, to urge removal of restrictions on Canadian agricultural products and to encourage US cooperation on the St. Lawrence Seaway and power project.

May 15 Jazz immortals Charlie Parker, Dizzie Gillespie, Charlie Mingus, Bud Powell and Max Roach electrified Toronto's Massey Hall in what was billed as "The Greatest Jazz Concert Ever." Because of the Rocky Marciano–Jersey Joe Walcott fight broadcast the same evening, Massey Hall was only 1/4 full. The concert would have been forgotten had Charlie Mingus not had the foresight to preserve the modern classic through a portable recorder borrowed just prior to the show.

May 21 Sarnia, Ont., was ravaged by a tornado that caused 5 deaths and $4 million in damage.

May 25 Alexander W. Matheson (1903–1976) became Liberal premier of PEI.

Also in May

• Geologists Franc Joubin (1911–1997) and Joseph Hirshhorn (1900–1981) staked claims to the largest uranium discovery in Canadian history near Blind R., Ont. The site would become home to Denison Mines Ltd. Financed and built by Slovakian immigrant Stephen B. Roman (1922–1988), Denison would also become a major potash, oil, gas and coal producer.

June 2 Official ceremonies were conducted at Ottawa and other Canadian cities to honour the coronation of Queen Elizabeth II. PM St. Laurent and his wife were in attendance in London, England. Healey Willan (1880–1968), organist and choirmaster of St. Mary Magdalene Anglican Church in Toronto, composed the *Coronation Suite.* He was the 1st non-British resident to compose music for a British coronation.

June 3–9 PM St. Laurent attended a meeting of Commonwealth PMs in London, England.

June 4 The Potash Corporation of Sask. was incorporated.

July 13 The Stratford Festival established in Stratford, Ont. by Tom Patterson (b 1920) opened for its 1st season, in a tent, with Alec Guinness starring in *Richard III.* The season ran for 6 weeks. British director Tyrone Guthrie mounted two plays, *Richard III* and *All's Well That End's Well.* In July 1957, the tent theatre was replaced by the $2 million Festival Theatre, designed by Robert Fairfield.

July 27 The Korean War ended with UN and North Korean delegates signing an armistice at Panmunjom; 26,791 Canadians had served in Korea in the army; 22 Canadian fighter pilots flew with the US Air Force; in addition, 7,000 Canadians served in Korea with UN forces after the end of the war, until Nov. 8, 1954. Canadian casualties amounted to 516 killed,1,211 wounded and 33 captured.

Aug. 10 Louis St. Laurent's Liberals won the federal general election with 171 seats. The PCs took 51, the CCF 23, Social Credit 15 and independents 5. Voter turnout was 67.5%.

Aug. 15 A riot at Kingston Penitentiary resulted in 3 buildings burned and $2 million in damage.

Also in Aug.

• Fifty-three Inuit from Port Harrison, Que., and Pond Inlet, Baffin Is., were relocated to Cornwallis Is. and Ellesmere Is. in the High Arctic on grounds that the area would provide more game to sustain a traditional lifestyle. Inuit would later argue they were used as sovereignty markers in the internationally disputed region.

Sept. 6 Thirty Canadians were freed in the final exchange of war prisoners in Korea.

Sept. 15 A professional exterminator hired to protect Alb. from the Norway rat — a disease-carrying agricultural pest — declared the province rat-free.

Oct. 15 The Trans-Mountain Oil Pipeline from Edmonton, Alb., to Vancouver, BC, was completed.

Oct. 16 Federal authorization was given to establish Canada's 1st peacetime regular army division, the 1st Canadian Infantry Division, which had disbanded after WW II. A brigade of the division was stationed in Germany.

Oct. 20 Canada's 1st privately owned television station, CKSO, went into operation in Sudbury, Ont.

Nov. 13 US President Eisenhower and his wife, Mamie, visited Ottawa. The president assured PM St. Laurent that joint construction of the long-awaited St. Lawrence Seaway and Power project was "inevitable and certain." The president also addressed the House of Commons.

Also in Nov.

• Nancy (Austin) Hodges, former speaker of the BC legislature, was appointed to the Senate.

Dec. 7 The Mercantile Bank of Canada began operations, with head offices in Montreal. A subsidiary of First National City Bank of New York, it was the 1st foreign-owned bank to be incorporated in this country.

Dec. 16 A bill to establish the Dept. of Northern Affairs and Natural Resources was given Assent.

Also in 1953

• The US army secretly sprayed zinc cadmium sulphide over Winnipeg to test its usefulness against possible US-bound guided missiles from Russia. A 29-page US military report, made public July 15, 1994, stated that subsequent tests on the material showed no associated health risks.

• Paul-Émile Léger (1904–1991), Archbishop of Montreal, was elected a cardinal of the Roman Catholic Church, noting "…to be a cardinal is very convenient in a certain way, it gives you a little bit of authority." Léger established the Fame Pereo organization in Africa to aid leprosy sufferers on that continent. Later, at age 75, he was named co-chair of the Canadian Foundation for Refugees, established to help Vietnamese boat people flee to Canada.

• The capital of Yukon Territory was moved from Dawson to Whitehorse.

• A radical splinter group of Doukhobors known as the Sons of Freedom burned down several schools in the Kootenay region of BC in a dispute over the education of their children. The BC govt subsequently rounded up some 100 Doukhobor children under the age of 15 and sent them to be re-educated at a residential school in New Denver.

• The annual International Canada Cup golf tournament of 2-man teams was 1st played at Beaconsfield Golf Club in Montreal. It was won by the Argentinean team of Roberto De Vicenzo and Antonio Cerda. The cup was a donation of industrialist John Jay Hopkins. The tournament was re-named the World Cup in 1967.

• The RCAF became the world's 1st air force to acquire jet transports — 2 Comets brought from England.

• At the age of 19, Fred Sasakamoose (b 1933) of Sask. became the 1st treaty Aboriginal to play in the NHL. He played for the Chicago Blackhawks.

• 8,700 cases of polio were reported in Canada, a disease that resulted in 500 cases of paralysis and 500 deaths for the year.

• Despite a club foot, no coaching and almost no money, Doug Hepburn (1926–2000) won the world heavyweight weightlifting championship in Stockholm, Sweden. His lifts were 168 kg (371.25 lb) press, 58.7 kg (297.5 lb) snatch, and 165 kg (363.75 lb) clean and jerk.

• Wardair was incorporated in Alb. by bush pilot and WW II aviation instructor Max Ward (b 1921). The bush service initially flew out of Yellowknife with a De Havilland Canada DHC-3 Otter. In 1966, Wardair purchased a Boeing 727, launching an internationally recognized, service-oriented passenger-jet service that would branch across Canada and into foreign markets. In 1989, Wardair was sold to Calgary-based PWA Corporation, parent company of Canadian Airlines, for $250 million.

• John Angus McDougald's (1908–1978) Argus Corporation paid $16 million to acquire Massey-Harris-Ferguson. The purchase price was determined by the flip of a coin between McDougald and Massey-Harris-Ferguson owner Harry Ferguson (1884–1960).

• Hard-hitting Scottish journalist Jack Fraser (1918–1999), recent Canadian immigrant, joined CJOR radio in Vancouver, broadcasting two shows a day, *Spotlight at Noon* and *City Mike*. In 1963, he moved to CKNW as a talk-show host, in addition to appearing on CBC-TV's *This Hour Has Seven Days*. In 1972, he rejoined CJOR, establishing himself as one of the pre-eminent radio journalists in the field, before moving on to BCTV in 1978 to host "*Webster*" five days a week. Fraser was awarded the Order of Canada in 1988.

• Paul-Émile Borduas working in New York, completed *Les Signes s'envolent*, now in the Musée des beaux arts (Montreal), and *Figure aux oiseaux*, now in the Agnes Etherington Art Centre (Queen's U. Kingston).

• Abstract artist Jack Leonard Shadbolt (1909–1998) painted *Presence after Fire*, now in the National Gallery of Canada.

• Educator Hilda Marion Neatby (1904–1975) published *So Little for the Mind*, an indictment of Canadian pre-university training and a condemnation of progressive education.

• Que. poet Robert Choquette published *Suite marine*, one of the works that earned him the title "prince of poets," given by the French-Canadian Poetry Society in 1961.

• Poet Anne Hébert published *Le tombeau des rois*.

• Poet Gilles Hénault (1920–1996) published *Totems*.

• Irving Layton published *Love the Conqueror Worm*, a volume of poems.

• Douglas Valentine Le Pan published his 2nd volume of poetry, *The Net and the Sword*, for which he received the Gov-Gen.'s Award.

• *Deux Sangs*, by Que. nationalist poets Gaston Miron (1928–1996) and Olivier Marchand (b 1928), was published.

1954

Jan. 1 Metropolitan Toronto, consisting of the City of Toronto and 12 suburban towns, villages and townships, was the 1st grouping of Canadian municipalities to adopt a formal metropolitan organization.

Feb. 4 PM St. Laurent began a round-the-world goodwill tour visiting 11 countries, including Asian members of the Commonwealth, until Mar. 17.

Feb. 5 The most northerly group of Canada's Arctic islands was named the Queen Elizabeth Islands.

Feb. 23 PM St. Laurent addressed a joint session of the 2 chambers of the Indian Parliament and praised NATO and the US for its defence of the free world, contrary to the feelings of Prime Minister Jawaharlal Nehru who believed the US and NATO held expansionist designs.

Feb. 26–27 Sec-Gen. of the UN, Dag Hammarskjöld, visited Ottawa.

Also in Feb.
• Painters Eleven exhibited their combined works for

the 1st time at Robert's Gallery in Toronto. Painters Eleven was founded in Oshawa/Whitby, Ont., in 1953, to support and exhibit abstract art. Members were Jack Bush, Oscar Cahen (1916–1956), Hortense Gordon (1887–1961), Tom Hodgson (b 1924), Alexandra Luke (b 1922), Jock Macdonald (1897–1960), Ray Mead (1921–1998), Kazuo Nakamura (b 1926), William Ronald (b 1926), Harold Town (1924–1991) and Walter Yarwood (1917–1996).

Mar. 30 The 7.4-km Yonge St. subway, the 1st subway line in Canada, was opened by the Toronto Transit Commission (TTC) at a cost of $67 million. The subway, which ran between Union Station and Eglinton Ave., was largely dug by hand and resulted in much new information regarding the glacial history of the area. Construction had started Sept. 8, 1949. A 13-km, $200-million east-west (Bloor St.) line was opened by PM Lester B. Pearson on Feb. 25, 1966.

Apr. 1 Woodside, Mackenzie King's former boyhood home in Kitchener, Ont., was made a national historic park. Situated on a 4.5-ha plot, the large grey-brick house held relics of the King family and furniture of the late 19th century.

Apr. 8 A TCA airliner crashed at Moose Jaw, Sask., killing 37 people.

Apr. 24 Former Director Gen. of Economic Development in Nfld., Alfred Valdmanis, was convicted of defrauding the govt while in the public service, and sentenced to 4 years in jail.

Apr. 26 The Far Eastern Conference for the settlement of the Korean question opened in Geneva. External Affairs Minister Lester B. Pearson led the Canadian delegation.

May 13 Six railway companies, the largest of which was the National Transcontinental Railway Branch Lines Co., amalgamated with the CNR.

May 31 The 1st prairie television station, CBWT, in Winnipeg, went on the air.

Also in May
• The Alb. Petroleum and Natural Gas Conservation Board granted TransCanada PipeLines an export permit to sell gas to the US.

June 3–7 The Emperor of Ethiopia, Haile Selassie I (Lion of Judea), visited Canada.

June 29–30 British PM Churchill and Foreign Secretary Anthony Eden visited Ottawa.

July 21 Biologists for the Canadian Wildlife Service announced they had discovered the summer nesting grounds of the whooping crane, in Alb.'s Wood Buffalo National Park. Only 24 birds were known to exist in the world at the time, and 6 of those (with young) were spotted as the Wildlife Service conducted a survey of the park's buffalo population.

July 28 Canada agreed to participate in the International Commissions for Supervision and Control of Vietnam, Laos and Cambodia, inaugurating a 20-year peacekeeping endeavour in the region.

July 30 The 5th British Empire and Commonwealth Games were opened in Vancouver by Earl Alexander, former Gov-Gen. of Canada. Canada came away with 9 gold medals. The games were 1st played in Hamilton in 1930.

Aug. 10 An international ceremony for the groundbreaking of the St. Lawrence Seaway project was held at Cornwall, Ont., and Massena, New York, although the massive, 3,700-km project would not officially be opened until June 26, 1959. The St. Lawrence Seaway Authority oversaw construction and upkeep of Canadian facilities, while the St. Lawrence Seaway Development Corporation managed US facilities.

Aug. 19 C.D. Howe who, as minister of transport under PM King helped create Trans-Canada Airlines, was awarded the Daniel Guggenheim Medal for his "great achievements in aeronautics."

Also in Aug.
• Lt-Gen. E.L.M. Burns (1897–1985) was named chief of staff of the UN Truce Supervision Organization in the Middle East.

Sept. 9 Sixteen-year-old Marilyn Bell (b 1937) became the 1st person to swim across L. Ont., completing the 51-km crossing from Youngstown, New York, to Toronto in 21 hours.

Sept. 27–28 Shigeru Yoshida, PM of Japan, visited Ottawa.

Sept. 30 Henry Davies Hicks (1915–1990) was appointed Liberal premier of NS after winning the provincial leadership convention in Halifax. At 30, he was the youngest premier in the country.

Oct. 3 In Calgary, crowds gathered around demonstration TV sets in appliance stores to see the new medium of television as Calgary's CHCT-TV went on air for the first time.

Oct. 15 Hurricane Hazel, which formed in the Caribbean on Oct. 6, struck Toronto with 124-km/h winds and 10.1 cm of rain in 12 hours. Low-lying areas flooded, 83 people died and damage was in excess of $25 million.

Oct. 28 The RCMP patrol vessel *St. Roch* arrived in Vancouver on its last voyage. The ship was transferred to the Vancouver Maritime Museum.

• 37-year-old Jean Drapeau (1916–1999) became mayor of Montreal upon the retirement of Camillien Houde.

Nov. 12–17 Queen Elizabeth II and the Queen Mother visited Ottawa and Hull, Que.

Nov. 14–17 French Premier Pierre Mendès-France visited Quebec City and Ottawa.

Nov. 21 The *Labrador* arrived in Halifax, after completing a 29,000-km voyage through the Northwest Passage and around North America via the Panama Canal.

Nov. 27 With his Edmonton Eskimos team trailing the Montreal Alouettes 25–20 in the final minutes of the Grey Cup, Jackie Parker (b 1932) picked up a fumble and ran 92 yards for a touchdown, to give the Eskimos victory. The game was won with Edmonton centre Eagle Keys playing his career last, on a broken leg.

Dec. 10 The 1,280-m $22-million Canso Causeway, linking Cape Breton Is. and the NS mainland over the Strait of Canso, was completed. Construction had begun Sept. 16, 1952.

Also in 1954

• The Pinetree Line of early-warning radar stations running along the 49th parallel went into operation. Eleven of the 33 stations were located in Canada. The line was a joint Canada–US operation designed to counter possible Soviet air strikes in North America. Pinetree was complemented by the Mid–Canada radar line, or "McGill Fence", which ran from Labrador to the Peace R. region and began operations in 1957, and the DEW Line, which went into operation July 31, 1957. Altogether the system ran from Alaska to Greenland. As part of the US–Canadian venture, the US agreed to recognize Canada's sovereignty in the Arctic.

• Women in NB were 1st permitted to serve on juries.

• Pat Fletcher (1916–1985), representing the Saskatoon Golf and Country Club, was the last Canadian golfer to win the Canadian Open Championship (established in 1904). He carded 280 over 4 rounds at Vancouver's spectacular Point Grey Golf and Country Club.

• Robert Weaver (b 1921) pioneered the CBC's radio program *Anthology*, which gave 1st exposure to many Canadian writers, including Alice Munro (b 1931).

• The Que. govt of Maurice Duplessis, implemented a provincial income tax plan for the province.

• A consortium of Canadian publishers formed the library wholesaler Co-operative Book Centre. The wholesaler was purchased by Maclean Hunter in 1970.

• Hudson Motors, located at Tilbury, Ont., and Nash–Kelvinator, Toronto, merged to form American Motors Canada Ltd.

• An image of Satan appeared in the Queen's hair on all replacement notes issued by the Canadian Mint. Known to collectors as the "Devil's Face portrait," these rare bills fetch upward of 5 times their stated value.

• Montreal-born artist Jean-Paul Riopelle painted *Pavane (triptych),* oil on canvas. The work, held in the National Gallery of Canada, Ottawa, represents the Spanish dance the Pavane.

• LeMoine FitzGerald painted the abstract *Green and Gold*, his last major canvas. It is now in the Winnipeg Art Gallery.

• *Woman with Child*, green stone and ivory carving by Johnny Inukpuk (b 1911), was completed. The carving is with the Canadian Museum of Civilization.

• Novelist Thomas Costain published *The White and the Gold*, a history of New France.

• Nature writer Fred Bodsworth (b 1918) published his 1st and best-known book, *The Last of the Curlews*, a look at traditional Inuit life in decline.

• Folklorist and music collector Edith Fowke (1913–1996) published the collection of 76 popular songs *Folk Songs of Canada*. A second printing was made in 1955.

• Poet P.K. Page (b 1916) published *The Metal and the Flower*.

• Editor Malcolm Ross published *Our Sense of Identity: A Book of Canadian Essays*, which included works by Emily Carr, Sarah Jeanette Duncan, Thomas Chandler Haliburton, Harold Innis, Northrop Frye and many others.

• Ethel Wilson (1888–1980) published the novel *Swamp Angel*.

• Novelist and editor Ralph Allen (1913–1966) published the novel *The Chartered Libertine*, a wry take on the CBC.

1955

Jan. 7 The 2nd session of the 22nd Parliament met until July 28. Opening ceremonies were broadcast on television for the 1st time.

Jan. 26 The House of Commons passed a resolution by a vote of 213–12 calling for the entry of West Germany into NATO.

Jan. 27 Pakistan PM Mohammad Ali made an official visit to Ottawa.

Jan. 31 A 109-day strike by Ford workers at Windsor, Oakville and Etobicoke, Ont., ended.

Feb. 1 During a Commonwealth Conference in London, England, PM St. Laurent was presented with the Freedom of the City of London.

Mar. 17 The suspension of Montreal Canadiens captain Maurice "Rocket" Richard on Mar. 16 by NHL president Clarence Campbell (1905–1984) triggered a riot at the Montreal Forum, which then spilled onto Rue Ste. Catherine. Richard, suspended for the final 3 games of the season and the playoffs for attacking Boston's Hal Laycoe with his stick, was forced to go on radio the next day and plead for calm.

Mar. 21 Fire destroyed 55 buildings at Nicolet, Que.

Mar. 22 A fire at Toronto's Malton Airport caused $5 million in damage.

Apr. 2 The Angus L. Macdonald suspension bridge, linking Halifax and Dartmouth, was opened. It was the 2nd longest suspension bridge in the country after Vancouver's Lion's Gate Bridge.

June 3 CP Airlines inaugurated the 1st service between Vancouver and Amsterdam over the North Pole.

Also in June
• The Galérie l'Actuelle, a small avant-garde showplace dedicated exclusively to the exhibition of non-figurative art, opened in Montreal under the directorship of Guido Molinari (1933-2004).

• Musical genius Glenn Gould (1932–1982) recorded J.S. Bach's *Goldberg Variations*, at CBS studios, New York City. The interpretation was instantly hailed a classic, placing Gould among the greatest — and some critics argued *the* greatest — pianists of the 20th century. Gould would go on to produce dozens of albums to international acclaim, including works by Beethoven, Debussy, Grieg, Haydn, Pavel and many others. Devoting much of his later career to the recording studio, Gould exclaimed,

"A record is a concert without halls and a museum whose curator is the owner." Gould died of a stroke Oct. 4, 1982, and is buried at Mount Pleasant Cemetery in Toronto.

Aug. 22 Rhodesia PM Garfield Todd visited Ottawa.

Aug. 25 Agricultural experts from the Soviet Union toured Canada's farming areas, until Sept. 10.

Aug. 26 The last steamboat left Dawson, Yukon Territory. The advent of all-weather trucks and airplanes had put an end to the traditional, water-based form of transportation.

Sept. 30 Operation Franklin, a geological survey of Canadian Arctic islands, was completed. It proved the potential for oil in Canada's Arctic.

Oct. 11 An agreement with the USSR was negotiated by External Affairs Minister Lester B. Pearson. It granted the USSR most-favoured-nation trade privileges and provided co-operation in Arctic research.

Oct. 29 The 1st of 14 new destroyer escorts, the *St. Laurent*, was commissioned in Montreal, for the Canadian navy.

Nov. 1 Lester B. Pearson opened the hydroelectric "Canada Dam" in India, built on the Mayurakshi R. with Canadian aid.

Nov. 14 A 4-month strike of 2,000 De Havilland aircraft workers in Toronto ended.

1955–1965 Jack Sissons (1892–1969) served as 1st judge of the NWT Territorial Court; his mandate — to try people in their own communities. To that end, his court travelled over 32,000 km annually across the NWT in the pursuit of justice. Judge Sissons published his memoirs in 1968.

Also in 1955

• David Arnold Croll (1900–1955) became Canada's 1st Jewish senator.

• Construction began on the Frederick G. Gardiner Expressway between downtown Toronto and L. Ontario. When completed in 1966 it stretched from the Don Valley Parkway (completed in 1960) westward to the Queen Elizabeth Way. The imposing Expressway visually and along many stretches isolated Toronto from its lakeshore and has been criticized as one of the great urban design blunders of the 20th century.

• Norris Roy Crump (b 1904) became president of the CPR.

• A Buick Century 60 cost $2,565.

• Restrictions on married women in the federal public service were removed. Previously, women public service employees were fired upon marriage.

• 800,000 Canadian children were immunized against polio with the new Salk vaccine injections.

• Dinosaur Provincial Park was established in Alberta. The 90 km² park is home to the world's largest deposit of late Cretaceous dinosaur fossils, and has been designated a World Heritage Site by the UN.

• Canadian Pacific, Bell Canada and Alcan ranked as the top 3 most valuable non-financial corporations in Canada. They held the same position in 1980.

• Aylmer, Que., passed a law regulating "peace, order and good morals," which banned, among other things, swearing, fortune-telling and roller skating.

• Painters Eleven artist Tom Hodgson painted the abstract work, *Red Lanterns*, now in the National Gallery of Canada.

• Jack Bush painted the abstract *Reflection*, now in the Robert McLaughlin Gallery, Oshawa, and *Theme Variation No. 2*, now in the Art Gallery of Ont., Toronto.

• James Archibald Houston (b 1921) published *Canadian Eskimo Art*, which helped bring Inuit art to national attention.

• Belfast-born novelist Brian Moore (1921–1999) published *The Lonely Passion of Judith Hearne*.

Although he lived in Canada for only 12 years, Moore wrote some of the most celebrated books ever produced by a Canadian citizen, including *The Luck of Ginger Coffey* (1960), *Catholics* (1972) and *Black Robe* (1985).

• Mordecai Richler (1931–2001) published the novel *Son of a Smaller Hero*.

• Earle Birney published his 2nd novel, *Down the Long Table*, a semi-autobiographical work.

• Wilfred Watson (1911–1999) published his 1st book, *Friday's Child*, for which he won the British Council and the Gov-Gen.'s Award for Poetry. Watson would later delve into theatre, finishing his 1st play, *Cockrow and the Gulls*, in 1960.

• Irving Layton published *The Cold Green Element*, a volume of poems.

• The play *Teach Me How to Cry*, by Patricia Joudry (1921–2000), was staged in New York and later won the Dominion Drama Festival Best Play Award in 1956.

• Hy Aisenstat (d 1988) founded Hy's Steakhouse Restaurant in Calgary, Alb., as the 1st in his chain of 7 Canadian restaurants.

1956

Jan. 10 The 3rd session of the 22nd Parliament met until Aug. 14. The Female Employees Equal Pay Act, guaranteed equal pay for equal work for women working in the federal govt, its agencies or Crown corporations.

Feb. 3 The Imperial Bank of Canada absorbed Barclays Bank (Canada).

Feb. 10 Wilbert Coffin, a local Gaspé prospector, was hanged for the murder of Richard Lindsay, 1 of 3 American hunters found dead in the Gaspé forest in the summer of 1953. Many believed Coffin was innocent. In 1964, a Que. Royal Commission, chaired by Justice Roger Brossard (b 1937), was established to address the issue; its 750-page report, issued in Dec. 1964, concluded that Coffin was guilty and dealt with in accordance to the law.

Feb. 14 A 148-day strike by 17,000 General Motors workers in Ont. ended. With 1.5 million person-days lost, it was one of the costliest strikes in Canadian history.

Also in Feb.
• The Nonfigurative Artists' Association of Montreal was founded. Fernand Leduc (b 1916) became president.

Mar. 4 Giovanni Gronchi, president of Italy, addressed a joint session of the Senate and House of Commons in Ottawa.

Mar. 26–27 PM St. Laurent met with US President Eisenhower and President Cortines of Mexico at White Sulphur Springs, Virginia, for talks on hemispheric solidarity and the expansion of Communism.

Apr. 8–May 20 Painters Eleven exhibited with American Abstract artists at the Riverside Museum in New York, to generous praise from US critics.

Apr. 10 The Montreal Canadiens beat the Detroit Red Wings to win their 1st of 5 consecutive Stanley Cups. The team included hockey legends Dickie Moore (b 1931), Jean Béliveau (b 1931), Bernard "Boom Boom" Geoffrion (b 1931), Jean-Guy Talbot (b 1932), Henri "Pocket Rocket" Richard (b 1936) and Maurice "Rocket" Richard (1921–2000).

Apr. 23–27 At a Toronto convention, the Trades and Labour Congress of Canada merged with the Canadian Congress of Labour to form the Canadian Labour Congress, as of May 1.

May 14 Liberal Minister of Trade and Commerce C.D. Howe tabled a bill in the House to provide an $80 million loan to the predominantly US-owned TransCanada PipeLines. TransCanada was incorporated Mar. 9, 1951, to build a natural gas pipeline from Alb. to Ont., and then to US markets. It required the loan by June 7. To keep debate on the issue within the 14 days available to the Commons, the govt announced it would invoke closure at each stage of the debate, the 1st time closure had been used in this way. The bill was passed on June 6 (termed "Black Friday" by Conservative MP Thomas M. Bell [1923–1996]) and received Assent on June 7. TransCanada repaid the loan in Feb. 1957.

The incident contributed to the fall of the St. Laurent govt in the June 10, 1957, election.

June 4–5 Achmed Sukarno, president of Indonesia, visited Ottawa.

June 19 Canada recognized the independence of Tunisia and Morocco.

July 26 The Suez Crisis began as Egyptian President Gamal Abdel Nasser announced intentions to nationalize the predominantly Anglo-French Suez Canal Company, which had operated the Suez Canal since 1869. The Egyptian Canal Authority was organized to manage the canal. On Oct. 29, Israel, with France and England, attacked Egypt in retaliation for the takeover. France and England would begin bombing operations Oct. 31.

Aug. 18 The Alexander Graham Bell Museum at Baddeck, NS, was dedicated.

Aug. 23 Toronto's 18-year-old Marilyn Bell swam Juan de Fuca Strait from Port Angeles, Washington, to Victoria, BC, in a record 10 hours, 33 minutes.

Sept. 21 The federal govt agreed to grant a permit for the export of 24 jet fighters to Israel with the assurance that the fighters would be used solely for defence against aggression. St. Laurent suspended the permit Oct. 30.

Sept. 25 The transatlantic telephone cable was inaugurated, creating the 1st 3-way telephone service between Ottawa, London, England and New York.

Oct. 30 The Conservatives under Robert Lorne Stanfield (1914–2003) won the NS election.

Nov. 1 Springhill, NS, suffered its 2nd major coal mine tragedy since 1891. A disastrous explosion entombed 112 miners. In spite of heroic rescue efforts, 39 lives were lost.

Nov. 2 A US resolution calling for the prompt withdrawal of French, English and Israeli forces from Egyptian territory and the end of military shipments to the area was passed by the UN General Assembly. Canada abstained.

Nov. 4 At the UN, Lester B. Pearson proposed the Canadian Plan, involving a special UN police force to serve in the Suez, to separate Egyptians from invading British, French and Israeli forces. The plan was adopted 57–0 with 19 abstentions. On Nov. 23, the British agreed to admit an advance party of the UN Emergency Force into Port Said, Egypt, in accordance with the Canada Plan, bringing an end to the Suez Crisis.

Nov. 5 Canadian Maj-Gen. Eedson Louis Millard Burns (1897–1985) was appointed commander of the UN Emergency Force.

Nov. 24 The 1st 20 Canadian peacekeeping troops arrived in Egypt. On Nov. 29, the main body of the UN Emergency Force (UNEF), made up of Canadians, Colombians and forces from 4 Scandinavian countries, took up positions in Egypt separating French, British and Israeli forces from Egyptian. On Jan. 11, 1957, the Canadian aircraft carrier *Magnificent* arrived in Port Said, Egypt, with peacekeepers and supplies to bring the Canadian strength in Egypt to approximately 1,000.

Nov. 26 The 4th session of the 22nd Parliament met until Jan. 8, 1957, to authorize the necessary expenditures for the Canadian contingent of the UNEF in Egypt.

Nov. 28 The federal govt granted refugees from the Hungarian Revolution $1 million and free passage to Canada. The violent suppression of the Hungarian uprisings of Oct. and Nov. by the Soviet army caused an outpouring of Western sympathy — and also fuelled Cold War tensions.

Dec. 9 A TCA passenger flight crashed at Mount Sclesse, BC, killing 62 persons.

Dec. 14 At the national convention of the Progressive Conservative Party in Ottawa, John George Diefenbaker (1895–1979) was chosen to succeed George Drew as leader, taking 774 votes to Donald Fleming's (1905–1986) 393, and Davie Fulton's 117. Drew had announced his retirement due to illness, Sept. 20. On June 25, 1957, Drew was appointed Canada's high commissioner to the UK, effective Aug. 1 of that year.

Dec. 19 A Canadian–West German air training agreement was announced, providing for the training of 360 West German aircrew in Canada.

Dec. 21–23 PM of India Jawaharlal Nehru visited Ottawa.

Also in 1956

• Pianist Glenn Gould (1932–1982) travelled to the Soviet Union on a concert tour.

• 607 cases of polio were reported nationwide.

• Canada won 6 medals, including 2 gold, at the Olympic Summer Games in Melbourne, Australia. U. of BC crews won gold and silver in the eights and fours; Gerald Ouellette (b 1934) won gold in the small-bore rifle-prone event.

• Louis Melzack opened an all-paperback shop, Classic's Little Books, in Montreal. By 1968, Classics would operate more than 20 stores.

• William Ronald (1926–1998) painted *J'accuse,* oil on canvas. A student of Jock MacDonald's at the Ontario College of Art, Ronald was one of the 1st Canadian artists to engage abstract expressionism. *J'accuse* is now in the Robert McLaughlin Gallery in Oshawa, Ont. Ronald also completed the abstract canvas *Central Black,* also in the Robert McLaughlin Gallery.

• Jean-Paul Lemieux (1904–1990) painted *Le Visiteur du Soir,* oil on canvas, showing a priest, representing death, moving across a snow-covered landscape. The painting is in the National Gallery of Canada.

• Cyrus MacMillan's classic children's book *Glooscap's Country and Other Indian Tales* was posthumously published and awarded the Canadian Library Association book of the year for children in 1957.

• The literary magazine *Tamarack Review* was founded by Robert Weaver (b 1921).

• Historian Donald Creighton published *The Empire of the St. Lawrence.*

• The novella *The Other Paris,* by Mavis Leslie Gallant, née Young (b 1922), was published.

• Anne Wilkinson (1910–1961) published *Lions in the Way: A Discursive History of the Oslers.*

• Adele Wiseman (1928–1992) published the novel *The Sacrifice,* for which she won the Gov-Gen.'s Award for Fiction.

• Charles Trick Currelly (1876–1957) published his autobiography, *I Brought the Ages Home,* the story of how the Royal Ontario Museum developed from one man's dream into one of the world's great collections.

• Left-wing poet Milton Acorn's (1923–1986) 1st collection of verse, *In Love and Anger,* was privately issued in Montreal.

• Leonard Cohen (b 1934) published his 1st book of poetry, *Let Us Compare Mythologies.*

• Playwright Lister Shedden Sinclair (b 1921) published *The Blood Was Strong: A Drama of Early Scottish Settlement in Cape Breton.*

• Paul-Emile Borduas completed *Le chant de la pierre,* oil canvas, now owned by the TD Canada Trust.

• Joseph Lister Rutledge was awarded the Gov-Gen.'s Award for non-fiction for the bestseller, *Century of Conflict: The Struggle Between the French and British in Colonial America.*

• Doo-wop vocal quartet The Four Lads recorded the hit single "Standing on the Corner." Each member of the group was a graduate of the St. Michael's Cathedral Choir School in Toronto.

• Gerald Pratley, director of the Ontario Film Institute, inaugurated the Stratford International Film Festival in Stratford, Ont., a 1-week event riding on the coattails of the Stratford Theatre Festival. In 1973, Pratley was honoured by the Canadian Film Awards for his "outstanding contribution to the Canadian film industry," but the Stratford Film Festival was cancelled in 1976 for lack of public funding.

1957

Jan. 2–10 CPR employees were on strike.

Jan. 31 The federal govt proclaimed the 2nd Monday in every Oct. Thanksgiving Day, a statutory holiday.

Feb. 9 The 1st half-hour episode of CBC-TV's *Adventures of Pierre Radisson* aired, starring Jacques Godin in the title role. The series was also shown to American audiences under the title *Tomahawk.*

Feb. 17 Contralto Maureen Forrester (b 1930) made her Carnegie Hall debut with the New York Philharmonic, performing Mahler's *Second Symphony.*

Mar. 6 The Supreme Court of Canada nullified the Que. "Padlock Law" of 1937, which empowered the attorney general to close any building suspected to be used in the propagation of Communism, and confiscate and destroy any related material. The court ruled that jurisdiction in such an area was a federal, not a provincial, concern.

Mar. 10 Some 1,000 workers of Gaspé Copper Mines, at Murdochville, Que., a subsidiary of Noranda Mines, struck for the right to unionize. The 7-month protest ended without success.

Mar. 18 Canada took part in a disarmament conference in London, England, with Britain, France, the US and the Soviet Union.

• Brothers Harrison (1927–2004) and Wallace McCain opened the 1st McCain's Food Ltd. potato-processing plant in Florenceville, NB. The plant produced 8-oz (227-g) packages of French-fried potatoes for 39 cents. By the end of the century, McCain's frozen fries would be sold worldwide and constitute 50% of all fries eaten in Argentina, Australia, Brazil, Canada, Chile and Great Britain.

Mar. 28 The Canada Council was established in Ottawa to encourage Canadian arts, humanities and social sciences. The council pledged $10,000 to support Canadian scholarly writing and publishing. Not until 1968 would the Council fund trade publishing, with $25,000 in subsidies.

Mar. 31 The last tax rental agreement between the federal govt and the provinces expired, and the 1st structured system of equalization payments, the brainchild of economist John James Deutsch (1911–1976), came into effect.

Also in Mar.

• A Royal Commission on broadcasting, under the chairmanship of Robert MacLaren Fowler (1906–1980), released its report recommending the establishment of a Board of Broadcast Governors (BBG, the predecessor of the CRTC) to exercise the regulatory powers formerly exercised by the CBC. The Broadcast Act of 1958 was passed the next year, creating a 15-member Board of Broadcast Governors with authority to supervise and regulate all private and public radio and television broadcasters in the country. In 1960, the board announced that television programs must have 45% Canadian content from Apr. 1, 1961, and 55% from Apr. 1, 1962.

Apr. 2 Twenty-two-year-old Elvis Aaron Presley made his Canadian debut at Toronto's Maple Leaf Gardens. Elvis performed two shows in his gold lamé suit in front of a total of 38,000 fans. Elvis made his final Canadian performance on Aug. 31, at Empire Stadium in Vancouver before 26,500 fans. Tickets for the tour ranged from $2 to $3.50. The King's Canadian tour grossed over $125,000.

Apr. 4 Canadian Ambassador to Egypt, Norman Hebert (1909–1957), jumped to his death from the roof of a Cairo building. He had been accused of being a Communist sympathizer by the RCMP and the US Senate Subcommittee on Internal Security.

Apr. 10 Paul Martin (1903–1992), Liberal minister of national health and welfare, introduced the Hospital Insurance and Diagnostic Services Act to the House of Commons, where it was unanimously passed. The act gave the federal govt the authority to enter into agreement with provinces that established comprehensive, universal plans covering acute hospital care and laboratory and radiology diagnostic services. The act took effect July 1, 1958. BC, Alb., Sask., Man. and Nfld. joined on that date. By 1961, every province adopted a federal-provincial insurance plan to cover hospital care.

June 10 Progressive Conservatives under John Diefenbaker won the federal election, beating out Louis St. Laurent and the Liberals to form a minority govt. The Conservatives won 112 seats, the Liberals 105, the CCF 25, and Social Credit 19. Diefenbaker formed the 1st Conservative govt in 22 years. He served from June 21 to Apr. 22, 1963. He was the nation's 13th PM. Voter turnout was 74.1%.

June 21 Hamilton, Ont., accountant Ellen Louks Fairclough (b 1905) was appointed secretary of state by PM Diefenbaker, becoming Canada's 1st woman cabinet minister. She would become postmaster general in 1962.

June 24 *Front Page Challenge* debuted on CBC television with panellists Gordon Sinclair (1900–1984), Alex Barris (1923-2004) and Toby Robbins. Fred Davis (1921–1996) hosted the current-affairs quiz show that would include such panellists as Pierre Berton (b 1920), Betty Kennedy (b 1926), Allan Fotheringham (b 1932), and Jack Webster. *Front Page Challenge* ran uninterrupted until its cancellation in 1995.

July 7 Upon his return from a Commonwealth PMs' conference in London, England, PM Diefenbaker announced it was his govts "planned intention" to divert 15% of Canada's purchases from the US to the UK.

July 8 Weldwood of Canada opened its pulp mill in Hinton, Alb., the 1st pulp mill in Alb. to work under the province's inaugural Forest Management Agreement of 1951. The agreement committed Weldwood to sustainable forest management, and brought both the company and provincial govt under a co-operative program of cost sharing and forest management responsibilities.

Also in July

• The 1st Pugwash Conference on nuclear arms was held in Pugwash, NS, birthplace of financier and philanthropist Cyrus Eaton (1883–1979), who hosted the conference. Pugwash was inspired by the 1955 *Bertrand Russell–Albert Einstein Manifesto,* calling on the world's foremost scientists to "assemble in conference to appraise the perils that have arisen as a result of the development of weapons of mass destruction." The conference was held every 3 years. In 1960, Eaton was awarded the Lenin Peace Prize for his involvement. In 1995, both the

Pugwash Conference and founding member, Polish nuclear physicist Joseph Rotblat, were recognized with the Nobel Peace Prize.

Aug. 11 A chartered Maritime Central Airlines aircraft, returning from England with veterans and their families, crashed at Issoudun, near Quebec City, killing 79 people.

Aug. 17 William Ronald resigned from Painters Eleven because of a dispute with fellow artist Harold Town.

Aug. 23 Sask. Premier T.C. Douglas opened the 740-km stretch of Trans-Canada Highway through his province. Sask. was the 1st province to complete its portion of the highway.

Sept. 3 International Union of Geodesy and Geophysics scientists met at a conference in Toronto. The Union was established in 1919 to study the component parts of earth and their internal and solar-terrestrial relations.

Sept. 4 The HMCS *Labrador* passed through Bellot Strait, the 1st deep-draught ship to do so.

Sept. 7 PM Diefenbaker made his 1st public address in the US at Dartmouth College in Hanover, New Hampshire, where he received an honorary degree.

Sept. 9 Great Britain made a free-trade proposal to Ottawa, which was rejected the next day on grounds that it would undermine Canadian producers.

Sept. 15 Queen Elizabeth appointed PM Diefenbaker a member of the Imperial Privy Council, thereby conferring on him the designation of "Rt. Hon."

Sept. 16 A 4-month strike by 6,500 Aluminum Company of Canada employees at Arvida, Que., ended.

Sept. 23 PM Diefenbaker became the 1st Canadian PM to address the UN General Assembly. He stressed continuing Canadian support of the UN and the need for world disarmament.

Sept. 30–Oct. 1 Commonwealth finance ministers met at Mont Tremblant, Que., to discuss plans for a full-scale Commonwealth Trade and Economic Conference in 1958.

Also in Sept.

• Sidney Earle Smith (1897–1959), president of the U. of Toronto, was appointed federal minister of external affairs.

Oct. 12 Lester B. Pearson was awarded the Nobel Peace Prize for his UN peacekeeping plan to resolve the Suez Crisis. He accepted the Prize in Oslo, Dec. 10.

Oct. 14 The 1st session of the 23rd Parliament met until Feb. 1, 1958. Queen Elizabeth II opened Parliament, the 1st reigning monarch to do so.

Oct. 15 Queen Elizabeth II ignited the initial dynamite charge to begin construction of the 24-km-long Queensway Expressway, bisecting Ottawa. The western section of the expressway was opened to traffic in 1962.

Oct. 18 The *Montreal Herald* ceased publishing after 146 years.

Nov. 20 The Conservative federal govt introduced the Winter Works Program, designed to increase winter employment to alleviate the normal seasonal slump.

Nov. 22 The *Grenville* was the 1st ship to pass through Iroquois Lock, the 1st completed lock of the St. Lawrence Seaway. The Iroquois Lock was the first Seaway lock on the St. Lawrence when travelling east out of L. Ontario. The Seaway officially opened June 26, 1959.

Also in Nov.

• A Royal Commission on Canada's Economic Prospects, chaired by Walter Gordon (1906–1987), completed its final report, submitting more than 50 proposals and suggestions, nearly all of which were accepted. The commission expressed deep concern about the acquisition by foreigners, mostly American, of Canadian resources and business enterprises.

Dec. 17 Federal Minister of Transport George Harris Hees (1910–1996) announced the construction of 6 federal ships to commence in 1958 at a cost of approximately $10 million, thereby stimulating the Canadian shipbuilding industry and providing an estimated 3.5 million person-hours of work.

Dec. 26 Much of the Springhill, NS, business section was destroyed by fire.

1957–1958 The 10-volume *Encyclopedia Canadiana*, edited by John Robbins (b 1903), was completed. Edited and revised editions were issued in 1972 and 1975.

1957–1977 Doris Anderson (b 1921) served as editor of the woman's magazine *Chatelaine*. Anderson tackled controversial subjects during her tenure, and readers responded as *Chatelaine's* circulation rose from 480,000 to 1.8 million under her stewardship. In 1979, Anderson accepted a position as chair of the Canadian Advisory Council on the Status of Women (CACSW), and campaigned to secure women's rights through inclusions in the Canadian Charter of Rights and Freedoms.

Also in 1957

• Germany surpassed Canada as the world's 3rd largest trading nation.

• Les Grands Ballets Canadiens de Montréal was founded by Ludmilla Chiriaeff (1924–1996).

• Bookseller William Duthie (d 1984) opened W.J. Duthie at 901 Robson St., Vancouver.

• Frank Bazos and Robert Lowe founded the 1st of 5 neighbourhood Becker's convenience stores in Toronto. The local shops opened daily between 9 a.m. and 11 p.m. Each contained approximately 2,500 items. The Becker's chain would expand to include 500 Ont. stores by 1976.

• Terra Nova National Park, the most easterly national park in the country, was established along Bonavista Bay, Nfld. The park includes 200 km of rugged coastline, and 396 km^2 of interior boreal forest, and bogs and marshes along the Atlantic Uplands. The Terra Nova coast is replete with myriad bird species, including nesting puffins, razor-billed auks and Leach's storm petrels. Up to 400 icebergs float past coastal park waters between Mar. and July each year.

• Writing-on-Stone Provincial Park (1,780 ha) was established near Milk R., Alb. It is home to 50 rock art locations containing thousands of Plains Peoples petroglyphs and pictographs. The park also protects 265 known plant species, 22 types of mammals including the yellow-bellied marmot, Nutall's cottontail, also the Western rattlesnake and 2-tailed swallowtail butterfly.

• Calgary's Southern Alberta Jubilee Auditorium and Edmonton's Northern Alberta Jubilee Auditorium opened to commemorate the province's 50th year in Confederation.

• Restaurant owner Fernand Lachance (1917–2004) created a mixture of cheese curds and French fries, which even he described as a mess. Lachance named his new menu item "poutine," and charged patrons of his Warwick, Que., eatery 35 cents a portion, sans gravy. By the 1990s poutine was a popular snack in fast-food and mainstream restaurants across North America, although modern connoisseurs prefer gravy added to the mishmash (average fat content per serving 60 g).

• Ben Wicks (1926–2000) arrived in Canada from England with his wife and $25 in his pocket. Wicks worked at a number of jobs in Calgary before selling his first cartoon to the *Saturday Evening Post*. The self-taught artist parlayed his wit, his Cockney accent and his cartooning style into a career that saw his single-panel cartoons and a comic strip, *The Outcasts*, carried in more than 200 Canadian and US newspapers. He briefly had his own television show, *The World of Wicks*, and later opened his own English-style pub and restaurant in Toronto.

• Painters Eleven artist Kazuo Nakamura (b 1926) completed the abstract *Waves,* on masonite, now in the Norman Mackenzie Art Gallery, U. of Sask., Regina.

• Alex Colville painted *Couple on Beach*, now in the National Gallery of Canada.

• Painter Graham Coughtry (1931–1999) completed *Interior Twilight*, now in the Winnipeg Art Gallery.

• Literary critic Northrop Frye published *Anatomy of Criticism: Four Essays.*

• Eric Nicol (b 1919) published *Girdle Me a Globe*, which won the Leacock Medal for Humour.

• Jean Jay Macpherson (b 1931) published *The Boatman*, for which she received the Gov-Gen.'s Award for Poetry.

• John Marlyn (b 1912) published *Under the Ribs of Death*, a novel based on the assimilation of a Hungarian immigrant in inter-war Winnipeg.

• Mordecai Richler published the novel *A Choice of Enemies.*

• Toronto-born musician and composer Gil Evans (1912–1988) arranged and conducted *Miles Ahead*, the 1st of 3 Miles Davis large jazz ensemble masterpieces. The others composed by Evans were *Porgy and Bess* (1958) and *Sketches of Spain* (1959).

• Paul Albert Anka (b 1941), of Ottawa, gained international stardom with the release of his #1 song "Diana."

1958

Jan. 14–16 At the federal Liberal convention in the Ottawa Coliseum, Lester Pearson was chosen Liberal leader over Paul Martin. Seventy-four-year-old former PM Louis St. Laurent had announced his retirement as opposition leader Sept. 6, 1957, and his retirement from politics Feb. 17, 1958.

Jan. 31 The federal govt enacted legislation authorizing loans up to $30 million to NB for the completion of the Beechwood Power Project. Assent was given Jan. 31. Beechwood hydroelectric dam on the Saint John R. was the second of the 3 major NB power projects initiated this decade. The first was the Tobique River Dam, completed in 1952; the third was the Mactaquac Dam, the largest in the Maritimes, completed in 1967.

Feb. 1 PM Diefenbaker received permission from Gov-Gen. Vincent Massey to dissolve Canada's 23rd Parliament. The federal election was later set for Mar. 31.

• Blood James Gladstone (Akay-na-muka, meaning "Many Guns," [1887–1971]) was the 1st Native person appointed to the Senate. In his inaugural address in the Upper Chamber, the senator from Lethbridge, Alb., spoke in Blackfoot, breaking a parliamentary tradition of addressing the Speaker in either French or English.

Feb. 4 A Royal Commission headed by Supreme Court of Canada Justice Roy Lindsay Kellock (1893–1975) determined that firemen were unnecessary on CPR diesel railway engines.

Mar. 25 With PM Pearson in attendance, the delta wing Avro Arrow *CF–105* prototype, regarded as the most advanced fighter aircraft of its day, was test-flown for the 1st time at Malton, Ont., by test pilot Janusz Zurakowski (1914–2004). Altogether, 5 Arrow prototypes performed a total of 57 tests, with flights reaching speeds of over 2,100 km/h — Mach 1.98. (Test runs were powered by Pratt & Whitney J75 engines; the most powerful jet engines in production, the Avro Iroquois, had yet to be installed.) Due mostly to costs, the Diefenbaker administration scrapped the Arrow program on Feb. 20, 1959.

Mar. 31 John Diefenbaker was re-elected PM with the greatest election victory to date, winning 208 seats out of 265. The Liberals under Lester B. Pearson won 49 and the CCF 8. Voter turnout was 79.4%.

Apr. 5 The twin peaks of Ripple Rock were completely destroyed in what was the world's largest non-nuclear explosion. Located in Seymour Narrows, off Vancouver Is., near the town of Campbell R., Ripple Rock was one of the world's most treacherous navigational hazards, taking at least 120 ships and 114 lives. The explosion was set with 1,270 tonnes of Nitramex-2H explosives, which threw some 635,000 tonnes of shattered rock and water 305 m into the air. The explosion cut the twin peaks to 14 m below the waterline at low tide, where before they stood at just 3 m below water.

Apr. 15 The Queen Elizabeth Hotel opened in Montreal. The city's largest hotel — 1,039 rooms and over 4,600 m^2 of meeting space — is located in the heart of Montreal directly above the VIA train station.

May 12 The North American Air Defence Command (NORAD) was formally established to co-ordinate

and jointly administer an integrated US-Canada air defence.

May 28 Liberal Democrat Theodor Heuss, 1st president of the Federal Republic of Germany, was the 1st German head of state to pay an official state visit to Canada.

May 31 Former federal cabinet minister Jean Lesage (1912–1980) was elected leader of the Que. Liberal Party.

Also in May

• The National Film Board took first prize at the Cannes International Film Festival for *City of Gold*, a documentary about life in Dawson City during the Gold Rush. The film, narrated by Pierre Berton, won 21 international awards and garnered an Oscar nomination.

June 12 British PM Harold Macmillan addressed Parliament during a visit to Ottawa.

June 16 The Progressive Conservatives under Dufferin ("Duff") Roblin (b 1917) won the Man. election.

June 17 The collapse of the Second Narrows Bridge spanning Vancouver's Burrard Inlet killed 19 workers and injured 20.

July 1 The 1st annual observance of Dominion Day was established by the federal govt, with the secretary of state in charge of ceremonies. The celebration included the trooping of colours on Parliament Hill, followed by a sunset ceremony and fireworks. Although the July 1st holiday had been established by statute in 1879, it was not followed by an annual observance.

• A coffer dam in the St. Lawrence R. near Cornwall, Ont., was blasted away, allowing water to flow into an artificial 40 km by 6.4 km water body known as L. St. Lawrence. The lake was part of the St. Lawrence Seaway to provide a water source for hydroelectric generators. It also connected with a canal allowing ocean-going vessels to sail up the St. Lawrence to the Great Lakes. To accommodate the lakes, over 8,000 ha of north shore land were flooded: 6,500 people were relocated, many to the specially built towns of Ingleside and Long Sault. The business section of Morrisburg was relocated, and all of Iroquois. Many towns were lost to the flood waters. The "Lost Villages" were Aultsville, Dickinson's Landing, Farmer's Point, Maple Grove, Mille Roches, Moulinette, Wales, and Woodlands.

• The Trans-Canada Microwave Radio Relay Network went into operation from coast to coast. The 6,400-km network, begun in 1953, longest to date in the world, linked Halifax, St. John, Montreal, Ottawa, Toronto, Winnipeg, Regina, Edmonton and Vancouver. The new network was built to transmit telephone and teletype signals, in addition to instant live television relay. Bell Canada President Thomas Eadie was a prime mover in establishing the system. This same day, CBC TV broadcast its 1st cross-country television program, *Memo to Champlain*.

July 8–11 US President Eisenhower visited Ottawa for discussions, which resulted in the establishment of a Canada-US joint committee on defence on July 10.

July 14 PM Diefenbaker launched a nationally televised campaign, appealing to all who purchased Victory Bonds during the war years to reinvest them "for the greater development of a greater Canada."

July 16 The Man. Theatre Centre Company in Winnipeg, 1st of Canada's regional theatres, created by John Hirsch (1930–1989) and Tim Hendry, staged its 1st production.

July 18 Canadian External Affairs Minister Sidney Earle Smith (1897–1959), British Foreign Secretary Selwyn Lloyd and US Secretary of State John Foster Dulles met in Washington, D.C., to discuss problems in the Middle East.

July 19–23 Kwame Nkrumah, PM of Ghana, visited Montreal and Ottawa, where he addressed Parliament.

Aug. 3 The US nuclear submarine *Nautilus* was the 1st vessel to travel under geographic North Pole.

Aug. 8 The Canadian Chiefs of Staff Committee for the Armed Forces told the Cabinet Defence

Committee that the Avro Arrow project should be scrapped and new interceptor aircraft, most likely from the US, should be secured. On Aug. 21, the Cabinet Defence Committee was informed that the scrapping of the Arrow would put the A.V. Roe Company and Orenda Engines Limited out of business, eliminate 25,000 jobs, and cost $170 million in cancellation charges. PM Diefenbaker, however, cancelled the Avro Arrow project Feb. 20, 1959.

Aug. 21 African-American airmen stationed at the Ernest Harmon US Air Base in Stephenville, Nfld., complained to American military authorities that they experienced discrimination off the base, reporting that local white women who had fraternized with black Americans had been fired by their merchant employers.

Aug. 30 A broad national agriculture policy was announced in the House of Commons, promising a program to increase sales of wheat and other agricultural commodities, a comprehensive Crop Insurance program, a 4-H Bank program, farm credit expansion, an Agricultural Prices Stabilization Act and an Agricultural Rehabilitation and Development Act, which was passed.

Sept. 5 PM Diefenbaker introduced Bill C-60, an Act for the Recognition and Protection of Human Rights and Fundamental Freedoms. It would be reformed into the Bill of Rights, and passed in the House Aug. 4, 1960.

Sept. 15–26 The Commonwealth Economic Conference met at the Queen Elizabeth Hotel in Montreal. The British agreed to eliminate the greater part of their trade discrimination against "dollar countries."

Oct. 1 Canada House in New York City was opened by Canadian Secretary of State for External Affairs, Sidney Smith and New York Mayor Robert Wagner.

Oct. 10 The last section of the 3,700 km TransCanada PipeLine — the longest gas pipeline in the world to date — was completed to pipe Alb. gas to Ont., then Montreal. Gas was 1st piped into Toronto on Oct. 27. (A longer gas pipeline would be built in the 1980s between Western Europe and Siberia.)

Oct. 15 Israeli Foreign Minister Golda Meir visited Ottawa.

Oct. 22 Blanche Margaret Meagher (1911–1999) was appointed ambassador to Israel, becoming the 1st Canadian woman to be appointed an ambassador. The Halifax-born diplomat was later ambassador to Austria (1962-1966) and Sweden (1969-1973).

Oct. 23 A coal-mine explosion at Springhill, NS, trapped 174 miners, some as deep as 3,960 m underground. Rescue workers brought 81 men out on the 1st day, 12 on Oct. 30, and 7 more on Nov. 1. The remaining 74 miners died underground. It was the deepest rescue effort in Canadian history, and the 1st such rescue effort to be broadcast on television, by CBHT-TV.

Oct. 28–Dec. 19 PM Diefenbaker and his wife, Olive, left Ottawa on a 6-week marathon world tour. On Oct. 29 the PM met with Secretary Gen. of the UN, Dag Hammarskjold, in New York to discuss developments in the Middle East, disarmament, China and UN peacekeeping. On Nov. 3 he met with Britain's PM Macmillan in London to discuss the European Common Market, the export of arms to Israel, Cyprus, and other issues. Three days later, Diefenbaker met with Gen. Charles de Gaulle in Paris, expressing his opposition to a French plan to reorganize NATO so the security of Europe would fall under the exclusive control of France, Britain and the US. On Nov. 11 and 12, the PM met with Italian PM Fanfani in Rome. They mutually opposed Gen. de Gaulle's NATO triumvirate proposal. On the 7th Diefenbaker met with West German Chancellor Konrad Adenauer in Bonn, to discuss the European Economic Community and its rivalry, the British-led European Free Trade Association.

Nov. 15 PM Diefenbaker met with President Ayub Khan in Karachi, only weeks after Khan took power in Pakistan (Oct. 7) in a bloodless coup. Diefenbaker also opened the Warsak dam which was created with Canadian aid. On the 19th Diefenbaker was met by PM Jawaharlal Nehru in New Delhi, India. On the 28th the "Chief" met with Malayan PM Tunku Abdul Rahman in Kuala Lumpur, discussing Communist Chinese threats in the region. On Dec. 2 in Djakarta, Diefenbaker talked with Indonesian PM Ir. H. Djuanda concerning Communist political

subversion in his country. On the leg home Diefenbaker met with Australian Foreign Minister Richard Casey in Canberra, who expressed that Communist China was the greatest threat to his country and to Southeast Asia.

Dec. 9 Canadian and international peacekeepers successfully completed their UN Observation Group obligations in Lebanon.

Dec. 10 In one of the most exciting and brutal fights in boxing history, Yvon "The Fighting Fisherman" Durelle (b 1929), a NB fisherman, knocked down world light-heavyweight champ Archie Moore 3 times in the 1st round and once more in the 5th. Durelle faded in the later stages of the fight and Moore scored a technical knockout in the 11th round to retain his championship, before a frenzied crowd at the Montreal Forum.

Also in 1958

• Canadian photographer Roloff Beny (1924–1984) published the 1st of his 16 books, *Thrones of Heaven and Earth*, a photographic interpretation, with accompanying text, of the artistic and architectural treasures of the Mediterranean.

• Canadian flutist, saxophonist and clarinet maestro Moe Koffman (1928-2001) composed "Swingin' Shepherd Blues," a jazz classic that would be recorded by more than 100 different artists.

• Rockin' Ronnie "The Hawk" Hawkins (b 1935) immigrated to Toronto from Arkansas in a beat-up Chevy. He would spread the sound of rockabilly nationwide.

• The Civil Service Commission (CSC) report, *Personnel Administration in the Public Service* (Heeney Report) was issued by public servant Arnold Heeney (1902–1970), recommending that the CSC, established in 1918, retain exclusive control over the recruitment and advancement of civil servants. In 1961, the new Civil Service Act gave civil servants the right to appeal CSC decisions.

• The UK edition of Vladimir Nabokov's *Lolita* was stopped at the Canadian border by Customs officials, marking the beginning of a long era of Canada Customs' attempts to censor books.

• Canadian Tire began issuing its ubiquitous Canadian Tire money, which could be redeemed for merchandise at any Canadian Tire location. The corporate paper currency, sporting the image of the fictitious jovial Scotsman Sandy McTire, was part of a promotions ploy to lure patrons of competitors to Canadian Tire gas pumps.

• Vancouver's renowned Playland Roller Coaster was completed by 72-year-old American designer Carl Phare, creator of the first great thrill rides at Coney Is., New York, at the turn of the century. The Playland coaster's first peak reached 23 m. Once the cars had been mechanically assisted to this level, the rest was determined entirely by gravity and the grace of God. By 2004, the Vancouver Phare wooden design would be one of only a handful left on the continent.

• The Ford Motor Company of Canada refused a 1,000 car and truck order from the People's Republic of China because of a US law prohibiting trade with most Communist countries. The US ban extended to Canadian subsidiaries of US companies.

• Fredricton, NB-native William (Willie) O'Ree (b 1935), of the Boston Bruins, became the 1st African-Canadian, and the 1st black man, to play in the NHL.

• Comedians Johnny Wayne (1918–1990) and Frank Shuster (1916-2002) made the 1st of their 26 appearances on the *Ed Sullivan Show*.

• Canadian-born Harvard economist John Kenneth Galbraith (b 1908) published *The Affluent Society*.

• U. of BC professor Margaret Anchoretta Ormsby (1909–1996) published *British Columbia: A History*. It was revised in 1971.

• *The Penguin Book of Canadian Verse*, edited by Ralph Gustafson (1909–1995), was published.

• William Edwin Richer (1908-2001) published *Handbook of Computation for Biological Statistics of Fish Populations*. The book would become a major work in the management of fisheries, both nationally and internationally.

• *Canada Made Me*, a collection of autobiographical reflections by Norman Levine (b 1923), was published in the UK, and distributed in Canada through McClelland & Stewart. A Canadian edition would not appear until 1979.

• Colin McDougall published the novel *Execution*, a story of Canadian soldiers on the Italian front during WW II.

• Yves Thériault published the novel *Agaguk*, which was translated into 7 languages.

• Paul-Émile Borduas completed the abstract canvas *Fence and Defence*, now in the Martha Jackson Gallery, New York.

• U. of NB professor and literary critic, William Cyril Desmond Pacey (1917–1975) published *Ten Canadian Poets*.

• Acadian poet Ronald Després published *Silences à nourrir de sang*.

• Photographer Yousuf Karsh published *Portraits of Greatness*.

• Paul Anka followed his 1957 #1 song "Diana" with the hits "Crazy Love," "Let the Bells Keep Ringing" and "You Are My Destiny."

1959

Jan. 1 Fidel Castro's revolutionary forces took Havana as dictator Fulgencio Batista fled. On Jan. 8, Canada's formal recognition of Fidel Castro's provisional govt in Cuba was sent to the Canadian embassy in Havana.

Feb. 16 A deadly blizzard struck Nfld., taking 6 lives, leaving 70,000 without power and blocking roads with 5-m-high snowdrifts.

Feb. 20 PM Diefenbaker cancelled the Avro *Arrow* project: 14,000 employees lost their jobs in what became known as "Black Friday." All 5 finished planes, as well as the 6 in production, plus all tools, jigs, fixtures and assembly-line mechanisms, and all Iroquois jet engines in production were destroyed and scrapped for ingots by Lax Brothers Salvage of Hamilton, Ont. for $300,000. The Department of

Defence also ordered destroyed all traces of how the plane was designed and built, including all blueprints, moulds, dies and research. The Avro defence potential was to be replaced by a less expensive defence system of 56 American Boeing *Bomarc-B* guided missiles located at North Bay, Ont., and La Macaza, Que., under the control of the C-in-C of NORAD. Ever since destruction of the *Arrow*, various individuals and groups, including the Canadian navy, have searched for scale replicas tested over and sunk into L. Ontario in the 1950s. Two were found in 1999, 7 remained undiscovered in 2003.

Also in Feb.

• Nfld. premier Joey Smallwood pushed a bill through the Nfld. legislature decertifying the International Woodworkers of America, whose members were on strike against the Anglo-Nfld. Development Company for a 54-hour workweek at $1.22 per hour. The strike had started Jan. 1.

Mar. 6 The Richardson rink (brothers Ernie, Garnet and cousins Arnold and Wes) of Regina captured the 1st of 4 national curling titles, beating the Scottish team skipped by Willie Young at the Scotch Whisky Cup.

Mar. 10 The US govt imposed mandatory controls over oil imports. The new measures applied to Canadian imports on Apr. 30.

Apr. 8 Sask.-born tenor Jonathan Stewart Vickers (b 1926) joined the Metropolitan Opera Company in New York for a 2-month appearance.

Apr. 10 Canada's 1st university-based nuclear research reactor, the McMaster Nuclear Reactor (MNR) went operational at McMaster U. in Hamilton, Ont.

Apr. 26 Premier Fidel Castro of Cuba visited Montreal to drum up Canadian dollars for capital investment and to encourage tourism to the Caribbean country.

May 3 Marie-Marguerite d'Youville (1701–1771), one of the original Grey Nuns, was beatified by Pope John XXIII.

June 4 WW I veteran and anti-nuclear advocate Howard Charles Green (1895–1989) became secretary of state for external affairs.

June 15 Steven Truscott (b 1945) was arrested and charged with the rape and murder of 12-year-old classmate, Lynn Harper, in Clinton, Ont. The 14-year-old Truscott was tried, found guilty and sentenced to die by hanging for the crime, becoming the country's youngest death-row inmate, and the youngest person in Canada ever sentenced to hang. The verdict was later commuted to life in prison, and Truscott, who had insisted on his innocence throughout his trial, served 10 years behind bars before being paroled. The Supreme Court was authorized to review the case Apr. 26, 1966.

June 18 Queen Elizabeth and Prince Philip arrived at Torbay, Nfld., to begin a 45-day Canadian tour.

June 20 A storm in the Northumberland Str. killed 35 fishermen.

June 26 The St. Lawrence Seaway, a 3,700-km navigational route of open waters punctuated with artificial lock systems, dikes and channels linking the Great Lakes with the Atlantic Ocean, was officially opened by US President Eisenhower and Queen Elizabeth II at the St. Lambert Lock at Montreal. The cost of construction exceeded $1 billion. The 1st ship to cross the St. Lambert Lock was the icebreaker *Frontenac*. The Seaway had been open for navigation since Apr. 25. Total average sailing time between Montreal and Thunder Bay was 119 hours.

July 17 The federal govt initiated formation of the Emergency Measures Organization, established to deal with the possibility of a nuclear attack.

July 22 Queen Elizabeth II opened the natural gas-fired Queen Elizabeth Generating Station in Saskatoon. The Sask. Power Corporation station had 3 units, with a generating capacity of 221 net megawatts (MW).

July 30 In Vancouver, Edmonton-born communications theorist Marshall McLuhan (1911–1980) remarked publicly for the 1st time, "The medium *is* the message."

Aug. 1 Lawyer, WW II veteran and former Ambassador to France, Maj-Gen. Georges-Philéas Vanier (1888–1967) was appointed gov-gen. of Canada, succeeding Vincent Massey. He was the country's

1st French-Canadian gov-gen., and served from Sept. 15 to Mar. 5, 1967.

Aug. 7 *The Don Messer Show* (later called *Don Messer's Jubilee*) 1st aired nationally on CBC television. The annual summer series regularly featured old-time and country-musical guests and aired until its cancellation in 1969. The show was then placed into syndication through CHCH TV in Hamilton where it ran until Messer's death in 1973.

Also in Aug.

• American abstract expressionist painter Barnett Newman (1905–1970) led a workshop for artists at Emma L., Sask.

Sept. 1 Progressive Conservatives under Walter Russell Shaw (1887–1981) won the PEI provincial election.

Sept. 7 Que. Premier Maurice Duplessis died in Schefferville, Que. He was succeeded Sept. 10 by Joseph-Mignault Sauvé (1907–1960).

Sept. 22 Canadian scientists Dr. Wilder Penfield, director of the Montreal Neurological Institute, and Dr. Edgar William Richard Steacie (1900–1962), chairman of the National Research Council, were the 1st Canadian scientists to be honoured with membership in the USSR Academy of Science.

Oct. 6 PM Diefenbaker pledged $20,000 to the Japanese Red Cross for the victims of Typhoon Vera, which hit the island of Honshu Sept. 26, killing 5,000, injuring 15,000 and leaving 40,000 homeless.

Nov. 1 Jacques Plante (1929–1986) became the 1st goaltender to wear a mask during a regular season game. Andy Bathgate of the New York Rangers had hit Plante with a vicious shot, opening the goaltender's face and breaking his cheekbone. Plante left the game briefly to receive medical attention and returned to the crease wearing the now-famous mask. The great NHL goaltender, best remembered for his years with Montreal (1952–1963), played 19 seasons with 434 wins and 247 losses, and a career 2.38 goals against average. He won 5 Stanley Cups, 7 Vezina Trophies (5 consecutively) and 1 Hart Memorial. He was inducted into the Hockey Hall of Fame in 1978.

Nov. 4 The president of the National Research Council of Canada and the president of the Soviet Academy of Science signed an agreement in Moscow for the exchange of science experts.

Nov. 6 The federal govt established a new program to produce $1 billion in uranium by 1966.

Nov. 9 The 1st snowmobile, the Ski-Doo, rolled off the Bombardier assembly line at Valcourt, Que.; 250 Ski-Doos were sold in the 1st year of production.

Nov. 12 Barbara Arrington of New York State was denied entrance into the Kappa Kappa Gamma sorority at U. of Toronto because she was African-American. She was later asked to join the university's Beta Sigma Phi.

Nov. 16 In a speech before the Montreal Canadian Club, gov. of the Bank of Canada, James Elliott Coyne (b 1910) defended his tight money policy (price stability), stating that "inflation was particularly insidious...which in due course produced recession, loss of confidence and contraction."

Nov. 17 At the UN, the Soviet bloc agreed to study the effect of radiation from atomic-test explosions, as proposed by Canada.

Nov. 18 Poland's total grain purchases from Canada for the year to date exceeded $30 million.

Nov. 25 U. of Toronto professor Donald Grant Creighton was named to Britain's Monckton Commission, to examine the constitutional development of the federation of Rhodesia and Nyasaland in Africa.

Nov. 27 The Sask. govt under Tommy Douglas established an advisory planning committee to study Medicare, a provincial plan to create the nation's first universal health-care plan. The committee was chaired by Dr. Walter Palmer Thompson (1889–1970), president emeritus of the U. of Sask.

Dec. 15 As part of Canada's responsibility in the UN's World Refugee Year (1959–1960), Minister of Citizenship and Immigration Ellen Fairclough admitted into Canada 325 European tubercular refugees and 501 members of their families.

Altogether, 6,912 refugees were admitted to Canada during World Refugee Year.

Dec. 17 The National Housing Act increased the mortgage interest rate from 6% to 6.75%.

Dec. 16 During a radio talk show, Sask. Premier Tommy Douglas outlined 5 principles for bringing Medicare to Sask. They were: medicare should be paid on an insurance basis; there must be universal coverage; there must be a high quality of care; the program must be govt-sponsored and administered by a public body responsible to the legislature; and the program must be acceptable both to those providing service and those receiving it. The Sask. Medical Care Act, based on this criteria, went into effect July 1, 1962.

Also in 1959

• The National Ballet School was established in Toronto, combining ballet with academic training.

• Canada's longest tunnel, the 19-km-long Chute-des-passes hydroelectric tunnel in Que., was completed.

• The federal govt created the National Energy Board, with powers to regulate the oil, natural gas and electric power industries and their products, and to act in an advisory capacity to the federal govt.

• Prince Albert, Sask.-born Harry Jerome (1940–1982) tied a world record of 10 seconds for the 100-m dash, a record he would hold until 1968. In 1971, he was awarded the Order of Canada "for excellence in all fields of Canadian life."

• The Crash Position Indicator (CPI) was perfected by National Research Council engineer Harry Stevenson. The CPI produced signals in all conditions, including oceans and mountainous terrain, which allowed searchers to locate downed aircraft in most situations. Leigh Instruments of Carleton, Ont., built the units.

• Dennis Burton (b 1933) completed the painting, *Intimately Close-in*, now in the National Gallery of Canada.

• Ronald Bloore (b 1925) completed the abstract, *Painting No. 1*, now in the Norman Mackenzie Art Gallery, U. of Sask., Regina.

• Jack Shadbolt completed *Night Harbour Image*, oil and lucite, now with the Art Gallery of Ont., Toronto.

• Mordecai Richler published the novel *The Apprenticeship of Duddy Kravitz*.

• 20-year-old Marie-Claire Blais (b 1939) published the novel *La Belle Bête* (translated as *Mad Shadows*).

• Edmund Carpenter published *Anerca,* an anthology of Inuit songs and tales with sketches.

• Philosopher George Parkin Grant (1918–1988) published *Philosophy in the Mass Age*, exploring the dichotomy between Western mores and the rise of technology.

• Irving Layton published *A Red Carpet for the Sun*, for which he received the Gov-Gen.'s Award for Poetry.

• Morley Callaghan's *Stories by Morley Callaghan* was published.

• George Woodcock and the U. of BC established *Canadian Literature*, a quarterly presenting serious criticism of Canadian writing, past and present.

• U. of Toronto Press and Université Laval launched the multi-volume *Dictionary of Canadian Biography/Dictionnaire biographique du Canada,* with funds bequeathed by Toronto businessman James Nicholson. Published in both languages, the biographies of significant Canadians were organized by year of death. An online version was 1st published in 2003.

• Hugh Maclennan published the novel *The Watch That Ends the Night*, for which he received the Gov-Gen.'s Award.

• Sheila Watson, née Doherty (1909–1998), published her only novel, *The Double Hook*.

1960

Jan. 5 Charles Comfort succeeded Alan Jarvis (1915–1972) as director of the National Gallery of Canada. Comfort was the 1st artist to be appointed to the position. The new National Gallery complex was officially opened in Ottawa on Feb. 17 by PM Diefenbaker.

Jan. 7 Antonio Barrette (1899–1968) became premier of Que., following the death of Union Nationale leader Paul Sauvé.

Jan. 11 The 1st Canadian Conference on Uranium and Atomic Energy was held in Toronto. It focused on the future and feasibility of nuclear power in Canada.

• Canada met India's request for $25 million in aid under the Colombo Plan. On Apr. 27, the govt agreed to give Pakistan $15 million through the Colombo Plan.

Feb. 16 The Coyne Affair erupted when, at the request of James Coyne, gov. of the Bank of Canada (appointed by the Liberal govt in 1955), the bank's board of directors increased his pension to $12,500 a year — half his annual salary. By comparison, former PM St. Laurent's pension was $3,000 per annum. Coyne's outspoken denunciation of govt growth put him at odds with PM Diefenbaker and Finance Minister Donald Fleming. His pension allocation further angered the Conservatives, who requested Coyne's resignation in May 1961, prior to the next Bank of Canada board of directors meeting. Coyne refused, and in June, the bank's board voted 9 to 1 on the motion "that it was in the best interests of the Bank of Canada that the gov. do immediately tender his resignation." Canadian law, however, specified that only Parliament, and not the Executive, could fire the bank gov. In July 1961, a bill to remove Coyne (the Coyne Bill) passed the House and was sent to the Liberal-dominated Senate. After the Senate Banking Committee heard James Coyne's testimony, it passed a motion that the Coyne Bill not proceed, and "that the Gov. of the Bank of Canada did not misconduct himself in office." The Senate adopted the report on July 13, 1961. James Coyne was vindicated, and immediately submitted his resignation. He was succeeded by Louis Rasminsky

(1908–1998). Coyne went on to become president of the Bank of Western Canada, but on July 17, 1967 was unanimously voted out of office by the board of directors over policy disagreements.

Feb. 26 The Que. govt approved an amendment to a bill allowing Que. universities to accept $41 million in federal grants held in trust. Previously, Que. had refused to accept federal involvement in the area of education.

Also in Feb.
• Anne Heggtveit (b 1939) won the gold medal in woman's slalom skiing at the Olympic Winter Games in Squaw Valley, Idaho. The victory gave her the woman's combined and slaloms title. Canada's other Winter Olympic gold was won by Barbara Wagner (b 1938) and Robert Paul (b 1937) in figure skating pairs. One month later, on Mar. 25, the pair won the World Championship.

Mar. 10 Senator James Gladstone introduced amendments to the Indian Act and the Canada Elections Act to give Aboriginal women and men living on reserves the right to vote in national elections without losing their rights to income tax exemption. The federal franchise was extended July 1.

Mar. 28 The Ont. legislature approved the incorporation of Laurentian U., a bilingual university in Sudbury, Ont.

Mar. 29–Apr. 2 PM Antonio Segni of Italy visited Canada.

Mar. 31 RCMP Commissioner Leonard Hanson Nicholson resigned after PM Deifenbaker refused to allow 50 Montreal police reinforcements from other provinces to help assist in the 1959 Nfld. woodworkers' strike. Nicholson was succeeded by Charles Edward Rivett-Carnac.

Apr. 1 The federal govt approved a National Energy Board recommendation to export natural gas to the US.

Apr. 13 Under the Territorial Land Act, new oil and gas regulations came into effect, requiring Canadian citizenship and residence of those granted oil and gas leases.

Apr. 18 French President Charles de Gaulle arrived in Ottawa for a 4-day visit.

• Canada and the Soviet Union signed a 3-year trade agreement, whereby the Soviet Union agreed to buy $25 million worth of goods every year from Canada.

Apr. 21 PM Diefenbaker and his wife travelled to Mexico City as guests of President Lopez Mateos. Diefenbaker succeeded in promoting the sale of Canadian manufactured steel rails to the Mexican State Railways.

Apr. 22 British Field Marshal Bernard Montgomery arrived in Ottawa for a 4-day visit.

May 3 The 10th Commonwealth PMs' Conference commenced in London, England. Condemnation was voiced against apartheid in South Africa. Canada, represented by PM Diefenbaker, proposed extending the Colombo Plan beyond Asia so it would cover Africa. On Sept. 22, Commonwealth finance ministers met to create a Special Commonwealth African Assistance Plan (SCAAP). Canada's contribution was to be $105 million during the 1st 3 years.

June 15 BC Ferries began service with 2 vessels and 2 terminals, one at Tsawwassen (Vancouver) and the other at Sydney (Victoria). By 2003, the company had 25 routes with 90 ports of call, 35 vessels and more than 4,700 employees. The Crown corporation was commercialized in 2003 through the Company Act.

June 22 Que. Liberals, under Jean Lesage (1912–1980), won their 1st provincial election in over 20 years, with a narrow victory over Antonio Barrette's Union Nationale. The Liberal campaign slogan, "It's time for a change," spoke of the Quiet Revolution that followed.

June 23 The Kelsey Generating Station, the 1st on Man.'s Nelson R., went into service. By 1972, the station had a capacity of 224 megawatts (MW). The Kettle Generating Station, the 2nd and largest Nelson R. hydroelectric power generating plant was opened in 1970. It was made possible through

a $300-million Man.-Ottawa agreement (1966) to further exploit the potential of the Nelson waterway.

June 27 NB Liberal leader Louis Joseph Robichaud (b 1925) won the provincial election ending Conservative Hugh John Flemming's 8-year reign. Robichaud was sworn in July 12, becoming the 1st Acadian premier of the province.

June 30 PM Diefenbaker opened the new Ottawa International Airport, designed by architect W.A. Ramsay. The facility, also known as Jacques Cartier International Airport, was given the international aeronautical designation YOW.

Also in June

• Halifax International Airport 1st began operations under a temporary permit. Located 38 km north of Halifax, the airport was designed to handle some 180,000 persons per annum. Official opening of its Air Terminal Building was celebrated Sept. 10, 1960.

July 10 The 40 megawatt (MW) Canada-India Reactor, US (CIRUS), created in India with Canadian assistance, went into operation, ostensibly as a research reactor. CIRUS supplied the plutonium for India's 1st nuclear weapons test on May 18, 1974.

July 11 The NWT Council convened at Resolute Bay.

July 25–27 At a federal-provincial conference, premiers discussed constitutional amendments and tax issues. Que. Premier Jean Lesage called for an end to shared-cost programs and for appropriate compensation to the provinces.

Aug. 4 The House of Commons unanimously approved the Canadian Bill of Rights, which guaranteed civil liberties (the right to life, liberty and personal security), language, education and enjoyment of private property. The bill received Assent on Aug. 10.

Aug. 5 The federal cabinet gave "authority for the maintenance on active service of up to 500 officers and men of the Canadian Armed Forces in support of the UN operations in the Congo." The 1st group of Canadian army signallers assigned to UN forces in the Congo left for Leopoldville on Aug. 13. The

Soviets charged that the move constituted western aggression. On Aug. 18, Canadian peacekeepers were manhandled by Congolese troops. Three days later, Congo Premier Patrice Lumumba apologized for the abuses.

Aug. 11 Hazen Robert Argue (1921–1991) was chosen national leader of the CCF, succeeding James William Coldwell (1888–1974).

Aug. 26 The 40-m long *Keno*, built for service on the upper Yukon R. in 1922, made its last trip from Whitehorse to Dawson City, as the last sternwheeler to travel the waterway. The boat was beached in downtown Dawson City and turned into a museum.

Also in Aug.

• Parliament approved $142 million for acreage payments to western farmers as an alternative to the 2-price system for wheat.

Sept. 12 The Social Credit Party under W.A.C. Bennett (1900–1979) won the provincial election in BC.

Sept. 15 Maurice "Rocket" Richard announced his retirement from hockey. Richard played 1,111 regular and playoff games over his 18 seasons with the Montreal Canadiens, scoring a total of 626 goals and assisting on 465 others. He played on 8 championship Stanley Cup teams and participated in 13 All-Star games. In retirement, the great Canadiens captain sold fishing tackle from his home to make ends meet.

Sept. 16 A Royal Commission on Government Organization headed by businessman J. Grant Glassco was appointed to examine all aspects of the federal govt. The commission's report, released in 1962, noted "government operations can be improved by adapting methods that have proved effective in the private sector."

Sept. 19 The U. of Alb. opened its new 130-ha campus on the outskirts of Calgary.

Sept. 21 Canada decided to contribute more than $22 million over 10 years to an international fund for the development of the Indus R. basin in Pakistan.

Sept. 28 The "Seaway Skyway," a new bridge between Prescott, Ont., and Ogdensburg, New York, opened. Designed by the architectural firm Modjeski & Master, the 655-m suspension bridge's main span is 350.75 m.

Oct. 1 The O'Keefe Centre for the performing arts opened in Toronto. Opening night featured the world premiere of Lerner and Lowe's musical *Camelot* starring Julie Andrews, Robert Goulet and Richard Burton: top ticket price was $5. Owned by the O'Keefe Brewing Company, the 3,200-seat auditorium was designed by Earle C. Morgan in conjunction with Page and Steele.

Oct. 5 Gov. of the Bank of Canada, James Coyne, delivered an address to the Canadian Chamber of Commerce in Calgary concerning foreign investment in Canada: "We should...live within our means and increase our means by our own efforts...A country which has reached Canada's stage of development can make better progress, and retain more control over its own destiny, by relying on its own savings to provide the necessary capital."

• A Royal Commission in Que. was appointed to investigate the Union Nationale party.

Oct. 12 The federal govt declared that the unnamed body of water between Axel Heiberg Is. and Amund Ringnes Is. in the Arctic would be named Massey Sound, after the former gov-gen.

Oct. 14 Fidel Castro's Cuban govt nationalized all foreign banks except the Bank of Nova Scotia and the Royal Bank of Canada. Cuban assets of the Bank of Nova Scotia were purchased by the Cuban govt on Dec. 1 and those of the Royal Bank on Dec. 8.

Oct. 20 PM Diefenbaker opened Sir John A. Macdonald Hall, the new law school at Queen's U. (Kingston, Ont.).

Oct. 24 Jean Drapeau's Civic Party won the Montreal municipal elections.

Oct. 26 Canada and other UN countries sponsored a resolution inviting the UN's Food and Agriculture Organization to mobilize and distribute available surplus foodstuffs to needy countries.

Oct. 27 The federal and Que. govts signed an agreement for construction of the Que. section of the Trans-Canada Highway.

Oct. 28 The Banting and Best Department of Medical Research at U. of Toronto received a $1 million gift from Canadian industrialist Garfield Weston (1898–1978).

Also in Oct.
• The National Theatre School of Canada, founded by Tom Patterson, Mavor Moore and 14 others, opened in Montreal.

Nov. 3–4 A 2nd federal-provincial constitutional conference on the amendment of the BNA Act was held in Ottawa.

Nov. 4 Justice Minister E. Davie Fulton announced a 15-year program to rehabilitate prisoners in federal penitentiaries.

Nov. 10 Canada pledged $1 million to the UN Congo Fund.

• Calston, Canada's deepest oil and gas well to date, was rig-released at Fording Mountain, BC. Spudded in mid-Mar. by California Standard, drilling of the 5,041-m well was completed by the end of Oct.

Nov. 16 BC fishermen ended a labour dispute that had shut down the BC herring fishery for 12 months.

• Israel presented Lester B. Pearson with the Medallion of Valour of the State of Israel for his "outstanding role in the deliberations of the UN, which led to the judicious consideration of the differences between the State of Israel and the Arab nations."

Nov. 24 PM Diefenbaker told the Canadian Club of Ottawa that Canada would not make a decision on maintaining nuclear weapons so long as progress toward disarmament continued.

Dec. 1 The federal govt increased duties on cars imported from Europe, which raised individual car prices by as much as $160. The average, standard and equipped Volkswagen was increased from $1,595 to $1,645.

Dec. 2 The 1st Interprovincial Conference of Provincial Premiers was held in Quebec City to discuss national co-operation at the provincial level.

Dec. 3 The $25 million Edmonton International Airport opened. It was the world's most northerly 24-hour airport.

• The Netherlands received 17 Tracker anti-submarine aircraft from Canada under a NATO mutual-aid program.

Dec. 7 The RCMP informed Minister of Justice E. Davie Fulton and PM Diefenbaker of an affair between Associate Minister of National Defence Joseph-Pierre-Albert Sévigny (b 1917) and suspected spy Gerda Munsinger, an episode the RCMP considered a security risk. Details of the affair were made known to PM Pearson in Dec. 1964. The case exploded in the House of Commons and became public on March 4, 1966.

Dec. 15 Typographer Allan Fleming's stylistic "CN" became the new corporate logo of the Canadian National Railway, replacing the traditional maple leaf logo and English-language acronym "CNR."

• Montreal's $30 million International Air Terminal at Dorval was opened.

Dec. 20 The National Productivity Council was established, a result of a conference on unemployment held in Ottawa on Oct. 25.

• Minister of Finance Donald Fleming brought down his supplementary budget, which included a withholding tax of 15% imposed on dividends and interest payments to non-residents. The profits of unincorporated branches of American companies were also subject to a 15% levy, which made foreign investment in Canada less attractive.

Also in 1960
• Canada's population was 17,870,000.

• The federal External Aid Office was established to administer foreign aid and develop aid-related policy. The office was independent of the Department of External Affairs but was responsible to the external affairs minister. The office became the

Canadian International Development Agency (CIDA) in 1968.

• The Combines Investigation Act was amended to allow for the regulation of misleading advertising. The definitions of *merger* and *monopoly* were also separated.

• The York University Act received Assent, paving the way for the formation of Ont.'s 10th university. On Dec. 2, writer and educator Dr. Murray Ross (1910–2000), former vice-president of the U. of Toronto, was appointed president of York, which, at the time had neither buildings nor students. "York University will, in the 1st years of operation," he said, "concentrate on a program of liberal and general education... The aim of a liberal education is to liberate." By 1968, York had 5,400 students. By 2000, York was the 3rd largest university in Canada, with 40,000 full- and part-time students.

• Nfld. designer A.J.C Paine (1886–1965), in association with Lawson, Beites and Cash, completed Confederation Building in St. John's. The "modern" work featured a 200-m-wide expansive facade rising in steps from 3 storeys to a 12-storey central tower.

• Isadore (Issy) Sharp (b 1931), nicknamed "Razzle Dazzle Issy," founded the Four Seasons Hotel chain. The 1st hotel opened on Jarvis St., Toronto, in 1961. In 1963, Sharp opened the prestigious Inn on the Park in Don Mills, Ont. By 2004, the Four Seasons chain was responsible for 62 hotels in 29 countries. Sharp was named to the Order of Canada in 1993.

• Walter Susskind (1913–1980) founded the National Youth Orchestra, a non-professional performing unit of 100 members, aged 14 to 24, selected through an annual competition. Following 4 weeks of intense training from some of the world's leading conductors, the orchestra would tour Canadian and international venues.

• The National Research Council established the National Medical Research Council.

• The annual All Native Basketball Tournament was 1st held in Prince Rupert, BC. It was won by Port Simpson in the Intermediate Division, and Kitkatla

in the Senior Division. Kaien Is. won the Women's Division in 1993, the 1st year women played in the prestigious community-based amateur event.

• William Wuttunee (b 1932) founded the National Indian Council and became its 1st chief.

• Tillie Taylor (1922–1999) was the 1st woman appointed provincial magistrate in Sask.

• Harold Fine, a Toronto wholesale druggist, was charged, convicted and jailed under an 1892 obscenity law for distributing condoms through the mail.

• Ottawa's Paul Anka (b 1941) played 3 shows at the Copacabana nightclub in New York, and was touted in the entertainment media as the youngest star ever to play the club.

• McClelland & Stewart launched the New Canadian Library series of paperback reprints, under editor Malcolm Ross (1911–2002). In 1963, the firm started the Carleton Library series for books on the social sciences.

• Senator Grattan O'Leary's (1889–1976) Royal Commission on Publishing recommended an end to tax privileges for Canadian companies advertising in foreign-owned periodicals. *Time* and *Reader's Digest* were originally exempt.

• Seven hundred British and American publishing houses were represented in Canada by distributors or branch plants.

• The Canadian Voice of Women for Peace (VOW), a voluntary organization dedicated to world peace and nuclear disarmament, was established.

• RCAF Wing Commander Johnny Tett (b 1926) devised the 5BX exercise plan, which became a worldwide success. His subsequent book became a best-seller.

• The Volkswagen *Bug* constituted 20% of the Canadian automobile market share.

• Kenojuak Ashevak completed the print *The Enchanted Owl*, at Cape Dorset, NWT.

• Harold Town (1924–1991) painted *Banners*, oil and lucite on canvas, his take on emotions associated with patriotic banners. The work is now in the Norman Mackenzie Art Gallery in Regina.

• Jock Macdonald completed *All Things Prevail*, his final painting before his death from a heart attack.

• Ronald Bloore completed the abstract on board *Painting, June 1960*, now in the National Gallery of Canada, and *The Establishment*, on mason-ite, now in a private collection.

• Michael Snow (b 1920) completed *Lac Clair,* on canvas, now at the National Gallery of Canada.

• Dennis Burton painted *The Game of Life,* on canvas, now in the National Gallery of Canada.

• Marie-Claire Blais published her 2nd novel, *Tête blanche.*

• Jean-Paul Desbiens (b 1927) published *Les Insolences de Frère Untel*, an anticlerical interpretation of the Que. educational system, which became influential in the Quiet Revolution.

• Arthur Hailey (b 1920) published the best–selling novel *In High Places*. The popular British-born Canadian citizen would go on to publish such best-sellers as *Hotel* (1965), *Airport* (1968), *The Money Changers* (1975) and *Detective* (1997).

• Margaret Laurence (1926–1987) published her 1st novel, *This Side Jordan.*

• Brian Moore (b 1921) published *The Luck of Ginger Coffey*, a bittersweet tale of a down-and-out Irish immigrant living in Montreal.

• Gérard Tougas published *Histoire de la littérature canadienne-française.*

• Historian Frank Hawkins Underhill (1889–1971) published *In Search of Canadian Liberalism.*

• The anthology *The Oxford Book of Canadian Short Stories* was published by Robert Weaver. Three further collections followed.

• Anne Wilkinson (1910–1961) published *Swan and Daphne*, a children's fairy tale.

• Margaret Avison's (b 1918) 1st collection of poetry, *Winter Sun*, was published, for which she received the Gov-Gen.'s Award.

• Poet James Reaney began publishing his semi-annual literary magazine *Alphabet,* which continued through 1971.

1961

Jan. 2 Polish national treasures, held for safekeeping since Sept. 1939, in the Que. Provincial Museum, were returned to Poland. The works included the 1st Gutenberg Bible and the original scores of Chopin.

Jan. 17 PM Diefenbaker and US President Eisenhower signed the Columbia River Treaty in Washington, D.C. The agreement awarded Canada half the electricity generated from dams on the Canadian section of the Columbia R. and compensation for half of the dams' flood control over US regions downstream. Canada consented to build 3 dams — Duncan (completed 1967), Keenleyside (1968) and Mica (1973). The treaty would not be effective until Sept. 16, 1964, due to a jurisdictional conflict between the BC and federal govts. Construction officially commenced May 1, 1965.

Feb. 3 The federal govt approved the merger of the Canadian Bank of Commerce and the Imperial Bank of Canada, forming the Canadian Imperial Bank of Commerce (CIBC).

Feb. 20 PM Diefenbaker met with US President Kennedy at Washington, D.C., to discuss a wide range of international and bilateral trade and security issues. Diefenbaker was the 1st foreign leader to visit the newly elected president.

• The federal govt announced a federal-provincial program of aero-magnetic surveys over the next 12 years to pinpoint mineral wealth in the Canadian Shield. The program was administered by the Geological Survey of Canada and through 1975 included over 4.5 million line miles of research resulting in the creation of more than 7,000 maps.

Mar. 8–17 PM Diefenbaker attended the Commonwealth Prime Ministers Conference in London, England, where he outlined Canada's censure of South Africa's apartheid policy. Canada was supported by Ghana, Malaya (Malaysia), India and Ceylon (Sri Lanka). South Africa elected to leave the Commonwealth on May 31.

Mar. 16 Maj-Gen. Jean Victor Allard (1913–1996) became the 1st Canadian to head a British Army Division, when he was appointed to command the 4th Division of the British Army of the Rhine. Allard was promoted to gen. and chief of Canada's defence staff in 1966.

Also in Mar.
• Effective Mar. 1961, by amendment to the BNA Act, the retirement age of Supreme Court of Canada judges was set at 75.

Spring Canada agreed to buy 66 F–101 *VooDoo* interceptor aircraft from the US. In return, the US assumed operational responsibility of all radar stations which comprised Pinetree Line. Both govts agreed on a joint Mutual Air Program, which provided for the Canadian purchase of 200 Canadian-built F–104 *Starfighter* aircraft.

Apr. 1 The 45% Canadian-content rule for Canadian television programming established as part of the Broadcast Act, 1958, went into effect.

• Thalidomide was made legally available in Canada to help pregnant women deal with morning sickness and insomnia. The drug was quickly discovered to have devastating effects on the fetus, leading to miscarriage, stillbirths, and amongst newborns, deafness, blindness and characteristically, a disfigurement of the limbs known as phocomelia. On Mar. 2, 1962, the federal govt removed thalidomide from shelves a full 3 months after European nations banned it. (An estimated 8,000 children were affected by thalidomide worldwide). On July 31, 1962, the govts of Ont., Alb. and Sask. pledged their support for the care of children deformed by thalidomide. Federal govt co-operation in the program was announced in Aug. 1962. In Feb. 1990, the federal govt offered surviving Canadian victims (between 75 and 100 individuals) a further $75,000 to $100,000 each.

Apr. 5 The MacPherson Royal Commission on Transportation report was issued. It recognized the importance of intermodal competition in transport, and recommended the federal govt pay the CNR and CPR annual subsidies of $40 million as compensation for uneconomic services in an effort to reduce transportation costs and stimulate railway improvement. A 2nd commission report, issued Jan. 24, 1962, concluded that competition, not the govt, should determine the price of transportation.

Apr. 6 A cheque for $260,000, representing funds collected by Canadian children, was presented to UNICEF.

Apr. 9–10 British PM Harold Macmillan visited Ottawa for talks with PM Diefenbaker.

Apr. 13–15 Greek Premier Constantine Karamanlis paid an official visit to Ottawa.

Apr. 22 The Canadian Wheat Board signed a long-term agreement with Chinese authorities in Peking (Beijing) for the purchase of $362 million of grain, including 3 to 6 million tonnes of wheat and over 1 million tonnes of barley. China became Canada's 2nd largest market for wheat. Despite a temporary ban of grain exports to China, established Oct. 23, 1962, by the Diefenbaker govt to protest the Sino-Indian border war, Canada would continue to sell China hundreds of millions of dollars' of wheat through the 1960s.

May 1–2 Habib Bourguiba, president of Tunisia, visited Ottawa.

May 2 The *Empress of Canada*, the new flagship of the Canadian Pacific fleet, arrived at Montreal on its maiden voyage from Liverpool. The *Empress* was 198 m in length and powered by 6 steam turbines; it weighed 30,558 tonnes and was appointed with original artwork and etched-glass windows, sculptures and murals, and provided transatlantic voyagers use of its swimming pool, movie theatre, library, cocktail bars, smoking rooms and sundeck. Its cheapest berth, a 4-bunk inside cabin without facilities, cost $225. The last of the great CP Empress-line ships was withdrawn from service and sold to Carnival Cruises in 1971. It later sailed for Royal Olympic Cruises under the name *Apollon*.

May 4 The *Federal Maple I* was launched, the 1st of 2 Canadian passenger-cargo ships presented to the Federation of the West Indies under the Canada–West Indies Aid Program.

May 13 A new shipping policy called for govt subsidization of Canadian shipyards, and shipments between Canadian ports on the Great Lakes were to be reserved for Canadian vessels.

May 16–18 US President John F. Kennedy and Jacqueline Lee Bouvier Kennedy (1929–1994) arrived in Ottawa for a 2-day visit, Kennedy's 1st foreign visit as president. Discussion focused on Cuba and Southeast Asia. At the conclusion of the meeting, the president accidentally left a secret memorandum behind, which fell into the hands of Diefenbaker. It spelled out what the president wanted from Canada: increased commitment to the Alliance for Progress launched Mar. 13 to aid Latin American countries; Canada becoming a member in the Organization of American States (OAS); larger foreign aid contributions; and "active support at Geneva and beyond for a more effective monitoring of the borders of Laos and Vietnam."

May 24–27 David Ben-Gurion, PM of Israel, paid an official visit to Ottawa.

May 30 Buffalo Gap, Sask., received 250 mm of rain in less than 1 hour, and retains to this day the record of being on the wet end of Canada's most intensive rainstorm.

• A Canadian-Soviet transpolar ski expedition reached the North Pole, and was greeted by dignitaries from Canada and the Soviet Union. The multinational force was appropriately titled Operation Polar Bear Bridge.

Also in May

• The federal Agricultural Rehabilitation and Development Act (ARDA) was passed. The legislation, spearheaded by Agriculture Minister Francis Alvin George Hamilton (b 1912), promoted joint federal-provincial programs to aid farmers in seeking land-use alternatives, and soil and water conservation.

June 5 Earnscliffe, the Ottawa residence of John A.

Macdonald and home of Britain's high commissioner to Canada, was declared a National Historic Site.

June 6 CUSO (Canadian University Services Overseas) was founded by representatives of 21 universities and 22 organizations across Canada to co-ordinate their volunteer services. CUSO also sent skilled Canadians, placed in 2-year postings, to provide education and technical assistance in developing countries. The 1st CUSO volunteers left for service later in the year.

June 13 The National Capital Commission completed its expropriations for the 16,590-ha Green Belt surrounding Ottawa.

June 23 Forest fires along Bonavista Bay, Nfld., forced 3,000 people to evacuate their homes.

June 25–26 Japanese PM Hyato Ikeda visited Ottawa. The Canada-Japan Ministerial Committee was established. The 1st Committee meeting was held in Tokyo, Jan. 11–12, 1963.

June 26 Upper Canada Village, at Crysler's Farm, Battlefield Park, near Morrisburg, Ont., was opened. The popular tourist site featured more than 40 historic buildings, populated by farmers, retailers and artisans, all re-creating life as it was in 1860s rural Ont.

Also in June

• The federal govt set up a Royal Commission on Health Services under the chairmanship of Emmett Matthew Hall (1898–1994), chief justice of Sask., to make "a comprehensive and independent study of existing facilities and future need for health services for the people of Canada." The 1st volume of the report was issued in June 1964.

July 6 Robert Norman Thompson (1914–1997) of Red Deer, Alb., was elected president of the Social Credit Party on the 1st ballot. He succeeded Solon Earl Low (1900–1962).

July 21 Inuvik, NWT, a govt-built town on the Mackenzie Delta, 2 degrees above the Arctic Circle, was officially opened by PM Diefenbaker. Inuvik (Inuit for "place of man") became a major communication and trading centre in the Arctic. It replaced the existing settlement of Aklavik, which was threatened by floods and erosion. Aklavik ("place of the barren grizzly lands") remains in existence to this day, however, because many of its citizens refused to move. Located close to the western border of the NWT, it is home to the Aklavik Fur Factory, and the gravesite of the "Mad Trapper" Albert Johnson.

July 31 The CCF (Cooperative Commonwealth Federation) Convention began in Ottawa's Coliseum where 2,000 delegates assembled to witness the New Democrat Party (NDP) replace the CCF. The NDP supported the "2 nations" theory and bilingualism as part of its nationwide social democracy platform. On Aug. 3, Sask. Premier Tommy Douglas was elected national NDP leader. On Nov. 7, Woodrow Stanley Lloyd (1913–1972) succeeded Douglas as premier of Sask.

Also in July

• The federal govt issued Shell Oil Company an offshore exploration permit in the Pacific Ocean on the grounds that the federal govt had jurisdiction over all offshore waters in Canada. BC govt officials disagreed, claiming that Victoria, not Ottawa, should issue the permits and garner the royalties.

Aug. 2 Leslie Frost announced his resignation as premier of Ont. and head of the provincial Progressive Conservative Party. He would be succeeded by John Parmenter Robarts (1917–1982) on Nov. 8.

Aug. 3 The BC govt approved the takeover of the British Columbia Electric Co. as a Crown corporation.

Aug. 18 The 1st Mariposa Folk Festival (named for the community of Mariposa in Stephen Leacock's *Sunshine Sketches of a Little Town*) was founded at Orillia, Ont., and quickly developed into one of the largest annual folk events on the continent. Regulars included such folk notables as Stan Rogers (1949–1985), Gordon Lightfoot (b 1938), Joni Mitchell (b 1943), Ian (b 1933) and Sylvia Tyson (b 1940), Alan Mills (1912–1977) and The Travellers.

Aug. 26 PM Diefenbaker opened the Hockey Hall of Fame in Toronto, and announced the establish-

ment of $5 million annual grants for amateur sports in Canada. On Sept. 25, the Fitness and Amateur Sport Act was passed, establishing a long-term, federal commitment to fitness and amateur sport. Responsibility fell under the Ministry of National Health and Welfare. On Feb. 6, 1962, the 1st grants were given to the Canadian Wheelmen's Association (cycling) and the Canadian Amateur Ski Association.

Also in Aug.

• Lincoln Kirstein, founder and general director of the New York City Ballet, was invited to head a commission to assess ballet in Canada. The subsequent Kirstein Survey looked disapprovingly on all 3 major ballet companies — Les Grands Ballets Canadiens, the Royal Winnipeg Ballet and the National Ballet. Kirstein reserved his sharpest criticism for the National Ballet.

Sept. 1 The 1st oil-drilling rig in the Arctic was unloaded in preparation for drilling on Melville Is.

Sept. 6 The 1st recipients of the Canada Council Medals were selected: Vincent Massey, artists Lawren Harris and A.Y. Jackson, poet E.J. Pratt, writers Ethel Wilson, Charles Marius Barbeau and Abbé Lionel-Adolphe Groulx, musicians Healey Willan and Wilfrid Pelletier, and posthumously to Brooke Claxton, 1st chairman of the Canada Council. The actual medals had not yet been struck.

Sept. 7 The federal govt announced that the Canadian armed forces would be increased by 15,000 and that 100,000 Canadians would be trained in a national survival program.

Sept. 8 The Université de Montréal played host to an international delegation of French-speaking universities from around the world.

Sept. 15 PM Diefenbaker opened the Sir Alexander Campbell Building, the largest of the 3 buildings forming the new post office headquarters in Ottawa.

Sept. 18 An electronic survey of Canada was completed, outlining its legal boundaries and the polar continental shelf.

Sept. 22 An aerial survey of wildlife in the Canadian Arctic islands was completed.

Sept. 27 The Thompson committee interim report, studying medicare for Sask., was released. It called for a general comprehensive and prepaid medicare scheme, administered by a public commission responsible to the govt through the minister of public health.

Oct. 1 The Organization for Economic Co-operation and Development (OECD) was established as an international body of industrialized nations to promote social and economic welfare in both member and non-member countries. Canadian Finance Minister Donald Fleming was elected chairman.

• The Canadian Television Network (changed to CTV in 1962) began broadcasting from stations in Toronto, Montreal and Halifax.

Oct. 6 The Canadian Committee for the Control of Radiation Hazards presented petitions with 141,000 names to PM Diefenbaker. Parliament Hill was picketed by members of the Voice of Women and the Combined Universities Campaign for Nuclear Disarmament.

Oct. 9 Mrs. Eleanor Roosevelt, widow of former US President Franklin D. Roosevelt, officiated at the opening of Memorial U., St. John's, Nfld.

Oct. 11 The National Defence Medical Centre was opened in Ottawa to serve all 3 military services.

Oct. 13 The Canadian Maritime Union was established in competition with the Seafarers' International Union.

Oct. 14 Canada and the US conducted a test of North American air defences in a simulated nuclear attack.

Oct. 16 Negotiations were completed for the sale of $20 million worth of Canadian wheat to Poland.

Oct. 23–28 The federal govt-sponsored Resources for Tomorrow Conference, at Montreal, discussed problems related to Canadian forests, water, fish, wildlife and soil.

Oct. 24 PM Diefenbaker left Ottawa for a 6-day official visit to Japan.

Dec. 11 The assistant military attaché at the Soviet embassy in Ottawa was expelled from Canada for receiving secret Canadian documents.

Dec. 19 PM Diefenbaker and Queen Elizabeth II inaugurated a transatlantic cable, carrying voice, picture and teletype messages. It was the 1st link in a new round-the-world Commonwealth communications system.

1961–1968 Archaeologists excavated the ruins of Straumford near L'Anse aux Meadows, Épaves Bay, on the northern tip of Nfld. They found 8 Viking house sites and 4 boat sheds dating back to approximately 1000 CE. Leif Eiriksson had spent a winter at Straumford, and Greenland colonists had regularly visited the village. Unveiled as a National Historic Site by PM Trudeau on June 27, 1975, L'Anse aux Meadows was declared a UNESCO World Heritage Site in 1978.

Also in 1961

• The population of Canada was 18,238,247. The population of Ont., was 6,236,000; Que., 5,259,000; BC, 1,629,000; Alb., 1,332,000; Sask., 925,000; Man., 922,000; NS, 737,000; NB, 598,000; Nfld., 458,000; PEI, 105,000; and Yukon and NWT, 38,000.

• The population of Canada included over 1 million male war veterans: 188,234 had served in WW I or in a prior war; 833,680 had served in WW II; 35,649 had served in Korea; 33,000 had served in more than one war.

• Three separatist organizations were formed in Que.–the right-wing Alliance laurentienne, the left-wing Action socialiste pour l'independance du Québec and the moderate Rassemblement pour l'indépendance nationale.

• Sam Sniderman's (b 1920) flagship Sam the Record Man store opened at 347 Yonge St. in Toronto. By 1969, Sam the Record Man was a franchise chain operated by Sam and his brother Sidney. The business was so successful that during the mid 1980s, Sam's 130-plus stores accounted for over 15% of all retail record business in Canada.

By 2001, however, dramatic changes in the music industry had forced the chain into bankruptcy, only one year after Sam Sniderman's retirement. Sniderman was named to the Order of Canada in 1976.

• The C.D. Howe Memorial Foundation was established in honour of the late liberal cabinet member Clarence Decatur Howe. The foundation provided financial assistance to Canadian students showing leadership and achievement promise. In 1973, the foundation became the C.D. Howe Institute, an independent non-profit think tank that analyses Canadian social and economic policies of import.

• Gary Cowan (b 1938) won the Canadian Amateur Golf Championship, beginning one of the greatest amateur careers in Canadian history. In 1964, he was low amateur at the Masters in Augusta, Georgia; in 1965, he helped the national team win America's Cup; in 1966, and again in 1971, he won the US Amateur Championship; and in 1999, he was named Canadian Male Amateur Golfer of the Century.

• The 1st *Tonight Show* hosted by Johnny Carson went on the air with theme music written by Ottawa's Paul Anka (b 1941).

• Ten-year-old Janice Babson died of leukemia. Her eyes were donated to the Canadian Eye Bank as per her wish. Her act prompted a flood of donations.

• Bernie "Boom Boom" Geoffrion (b 1931) took up where Rocket Richard left off, becoming only the 2nd player in NHL history to score 50 goals in 1 season.

• Whiteshell Provincial Wilderness Park near Pointe du Bois, Man., was established. The park protects over 200 lakes, many accessible only by aircraft.

• The Canadian Book Publishers Council (CBPC), which allied a group of textbook publishers with members of the Book Publishers Association of Canada, was founded. The CBPC would later oppose the Canadian-owned firms' rival association (Association of Canadian Publishers — ACP) on many govt policies favouring Canadian ownership.

• Sask.-born artist Arthur Fortescue McKay (b 1926) painted *Effulgent Image*, a mandala image on a 1.2-m x 1.2-m sheet of masonite, now in a private collection.

• Guido Molinari (1933–2004) completed the painting, *Hommage à Jauran*, on canvas. The work, consisting of vertical bars of colour, is now in the Vancouver Art Gallery.

• Joyce Wieland (1931–1998) painted *Time Machine Series* on canvas, now in the Art Gallery of Ont., Toronto. She also produced *Heart-on*, now in the National Gallery of Canada.

• Anthony Morse Urquhart (b 1934) produced the allegorical landscape, *In Hiding*, now in the National Gallery of Canada.

• Painter Ronald Bloore arranged a show of 5 Regina painters who had been influenced by international encounters at Emma L., Sask. The group included Bloore, Ted Godwin (b 1933), Kenneth Lochhead (b 1926), Art McKay (b 1926) and Doug Morton (b 1926). They would exhibit across Canada as the Regina Five.

• *Tish* magazine was founded in Vancouver by writers Frank Davey (b 1940), George Bowering (b 1935), David Dawson, Jamie Reid and Fred Wah (b 1939). The avant-garde poetry newsletter was published intermittently until 1969.

• Pierre Berton (b 1920) published the children's story *The Secret World of Og*, illustrated by his daughter Patsy.

• Sheila Every Burnford's (1918–1984) 1st novel, *The Incredible Journey*, was published. It depicted the long and arduous trek that housepets (2 dogs and a cat) made across Canadian wilderness to return home. The best-selling tearjerker was brought to the screen twice, as *The Incredible Journey* in 1963 and as *Homeward Bound* in 1993. Both films were produced by Walt Disney Studios. Burnford went on to write *Bel Ria* (1977), another heart-wrenching dog story for children.

• Farley Mowat (b 1921) published the humorous and ever-popular children's novel *Owls in the Family*.

• Jacques Hébert (b 1923), in collaboration with Pierre Elliott Trudeau (1919–2000), published *Deux innocents en Chine rouge,* following a trip to communist China.

• Canadian-American writer Daryl Hine (b 1936) published the novel *The Prince of Darkness & Co.* Hine, who caused Northrop Frye to wonder "if any Canadian poet [had] potentially greater talents," served as editor of the prestigious literary magazine *Poetry* (Chicago) between 1968–1977.

• Jean Le Moyne (b 1937) published a collection of essays entitled *Convergences*, for which he won the Gov-Gen.'s Award.

• Journalist Ralph Allen published his history of Canada, *Ordeal by Fire.*

• *Hear Us O Lord from Heaven Thy Dwelling Place*, a collection of 7 interrelated stories and novellas by Malcolm Lowry (1909–1957), was posthumously published and won the Gov-Gen.'s Award.

• Hugh MacLennan published *Seven Rivers of Canada*, an historical survey of the St. Lawrence, the Mackenzie, the Red, the St. John, the Ottawa, the Saskatchewan, and the Fraser Rivers.

• Historian William L. Morton (1908–1980) published *The Canadian Identity.*

• The poetic work *The Spice-Box of Earth* was published by Leonard Cohen.

• An underground bomb shelter, dubbed the "Diefenbunker" after the PM, opened its doors. Construction of the site near Carp, Ont., had taken 2 years. The 4-storey structure was equipped to handle 300–500 people for 30-plus consecutive days.

• The Bank of Nova Scotia became the 1st Canadian bank to appoint women bank managers.

1962

Jan. 15 The famous Musical Ride became a permanent, full-time component of the RCMP.

Jan. 25 The Bank of Montreal purchased the Nfld. Savings Bank. Its single branch was located in St. John's.

Also in Jan.

• The newly founded, Toronto-based Canadian Arab Friendship Society issued the 1st edition of its quarterly *Middle East Digest and Newletter*. The publication promoted Arab-Canadian education and addressed anti-Arab bias in mainstream media. The Canadian Arab Friendship Society is the oldest secular Arab society in the country. The 1st notable wave of Arab immigrants to Canada came from present-day Syria and Lebanon (Ottoman Empire) in 1882. By 1990, approximately 200,000 Arabs from 20 countries lived in Canada, with nearly 85% in Montreal and Toronto.

Feb. 6 The Surveys and Mapping Building of the Department of Mines and Technical Surveys opened. It was Ottawa's largest govt building.

Also in Feb.

• Hazen Argue, former leader of the CCF, left the newly formed NDP and joined the Liberal party. Tommy Douglas had defeated Argue for the NDP leadership in 1961.

• An informal committee on French-English relations met at McGill U. in Montreal as many Quebecers found it increasingly necessary to address questions raised by the Quiet Revolution. Among those in attendance were: André Laurendeau, Maxwell Cohen, Pierre Elliott Trudeau, Claude Ryan and F.R. Scott (1899–1985).

• Artist Gregory Richard Curnoe (1936–1992) of London, Ont., arranged a "happening" at the London Art Museum — an audience-participation piece called *The Celebration.*

Mar. 6 An electric-power pylon near Riondel, BC, was destroyed by explosives placed by Sons of Freedom Doukhobors. Between May 10 and 11, 9 people were arrested on related charges and later sentenced to 15 years' imprisonment.

Mar. 15 At the World Men's Figure Skating Championships in Prague, Czechoslovakia, 21-year-old Donald Jackson (b 1940) of Oshawa, Ont., became the 1st Canadian to win the event, with 7 perfect marks for the free skate portion of his program, a feat never before equalled. Trailing the favoured Russian Karol Divin by 45 points at the end of compulsory figures, Jackson electrified

18,000 spectators and a television audience estimated at 250 million viewers, with the 1st triple lutz ever completed in world competition. Also at the Worlds, Otto (b 1940) and Maria Jelinek (b 1942), who had fled to Canada from Czechoslovakia with their family in 1951, returned to Prague to win the World Figure Skating Pairs Championships as Canadian representatives. The brother-and-sister team had won the 1961 and 1962 Canadian pairs title and also the 1961 North American pairs title.

Mar. 28 A meeting between the Sask. govt and the Sask. College of Physicians and Surgeons took place at Regina to discuss the impasse between the govt and the province's doctors concerning medicare. The College attempted to force the withdrawal of the Medicare Act.

Also in Mar.
• Pamela Anne Gordon (b 1943) of BC became Miss March and the 1st Canadian *Playboy* magazine Playmate of the Month.

Apr. 1 The 55% Canadian-content rule for television programming, as determined under the Canadian Broadcasting Act, 1958, became effective.

Apr. 2 The 640-km microwave system between Peace River, Alb. and Hay River, NWT, built by Alb. Govt Telephones and CN Telecommunications, was opened.

Apr. 3 Gen. Andrew McNaughton resigned as chairman of the Canadian section of the International Joint Commission, a position he had held since 1950. McNaughton's bitter opposition to the 1961 Columbia R. Treaty between Canada and the US alienated him from the Diefenbaker govt, and despite the gen.'s distinguished record of public service, he was forced from office.

Apr. 9 An 11-month strike of CPR employees of the Royal York Hotel in Toronto came to an end. On June 25, the Supreme Court of Canada ruled Toronto's Royal York Hotel engaged in illegal conduct when it discharged employees who had participated in the legal strike.

Apr. 17 Canada was elected to the UN Commission on Human Rights for a 3-year term, beginning Jan. 1, 1963.

Apr. 19 The National Capital Commission served notice to some 2,800 residents of Lebreton Flats that their land would be expropriated. The last residence of the largely working-class 62.3-ha community in central Ottawa was demolished in 1965, to provide an improved view of the Parliament Buildings.

Apr. 29 British PM Harold Macmillan arrived in Ottawa for talks with PM Diefenbaker and his cabinet on the European Common Market and to gather Conservative-govt reaction to Britain's application for membership.

May 2 The Canadian dollar was officially pegged at 92.5 cents US thereby giving rise to the term "Diefendollar." It would float again in 1970, and rise to as much as $1.07 US that year.

May 28 The federal and Man. govts signed an agreement for construction of the $63.2 million Greater Winnipeg Floodway, known affectionately as "Duff's Ditch," after Dufferin Roblin (b 1917), Conservative premier of Manitoba from 1958 to 1976. The project, designed to divert floodwaters of the Red R. around the Man. capital, was 1st conceived after 1950, when the Red R. crested at 9.24 m in downtown Winnipeg. Completed in 1968, the floodway, when used, guides river waters around the city through a flood-control channel before releasing it back into the main river flow below Lockport. The Winnipeg Floodway was the largest earth-moving project ever undertaken to date in Canada. On Apr. 13, 1969, the Greater Winnipeg Floodway went into operation for the 1st time, to divert the rising spring waters of the Red R.

May 30 Riots broke out at a Diefenbaker rally in Vancouver where 7,000 people were in attendance. Diefenbaker blamed the NDP for organizing the melee.

May 31 Bank of Canada gov. Louis Rasminsky warned Minister of Finance Donald Fleming that the govt was facing a major financial crisis.

June 4 Nuclear-generated electricity was 1st delivered to Canadian consumers from the 20 megawatt (MW), heavy water–moderated Nuclear Power Demonstration (NPD) plant at Des Joachims, Ont., on the Ottawa R., near Rolphton. The plant had gone critical Apr. 11. The NPD research facility illustrated the practical use of nuclear-generated power and inspired the spread of CANDU (Canada Deuterium Uranium) reactors in Canada and abroad.

June 7 Queen Elizabeth II and the Queen Mother arrived in Canada for a 10-day visit.

June 8 After 5 years and $10 million in expenses, the International Minerals and Chemical Corp. of Canada shaft struck potash north of Esterhazy, Sask. The site would become the largest potash mine in the world, and make Canada the leading exporter of potash.

June 11 A preliminary hearing began in BC against 72 members of the Sons of Freedom Doukhobors, in relation to a spate of incidents that occurred between 1958 and 1961. The hearing concluded on Aug. 7 with the dismissal of conspiracy charges.

June 15 Canada's 1st space vehicle, a 11.3-kg non-orbiting instrument package, was launched from Wallops Is., Virginia.

June 17 An estimated $2 to $3 million in damage was caused in a prison riot at St. Vincent de Paul Penitentiary in Montreal.

June 18 In the federal general election, PM Diefenbaker's Progressive Conservatives retained minority power with 116 seats. Lester Pearson's Liberals took 100 seats, the Social Credit 30 and the NDP 19. Voter turnout was 79%.

June 21 Due to a rapidly falling dollar, the federal govt was forced to seek foreign assistance in the form of temporary credits from Britain and the US, and $400 million from the International Monetary Fund. On June 24, PM Diefenbaker announced emergency measures to strengthen the economy and protect the dollar. The move included a 5% surcharge on $23 billion of imports, a 15% surcharge on luxury imports and a 10% surcharge on deferrable imports (these surcharges were dropped Nov. 15). Also, $250 million in govt expenditures was cut, and $1 billion of standby credit secured. The Bank of Canada simultaneously raised the bank rate to 6%, without announcement.

July 1 Sask.'s medicare plan came into effect officially, but implementation of the plan was delayed as the province's doctors went on strike in protest. The problem was solved when a special session of the legislature passed amendments satisfactory to both sides on Aug. 2: doctors would work under the universal health care scheme but would be allowed extra billing.

July 30 Britain agreed to purchase 10,886,400 kg of Canadian refined uranium.

Also in July

• Following 14 acts of violence and harassment, and the prevention of a ship's passage through a Seaway canal, Justice T.G. Norris of the Court of Appeal of BC was named to head an Industrial Inquiry Commission into shipping disruptions and labour strife on the Great Lakes. Justice Norris issued his report on July 15, 1963. He recommended the appointment of a board of trustees to control the major maritime transportation unions representing various Seaway workers. On Oct. 23, 1963, the Maritime Transportation Unions Trustee Act received Assent, placing Canadian maritime unions under the control of a 3-person board of trustees. Longshoremen had marched on Ottawa to protest the act a week earlier.

Aug. 1 The Ont. Construction Safety Act came into effect, making employers responsible for the safety of their employees.

Aug. 7 Fifteen Chinese refugees fleeing food shortages in their homeland arrived in Canada. They were the 1st members of 100 families allowed into the country from Hong Kong under a special policy initiated by PM Diefenbaker.

Aug. 9 A federal conciliation board report recommended a pay increase for 100,000 nonoperating railway employees, plus 1% per hour for a job-security fund. It was the 1st report of its kind to be unanimously accepted by both unions and railway companies, and broke new ground in labour relations by dealing with job security.

Aug. 27 Kenneth Carter was appointed chairman of a federal Royal Commission on Taxation. The commission's report of 1967 included such recommendations as a flat 50% taxation on corporate profits, the merging of personal and corporate income tax, the taxation of capital gains and the removal of estate and gift taxes.

Sept. 3 The 7,821-km Trans-Canada Highway stretching from St. John's, Nfld., to Victoria, BC, was officially opened by PM Diefenbaker at Rogers Pass in BC. The highway was initiated on Dec. 10, 1949, with the Trans-Canada Highway Act. Work officially began in 1950. Construction of the highway would continue until 1965. Total costs exceeded $1 billion.

Sept. 5 The Canada-US–sponsored World Food Bank was initiated with Canada's pledge of $5 million in cash and commodities.

• PM Diefenbaker speaking at the Commonwealth PMs' Conference in London, England, opposed the proposed entry of Britain into the European Economic Community (EEC).

Sept. 11 President Mohammad Ayub Khan of Pakistan arrived in Canada for a 5-day state visit.

Sept. 24 The Garden of the Provinces, across from the National Archives and the National Bank in Ottawa, was opened officially by PM Diefenbaker. Conceived as a celebration of Canada's provinces and territories, the garden is situated on the high bluff above the LeBreton Flats; it is open 24 hours a day and illuminated at night.

Sept. 25 Shell Oil, a British and Dutch–owned company, purchased Canadian Oil Companies and its "White Rose" brand name for $130 million.

Sept. 29 Canada's 1st satellite, *Alouette I*, was launched into orbit by the National Aeronautics and Space Administration (NASA) from Vanderberg Air Force Base, California. It cost $3 million, weighed 146 kg, and flew 1,000 km above Earth. The orbit made Canada the 3rd nation in space. A joint Canada-US project, the satellite was to gather information about the upper atmosphere and to improve radio transmission on earth. It was deactivated in the 1970s, yet remains in orbit.

Oct. 10 Two people were killed and 5 injured in a collision between a TCA Viscount and an RCAF fighter over Bagotville, Que.

Oct. 11 The 1st of 200 Canadian-built CF–104 *Starfighters* left for Zweibrucken, West Germany, to join Canadian NATO strike-reconnaissance squadrons.

Oct. 17 A 5% surcharge was removed on most imported industrial machinery.

Oct. 22 US President John F. Kennedy placed a "quarantine" around Cuba after Americans detected Soviet missile bases on the island. The nuclear weapons were reportedly pointed at North American targets. On Oct. 24, PM Diefenbaker officially put Canadian armed forces on alert after Defence Minister Douglas Harkness (1903–1999) showed him a communiqué indicating that the US had moved to a greater degree of readiness over the Cuban Missile Crisis. Fears of an imminent nuclear war were widespread. On Oct. 27, Soviet Premier Nikita Khrushchev announced that the USSR would remove the missile sites, easing one of the most stressful episodes in cold war history.

Oct. 23 Protesting the Sino-Indian border war, PM Diefenbaker's cabinet elected to ban all exports to China except wheat.

Oct. 25 The Bedford Institute of Oceanography (BIO) on the northeastern shore of Bedford Basin, NS, was officially opened. Established by the federal govt, largely as a result of lobbying by Dr. W.E. van Steenburgh, director-general of Scientific Services of the Department of Mines and Technical Services, the institute is dedicated to research and exploration of the oceanic ecosystem on a national and global scale. The institute's 1st director was Dr. W.N. English.

Oct. 30 Canada voted against UN membership for the People's Republic of China. On Dec. 6, Canadian transport aircraft were sent to India to help repel Chinese aggression in the Himalayas.

Oct. 31 The Sault Ste. Marie International Bridge, spanning the St. Mary's R. between Sault Ste. Marie, Ont., and Michigan, was opened.

Oct.–Apr. 1963 Thirteen RCAF personnel served as part of the UN Temporary Executive Authority in West New Guinea, maintaining peace and security in the territory during the transfer of power from the Netherlands to Indonesia.

Nov. 5 The Political Committee of the UN approved a Canadian-proposed formula for halting above-ground nuclear-bomb tests by 1963. President John F. Kennedy had previously expressed dissatis-faction with Canada's antinuclear-testing stance in a letter to PM Diefenbaker dated Oct. 30. On Aug. 8, 1963, Canada, Britain, the US and Soviet Union signed the Nuclear Limited Test Ban Treaty.

Nov. 12 Montreal's application to hold a world's fair, Expo '67, was approved by the International Exhibition Bureau.

Nov. 14 Sioux Rock, depicting Native legends, was discovered at Port Arthur, Ont.

• Liberal premier Jean Lesage was re-elected in Que. on a platform to nationalize Que. hydroelectric companies. "*Maîtres chez nous*" (Masters in our own house) was his political slogan.

Nov. 22 The British Commonwealth Games were held in Perth, Australia, until Dec. 1. Canada placed 4th with gold medals won by Bruce Kidd (b 1943) in track, Richard Pound (b 1942) and Mary Stewart (b 1945) in swimming, and Harry Mann (b 1943) in boxing.

Nov. 29 Public Works Minister Edmund Davie Fulton resigned (effective 1963) from federal politics to become Conservative leader of BC. He returned to Ottawa in 1965.

Nov. 30 More than 100 residents of Cornwall, Ont., required hospital treatment after chlorine gas escaped from a railway tank car.

Also in Nov.

• Liberal MPs Paul Theodore Hellyer (b 1923) and Julia "Judy" Verlyn LaMarsh (1924–1980) returned to Ottawa after visiting NATO and American NATO Commander Lauris Norstad in France. The MPs were convinced that Canada was not meeting its NATO commitments and was therefore endanger-ing the alliance. Both threatened to leave the Liberal opposition party if leader Lester B. Pearson did not establish a definite party position on

nuclear warheads. On Jan. 3, 1963, Norstad spoke at a news conference in Ottawa on the issue.

Dec. 1 The Grey Cup game at Varsity Stadium in Toronto, between the Hamilton Tiger-Cats and the Winnipeg Blue Bombers was halted with 9:22 left to play because of severe fog that rolled in from L. Ontario. Dubbed the "Fog Bowl," the game con-tinued the following day (the 1st Grey Cup to be played on a Sunday), with Winnipeg winning 28–7.

Dec. 5 Que. Liberal Marie-Claire Kirkland-Casgrain (b 1926) was appointed minister without portfolio in the Que. legislature, becoming the 1st woman to hold a Que. cabinet post.

Dec. 11 The last judicial hanging in Canada took place in Toronto's Don Jail. Ronald Turpin and Arthur Lucas were executed for murder. A partial ban on capital punishment was established in 1967, and the punishment removed from the Criminal Code in 1976.

Dec. 17 Opposition Leader Lester B. Pearson suggest-ed in the House of Commons that Canada should become a bilingual nation.

Dec. 18 The CNR board of directors decided to study ways of attracting more French-speaking Canadians into the organization.

Dec. 21 PM Diefenbaker arrived in the Bahamas for post–Cuban Missile Crisis talks with British PM Macmillan and US President Kennedy.

Also in 1962

• The Shaw Festival, the only theatrical festival in the world devoted to the works of Irish playwright George Bernard Shaw (1856–1950) was founded by Brian Doherty at Niagara-on-the-Lake, Ont. It opened in a renovated courthouse. On June 20, 1973 the new 869-seat Shaw Festival theatre, designed by architect Ronald James Thom (1923–1986), was officially opened. By 1998, Shaw Festival ticket sales were $11.75 million, with a paid attendance of 321,000 for 765 performances.

• The Department of Agriculture's Experimantal Farms in Morden, Man., issued the 1st in its Parkland series of hybridized, prairie-loving roses.

The 1st Parkland rose was the Assiniboine. Others in the series included: Cuthbert Grant (1967), Adelaide Hoodless (1973), Morden Amorette (1977), Morden Ruby (1977), Morden Cardinette (1980), Morden Centennial (1980), Morden Blush (1988), Morden Fireglow (1989), Prairie Joy (1990), Winnipeg Parks (1990), Hope for Humanity (1995), Morden Snowbeauty (1997) and Morden Sunrise (2000). The Experimental Farms' Ottawa division began issuing its famous Explorer roses in 1968.

• The Sask. govt established the Wascana Centre Authority to control 3.8 km² of land surrounding artificial Wascana L. in downtown Regina.

• Montreal's Place Ville Marie opened as the largest integrated office-shopping centre in North America. Owned by the Royal Bank of Canada and American real estate tycoon William Zeckendorf, the complex was designed by architect I. Mario Pei to fit on a 2.8-ha site. Total cost was $105 million.

• Artist Jean McEwen (1923–1999) completed the canvas *Meurtrière traversant le bleu*, now in the Montreal Museum of Fine Arts.

• Internationally renowned artist Michael Snow painted the oil on canvas and wood *Venus Simultaneous*, portraying 8 walking women, each in a different relationship to the canvas. It is now in the Art Gallery of Ontario, Toronto.

• London, Ont.–born artist, Jack Chambers (1931–1978) painted *Messengers Juggling Seed*, now in the National Gallery of Canada, Ottawa.

• BC artist, printmaker, and designer Takao Tanabe (b 1926) established Periwinkle Press to promote the works of poets John Newlove, Robin Matthews, Roy Koyooka and Gerry Gilbert.

• Marshall McLuhan published *The Gutenberg Galaxy: The Making of Typographical Man*, which his publishers touted as "the famed thinker's stunning analysis of the rise and fall of the tyranny of the printed word."

• American scientist Rachel Carson published the highly influential *Silent Spring*, which would lead directly and indirectly to a host of future Canadian environmental legislation, pesticide and pollution controls, and widespread environmental activism.

• André Laurendeau (1912–1968) published a collection of essays called *The Conscription Crisis, 1942*.

• Kildare Dobbs published the largely autobiographical *Running to Paradise*, which won the Gov-Gen.'s Award for fiction. It was his 1st book.

• Jacques Ferron (1921–1985) published *Contes du pays incertain*, for which he received the Gov-Gen.'s Award under the category Romans-et-nouvelles.

• Claire Montreuil (b 1914, pseud. Claire Martin) published the novel *Quand j'aurai payé ton visage*, a contemporary account of the tensions between church and state, family and women.

• Rudy Henry Wiebe (b 1934) published his 1st novel, *Peace Shall Destroy Many*, a story set in a pacifist Mennonite community during WW II.

• Poet Al Purdy (1918–2000) published *Poems for All the Annettes*.

• Poet Gatien Lapointe (1931–1983) published *L'ode au St. Laurent*, for which he received the Prix Du Maurier, the Prix du Québec and the Gov-Gen.'s Award.

• The play *Riel* written and produced in 1950 by John William Coulter (1888–1980), was 1st published as the 1st in a trilogy that included *The Crime of Louis Riel* (1968) and *The Trial of Louis Riel* (1968).

• Jacques Languirand (b 1931) published the play *Les Insolites*, 1st performed in 1956. It was awarded the prize for the Best Canadian play at the Dominion Drama Festival.

1963

Jan. 3 US Gen. Lauris Norstad, newly retired commander of NATO, held a news conference in Ottawa and sharply criticized the Diefenbaker govt's antinuclear stance. He argued that if Canada refused to equip its *Starfighter* squadrons with nuclear ammunition, it would not be fulfilling its NATO commitment. On Jan. 12, Leader of the Opposition

Lester Pearson stated that Canada should accept US nuclear weapons for its 2 Canadian *Bomarc* missile sites, and its Air Division in Europe. This policy was a reversal of earlier Liberal positions on nuclear arms, and caused Pierre Trudeau to label Pearson the "defrocked priest of peace."

Jan. 14 Canada and the Republic of Korea (South Korea) established diplomatic relations.

Jan. 25 PM Diefenbaker revealed secret details covered in negotiations with US President Kennedy concerning the deployment of *Bomarc* missiles on Canadian soil. Five days later, on Jan. 30, the Kennedy administration, under the auspices of the US State Department, released a scathing press release denouncing Diefenbaker as a liar on nuclear issues, and criticizing Canada for "not having made practical arrangements" to equip its forces with nuclear weapons. The next day, Diefenbaker denounced the criticism as "unwarranted intrusion" and recalled Charles Ritchie, Canada's ambassador to the US. Ritchie called the US news release "an absolute outrage, the most blatant, heavy-handed, intolerable piece of bullying." An aide to William Butterworth, US ambassador to Canada, noted that the reaction to the press release "was like tossing a match into dried hay."

Jan. 29 The British empire–bound Diefenbaker govt was much relieved when a French veto kept Britain out of the European Common Market.

Feb. 3 Minister of Defence Douglas Harkness, tendered his resignation over PM Diefenbaker's refusal to accept US nuclear warheads for its *Bomarc* missiles and *Voodoo* interceptors as part of the US-Canada joint defence of North America.

Feb. 4 Conservative minister George Hees and retiring MP Davie Fulton offered PM Diefenbaker the position of chief justice of the Supreme Court of Canada if he would resign. Diefenbaker indignantly refused.

Feb. 5 For the 2nd time in the 20th century, a vote in the House brought down a govt, when NDP and Social Credit members joined the Liberals to defeat the Diefenbaker govt on its antinuclear weapons policy. The vote was 142 to 111 against the Tories.

Parliament was later dissolved and a general election was set for Apr. 8.

Feb. 8 Conservative federal ministers George Hees and Pierre Sévigny resigned due a lack of confidence in PM Diefenbaker. On Feb. 18, veteran Conservative MP, Justice Minister Donald Fleming (1905–1986), resigned from politics after 25 years of public service.

Feb. 11 Three striking loggers were killed and 9 wounded in a shootout near Kapuskasing, Ont. The gunplay involved loggers and independent bush workers. Twenty-two non-capital murder charges were laid on Feb. 13. The men charged were acquitted on Oct. 2.

Feb. 18 The Canada Council received an anonymous gift of $4.25 million to provide scholarships and grants to eligible Canadians who wanted to pursue, in Canada, advanced studies in medicine, science and engineering.

Feb. 25 PM Diefenbaker was made a Freeman of the City of London, England, on the last day of a 3-day visit to the city.

Mar. 1 The BC govt established Victoria College as the U. of Victoria, with full degree-granting status. (Victoria College had been established in 1903.) UVic had a 2003–2004 student body exceeding 18,300 with 72% of students from off-island. The university, whose mottos are "Let there be light" and "A multitude of the wise is the health of the world," is Victoria's 4th largest employer.

• The BC govt established Simon Fraser U. in Burnaby. Named after 19th-century explorer and fur trader Simon Fraser, the Burnaby Mountain campus was designed by Arthur Erickson and is terraced atop Burnaby Mountain, some 365 m above sea level. The campus faces northwest over Burrard Inlet. The university opened Sept. 9, 1965.

Mar. 29 The Wolfe Monument on the Plains of Abraham in Quebec City was vandalized. The monument was erected in memory of British Gen. James Wolfe who defeated French Gen. Marquis de Montcalm on Sept. 13, 1759. The victory marked both the beginning of the English conquest of

Quebec and the slow retreat of France from North America.

Also in Mar.

• The revolutionary Front de libération du Québec (FLQ) was founded as a movement supporting Que. sovereignty and the establishment of an independent socialist state. The marginal group resorted to the use of propaganda, murder and terrorism to further its goals. The FLQ was trained by Belgium-born Georges Schoeters. Its leaders included Pierre Vallières (1938–1998) and Charles Gagnon. Through April and May, the FLQ set off a series of bombs in Montreal: on April 20, Wilfred O'Neill, a 65-year-old night watchman, was killed at a Montreal army recruiting centre. On May 17, the Que. govt offered a $50,000 reward for information leading to the arrest and conviction of the little-known terrorists. The Montreal police also announced the formation of a 200-person anti-terrorist unit. The same day, a series of FLQ bombs exploded in mailboxes in the Montreal anglophone community of Westmount. One of the bombs seriously injured Sgt-Maj. Walter Leja as he tried to dismantle it. Altogether, the FLQ would commit over 200 violent crimes, including the Oct. 1970 kidnapping of British Trade Commissioner James Cross and the execution of Que. Minister of Labour Pierre Laporte (1921–1970).

Apr. 8 Lester Pearson's Liberals won the federal election with a minority govt of 129 seats. John Diefenbaker's Progressive Conservatives took 95 seats, the Social Credit 24 and the NDP 17. The federal Liberal govt took office Apr. 22. Voter turnout was 79.2%, the highest turnout to date.

Apr. 10 New amendments to the Food and Drug Act increased federal jurisdiction over the testing, manufacturing and distribution of pharmaceuticals.

Apr. 23 Robert Taschereau (1896–1970) was appointed chief justice of the Supreme Court of Canada, replacing Justice Patrick Kerwin (1889–1963). Taschereau 1st became a member of the Supreme Court when appointed Feb. 9, 1940, and served a total of 27 years until his retirement Sept. 1, 1967.

May 1 Hydro-Quebec took over 11 private Que.

power companies to extend its reach across the province.

May 3 PM Pearson visited London, England, for consultations with British PM Harold Macmillan. The PM was received by Queen Elizabeth II and appointed to the British Privy Council, thereby acquiring the title "Rt. Hon."

• Hay River and Fort Simpson, NWT, were struck by severe floods; 1,600 residents were airlifted to safety.

May 8 Air evacuation began of Canadian citizens caught in the troubled nation of Haiti under President Dr. Francois "Papa Doc" Duvalier. (Duvalier declared himself Haiti's only and permanent president the following year.) On Feb. 11, 1964, 18 members of the Canadian Jesuit mission in Haiti were expelled.

May 10–11 PM Pearson visited Hyannis Port, Massachusetts, for talks with US President Kennedy. Pearson agreed to equip Canadian forces with US-supplied nuclear weapons. He also agreed to jointly establish the former F.D. Roosevelt home on Campobello Is., NB, as an international park. On Dec. 31, nuclear warheads for *Bomarc* missiles arrived at the RCAF base near North Bay, Ont. After 1965, American nuclear weapons were stored in BC and Que. for use by Canadian *VooDoo* fighters, and in Argentia Bay, Nfld., for use against submarines. US Air Force Mark IV nuclear bombs had been stored at the US air force base in Goose Bay, Labrador, since 1950.

• India agreed to purchase 16 Caribou transport aircraft from Canada.

May 27 The Northern Alberta Institute of Technology (NAIT) opened in Edmonton. By 2003, the college was producing 45% of the province's registered apprentices.

May 29 A new permanent exhibit at the National Museum of Canada, the Hall of Canadian Eskimos, opened.

June 13 Liberal Finance Minister Walter Gordon tabled his budget, imposing an 11% sales tax on machinery equipment and building machinery, and making other tax changes to reduce the deficit, stimulate investment and reduce unemployment. His proposal to tax corporate takeovers was later withdrawn under pressure from US and Canadian business. On Oct. 18, Parliament showed spending cuts of $228 million with a federal deficit estimated at $570 million.

June 25 A voluntary Alb. govt medical care program came into effect.

July 1 The Neptune Theatre, named after Canada's 1st theatrical production (Marc Lescarbot's *Théâtre de Neptune*, 1606), opened in Halifax, in a 525-seat former vaudeville house. Leon Major was founding artistic director. The 1st production was Jean Anouilh's *Antigone*. The Neptune was the 1st Canadian theatre to adopt the repertory system, and also the 1st Canadian theatre to hold performances all year long.

July 2 Canada provided 50,000 doses of polio vaccine to Barbados.

July 12 The Queen Victoria monument in Montreal was destroyed by a dynamite explosion.

July 17 Pilot John Hegland (1937–1965) founded Bearskin Lake Air Service, named where he headquartered at Bearskin L., a small northern Ont. community located northeast of Sioux Lookout (the service was later named Bearskin Airlines). By 2003, Bearskin operated a fleet of more than 30 aircraft and offered almost 200 scheduled departures daily from 37 locations across Ont. and Man.

July 21 A British freighter and a Bermudan ore carrier collided in the St. Lawrence R. At least 18 people died.

July 22 An act establishing the federal Department of Industry received Assent.

• As expressions of Que. nationalism spread throughout the province, the Pearson administration established the Royal Commission on Bilingualism and Biculturalism. It was chaired by André Laurendeau (1912–1968) and Arnold Davidson Dunton (1912–1987). (Laurendeau, an editor with *Le Devoir*, had proposed such an inquiry on Jan. 20, 1962, but the idea was dismissed by PM

Diefenbaker.) The commission's goal was to assess the state of bilingualism and biculturalism in Canada and determine whether the promotion of French outside Que. might be acceptable to ordinary citizens. The Laurendeau-Dunton interviews began in Winnipeg Jan. 20, 1964, and a preliminary report tabled in the House on Feb. 25, 1965.

• Zafrulla Khan, president of the UN General Assembly, visited Ottawa.

July 24 *Bluenose II*, a replica of the storied original racing schooner, was launched in Lunenburg, NS, from the same yard in which the original was launched on Mar. 26, 1921.

Aug. 2 The Economic Council of Canada, a Crown corporation responsible to the PM, was established under the chairmanship of John J. Deutsch to assess medium- and long-term economic prospects; to consider ways of strengthening Canada's international finances and trade position; to study the effects of economic growth and technical change on employment and income; to explore policies to foster regional development; and to study means of increasing Canadian ownership, control and management of industries in Canada.

Aug. 7 Canada donated $1 million worth of food to Greece.

• Algonquin Park, Ont., held its 1st public wolf howl. Between this date and 2003 the annual event has drawn close to 100,000 people, half of whom have heard wolves respond to human howls.

Aug. 8 Canada, Britain, the US and Soviet Union signed the Limited Test Ban Treaty, banning nuclear weapons testing in the atmosphere, underwater and in outer space. Its goal was to end "the contamination of man's environment by radioactive substances." The treaty, which entered into force Oct. 10, 1963, did not ban underground testing.

Aug. 13 One thousand delegates from 78 countries attended an Anglican congress in Toronto.

Sept. 6 The federal govt designated 35 high-unemployment areas as tax-free regions for 3 years to help attract new industries.

Sept. 16 The Soviet Union agreed to purchase $500 million worth of Canadian wheat. On Oct. 4, a shipment of wheat to the Soviet Union was temporarily delayed by a strike of 3,800 longshoremen at 3 St. Lawrence R. ports.

Sept. 17 PM Pearson addressed the UN General Assembly, outlining proposals to strengthen UN peacekeeping forces.

Sept. 21 The 2,982-seat Grande Salle, later named the Salle Wilfrid Pelletier, the 1st of 5 concert halls comprising Place des Arts (PDA) performing arts complex in downtown Montreal, was inaugurated with a performance by the Montreal Symphony Orchestra. The last PDA hall — La Cinquième Salle — was completed in 1993.

Sept. 26 Premier John Robarts's Progressive Conservative govt was returned to power in Ont.

Oct. 7 Sixteen FLQ members pleaded guilty to terrorist activities. Gabriel Hudon and Raymond Villeneuve received 12 years for the death of Wilfred O'Neill on Apr. 20. Villeneuve spent 4 years in prison, and 17 overseas, before returning to Que. in 1984. The nominal leader of the FLQ, Georges Schoeters, received 2 five-year sentences.

Oct. 15 Canada doubled its UN Special Fund contribution to $5 million.

Oct. 16 Old age security pensions were increased to $75 per month.

Nov. 5 Seafarers' International Union leader Hal C. Banks was charged with conspiring to cause bodily harm by assaulting ship captain H.F. Walsh in 1957. Banks was sentenced by a Canadian court to 5 years on May 5, 1964, but fled to his native US. The US refused to extradite Banks to Canada. The story of Banks, who came to Canada in 1949 to rid the seaman's union of Communists, was documented in the Donald Brittain (b 1928) film *Canada's Sweetheart: The Saga of Hal C. Banks* (1985), which was awarded 2 Geminis and named Best Canadian Production.

Nov. 10 In a 2–0 victory over the Montreal Canadiens, Detroit Red Wings star Gordie Howe scored his 545th career goal, passing the record set by Maurice "Rocket" Richard. In the same game, Detroit goaltender Terry Sawchuk (1929–1970) recorded his 94th career shutout, tying George Hainsworth's (1895–1950) career record.

Nov. 18 The last segregated school in NS closed.

• A National Fitness grant of $25,000 was given to Canada's 1964 Olympic hockey team, the 1st federal grant given to a Canadian hockey team travelling abroad.

Nov. 22 US President John F. Kennedy was assassinated in Dallas, Texas. He was succeeded by Vice-President Lyndon Baines Johnson, who would, on April 3, 1965, have an infamous physical quarrel with PM Pearson.

Nov. 23 Two Canadians, R.P. Lippert and W.D. Milne, who had been arrested in Cuba in Oct., were tried for smuggling explosives and endangering the security of Cuba. Milne was acquitted but Lippert was given 30 years. Lippert, who Fidel Castro charged was a CIA agent, was released in 1973.

Nov. 25–29 A federal-provincial conference was held in Ottawa, with federal revenue concessions offered to the provinces.

Nov. 29 A Trans-Canada Air Lines (TCA) DC-8 airliner with 111 passengers and a crew of 7 crashed near Ste. Thérèse de Blainville, Que. The speed at impact was over 800 km/h. There were no survivors. It was Canada's worst air disaster.

Dec. 3 The Toronto Symphony Orchestra made its debut at Carnegie Hall under the baton of Walter Susskind.

Dec. 10 Canada's 1st permanent research laboratory north of the Arctic Circle, the Inuvik Research Centre, was completed in Inuvik, NWT. The centre, which began publishing research material in 1964, includes chemical and biological laboratories and a scientific library. It can accommodate 24 people and offers, on loan, tents, snowmobiles, toboggans, firearms and other necessities. The centre is maintained by the Aurora Research Institute.

Dec. 13 FLQ member Mario Bachand (d 1971) was sentenced to 4 years in prison for his part in a May 17 bomb explosion in Montreal that injured Sgt-Maj. Walter Leja. Bachand was mysteriously murdered in a Paris apartment in Mar. 1971. On Mar. 19, 1964, Sgt-Maj. Leja was awarded the George Medal for heroic conduct.

Dec. 27 Minister of Defence Paul Hellyer sent a copy of his white paper on the integration of the armed forces to PM Pearson. It proposed increasing civilian control, reducing waste and duplication, and making the services work together more efficiently. The paper, calling for "a single unified defence force," led to the Act to Amend the National Defence Act, which passed Parliament July 16, 1964.

Also in 1963

• Thelma Forbes (b 1910) became the 1st woman Speaker in the Man. legislature.

• Deuterium of Canada Ltd. and the Atomic Energy Council of Canada Limited (AECL) agreed to build at Glace Bay, NS, the nation's 1st full-scale heavy-water plant for CANDU reactors. Other large-scale heavy-water plants were built at Port Hawkesbury, NS, in 1971, and La Prade, at Bécancour, Que., near the Gentilly reactors in 1982.

• Massey College, the graduate students' college at the U. of Toronto, was completed and opened. The institution had been established with funds from the Massey Foundation.

• Professor Andre Robert (d 1993) of the U. of Québec at Montreal released the 1st Canadian computer-simulated weather patterns.

• Canada bought 41 single-rotor American-made Sikorsky CH–124 helicopters, known as Sea Kings. Twenty-nine of the military units remained in active service in 2004, by which time the once-acclaimed but much-outdated aircraft had been renamed "flying coffins."

• The Social Credit Party split into 2 groups: a national group under leader Robert Thompson and a Que. group — the Ralliement des Créditistes — under David-Réal Caouette (1917– 1976). Of the 30 Social Credit Party members elected in 1962, 26 were from Quebec; of the 20 elected in 1963, 13 joined the new Créditistes.

• The Nfld. govt sought to move the province into the Atlantic time zone, thereby eliminating its half-hour time separation from Atlantic Canada. The initiative was defeated by local opposition.

• Dr. Jacques Ferron (1921–1985) founded the Rhinoceros Party, a satirical federal party whose policies were developed to mock politicians and the electoral process. Over the years, Rhino candidates campaigned to repeal the law of gravity, pave the Bay of Fundy, use bubble gum as currency and put acid rain to good use by collecting it in swimming pools, which would then serve as giant batteries. The Rhino Party was dissolved in 1993.

• Volvo (Canada) Ltd. became the 1st non–North American vehicle producer to establish a Canadian assembly plant. It was located at Dartmouth, NS.

• U. of Toronto geophysicist John Tuzo Wilson (1908–1993) published a landmark paper on plate movements, volcanic hot spots and the origins of the Hawaiian Islands and other volcanic chains in the *Canadian Journal of Physics*. The theory was considered so radical (but later verified) that his paper was rejected by every major scientific journal of the day. Wilson's theory of plate tectonics and the origins of oceans and continents would further be reformed in landmark papers published in 1965 and 1967. Wilson was made a Companion of the Order of Canada in 1984.

• The Vicky Metcalf Awards were established by librarian Vicky Metcalf to "stimulate writing for children by Canadian writers." Three awards were given annually: $10,000 for the Best Body of Work; $3,000 for the Best Short Story in English; and $1,000 to the editor of the Best Short Story.

• The Ontario Council for the Arts, later the Ontario Arts Council (OAC), was established. In 1970, the OAC awarded its 1st publishing grants: 4 companies shared $27,500.

• Jean Palardy (1905–1991) published the illustrated survey *Les Meubles anciens du Canada Francais*, and its English counterpart, *The Early Furniture of French Canada*.

• Morley Callaghan published the memoir *That Summer in Paris*.

• Historian William L. Morton published a definitive survey of Canadian history, *The Kingdom of Canada*.

• Critic Northrop Frye published *The Educated Imagination*.

• Herbert Kairley Wood (1914–1967) published *Forgotten Canadians*.

• Gwendolyn MacEwen (1941–1987) published her 1st novel, *Julian the Magician,* about a medieval miracle worker who thinks he is Jesus.

• Louise Maheux-Forcier (b 1929) published her 1st novel, *Amadou,* which dealt with lesbianism. The book won the Prix de Cercle du livre de France.

• Suzanne Martel published the children's book *Quatre Montréalais en l'an 3000* (translated in 1982 as *The City Underground*).

• Farley Mowat published the best-selling novel *Never Cry Wolf*.

• Kenojuak Ashevak (b 1927) completed *Sun Owl*, a 46 x 60 cm stone-cut image. The relief print was made from Ashevak's drawing and then traced on a large flat stone, which was then cut. Fifty limited-addition prints were then produced. The West Baffin Eskimo Co-operative Ltd. owns the original drawing.

• Kenneth Lochhead (b 1926) painted *Dark Green Centre*, now in the Art Gallery of Ont., Toronto.

• Charles Gagnon (1934–2003) painted *Hommage à John Cage*, now displayed at the Department of External Affairs in Ottawa.

• Michael Snow produced the painting *Beach–hcaeb*, on canvas, now in the Alumni Collection at the U. of Western Ont., London.

• Kenneth Edison Danby (b 1940) painted *Fur and*

Bricks, with egg tempera. The work is now in a private collection.

• The Canadian govt sponsored an exhibition of painter James Fenwick Lansdowne (b 1937) at the Smithsonian Museum in Washington, D.C. The show was so successful that a 2nd exhibition of Lansdowne's work was staged at the same location in 1969.

• Ian and Sylvia Tyson recorded the single *Four Strong Winds*.

• Pierre Mercure (1927–1966), Montreal Symphony Orchestra bassoonist, composed *Psaume pour abri*, a work for choir and orchestra, which merged traditional folk melodies with modern electronic creations.

1964

Jan. 1 A new electoral act went into effect in Que., reducing the minimum voting age in provincial elections to 18 years. The age to vote in federal elections for all Canadians was lowered from 21 to 18 on June 26, 1970.

Jan. 15 PM Pearson arrived in France. He was the 1st Canadian PM to make an official visit. He discussed Que. with President Charles de Gaulle, who indicated it was in France's interest that Canada remain united and strong. On Jan. 21, the PM visited Washington D.C. for talks with US President Johnson.

Jan. 17 The Winnipeg International Airport terminal, designed by the prominent Winnipeg architectural firm Green, Blankstein, Russell (GBR), opened.

Jan. 30 A Montreal armoury was robbed of weapons and ammunition by a group calling itself the Comité révolutionnaire du Québec. On Feb. 20, an armoury in Shawinigan, Que., was raided. On July 3, 4 members of the L'Armée de libération du Québec (ALQ), an FLQ splinter group, received 8-year sentences for stealing weapons from the two armouries.

Feb. 3 PM Pearson appointed Guy Favreau (b 1917) of Montreal, minister of justice and attorney gen., as well as Liberal house leader.

Feb. 14 A new $6.5 million, 90-m oceanographic research vessel, the *Hudson*, was commissioned in Halifax as part of the Bedford Institute of Oceanography fleet at Dartmouth. The ship could accommodate 86 people and had provisions for 2 helicopters and 3 launches.

Feb. 22 Police in Montreal seized millions of dollar's worth of smuggled heroin.

Feb. 24 Editor-publisher Walt Grealis founded Canada's music trade magazine in Toronto. In Dec., the magazine, *RPM Weekly*, asked readers to select their favourite Canadian artists, and ran the results in the Dec. 28 issue. In 1970, this annual poll had become the RPM Gold Leaf Awards, presented for the 1st time in front of a live audience at Toronto's St. Lawrence Hall. In 1971, the awards were renamed the Junos.

Feb. 28 The $27.5 million Toronto International Airport, Terminal 1, was opened by PM Pearson. It replaced the original Malton Airport, which was 1st established in 1938. Terminal 2 opened in 1972, and the airport was renamed Lester B. Pearson International Airport on Jan. 1, 1984. Terminal 3 was completed in 1991.

Mar. 13 The federal govt approved a Canadian contribution to the UN international peacekeeping force in Cyprus. Canadians began serving in Cyprus on Mar. 27. The mission ended June 15, 1993, 29 years later.

Mar. 15 Foreign film stars Richard Burton and Elizabeth Taylor were married in Montreal. It was their 1st marriage — together.

Mar. 20 BC became the 1st province to prohibit workplace discrimination based on age, with amendment to its Fair Employment Practices Act. The amendment covered all employees between ages 45 and 65.

Mar. 31 Historian Donald Creighton and poet Alain Grandbois (1900–1975) were the 1st recipients of the Canada Council's Molson Prize. They received $15,000 each. The annual award was established with a $1 million endowment given to the council by the Molson Family Foundation. Awards were presented for outstanding achievement in the arts, humanities, and social sciences.

Apr. 6–25 Actors and crew from Canada's Stratford Festival performed in Chichester, England, to celebrate the 400th anniversary of William Shakespeare's birth.

Apr. 17 A major copper–zinc–silver discovery near Timmins, Ont. was confirmed by Texas Gulf Sulphur Co., sparking one of the largest stock-gambling sprees in Canadian history.

Apr. 18 Astronomer Helen Hogg (1905–1993) became the 1st woman president of the Royal Canadian Institute for the Advancement of Science. The Institute, founded in Toronto in 1849, was incorporated Nov. 4, 1851. Its goal was to encourage and further the "Physical Sciences, the Arts and Manufactures…Surveying, Engineering and Architecture." The Royal Institute is the oldest scientific society in the country.

Apr. 20–24 The PM of Trinidad and Tobago, Eric Williams, visited Ottawa.

Apr. 22 Liberals under W. Ross Thatcher (1917–1971) won the Sask. provincial election, displacing the CCF–NDP, which had held power for 20 years.

Apr. 28 Vasily Vasilievich Tarasov, Ottawa correspondent for the Soviet newspaper *Izvestia*, was expelled from Canada as a spy.

Apr. 29 The Ont. govt established a province wide minimum wage of $1 an hour, effective incrementally from June 29. Agriculture workers were not covered by the minimum.

Also in Apr.

• Under the Social Insurance Number (SIN) program, Social Insurance Number cards were 1st issued by the federal govt to assist record-keeping and administration. In 1985, the govt began charging $10 for replacement SIN cards.

• US Secretary of State Dean Rusk visited Ottawa. He told PM Pearson that a Canadian should be assigned in Vietnam to mediate between Hanoi and Washington. Pearson agreed, and Blair Seaborn (b 1924), senior Canadian diplomat on the International Control Commission (ICC), was given the task.

• Federal Minister of Justice, Attorney Gen. and Liberal House Leader Guy Favreau (1917–1967) was appointed Que. Liberal party leader.

May 2 Northern Dancer, a Canadian-bred colt owned by Edward Plunkett (E.P.) Taylor, won the 1 1/4-mile Kentucky Derby in a record 2 minutes flat. The horse won the 2nd leg of the US Triple Crown 2 weeks later — the Preakness at Pimlico, Maryland — but came in 3rd at the Belmont in New York. The famed thoroughbred entered his last race Sept. 16 that year.

May 11 The CNCP Telecommunications microwave network extending from Montreal to Vancouver began operations.

May 13 The Que. National Assembly passed Education Bill 60, which established the Department of Education.

May 14 The Canadian Post Office released a maple-leaf stamp, which 1st suggested to PM Pearson that the symbol would make a fitting emblem for a Canadian flag. On Sept. 10, the House of Commons agreed to appoint a special 15-member committee to study the issue of establishing a new Canadian flag.

• The Department of University Affairs was established in Ont., with Education Minister William Grenville Davis (b 1929) assuming the portfolio.

May 26 UN Secretary-Gen. U Thant addressed a joint sitting of the House of Commons and Senate.

May 31 Canadian Press's 1st resident correspondent in the Soviet Union arrived in Moscow.

Also in May
• Radio-Canada broadcast *Les grands phoques de la banquise* (Seals of the Floes), a graphic documentary on the Îles-de-la-Madeleine seal hunt. The film generated international outrage due to the vivid scenes of slaughter.

June 1–3 President of Ireland Eamon de Valera visited Ottawa.

June 7 *Le Train*, a play by Michel Tremblay (b 1942), which won 1st prize in the Concours des jeunes auteurs sponsored by Radio-Canada, was broadcast on that station.

June 8 Chancellor Ludwig Erhard of West Germany arrived in Ottawa for talks with PM Pearson.

June 11 The Pearson cabinet gave its approval for negotiations with the US that would guarantee Canada a specified share of the auto market and see both countries agree to cut tariffs on cars and auto parts. The final text of the Auto Pact was signed Jan. 16, 1965.

• Canada and the Hungarian People's Republic signed a 3-year trade agreement, the 1st between the 2 countries in the postwar period.

Also in June
• The 1st volume of the report of the Royal Commission on Health Services, under the chairmanship of Chief Justice of Sask. Emmett Hall, was tabled in Parliament. The report dealt with all aspects of medical and dental care and pharmaceutical needs, and called for a nationwide medicare program based on the principle of universality. The 2nd report, tabled Feb. 18, 1965, outlined the administrative framework for the proposed prepaid medical care plan. Commission recommendations influenced creation of the Medical Care Act, passed in the House Dec. 8, 1966.

July 9 Two hundred and twenty-five members of the Toronto Mailers Union went on strike against 3 Toronto daily newspapers: the *Toronto Star*, *Telegram* and *Globe and Mail*. The strike was not settled until May 7, 1965.

July 16 The Act to Amend the National Defence Act was passed by Parliament. It placed the entire Canadian military service under the single command of the chief of the defence staff. The positions of chairman of the chiefs of staff, chief of the naval staff, chief of the gen. staff, and chief of the air staff were eliminated. The act, the 1st major step toward unification of the Canadian Armed Forces, went into effect Aug. 1. On Nov. 3, the Defence Department announced that 60 units of the militia would also be disbanded. The 2nd major step toward military unification was unveiled June 7, 1965.

• The Territorial Sea and Fisheries Zone Act, extending Canada's coastal fishing limits to 19.3 km, received Assent.

July 24 The 1st reporter from the New China News Agency arrived in Canada.

July 27–29 Malaysia's PM Tunku Abdul Rahman visited Canada. Canadian aid to Malaysia under the Colombo Plan was increased by $4.5 million.

July 28 The Senate Banking Committee approved charters to the Bank of Western Canada and the Laurentide Bank.

• A federal act providing interest-free loans to university students received Assent.

July 30 A fire at the Beacon Arms Hotel in Ottawa killed 3 and injured 17.

Aug. 5 Jean Vanier (b 1928) founded L'Arche (The Ark) in France, an international network of family-based communities for the mentally and physically challenged. In 2004, there were 120 L'Arche communities in 30 countries worldwide.

Aug. 20 The Roosevelt Campobello International Park on Campobello Is., NB, was opened by Maryon Pearson and Lady Bird Johnson. The 11.33-km² park is jointly administered and funded by the US and Canada. It is part symbol and celebration of Canada-US relations, and preservation of Roosevelt Cottage, the late President Franklin D. Roosevelt's summer home.

Aug. 21 Eight people were killed when a truck and a passenger train collided at Leonard, Ont.

Sept. 6 The Riot Act was read at Grand Bend, Ont., as mobs of young people created a disturbance. More than 120 people were charged by police.

Sept. 9 Que. borrowed $100 million from BC, the 1st time a province borrowed money from another. The loan was repaid Oct. 15, 1968.

Sept. 11 The Canadian Imperial Bank of Commerce was ordered by the Ont. Supreme Court to pay $960,000 and $415,000 in interest to Brilund Mines Ltd., which had been defrauded by 3 New York men

who had completed a fraudulent Brilund share transaction through the bank.

Sept. 16 Northern Dancer of E.P. Taylor Farms, Oshawa, Ont., ran his last race, winning the 1 1/4-mile Queen's Plate in a time of 2:02. The horse won 14 of 18 starts over his career. At stud, Northern Dancer sired 70 stakes winners.

Sept. 21 Blanche Margaret Meagher (1911–1999), Canadian ambassador to Austria, was elected chairman of the board of govs. of the International Atomic Energy Agency.

Oct. 4 The controversial CBC television public affairs program *This Hour Has Seven Days*, with hosts Laurier LaPierre and Patrick Watson, was 1st broadcast. The show was discontinued after May 8, 1966.

Oct. 6 Mount St. Laurent at Rogers Pass in the BC Rockies was named in honour of the former PM. Other Rogers Pass peaks named after the former PM's are Mount Macdonald, Mount Mackenzie, and Mount Tupper.

Oct. 7 The Eastern Ont. Institute of Technology in Ottawa was opened.

Oct. 10–11 Queen Elizabeth II visited Que. to commemorate the Quebec Conference of 1864. She found the city's streets largely deserted but for a few hundred jeering student protestors, who were attacked by police and beaten with nightsticks. On Oct. 20, a report released by Acting Attorney Gen. Claude Wagner (1925–1979) dismissed as exaggerated related charges of police brutality.

Oct. 12 The federal govt announced plans to build the Queen Elizabeth II Observatory on Mount Kobau, near Osoyoos, BC. The project was cancelled Aug. 29, 1968, while the observatory was under construction. The govt cited financial problems. The ideal stargazing location is now home to the annual, week-long Mount Kobau Star Party, where astronomers of every description gather to swap stories and peer into the universe from portable telescopes.

Oct. 14 A federal-provincial constitutional conference began at Ottawa, and an amending formula to bring the Constitution under exclusive Canadian control was accepted. Called the Fulton-Favreau Formula (after former and current Justice Ministers Davie Fulton and Guy Favreau), it spelled out that Canada could amend its own Constitution only with the unanimous consent of all provinces, thereby giving each province a veto over any constitutional amendment. Que. later opposed the formula because Quebecers could not effectively control their own destiny — any constitutional change affecting Que. would have to be accepted by 9 other provinces. The Fulton-Favreau Formula was dropped in Jan. 1965. Power to amend federal elements of the Canadian Constitution (BNA Act) remained in the hands of British politicians until PM Trudeau repatriated the Constitution in 1982.

Oct. 16 The Mendel Art Gallery opened on the banks of the South Saskatchewan R., Saskatoon, with a wide-ranging focus on contemporary and traditional works of art. The municipal institute was named in honour of Frederick Mendel (1888–1976), a patron of the arts who fled Nazi Germany in 1939 with his collection of 20th-century German Expressionist paintings, many of which were donated to the gallery. In 1974, Frederick Mendel was named a member of the Order of Canada for his contributions to the cultural life of Saskatoon.

Oct. 17 Trent U., established at Peterborough, Ont., opened its doors. It occupied 2 sites in downtown Peterborough — Peter Robinson College for men and Catharine Parr Traill College for women. It was Canada's 14th university. Trent would offer the nation's 1st Native Studies program in Sept. 1969.

Oct. 19 Brock U., named after Maj-Gen. Issac Brock, opened its doors in St. Catharines, Ont.

Oct. 29-30 The Federal-Provincial Ministerial Conference on Native Affairs was held in Ottawa. Delegates agreed to the creation of regional Indian advisory councils and a national Indian advisory board, all incorporating Native representation. The National Indian Advisory Board 1st convened in Ottawa on Jan. 10, 1966.

Also in Oct.
• The most detailed mapping of Canada ever made, on a scale of 4 miles to the inch, was completed after 19 years of work by the Canadian Department of Mines and Technical Surveys and the Army Survey Establishment.

Nov. 2–6 Representatives of 23 nations attended a conference at Ottawa to review UN peacekeeping operations.

Nov. 13 The federal govt ratified the International Labour Organization Convention to stop discrimination in employment on the basis of colour, race, sex, religion, political views, national extraction or place of birth.

Nov. 18 The 1st shipment of lead-zinc ore left Pine Point, NWT, for smelters in Trail and Kimberley, BC, over the recently completed Great Slave Lake Railway.

Nov. 20 One of the highest unnamed mountains in Canada, located on the Alaska-Yukon border, was named Mount Kennedy in memory of the late US president.

• The Redistribution Bill received Assent. It established commissions to assess each decennial census by which provincial electoral boundaries were adjusted according to the number of Parliament seats each province was allowed — by no more or less than 25% of the provincial quota.

• The report of the Que. Royal Commission on Education recommended a major transformation of the school system–including govt control over the Catholic church–run classical college system.

Dec. 14 After weeks of debate, closure was imposed in the House of Commons to bring debate over the new Canadian flag to an end, and on Dec. 15, Canada's new maple leaf flag was adopted 163–78 with 1 Liberal, 1 NDP and 3 Social Credit Party members joining Diefenbaker's Conservatives in opposition. The new national flag replaced the Red Ensign. The maple leaf was 1st flown on Parliament Hill on Feb. 15, 1965. On Dec. 17, the House of Commons voted to continue flying the Union Jack, the national flag of the United Kingdom, as a symbol of Canada's membership in the Commonwealth.

Dec. 19 *Annapolis,* the 20th ship in the RCN's destroyer escort program, was commissioned in Halifax.

Dec. 21 Defence Minister Paul Hellyer unveiled a $1.5 billion military-equipment procurement plan, which included 200 ground-support aircraft, 4 helicopter-equipped destroyers and 155-mm howitzers.

Also in Dec.

• Canada agreed to make up to $10 million available to Latin America through the Inter-American Development Bank.

• Robert Samuel McLaughlin (1871–1972), chairman of General Motors of Canada, donated $1 million to the Royal Ontario Museum (ROM) for construction of a planetarium. Completed beside the ROM in 1968, the McLaughlin Planetarium hosted innumerable educational demonstrations and also popular rock-music light shows. It was shut down in 1995.

Also in 1964

• At the Summer Olympics in Tokyo, Canada won 4 medals, including 1 gold by George Hungerford (b 1944) and Roger Jackson (b 1942) in coxless pairs rowing. At the Winter Olympics at Innsbruck, Austria, Canada won 3 medals, including its only gold by Vic Emery, a former pilot in the military, who steered Canada to victory in the 4-man bobsled.

• Designer Louis Poirier of the Canadelle bra company in Montreal invented the 1st push-up and plunge Wonderbra. It became the best-selling specialty bra in the world.

• Arthur Wightmann, NB member of the Canadian Permanent Committee on Geographical names, designated a 210-m hill North Pole Mountain in honour of Santa Claus's mythical home. Pleased with the result, Wightmann had 8 nearby peaks named after Santa's reindeer — Dasher, Dancer, Prancer, Vixen, Comet, Cupid, Donder and Blitzen. The small range in central NB is known as the Christmas Mountains.

• The Second Vatican Ecumenical Council (Vatican II) agreed to allow elements of the Roman Catholic Mass to be celebrated in the vernacular. By 1969, Latin had all but disappeared from Mass in Canada.

• Ont. amended the Separate Schools Act to eliminate legislation, that had allowed race-based school segregation.

• The Quebec Civil Code was amended to extend full legal and property rights to married women. The province also established fair employment legislation to prohibit hiring and workplace discrimination based on colour, creed, ethnicity, national origin and race.

• NB passed legislation giving women the right to take maternity leave.

• The $5.6 million Confederation Centre of the Arts was completed in Charlottetown PEI, as a national memorial to the Fathers of Confederation. The centre, which boasts 3 theatres — the 1,102-seat Mainstage, the 180-seat Studio, and 190-seat MacKenzie — and also an art gallery, was partly funded by every provincial govt in the country, a precedent for such an undertaking.

• Popular Toronto Maple Leafs defenceman Tim Horton (1930–1974), with Ron Joyce (b 1930), a former Hamilton policeman, founded Tim Hortons — a franchised series of coffee and doughnut shops. The 1st outlet opened in the Hamilton area. The 1,000th Tim Hortons would also be opened in the same area — in 1995.

• The gravestone marking the burial place of the 5 Donnellys who were violently murdered by vigilantes in 1880 was removed from the Catholic cemetery in Lucan, Ont. It carried the word "murdered" after each name, and attracted so many tourists that the cemetery was experiencing damage.

• Pianist Glenn Gould gave up his stellar concert career to concentrate on recording.

• The Alb. govt licenced Sun Oil Co. to begin work on the $300 million Great Canadian Oil Sands plant at Fort McMurray, Alb.

• Man. native William Kurelek (1927–1977) completed *In The Autumn of Life,* oil on masonite, portraying a family reunion with an atomic explosion occurring far off at the horizon. The painting is in the Art Gallery of Ont., Toronto.

• St. Lambert, Que., native Graham Coughtry (1931–1999) painted *Two Figure Series XIX,* oil on canvas, portraying a male and female figure fused together. It is now in a private collection.

• Sask. artist Ernest Lindner (1897–1988) painted *Decay and Growth,* watercolour studies of tree stumps, now in the Norman Mackenzie Art Gallery, U. of Sask., Regina.

• Roy Kenzie Kiyooka (1926–1994) painted *Barometer No. 2,* on canvas, now in the Art Gallery of Ont., Toronto.

• Claude Tousignant (b 1932) painted *Ciel de boeuf,* now in the National Gallery of Canada, Ottawa.

• Nfld. artist John Christopher Pratt (b 1935) painted *Woman at a Dresser,* oil on masonite, now in the CIL Art Collection, Toronto.

• Iqaluit Manno (1923–1973) carved the soapstone *Bear on Ice.* The 9 x 17 x 80.5-cm sculpture portrays the sacred animal, looking at its own reflection in the ice. It is now in a private collection.

• Margaret Laurence published one of her most acclaimed novels, *The Stone Angel,* a dark, disturbing story of Hagar Shipley, who looks back over her 91 years of proud prairie life as she moves ever closer to its end.

• Jacques Renaud (b 1943) published his most popular work, the novella *Le Cassé.*

• Former U. of BC professor Jane Vance Rule (b 1931) published the novel *Desert of the Heart,* which was adapted to film as *Desert Hearts* (1986).

• Roch Carrier (b 1937) published the short-story collection *Jolis devils,* for which he received Les Concours littéraires du Québec award.

• Leonard Cohen published the book of poetry *Flowers for Hitler.*

• Claude Jasmin (b 1930) published the novel *Ethel et le terroriste,* which won the Prix France-Québec.

• Douglas Le Pan (1914–1998) published the war novel *The Deserter,* for which he received the Gov-Gen.'s Award.

• Conservationist Roderick Haig-Brown published the classic *A Primer of Fly Fishing.*

• Marshall McLuhan published *Understanding the Media: The Extension of Man.*

• Poet Suzanne Paradis (b 1936) published *Pour les enfants des morts: Poèmes,* for which she received the Prix France-Québec.

• Poet Raymond Souster published *The Colour of the Times,* for which he received the Gov-Gen.'s Award.

• The song *Mon Pays* was written by Gilles Vigneault (b 1928) for the NFB film *Il a neigé sue a Manicougan.* The song includes the refrain *"Mon pays, ce n'est pas un pays, c'est l'hiver"* (My country isn't a country, it's winter).

• Ottawa-born Lorne Greene (1915–1987) (patriarch Pa Cartwright of television's *Bonanza* series) hit No. 1 on *Billboard* magazine's Top 100 chart with "Ringo," a ballad many considered a novelty song.

• Twenty-one-year-old Roberta Joan Anderson (b 1943), while visiting from Lethbridge, Alb., sang at The Penny Farthing in Toronto's Yorkville district. There she met folksinger Chuck Mitchell, married him several months later in Detroit and became Joni Mitchell.

1965

Jan. 1 The name Trans-Canada Airlines was changed to Air Canada by Act of Parliament.

Jan. 4 The Montreal newspaper *La Presse* resumed publication after a 7-month strike.

Jan. 6 Letters from former US President Kennedy's widow, Jacqueline, and mother, Rose Kennedy, were released to the media. They thanked Canada for naming a mountain in former President Kennedy's honour and for a $100,000 contribution to the John F. Kennedy Memorial Library to be built in Boston, Massachusetts.

Jan. 9 A massive landslide near Hope, BC, covered a 3-km stretch of the Hope-Princeton highway with 47 million m^2 of rubble from Johnson Peak.

Some of the debris was 85 m thick. Four people were killed.

Jan. 13 An avalanche at the northern pulp-and-paper town of Ocean Falls, BC, killed 7.

Jan. 16 The final text of the Canada–United States Automotive Products Agreement, or Auto Pact, was signed in Texas by PM Pearson, External Affairs Minister Paul Martin (1903–1992), US President Johnson and Secretary of State Dean Rusk. The pact eliminated tariffs on automobiles and vehicle parts between the 2 countries and included 2 significant protections for Canada: that all cars built in Canada contain 60% Canadian parts and be the product of 60% Canadian labour; and Canadian imports of US cars must not exceed the number manufactured in Canada. Seventy thousand six hundred people were employed in the Canadian auto industry in 1965; 125,000 in 1978. On May 13, 2000, a World Trade Organization (WTO) appeal panel ruled the Auto Pact a violation of international treaty practices.

• Winnipeg-based Chad Allan & the Expressions released the single "Shaking All Over," which bumped the Beatles' "Eight Days A Week" off the *RPM* singles chart. Chad Allan was replaced by Burton Cummings in 1966 and the Guess Who was born. The band defined prairie rock with such classic albums as *Canned Wheat* (1968), *Share the Land* (1970) and *The Guess Who Live at The Paramount* (1972). Guess Who singles included "These Eyes" (1969), "American Woman" (1970), "Running Back to Saskatoon" (1972) and "Orly" (1973).

Jan. 18 Canada and Nepal established diplomatic relations. On Jan. 21, Canada and the Malagasy Republic established diplomatic relations.

Jan. 20 The Electoral Boundaries Commission was established to report to the House of Commons on provincial representation boundaries and adjustments.

Jan. 25 Canada pledged $4 million in military assistance to Malaysia, which included 4 transport aircraft, motorcycles and training facilities.

Feb. 1 Hamilton R. in Labrador was renamed Churchill R., in honour of late British statesman Winston Churchill, who died Jan. 24.

• Canada agreed to give Trinidad and Tobago $3 million in grants and loans over 50 years.

Feb. 1–2 Indian Minister of Information and Broadcasting, Indira Gandhi, visited Canada.

Feb. 5 The federal govt established a Fine Art Policy for new public works: an amount equalling 1–3% of the construction costs of any new federal building would be used to purchase or contract out for Canadian art to embellish the same.

Feb. 10 Harvey Reginald MacMillan of Vancouver donated $8.2 million to U. of BC for postgraduate education.

Feb. 13 A strike by Que. Liquor Board employees that had kept the province's 204 liquor stores closed since Dec. 4, 1964, ended with an agreement giving workers $18 more a week over 3 years.

• Canadian research scientists, under Dr. Stanley Skoryna of McGill U., left Easter Is. in the South Pacific after 2-months' research on diseases in an isolated environment.

Feb. 15 Canada's new red and white maple leaf flag was raised for the 1st time on Parliament Hill. Maurice Bourget, Speaker of the Senate, addressed the audience which included the PM, the cabinet and the parliamentarians: "The flag is the symbol of the nation's unity, for it, beyond any doubt, represents all the citizens of Canada without distinction of race, language, belief or opinion."

Feb. 18 An avalanche buried a Granduc Mines coppermine camp 48 km north of Stewart, BC, killing 18.

Feb. 23 Jacques Hébert was sentenced to 30 days in jail and fined $3,000 after being convicted of contempt of court for statements in his 1963 essay *J'accuse les assassins de Coffin,* an indictment of the Que. jurisdictional system that sentenced convicted murderer, Gaspé prospector Wilbert Coffin to death in 1956. Hébert's conviction was reversed by the Que. Court of Appeals on Jan. 31, 1966. Hébert's essay led to a 1964 Que. Royal Commission into the matter, which concluded that Coffin was, in fact, guilty.

Feb. 24 The new flag of NB was proclaimed. The striking yellow lion, and ship, was based on the provincial shield of arms, which was approved by Queen Victoria in 1863.

Feb. 25 The preliminary report of the Royal Commission on Bilingualism and Biculturalism was tabled in the House of Commons. It stated that there was a "deep gulf of unawareness dividing French and English Canada, and this ignorance was pushing Canada" into the "greatest crisis" in its history. A 2nd report, with proposals, was tabled Dec. 9, 1968.

Feb. 27 Que. and France signed an entente on educational and cultural exchanges.

Mar. 1 A natural-gas explosion in Ville LaSalle, a Montreal suburb, destroyed an apartment building, killed 26 and injured 32.

Mar. 2 Que. native Lucien Rivard (b 1915), a key figure in the Dorion Inquiry (its report released June 29), escaped with a companion from Bordeaux Prison, Montreal, where he had been held pending US narcotics-trafficking charges. He received permission to water the prison rink, but tossed the hose over the wall and scampered off. A continent-wide manhunt was initiated. Rivard was captured near Montreal 4 months later, on July 16. On July 28, 1965, Rivard was extradited to the US to face narcotics charges. He was convicted and sentenced to 20 years. He served 9 and was then deported to Canada.

Mar. 5 Bylot Is. was declared a migratory-bird sanctuary, the 15th such sanctuary established in the Arctic.

Mar. 8 The Nfld. govt announced free tuition for all of Nfld. 1st-year students enrolled at Memorial U., St. John's, establishing a Canadian precedent.

Also in Mar.
• The RCMP seized $25 million worth of pure heroin in Montreal.

• The U. of Waterloo, founded in 1959, inaugurated a bilingual course in honours French and political science for students preparing to enter the federal civil service.

Apr. 1 Prosthetic services of the Department of Veterans' Affairs were made available to all Canadians through the Department of National Health and Welfare.

• The National Employment Service was transferred from the Unemployment Insurance Commission to the Department of Labour.

Apr. 2 PM Pearson delivered a convocation address at Temple U., in Philadelphia, where he suggested that if the US stopped its air strikes against Vietnam, Hanoi might "inject some flexibility into their policy." Pearson was awarded the Temple U. Peace Award for making "a singular contribution to the cause of peace and understanding among nations and men."

Apr. 3 PM Pearson arrived at Camp David where he was met by President Johnson who was furious over Pearson's Apr. 2 Temple U. speech. At one point, the president shouted and grabbed the PM by the shirtfront.

• Toronto lawyer Joseph Sedgwick tabled a report in the House of Commons alleging that the Department of Citizenship and Immigration unlawfully jailed and denied counsel to aliens facing deportation.

Apr. 6 The federal govt initiated a program to equip and train an air force in the newly established Tanzania, formed in 1964 when Tanganyika merged with the islands of Zanzibar and Pemba.

• Leonard S. Marchand (b 1932) was appointed special assistant to the minister of citizenship and immigration. Marchand became the 1st Native person appointed to the staff of a federal cabinet minister.

Apr. 10 The Dutch ship *Hermes* collided with the German *Transatlantic* in the St. Lawrence near Trois-Rivières. The *Transatlantic* sank, killing 3 people. On Sept. 11, 1968, the federal govt was found liable by the Exchequer Court of Canada for the collision.

The ruling placed, for the 1st time, "an unqualified duty" on the Crown to ensure that navigational aids on Canadian waterways were fulfilling their intended purposes.

Apr. 13 The federal govt pledged $3.3 million for a nationwide festival of the performing arts to celebrate Canada's centennial year.

Apr. 17 A CPR passenger train derailed near Terrace Bay, Ont., killing 1 and injuring 47.

Apr. 21 Toronto journalist Gregory Clark (1892–1977) became the 1st honorary member of the newly established Canadian News Hall of Fame. (A week later, on the 29th, he was awarded the Stephen Leacock Medal for Humour.) The Hall of Fame was established by the Toronto Press Club (founded in 1882) to honour writers who made significant contributions to Canadian journalism. Over 100 people have been singled out for recognition, including Ray Guy, Lise Bissonette, Allan Fotheringham, Joe Schlesinger (b 1928), John W. Dafoe, Grattan O'Leary, Ross Munro (1913–1990), Treffle Berthiaume, Borden Spears, Doris Anderson (b 1921), and Bruce Hutchinson.

Apr. 30 The Vanier Institute of the Family received a charter. Established under the patronage of Gov-Gen. Georges Vanier and Madame Pauline Vanier, the institute studies the social, economic and statistical characteristics of the Canadian family to provide family support, information and policy advice. Montreal neurologist Wilder Penfield was elected its president. On July 16, 1966, the federal govt approved a $2 million grant for endowment of the institute.

May 7 Two Soviet diplomats were expelled from Canada after a plot to establish an espionage network was discovered.

May 12 The terms of an 1876 treaty with Sask. Native Peoples were upheld in a Battleford, Sask., court, making the federal govt responsible for the provision of free medical care.

May 15 The United Nations presented a special medal to the Canadian film industry commemorating International Co-operation Year and drawing attention to the "common interest and purpose of humanity in achieving peace and human dignity." Dr. J. Roby Kidd, founding director of the Canadian Film Awards, presented the medal to cinematographer Roy Tash at the 17th annual Canadian Film Awards in Toronto. Tash accepted the award on behalf of the film industry.

May 19 Toronto's new city hall, designed by Finnish architect Viljo Revell, opened. The 48,000-m² building cost $31 million to construct and could provide office space for 2,500 people. It also featured an outdoor skating rink. Many were offended that the building was not designed by a Canadian.

• The Shah of Iran, Muhammad Reza Shah Pahlevi, and Empress Farah, arrived in Ottawa for an 8-day state visit.

May 20 The highly manoeuvrable De Havilland Twin Otter (DHC-6) turboprop was 1st test-flown in Toronto. It would be shipped to customers the following year and in various versions for 22 years after that.

May 21 Ont.'s flag, displaying the United Kingdom's Union Jack and the Ont. coat of arms, was proclaimed. It resembled the displaced Red Ensign.

• George Drew was installed as chancellor of the U. of Guelph, Ont., at its 1st convocation.

May 24 A Que. nationalist demonstration was held in Montreal to coincide with the Victoria Day holiday; 25 were arrested.

June 1 The Anglican and United Churches of Canada published *Principles of Union*.

• The CCGS *John Cabot*, the world's 1st icebreaker-cable-repair ship, was commissioned in Montreal for the Canadian Coast Guard. The 91.44-m-long ship was built by Vickers of Montreal. It became part of the Canship Limited line and laid cable for Teleglobe Canada between 1994 and 1996.

• Federal legislation was approved setting the retirement age of senators at 75, ending lifetime appointments.

June 2–Aug. 16 Grain handlers in the Port of Vancouver were on strike.

June 7 The 2nd step toward the unification of the Canadian military was made public by Defence Minister Paul Hellyer. Six major commands would replace the existing 11. The new commands were: Mobile Command; Maritime Command; Air Defence Command; Air Transport Command; Training Command; and Material Command. Full unification of air force, army and navy was complete when the Canadian Forces Reorganization Bill was proclaimed Feb. 1, 1968.

June 14 Dr. Ernest Frederick Roots (b 1923) of Ottawa was awarded the Patron's (H.M. Queen Elizabeth) medal of the Royal Geographic Society for his work in polar exploration and research.

June 16 Dr. Wilder Penfield, founder of the Montreal Neurological Institute, received the Canadian Medical Association's highest honour, the Frederick Newton Gisborne Starr Award. On May 24, 1967, Dr. Penfield was awarded the 1st Royal Bank Centennial Medal.

June 16–Aug. 10 Grain handlers in the Port of Montreal were on strike.

June 18 Construction began on Katimavik (Inuit for "meeting place"), a huge inverted pyramid, which became the focal point of the Canadian Pavilion at the 1967 World Exhibition (Expo '67) held in Montreal.

June 21 Canada pledged $4 million to the UN to ease its financial difficulties.

June 29 The Dorion Report, prepared by Que. Chief Justice Frédéric Dorion (b 1909), was released. It resulted in the resignation of Guy Favreau (1917–1967) as justice minister. The report revealed that federal govt officials had attempted — through bribery — to free suspected drug smuggler Lucien Rivard from Montreal's Bordeaux Prison (he escaped Mar. 2). On July 7, PM Pearson appointed Favreau president of the Privy Council. On July 14, former Executive Assistant to the Minister of Citizenship and Immigration Raymond Denis was charged with attempted bribery and obstruction of justice in the affair.

June 30 In a dispute between the Canadian Actors' Equity Association (an affiliate of Actor's Equity, New York), and the Montreal-based Union des Artistes (CLC), Justice François Chevalier of Hull, Que., divided jurisdictional representation in Canada on the basis of language.

July 1–2 Fifty-five people were arrested during separatist demonstrations in Montreal and Sherbrooke, Que.

July 6–8 A strike by the Gasoline Retailers Fraternity of Que. against their oil-company suppliers kept most of Montreal's service stations closed.

July 8 The federal govt agreed to give Que. responsibility over all municipal services in the Inuit community of Great Whale River, beginning a new jurisdictional pattern in Que.'s Arctic.

• Canadian Pacific airliner Flight 21 crashed into Gustafsen L., BC, after a bomb exploded on board, killing 52 people. Officials speculated that a passenger ignited a gunpowder mixture in a suicide–life insurance scheme.

July 16 The federal govt announced plans to purchase the multi–purpose Canadair CF–5 *Freedom Fighters* for the RCAF for $215 million. Successors to the *Starfighters*, the 1st of 135 CF–5s was acquired by the air force in 1968. The twin-engine, supersonic fighters carried 500-pound (227-kg) bombs and/or pods of 70-mm aerial rockets. The planes were taken out of service Mar. 31, 1995, and replaced with CF–18 *Hornets*.

July 20 At a federal-provincial conference of premiers, PM Pearson announced that the federal govt would contribute funds to any provincial medicare scheme that was universal and portable, so long as it covered all general and specialist services without using private firms or groups. The proposal preceded the federal-provincial Medical Care Act passed in the House Dec. 8, 1966. Economic growth and offshore mineral rights were also discussed. Representatives from Yukon and NWT attended the conference of premiers for the 1st time.

July 22 The Ontario Court of Appeal, which had previously denied Canadian citizenship to Ernest and Cornelia Bergsma of the Netherlands because they were atheists, reversed its decision.

• About 10,000 postal workers in Ont., Que. and BC went on strike for higher wages. An agreement was reached on Aug. 3, with Montreal workers returning to work last, on Aug. 7.

July 27 *Anne of Green Gables — The Musical* premiered at the Charlottetown Festival, on stage at the Confederation Centre for the Arts. It was written by Don Harron (b 1924) and Norman Campbell (b 1924), with lyrics by Elaine Campbell and Mavor Moore.

July 28 Que. Liberal Thérèse Casgrain was elected to the 100-member presidium of the World Peace Congress.

July 30 Ont. Supreme Court Justice Samuel H.S. Hughes was appointed commissioner to investigate the collapse of Atlantic Acceptance Corporation Ltd., which went into receivership in June with debts estimated at $115 million.

Aug. 5 The city of Laval was created by Que. provincial legislation.

• The Canadian Wheat Board announced the sale of 27 million bushels of wheat to the Soviet Union. Another sale of 4.45 million tonnes was announced Aug. 11.

Aug. 13 Mr. Justice Kelly was appointed as a 1-man committee to investigate questionable activities at the Toronto Stock Exchange (TSE) involving Windfall Oils and Mines Ltd. On Oct. 12, John Hunter Campbell, former director of the Ontario Securities Commission, was charged with breach of trust, a result of Justice Kelly's Windfall report. Campbell was later acquitted Mar. 7, 1966.

Aug. 16 A 6-member Soviet delegation, specialists in northern development and construction, began an 18-day tour of Canada.

Aug. 17 Rob Restall, his son and 2 co-workers were accidentally killed at Oak Is., NS, while working in the shaft of the mysterious "Money Pit," 1st discovered in 1795, and rumoured to contain a wealth of pirate booty .

• Toronto Maple Leafs owner Harold Ballard (1903–1990) ordered Maple Leaf Gardens workers to turn up all furnaces and shut off all drinking fountains in a successful effort to stimulate soft-drink sales at a sold-out Beatles concert.

Aug. 21 The $2 million Swift Rapids Lock on the Severn R., in Ont., was opened. The 14.2-m lock is the deepest in the Trent-Severn Waterway. It replaced a marine-railway system, which had been in place since 1920.

Aug. 23–28 The U. of Alb. and the Canadian Institute of International Affairs sponsored a conference on world development at Banff, Alb. The main area of discussion was the role of Canada as a middle power.

Sept. 3 The federal govt unveiled plans to spend $1 million in 1965 and 1966 on cultural exchanges with French-speaking countries. On Nov. 17, the 1st general cultural agreement was signed between Canada and France.

Sept. 7 PM Pearson dissolved Parliament and called an election for Nov. 8.

Sept. 8–18 The 54th Conference of the Inter-Parliamentary Union was held in Ottawa with 800 delegates from 61 countries in attendance.

Sept. 16–Oct. 2 The Commonwealth Arts Festival was held in Britain where 4 Canadian artistic groups performed: the Toronto Symphony Orchestra, the Royal Winnipeg Ballet, le Théâtre Nouveau Monde and Les Feux Follets.

Sept. 20 Federal authorities announced that Canada and Britain would share the cost of a survey for the Zambia-Tanzania railway.

Sept. 24 The British-made *Ojibwa*, the 1st of the Canadian navy's 3 Oberon- class submarines, was commissioned at Chatham, England. It was decommissioned May 21, 1998. The other 2 diesel-electric 6,000-hp Oberon subs were the *Okanagan*, decommissioned Sept. 1998, and the *Onandaga*, still in service out of Halifax.

• Bruce F. Macdonald (b 1917) was appointed to command the UN India-Pakistan Observation Mission.

Oct. 4 Hilton of Canada Ltd. was convicted of discriminating against an African-Canadian person who had applied for a job at the Queen Elizabeth Hotel in Montreal. The conviction set a Canadian legal precedent.

Oct. 8 The provincial flag of Man. was proclaimed — the Red Ensign with the provincial shield showing a bison standing on a rock against a green back ground.

Oct. 13 The Canadian Film Development Agency was formed as a Crown corporation to help the Canadian private film industry produce feature films.

• Canada established diplomatic relations with Ethiopia.

Oct. 15 The $13 million Macdonald-Cartier Bridge spanning the Ottawa R. was opened by PM Pearson, Ont. Premier John Robarts and Que. Premier Jean Lesage.

Oct. 18 Abraham Allen Okpik (1929–1997) of Yellowknife became the 1st Inuit person appointed to the NWT Council.

Oct. 27 Canadian contributions to the UN High Commission for Refugees were increased to $350,000, making Canada the world's 2nd largest contributor.

Nov. 1 The organically cooled (oil-cooled) thermal nuclear reactor WR–1 went critical at the Whiteshell Nuclear Research Establishment (WNRE), on the Winnipeg R., northeast of Winnipeg. The WNRE was the 2nd Atomic Energy of Canada Limited (AECL) nuclear research facility after Chalk R., Ont. WR–1 stopped functioning as a research reactor in 1972, and was permanently shut down May 17, 1985.

Nov. 8 Liberals under Lester B. Pearson were re-elected with a minority govt, taking 131 seats. Diefenbaker's Conservatives took 97, the NDP 21, the Ralliement des Créditistes 9, Social Credit 5, and others 2. The "Three Wise Men" — Liberals Jean Marchand (1918–1988), Gérard Pelletier and Pierre Elliott Trudeau — were elected in Que. ridings, marking their entry into federal politics. Voter turnout was 74.8%.

Nov. 9 The Great Northeast Blackout began at 5:16 p.m. and lasted approximately 13 hours. Thirty million people in northeastern Canada and 8 northeastern US states were plunged into complete darkness. The blackout was the largest-single power failure in North America to that time. It took 6 days for Federal Power Commission investigators to locate the cause: a single faulty relay at Sir Adam Beck Station No. 2 in Ont. Despite widespread belief (urban legend), statistical evidence shows that the blackout had no measurable impact on the 1966 birth rate.

Nov. 10 The Citadel, Alb.'s 1st professional theatre, opened for business in a converted Salvation Army building in Edmonton, with an intentionally controversial production of Edward Albee's *Who's Afraid of Virginia Woolf?* The Citadel was founded by Joseph Harvey Scoctor (b 1922).

Nov. 13 A $117 million Man. Hydro power station began operation at Grand Rapids on the Saskatchewan R. Construction began on the 4-turbine, 479-megawatt (MW) facility in Jan. 1960.

Nov. 17 The 1st general cultural agreement was signed between Canada and France.

Dec. 15–18 Canada agreed to act as diplomatic intermediary between Britain and the United Arab Republic (Egypt) at Cairo, and also between Tanzania and Britain at Dar es Salaam. The United Arab Republic and Tanzania broke relations with Britain to protest Britain's failure to oust the white-minority regime in Rhodesia. On Nov. 11, Canada refused to recognize the independent state of Rhodesia (Zimbabwe) because it had unilaterally declared independence from Britain. On Nov. 20, Canada placed an embargo on the export of oil and arms to Rhodesia.

Dec. 16 Mitchell William Sharp (b 1911) became minister of finance, replacing Walter Gordon who resigned Nov. 11.

Dec. 17 PM Pearson announced creation of the new Department of Manpower, merging the National Employment Service with sections of the Department of Labour and Immigration Services. The department began operations in 1966.

Dec. 20 Otto Scholton, a member of a 4-man survey party from Burnaby, BC, was killed in captivity by Viet Cong guerrillas near Saigon.

Dec. 22 A report of the Organizing Committee for the Company of Young Canadians recommended the establishment of the Company as a Crown corporation. In 1966, the Canadian govt established the Company as a volunteer organization committed to community development.

Dec. 29 The federal govt pledged $15 million worth of food to India, in addition to the $10 million worth of wheat shipped under the 1965–1966 food-aid program.

Dec. 30 Madame Pauline Vanier was selected Canada's Woman of the Year in the annual Canadian Press year-end poll.

Also in 1965

• CBC television launched *The Tommy Hunter Show*, which, proving the appeal of country music in Canada, ran an unprecedented 27 years, thereby becoming the longest-running music show on North American television. Hunter (b 1937), of London, Ont., became known widely as a country gentleman and his theme "Travellin' Man" became his trademark tune with audiences during his many tours across Canada. Ironically, CBC cancelled his show in 1992, the same year it won a Gemini Award for Best Varitey Series. Hunter was named to the Order of Canada in 1986, and became a member of the Order of Ontario in 1996.

• Canada implemented the Seal Protection Regulations, which 1st set dates to the seal-hunt season, seal quotas, methods of slaughter, a ban on adult seals, and regulations covering the use of aircraft in the seal hunt.

• Less than half of all houses on Native reserves had electricity; only 1 in 6 had access to safe water supplies.

• The 137.5-ha Sheridan Park Research Community was opened as the 1st science-and-technology research community in the world developed by a community of private interests. Located in Mississauga, Ont., the community was founded by Abitibi, AECL, Cominco Ltd. Dunlop Research Centre, Gulf Oil, Inco Ltd., Mallory Batteries and others, who in 1960, all purchased land on the site and began work on a diverse range of fields including pharmaceuticals, chemicals and film-making. The park's name was later changed to Sheridan Science and Technology Park, and by 2003, its occupant companies employed a total of more than 2,700 engineers, scientists and associated professionals.

• The federal govt established an embassy in Dakar, Senegal. The embassy would grow to serve interests in Senegal's Cape Verde, Gambia, Guinea-Bissau and Mauritania.

• Construction was completed on the 222.5-m Canadian Steamship Lines (CSL) self-unloader, the *Tarantua*. The Collingwood Shipyards–built vessel had 2 boilers, 2 turbines and could produce 9,900 horsepower. The *Tarantua* was the last steam-driven ship in the CSL line.

• US-owned Merck and Co. acquired the major Canadian pharmaceutical company Charles E. Frosst & Co., thereby becoming Merck Frosst Canada Inc.

• The Norman Paterson School of International Affairs, at Carleton U. in Ottawa, was established on a grant of $400,000 from Senator Norman M. Paterson. The school is the only in Canada offering master of arts degrees in international affairs.

• Lakehead U. was founded at Thunder Bay, Ont., as an amalgamation of the Lakehead College of Arts, Science and Technology and the Lakehead Technical Institute. The 1st chancellor was Senator Norman Paterson.

• The Killam Trusts were established on $100 million from the will of Dorothy J. Killam (1899–1965), widow of the late NS-born financier and industrialist Izaak Walton Killam (1885–1955). Benefactors included 5 institutions: Dalhousie U. ($10 million), U. of Alb. ($6 million), U. of BC ($4 million), the Izaak Killam Hospital for Children in Halifax ($8 million) and the Montreal Neurological Institute. These institutions in turn awarded Killam graduate and postgraduate scholarships. The Canada Council was also given funds, which it transformed into annual professorial Killam Fellowships ($65,000 a year in 2003) and prestigious Killam Prizes ($100,000 each in 2003).

• Petra Burka (b 1946) won the world championships in figure skating and in the process became the 1st woman to complete a triple salchow in competition. She was also awarded the Lou Marsh Trophy for Canadian Athlete of the Year, and the Belma Springstead Award for Outstanding Female Athlete of the Year.

• Bill Crothers, a pharmacist from Markham, Ont., defeated 2-time defending Olympic champion and world record holder Peter Snell of New Zealand in an 800-m race at Toronto's Varsity Stadium. It was Snell's 1st significant defeat in international competition and one that sent him into retirement. Crothers had finished 2nd to Snell at the Olympics in Tokyo the previous year.

• The federal govt established grants to help relocate workers from economically depressed regions of the country.

• Seven hundred and forty-three Japanese-made Toyotas and 1,208 Datsuns were sold in Canada.

• Grace MacInnis (1905–1991), NDP representative for Vancouver-Kingsway, became BC's 1st woman MP. MacInnis (daughter of Methodist minister and 1st leader of the CCF, J.S. Woodsworth) was a popular supporter of women's and social issues. She served in the House until her retirement in 1974.

• The Beatles Fan Clubs International office in England announced that Canada had some 50,000 members, more than any other country.

• Arts philanthropist Robert McMichael (1921–2003) and Signe McMichael donated 200 artworks (most painted by Tom Thomson and the Group of Seven), their log-cabin home and the 6 ha in Kleinburg on which it is situated, to the Ont. govt. This collection would evolve into the world-famous McMichael Gallery.

• The humidex was both developed and 1st used in Canada. The measurement combines temperature and humidity to describe how hot these factors feel to the average human being.

• The painting *To Prince Edward Island*, by Alex Colville (b 1920), was completed. It hangs in the National Gallery of Canada, Ottawa.

• Jack Bush completed the masterpiece *Dazzle Red*, now in the Art Gallery of Ont., Toronto.

• Gordon Rayner painted *Magnetawan No. 2*, on canvas, now in the National Gallery of Canada, Ottawa.

• Polish-born painter Gershon Iskowitz (1921–1988) completed the landscape painting *Summer Sound*, now in the Art Gallery of Ont., Toronto.

• Ivan Kenneth Eyre (b 1935) painted *Mythopoeic Prairie II*, now in the Winnipeg Art Gallery.

• Claude Herbert Breeze (b 1938) painted the 3.5-m-tall *Sunday Afternoon: from an Old American Photograph*, depicting lynched African-Americans hanging from a tree, with legs consumed by fire. The painting is with the Department of External Affairs, Ottawa.

• Coach House Press was inaugurated in Toronto. It would be the 1st to publish Matt Cohen (1943–1999) and Michael Ondaatje (b 1943).

• Stephen Vizinczey's (b 1933) self-published book *In Praise of Older Women: The Amorous Recollections of Andras Vayda* sold 5,000 copies (at $4.95 for the hardcover) in 2 months.

• Philosopher George P. Grant published *Lament For A Nation*, contending that Canada would fall victim to American continentalism (imperialism).

• Walter Gordon, president of the CNR, former minister of finance, and future president of the Privy Council, published *A Choice for Canada: Independence or Colonial Status*.

• Sociologist John Arthur Porter (1921–1979) published *The Vertical Mosaic: An Analysis of Social Class and Power in Canada*, arguing that Canada consisted of a mosaic of different ethnic, linguistic, regional and religious groupings, each with varying relations to status and power.

• Stanley Mealing published "The Concept of Social Class in the Interpretation of Canadian History" in the *Canadian Historical Review*, igniting new scholarly interest in the Canadian working class.

• Carl Klinck (b 1908) edited *Literary History of Canada.*

• Popular historian Pierre Berton published *The Comfortable Pew.*

• Hubert Aquin's (b 1929) 1st novel, *Prochain Épisode,* was published, launching his career as one of Que.'s leading thinkers.

• Marie-Claire Blais published her most noted novel, *Une saison dans la vie d'Emmanuel,* for which she received the Prix France-Québec and the Prix Médicis. The book was translated into 13 languages.

• Poet Gilles Vigneault (b 1928) published *Quand les bateaux s'en vont.*

• BC poet Phyllis Webb (b 1927) published *Naked Poems.* In 1982, Webb's selected poems, *The Vision Tree,* was selected for a Gov-Gen.'s Award.

• Poet Jacques Brault published *Mémoire,* for which he received the Prix de poésie du Québec.

• Buffy Sainte Marie (b 1941) recorded the album *It's My Way,* which included the song "Universal Soldier," a hit for Scottish pop star Donovan and the unofficial anthem of the 1960s counterculture. Sainte Marie said she wrote the song during a stint at the Purple Onion coffee house in Toronto's Yorkville. The Sask.-born Cree singer would continue her singer-songwriting success into the next century, taking with her the Order of Canada, awarded July 3, 1997.

• Architect Moshe Safdie (b 1938), with associates David, Barott, and Boulva, completed the experimental prefabricated housing project Habitat '67 in Montreal along the St. Lawrence R. The design was Safdie's master's thesis at McGill U. Built for the 1967 International World Exposition (Expo '67), the high-density housing complex was constructed of

precut 55-m² elongated cubes that were built on the ground and then lifted into place by cranes. For the design, Safdie was awarded the 1967 Construction Man of the Year Award from the *Engineering News Record,* and the Massey Medal for Architecture in Canada. By the turn of the century, Habitat '67 was habitat for the nouveau riche, boasting some of the most sought-after condominiums in the city.

• Robert Goulet (b 1933), dubbed the "American Baritone from Canada," gained a measure of infamy when he mangled the "Star Spangled Banner" prior to a heavyweight boxing rematch between Muhammad Ali (then Cassius Clay) and Sonny Liston, in Lewiston, Maine.

1966

Jan. 1 The Canada Pension Plan Act, Bill C–136, came into effect, providing a wage-related supplement to the $75-a-month Old Age Security, including a cost-of-living allowance. The act was passed in the House in Mar. 1965. It was to be phased in over 10 years, and would cover 91% of the Canadian labour force. By month's end, some 100,000 Canadians over the age of 69 became eligible for the monthly pension. The age requirements progressively dropped to 65 one year at a time. The Canada Pension Plan (CPP) was followed by the Guaranteed Income Supplement (1966), which guaranteed CPP recipients an adequate living standard, not just subsistence. Que., however, opted out of the CPP. In June 1965, legislation to establish the Quebec Pension Plan (QPP) was passed in Que.'s National Assembly.

Jan. 6 *The Drum,* a multilingual Arctic newspaper published in English, Inuktituk and Loucheux, a Native dialect, was 1st issued. It was the 1st of its kind in the Arctic.

Jan. 7 Approximately 200 passengers were airlifted from a CNR train stranded by snow and mudslides in the Fraser Valley, BC.

• Federal authorities pledged Canadian emergency-food supplies for the drought-stricken African countries of Zambia, Rhodesia (now Zimbabwe), Bechuanaland (now Botswana) and Basutoland (now Lesotho).

Jan. 7–8 Financial aid to provinces was increased by agreement at a federal-provincial welfare ministers' conference at Ottawa.

Jan. 11–12 Commonwealth PMs met at Lagos, Nigeria, to discuss Rhodesia's Unilateral Declaration of Independence from Britain. The move was declared illegal. PM Pearson placed sanctions on all imports to and exports from Rhodesia on Feb. 3, joining other international sanctions, which remained through 1980, at which time Rhodesia became Zimbabwe, free elections were held and Robert Mugabe became president.

• The federal govt pledged $1 million in long-term loans to Ceylon (now Sri Lanka) for the purchase of industrial raw materials. The aid was made through the External Aid Office.

Jan. 18 Agriculture Minister John Joseph Greene (b 1905) was appointed chairman of the pledging committee of the World Food Program in New York. Canada's contribution to date was $27.5 million.

Jan. 25 The Supreme Court of Canada ruled that Aboriginals living on reserves did not have un-restricted year-round hunting rights.

• The federal govt confirmed its decision to raise grants to Canadian universities, from $2 to $5 per capita per province.

Also in Jan.
• Que. Liberal MP Jean Marchand persuaded PM Pearson to promote Pierre Trudeau to parliamentary secretary.

Feb. 2 The report of the Senate Committee on the Elderly recommended a guaranteed annual income at age 65, and the opportunity for senior citizens to maintain themselves as productive members of society.

Feb. 9 Ont. provincial sales tax was increased from 3% to 5%.

Feb. 12 Nancy Greene (b 1943) of Rossland, BC, won the women's slalom title at the Canadian International Ski Championships at Banff, Alb., the 1st held in Canada sanctioned by the International Ski Federation.

Feb. 15 After a 7-week strike, 354 Roman Catholic schoolteachers signed a new collective agreement and returned to work in Hull, Que.

Feb. 18 Ont.'s noncompulsory medical care plan was given Assent, effective July 1.

• The federal govt announced that armed forces personnel would receive interim pay increases and bonuses for re-enlistment.

Feb. 21 Que. Lt-Gov. Paul Comtois died in a fire that destroyed the historic vice-regal residence of Bois de Coulonge, Quebec City. He was succeeded the next day by Agent Gén. of Que. in London, Hugues Lapointe.

Also in Feb.
• Harold Town exhibited *Great Divide*, one of his most celebrated paintings, in the Morris portion of Jerrold Morris and Mazelow Galleries in Toronto. The painting is now in the Art Gallery of Ont., Toronto.

Mar. 1 Gold bars valued at $450,000 were stolen from the Winnipeg International Airport. All but 1 were recovered.

Mar. 3 George Bain (b 1920), Ottawa columnist for the *Globe and Mail*, was awarded the 1965 Stephen Leacock Memorial Medal for Humour for his book *Nursery Rhymes to be Read Aloud by Young Parents with Old Children*.

Mar. 4 Canadian Pacific DC-8 Flight 402 crashed in Japan, killing 64 people, including 18 Canadians. Tragically, the plane struck the approach lights while attempting a landing in heavy fog.

• Demonstrations against war in Vietnam were staged on Parliament Hill, Ottawa.

• Canada's "Munsinger Affair" became public when Liberal Justice Minister Lucien Cardin (1919–1988), under fire in the House on matters of security breaks, lashed out at Conservative opposition members by claiming that the security risks they were talking about paled in comparison with what he called the "Munsinger" case. Within hours, Canadians began hearing about a German prostitute and alleged KGB spy, Gerda Munsinger, who was rumoured to have met, lunched and had affairs with senior members of the former Diefenbaker administration. The most serious allegation involved a lengthy affair between Munsinger and then Minister of National Defence Pierre Sévigny. On Mar. 9, Supreme Court of Canada Judge Wishart Flett Spence was appointed to head a Royal Commission into the case. The Spence report was tabled in the House Oct. 5, calling the whole affair a "startling" national-security risk.

Mar. 12 Bobby Hull (b 1939) became the 1st NHLer to score more than 50 goals in a season. (Maurice Richard set, but never exceeded, the 50-goal mark during the 1944–1945 season. Bernie "Boom Boom" Geoffrion also reached the 50-goal mark in 1960–1961). The Chicago left-winger beat Rangers goalie Cesare Maniago for his 51st goal, ending the season with 54, winning the Art Ross and Hart Trophies and setting a league scoring record with 97 points.

Mar. 17 The govt unveiled a $112 million program to improve housing, water supplies, sanitation and roads on Aboriginal reserves.

Mar. 26–27 The Que. Liberal Federation adopted a resolution, drafted by federal Parliamentary Secretary Pierre Trudeau, calling for Ottawa to retain monetary, fiscal and tariff powers, while the provinces exercised responsibility over social security. The resolution also called for facilities to support bilingualism coast to coast.

Mar. 27 The 1st all-Canadian space project, a 158-kg instrument package to study the aurora borealis and upper atmosphere, was launched from the Churchill, Man., rocket-research range.

Mar. 29 In one of the greatest displays of sporting courage and stamina, Canadian heavyweight boxer George Chuvalo (b 1937) lost a 15-round decision at Maple Leaf Gardens to Cassius Clay (Muhammad Ali). The great Canadian heavyweight champion Chuvalo finished his career with a 73–18–2 record; he was never knocked out.

• Following the death of 16 people in the Quebec City area who had died after drinking large amounts of beer, Dow Brewery announced it would destroy 4.546 million litres of the brew at its Quebec City plant and withdraw existing supplies at bars and taverns.

Mar. 30 France demanded the removal of all Canadian and US military installations from French soil by Apr. 1, 1967, after announcing plans to give up its membership in NATO. NATO headquarters were moved from Versailles and Fontainbleau on Apr. 1, 1967 to Brussels and Mons, Belgium. France then pursued an independent nuclear weapons program.

Apr. 4 Canada established a 5-year, $350,000 plan to help increase wheat production in Kenya.

• External Affairs Minister Paul Martin announced that India's remaining payments on 2 loans made in 1958 for the purchase of Canadian wheat and flour would be considered an aid measure and forgiven.

Apr. 6 PM Pearson furthered the course toward bilingualism with a policy announcement in the House calling for widespread bilingualism among civil servants "within a reasonable period of years." In 1966, financial incentives were given to civil servants, in specified occupations, who proved to be somewhat fluent in both languages. Language-training programs were also offered to executive officers. A bilingual bonus system was established in 1977 with plans for its eradication unveiled Feb. 16, 1979.

Apr. 13 The Soviet Union inaugurated its North Atlantic passenger liner service, with the departure of the *Alexander Pushkin* from Leningrad for Montreal.

Apr. 20 After an open competition completed Mar. 31, 1965, to select reversal coinage designs for its upcoming 1967 centennial coinage, the Canadian Mint announced that artist Alex Colville had won in each of the 6 categories. The designs were a rock dove for the penny, a rabbit for the nickel, a mackerel for the dime, a bobcat for the quarter, a wolf for the 50-cent piece and a Canada goose for the dollar coin. Colville received $2,500 for each winning design.

Apr. 22 Former federal Minister without Portfolio Yvon Dupuis, of St. Jean, Que., was found guilty of influence peddling by a Que. Court of Queens Bench jury. He had been charged with accepting a $10,000 bribe to help a constituent obtain a race-track permit. Dupuis had resigned his cabinet post Jan. 20, 1965, after details of the incident became public.

Apr. 24 Central standard time was implemented in Sask. The Lloydminster area and the far northwest of the province were exempt. Sask. is the only province that does not change to daylight savings in late spring.

Apr. 26 The Supreme Court of Canada was authorized to review the Steven Truscott case. Truscott had been sentenced to death in 1959 for the murder of 12-year-old Lynne Harper. Because Truscott was only 14, his sentence was commuted to life imprisonment. The Supreme Court rejected his appeal on May 4, 1967, and Truscott was eventually paroled in 1969. The case became the subject of a book by Isabel LeBourdais, *The Trial of Steven Truscott*, who contended that Truscott was a victim of a miscarriage of justice. LeBourdais was later named 1966 Woman of the Year by Canadian Press women editors.

May 1 Military camps, stations and the navy's land-based "ships" were reconfigured into 39 Canadian Forces Bases (CFBs). Unified training and a single pay system went into effect.

• A 14-week Ont. teamsters' strike that had disrupted transport across the province ended. Teamsters received a pay increase of 70 cents an hour and a 40-hour workweek.

May 3 Dr. Alf Erling Porsild (1901–1977), chief botanist for the National Museum of Canada, was presented with the Massey Medal for his studies of the Canadian Arctic.

May 4 Jean Sutherland Boggs (b 1922) was appointed and became the 1st woman director of the National Gallery of Canada.

May 6 One person was killed and 3 injured when a bomb exploded at a strike-bound shoe–manufacturing plant in Montreal. Six members of the FLQ were arrested on non-capital murder charges.

May 7 The report of the Parent Royal Commission on Education in Que. recommended provision for non-denominational education, local school reorganization and creation of an Aboriginal education service.

• "Monday, Monday" by The Mamas and the Papas hit number one on *Billboard* magazine's Top 100 singles list. The group, made up of Halifax native Denny Doherty (b 1940) and Americans John and Michelle Phillips, and Cass Elliott, was founded in Los Angeles in 1965.

May 9 Approximately 1,600 Que. civil servants went on strike for increased wages, until July 29.

May 12 Assent was given to an Act establishing the Science Council of Canada.

May 18 Paul-Joseph Chartier (1921–1966) was killed in a washroom at the Parliament Buildings by the bomb which, it was believed, he intended to throw into the House of Commons.

May 19 Dalton Camp (1920–2002), the Progressive Conservative party's national president, told a private gathering of Conservatives at Toronto's Albany Club that a new leader must replace John Diefenbaker before the next election. On Sept. 20, Camp publicly called for an assessment of John Diefenbaker's leadership of the party.

May 30 Liberals, under Alexander Bradshaw Campbell (b 1933), won the PEI provincial election, taking 17 seats. The Progressive Conservatives took 15. Campbell became Canada's youngest premier.

June 5 In the Que. provincial election, Daniel Johnson's (1915–1968) Union Nationale won 56 seats to narrowly defeat Jean Lesage's Liberals, who took 50 seats.

• Edwin Godfrey Newman became the 1st Native person to be appointed a magistrate.

June 7 The Presbyterian Church voted 133 to 72 in favour of the ordination of women.

June 9 Dora Alencar de Vasconcellos of Brazil arrived in Ottawa, as the 1st woman to hold the position of foreign ambassador to Canada.

June 10 The CPR and the National Harbours Board signed an agreement to end a 30-year argument over the ownership of Vancouver's waterfront, enabling future development of the area. Title was divied up between interests, with the Harbours Board buying Pier BC for nearly $4 million, then leasing it to the CPR.

• NB Premier Louis Robichaud's Liberal govt passed the Municipalities Act, transferring municipal responsibilities for health, welfare, education and justice to the province.

June 11 At Springfield, Illinois, PM Pearson was presented with the 1966 Atlantic Union Pioneer Award for his leadership in bringing NATO countries together into a defensive alliance.

• David Bailey (b 1945) became the 1st Canadian to break the 4-minute mile (3:59.1) at a race in San Diego, California.

June 13 Dr. Geoffrey Hattersley-Smith of the Defence Research Board was awarded the Royal Geographical Society gold medal for his glaciologies work in the Canadian Arctic.

June 14 The 39-day strike of Que. longshoremen ended, with strikers getting a 34% wage increase.

June 20 The Soviet Union agreed to buy $800 million worth of Canadian wheat and flour.

June 21 The Guelph, Ont., birthplace of John McCrae, author of "In Flanders Fields," was designated a national historic site. The renovated house opened Sept. 8, 1968.

June 23 A Man. provincial election returned Premier Duff Roblin and his Progressive Conservative govt to power for a 4th term.

July 6 PM Pearson pledged grants and development loans to Caribbean Commonwealth countries totalling approximately $71 million over the next 5 years.

July 12 The Tri-Services Identities Organization (TRIO) was founded to stop the unification process of the Canadian military, at least until a full inquiry was convened. On July 19, Rear Admiral William Moss

Landymore (b 1916) was given an honourable discharge by Minister of National Defence Paul Hellyer. Landymore was a leading critic of Hellyer's armed forces unification plans. The integration process began with an Act to Amend the National Defence Act, passed July 16, 1964, and the replacement of military commands, announced June 7, 1965. On Nov. 6, Defence Minister Hellyer introduced unification Bill C-243.

July 14 Allie Ahern was appointed judge of the Canadian Citizenship Court in Halifax, the 1st woman to hold the position in Canada.

July 15 Assent was given to an Act to establish a Crown Agency — the National Arts Centre Corporation — to operate the multimillion-dollar National Arts Centre in Ottawa. On Mar. 9, 1967, Gordon Hamilton Southam (b 1916) was appointed the 1st director of the centre, which officially opened June 2, 1969.

July 22 It was declared Gordie Howe Day in Saskatoon, Sask.

July 25 Martine van Hamel (b 1945) of Toronto won the junior-class category at the International Ballet Competition in Bulgaria.

July 31 Union Station in central Ottawa ceased operations. It was replaced by a new station in the suburb of Alta Vista. The Doric Roman Revival, multi-pillar Union Station, completed in 1912, was later classified a Federal Heritage Building and transformed into a conference centre.

Aug. 1–2 The provincial premiers' conference was held in Toronto. Six of 8 provinces rejected the proposed federal medicare scheme (July 20, 1965) of sharing medical-care insurance-plan costs with the federal govt. Nlfd and BC were not present.

Aug. 3 In Delhi, Ont., more than 250 migrant tobacco workers were read the Riot Act for demonstrating against worker accommodations. Nine were arrested for unlawful assembly and causing a disturbance.

Aug. 4–8 Some 16,000 Stelco workers in Hamilton staged a wildcat strike to protest slow contract negotiations, despite an offer that would have made them the highest-paid steelworkers in the world by Aug. 1, 1967.

Aug. 10 The newly formed Armed Forces Council, composed of senior headquarters officers and commanders of all 6 military commands, met to plan steps for the integration and unification of the forces.

• Eight were killed and more than 50 injured when the Heron Road Bridge, under construction in Ottawa, collapsed. On Mar. 3, 1967, the O.J. Gaffney Construction Company of Stratford, Ont., was found responsible for the collapse and fined the maximum $5,000 for negligence.

• Brian Parks of Winnipeg won the world bridge trophy.

Aug. 13 The 8th British Commonwealth Games closed in Kingston, Jamaica. Canadian athletes won 14 gold medals, 20 silver and 23 bronze, and set 2 world records. Elaine Tanner (b 1951), known as "Mighty Mouse," won 4 gold and 3 silver in swimming.

Aug. 16 *Rose Latulippe*, the 1st full-length Canadian ballet, premiered in Stratford, Ont. It was written by Brian Macdonald (b 1928), with music by Harry Freedman (b 1922).

Aug. 26 A strike of 118,000 Canadian railway workers from various unions shut down telecommunications, air express, all but 1st class mail and ferry service to PEI. Parliament was recalled on Aug. 29 to end the strike. On Sept. 1, a bill was passed ending the stoppage, with an interim wage hike of 18% and a provision for compulsory arbitration.

Also in Aug.
• *The Cat's Whiskers*, the 1st topless bar in Canada, opened in Vancouver.

• The Globe Theatre in Regina, Sask., was founded by Ken and Sue Kramer. It was Sask.'s 1st professional theatre company.

Sept. 8 Liberal premier Joey Smallwood was returned to office for the 6th time (with his greatest majority) in the 6th Nfld. provincial election. His party won 39 of 42 seats.

• The Essential Services Act was passed by the Sask. legislature, providing for compulsory arbitration, without appeal, in labour disputes involving workers in essential services.

Sept. 12 BC Social Credit Premier W.A.C. Bennett was returned to office in the provincial election, taking 33 of 55 seats.

Sept. 19 Leopold Senghor, president of Senegal, arrived in Ottawa for a 10-day visit.

Sept. 20 The federal and NB govts signed an agreement providing an expenditure of $114 million to fight rural poverty over the next 10 years.

Sept. 22 The 21st session of the UN General Assembly opened in New York under the chairmanship of Canadian External Affairs Minister Paul Martin.

• The Cuban embassy in Ottawa was hit by a bazooka-type rocket, believed to have been fired by Cuban nationalists.

Sept. 29 Eight people were arrested in connection with the seizure of $3 million worth of heroin in Montreal.

Oct. 1 Colour-television broadcasting was inaugurated by the CBC.

Oct. 6 The Que. govt approved a 40-year agreement between Hydro-Que. and the British Nfld. Corp., allowing Que. to buy power from the planned Churchill Falls hydroelectric project in Labrador. The power project went on line Dec. 6, 1971.

Oct. 11 A report of the committee study on election expenses recommended the full disclosure of election spending by parties and candidates, and equal free broadcast time to all national parties within 4 weeks of an election.

Oct. 13 A $1 million mail robbery was orchestrated at Montreal International Airport.

Oct. 14 Montreal's subway, le Métro, began operations. It consisted of 3 lines connecting 26 spacious stations filled with public art. It was the 1st subway to run on rubber tires. Drilling had begun May 23, 1962.

Oct. 17 Centennial College of Applied Arts and Technology, Ont.'s 1st community college, opened in Scarborough.

Oct. 19 Canada agreed to sell Britain Canadian uranium oxide through the next decade.

Oct. 24 SATCOM, Canada's 1st satellite communications earth station, began operations near Mill Village, NS.

Nov. 1 International Nickel Co. (Inco) announced plans to more than double the production of nickel at Thompson, Man., with capital expenditures estimated at $100 million.

• The Canadiana Room in the PM's official residence was opened by Maryon Pearson. The room featured a collection of early Canadian art, handicrafts and furniture collected by the Pearsons.

Nov. 4 Direct air service began between Montreal and Moscow.

Nov. 6 Defence Minister Hellyer introduced Bill C–243, the Canadian Forces Reorganization Act, in the House of Commons, amending the National Defence Act to unify the army, navy and air force into a single organization — the Canadian Armed Forces. The act came into effect Feb. 1, 1968, after much heated debate.

Nov. 11 Canada was elected to a 2-year term on the UN Security Council.

Nov. 14–28 Machinists and auxiliary workers forced the 1st strike in the 29-year history of Air Canada.

Nov. 15 At the National Progressive Conservative Association meeting at Ottawa, Dalton Camp was re-elected national president of the party. The association also instructed its executive to hold a leadership convention before the end of 1967, placing Diefenbaker's future as Tory leader in doubt.

Nov. 25 Canada pledged $500,000 toward a Canadian fund for flood relief in Italy.

Nov. 26 The Sask. Roughriders won their 1st Grey Cup, defeating Ottawa 29–14.

Dec. 8 The House of Commons passed the national Medical Care Act. It received Assent Dec. 21. Under the act, the federal govt would share general medical-care insurance-plan costs with the provinces. The act was effective July 1, 1968. By 1972, all provinces had in place federal-provincial insurance-plan programs extending free, universal coverage beyond in-patient hospital care, to include free access to the general services of physicians.

• A 3-week longshoremen's strike in BC ended.

Dec. 14 Assent was given to an act that incorporated the Bank of BC, Canada's 10th chartered bank. The bank opened in Vancouver on July 18, 1968.

Dec. 19 Finance Minister Mitchell Sharp announced a 1% increase in the federal sales tax and an Old Age Security Tax increase for people in higher income brackets. On Dec. 21, an amendment to the Old Age Security Act received Assent, providing needy recipients of the $75 Old Age Pension an additional $30 a month.

Dec. 20 A Commons-Senate Special Joint Committee on Credit and Prices released its report, which included a recommendation for the establishment of a federal department of consumer affairs. A Senate-Commons Committee made the same recommendation on Feb. 15, 1967, as did an Economic Council of Canada report on July 17, 1967. The Department of Consumer and Corporate Affairs was established in 1968.

Dec. 23 Sask. Premier Wilbert Ross Thatcher announced that the farm home of former PM Diefenbaker located near Borden, Sask., would be moved to Regina and restored as part of the Wascana Centre.

Dec. 31 A report on graduate studies and research in Ont. recommended the amalgamation of Ont.'s 14 provincially supported universities into 1 institution with many campuses. The recommendation was not realized.

• Former Finance Minister Walter Gordon retired from the presidency of the CNR after 17 years in that capacity.

Also in 1966

• Halifax-born Acadia U. graduate Dr. Charles Brenton Huggins (1901–1997) was co-recipient of the Nobel Prize in Medicine for his discovery of hormonal therapy in the treatment of prostate cancer. The U. of Chicago instructor shared the prize with American Rockefeller U. pathologist F. Peyton Rous.

• Women in PEI were 1st permitted to serve on juries.

• Caisse de Dépôt et Placement was established to manage the Que. Pension Plan. By 2000, the Caisse de Dépôt would manage retirement funds worth $88.3 billion.

• Divers collected $700,000 in gold from the French pay-ship *Chambeau*, wrecked off NS in 1725.

• The Château Lacombe opened in Edmonton. It was the 1st of 2 CPR hotels built in the 1960s. The 2nd was the Château Champlain, opened in Montreal on Jan. 11, 1967. At 36 stories, the Château Champlain was the nation's tallest hotel — and referred to as the "cheese grater" because of its half-moon window configuration.

• The NHL announced that the league would expand to 12 teams for the 1967–1968 season. Added to the "original six" were the St. Louis Blues, Minnesota North Stars, Philadelphia Flyers, Oakland Seals, Los Angeles Kings and Pittsburgh Penguins. Each franchise cost $2 million.

• Ken Weis reached New Zealand in a 6-m sailboat after a 6-month voyage from Vancouver.

• The RCMP discontinued equestrian training for recruits.

• Singer-songwriter Murray McLauchlan (b 1948) made his 1st appearance at the Mariposa Folk Festival.

• Anne Murray (b 1945) took a job as a gym teacher at a Summerside, PEI, high school.

• While vacationing in France, Paul Anka bought world rights to a French ballad ("Comme d'Habitude" by Claude François), wrote English lyrics to the tune and titled it *My Way*. The song became synonymous with Frank Sinatra and went on to become one of the most covered songs in the history of popular music.

• Fitzhenry & Whiteside was established in Toronto, by Robert I. Fitzhenry and Cecil L. Whiteside (1911–1989).

• Greg Curnoe completed the painting *Camouflaged Piano or French Roundels*, on panel, now in the National Gallery of Canada, Ottawa. He also completed *Family Painting No. 1 — In Labour*, on board, now in a private collection.

• John Meredith (b 1933) painted the huge triptych *Seeker*, now in the Art Gallery of Ont., Toronto.

• Montreal-born Yves Gaucher (1934–2000) painted *Triptych*, acrylic on canvas, representing music and mathematics. The painting is now in the Art Gallery of Ontario, Toronto.

• Alex Colville painted the strikingly realistic *TruckStop*, an acrylic polymer emulsion, now in the Museum Ludwig, Köln, Germany.

• Charles Gagnon completed *November Steps (For Turu Takemitsu)*, oil on canvas. *November Steps* was inspired by the song of the same name composed by Gagnon's close friend, Toru Takemitsu, whom Gagnon had recently visited in Japan. The painting is in the National Gallery of Canada, Ottawa.

• Guido Molinari painted *Mutation Sérielle Vert-Rouge*, acrylic on canvas, now in the Art Gallery of Ontario, Toronto.

• Montreal native Claude Tousignant painted *Gong 88, No. 1*, a 223.5-cm (diameter) acrylic on canvas. The painting is with the National Gallery of Canada, Ottawa.

• Otto Donald Rogers (b 1935) painted *Sunset Stillness*, on canvas, now in the Mendel Art Gallery, Saskatoon.

• Victoria artist Michael Morris painted *The Problem of Nothing*, on canvas, now in the Vancouver Art Gallery.

• Master carver John Tiktak (1916–1981) completed *Mother and Child,* a 48 x 12 x 21–cm soapstone sculpture. Tiktak was born near Eskimo Point, Nunavut, and later moved to Rankin Inlet in 1958 where he worked in a nickel mine until his leg was crushed in an accident. He then turned to sculpture. The masterpiece is now in a private collection.

• Dave Godfrey (b 1938) and Dennis Lee (b 1939) established the literary press House of Anansi Press, in Toronto, which published such authors as Northrop Frye and Margaret Atwood.

• George Woodcock (1912–1995) received the Gov-Gen.'s Award for *The Crystal Spirit,* a biography of British writer George Orwell. Born in Winnipeg, Woodcock became a renowned editor, critic, writer, historian, philosopher, essayist, biographer, political activist and professor, with as many as 150 works accredited to him. In 1959, Woodcock founded the *Canadian Literature* journal and remained its editor for 18 years. In the 1970s he was awarded 6 honorary university degrees; he also refused many awards, including the Order of Canada, accepting only those honours given by his peers. In 1994, Vancouver declared May 7th George Woodcock Day.

• The League of Canadian Poets was established for the support and promotion of Canadian poets.

• Leonard Cohen published the novel *Beautiful Losers.*

• Writer and illustrator James Houston (b 1921) published his 1st children's book, *Tikta'liktak: An Eskimo Legend.*

• Christie Harris, née Lucy Christie Irwin (1907–2002), published her children's novel about the Haida First Nation, *Raven's Cry.*

• Historian George Ramsay Cook (b 1931) published *Canada and the French Canadian Question.*

• Historian Fernand Ouellet (b 1926) published the highly influential *Histoire économique et sociale du Québec, 1760–1850,* translated as *Economic and Social History of Quebec* in 1980. Ouellet, who ran against the grain of Que.'s growing "nationalist" interpretation of history, was made an Officer of the Order of Canada in 1978. He was also a founding

member of the Société Charlevoix, organized in 1992 to study the history of Franco-Ontarians.

• The 1st volume of the *Dictionary of Canadian Biography,* edited by George W. Brown (1894–1963), was published by the U. of Toronto Press.

• Harold Andrew Horwood (b 1923) published the popular novel *Tomorrow Will Be Sunday.*

• Margaret Laurence published her classic novel *A Jest of God.*

• Claire Martin published *La joue droite.* The novel won the Prix du Québec.

• Novelist Réjean Ducharme published his 1st novel, *L'Avalée des vales,* which won the Gov-Gen.'s Award.

• Margaret Atwood (b 1939) won the Gov-Gen.'s Award for her book of poems *The Circle Game.*

• Gwendolyn MacEwen's collection of poetry, *A Breakfast for Barbarians,* was published.

• CBC cancelled the popular television program, *The Juliette Show,* featuring the vivacious musical talents of host "Our Pet" Juliette Cavazzi (b 1927). The show had been viewed every Saturday night by over 1 million people since 1st hitting the airwaves in 1956.

• Allan King directed *Warrendale,* a feature-length documentary film he described as an "actuality drama." The controversial film about emotionally disturbed children at the Warrendale Treatment Centre won the New York Critic's Award for Best Documentary and the Canadian Film Award for Film of the Year and Best Feature Film. It also shared both the British Academy's Best Foreign Film Award (with Luis Buñuel's *Belle de Jour*) and the Critics' Prize at the Cannes International Film Festival (with Michelangelo Antonioni's *Blow-Up*).

1967

Jan. 1 Canada's centennial year (1967) was welcomed with a ceremony in Ottawa. PM Pearson was 1st to light the Centennial Flame at Parliament Hill as the seconds ticked in 1967. The Centennial Flame is located at the foot of the walkway leading into the central entrance of Centre Block at the base of the Peace Tower. The flame constantly burns above a fountain with water representing the nation's 3 oceans. The shields and floral emblems of all provinces and territories, including the dates they joined Confederation, are also displayed on the Centennial Flame unit.

Jan. 4 Astronomer Dr. Helen Hogg of the U. of Toronto was presented with the Rittenhouse Silver Medal by the Rittenhouse Astronomical Society, Philadelphia, for her work on variable stars. She was the 1st Canadian and the 2nd woman to win the honour.

Jan. 5 In this centennial year, a federal proclamation stated that Jan. 11, the birthday of John A. Macdonald, should be observed across the country.

Jan. 9 The Centennial Train left Victoria, BC. A travelling museum of Canadiana, it made 83 stops across the country over 1967.

• Walter Gordon, former minister of finance who resigned in Nov. 1965, rejoined the Pearson cabinet as president of the Privy Council on the condition that something be done to regulate foreign investment. On Jan. 23, Gordon was placed in charge of a special ministerial committee to study the implications of foreign ownership in Canada. This would lead to the Watkins Report, tabled in the House Feb. 15, 1968.

Jan. 14 Hundreds of schools in Montreal and Trois-Rivières, Que., were closed when Catholic elementary– and secondary–school teachers went on strike. The strike ended with the Que. govt's passage of controversial Bill 25, on Feb. 17, which ordered teachers to return to the classroom within 48 hours. It also suspended their right to strike until June 30, 1968.

Jan. 18 Yellowknife became the official capital of the NWT. Administrative functions were transferred from Ottawa on Sept. 15.

Jan. 27 Canada signed the UN Treaty on Principles Governing the Activities of States in the Exploration and Use of Outer Space (Outer Space Treaty), at London, Moscow and Washington, D.C.

The treaty was based on the principle that outer space was to be free from claims of ownership and sovereignty and its exploration and use must be carried out in the interests and for the betterment of all humanity.

Jan. 29 Yugoslavia's embassy in Ottawa and Yugoslav consulates in Toronto were rocked by bomb explosions. There were no injuries.

Also in Jan.
• Laura Sabia (1916–1996), founder of the Committee for the Equality of Women in Canada (CEWC), threatened PM Pearson with a march of 2 million women in Ottawa if a Royal Commission was not established to inquire into the status of women in Canada. On Feb. 16, Pearson established the Royal Commission on the Status of Women (RCSW). The 7-member commission, 5 of whom were women, was chaired by CBC journalist Florence Bird (1908–1998). In Apr. 1968, the commission held hearings in 14 communities in all 10 provinces, met with 890 witnesses, received 468 briefs and 1,000 letters. Its report tabled Dec. 7, 1970, recommended the provision of daycare services for children, qualified abortion on demand, provision of birth control information, restriction of the marriage age to 18 and a loosening of divorce laws.

Feb. 11–18 The 1st Canada (Winter) Games were held in Quebec City. The Games include competitions in a number of sports, including basketball, wrestling and volleyball. Competitors represent every province and territory. The Canada Games alternate between Winter Games and Summer Games every 2 years, and move from province to province. The 1st Canada Summer Games were held in Halifax-Dartmouth from Aug. 16–24, 1969. It was during the 1967 Quebec Games that Yukon official Cal Miller developed the idea for the Arctic Winter Games, a circumpolar sporting event to include only Arctic and Northern athletes. Miller came up with the idea as he watched representatives of richer, more populous southern communities trounce his Northern teams. The 1st Arctic Winter Games were held Mar. 9–14, 1970.

Feb. 13–22 A controversy involving the terms under which US-owned Mercantile Bank of Canada could operate in Canada was resolved when parent company City Bank of New York was given an extra 5 years to sell 75% of its Mercantile stock to Canadian interests. Mercantile had operated in Canada as a wholly Dutch-owned company without issue. Controversy erupted when City Bank of New York began its takeover of the bank in 1963. In 1971, the Department of Finance agreed to give Mercantile Bank until 1980 to become at least 75% Canadian-owned.

Feb. 17 Assent was given to an Act establishing the Canada Deposit Insurance Corporation, under which all federally incorporated trust and loan companies were required to insure their deposits.

Also in Feb.
• Twenty top English-speaking civil servants moved to Que. for a year of intensive schooling in French as part of a federal govt bilingualism program.

• The Royal Netherlands Air Force agreed to purchase 105 Canadian-built CF–5 *Freedom Fighter* ground-attack aircraft. The contract was worth approximately $100 million.

Mar. 4 A 34-day strike of 4,500 Montreal civic clerical workers ended with the acceptance of a 2-year contract. On Jan. 30, the strikers had closed down Montreal's municipal courts, the social welfare department and City Hall.

Mar. 5 Gov-Gen. Georges P. Vanier died in Ottawa. The WW I veteran was the 1st French Canadian to hold the office and only the 2nd Gov-Gen. to die in it. His state funeral was held at Notre Dame Cathedral in Ottawa on Mar. 8. Vanier was succeeded by Daniel Roland Michener (1900–1991) on Mar. 29. Michener officially assumed office Apr. 17.

Mar. 13 The Public Service Staff Relations Act took effect, providing collective bargaining rights for more than 20,000 public employees. The Public Service Employment Act and the revised Financial Administration Act established the Treasury Board as the central management agency for the public service.

Mar. 16 Que. provincial sales taxes increased from 6% to 8%, the highest in the country. Que. also introduced a family allowance program to supplement the federal allowance.

Mar. 17 *Globe and Mail* columnist Richard J. Needham (b 1912) was awarded the 1966 Stephen Leacock Memorial Medal for Humour for his book *Needham's Inferno*.

• M.M. Bienvenu of Montreal acquired controlling interest in Sinclair Stevens's Toronto-based British International Finance (Canada) Ltd. Control over the Bank of Western Canada, from which Stevens resigned Feb. 17, was included.

• Leader of the National Social Credit Party, Robert Thompson, MP representing Red Deer, Alb., resigned, citing lack of support from provincial-party organizations.

Mar. 29 The 1st debentures in Canadian banking history were offered by the Toronto-Dominion Bank under authorization of the new Bank Act amendment of 1967, which reduced cash-reserve measurements for Canadian banks, removed the 6% ceiling on loans and allowed banks better access to the mortgage and consumer loan markets.

Mar. 31 Gordon Lightfoot performed his 1st annual concert at Toronto's Massey Hall, a tradition that ran until 1984 and every 18 months after that.

Early Apr. As Montreal prepared for Expo '67, Victoriatown — a working-class neighbourhood in Montreal — was demolished to make way for a parking lot to serve the event. In the Centre-Sud district, east of Old Montreal, fences were erected to hide the area from tourists. Social activists covered the fences with slogans such as "Visitez les slums!"

Apr. 1 Bush pilot Robert Gauchie was rescued 58 days after being forced down in a remote section of the NWT.

Apr. 3 A coal mine explosion near Natal, BC, killed 15 and injured 9.

• Guy Favreau resigned from the presidency of the Privy Council and as registrar gen. and member of

Parliament. He was appointed to the Que. Superior Court.

Apr. 4 Pierre Trudeau was sworn in as Justice Minister under Lester B. Pearson.

Apr. 6 George Brinton McClellan (b 1908), Commissioner of the RCMP, was named ombudsman of Alb., the 1st such position in Canada.

Apr. 11 Bower Edward Featherstone, a federal civil servant, was convicted under the Official Secrets Act of acquiring a confidential naval chart. He was sentenced on Apr. 24 to 2.5 years in prison.

Apr. 12 The House of Commons recommended the adoption of "O Canada" as the national anthem, and "God Save the Queen" as the Royal anthem. The anthem would not be made official until June 27, 1980.

Apr. 18 The Union of Que. Specialized Education Teachers was convicted of contempt after its 2,300 members rejected a 1966 court injunction forbidding them to strike. The union was fined $2,000 and each executive member sentenced to 20 days in prison.

• The Man. govt approved imposition of a 5% sales tax, effective June 1.

Apr. 27 Expo '67 opened in Montreal under the theme "Man and his World." The World's Fair was held on the Cité du Havre peninsula at Montreal, and on the St. Lawrence islands of Sainte-Hélène and Notre-Dame. Both islands had been artificially augmented with over 6 million tonnes of fill. Expo included over 90 international, regional, commercial and theme pavilions, including the US Pavilion — a geodesic dome designed by Buckminster Fuller; the Canada Pavilion — the huge Katimavik inverted triangle; and the interconnected "Man the Explorer" complex. The World's Fair closed on Oct. 29, having hosted 50,306,648 visitors. Admission was $2.50 per day; $12 for the week; or $35 for unlimited entry. Total cost of Expo was $432 million.

Apr. 30 Ian Tyson (b 1933) and Sylvia Tyson (b 1940) played New York's Carnegie Hall for the 1st time.

Also in Apr.
• French President Charles de Gaulle refused to attend ceremonies at Vimy Ridge because Canadians had invited Prince Philip of England.

May 2 Dave Keon (b 1940) scored 2 short-handed goals and George Armstrong (b 1930) a clinching empty-netter against the Montreal Canadiens to take the 6th and deciding game of the Stanley Cup finals in Toronto. It was the Maple Leafs' 11th and last Stanley Cup of the century.

May 12 Queen Elizabeth II had white swans flown from England to Canada as a Confederation gift.

May 16 A $1 million federal program was unveiled to help Native Peoples buy or build homes off their reserves and closer to places of employment.

May 18 Canadian Pacific Airlines presented a reconstructed Fairchild Model 82 aircraft to the Canadian National Aviation Museum in Ottawa.

May 20 Three veteran pilots were killed when an Air Canada DC-8 crashed near Ottawa during a training flight.

May 23 Alb.'s Social Credit govt, under Ernest Charles Manning, was returned to power for the 7th consecutive time. Manning retired in 1968.

May 24 For the 1st time, the doors of Centre Block were locked when more than 10,000 Ont. and Que. dairy farmers demonstrated on Parliament Hill demanding better prices for their milk.

• Bellevue House, the Kingston, Ont., home of John A. Macdonald, was opened as a museum.

• The Centennial Voyageur canoe pageant began at Rocky Mountain House, Alb. Teams representing 8 provinces and 2 territories paddled 5,283 km to arrive at Expo '67 in Montreal on Sept. 4.

May 25 The Great Ring of Canada — a large crystal and steel sculpture presented as a centennial gift to Canada by the US — was unveiled at Expo '67 by US President Lyndon B. Johnson.

May 27 Egypt demanded the immediate withdrawal

of Canadian peacekeeping troops from Egypt. The troops were airlifted out within 48 hours.

May 29 The Royal Architectural Institute of Canada presented Montreal Mayor Jean Drapeau with the 1967 Gold Medal for distinguished service to the arts and architecture.

May 30 NS Progressive Conservative Premier Robert Stanfield was returned to power for the 4th consecutive time.

May 31 The Sir John Carling Building opened in Ottawa to serve as the new headquarters for the Department of Agriculture. Named after the late Minister of Agriculture John Carling (1823–1911), the 10-storey precast-concrete building is located at the eastern boundary of Ottawa's Central Experimental Farm and was awarded the Vincent Massey Medal for Architecture.

Also in May

• SEDCO 135, the 1st semi-submersible drilling vessel built in Canada, and the largest in the world, began drilling for oil and gas off Vancouver Is. SEDCO worked off the BC coast until 1969, and then in Australia, the North Sea and South America.

June 1 Parliament removed a federal sales tax on drugs, effective Sept. 1.

June 10 The Bruce Trail in southern Ont. was officially opened. The 800-km footpath, which runs along the Niagara Escarpment from Niagara to Tobermory, was designated a UNESCO World Biosphere Reserve in 1990. Work on the trail began in 1960. The Bruce is the oldest and longest single recreational hiking trail in the country.

June 20 PM Pearson officially opened the National Library and Archives Building on Wellington St. in Ottawa. The cornerstone was laid by Gov-Gen. Vanier on May 10, 1965. The library was established by Parliament in 1953 with a mandate to collect, preserve and provide access to Canada's published cultural heritage. The first national librarian was W.K. Lamb (b 1904), who served until 1968.

• The US Federal Power Commission approved plans by TransCanada PipeLines to carry Western Canadian natural gas to eastern Canadian and US markets via the US.

June 30 Dosco Industries Limited closed the Bell Is. iron mine in Nfld. after 72 years of operation.

June 30–July 1 President Zakir Hussain of India opened a hardboard factory to be operated by Indian interests at East R., near Halifax. It was India's 1st industrial investment in the western hemisphere.

Also in June

• CKYK-TV in Yellowknife, NWT, became the 1st television station to subscribe to CBC's "frontier package" service, which consisted of 4-hour videotapes delivered daily by air.

July 1 Canada's centennial was marked by a mass celebration on Parliament Hill. PM Pearson addressed the nation: "Every Canadian before you has had some part, however humble and unsung, in building the magnificent national structure of Confederation that we honour and salute today… Ours is a good land. Our Centennial resolve must be to make it better for our children and our children's children."

• The Order of Canada, the country's most prestigious honour, was officially established to coincide with Canada's centennial. It was awarded for merit, in the service of Canada or humanity at large. There were initially 2 ranks of merit: Companion and Medal of Service. There are now 3 hierarchical ranks (in order of highest achievement): Companion, Officer, and Member. Gov-Gen. Roland Michener was 1st recipient of the Order of Canada.

• Actress and model Pamela Denise Anderson (better known as Pamela Anderson Lee or C.J. Parker on the syndicated TV series *Baywatch*) was born in Ladysmith, BC. She was the 1st baby born on Canada's 100th birthday and was promptly named the country's "Centennial Baby."

• United College became the U. of Winnipeg.

July 3–6 The NDP held its national convention in Toronto and returned Tommy Douglas as national leader by acclamation.

July 7 St. Patrick's College, formerly part of the U. of Ottawa, merged with Carleton U. (founded in 1942).

July 23 French President Charles de Gaulle arrived in Quebec aboard the French warship *Colbert* for Canada's centennial celebrations.

• Winnipeg played host to the Pan-American Games until Aug. 6. Canada won 92 medals, including 12 gold. Elaine "Mighty Mouse" Tanner set world records in the 100- and 200-m backstroke.

July 23–25 Windsor, Ont., fire crews were called to assist their American colleagues in the Detroit Race Riots, which resulted in 43 dead and 1,189 injured. Windsor residents lined the banks of the Detroit R. and watched with a mixture of horror and heartsickness as much of Detroit, less than 1 km away, burned to the ground.

Also in July

• The Cunard Line sold its 311-m steamship *Queen Mary* to Long Beach, California, interests who planned to use the ship as a maritime museum and hotel. The *Queen Mary,* 41 m longer than the *Titanic,* was commissioned in 1936. Cunard's *Queen Elizabeth* was sold to private interests on Apr. 5, 1968.

Aug. 15 Nfld. Premier Joey Smallwood opened the $62 million hydroelectric project at Baie d'Espoir, and a highway connecting the area to Grand Falls.

Aug. 17–Sept. 24 Some 5,400 members of the Seafarers' International Union of Canada struck against the Canadian Lake Carriers Association for better pay, premiums and leave allotments based on hours worked.

Aug. 23 The Anglican Church of Canada agreed to permit the remarriage of divorced persons in its churches.

Sept. 9 NS Premier Robert Stanfield was elected leader of the national Progressive Conservative Party on the 5th ballot at a Toronto convention. He was John Diefenbaker's successor. On Sept. 13, George Isaac Smith (b 1909) succeeded Robert Stanfield as Conservative premier of NS. On Nov. 6, Stanfield was elected to the House of Commons in a by-election held in the riding of Colchester-Hants, NS.

Sept. 18 Que. Liberal MP René Lévesque (1922–1987), speaking to his riding association in Montreal-Laurier, issued "Option Québec," an argument for Que. sovereignty as the only future course for Que. Lévesque's Option Québec would be tabled at the Que. Liberal convention Oct. 15.

Sept. 21 Bass-baritone Peter van Ginkel, a Canadian with the Metropolitan Opera Company in New York, was appointed affiliate artist at Waterloo Lutheran U. (Wilfrid Laurier U.) — the 1st appointment of its kind in Canada.

Sept. 30 The $235-million Great Canadian Oil Sands Ltd. (Suncor Energy in 1979) plant began commercial extraction of oil from the Athabasca oil sands north of Fort McMurray, Alb. The plant was the 1st large-scale commercial producer on the tar pitch. Syncrude, the 2nd major player in the region, would ship its 1st barrel of oil-sands petroleum on July 30, 1978.

Oct. 4 Approximately 4,500 BC lumber workers went on strike for higher wages. They returned to work May 11, 1968, with a settlement that included a 72 cents-an-hour wage increase.

Oct. 6 W.T. Ross Flemington (b 1916), former president of Mount Allison U., was appointed NB ombudsman.

• Ucluelot Brynnor Mines, BC, received the highest precipitation to fall in Canada over a 24-hour period — 489.2 mm.

Oct. 7 Arctic lupines, grown in the National Museum's herbarium from 10,000-year-old seeds found in the Yukon, were placed on display.

Oct. 11 Sask. Liberal Premier Thatcher's govt was returned to power with 35 seats, 11 more than the CCF.

• Que. Justice Frédéric Dorion ordered 6,000 Montreal Transportation Commission employees back to work, ending an 80-day strike. Service was restored Oct. 13.

Oct. 15 A 3-day Que. Liberal convention in Quebec City supported special status for Que. within

Canada, but rejected René Lévesque's "Option Québec" (separatism). Lévesque resigned from the party in Nov. to pursue a campaign for an independent Que. through formation of the Mouvement Souverainété-Association (MSA), which would merge (Oct. 11–15, 1968) with the Railliement National to form the Parti Québécois.

Oct. 17 Ont. PC govt, under Premier John Robarts, was returned to power for the 8th consecutive time but with a reduced majority.

Oct. 19 The Cunard Steamship Co. announced the cancellation of its Canadian passenger service. The storied shipping company had been established by Nova Scotian Samuel Cunard in 1839 as the British and North American Royal Mail Packet Company.

Oct. 22 A 44-day company-wide strike of 150,000 members of the United Auto Workers Union against the Ford Motor Company came to an end with a new contract agreement, increasing workers' pay and providing a form of guaranteed annual income.

Oct. 23 The NB Liberal govt of Premier Robichaud was returned to power for the 3rd consecutive time.

Oct. 24 Montreal's payment of over $22 million to the federal govt for Expo '67 was deferred for 2 years to enable Mayor Drapeau to turn the Expo site into a permanent exhibition. On Apr. 2, 1968, Drapeau established a provincial lottery — the 1st such scheme in the country — to help cover the costs of Expo '67. (On May 30, 1968, the 1st winner of the $100,000 grand prize in Montreal's "voluntary tax" lottery was Venetia Barrette of Longueuil.) On May 17, 1968, "Man and his World" opened as an annual fair on the old Expo '67 site.

Also in Oct.
• The amphibious Canadair CL-215 water-bomber was flown for the 1st time. The craft was capable of skimming over the surfaces of large bodies of water and filling its hollow belly with as much as 5,000 litres of water in 10 seconds.

Nov. 7 The Supreme Court of Canada ruled that offshore mineral rights on Canada's West Coast belonged to the federal not the BC govt.

Nov. 9 Cardinal Paul-Émile Léger (1904–1991) retired as Archbishop of Montreal to work as a missionary among lepers in Africa.

Nov. 15 Secretary of State Judy LaMarsh opened the new national Museum of Science and Technology in Ottawa. The new institution's mandate was to study and preserve the "transformation of Canada." The museum's collection includes a Mclaughlin–Buick automobile, survey equipment, early televisions, sound equipment, threshing machines, and a host of other scientific and technological objects that helped change the nation.

Nov. 16 Canadian Coast Guard ship *John A. Macdonald* completed a voyage from Montreal through the Northwest Passage and the Bering Strait to Vancouver, and then south, through the Panama Canal, then north, docking at Dartmouth, NS.

Nov. 19 Ukrainians from all over the world presented former PM John Diefenbaker with the Shevchenko Freedom Award in New York.

Nov. 21–27 PM Pearson visited Britain where he received an honorary degree from the U. of London.

Nov. 23 The House of Commons voted to ban capital punishment for 5 years, except for the murders of police officers or prison guards. The ban would be continued until capital punishment was removed from the Criminal Code and replaced with mandatory life imprisonment on July 14, 1976. Capital punishment was removed from the Canadian National Defence Act (Armed Forces) in 1998.

Nov. 26–30 The provincial premiers' Confederation of Tomorrow Conference was held in Toronto, where delegates reached an agreement on the need to alter Canada's economic and constitutional structure.

Nov. 27 Walter C. Weir (b 1929) succeeded Duff Roblin as Conservative Premier of Man.

Dec. 6 The world's largest underground walkway opened in Montreal: 4.8 km of walkways linked Place Bonaventure with Place Ville Marie and Central Station. The walkway serviced 10 office buildings, 240 shops, 36 restaurants and 4 cinemas.

Dec. 14 PM Pearson announced his intention to resign as leader of the Liberal party after a successor was chosen at the Apr. 6, 1968 national party convention.

Dec. 21 The Royal Mint reduced the silver content of 1967 centennial coins to 50% as a result of rising silver prices.

Dec. 22 Justice Minister Pierre Trudeau proclaimed, "There's no place for the state in the bedrooms of the nation" as he introduced the Omnibus Bill designed to loosen the Canadian Criminal Code's stringent laws on homosexuality and other regulations regarding sex. The bill would go before the House for the last time on May 14, 1969.

Dec. 28 Toronto's 116-year-old St. Lawrence Hall was re-opened after undergoing centennial-project renovations.

Dec. 29 The 10,324-seat Ottawa Civic Centre was completed at Landsdowne Park. Home to the Ottawa 67s, it is the largest rink in the Ontario Hockey League (OHL). The arena was built directly under the sloping grandstands of Landsdowne Park (home to the CFL Ottawa Roughriders), which forced designers to place most of the seats on the opposite side of the rink.

Also in 1967

• The South Saskatchewan River Project was completed. The massive irrigation and hydroelectric project includes the 64-m-high, 5-km-long Gardiner Dam and the 27-m-high, 3.3-km-long Qu'Appelle River Dam. The project blocked and regulated South Sask. waters to form L. Diefenbaker, which covers 43,000 ha of previously arid land. The lake shoreline totals 760 km and has a storage capacity of 9.4 billion m³. Three provincial parks — Douglas Park, Danielson Park and Saskatchewan Landing Park — and 4 municipal parks, are located on L. Diefenbaker shores. The lake is the largest in the province.

• Originally organized as a community heritage project during Canada's Centennial year, Toronto's "Caribana" quickly grew to become the largest Caribbean festival in North America. Featuring a 1.5 km parade, the crowning of the "King and Queen of the Bands," calypso harbour cruises, outdoor concerts, and a 2-day Caribbean arts festival, the event, by the mid-1990s was attracting over 1 million people, hundreds of thousands of them from the US and the islands of Caribbean.

• The waters surrounding Portland Is., north of Sydney, Vancouver Is., were designated as the Princess Margaret Provincial Marine Park. The park is home to river otters, black-tailed deer, mink, bald eagles and oystercatchers. It also includes the wreck of the *G.B. Churde*, deliberately sunk to form BC's 1st artificial reef.

• The not-for-profit Canadian Arab Federation was established in Toronto to address the political interest of Arab-Canadians at the municipal, provincial and federal levels, assist newcomers, provide educational resources, promote Arab cultures and eliminate all forms of anti-Arab prejudice across the country. The national organization has 22 member organizations across the country.

• Everett Klippert was imprisoned as a "dangerous sex offender" after announcing to police in 1965 that he was gay and unlikely to change. The Supreme Court of Canada supported the sentence. Klippert was released from jail on July 20, 1971.

• Mushuau Inuit families were relocated to a permanent settlement of 33 prefabricated homes in Davis Inlet, a small island in the Labrador Sea. Built by the Nfld. govt., and supported by the Catholic Church, Davis Inlet was designed to woo the Inuit away from nomadic traditions. The new community featured a deep-water harbour that was supposed to facilitate delivery of supplies, but the houses had no plumbing, and the remote northern location was inaccessible to all outside aid for a minimum of 3 months every year.

• The Ontario Games for the Physically Disabled were 1st held, in Cambridge, to provide participants with a venue to compete and prepare for national and international events.

• The centennial song *CA-NA-DA* written by Bobby Gimby (b 1919) and recorded by Gimby and The Young Canada Singers, was heard from sea to sea and became Canada's top-selling single of the year.

• Toronto-born composer Harry Somers (1925–1999) composed *Louis Riel*, the opera created for Canada's 1967 centennial. Somers entered the Royal Conservatory of Music at age 16. He was a founding member of the Canadian League of Composers, established in 1951, and a versatile artist who created works for orchestra, voice and piano, and also music for schools, television, films and theatre. Somers was named a Companion of the Order of Canada in 1971.

• The Nikka Yuko Japanese Garden opened in Lethbridge, Alb., as a celebration of Japanese-Canadian friendship. Designed by Dr. Tadashi Kubo of Osaka U., the garden features traditional Japanese structures in a 1.62-ha landscape.

• St. Joseph's Oratory on Mount Royal, Montreal, was completed. Construction had begun in 1924. The 1,000-seat Oratory is considered one of the great world temples, and is visited each year by thousands of pilgrims. It is located on the site of a chapel built by Brother André (Alfredo Bessette [1845–1937]) in 1904. Pope Paul declared Brother André venerable on July 12, 1978.

• The cultural variety show *Les beaux dimanches* premiered on TV Radio-Canada, hosted by Henri Bergeron (1925–2000). The program's lively mixture of politics and the arts, coupled with the gracious and informed commentary of its host, made *Les beaux dimanches* a Que. institution.

• The National Film Board's munificent full-colour centennial portrait of the country was published by McClelland & Stewart as *Canada: A Year of the Land*. Seventy-seven photographs and 260 images were featured in the work. Text was written by journalist Bruce Hutchinson.

• Celebrated Aboriginal painter, Arthur Shilling (1941–1986) held his first solo exhibition in Ottawa.

• Bill Bissett (b 1939) established Blewointment Press. It remained in existence through 1983 as one of Canada's earliest and most influential literary presses.

• *The Georgia Straight,* Vancouver's only independent newspaper, began publication, with Dan McLeod as publisher; 2004 circulation was 122,000 copies per week.

• Novelist Austin Chesterfield Clarke (b 1934) published *The Meeting Point*, the 1st in the "Toronto trilogy" about the life and struggles of West Indians. Other books in the trilogy were *Storm of Fortune* (1973) and *The Bigger Light* (1975).

• Historians JMS Careless and Robert Craig Brown published *The Canadians 1867–1967*.

• West Coast Native artist and author George Charles Clutesi (1905–1988) published *Son of Raven, Son of Deer: Fables of the Tse-shaht People*.

• Louis Dudek published the long poem *Atlantis*.

• Timothy Findley (1930–2002) published his 1st novel, *The Last of the Crazy People*.

• Dave Godfrey, cofounder of the House of Anansi, published the short novel *Death Went Better with Coca-Cola*.

• John Herbert's drama *Fortune and Men's Eyes* opened in the Actor's Playhouse, New York City. The play, set in a single prison cell, addressd the relationship between masculinity and homosexuality. Since its 1st production, the play has been through over 400 productions in over 100 countries. A film version was released in 1971.

• Photographer Roloff Beny (1924–1984) published *To Everything There Is a Season: Roloff Beny in Canada*.

• Alden Nowlan (1933–1983) published a collection of poetry, *Bread, Wine and Salt*, which received the Gov-Gen.'s Award.

• P.K. Page's book of poetry, *Cry Ararat!*, was published.

• Playwright Leonard Byron Peterson (b 1917) published the drama *The Great Hunger,* a 3-act Inuit spinoff of Shakespeare's *Hamlet*.

• Audrey Grace Thomas, née Callahan (b 1935), published her collection of short stories, *Ten Green Bottles*.

• *Alberta: A Natural History*, edited by W.G. Hardy, was published, complete with colour photographs, maps and drawings.

• Sixty-nine-year-old Margaret Craven published her 1st novel, *I Heard the Owl Call My Name*, an international best-seller.

• Dr. James Healey Willan, composer of religious and classical music, was made a Companion of the Order of Canada. The influential composer and teacher wrote over 700 original operas, symphonies, concerts and other works.

• The quarterly journal *Malahat Review: an international magazine of life and letters* was established at the U. of Victoria. Its founders and initial editors were John Peter and Robin Skelton (1925–1977).

• Anne Murray began appearing on the Halifax television music show *Let's Go*.

• Singer-songwriter Bruce Cockburn (b 1945) made his 1st appearance at the Mariposa Folk Festival.

1968

Jan. 2 Canada's 1st indoor track-and-field stadium, built by the Edmonton Kinsmen Club with city and provincial help, opened in Edmonton, Alb.

Jan. 8 Canada pledged $21.6 million to the world food program for 1969 and 1970 at a UN Food and Agricultural Organization conference.

Jan. 22 The bank rate was increased from 6% to 7% in an effort to tighten Canada's money supply.

Jan. 25 Charles F. Wilson, a member of the gang that took part in England's Great Train Robbery, was arrested at Rigaud, Que., more than 3 years after he escaped from prison. Wilson was returned to Britain in the custody of the Scotland Yard.

• The Divorce Act, C–187, Canada's 1st unified divorce law, was given Assent. The new law no longer restricted grounds for divorce to adultery alone. The 16 new grounds for divorce included physical and mental cruelty, desertion and separation of at least 3 years. The annual number of divorces increased from 11,343 in 1968 to 26,079 in 1969. The act was later amended through Bill C–47 (passed into law in 1986), which authorized the granting of divorce solely on the grounds of marital breakdown.

Feb. 14 Pierre Trudeau announced he would run for leadership of the national Liberal party, whose leadership convention was held April 16.

Feb. 15 The Watkins Task Force Report on Foreign Ownership and the Structure of Canadian Investment was tabled in the House of Commons. It recommended a new national policy to protect against the spread of US ownership in Canadian industry, and the creation of the Canadian Development Corporation, which was established by legislation passed June 9, 1971, to provide investment capital to new Canadian ventures. The report led to the creation of the Foreign Investment Review Agency (FIRA), which, in 1975, was given power to screen and prescribe conditions for new investments by foreign-owned companies. The Watkins Task Force was created under the influence of Privy Council president Walter Gordon, who resigned from the council less than a month (Mar. 11) after the task force report was tabled.

Feb. 17 Nancy Greene of Whistler, BC, won gold in the giant slalom, and silver in the slalom at the Winter Olympics in Grenoble, France. Canada's only other Winter Olympic medal was a bronze, awarded to the national men's hockey team.

Feb. 19 The opposition combined in the House of Commons to reject a proposed income tax bill by a vote of 84 to 82, and in the process, blocked all parliamentary business for 3 days. Progressive Conservative MP Gordon Minto Churchill (1898–1985) resigned from the PC caucus on Feb. 27, protesting the Opposition's decision not to pursue a non-confidence motion with defeat of the bill. An amended bill passed Parliament by a vote of 122 to 106 on Mar. 15; it placed a 3% surcharge on corporate and personal income taxes.

• More than 1,000 uranium prospectors staked claims in a 40,470-ha area near Elliot L. Ont., precipitating a uranium-mining boom.

Feb. 22 Que. Union Nationale premier Daniel Johnson constituted, by decree, the Que.-owned television-radio network, to be known as Radio-Québec, for the promotion of education and culture.

Feb. 26 Finance Minister Mitchell William Sharp announced the repatriation of $426 million (US) in money and gold on deposit with the International Monetary Fund to help inflate the dollar.

Feb. 28 Lester Pearson's Liberal govt survived a non-confidence motion by 138 votes to 119.

Mar. 5 The McRuer Royal Commission on Civil Rights in Ont., chaired by Chief Justice James McRuer, tabled its report. The commission noted that although all statutes entering law were debated through the legislative process, the regulations governing the statutes were not. The process there-by placed civil liberties at risk. The commission recommended establishment of independent com-mittees to analyze statute regulation; such commit-tees were established in 1969 through Section 12 of the Ont. Regulations Act.

Mar. 7 External Affairs Minister Paul Martin announc-ed that Canada would participate with the US in developing an airborne radar system (AWACS — Airborne Warning and Aircraft Control System) to replace all or part of the Distant Early Warning (the DEW Line) radar stations in northern Canada.

Mar. 13 Canada Post issued a 5-cent stamp depicting a weather map and instruments in celebration of the bicentenary of the 1st meteorological readings in Canada.

Mar. 15 Gold trading by Canadian banks and other dealers was suspended by the federal govt as inter-national demand for gold skyrocketed. Restrictions were removed on Apr. 3.

Also in Mar.
• McMaster U. in Hamilton, Ont., purchased the collection of letters and papers of English philoso-pher and mathematician Bertrand Russell.

Apr. 1 The Canadian Radio-Television Commission (CRTC) was formed under the Broadcasting Act. The CRTC was to act as a regulatory body for broadcasting, with control over such arenas as licencing and program standards. The agency replaced the Board of Broadcast Governors in the communications industry. The 1st chairman was Pierre Juneau (b 1922), who held the position until 1975.

Apr. 5 The liner *Queen Elizabeth* was sold by Cunard to a Philadelphia businessman for £3.25 million. The ship was taken to Port Everglades, Florida, where it was berthed and opened to the public as a hotel and museum. A money loser, the *QE* was then sold in 1970 to a group headed by C.Y. Tung and renamed the *Seawise University*, planned for use as a mobile university. On Jan. 9, 1972, the ship caught fire and sank in the Hong Kong Harbour before the new *Seawise* could complete its maiden voyage.

Apr. 6 Pierre Elliot Trudeau was elected leader of the Liberal party at the National Liberal Convention in Ottawa on the 4th ballot. Trudeau was sworn in as Canada's 15th prime minister on Apr. 20, succeeding Lester B. Pearson.

Apr. 19 At Massey-Ferguson Industries Ltd. in Toronto and Brantford, Ont., 5,700 workers went on strike for parity with their US counterparts. The strike ended June 29, with workers accepting wage increases without parity.

Apr. 20 A Canadian-US expedition led by Ralph Plaistead of St. Paul, Minnesota, reached the North Pole after 42 days on 4 snowmobiles. Sponsored by the American CBS network, it was the 1st indis-putable arrival at the Pole over sea ice, as the expedition's position was verified by a US Air Force weather aircraft.

Apr. 22 A 6-day strike involving more than 11,000 Ford of Canada workers came to an end as workers accepted wage parity with their Detroit counter-parts.

Apr. 26 The federal govt pledged a long-term inter-est-free loan of $11.3 million for the building of a major electric-power transmission system in Ghana, Togo and Dahomey. This was the largest financing project to date that Canada had under-taken with African nations.

May 3 Canadian Ambassador to France Paul Beaulieu delivered a note of protest to the French govt for treating Que. as an independent state at the Apr. 22–26 international education conference in Paris. (France had asked Que., not Canada, to attend the conference).

May 9 Lester B. Pearson was appointed professor of international affairs at Carleton U. in Ottawa.

May 10 President of Tunisia Habib Bourguiba visited Ottawa.

May 13 The federal govt borrowed more than $262 million from West Germany, the US and Italian sources, to cash reserves, allow payments to the federal reserve board and extend the govt foreign debt.

May 14 The tallest building in Canada to date, the 56-storey Toronto-Dominion Tower in Toronto, part of phase 1 of the Toronto-Dominion Centre in Toronto, was opened. Begun in 1963, the building was designed by German-born architect Ludwig Mies van der Rohe (1886–1969).

May 15 The Centennial Planetarium in Winnipeg opened. The structure was centered around the opto-mechanical Zeiss Model Vs Star Projector, a 154-unit projector that could broadcast images of over 9,000 different stars, the Milky Way, the sun, moon and planets. The Zeiss cost $125,000.

May 17 Mike McIntosh became the 1st undergraduate appointed to a board of govs. of a Canadian university, at St. Francis Xavier U. in Antigonish, NS.

May 23 The British Broadcasting Corp. (BBC) invited former PM Lester Pearson to give the year's prestigious Reith Lectures.

May 24 The American consulate in Quebec City was damaged by an FLQ bomb.

May 27 Montreal was awarded a National League baseball franchise, to be known as the Montreal Expos. The Expos played their 1st official season game Apr. 8, 1969.

May 31 Dr. Pierre Grondin (b 1925) and 21 heart specialists of the Montreal Heart Institute performed Canada's 1st heart transplant on 58-year-old Laval grocer, Albert Murphy.

June 3 The federal govt announced that silver in all new Canadian coinage would be replaced by nickel alloy beginning in Aug. 1968.

June 9 The 3 leaders of the major federal political parties engaged in a CBC/CTV–produced televised debate before the June 25 general election. It was the 1st televised political debate in Canada. The leaders were PM Trudeau (Liberal), Robert Stanfield (Progressive Conservative) and Tommy Douglas (New Democrat Party).

June 10 Members of a Catholic school commission, who promised to force children of non–English speaking immigrants to attend French-language schools, were elected in Montreal's suburban St. Léonard district. On July 11, Que. premier Daniel Johnson affirmed that provincial policy providing immigrants with a schooling choice could not be overturned by local referendums or elections of school board officials. The status quo was upheld until the provincial govt could set a long-term policy for all Que. schools.

June 12 The report of a committee to examine the Ont. educational system (*Living and Learning*) recommended the abolition of grades, percentage marks and corporal punishment, and the reorganization of general subjects such as communications, humanities and environmental studies.

June 13 The Que. La Haye Commission on Urbanization recommended the reorganization of the Municipal Affairs Department, and the appointment of an urban affairs expert.

June 22 The day after summer solstice was marked by labour strife: in Toronto, as some 3,700 city outside workers, including garbage collectors, went on strike until June 27. Across Ont., 2,700 brewery workers went on strike until July 17. In Montreal, 1,200 employees of the St. Lawrence Seaway Authority walked off the job. All received pay increases.

June 23 Auto workers at the American Motors Canada Ltd. plant at Brampton, Ont., were promised wage parity with their US counterparts as part of a 16-month contract.

June 24 Riots broke out in Montreal during St. Jean Baptiste Day celebrations; 290 persons were arrested and 130 injured, including 43 policemen. PM Trudeau was showered with rocks and bottles while watching festivities from a viewing stand.

Four hundred and fifty criminal charges were laid against 210 individuals the next day.

• Oakville, Ont., golfer Sandra Post (b 1943) became the 1st rookie and 1st foreign player to win the US Ladies' PGA Championship. She was 19. Post would go on to win 7 more times on the tour, her last victory coming in 1981.

June 25 Federal Liberals under Pierre Elliott Trudeau retained office in the general election, winning 155 seats; Tories under Robert Stanfield won 72; the NDP under Tommy Douglas won 22; and the Ralliement des Créditistes, under Réal Caouette, 14. There was 1 Independent. Voter turnout was 75.7%.

• Liberal Leonard Marchand (b 1933) became the 2nd Native person after Louis Riel to become a member of federal Parliament after being elected in the riding of Kamloops-Caribou.

• Lincoln MacCauley Alexander (b 1922) was elected MP in Hamilton, Ont., to become Canada's 1st African-Canadian MP.

June 29 Alb. premier Ernest Manning officially opened Calgary's 190-m, $3.5 million Husky Tower, whose top is 1,228 m above sea level.

Also in June
• The *Lady Grenfell*, the last Grenfell Mission ship, was retired. The decision marked the end to the Mission's hospital and nursing services to northern Nfld. and Labrador, which had begun in 1832.

July 1 The federal Medical Care Act, which passed Parliament Dec. 8, 1966, went into effect.

• A bronze statue of former PM W.L. Mackenzie King was unveiled on the lawn of Parliament Hill by Gov-Gen. Michener. The work was created by Que. sculptor Raoul Hunter.

July 3 Sunday horse racing was legalized in Ont.

July 4 The radical El Poder Cubano group exploded a bomb at the offices of the Canadian consulate gen. in New York. There were no casualties.

July 11 Forty Canadian university presidents met at Ottawa to discuss the state of nationwide campus unrest.

July 15 It was announced that the Nfld. railway, the "Newfie Bullet," the 900-km narrow-gauge (3'6") train service operating between St. John's and Port aux Basques, would be retired on Apr. 15, 1969. The train's 1st passenger service commenced June 1898. On Nov. 18, Nfld.'s Board of Public Utilities Commissioners granted permission to the CNR to operate a trans-island, modern, air-conditioned bus service to replace the train. "Newfie Bullet" train cars were donated to the National Museum of Science and Technology in Ottawa.

July 17 Former PM Pearson became president of the Institute for Strategic Studies, a defence and disarmament research centre in London, England.

July 18 A nationwide postal strike involved 24,000 workers, until Aug. 9. Workers returned to work with the Rand Formula, an employee dues scheme 1st used by Ivan Rand in 1945 to settle a strike.

July 22 A fire caused $2.5 million in damages to the historic Basilica of St. Boniface, Man., destroying priceless items of early western Canadian history.

• Canada signed the Nuclear Non-proliferation Treaty at Moscow, London, England, and Washington, D.C. The treaty restricted the possession of nuclear weapons to China, Russia, France, the UK and the US. These nuclear-states agreed not to share or transfer weapons or related material to non-nuclear states; non-nuclear states agreed not to acquire or produce nuclear weaponry. On Jan. 8, 1969, Canada became the 6th of 80 countries to ratify the treaty.

Aug. 2 A surgical team headed by Dr. André Gilbert successfully performed the 1st kneecap transplant in Quebec City.

Aug. 16 Air Canada acquired 40% of Air Jamaica stock.

Aug. 18 The Ont. govt proclaimed the Moosonee Development Area Board Act, creating Canada's 1st Aboriginal self-governing municipality — a community of approximately 1,500 residents on the shores of James Bay.

Aug. 19 Lester Pearson was appointed to head a World Bank international commission to study future economic aid to developing countries.

• The Post Office announced the closing of the Post Office Savings Banks, after a century of operation.

Aug. 21 The Soviet Union invaded Czechoslovakia. The move was censured by the Canadian govt, which quickly established a 4-month program (at a cost of between $8– $10 million), to take in Czechoslovakian refugees. The 1st of more than 10,000 refugees arrived in Canada Sept. 8.

Aug. 26 The good ship *Nonsuch II* was launched in Appledore, England. It was a replica of the original 17th-century Hudson's Bay Company *Nonsuch*, which sailed out of London on June 5, 1668. The new ship was built to commemorate the 300th anniversary of the HBC.

Aug. 28 Playwright Michel Tremblay's *Les Belles-Soeurs* premiered in Quebec City, one of the 1st plays to incorporate Que.'s colloquial "joual."

Aug. 30 PM Trudeau cancelled the make-work Winter Works Program, started in 1958–1959.

Sept. 1 In Toronto, about 2,000 striking employees of the Goodyear Tire and Rubber Company of Canada agreed to return to work since striking May 3. The new 3-year contract gave workers a wage increase of about $1.05 an hour, plus benefits.

Sept. 6–8 Jamaica PM Hugh Shearer visited Ottawa.

Sept. 11 Charles Lavern Beasley of Texas attempted the 1st air hijacking in Canada, when he ordered a Toronto-bound flight from Moncton, NB, to Cuba. Beasley gave himself up during a refuelling stop at Dorval Airport, Montreal, and was sentenced to 6 years' imprisonment on Dec. 10.

Sept. 12 Lakehead grain handlers ended an 8-week strike, agreeing to a wage increase of over $1 an hour over 3 years, plus improved benefits.

Sept. 20 The federal govt cancelled development of the $150 million Intense Neutron Generator (ING), an ambitious plan by Chalk R. physicists to build a

thermal nuclear facility designed to outperform all existing nuclear power generators.

Sept. 26 The 220-megawatt (MW) Douglas Point, Ont., nuclear power plant went into commercial operation. It was the 1st CANDU (Canada Deuterium Uranium) reactor to go into commercial operation in the country.

• Que. Union Nationale premier Daniel Johnson died of a heart attack while en route to inaugurate what is now the Hydro-Quebec Daniel Johnson Dam, a giant 214-m-tall concrete structure spanning the Manicouagan R. north of Comeau. The dam was dedicated to the late premier Sept. 26, 1969. On Oct. 2, Jean-Jacques Bertrand succeeded Johnson as Union Nationale premier of Que.

Sept. 28 BC Premier W.A.C. Bennett opened the 2,730-megawatt (MW) capacity Dr. Gordon M. Shrum Powerhouse, part of the $485 million Peace R. hydroelectric project at Hudson Hope, BC. The powerhouse is part of the W.A.C. Bennett Dam, which was completed in 1967. The dam holds back the waters of BC's largest body of water — Williston Reservoir — which has over 1,600 km of shoreline.

Also in Sept.

• Rochdale College opened in downtown Toronto as Canada's 1st free university, where students organized their own classes and curriculum. A BA could be obtained for $25, an MA for $50 and a Ph.D. for $100. Rochdale was also U. of Toronto's 1st co-op residence, and a lightning rod for radical thought and alternative living. The residence attracted a mixed crowd of students, American draft dodgers, drug dealers, bikers and street people, and was soon considered one of the city's greatest dens of iniquity. A July 30, 1974, riot between Rochdale residents and police precipitated the college's demise. The last tenants were removed May 30, 1975, and Rochdale's doors were spot welded closed.

Oct. 2 PM Trudeau unveiled a statue of Louis Riel in Regina, Sask.

Oct. 4 Southern Ont. farmers demonstrated on Parliament Hill against the price of corn.

Oct. 6 MPs David MacDonald and Andrew Brewin released a report on war and starvation in Biafra. (The short-lived [1967–1970] breakoff state of Nigeria.) As a result, Canada agreed to fly relief supplies to Biafra for the International Red Cross. On Nov. 15, after 11 successful trips by Canadian relief planes, the Canadian govt cancelled the airlift program. The govt then announced that Canadian families and institutions would be allowed to adopt children orphaned in the Nigeria-Biafra Civil War.

Oct. 7 Students occupied Lionel Groulx College in Ste. Thérèse, Que., demanding a 2nd French-language university in Montreal (after the Université de Montréal), better job preparation in schools and a govt program to create more jobs.

Oct. 9 Acadia U. at Wolfeville, NS, established a Canada-Commonwealth Caribbean Centre for the study of matters of interest to both Canada and Caribbean members of the Commonwealth.

Oct. 11 The US govt awarded Canada $52 million as payment to BC for Canadian flood control of US territory through the Columbia R. project.

Oct. 11–15 At a convention in Que., the Mouvement Souverainété-Association and the Ralliement Nationale amalgamated to form Le Parti Québécois with a membership of 20,000. Former journalist and Que. Liberal MPP René Lévesque was chosen leader of the new party.

Oct. 14 CF-TCA No. 1112, the 1st aircraft acquired by Trans-Canada Airlines (Air Canada) in 1937, was presented to the National Museum of Science and Technology.

Oct. 15 Atomic Energy of Canada Limited (AECL) signed a 5-year agreement with the Commissariat à l'Énergie Atomique of France to share nuclear information.

Oct. 17 Ont. increased its minimum wage from $1 to $1.30 an hour for workers involved in general industry, and from $1.25 to $1.55 for those in construction, effective on Jan. 1, 1969.

Oct. 25 The $32 million international airport terminal in Vancouver officially opened.

Oct. 26 The $35 million Centennial Museum–MacMillan Planetarium complex opened in Vancouver as a gift from lumber baron Harvey MacMillan (1885–1976), whose H.L. MacMillan Export Co. merged in 1951 to become MacMillan-Bloedel. The planetarium was renamed the Pacific Spruce Centre in 1997, and the H.R. MacMillan Space Centre in 2000.

Oct. 28 Canada's only gold medal at the Olympic Summer Games in Mexico City was won by the equestrian team of Tom Gayford (b 1928), Jim Day (b 1946) and Jim Elder (b 1934).

Nov. 1 Postage for a 1st class letter broke the nickel mark, increasing from 5 cents to 6 cents.

Nov. 4 The federal govt announced its intention to drop out of the federal-provincial medicare program in 5 years, at which time additional taxation powers would be turned over to the provinces to pay for the system.

Nov. 17 The World Cup golf tournament (now the Canada Cup) was won by Al Balding (b 1924) and George Knudson (b 1937), who defeated 41 other national teams in Rome, Italy. It was the 1st Canadian victory since Canada donated the cup in 1953.

Nov. 20–22 Canada's Finance Minister Edgar J. Benson and Bank of Canada Gov. Louis Rasminsky attended a financial meeting in Bonn, Germany, a Group of 10 ministers to discuss how to restore equilibrium in the international monetary system, disrupted by massive speculative ventures and related European-currency devaluations.

Nov. 25 Students ended a 3-day occupation of the administration building at Simon Fraser U. in Vancouver. The protest followed failed student–administration talks on education costs. Police charged 114 people.

Nov. 26 Que. Liquor Board employees ended a strike, which began June 26.

Nov. 27 The International Dance Festival in Paris, France, gave Gold Star awards to the Royal Winnipeg Ballet, as best ballet company at the festival, and to Christine Hennessy, its prima ballerina, for best female interpretation.

Also in Nov.

• Wheelchair racer Hilda May Torok Binns became the 1st Canadian physically challenged gold medallist, winning 2 gold medals and a silver medal at the Tel Aviv Paralympic Games, then called the International Stokes Mandeville Games for the Paralyzed.

Dec. 2 The federal govt offered Canada's coastal provinces a 9% share of the Canadian continental shelf, while retaining control of the area beyond the 800 m–1.6 km offshore line.

Dec. 6 Harry Edwin Strom (1914–1984) was elected leader of the Social Credit Party in Alb., succeeding Ernest C. Manning who had announced his retirement Sept. 27. Manning had served as Alb. premier for 25 uninterrupted years. Strom assumed his new position Dec. 12.

Dec. 9 The 2nd report of the Royal Commission on Bilingualism and Biculturalism recommended that all children in Canadian schools be required to study the 2nd official language, and the federal govt make available grants to implement the recommendation.

• Bill 85, guaranteeing the right to English-language education, was introduced in the Que. legislature by the Union Nationale govt. On Mar. 19, 1969, Que. premier Jean-Jacques Bertrand announced that the language bill would not be pursued because of continued opposition.

• Transport Minister Paul Hellyer made the controversial announcement authorizing Crown corporation Air Canada to sell its Winnipeg overhaul base and move to Montreal.

Dec. 13 Que. passed legislation to abolish its appointed upper chamber, the Legislative Council, effective Dec. 31. The name of the Legislative Assembly was changed to the National Assembly (Assemblée Nationale) of Que.

Dec. 18 Native Peoples of the St. Regis Reserve blocked the Seaway International Bridge at Cornwall,

Ont., to protest the imposition of customs duties on their purchases in the US. The protesters claimed exemption under the Jay's Treaty of 1794.

Dec. 26 The NS govt transferred management of the Dominion Steel and Coal Corporation (Dosco) to Sidbec, a Que. Crown corporation.

Dec. 30 H.P. MacKeen, (b 1909) former lt-gov. of NS, was appointed Acadia U.'s 1st chancellor.

1968–1969 Three NHL players — Phil Esposito (b 1942) of the Boston Bruins, Gordie Howe of the Detroit Red Wings and Bobby Hull (b 1939) of the Chicago Blackhawks — each scored 100 points in 1 season, an NHL record.

1968–1970 Abe Okpik (1929–1997) served as director of Project Surname in the NWT, designed to replace the Canadian govt's policy (introduced in the 1940s) of assigning numbers rather than names to residents of the territory. Okpik travelled extensively through the NWT interviewing every inhabitant, in order to ascertain what official surname each individual wanted to be known by.

Also in 1968

• Aboriginals in Que. were allowed to vote in provincial elections for the 1st time.

• CBC Radio's *As It Happens* went on the air as hosts William Ronald (1926–1998) and Harry Brown (1932–2002) interviewed newsmakers, politicians, and frequently, eccentric individuals from across Canada and around the world. In 1971, Barbara Frum (1937–1992) joined the show as a host until 1982 when she became anchor for a new CBC-TV nightly show *The Journal*.

• The McGill Student Society released *The Birth Control Handbook*, a controversial and dangerous publication (because distribution of information on birth control was illegal in Canada). The handbook rapidly became an underground best-seller and, is published today through the Montreal Health Press.

• Sydney Steel Corp., with an annual production of 910,000 tonnes — one of the largest in the nation — was purchased by the province of NS.

• Archaeologists uncovered 12, 1,000-year-old Native burial mounds on a hillside near Crooked L., Sask. The dead had been wrapped in buffalo hides and placed on scaffolds with food and tools. The skeletal remains had been rubbed with ochre and covered with mounds of earth.

• The Department of Agriculture's Experimental Farms in Ottawa issued the 1st in its Explorer series of hardy hybridized, Canadian climate-tolerant roses. The 1st rose was the Martin Frobisher. The other 24 in the series were: Jens Munk (1974), Henry Hudson (1976), John Cabot (1978), David Thompson (1979), John Franklin (1980), Champlain (1982), Charles Albanel (1982), William Baffin (1983), Henry Kelsey (1984), Alexander Mackenzie (1985), John Davis (1986), J.P. Connell (1987), Captain Samuel Holland (1992), Frontenac (1992), Louis Jolliet (1992), Simon Fraser (1992), George Vancouver (1994), Lambert Closse (1995), Royal Edward (1995), Quadra (1995), Nicholas (1996), De Montarville (1997) and Marie-Victorin (1998). The last in the series was William Booth (1999), after which the rose program in Ottawa shut down due to budget restraints.

• The Canadian Film Awards was reorganized to recognize the contributions of craftspeople and performers. An executive committee that included representatives of key industry associations, guilds and unions was established. The group commissioned an awards statue created by Romanian-born sculptor Sorel Etrog. Known as the Etrog until 1979, the award would be renamed the Genie in that year.

• The 1st Canadian-designed telephone, the Contempra, was introduced to the marketplace.

• Carrol Baker (b 1949) said she gave up her dream of being a rock and roll singer when she heard a country and western song in a club while on her honeymoon. Born in Medway, NS, Baker released her 1st record — Mem'ries of Home — in 1970. The song remained on Canadian country charts for 26 weeks. From 1975 to 1982, Baker had 22 top 10 recordings among her songs, including "I've Never Been This Far Before," which went on to become a No. 1 hit in the US for Conway Twitty.

• Royal Bank, Toronto-Dominion Bank, Canadian Imperial Bank of Commerce and Banque Canadienne Nationale introduced the Chargex (Visa) credit card to Canada.

• Contemporary artist Greg Curnoe (1936–1992) had a section of his mural at Dorval Airport in Montreal censored and removed by Transport Canada, who claimed it was anti-American. The section in question showed Muhammed Ali, stripped of his World Heavyweight title, refusing to take an entrance oath into the US military. Curnoe offered to paint the word "Censored" over the scenes rather than see them removed. His offer was rejected. Curnoe died in 1992 in a collision with a pickup truck while cycling near his home in Windsor, Ont. He was 55.

• The teepee-style Église du Précieux Sang, designed by Métis Étienne Gaboury (b 1930), was completed in St. Boniface, Man. The conical-shaped Roman Catholic church featured 11 interior wood beams spiralling upward to form a smoke-hole-like skylight 30 m above the altar.

• Alb.-born architect Douglas Cardinal (b 1934) completed his 1st public commission, the complex, curvilinear St. Mary' Roman Catholic Church, in Red Deer, Alb.

• Anne Murray recorded her 1st album, *What About Me*.

• Leonard Cohen recorded the single "Suzanne."

• The Boss Brass, a 16-piece, all-brass jazz orchestra with rhythm section, was formed under the leadership of valve trombonist Rob McConnell (b 1935). With its self-titled recording of the same year, Boss Brass established itself as one of the most innovative jazz ensembles on the continent.

• William Kurelek (1927–1977) completed, in oil, *Manitoba Mountain*.

• Novelist Hubert Aquin published the novel *Trou de mémoire*, for which he declined the Gov-Gen.'s Award.

• Roch Carrier published the novel *La Guerre, Yes Sir!*

• Robert Gurik produced the play, rich in political satire, *Hamlet, Prince du Québec.*

• Poet Don Gutteridge (b 1937) published *Riel.*

• Journalist Edna Staebler (b 1906) published her best-selling cookbook *Food that Really Schmecks*, a combination of Dutch-Mennonite, German and modern Canadian culinary traditions. Staebler followed her 1st offering with *More Food that Really Schmecks* (1998) and *Schmecks Appeal* (2002).

• Short-story writer Alice Munro (b 1931) published *Dance of the Happy Shades and Other Stories*, for which she received the Gov-Gen.'s Award.

• FLQ member Pierre Vallières (b 1938) published *Nègres blancs d'Amérique* (translated as *White Niggers of America*, 1971) while awaiting trial on charges related to terrorist bomb blasts in Montreal. On Dec. 15, 1969, Vallières was found guilty of manslaughter in the death of Thérèse Morin of Montreal, the result of a May 1966 bombing.

• Vancouver architect Arthur Erickson (b 1924) designed the 1st buliding of Lethbridge U.: University Hall, located in Old Man River Valley, outside Lethbridge, Alb. The structure, which cost $12.2 million to build, covers an area of 41,806 m², stands 9 stories high, and is 277.9 m long.

1969

Jan. 1 The cities of Ottawa and Eastview, the county of Carleton and township of Cumberland, were unified into the Regional Municipality of Ottawa-Carleton. Ont. govt approval for the move was given Feb. 2, 1968.

• Halifax annexed 5 western suburbs, increasing the city's population to 123,000.

Jan. 7 Native Peoples and Métis groups met with the Man. Natural Resources minister to oppose a $29 million Man. Hydro project, slated to raise the Southern Indian L. 10.7 m and divert 80% of the Churchill R. waters, causing potential damage to the trapping and fishing industry, while displacing hundreds of local residents. On Sept. 15, the Man. govt backed away from the plan.

Jan. 19 The Soviet national hockey team played the 1st game of its Canadian tour with a Canadian national team composed almost entirely of juniors. The Soviets won all 8 games.

Jan. 24 An agreement between France and Que. to study the development of a communications satellite system was criticized in the House of Commons because of Que.'s failure to inform the federal govt of its intentions.

• The International Satellites for Ionospheric Studies (ISISA), Canada's 3rd space satellite, was launched from Vandenberg Air Force Base in California as a communications satellite.

Jan. 29 Recommendations of the final report of the federal Task Force on Housing included the elimination of down payments on homes for middle- and lower-income earners, the abolition of sales taxes on building materials for residential construction and a halt to the building of large public-housing projects.

• The computer centre of Sir George Williams U. in Montreal was occupied by Canadian and West Indian students to protest the manner in which the university was handling charges of racism levelled against one of its professors. On Feb. 11, demonstrators destroyed the $1.4 million computer centre and set fire to the university's data centre. Ninety adults and 7 juveniles were charged with conspiracy to commit mischief and arson when the occupation ended Feb. 12. On Mar. 14, eight Trinidadian students were convicted of conspiracy to obstruct the use of the computer centre and fined a total of $32,500, or up to 4 years in prison. They were also ordered deported.

Jan. 31 The Council of the NWT selected its new flag, which featured blue borders at each end of a white field, with the NWT coat of arms in the centre.

Feb. 1 Canada Post eliminated Saturday mail-delivery service and closed its post offices to Saturday service.

• Joni Mitchell played New York's Carnegie Hall.

• A new program of medical care came into effect in northwestern Ont. as U. of Toronto teaching-hospital doctors began rotating shifts at the Sioux Lookout govt hospital and in 5 nursing stations in outlying communities.

Feb. 3 A painting of the Fathers of Confederation by Toronto artist Rex Woods was unveiled on Parliament Hill. Commissioned by the Confederation Life Association as a centennial project, it replaced the original work by Robert Harris that had been destroyed in the Parliament Hill fire of 1916.

Feb. 10–12 Delegates at a federal-provincial constitutional conference in Ottawa reached agreement to study constitutional reforms and the recommendations set out by the Royal Commission on Bilingualism and Biculturalism Feb. 25, 1965 and Dec. 9, 1968.

Feb. 11–Mar. 4 The 1st official state visit undertaken by a Canadian gov-gen. was made by Gov-Gen. Roland Michener and his wife, Norah, when they visited 4 Caribbean countries.

Feb. 13 A bomb explosion injured 27 people and caused an estimated $1 million in damages to the Montreal and Canadian Stock Exchanges. Rewards totalling $50,000 were offered for information leading to the arrest of the guilty parties. Police suspected the bombing to be the work of the FLQ.

Feb. 20 Health Minister John Munro (b 1931) announced the formation of Hockey Canada, a federal corporation to develop a competitive national hockey team for international competition. Hockey Canada would also lobby unsuccessfully for the incorporation of Canadian professional players in Olympic and World Championship play.

Feb. 21 Réjane Laberge-Colas (b 1923) was appointed to the Que. Superior Court, the 1st woman in Canada to be named to a Superior Court bench.

Feb. 23 Pacific Hovercraft began the 1st scheduled hovercraft service in Canada between Vancouver and Nanaimo.

Mar. 5 The Trudeau govt pledged to PEI and NB improved ferry services and terminals, and a 15-year $225 million program to upgrade the PEI agriculture, tourist, fishery and forest industries in place of a previously committed causeway linking PEI and NB.

Mar. 6 The papers and memorabilia of Wilfrid Laurier were displayed at the National Library in Ottawa.

Mar. 7 FLQ member Pierre-Paul Geoffroy (b 1941) of Berthier, Que., pleaded guilty to 129 charges of making and placing bombs, conspiracy, theft and possession of dynamite in connection with 31 bombings in the Montreal area. Geoffroy was sentenced to life imprisonment on Apr. 1.

Mar. 11–Apr. 5 An RCMP dogsled was driven from Old Crow, Yukon, to Fort McPherson, marking the end to the RCMP's use of dogsleds. The snowmobile was adopted instead, as a more modern solution to northern transport.

Mar. 25 PM Trudeau explained to an American audience at the National Press Club in Washington that, "Living next to you is like sleeping with an elephant; no matter how friendly and even-tempered is the beast, one is affected by every twitch and grunt."

Mar. 27 Que. lawyer Louis Marceau was appointed Que.'s 1st ombudsman. He sat from May 1, 1969 to Jan. 15, 1976.

Mar. 29 Some 6,000 demonstrators marched on McGill to demand that the university be made a French-language institution. About 25 persons were later arrested and charged with disturbing the peace, carrying offensive weapons and assaulting policemen.

• The Government Organization Act, 1969, to eliminate govt duplication, simplify administrative structure and provide better service to the public, received Assent.

Mar. 31 The Sask. legislature adopted its official flag from design submissions in a province-wide contest. Based on the design of Anthony Drake, the flag is divided into 2 horizontal bands: the top green band represents northern forest; the bottom gold band represents fields of grain. Included at top left is the provincial shield of arms, and at the right, the provincial floral emblem, a single western red lily.

Also in Mar.

• Montreal recorded 64 terrorist bombings of armouries, public buildings and businesses.

Apr. 1 Que. legalized civil marriages.

Apr. 2 The Ont. govt announced that ores mined in the province after Jan. 1, 1970, must be processed in Canada.

Apr. 3 PM Trudeau unveiled plans to reorient Canadian defence priorities, placing Canadian sovereignty and the defence of North America at the top of the list. The reorganization included a reduction in the size of both the regular force and the reserves. Trudeau also announced that the country's commitment to NATO would be downgraded, his cabinet having decided just days before to cut the number of soldiers in Europe from 10,000 to 5,000. The cuts were made in Aug., and remaining ground forces were transferred from British to American command. More changes were announced in Sept: the Canadian Guards to be disbanded (1970), and the Queen's Own Rifles and the Black Watch (Royal Highland Regiment) reverted to reserve (1970); the aircraft carrier HMCS *Bonaventure* to be retired early in Halifax on Dec. 12, after 12 years of service; and 41 armouries closed across the country.

Apr. 8 The Montreal Expos of the National Baseball League played their 1st game, defeating the New York Mets 11–10 at Shea Stadium. Dan McGinn hit the Expos 1st home run in the 3rd inning off future Hall-of-Famer Tom Seaver.

Apr. 14 Former PM and ardent baseball fan Lester Pearson threw out the 1st pitch on the Montreal Expos' Opening Day at Jarry Park. It was the 1st Major League Baseball game played outside the US. The Expos defeated the St. Louis Cardinals 8–7 before a sellout crowd of 29,184. Three days later, on Apr. 17, the Expos' Bill Stoneman threw the team's 1st no-hitter, blanking the Philadelphia Phillies 7–0 in Philadelphia.

Apr. 17 A 32-page, hand-written account of the 1870 Northwest Rebellion, by Louis Riel, was purchased by the govt for $16,000.

• Economist Dr. Sylvia Ostry (b 1927) was appointed director of the Economic Council of Canada, the highest post ever held by a woman in govt service.

Apr. 20 Air Canada was grounded when 6,200 members of the International Association of Machinists and Aerospace Workers went on strike for wage parity with their US counterparts. They demanded a 20% increase in wages in a 1-year contract, and returned to work May 19, with wages increased 16% over 26 months, plus benefits.

Apr. 21 George Knudson, the best Canadian golfer of his generation and one of the best ball-strikers on the Professional Golf Association tour, finished 2nd to George Archer at the Masters, missing a putt on the 72nd hole that would have led to a playoff. It was the closest a Canadian would ever come to winning the prestigious event, until Apr. 3, 2003. Knudson won 8 PGA events over his career and was a 5-time Canadian PGA champion. He died in 1989 after a lengthy battle with cancer.

Apr. 24 Transport Minister Paul Hellyer resigned his cabinet post disputing a policy giving priority to constitutional reform over housing legislation.

Apr. 28 Donald Johnston and Sidney Durward were sentenced to 14 years in prison, in what is believed to be the harshest penalty ever handed down in Canada for possession of marijuana for the purposes of trafficking.

Also in Apr.

• A 4.8-km causeway to the artificial island of Roberts Bank, south of Vancouver, was opened, providing access to a deep-sea port developed for shipping BC and Alb. coal to Japan. On Apr. 30, 1970, the 1st new CP Rail computer-commanded coal train reached Roberts Bank from Alb. Mines.

May 2 The federal govt and Trans-Canada Telephone Systems concluded an agreement to form Telesat Canada, for the development of communications satellites.

• Gatherings were held in cities across Canada to commemorate the 50th anniversary of the Winnipeg General Strike.

• The Political Action Committee of the Confederation of National Trade Unions urged affiliated unions to form a "second front," a social conscience that would serve as a guardian over public interests.

• The Agriculture Department recommended a 14% reduction in wheat acreage to help ease the world wheat surplus.

May 3 Majestic Prince became the 2nd Canadian horse to win the Kentucky Derby. Northern Dancer was 1st in 1964. Thoroughbred fans would have to wait until May 7, 1983, to see another Canadian horse take the grand event.

• The Union Nationale caucus in Que. declared its allegiance to Premier Jean-Jacques Bertrand, who reaffirmed his faith "in a renewed federal structure" consisting of "10 federal states and 2 nations."

May 4 The federal govt banned herring fishing and the export of fish from the waters around Placentia Bay, Nfld., because of mass deaths of fish due to pollution.

• Forillon National Park was created along the eastern tip of the Gaspé Peninsula, Que. the 1st national park in the province. It covers 244 km² of striking coastal cliff, and protects the northernmost extension of the Appalachian Mountains, which roll into the Atlantic. Ninety-five percent of the park is forested. The park also included the Pointe-au-Père lighthouse, a National Historic Site that rises 30 m above the St. Lawrence.

May 5 *Miles for Millions* community walk, organized by volunteers across Canada, raised nearly $3 million for 15 major charitable organizations. Over 55,000 participants from coast to coast joined in what was the biggest charity walk in the country to date.

May 7 The CBC banned all new tobacco-advertising contracts with its radio and television networks, and announced that its existing tobacco-advertising contracts would run out as scheduled.

May 8 Plans were released for establishment at Canso, NS, of Canada's 1st commercial plant to produce fish protein to help alleviate the world's protein shortage. The $4.6 million Cardinal Protein Ltd. plant was completed in 1970, but the firm soon went bankrupt and the plant sold at a sheriff's sale in 1973.

May 12 The federal and US govt agreed to accept a proposal made by an International Joint Commission to establish pollution controls on the Red R.

May 14 The House of Commons passed the Liberal govt's Omnibus Bill (Bill C–150) 149–55. The bill liberalized laws on abortion for the 1st time since Confederation. It also legalized the dissemination of birth control information and birth control itself, as well as homosexual acts between consenting adults.

May 26–June 2 John Lennon and Yoko Ono held their 2nd week-long "Bed-In" for peace in suite 1742 of the Queen Elizabeth Hotel, Montreal, at which time they recorded the hit song "Give Peace A Chance." (The Bed-In was originally planned for the Caribbean, but Lennon found the warm climate unaccommodating.) The Queen Elizabeth subsequently offered "John and Yoko Getaway" packages, which included a night's stay in the same suite, a bottle of wine, lyrics to "Give Peace a Chance" and the same breakfast had by the famous pair — starting at $230.

May 28 Alb. Premier Harry Strom (b 1914) opened the Alb. Resources Railway, a 378-km line from Grande Prairie north to Solomon.

May 29 A Commission of Inquiry into the non-medical use and abuse of drugs and substances was established by the federal govt with Gerald LeDain chief commissioner. Its 1st report was issued Jan. 26, 1972.

June 2 The 107,582-m² hexagonal National Arts Centre (NAC) designed by Fred Lebensold, officially opened in Ottawa as the only bilingual performing arts centre in North America. Brainchild of PM Pearson, the $46 million (approximately) NAC, with its 3 theatres — Southern Hall (2,326 seats), Theatre (967 seats) and Studio (300 seats) — is home to the NAC orchestra, also established in 1969, and over 130 works of Canadian art. PM Trudeau, with date, was on hand for the inaugural, and premiere performance of Roland Petit's *Kraanerg*, with futuristic music by Greek Iannis Xenakis.

June 4 Premiers Robarts of Ont. and Bertrand of Que. agreed to establish a permanent Commission for Ont.-Que. Co-operation, providing public services in English and French languages and education to minority-language groups wherever feasible.

June 11–12 The 3rd Federal-Provincial Constitutional Conference was held in Ottawa in private, the press being excluded for the 1st time. An agreement was reached permitting provinces to block federal spending in areas of provincial jurisdiction and granting provinces access to all fields of taxation.

June 12–13 The Canadian Progress Club sponsored the Canadian Special Olympics for mentally and physically challenged athletes, in Toronto.

June 19 The Prices and Incomes Commission was formed to study the causes and effects of inflation and suggest means to stabilize prices. The chairman was Dr. John Young of BC.

June 25 Indian Affairs Minister Jean Chrétien tabled his White Paper on Indian Affairs, proposing assimilation of Native Peoples through the gradual elimination of Native rights, and termination of treaties. The paper also proposed to phase out the Indian Affairs Department. Native Peoples across the nation were outraged. On June 4, 1970, Native representatives met with PM Trudeau.

• Man. NDP leader Edward Richard Schreyer (b 1935) won the provincial election, beating Premier Walter Weir's Progressive Conservatives. The NDP took 28 of 57 seats, becoming the 1st NDP govt in the province's history.

June 26 Among the recommendations in the report of the Royal Commission into the operation of Canadian security methods was the restructuring of the RCMP directorate of security and intelligence, and the establishment of an independent review board to hear complaints about security decisions.

June 27 US President Richard M. Nixon visited the Place des Nations at Man and His World in Montreal, to commemorate the 10th anniversary of the St. Lawrence Seaway.

July 2 The 1st college of veterinary medicine in western Canada opened at the U. of Sask., Saskatoon.

• The House of Commons passed amendments to the Canada Shipping Act providing for govt regulation of air-cushion vehicles on navigable waters, and giving Parliament jurisdiction over ship-related water pollution.

July 10 More than 17,000 members of the United Steel Workers of America went on strike against Inco plants in Ont., causing a world shortage in nickel. Strikers returned to work after 128 days, on Nov.14.

July 19 In Lethbridge, Alb., PM Trudeau announced that western farmers would receive interest-free cash payments for farm-stored grain to a total amount of $250 million, to start on Aug. 1.

July 20 Neil Armstrong, the 1st person to walk on the moon, left there a disk of miniaturized messages from 73 world leaders. PM Trudeau's was, "Man has reached out and touched the tranquil moon."

July 23 Sask. increased its minimum hourly wage requirements from $1.05 to $1.25 for urban workers and from 95 cents to $1.15 for rural workers.

July 24 Controversial Standing Orders 115, 116 and 117 were passed, establishing new procedures by which the House of Commons could set a time schedule for a bill at one or more stages of the legislative process.

July 25 At the Fillmore East in New York, Neil Young (b 1945) made his 1st concert appearance with Crosby, Stills and Nash. In 1970, the band became known as Crosby, Stills, Nash and Young (CSNY).

Aug. 1 Sask. Premier Ross Thatcher announced that feed grain would be accepted as payment for university tuition for children of Sask. farmers.

Aug. 5 The Department of Energy, Mines and Resources completed a series of 918 topographical maps of Canada, on a scale of 4 miles to the inch.

Aug. 9 Indian Affairs and Northern Development Minister Jean Chrétien officially opened Kejimkujik National Park, 170 km southwest of Halifax, NS. The 381-km^2 inland park preserves typical Atlantic Coast plain, characterized by exposed metamorphic rock, eskers, drumlins, kames, outwashes and lakes, all formed during the last glaciation. The forest is refuge to moose, white-tailed deer, hare, black bear, bobcat, fox and porcupine. A separate 22-km coastal strip, the Seaside Adjunct, was established as part of the park in 1988.

Aug. 13 Defence Minister Léo Cadieux announced the closure of the military base at Clinton, Ont., supply depots at London and Cobourg, Ont., as well as Ville LaSalle, Montreal, and a reduction in the operations at St. Hubert, Que.

• Govt expenditures were frozen by the federal govt in an attempt to halt inflation.

Aug. 24 The US oil tanker *Manhattan* left Chester, Pennsylvania, on a trial voyage through the Northwest Passage to prove the feasibility of the route for transporting Arctic oil. With the assistance of the Canadian icebreaker CCGS *John A. Macdonald* and the USCG *Westwind*, the *Manhattan* reached Sachs Harbour, NWT, on Sept. 15.

Aug. 27 A general election in BC returned Social Credit Premier W.A.C. Bennett to power with 39 seats. The NDP took 11, the Liberals 5.

Aug. 28 The govt of BC passed legislation ordering compulsory mediation in a strike of 550 oil workers employed by 6 companies.

Aug. 29 A 2-year dispute between 70,000 Que. elementary and secondary teachers and the Que. govt and local school boards ended on a renewed collective agreement.

Sept. 7 The Official Languages Act (An Act Respecting the Official Languages of Canada), passed in the House in July, received Assent, extending the minimal guarantees already established in the BNA Act and asserting that Canada was one nation with 2 languages. English and French became official languages of the federal administration. Bilingual districts were created in all provinces except Nfld. and BC.

Sept. 10 The Riot Act was read to French-speaking students at St. Léonard, a suburb of Montreal, following explosive demonstrations and demands that instruction in schools be provided in French only. Raymond Lemieux, president of the Ligue pour l'intégration scolaire, was arrested. The conflict started in 1968 when the St. Léonard Catholic School Board announced it would phaseout its English-language schools. The Que. Superior Court supported the action, which sparked angry opposition from the St. Léonard Italian community, which demanded that their children be taught in English. In Aug. 1970, the St. Léonard School Board reversed its French-only stand.

Sept. 11 A college for advanced aerospace studies was opened at the Space Research Institute on the Canada-US border, at Highwater, Que., and North Troy, Vermont.

Sept. 13 The Toronto Rock 'n' Roll Revival was held at Varsity Stadium. Performers included The Doors, John Lennon & The Plastic Ono Band, Chuck Berry, Little Richard, Jerry Lee Lewis and Bo Diddley. During a set by a then little-known Alice Cooper, an alleged live chicken was thrown onstage and never made it back to roost.

Sept. 16 Atomic Energy of Canada Limited (AECL) sold a nuclear research reactor to Taiwan for $35 million. The reactor went on line in 1971.

Sept. 18 In Winnipeg, John Diefenbaker was presented with a human relations award from the Canadian National Council of Christians and Jews, for promotion of civil liberties and human rights.

Sept. 22 The highest mountain (2,670 m) in the Canadian Arctic, located on Ellesmere Is., was officially named after noted Canadian anthropologist, ethnologist and folklorist, Dr. Charles Marius Barbeau (1883–1969).

Sept. 25 Approximately 3,200 members of the West Coast International Longshoremen's and Warehousemen's Union went on strike, tying up grain shipments from West Coast terminal elevator companies. On Oct. 9, the federal govt ordered the National Harbours Board and the Board of Grain Commissioners to start shipping grain through the strikebound ports, bypassing West Coast terminal elevator companies. The strike ended Oct. 17, with workers agreeing to a 2-year contract.

Sept. 27 Ont. Premier John Robarts opened the Ontario Science Centre in Don Mills, the 1st science centre in the country. Designed by Raymond Moriyama (b 1929), the 3 main structures are connected with long glass stairways overlooking Don Valley cliffs. The centre includes a host of permanent, hands-on exhibits and regularly produces some of the world's most innovative science displays, such as "Native Heritage" (1976), "China: 7,000 Years of Discovery" (1982), "Mindworks" (1991), and "Candy Unwrapped" (2003). The Science Centre attracted over 35 million people between 1969 and 2003.

Sept. 29 Montreal Mayor Jean Drapeau's home was bombed. There were no injuries.

Oct. 2 The US tested a 1-megaton nuclear device underground at Amchitka Is. in the Alaska Aleutian chain, in the face of international protests that included Canadian condemnation. Opponents feared the blast could trigger earthquakes in an area of unstable faults and contaminate the Gulf of Alaska with radiation, damaging fish stocks and other marine life. The Don't Make A Wave Committee, organized in Vancouver by Jim Bohlen, Paul Côté and Irving Stowe, sailed to the region to protest the test. The group would soon become Greenpeace, the international conservation organization with a focus on whaling, acid rain, sealing, leg-hold traps and a number of other environmental concerns.

Oct. 2–3 Soviet Foreign Minister Andrei Gromyko visited Canada for official talks. It was the 1st visit of a Soviet foreign minister to Canada.

Oct. 5 Leaside, Ont., native Ron Taylor became the 1st Canadian pitcher to win a Major League post-season game, relieving Jerry Koosman in the 5th to move the "Miracle" Mets 2 games ahead of Atlanta in the National League playoffs. The only other Canadian post-season winners were John Hiller of the Detroit Tigers, who won against the Oakland A's in 1972 and Rich Harden of the A's, who beat Boston in the 2003 American League playoffs. The great Fergie Jenkins never made it to post-season. Ron Taylor would retire and become one of the most respected physicians in Toronto, and also,

a medical consultant to the Toronto Blue Jays.

Oct. 7 Montreal police and firefighters went on a 16-hour wildcat strike to protest an arbitration board ruling on salary negotiations. Violence, looting, 2 deaths and much property damage resulted. On Oct. 8, the Que. National Assembly was forced to pass emergency legislation ordering police and firefighters back to work; a state of emergency was declared and the govt requested help from the army, the RCMP and the Sureté de Québec. Police and firefighters returned to work that day and order was restored. On Mar. 24, 1971, the report of the Que. Police Commission examining the police walkout recommended the formation of a contingency plan for emergencies and the separation of the Montreal Policemen's Brotherhood into units for officers and men.

Oct. 10 Man. passed legislation reducing the voting age in provincial elections from 21 to 18.

Oct. 11 The city of Montreal and the vice-president of the Que. section of the Liberal Federation of Canada charged that the Company of Young Canadians was linked with groups financed by Communist countries, and that the Company promoted separatist and subversive activities. On Nov. 27, Lucien Saulnier, Executive Committee Chairman of the city of Montreal, testified to a House of Commons committee that the Company posed a danger to the entire country because it engaged in revolutionary activities. On Dec. 17, the finances and placement of Young Canadian workers came under close govt supervision through federal legislation enacted for that purpose.

Oct. 14 A 75-day strike by 14,500 Ont. and Que. Stelco employees ended.

• The federal and NB govts agreed to establish a new national park north of Moncton, to be known as Kouchibouguac. The 238-km² park at the northern part of the Northumberland Str., along the shores of the Kouchibouguac R., protects a unique maritime lowland ecology, a mix of coastal estuaries, lagoons, saltwater marshes and intertidal flats. It also preserves an interior Acadian forest, with cedar swamps, bogs and freshwater streams. The eclectic mix of ecosystems is home to an extensive and varied array of fauna, from colonies of grey and harbour seals, to moose and black bears.

Oct. 15 Former president of Brandon U., Dr. John Everett Robbins (b 1903), was appointed Canada's 1st ambassador to the Vatican.

Oct. 21 A Sask. govt program designed to help prairie farmers get into the cattle business with subsidized rates of interest, was announced and took effect on Nov. 1.

• The govt banned the use of the artificial sweetener cyclamate, after tests indicated that the chemical could cause tumors in rats and mice.

Oct. 23 Nine men were killed when a faulty bearing caused an explosion in the engine room of the destroyer HMCS *Kootenay*. The ship was engaged in training exercises off the coast of England.

• In Quebec City, the Union Nationale govt tabled Bill 63, allowing Quebecers the choice of education in French or English. Riots ensued, resulting in the arrests of 34 people. The bill was adopted in the National Assembly on Nov. 20, with 67 for and 5 against, with 2 abstentions.

Oct. 26 Former PM Diefenbaker was installed as chancellor of the U. of Sask.

Also in Oct.
• Canada's largest icebreaker, the 11,800 tonne CCGS *Louis St. Laurent*, was completed by Canadian Vickers Ltd. in Montreal.

Nov. 3 For economic reasons, federal authorities announced that 3 Canadian diplomatic missions in Latin America, and others in Cambodia, Laos, Cyprus and West Berlin, were to close.

Nov. 4 Striking workers of the Algoma Steel Corporation voted to return to work after being out since Aug. 28. The settlement included increased pay and fringe benefits.

• The 1st conference of the Users of the Great Lakes met at Toronto to discuss pollution.

• The report of the task force on govt information

services recommended the formation of Information Canada to co-ordinate govt-information programs.

Nov. 6 The federal govt initiated a $50 million program to promote language training for minority groups and for 2nd-language training in French and English.

Nov. 7 Man. established a lottery for 1970, in conjunction with the running of the Man. Derby on July 15, 1970.

Nov. 12 Montreal City Council passed a bylaw prohibiting marches, meetings or public demonstrations on public ground that could result in acts of violence. Violation of the bylaw was punishable by fines and/or jail terms. Two days later, the annual Santa Claus parade in Montreal was cancelled because of growing tensions and increased violence in the city.

Nov. 19 The Canadian scientific vessel *Hudson* left Halifax for an 11-month voyage of the Atlantic, Antarctic, Pacific and Arctic Oceans to examine ocean currents and resource potential. It arrived back in Halifax Oct. 16, 1970.

Nov. 20 The Supreme Court of Canada overturned the conviction of Treaty Native Joseph Drybones for being intoxicated off the reserve. The Court ruled that under the Canadian Bill of Rights, 1960, Drybones had been denied equality before the law.

Nov. 23 Workers of Falconbridge Nickel Mines Ltd. ended a 3-month strike for increased wages.

Dec. 1 The use of the Breathalyzer to test the blood-alcohol levels of suspected impaired drivers took effect.

Dec. 2 Canada, the US, Denmark and the USSR agreed to participate in a permanent secretariat to consider issues involving Inuit.

Dec. 8–10 A federal-provincial constitutional conference was held in Ottawa.

Dec. 15 Red River Community College was opened at Winnipeg; 10,000 students were enrolled in

1970. In 1993, the college opened the Aboriginal Education and Institutional Diversity Division to provide programs and services to local First Nations students.

• A new series of banknotes was unveiled by the Bank of Canada, with portraits of former PMs instead of the queen of England on most bills. Wilfrid Laurier was shown on the $5 bill, John A. Macdonald on the $10 bill, W.L. Mackenzie King on the $50 bill, and Robert Borden on the $100 bill. The English monarch remained on the $1 and $20 bills. The new 1969 series included swirling multi-coloured tints and patterns to thwart counterfeiting. Also, to reflect that Canada had been off the gold standard since 1931 and would no longer redeem currency in gold, the promise "will pay to the bearer on demand" was replaced with the phrase "this note is legal tender."

Dec. 22 The Supreme Court of Canada ruled that Montreal's lottery, established on Apr. 2, 1968 to help pay off the municipal deficit, was illegal under Canada's Criminal Code. The next day, the Que. govt announced the formation of a corporation to run lotteries and races in the province. The 1st lottery took place Mar. 14, 1976.

Also in 1969

• An oil and gas report estimated that Alb.'s petroleum reserves would be exhausted in 55 years.

• "Africville," a predominantly black suburb of Halifax, NS, founded by former American slaves after the War of 1812, was razed. Home, at its height, to a population of 400, the suburb was a tightly knit community of large extended families of colour. In 1964, Halifax officials ordered the town destroyed, over the vigorous protests of Africville's residents. Demolishing the settlement took 5 years.

• The Special Committee on Corrections, established in 1965 and headed by Justice Roger Orimet, tabled its report recommending the Canadian penal system focus on rehabilitation rather than punishment. It also recommended the creation of a dangerous-offender category for the dangerously incorrigible; those convicted as such would receive indefinite sentences and require mandatory psychiatric care.

• The Que. Department of Cultural Affairs was established. In 1972 it issued its Orders-in-Council, establishing rules for the ownership of Que. publishing houses, accredited bookstores to sell books to provincial institutions and fixed prices on French- and English-language books.

• Dr. Donald Chant (b 1928), head of the U. of Toronto's Zoology Department, founded Pollution Probe to monitor human impact on the environment. The Toronto-based organization provides programs, initiatives, research and publications in the areas of air pollution, water quality, alternative energies and indoor building environments.

• The Acres Consulting Services, a leading engineering, research and development firm based in Toronto, paid 6 forward-thinking intellectuals $10,000 each to "think about the future."

• N.E. Thing Company Ltd. (founded by copresidents Ian and Ingrid Baxter) produced *Reflected Landscape: The Arctic Sun*. The image produced in various forms, including 35mm slides, lithographs and transparencies, was created during a visit to Inuvik, in the Canadian Arctic, with a mirror set up on the darkened tundra to reflect the setting Arctic sun. It is now in a private collection.

• Don Shebib (b 1938) produced and directed *Goin' Down the Road*, a feature film about two Maritime drifters who end up in the big city of Toronto. Produced for $87,000, the film was both a critical and commercial success, earning a best feature film award from the Canadian Film Awards in 1970. Actors Paul Bradley and Doug McGrath (b 1935) shared the Best Actor Award and William Fruet won for Best Original Screenplay.

• Calgary bartender Walter Chell (d 1997) developed the Bloody Caesar, a combination of tomato juice, vodka, celery, a lime wedge, pepper sauce, celery salt and ice all mixed in with his pièce de résistance, mashed clams. The Bloody Caesar became one of the most popular cocktails in Canada.

• Cognos (originally Quasar) was founded to act as an information-systems consultant to the federal govt. Based in Ottawa, the firm specialized in management software, with special emphasis on business and intelligence development, and performance planning.

• Canadians coast to coast got their 1st glimpse of Anne Murray on the CBC network's TV show *Singalong Jubilee.* She had been a member of the chorus since 1966, after being turned down during an audition in 1964.

• Bernie Finkelstein founded *True North Records,* the country's oldest independent record label and recorded such artists as Blackie and the Rodeo Kings, Bruce Cockburn (b 1945), Lighthouse, Randy Bachman (b 1943) and Lorraine Segato. By 2003, the Toronto-based recording and distribution firm had produced 37 gold and platinum records and 38 Juno Award winners.

• McGill–Queens University Press opened.

• Joanna Ruth Nichols (b 1948) published the children's adventure book *A Walk Out of the World,* an adventure in which children were transported to alternate universes.

• Margaret Laurence published the novel *The Fire Dwellers.*

• Margaret Atwood published her 1st novel, *The Edible Woman.* The humorous 1st Atwood classic involves the collapse of protagonist Marian McAlprin, whose eating disorder and gender relations merge to provide crisp reflections on roles of women and consumerism.

• Robert Kroetsch (b 1927) published the novel *The Studhorse Man,* for which he received the Gov-Gen.'s Award.

• Réjean Ducharme published the novel in verse *La fille de Christophe Colomb.*

• Milton Acorn published his 1st major collection of verse, *I've Tasted My Blood.*

• Phyllis Fay Gotlieb, née Bloom (b 1926), published *Ordinary Moving,* one of her 4 volumes of poetry. She also published the novel *Why Should I Have All the Grief,* an exploration of her Jewish roots.

• Canadian Ambassador to the USSR Robert Arthur Douglas Ford (b 1915) published the collection of verse *The Solitary City.*

• Poet George Bowering (b 1935) published *The Gangs of Kosmos,* for which he was awarded the Gov-Gen.'s Award.

• The poem *Speak White,* by Michèle Lalonde was published. It portrayed a francophone Quebecer in an anglophone world.

• Gwendolyn MacEwen published the collection of poems *The Shadow-Maker,* for which she received the Gov-Gen.'s Award.

• Native leader Harold Cardinal (b 1945) published *The Unjust Society: The Tragedy of Canada's Indians.*

• The anthology of Native writing *I Am an Indian,* edited by non-Aboriginal Kent Gooderham, was published.

• The National Museum of Canada published the anthology of Inuit stories with photographs of soapstone carvings *Stories from Povungnituk, Quebec,* by Zebedee Nungak and Eugene Arima.

• *The Peter Principle: Why Things Always Go Wrong* was published by Laurence J. Peter and Raymond Hull. The book rested on the premise that within a business hierarchy employees will be promoted to a level at which they are incompetent, and will rise to even greater degrees of incompetence with each promotion.

• The musical *Hair* scored by Galt MacDermot (b 1928) of Montreal, premiered in Canada at Toronto's Royal Alexandra Theatre.

• *Crabdance,* the best-known and most widely produced play by Beverley Simons, née Rosen (b 1938), was 1st produced. It was a ritualistic treatment of women as elders.

• Ray Smith published the collection of short stories *Cape Breton Is the Thought Control Centre of Canada.*

• The drama *Let's Murder Clytemnestra, According to the Principles of Marshall McLuhan* was produced by Wilfred Watson.

• Ont.-born artist John Boyle (b 1941) painted *Midnight Oil: Ode to Tom Thomson*, now in the London Regional Art Gallery collection.

• *Shop on An Island*, oil on board, by Christopher Pratt (b 1935), was completed

• Clark McDougall completed *A & A Music*, enamel and acrylic.

1970

Jan. 1 The Ont. cities of Fort William and Port Arthur, and the townships of Neebing and McIntyre, merged to form Thunder Bay.

• Canada placed a qualified ban on the use of the pesticide DDT (dichloro-diphenyl-trichloroethane). By 1974, most uses of DDT were banned through-out Canada. The presticide is known to severely effect bird populations and was a suspected human carcinogen. DDT use would not be completely discontinued until 1985.

Jan. 4 Canada withdrew from an international men's hockey tournament, set for Montreal and Winnipeg, to protest rules barring Canadian professionals from competition.

Jan. 15 George Maltby, police chief of St. James–Assiniboia, was appointed Man.'s 1st ombudsman.

Jan. 23 Canada pledged $30 million to the UN World Food Program for 1971–1972.

Also in Jan.
• The federal govt tabled the White Paper on Metric Conversion, which was supported by all House leaders. The paper established the Metric Commission in June 1971 to implement conversion of the country's imperial system of measurement to the metric system (International System of Units). Metric product labelling began Jan. 1975; road signs went metric Sept. 1977, and beginning in Jan. 1981, all gas and diesel fuel was sold by the litre.

Feb. 4 The Liberian-registered tanker *Arrow*, owned by Greek shipping tycoon Aristotle Onassis and carrying 108,000 barrels of Bunker C Oil, ran aground in Chedabucto Bay, NS, spilling massive amounts of oil, and contaminating water and nearby beaches.

Feb. 12 A 3-month-old baby was the recipient of Canada's 1st successful liver transplant, at Montreal's Notre-Dame Hospital.

Feb. 23 Canada's music trade magazine *RPM Weekly* presented its 1st RPM Gold Leaf Awards at Toronto's St. Lawrence Hall. One year later, the awards were renamed the Juno Awards in honour of Pierre Juneau, the 1st CRTC chairman and the man who had spearheaded the introduction of Canadian-content policies that governed radio content in Canada.

Mar. 2 Keith Spicer (b 1934) was appointed Canada's 1st commissioner of official languages.

• The federal govt prevented the foreign takeover of Denison Mines Ltd., Canada's largest uranium-mining company. On Mar. 19, the federal govt established rigid regulations on foreign ownership of uranium operations in Canada, limiting foreign ownership of such companies to 33%.

Mar. 3 Queen Elizabeth II and Princess Anne visited Ottawa and Vancouver.

Mar. 9–14 PM Trudeau opened Canada's 1st Arctic Winter Games in Yellowknife, NWT. The annual event involves athletes from the NWT (and now Nunavut), the Yukon and Alaska competing in traditional Inuit and Native games.

Mar. 20 Canada signed an agreement with 19 other countries to establish the Francophone International Cooperation Society, to promote and facilitate cultural and technological exchange among French-speaking nations.

Mar. 24 The federal govt banned commercial fishing on L. St. Clair, and the sale of pickerel and perch from western L. Erie, because of mercury contamination.

Apr. 1 Responsibility for governing the eastern and upper Arctic was transferred to the NWT govt, from the federal Department of Indian Affairs and Northern Development (DIAND).

• The NWT hamlet of Tuktoyaktuk (Inuktituk for "looks like caribou"), population 600, was incorporated. The town is situated on the Tuktoyaktuk

Peninsula along the Beaufort Sea, home to an estimated 1,450 pingos (conical, ice-cored hills that can grow to 50 m in height), more than anyplace on earth.

Apr. 2 The BC Supreme Court declared the federal law allowing use of compulsory breath tests in cases involving suspected drunk drivers null and void. On June 26, however, the Supreme Court of Canada overturned the ruling and upheld the breath-test legislation.

• The Medical Research Council and the U. of Alb. agreed to establish Canada's 1st organ transplant research group, at the U. of Alb.

Apr. 17 The Que. Savings Bank, founded in the 1840s as La Banque Populaire, was granted full chartered-bank status.

• The Ministry of National Defence made Yellow-knife, NWT, the permanent headquarters for Canadian military activities in the North.

Apr. 22 Ottawa provided Nfld. and NB $41.2 million and $32.5 million, respectively, in an effort to mini-mize regional disparities across the country.

Apr. 29 The Que. Liberal Party, led by Robert Bourassa (1933–1996), defeated the Union Nationale govt under Jean Jacques Bertrand in the provincial elec-tion. The Liberals won 72 seats, the Union 17. Seven members of Réne Lévesque's Parti Québécois were elected to the National Assembly. Bourassa was sworn in May 12.

May 2 The International Olympic Committee voted in Amsterdam to give Montreal the 1976 Summer Olympics Games. It would be the 1st Olympics held in Canada.

May 9 The Guess Who's *American Woman/No Sugar Tonight* hit No. 1 on *Billboard* magazine's Hot 100 chart and remained there for 3 weeks.

May 10 Twenty-two-year-old Boston Bruin Bobby Orr (b 1948), of Parry Sound, Ont., scored the Stanley Cup–winning goal in overtime against the St. Louis Blues, capping a season in which he became the 1st defenceman to win the Art Ross Trophy as the league's leading scorer. He also won the Hart

Trophy as the NHL's most valuable player, and the Conn Smythe for most valuable player in the play-offs. Number 4 had 33 goals and 87 assists during that brilliant 1969–1970 season, with 9 goals and 11 assists in the playoffs.

May 10–29 PM Trudeau visited New Zealand, Australia, Malaysia, Singapore and Japan, where he took part in Expo '70 ceremonies in Osaka.

May 11 PEI Liberal premier Alex Campbell was re-turned to power in the provincial election, winning 27 seats. The Progressive Conservatives took 5.

May 15 In Holland, work began on a 1,500-pipe organ to be installed in the National Arts Centre in Ottawa. The organ was a formal thank-you gift offered 25 years after Canada's liberation of Holland during WW II.

May 22 The CRTC bumped up Canadian-content requirements for television from 55% to 60% effec-tive Oct. 1, 1970, for the CBC, and Sept. 30, 1971, for the private sector.

May 29 The head office of the Hudson's Bay Com-pany (HBC) was transferred from London, England, to Winnipeg, Man. The Great Seal of Canada was applied to the Company's 300-year-old charter, making the oldest established firm in North America officially Canadian.

Also in May
• Calling for free abortion on demand, the Vancouver Women's Caucus organized a cross-country "Abortion Caravan" to protest Section 251 of the Criminal Code that allowed for abortions but only under qualified circumstances. The caravan left Vancouver for Ottawa, and picked up support-ers along the way. As part of the protest, several women chained themselves to seats in the House of Commons Visitors' Gallery.

June 1 The Que. govt offered a $50,000 reward for information leading to the arrest of those responsi-ble for 5 bombings that occurred in Montreal on May 31.

June 3 The last Canadian aircraft carrier, the HMCS *Bonaventure*, was decommissioned at Halifax. Commissioned on Jan. 17, 1957, the 192-m-long carrier had a 215 m x 34 m flight deck and could carry approximately 21 aircraft and a wartime crew of 1,370. The ship had a maximum speed of 24.5 knots.

June 4 PM Trudeau and other federal ministers met with approximately 200 Native representatives. All rejected the govt's Indian policy as outlined in the white paper of June 25,1969. Native leaders protested that the paper promoted assimilation through its support of individual, not collective, rights, and instead, argued for self-govt. PM Trudeau withdrew the white paper in 1971.

June 5–6 Federal and provincial finance ministers, meeting in Winnipeg, discussed a federal, voluntary guideline to increase wages by 6% over 12 years and agreed to limit inflation by upholding wage restraints, and also to provide more money to the provinces most in need. Federal plans for tax reform were rejected by provincial finance ministers.

June 16 Parliament passed the Arctic Waters Pollution Prevention Act in an attempt to make all ship owners liable if found polluting Arctic waters north of 60° parallel. The act also made polluters vulnerable to civil and criminal charges in Canada. Foreign states, the US in particular, opposed the act, declaring it a unilateral effort to assert jurisdiction over international waters. The act was passed after the US oil tanker *Manhattan* made a successful trip through the Northwest Passage from Aug. 24 through Sept. 15, 1969.

June 18 An exhibition of 203 Group of Seven paintings opened at the National Gallery of Canada, Ottawa, to commemorate the 50th anniversary of the Group's 1st exhibition.

June 24 A female employee was killed when a bomb exploded in a Department of National Defence building in Ottawa.

June 25 The white paper on foreign policy, "Foreign Policy for Canadians," set out policies and objectives for safeguarding Canada's sovereignty; increasing economic growth; securing peace; supporting social justice; improving the quality of life; and enhancing the natural environment.

June 26 Assent was given to a revised Canada Elections Act, reducing the minimum voting age in federal elections from 21 to 18. Other provisions included the right to place party labels on ballots and to vote by proxy under select circumstances.

Also in June

• The federal govt allocated approximately $1 million in emergency-relief assistance to earthquake victims in Peru, including an aircraft-ferrying service, tents and flour. Canada also sent $7.5 million in relief assistance to flood-ravaged Romania.

July 2–15 Queen Elizabeth II, Prince Philip, Prince Charles and Princess Anne visited Man. for its centennial celebrations, and also visited the NWT.

July 5 An Air Canada DC–8 crashed near Toronto International Airport while en route from Montreal to Los Angeles. All 109 aboard were killed. The pilot had prematurely deployed the rear spoilers at landing, which caused the plane to bounce off the runway and rupture a fuel line. The landing was aborted, the pilot attempted to gain altitude, but the plane exploded and crashed to the ground. It was the 2nd worst Canadian air since the TCA tragedy of Nov. 29, 1963.

July 10 The Que. govt passed the Quebec Health Insurance Act to fall in line with the national Medical Care Act. Que. medical specialists went on strike Oct. 8 to protest associated controls over physician-service fees, but returned to work Oct. 18.

July 14 A mountain in the St. Elias Range in the Yukon Territory was named Mount Leacock in honour of Canada's great humorist.

• Nine lives were lost when a Canadian lake freighter, the *Eastcliffe Hall*, sank in the St. Lawrence Seaway, near Cornwall, Ont., after striking a shoal. The captain was later held responsible for the accident.

July 16–26 At the 9th British Commonwealth Games in Edinburgh, Scotland, Canada finished 3rd among 41 nations, with 18 gold medals, 24 silver and 2 bronze.

July 22 A 3-month-old strike in BC's construction industry came to an end when BC Attorney Gen.

and Labour Minister Leslie Raymond Peterson forced workers to return to work under threat of fines and imprisonment.

July 30 The Alb. govt established oil pollution standards, effective Nov. 1. The standards required regular reports on volume of raw gas produced at plants, and the installation of automatic closing gates in conduits to prevent discharges in the event of leaks.

Aug. 1 The several hundred people who celebrated Toronto's 1st "Gay Day Picnic" at Hanlan's Point on the Toronto Islands set in motion a series of events that led to the 1st Gay Pride Week in 1972. After years of lobbying by gay and lesbian groups and individuals, the annual celebration was eventually recognized by City Council in 1991. By the 2000s the annual week-long celebration with its focal point parade was attracting more than 1 million visitors to the city each year.

Aug. 2 Three people were killed and 2 injured when the BC ferry *Queen of Victoria* and the Soviet freighter *Sergey Yesenin* collided in the Active Pass between the mainland and Vancouver Is.

Aug. 10 The Que. National Assembly legislated 40,000 striking construction workers back to work.

• Judith Merrill (1923–1997) donated her collection of 5,000 items of science fiction, fantasy and related non-fiction to the board of directors of the Toronto Public Library. The collection was named The Spaced-Out Library. In 1990, the collection was renamed the Merril Collection of Science Fiction, Speculation and Fantasy. It now includes more than 32,000 books, 25,000 periodical works, as well as graphic novels and role-playing games.

Aug. 13 Archaeologists discovered an ancient burial ground at Cow Point, near Grand L., NB, estimated to be more than 3,735 years old.

• The Man. govt assumed control over the province's automobile-insurance industry.

Aug. 17 The top architectural award at Expo '70 in Osaka, Japan, was given to the Canadian pavilion, designed by Arthur Erickson (b 1924).

Aug. 19 Canada sent $3.54 million in relief assistance to flood victims in Pakistan.

Aug. 20 A windstorm near Sudbury, Ont., caused 4 deaths and $6 million damage.

Aug. 21 BC Shuswap Chief George Manuel (1921–1989) was elected the 1st president of the newly formed National Indian Brotherhood (NIB). The NIB represented a cross-national group of Status and Treaty Aboriginal groups that lobbied for structural changes to provincial and federal Native policies. The NIB was the 1st truly national First Nations political body. (It became the Assembly of First Nations in 1982.) George Manuel went on to become president of the World Council of Indigenous Peoples from 1975 to 1981. The great chief spent a lifetime fighting govt aims toward Native assimilation, and inspired not only Canadian but world Aboriginal peoples toward self-govt and freedom. Manuel was buried at the Neskomlith Cemetery on the Neskomlith Reserve, BC, on Nov. 20, 1989.

Aug. 23 The federal and Que. govt agreed on the creation of St. Maurice National Park. The 544-km^2 park is located in the Laurentian Mountains on the southern portion of the Canadian Shield. It embraces a forest transition zone of deciduous trees and the boreal forest, including the nation's oldest and largest white spruce plantation, planted by a forestry firm in the early 1930s. St. Maurice was home to the Paleolithic Attikamek Peoples some 8,000 years ago. Thirty-four archaeological sites, including the famous rock paintings at L. Wapizagonke, provide evidence of ancient Aboriginal habitation.

Aug. 24 Gov-Gen. Michener opened the $7.7 million Sask. Centre of the Arts in Regina. At the heart of the centre is the 2,033-seat Shirley Bell Theatre; its orchestra pit can accommodate up to 100 musicians.

Sept. 2 BC pulp industry workers, on strike since July 24, returned to work with a 22.5% wage increase.

Sept. 4 The 27,000-member Council of Postal Unions and the federal govt reached an agreement providing for a 55 cent-an-hour wage increase over 2.5

years based on a basic salary of $3.06 per hour. The agreement ended an 11-month postal dispute.

Sept. 9 The 1st deep-water supertanker terminal in North America was opened at Mispec Point, NB.

Oct. 1 Soviet vessels were prohibited from fishing the Big Bank region off the west coast of Vancouver Is. following several collisions between Soviet and Canadian ships.

Oct. 5 The Oct. Crisis began as British trade commissioner in Montreal James Cross was kidnapped from his home by FLQ terrorists. Their demands for his release included a ransom of $500,000 in gold, the release and safe passage out of the country of 23 convicted FLQ "political prisoners" and publication of the FLQ manifesto. The govt refused to comply.

Oct. 10 Que. Minister of Labour and Immigration Pierre Laporte (1921–1970) was kidnapped outside his home in the Montreal suburb of St. Hubert by a cell of the FLQ. He had been playing ball with his children.

Oct. 12 Troops left Camp Petawawa, Ont., for Ottawa, to guard govt buildings, officials and the diplomatic community from possible FLQ terrorist attack. Three days later (Oct. 15), soldiers from the 22nd Regiment arrived in Montreal to bolster civil authorities as growing FLQ support culminated in a mass rally of some 3,000 students and unionists at Montreal's Paul Sauvé Arena. The "Van Doos" were later joined by other armed forces units, all of whom took up positions throughout Que.

Oct. 13 The federal govt and the People's Republic of China agreed to establish diplomatic relations that would include a Chinese embassy established in Ottawa in 1971. Official ties with Taiwan were ended. The 1st Chinese ambassador to Canada, Huang Hua, arrived in Ottawa July 23, 1971.

• The Liberal Party, under Gerald Augustine Regan (b 1929), won the NS provincial election, defeating the Conservative govt of George Smith.

Oct. 16 At 3 a.m., PM Trudeau proclaimed the War Measures Act, declaring that an "apprehended

insurrection" existed in Que. Police were given extraordinary powers of arrest and detention against anyone suspected of belonging to, or sympathizing with, the FLQ. Membership in the FLQ became a criminal offence and political rallies were banned. *Habeas corpus* was suspended. Overnight, 465 people were arrested. Only 18 of the arrested were convicted of any crime. It was the 1st time such powers had been used in Canada in peacetime. NDP leader Tommy Douglas responded to the War Measures Act proclamation, stating, "We are not prepared to use the preservation of law and order as a smoke screen to destroy the liberties and the freedom of the people of Canada… The govt, I submit, is using a sledgehammer to crack a peanut."

• Montreal police ransacked the home of Gérard Pelletier (1919–1997), secretary of state for external affairs, in search of FLQ literature. They produced official stationery with Pelletier's name and ministerial title, which convinced them of their mistake.

Oct. 17 Pierre Laporte's strangled body was found in the trunk of a car at St. Hubert Airport in Que. On Nov. 2, the federal and Que. govts offered rewards of up to $75,000 for information leading to the arrest of the kidnappers and murderers of Pierre Laporte, and for information leading to the arrest of James Cross's kidnappers.

Oct. 19 The House of Commons approved the Oct. 16 proclamation of the War Measures Act, 190 votes to 16.

Oct. 22 Former PM Pearson was named the 1st chairman of the board of govs. of the Canada-based International Development Research Centre.

Oct. 25 Jean Drapeau and his Civic Party won all 52 council seats in the Montreal election, while his Front d'Action Public (FRAP) opponent was locked up with 464 others under the War Measures Act.

Oct. 26 The Progressive Conservatives, led by Richard Hatfield (1931–1992), won the NB provincial election, defeating the Liberal govt of Louis Robichaud.

Oct. 30 FLQ member Robert Hudon was sentenced to 25 years in prison for armed robberies and conspiracy to commit holdups to finance FLQ subversive activities.

Nov. 6 Bernard Lortie was arrested in a Montreal apartment in connection with the kidnapping of Pierre Laporte. His FLQ-cell accomplices escaped after hiding in a specially built compartment built behind a wardrobe.

Nov. 10 Anne Murray became the 1st Canadian female singer to top 1 million sales in the US with her smash hit "Snowbird." She was also awarded a gold record while appearing on *The Merv Griffin Show.* "Snowbird" was written by Gene MacLellan (1940–1995), who also wrote the hit song "Put Your Hand in the Hand."

Nov. 16 Canada arranged a $20 million development loan for the African country of Botswana.

Nov. 20 In the United Nations Gen. Assembly, Canada voted in favour of giving the People's Republic of China membership in the United Nations. The Assembly vote was 51 to 49 in favour. China took a seat at the UN, displacing Taiwan, in 1971.

Nov. 24 Opera soprano Pierrette Alarie (b 1921) performed Handel's *Messiah* in her farewell concert, in Montreal, with tenor husband Léopold Simoneau (b 1916).

Dec. 1 The Public Order (Temporary Measures) Act was passed in the House of Commons to replace the War Measures Act. The new act continued to outlaw the FLQ and allowed police to arrest without warrant and hold suspects for as long as 1 week without laying charges. The act was allowed to lapse on Apr. 30, 1971. The FLQ, however, remained an illegal organization under the Criminal Code.

Dec. 2 The federal govt declared a 10% increase to military pensions involving disability and death, and a 15% increase in veterans' allowances, effective Apr. 1, 1971.

Dec. 3 James Cross was freed by police from a room on Rue des Recollets in north Montreal. In return, the kidnappers and their families received safe conduct and transport to Cuba. The next day, Justice Minister John Turner (b 1929) declared that

the exiles would remain so for the rest of their lives. However, most FLQ members in exile eventually returned to Canada to face charges. Jacques Cossette-Trudel and Louise Lanctot returned in Dec. 1978; Jacques Lanctot, Michel Lambert, Alain Allard and Pierre Charrette in 1979; Marc Charbonneau in 1981; Yves Langlois in 1982; and Raymond Villeneuve in 1984. The maximum sentence was 3 years' imprisonment.

Dec. 16 A 3-month strike begun Sept. 14 by 23,500 General Motors of Canada workers was settled with a 34-cent-an hour raise and a compromise on the issue of parity with US counterparts.

Dec. 28 Suspected Pierre Laporte kidnappers Paul Rose (b 1943), Jacques Rose (b 1942) and Francis Simard (b 1943) were captured in a tunnel under a farmhouse near Montreal. On Jan. 5, the Roses, Simard and Bernard Lortie (arrested Nov. 6) were charged with the kidnapping and non-capital murder of Pierre Laporte. When convicted, Paul Rose was sentenced to 2 life terms in prison, Francis Simard to life imprisonment, Bernard Lortie to 20 years, and Jacques Rose to 8 years. Jacques Rose and Bernard Lortie were granted parole in 1978. Francis Simard and Paul Rose were granted parole in 1982. On June 14, 1971, Michel Viger received 8 years imprisonment for his part in hiding Pierre Laporte's murderers.

Also in 1970

• Canada's population was 21,297,000.

• The NWT began issuing its distinctive polar bear–shaped licence plates.

• The federal govt applied a "quota management" system to the harp seal hunt. The average annual seal catch in the Gulf of St. Lawrence and off Nfld. and Labrador dropped from 287,000 animals in the 1960s to 172,000 in the 1970s.

• The US held 80% and the UK 9% of the total foreign capital invested in Canada. In 1900, the investment figures were nearly reversed: the US held 14% and the UK 85%.

• The average single or semi-detached house retailed in Montreal for $19,000. In Toronto, the same house retailed for $37,000, and in Vancouver $30,000.

• The United Church of Canada sold Ryerson Press to US-owned McGraw-Hill, raising fears that Americans were taking over the Canadian book business.

• Canada's 1st undergraduate program in dance opened at York U., Toronto.

• A 381.3-m smokestack — the tallest in the world — was completed by Inco in Copper Cliff, near Sudbury, Ont.

• Shell Canada became the 1st oil company in the country to offer unleaded gasoline — the Shell Ultra brand. By 1990, leaded gasoline was phased out and no longer available at service stations.

• The Pierre Laporte Bridge, crossing the St. Lawrence at Quebec City, was completed. At 667.5 m, it was Canada's longest bridge span.

• The International Standard Book Number (ISBN) was 1st applied in Canada. The system provided each book, including paperback and hardcover editions of the same title, a unique number in order to facilitate customer orders, book tracking and traceability.

• Canadian book publishers James Lorimer & Co. and NC Press opened for business.

• The Ont. Educational Communications Authority (TV Ontario), a provincially owned television network, began broadcasting.

• Kwakiutl carver Tony Hunt (b 1942) opened the Arts of the Raven Gallery in Victoria, BC.

• Niagara Falls native Tony Urquhart (b 1934) fashioned *Rocamadour I*, a 162 x 51 x 41 cm skeleton box constructed with wire and wood on a pedestal. It is now with the National Gallery of Canada.

• Prairie artist Ivan Eyre (b 1935) painted *Black Woman*, now in the Musée des beaux-arts de Montréal.

• Moose Jaw, Sask.-born Roy Kiyooka (1926–1994), artist, writer, poet, painter, sculptor, photographer and filmmaker, completed the 69 x 101 cm photographic print *Stone Gloves*, now with the Vancouver Art Gallery.

• Margaret Atwood published the major poetic achievement *The Journals of Susanna Moodie*.

• Ceylon-born poet Michael Ondaatje (b 1943) published *The Collected Works of Billy the Kid*, for which he won the Gov-Gen's Award.

• Fernand Ouellette (b 1930) published *Les Actes retrouvés*, on poetry and poetics, power, violence and tolerance, for which he was offered the Gov-Gen.'s Award, and refused.

• Experimental language poet Barrie Phillip "bp" Nichol (b 1944) published *The Cosmic Chef An Evening of Concrete*, for which he received the Gov-Gen.'s Award for poetry.

• Historian Donald Creighton published *Canada's First Century 1867-1967*.

• *Trappings of My Life*, the autobiographical account of Slavey trapper John Testo (1912-1964) was posthumously published.

• Farley Mowat (b 1921) published *Sibir*, an account of his travels through Siberia.

• Aboriginal writer Markoosie (b 1941) published *Harpoon of the Hunter*. The autobiographical novel has been translated into more than 10 languages.

• Madame Jehane Benoit (1904–1987) published *Canadiana Cookbook: A Complete Heritage of Canadian Cooking*. Benoit, who was born in Montreal and studied at the Cordon Bleu cooking school in Paris, wrote more then 30 cookbooks and once stated, "If you're interested in cooking, you're also interested in art, in love, and in culture."

• George Woodcock (1912-1995) published *Canada and the Canadians*.

• Robertson Davies published his masterpiece novel *Fifth Business*, the 1st in his Deptford trilogy. He would follow the Jungian thread developed in the book through sequels *The Manticore* (1972), which won the Gov-Gen's Award, and *World of Wonders* (1975).

• Dave Godfrey (b 1938) published the novel *The New Ancestors*, set in Africa, where Godfrey served with CUSO.

• The Canadian govt acquired the W.H. Coverdale Collection of Canadiana. Assembled by William Hugh Coverdale (1871–1949), president of Canada Steamship Lines, the 2,482 Canadian historical artworks (previously known as the Manoir Richelieu Collection), were transferred to the Canadian National Archives and the National Gallery, where they became the backbone of both collections.

• Folklore collector Edith Fowke published *Sally Go Round the Sun: 100 Songs, Rhymes and Games of Canadian Children*.

• Anne Hébert published the great novel *Kamouraska*, set in 19th-century Que. The novel won Hébert France's Prix des Libraries and was later made into a film by Canadian director Claude Jutra (1930–1986).

• *Le Réel et le théâtral*, a collection of essays by Iraq-born writer Naim Kattan (b 1928), was published and won the Prix France-Canada.

• The feature film *Mon Oncle Antoine*, directed by Claude Jutra, became the 1st French-language drama to attract a significant English-speaking audience. It swept the 1971 Canadian Film Awards, winning a total of 8 Etrogs. Telling the story of a rural-Que. adolescent boy's sexual, moral and social awakening, *Mon Oncle Antoine* became an enduring Canadian masterpiece and went on to win 14 international awards.

• The feature film *Act of the Heart*, written and directed by Paul Almond, was released. It starred Genevieve Bujold, Donald Sutherland, Gilles Vigneault and Monique Leyrac.

• Joni Mitchell recorded the album *Ladies of the Canyon* which included Mitchell classics, "Big Yellow Taxi," "Woodstock" and "The Circle Game."

1971

Jan. 4 Troops stationed in Que. during the October Crisis were withdrawn from Montreal and other points in the province.

Jan. 8 Montreal labour leader Michel Chartrand (1916–1967), charged with seditious conspiracy and membership in the FLQ, was sentenced to a year in jail for contempt of court.

Jan. 9 The federal govt pledged $2.25 million in relief aid for both factions in the Nigerian civil war.

Jan. 14–22 At the Commonwealth heads of govt conference in Singapore, PM Trudeau was credited with preventing a breakup of the Commonwealth by suggesting the formation of an 8-nation study group to analyze the UN arms embargo on South Africa. The UN had passed a resolution Nov. 2, 1970 advancing a previous ban on arms sales to the apartheid regime.

Jan. 18 The Que. govt adopted regulations requiring English-language schools to teach French as a 2nd language.

Jan. 20 Radio Tuktoyaktuk (NWT) began broadcasting in Inuit and English for the 1st time.

Feb. 1 Canada Post began an "assured mail delivery program," with next-day delivery of letters posted before 11 a.m., in most major Canadian cities.

• The Que. Press Council was formed out of 4 news organizations, representing more than 700 reporters.

Feb. 4 William (Billy) Mills, the last surviving participant in the Red R. Rebellion, died in London, Ont., at the age of 104.

Feb. 5 David Freeman's (b 1945) critically acclaimed play *Creeps* premiered at the Factory Theatre, Toronto. The comic drama focused on the lives and thoughts of 4 men with cerebral palsy.

Feb. 13 William G. Davis was chosen Progressive Conservative premier of Ont., on the 4th ballot at the Ont. Progressive Conservative Party convention, succeeding John Robarts, who retired. Davis took office on Mar. 1.

Feb. 16 Conservative MP John Lundrigan (b 1939) accused PM Trudeau of mouthing a 4-letter obscenity during a debate over training programs for the unemployed. Fellow Conservative Lincoln Alexander (b 1922) supported his colleague's claim, stating that the PM had in fact mouthed 2 words: "The 1st started with the letter F, the 2nd with the letter O." Pressed by journalists outside the Commons as to what he'd actually said, the PM shrugged off the accusations, suggesting he might have muttered, "fuddle duddle." The term has since become a Canadian euphemism.

Feb. 25 American Chapin Scott Paterson hijacked a US Boeing 747 and landed it in Vancouver. Paterson was turned over to US authorities the same day.

Feb. 26 The federal govt initiated a program to push francophone representation in the Canadian Armed Forces to 28%.

Mar. 2 The Canadian Transport Commission ordered CN to continue Super Continental passenger service, despite financial losses. The cross-country service provided lounges and sleeping cars, and a diner; some cars even had domed-glass ceilings that afforded views of mountaintops by day and stars by night.

Mar. 4 PM Trudeau married 22-year-old Margaret Sinclair (b 1948) in North Vancouver, thereby becoming the 1st PM to wed while in office.

Mar. 12 The Que. govt pledged compensation for those who were arrested during the Oct. Crisis but not charged. Police files and fingerprints of those not charged were also to be destroyed.

Mar. 16 PM Trudeau announced plans in the House of Commons to establish the Opportunities for Youth (OFY) program to help the flood of baby-boomer youth, particularly students, locate employment. The program was cancelled in Dec. 1975 as a cost-cutting measure.

Mar. 22 The federal govt established a $2 million program to hire 276 francophone university graduates for jobs in the public service where French was the "language of work."

Mar. 29 Ralph E. Collins (b 1922) was appointed Canada's 1st Ambassador to the People's Republic of China.

Apr. 5 Fran Phipps became the 1st woman to set foot on the North Pole after she and her Arctic pilot husband, Wilfred "Weldy" Phipps, touched down during a flight to service a fixed radio transmitter.

• The 250 megawatt (MW) Gentilly 1 nuclear reactor, the 1st in the world fuelled by natural uranium and cooled by ordinary water, began service at Bécancour, near Trois-Rivières, Que. It was shut down in Oct. 1981, to be followed by the 635 megawatt (MW) Gentilly 2, which went into commercial operation Oct. 1983. Gentilly 2 is the only commercial nuclear reactor in Que. and Hydro-Quebec's most powerful power-generating plant.

Apr. 15 Harry Douglas Smith, former president of King's College, Halifax, was appointed NS's 1st ombudsman.

Apr. 18 Two convicts were murdered and 11 injured when Kingston Penitentiary inmates rioted for 4 days, during which 5 guards were held hostage. On Nov. 22, 12 inmates were convicted of manslaughter in the beating deaths of the 2 inmates. Their sentences ranged from 2 to 15 years, which were added to their previous sentences.

Apr. 22 Former Métis member of Parliament Gene Rhéaume purchased at auction, for $26,500, the 48-page diary of Louis Riel, covering the 1885 Battle of Batoche.

• Consumers' Gas Co. of Toronto agreed to buy a controlling interest in struggling Home Oil Ltd. of Calgary, the last major Canadian petroleum company. The federal govt had expressed interest in Home Oil on Mar. 11.

Apr. 24 David Lewis (1909–1981) succeeded "Father of Medicare" Tommy Douglas as national leader of the NDP. Douglas assumed the role of NDP energy critic until his retirement in 1979.

Apr. 29 Federal minister of communications, the controversial "economic nationalist" Eric William Kierans (1914–2004), resigned his cabinet portfolio over the govt's unwillingness to scare off foreign ownership of Canadian resources.

• The Que. govt outlined plans to build a $6 billion hydroelectric power project in the James Bay region, the largest such development ever undertaken in the western hemisphere. In May 1972, the Indians of Quebec Association filed legal action to stop the James Bay project, claiming compensation for the northern part of Que., which had been acquired by the province through the 1912 Transfer Act. Native Peoples, the federal and Que. govts came to agreement on phase one of the James Bay project on Nov. 11, 1975.

Apr. 1971–Nov. 1973 The Canadian Post Office introduced a 6-digit postal code to facilitate mechanical sorting of mail.

May 1 The Dominion Bureau of Statistics became known as Statistics Canada.

May 3 Gordon Lightfoot (b 1938) became the 1st non-classical singer to perform at the Lincoln Center's Philharmonic Hall in New York.

May 3-12 Queen Elizabeth II, Prince Philip and Princess Anne visited BC for the province's centennial.

May 4 Part of St. Jean Vianney, Que., was destroyed by a landslide, killing 31 people.

• The federal govt established 37 bilingual districts across Canada in which federal govt services would be made available in both official languages.

May 7 Mr. Robert Andras (1921–1982) was appointed 1st Minister Responsible for the Status of Women, a new federal cabinet portfolio.

May 17–28 PM Trudeau, Margaret Trudeau and a 21-member official party visited the Soviet Union, where a protocol was signed providing for consultation and co-operation in economic, scientific and cultural spheres. Political consultation on problems of northern development was also discussed.

May 22 The $23 million amusement and entertainment showplace Ontario Place opened on the shore of L. Ontario south of the CNE grounds in Toronto.

• The Norwegian cruise vessel *Meteor* caught fire in the Strait of Georgia while en route to Vancouver. Thirty-two crew members died.

May 25 Former Liberal MP and Defence Minister Paul Hellyer (b 1923) launched Action Canada, a new political movement to exert pressure on the federal govt over such issues as tax cuts, unemployment, and wage and price guidelines. Hellyer resigned from the Liberal caucus May 21, to sit as an independent Liberal.

June 3 The Ont. govt halted construction of the Spadina Expressway in Toronto because of citizen opposition. Construction had begun in 1964, with the highway extending south from highway 401 to Eglinton Ave. The half-built highway was renamed the W.R. Allen Road, or Allen Expressway.

June 9 The House of Commons passed legislation establishing the Canada Development Corporation, with a mandate to help develop and maintain strong Canadian-owned and -operated corporations in the private sector, and to create a climate in which Canadians were provided greater opportunities to invest in the economic development of the country.

June 10 Assent was given to legislation creating the Department of the Environment and the appointment of a minister of state.

June 14–18 A federal-provincial constitutional conference was held at Victoria, BC. A proposed constitutional charter was subsequently rejected by Que. Premier Robert Bourassa for not giving his province "legislative primacy" in the field of income security.

June 15 A letter was circulated to cabinet members by Solicitor-Gen. Jean-Pierre Boyer, warning against federal civil servants engaged in "extra-Parliamentary opposition," those thought to be involved in social movements considered dangerous to democratic institutions.

June 21 Toronto publisher McClelland & Stewart received an Ont. govt loan of $351,000, part of a $961,000 loan to maintain Canadian ownership of the prestigious firm.

June 23 The NDP under Allan Emrys Blakeney (b 1925) won the Sask. provincial election, defeating the Liberal govt of Ross Thatcher (1917–1971).

• Assent was given to a new Unemployment Insurance Act, increasing coverage and rates of benefit and more than doubling the federal govt's contribution.

• The federal govt pledged a $1.5 million assistance program to compensate Canadian Atlantic fishers and processors for losses incurred as a result of mercury contamination of fish in Atlantic and inland waters.

July 1 At BC's centennial celebration, PM Trudeau presented, "on behalf of the people of Canada," $2.5 million for the construction of a new museum of anthropology at U. of BC. The new building, designed by Arthur Erickson, opened in 1976. Trudeau also provided a $4.5 million "2nd Century Fund" to develop natural conservation areas in the province.

• After 729 performances, the love-rock musical *Hair,* its score and direction by Montreal-born composer Galt MacDermot, closed on Broadway in New York.

July 1–Aug. 8 The National Gallery displayed "True Patriot Love," an exhibition by artist Joyce Wieland (1931–1998). It was the gallery's 1st solo exhibition by a living Canadian woman.

July 2 The 1st Canadian ministerial mission ever to visit the People's Republic of China was received by Premier Chou En-lai.

July 11 Acclaimed armed forces aeronautical ambassadors, the Snowbirds, performed their 1st official exhibition at the Sask. Homecoming Airshow.

July 12–13 Federal and provincial finance ministers met in Ottawa, where the federal govt agreed to extend provincial equalization payments, and a 2-year continuation of federal post-secondary education aid.

July 29 The 515 megawatt (MW) Pickering 1 CANDU reactor was the 1st of 8 plus-500 MW Pickering nuclear plant reactors to enter commercial operation. Pickering 8 went into operation Jan. 21, 1986. The 1st 4 reactors were housed in Plant A, the rest in Plant B. They are situated some 48 km east of Toronto. Together, all 8 reactors had a total capacity

of 4,120 MW. Plant A was mothballed in 1997 with its reactor No. 4 returning to commercial operation in Sept. 2003.

• The Oland family of Halifax presented the *Bluenose II,* a replica of the original *Bluenose,* to the NS govt as a floating museum.

Aug. 13 The Crown suspended charges laid under the War Measures Act against 32 people, including labour leader Michel Chartrand, lawyer Robert Lemieux and teacher Charles Gagnon.

• The federal and Ont. govts pledged $262 million for a 4-year program to clean up pollution in L. Erie, L. Ont. and the international region of the St. Lawrence.

Aug. 15–21 The 1st Banff Festival of the Arts was held in Banff, Alb.

Aug. 16 The coast of NS was severely damaged by Hurricane Beth. Twenty-five mm of rain fell in Halifax. Extensive flooding caused an estimated $35 million in damage.

Aug. 17 The federal govt initiated an experiment in bilingualism requiring 29,000 of the country's 196,000 federal civil servants to conduct services in French.

Aug. 24 A gay-liberation demonstration took place in the rain on the steps of the Parliament Buildings. Demonstrators demanded equal rights and an end to societal prejudice against homosexuality.

• The federal Liberal govt issued its white paper "Defence in the 70s," emphasizing "the protection of our sovereignty," including increased surveillance of coastal waters for pollution control, the policing of territorial seas and fishing zones, and the maintenance of Canada's NATO forces. Under the paper, a freeze on military spending would be removed and spending increased to nearly $2 billion for 1972–1973. The number of armed forces personnel in 1971 was approximately 87,500.

Aug. 26 The Special Committee on Youth recommended the disbanding of the Company of Young Canadians, increased federal jurisdiction over education, termination of the cadet program and legalization of marijuana.

Aug. 30 The Progressive Conservatives under Edgar Peter Lougheed (b 1928) won the Alb. provincial election, defeating the Social Credit govt of Harry Strom. It was Alb.'s 1st Conservative govt. Premier Lougheed would serve from Sept. 10 to Nov. 1, 1985.

Aug. 31 Ont. Premier William Davis announced that his govt would not extend full funding to grades 11, 12 and 13 in Roman Catholic schools. Davis reversed his decision in 1984.

Sept. 1 A law banning alcohol and tobacco advertising went into effect in the province of BC.

Sept. 10 A 400-km BC Railway extension from Fort St. John to Fort Nelson was completed. By the turn of the century, BC Railway had 1,557 km of mainline and more than 2,000 employees.

Sept. 13 The Ont. govt established free hospital and medical care for those 65 and over, effective Jan. 1, 1972; and for low-income earners, effective Apr. 1, 1972. The program was extended to dependents of persons 65 years of age or older on Sept. 25, 1972.

• The Ont. govt unveiled an aid program to help prevent foreign ownership of Ont.-based Canadian publishing houses.

Sept. 25 The International Typographical Union ended a 7-year strike against 3 Toronto newspapers — the *Star*, *Telegram* and *Globe and Mail*.

• British Princess Margaret, Countess of Snowdon, opened the Winnipeg Art Gallery. Hometown architect Gustavo da Roza (b 1933) and the Number Ten Architectural Group completed the distinctive, grey Tyndall limestone-over-concrete building, which features 8 galleries, a 320-seat auditorium, a rooftop restaurant and a sculpture garden.

Sept. 28 The federal govt passed legislation providing for subsidies to manufacturers and processors whose exports were threatened by a new US surcharge.

Oct. 9 A federal Court of Appeal ruled that under the 1960 Bill of Rights, a Native woman could not be denied Indian status after marrying a non-Native. The ruling was made in the case of Jeannette Vivian Corbiere Lavell (b 1942), a member of the Nishnawbe Peoples of Manitoulin Is. Ont., whose Indian status was terminated after she married David Lavell, a non-Native, in 1970. Corbiere Lavell took the case to county court in June 1971, but lost. The case was eventually taken to the Supreme Court of Canada, which heard it in Feb. 1973. Its final verdict was delivered Aug. 27, 1973.

Oct. 10 The national Social Credit Party re-elected Réal Caouette as leader.

Oct. 14 With unemployment in Canada at 7.1% — equalling its highest level since 1961 — the govt reduced personal income taxes by 3%, and corporate taxes by 7%, retroactive from July 1 to Dec. 31, 1971.

Oct. 17–26 Soviet Premier Alexei Kosygin became the 1st Soviet head of state to visit Canada. On Oct. 18, Kosygin was assaulted by Hungarian immigrant Geza Matrai in Ottawa. Kosygin was not injured and Matrai was sentenced on Jan. 7, 1972, to 3 months in jail.

Oct. 21 In an Ont. general election, the Progressive Conservative govt of William Davis was returned to power, winning 78 seats. The Liberals took 20, the NDP 19.

Oct. 28 In the Nfld. provincial election, the Progressive Conservatives under Frank Duff Moores (b 1933) won a tight victory with 21 seats. Joey Smallwood's Liberals took 20 seats, and the New Labrador Party 1. Moores took office as premier on Jan. 18, 1972, but could not hold on to power. The legislature was dissolved in 1972 and another election held Mar. 24, 1972. Joey Smallwood resigned before the 1972 election (Jan. 18, 1972) and was succeeded by Edward Roberts, Feb. 15, 1972.

• A labour-organized protest against the Montreal newspaper *La Presse* turned into a riot, leaving 160 people injured. Workers had been on strike since Oct. 27. They returned to work Feb. 7, 1972.

Oct. 30 The Toronto *Telegram*, published by John Bassett (1915–1998), ceased publication after 95 years. On Nov. 1, a new Toronto daily newspaper, *The Sun*, began publication, filling the vacancy. *The Sun* was staffed mainly by former *Telegram* employees.

Nov. 2 Dr. Gerhard Herzberg (1904–1999), of the National Research Council of Canada, received the Nobel Prize in chemistry for his work in molecular spectroscopy.

• The federal govt mothballed the experimental hydrofoil antisubmarine vessel *Bras d'Or* because of costs.

Nov. 2–7 President Joseph Tito of Yugoslavia visited Canada for the 1st time. Agreements were reached on updating trade relations, establishing contacts and exchanges in science and technology, and the encouragement of travel between the countries.

Nov. 3 Quebec City's last English-language newspaper, the *Quebec Chronicle-Telegraph,* went from a daily to a weekly. The paper was established in 1925 when the *Morning Chronicle* and *Daily Telegraph* merged.

Nov. 10 The Senate Committee on Poverty recommended that a family of 4 be guaranteed a minimum annual income of $3,500.

Nov. 12 Paul Joseph Cini, with 54 sticks of dynamite and a shotgun, hijacked an Air Canada aircraft over the prairies, but was subdued and arrested. He was sentenced to life imprisonment for the crime Apr. 11, 1972.

Nov. 13 Cree Helen Betty Osborne was forced into a car in La Pas, Man., driven outside of town, brutally violated and murdered by 4 white men. It wasn't until 1987 that 1 member of the tight-knit community, Dwayne Archie Johnson, was charged and later convicted of second-degree murder. He was paroled Oct. 1997. On July 14, 2000, Man. Justice Minister Gord Mackintosh formally apologized to the Osborne family for the way the former govt responded to the murder. On July 16, 2000, a bronze Celebration of Life plaque was set in Guy Hill Park, the site of the murder, to commemorate Helen Osborne's 48th birthday.

Dec. 2 Canada and Norway signed fishing and sealing agreements ending Norway's right to fish within Canada's 19.3-km (12-mile) limit, except in the Gulf of St. Lawrence. The regional seal harvest was also split between Canada and Norway.

Dec. 3 A Canada-US extradition treaty was signed in Washington, D.C., with conspiracy to commit assault and unlawful seizure of aircraft added as grounds for extradition.

Dec. 6 The 1st two units of the 296-m-long Churchill Falls powerhouse, on the Churchill R., Labrador, went on line to Hydro-Quebec. The $946 million project — the largest single-site hydroelectric power project in the world — reached full operation in 1972.

Dec. 9 Two Montreal subway trains collided, killing 1 person and destroying 36 subway cars.

Dec. 18 The Group of Ten, a selection of bank governors from 10 major non-Communist trading countries, including Canada, met in Washington, D.C. The group agreed to eliminate a US 10% import surcharge, to devalue the US dollar through an increase in the price of gold and to continue to float the Canadian dollar.

• More than $1 million was stolen from a Windsor, Ont., branch of the Royal Bank of Canada. Six people were arrested several days later.

Dec. 23 New federal income tax legislation was passed: a tax on capital gains was established for the 1st time, effective Jan. 1, 1972. Gains subject to the tax were measured from Dec. 22, 1971 (known as Valuation Day) for publicly traded securities, and from Dec. 31, 1971 for all other assets.

Dec. 25 Justin Pierre Trudeau was born, the 2nd child born to a PM while in office. Mary Macdonald, daughter of PM John A. Macdonald, was the 1st, in 1869.

Dec. 26 Air Canada Flight 932 from Thunder Bay to Toronto was hijacked, flown to Toronto then Cuba. The hijacker, American Patrick Dolan Critton, a suspected member of a Black Panther affiliate, was caught 3 decades later in the US. He pleaded guilty to kidnapping and extortion in a Toronto court, and on June 12, 2002, was sentenced to 3 years' imprisonment.

c 1971 Janet Kigusiuq (b 1926) of Baker L., now in Nunavut, completed the graphite and colour pencil *A Giant, Half Human, Half Animal, Attacks,* inspired by figures from the Qiviug Cycle. The drawing is now with the Winnipeg Art Gallery.

1971–1972 A 4-foot-4, 10-year-old Wayne Gretzky (b 1961) scored 378 goals in 68 games for his Minor Pee Wee Brantford, Ont., hockey team.

• The greatest seasonal snowfall in Canada was recorded at Revelstoke/Mount Copeland, BC, at 24.4 m during the winter.

Also in 1971
• The population of Canada was 21,568,310.

• Oil and natural gas was discovered on Sable Is., 280 km from Halifax.

• Dr. James Guillet (b 1927) of the U. of Toronto invented UV-biodegradable plastic.

• The Ont. govt appointed the Royal Commission on Publishing, led by Richard Rohmer, Dalton Camp and Marsh Jeanneret. The commission recommended policies to increase the strength of Canadian-owned Ont. publishers through the elimination of sales tax on magazines and periodicals, a recommendation that was rejected by the Ont. govt.

• The Molson family sold the Montreal Canadiens and the Montreal Forum for $15 million to Placements Rondelle, a consortium comprising John Bassett, the Bank of Nova Scotia, and Edward and Peter Bronfman. The deal was consummated before the new capital gains tax measure took effect.

• Debbie Brill (b 1953) became the 1st North American woman high jumper to clear 6 feet (6' 3/4" or 1.85 m), giving her gold at the Pan Am Games in Cali, Colombia.

• Peter Gzowski (1934–2002) began a 3-year stint as host of CBC Radio's *This Country in the Morning,* a 3-hour morning program (9 a.m. to noon), connecting all kinds of Canadians from all over the country with a mixture of music, talk, interviews, quizzes, monologues and just plain fun.

• Tagak Curley (b 1944) founded the political organization Inuit Tapirisat of Canada (ITC) to promote Inuit land issues and to promote Inuit culture.

• The Irish Rovers were given their own TV show on CBC in Vancouver.

• The Juno Awards, honouring excellence in the Canadian music industry, were established. The 1st awards went to Gordon Lightfoot (b 1938) for Male Vocalist of the Year, and to Anne Murray for Female Vocalist of the Year.

• Production began on the comedy television series for kids *The Hilarious House of Frightenstein,* at CHCH studios in Hamilton, Ont. One hundred and thirty episodes were made in less than a year. Hosted by the Count (Billy Van [1934–2003]) and Igor (Fishka Rais), the *Hilarious House* introduced an entire generation of Saturday-morning couch potatoes to the likes of the psychedelic record-spinning Wolfman, Grizelda the Ghastly Gourmet, the cobwebbed Librarian, The Maharishi, Dr. PetVet and Superhippy.

• Acclaimed Jamaican jazz pianist Wynton Kelly suffered an epileptic attack at a concert in Toronto and died from lack of medical assistance.

• An exhibition of Inuit art, assembled by the Vancouver Art Gallery, began a tour of Copenhagen, Moscow, Leningrad, London, Philadelphia, and then Ottawa. It was the largest exhibition of Canadian sculpture shown abroad, and for the majority of viewers, the 1st Inuit art they had ever seen in person.

• Christopher Pratt (b 1935) painted *Night Window,* oil on masonite, now at York U., Toronto.

• Mary Pratt, née West (b 1935), painted *Eviscerated Chickens,* a kitchen still life, now in the Memorial U. Art Gallery, St. John's.

• Yves Gaucher (1934–2000) completed *Rouge/Bleu/Vert,* on canvas, now in the Art Gallery of Ontario, Toronto.

• Ottawa native Kenneth Lochhead (b 1926) completed *Inner Release*, acrylic on canvas, using a spray gun while the canvas lay flat on the floor. The work is in a private collection.

• Winnipeg playwright Carol Bolt (b 1941) produced the critically acclaimed play *Buffalo Jump*. It would be published in 1972.

• Publishers New Press, Anansi, Hurtig, Oberon Press and Sono Nis became the founding members of the Independent Publishers Association (IPA), established to lobby for Canadian-only policies. The IPA became the Association of Canadian Publishers (ACP) in 1976.

• Book publishers Black Rose Books, Douglas & McIntyre and U. of BC Press began operations.

• Pierre Berton published *The National Dream: The Great Railway, 1871–1881*.

• James Houston published the novel *White Dawn: An Eskimo Saga*, about a group of whalers forced to winter in the Arctic and the trouble they create for themselves and the Inuit who have so generously offered to save them. The book was published in 11 languages, went through 31 editions and was adapted into a Hollywood movie.

• Gérard Bessette (b 1920) published the novel *Le Cycle*, for which he received the Gov-Gen.'s Award.

• Sask. native Max Braithwaite (1911–1995) published *The Night He Stole the Mountie's Car*, which won the 1972 Stephen Leacock Medal for humour. The fictional town Winnego was modelled on the Sask. towns Aberdeen and Vonda, where Braithwaite taught during the 1930s.

• Antonine Maillet (b 1929) published the Acadian novel *La Sagouine*.

• Alice Munro published the novel *Lives of Girls and Women*, for which she received the Canadian Booksellers Association International Book of the Year Award.

• The children's picture-storybook *Mary of Mile 18*, written and illustrated by Ann Blades (b 1945), was published. The work, which depicted life on a remote Mennonite settlement in northern BC, became an instant, enduring classic.

• Mordecai Richler published the classic novel *St. Urbain's Horseman*.

• George Ryga (1932–1987) vaulted to literary prominence with publication of *The Ecstasy of Rita Joe and Other Plays*.

• Bill Bissett published the book of poetry *Nobody Owns the Earth*.

• John Glassco (1909-1981) published the critically acclaimed, *Selected Poems*.

• Poet Paul-Marie Lapointe (b 1929) published *Le Réel absolu*, for which he received the Gov-Gen.'s Award.

• Toronto-born Michael Snow completed the 16-mm, 3-hour colour concept film *La Region Centrale*, portraying a prehistoric landscape untouched by human life.

• Leonard Cohen supplied the songs for the Robert Altman film *McCabe and Mrs. Miller*.

• Gordon Lightfoot recorded the single "If You Could Read My Mind."

• Joni Mitchell released the album *Blue*, containing the song "Little Green." In 1997, Mitchell explained that Little Green was a coded wish of love and happiness to the infant daughter she had named Kelly and given up for adoption in 1965.

• Neil Young recorded the folk-rock classic *Harvest*, which included the hit song "Heart of Gold," with backing vocals by James Taylor and Linda Ronstadt.

• Rita MacNeil moved to Toronto from Big Pond on Cape Breton Is. and supported herself with odd jobs while working on her 1st album, *Born a Woman*.

1972

Jan. 1 The Canadian Tobacco Manufacturers Council's Cigarette Advertising Code came into effect, placing a voluntary ban on all cigarette advertising on Canadian television and radio.

Jan. 17–29 Canadian air traffic controllers went on strike over salaries and hours, grounding most commercial flights in the country. On Mar. 10, the controllers were awarded a 17.4% salary increase over 27 months, by arbitration.

Jan. 18 Seal hunting in the Gulf of St. Lawrence was banned to large fleet-sized vessels and aircraft.

• The CRTC implemented the 1st Canadian-content requirements for music selection on AM radio, at 30% between 6:00 a.m. and midnight.

Jan. 19 The minutes and documents of the Canadian Cabinet War Committee of Dec. 5, 1939, became public. The material revealed decisions refusing a US proposal to assume supreme command of Canadian forces, a concern over possible violent demonstrations against Japanese Canadians, and PM King's determination to avoid conscription.

Jan. 24 FLQ leader Pierre Vallières, wanted for seditious conspiracy and for providing counsel to kidnapping and murder, surrendered to police. On Oct. 4, 1972, he received a 1-year suspended sentence for giving counsel to kidnapping.

Jan. 25 Ont. Supreme Court Justice A.H. Lieff granted an injunction to prevent a woman from having an abortion. The injunction was granted in Ottawa to the husband (the family name was protected by the judge), who was recognized in court as guardian of the "infant plaintiff." The injunction was possibly the 1st of its kind in North America.

Jan. 26 Part 1 of the report of the LeDain Commission on the non-medical use of drugs chaired by Gerald LeDain (b 1924), was published, recommending the legalization of heroin for drug-addiction treatment. Part 2 of the report, issued May 17, recommended eliminating penalties for possession of marijuana and hashish. The govt rejected both recommendations.

Feb. 2 Canada's application for official status as a permanent observer to the Organization of American States (OAS) was approved. In 1990, Canada officially joined the OAS after having enjoyed observer status since 1972. By 1991, all 35 independent nations in the Americas were members. The goal of the OAS was to advance democracy and human

rights, fight poverty, drugs and corruption and expand trade throughout its membership.

Feb. 5 Que. prison guards, game wardens and other peace officers went on strike until Mar. 4. The strike closed 22 of Que.'s 35 jails.

Feb. 6–Mar. 2 Airport radar and communications technicians went on strike, which all but halted commercial air traffic across the country. The dispute was settled Mar. 2 with a new contract that increased workers' wages by up to 15.1%.

Feb. 8 The Canadian Transport Commission refused a request by the CNR and CPR to discontinue passenger service between Montreal and the Maritime provinces. The railways had argued that the routes were uneconomical.

Feb. 9 The Canadian Telecommunications Carriers Association, representing Canadian telephone companies, railway telecommunications operations, the Canadian Overseas Telecommunication Corporation, and Telesat Canada, was established.

Feb. 11 The federal govt pledged $1.7 million to bolster the Canadian book publishing industry.

Feb. 14 Canada recognized the independence of Bangladesh, formerly East Pakistan.

Feb. 21 Canada agreed to allow the Vienna-based International Atomic Energy Agency to verify that Canada's nuclear power was used for peaceful purposes only.

Feb. 22 Canadian light-heavyweight Stewart Gray died in a Winnipeg hospital after a match with Canadian champion Al Sparks.

Also in Feb.
• Panarctic Oils Ltd. discovered oil on Ellesmere Is. in the Canadian Arctic.

• Responsibility for all canals, other than those under the St. Lawrence Seaway Authority, was transferred to the Conservation Program of the Natural Historic Sites Branch of the Department of Indian Affairs and Northern Development.

Mar. 2 The federal govt announced plans to build a

new international airport in Pickering Township, about 48 km east of Toronto. The federal govt spent $120 million to expropriate approximately 7,350 ha for the purpose, a move vehemently opposed by residents and environmental groups. The federal govt abandoned its proposal Sept. 25, 1975, after the Ont. govt refused to contribute roads, water and services. The land remained under the stewardship of the federal govt and the area designated an airport site for future use on Aug. 1, 2001.

Mar. 7 The Yukon transferred 13 km^2 to the NWT as compensation for a surveying error. The new land, on Mount Logan, was used to create the Norah Willis Michener Game Preserve.

Mar. 12 The federal govt allowed Que. qualified control over the distribution of family allowances.

Mar. 24 Frank Moores' Conservatives were re-elected in the Nfld. provincial election, gaining a majority govt with 33 seats. Edward Roberts' Liberals took 9. The election win marked Nfld.'s 1st Conservative majority govt.

Mar. 27 France, Britain, Portugal and Denmark signed agreements with Canada to eliminate traditional and treaty fishing rights within Canadian waters off the East Coast, on a gradual basis.

Mar. 30 Canadian naval personnel were issued their last daily rum rations. The Canadian navy had borrowed its rum ration tradition from the English, who initiated the custom after conquering Jamaica in 1655.

Also in Mar.
 • Gordon Lightfoot's album *Don Quixote* was released, which included the classic songs "Alberta Bound," "Christian Island," "Beautiful" and the title cut, "Don Quixote."

Apr. 3 Dr. Gustave Gingras (1918–1996), of the Rehabilitation Institute of Montreal, won the Royal Bank Award for his work with physically challenged children and adults.

Apr. 5 China's championship ping-pong team visited the Norman Bethune House in Gravenhurst, Ont., to pay tribute to the great doctor who died in China

Nov. 12, 1939, while tending to the wounds of fallen Chinese soldiers. The house was made a National Historic Site on Aug. 30, 1976.

Apr. 6 A bomb planted by unknown perpetrators exploded at the Cuban Trade Commission in Montreal, killing 1 person.

 • A large peninsula on Victoria Is. in the NWT was named after the renowned anthropologist Diamond Jenness.

Apr. 11–24 Some 200,000 Que. employees, including Hydro-Que. workers, teachers and hospital staff, staged the largest strike in Canada's history. Back-to-work legislation ended the walkout, but 3 strike leaders were sentenced to 1 year in jail.

Apr. 15 While in Canada, US President Richard Nixon and PM Trudeau signed the Canada-US Great Lakes Water Quality Agreement, committing the countries to cleaning up industrial and non-commercial waste in the Great Lakes. The agreement was renewed in 1978, and amended to enhance antipollution programs and practices and establish specific timetables.

Apr. 24 The federal govt temporarily banned commercial salmon fishing in NB and the Port aux Basques area of Nfld. in order to conserve depleted stocks. On May 29, the Que. govt banned all commercial salmon fishing off the Gaspé Peninsula for the same reason.

Apr. 28–July 22 BC contractors locked out union members of 18 building trades because of escalating labour strife.

Also in Apr.
 • The National Ad Hoc Action Committee on the Status of Women was founded at the Strategy for Change Conference in Toronto, attended by more than 500 people. The body would later become the National Action Committee on the Status of Women (NAC).

May 1 George Davidson, president of the CBC, was appointed undersecretary-gen. of the UN. He assumed his new role on Aug. 1.

May 10 Canada joined the Inter-American Development Bank, becoming its 24th member. Headquartered in Washington, D.C., the bank provides financing to social- and economic-development projects in Latin America and the Caribbean.

May 24–25 Kurt Waldheim, secretary-gen. of the UN, visited Canada.

June 8 Former PM Lester B. Pearson received the Order of Merit from Queen Elizabeth II.

June 13–Sept. 13 Steelworkers at Iron Ore Company of Canada plants in Schefferville, Que., and Labrador City, Nfld., conducted a 3-month strike that ended with the appointment of a commission to investigate the dispute.

June 19 The 2,000-member Canadian Airline Pilots Association participated in an international, 24-hour strike to protest worldwide escalations in airliner hijackings.

June 23 A 5-month strike of 2,200 CBC broadcasting technicians ended.

June 29 The Supreme Court of Canada ruled that motorists could seek legal advice before submitting to breath tests.

Also in June
 • The RCMP burned a barn near Montreal to prevent a suspected meeting between the FLQ and the US-based Black Panthers organization.

July 5 The National Ballet of Canada ended its 1st European tour, having performed in Monte Carlo, London, Glasgow, Paris, Stuttgart and Lausanne.

July 7 The govt legislated an end to a 7-week longshoremen's strike in St. Lawrence R. ports.

July 14 Canadian Labour Congress President Donald Macdonald (b 1932) was elected the 1st non-European president of the 91-nation International Confederation of Free Trade Unions.

July 17 The federal govt pledged $587,000 to establish the New Horizons program, designed to keep retired people active and help alleviate loneliness and isolation.

 • The new St. Boniface, Man., cathedral, designed by Étienne Gaboury (b 1930), was dedicated on the former site of the 4 previous churches. The 1st was a log-cabin chapel built Nov. 1, 1818, by Father Joseph-Norbert Provencher. It was replaced by a more impressive twin-spired cathedral in 1832, which was replaced by an even grander stone cathedral in 1862. Then, on Aug. 15, 1906, Archbishop Langevin laid the cornerstone for the striking Marchand- and Haskell-designed cathedral, which was destroyed by fire July 22, 1968. The newest cathedral incorporated whole sections of the earlier cathedral walls, facade and sacristy.

July 31 The federal govt announced that 1st-time marijuana possession offenders would not be sent to jail.

Also in July
 • Man.'s Planetarium (opened May 1968) and Museum (opened July 1970) were merged by provincial legislation to become the Manitoba Museum of Man and Nature (changed to the Manitoba Museum in 1996). The largest Man. heritage centre includes a 3-dimensional tour through the province's past, a replica of the 17th-century Hudson's Bay Company *Nonsuch* and a gallery devoted to the history of the Hudson's Bay Company.

Aug. 3–4 The 13th provincial premiers' conference met at Halifax, with offshore mineral rights and winter employment programs the main topics of discussion.

Aug. 14 The PEI govt created a Royal Commission to investigate land use in the province, and land sales to non-islanders.

Aug. 15 Irascible Harold Ballard (1903–1990), president of Maple Leaf Gardens, was convicted in Toronto of 47 charges of fraud, and theft of $205,000 in Gardens' funds. On Oct. 20, he was sentenced to 3 years in prison.

Aug. 17 The Dennis Study on housing, established in 1971 through the Central Mortgage and Housing Corp., revealed that more than half the land required for new housing in 10 of the nation's largest cities was owned by each city's 6 largest developers.

Aug. 21–Sept. 2 The Canadian Trade Exposition, largest trade fair in Canadian history, was held in Beijing, China.

Aug. 22–Sept. 10 The Commonwealth Institute in London, England, showcased an exhibition of Emily Carr paintings.

Aug. 24 The federal govt agreed to allow Asians holding British passports, who had been expelled from Idi Amin's Uganda on Aug. 5, to enter Canada. By Nov. 8, 4,420 Ugandan Asians had immigrated to Canada.

• In the BC general election, Premier W.A.C. Bennett's Social Credit govt was defeated after 20 years in power. The NDP, under David Barrett (b 1930), won 38 seats, the Social Credits 10 seats, the Liberals 5 and the Progressive Conservatives 2. On June 5, 1973, Bennett retired from politics.

Aug. 30 Rosemary Brown (1930–2003) of Vancouver became the 1st black woman elected to a provincial legislature in Canada. She later became the 1st woman to run for the leadership of a major Canadian political party, losing the national NDP leadership race to Ed Broadbent (b 1936) in 1975. Brown was re-elected to the BC legislature in 1975, 1979 and 1983.

Sept. 1 The BC legislature ordered striking longshoremen back to work to keep wheat shipments moving to China, Japan and the USSR. The 6-month dispute ended Jan. 24, 1972, with workers accepting an hourly-wage increase of $1.05, plus improved benefits.

• In Montreal's worst blaze since Jan. 9, 1927, 37 people were killed and 54 injured when an arson fire ravaged the Blue Bird nightclub.

Sept. 2 Summit Series, Game 1, Montreal: Phil Esposito (b 1942) and Vladimir Petrov faced off at centre ice at the Montreal Forum, beginning one of the most storied sporting events in Canadian history: Team Canada '72 versus Team USSR in the 8-game Summit Series. The Canadian team consisted of such greats as Yvan Cournoyer (b 1943), Brad Park (b 1948), Bill White (b 1939), Bobby Clarke (b 1949) and Ken Dryden (b 1947). The Russian

squad boasted Valery Kharlamov, Alexander Yakushev, Boris Mikhailov, Yuri Liapkin and Vladislav Tretiak. Despite scoring 2 quick goals in the 1st period, Canada fell to the agile Russians 7–3 before a crowd of 18,818. Game 2 was held in Toronto Sept. 4: Team Canada tied the Summit Series at one game apiece by beating the Russian squad 4–1. Phil Esposito opened the scoring at 7:14 in the 2nd period. Game 3 was held Sept. 6

Sept. 4 The Musée des beaux-arts de Montréal was robbed of $3 million in paintings and art objects, including the $1 million 1654 Rembrandt *Landscape with Cottages*. The thieves had entered through the museum's skylight. The art was not recovered.

Sept. 5 The Immigration Act was modified to allow aliens who had entered Canada as visitors to apply for landed-immigrant (permanent-resident) status. These Immigration Act modifications were suspended Nov. 3.

Sept. 6 Game 3, Winnipeg: Vladislav Tretiak stopped 38 shots in a 4–4 tie, and was chosen his team's MVP (Most Valuable Palyer). Team Canada's MVP was Paul Henderson (b 1943). Game 4 was held Sept. 8 in Vancouver: Ken Dryden faced 41 shots in a 5–3 loss to the Soviets. A frustrated and impassioned Phil Esposito explained in a post-game interview, "We're trying our best. I can't believe people are booing us. We're all here because we love Canada. Let's face facts. They've got a good team." The Summit Series moved to Moscow Sept. 22–28 for the remaining games.

Sept. 15 In Toronto, striking De Havilland Aircraft Company of Canada Ltd. workers ended an 8-month walkout, agreeing to a new contract providing for an average pay increase of $1.05 per hour over 3 years.

Sept. 17 Cartier-Brébeuf National Historic Site was opened in Quebec City in honour of explorer Jacques Cartier and missionary Jean de Brébeuf. The site provides a number of exhibits that commemorate Cartier's 1st winter in Canada, 1535–1536, and also the 1st Jesuit residence in Que., built in 1625–1626.

Sept. 20 Letter bombs intended for the Israeli

embassy in Ottawa and the Israeli consulate in Montreal were intercepted without incident.

• Inuit artist Pitseolak Ashoona (1904–1983) published *Pictures Out of My Life*, incorporating recorded interviews edited by Dorothy Eber. The book was profusely illustrated in colour, with prints of Pitseolak's works.

Sept. 21–Oct. 23 Steelworkers at Sydney, NS, walked off their jobs. The strike ended with workers agreeing to a 33.5% increase in the basic rate of pay.

Sept. 22-28 The Summit Series moved to Moscow for the remaining 4 games. Canada lost game 5 by a score of 5-4 on Sept. 22, but won game 6 on Sept. 24 by a score of 3–2 — a game best remembered for Bobby Clarke's grim assault on the ankle of Valery Kharlamov. Canada went on to take game 7 on Sept. 26 by a score of 4–2, knotting the series at 3 games apiece, with 1 tie. The rubber match was played Sept. 28. At 12:56 of the 3rd period of the 8th game, Cournoyer tied the score at 5–5. In the last minute, Esposito intercepted a pass and shot at the net; Paul Henderson met the puck, and with 34 seconds left, scored on his 2nd attempt. Team Canada won the inaugural Summit Series. In Dec. 2000, the Hockey Hall of Fame declared Team Canada '72 the greatest hockey team of the 20th century.

Oct. 11 *In the Ward*, oil on canvas, by Lawren Harris, sold for $48,000 at Maynard's in Vancouver.

Oct. 12 An International Joint Commission blamed the US for more than 90% of the air pollution in Windsor, Ont. Pollution had reduced air quality in the city to below Ont. standards.

• More than 100 people were arrested for drug trafficking in Vancouver, Victoria, Toronto, Moncton and Hull in a nationwide drug sweep. The raid was the result of a 6-month RCMP investigation.

Oct. 13 A plaque honouring the late Plains Cree chief Poundmaker was unveiled by his great-grandson Jimmy Poundmaker on the Poundmaker Indian Reserve near Cut Knife, Sask.

• Approximately 12,000 Ont. Hydro employees ended a 122-day strike, agreeing to submit unresolved issues to arbitration.

Oct. 20 The Canadian Transport Commission announced the beginning of air charter service for destinations outside Canada, requiring booking in advance with a deposit, effective Apr. 1, 1973.

Oct. 27 BC passed legislation to provide $200 a month to the physically challenged and to old-age pensioners.

Oct. 30 PM Trudeau's Liberals were returned to power in the general election with a minority govt. Liberals took 109 seats, Progressive Conservatives under Robert Stanfield won 107, the NDP under David Lewis 31, Social Credit 15, and Independents 2. Voter turnout was 76.7%.

• Monique Bégin (b 1936) became the 1st woman from Que. to be elected to the House of Commons. Bégin was re-elected in 1974, 1979 and 1980. She served as parliamentary secretary to the minister of foreign affairs in 1975, as minister of national revenue in 1976 and as minister of national health and welfare from 1977 until her leave from politics in 1984.

Nov. 9 *Anik-I*, Canada's (and the world's) 1st geostationary domestic communications satellite, was launched from Cape Canaveral, Florida. Operated by Telesat Canada, it was designed to improve telephone and radio service, and provide television to communities in the Far North.

Nov. 14 Approval was given for the installation of SAMSON — Strategic Automatic Message Switching Operation Network — a computer-controlled message-handling network connecting Canadian Armed Forces bases in Canada and Europe.

Nov. 15 Que. legislated 8,500 striking Hydro-Quebec employees back to work.

• Peter Lougheed's Alb. Progressive Conservatives passed the Alberta Bill of Rights. The legislation outlawed discrimination based on race, national origin, colour, religion and sex, and provided the right to liberty, security, enjoyment of property and freedom of religion, speech, assembly and press.

Nov. 16 The Unity National Bank was chartered as Canada's 11th bank, with head offices in Toronto.

Nov. 20–21 The 1st federal-provincial-municipal govt conference was held in Toronto.

Nov. 23 Ont. introduced legislation allowing people access to credit-agency information banks.

Nov. 24 The Que. National Assembly introduced legislation to create 13 electoral districts in northern Que., providing the vote to 1,500 Inuit, 3,500 Native Peoples and several hundred of European descent.

Nov. 29 The federal govt approved a $74 million plan to computerize and automate air traffic control to improve safety and efficiency, and help ease air traffic congestion at Canada's larger airports.

Also in Nov.
• CBC television's comedy-drama the *Beachcombers,* starring Bruno Gerussi (1928–1995) as Nick Adonidas, and Robert Clothier (1921–1999) as Relic, was 1st aired. The unfolding hijinks of the 2 rival timber scourers was the cause of mirth and mayhem in Gibson's Landing, a fictional setting on BC's Sunshine Coast. The show aired until Apr. 1990. It was the longest-running series in Canadian television history.

Dec. 4 The federal govt pledged $350 million toward a program to help provinces and municipalities create more jobs over the next 3 years. An additional $150 million was granted for federal job-creation programs.

Dec. 9 Bush pilot Martin Hartwell was found alive 32 days after his plane crashed in the Arctic. Three passengers had died in the crash.

Dec. 20 The federal govt prohibited Canadian vessels from whaling on the East Coast because of diminishing whale numbers.

Dec. 27 Former PM Lester B. Pearson died in Ottawa of cancer. He was 75.

1972–1973 The NFB produced a series of 12 documentary films exploring contemporary Que. society and English-Canadian stereotypes about the province.

1972–1976 Canada Post issued 20 new stamps honouring the heritage of First Nations peoples. Denominations were 8 cents and 10 cents.

• CBC television aired *This Is the Law*, a game show involving a bumbling character played by actor Paul Soles (b 1931) performing a number of seemingly innocuous activities, only to be arrested at the end of each vignette. Panellists (including humorist/lawyer Hart Pomerantz) were then challenged to determine which Canadian law was in fact broken. Veteran Canadian actor Austin Willis (1917–2004) hosted the popular show.

Also in 1972
• Following the federal general election, 20-year-old Sean O'Sullivan (1952–1989), representing Hamilton (Ont.) West, became the youngest MP to ever sit in the Commons. Sullivan retired from politics in 1977 and entered the Roman Catholic priesthood. In 1989, O'Sullivan became editor of the *Catholic Register* and published his autobiography, *Both My Houses: From Politics to Priesthood.* He was named Companion of the Order of Canada in 1987 for promoting the rights of the elderly and disabled. O'Sullivan died of leukemia in 1989. A Hamilton-area park was named in his honour on May 25, 1993.

• The multi-million dollar Rodney (shipping) Container Terminal was completed on the west side of the Saint John, NB, harbour, making Saint John a major-container shipping centre.

• The spectacular Nahanni National Park Reserve (300 km²) was established in the South Mountains at the southwest end of the NWT. The park is home to the 92-m-tall Virginia Falls, 4 canyons that rise up to 1,500 m above the turbulent South Nahanni R., and a host of boreal forest wildlife including moose, black bear, mule bear, mountain goats, dall sheep and the occasional grizzly bear. Nahanni was designated a UNESCO World Heritage site in 1978. In 1987, the South Nahanni R. was designated a Canadian Heritage River.

• The Canadian govt established Kluane National Park and Reserve (21,980 km²) in the southwestern Yukon. Kluane is dominated by the St. Elias Mountains and the world's largest non-polar icefield. Canada's highest peak, Mount Logan

(5,950 m), is located in the park, which is not accessible by road.

• The Richmond Hill (Ont.) Dynes won the World Softball Championships, defeating the US 1–0 in 11 innings.

• Gordie Howe received the President's Cabinet Medallion from the U. of Detroit.

• Winnipeg and surrounding municipalities merged under the Unicity plan, forming 1 city, with a population of 550,000, run by a central 50-member city council.

• Terry Mosher (b 1942) joined the *Montreal Gazette* as editorial cartoonist. Mosher, who chose his daughter's name — Aislin — as his *nom de plume*, is known by policitians and newspaper editors alike as "Canada's nastiest cartoonist." Through syndication, Aislin's cartoons appear in newspapers throughout Canada and are frequently published as collections in book form.

• Three new Decorations of Bravery were instituted by the federal govt: the Cross of Valour, "for acts of the most conspicuous courage in circumstances of extreme peril;" the Star of Courage, "for acts of conspicuous courage in circumstances of great peril;" and the Medal of Bravery, "for acts of bravery in hazardous circumstances."

• Tillie Taylor became the 1st chairperson of the Sask. Human Rights Commission.

• The country's 2 reigning national curling champions, Vera Pezer's (b 1939) Sask. rink and Orest Meleschuk's (b 1940) Man. rink, faced off in a CBC event to determine which was the best. The Sask. women's team took the crown.

• ACTRA (Association of Canadian Television and Radio Artists) presented its 1st Canadian industry awards. The 1st ceremony included only 3 award presentations. In 1986, the ACTRA Awards were replaced by the Gemini Awards for Canadian Television. In celebration of the 60th anniversary of ACTRA, the awards were revived Feb. 27, 2003; Gordon Pinsent received the Award of Excellence.

• Venerable Canadian publisher McClelland & Stewart (M&S) reported liabilities of more than $1 million. M&S printed 89 titles in 1972, including books by historian Pierre Berton (*The Great Railway*), novelist Brian Moore (*Catholics*), Eric Arthur (1898–1982) (*The Barn*), Jerry Goodis (b 1929) (*Have I Ever Lied to You Before?*), Farley Mowat (*A Whale for the Killing*), Mordecai Richler (*Shovelling Trouble*) and George Swinton (b 1917) (*Sculpture of the Eskimo*).

• Jack Shadbolt completed the ink, latex, crayon and acrylic *To Old Gardens,* now in a private collection.

• Gershon Iskowitz (1921–1988) produced *Uplands H,* on canvas, now in the Art Gallery of Ontario, Toronto.

• Ken Danby painted *At the Crease*, the unmistakable goaltender in net, now in a private collection.

• Sask.-born artist William Perehudoff (b 1919) completed *Prairie No. 4*, now with the Edmonton Art Gallery.

• Beverley Slopen established the Beverly Slopen Literary agency, joining high-profile agents such as Bella Pomer and Lucinda Vardey, who represented the growing number of published Canadian authors. Until the 1970s, only Matie Molinaro, of the Canadian Speakers and Writers Service, represented authors. Her clients included Marshall McLuhan.

• Longhouse Book Shop, an all-Canadian bookstore owned by Beth Appeldoorn (b 1940), opened on Yonge St. in Toronto.

• The Women's Press was launched in Toronto. It would become the oldest English-language feminist publisher in the nation.

• Margaret Atwood published the novel *Surfacing*, and *Survival: A Thematic Guide to Canadian Literature.*

• Historian and poet Alfred Goldsworthy Bailey (1905–1997) published a collection of essays, *Culture and Nationality.*

• Matt Cohen (1942–2000) published the collection of short fiction *Columbus and the Fat Lady.*

• Novelist Robert Harlow (b 1923) published the popular novel *Scann*.

• David Gordon Helwig (b 1938) published *A Book About Billie,* a non-fiction work stemming from a series of interviews with a convict.

• The novel *L'Elan d'Amérique*, by André Langevin (b 1927), was published.

• James Houston published the anthology *Songs of the Dream People*.

• Comedienne Beatrice Lillie (1894–1989) published her autobiography, *Every Other Inch a Lady*.

• John Metcalf published his 1st novel, *Going Down Slow*.

• U. of Toronto professor of philosophy Francis Edward Sparshott (b 1926) published *Looking for Philosophy*.

• Dennis Lee published *Civil Elegies and other Poems,* for which he received the Gov-Gen.'s Award for Poetry.

• *Driving Home*, Miriam Waddington's 7th volume of poetry, was published, for which she won the J.I. Segal Prize.

• Gilles Hénault (1920–1996) published *Signaux pour les voyants*, which won the Gov-Gen.'s Award for poetry in French.

• Playwright Ann Henry's *Lulu Street* was performed at the opening of the Festival Lennoxville, at Bishop's U. in the Eastern Townships, Que.

• The National Ballet of Canada's production of *The Sleeping Beauty*, which featured Rudolph Nureyev, was the most lavish Canadian ballet production to date. Costing $375,000, it nearly bankrupted the company.

• Avant-garde jazz pianist Paul Bley (b 1932) record-ed his 1st solo album, *Open, To Love*.

• The largest French-language broadcasting production centre in the world, Maison de Radio-Canada, opened in Montreal. Construction had begun on the CBC building May 24, 1968.

1973

Jan. 5 The federal govt officially condemned US air raids on Hanoi and Haiphong, North Vietnam, and urged the US to refrain from further action.

Jan. 14 The Unité-Québec reverted to its original name, Union Nationale. The Que. political party, formally established in 1936, had changed its name to Unité-Québec Oct. 25, 1971.

Jan. 20 Approximately 240 Nordair Ltd. ground-personnel workers returned to work after a 9-week strike, accepting an 18% wage increase over 2 years.

Jan. 22 Istvan Meszaros, Marxist scholar and former Hungarian culture minister, was granted landed immigrant status. He had been refused twice before as a security risk.

Jan. 24 Canada, together with Hungary, Poland and Indonesia, joined the International Commission for the Control and Supervision (ICCS) of the truce between North Vietnam and South Vietnam, for a 60-day trial period. On Jan. 29, the 1st 130 Canadian ICCS members arrived at Saigon, South Vietnam. Canada officially recognized the Communist govt of North Vietnam of Feb. 7. The last American troops left Vietnam Mar. 29, but battle still raged. The Canadian ICCS members left July 31. On Apr. 30, 1975, Saigon fell, marking the end of the war and the re-unification of the country under Communist rule.

Jan. 25 The freighter *Irish Stardust* ran aground north of Vancouver Is., spilling 378,000 litres of fuel oil. The spill spread south for more than 320 km.

Jan. 31 The Supreme Court of Canada ruled that the Nisga'a peoples had no rights over land in the Nass R. Valley in BC. It would take 26 years (Apr. 27, 1999) until the Nisga'a received control over the Nass, their traditional territory.

Also in Jan.
• The RCMP broke into Parti Québécois offices, stealing a 2-m stack of computerized PQ membership lists. A number of active and former RCMP were charged in connection with the crime on June 11, 1981.

• Elijah Smith (1912–1992), Chairman of the Council for Yukon Indians, presented PM Trudeau with the document *Together Today for Our Children Tomorrow*, which outlined Aboriginal rights, and the concept of Aboriginal title to land.

Feb. 6 Construction began on Toronto's 553.34-m CN Tower, the world's tallest free-standing structure to date. Used as a communications transmission mast and observation post, the tower opened June 26, 1976.

Feb. 13 The central recommendation of the report of the Que. Royal Commission on the French Language (Gendron Report) was that French be made the official language of Que., with both French and English the national languages.

Feb. 16 Canada and Cuba signed an anti-hijacking agreement, requiring each country to prosecute airliner hijackers in their own courts or return them to the country in which the crime was committed.

Feb. 19 The Trans-Canada Telephone System inaugurated Data-route, the world's 1st national digital system for commercial use.

Feb. 25 René Lévesque was re-elected president of the Parti Québécois by acclamation.

Mar. 15 Alb. Native Peoples won a $190,000 settlement in back payment of "ammunition money." According to an 1877 treaty, a sum of $2,000 was to have been paid annually.

• Approximately 50 Native Peoples left Winnipeg with supplies for members of the American Indian Movement, who had begun the 71 day "Siege at Wounded Knee," South Dakota, on Feb. 27.

Mar. 22 The St. Lawrence Seaway Authority granted $1.5 million and 321.7 ha to the Caughnawaga as compensation for 526 ha of land expropriated in 1955.

Mar. 29 Mexican President Luis Echeverria visited Canada until Apr. 1.

Also in Mar.
• Crude-oil exports were restricted due to soaring US demand; by Sept., the cost of Canadian crude was frozen below world prices. In June, gasoline exports were restricted, and in Oct., propane and butane exports were restricted.

Apr. 6–8 The 1st National Congress of Black Women was held in Toronto, under the auspices of the Canadian Negro Women's Association (CANEWA). The association was led by President Kay Livingstone (1918–1975).

Apr. 7 Four members of an ICCS truce-observance team in South Vietnam, including 1 Canadian, were killed when their helicopter was shot down.

Apr. 12 Heritage Canada Foundation, a non-profit national registered charity founded Mar. 28, began operations with a $12 million fund. Its mandate was to preserve, demonstrate and encourage the preservation of the nation's historic, architectural, natural and scenic heritage. In 1974, Heritage Canada acquired its 1st property, the stone Louis-Joseph Papineau Chapel, built in the woods of Montebello, Que., in 1951.

Apr. 20 Canada's 2nd communications satellite, *Anik II*, was launched from Cape Kennedy, Florida.

Apr. 29 The St. John R. in NB flooded, causing an estimated $25 million damage.

Also in Apr.
• Alb.'s Rosella Bjornson (b 1947) became the 1st woman airline pilot in North America when she was hired as 1st officer by Transair. She was inducted into Canada's Aviation Hall of Fame in 1987.

• The Food Prices Review Board, headed by Beryl Plumptre (b 1908), was formed by the federal govt. Its mandate was to investigate the rising cost of food. Periodic board reports blamed supply-and-demand factors and the influence of commodity marketing boards.

May 1 The Ont. govt awarded a $16 million contract to a West German firm to build a 4-km experimental elevated transit system at the Canadian National Exhibition (CNE) in Toronto. The Ont. govt cancelled the contract Nov. 13, 1974.

May 5 The great NB jockey Ron Turcotte (b 1941) rode Secretariat to a stunning Kentucky Derby victory, breaking Northern Dancer's track record and becoming the 1st jockey to win back-to-back Kentucky Derbies. (Turcotte had won the Derby aboard Secretariat's stablemate, Riva Ridge, in 1972.) Turcotte completed the American Triple Crown the same year, riding Secretariat to wins at the Belmont and Preakness.

May 7 Canada's mayors agreed to seek additional funds from the federal and provincial govts, at a "Cities for the 70s" conference in Toronto.

May 18 Former PM John Diefenbaker donated his Prince Albert, Sask. family homestead to the U. of Sask. on the condition that its lease provided public-speaking scholarships, and the land be permanently maintained in the memory of the early 19th-century prairie homesteaders.

June 1 Marshall McLuhan was appointed to the Papal Commission for Social Communication, to examine the relationship between the Vatican and the media.

June 6 Parliament passed a resolution supporting the 1969 Official Languages Act and stating further support for the equality of French and English within the civil service.

• A program to help illegal immigrants become Canadian citizens was launched. About 50,000 people applied for landed immigrant status before the Oct. 15 deadline.

• Canada prohibited US oil tankers from sailing through Canadian waters to reach a planned oil refinery at Eastport, Maine.

June 16 Prime Minister of India Indira Gandhi visited Canada for 8 days.

June 19 At the International Ballet Competition in Moscow, Karen Kain (b 1951) and Frank Augustyn (b 1953), of the National Ballet of Canada, won 1st prize for duet ensemble.

June 26 The International Association of Machinists accepted a new contract, ending rotating strikes against Air Canada.

June 28 NDP Premier Edward Schreyer was returned to power with 31 seats in the Man. election. The Conservatives took 21 seats and the Liberals 5.

June 29 The federal govt placed controls on the export of oilseeds and related products, to prevent a shortage of animal feeds. The controls were extended by July 9 to include edible oils, animal fats and livestock protein feeds.

June 30 The 1st National Lesbian Conference in Canada was held in Toronto at the YWCA on McGill St. Lesbians gathered together to discuss organizing strategies. Subsequent conferences were held in Montreal in 1974 and Ottawa in 1976.

July 6 The federal govt approved a $65 million plan to increase the crude-oil capacities of the Interprovincial Pipe Line from Alb. to Ont., and a $35.5 million plan to increase capacity of the natural gas pipeline from Alb. to BC. The capacity increases had been recommended by the National Energy Board.

July 12 Ont. Supreme Court Justice John Osler ruled the federal Indian Act inoperative in a case testing the legality of the elected council on the Six Nations Reserve, Brantford, Ont. The Supreme Court of Canada upheld the act on Aug. 27.

• The final report of the task force on Ocean Industry, Science and Technology recommended measures to stimulate offshore resources development, as well as the review of all existing legislation related to off-shore resource exploration.

July 14 Approximately 6,500 striking BC salmon fishers, shoreworkers and tendermen returned to work after accepting a contract providing higher prices for catches and better fringe benefits.

July 18 Former fashion model Christine Demeter was found bludgeoned to death in her Mississauga, Ont., home. In Dec. 1974, her husband, Peter Demeter, was sentenced to life imprisonment for ordering the hit on his wife so he could collect a $1 million insurance claim.

July 23 The federal and BC govts agreed to invest $325 million in rail, port and resource projects to encourage development in northwestern BC.

July 25 Former PM Louis St. Laurent died of heart failure in Que. He was 91.

Aug. 2–10 The 19th Commonwealth Heads of Govt Conference opened in Ottawa. Discussions included minority rights in South Africa, and a moratorium on nuclear weapons testing.

Aug. 8 The federal govt established 2 policies to facilitate Native land claims. Specific Claims Policy involved claims related to existing but unfulfilled treaties; Comprehensive Claims Policy involved claims to traditional territory not covered or surrendered by existing treaty. The Comprehensive policy also involved Aboriginal rights within the territory in question.

Aug. 27 Cedoux, Sask., was buffetted by a fierce hailstorm that produced the largest hailstone ever documented in Canada: it weighed 200 g and had a diameter of 144 mm. Mass on impact was estimated to be 450 g — and no one was hurt.

• The Supreme Court of Canada ruled 5–4 against Jeannette Corbiere Lavell, a member of the Nishnawbe Peoples, who lost her treaty rights when she married a man of European descent in 1970. She had won her case Oct. 9, 1971, but the ruling was eventually appealed to the Supreme Court, which argued section 12 of the Indian Act did not discriminate against women, even though Indian women who married non-status men lost their Indian status, while Indian men not only maintained their status, but conferred it on non-status wives. On Dec. 29, 1977, Section 12 of the Indian Act was brought before the UN Human Rights Committee.

Aug. 30–31 Some 200 Native Peoples occupied the Indian and Northern Affairs building in Ottawa to demand a halt to the James Bay power development project until the settlement of land claims. Agreement was eventually reached Nov. 11, 1975.

Sept. 7 The 1st report on the Canada-US Agreement on Great Lakes Water Quality, signed Apr. 15, 1972, blamed both countries for delaying the enforcement of anti-pollution rules, and suggested that the US spend more money to meet Agreement obligations.

Sept. 11 Helen Hunley (b 1920) was appointed Alb.'s 1st woman solicitor gen.

Sept. 13 Ottawa placed a 40-cent per-barrel tax on crude-oil exports, setting in motion a jurisdiction battle with Alb. involving price freezing and taxation. Premier Lougheed declared the tax an unconstitutional invasion into Alb. resource control, and on Oct. 4, flexed provincial muscle and declared an increase in provincial oil royalties. The announcement caused an immediate decline in the price of oil refinery shares: on Oct. 5, Texaco Canada dropped $3.87 to $55.35; Gulf Canada, $3.50 to $31.25; and Imperial Oil, $3.37 to $42.50.

Sept. 23 The United Auto Workers (UAW) and Chrysler Corp. agreed to a contract that gave Canadian auto workers wage parity with their American colleagues.

Oct. 2 A ruptured gas main near Red Deer L., Alb., forced the evacuation of 500 people from 3 communities.

Oct. 5 Jules Léger (1913–1980) was appointed gov-gen. of Canada, serving from Jan. 14, 1974 to Jan. 22, 1979. His wife, Gabrielle Carmel (d 1998), aided Léger with throne speeches after he suffered a stroke in 1974.

Oct. 10 A US federal court prevented the Canadian Development Corporation's (CDC) hostile takeover of Texasgulf Inc. The CDC attempted to gain a controlling interest in the firm, offering to buy 10 million shares for $29 a share. The CDC eventually purchased approximately 30% of the firm's stock. Texasgulf derived approximately two-thirds of its income from Canadian resources.

• The $198 million New York-based Shaheen Natural Resources oil refinery at Come By Chance, Nfld., opened. Owner John Shaheen hired the ocean liner *Queen Elizabeth II* at $97,000 a day to accommodate the 4,000 guests invited to the opening ceremonies. The refinery had a capacity of 17 million litres (100,000 barrels) per day. It was declared bankrupt a little less than 3 years later, on Mar. 12, 1976, with a total debt of more than $500 million. The collapse ranked as one of the biggest bankruptcies in Canada to that time.

• PM Trudeau began a 3-day visit to China, where he met with Chairman Mao Zedong.

Oct. 17 The Organization of Arab Petroleum Exporting Countries (OPEC) cut back oil supplies to Western nations following the Arab defeat in the Six Day War (Yom Kippur War), which Israel won on Oct. 24 with Western backing. The cut backs dramatically increased world prices, which tripled between 1973 and 1974. The "oil crisis" or "energy crisis" was on. Canada had already ensured domestic supply through export controls, and was not as immediately hard hit as other Western nations. However, the crisis led to plus-10% inflation in 1974 and 1975 and 7% unemployment in 1975. The one-two inflation-unemployment punch was termed "stagflation," and lingered through the 1970s.

Oct. 25 The United Nations Emergency Force (UNEF) II was established to supervise the ceasefire between Egyptian and Israeli forces following the Six Day War. On Nov. 2, Canada agreed to share a support role with Poland on the UN Middle East peacekeeping force.

Also in Oct.
• China signed a contract to purchase 220 million bushels of Canadian wheat over 3 years.

Nov. 1 The federal govt imposed a $1.90-per-barrel export tax on crude oil.

Nov. 13 Dr. Henry Morgentaler (b 1923) was acquitted in Montreal of having performed an illegal abortion, despite admitting to having carried out 6,000 others. His acquittal was overturned by the Que. Appeal Court, whose judgment was upheld by the Supreme Court of Canada on Mar. 26, 1974. On July 25, 1975, Morgentaler was sentenced to 18 months in jail. He served 10 months when a retrial was ordered, which resulted in another acquittal. As a result, the House of Commons passed legislation (the "Morgentaler Amendment") in 1975 to amend the Criminal Code to prevent appeal courts from reversing "not guilty" jury decisions. On Sept. 18, 1976, the Que. govt dropped all further charges against Morgentaler, ending one of the most controversial legal cases in Canadian history.

Nov. 26 As the oil crisis continued, Denison Mines Ltd. agreed to sell Tokyo Electric Power Co. $800 million worth of uranium oxide. In Dec., South Korea purchased a $250 million CANDU nuclear reactor.

Nov. 29 The federal govt established an aid program for Chilean refugees facing rampant human rights violations and wholesale assassinations under the military regime led by Augusto Pinochet. The new program included relaxed immigration regulations, job training and placement. The Pinochet govt came to power under US support and that of its Central Intelligence Agency (CIA). Canada officially recognized the Pinochet govt on Sept. 24, 1973.

Dec. 6 PM Trudeau announced on television the establishment of a new national oil policy to make Canada self-sufficient before the end of the 1970s. The part oil-crisis-inspired-policy included extension of existing oil pipelines eastward; a single national oil price; a program to further develop Alb.'s tar sands; and a nationalized petroleum company (Petro-Canada) in 1975.

Dec. 12 The Canadian Mint issued its 1st commemorative silver $5 and $10 coins to help finance the 1976 Montreal Olympics. The Olympic series would run to 1976 and include 14 designs in each denomination.

Dec. 18 PM Trudeau introduced a conflict-of-interest code for members of the House of Commons, requiring public servants to reveal business, financial or commercial interests that might conflict with performance of official govt duties.

Dec. 19 The Montreal Orchestra announced that financial aid from citizens, businesses and govt would allow it to continue operations.

1973–1974 Jessie Oonark (1906–1985) hand-stitched the 396.2 x 640.1–cm *Untitled Wall Hanging* with wool, felt and embroidery floss. The hanging includes traditional Inuit hunting scenes with sleds, animals and a woman's knife called the ulu. Oonark was born in the Back R. region about 240 km north of Baker L. She was elected to the Royal Canadian Academy of Arts in 1975 and was named an Officer in the Order of Canada in 1984. *Untitled Wall Hanging* is with the National Gallery of Canada.

Also in 1973

• Paul Martin Jr. was named president of Canadian Steamship Lines (CSL), a subsidiary of the Power Corporation. Seven years later, he and partner Laurence Pathy purchased CSL outright for $180 million. Martin bought out his partner's interests and assumed full control of the dry-bulk shipping corporation in 1988. By 2000, the company employed some 600 persons and operated a fleet of more than 40 vessels.

• A *caveat emptor* (buyer beware) was issued for all NWT land in the Mackenzie Valley after the Dene submitted a land claim with the NWT Supreme Court. Justice Morrow held that the Dene had standing to make the claim. The case was part of the political-legal process that led to the creation of Nunavut (Apr. 1, 1999).

• The federal govt placed a 5% maximum on the amount of phosphates allowed in laundry detergent. The amount of phosphates in other cleaners, including dishwashing soap, was not restricted. The regulation followed environmental studies linking phosphates to increased rates of algae growth in lakes, which caused freshwater eutrophication (the loss of essential dissolved oxygen).

• The Olympic Lottery Corporation of Canada was chartered and began selling lottery tickets to offset the costs of the 1976 Montreal Summer Olympic Games. Participating provinces and territories were Alb., NWT, Ont., Que., NB, PEI and Nfld. In 1976, the lottery was extended to 1979 to help cover Olympic-cost overruns.

• In a case involving matrimonial property law, the Supreme Court of Canada ruled that Irene Murdoch, an Alb. rancher seeking a divorce from her husband, James Murdoch, was not entitled to a share of the ranch she and her husband had built over 25 years because the work she had invested in the property was "the work done by any ranch wife."

• Gros Morne National Park (2,978 km²) was estab-

lished on the west coast of Nfld. Declared a UNESCO heritage site in 1987, the park contains coastal lowlands and alpine plateau, glaciated fjords, sea stacks and a plethora of animals, including black bear, marten, caribou, lynx, hare and 239 species of birds.

• The improvisational comic-theatre group Second City Company was established in Toronto. (The original comedy troop was 1st established in Chicago, America's "Second City," in 1959.) The 1st Toronto cast included Dan Aykroyd (b 1952), Jayne Eastwood, Joe Flaherty (b 1941) and Gilda Radner (1946–1989). Other Second City veterans would include Mike Myers (b 1963), Sandra Shamas (b 1957), John Candy (1950–1994), Martin Short (b 1950) and Catherine O'Hara (b 1954). The theatre group spawned the spectacularly popular *SCTV* television series in 1976.

• Ojibway Norval Morriseau (b 1932) painted *Warrior with Thunderbirds*, oil on canvas, representing the transformation of humankind into the almighty spirit Thunderbird. Morriseau received the Order of Canada in 1978, was presented with honorary doctorates from McGill and McMaster in 1980 and was honoured by the Assembly of First Nations in 1995. *Warrior with Thunderbirds* is in a private collection.

• Ivan Eyre (b 1935) completed the landscape paintings, *Manitou*, now owned by the province of Man., and *Touchwood Hills*, presently in the National Gallery of Canada.

• Montreal's Louis de Niverville (b 1933) completed the acrylic airbrush on canvas *Funk*, by combining 2 like photographs. The work is currently held in La Médiathèque du Musée d'art contemporaine du Montréal.

• Vancouver-born Robert Murray (b 1936) fashioned *Swing*, a yellow 84 x 58 x 284 cm aluminum abstract formalist sculpture. It is now with the Art Gallery of Ontario, Toronto.

• Master craftsman Bill Reid (1920–1998) of Victoria, BC, fashioned *Box: Haida Myth of the Bear Mother*, an intricately detailed 7.3 x 7.0 x 5.2 cm gold box. The work incorporated scenes of the Haida legend of a beautiful young girl who mates with a bear and gives birth to bear-human children. The piece is with the Canadian Museum of Civilization, Ottawa.

• Montreal writer Don Bell (d 2003) received the 1973 Stephen Leacock Memorial Medal for humour for his work *Saturday Night at the Bagel Factory*.

• The Canadian Periodical Publishers Association, later the Magazine Publishers of Canada, held its founding meeting. The association would later lobby to remove tax exemptions for advertisers in foreign publications, and for postal subsidies for Canadian-owned magazines.

• Constance Beresford-Howe (b 1922) published the novel *The Book of Eve*.

• Clark Blaise (b 1940) published his 1st book of stories, *A North American Education*.

• Horatio Henry Lovat Dickson (1902–1987) published *Wilderness Man: The Strange Story of Grey Owl*.

• Poet Roland Giguère (b 1929) published *La Main au feu*, for which he refused the Gov-Gen.'s Award.

• The children's book *A Prairie Boy's Winter*, by William Kurelek (1927–1977), was published.

• Rudy Wiebe published *The Temptations of Big Bear*, the tragic historical novel about Plains Cree Chief Mistahimoskwa.

• The *OptiMSt*, a periodical for Yukon women, was 1st published.

• Maclean Hunter bought Macmillan of Canada. The magazine conglomerate would sell the venerable publishing house to Ron Besse, president of Gage publishers, in 1980.

• Breakwater Books was founded in Nfld. Other start-up publishers included Lester & Orpen, later Lester & Orpen Dennys.

• Don Gutteridge published the poetic work *Coppermine*, about fur-trading explorer Samuel Hearne.

• Herschel Hardin published the play *Esker Mike and His Wife Agiluk*.

• Roots was cofounded by Michael Budman and Don Green in Toronto. They started the company with a single store with a single product, Roots negative-heel shoes. By 2003, this privately held company employed thousands worldwide, with 140 stores in Canada, 7 in the US, 68 in Korea and 12 in Taiwan.

• Traffic fatalities resulted in a record 6,706 deaths.

• Vancouver-born architect Raymond Moriyama (b 1929) completed the Scarborough (Ont.) Civic Centre, built as the centerpiece of the new town centre of Scarborough.

• Yukon Territory switched from Yukon standard time — Canada's most western time zone — to Pacific time, leaving the country with 6 time zones: Pacific, Mountain, Central, Eastern, Atlantic and Newfoundland Is.

• Water-skiing superstar George Athans Jr. (b 1952) of Kelowna, BC, won his 2nd World Overall water-skiing championship. The 28-time Canadian record holder won 10 consecutive national titles (1965–1974) during his career and was inducted into the International Water Ski Federation Hall of Fame in 1993.

• The Women and Film International Festival (WFIF) was staged in Toronto over 10 days with 182 films by and about women. The festival then toured 18 cities across the country.

• Northern Electric made its 1st public offering of 2.6 million common shares, reducing Bell Telephone's share of the firm to 90%.

• The 1st rape crisis centres in Canada opened in Vancouver and Toronto. In the same year, Interval House, one of the 1st shelters for abused women, opened in Toronto. By 1975, there were 5 such transition houses in BC.

• Okanagan vintner Walter Hainle produced Canada's 1st icewine from frozen Reisling grapes. Icewine was 1st commercially produced in 1978 by

Tilman and Sandra Hainle of BC's Hainle Vineyards. Retail price was $28 per bottle.

• The Consumer Packaging and Labelling Act came into force, requiring bilingual labelling on all consumer products.

1974

Jan. 1 The Montreal and Canadian Stock Exchanges merged to become the Montreal Stock Exchange.

Jan. 6 Global Television was established in southern Ont. It joined CBC and CTV as Canada's 3rd television network.

Jan. 7 Bora Laskin (1912–1984) was sworn in as chief justice of the Supreme Court of Canada, succeeding Joseph-Honoré-Gérald Fauteux (1900–1980).

Jan. 11 After 23 years, Celia Franca (b 1921) retired as artistic director of the National Ballet of Canada. She was succeeded on July 1 by David Haber (b 1927).

Jan. 12 Jacques Francoeur sold the Quebec City newspaper *Le Soleil* to Unimedia Inc. for an estimated $8 million. The French-language daily had a circulation of 155,000.

Jan. 14 Assent was given to 4 new acts, including the Energy Supplies Emergency Act, and the Oil Export Tax Act.

Jan. 17 Pauline McGibbon (1910–2001) was appointed lt-gov. of Ont., the 1st woman ever appointed to a vice-regal post in Canada. She was sworn in Jan. 17, 1975.

• Lake Louise, Alb., received the most snow to ever fall in Canada in one day: 118.1 cm.

Jan. 22–23 The federal-provincial National Energy Conference was held in Ottawa. Agreement was reached to subsidize oil prices in Eastern Canada while stabilizing prices in the rest of the country. On Mar. 27, the federal and provincial govts reached an interim oil policy agreement changing the price of domestic crude oil from $4 and freezing it at $6.50 per barrel, by Apr. 1.

Jan. 24 A NB court found K.C. Irving Ltd. and 3 K.C. Irving newspaper companies guilty of forming a NB newspaper monopoly. The companies were fined $150,000 and the Moncton newspapers ordered onto the auction block. On June 4, 1975, the NB Supreme Court ruled that Irving's ownership of all 5 English dailies in the province was not injurious to the public and reversed the ruling.

Feb. 1 Canada established diplomatic relations with Bahrain, Oman, Qatar and the Union of Arab Emirates.

Feb. 2 Canada finished 3rd among competing countries at the close of the 10th Commonwealth Games at Christchurch, New Zealand, taking 25 gold medals, 19 silver and 18 bronze.

Feb. 13 The Que. Court of Appeal refused to allow a First Nations–Inuit coalition to proceed in its quest for a permanent injunction against the James Bay hydroelectric development, while it awaited the outcome of an earlier appeal. The dispute over the James Bay project was quelled temporarily when the James Bay and Northern Que. Agreement was signed Nov. 11, 1975.

Feb. 14 The federal govt pledged $50 million to the Accelerated Coverage Plan to extend CBC radio and television services to regions in the North.

Mar. 1 The BC Court of Appeal ruled that a Native child could be adopted by non-Native parents without the child losing Indian status.

Mar. 7 The federal govt initiated a 5-year plan to provide 50,000 housing units to rural and Native families, with payments geared to incomes.

Mar. 13 Jean Chrétien (b 1934), minister of Indian and Northern Affairs, halted offshore drilling plans in the Beaufort Sea until completion of environmental-impact studies by 1976. On Apr. 15, 1976, the federal govt gave final approval to Dome Petroleum Ltd. of Calgary to drill the 1st offshore wells in the sea. Dome discovered huge new oil deposits in the Beaufort Sea, about 109 km north of the Mackenzie R. delta, in 1981.

Mar. 17–19 Robert Stanfield was confirmed leader of

the national Progressive Conservative party at a Conservative party convention in Ottawa.

Mar. 20 Construction workers rioted at the James Bay Hydro-Que. site, causing a closedown of the project. Millions of dollars' worth of buildings and equipment were destroyed. On Aug 23, union representative Yvon Duhamel was sentenced to 10 years in prison for arson and mischief in connection with the riot.

Apr. 2 NS Liberal Premier Gerald Regan was re-elected. His party won 31 seats, the Progressive Conservatives 12, and the NDP 3.

Apr. 5 The last, living original member of the Group of Seven, A.Y. Jackson, died in Kleinburg, Ont. He was 91.

Apr. 8 Canada banned the importation of cattle treated with the growth hormone diethylstilbestrol (DES), suspected to cause cervical cancer in children whose mothers consumed the synthetic estrogen-treated meat.

Apr. 23 The Ont. Ministry of the Environment ordered Falconbridge Nickel Ltd. of Sudbury to close temporarily after the Sudbury area air pollution index reached 102. The incident marked the 1st time an Ont.-based industry had been closed for exceeding air pollution guidelines geared against the air pollution index.

Apr. 25 The federal govt extended Canada's involvement in the UN Middle East Emergency Force for 6 months. On Aug. 9, nine Canadian members of the UN peacekeeping force in the Middle East were killed when their aircraft was shot down by a missile launched from Syrian territory. On Dec. 12, 1975, the govt further extended Canadian involvement into 1976.

Apr. 29 Federal Consumer and Corporate Affairs Minister Herb Gray (b 1931) introduced an anti-profiteering bill, designed to halt "gouging" of consumers by giving govt the power to roll back price increases that produced "above customary profits."

• Liberal Premier Alex Campbell was returned to power in PEI. His party won 26 of 32 seats, with the Progressive Conservatives taking the remaining 6 seats.

Apr. 30 Ralph Steinhauer (1905–1987), former chief of the Saddle L. Native band, was appointed lt-gov. of Alb., becoming the 1st Native lt-gov. in the country.

May 1 The Que. govt implemented a provincial program providing free dental care to all children under 8.

May 8 On an NDP non-confidence vote, John Turner (b 1929) became the 1st finance minister in Canada to see his budget defeated. The Liberal minority govt was defeated 137 to 123, forcing a federal election July 8.

May 10 The Sask. govt passed the Prescription Drug Act, providing all qualified residents free prescription drugs, not including dispensing fees, beginning Sept. 1, 1975.

May 17 Joe Morris (1913-1996) was elected president of the Canadian Labour Congress, at its Vancouver convention.

May 23 NB became the 1st province to draft statutes in both official languages.

Also in May

• Spring floods devastated dozens of communities along the Ottawa and Gatineau Rivers and their immediate vicinities, causing millions of dollars' damage and thousands of evacuations. On May 16, the main street in Manawaki, Que., completely disappeared underwater, forcing 3,000 from the community. On June 11, the federal govt pledged $55 million in aid to victims.

• The municipal Montreal Citizens' Movement (MCM) party, established by union representatives and left-leaning politicians and intellectuals, was formed. The party won 18 out of 52 council seats in the Nov. 1974 municipal election.

June 10 Canadian Greenpeace co-founder David McTaggart (d 2001), captain of *Greenpeace III*, served a writ on the French govt, charging civil and criminal liability of 100,000 francs ($21,000) in the

1972 ramming of his ship by a French vessel. *Greenpeace III* was struck when it entered a security zone around Mururoa atoll in the South Pacific; Greenpeace was protesting French nuclear testing in the region. (McTaggart was severely beaten by French sailors in a similar incident in 1973.) On June 17, a French court ordered the French govt to pay McTaggart damages.

June 19 An exchange of notes between Canada and the US established the Joint Marine Pollution Contingency Plan for controlling oil and other noxious spills by ocean-going vessels. The plan came into force the same day.

June 25 Canada sold China $50 million of wheat.

June 30 The federal Protection of Privacy Act went into effect, allowing qualified use of police wire-tapping.

• Soviet ballet dancer Mikhail Baryshnikov defected in Montreal during the Kirov Ballet's tour of North America. He was granted permission to stay in Canada July 2.

July 1 Regina College received university status, becoming the U. of Regina.

July 3 At the Law of the Sea Conference in Caracas, Venezuela, Environment Minister Jack Davis (1916–1991) called for the restriction of deep-sea salmon fishing and the extension of Canada's coastal jurisdiction to 200 nautical miles (370 km). Canada established its 200-mile coastal zone in 1977, providing domestic and foreign fish quotas within that jurisdiction, after Dec. 13, 1976, when the International Commission for the Northwest Atlantic Fisheries accepted the 200 nautical-mile fishing limit. The zone was further recognized through the international Law of the Sea Convention, signed Dec. 10, 1982.

July 8 In the general election, Liberals under Pierre Trudeau were returned to power with a majority govt (141 seats). The Progressive Conservatives under Robert Stanfield took 95 seats, the NDP under David Lewis won 16 seats. The Social Credit under Réal Caouette won 11 seats, 1 short of obtaining official party status. There was 1 Independent. Voter turnout was 71%.

July 17 Following a dismal federal election showing, the NDP elected John Edward Broadbent (b 1936) interim party leader, to succeed David Lewis. Broadbent was elected official leader of the federal NDP at a Winnipeg leadership convention July 7, 1975.

July 23 The prime lending rate increased to 9.25%, but was lowered to 8.75% on Nov. 15.

July 25 Canada raised the number of personnel in its UN peacekeeping force on Cyprus from 486 to 950, by UN request. On Aug. 6, a Canadian peacekeeper was killed during the Greek-Turkish conflict. Despite the tragedy, Canadian peacekeepers remained on the island until June 15, 1993.

July 30 Que.'s Official Language Act, Bill 22, passed the National Assembly, 92 to 10, making French the only official language of Que. The bill was drafted by Robert Bourassa's Liberals. It gave priority to French in govt, business and advertising, and required that children demonstrate a knowledge of English before given entrance into English schools.

Aug. 16 Cindy Nicholas (b 1957) of Scarborough, Ont. swam L. Ontario in 15 hours, 10 minutes, breaking by nearly 2 hours the previous record set by American Jim Woods.

Aug. 24 The 1st Francophone International Youth Festival, with 25 French-speaking countries participating, ended at Quebec City.

Sept. 12 Que. Senator Louise Marguerite Renaude Lapointe (1912-2002) became Speaker of the Senate, the 1st francophone woman Speaker in Parliament.

Sept. 16 US President Gerald Ford offered amnesty to American draft dodgers residing in Canada, on the condition they swear allegiance to the US and agree to work at low-paying public service jobs for 2 years. Draft dodgers' organizations rejected the offer. Between 1965 and 1974, some 30,000–50,000 Americans immigrated to Canada to resist the war in Vietnam. American women accounted for more than half of these estimates.

Sept. 17 The 1st female RCMP recruits began training at Regina, Sask.

Sept. 20 The National Energy Board ordered an increase to the cost of natural gas exported to the US from 61 cents per 1,000 cubic feet to $1. The next day, BC raised the price of its US-bound natural gas by 50%.

Sept. 24 The 1st students arrived at Lester Pearson United World College of the Pacific, located near Victoria, BC. One of the 10 World Colleges located on the 5 continents, Pearson offers up to 200 students from 80 countries post-secondary education based on the ideals of internationalism, civic responsibility, environmentalism, co-operation, peace and justice. The 1st World College was opened in Wales in 1962.

Sept. 29 The RCMP prevented approximately 200 Native protestors from entering the Parliament Buildings. Fighting erupted when protestors attempted to break through the police barricade. The protestors were part of the Native Peoples Caravan, organized to help bring international attention to Canada's treatment of Aboriginal Peoples.

Oct. 3 The Sony Corporation was listed on the Montreal Stock Exchange, becoming the 1st Japanese corporation to be listed on a Canadian stock exchange.

Oct. 6 Team Canada, comprising of World Hockey Association (WHA) players, finished an 8-game Canada-Russia Hockey series with the USSR in Moscow. Altogether, Team Canada won 1 game and tied 3. The Canada squad included Bobby Hull, 46-year-old Gordie Howe and his 2 sons, Mark (b 1955) and Marty (b 1954).

Oct. 21–22 PM Trudeau paid an official visit to France for trade talks with President Giscard d'Estaing.

Oct. 25 Political scientist Pauline Jewett (1922–1992) became president of Simon Fraser U. in Burnaby, BC, becoming the 1st woman to head a major Canadian university. Jewett had previously been a professor of political science at Carleton U. and a Liberal MP for Northumberland, BC. She would go on to become chancellor of Carleton, an NDP MP for New Westminster, BC and a member of the Privy Council.

Oct. 26 Former premier of Nfld. Joseph Smallwood was unsuccessful in regaining the leadership of the provincial Liberal party. Smallwood lost to Edward Roberts, who had succeeded Smallwood as party leader in 1972.

• The Henry Moore Centre opened at the Art Gallery of Ontario, Toronto, home to the world's largest collection (more than 900) of the British sculptor's works. Moore had donated more than 400 of his works to the Gallery in Dec. 1968.

Oct. 30 PM Trudeau and the 10 provincial premiers attended a special 1-day conference on inflation in Ottawa.

Also in Oct.
• The large canvas *Lake Superior (No. 9)* by Lawren Harris was sold from the John A. MacAulay Collection, Winnipeg, by Sotheby's in Toronto, for $45,000.

Nov. 5 A collection of works by Haida artist and master sculptor Bill Reid was put on exhibit at the Vancouver Art Gallery.

Nov. 6 External Affairs Minister Allan Joseph MacEachen (b 1921) pledged $785 million in international food aid over a 3-year period at the World Food Conference in Rome.

Nov. 8 Assent was given to Canada Pension Plan (CPP) amendments providing equal treatment to all contributors regardless of gender.

• An Ont. govt report showed that fish containing more than 1 part per million of mercury could present a health hazard, and that fish in a number of lakes in northwestern Ont. exceeded that level.

Nov. 10 Montreal Mayor Jean Drapeau was elected to a 6th term.

Nov. 16 The US govt cut Canadian beef imports to 30% of the previous 5-year average, and pork to 50%.

Nov. 18 NB Progressive Conservative Premier Richard Hatfield was returned to power with another majority, taking 33 of 58 available seats; the Liberals, under Robert Higgins, won 25 seats.

Also in Nov.

- Artist Vincent Trasov (b 1947) ran as Mr. Peanut in the Vancouver mayoralty election. His campaign platform was: P for performance, E for elegance, A for art, N for nonsense, U for uniqueness and T for talent. American novelist William S. Burroughs visited Vancouver and made a formal endorsement of the candidate. Trasov received 3.4% of the vote.

Dec. 20 Assent was given to legislation increasing the number of seats in the House of Commons from 264 to 282, effective the next federal general election.

Also in Dec.

- PM Trudeau pledged to reduce Canada's economic ties with the US "by more trade with other countries."

1974-1975 Canadian pianist Anton Kuerti (b 1938) recorded the *Complete Piano Sonatas & Diabelli Variations by Beethoven*, on the Canadian Aquitane label.

Also in 1974

- Canada's trade surplus was $472 million, the lowest since 1966.

- A record $2.19 billion was paid out for unemployment insurance benefits over the year.

- The federal govt purchased struggling Toronto-based De Havilland Aircraft of Canada Ltd. from the British company Hawker Siddeley Aviation. Hawker Siddeley had purchased the storied manufacturer of such legendary planes as the Beaver, Caribou and Otter in 1960.

- The Hay R. Reserve, the 1st Native Peoples reserve in the NWT, was established at the request of the local Dene population.

- The CBC opened its French-language FM stereo network. The English FM stereo network opened in 1975.

- The 1st registered Holstein embryo-transfer calf was born in Canada.

- Donald Ziraldo and Karl Kaiser received a licence from the Liquor Control Board of Ont. to open a new winery in the Niagara region. Inniskillin, as the new venture was called, was the 1st new winery to be licenced by the province since Prohibition.

- Canadian Pacific Archivist and historian Omer Lavallée published, *Van Horne's Road: An Illustrated Account of the Construction and First Years of Operation of the Canadian Pacific Transcontinental Railway*.

- The 1st Winnipeg Folk Festival was held to celebrate the 100th anniversary of Winnipeg. Situated in Birds Hill Park, 34 km northeast of Winnipeg, the 3-day festival featured over 50 acts on 4 stages and drew 20,000 folk-music fans. By 2003, the festival featured over 250 artists on 7 stages, with attendance reaching 50,000. The Winnipeg Folk Festival has since become one of the world's leading outdoor music festivals.

- Paterson Ewen (1925–2002) created the 244 x 336 cm acrylic on plywood *Rain Over Water*. The piece was made with three, 122 x 91 cm plywood sheets, laid flat then carved with a chisel. The work is now in the London Regional Art Gallery, Ont. Ewen also painted *Portrait of Vincent*, based on a slide of his eldest son, now in the Vancouver Art Gallery.

- Mary Pratt painted *Cod Fillets on Tinfoil*, now in a private collection.

- The Writers Union of Canada (TWUC) held its 1st annual meeting. TWUC would do much to support Canadian writers, including establishment of the Public Lending Right to compensate authors for circulation of their books in libraries (Feb. 10, 1987).

- Donald Jack (1924–2003) won the Stephen Leacock Medal for humour for his work *That's Me in the Middle*.

- Margaret Laurence published the novel *The Diviners*. The sexual content and earthy language led to its banning by some Ont. school boards. In 1976, the book was removed from a Grade 13 Lakefield, Ont. highschool reading list, and also from an approved highschool reading list in Dufferin County, Ont. In 1978, the novel was banned from Grade 13 reading lists by the Huron Board of Education, Ont.

• Dennis Lee published the children's classic *Alligator Pie*.

• Adele Wiseman (1925–1992) published *Crackpot*, for which she was presented the J.I. Segal Award for the best Canadian novel in English on a Jewish theme.

• Diplomat and diarist Charles Ritchie (1906–1995) published *The Siren Years: A Canadian Diplomat Abroad, 1937–1945*. The book recalled Ritchie's years in London, England, during WW II.

• McGill U. professor Dr. Hans Selye (1907–1982), published the highly successful self-help guide *Stress Without Distress*.

• Shuswap Chief George Manuel (1920–1989) and Michael Posluns published *The Fourth World: An Indian Reality*, arguing that the worldwide indigenous population comprised a "fourth world" that was dominated and manipulated by non-indigenous powers.

• The Book Award of the City of Toronto was established to honour authors whose works were evocative of Toronto, 1st winners were William Kurelek for *O Toronto*, Desmond Morton (b 1937) for *Mayor Howland* and Richard Wright (b 1937) for *In the Middle of a Life*.

• John Robert Colombo (b 1936) published *Colombo's Canadian Quotations*.

• Poet Nicole Brossard (b 1943) published *Mécanique jongleuse suivi de masculin grammatical* (translated as *Daydream Mechanics*), for which she received the Gov-Gen.'s Award.

• Ralph Gustafson (1909–1995) published a collection of poems, *Fire on Stone*, for which he received the Gov-Gen.'s Award.

• Michael Cook (1933–1994) published the major contemporary Nfld. play *The Head, Guts and Soundbone Dance*.

• Classical guitarist Liona Boyd (b 1950) cut her 1st album, *The Guitar*.

• Peter Gzowski premiered as host of CBC Radio's early-morning show, *Morningside*, a role he and the country would relish for the next 15 years.

• Led by executive producer Kathleen Shannon (1935–1998), the National Film Board of Canada launched Studio D, the 1st English-language film studio in the world to produce and promote films by and about women.

• *The Apprenticeship of Duddy Kravitz*, the movie adapation of Mordecai Richler's 1959 novel, cost less than $1 million to make and became the 1st commercially successful English-Canadian feature film. Produced by John Kemeny and directed by Ted Kotcheff (b 1931), the film starred Richard Dreyfuss as the ruthlessly ambitious Duddy. It won the Canadian Film Awards 1974 Film of the Year prize.

1975

Jan. 6 Ont. separate schools in Carleton, Elgin County, Ottawa, Middlesex, Wellington, Durham and Sudbury were closed because 4,170 teachers resigned over salary disputes. Approximately 89,200 students were affected.

• Management of all CN hotels was turned over to US-based Hilton International, although CN and Air Canada retained financial control. Hilton operated the Canadian hotels as a subsidiary of Trans World Airlines.

Jan. 14 The Canadian Egg Marketing Agency showed a surplus of 40 million eggs, which was increasing by approximately 15 million per week. Previously on Sept. 12, 1974, the Egg Marketing Agency confessed that 28 million eggs had been destroyed because they had rotted due to improper storage.

Jan. 15 At a federal-provincial meeting of health ministers, the federal govt agreed to ban foreign doctors from immigrating to Canada unless they 1st secured a job in the country or agreed to practice in areas suffering a doctor shortage. The decision was based on provincial concerns that a surplus of doctors increased medical costs. In 1973, 1,170 doctors immigrated to Canada, only 156 less than graduated from Canadian medical schools.

Jan. 20 The CRTC drafted new rules for FM radio stations, calling for a broader range of programs with less advertising.

Jan. 21 A 1-million tonne earth landslide at Asbestos, Que., caused 250 people to flee their homes.

Jan. 22 In the House of Commons, PM Trudeau declared the nation's respect for International Women's Year 1975. Created by the UN and other organizations, Women's Year included conferences held worldwide on issues relevant to women. On June 19, Canada was represented at the World Conference on International Women's Year, which opened in Mexico City.

Jan. 30 The Ont. govt created the new Ont. lottery Wintario, to raise money for recreational and cultural activities and related facilities. The 1st official lottery was held May 15.

Also in Jan.

• Artist Ron Martin (b 1943) began work on his canvas, *Lovedeath Deathlove, No. 15*, using black paint. The work is now in the National Gallery of Canada.

• Grace Hartman (1918–1993) became the 1st woman president of a national labour union, the Canadian Union of Public Employees (CUPE).

Feb. 4 The federal govt and the provinces of Alb. and Ont. agreed to invest $600 million into Syncrude Canada Ltd. to facilitate development of the Alb. Athabasca oil sands project. Ottawa received a direct share of 15%, Alb. 10% and Ont. 5%. Syncrude began shipping oil from the Athabasca oil sands on July 30, 1978.

Feb. 6 Energy Minister Donald Macdonald pledged $13 million toward a natural energy conservation program to include national advertising and a 55 mph (88 km/h) speed limit for federal vehicles.

• The Alb. budget called for a 28% decrease in personal income tax, making Albertans the least-taxed population in the country.

Feb. 17–Mar. 19 Nearly 11,000 federal blue-collar members of the Public Service Alliance of Canada conducted a strike after mediation talks failed. Agreement was reached when wage increases totalling 29.25% over 26 months were offered.

Feb. 24 Conservative House leader William Marshall quit the Nfld. cabinet over a conflict with Premier Frank Moores concerning the govt's agreement to rent a building for $900,000 without 1st calling tenders.

Feb. 26 Federalist Jean Marchand (1918–1988) resigned as Que. leader of the federal Liberal party, but remained as minister of transport. He resigned that position in 1976 to run (unsuccessfully) against the Parti Québécois in the Que. provincial election of that year.

Feb. 28 Legislation was passed to grant the NWT a 2nd Member of Parliament.

Mar. 3 Public hearings into the implications of a planned Mackenzie Valley gas pipeline opened in Yellowknife, NWT, under BC Supreme Court Justice

Thomas Berger (b 1933). The proposed plan involved a gas line from the Beaufort Sea, Yukon, down the Mackenzie R. delta to Alb. and markets south. The Berger hearings ended June 8, 1976, and a report released May 9, 1977.

Mar. 12 Thirteen companies and 14 people were charged in Ottawa with conspiring to defraud the federal and Ont. govts and the Hamilton Harbour Commission of more than $4 million between 1969 and 1973, through bid rigging and other practices.

Mar. 15 PM Trudeau returned from a 16-day European tour, having established closer ties with the European Economic Community (EEC).

Mar. 24 Assent was given to legislation making the beaver (*Castor canadensis*) the official symbol of Canada.

Mar. 26 Alb. Progressive Conservative Premier Peter Lougheed was re-elected with one of the most powerful mandates in Canadian provincial politics, winning 69 of 75 seats and decimating the Social Credit Party.

• The minimum wage for federal employees was increased from $2.20 to $2.60 per hour.

Apr. 8 *The Man Who Skied Down Everest*, produced by Crawley Films of Ottawa, became the 1st Canadian feature-length documentary to win an Oscar. The film followed Japanese skier Yuichiro Miura, who climbed Everest to the 8,000-m level and attempted to ski down at a 40–45-degree angle. Miura flew 180 m at about 160 km/h — only to skid to a stop, on his stomach, just short of a huge crevasse.

Apr. 9–10 The federal-provincial premiers conference convened in Ottawa. No agreement was reached on future domestic oil prices.

Apr. 11 The federal govt pledged $280 million in food aid abroad over 1975–1976.

Apr. 15 Parliament approved a measure to increase MPs' salaries by 33%, effective immediately.

Apr. 18 Bill C-58, the Income Tax Act amendment to end tax concessions for Canadian companies advertising in Canadian editions of foreign-owned magazines, and for Canadian businesses advertising on US-border television stations, was introduced. It went into effect in 1976.

Apr. 24 Ottawa closed its embassy in Saigon, Vietnam, and evacuated its consular staff and citizens after Communist forces completed the takeover of the country. The Canadian embassy had been in Saigon more than 20 years. Immigration Minister Robert Andras (1921–1982) offered to admit 14,000 relatives of Vietnamese and Cambodians already living in Canada. On May 1, the federal govt announced that it would allow 3,000 South Vietnemese refugees into Canada.

Apr. 26 *Saturday Night* magazine, established 1887, recommenced publication under editor Robert Marshall Blount Fulford (b 1932), and publisher Ed Cowan (b 1937), thanks to a successful bailout by private investors and subscribers. The magazine suspended publication in Oct. 1974 due to financial difficulties.

Apr. 30 The Petroleum Administration Act was approved by the House of Commons, giving the federal govt power to establish the domestic price of oil and natural gas without agreement of energy-producing provinces.

Also in Apr.
• Canadian weather reports began using Celsius as a measure of temperature. Metric rainfall and snowfall measurements were instituted 5 months later, on Sept. 1.

May 1 The Ont. legislature passed the Redistribution Act, which added 8 seats to its 117-member legislature, and a bill that limited election spending for each party to a maximum 50 cents per voter.

May 7 The Canadian Labour Congress rejected the federal govt's working proposal for voluntary wage and price restraints that would limit wage increases to 12%.

May 20 The Supreme Court of Canada upheld the right of citizens to challenge provincial movie-censorship laws. The decision was made in the case of Dartmouth, NS, newspaper editor Gerard McNeil, who took the province's censorship board to court over its decision to ban the Marlon Brando movie *Last Tango in Paris*. On Feb. 4, 1976, the Supreme Court of NS ruled that the province did not have the right to censor motion pictures.

• The federal govt approved construction of a 840-km crude-oil pipeline extension (Line 9) from Sarnia, Ont., to Montreal, to be built by Inter-Provincial Pipeline Ltd. The line was completed in 1976 at a cost of nearly $250 million.

May 22 Former Progressive Conservative MPP Arthur Maloney (1919–1984) was appointed Ont.'s 1st ombudsman.

May 30 Federal legislation was passed to increase the Senate from 102 to 104 seats, giving the Yukon and the NWT 1 new seat each. On Oct. 23, 1975, Paul Lucier (1930–1999), mayor of Whitehorse, was named the 1st senator from the Yukon. On Apr. 5, 1977, Willy Adams (b 1934), of Rankin Inlet, was appointed the 1st senator for the NWT. Adams became the 1st Inuit to sit in Parliament.

Also in May
• *North Shore, Lake Superior*, oil on canvas, by Arthur Lismer, sold at Sotheby's in Toronto for $32,000. Also sold was *Rapid in the North*, on canvas, by J.E.H. Macdonald, for $31,000.

• Canada's communications satellite, *Anik III*, was successfully launched. It assumed the main functions of *Anik I*. on Nov. 1.

June 3 NB established a new provincial holiday called New Brunswick Day, to be celebrated every 1st Monday of Aug.

June 5 TransCanada PipeLines Ltd. of Toronto became the 1st Canadian firm to purchase gas from the Mackenzie R. delta when the firm signed a 20-year contract for 4 trillion cubic feet of natural gas with supplier Imperial Oil Limited.

June 11 The Sask. NDP under Premier Allan Blakeney won 39% of the popular vote to win the provincial election. The party had captured 55% of the vote in 1971.

June 18 The Anglican Church of Canada voted in favour of ordaining women to the priesthood.

June 26 The Supreme Court of Canada upheld a PEI law forbidding nonresidents from owning more than 4 ha of land on the Island.

June 30 The Canadian vessel *Greenpeace V* succeeded in disrupting a whale hunt by a Russian fleet off Canada's West Coast.

July 1 Federal prison guards staged a "day of mourning" to protest Solicitor Gen. Warren Allmand's refusal to reinstate capital punishment. Military personnel and the RCMP guarded the prisons during the walkout. The ban on capital punishment had existed since 1967, and punishment by death was removed from the Criminal Code on July 14, 1976.

July 5 Former Nfld. premier Joey Smallwood was elected leader of the new Liberal Reform Party of Nfld. and Labrador.

July 9 Canada and Iran signed trade agreements worth $1.3 billion; another $650 million remained on the negotiation table.

July 20 An early-morning fire destroyed the main street of Springhill, NS.

July 23 The federal govt barred the Soviet Union's Atlantic fishing fleet from Canadian ports because it had overstepped quotas. On Sept. 26, the bar was lifted when the Soviets agreed to support Canadian efforts to achieve a 14% reduction in foreign fishing off the Canadian East Coast.

July 24 A vicious tornado struck St. Bonaventure, Que., killing 3 and injuring 45. A 4.8-km section of town was destroyed.

Aug. 1 The price of natural gas exported to the US increased from $1 per 1,000 cubic feet to $1.40, and to $1.60 on Nov. 1.

Aug. 19 Que. Solicitor Gen. Fernand Lalonde (b 1932) introduced new rules governing language usage in advertising and labelling. The legislation prohibited companies operating in the province from distributing catalogues in English only, without written requests from recipients. Violators were subject to fines. Also, English-only placards and handbills carried or distributed by demonstrators or strikers were made illegal.

Also in Aug.

• Consultant and former Pearson appointments secretary James "Jim" Allan Coutts (b 1938) succeeded Jack Austin (b 1932) as PM Trudeau's chief of staff.

• Canada's unemployment rate for the month was 7.3%, the highest since 1961 and 1971, when the average unemployment rate was 7.1%.

Sept. 11 Future PM John Turner resigned as federal finance minister for unspecified reasons. On Feb. 12, 1976, Turner resigned his seat in the House and returned to the practice of law in Toronto.

Sept. 12 A federal govt study revealed that a growing number of Canadians were moving out of Toronto and Montreal, while a growing number of immigrants were moving into those cities.

Sept. 16 Progressive Conservative Frank Moores was re-elected premier of Nfld., as his party won 30 of 51 seats in the House.

Sept. 18 The Ont. Progressive Conservative Party was returned to power with its 1st minority govt in 30 years. Premier William Davis's Conservatives won 51 of 125 seats in the legislature. The Liberals under Robert Nixon (b 1928) took 36 seats, but were replaced by Stephen Lewis's NDP (38 seats) as the Official Opposition.

Sept. 29 Striking Montreal transit workers voted to return to work when threatened with fines and union decertification. The strike began Sept. 18.

Also in Sept.

• Pierre Berton's *Hollywood's Canada: The Americanization of Our National Image* was published. Berton claimed that Hollywood films perpetuated false stereotypes about Canada, with singing Mounties and French-Canadian woodsmen. Between 1907 and 1975, Hollywood studios and filmmakers made 575 movies set (although not usually filmed) in Canada. These flicks defined the image of Canada for the rest of the world.

• The Bricklin Vehicle Corp., established by American Malcolm Bricklin and manufactured in Saint John and Minto, NB, went into receivership.

The Bricklin was a small futuristic gull-wing sports car with state-of-the-art safety features; 2,857 were produced; all were shipped to the US. Bricklin had been lured to NB with guaranteed loan investments worth 51% of Bricklin stock; the company went bankrupt owing the NB govt $23 million.

Oct. 2 Approximately 100 members of the NB Maliseet band blocked a CP rail line that crossed reserve lands, in a dispute over right-of-way ownership. CP Rail had taken over the disputed area from NB Railway without Maliseet approval.

Oct. 4 Mirabel International Airport, 55 km from Montreal, was officially opened. It was the most sprawling airport in the world, covering 6,556 ha. Traffic and service at Montreal's Dorval Airport was split with Mirabel, with many passengers (and luggage) forced to transfer planes between airports. Mirabel soon became one of Canada's grandest white elephants; in 1997, all its international and domestic passenger flights were rerouted back to Dorval.

• Approximately 750 Americans, with colonial costumes and flintlocks, re-enacted the unsuccessful 1775 American attack on Quebec City as part of a lead-up to the US Bicentennial celebrations.

Oct. 7 The BC legislature passed emergency measures forcing striking forest, railway, propane and food industry workers back to work.

Oct. 10 The Soviet Union purchased 304,814 tonnes of barley, 152,407 tonnes of wheat and 50,802 tonnes of oats from the Canadian Wheat Board. The deal was worth some $100 million.

Oct. 12 Michel Brault (b 1928) won 4 Etrogs at the Canadian Film Awards for *Les Ordres*, a dramatized documentary of the October Crisis. The film also won the Director's Prize at the Cannes Film Festival on May 25, 1975. Brault, a respected cinematographer and producer, was among the pioneers of *cinéma vérité* techniques and received a Gov-Gen.'s Award in 1996 for his body of work, which included more than 200 productions and a number of technical innovations.

Oct. 13 The Que. National Assembly approved the abolition of union halls in the province by July 1976. The move followed a report of the Cliche Commission of Inquiry into Que. construction industry violence.

Oct. 14 The Anti-Inflation Board, an administrator and an Anti-Inflation Tribunal were established to administer wage-and-price controls. Jean-Luc Pépin (b 1924) was appointed chairman of the board, and Beryl Plumptre his assistant. The 1st meeting of the board was held in Ottawa on Oct. 28. Legislation establishing wage-and-price control was passed Dec. 3.

• Métis and non-status Native Peoples demonstrated on Parliament Hill to protest the federal govt's refusal to recognize Aboriginal rights.

Oct. 21 The 22,000-member Canadian Union of Postal Workers (inside workers) began a 43-day strike. Union members accepted a govt-offered pay increase and returned to work Dec. 2. The strike caused the largest disruption of mail service in Canadian history.

Oct. 23 Que. Education Minister and ardent nationalist Jérôme Choquette (b 1928) resigned his portfolio from the Que. Liberal Party in frustration over the province's inability to enforce language Bill 22 (1974). In Dec., Choquette and Ralliement Créditiste member Fabien Roy formed the new provincial Parti National Populaire, which took 14.2 % of the Nov. 15, 1976, Que. election.

• Holger Peterson (b 1949) and Alvin Jahns founded Stony Plain Recording Co. Ltd. in Edmonton, Alb. Since its 1st release in 1976, the roots-music label has released more than 300 CDs, received 9 Juno Awards, the Canadian Country Music Independent Record Label of the Year award (8 years in a row), and a 2001 Grammy nomination for Maria Muldaur's *Richland Woman Blues*. Artists signed with the label have included Ian Tyson, Gillian Welch, Duke Robillard, Jay McShann, the Corb Lund Band, Ray Bonneville and David Wilcox.

Oct. 24 The BC govt imposed a 68-day price freeze on hundreds of basic commodities and essential services.

Oct. 26–31 The 1st World Conference of Indigenous Peoples was held in Port Alberni, BC. Aboriginal representatives from Canada and 19 other countries attended. Concerns included cultural genocide, traditional land rights, the environment and natural resources.

Oct. 28 The Indian Association of Alb. filed a notice of intention to make a claim for 259,000 km^2 of land encompassing the Athabasca tar sands.

Nov. 3 The Galloway family of Deloro, Ont., were forced to evacuate their home, which bordered an abandoned Deloro Stellite mine site that contained hazardous wastes, including radioactive slag and cobalt. The evacuation notice was given by the Ont. Ministry of Health following an Atomic Energy Control Board–initiated environmental investigation. Mr. Galloway died of cancer the following year; a coroner's inquest determined that radiation exposure was at least a contributing factor.

Nov. 7 The Alb. govt issued shares in Alb. Energy Company Ltd. to Alb. citizens and corporations, with the intent that the Alb. Energy Company Ltd. would ultimately be 50% owned by the Alb. govt and 50% owned by the Canadian public, with Alb. citizens getting priority access to shares.

Nov. 10 The 218-m ore carrier *Edmund Fitzgerald*, sailing from Superior, Wisconsin, broke apart and sank in a storm on L. Superior. Twenty-nine crew members were lost. There were no survivors. The tragic story was made famous by Gordon Lightfoot in his song "The Wreck of the Edmund Fitzgerald."

Nov. 11 The James Bay and Northern Quebec Agreement was signed in Quebec City by representatives of the Grand Council of the Cree, the Northern Quebec Inuit Association, the federal and Que. govts and other organizations involved in the James Bay hydroelectric development project. A related Northeastern Quebec Agreement was signed in 1978. Together, the complex deals provided 19,000 northern Que. Cree, Inuit and Naskapi with $225 million in federal and Que.-govt funds, and qualified ownership and exclusive hunting, fishing and trapping rights over specified areas of land in the region. In return, Aboriginals surrendered title to approximately 981,610 km^2 of the previously disputed James Bay-Ungava territory, which allowed the Que. govt to proceed with Phase I of the James Bay hydroelectric project. The deal came into effect Oct. 31, 1977. The agreement was Canada's 1st modern land claim settlement.

Nov. 12 In Toronto, 8,800 Ont. secondary-school teachers went on strike at 135 high schools, affecting 130,000 students. The strike was ended by provincial legislation on Jan. 15, 1976.

Nov. 14 The Que. govt declared it would assume complete control of finance and construction of the main stadium (Olympic Stadium) for the 1976 Summer Olympics in Montreal, to begin July 17 of that year. On Nov. 19, an Olympics Installation Board was established to supervise construction and site facilities. With an exterior perimeter of 885 m, the elliptical plastic, concrete and steel structure cost Que. taxpayers $1 billion, and was quickly dubbed "the Big Owe." The 60,000-seat stadium was never fully completed for the Olympic Games.

Nov. 18 The Potash Development Bill and the Potash Corporation of Sask. Bill were introduced in the Sask. legislature to bring the potash industry in the province under provincial ownership. The legislation was passed Jan. 28, 1976.

• The Ont. govt took over the administration of Ignace Township in northern Ont. because the township did not have the tax base to recover from its deficit.

Nov. 20 The 1st credit union in Canada to serve women only opened in Toronto.

Nov. 24 Nfld. raised its sales tax to 10%, the highest in Canada, to help cope with a $30 million deficit.

• The CRTC ordered cable companies to black out US television programs that were simultaneously available on local channels.

Nov. 28 Members of Parliament gave approval in principle to a private member's bill, proposed by Ken Robinson, requiring railways, planes and buses under federal jurisdiction to provide non-smoking areas for its passengers.

• The federal govt purchased Canadair Ltd. of Montreal, and turned the aircraft manufacturer into a Crown corporation.

Dec. 3 Federal anti-inflation legislation, Bill C-73, passed in the House of Commons by a vote of 111 to 96, providing the govt with power to apply selective wage controls on 4.3 million workers and price controls on 1,500 of the largest Canadian companies. The controls were established to combat the rising rates of inflation, and affected all firms with more than 500 employees, construction firms with more than 30 employees and all federal and Crown employees. All provinces but Sask. and Que. placed their public sector employees under the controls. It was the 1st time such wage-and-price controls had been implemented in peacetime. The controls were eliminated Apr. 14, 1978.

Dec. 5 A representative for 125,000 female members of the Que. Federation of Labour, the Confederation of National Trade Unions and the Que. Teacher Corporation established a common front to fight sexual discrimination in provincial govt contract proposals.

Dec. 7 Crazy Canuck Ken Read (b 1955) won Canada's 1st World Cup Ski race, at Val d'Isère, France, in a time of 2:04.97. The win also marked the 1st by a North American skier.

Dec. 11 The Social Credit Party, under the leadership of William Richards Bennett (b 1932), won 36 of 55 seats in the BC election. NDP leader David Barrett lost his seat.

Dec. 11–12 A federal-provincial conference on human rights was held in Ottawa. Involved were 4 federal departments: Secretary of State, Justice, External Affairs and Labour.

Dec. 13 The federal govt initiated a gradual phase-in of bilingual air communications at Que. airports.

Dec. 18 The federal govt placed a 10% surtax on the portion of any personal taxable income in excess of $30,000, as part of an effort to combat the effects of inflation. The tax applied to 1976 earnings.

Dec. 31 The federal govt confirmed that a program protecting 10,112 km of prairie rail lines from abandonment would be extended to the end of 1976. On May 26, 1977, the govt added another 2,900 km of prairie line to the program.

1975–1978 The federal and Man. govts jointly implemented the Man. Basic Annual Income Experiment to guarantee annual incomes to more than 1,000 families. The program was designed to establish a relationship between fixed income and the willingness of recipients to find paid work.

Also in 1975

• Former CBC television producer Lorne Michaels (b 1944) launched *Saturday Night Live*, the longest-running late-night TV show in the history of television. The 90-minute NBC hit series has included such comedic Canadian actors as Dan Aykroyd, Martin Short, Phil Hartman, Robin Duke, Norm MacDonald (b 1962), Mark McKinney (b 1959), Mike Myers (b 1963) and Tony Rosato (b 1954).

• Parliament passed the Petro-Canada Act, founding Petro-Canada as a Crown corporation. The new Crown corporation would assume control of the federal govt's interests in Syncrude and Panarctic Oils. The act was established partly in response to the OPEC oil crisis and the rising need for energy self-sufficiency.

• Strikes, work stoppages and lockouts accounted for 10,829,000 lost person-days for the year.

• Consolidated-Bathurst Packaging Ltd. sold the 217-km-long Anticosti Is., located at the mouth of the St. Lawrence R., to the Que. govt.

• The number of Canadian drive-in theatres peaked at 315. Urban growth, rising realty prices and the compact car helped shave this number to 123 by 1989.

• Canada's population of nesting peregrine falcons totaled 34 pairs.

• Preeminent wood-duck carver Bill Cooper (1886–1975) died in Verdun, Que., leaving a legacy of approximately 6,000 ducks praised for their elegant wing detail and durability. Many are still used every fall.

• Jack Bush completed the canvas *Arabesque*, now in the Hirshhorn Museum, Washington, D.C.

• Torstar, owner of the *Toronto Star*, purchased Harlequin books, whose sales had reached $19 million. By 1986, Harlequin sales hit $206 million annually; by 1993, $443.8 million.

• CBC TV launched *The John Allen Cameron Show*, and the Celtic rhythms of Cape Breton Is. went mainstream. Cameron (b 1938) grew up in Inverness County, Cape Breton, and is regarded by many as the singer and musician who paved the way for such Cape Breton entertainers as the Rankin Family, Ashley MacIsaac, the Barra MacNeils and Natalie McMaster. Cameron was named to the Order of Canada in 2003.

• The country band Prairie Oyster was founded in Toronto where they performed for fans mainly at The Horseshoe Tavern. Hit songs like "Man in the Moon," "Goodbye, So Long, Hello" and "Play Me Some Honky Tonk Music" earned them a loyal following. The band went on to win Juno Awards as Best Country Group or Duo of the Year in 1986, 1987, 1991, 1992, 1995 and 1996.

• The Writers Union of Canada picketed a Coles store in Ottawa, protesting the chain's practice of selling dumped American editions of its members' books.

• Canadian publishers Black Moss Press, Kids Can Press and Thistledown Press were founded.

• The Canadian Authors' Association (CAA) re-established its literary awards. (The CAA had established the Gov-Gen.'s Awards in 1937, but passed responsibility for them on to the Canada Council in 1959.) Recipients of the new CAA awards in the categories of fiction, non-fiction, poetry and drama were each given $5,000 and a silver medal.

• Inuit photographer Peter Pitseolak's (1902–1973) *Peoples from Our Side: A Life Story with Photographs and Oral Biography*, an Inuit record of Seedkoseelak — the land and the people of Cape Dorset, was published posthumously. Peter Such (b 1939) described the work in his *Books in Canada* review "as close to the real experience of the Cape

Dorset Inuit as the eye can glean from print and picture. And as close to the experience of meeting a true human heart as any novel you might have read." Pitseolak's manuscript was originally written in syllabics, and accompanied by his photographs.

• Playwright Michael Cook (1966–1997) published *Quiller and Jacob's Wake.*

• Hugh John Hood published the novel *The Swing in the Garden,* the 1st of 12 volumes in his New Age series.

• Twelve-year-old Gordon Korman wrote his 1st novel for a Grade 7 English class, *This Can't Be Happening at MacDonald High.* The novel received a B+ from Korman's teacher but was soon published.

• Robert Kroetsch published the comic novel *Badlands,* a daughter's account of her fossil-hunting father, set against Alb.'s Badlands.

• Mordecai Richler published the popular children's book *Jacob Two-Two Meets the Hooded Fang,* which was twice made into a film.

• Peter Charles Newman (b 1929) published *The Canadian Establishment,* an account of Canada's rich and powerful.

• Folklorist and song collector Helen Creighton (1899–1989) published her autobiography, *A Life in Folklore.* Creighton dedicated her life to the collection and preservation of Maritime folklore and music.

• Jane Rule (b 1931) published *Lesbian Images,* a study of lesbian writers.

• Inuit Anglican minister Armand Tagoona published his illustrated description of Arctic life, *Shadows.*

• George Woodcock published *Gabriel Dumont,* an account of the fabled Métis leader.

• Neurosurgeon Wilder Graves Penfield published *The Mystery of the Mind.*

• Milton Acorn (1923–1986) won a Gov-Gen.'s Award for his collection of poems, *The Island Means Minago.*

• Earle Birney (1904–1995) published his *Collected Poems.*

• Poet Jacques Brault (b 1933) published *Poèmes des quatre côtés.*

• Toronto-born trumpeter Kenny Wheeler (b 1930) recorded one of the most memorable jazz albums of the 1970s, *Gnu High.*

1976

Jan. 1 Former PM John Diefenbaker was appointed a Companion of Honour by Queen Elizabeth.

Jan. 17 A $60 million Canada-US communications technology satellite was launched from Cape Canaveral, Florida, as part of a 2-year experimental program to provide television and telephone reception to isolated North American communities.

Jan. 25 Dr. Stuart Smith (b 1938) was elected leader of the Ont. Liberal Party, succeeding Robert Nixon.

Feb. 1 Ont. lowered its speed limits on provincial highways from 60 mph to 50 mph, and from 70 mph to 60 mph on expressways.

Feb. 13 Eighteen-year-old Kathy Kreiner (b 1957) of Timmins, Ont., won Canada's only gold medal at the Winter Olympics in Innsbruck, Austria, taking the women's giant slalom event in a dazzling time of 1:29:13. The unexpected win came on the last day of the Games. She was 1st out of the gate. Only 1 Canadian reporter was on hand to witness the triumph. Canada won only 2 other medals: silver by Cathy Priestner (b 1956) in the 500-m speed-skating event; and bronze in figure skating by Toller Cranston (b 1949), the controversial skater whose artistic interpretations revolutionized the sport.

Feb. 22 Charles Joseph "Joe" Clark (b 1939) was elected national leader of the Progressive Conservative party on the 4th ballot, beating out Claude Wagner (1925–1979), Brian Mulroney (b 1939) and Flora Isabel Macdonald (b 1926), who was the 1st woman to seek the leadership of the Progressive Conservative party. Clark succeeded Robert Stanfield.

Feb. 27 The Canadian Wheat Board sold 35.4 million bushels of wheat to China. China purchased another 110 million bushels, valued at $330 million, in May 1977.

Mar. 2 The last issue of the Canadian edition of *Time* was distributed. In 1975 (Apr. 18), the federal govt eliminated tax concessions to Canadian firms that advertised in Canadian editions of foreign-owned magazines. The subsequent loss of revenue forced *Time* to abandon the Canadian edition.

Mar. 5 Following years of federal-provincial talks on patriation of the BNA Act, PM Trudeau announced that Ottawa would unilaterally bring home the Constitution. He stated before reporters, "This is the Canadian Constitution. What's it been doing in Britain for the last 109 years?"

Mar. 25 Recommendations of the Law Reform Commission of Canada included a reconsideration of whether abortion, indecency, bigamy, incest, obscenity and gambling should remain part of the Criminal Code.

Apr. 1 The Canadian Radio-Television and Communications Act was implemented, moving regulation and supervision of all federally regulated tele-communications from the Canadian Transport Commission to the Canadian Radio-Television and Communications Commission (CRTC). The CRTC continued to regulate and supervise traditional broadcast carriers.

• The federal minimum wage was increased to $2.90 per hour.

Apr. 6 The Que. Superior Court ruled against a submission by 10 Protestant Que. school boards that Que.'s Official Language Act was unconstitutional.

Apr. 7 Nanaimo-born Jean Lumb (1919–2002) became the 1st Chinese-Canadian woman to be invested as a member of the Order of Canada. Lumb's contributions reached far and wide: she was an ardent anti–Exclusion Act advocate, president of the Women's Association of the Toronto Chinese Community Centre, citizenship judge, owner of Kwong Chong, one of Toronto's original Chinatown restaurants, and tireless defender of Chinatowns in Vancouver, Calgary and Toronto.

Apr. 13 Ninety thousand Que. teachers staged a 24-hour walkout during a contract dispute with the govt; 100 teachers' union locals were served with summonses the next day.

Apr. 20 The House of Commons approved legislation giving unions the right to appeal Anti-Inflation Board rulings.

May 4 The Ont. govt confirmed that foreign student fees at Ont. universities would be raised from $585 to $1,500.

May 10 Windsor high schools opened for the 1st time since the end of Mar. after the Ont. govt passed back-to-work legislation on May 7, forcing striking teachers to capitulate.

May 14 Six provincial govt employees' associations amalgamated to form the National Union of Provincial Government Employees, Canada's 5th largest union.

May 19 The Alberta Heritage Savings Trust Fund Act was given Assent. The Heritage Fund included the stewardship of investments gained from the province's non-renewable resource revenues, and injected the returns back into capital projects and social programs, including health care, education, tax reduction and debt repayment. Between 1976 and 2002, the trust fund re-invested more than $25 billion into the province.

Also in May
• The Sask. Indian Federated College, an independent affiliate of the U. of Regina, opened, becoming the 1st college in Canada directed by Native Peoples.

June 10 The price of natural gas exported to the US was increased by 21%. The next day, the National Energy Board declared a 12% reduction in US oil exports.

June 11 The UN's Habitat conference on Human Settlements ended in Vancouver. The meeting focused attention on the relations between people, settlement, environment and development. The conference site comprised 5 WW II seaplane hangars converted by 38 artists, including Bill Reid and Evelyn Roth. UN delegates included PM

Trudeau, Mother Teresa, Margaret Mead and Buckminister Fuller.

June 16 PM Trudeau visited Washington, D.C., where he reaffirmed Canada's commitment to NATO and presented President Ford with the book *Between Friends — Entre Amis*, commissioned by Canada to commemorate the US bicentennial.

June 26 The $63 million, 553.34-m-high CN Tower, the world's tallest free-standing structure, was opened in Toronto. It contains a glass-floored observatory at 342 m, a lookout at 346 m and a sky pod at 447 m. Broadcast facilities include UHF, VHF television, FM radio and microwave. Construction had begun Feb. 6, 1973 and was completed Apr. 2, 1975.

June 27–28 Canada, with 6 western nations, attended the G-7 economic summit in San Juan, Puerto Rico. Attending nations were the US, West Germany, Japan, France, Britain and Italy. Canada was not invited to the 1st meeting of major economic western powers held Nov. 1975 at Château de Rambouillet, France. G-7 meetings were held annually on such international issues as trade tariffs and protectionism, crime, terrorism, globalization, employment and development. The Soviet Union (later Russia) joined the group in 1997.

June 29 A 9-day strike by anglophone air traffic controllers over the expansion of French and its effect on safety at Que. airports ended, when the federal govt halted the French-language expansion. A federal commission was subsequently established and reported in 1979 that use of both French and English in air traffic control did not constitute a safety risk. The govt accepted the conclusions of the commission and provided for total bilingual air traffic control systems in Que. for 1980.

June 30 The last US Air Force personnel pulled out of Goose Bay, Labrador, as the lease on the US Air Force base expired. The 32-km² military site had been developed by the US military during WW II, and contained facilities for 9,000 people. The base included schools, a hospital, a theatre, barracks, homes, hangars and a bowling alley. Its 3,382-m runway was the longest in the western world until completion of Mirabel Airport in Montreal in 1975.

• The BC Court of Appeal rejected federal claims to the mineral resources on the sea bottom between Vancouver Is. and the mainland, ruling that the resources fell under provincial authority.

July 7 Canada signed an inaugural trade framework with the European Economic Community (EEC) establishing mutual commercial and economic co-operation over 5 years.

July 14 Parliament abolished the death penalty for all civilian offences and removed it from the Criminal Code. Although the death penalty had been banned in Canada since 1967, the Supreme Court of Canada ruled on Oct. 5, 1976, that it was not a cruel and unusual punishment within the meaning of the Canadian Bill of Rights. The Supreme Court ruling had no effect on the legislation.

July 17 The 21st Summer Olympic Games officially opened in Montreal as the 1st Olympics ever hosted by a Canadian city. Teams from 92 participating countries filed into Olympic Stadium, an uncompleted 60,000-seat clamshell-like structure designed by French architect Roger Taillibert. The Olympic torch was lit by 15-year-olds Sandra Henderson and Stéphane Préfontiane (who later married). Canada established the dubious distinction of being the 1st host country not to win a single Olympic gold, as Canadian athletes took 5 silver and 6 bronze in the competition. The Montreal Olympics introduced women's basketball, rowing and team handball, and 14-year-old Romanian gymnast Nadia Comaneci, the 1st Olympic gymnast to score 7 perfect marks of 10.0. The only security incident involved a single streaker crashing the closing ceremonies. The Games ended Aug. 1. The Olympics put Mayor Jean Drapeau's Montreal into debt for $1.5 billion.

July 21 Canada signed a $1 billion contract with US-based Lockheed Aircraft for 18 long-range patrol aircraft to be used by the Canadian Armed Forces. Known as the turbo-prop CP-140 *Auroras*, the planes would replace Canadian-built Argus aircraft in 1979.

Aug. 18–20 The 17th annual premiers conference was held in Banff, Alb. No agreement was reached on repatriating the Canadian Constitution. On Oct.

1 and 2, a provincial premiers conference was held in Toronto. Again, leaders failed to reach an agreement on an amending formula to the BNA Act.

Aug. 19 The Science Council of Canada suggested that urbanization and immigration jeopardized the nation's standard of living.

Aug. 30 The Man. Liquor Commission was ordered to pay the federal govt $300,000, the 1st case of a provincial agency fined for violating federal wage-and-price controls.

• A delegation of 17 Chinese govt officials attended the official opening of a new National Historic Site — the restored 1890 birthplace of Dr. Norman Bethune in Gravenhurst, Ont. The federal govt declared Bethune a Canadian of national historic significance in 1972. Bethune sacrificed his life helping Chinese soldiers repel the invading Japanese army in 1939.

Also in Aug.
• Canada hosted its 1st Paralympic Games in Toronto. More than 1,500 athletes from 38 countries attended. Canada placed 5th. Federal funding was withdrawn due to the participation of South African athletes. The Polish team withdrew from competition after several of its members defected. Saskatoon's track-and-field star Arnie Boldt (b 1957) was named Outstanding Athlete after he won gold medals in both the high jump and the long jump. Boldt was inducted into the Canadian Sports Hall of Fame on Aug. 27, 1977.

Sept. 1 Environment Canada began reporting weather statistics in metric. The change affected its accounting of precipitation, reported in mm's, and snowfall, reported in cm's. The agency began reporting wind speed in metric units in 1977.

Sept. 15 Arguably the strongest team to represent Canada in international hockey — and the only one featuring Bobby Orr — won the 1st Canada Cup by defeating Czechoslovakia 5–4 in overtime. Darryl Sittler (b 1950) scored the winning goal. Participating countries included Canada, the US, the Soviet Union, Sweden, Finland and Czechoslovakia. The 1st series game between the Soviet Union and Canada was played in Montreal and was opened by legendary Forum singer Roger Doucet (1919–1981), who sang renditions of both national anthems. Lyrics to the "Hymn of the Soviet Union" had been removed by that state in 1956 due to an overabundance of Stalin references. Doucet had members of the Russian Department at the Université de Montréal modernize them so he had something to sing. Not only were the Soviets not offended, but the Kremlin officially accepted the new lyrics in 1977.

Oct. 14 More than 1 million Canadian Labour Congress members participated in a Day of Protest strike against federal wage-and-price controls. The protest included a massive demonstration on Parliament Hill.

Oct. 15 The govt signed a $184 million contract for 128 West German–made tanks, with deliveries beginning in July 1978.

Oct. 24 Jan Kadar's (1918–1979) 1975 film, *Lies My Father Told Me*, received the Canadian Motion Picture Distributors' Association's (CMPDA) 1st Golden Reel Award as the highest-grossing Canadian feature film of the year. It also won best feature film, best actress (Marilyn Lightstone [b 1941]) and best adapted screenplay (Ted Allen [1910–1993]), as well as awards for overall sound and sound editing at the Canadian Film Awards.

Also in Oct.
• Bill Marshall, Dusty Cohl (b 1929) and Henk van der Kolk (b 1940) launched the Festival of Festivals in Toronto, a non-competitive event to present the best films from other festivals. The 1st festival showed 140 films from 30 countries and drew 7,000 people a day. The festival was renamed the Toronto International Film Festival in 1994.

Nov. 1 Japan agreed to buy 1 million tonnes of Canadian wheat and 900,000 tonnes of barley in 1977. On Nov. 24, Poland struck a deal with the Canadian Wheat Board to buy up to 1.2 million tonnes of wheat, barley and oats over 3 years.

Nov. 8 In Oakville, Ont., a US-Canadian syndicate paid $235,000 for "Hanover Hill Barb," the highest price ever paid in the world for a cow.

Nov. 12 Jockey Sandy Hawley's (b 1949) total earnings reached $4,255,912, breaking thoroughbred racing's all-time money-winning record for a single year. Hawley retired in 1998 with career earnings exceeding $88 million. His record was 6,449 wins, 4,825 places and 4,158 shows, including 4 Queen's Plates and 8 Canadian Oaks. Hawley was made a member of the Order of Canada Oct. 20, 1976.

Nov. 15 René Lévesque and the Parti Québécois defeated Robert Bourassa's Liberals in the Que. election by winning 69 seats. The Liberals garnered 28, and the Union Nationale 11. Liberal Premier Robert Bourassa lost his own seat, then resigned as Liberal leader Nov. 19.

Nov. 26 PM Trudeau, responding to a press question on the Parti Québécois, exclaimed, "The French won't take us over and neither will the pope, although he's not the menace he used to be."

Also in Nov.

• The roots-rock group The Band performed a farewell concert at Winterland in San Francisco, along with an all-star lineup including Neil Young, Joni Mitchell, Emmylou Harris and Muddy Waters. The 4–hour concert was filmed by Hollywood director Martin Scorsese and sold as *The Last Waltz*. Band members included Canadians Rick Danko (1942–1999), Richard Manuel (1943–1986), Garth Hudson (b 1937) and Robbie Robertson (b 1943), backed on drums by Arkansas native Levon Helm.

Dec. 5 The 1st 4 Canadian women Rhodes Scholars were chosen.

Dec. 14 A federal-provincial premiers conference in Ottawa resulted in the provinces gaining $680 million in new taxing powers.

Dec. 20 Dr. Hsio-Yen Shih (1933–2001), a professor of East Asian studies at the U. of Toronto, was appointed director of the National Gallery of Canada. She replaced Dr. Jean Sutherland Boggs.

Also in 1976

• Ont. became the 1st provincial govt to make wearing seat belts mandatory.

• More than 1.5 million Canadian workers were involved in strikes and lockouts during the year.

• The Canadian dollar was stronger than the US dollar for the last time.

• Roberta Jamieson (b 1953) graduated from the U. of Western Ontario, becoming the 1st Aboriginal woman to receive a law degree in Canada.

• The Eaton's department store discontinued its catalogue operation after 92 years of publication.

• The Museum of Anthropology Building, U. of BC, was completed. The Haida longhouse-inspired concrete-and-glass museum was designed by Arthur Erickson and is home to a stunning collection of Northwest coastal artifacts and contemporary artworks, including totems, jewelry, bone carvings and ceremonial masks. The museum is also the largest teaching museum in Canada, with 5,465.6 m² of usable space, 1,494.9 m² of academic area and 3,612.8 m² of space available to the public (galleries, exhibitions, shops, etc).

• The 7,000-yard Jack Nicklaus-designed Glen Abbey Golf Course in Oakville, Ont., was completed, becoming the pre-eminent site for the Canadian Open. The course required movement of more than 28,000 m² of earth to bring its design to Nicklaus' standards.

• The Toronto Metros-Croatia soccer team beat the Minnesota Kicks 3–0 at the Kingdome in Seattle, Washington, to win the 1976 North American Soccer League (NASL) Championship. The Metros-Croatia, led by Portuguese star Eusebio, was the 1st Canadian team to take an NASL title.

• A domestic 1st class letter cost 10 cents.

• Canadians spent $3.12 billion abroad, establishing a record 1-year travel deficit of $1.18 billion.

• Toronto's Second City theatre company moved its unique brand of sketch comedy from the stage to television. The fictional Second City television station, with call letters SCTV, began broadcasting on Global television with a cast that included John Candy, Joe Flaherty, Eugene Levy (b 1946), Andrea Martin (b 1947), Rick Moranis (b 1954), Catherine O'Hara, Dave Thomas (b 1949) and later Martin Short. The show parodied film and television, creating memorable characters such as Johnny LaRue,

The Schmenge Brothers, Edith Prickley and Bob and Doug Mckenzie of the "Great White North." The series won unqualified praise and ran for 7 years in Canada, and in syndication in the US. *SCTV* garnered 13 Emmy nominations, winning 2 for best writing.

• Buffy Ste. Marie and her son, Dakota Starblanket Wolfchild, began their 5-year association with the popular children's TV program *Sesame Street.*

• St. John's Christopher Pratt painted *March Night,* oil on masonite, showing a windowsill partially blocking Pratt's childhood memory of the Salmonier R. on a cool March night. The work is now in the Art Gallery of Ont., Toronto.

• Don Proch (b 1944) fashioned *Rainbow Mask,* a 34 x 21 x 29 cm silverpoint and graphite piece on fiber-glass. The work incorporates a number of magical and spiritual elements shocked to life with a heat-sensitive neon rainbow light — one of Proch's most daring creations. It is with the Glenbow Museum, Calgary.

• Greg Curnoe produced his watercolour, *Corner,* now in the National Gallery of Canada.

• Paterson Ewen painted *The Great Wave: Homage to Hokusai,* on panel, now in the Art Gallery of Windsor, Ont.

• Charles Gagnon completed *Cassation/Dark/ Sombre,* on canvas, now in the Art Gallery of Ontario, Toronto.

• David Bolduc (b 1945) painted *Wo,* on canvas, now at Concordia U., Montreal.

• Marian Engel, née Passmore, published the novel *Bear,* for which she received the Gov-Gen.'s Award.

• Phyllis Gotlieb published her science fiction novel *O Master Caliban.*

• André Major (b 1942) published the novel *Les Rescapés,* for which he received the Gov-Gen.'s Award.

• Michael Ondaatje published *Coming Through Slaughter,* a fictional account of New Orleans jazz cornetist Buddy Bolden.

• Carol Shields (b 1935) published the novel *Small Ceremonies,* one of her most cherished works.

• Astronomer Helen Hogg published *The Stars Belong to Everyone.*

• Poet Irving Layton published *For My Brother Jesus.*

• Gary Geddes published *War Measures & Other Poems.*

• The drama *The Donnellys, parts I and II,* by James Reaney, was published. Part III appeared in 1977.

• Rick Salutin (b 1942) published the play *1837: The Farmers' Revolt.*

• Toronto-born silent- and sound-screen star Mary Pickford, known as "America's Sweetheart," was awarded a Lifetime Achievement Award from the Academy of Motion Picture Arts and Sciences. Pickford starred in dozens of films, including *New York Hat* (1912), *Daddy Long Legs* (1919) and *Coquette* (1928).

• The 1st 4 Canadian pop singles to reach "Gold" in Canada (selling more than 50,000 copies) were recorded this year: Hagood Hardy's "The Home-coming," Sweeney Todd's "Roxy Roller," André Gagnon's "Wow" and René Simard's "Fernando."

1977

Jan. 10 Canada expelled 4 Cubans, including 2 diplomats, on evidence gathered in the wake of an RCMP spy investigation.

Jan. 12 In an effort to offset 1976 operating losses, Air Canada suspended regular flights to Moscow, Prague and Brussels, revised domestic flight schedules and increased fares.

• Karen Kain and Frank Augustyn of the National Ballet of Canada performed with the Bolshoi Ballet in Moscow, the 1st Canadian dancers to do so.

Jan. 14 The 1st of 8 Bruce plus-750-megawatt (MW) CANDU reactors went into commercial service on L. Huron near Kincardine, Ont.; number 8 started on Mar. 9, 1987. Operations were later moth-balled, and the plant leased by Ontario Power Generation to British Energy in 2002. British Energy then formed Bruce Power, the province's largest independent producer of energy, which by Oct. 7, 2003, had 6 of the 8 reactors back in operation.

• A Northern Thunderbird Airlines aircraft crashed at Terrace, BC, killing 12 people.

• The Metropolitan Toronto Police formed a special ethnic squad to deal with problems within the urban Asian community.

Jan. 18 Seal Books was established by a joint venture between McClelland and Stewart Ltd. and Bantam Books of Canada Ltd. to publish inexpensive paperbacks written by Canadian authors.

Jan. 25 Que. Premier René Lévesque told an audience at the Economic Club of New York that Que. independence was inevitable. On Feb. 15, the Royal Bank of Canada announced the transfer of 3 head office departments from Montreal to Toronto. More than a year later (Mar. 22, 1978), PM Trudeau told 2,000 top-ranking US businesspeople at the club that Quebecers would never vote for independence.

Also in Jan.
• Prince Andrew, 2nd in line to the British throne, entered Lakefield College School near Peterborough, Ont., for 2 terms.

Feb. 1 Maritime provinces and the federal govt signed an agreement giving the provinces 100% of royalties from future offshore mineral discoveries within 5 km of their respective coasts, and 75% from coastal resources beyond that.

Feb. 14 The Unity Bank of Canada merged with the Provincial Bank of Canada to form the National Bank of Canada. The number of chartered banks in the country was reduced from 12 to 11.

Feb. 15 The Citizenship Act, which set out criteria by which Canadian citizenship was determined, acquired and lost, went into effect.

Feb. 22 PM Trudeau told a joint session of the US Congress that Canada would remain united, despite growing US concerns about Que. separation. It was the 1st time a Canadian PM addressed the US Congress.

Also in Feb.
• The federal Canadian Works program began allocating funds to create job opportunities for the unemployed. A successor to the Local Initiative Program established in 1971, Canada Works spent $253.8 million over 1977–1978; 27% of the jobs created by the program over that period went to women. Canada Works was replaced by Canada Community Development Program in 1980.

Mar. 2 Solicitor Gen. Francis Fox (b 1939) signed an agreement in Washington, D.C., for an exchange of prisoners with the US. The deal allowed Canadians incarcerated for crimes in the US to serve their terms in Canada, and vice versa. On Nov. 22, the federal govt signed a similar prisoner-exchange treaty with Mexico.

Mar. 4–5 The Rolling Stones played 2 low-key gigs at the legendary El Mocambo club in Toronto. Mainstream media joined the tabloid press in reporting that Margaret Trudeau and Mick Jagger had arrived at the tavern together. (It was during this 2-day concert stop that Stones guitarist Keith Richards was arrested for heroin possession.) On May 27, PM Trudeau and his wife, Margaret, agreed to separate. The PM retained custody of the couple's 3 children.

Mar. 14 Renowned Ojibwa artist Benjamin Chee Chee (1944-1977) committed suicide in an Ottawa jail at the height of his success. Chee Chee's sparse, elegant drawings and paintings reside in collections across the country, including the Glenbow Museum, Alb., Thunder Bay Art Gallery, Ont., Woodland Cultural Centre, Brantford, Ont., and the McMichael Canadian Art Collection, Ont. His linear depictions of geese were mass-marketed as prints and on greeting cards.

Mar. 21 Foul weather, icy conditions and lack of money forced the Greenpeace Foundation to abandon its protest of the annual seal hunt off the coast of Nfld.

Also in Mar.
• National unemployment figures for Mar. were 944,000, or 8.1% of the workforce — the highest since figures were 1st collected in 1953. By Nov., the unemployment rate reached 8.4%.

Apr. 2 Vancouver's restored Orpheum Theatre was opened as the new permanent home of the Vancouver Symphony Orchestra (VSO). The theatre's 1st incarnation was in Nov 1927, as a vaudeville house.

Apr. 7 44,649 new Toronto Blue Jays fans braved a snowstorm at Exhibition Stadium to watch Canada's American League representative beat the Chicago White Sox 9–5 in their 1st regular season game. The Blue Jays' Doug Ault stole the show with 2 home runs. With good humour, American newscasts showed the snow-clad crowd, many wearing toques and winter jackets, chanting, "We want beer! We want beer!" in protest to the stadium's ban on the sale of suds.

Apr. 18 Jerome Drayton (b 1945) became the 8th Canadian to win the Boston Marathon.

Apr. 20 The govt pledged $41 million toward a program to upgrade East Coast fisheries.

• The Federal Court of Canada upheld a ban on the May issue of *Penthouse* magazine on the grounds it was indecent.

Apr. 27 Que.'s PQ govt, under Premier René Lévesque, introduced Bill 1, the Chartre de la langue française (Charter of the French Language), extending the use of French as the province's only official language. English was banned from most govt and legal proceedings, and from businesses of 50 or more employees. Que. signs were to be posted in French, and only those children who had a parent who attended English elementary school in the province could attend school in English. The bill was opposed in the legislature but re-introduced as Bill 101 on July 12 and passed by the National Assembly Aug. 26, 1977.

May 9 A federal Royal Commission, led by BC Supreme Court Justice Thomas Berger, released its report (*Northern Frontier, Northern Homeland*) on the proposed Mackenzie Valley gas pipeline and its potential impact on the North. The report agreed with the feasibility of the project, but recommended a 10-year moratorium, during which further study and Native land claims could be addressed.

It also suggested a permanent ban on any pipeline from Alaska across northern Yukon. The Mackenzie pipeline was subsequently stalled, and a deal eventually signed between Aboriginal and corporate oil interests on Oct. 15, 2001. The popular 1977 Berger Report was published in book form with photographs and distributed through local bookstores.

May 14 The Montreal Canadiens, dominant NHL team of the era, lost only 8 games in their 80-game regular season schedule, coasting to their 2nd of 4 consecutive Stanley Cups, beating the Boston Bruins for their 20th Stanley Cup. Steve Shutt (b 1952) scored 60 goals during the season, the most to date by a left-winger, and Guy Lafleur (b 1951) accumulated 136 points, a NHL season record.

May 16 Recommendations of the Hall Commission report on grain handling and transportation included the formation of a prairie rail authority, construction of a new Arctic railway, abandonment of more than 3,200 km of branch rail lines and retention of subsidized Crow's Nest Pass rates.

May 24 The Liberals won 5 of 6 federal by-elections.

Also in May
• A group of 18 haunting sketches by Clarence Gagnon, based on the 1911 Louis Hémon novel *Maria Chapdelaine*, was sold in Toronto for $58,000.

June 2 Que. raised its provincial minimum wage from $3 to $3.15 per hour, the highest in the country.

June 15 The report of the Ont. Royal Commission on Violence in the Communications Industry, established Apr. 1975 and chaired by Judy LaMarsh (1924–1980), was issued. It pointed to a relationship between media violence and violent social behaviour, and recommended a Freedom of Expression Act that would set the boundaries of free expression within the realms of such categories as libel, obscenity, sedition, treason and material that might cause violence or crime.

June 21 A fire in the cell block of the St. John's, Nfld., police headquarters killed 20 prisoners and injured 12 police officers who attempted rescue.

July 1 The federal health department barred use of the artificial sweetener saccharin in soft drinks, with a phase-out in food complete Nov. 1, and as a sweetener in drugs Dec. 31. The ban was based on concerns that saccharin was potentially carcienogenic.

July 5 PM Trudeau established a special organization to examine national unity, headed by Jean-Luc Pépin (b 1924) and John Robarts (1917–1982). The Pépin-Robarts Task Force on Canadian Unity report was issued Jan. 26, 1979.

July 8 All parties in the House of Commons, the Canadian Air Traffic Controllers Association and the Canadian Airline Pilots Association supported motions to increase the use of French in air traffic control of small planes under visual flight rules in Que.

July 14 The Canadian Human Rights Act received Assent, prohibiting discrimination on grounds such as gender, race, religion and disability in all federal jurisdictions. A new Human Rights Commission was also established. Headed by former Progressive Conservative MP Gordon Fairweather (b 1923), it began to administer the act in 1978.

July 15 The federal govt pledged to strengthen the Armed Forces by 4,700 members, bringing the total to 83,000.

July 19 Federal legislation was passed to increase the qualifying period for unemployment benefits from 8 weeks to 10–14 weeks, and bring the benefit payment period to between 10 and 50 weeks.

July 20 After investigation, the CRTC failed to find a separatist bias in the CBC's French-language service.

July 29 Following the sexual abuse and murder of 12-year-old Emanuel Jacques in an apartment above a Toronto body-rub parlour, police and political action virtually eliminated such establishments from the Yonge Street Strip.

Aug. 1 The federal govt made more than 400 million ha of land available for exploration and development in northern and offshore areas, ending a 5-year freeze.

Aug. 5 Bill C–51 received Assent, requiring Firearms Acquisition Certification (FACs) for the purchase of guns and where applicable, Firearms and Ammunition Business Permits. Fully automatic weapons not registered before Jan. 1, 1978, were categorized prohibited. Bill C-51 was effective 1978.

Aug. 10 A 3–day strike by air traffic controllers over wages was terminated by federal legislation.

Aug. 19 Que. Premier René Lévesque's offer of English-language education guarantees in Que., in return for French-language education guarantees in the other provinces, was rejected by the other 9 provincial premiers.

• Serge Losique (b 1931) launched the 1st edition of the Montreal World Film Festival (Festival des Films du Monde). The inaugural festival was opened by Ingrid Bergman and attended by cinema legends Howard Hawks, Jean-Luc Godard, Gloria Swanson, Fay Wray and the Taviani brothers. In 2002, awards were presented in over 20 categories and films from more than 70 countries were screened.

Also in Aug.
• The Immigration Act (1976) received Assent. The act enshrined in law the humanitarian principles of non-discrimination, family reunion and compassion and protection for refugees. It also provided the provinces with joint responsibility over education and immigrant recruitment.

Sept. 6 Vietnam purchased 120,000 tonnes (4,400,000 bushels) of wheat from the Canadian Wheat Board, the 1st time Vietnam had purchased wheat from Canada.

• Road signs in all areas of Canada except Que. and NS were converted to metric. Also, all new cars in Canada were required to have metric speedometers and odometers.

Sept. 7 Toronto-born Cindy Nicholas became the 1st woman to complete a return, nonstop swim of the English Channel. Nicholas beat the male record by 10 hours.

Sept. 30 The Supreme Court of Canada upheld a NB court ruling stipulating that an individual must fail

2 or more breath tests before being convicted of impaired driving.

Oct. 6 The Que. Superior Court ruled a section of the Que. Charter of the French Language requiring all court documents to be in French only unconstitutional under the BNA Act. The BNA Act required use of both English and French in Que. courts.

Oct. 11 The Progressive Conservatives under Sterling Lyon (b 1927) defeated the NDP govt under Ed Schreyer in the Man. provincial election. The Conservatives took 33 of 57 seats; the NDP took 23 seats, and the Liberals 1.

Oct. 18 The 3rd session of the 30th Parliament opened, until Oct. 10, 1978. The throne speech was read by Queen Elizabeth II for the 1st time since 1957.

Oct. 20 Toronto-based Inco Ltd. announced cutbacks to its northern mining industry, including the layoff of 3,500 workers by mid-1978. Sudbury was hardest hit, with 2,800 nickel jobs slated for elimination.

Oct. 24 For the 1st time since 1939, the Canadian dollar dropped to under 90 cents US (89.88 US). Standby credit of $1.5 billion (US) was arranged by the federal govt to help bolster the dollar.

Oct. 27 Charles Marion, a Que. credit union manager, was released on the payment of a $50,000 ransom. He had been held for 83 days in Canada's longest kidnapping.

Nov. 2 The new 36,404-m² Toronto Reference Library, a 6-floor, open-concept structure designed by Raymond Moriyama (b 1929), opened on Yonge St. and Asquith Ave. The library began as the York Mechanic's Institute in 1830 to provide workers with books and reading space, lectures and after-work literacy classes. It became the Toronto Public Library (the city's 1st public library) on Mar. 6, 1884, then moved to College and George Streets in 1904. By 2003, the library contained 4.5 million items, including 1.5 million books, on 82 km of shelving.

Dec. 1 The federal govt cut footwear imports by 32.5 million pair a year to help the ailing domestic shoe and boot industry.

Dec. 6 The Canadian Transport Commission (CTC) gave permision to Air Canada, CP Air and 5 regional carriers to offer advance booking and charters within Canada on a trial basis in 1978.

Dec. 16 Que. became the 1st province to pass a gay civil rights law when it included sexual orientation in its Human Rights Code. By 2001, the only provinces and territories that had not taken this step were Alb., PEI and the NWT.

• The federal govt dropped its support of commercial relations with South Africa in opposition to that country's racial policies and apartheid regime. It also began plans to withdraw its commercial attachés from South Africa. Canada adopted full-blown economic sanctions against South Africa in 1986.

Dec. 29 Sandra Lovelace (b 1947), a Maliseet woman from the Tobique reserve in NB, submitted a communication to the United Nations Human Rights Committee (UNHRC) to challenge the Canadian Indian Act. Along with Jeannette Corbiere Lavell (Aug. 27, 1973), Lovelace argued that the act was discriminatory on the grounds of gender and contrary to the Covenant on Civil and Political Rights. On July 30, 1981, the UNHRC found Canada in breach of the covenant. Section 12 of the Indian Act was subsequently repealed in 1985.

1977–1992 The *Canadian Tax Journal* reported that Alb. had a net federal tax payout of $32.9 billion and Que. a net federal gain of $95.1 billion.

Also in 1977
• Canada banned the sale, import and manufacture of all polychlorinated biphenyls (PCBs), a compound used primarily in electrical machinery such as transformers, heat exchangers and hydraulic systems. PCBs were found to increase risks of cancer, cause damage to the fetus, and were slow to degrade in the environment after spills or intentional release.

• VIA Rail was founded as a Crown corporation with headquarters in Montreal. It assumed the slumping passenger service of CN and CPR. In 1978, VIA received 31 Bombardier LRC (light, rapid and comfortable) power cars, which could run at a top speed of 200 km/h. However, track upgrades were scrapped soon after and the cars' operational speed limited to 155 km/h maximum on the best of existing track. By the turn of the century, VIA moved 480 trains a week and connected 450 Canadian communities.

• The Badgley Report of the Committee on the Operation of the Abortion Law was released. Commissioned by the federal govt, it confirmed widespread concerns that abortion was not equally available across the country.

• Ojibwa Tommy Prince (1915–1977), Canada's most highly decorated Aboriginal soldier, died in Winnipeg. His funeral was attended by over 500, including soldiers and members of the Princess Patricia's Light Infantry Brigade (who attended as pallbearers), Man. Lt-Gov. Jobin, trappers, fishermen and consuls from France, Italy and the US. Prince fought in World War II (as a member of the famous Canadian Devil's Brigade), and in the Korean War. He was awarded 11 medals, including the King George Military Medal and the US Silver Star. A bronze bust of Prince on marble was installed in his honour in 1994 at the Brokenhead Ojibway Nation, Man.

• The Medicine Hat Blue Jays of the Pioneer League were established as an affiliate of the Toronto Blue Jays.

• The $250 million Eaton Centre was built on the original Eaton's Department Store site in Toronto. Architect Eberhard Heinrich (b 1926) oversaw the design, which spread over 5.6 ha and contained almost 278,709.12 m^2 of office and retail space.

• American investors owned 24% of all Canadian industrial assets.

• Sam Johnston (b 1935) and his family founded the Teslin Tlinglit Dancers of the Yukon.

• Paterson Ewen painted *Moon Over Water* on panel, now part of the collection of the Canada Council Art Bank.

• *Seagulls and Sharks*, enamel on canvas, by acclaimed folk artist Joseph Norris (1924–1996), was completed.

• Clark Blaise and his wife, Bharati Mukherjee (b 1940), co-authored *Days and Nights in Calcutta*, an autobiographical account of Blaise's year in India.

• Photographer Roloff Beny published *Roloff Beny interprets in photographs Pleasures of Ruins,* a photographic essay of Rose Macauley's 1953 book. The book was the 1st to present Beny's colour work.

• Novelist and critic Gérard Bessette (b 1920) published the novel *Les Anthropoides*.

• George Bowering published the novel *A Short Sad Book*.

• The novel *L'Emmitouflé*, by Louis Caron (b 1942), was published.

• Inuit writer Alice French (b 1930) published *My Name is Murak*, a story set in Aklavik, NWT.

• Jack Stanley Hodgins published the novel *The Invention of the World*.

• Neurosurgeon Wilder Graves Penfield published *No Man Alone*, an autobiographical account of his early career.

• Novelist Josef Skvorecky (b 1924) published *The Bass Saxophone*, a translation of his 1963 novel written in Czechoslovakian.

• Timothy Findley published the novel *The Wars*, for which he received a Gov-Gen.'s Award and an international reputation. He also published the play *Can You See Me Yet?*, which had been performed the previous year at the National Arts Centre (NAC) in Ottawa.

• Audrey Grace Thomas's (b 1935) collection of short stories, *Ladies and Escorts*, was published.

• Rudy Wiebe published *The Scorched Wood People*, a novel of Louis Riel as seen through the eyes of the Métis.

• Elizabeth Smart (b 1913) published her prose poem *The Assumption of Rogues and Rascals*.

• *The Fat Man: Selected Poems 1962-1972* by John Newlove, (1938-2003) was published.

• Monique Mercure (b 1950) won international recognition for her work in Jean Beaudin's *J.A. Martin, Photographe,* taking the Best Actress award at the 1977 Cannes International Film Festival. The story of a 19th-century itinerant photographer and his wife, the film won 7 Etrogs at the 1977 Canadian Film Awards, including Best Actress for Mercure and Best Director for Jean Beaudin.

• English-born architect Peter Hemingway (1929–1995) completed Muttart Conservatory along the North Saskatchewan R. in Edmonton. The concrete walls of the 4 connected botanical gardens are buried underground, with 4 large glass pyramids protruding above. The Pyramids, as the conservatory is known, boasts more than 700 species of plants.

1978

Jan. 5 After publishing an article in Dec. 1976 entitled "Men Loving Boys Loving Men," Pink Triangle Press of Toronto was charged with possession of obscene material and use of the mail for distribution of obscene, indecent or scurrilous material. In June 1982, Ont. Court Justice Judge Thomas Mercer ruled that the article did advocate "pedophilia" but submitted that it was legal to advocate something that most Canadians would find unacceptable.

Jan. 16 Canada signed an agreement with the European Economic Community (EEC) to resume uranium shipments. Canada had banned the export of uranium to Europe Jan. 1, 1977, when the EEC could not guarantee the material would not be used in nuclear weaponry; the new agreement did make that guarantee.

Jan. 19 PM Trudeau appointed Joseph-Georges-Gilles-Claude Lamontagne (b 1919) to cabinet as postmaster gen., increasing the number of cabinet members to a record 34.

Jan. 24 *Cosmos 954*, a nuclear-powered Soviet satellite, re-entered earth's atmosphere and crashed in the NWT. On Feb. 1, fragments were recovered by Canadian and US military personnel in various areas of the NWT. On Jan. 23, 1979, the federal govt presented the Soviet ambassador to Canada with a $6 million cleanup bill. At first, the Soviets failed to acknowledge the debt, but on Nov. 21, 1981, agreed to pay $3 million, or half the requested amount.

Jan. 30 Solicitor Gen. Francis Fox (b 1939) resigned his seat in the federal cabinet after a disclosure indicated he forged a signature on a hospital document to secure an abortion for a woman with whom he had had an affair several years earlier. Fox later became a lobbyist for Rogers AT&T and principal secretary to Paul Martin Jr. in 2003.

Feb. 1 On tour in China, the Toronto Symphony played to a crowd of 18,000 people in Peking (Beijing), its largest audience to date.

Feb. 5 Former financial journalist Michael Cassidy (b 1937) succeeded Stephen Lewis (b 1937) as NDP Leader of the Official Opposition in the Ont. legislature.

Feb. 11 A Pacific Western Airlines aircraft crashed at Cranbrook, BC, killing 43 people.

Mar. 1 Revised regulations under the Canada Elections Act came into effect, ending political party status for 7 groups, including the Nude Garden Party. Twelve parties remained officially registered.

Mar. 16 The Family Law Reform Act (Bill 59) was passed by the Ont. legislature. Effective date was Mar. 31. The act provided reforms to property rights and support obligations between spouses entering into a divorce, including equal division of family assets.

Mar. 17 *Toronto Sun* editor Peter John Vickers Worthington (b 1927) and publisher Douglas Creighton were charged for violating the Official Secrets Act for publishing top-secret information from an RCMP report on Soviet espionage activities in Canada. A parliamentary hearing was held but no more action was taken against the accused.

Mar. 18 Five members of Greenpeace, under the leadership of Greenpeace president Patrick Moore (b 1947), visited a seal hunt off the Labrador coast. Moore was arrested for interfering with the annual hunt.

Mar. 24 The Que. govt ordered its liquor corporation (SAQ) to stop importing wines and liquor from South Africa. The move was a protest of that country's human rights violations.

Apr. 2 The 1st issue of the *Edmonton Sun* hit the streets. The 1st Saturday edition was produced Sept. 17, 1994.

Apr. 3 Gerald K. Bouey, gov. of the Bank of Canada, raised the bank rate to 8.5% from 8% after the Canadian dollar fell below 88 cents US.

Apr. 14 PM Trudeau ended wage-and-price controls but set up the Economic Council as a watchdog agency. Wage-and-price controls were established for the 1st time in Canada during peacetime under anti-inflation legislation of Dec. 3, 1975, to curb escalating inflation rates. The effectiveness of the controls is not clear.

May 11 At the Law of the Sea conference in Geneva, Switzerland, Canada and the US agreed to place ceilings on seabed nickel production. Canada and the US, the world's 2 largest producers and consumers of nickel, were both interested in preventing a possible glut in the world nickel market.

May 15 A 450-page report of the Royal Commission on Corporate Concentration was tabled in the House of Commons. Recommendations included that the govt not tax business profits of those firms that reflowed profits back into their businesses. It also recommended the elimination of federal screenings of proposed corporate mergers.

Also in May
• *Portage Past the Rapids*, oil on canvas, by Cornelius Krieghoff, brought $41,000 at Sotheby's, a record auction price for a Krieghoff. Also selling was *Evening, North Shore, Lake Superior*, by Franklin Carmichael, which went for $36,000, an auction record for the Group of Seven artist.

June 1 Ont. Premier William Davis rejected a bill to enshrine French-language rights in provincial law.

The bill had passed 2nd reading. Davis also stated that his govt would not declare French an official language of the province.

June 2 The federal govt ordered all US fishing vessels out of Canadian waters; the US retaliated with similar measures against Canadian vessels. The moves followed the collapse of an interim fisheries agreement between the 2 countries that exacerbated jurisdictional and catch-quota conflicts along both coasts.

June 12 The govt tabled a white paper entitled "A Time For Action," outlining federal plans for a renewed federation. The plan involved a new constitutionally entrenched charter of rights and the free use of English and French, the establishment of a 118-member House of the Federation to replace the Senate, provincial voice in appointments to both the Supreme Court of Canada and House of the Federation, a redefinition of federal and provincial jurisdictions, repatriation of the Constitution from Britain, and the creation of an amending formula. Proposed Bill C–60, the constitutional amendment bill, was rejected by provincial premiers in 1979, and several of its proposals were ruled outside federal jurisdiction by the Supreme Court of Canada on Dec. 24, 1979.

June 19 The federal govt prohibited the importation and sale of cut-rate US editions of Canadian books. Such books had been sold in Canada below Canadian-edition costs, thus cutting into author royalties.

June 23 The Referendum Act came into effect in Que., establishing the procedure for Que.'s referendum on sovereignty.

Also in June
• Greg Curnoe began work on a large watercolour, *Homage to van Dongen (Sheila) No. 1*, which he completed late the following year. The work hangs in Hart House, U. of Toronto.

July 6 The govt prohibited all new development in a 38,850-km² region of northern Yukon so that a national wilderness area might be established. The area formed part of the migratory route of the porcupine caribou herd, numbering between

110,000–140,000 animals. The development freeze eventually led to establishment of Vuntut National Park in 1995.

• The Black brothers, Conrad (b 1944) and Montague (1940–2002), bought a controlling share of J.A. McDougald and Eric Philips's Ravelston Holding Company from its founders' widows. Price paid was $18.4 million, and much of the money was borrowed. Ravelston controlled the Argus Corporation, which in turn had interests in Massey-Ferguson Ltd., Dominion Stores (the largest grocery chain in Canada at the time), Norcen Energy Resources, Domtar Inc., Hollinger Mines Ltd. and the Standard Broadcasting Corporation. Argus had a book value of $4 billion.

July 15 In negotiations with the Committee for the Original Peoples' Entitlement (COPE), the federal govt offered $45 million to 2,500 Inuit in the western Arctic from 1981 to 1994. The Inuit would own surface and subsurface rights to more than 10,360 km^2 of land, and surface rights to another 82,880 km^2. In return, the Inuit would relinquish rights to a 435,120-km^2 region. On Oct. 31, COPE signed the agreement (Inuvaluit Land Rights Settlement) in principle, which was an initial, major step in the development of Nunavut (Apr. 1, 1999).

July 19 The US initiated a 10-year program to pave and rebuild the Alaska and Haines Highways in the Yukon. The Alaska Highway had opened Nov. 20, 1942.

July 20 The A.J. Casson Retrospective art exhibition opened at the Art Gallery of Ontario in Toronto, featuring the work of the last living member of the Group of Seven.

July 30 Syncrude shipped its 1st barrel of oil from the Athabasca oil sands, thereby becoming the 2nd major commercial producer to extract oil from the sands. Suncor was the 1st, with its Great Canadian Oil Sands plant, which had opened in 1967.

Aug. 3–11 The 11th Commonwealth Games opened in Edmonton, attended by nearly 1,500 athletes from 46 countries. Eleven sports were featured, including track and field, badminton, boxing, cycling and gymnastics. Canada won a total of

109 medals (45 gold, 31 silver, 33 bronze), more than any other country. Swimmer Graham Smith (b 1958) won 6 golds, a Games record.

Aug. 4 A chartered bus plunged into a lake near Eastman, Que., after its brakes failed. Forty-one mentally and physically challenged passengers were killed. It was the worst bus disaster in North America.

Aug. 15 The Department of Communication's Telidon system was put through its paces for the 1st time in public. The innovative, 2-way, 2nd-generation videotex system incorporated a modified television set, keypad and a Telidon transmission link to a central data bank. Experimental work on this precursor to the Internet was dropped on Mar. 31, 1985, as costs and information access limitations, coupled with development of personal computers, made mass marketing of the system impractical.

Sept. 18 W.B. Campbell (b 1943) assumed office as Liberal premier of PEI, succeeding Alex Campbell, who resigned after 12 years in office.

Sept. 19 The Progressive Conservatives under John MacLellan Buchanan (b 1931) won the NS provincial election with 31 seats to defeat the Liberal govt of Gerald Regan (b 1929), which took 17 seats. In the previous election, the Liberals won 31 seats, the Conservatives 12.

Sept. 28 The Bank of NS and the Canadian Union of Public Employees signed a collective agreement in Toronto, the 1st such agreement between a Canadian bank and a union.

Oct. 8 Gilles Villeneuve (1952–1982) won his 1st Formula One victory, in a red Ferrari 312 T-3 at the Canadian Grand Prix in Montreal. Villeneuve would win 5 more races on the F1 circuit before dying in a crash during training for the Belgian Grand Prix on May 8, 1982. The tragedy cut short one of the brightest futures in the sport.

Oct. 14 Cathy Sherk of Fonthill, Ont., won the women's world amateur golf championship in Fiji. She was later awarded the 1978 Velma Springstead Award for outstanding Canadian female athlete of the year.

Oct. 25 Jean-Claude Parrot, national president of the Canadian Union of Postal Workers, ordered his members back to the job after a week of defying federal back-to-work legislation, during which time 5 union leaders were charged under section 115 of the Criminal Code for contravening the parliamentary legislation; others were threatened with dismissals if they did not return to work. On May 7, 1979, Parrot began a 3-month sentence followed by 18-months' probation for defying the back-to-work order.

Also in Oct.
• Public Archives of Canada researchers announced they had discovered a Spanish galleon off the coast of Labrador, which had sunk in 1525.

Nov. 3 Kenneth Swan, appointed referee under Ont.'s Employment Standards Act, ordered Abitibi Forest Products to pay $300,000 to 135 former employees who had been dismissed without severance pay.

• *Billy Bishop Goes to War*, with music and lyrics by John Gray (b 1946) and Eric Peterson (b 1946), premiered at the Vancouver East Cultural Centre. The show moved to off-Broadway under director Mike Nichols, and later to Broadway (1980). It has been revived over 150 times with a plethora of actors, and was made into a controversial CBC movie. *Billy Bishop* also won the Gov-Gen.'s Award, the Chalmers Award and the Los Angeles Drama Critics Award.

Nov. 20 Progressive Conservatives won 11 out of 16 seats in the 1st Yukon election contested by political parties. PC leader Hilda Watson, however, lost her seat.

Dec. 1 *Lumber Camp at Gaspé*, a stolen A.Y. Jackson oil painting worth an estimated $30,000, was recovered at a Halifax art gallery. It had been snatched from the Windsor Western Hospital Centre in Ont.

Dec. 6 The federal govt pledged $200 million toward a NATO fleet of Boeing 707s, which would form a $25 billion, continuously airborne warning system across Western Europe.

Dec. 7 Edward Schreyer (b 1935) was appointed gov-gen. of Canada, assuming office on Jan. 22, 1979.

Dec. 13 Former FLQ members Jacques Cossette-Trudel and his wife, Louise Lanctot, returned to Montreal after an 8-year exile following the kidnapping of British trade commissioner James Cross. They were charged with kidnapping and sentenced to 2 years less a day. On Jan. 3, the couple had published a letter in Montreal's *Le Devoir* calling for an amnesty on all FLQ members either serving time or still in exile.

Dec. 14 The Ont. govt agreed to sell its 5% share in the Syncrude oil sands project to Canadian-owned PanCanadian Petroleum Ltd. for $160 million.

Dec. 15 *ANIK-IV*, Canada's 4th communications satellite, was launched from Cape Canaveral, Florida.

Also in 1978
• Simpson-Sears broke into 2 companies, Sears (Canada) and Simpson's. In 1980, Simpson's was acquired by the Hudson's Bay Company and all its stores were converted into The Bay stores by 1991.

• Air Canada hired its 1st woman pilot — Judy Cameron. The former bush pilot and 1st Canadian woman to obtain a certificate in aviation technology flew Air Canada Boeing 767 jetliners.

• The Ford Motor Company of Canada established its $500 million–plus engine plant in Windsor, Ont., helped by federal and provincial incentives of $68 million.

• Pukaskwa National Park was founded on the north shore of L. Superior as Ont.'s only wilderness park. At 1,880 km², it was also Ont.'s largest national park. Pukaskwa covers an eclectic mix of shoreline, sand dunes, towering boreal forest pines, exposed outcrops of the Canadian Shield, whitewater, bogs and rock-rimmed lakes. Fauna include rookeries of herons, woodland caribou, loons, shorebirds, wolves, moose, hare, grouse, lynx and black bear. The park also protects the Pukaskwa Pits, ancient rock structures believed to have been made by Aboriginal Peoples some 5,000–10,000 years ago, as either lookout posts or hunting shelters.

• The Etienne-Joseph Gaboury–designed Royal Canadian Mint at Winnipeg was completed. A Winnipeg landmark, the principal glass-clad triangular building was made from slick, gleaming, high-tech materials. The Royal Canadian Mint's Ottawa headquarters, and the Winnipeg production facility are some of the largest and most advanced minting operations in the world. By 2003, the Royal Canadian Mint was pressing coins for 40 other countries.

• Gordie Howe of the WHA's New England Whalers became the 1st 50-year-old to play professional hockey. On Oct. 3, 1997, the 69-year-old became the 1st player to play professional hockey over 6 decades, when he took a 46-second shift with the IHL Detroit Vipers.

• The Sun Life Assurance Co. of Canada moved its head office from Montreal to Toronto as a result of Que.'s unstable political climate and volatile language laws.

• Dr. Patricia Baird was appointed head of the U. of BC Department of Medical Genetics, the 1st women to hold the post. The internationally renowned geneticist and University Distinguished Professor entered the Order of British Columbia in 1992, and became an Officer of the Order of Canada in 2000. Her groundbreaking Royal Commission report, *Handle with Care*, was tabled in the House of Commons Nov. 15, 1993.

• The Book and Periodical Development Council established a Freedom of Expression Committee to stifle the growth of censorship in schools and libraries.

• Female flight attendants won the right to continue working after marriage and past the age of 32.

• The Canada Labour Code was amended to ensure that women could no longer be fired for pregnancy in federally regulated industries.

• Nicola Schaefer (b 1939) published *Does She Know She's There?: The Courageous and Triumphant True Story of a Woman and Her Handicapped Child*, which chronicled her family's fight to raise their severely challenged daughter, Catherine, at home, in Winnipeg. Eight years after the publication of this 1st edition, Catherine was successfully living in her own apartment.

• Colette Whiten (b 1945) completed *Family*, 3 life-like plaster, wood, burlap and metal sculptures representing her 2 daughters, Shauna and Carmen, and artist/teacher Gernot Dick. The work is in a private collection.

• Otto Rogers painted *Mondrian* and *Prairie Landscape*, now in the Edmonton Art Gallery.

• Edmonton-born artist John Scott Hall (b 1943) painted *Trogon*, on canvas, now in the Mendel Art Gallery, Saskatoon.

• Toronto-born Shirley Wiitasalo painted *The Shortest Route*, on canvas, now in the Art Gallery of Ontario, Toronto.

• The National Film Board produced its prize-winning documentary, "The Beauty of My People," the life and times of Arthur Shilling.

• The federal govt funded the 1st week-long National Book Festival.

• Peter Such published *Vanished Peoples: The Archaic Dorset & Beothuk People of Newfoundland*.

• René Lévesque published *La Passion du Québec*, issued in English in 1979 as *My Quebec*.

• Kevin Major published the children's novel *Hold Fast*, about troubled adolescents in Nfld.

• Short-story writer Alice Munro published the critically acclaimed *Who Do You Think You Are?* The US edition was called *The Beggar Maid*.

• Robin Mathews published *Canadian Literature: Surrender or Revolution*.

• Al Purdy published his selection of verse, *Being Alive*.

• Patrick Lane (b 1939) published *Poems New and Selected,* for which he received the Gov-Gen's Award.

• Poet A.J.M. Smith published *The Classic Shade*.

• Sharon Pollock published the play *The Komagata Maru Incident*, based on the 1914 Vancouver Sikh-immigration debacle.

• *Touchstone*, the 1st newspaper for the blind, was published.

• The 1st 2 Canadian pop singles to reach platinum in Canada (selling over 100,000 copies) were recorded this year: The Irish Rover's "The Unicorn" and Alain Barrière's (b 1935) "Tu t'en vas."

1979

Jan. 4 Canadian planes were dispatched to Iran to airlift 350 Canadians and other nationals from the country, in a period of political instability marked by widespread violence, looting, anti-American sentiment and anti-Shah rioting.

Jan. 5 Canadian chartered banks raised their prime lending rate to 12%, the highest since 1934.

• A new dinosaur gallery featuring 3 dinosaur skeletons found around Drumheller in southern Alb. opened in the Provincial Museum of Alb. in Edmonton.

Jan. 17 The Canadian Institute of Economic Policy was founded by a group of businesspeople and academics to promote solutions to Canadian economic problems. Former Liberal cabinet minister Walter Gordon was founding chairman.

Jan. 26 The Pépin-Robarts Task Force on Canadian Unity, appointed by PM Trudeau in 1977, issued its report, *A Future Together*. It concluded that Canadian unity had worsened because of "costly and relatively ineffective" policies such as institutional bilingualism and the failure of such policies to recognize Canada's defining characteristics of "duality and regionalism." Recommendations included that Que. be given "distinctive" though not special status; all provinces be given increased powers over their residents' cultural and social well-being; and the provinces be given authority to negotiate treaties in areas under their own jurisdiction.

Jan. 29 Defence Minister Barnett Danson (b 1921) issued a policy paper providing women with a greater range of assignments in the Canadian Armed Forces, stopping short of actual combat roles. There were 4,000 women (5.9%) in the 80,000-member Canadian Armed Forces, the highest inclusion rate next to the US and Israel.

Feb. 7 The 1st Ministers' Constitutional Conference ended. Complete or partial agreement was reached on provincial control over family law, including marriage and divorce; retention of the British monarchy; the entrenchment of the Supreme Court of Canada in the Constitution and consultation with the provinces on appointments; the provincial right to levy indirect taxes on natural resources and the constitutional enshrinement of the principle of regional financial equalization.

• Striking *Montreal Star* workers from 3 unions ratified a new contract and returned after an 8-month work stoppage.

Feb. 14 North York, part of Metropolitan Toronto, officially became a city. Former mayor of the borough of North York, the irrepressible Mel Lastman (b 1933), became the 1st mayor, a position he held until the city merged with Toronto on Jan. 1, 1998, when he was elected mega-Toronto's 1st mayor.

Feb. 16 During the worldwide oil shortage, the federal govt strongly criticized Toronto-based Imperial Oil for arranging oil swaps with Exxon, its US parent company. Exxon planned to divert Venezuelan oil destined for Canada to the US, which would have undercut supplies and exacerbated shortages in Eastern Canada.

• The federal govt unveiled plans to discontinue its $800 annual bilingual bonuses to some 47,000 federal civil servants, effective Mar. 31. The deadline was later extended due to a threatened boycott by civil servants, supported by union representatives from the Public Service Alliance. The bonus system had been implemented in Oct. 1977, for those who could communicate in both national languages. The system was immediately riddled with abuse and remained a source of internal civil servant conflict until the bilingual bonus was eventually phased out in 1983.

Feb. 17 Federal Bill C–42, the Energy Supplies Emergency Act, was introduced to control the distribution of oil and its rationing, if necessary. Western nations faced oil disruptions due in part to revolution in Iran.

Feb. 24 A mine explosion at Dominion Coal Co.'s

No. 26 colliery in Glace Bay, NS, killed 10 men and injured 6.

Mar. 14 The Dene-Métis of the NWT presented land claims to the federal govt, calling for autonomy over a large eastern portion of the Territory. The move marked the early beginnings of Nunavut. The presentation was followed by a land claims publicity tour through southern Canada by members of the Dene, the Nisga'a of BC, the Council of Yukon Indians and the Naskapi-Montagnais of Labrador.

Mar. 15 The British oil tanker *Kurdistan* broke in half in heavy seas, spilling over 6,350 tonnes of heavy bunker oil in the Cabot Str. between Nfld. and Cape Breton. On Mar. 22, its British owners agreed to a Canadian request that a $150 million bond be deposited against damages and costs of cleaning up the spill.

Mar. 19 Alfred Brian Peckford (b 1942) won the provincial leadership of the Progressive Conservative party in Nfld. He became premier on Mar. 26, succeeding retiring Frank Moores.

Mar. 27 OPEC nations raised the price of crude oil by almost 9% to $15.74 US per barrel. The federal govt announced that it would continue to use a federal tax of 10 cents per gallon to keep energy costs uniform across the country.

Also in Mar.
• Programs implemented under the Agricultural Rehabilitation and Development Act (ARDA), 1961, created to ease rural poverty and to keep small farmers on the land, came to an end.

Spring James Picard became the nation's 1st commercial peanut farmer after successfully harvesting a variety of valencia peanuts from a 2-ha plot in southern Ont. In 1980, he expanded to 34 ha and started Canada's 1st peanut shelling and cleaning processing plant in Windham, Ont.

Apr. 1 The National Energy Board raised the export tax on light crude oil $1 per barrel to $8, and on heavy crude $1.35 per barrel to $5.70. The National Energy Board also raised the export price of natural gas to $2.30 US per thousand cubic feet, to take effect May 2. On July 13, the export price of

Canadian natural gas was raised to $2.80 per thousand cubic feet, effective Aug. 11.

Apr. 9 *Every Child*, an animated film by Eugene Fedorenko, won an Oscar at the 52nd Academy Awards ceremony in Los Angeles. The NFB-produced film told the story of a baby who appeared mysteriously, only to bounce from one family to the next.

Apr. 11 The Academy of Canadian Cinema was formed as a "vehicle for greater exposure for the industry in Canada and abroad." As a result, the Genie Awards were established, replacing the Canadian Film Awards; the Etrog sculpture that had been created in 1968 for the Canadian Film Awards was renamed the Genie.

Apr. 23 The Progressive Conservatives under John Angus MacLean (1914–2000) won 21 seats in the PEI provincial election to defeat the Liberal govt, under Bennett Campbell, which won 11 seats. The Campbell govt had been the 1st provincial Liberal govt.

Apr. 25 The Man. govt ordered the evacuation of 10,000 people from the Red R. Valley because of rising water and threatening floods.

May 1 Leader of the Que. Liberal Party and former publisher of *Le Devoir*, Claude Ryan (1925–2004), won his 1st seat in Que.'s National Assembly, in a by-election in the riding of Argenteuil.

May 10 Premier William Bennett's Social Credit govt retained power in BC's provincial election, winning 31 seats. David Barrett's NDP won 26 seats; both the Liberals and Conservatives were shut out.

May 22 The Progressive Conservatives under Joe Clark won 136 seats in the federal general election, defeating the Liberal govt under Pierre Trudeau, which took 114 seats. The NDP under Ed Broadbent won 26 seats, and the Social Credit under Fabien Roy, 6. Voter turnout was 75.7%. Twelve Trudeau cabinet members lost their seats. On June 4 (to Mar. 3, 1980), Joe Clark served as PM. He entered office the youngest PM in Canadian history, 1 day short of 40 years of age. On Aug. 15, he confirmed a campaign promise to eliminate 60,000 federal civil servant positions over 3 years.

May 24 After an 8-month inquiry into the cost of Montreal's Olympic Games, which left Montreal tax-payers with a $1 billion debt, Que. Superior Court Justice Albert Malouf (1916–1997) released a 60-page summary, revealing scandals involving a number of Que. Liberals and hired contractors who received illegal benefits from their association.

Also in May

• The RCMP made its largest drug seizure to date: 27 tonnes of Colombian marijuana worth $50 million nabbed at Sidney Inlet on Vancouver Is.

• The Sask. legislature unanimously supported the proclamation of the Sask. Human Rights Code, which included provisions for rights to freedom of conscience, expression, association, election and from arbitrary imprisonment; and prohibitions against discrimination based on religion, creed, marital status, gender, sexual orientation, disability, age, race, ancestry and receipt of public assistance.

June 3 Members of the United Steelworkers of America ended an 8.5-month strike against Inco Ltd. in Sudbury, Ont., after winning a landmark labour bargaining deal with a $4.07 per hour increase in wages and benefits.

June 6 Ambassadors to Canada from Arab League countries protested the new Conservative govt's plan to move the Canadian embassy, in Israel, from Tel Aviv to Jerusalem. The Palestinian Liberation Organization (PLO) called PM Clark's plan "an act of aggression." On June 9, the govts of Saudi Arabia and several gulf oil states subsequently threatened to boycott Canadian companies in the Middle East. On June 19, the Arab Monetary Fund announced it would make no further deposits with Canadian banks. Clark's plan, which would have given Canadian recognition to Jerusalum as the capital of Israel and thereby discount Arab claims to the city, was abandoned on Oct. 29. No such attempt has been made by a PM since.

June 6–18 BC longshoremen went on strike, disrupting wheat shipments.

June 8 The federal govt initiated a 2-month hiring freeze for the public service. The freeze was lifted Aug. 15.

June 10 The ambitious Project Lorex, or the Lomonosov Ridge Experiment, was dismantled. It had been financed by the Department of Energy, Mines and Resources, and involved a temporary scientific station built on a permanent ice floe, which drifted 240 km across the Arctic from mid-Mar. to June 10. On May 17, it came within 35 km of the North Pole. Gov-Gen. Schreyer, Prince Charles and PM Trudeau made scuba dives near the North Pole from the Lorex. The multi-study project was designed to uncover the origins of the underwater Lomonosov Ridge.

• The Feminist Party of Canada was launched in Toronto. Its goal, to increase women's involvement in Canadian politics. The inaugural meeting was attended by 700 women. Members estimated that at 1970s rates, gender equality would not be reached in the House of Commons for another 843 years. The party ceased to function in 1982, never having run a candidate for political office.

June 18 Brian Peckford and his Progressive Conservatives were returned to power in Nfld., winning 33 of 52 seats.

June 28–July 1 The 1st International Gathering of the Clans, an international celebration of Scottish heritage, was held in Pugwash, NS. The event included a Thinker's Conference dubbed "The Scottish Role in the Development of Canada."

July 2 A delegation of 300 Canadian Native leaders held a press conference in London, England, after failing to obtain an audience with the British queen and to gain access to the House of Commons and House of Lords. The leaders protested the repatriation of the BNA Act before Native Peoples were assured founding nation status in the Constitution.

July 11 The federal govt began a 40% reduction of tariffs on imported manufactured goods over a period of 8 years as a result of GATT negotiations in Tokyo, June 28th and 29th. Canadian GATT partners were West Germany, France, Italy, Japan, the United Kingdom of Great Britain and Northern Ireland, and the US. The negotiations marked a significant step toward the elimination of international trade barriers and a movement toward corporate globalization.

July 16 About 135 pothead whales beached themselves at Point au Gaul, Nfld., for no known reason. Efforts to tow the whales back to sea were unsuccessful.

July 19 In what she would recall years later as the most vital speech of her political career, Canada's Secretary of State for External Affairs, Flora Macdonald, stood before an international gathering in Geneva, Switzerland, and outlined Canada's response to the plight of south Asians caught up in the aftermath of the Vietnam War. The response was a refugee program (unveiled to the Canadian people July 18) that committed the Canadian govt to match the number of Vietnamese, Cambodian and Laotian refugees adopted by private sponsors. Canada's decision to lead the way and the humanitarian outpouring of more than 7,000 church groups, community centres, employee groups and individual Canadian sponsors saw the country offer a safe haven to upwards of 60,000 refugees and "boat people" by Dec. of 1980, a per capita number unmatched by any other country in the world.

Aug. 7 A freak tornado struck Oxford County in southwestern Ont., causing at least 3 deaths and millions of dollars' damage. The region around Woodstock, Ont., was declared a disaster area by the Ont. govt.

Aug. 15 Que. Lands and Forests published a map showing an area of some 19,424 km^2 of Labrador as part of Que.

Aug. 16 Former PM John Diefenbaker died in Ottawa at age 83. On Aug. 19, following a state funeral in the capital, his body was taken in a special Funeral Train, which made many stops en route to Saskatoon, where on Aug. 22, Diefenbaker was buried on the banks of the South Saskatchewan R.

Aug. 18 The 736-km Dempster Highway, running northwest from Dawson, Yukon (km 0), to Inuvik, in the Mackenzie R. delta, NWT, was opened. The highway crosses the Arctic Circle at km 405; at km 608, travellers cross the mighty Mackenzie R. by ferry, between June and Oct., and by icebridge between Nov. and Apr.

Sept. 3 Canadian fisheries officials seized a number of US fishing boats along with their cargoes, charging the captains with violating Canada's 200-mile (322 km) territorial limit. In retaliation, the US banned further imports of Canadian tuna and threatened to extend the embargo on other fishery products if charges against their fishers were not withdrawn.

Sept. 5 The Banque Canadienne Nationale merged with La Banque Provinciale du Canada, forming the Banque Nationale du Canada.

• Canada's 1st gold-bullion coin, the Canadian gold maple leaf, produced at the Royal Canadian Mint in Winnipeg, went on sale to stimulate the domestic gold industry.

Sept. 14 Ont. Minister of Education Bette Stephenson ordered the Toronto Board of Education to reinstate the Lord's Prayer in its schools on the grounds that suspension of the Christian petition contravened the Education Act.

• Alb. Premier Peter Lougheed offered to lend the federal govt money from the Alb. Heritage Trust Fund if a mutually acceptable agreement on oil and gas prices, and natural gas exports could be reached.

• China signed an agreement to purchase 2 million tons of Canadian wheat for $400 million.

Sept. 16 Toronto's newest television station, CFMT, the 1st in Canada to offer predominantly ethnic multilingual broadcasting, officially began broadcasting.

Sept. 22 Citytv's *The New Music* station 1st aired, with hosts Jeanne Beker and J.D. Roberts (b 1956). The topical television music and music-video magazine was forerunner to *MTV* and the 24-hour music-video *MuchMusic*, which went on air Aug. 31, 1984.

Sept. 24 A family court in Halifax, NS, gave guardianship of an unborn child to an anti-abortion group after the pregnant woman was unable to secure an abortion at a local hospital. The hospital refused to perform the operation because the woman's estranged husband threatened an injunction against it.

Sept. 25 The *Montreal Star* went out of business after 110 years of publishing due to an 8-month strike that impacted on circulation and advertising revenues.

Oct. 4 For the 1st time Native Peoples won a majority of seats on the NWT Council in the territorial elections, capturing 13 of the council's 22 seats.

Oct. 6–7 One thousand seven hundred Acadians converged on Edmundston, NB, to discuss their place in North America. They rejected a new union with the US and separation with Canada, and instead favoured forming an 11th province.

Oct. 30 PM Clark aggravated strained relations between Alb., Ottawa and the provinces by threatening in the House of Commons that federal constitutional powers would be used, if necessary, to make inexpensive Alb. oil available to Eastern Canada. The comments came after Alb. Premier Lougheed demanded (Oct. 29) that other provinces pay Alb.-set prices for Alb. oil. The battle over the pricing of Alb. oil peaked with PM Trudeau's National Energy Program (Oct. 28, 1980).

Nov. 1 René Lévesque's Parti Québécois tabled a white paper entitled *Québec-Canada: A New Deal*, spelling out a proposed semi-succession with Canada referred to as "sovereignty-association." The paper explained that federalism undermined Que.'s control over its own social, cultural, fiscal and financial institutions, and also its land resources, and called for a new deal that would see Que. achieve political independence but at the same time maintain an economic union with what remained of Canada. On Dec. 20, Lévesque announced that a referendum on sovereignty-association would be held in Spring 1980 (May 20, 1980).

Nov. 1–Dec. 31 An exhibition of the "Treasures of King Tutankhamen" at the Art Gallery of Ontario in Toronto attracted 750,000 people.

Nov. 5 Ont. Premier Davis condemned the Parti Québécois white paper on sovereignty-association,

stating he would take no part in any negotiations on the subject. Davis's condemnation received all-party approval in the legislature.

• The Métis Association of the NWT offered $160 million for the govt's one-third interest in Imperial Oil's Norman Wells operation. The offer, which was not accepted, included a $1,000 down payment for the govt share. The remainder, the offer proposed, would come from money owed the Métis on existing unsettled land claims in the area.

Nov. 6 The Clark govt survived a non-confidence vote by a mere 2 votes on the issue of energy supplies. The govt had also survived, by 9 votes, a non-confidence vote Oct. 15.

Nov. 10 A CP train spun off the tracks in Mississauga, Ont., while en route from Windsor to Agincourt. Of the 24 cars derailed, 19 contained dangerous materials, including propane, inflammable liquids and caustic soda. Also involved was chlorine, which leaked into the atmosphere from a punctured tanker. Within 24 hours, 220,000 people — most of the city's population — was evacuated. Residents began returning Nov. 16 after work crews drained the liquid chlorine into tank trucks. No one was killed or injured. The evacuation was the largest single movement of people in Canada during peacetime.

Nov. 12 A federal-provincial conference was held in Ottawa, where energy prices were discussed. Premiers agreed on the need to increase the price of domestic oil by $2 per barrel over the objections of Ont. Premier Davis, leader of the nation's most industrialized province.

Nov. 14 Liberals won all 3 seats contested in Que. provincial by-elections, dealing a blow to the Parti Québécois.

Dec. 11 Federal minister of finance John Crosbie (b 1931), delivered his Tory budget address, which included a 4-cent per-litre excise on gasoline, a $4-per-barrel increase in oil in 1980, followed by annual increases of $4.50, and decreases to the total amount of foreign oil imported. Altogether, the 1979–1980 deficit of $9.4 billion was projected to decrease to $4.4 billion by 1983–1984. Crosbie tabled the budget in mukluks, continuing the tradition of wearing new shoes when delivering the federal budget.

Dec. 12 NS MP Allan MacEachen told Liberals, assembled for their weekly caucus, that the time had come to vote against Crosbie's budget and bring down the Clark govt.

Dec. 13 Joe Clark's minority Tory govt was defeated in a non-confidence vote over the budget, 139 votes to 133. Parliament was dissolved and an election called for Feb. 18, 1980.

• The Supreme Court of Canada struck down Que. and Man. laws that had created unilingual legislatures and courts, and ruled that the provinces did not have the constitutional powers to impose only 1 official language in these areas. The Que. National Assembly was forced to pass legislation creating 311 new bilingual laws, replacing French-only laws passed in the wake of language Bill 101 (1977). On July 8, 1980, the Man. legislature passed Bill 2, which provided for French and English versions of all provincial statutes, following the Court's ruling that the province's 90-year-old Official Language Act was unconstitutional.

• The NS govt reintroduced an amendment (dubbed the "Michelin Bill," based on efforts by NS Michelin tire employees) to the Trade Union Act, which would only recognize unions that covered entire companies, not individual plants or branches. The NS Federation of Labour threatened a general strike and total noncommunication with the labour minister if the bill became law. The legislation was not passed.

Dec. 15 The 36-member National Liberal Executive met in Ottawa and overwhelmingly endorsed Pierre Trudeau as their candidate for the Feb. 18, 1980, election. Previously, on Nov. 20, Trudeau announced he was stepping down as Liberal leader and called for a leadership convention in Mar. 1980. However, he reconsidered his options in the wake of the Tory collapse (Dec. 13) and ran as Liberal leader in the 1980 election.

Dec. 18 The United Nations General Assembly adopted the Convention on the Elimination of all Forms of Discrimination Against Women. Canada was an early signatory to the document, which came into force as an international treaty on Sept. 3, 1981.

Dec. 31 A federal amendment to the Criminal Code, giving the right to anyone charged under the Code to opt for trial by judge or jury in either French or English, was proclaimed effective in Ont. Ont. was the 1st unilingual province — and the 2nd province after officially bilingual NB — to proclaim the amendment.

Also in Dec.

• An Ont. program begun in 1978 to locate lost and abandoned waste-disposal sites was completed: 787 sites previously unknown to the Ont. environment ministry were discovered.

Also in 1979

• The population of Canada was 23,671,500.

• The 1st Canadian case of AIDS (acquired immune deficiency syndrome), the most advanced stage of HIV (human immunodeficiency virus), was reported in Canada. The disease emerged as an epidemic strain in Africa in 1930; the 1st AIDS-related death occurred in the Congo in 1959. In 1980, there were 5 reported AIDS cases in Canada. By 2001, 55,000 Canadian men, 14,000 women and more than 500 children would be living with either HIV or AIDS. There was no known cure.

• The Commission de toponymie du Québec began a systematic undertaking to restore place names, in the northern part of the province, to traditional Aboriginal use or preference. Initial efforts of the commission led to 7 official Canada Post redesignations in 1981: Port Harrison and Inoucdjouac became Inukjuak; George R. and Port-Nouveau-Quebec became Kangiqsualujjuaq; Wakeham Bay and Maricourt became Kangiqsujuaq; Payne Bay and Bellin became Kangirsuk; Fort Chimo became Kuujjuaq; Koartak and Notre-Dame-de-Koartac became Quaqtaq; and Sugluk and Saglouc became Salluit.

• Polish WW II hero Romuald Nalecz-Tyminski moved to Toronto and was made an honorary member of the Royal Regiment of Canada. The naval commander was part of the Polish Flotilla stationed in Great Britain during WW II. During the invasion at Dieppe, Nalecz-Tyminski defied British orders and German artillery, and with guns blazing, spearheaded his destroyer *Slaza* through the surf, and saved the lives of 85 Canadian soldiers stranded on the beach.

• Claudja Barry recorded Canada's 1st single to sell over 1 million copies, "Boogie Woogie Dancin' Shoes."

• UNESCO declared Dinosaur Provincial Park in Alb. a World Heritage Site. Located in the Badlands of southeastern Alb., the 75-km² park protects fossil beds containing bones that date back 75 million years. One hundred and fifty complete dinosaur skeletons have been found in the park, making it one of the most important study sites in the world.

• Aboriginal women organized a 100-km march to Ottawa from Oka, Que., to protest housing conditions on reserves and to demand changes to the Indian Act.

• The long standing 10% duty on the importation of Canadian books printed abroad was lifted.

• Philadelphia jazz bassist Charlie Biddle (1926–2003), who immigrated to Montreal in 1948, organized the Montreal Jazz de chez nous, forerunner to the Montreal International Jazz Festival. Also this year, "Monsieur Jazz Montreal," as he was called, opened the internationally renowned Biddle's Jazz and Ribs club in downtown Montreal. In 2003, Biddle was invested as a member of the Order of Canada and received the Prix Calixa Lavalée for outstanding contributions to Canadian jazz.

• Montreal architect Peter Rose (b 1943) completed the 3-storey postmodern Bradley House, located in North Hatley in the Eastern Townships, Que.

• *Women Holding Fish*, an elegant black stone carving by Matthew Aqiguq (b 1940), was completed.

• Paterson Ewen painted *Cloud Over Water*, on panel, now in the Art Gallery of Ontario, Toronto.

• John Hare published *Anthologie de la poésie québécoise du XIXe siècle*.

• Roch Carrier published the comic classic *Les enfants du bonhomme dans la lune*. It was translated into English as *The Hockey Sweater and Other Stories*. The main story involves the trials and tribulations of a rural Que. youth forced by his mother to wear a Toronto Maple Leafs hockey sweater mistakenly ordered through Monsieur Eaton's catalogue.

• Matt Cohen published the novel *The Sweet Second Summer of Kitty Malone*.

• Acclaimed children's writer Robert Munsch (b 1945) published his 1st children's book, *Mud Puddle*. Munsch would go on to publish more than 35 titles by century's end.

• Antonine Maillet published the novel *Pélagie-la-charrette*, for which she won the Prix Goncourt.

• Michael Ondaatje published his collection of poems, *There's a Trick with a Knife I'm Learning to Do*, for which he received his 2nd Gov-Gen.'s Award.

• Garth Drabinsky (b 1949), along with partner Nathan Taylor, opened Cineplex in the Eaton Centre, Toronto, an 18-screen movie theatre that marked the beginning of an entertainment empire. Eighteen months later, Drabinsky acquired the Canadian Odeon theatre chain that gave Cineplex control of 446 movie screens in 185 locations. In 1984, Drabinsky took over the 4th largest theatre chain in the US, giving him another 574 screens in 22 states. He continued to acquire movie theatres in Canada and the US, eventually controlling 1,800 screens in more than 500 locations.

1980

Jan. 7 A 19-year-old dispute was settled between the Fort Nelson Slave Native Peoples and the govt of BC at Fort Nelson, BC, when both parties agreed to an equal share of revenues from natural gas production beneath reserve lands.

Jan. 8 BC Premier William Bennett unveiled a $200 million plan to subsidize mortgages on new BC homes in the hope of setting a national trend toward lower interest rates.

Jan. 9 Consumers' Gas Co. of Toronto and Hiram Walker-Gooderham and Worts Ltd. agreed in principle to a $1.3 billion merger in a bid to diversify holdings. The firms amalgamated later in the year.

Jan. 10 Que. Liberal leader Claude Ryan (1925–2004) presented a policy paper on constitutional reform entitled *A New Canadian Confederation*. Recommendations included a shift of more power to the provinces, abolishing the Senate and English monarchy in Canada, and increased bilingualism throughout the country. It also recommended development of a new Constitution.

• Brazil contracted to buy at least 3 million metric tonnes of Canadian wheat over the next 3 years.

• Canadian-Soviet relations cooled in the wake of the 1979 Soviet invasion of Afghanistan: PM Clark initiated trade restrictions with the Soviet Union and launched a campaign against the 1980 Summer Olympics in Moscow, which Canada eventually boycotted, along with 60 other nations, including the US, Japan, China and West Germany. Traditional Western allies Great Britain and France attended.

• The McDonald Royal Commission, set up July 1977 to investigate allegations of spy activities within the RCMP, released its 1st report in Ottawa. It recommended a major overhaul of the 1939 Official Secrets Act to increase the penalty for espionage to life imprisonment and reduce the penalty for leaking sensitive secrets to 7 years. The commission's 2nd report was released Aug. 25, 1981.

Jan. 11 Thomson Newspapers Ltd. of Toronto purchased FP Publications Ltd., owner of 8 Canadian newspapers, including the *Globe and Mail*, for $165 million. The move gave Thomson over 100 dailies across North America.

Jan. 12 Liberal leader Pierre Trudeau outlined his party's multi-point economic platform: more effective use of tax money, energy security, stimulation of economic growth, job creation and increased Canadian ownership and economic control, and protection of low and middle-income Canadians.

• Ken Read became the 1st Canadian to win a World Cup ski event on Austria's legendary Hahmenkamm at Kitzbuhel, downhill skiing's greatest and most terrifying test.

Jan. 21 The federal govt expelled 3 Soviet embassy employees for spying. On Feb. 1, Canada's top military attaché in Moscow, Harold Gold, was expelled by the Soviet Union in retaliation. Canada then expelled Soviet embassy worker V.F. Trofimov on Feb. 7.

Jan. 28 Canada's ambassador to Iran, Kenneth Taylor (b 1934), arranged the escape of 6 US embassy employees from Tehran. The 6 had fled from the US embassy when it was occupied by Iranian students in Nov. 1979, during the revolution against the Shah. By Nov. 22, the Americans were safely housed with Canadian embassy staff. Afraid Iranians had learned of the whereabouts of the Americans, Canadians drove the 6 to Tehran airport where they left the country under non-diplomatic Canadian passports. Taylor and 4 other Canadians left Iran a few hours later. It was later revealed that the CIA, which had supported the brutal regime of Shah Mohammad Reza Pahlavi, had been closely involved with the escape effort.

• More than 70,000 striking teachers closed Que. schools, which affected nearly 1 million students. Teachers were seeking strict limits on class size and a clear definition of teachers' jobs as differentiated from support staff. Teachers returned to work Feb. 21, after a settlement providing a minimum wage of $265 per week and improved job security and working conditions.

Jan. 31 In a telephone call to PM Joe Clark, US President Jimmy Carter officially thanked Canada for smuggling American diplomats out of Iran. On June 16, 1982, in Washington, D.C., Taylor became the 1st foreigner to receive the US Congressional Medal for his role in sheltering and helping the American diplomats escape Iran.

• Ont. offered a rebate of up to $700 on its provincial sales tax for those who purchased 1979-model cars, in an effort to help the slumping automobile business.

Feb. 11 The federal govt unveiled subsidy programs to help northern residents meet rising electricity and home-heating oil prices.

Feb. 18 Liberals under Pierre Trudeau won the general federal election, taking 146 seats. Joe Clark and the Progressive Conservatives won 103 seats, the NDP under Ed Broadbent won 32. One seat remained vacant. Trudeau reigned as Liberal PM from Mar. 3 to June 30, 1984. Voter turnout was 69.3%.

Feb. 24 At the close of the Winter Olympic Games in L. Placid, New York, Canada won 2 medals — a silver in the 1,000-m speed-skating event by Gaétan Boucher (b 1959), and a bronze in downhill skiing by Steve Podborski (b 1957). Crazy Canuck Ken Read was the favourite to win the downhill: faced with intense Canadian and European media pressure, Read sprang from the starting gate only to fall victim to a failed binding 8 seconds later. He lost a ski and did not finish the race.

Feb. 27 The BC govt declared a 7-year moratorium on uranium mining and exploration in the province in response to public concern that the activity might do irreversible harm to the environment.

• In Hollywood, California, Oscar Peterson won a Grammy in the jazz solo category for his album *Jousts*.

Feb. 29 Outgoing PM Clark released the final report on the Middle East by Ambassador-at-Large Robert Stanfield. It recommended that Canada broaden its links with the Palestinian Liberation Organization (PLO) to facilitate peace in the Middle East.

Mar. 6 Canada protested proposed US legislation requiring American utilities to begin burning coal by 1985, despite warnings by environmentalists that such action would contribute to acid rain. Coal consumption in the US steadily increased from that time through the end of the 20th century, making the US 2nd to China as the world's largest consumer of coal. Most US coal was burned to generate power.

Mar. 7 Clarence Campbell, former president of the NHL, and businessman Gordon Brown, were each sentenced to 1 day in prison and fined $25,000 for

conspiring to bribe Senator Louis Giguère (1911-2002) in 1972 in an effort to acquire a lease extension on a Sky Shops duty-free store at Dorval Airport in Montreal. The press referred to the case as the "Sky Shops Affair."

Mar. 13 The Bank of Canada interest rate (14%) was allowed to float.

Mar. 15 The Que. Labour Federation (QFL) urged its 320,000 members to vote yes on sovereignty-association in the upcoming Que. referendum (on Apr. 15, the Que. govt would set the referendum date for May 20). On Apr. 11, the 200,000-member Confederation of National Trade Unions (CNTU) also voted to back the yes side of the Que. referendum. On Apr. 18, the Que. Council of the Canadian Union of Public Employees voted almost unanimously to support the yes side.

Mar. 19 The Alb. govt reached an agreement with PEI to lend that province $29 million from the Alb. Heritage Savings and Trust Fund. Interest was 13.95%.

• The 1st annual awards ceremony of the Academy of Canadian Cinema was held in Toronto. The horror film *The Changeling*, was awarded Best Picture. Christopher Plummer (b 1929) received the Best Actor award in *Murder by Decree*; Kate Lynch was awarded Best Actress for her role in *Meatballs*.

Mar. 21 The Canadian International Development Agency (CIDA) offered a $25 million loan to India so that country could extend credit to small farmers and landless labourers.

Mar. 24 Canada signed a new agreement with the US on Canadian gas export prices, linked to world prices and calculated monthly. Price changes would become effective 90 days after notification.

Also in Mar.

• The National Archives of Canada, Ottawa, placed on display a collection of more than 2,000 Canadian historical documents that had been purchased for approximately $500,000 in 1980 from renowned book and manuscript collector Lawrence Lande (1906–1998). The collection included the 1757 order for the expulsion of the Acadians from NS, George Washington's order for the 1778 invasion of Canada and the score to Beethoven's canon *Freu Dich Des Lebens*, with an autographed dedication from the master to Montreal music teacher Theodore Molt.

Apr. 1 The Alb. Petroleum Marketing Commission assumed control of crude-oil sales from Crown land and informed Ont.-based Petrosar, a federally owned company, to seek other sources. The move followed a Mar. 28 announcement by federal Energy Minister Marc Lalonde (b 1929), who declared that due to rapid escalations in world energy prices, the 2 Alb. tar sands exploiters — Syncrude and Suncor — would not be allowed to sell oil at world prices. On May 23, the Alb. legislature passed Bill 50, an amendment to the province's Mines and Minerals Act, which gave cabinet power to restrict production of oil from Crown leases.

• Que.'s hourly minimum wage increased to $3.65, the highest minimum wage in the country.

• *The Raven and the First Men,* a 4.5-tonne yellow cedar sculpture by Bill Reid (1920–1998), was dedicated at U. of BC's Museum of Anthropology. The carving depicts the Haida Creation legend, with Raven atop a partially opened clamshell full of human figures struggling to be free.

Apr. 6 Gordie Howe of the Hartford Whalers scored his last NHL goal, number 801, against the Detroit Red Wings, the same team for which he scored his 1st NHL goal in 1946.

Apr. 8 Alain Allard, a former member of the FLQ who had lived in exile in Cuba for 11 years, was sentenced to 3 months and an additional 30 weekends in prison for planting 3 bombs at political clubs and a liquor outlet in 1968.

Apr. 12 Terrance "Terry" Fox (1958–1981), who had lost a leg to cancer in 1977, began his cross-country "Marathon of Hope" to raise money for cancer research. The trek began in St. John's, Nfld. Fox was greeted by thousands who lined the streets in every town he entered. On Sept. 2, in Thunder Bay, Ont., Fox was forced to cancel his odyssey when it was learned that cancer had spread to his lungs. He spoke to the country, "I tried as hard as I could,

I said I'd never give up and I didn't." A national telethon raised more than $10 million on Sept. 7, and on Sept. 19, Fox was invested as the youngest Companion of the Order of Canada. Terry Fox died on June 28, 1981.

Apr. 14 Jeanne-Mathilde Sauvé (1922–1993) was elected the 1st women Speaker of the House of Commons. Sauvé was appointed the 1st woman gov-gen. in Canada on Dec. 23, 1983.

Apr. 15 Que. Premier René Lévesque declared in the National Assembly that the referendum on sovereignty-association would be held May 20. A *oui* (yes) vote to the carefully constructed referendum question would give the Que. govt the right to negotiate sovereignty-association but would not result in an outright, unilateral declaration of Que. independence. PM Trudeau had declared in the House a day earlier that neither Ottawa nor the provinces would negotiate with Que. should it vote for sovereignty-association.

Apr. 17 Lt-Gen. Ramsay Muir Withers (b 1930), vice-chief of the defence staff, was named chief of defence staff, succeeding Admiral Robert Hilborn Falls (b 1924), who was appointed chairman of the military arm of NATO.

Apr. 18–27 Approximately 6,000 members of the United Nurses of Alb. were on strike for higher wages, despite back-to-work legislation. They returned to work after accepting an average pay increase of 37.8% over 2 years.

Apr. 21 Denver-based Oil, Chemical and Atomic Workers International Union, and the Canadian Chemical Workers Union, merged to create the Energy and Chemical Workers Union (ECWU).

Apr. 23 Canada expelled 1 of the 2 Iranian diplomats in Ottawa and strengthened economic sanctions against that country in an effort to speed the release of 52 American hostages held in Tehran. The hostages were released Jan. 20, 1981, after 444 days in captivity. Canadian economic sanctions against Iran were lifted Mar. 3, 1981.

Apr. 25 The Unionist Party, dedicated to the union of western Canada and the US, was formed in Sask. It was led by former provincial Progressive Conservative leader Dick Collver, who resigned from the Tory party Mar. 11.

May 1 PM Trudeau released tough conflict-of-interest guidelines for his ministers. The new roles gave ministers 120 days to sell or put into blind trusts (over which ministers or their families could have no control) publicly traded shares or speculative investments.

May 2 Bill C–242 received 1st reading in the House of Commons by Conservative MP Pat Carney, representing Vancouver Centre. The bill proposed prohibition of discrimination on the basis of sexual orientation through amendments to the Canadian Human Rights Act. The bill did not pass.

May 9 The House of Commons unanimously approved a patriation motion to transfer British control of the country's Constitution to Canada.

• The Nfld. legislature established a fisheries loan board with access to $22 million, to be loaned to fishers at 8% interest for the purchase of new boats and equipment.

• Sask. passed legislation ordering approximately 800 striking dairy workers back to work, with an immediate $100-a-month wage increase.

May 10 The federal govt provided $200 million in loan guarantees, and the Ont. govt a $10 million grant, as part of a US-Canada program to save Chrysler Corp. from bankruptcy. The US provided $1.5 billion in loans. Approximately 8,500 workers were employed at Chrysler's Windsor, Ont., plant.

May 13 Canada pledged to meet NATO's goal of increasing defence spending by 3% or more.

May 18 People in BC and southern Alb. claimed to have been roused from their beds by the early morning eruption of Mount St. Helens in Washington State.

May 20 In the Que. referendum, 59.5% of Quebecers voted against proceeding with sovereignty-association. PM Trudeau had promised throughout the campaign that a *non* (no) vote would mean a vote

for a renewed Canadian federation. Ottawa and the provinces began serious discussions on the new Constitution June 9.

• The NS Progressive Conservative govt passed the Petroleum Resources Bill, which claimed provincial jurisdiction over federally disputed offshore oil and gas resources. On Mar. 2, 1982, the federal and NS govts signed an agreement on offshore resources, which gave the federal govt management of the oil and gas, and NS more than double Ottawa's percentage of the revenue. Ownership of the resources, however, was still not settled. The agreement paved the way for the 1st commercial offshore energy project in Canada — the Cohasset-Panuke oil project off Sable Is., NS, which was initiated in June 1992.

May 26 The Nfld. legislature gave final approval to the province's new flag: a complicated arrangement of Christian, Beothuk and Naskapi designs with blue (representing the sea), red (representing human effort) and gold (representing confidence) against a white background (representing snow and ice). The triangular arrangement forms a Union Jack impression, pointing to a bright future. The new flag replaced the UK's Union Jack.

May 27 Final approval was given to legislation introduced on Apr. 18, in the House, increasing the supplement paid to pensioners from $153 to $188 a month.

• In Ottawa, Mexican President Jose Lopez Portillo and PM Trudeau signed a new industrial and energy co-operation pact, whereby Mexico agreed to sell Canada 50,000 barrels of oil a day by the end of 1980.

• More than $1.1 million was netted and 10 records broken at a Sotheby Parke Bernet (Canada) art auction. *Summer in the Arctic* (1939), by F.H. Varley, sold for $170,000, a record for a Canadian painting. Other highlights included $50,000 for *Summer Morning* (1948), by A.J. Casson, and $68,000 for *Forest Landscape* by Emily Carr.

May 31 The BC govt closed the Crown-run paper mill in the isolated coastal town of Ocean Falls, located nearly 500 km north of Vancouver. All but 50 residents moved. Ocean Falls was established in 1909 in anticipation of the Bella Coola Pulp and Paper Company mill, completed less than 2 years later. Ocean Falls had a school, store and a 1-bed hospital. In 1973, the BC govt purchased the struggling mill — and the entire town — for $1 million from its new owners, Crown Zellerbach, but failed to make the necessary margins.

June 5 The Toronto Sun Publishing Co. purchased the *Albertan*, a morning tabloid, from Thomson Newspapers Ltd., and renamed the paper the *Calgary Sun*. The *Albertan* had 50,000 subscribers. The *Toronto Sun* established the *Edmonton Sun* in 1978.

June 9 PM Trudeau and the 10 premiers agreed that a committee of federal and provincial ministers would negotiate a list of 12 constitutional reform items, which included a statement of principles; an amending formula; Senate and Supreme Court reform; increased provincial controls over respective natural resources; increased federal control over the economy; and Aboriginal representation at constitutional-reform discussions. Provincial premiers met Sept. 8 over the matter. Debate over the new Constitution was hot and lively throughout the country until its proclamation Apr. 17, 1982.

June 13 The federal govt pledged $7 million in aid to drought-stricken western farmers who had little feed for their cattle.

June 16 The Council of Maritime Premiers agreed that the benefits of offshore mineral resources should go to the provinces as though they were onshore resources.

June 22 Pope John Paul II beatified Mohawk religieux Kateri Tekakwitha (1656–1680). Orphaned at 4 years of age, and raised by her Iroquois relatives, Tekakwitha was introduced to Christianity in 1667 by Jesuit missionaries Fremin, Bruyas and Pierron. Baptized at age 18, she lived with Anastasia Tegonhatsihonga, an Aboriginal woman of similar faith. Known largely for her chastity, Tekakwitha's devotion to God inspired many others. In 1884, a monument was erected to her memory in Caughnawaga (Kahnawake), Que. Tekakwitha became the 1st North American Aboriginal candidate for sainthood.

June 25 PM Trudeau met with British PM Margaret Thatcher in London, England, to discuss Canadian plans for patriation of the Constitution.

June 27 The Alb. govt provided Hydro-Que. with a $110 million loan at 11.75% over 25 years. The move made the Que. Crown corporation the largest single borrower of money from the Alb. Heritage Savings and Trust Fund to date.

• Parliament passed the National Anthem Act, officially declaring *O Canada,* by Adolphe-Basile Routhier and Calixa Lavallée, the national anthem. The new English lyrics (by Stanley Weir) included the phrases "from far and wide" and "God keep our land" in place of 2 of the 5 "stand on guard" phrases.

• The US Senate approved the $97 million Garrison irrigation project to irrigate over 40.5 million ha in North Dakota, in spite of Canadian charges that the massive water-diversion project might devastate the Manitoba ecology. On Oct. 6, the Canadian embassy in Washington, D.C., delivered a stiff note to the US State Department, stating that the US risked violating the Boundary Waters Treaty if it permitted further construction on the project. A US federal judge halted the project on May 6, 1981, pending re-authorization of a new scaled-down plan by Congress, which occurred in 1986.

July 2 A group of British Labour MPs threatened to impede passage of a British bill that gave Canada the power to amend its own Constitution, unless Canada's 300,000 status Native Peoples were assured a voice in future federal-provincial constitutional talks. Native Peoples furthered the issue in Canada, Nov. 19, 1981.

July 4 Canada Post issued a stamp bearing the portrait of composer and musician Healey Willan, the 1st such tribute to a Canadian musician. Willan produced more than 700 original compositions, including *The Beggar's Opera* (1928) and *Hymn for Those in the Air* (1942).

June 5 Liberal delegates gave PM Trudeau an overwhelming vote of confidence at their national party-policy convention in Winnipeg, voting almost 87% against holding a leadership convention.

July 9 Alb. and BC govts formed a joint committee to plan strategy for fighting any federal attempt to assume a larger share of provincial resource revenues.

July 14 Fire in a Mississauga, Ont., nursing home claimed the lives of 21 pensioners and injured 35 others.

July 16 The BC govt unveiled a new policy permitting the sale of agricultural land to Canadian citizens only.

• The 28 women MPs and senators in Parliament formed a coalition called Sisters of All Women in Canada, to fight for the equality of Native women.

July 20–24 The World Future Society and the Canadian Futures Society organized the 1st Global Conference on the Future in Toronto. The meeting attracted 4,000 intellectuals from all over the world.

July 22 The House of Commons passed legislation outlawing loan-sharking and removing outdated limits on credit union interest charges.

July 29 NB borrowed $110 million from Alb.'s Heritage Savings Trust Fund, bringing NB's total amount borrowed from the fund to $300 million.

• Canada voted no as the UN General Assembly approved a resolution calling for Israel to withdraw from all occupied territories.

July 30 The CRTC approved the merger of Canadian Cable-Systems Ltd. of Toronto with Premier Communications Ltd. of Vancouver, the 2 largest cablevision companies in Canada.

Also in July
• Petro-Canada purchased the oil refinery at Come By Chance, Nfld., which had opened in 1973, and declared bankruptcy on Mar. 12, 1976.

Aug. 13 Oceanographer Joseph MacInnis discovered the sunken barge HMS *Breadalbane*, which had been crushed by ice at Beechey Is. in the NWT in 1853. The ship had been largely preserved by the extremely cold water; sonar pictures showed that even some of the vessel's sails and rigging had

been preserved. The ship had been sent to locate the missing crew of the 1845 John Franklin expedition.

Aug. 16 Rev. Lois Miriam Wilson, née Freeman (b 1927), was elected the 1st woman moderator of the United Church of Canada at the 28th General Council meeting in Halifax. On Aug. 17, a United Church of Canada task force released its report on sexual ethics *In God's Image*, recommending the liberalization of traditional sexual "taboos." Included were recommendations for the admission of homosexuals into the ministry and tolerance of premarital sex. The report also rejected abortion on demand, but accepted it under qualified circumstances.

Aug. 27 The Thomson-owned *Ottawa Journal* and Southam-owned *Winnipeg Tribune*, both century-old newspapers, were shut down as Canada's 2 largest newspaper chains cut losses. The closures eliminated 745 jobs. On Oct. 9, the thrice-weekly morning tabloid the *Winnipeg Sun* was 1st published, replacing the *Winnipeg Tribune*.

Aug. 28 A 31-day Halifax transit strike ended as bus drivers and mechanics agreed to a 79 cent-an-hour raise.

Sept. 8–13 Constitutional talks between the federal and provincial govts resulted in no agreement over tabled Constitutional reforms. PM Trudeau subsequently announced on Oct. 2 he would "unilaterally" patriate the Constitution (pushing the reforms through Parliament and presenting an Address to the British Parliament). Included in the new reforms platform was a "Peoples' Package" which involved a Canadian Charter of Rights and Freedoms and a commitment to the principles of provincial equalization. Canadian premiers met in Toronto on Oct. 14, to discuss the new constitutional scenario.

Sept. 12 Que. Cree filed a $64 million lawsuit in the Que. Superior Court against the provincial govt for alleged failure to provide adequate health care in northern Cree villages.

Sept. 17 The Que. govt unveiled a $23 million program designed to put able-bodied welfare recipients back to work.

Sept. 19 In Ottawa, Canada and Britain signed an agreement giving Air Canada and CP Air access to terminals in Africa, the Middle East and the Far East. British Airways was allowed to expand its services to Calgary, Edmonton and Vancouver.

Sept. 25 Native Peoples in BC filed a suit in federal court in Vancouver to prevent patriation of the BNA Act without Native Peoples' consent.

Sept. 29 Approximately 47,000 federal clerks belonging to the Public Service Alliance of Canada (PSAC) walked off the job across the country for higher wages, a cost of living allowance and a workweek reduced from 37.5 to 35 hours. On Oct. 14, the clerks returned after winning a 24.7% raise with fringe benefits.

Oct. 13 Approximately 700 BC Native Peoples protested the apprehension of an estimated 1,700 Native children by the provincial govt in 1978 for what welfare officials had termed neglect, abuse, orphaning and abandonment by their parents.

Oct. 14 The provincial premiers met in Toronto. BC, Alb., Man., Que. and Nfld. decided to challenge in provincial courts the legality of PM Trudeau's goal to unilaterally patriate the Constitution. They were supported by PEI, NS and Sask. Only Ont. and NB supported PM Trudeau's unilateral position. On Feb. 3, the Man. Court of Appeal ruled that Ottawa's constitutional proposals were legal, as did the Que. Court of Appeal on Apr. 15. The Nfld. Court of Appeal voted against Ottawa Mar. 30. However, in a reference case initiated by PM Trudeau, the Supreme Court of Canada ruled on Sept. 28 that Ottawa could legally and unilaterally request patriation of the Constitution from the British Parliament.

Oct. 15 Television newsman Ralph Klein (b 1942) defeated incumbent Ross Alger (1920–1992) by 15,000 votes to become mayor of Calgary.

Oct. 18 The 1st African elephant born in Canada was born at the Metro Toronto Zoo.

Oct. 21 The Alb. govt effected a 4-year-old law, giving it the power to unilaterally set the price of natural gas produced in the province and sold in Canada.

Oct. 23 The *Globe and Mail* became Canada's 1st newspaper to employ satellite technology. It used the *Anik-III* satellite to send computerized microwave signals of each newspaper page from Toronto to Montreal, where the "national edition" was published. The system extended to begin publishing editions in Calgary on Oct. 29, and Vancouver Oct. 5, 1981.

• The Que. National Assembly approved legislation ordering some 2,000 striking teachers in the Trois-Rivières area back to work by Oct. 27.

• Agnes Richardson Benidickson (b 1920), of Winnipeg, was installed as the 1st woman chancellor of Queen's U., Kingston, Ont.

Oct. 26 Canada signed a treaty at The Hague to curb the abduction of children by their separated, non-guardian parents.

Oct. 27 The federal govt sent a note of protest to the Chinese govt in Beijing over nuclear explosion experiments conducted there in early Oct.

Oct. 28 Liberal Finance Minister Allan MacEachen tabled the budget, which ushered in the National Energy Program (NEP). Created in the wake of the 1970s oil crisis, the program aimed to achieve oil self-sufficiency; greater federal control of the domestic oil industry; and sharing of oil and gas revenues among provinces. The program was adamantly opposed in the West and gave rise to one of the country's clearest expressions of regional discontent — thousands of Alb. bumper stickers reading, "Let the Eastern bastards freeze in the dark!" The NEP was eliminated as energy prices dropped through the 1980s.

Nov. 5 Carl and Jack Cole opened The World's Biggest Bookstore in Toronto. The store occupied nearly 6,500 m^2, with 1.5 million books on 27.3 km of shelves.

Nov. 6 A 25-member parliamentary committee began hearings on constitutional proposals. They were televised over a 3-month period, during which time more rights for women, Native Peoples, the handicapped, Acadians and those accused of crimes were added to the Charter of Rights. The report was tabled Feb. 13, 1981, recommending some 65 amendments to the original constitutional package.

Nov. 11 The Que. National Assembly voted 48–26 to suspend regular Assembly business and concentrate on fighting PM Trudeau's plan to unilaterally patriate the Constitution. On Dec. 7, Que. Premier Lévesque called PM Trudeau's constitutional plan a "coup d'état."

• *Algoma Lake*, by Group of Seven member A.Y. Jackson, was sold at auction for $210,000, a record for a Canadian painting. The record was broken May 26, 1981, when *South Shore, Baffin Island*, by Lawren Harris, sold at auction in Toronto for $240,000.

Nov. 16 Alexa McDonough (b 1944) was elected leader of the New Democratic Party of NS, becoming the 1st women leader of a Canadian provincial political party. She won a seat in the provincial legislature in 1981.

Nov. 20 Author Margaret Laurence was appointed chancellor of Trent U. in Peterborough, Ont., effective Jan. 1, 1981.

Nov. 24 Canadian Native Peoples began a journey across Canada by train caravan, starting at Vancouver and picking up people as the train progressed toward Ottawa, where they planned to lobby the federal govt to include treaty and Aboriginal rights in the Constitution. The train was dubbed the "Constitutional Express." On Dec. 8, a group of Canadian Native Peoples took their constitutional grievances to the UN in an effort to gain international support for the reinstatement of their rights.

Nov. 26 Assent was given to the new Bank Act, which replaced the 1967 Bank Act. The new act established operating rules for chartered banks in the next decade, and allowed foreign banks to open branches in Canada.

Nov. 28 Canada pulled out of the US-led embargo on grain exports to the Soviet Union. The embargo had been established as a protest against the Soviet invasion of Afghanistan in 1979. Countries were directed not to sell grain to the Soviet in excess of what was "normal and traditional." After pulling out,

Canada sold the Soviet Union an additional 2 million tonnes of wheat worth about $450 million. The Soviets withdrew from Afghanistan in 1989.

Also in Nov.

• The world's 1st heavy icebreaking cargo vessel, the *Arctic*, arrived in Churchill, Man., to take on wheat for Italy.

Dec. 1 The BC govt submitted a brief in London to the Foreign Affairs Committee of the British House of Commons requesting that the British Parliament not act on the request of Ottawa for patriation of the BNA Act. On Dec. 9, British PM Margaret Thatcher declared the British govt would deal with a patriation request "expeditiously and in accordance with precedent."

Dec. 16 Que. Premier Lévesque and French Premier Raymond Barre completed 2 days of talks in Paris and announced plans for increased co-operation, particularly in economic and scientific matters.

Dec. 31 PM Trudeau's New Year's message to the nation was: "We peer so suspiciously at each other that we cannot see that we Canadians are standing on a mountaintop of human wealth, freedom, and privilege."

Also in Dec.

• Urea-formaldehyde foam insulation was banned in Canada following widespread complaints that improperly cured foam produced harmful gases leading to headache, respiratory distress, nausea and other complications. Up to an estimated 100,000 Canadian homes had been insulated with the foam during the 1970s, many through financial incentives administered through the federal Canadian Home Insulation Program (CHIP).

Also in 1980

• Canada's population was 24,516,000.

• The De Havilland Dash-8, which would become the most successful regional commercial aircraft series in the world, was 1st launched. It succeeded the Dash-7 and Twin Otter.

• Canadian ballerina Evelyn Anne Hart (b 1956) was awarded the women's gold medal for solo performance at the International Ballet Competition at Varna, Bulgaria.

• The stellar team of Dan Halldorson and Jim Nelford won the annual World Cup golf tournament in Bogotá, Colombia.

• *La vie en rose*, the Que. feminist magazine, began publication.

• A record-high 40,638 people entered Canada as refugees.

• Researchers located only 3 surviving pairs of nesting bald eagles in the Great Lakes region. They were found along the shores of L. Erie and were not reproducing. The diurnal birds of prey were once common throughout the eastern and Maritime Provinces.

• Jack McClelland, head of McClelland & Stewart Publishers and a known leader in book promotions, launched Sylvia Fraser's (b 1935) novel *The Emperor's Virgin*. In a stunt organized by marketing director Peter Taylor (b 1939), the McClelland & Stewart staff, including McClelland and Fraser, were outfitted in togas, and arrived — during a snowstorm — at Coles Books on Yonge St. in Toronto in a Roman chariot.

• The Canadian pacer Niatross won 37 of 39 races and shattered the world record for the mile by almost 3 seconds.

• Novelist Gérard Bessette was awarded the Prix David for his lifetime contributions to Que. literature.

• Paterson Ewen painted *Gibbous Moon*, on panel, now in the National Gallery of Canada.

• Dave Godfrey (b 1938) and Douglas Parkhill published *Gutenberg Two: The New Electronics and Social Change*.

• George Bowering published *Burning Water*, a novel about Captain George Vancouver, for which he received his 2nd Gov-Gen.'s Award.

• Mary di Michele (b 1949) published *Mimosa and Other Poems*, on the nature of Italian immigration in Canada.

• David Fennario (b 1947) published Canada's 1st bilingual play, *Balconville*, for which he won the Chalmers Award.

• Jack Stanley Hodgins published the novel *The Resurrection of Joseph Bourne*, for which he received the Gov-Gen.'s Award.

• Journalist Richard Gwyn (b 1934) published the best seller, *The Northern Magnus: Pierre Trudeau and Canadians*.

• Mordecai Richler published the popular novel *Joshua Then and Now*.

• Monica Hughes (1925–2003) published her children's fantasy novel *Keeper of the Isis Light*. It would become the 1st in a trilogy.

• Acclaimed children's writer Robert Munsch published his second children's book, *The Paperbag Princess*, with illustrations by Michael Martchenko.

• The novels *Fat Woman* (short-listed for the Gov-Gen.'s Award) and *Cry Evil*, by Leon Rooke (b 1934), were published.

1981

Jan. 1 Wellhead prices for Canadian crude oil were raised $1 per barrel to $17.75. The federal govt imposed an extra $2.50 per barrel for the Petroleum Compensation Charge, a new levy to pay for imported oil.

Jan. 7 The Toronto Stock Exchange (TSE) 300 Index dropped 54.04 points because one investment adviser, American Joseph Granville, advised his clients in the US to sell all classes of shares.

Jan. 14 PM Trudeau paid an official visit to Brazil, where he urged authorities to join Canada in bridging the growing economic disparities between rich and poor nations. On Oct. 24, 1981, PM Trudeau was co-chair of a summit conference of 22 world leaders at Cancún, Mexico, organized over problems of growing international economic disparities.

Jan. 25 BC signed a deal in Tokyo to supply a consortium of Japanese steel firms with 60 million tonnes of coal a year from northeastern BC over a 15-year

Year

1981

period. The deal hastened exploitation of vast coal fields in northern BC in the Peace R. region and the creation of the town of Tumbler Ridge and adjacent mines Quinette and Bullmoose. On Jan. 7, 1984, the 1st shipment of BC coal from Bullmoose and Quintette mines was placed aboard the Shorya Maru at Ridley Island Terminal, south of Prince Rupert, for shipment to Japan. To facilitate the supply of Peace R. coal to Japanese steel mills, BC Railway constructed a 129-km branch line out of isolated Tumbler Ridge to the main line north of Prince George. The Ridley Island Terminal was also constructed for Japanese coal export. Its facilities could load up to 8,000 tonnes of coal onto ships every day. By 2003, nearly 50% of all BC metallurgical coal was shipped to Japan.

Jan. 28 The federal govt proposed an amendment to the Charter of Rights to protect the mentally and physically disabled from discrimination under the law.

Jan. 29 In Calgary, Dome Petroleum Ltd. agreed to form Dome Canada Ltd., a new company having 75% Canadian ownership. It would function as the parent firm's exploration arm and benefit from new financial incentives — given only to Canadian-owned energy firms — that were set out in the National Energy Program.

Also in Jan.
• Gasoline and diesel fuel was legislated to be sold in metric units only.

Feb. 5 Under "bawdy-house" laws, over 300 men were arrested during violent police raids at 4 gay bathhouses in Toronto. At midnight, Feb. 6, over 1,500 protestors confronted police on a march to the station where the arrested men where held. Sporadic violence ensued; 11 were arrested. On Feb. 20, over 2,000 gay and straight Torontonians protested police brutality at Queen's Park. In all, the bathhouse raids helped solidify Canada's largest gay community and sparked a movement toward open, community-based gay activism.

Feb. 6 Delegates to the annual convention of the Alb. Federation of Labour, which met in Edmonton, voted in favour of a resolution supporting

Canadian unity and another deploring the growing western separatist movement.

Feb. 17 The final round of constitutional debates began in the House of Commons. On Mar. 11, Alb. Progressive Conservative MP Bill Yurko (b 1926) broke party ranks by announcing that the Charter of Rights proposed by PM Trudeau represented "a great leap in freedom" for Canadians. Yurko, however, did not sway his colleagues, who on Mar. 24 began to filibuster in the House of Commons in an effort to halt the constitutional package.

Mar. 1 Alb. opposed the federal energy policy and cut back its oil production. The federal govt imposed a compensation charge, or "Lougheed Levy," of 75 cents per barrel to help pay for additional oil imports necessitated by the cutbacks. On June 3, the Lougheed Levy was increased $1.10 per barrel because of a 2nd Alb. oil-production cutback of 60,000 barrels per day.

Mar. 4 An 8-year federal Combines Report of the Department of Consumer and Corporate Affairs was released, charging that big oil companies cheated consumers out of $12 billion between 1958 and 1973 by consorting to fix prices and limit competition. The oil companies denied the allegations.

• For the 1st time in Canada, the Ont. Labour Relations Board ruled that employers had the right to lock out employees and hire replacements to maintain plant operations. The ruling was made in the case of Westroc Industries of Mississauga, which locked out and replaced its employees in July 1980.

Mar. 6 The US Reagan administration scrapped the East Coast Fisheries Treaty with Canada on fish quotas and boundaries, which had been signed Mar. 29, 1979, but never ratified by the US Senate.

Mar. 10–11 US President Ronald Reagan visited Ottawa for talks with PM Trudeau. An agreement was signed to make it easier for people who had worked in both countries to become eligible for social security benefits. Reagan also addressed a joint session of Parliament.

• In Ottawa, the Canadian Labour Congress (CLC) suspended 12 US-run international building trade unions for what it considered autocratic, authoritarian and undemocratic practices, effective Apr. 30.

Mar. 25–27 Susan Nelles, a nurse at Toronto's Hospital for Sick Children, was charged with the murder of 4 infants. Between June 1980 and Mar. 1981, 33 babies and 3 older children died in cardiac wards 4A and 4B of Sick Kids Hospital between midnight and 6 a.m. Nelles was later released for lack of evidence and instituted proceedings for malicious prosecution, which were settled with a considerable payment to her by the Ont. govt. A Royal Commission, established to look into the tragedy, released its report Jan. 3, 1985.

Mar. 30 U. of Toronto received court approval to prosecute a former student charged with plagiarizing parts of his Ph.D. thesis. The case was believed to be the 1st of its kind in Canada. On June 22, Guillaume T. Uyidi was stripped of his Ph.D.

Apr. 13 Premier René Lévesque's Parti Québécois won the provincial election, taking 80 of 122 seats in the National Assembly. The Liberals under Claude Ryan captured 42 seats, while the Union Nationale was shut out.

Apr. 15 A Sask. provincial court ruled that Rev. André Mercure did not have a right to have his court case, involving a speeding charge, conducted in French, setting a precedent for future cases in both Sask. and Alb. courts.

Apr. 16 All provincial premiers except NB's and Ont.'s signed a pact (Premiers' Accord) to patriate the Constitution at once with no changes, but with an amending formula different from that contained in the federal proposal. The premiers' amending formula provided no veto powers to any one province, but instead established a single block comprising of all provinces with which the federal govt would have to negotiate. The federal govt refused to sign the proposed accord.

Apr. 23 The House of Commons voted on final amendments to the govt's constitutional proposals. The Senate ended its deliberations the following day; 8 Liberals abstained from voting. On Nov. 5, PM

Trudeau and all provinces except Que. reached a constitutional agreement for the patriation of the Constitution from Britain, an amending formula and a 2-tired Charter of Rights, based on a proposal put forward by Nfld. Premier Brian Peckford. On Nov. 9, Que. Premier René Lévesque protested the new constitutional agreement by boycotting all but the most essential federal-provincial meetings. Que. lifted the partial boycott Feb. 19, 1982.

Apr. 30 John Lauchlan and James Blench, both of Seebe, Alb., reached the summit of the 7,454.5-m Mount Gangapurna in the Nepalese Himalayas by a new route, the south face.

May 1 The federal govt charged Canada's 2 largest newspaper chains, Thomson Newspapers Ltd. and Southam Inc., with illegally conspiring to reduce competition, and merge and monopolize the production and sale of major English-language newspapers. A Royal Commission on Newspapers was issued Aug. 18, 1981.

May 11–31 Nineteen theatres staged 34 plays in the 1st Toronto Theatre Festival.

May 12 A Special Parliamentary Report was released in Ottawa. It recommended that Canada adopt a non-traditional energy system within the next 50 years, to be based on hydrogen rather than oil, gas or coal; these traditional energy supplies were instead recommended for use in non-energy commodities such as petrochemicals.

• The North American Defence Command (NORAD) was renamed and became the North American Aerospace Defence Command to reflect its involvement with space surveillance.

May 14 The Bank of Canada lending rate was raised to a record-high 18.98%.

May 21 Canada agreed to a $15 million fisheries project with Association of Southeast Asian Nations countries. The project provided the Philippines, Thailand, Indonesia, Malaysia and Singapore with technical assistance, training awards, equipement and project evaluation.

May 25 The federal govt initiated a $22 billion program to reimburse Canadians for half the cost of converting their building heating systems from oil to other energy sources, to a maximum of $800.

• A 7-month strike at Domtar Fine Papers Ltd., of Cornwall, Ont., ended when 1,200 striking employees returned to work after agreeing to lump-sum payments and a 25% wage increase along with other benefits.

May 26 Canada and the US signed a treaty allowing both countries free and unlimited fishing for albacore tuna off the Pacific Coast.

• The Soviet Union signed an agreement to purchase $5 billion worth of Canadian prairie grain.

May 27 Saint John, NB, police returned to work after a 27-hour strike sparked violence and looting in the city's downtown core.

June 4 Japanese automakers agreed to cut automobile exports to Canada by 6% during the 1981–1982 fiscal year, providing a breathing space for the domestic auto industry to become more competitive and produce more fuel-efficient cars.

June 11 The House of Commons defeated a motion to restore capital punishment by a vote of 153–82.

• As a result of information revealed by the Keable Commission (established May 1977), 44 charges were laid against 17 active and former RCMP officers for alleged illegal police activities in Que. in the early 1970s. The charges included conspiracy and breaking and entering in connection with the Jan. 1973 theft of Parti Québécois membership lists.

June 12 The House of Commons gave final approval to legislation to cut off air service to countries that condoned hijacking.

June 14 The Western Canada Concept Party received official party status in Alb. Led by Doug Christie, the party was dedicated to creating an independent western nation.

June 19 The federal govt extended import quotas to protect the clothing and textile industry from low-cost foreign imports for at least 5 years.

June 23 The Ont. govt announced that pensioners, the poor, and hard-pressed farmers would receive about $100 million in emergency aid to offset inflation and high interest costs.

June 25 Striking CBC journalists in Que. voted to accept a new contract. They had been off the job nearly 8 months. It was the longest strike in CBC history. On Sept. 3, the CBC and 2,100 of its broadcast technicians signed a tentative agreement, ending the 14-week strike.

June 26 BC banned extra billing by its 3,700 doctors.

July 3 The *Arctic Explorer*, chartered by Geophysical Services Inc. of Dallas, Texas, sank off Cape Bauld on Nfld.'s Great Northern Peninsula, with the loss of 11 lives. Fifty-two hours after the *Arctic Explorer* sank, 19 survivors were rescued from a life raft.

July 6 The BC govt named a 2,650-m mountain 21 km southwest of Mount Robson after Terry Fox as an everlasting symbol of his "Marathon of Hope."

July 7 Six companies, including the Crown corporations Eldorado Nuclear Ltd. and Uranium Canada Ltd., were charged with violating the Combines Investigation Act by criminally conspiring to fix domestic uranium prices between Sept. 1, 1970, and Apr. 1, 1978.

• In 2 new Acts, PEI police received wide-reaching powers, including the authority to take citizens from their homes without warrant, and hold them in drug- or alcohol-treatment centres without laying charges.

July 9 A report by a Senate-Commons Committee recommended that all designated bilingual positions in Canada be filled by bilingual staff by Dec. 31, 1983, and that unilingual workers presently filling those offices be barred from moving up into many senior positions within the federal civil service.

• Members of Parliament voted 159–10 to raise their pay by 31%, effective immediately. The vote increased the minimum MP salary to $40,200.

July 10 The House of Commons approved legislation

that provided pensions for about 23,000 widows and dependants of disabled war veterans.

July 12 The BC forest industry was shut down when 48,000 woodworkers went on strike. By July 20, the total number of workers off the job had reached 60,000.

July 16 The 530-million-year-old fossil deposit known as the Burgess Shale was dedicated the 86th UNESCO World Heritage Site, and 5th in Canada. It is located about 74 km west of Banff, Alb.

July 19 Ontario Hydro closed 2 of its nuclear power stations. The Douglas Point plant was closed when a cooler was found leaking radioactive heavy water into L. Huron. Douglas Point was eventually shut down May 4, 1984. The NPD reactor near Rolphton, northwest of Ottawa, Canada's 1st to provide electricity to a grid, was closed because of flooding in the reactor's boiler room. NPD was shut down Aug. 1, 1987.

July 20 Canada hosted the G-7 Economic Summit involving leaders from the major western trading nations–the US, Japan, West Germany, France, Britain, Italy and Canada — amid tight security at Montebello, Que. Also on hand were representatives of the European Economic Community (EEC).

• The federal govt pledged $12 million for rural development in Nepal over 3 years.

July 22 In Halifax, NS, 196 policemen ended a 53-day strike with a 3-year agreement that boosted their salaries to $29,000 by July 1983.

July 27 The federal govt announced the sale of a 2nd 600-megawatt CANDU reactor to Romania.

July 28 The historic St. Paul's Anglican Church in Saint John, NB, built in 1871, was destroyed by fire.

July 30 The US established a new immigration policy that included higher quotas for Canadians and Mexicans.

Also in July
• All Que. taverns licenced after 1979 were forced by provincial law to admit women. Taverns licenced

before this date could continue to ban women if they so desired.

Aug. 3 The Canadian dollar dropped to its lowest rate of exchange with the US dollar since Dec. 1931. The dollar held at 80.53 cents US, after dropping as low as 80.43. The 1931 low was 80.08.

Aug. 10 A 42-day postal strike by 23,000 Canadian Union of Postal Workers members ended.

Aug. 12 PM Trudeau addressed a United Nations conference in Nairobi on new and renewable energy sources. Trudeau stated Canada would give an extra $40 million for energy-related foreign aid in addition to $1 billion in bilateral aid over the next 5 years to be spent on energy projects in developing countries.

• Canadian air traffic controllers disrupted flights between the US and Canada and between North America and Europe in a sympathy strike with US air traffic controllers fired by President Ronald Reagan. Canadian controllers returned to work after Transport Canada officials threatened them with jail or dismissal.

Aug. 18 The Royal Commission on Newspapers (Kent Report) was issued. Recommendations included that Thomson Newspapers be required to sell either the *Globe and Mail* or its other 39 newspapers; a breakup of regional newspaper monopolies; a prohibition on the ownership of radio or television stations by newspapers in the same region; and the establishment of a press-rights panel within the Canadian Human Rights Commission.

Aug. 24 The *Toronto Star* introduced a Monday to Friday morning edition.

Aug. 25 The final report of the McDonald Commission on RCMP wrongdoing recommended that security officials be allowed to open mail with a warrant approved by the solicitor-gen. and a federal court judge, and that police powers be expanded to allow surreptitious searches and access to confidential information held by other govt departments.

Aug. 26 A 5-week strike by Vancouver transit workers ended.

Aug. 31 Mass murderer Clifford Robert Olson of Coquitlam, BC, was charged with 9 counts of 1st-degree murder after the RCMP paid $100,000 into an Olson family trust so Olson would tell them where the bodies were located. He was eventually charged on 11 counts of 1st-degree murder and sentenced to life imprisonment Jan. 14, 1982. On Dec. 8, 1984, Justice William Trainor of the BC Supreme Court ruled that the $100,000 paid by the RCMP must be returned to the court.

Sept. 1 A ban on non-French storefront signs became effective in Que. Violators faced fines of up to $500.

• The federal and Alb. govts signed an energy agreement. Included in the deal was a 2-tiered price system, with one price for oil produced from existing fields, and another for production from new fields, oil sands and frontier areas. In 1986, old oil would cost $57.75 per barrel, while new oil would be at or near world prices. The federal govt would withdraw its export tax on natural gas in 1982, while the federal tax on oil and gas revenues would double from 8% to 16%. Another pricing agreement was signed June 30, 1983.

Sept. 13 More than 880 Canadian communities held 10-km runs in the 1st Terry Fox Run to raise money for cancer research.

• The Soviet Union won the Canada Cup hockey tournament by humiliating Wayne Gretzky and Team Canada 8–1 in the final game in Montreal.

Sept. 15 The largest shopping centre in the world, the West Edmonton Mall, opened. Constructed in 4 phases between 1981 and 1988, the mall would contain 800 stores, 100 restaurants, a skating rink, a water and amusement park, an aquarium and a hotel. The mall spans the area equivalent to 48-city blocks and reaches 1.6 km from one end to the other.

Sept. 18 The Canadian Association of Sexual Assault Centres (CASAC) organized the 1st cross-country "Take Back the Night" marches across Canada to protest violence against women and demand that women be able to walk the streets at night in safety.

Sept. 22 The Reagan administration threatened Canada over its nationalist energy and economic policies, suggesting Canada risked a crisis in US relations and possible loss of world commercial status unless it liberalized those policies.

Sept. 26 Canada and the Soviet Union signed a 5-year agricultural agreement that included scientific co-operation, crop-data exchanges and the formation of a Canada-Soviet commission on agricultural issues.

Sept. 30 The International Olympic Committee (IOC) announced that Calgary won the right to host the 1988 Olympic Winter Games.

Oct. 6 The federal govt pledged $288 million over 5 years toward a 3-point training program aimed at increasing third World food production.

Oct. 9 The Man. Communist Party was granted official status in the province.

Oct. 15 The RCMP seized $200 million worth of methaqualone at the Collingwood, Ont., airport, the largest drug seizure in Canada to date.

• The federal govt declared that visitors from India would no longer be admitted to Canada without visas. The action was taken to curtail an influx of Indian nationals, mainly Sikhs, who came to Canada as visitors and then claimed refugee status.

Oct. 19 "Blue Monday": Los Angeles Dodgers outfielder Rick Monday ripped a 9th-inning, game-winning home run off Montreal Expos pitcher Steve Rogers, a stellar starter who had been called in for relief duty. The win gave the Dodgers the 5th and deciding game of the National League Championships. They would go on to beat the New York Yankees to win the World Series. Blue Monday was the closest the Expos ever came to the World Series.

Oct. 23 Pearl McGonigal (b 1930) became Man.'s 1st woman lt-gov. and the 2nd in Canada after Ont.'s Pauline McGibbon, who was appointed in 1974.

Nov. 3 For the 1st time since 1874, the Ont. govt invoked closure to end debate in the legislature, thereby enabling it to gain access to tax funds (supply) to pay its bills.

Nov. 7 James Matthew Lee (b 1937) was chosen Progressive Conservative premier of PEI, succeeding Angus MacLean on Nov. 17.

Nov. 9 Que. purchased controlling interest of Asbestos Corp. for $16 million from US-based General Dynamics Corp.

Nov. 12 The federal budget altered the tax system to increase the taxes of corporations and high-income earners by an additional $25 billion. Changes were effective Jan. 1, 1982.

Nov. 13 Motorcycle enthusiast Chris Simons of Port Dover, Ont., and about 25 friends celebrated Friday 13th with a gathering of motorcycle enthusiasts. The party marked the 1st in what would become a biker tradition. Motorcycle owners from Canada, the US, and many from Europe now gather every Friday the 13th in Port Dover to celebrate the "joys of the open road." By 2003, the event had grown to a point where the population of the town (approximately 5,000) swelled to 40,000 for the weekend gathering.

Nov. 15 VIA Rail cut 18% of its train kilometreage, from 24,444 to 19,783. The percentage of passengers riding VIA Rail dropped only 5% from 7,586 to 7,223.

Nov. 17 The NDP under Howard Russell Pawley (b 1934) won the Man. provincial election, defeating Sterling Lyon's Progressive Conservative govt.

Nov. 19 Canadians across the country staged demonstrations, including a march on Parliament Hill by about 3,000 Native Peoples, to protest the exclusion of Native- and gender-equality rights in the new Constitution. On Nov. 23, Ottawa and the provinces, except Que., reached an agreement on the rights issues: on the 24th, the House gave unanimous approval to remove limits on gender-equality guarantees, and recognize existing Native and treaty rights in the new Constitution. On Dec. 2, the House of Commons voted 246–24 to approve a resolution to patriate the BNA Act from Britain, with an amending formula and a Charter of Rights. And on Dec. 8, the Senate voted 59–23 in favour of the constitutional package. The British govt voted on the bill to patriate the Canadian Constitution on Mar. 8, 1982.

Nov. 24 Metric Commission Canada declared that scales in 35,000 stores across the country must be altered from imperial units to metric, beginning Jan. 4, 1982, and that the changeover be completed by the end of 1983. Advertising would be allowed only in metric after Dec. 31, 1983.

Also in Nov.
• VIA Rail cancelled La P'tit (Petit) Train du Nord, the popular 200-km Que. tourist train linking St. Jerome with Mount Laurier in the Laurentians. The abandoned route would later be turned into a bicycle trail.

Dec. 4 Twelve thousand five-hundred United Steelworkers of America members from Stelco's Hamilton, Ont., Hinton Works returned to the job, ending a 125-day strike — the longest at Stelco to date. The average hourly wage of $10.24 an hour was increased by $1.65 over 3 years.

Dec. 5 Que. Premier René Lévesque appealed to the "social conscience" of Que. govt employees by asking them to renounce part of their next wage increase to help ease the province's budgetary problems.

Dec. 10 The Sask. NDP govt passed the Homeowners' Protection Act, the 1st legislation of its kind in Canada, to protect homeowners facing foreclosure because of high interest rates. The act allowed homeowners to renew their mortgages in 1982 at a rate agreed upon with the lending company, continue paying at the existing rate of the mortgage or pay nothing at all for 1 year. In July 1982, the Sask. Progressive Conservative govt passed Bill 1, which reduced mortgage interest rates to 13.25%. The average Sask. mortgage was $34,000 at 19% interest over 25 years. The new bill was effective for 3 years only.

Dec. 11 Trevor Berbick (b 1953), Canadian and Commonwealth heavyweight boxing champion, defeated the aging 3-time world champion Muhammad Ali in Nassau, Bahamas, in a 10-round unanimous decision.

Dec. 14 The House of Commons approved labour legislation which included: "last resort" income help to laid-off older workers unable to find new jobs;

improved severance pay; and early advance notice of mass layoffs.

Dec. 17 The federal govt pledged $100 million to help Canadian co-operatives obtain shares in the oil and gas industry.

Dec. 30 Wunderkind Wayne Gretzky shattered the record of 50 goals in 50 games set by Maurice "Rocket" Richard in 1944–1945 and tied by Mike Bossy (b 1957) during the 1980–1981 season. The Edmonton Oiler scored 50 goals in 39 games and set the mark with style, scoring 5 times in game number 39 against the Philadelphia Flyers. Gretzky also established a new NHL scoring mark during the 80-game 1981–1982 season with 92 goals and 120 assists for 212 points. Incredibly, Gretzky topped this total point record in the 1985–1986 season: over 80 games he scored 52 goals and a nearly incomprehensible 163 assists for 215 regular season points.

Also in Dec.

• 987,000 people, or 8.6%, of the workforce, were unemployed — the most since figures were 1st regularly recorded in 1946.

Also in 1981

• The population of Canada was 24,343,181. The population of Ont. was 8,625,107; Que., 6,438,403; BC, 2,744,467; Alb., 2,237,724; Man., 1,026,341; Sask., 968,313; NS, 847,442; NB, 696,403; Nfld., 567,681; PEI, 122,506; NWT, 45,741; and Yukon, 23,153.

• Canada withdrew from the International Whaling Commission (IWC) after 35 years' involvement. Canada had stopped commercial whaling in 1972.

• Convinced that World War III was imminent, Bill and Barbara Curtis decided to move to what they described as "an island in the middle of nowhere" and, with their 2 children, left a home in Mission, BC, for the Falkland Islands. By May of 1982, the family found themselves living in Port Stanley while the Falklands War raged around them.

• Petro-Canada purchased Belgian-owned Petrofina SA, taking over 12 million $120 shares. The purchase gave the Crown corporation refining operations in eastern Canada. Petro-Canada furthered expansion in 1983, buying the marketing and refining operations of British-owned BP Canada Inc. for $350 million.

• Bombardier Inc. of Montreal sold $150 million worth of subway cars to Mexico.

• The Inuit Broadcasting Corporation, the 1st Inuktitut-language television service, was licenced by the CRTC to begin broadcasting across the NWT, northeastern Que. and Labrador.

• Dr. David Hubel (b 1926), a McGill graduate working out of Harvard U., won the Nobel Prize in medicine for his research on the visual system and cerebral cortex.

• Sudbury, Ont., MP Judy Erola (b 1934) was appointed the 1st woman Minister Responsible for the Status of Women. The department was created in 1971.

• Interest rates reached a post-war high of 22.5%.

• The inflation rate for the year hit 12.5%, a 33-year high.

• The International Labour Office (ILO) revealed statistics showing Canada led the industrialized world in working days lost through strikes.

• 13.6% of Ont.'s population was born in the Atlantic provinces.

• 17% of all physicians and surgeons working in Ont. were women.

• *Three Walrus on a Boat*, bone and ivory carving by Alooloo Imity (b 1932), was completed. It is now in the National Gallery of Canada.

• Judas Ullulaq (1937–1999) completed *Narwhal* a green stone and ivory sculpture, now in the collection of the National Gallery of Canada.

• Bernice Thurman Hunter (b 1922) published the Canadian best-seller, *That Scatterbrain Booky,* a fictionalized autobiography for young adults. It was the 1st in a trilogy, which included *With Love From Booky* (1983) and *As Ever, Booky* (1985). The prolific, multi-award winning children's author was made a member of the Order of Canada Oct. 26, 2002.

• Janet Lunn (b 1928) published *The Root Cellar*, a young-adult novel about an orphan who travels back in time through a root cellar.

• W.O. Mitchell published the novel *How I Spent My Summer Holidays*.

• *The Game of Our Lives*, by Peter Gzowski, was published.

• Joy Kogawa (b 1935) published *Obasan*, the 1st novel to trace the internment and dispersal of 20,000 Japanese Canadians from the West Coast during WW II.

• *Miramichi*, the collected poetry of Alfred Goldsworthy Bailey, was published.

• Michel Beaulieu (1941–1985) published his collection of poetry, *Visages*, for which he received the Gov-Gen.'s Award.

• Acclaimed poet P.K. Page (b 1916) published *Evening Dance of the Grey Flies*.

• *The Collected Poems of F.R. Scott* was published and won the Gov-Gen.'s Award.

• Fred Wah's (b 1939) book of poetry *Breathin' My Name with a Sigh* was published.

• Charlemagne, Que., native Céline Dion (b 1968) vaulted into Que. stardom with the release of her 1st album, *La Voix du bon Dieu* (The Voice of God). Dion would go on to international success, recording over 25 albums, most notably the 1996 release *Falling into You*, which won 2 Grammys and sold over 25 million copies.

1982

Jan. 1 The Post Office Department became a Crown corporation. It had been incorporated Oct. 16, 1981. Postal rates nearly doubled at the same time: the cost of sending a domestic 1st class letter was increased from 17 cents to 30 cents.

Jan. 5 The federal Employment Department declared a ban on the hiring of certain types of skilled workers from abroad, especially in the mining, manufacturing and construction sectors, to protect Canadian jobs.

Jan. 9 Two earthquakes, measuring 5.5 and 4.9 on the Richter scale, shook NB. No serious damage or injuries occurred.

Jan. 11 Barbara Frum (1937–1992), born in Niagara Falls, New York, became host of CBC Television's nightly current-affairs show *The Journal*, the most watched current-events program in the nation. She would remain host until her untimely death.

Jan. 15 The Que. National Assembly adopted legislation to force 2,200 striking Montreal transit workers back to work. The strike continued until Jan. 21.

Jan. 17 Canada and Egypt signed a joint statement in Cairo signifying intentions to co-operate in the peaceful use and exchange of nuclear energy. The agreement included the Egyptian purchase of Canadian CANDU reactors and the technology, uranium, heavy water and services required to operate the power generators. A 30-year nuclear co-operation agreement was signed between the countries on May 17.

Jan. 27 The Man. Court of Appeal ruled that mandatory retirement at age 65 contravened the province's Human Rights Act.

Jan. 28 The British Court of Appeal ruled that Britain no longer held legal responsibility toward Canadian Aboriginals. The ruling stifled an attempt by Native groups to take their case for increased constitutional rights to the British House of Lords.

Jan. 31 On the US-based *Let Poland be Poland* television program, PM Trudeau urged Poland to put an end to martial rule and instead support its Solidarity movement. Martial law had been declared in Poland on Dec. 13, 1981, following a popular Solidarity movement initiated by striking trade workers against the state. On Feb. 23, Ottawa placed sanctions on the Soviet Union and Poland to protest the martial law. Sanctions did not include a ban on food exports.

Feb. 1 The Point Lapreau, NB CANDU nuclear reactor power went into commercial operation. By 2003, the single 635-megawatt (MW) unit supplied 30% of NB's energy requirements.

• Amoco Canada and Chevron Standard Ltd. withdrew from a consortium to develop the $13.5 billion Alsands oil project in northern Alb. Dome Petroleum Ltd. and its Hudson's Bay Oil and Gas Co. Ltd. withdrew on Feb. 24; Shell Exploration Ltd. left on Feb. 25. Together, these companies held 50% of the project. The Alsands project finally collapsed on Apr. 30 when its surviving investors turned down an aid package from the federal and Alb. govts.

Feb. 2 Canadian physicist Wilfred Bennett Lewis (1908–1987) was named recipient of the US govt's Enrico Fermi Award for contributions to the peaceful use of atomic energy in the development of the Canadian nuclear energy industry, and also for his promotion of nuclear energy internationally.

Feb. 4 Gerry Sorensen (b 1958) won the Women's Alpine World Ski Championship in Schladming, Austria, becoming the 1st Canadian skier to win the Worlds since Nancy Greene in 1968. Sorensen was later named 1982 Canadian Press Athlete of the Year.

Feb. 7 Bob Rae (b 1949) won the Ont. NDP leadership over Richard Johnston and Jim Foulds at the party's leadership convention at Toronto. Rae replaced Michael Cassidy (b 1937).

Feb. 9 The Supreme Court of Canada upheld the Ont. Human Rights Code ruling that Ont. municipalities could not impose a mandatory retirement age of 60 on firefighters.

Feb. 15 The 35-storey, self-propelled oil drilling rig *Ocean Ranger* sank off Nfld. during a fierce storm, killing all 84 aboard. Winds were clocked at over 100 km/h; waves reached as high as 27 m. It was the worst marine disaster in Canada since WW II.

Feb. 21 Ont. Liberals elected David Robert Peterson (b 1943) leader of the party on the 2nd ballot. Peterson beat out Sheila Copps (b 1952) and Richard Thomas. Peterson succeeded Stuart Smith.

Feb. 23 Claude Charron (b 1947) resigned as Parti Québécois govt House leader after admitting he stole a sports jacket from a Montreal Eaton's store.

Feb. 24 Canada pledged to cut 50% of its sulphur dioxide emissions in the East by 1990 if the US agreed to do the same. There was no US response to the proposal. Canada and the US eventually signed a comprehensive sulphur dioxide emission agreement, the Acid Rain Accord, on Mar. 13, 1991.

Feb. 25 Canadian magazine publisher, Maclean Hunter Ltd. acquired controlling interest in the *Toronto Sun* and its 2 Alb. tabloids, the *Edmonton Sun* and *Calgary Sun*, from Sun Publishing Corp., for $54 million.

Feb. 27 Doug Young (b 1946) was elected leader of the NB Liberal Party, succeeding Joseph Daigle, who retired Nov. 1981.

Mar. 3 Statistics Canada confirmed that Canada entered a recession in 1982.

Mar. 4 Ont. Court of Appeal Justice Bertha Wilson (b 1923) was appointed to the Supreme Court of Canada, becoming the 1st woman to sit at the country's highest court. Wilson retired from the Court on Jan. 4, 1991.

Mar. 5 The Canada Oil and Gas Act became law. Intended to speed oil and gas development off the north, east and west coasts of Canada, the legislation also gave Petro-Canada an automatic 25% of all new offshore oil and gas discoveries.

• Steve Podborski won the overall men's downhill World Cup title (1981–1982) with a win in Aspen, Colorado. Over the incredible season, he had 3 wins, 2 seconds and 2 fourths to become the 1st Canadian — and the 1st non-European — to win the coveted title (Podborski went into Aspen in the lead during the previous season but lost the final race — and the overall World title — by 22/100th of a second). Podborski's win was the crowning achievement for the Crazy Canucks — a super-skilled assembly of go-for-broke downhillers who began breaking the European monopoly on downhill in the mid-1970s. Canucks included Podborski,

"Jungle" Jim Hunter, Dave Irwin, Dave Murray and Ken Read.

• The Nfld. Court of Appeal ruled that Nfld. had the legislative authority to take back all water rights along the Northern Churchill, which would allow the province to cut off power supply to Churchill Falls (Labrador) Corp., jointly owned by Que. and Nfld. At stake was a 1969, 65-year contract involving the sale of Labrador hydro to Que. at pre-energy crisis prices.

Mar. 8 The Canada Bill, which allowed Canada to patriate its Constitution, was passed by the British House of Commons. Final approval was given in the House of Lords on Mar. 25, thereby ending Canada's last colonial and legal tie with Britain. PM Trudeau and Queen Elizabeth II signed the Canadian Constitution in Ottawa Apr. 17.

• West-Fed, a political organization promoting western secession, disbanded and joined the Western Canada Concept movement to concentrate western separatist forces.

Mar. 19 Que. signed a 13-year, $6 billion agreement to export hydro-electric power to New York State.

Mar. 26 The Sask. legislature passed a bill ordering 5,000 non-medical hospital employees back to work, ending a 16-day strike that affected 67 of the province's 78 hospitals.

Mar. 31 The House of Commons passed a bill, 174–26, offering limited mortgage renewal aid to hard-pressed homeowners.

Also in Mar.
• Following widespread protest, the European Parliament voted to ban the importation of Canadian harp and hooded seal-pup skins. The temporary ban was effective to Oct. 1, 1983, at which time it was extended another 2 years. The ban destroyed the commercial-sealing industry, which was virtually shut down in 1985 and 1986. On Dec. 17, 1986, the Royal Commission on Seals and Sealing tabled its report recommending elimination of the hunt. A temporary federal ban was instituted on whitecoat and blueback seals Jan. 1, 1988.

Apr. 5 The federal govt placed an embargo on arms sales to Argentina because of its Apr. 2 occupation of the British-governed Falkland Islands. On Apr. 12, the federal govt placed a ban on Argentinean imports.

Apr. 6 The Progressive Conservatives, under Premier Brian Peckford, were re-elected in Nfld., winning 44 of 52 seats.

Apr. 13 The Alb. govt overhauled its oil and gas royalty structure to increase oil industry revenues an estimated $54 billion over a period ending in 1986.

• A commemorative stamp honouring the late Terry Fox and his "Marathon of Hope" run for cancer research was unveiled in his hometown of Port Coquitlam, BC.

Apr. 17 PM Trudeau and Queen Elizabeth II signed the Canadian Constitution, which incorporated the Charter of Rights and Freedoms, and ended the last traces of British authority in the country. Que. Premier René Lévesque, who had rejected the Constitution, boycotted the ceremony, and instead led an estimated 20,000 marchers in Montreal to protest the signing ceremonies.

Apr. 26 The Progressive Conservatives, under Grant Devine (b 1934), defeated the NDP govt under Premier Allan Blakeney in the Sask. general election. The PCs won 57 of 64 seats.

• About 80% of Ont.'s 14,000 doctors staged a 2-day walkout in a dispute over fee schedules. A new fee plan was agreed to on May 7.

May 5 The Canadian Wheat Board signed a deal with China to provide that country with a record $2.25 billion worth of wheat over 3 years.

May 10 The Departments of Energy and Northern Affairs initiated a $600 million oil and gas exploration program in the Beaufort Sea.

May 12 The House of Commons responded with laughter when NDP MP Margaret Mitchell (b 1925) raised the issue of violence against women. The parliamentary response disgusted much of the nation and helped galvanize attention toward the problem.

May 17 The House of Commons approved the Young Offenders Act. The act applied to youth 12 to 18 years of age and gave the offender the same rights to due process of law as adults. Maximum sentence under the act was 3 years.

May 18 Bombardier Inc. was awarded a contract to build 825 subway cars for New York City. Worth nearly $1 billion, it was the largest-ever export contract for a Canadian manufacturer.

May 26 The UN Security Council extended the mandate of the UN observer forces stationed between Syria and the Israeli-annexed Golan Heights. The 219 members of the force included Canadian, Finnish, Polish and Austrian troops.

May 28–30 Alliance Québec, a non-profit organization geared toward the support and promotion of anglophone institutions in Que., held its 1st major convention; 300 delegates attended, and elected a 30-member executive.

May 30 Delegates to the BC Liberal party convention called on PM Trudeau to prohibit testing of US cruise missiles in Canada and to press for an immediate freeze on the production of nuclear arms. The 1st US cruise missile tested over Canada was deployed Mar. 8, 1984.

May 31 The federal govt pledged more than $2 billion toward a program to help the struggling domestic-energy industry.

June 17 Five thousand, five hundred Que. doctors began a 5-day strike to press for a 38.5% increase in fees. The GPs were legislated back to work June 21, with an 11.4% fee increase over the next year.

June 18 A federal bill established Co-Enerco, a Crown corporation, to enter joint oil and gas ventures with co-operating energy companies. The firm was privatized in 1992.

June 23 The Supreme Court of Canada ruled that the federal govt did not have the power to tax natural gas exported to the US from provincially owned wells.

June 28 The federal budget released on this date included the "6 and 5" wage-restraint program for federal employees, limiting salary increases to 6% in 1983 and 5% in 1984. Despite tax increases and govt restraint, the federal deficit was projected to rise to $19 billion, from a 1981 figure of $10 billion.

July 13 Montreal hosted the 1st Major League Baseball All-Star game played outside the US. The hometown's National League beat the American League 4-1 for its 11th consecutive All-Star win.

July 20 Canada agreed to sell Brazil between $600 million and $900 million worth of grain over 3 years.

July 26 An unsuccessful prison break at Archambault maximum-security prison near Montreal resulted in 3 murdered guards, 7 injured guards, 2 inmate ringleaders dead by suicide, and a riot.

Aug. 3 The federal govt announced that the Naval Reserve headquarters would be moved from Halifax, NS, to Quebec City, in order to encourage more French-speaking Quebecers to join the Canadian navy. The move was complete Feb. 1983.

Aug. 4 Que. legislation allowing credit unions and caisse populaires to accept govt deposits was passed into law.

• Four thousand, two hundred Montreal transit drivers were ordered back to work by the province following a 5-day strike.

Aug. 8 Protestors waving placards and shouting on a railway-station platform became enraged when PM Trudeau gestured rudely from the window of a private rail car — not once, but several times during a late-night whistle stop in Salmon Arm, BC. The single-digit gesture, immediately dubbed "the Salmon Arm Salute" by the media, made headlines across the country. Within weeks, local entrepreneurs were selling T-shirts emblazoned with the extended finger gesture and the slogan, "PM Says We're Number 1."

Aug. 10 Claude Ryan announced his resignation as leader of the Que. Liberal Party, effective Aug. 31, because of increasing criticism of his leadership. Ryan was replaced by interim leader Gérard-D. Lesque, who was succeeded by former leader Robert Bourassa on Oct. 15, 1983.

Aug. 28 *Today* magazine, distributed in 18 Canadian newspapers with a circulation of 3 million, published its last issue.

Sept. 1 Statistics Canada revealed that the Canadian economy shrank 2.1% in the 2nd quarter of 1982, leading to the deepest economic decline since WW II.

Sept. 5 The World Bank and International Monetary Fund (IMF) met in Toronto to discuss international economic problems, until Sept. 9.

Sept. 8 The Que. Superior Court ruled that language-of-education clauses in the province's French-language law Bill 101 were unconstitutional. On July 26, 1984, the Supreme Court of Canada ruled that sections of Que.'s Bill 101 restricting access to English-language schooling violated the Canadian Charter of Rights and Freedoms.

Sept. 27 General Motors of Canada was awarded a 5-year contract worth over $625 million to build armoured vehicles for the US Army and Marine Corps.

• The Progressive Conservative govt, under James Lee, was re-elected in PEI, taking 22 of 32 seats.

• *L'Évangéline*, a 95-year-old Moncton, NB, newspaper — and the country's only French-language newspaper east of Quebec City — ceased publication.

Also in Sept.
• The Toronto Symphony Orchestra (TSO), under the direction of Andrew Davis, moved to Roy Thompson Hall where, in its 1st season, it performed over 150 concerts for nearly 1/2 million people. The TSO had played in Massey Hall since 1923.

Oct. 5 A team of Alb.-based climbers launched a successful assault on Mount Everest. Team member Laurie Skreslet (b 1949) of Calgary became the 1st Canadian to stand on top of the world's highest mountain, at an elevation of 8,848 m.

Oct. 7 The US lumber industry advanced its 1st petition on Canadian softwood lumber imports, charging that Canadian provinces unfairly subsidized the softwood export industry by charging minimal stumpage fees on Crown land. US producers demanded countervailing tariffs on Canadian softwood to exceed $2 billion. The petition set off a usually volatile trade dispute between the countries that ebbed and flowed through 2004.

Oct. 9 Canada finished 3rd at the close of the Commonwealth Games in Brisbane, Australia, with a total of 26 gold, 23 silver and 33 bronze medals.

Oct. 12 The Progressive Conservatives under Richard Hatfield were re-elected in the NB provincial election, winning 39 of 58 seats.

Oct. 14 A car-bomb explosion outside the Litton Systems Canada Ltd. plant in Toronto injured 7, including 3 police officers. The blast caused heavy damage at the plant, which produced guidance systems for US cruise missiles. On Jan. 20, 1983, members of the militant activist collective "Direct Action" (also known as the "Squamish Five") were arrested on the Sea to Sky Highway near Squamish, BC, as suspects in the bombing. Direct Action member Gerry Hannah served 5 years for his participation in what was termed "terrorist" activities.

Oct. 18 Former Ont. Premier John Robarts was found dead in his Toronto home, after having taken his own life. He had suffered a series of strokes since Aug. 1981.

Oct. 26 Legislation was passed renaming Dominion Day (July 1) Canada Day.

Oct. 31 Marguerite Bourgeoys (1620–1700), founder of the Congrégation de Notre-Dame de Montréal, was canonized by Pope John Paul II, becoming the 1st Canadian woman to be officially recognized as a saint.

Nov. 2 In the Alb. provincial election, Peter Lougheed's Progressive Conservatives won 75 of 79 seats.

Nov. 12 The $50 million *Anik C3*, Canada's most powerful satellite, was successfully launched into space from the American space shuttle *Columbia*.

Nov. 15 PM Trudeau attended the funeral of Soviet President Leonid Brezhnev in Moscow, and discussed the arms race and detente with Soviet officials.

Nov. 16 The Applebaum-Hébert report on Canadian cultural policy was released, recommending greater funding for the arts and more Canadian content in film and television production.

Nov. 22 In Vancouver, a group calling itself the Wimmin's Fire Brigade firebombed 3 Red Hot Video stores that were allegedly dealing in pornographic video cassettes. The stores were at the centre of a controversy surrounding the legality, meaning and sale of pornographic materials in BC.

Dec. 6 The Supreme Court of Canada denied Que.'s claim of a veto over constitutional amendments, maintaining that the Constitution was unassailable.

Dec. 7 In London, England, Laval U. professor Hugh Hambleton (b 1922) was convicted of spying for the Soviet Union during the 1950s.

Dec. 10 Canada, along with 118 other countries, signed the Law of the Sea Convention. The Convention gave international recognition to Canada's 200-mile (322-km) offshore-fisheries zone and established Canadian sovereignty over the Continental Shelf for 350 miles (568 km) offshore. It also provided agreements on pollution and environmental controls, and seabed mining and exploration.

Dec. 15 Ont. legislation was passed placing a 5% wage-increase limit on 500,000 public employees, from Oct. 1, 1982, to Sept. 30, 1983.

Also in 1982
• Canada's population broke the 25-million mark, reaching 25,117,442.

• Statistics Canada reported that the Gross National Product (GNP) fell 4.8%, the sharpest decline since 1933.

• 98% of Canadian homes had at least 1 television; 58% had cable TV.

• Discovery of gold at Hemlo, Ont., sparked the biggest gold rush in North America since the 1920s.

• Toronto entrepreneur "Honest Ed" Mirvish purchased London's historic "Old Vic" theatre for $550,000. The building was opened in 1983 after $2.5 million was spent on restoration and renovation. In 2000, the Mirvish family sold the building to the Old Vic Theatre Trust, a non-profit organization.

• Belgium-born chocolatier Bernard Callebaut founded Chocolaterie Bernard Callebaut in Calgary; $700 worth of chocolates were sold that day; $200,000 worth were sold over the 1st year of production. The company handcrafts all its delicacies using imported chocolate from the generations-old Callebaut Chocolate Factory in Wieze, Belgium. By 2004, there were 31 Callebaut stores from BC to Ont., plus 6 in the US. In 1998, Bernard Callebaut became the 1st North American to be named "Grand Prix International Artisan Chocolatier" at the International Festival of Chocolate in Roanne, France.

• The Edmonton International Fringe Festival was established to provide a place where artists could perform before audiences in an uncensored, free-form environment. It was the 1st and biggest fringe festival on the continent. Canada has had more fringe festivals per capita than any other country in the world. In 2002, fringe festivals took place in Montreal, Saskatoon, Vancouver, St. John's, Halifax, Peterborough, Lloydminster, Kelowna, Abbotsford, Duncan, Nanaimo, Toronto, Winnipeg, Ottawa, Victoria, Calgary, Thunder Bay, Prince George and Athabasca.

• Nfld.-born Shannon Tweed (b 1957) became Canada's 1st Playboy Playmate of the Year. She had placed 4th in the 1978 Miss Canada Pageant, representing Ottawa Valley.

• Iona Campagnola, née Hardy (b 1932), was the 1st woman elected president of the federal Liberal party.

• Renowned Inuit artist Kenojuak Ashevak (b 1927) was named Companion of the Order of Canada for her contribution to Canadian art. Born in an igloo and raised in the art of traditional Inuit survival skills, Ashevak was 1st encouraged to make simple soapstone carvings by Cape Dorset's federal administrator, James Houston, in 1950. Ashevak quickly became known for her carved stone sculptures and sealskin wall hangings and appliqués.

At 30, she gained national attention for her striking pencil representations of subjects such as birds, fish and human faces. In 1995 she received the Aboriginal Arts Foundation Award for Lifetime Achievement.

• Financial troubles brought the influential Canadian literacy quarterly *The Tamarack Review* to a close after 25 years of publication.

• Toronto's Tarragon Theatre premiered Mavis Gallant's 1st play, *What Was To Be Done?*

• Northrop Frye published *The Great Code: The Bible and Literature*, an examination of the literary aspects of the Bible and its influence on Western art, literature and imagination.

• The *Dictionary of Newfoundland English*, edited by G.M. Story, W.J. Kirwin and J.D.A. Widdowson, was published. It was revised for a 2nd edition in 1998.

• *Kicking against the Pricks*, a book of literary criticism by John Metcalf, was published.

• Anne Hébert published *Les Fous de Basson* (translated into English as *In the Shadow of the Wind*), for which she received the Prix Fémina.

• W.P. Kinsella published the highly popular baseball novel *Shoeless Joe*, which won both the Houghton Mifflin Literary Fellowship and the Books in Canada Award for 1st novel.

• Novelist Antonine Maillet published *Christophe Cartier de la noisette dit Nounours*.

• Short–story writer Alice Munro published the highly acclaimed *The Moons of Jupiter*.

• Guy Clarence Vanderhaeghe (b 1951) published the collection of short stories *Man Descending*, for which he received the Gov-Gen.'s Award.

• Mervyn J. Huston (b 1912) of Edmonton won the Stephen Leacock Award for Humour for the book *Gophers Don't Pay Taxes*.

• Poet Irving Layton published *A Wild Peculiar Joy*.

• St. Stephen's Byzantine Ukrainian Catholic Church was completed in Calgary. McGill U. professor of architecture Radoslav Zuk, a renowned designer of many distinct Ukrainian churches throughout North America, received the Gov-Gen.'s Medal for Architecture for the work.

1983

Jan. 2 Joe Clark resigned as federal Opposition leader, following a lack of support at a Progressive Conservative party convention. Erik Hersholt Nielsen (b 1924) became interim leader of the Opposition. Clark resigned as PC party leader on Feb. 19, but vowed to fight for the leadership at the next party convention held June 9–11.

• PM Trudeau embarked on an 18-day tour to promote Canadian trade with Pacific Rim countries. The PM visited Hong Kong, Thailand, Singapore, Malaysia, Indonesia, Brunei, the Philippines and Japan before returning Jan. 19.

Jan. 4 A new Criminal Code amendment came into effect which replaced rape with 3 categories of sexual assault. The new law gave equal protection to men and women, and allowed wives and husbands to charge each other with sexual assault.

Jan. 5 Roman Catholic Bishops of Canada released a New Year's message calling unemployment a "serious moral as well as an economic crisis in this country."

Jan. 7 The Ont. govt seized the assets of Greymac Trust Company, Crown Trust Company and Seaway Trust Company. The 3 firms were charged with helping finance the sale of nearly 11,000 Toronto-area apartment units to Saudi investors in Nov. 1982, when the price of the former Cadillac-Fairview buildings rose from $270 million to $500 million in a matter of weeks.

Also in Jan.
• Under Bill 141, the Canadian Human Rights Act was amended to prohibit sexual harassment in workplaces under federal jurisdiction, and to ban discrimination on the basis of pregnancy and family or marital status.

Feb. 10 The US signed an agreement with Canada allowing it to test military equipment in Canada, including cruise missiles. On June 15, Ottawa accepted a June 13 request to test the cruise missile over Canada in 1984. On Nov. 28, a Federal Court of Appeal panel ruled that the decision to allow cruise testing was constitutional and did not infringe on the Charter of Rights and Freedoms. The 1st US cruise missile was deployed over Canadian territory Mar. 8, 1984.

Mar. 23 *Porky's*, a comic film about teenage lust and hijinks, was awarded the Golden Reel Award at the 1983 Genie Awards. It was the highest-grossing movie in Canadian history, eventually earning over $100 million (US).

Mar. 28 North York Mayor Mel Lastman proposed that North York switch to daylight savings time in Mar. instead of Apr. (when the rest of Ont. did) because "there are more car accidents at night."

Also in Mar.
• The unemployment rate in Mar. was a record 13.6%, or 1,658,000 unemployed.

Apr. 19 The federal Liberal budget was dropped. It included higher taxes to cover a 4-year, $4.8 billion economic-recovery program. The projected deficit for 1983–1984 was $31.3 billion.

Apr. 26 *Skyship 500* "the 1st Canadian-built airship," made its inaugural flight at Toronto International Airport. The airship could carry 10 people and was held aloft by non-flammable helium.

Apr. 28 Ont. and New York State signed an acid rain agreement to exchange information, conduct joint research and lobby the US govt to place greater controls on sulphur dioxide emissions. The Reagan administration had stalled gains on acid rain controls through a "research before action" policy. The Canada-US Acid Rain Accord was eventually signed Mar. 13, 1991.

May 5 The BC provincial election was won by William Bennett's ruling Social Credit Party, which won 35 seats. The NDP, under David Barrett, won 22 seats.

May 7 Sunny's Halo, owned by Toronto stockbroker David Foster, became the 1st Canadian horse to win the Kentucky Derby since Majestic Prince in 1969.

May 10 After serving 11 years in federal prison on murder charges, Mi'kmaq Donald Marshall, from the Shubenacadie Reserve near Sydney, NS, was found innocent after a re-examination of the evidence, and acquitted. On May 12, Roy Ebsary was charged with the offence for which Marshall had spent so much time in jail, the May 28, 1971, stabbing death of Sandy Seale. The province of NS subsequently established a Royal Commission to investigate the case. Its report was released Jan. 26, 1990.

May 11 Approximately 100 Atlantic fishers burned and sank 2 federal fisheries patrol boats at West Pubnico, NS, to protest recent lobster conservation enforcement. On May 13, nine of the men were charged with piracy in the incident.

May 22 A CF-104 participating at an air show near Frankfurt, West Germany, crashed into a crowded highway, killing Canadian pilot Captain Allan Stephenson and 5 civilians on the ground.

May 25 The Société Franco-Manitobaine ratified a deal with the provincial govt, restoring French-language rights, making French an official language of the legislature and courts and providing French services at head offices of govt departments and agencies. The Supreme Court of Canada last ruled against French-language rights in both the courts and provincial legislature in 1890.

June 2 Canadian folksinger and songwriter Stan Rogers (1949–1983) was killed when an Air Canada DC-9 on a flight from Texas to Toronto caught fire in midair and was forced to make an emergency landing at Cincinnati, Ohio. Rogers, best known for his songs "Fogarty's Cove," "Mary Ellen Carter" and "Barrett's Privateers," was among 23 of 46 passengers and crew who died of smoke inhalation and burns. Rogers was at the peak of his success.

June 3 Police raided Henry Morgentaler's Winnipeg abortion clinic and charged him and 7 employees with performing illegal abortions. On July 5, police raided a Morgentaler clinic in Toronto and charged Morgentaler and 2 associates with violating Ont. abortion laws. The Toronto clinic was reopened Dec. 10 after Morgentaler was acquitted of the charges on Nov. 8. However, in Oct. 1985, the

Ont. Court of Appeal overturned Morgentaler's Nov. 8, 1984 acquittal and ordered a new trial. Morgentaler appealed this decision to the Supreme Court of Canada, which ruled on the legality of abortion Jan. 28, 1988.

June 11 Brian Mulroney (b 1939), former president of Iron Ore Canada, was chosen new leader of the federal Progressive Conservative Party, beating out Joe Clark 1,584–1,325 on the 4th ballot. On Aug. 29, Mulroney won a seat in the House with a by-election victory in the NS riding of Central Nova.

June 19 Vancouver's 60,000-seat, $126 million BC Place officially opened. The domed stadium became home to the BC Lions of the CFL.

June 22 The US space shuttle's Canadarm was 1st used to release and retrieve a satellite in space. The unit was 1st tested on shuttle *Columbia* in Nov. 1981. Known officially as the Shuttle Remote Manipulator (SRMS) the Canadarm measures 15.2 m, weighs 410 kg (on Earth) and is capable of maneuvres even more complex and finite than those of the human arm. Its maneuverability, at speeds of 60 cm/sec. (unloaded) and 6 cm/sec. (loaded) is made possible by a shoulder, elbow and wrist with closed circuit cameras in both shoulder and wrist joints. Whether knocking ice from the shuttle's fuselage, repairing the Hubble Space Telescope, or assisting in the assembly of the International Space Station, the Canadarm has never malfunctioned, performing on more than 50 missions and some 7,000 orbits of Earth.

June 29 Contracts were let for 6 new patrol frigates for the Canadian navy, worth $3.2 billion. Saint John Building and Dry Dock Co. received the bulk of the order.

• Que. and the French-owned Picheney-Ugine-Kuhlman signed an agreement to build a jointly financed $1.5 billion aluminium smelter at Bécancour, 130 km northeast of Montreal. The deal gave Picheney preferential, inexpensive power from Hydro Que.

June 30 C-Channel, the nations's 1st pay-TV arts network, went off the air after beginning operations Feb. 1.

• A new oil-pricing agreement was signed by the federal and Alb. govts: Canadian oil prices were frozen at $29.75 per barrel (approximately 83% of the world price) for 18 months. Producers would get world prices for oil discovered between 1974–1980.

• The Simpson-Sears retailing chain was fined $1 million for misleading advertising, the largest such fine in Canadian history. The company was found to have sold approximately 35,000 diamond rings, each given an exaggerated appraisal value to make the retail price more attractive.

July 1 The Access to Information Act (Freedom of Information Act) went into effect, entitling Canadian citizens and permanent residents to examine information under control of the federal govt. The act was passed in the House of Commons June 28, 1982. The Privacy Act also went into effect, giving Canadians the right to access govt records about themselves. It also established criteria governing the collection and dissemination of personal records.

• The World University Games were held in Edmonton, until July 11. Canada finished 3rd behind the US and USSR, its best-ever showing. The Canadian men's basketball team won gold, beating Yugoslavia 83–68. In the right to advance to the gold round, Canada upset the seemingly unstoppable US squad 85–77, despite the Americans fielding such future NBA superstars as Charles Barkley, Karl Malone, Johnny Dawkins and Ed Pickney.

July 23 An Air Canada 767 ran out of fuel in midair but managed a remarkable emergency landing on an abandoned air-force strip at Gimli, Man. Blame was traced to faulty gauges and a mixup in metric conversion.

July 27 Judge Rosalie Abella (b 1946) was appointed to lead a one-woman Royal Commission on Equality in Employment. Abella coined the expression "employment equity" to describe those programs and practices necessary to bring about workplace equality for women and other disadvantaged groups. Her report was tabled in the House of Commons on Nov. 29, 1984.

Also in July

• The GATT in Geneva ruled that the Foreign Investment Review Agency's (FIRA) practice of obliging foreign firms to buy quantities of Canadian-made goods when they expanded operations in Canada or acquired Canadian companies, violated the International GATT agreement. The ruling was the result of a US complaint lodged with GATT Jan. 5, 1982.

Aug. 31 It was declared "Oscar Peterson Day" in Baltimore, Maryland.

• Canada finished 3rd with 108 medals, behind the US and Cuba, at the end of the Pan-American Games in Caracas, Venezuela. Two Canadian weightlifters were disqualified for anabolic steroid use.

Sept. 2 The Russian airline Aeroflot had its landing rights cancelled at Montreal's Mirabel Airport after the Soviets shot down Korean Air Lines Boeing 747 (Flight 007) on Sept. 1, killing 269 people, including 10 Canadians. Flight 007 had strayed over Soviet airspace. On Dec. 21, the federal govt formally claimed $2.1 million in damages from the Soviet Union on behalf of Canadian victims of the tragedy.

Sept. 12 Canada expelled 2 Soviet diplomats for trying to obtain prohibited high-technology equipment.

Oct. 17 The Toronto Sun Publishing Corporation bought the *Houston Post*, the 17th largest newspaper in the US, for $100 million.

Oct. 24 Canadian immigration policy was altered to give precedence to those wanting to open businesses or invest money in the country.

Oct. 26 Plebiscites to expand bilingual services were defeated in all 20 Man. communities where they were held.

Oct. 27 At a "Peace and Security in a Nuclear Age" conference at the U. of Guelph, PM Trudeau presented his peace initiative, which included a ban on nuclear arms testing, a ban on high-altitude weapons testing, a nuclear arms control conference between the major world powers, and a mediation program between NATO and Soviet bloc countries.

From Nov. 8–11, PM Trudeau travelled through Europe on a peace mission, meeting with the leaders of France, Holland, Belgium, West Germany, Britain, and with Pope John Paul II. On Nov. 28, Trudeau took his peace initiative to China for discussions with PM Zhao Ziyang and Chairman Deng Xiaoping. On the same trip abroad, Trudeau pushed his plan in Japan, Bangladesh and at the Commonwealth Conference in India. The 19-day peace trip brought the PM home Dec. 5. On Jan. 11, 1984, the PM discussed his peace initiative with UN Sec-Gen. Javier Perez de Cuellar.

Also in Oct.

• Donna Carrière, a Cree, was placed in charge of a Hudson's Bay Company (HBC) store at Weagamow L. in northwestern Ont., becoming the 1st woman manager of a northern HBC post.

• Statistics Canada announced that the inflation rate in Oct. was 4.9%, the lowest since Aug. 1972.

Nov. 14 BC govt employees and union workers ended a 13-day strike called to protest govt pay and job-restraint programs.

• The House of Commons gave 3rd reading to legislation amending the 1897 Crow's Nest Pass grain freight rates. The new rates would increase shipping costs for farmers but inject $3.7 billion into western railways. The bill was given Assent Nov. 17. (After the 1982 patriation of the Canadian Constitution, Royal Assent remained a symbolic last stage of the legislative process, given by either the gov-gen. or a Supreme Court justice.) The Crow's Nest agreement was eventually abolished Aug. 1, 1995.

Nov. 16 Ont.-born Lynn Williams (b 1924) was elected acting president of the United Steelworkers of America.

Nov. 27 The Toronto Argonauts defeated the BC Lions 18–17 in Vancouver, to win the Grey Cup for the 1st time in 31 years.

Dec. 5 Marc Garneau (b 1949), Bjarni Tryggvason (b 1954), Steven MacLean (b 1953), Robert Thirsk (b 1953), Kenneth Money (b 1952) and Roberta Bondar (b 1951) were chosen to become Canada's

1st astronauts. On Mar. 14, 1984, Garneau was named the 1st to go into space. He would take off aboard space shuttle *Challenger* Oct. 5, 1984.

Dec. 10 Romanian President Nicolae Ceausescu became the 1st Eastern bloc leader to endorse PM Trudeau's peace initiative. US President Reagan announced his support of the initiative on Dec. 15.

Dec. 11 Gary Filmon (b 1945) was elected leader of the Man. Progressive Conservative Party, succeeding Sterling Lyon.

1981–1983 1,000 Canadian farms went bankrupt.

Also in 1983

• Canadian immigration numbers were reduced about 25% to 105,000–110,000 immigrants.

• Queen's U. graduate student Rainer Wolf (working under Professor Robert Dalrymple) found a series of fossil trackways (footprints) while investigating the reddish sandstone Potsdam formation north of Kingston, Ont. In 2001, Queen's scientists published an article in *Geology* magazine, "First Steps on Land: Arthropod Trackways in Cambrian-Ordovician Eolian Sandstone, Southeastern Ontario…" arguing that these trackways were made by animals abandoning their aquatic homes for land. The arthropod involved was the now-defunct Euthycarcinoid.

• The Experimental Studies Division of the Meterological Service of Canada invented the Brewer spectrophotometer, which measures atmospheric ozone and ultraviolet irradiation. The unit is used in 40 countries, with 12 Brewer stations in Canada.

• Bad times for Canadian publishers were signalled with the demise of Clarke Irwin, a venerable Canadian publisher of poetry, fiction, non-fiction and educational material. The firm was founded in 1930.

• Montreal native Jim West founded Justin Time Records Inc., out of Montreal. The jazz-based label's 1st recording was Montreal pianist Oliver Jones's *Live at Biddles*. The label has since developed an important catalogue of more than 300 recordings,

including works by such important Canadian jazz musicians as Guido Basso (b 1937), Pat LaBarbera (b 1944), Kirk MacDonald, P.J. Perry, Carol Welsman and Dave Young (b 1940). Justin Time has received the Jazz Label of the Year Award from *Jazz Report* every year from 1994–2000.

• The Duguld Costume Museum in Duguld, Man., opened. It was the 1st costume and fashion museum in Canada and boasted over 12,000 pieces of men's, women's and children's fashions and accessories, some dating to 1765.

• Former Montreal Canadiens goalie Ken Dryden published *The Game*, about his life in hockey, its history and the great "Habs" teams of the 1970s, which included Guy Lafleur, Larry Robinson, Guy Lapointe and coach Scotty Bowman. The book was reissued in a 20th-anniversary edition in 2003.

• Alden Nowlan published *Nine Micmac Legends*.

• *Dig Up My Heart: Selected Poems 1952–1983*, by Milton Acorn, was published.

• Morley Callaghan published the novel *A Time for Judas*, a fictionalized account of the trial of Christ.

• Native author Beatrice Cullerton published the children's book *In Search of April Raintree*, a story about the separation of 2 Métis children.

• Leon Rooke published the novel *Shakespeare's Dog*, for which he received the Gov-Gen.'s Award.

• Eric Stanley Wright (b 1929) published the crime novel *The Night the Gods Smiled*, which introduced fans of the genre to Inspector Charlie Salter.

1984

Jan. 7 A faulty brake in a CP freight train caused a 62-car derailment in Medicine Hat, Alb. The accident killed the engineer, the subsequent sulphur car fires caused the evacuation of approximately 800 residents.

Jan. 13 Anne Clare Cools (b 1943) was appointed Liberal Senator from Ont., becoming Canada's 1st African-Canadian Senator. In 1974, Cools founded

Women in Transition Inc. in Toronto, one of the 1st battered women's shelters in the country. In 1997, she was named Spiritual Mother of the Year by NA'AMAT, the international Jewish women's organization; in 1999, she was named Real Woman of Canada's Person of the Year; and in 2001 she was the recipient of Toronto's Bob Marley Day Award.

Jan. 17 Ralph Cross (b 1929), who defected to East Germany from the Canadian Armed Forces in 1955, was sentenced to 60 days in a Canadian military prison. He had been expelled from East Germany in 1983.

Jan. 23 Chinese Premier Zhao Ziyang ended a 7-day visit to Canada.

• Stuart (1927–1984) and Lillian Kelly (b 1930) of Brantford, Ont., collected $13,890,588.80 for the winning Lotto 649 ticket. It was the largest lottery prize in North America to that date.

Jan. 24 The ABC network agreed to pay $309 million US for the American television rights to the 1988 Winter Olympics in Calgary. The Olympic Organizing Committee would receive 26.6% of the money, with the rest going to Calgary Olympic organizers. US rights to the 1976 Olympics in Montreal were sold to ABC for $25 million.

Also in Jan.
• Alex Tilley founded Alex Tilley and Family's Nautical gear, now Tilley Endurables Inc., as a small mail-order company out of his home in suburban Toronto. By 2003, Tilley had stores all over Canada, the US and UK.

• Architects Barton Myers Associates completed Unionville Library in Markham, Ont. The urban design reflects Unionville's Victorian origins, yet with a modern half-completed tower and copper roof.

Feb. 14 PM Trudeau attended the funeral of gen. sec. of the Communist Party of the Soviet Union (CPSU), Yuri Andropov, in Moscow, and held discussions with Soviet leaders regarding his peace initiative.

Feb. 16 Speed skater Gaétan Boucher (b 1958) became the most decorated Canadian in Winter Olympic competition, winning gold medals in the 1,000-m and 1,500-m and a bronze in the 500-m race in Sarajevo, Yugoslavia. Boucher had won silver in the 1,000-m at the 1980 Olympics in L. Placid, New York. By the end of the games on Feb. 19, Canada won a total of 4 medals, with Brian Orser (b 1962) taking silver in figure skating.

Feb. 29 Following a contemplative walk in the snow, PM Trudeau announced his retirement from federal politics after 16 years in office. He officially resigned June 27, the same day he was awarded the 1984 Albert Einstein Peace Prize. Trudeau was succeeded by John Turner (b 1929), who was elected leader of the Liberal party at an Ottawa convention June 16. Turner was sworn in as Canada's new PM June 30.

Also in Feb.
• Telefilm Canada was created from the ashes of the Canadian Film Development Corporation in an effort to increase the creation and distribution of Canadian-made feature films. Formed as a Crown corporation, Telefilm acted primarily as a banker to independent Canadian film producers.

Mar. 8 The cruise missile was 1st tested in Canada over Alb. The unarmed missile was attached to a B–52 bomber during its 2,500-km flight. The test was followed (Mar. 10–11) by a weekend of mass anti–cruise missile rallies in cities coast to coast.

• The Supreme Court of Canada ruled that the federal govt owned the Hibernia oil field resources off the Nfld. coast. A revenue-sharing pact, however, was signed between Nfld. and Ottawa on Feb. 11, 1985.

Mar. 11 Seal-hunt supporters in the Magdalen Islands badly damaged a helicopter chartered by the International Fund for Animal Welfare, a seal-hunt opponent.

Mar. 12 King Juan Carlos and Queen Sofia of Spain arrived in Canada for a 6-day state visit.

Mar. 21 Canada and 9 European countries signed an agreement to cut sulphur dioxide emissions by at least 30% by 1993, and to reduce nitrogen oxide emissions, both key components of acid rain.

Mar. 26 Chief Justice of the Supreme Court of Canada Bora Laskin died. On Apr. 16, Supreme

Court Justice Brian Dickson (1916–1998) was sworn in as new chief justice.

Mar. 28 An Eaton's store in Brampton, Ont., gained union certification, a 1st in the company's history.

Apr. 1 The Canada Health Act was given Assent. The act was based on 5 health-care pillars to ensure preservation of the Canadian health-care system: full access, universality, comprehensive coverage, portable coverage, and public not-for-profit administration. The act included penalty provisions for provinces not fulfilling Act requirements. Effective July 1, any province allowing health care user fees or extra billing would lose $1 of federal medicare money on a dollar-for-dollar basis.

Apr. 10 BC pulp and paper workers returned to work after a lockout and strike that began on Feb. 2. The day before (Apr. 9), the BC Labour Relations Board ruled that the strike, by members of the Canadian Pulpworkers Union and Canadian Pulp, Paper and Woodworkers Union, was illegal.

Apr. 15 A fleet of tall ships left St-Malo, France, on a race to Canada, arriving in Halifax June 9. The tall ships spent the summer visiting several Canadian cities, including Quebec City, Montreal and Toronto, to celebrate the 450th anniversary of Jacques Cartier's discovery of Que., and also, Ont.'s bicentennial.

Apr. 25 Canada and the Soviet Union signed a 5-year agreement for co-operation in scientific research in the Arctic, including areas involving resource development and environment.

May 1 The federal govt's Sport Select baseball betting pool began, despite opposition from all provinces and Major League Baseball. The program was cancelled by the new Conservative govt following the Sept. 4 election. Its biggest ticket was also its last ticket drawn — $4.8 million on Sept. 30, 1984.

May 8 Canadian soldier, Corporal Dennis Lortie (b 1959), killed 3 and wounded 13 in the Que. National Assembly with submachine gunfire. Lortie, who wanted to destroy the Parti Québécois govt, was talked into surrendering. On Feb. 13, 1985,

Lortie was found guilty in a Que. Superior Court on 3 counts of 1st degree murder and given a life sentence. He was granted full parole on June 19, 1995.

May 10 The Ministry of Transport declared that qualified airline deregulation policies would be introduced within 2 years, which would allow airlines to offer lower fares, more routes and greater competition. On May 18, permission was given to loosen restrictions on domestic air-fare rates as of June 1.

May 11 Legislation was introduced to establish the Canadian Security Intelligence Service (CSIS). This civilian security agency replaced the RCMP in dealing with espionage, terrorism, subversion and threats to Canadian security. Assent was given June 21. Headquartered in Ottawa, the self-proclaimed "organization with secrets to protect, not a secret organization," serves as the principal adviser to Ottawa on matters of national security. On Nov. 29, Ron Atkey (b 1942), former Conservative MP and cabinet member, was appointed to head the security intelligence review committee that monitored CSIS activities.

May 19 Wayne Gretzky led the Edmonton Oilers to the 1st of his 4 Stanley Cup victories with the team, defeating the 4-time champion New York Islanders 4 games to 1, with a final-game 5–2 win at Edmonton's Northlands Coliseum. The Oilers set an NHL record with 446 goals for the season, and Paul Coffey (b 1961) broke Bobby Orr's record for points by a defencemen in a season with 126.

June 14 PM Trudeau bade farewell to the Liberal party and the nation in a televised tribute in Ottawa.

June 18 NB officially celebrated the bicentennial of its founding as a British colony.

June 19 The Raymond Moriyama–designed $15 million Science North science centre opened in Sudbury, Ont. It was jointly funded by Inco, Falconbridge, the Ont. govt and private interests. The centre includes access to an old Inco mine cut into 2.3-billion-year-old bedrock; the 1-billion-year-old Creighton Fault, which actually runs through the centre (and all the way to Sault Ste. Marie); the F. Jean Macleod free-flying Butterfly Gallery; a beaver pond; theatres; and numerous hands-on exhibits. Science North has since become one of Northern Ont.'s leading tourist destinations.

June 20 A cave-in killed 4 miners in a Falconbridge Nickel mine in Sudbury, Ont.

June 21 The Constitution Proclamation, created in 1983 as the 1st amendment to the new Constitution, became effective to guarantee Native rights acquired — or to be acquired — through land claim agreements.

Also in June.
• Canadair Ltd. reported a year-end loss of $1.4 billion, a record loss for a Canadian corporation.

July 1 The 4,180-m² Edmonton Space Sciences Centre, designed by internationally renowned architect Douglas Cardinal (b 1934), opened in Coronation Park. It reopened as Odyssium on July 1, 2001 after undergoing a $14 million expansion. It is home to 6 galleries, a 250-seat star theatre and a 275-seat IMAX theatre. Odyssium includes an outdoor observatory, which closes when temperatures dip below –15°C.

July 6 GM of Canada pledged an investment of more than $1 billion for new facilities in Oshawa, Ont., which included 125 industrial robots.

July 11 The Canadian dollar sank to 74.86 cents US, an all-time low.

July 24 Major federal party leaders — John Turner, Brian Mulroney and Ed Broadbent — met for the 1st time in a French-language television debate.

Aug. 12 Canada made its best Olympic showing ever at the close of the Summer Games in Los Angeles (boycotted by Soviet bloc countries). Canada won a total of 44 medals, including 10 gold, 18 silver and 16 bronze. Canada did especially well in the pool, where Alex Baumann (b 1964) won 2 gold (200-m and 400-m individual medley) and Victor Davis (1964–1989) and Anne Ottenbrite (b 1966) a gold each in the 200-m breaststroke. Sylvie Bernier won a gold in 3-m diving and Larry Cain the 1st Canadian canoeing gold since Francis Amyot in 1936. Linda Thom (b 1943) began the windfall with

gold in sport pistol on the 1st day of the games. The last gold medals Canada won in swimming were by George Hodgson of Montreal in the 1912 Stockholm Olympics.

Aug. 15 The 1st televised debate on women's issues by the 3 major federal political parties took place. The seminal event was organized by the National Action Committee on the Status of Women (NAC).

Aug. 17 The Alb. govt sold Pacific Western Airlines, which it had owned since 1974, to PWA Corp., a holding company that in 1987 amalgamated PWA with CP Air, CP-owned Eastern Provincial Airlines and Nordair to form the single airline Canadian Airlines International (later Canadian Airlines). Canadian became a chief rival to Air Canada, but floundered in the 1990s, only to be taken over by rival Air Canada in Dec. 1999.

Aug. 31 Muchmusic, Canada's 1st all-music video network, went on air. The CRTC had issued it a licence earlier in the year. The 1st video was an early music-to-film synchronization short from the 1920s featuring Eubie Blake performing "Snappy Songs." The 2nd was Rush's "The Enemy Within." The CRTC also granted licences this year to the Sports Network (TSN), Telatino, Chinavision and Cathay.

Sept. 3 A bomb in Montreal's Central Station killed 3 and injured 47. Thomas Brigham (b 1919) of Rochester, New York, was sentenced to life imprisonment in connection with the blast. He had a history of mental illness.

Sept. 4 In the general federal election, the Progressive Conservatives under Brian Mulroney won 211 seats, the Liberals under John Turner 40, and the NDP under Ed Broadbent 30. One Independent was elected. It was the largest federal majority to date. Voter turnout was 75.3%. On Sept. 17, Brian Mulroney was sworn in as PM, along with a 40-member cabinet. The Conservative govt's Nov. 5 Speech from the Throne promised to bring Que. into a constitutional accord amenable to the other provinces and to "purge the spirit of confrontation from the conduct of the nation's affairs."

Sept. 9–20 Pope John Paul II arrived in Quebec City to begin the 1st papal visit to Canada. The pontiff continued to Montreal, St. John's, Moncton, Halifax, Toronto, Midland, Ont., Winnipeg, Edmonton and Vancouver, before leaving from Ottawa. Fog prevented a planned visit and Mass at Fort Simpson, NWT, an island where the Mackenzie meets the Liard R. On Sept. 20, 1987, the pope fulfilled a promise given to the Dene and arrived in Fort Simpson for a 5-hour visit while en route to the US.

Sept. 13 Canada defeated the USSR 3–2 in overtime of a semifinal match of the Canada Cup. Mike Bossy deflected a shot by Paul Coffey for the winner. Canada won the championship final over Sweden 6–5 on Sept. 18. John Tonelli was named Most Valuable Player. It was Canada's 2nd Canada Cup since the Bobby Orr team won the inaugural cup in 1976.

Sept. 20 On behalf of the Inuit people of Canada, artist Jessie Oonark's (1906–1985) print *Giver of Life* was presented to Pope John Paul II during a Mass held in Ottawa.

Sept. 26 The Ont. govt authorized the extension of a $500,000 line of credit to ailing independent Canadian publisher McClelland & Stewart.

Oct. 5 7:03 a.m. Marc Garneau, crew member of NASA's flight 41-G, became the 1st Canadian astronaut to be launched into space. Eight days, 5 hours and 24 minutes later, he and the rest of the *Challenger* crew landed safely at the Kennedy Space Center, Florida, after 132 1/2 orbits of the Earth. Garneau went into space twice more, on Space Shuttle *Endeavor* May 19, 1996, and on *Endeavor*, Nov. 30, 2000.

Oct. 9 Peter Fenwick (b 1944), leader of the provincial NDP, was elected the 1st NDP member of the Nfld. House of Assembly in a Labrador by-election.

Oct. 12 The Que. Environment Department reported that provincial workers and Inuit had cleaned up approximately 10,000 caribou carcasses along the Caniapiscau R. The migrating animals had drowned Oct. 5 while trying to ford unusually high waters caused by a hydroelectric dam.

• The International Court of Justice at The Hague, Netherlands, ruled that Canadian fishers could still work a disputed sector of Georges Bank in the Gulf

of Maine. Delimitation of the area had been referred to the international court on Nov. 25, 1981, which used coastal geography to project maritime boundaries over the disputed Gulf of Maine. Both countries accepted the ruling.

Oct. 13 Leo Barry (b 1943), a Yale-educated corporate lawyer, was elected leader of the Nfld. Liberal Party. Barry, who had previously been a provincial Conservative cabinet minister, succeeded Stephen Neary (1925–1996).

Oct. 19 Six people were killed, including Grant Notley (1929–1984), leader of the Alb. NDP, in a plane crash near High Prairie, Alb. Four people survived the accident.

• The Ont. Supreme Court awarded Norris Walker and Walker Brothers Quarry, a waste-disposal company, $908,000 in a libel suit against CTV Television Network. In 1980, the *W5* news program alleged the company secretly disposed of liquid waste. It was the largest libel award ever granted by a Canadian court.

Oct. 26 NB Premier Richard Hatfield was charged with marijuana possession after 35 g of the substance were found in an outside pocket of his suitcase at an airport security check during Queen Elizabeth II's visit to Fredericton. On Jan. 29, 1985, Hatfield was acquitted of the charge in a Fredericton court following a 2-day trial.

Oct. 28 Western Canadian Métis leaders ended a meeting at Spruce Grove, Alb., with a pledge to pursue constitutional rights for Métis, a land base in western Canada and self-governing powers.

Oct. 30 The new federal Conservative govt declared it would sell off at least $2.2 billion worth of Crown-owned assets during its mandate.

Nov. 6 Premier John Buchanan led his Conservatives to an overwhelming victory in the NS general election. The Tories captured 42 seats, leaving the Liberals with 6 members, the NDP with 3 and the Cape Breton Labour Party with 1.

• Colin Thatcher (b 1938), a wealthy Moose Jaw rancher, ex-provincial Conservative cabinet minister and only son of former Liberal Premier Ross

Thatcher, was found guilty of murder in the death of JoAnn Wilson, his former wife. He was sentenced to a mandatory life term without parole eligibility for 25 years.

• Stephen Lewis, former Ont. NDP leader and the federal Conservatives' surprise appointment as Canadian ambassador to the UN, made his maiden speech in New York City, an impassioned plea for international aid to help Ethiopian victims of famine and civil war.

Nov. 9 The Ont. legislature passed legislation to send 7,500 striking community colleges teachers back to work. The teachers had been on strike over pay and workload since Oct. 17.

Nov. 13 The External Affairs Department announced that, in order to cut costs, it would close the Canadian embassy in Ougadougou, Burkina Faso (the African nation formerly called Upper Volta), as well as consulates in Rio de Janeiro, New Orleans, Birmingham, England, and Bordeaux, France.

Nov. 26–27 After the Parti Québécois suffered its 22nd consecutive by-election defeat, this one at the hands of the Liberals, Que. Premier René Lévesque shuffled his cabinet. Many of his Parti Québécois cabinet ministers and backbenchers had crossed the floor of the legislature to sit as Independents. The dissidents believed that sovereignty-association should have a higher priority for the party when it fought the next provincial election.

Nov. 29 PM Brian Mulroney condemned the actions of a federal aide who had surreptitiously taped a conversation between Finance Minister Michael Wilson (b 1937) and his Man. counterpart. The federal govt was further embarrassed after Wilson's Winnipeg visit, when it was revealed that a newspaper reporter had picked up federal briefing notes that suggested Wilson not build up the province's hopes of receiving more transfer payments. During a week of communication foul-ups, a staff member in Joe Clark's External Affairs Department inadvertently sent to a radio station a tape containing confidential information about establishing a Canadian embassy in Nicaragua.

• The Royal Commission on Equality in Employment, chaired by Justice Rosalie Abella, recommended that the federal govt impose mandatory legislation to ensure employment equity in all federally regulated private and public sectors. It also recommended that better employment opportunities be provided to women, as well as to Native Peoples, people with physical disability and other minorities. Recommendations of the report were partly incorporated in the Employment Equity Act, given Assent June 27, 1986.

Dec. 5 Bryan Adams (b 1959) swept the 1984 Juno Awards for Canadian music, taking 5 awards for his international hit album *Cuts Like a Knife*: Album of the Year, Male Vocalist of the Year, Composer of the Year, Best Songwriter, and Best Producer of the Year.

Dec. 10 Citizens of the Baffin Is. community of Frobisher Bay voted 310 to 213 to change the name of the town back to Iqaluit, meaning "where the fish are" in Inuktitut. The name was officially changed Jan. 1, 1987. Frobisher Bay had been established as a Hudson's Bay post in 1914.

Dec. 11 The CBC announced it would cut 1,500 staff positions, effective Apr. 1, 1985, as part of a move to reduce the Crown corporation's budget by $75 million. The network's budget cut had been ordered in Finance Minister Michael Wilson's economic statement to the Commons Nov. 8. Nearly 3,000 CBC jobs were eliminated between 1985 and 1989.

• Ont. banned the sale of cheap drinks in bars during "Happy Hour" in an attempt to cut down on drinking and driving. The move was made after a successful lobby campaign by Mothers Against Drunk Driving (MADD).

Also in 1984
• The 11,965-km, 1,380-channel, 14-MHz ANZAC Communications analog cable, connecting Port Alberni, BC, to Sydney, Australia (through Hawaii, Fiji and New Zealand) went into service, until May 15, 2002.

• The federally funded Canadian Institute for International Peace and Security was established in Ottawa by act of Parliament to provide annual reports to the House on disarmament issues and to raise issues regarding world peace.

• The Annapolis, NS, Tidal Generating Station was completed to generate electrical energy from Bay of Fundy tides. The $46 million–plus project was funded by the NS federal govt. It was the 1st such generating plant in North America, and 3rd in the world (La Rance, St. Malo, France and Kislaya Guba, White Sea, Russia). Bay of Fundy tidal extremes can exceed 6.096 m every 12 hours and 25 minutes.

• Commercial fishing was banned on NB's Miramichi R., home to Canada's largest population of Atlantic salmon. Although sport fishing was still allowed on the river, NB law required that all salmon over 61 cm be released, and that out-of-province anglers be accompanied by local guides.

• The body of English petty officer John Torrington, a member of Englishman John Franklin's ill-fated 1845 expedition, was found on Beechey Is., NWT, by U. of Alb. anthropologist Owen Beattie. Hair analysis showed inordinate lead levels in the body, suggesting Franklin's crew may have succumbed to lead poisoning caused by eating tinned food sealed with lead solder.

• Science fiction novelist William Gibson (b 1948) coined the term "cyberspace" ("a graphical [3D] representation of data abstracted from the banks of every computer in the human system") which he used in his book *Neuromancer*, published the same year. The controversial novel won international praise, taking the Hugo, Nebula and Philip K. Dick Awards. American-born Gibson immigrated to Canada's West Coast in 1968.

• 41.8% of Canadian workers were covered under some form of collective bargaining agreement. The rate declined to 32.2% by 2002.

• The Environmental Defence Fund (changed to Environmental Defence Canada in 2002) was founded as a national charitable organization to raise awareness of, and provide legal assistance and funding to, Canadian environmental issues.

• Pauktuutit, the Inuit Women's Association of Canada, was incorporated.

• Daurene Lewis was elected mayor of Annapolis Royal, NS. She was the 1st African-Canadian woman to lead a Canadian city. She held the mayoral position until 1988.

• CTV London bureau chief Todd Clark was killed while on assignment in Lebanon.

• Robert Cooper's film *The Terry Fox Story* won 5 Genie Awards, including Best Picture.

• The sketch-comedy series *Kids in the Hall* (1984–1994) 1st aired on CBC Television. Featuring Dave Foley (b 1963), Bruce McCulloch (b 1959), Kevin McDonald (1961), Mark McKinney (b 1959) and Scott Thompson (b 1959), and produced by Lorne Michaels, *Kids in the Hall* quickly became a Canadian comedy classic, with a catchy theme song and such memorable reoccuring characters as Chicken Lady, It's a Fact Girl, Headcrusher, Cabbage Head, the Apathetic Cops, and Darrill.

• The 1st Inuit Circumpolar Conference (ICC) comprising Native Peoples from Canada, Alaska and Greenland was held at Barrow, Alaska. Representatives agreed to officially replace the term "Eskimo" with the designation Inuit. The ICC would later include Russia to represent a total of 150,000 Arctic Inuit. Conference goals are to strengthen ties between Arctic peoples and promote Inuit human, cultural, political and environmental rights and policies at the international level.

• Tatshenshin-Alesk Wilderness National Park in northern BC was declared a World Heritage Site by UNESCO. The park is comanaged by the provincial govt and the Champagne and Aishihik First Nations. Dominated by the rugged St. Elias Mountains, the park connects neighbouring parks Kluane in the Yukon, and Glacier Bay and Wrangell-St. Elias in Alaska, thereby forming the world's largest protected international region.

• The Canadian Rocky Mountain Parks, which include the contiguous national parks Yoho, Kootenay, Banff and Jasper, and also the Burgess Shale fossil deposit and Mount Robson, Mount Assiniboine and Hamber Provincial Parks, were declared a World Heritage Site by UNESCO.

The parks range over the Alb.-BC border, and boast spectacular mountain scenery, flora and fauna.

• Mingan Archipelago National Park was established off the north St. Lawrence shore between Havre-Saint-Pierre and Anticosti Is., Que. The unique archipelago comprises 40 islands and 800 islets, which include fantastic water- sculpted limestone formations, grottoes, arches, sea stack monoliths and 15-m cliffs. Common eiders, Atlantic puffins and kittiwakes are common, as are grey, harbour and harp seals. Nine types of whale feed off the archipelago, including minke, humpback, fin and the fabled blue whale.

• Ivvavik National Park in northwestern Yukon, on the Beaufort Sea, was established. It was the 1st national park created through a lands claim agreement — and a 16,999-km² gift to Canada by the Inuvialuit people. The park includes the British Mountains — Canada's only non-glaciated mountain range, and also, the most northern-ranging populations of moose and Dall's sheep.

• Korean-Canadians owned 85% of all Ont. corner stores.

• There were 9 potash mines in Sask.

• Lithoprobe, the largest geoscientific research program ever undertaken in Canada, began to probe deep within the earth's crust to develop a 3-dimensional understanding of how North America evolved.

• Canada joined the international Ocean Drilling Program to study geological processes deep within the world's oceans.

• The Gardiner Museum of Ceramic Art was established in Toronto by philanthropists George R. and Helen Gardiner. Featuring over 2,600 works, the museum specializes in 15th- and 16th-century Italian majolica, 17th-century English Delftware, and 18th-century Meissen.

• Paulette Jiles (b 1943) published *Celestial Navigation*, for which she received the Gov-Gen.'s Award for Poetry.

• Czech-born novelist Josef Skvorecky (b 1924) published *The Engineer of Human Souls*, for which he received the Gov-Gen.'s Award.

• Nicole Brossard (b 1943) published the collection of poetry *Journal Intime*, for which she received the Gov-Gen.'s Award.

1985

Jan. 1 Nancy Eaton (1961–1985), the great-great-granddaughter of department–store tycoon Timothy Eaton, was found dead in her Toronto apartment, a victim of multiple stab wounds. The victim's childhood friend, Andrew Leyshon-Hughes, was charged with the murder. CTV capitalized on the sensational crime with the television movie *The Death and Life of Nancy Eaton* (2003).

Jan. 2 The Que. Superior Court overturned provisions of Bill 101, which outlawed the use of languages other than French on commercial signs, ruling that the law violated Que.'s Human Rights Charter guaranteeing freedom of expression.

Jan. 3 Justice Samuel Grange (b 1920), head of an exhaustive Royal Commission into baby deaths at Toronto's Hospital for Sick Children, released a report that affirmed that nurse Susan Nelles, part of a 5-member nursing team on duty for most of the deaths and the only person ever charged, should not have been prosecuted. He recommended she receive compensation for her legal costs. The commission concluded that 8 of the 36 children who died at the hospital between June 1980 and Mar. 1981 were given deliberate overdoses of the heart drug digoxin by an unknown person or persons.

Jan. 15 For the 1st time, a special guard of the House of Commons was armed. The move was made as a precaution in the wake of the May 8, 1984, shooting in Que.'s National Assembly, which left 3 people dead and 13 injured.

Jan. 23 Que.'s acting Premier Bernard Landry (b 1937) announced that a retractable roof canopy would be built over Olympic Stadium in Montreal for a total cost of $125 million. The roof was part of the original plan of French architect Roger Taillebert, who designed the stadium. The orange and silver

Kevlar roof was completed in 1987 and draped from the 169-m tower overhang. Upkeep was $700,000 a year. It did not fully retract and remained capped on the stadium until 1997 when it was removed and then replaced with a permanent roof in 1999.

Jan. 26 Industry Minister Frank Miller won the Ont. Conservative leadership over Larry Grossman in a dramatic and close 3rd balloting.

Jan. 30 Consumer and Corporate Affairs Minister Michel Côté (b 1942) outlined the federal govt's new metric policy. It required businesses to sell and advertise food, gasoline and home furnishings in metric, although imperial measures might also be provided in certain circumstances. Ottawa had suspended its enforcement of metric laws on Nov. 29, 1983, after 2 Toronto gas station owners were cleared in an Ont. court of violating the Weights and Measures Act for selling gasoline by the gallon.

• Canadian tax collection laws were changed so individuals whose taxes were in dispute did not have to pay before going through an impartial appeal process. The change was retroactive to Jan. 1.

Feb. 7 Justice Minister John Crosbie initiated formation of an independent commission under Justice Jules Deschênes (1923–2000), former chief hustice of the Que. Superior Court, to investigate the presence of Nazi war criminals in Canada and the question of whether they could be prosecuted, extradited or deported. The report of the Commission of Inquiry was submitted to the govt Dec. 30, 1986.

Feb. 11 PM Brian Mulroney and Nfld. Premier Brian Peckford signed an offshore energy pact giving Nfld. $225 million to develop its petroleum industry, and much of the potential revenues from the oil fields. The deal paved the way to the July 18, 1988, Hibernia oil agreement.

Feb. 12 Minister of Defence Robert Coates (b 1928) resigned after it became known that on Nov. 29, 1984, he had visited a West German bar that featured nude dancers and pornographic movies. An *Ottawa Citizen* story suggested the visit might have posed a security threat.

Feb. 13 External Affairs Minister Joe Clark pledged another $15 million to Ottawa's African famine relief fund to keep pace with a huge outpouring of private donations. The fund was created in Nov. 1984 through a program where Ottawa matched private donations to drought and famine-stricken Ethiopians. The govt contribution marked Ottawa's last to the fund on a match basis.

Feb. 16 Guy Lafleur (b 1951) took to the Forum ice for the last time in a Montreal Canadiens uniform and was met with a 5-minute standing ovation from a full house of 18,000. The great right-winger was the 1st to score 50 goals and 100 points in 6 consecutive seasons. He retired from the Habs as the team's all-time leading scorer, with 518 goals and 1,246 points. He won 5 Stanley Cups with Montreal, and also 3 Art Ross Trophies (1976, 1977, 1978), 2 Hart Memorial Trophies (1977, 1978), 3 Lester Pearson Trophies (1976, 1977, 1978) and 1 Conn Smythe (1977). His number 10 was the 6th Canadiens number to be retired. Lafleur returned to the ice (after being inducted into the Hockey Hall of Fame in 1988) with the New York Rangers for the 1988–1989 season, then played 2 seasons with the Quebec Nordiques, finally retiring with that team after the 1990–1991 season.

Feb. 20 American relief pitcher Bill Caudill signed a 5-year contract with the Toronto Blue Jays worth $10.5 million, making Caudill the highest-paid athlete in the country. Picked up to help the highly competitive team over the hump, Caudill saved only 16 games over the next 2 seasons. He was released with a blown-out arm after the 1986 season and collected the remainder of his contract from home.

Mar. 12 Armenian terrorists carrying shotguns, revolvers and explosives attacked the Turkish embassy in Ottawa. A Canadian security guard, Claude Brunelle, was killed. Twelve hostages were held for more than 4 hours.

Mar. 17–18 PM Mulroney and US President Ronald Reagan held the "Shamrock Summit" in Quebec City. It produced a call for a new liberal trade agreement between the countries (during the 1983 Tory leadership campaign, Mulroney spoke against free

Year
1985

trade: "It effects Canadian sovereignty and we'll have none of it.") It also produced the Joint Canada–United States Statement on Acid Rain, to examine the issues and appoint a Special Envoy from each country to assess the problem. The new era of amiable Canada-US relations hit its stride when both leaders and their spouses completed the summit with a rendition of "When Irish Eyes Are Smiling."

Mar. 21 Ivan Reitman (b 1946) received a special achievement award from the Academy of Canadian Cinema for his "outstanding contributions to the Canadian and international world of film comedy." Reitman made his 1st film, *Orientation*, in 1969, a student piece about freshman orientation. He later made *Animal House* with John Belushi, a Hollywood film that grossed $200 million. He produced and directed *Meatballs* in 1979 and *Ghostbusters* in 1984.

Mar. 26 William Davis was succeeded by Frank Miller (1927) as premier of Ont. Davis, who unexpectedly announced his retirement Oct. 8, 1984, had been premier since 1971.

Mar. 28 Federal Energy Minister Pat Carney (b 1935) tabled in the Commons an energy accord reached between Ottawa and BC, Alb. and Sask. The accord gave the oil industry at least $800 million in extra revenue for 1985. On Dec. 20, Carney introduced legislation in the Commons to provide new incentives for frontier and offshore oil exploration. Together, these moves effectively wiped out the last vestiges of the former Liberal govt's 1980 National Energy Program.

Mar. 29 Nine Canadian airmen and 1 US exchange officer were killed when 2 Canadian Forces C–130 Hercules transport planes collided and exploded at CFB Edmonton.

Apr. 2 The Progressive Conservatives under Premier Brian Peckford won the Nfld. provincial election. The Tories captured 36 of 52 seats; the Liberals took 15 and the NDP 1.

Apr. 12 A Canadian satellite was launched from the US space shuttle *Discovery* on behalf of Telesat Canada.

Apr. 17 Section 15 of the Canadian Charter of Rights and Freedom, which banned discrimination on the basis of sex, age, colour, religion, race, national or ethnic origin and physical or mental handicaps, was proclaimed 3 years after the rest of the charter came into effect (Apr. 17, 1982).

• The Women's Legal Education and Action Fund (LEAF) filed its application for incorporation as a non-profit organization to intentionally coincide with the enactment date of Section 15 of the Canadian Charter of Rights and Freedoms. LEAF had its founding meetings Apr. 13 and 14.

Apr. 24 The Supreme Court of Canada ruled that the federal Lord's Day Act, used by some provinces to restrict or ban Sunday shopping, was unconstitutional.

May 2 After holding power since 1943, the Ont. Conservative Party lost the provincial election. The Liberals, under David Peterson, and the NDP, led by Bob Rae, toppled the Tories, led by Frank Miller. Neither the Liberals nor the NDP won a clear majority. The final tally was 52 Conservatives, 48 Liberals and 25 NDP. On May 28, after almost 4 weeks of closed-door meetings, Liberal leader David Peterson and his NDP counterpart, Bob Rae, signed a 2-year agreement paving the way for a Liberal minority govt in the province. Peterson was sworn in as premier on June 26.

May 3 Delegates attending the annual convention of the Alb.-BC District of the Lutheran Church–Missouri Synod voted to form an autonomous Canadian church — the Evangelical Lutheran Church of Canada.

May 4 Sask. Métis elected an administration to negotiate their rights with Ottawa. The Métis government of Sask. was the 1st Métis governing body since 1885, when Louis Riel established the provincial Métis govt at Batoche.

May 9 The Supreme Court of Canada unanimously ruled that Operation Dismantle had no legal grounds on which to challenge testing of US cruise missiles over northwestern Canada.

May 13 The NDP, led by Tony Penikett (b 1945), won an upset victory in the Yukon territorial elections by taking 8 of the 16 seats. The Conservatives won 6 and the Liberals 2.

• A strike lasting more than 5 months by Eaton's employees at 6 southern Ont. stores ended when officials of the Retail, Wholesale and Department Store Union accepted the company's offer without a vote by union members.

May 17 Que. Premier René Lévesque summarized the requirements necessary for Que. to rejoin the Constitution framework: exception from the bulk of clauses forming the Charter of Rights and Freedoms, recognition that Que. is a distinct society, and exclusive power over provincial language matters.

May 23 The Supreme Court of Canada ruled that Breathalyzer evidence was inadmissible if police failed to inform drivers promptly of their right to call a lawyer. The ruling meant that police had to tell the driver of this right the moment he or she agreed to a breath test. In a related case, the Supreme Court of Canada, in a 4–3 decision, ruled on July 31 that random stops by police to curb impaired driving were reasonable and acceptable.

May 24 Simpson's Ltd. and the Retail, Wholesale and Department Store Union reached a tentative agreement, marking the 1st labour contract in the history of the department store chain.

May 29 Steve Fonyo (b 1965), a 1-legged cancer victim, completed his 14-month cross-Canada "Journey for Lives," when he dipped his artificial leg in the Pacific Ocean at Mile 0 of the Trans-Canada Highway.

May 30 Academy of Canadian Cinema chairman Robert Lantos (b 1949) announced the creation of a national television awards program for English- and French-language television production. The 1st Gemini Awards ceremony, recognizing excellence in craft and technical categories, was held in Toronto on Dec. 3 and 4, 1986. The Prix Gemeaux, honouring French-language television production, was launched in Montreal on Feb. 15, 1987.

May 31 Twelve people, including 4 children, died in a tornado that swept across central Ont., leaving damage estimated in the hundreds of millions of dollars. Barrie was hardest hit, where as many as 200 homes, several businesses and a racetrack were destroyed.

Also in May

• Robert Lantos and Stephen Roth were the 1st Canadian producers to have 2 movies entered in the official program of the Cannes International Film Festival in 1 year: *Joshua Then and Now*, directed by Ted Kotcheff (b 1931) from Mordecai Richler's 1980 novel, and *Night Magic*, a Canada-France co-production directed by Lewis Furey, and written by Furey and Leonard Cohen.

June 6 The Commons passed legislation raising the dollar threshold on foreign investment necessary for scrutiny by the Foreign Investment Review Agency (FIRA), and changing the name of FIRA to Investment Canada.

June 12 The Commons approved changes (Bill 31) to the Indian Act that would return Indian status and band membership to some 16,000 women who, because of a clause in the act, lost their status when they married non-Native peoples. Introduced by Indian Affairs Minister David Crombie, the new legislation also aimed to eliminate discrimination by making the Indian Act conform to the Canadian Charter of Rights and Freedoms. (The amendment followed the case of Jeannette Corbiere Lavell Oct. 9, 1971). The amendments were proclaimed June 28. However, the legislation failed to define how band membership was determined, so many women were subsequently denied the right to return to bands. On July 7, 1995, the Federal Court ruled that band chiefs could not deny membership to women who had previously lost band status after marriage.

June 13 The Supreme Court of Canada ruled that English-only laws passed by the Man. legislature over most of the previous 100 years "are and always have been invalid and of no force or effect" because they did not follow the Man. Act of 1870, the federal bill which stated that all acts of legislation "shall" be in both French and English. Because of the havoc that dissolution of the laws would cause, the court ruled that the laws would remain in force while documents were translated into French. The court also overturned an 1890 provincial law making English the only official language.

June 20 Que. premier René Lévesque announced his resignation as leader of the Parti Québécois. Lévesque would remain premier until a successor was chosen Sept. 29.

June 23 Three hundred and seven passengers and 22 crew members died aboard Air India flight 182 from Toronto to Britain. No one survived the crash, caused by a bomb exploding inside the plane 150 km off the coast of Ireland. The same day a bomb in luggage aboard a CP plane en route from Vancouver to Bangkok killed 2 baggage handlers at Tokyo's Narita Airport. Authorities linked both events to Sikh terrorists. On Apr. 28, 2003, Vancouver businessman Ripudaman Singh Malik and Kamloops labourer Ajaib Bagri stood trial in a BC court for the murder of all 329 passengers.

June 25 Justice André Brossard of the Que. Superior Court ruled unconstitutional the Que. govt's law realigning the provincial school system along linguistic rather than religious lines. The law had been challenged by Protestant school boards.

June 27 The federal govt gave in to public pressure and agreed not to stop the full indexing of old age security payments to the rate of inflation.

June 29 The city of St. Thomas, Ont., marked the 100th anniversary of the death of Jumbo the elephant by erecting a life-sized, concrete-and-steel monument to the star of the Barnum and Bailey Circus killed in the town when struck by a train. Jumbo was said to have been the largest African elephant in captivity ever and has been credited with lending his name to everything from jet aircraft to ice-cream cones.

Also in June

• The Disabled Women's Network (DAWN) was founded to provide support, information and resources to women with disabilities.

July 9 Richard T. Price, a senior bureaucrat in the federal Indian Affairs Department and an ordained United Church minister, was charged in Vancouver with breach of trust in connection with the alleged leak of a cabinet document outlining proposed cuts of $312 million in funding to Native programs.

July 20 After 30 hours of deliberation, a jury in Red Deer, Alb., found former Eckville high school teacher Jim Keegstra guilty on a charge of willfully promoting hatred against Jews. Keegstra was fined $5,000. The Alb. Court of Appeal overturned the verdict on June 6, 1986, and on Dec. 13, 1990, the Supreme Court of Canada ruled there should be a new trial. A 2nd Alb. jury convicted Keegstra on July 10, 1992, but the Alb. Court of Appeal overturned the conviction on Sept. 7, 1994. The case again went back to the Supreme Court of Canada, which, on Feb. 28, 1996, upheld the 1992 conviction on the grounds that hate propogation was not protected under freedom of expression laws in the Canadian Charter of Rights and Freedoms.

Aug. 11 The American icebreaker *Polar Sea* challenged Canada's Arctic sovereignty by completing a voyage through the Northwest Passage without permission of the Canadian govt.

Sept. 1 A joint US-French expedition discovered the wreck of the *Titanic*, 590 km southeast of Nfld. at a depth of 3,810 m. Claims to the ship came to a head July 22, 1987.

Sept. 3 Toronto-based De Havilland Aircraft agreed to sell 10 Dash–8 commuter planes, and options for 10 more, to Horizon Air of Seattle, Washington. The $200 million deal was the largest commercial contract signed by the Canadian company to date.

Sept. 4 Daniel Nicolas Dimitri was born to Mila and PM Brian Mulroney, their 4th child.

Sept. 5 A 13-member Royal Commission on the economy headed by Donald Macdonald, a former Liberal finance minister, presented a 2,000-page report calling for free trade with the US and for other extensive changes to Canada's social and political structure. The report also recommended that tax breaks and other social programs, such as family allowances, be replaced by a Universal Income Security program. The commission had been established Nov. 5, 1982.

Sept. 9 PM Brian Mulroney told cabinet ministers not to award govt jobs or contracts to immediate relatives, and initiated a code to prevent conflict of interest in the public service. Opposition leader John Turner had earlier attacked the govt for filling 1,200 govt-related posts with Tories.

Sept. 23 Federal Fisheries Minister John Fraser (b 1931) resigned his cabinet post after a public disagreement with PM Mulroney. Fraser had approved the release of more than 1 million cans of tuna tested as potentially unfit for human consumption.

Sept. 25 The $30 million, 4,400-m^2 Tyrrell Museum of Palaeontology opened in the Badlands region near Drumheller, southern Alb. Canada's only museum dedicated solely to the study of dinosaurs keeps a permanent display of more than 800 prehistoric fossils. The museum is located on the spot where Joseph Burr Tyrrell, on an 1884 coal expedition with the Geological Survey of Canada, discovered a vast deposit of dinosaur bones.

• Federal Communications Minister Marcel Masse (b 1936) resigned from cabinet after learning he was under investigation for alleged overspending in the 1984 federal election campaign. On Nov. 30, Masse returned to cabinet after he was cleared of all charges.

Sept. 29 Pierre Marc Johnson (b 1946), son of former Que. Union Nationale premier Daniel Johnson, won a 1st-ballot victory at the Parti Québécois leadership race. He pledged that the next election would not be fought on the issue of Que. independence. Hours before Johnson's victory, Premier René Lévesque announced he was resigning his seat, which left the PQ with a working majority of 1 in the National Assembly. Lévesque, a former journalist and broadcaster, founder of the Parti Québécois, had served as its leader since 1968, and was Que. premier from 1976 to 1985. He died from a heart attack Nov. 1, 1987.

• Lincoln Alexander was named lt-gov. of Ont. The 1st African-Canadian to hold a vice-regal position in Canada, he had also been the 1st black federal MP and cabinet minister (June 25, 1968).

Sept. 30 Agriculture Minister John Wise planned a

moratorium on foreclosures by the Farm Credit Corp., the 2nd such moratorium in less than a year.

• Calgary-based Northlands Bank closed, becoming the 2nd western bank to collapse within a month. On Sept. 1, Edmonton-based Canadian Commercial Bank closed its doors to customers, marking the 1st time in 62 years a Canadian bank had failed. The failures, despite the relative size of the 2 banks, created the worst banking crisis in the country since the Great Depression. On Oct. 24, 1986, Supreme Court of Canada Justice Willard Estey (b 1919) absolved the govt of any blame for the bank collapse but stated the bank regulators had been too slow to respond to signs of the banks' demise.

Oct. 13 Don Getty (b 1933), once a quarterback for the Edmonton Eskimos, was elected leader of the Alb. Conservative Party, and became the new premier of the province, succeeding Peter Lougheed, who announced his retirement June 26.

Oct. 14 A large piece of wall, part of Lock 7 in the Welland Canal, collapsed, trapping dozens of vessels in L. Erie and beyond, and also stranding others due to pass through the canal into the upper Great Lakes.

Oct. 16 The Toronto Blue Jays, in post-season play for the 1st time, lost the American League Championship (ALC) series to the Kansas City Royals, 4 games to 3. This was the 1st year the ALC series was expanded from 5 games to 7. The Blue Jays were leading 3 games to 1 before they dropped the final 3.

Oct. 21 Nick Sibbeston (b 1943), the 1st Native northerner to become a lawyer, was elected govt leader of the Northwest Territories.

Oct. 22–23 Opposing the views of British PM Margaret Thatcher at the Commonwealth leaders' conference in Nassau, PM Brian Mulroney urged that mandatory economic sanctions be used against South Africa because of its apartheid policies. The next day, speaking before the UN General Assembly, Mulroney stated that Canada might sever relations with Pretoria unless South Africa took measures to dismantle apartheid. Canada, with other Commonwealth nations, placed economic sanctions on South Africa Aug. 5, 1986.

Oct. 25 A report by a special parliamentary committee aimed at bringing federal laws into line with the Charter of Rights and Freedoms, recommended that mandatory retirement be abolished, that women be permitted combat roles in the armed forces, and that discrimination against homosexuals be outlawed by law.

Oct. 31 The federal govt announced that Canada would accept up to 115,000 immigrants in 1986, about 30% more than in 1985.

Nov. 8 Simon Reisman (b 1919), the man who negotiated the Auto Pact with the US in 1965, was named Canada's chief negotiator in the free trade talks with the US. The appointment was made following PM Mulroney's Sept. 26 request to the US to begin negotiations on a free trade deal. President Reagan notified Congress of his intent to pursue a deal on Dec. 10. Official negotiations began June 17, 1986. By Oct. 3, 1987, a trade agreement was established and initiated, and ready to be signed by President Reagan and PM Mulroney on Jan. 2, 1988.

Nov. 12 Standard and Poor's Rating Service announced that Ont. had lost its prized Triple-A credit rating and was downgraded to a rating of Double-A.

Nov. 18 Michel Côté, minister responsible for Canada Post, tabled an independent report in the Commons recommending that the Crown corporation be ordered to provide acceptable mail service without govt subsidies by 1990, or be taken over by the private sector.

Dec. 2 Que. Liberals, led by Robert Bourassa, easily defeated the ruling Parti Québécois. The Liberals won 99 seats and the Parti Québécois 23. Bourassa lost his own seat in the election, but regained his place in the National Assembly Jan. 20, 1986, by taking the Montreal riding of St.-Laurent.

• De Havilland Aircraft, a Crown corporation, was sold to the US Boeing Corp. for an estimated $155 million.

Dec. 10 Swedish diplomat Raoul Wallenberg, missing since 1945 and last seen in Berlin seeking the

release of imprisoned Jews, was declared by the Commons Canada's 1st honorary citizen. The move enabled the federal govt to demand disclosure of his whereabouts from the USSR.

Dec. 12 All 256 passengers died as a DC-8, chartered by the US military, stalled and crashed after takeoff near Gander, Nfld. It was the worst air disaster on Canadian soil. The soldiers and crew were returning home to the US for the Christmas holidays.

Dec. 20 Ont. Premier David Peterson announced the end of Queen's Counsel appointments, stating that the practice was being abolished because it had been used by previous govts as a form of political patronage.

Dec. 21 Assent was given to a Commons bill under which prostitutes would be prohibited from stopping motor vehicles, interrupting pedestrian or vehicular traffic and making any other public attempts to solicit customers. The bill also aimed to prevent customers from propositioning prostitutes in public places.

Dec. 30 McClelland & Stewart, the prominent but money-losing Canadian publisher, was sold for an undisclosed sum to Toronto real estate developer Avie Bennett. The country's most ardent supporter of Canadian authors was founded in 1906. Its backlist contained a virtual who's who of great writers, including Lucy Maud Montgomery, Stephen Leacock, Brian Moore, Bliss Carman, Marie-Claire Blais (b 1939), Margaret Laurence, Pierre Berton, Margaret Atwood, Leonard Cohen, Farley Mowat and Mordecai Richler. Publisher Jack McClelland remained with the firm as a consultant until Feb. 1987.

Also in Dec.

• Old Town Lunenburg, NS, was declared a United Nations World Heritage Site. The town had been created by the British in 1753, based on a standard grid pattern with 7 streets running north-south and 9 running east-west. Old Town is home to 400 brightly painted wooden buildings, all built during the 1700s and 1800s.

• Hydro Que., with US-based engineering and project management firm Bechtel Corporation, completed Phase I, La Grande hydroelectric project in the James Bay watersheds, in northern Que. The $13.8 billion project included 4 major dams and diversion works, which redirected waters of the Caniapiscau, Eastmain, Opinaca and Petite Opinaca Rivers into La Grande R. Phase I flooded nearly 10,000 km^2 of pristine natural land and created a total hydroelectric capacity of 10,300 megawatts (MW).

Also in 1985

• PEI, NS, Nfld., NB, Que., Ont. and Man. joined forces in the new Canadian Acid Rain Control Program, agreeing to cut SO_2 emissions by 2.3 million tonnes by 1994. The goal was reached in 1993.

• The Great Lakes Charter was signed by the 8 US Great Lakes states — Minnesota, Wisconsin, Illinois, Indiana, Michigan, Ohio, Pennsylvania and New York — and Ont. and Que. The good-faith agreement committed the signatories to safeguard Great Lakes Basin waters from deterioration caused by water diversion and consumption. The same signatories signed the Annex to the Charter on June 18, 2001, reaffirming their commitment protecting the international resource.

• The Ont. govt passed Bill 30, providing full funding to Grades 11, 12 and 13 in Catholic schools. The Ont. Court of Appeal ruled the bill constitutional in 1986, as did the Supreme Court of Canada in 1987.

• The Canadian Missing Children Program was launched as a joint initiative involving the RCMP, Canada Customs and Revenue Agency, Citizenship and Immigration, and the Department of Foreign Affairs. Renamed Our Missing Children in 1993, the program was established to prevent abductions of Canadian children in and across international borders, and to prevent other crimes against youth. In Aug. 1986, the program opened Missing Children's Registry (later the National Missing Children Services), which between 1988 and 2004 opened 8,052 missing children cases, and closed 6,052 of these. The National Missing Children Services' 2004 caseload was 2,000 cases.

• Imperial Oil's Cold L. oil sands project in northern Alb. started up. By 2003, it was producing approximately 120,000 barrels of bitumen a day, accounting for nearly half of Imperial's total daily hydrocarbon production.

• Lynn Johnston (b 1947), the wit, wisdom and conscience behind the popular cartoon strip *For Better or For Worse*, won the National Cartoonists Society's Reubens Award as Cartoonist of the Year. The award, named after Rube Goldberg, saw Johnston join a list of creators spanning cartoon history from Al Capp (*L'il Abner*) and Milton Caniff (*Steve Canyon*) to Bill Watterson (*Calvin & Hobbes*) and Gary Trudeau (*Doonesbury*). The strip (launched in 1979) appeared in more than 2,000 daily and Sunday papers by 2003, despite newspapers occasionally dropping it whenever Johnston delved into "controversial areas." (Because of a sequence in which one of her characters announced his homosexuality, 19 editors dropped the strip permanently.)

• The Canadian federal debt climbed to $250 billion.

• Library worker Karen Andrews began a struggle for family coverage under the Ontario Health Insurance Plan (OHIP) to have herself, her same-sex partner and the children they co-parented deemed a family under health benefit legislation. In 1988, an Ont. court upheld the Ministry of Health decision not to grant Andrews family benefits, on the grounds that a relationship between same-sex partners could not lead to procreation, and therefore, the need to support children.

• The Historic Area of Quebec City, including much of the walled interior and Lower Town along Boulevard Champlain, was declared a United Nations World Heritage Site. The city was founded by Champlain in 1608. Almost half the buildings in the Historic Area were built before 1850.

• Fred Wheatley (1913–1990), linguist and leading expert on the Ojibwa language, was made Professor Emeritus at the University of Toronto.

• Coles bookstores began discounting best-selling titles. The practice was twinned with demands for deeper discounts on books from Canadian publishers.

• Artist Jack Shadbolt completed the acrylic *Elegy for an Island*.

• Timothy Findley published the novel *Not Wanted on the Voyage*, a fantastic version of Noah and the Flood.

• Margaret Atwood published the novel *The Handmaid's Tale*, for which she received the Gov-Gen.'s Award and furthered her international reputation as a leading contemporary writer.

• Novelist Wayne Johnston (b 1958) published his 1st book, *The Story of Bobby O'Mally*, which won the W.H. Smith/Books in Canada First Novel Award.

• Victor-Lévy Beaulieu (b 1945) published the novel set in post-referendum Que., *Steven le hérault*.

• Jacques Brault published the novel *Agonie*, for which he received the Gov-Gen.'s Award.

• Cora Taylor (b 1936) published the classic teen novel *Julie*.

• Jean Little (b 1932) published her classic children's novel *Mama's Gonna Buy You a Mockingbird*.

• The collection *Overhead in a Balloon: Stories of Paris*, by Mavis Gallant, was published. It depicted French life in the post-war period.

• Brian Moore published the popular historical novel set against the Jesuit missions of New France *Black Robe*.

• Bharati Mukherjee (b 1940) published the book of short stories *Darkness*.

• Fernand Ouellette published the controversial novel *Lucie ou Un midi en novembre*, for which he received the Gov-Gen.'s Award.

• Novelist Henry Kreisel's internment diary (concerning events that occurred during his 18-month internment in England during WW II) and other autobiographical materials were combined with essays on his work by 8 critics in *Another Country: Writings By and About Henry Kreisel*. Kreisel was named University Professor at the U. of Alb. in 1975.

• U. of Toronto historian Allan Greer published *Peasant, Lord, and Merchant: Rural Society in Three Quebec Parishes, 1740–1840*, characterizing the seigniorial system in early Que. as feudal and fundamentally exploitive. The book received the Canadian Historical Association's 1986 Sir John A. Macdonald Prize.

• Yolande Villemaire (b 1949) published *La Constellation du cygne*, for which she won the Grand Prix of the *Journal de Montréal*.

• Terence Dickinson published *Night Watch*, a best-selling introductory guide for the amateur astronomer.

• Mel Hurtig published the exhaustive *Canadian Encyclopedia*, in 3 volumes, which he would later sell to McClelland & Stewart.

• Margaret Hollingsworth published 5 of her plays in the collection *Wilful Acts*.

• Poet Irving Layton published the 1st volume of his memoirs, *Waiting for the Messiah*.

• Poet Fred Wah published *Waiting for Saskatchewan*, for which he received the Gov-Gen.'s Award.

• Jazz guitarist Peter Leitch (b1944) recorded the critically acclaimed album *Exhilaration*, which included saxophone great Pepper Adams. The album was reissued on CD in 1993.

1986

Jan. 1 Finance Minister Michael Wilson placed a minimum tax of 24% on incomes over $50,000. The move was designed to prevent high-income earners from exploiting possible tax breaks.

Jan. 4 US President Reagan stated in his weekly radio address that ties between the US and Canada were so strong that "we're not only friends and neighbours, we're cousins."

Jan. 10 The federal govt cut off all assistance to companies seeking business with Libya because of Libya's occupation of northern Chad and its support of international terrorism.

Jan. 21 The day after passing a bill limiting cost-of-living increases to family allowances, the federal Conservative govt approved major income tax changes that included a $500,000 lifetime capital gains exemption and the elimination of the Registered Home Ownership Plan (RHOSP).

Jan. 23 James Morrison, a former RCMP corporal, ended a protracted legal battle when he interrupted his own jury trial in an Ottawa court and admitted his guilt. Morrison, known as "Long Knife," admitted he breached the Official Secrets Act in 1955 when he turned a prized double agent over to the Soviets.

Jan. 28 Brazil signed a 3-year agreement to purchase up to 4.5 million tonnes of Canadian wheat.

Jan. 29 The US National Geographic Society announced that the largest collection of fossils in North America had been unearthed in NS along the shore of the Bay of Fundy's Minas Basin. The regional rock formations reveal ancient forest and plant life, extinct amphibians, worms, anthropoids, corals, bryozoa, cephalopods, trilobites and a large cast of other long-dead creatures, including evidence of the now-famous *Pachygenelus*, an odd mammal-like reptile. Preservation of the Fundy fossil record is the responsibility of the Fundy Geological Museum in Parrsboro, NS.

Jan. 31 The value of the Canadian dollar fell to an all-time low 70.20 cents US.

• An earthquake measuring 5.5 on the Richter scale struck Ont. and much of eastern Canada and the US at 11:47 a.m. EST. Although people from Barrie, Ont., to Washington, D.C., felt the ground shake beneath them, there were no deaths or injuries reported.

• A back-to-work order was passed in Sask. to end a 16-month labour dispute involving rotating strikes by 12,500 members of the Sask. govt employees union.

Feb. 3 After a month-long uproar in the Commons, Deputy PM Erik Nielsen (b 1924) apologized for having eavesdropped on Liberal party caucus meetings during the mid-1960s.

Feb. 8 A VIA Rail Supercontinental passenger train and a CN freight train collided near Hinton, Alb., killing 26 people. The freight train had passed a warning light and a red stop signal and jumped a closed switch into the path of the oncoming Supercontinental.

Feb. 14 PM Mulroney arrived in Paris for the start of the Francophone summit (Feb. 17–19), which was attended by representatives from 40 countries. Also present was Que. Premier Bourassa.

Feb. 17 The interest rate on Canada Savings Bonds was increased to 10% from 8.5% for a period of 4 months in an attempt to dam a flood of redemptions.

Feb. 19 The Canadian Armed Forces ordered compulsory urine tests to check for drug abuse among its 82,000 members.

Feb. 22 The Canadian Ultraviolet Images (UVI) was launched around Swedish Satellite Viking to provide Canadian scientists with their 1st images of the entire spectrum of the aurora.

Feb. 27 Veteran Liberal MP and former cabinet minister Jean Chrétien, runner-up to John Turner at the previous Liberal leadership convention, resigned his Commons seat to return to private life.

Feb. 28 The Supreme Court of Canada ruled that police could enter a citizen's home to make an arrest without a warrant if a serious offence was involved and they had reasonable grounds to believe the occupant had committed the offence. The Court also ruled on a section of the Narcotic Control Act, which allowed police to assume that anyone possessing narcotics was also trafficking those narcotics. The Court ruled this unconstitutional, forcing the police to provide evidence of trafficking before that charge was laid.

Also in Feb.
• The world price of crude oil dropped sharply after OPEC failed to agree on a uniform price. Oil sold in New York for $31.70 a barrel in Nov. 1958 and for $13 in late Feb. of this year. The Canadian petroleum industry was shaken as domestic oil prices were pegged to world levels.

Mar. 9 Senator Jacques Hébert (b 1924) began a hunger strike to protest the govt's decision to eliminate the Katimavik Youth Program. The senator ended his hunger strike on Mar. 31, satisfied he had made his point. Senator Hébert had established the Katimavik (KATI) youth training and community service program in 1977; 15,000 Canadian youth served in the program in regions throughout the country until its budget was withdrawn in 1986. It would resurface as a program in 1994 through Youth Services Canada and regain federal support in 1999.

Mar. 11 The Task Force on Program Review, headed by Deputy PM Erik Nielsen, reported that 1,000 govt programs worth $92 billion were burdened with overregulation, unneeded duplication, bureaucratic confusion and pervasive waste.

Mar. 12 The federal govt approved the takeover of publishers Prentice-Hall Canada and Ginn and Co. by the US conglomerate Gulf & Western.

Mar. 18 Man. voters re-elected the NDP, under Premier Howard Pawley, which defeated Gary Filmon's Conservatives in a race that saw both sides capture 41% of the popular vote. Before recounts, the NDP won 30 seats, the Conservatives 26. Liberal leader Sharon Carstairs (b 1942) won her seat and became the 1st Liberal to sit in a provincial legislature west of Ont. since 1981.

Mar. 19 Sondra Gotlieb (b 1936), journalist and wife of Allan Gotlieb (b 1928), Canadian ambassador to the US, slapped her social secretary in the face at a black-tie dinner for PM Brian Mulroney at the embassy in Washington, D.C. The incident was reported internationally and was a national embarrassment.

Mar. 24 A feature-length documentary by Brigitte Berman, *Artie Shaw: Time Is All You've Got*, received the Oscar at the 59th Academy Awards. Although the film was not a financial success, Shaw sued Berman in an Ont. court after the Oscar win, claiming a 35% interest in the film's profits. The judge refused the claim.

Apr. 14 PM Brian Mulroney publicly supported the US bombing of suspected terrorist positions in Muammar Gadhafi's Libya. The bombing was a response to an Apr. 5 terrorist attack in Berlin that killed an American. US President Reagan referred to

the strike as "pre-emptive" and a form of "self-defence."

Apr. 21 Voters in PEI ended 7 years of Tory rule and swept Conservative premier James Lee out of office. The Liberal party led by Joe Ghiz (b 1945) won with a majority of the seats, taking 21 in the 32-seat house.

May 1 Shirley Carr was unanimously elected president of the Canadian Labour Congress at its bi-annual meeting in Toronto. She was the 1st woman and the 1st candidate from the public service sector to lead the 2-million-member congress.

May 2 PM Brian Mulroney, with Prince Charles and Princess Diana, opened Expo '86 in Vancouver. The World's Fair had participants from 54 nations and focused on transportation and communication. It was the last world's fair in North America. The exhibition closed Oct. 13. Attendance exceeded 22 million.

• Assisted only by dogs, 6 Canadian and American explorers became the 1st since Robert E. Peary in 1909 to reach the North Pole without mechanical assistance. They completed the 805-km trek in 56 days. Brent Boddy and Richard Weber (b 1959) were the Canadian members, and Will Steger, Paul Schurke, Ann Bancroft and Geoff Carroll the Americans. The group began their trip from Ellesmere Is.

May 8 Don Getty's Conservatives were re-elected in the Alb. provincial election, but with 14 less seats than after the last election. The Tories won 61 seats, the NDP 16, the Liberals 4 and the Representative Party 2.

May 9 Communications Minister Marcel Masse unveiled a 5-year, $25-million program in support of the Canadian music and recording industry.

May 12 Sinclair Stevens resigned as federal minister of regional industrial expansion because of conflict-of-interest allegations regarding a $2.6 million loan arranged by his wife. The money was used to rescue a holding company they owned that was securing federal grants. A report of a judicial inquiry into the matter was tabled in the House Dec. 3, 1987. Written by Justice William Parker (b 1914) of the Ont. Supreme Court, it stated Stevens had broken conflict of interest guidelines and demonstrated "complete disregard" for the code of conduct expected of him. His blind trust, it read, had 20–20 vision.

May 20 Halifax-born Sharon Wood (b 1957) became the 1st North American woman to reach the summit of Mount Everest.

May 21 Keith Alexander, millionaire president of Toronto-based Jetco Manufacturing Ltd., became the 1st company executive sentenced to jail by a Canadian court for a pollution-related offence: dumping illegal levels of toxins into the Metropolitan Toronto sewer system.

May 22 The US govt imposed heavy tariffs on imported cedar shakes and shingles to reduce what it termed unfair, low-priced competition from Canadian producers.

May 24 Rookie goaltender Patrick Roy (b 1965) led a lightly considered Montreal Canadiens team to victory over the Calgary Flames in the Stanley Cup final. At 20 years of age, Roy was the youngest goalie to win the Stanley Cup.

May 25 A Punjabi cabinet minister, Malkiat Singh Sidhu, was shot while on a visit to Vancouver Is. Four members of the International Sikh Youth Federation were charged in connection with the attempted murder and later sentenced to 20 years in prison. Sidhu returned to India, where he was later assassinated.

May 30 Five Montreal-area members of the Sikh separatist organization Babbar Khalsa were charged with conspiring to possess explosives to cause bodily harm. The arrests were linked to an Air India jet that was scheduled to leave New York City on June 1, 1985, 22 days before ill-fated Flight 182. Only 2 of the 5 men were convicted.

Also in May

• The North American Waterfowl Management Plan was signed by both the US and Canadian govts. To be implemented over 15 years, the plan aimed to bring waterfowl populations back to 1970s levels by restoring and protecting habitat and wetlands.

• Denys Arcand's (b 1941) *The Decline of the American Empire (Le Déclin de l'Empire Américain)* was shown in the prestigious Directors' Fortnight of the Cannes International Film Festival and won the International Critics' Prize. It was also nominated as Best Foreign Film of 1986 by the Academy of Motion Picture Arts and Sciences but lost the Oscar to *The Assault*, a Dutch film about the Nazi occupation. *Decline* was made for $1.6 million and earned more than $20 million internationally. It also won several Genie Awards, including Best Picture, Best Director and Best Screenplay, and at the Toronto Festival of Festivals, Most Popular Film and Best Canadian Film.

June 1 The new Divorce Act went into force, making divorces quicker, cheaper and easier to get, and making it harder to default on court-ordered family-maintenance payments. Couples could get divorced after living separately for 1 year, and partners who claimed they had suffered mental or physical cruelty or that their spouses had indulged in adultery could file for divorce at once.

• Canada played its 1st World Cup soccer game, losing 1–0 to France in Léon, Mexico.

June 9 Two US bounty hunters were sentenced by an Ont. court to 21 months in jail for the kidnapping of Toronto businessman and US bail-jumper Sidney Jaffe, who was wanted by police in Florida on several accounts of land fraud.

June 12–July 7 Ont. Medical Association doctors conducted a strike to protest a provincial ban on extra billing as outlined in the newly approved Bill 94.

June 19 The Competition Act came into effect, replacing the outdated Combines Investigation Act. The new act contained powers to preserve competition by restraining mergers. It also provided the Bureau of Competition Policy with powers to scrutinize and approve any acquisition, or bring matters to a tribunal.

June 20 Jean Drapeau, who was 1st elected mayor of Montreal in 1954, announced he was stepping down from the civic post after suffering a stroke. The always controversial and often tough-handed statesmen brought Montreal its subway (1966), the 1967 World Exposition, the Montreal Expos (1969) and the 1976 Olympic Games. In Dec., PM Mulroney appointed him special ambassador to UNESCO, in Paris.

June 27 Assent was given to the Employment Equity Act, effective Aug. 13, designed to establish equal employment opportunities and benefits to all Canadians "for reasons unrelated to ability," and "correct the conditions of disadvantage in employment experienced by women, Aboriginal Peoples, persons with disabilities, and persons who are, because of their race or colour, in a visible minority in Canada." The act applied to firms employing 100 or more people or in connection with federal work.

June 30 PM Brian Mulroney shuffled his cabinet, moving approximately half of his ministers into new positions, retiring 2, firing 4, adding 8 and increasing representation from Que. Among those dropped was former Deputy Prime Minister Erik Nielsen, who was replaced by former Transport Minister Don Mazankowski, who also became president of the Privy Council and govt House leader.

Also in June

• A govt evaluation team, in its final recommendation to cabinet, recommended that the Winnipeg-based Bristol Aerospace Group be awarded the maintenance contract for the new McDonnell-Douglas CF-18 Hornet fighter jets. The recommendation was based on cost and technical criteria. The Hornets replaced the Armed Forces not always reliable *Starfighter* jets, known in military circles as "Widow Makers." The new Hornets carried Sidewinder and Sparrow air-to-air missiles, Maverick air-to-ground missiles, conventional and electronically guided bombs, and M–61 20-mm cannon. The planes could reach a speed of Mach 1.8. Procurement of the jets ended in 1988. By 2003, the Armed Forces had 60 operational Hornets and 62 for training, testing and rotation. The govt awarded its CF–18 maintenance contract Oct. 31.

July 8 Declared "Tax Freedom Day" by the Fraser Institute, this was the day that all Canadians had earned enough money, since Jan. 1, to pay all their taxes.

July 13 Gail Greenough of Edmonton became the 1st Canadian, the 1st woman, and at age 24, the youngest competitor to win the World Show Jumping Championship, at a horse show in Aachen, Germany. Riding her 10-year-old chestnut gelding, Mr. T., she completed 4 rounds on an 8-obstacle course with no faults and no time violations.

July 14 The Ont. Supreme Court handed down a ruling upholding a provincial regulation allowing for prayer in public schools, despite arguments that the regulation compelled children to participate in religious observances.

July 17 Gerry Weiner (b 1933), federal minister of state for immigration, declared that all visitors from Portugal would require visas to enter Canada, making the Portuguese the only members of the European Union (EU) to require visas to enter Canada. The move was made to stifle an alleged trend of illegal immigration from the country.

July 21 Nordair bought Quebecair from the Que. govt for $10 million.

July 24 In an emergency sitting of Parliament, Assent was given to authorize the National Parole Board to keep dangerous criminals in prison to complete their sentences, rather than be released into mandatory supervision after completing two-thirds of their time.

July 30 Bill Vander Zalm (b 1934) defeated 11 other candidates to become leader of the BC Social Credit Party. He succeeded Bill Bennett, who stepped down.

July 31 In the case of *Sorochan vs Sorochan*, the Supreme Court of Canada ruled that Alb. farmer Alex Sorochan had to share his wealth with his common-law wife, Mary, who had raised their 6 children and had worked on "his" farm for 42 years.

Aug. 2 The 1986 Commonwealth Games, held in Edinburgh, Scotland, and boycotted by African nations, ended. Canada came 2nd in the medal count with 51 golds. Highlights included 3 golds in swimming by Alex Baumann and, in track and field, a gold in the 110-m hurdles by Mark McKoy (b 1961), a gold in the 100-m by Ben

Johnson (b 1961) and a gold in the 200-m by Angella (Taylor) Issajenko (b 1958).

Aug. 5 Canada joined other Commonwealth nations (Australia, the Bahamas, India, Zambia and Zimbabwe) in adopting economic sanctions against South Africa and its apartheid policy. Sanctions included bans on air links, new bank loans and govt contracts with majority-owned South African companies. Canadian sanctions were lifted Sept. 24, 1993, after the segregation system had been dismantled.

Aug. 11 One hundred and fifty-five Tamil refugees from Sri Lanka were found drifting in lifeboats off the coast of Nfld. Despite misleading officials by claiming they had begun their voyage in southern India and not West Germany, their actual point of embarkation, all were granted refugee status.

• The Crown corporation Canadair was sold to Bombardier Inc. of Montreal for $120 million. Bombardier rightly anticipated Canadair being awarded the federal govt's $1.2 billion CF–18 Hornet maintenance contract (Oct. 31). On Dec. 19, Assent was given to the Canadian Authorization Act, sealing the deal for Bombardier. In 1985, Bombardier had $420 million in assets with a profit of $16.1 million; Canadair had $478 million in assets and a profit of $19.6 million.

Aug. 25 PM Mulroney appointed Dalton Camp senior adviser to the cabinet in a move to help seal the leaks in the Conservative ship.

Also in Aug.
• Alb. and NB each reached agreements with their respective medical associations to end extra billing before the issues resulted in strikes.

Sept. 16 PM Brian Mulroney declared that voters would have the final say on accepting a free trade deal with the US. Voters did not get that opportunity.

Sept. 18 A bronze statue of former Conservative PM John Diefenbaker was unveiled on Parliament Hill. Over 3,000 people attended the ceremony.

Oct. 1 John Fraser (b 1931) was elected to replace John Bosley, who had resigned as Speaker of the Commons. It was the 1st such election completed under secret ballot. Previous Speakers had been appointed by the PM with the nod from opposition parties.

Oct. 2 The Continental Bank sold most of its assets to Lloyds Bank PLC of London. Investor confidence in Continental had been shaken following the collapse of 2 western banks in the fall of 1985 (Northlands Bank and Canadian Commercial Bank). The new Lloyds Bank Canada became the largest Schedule B (foreign-owned) bank in the country.

Oct. 6 The Que. Statistics Bureau released figures showing that the population of the city of Montreal had dropped below the 1-million mark for the 1st time since 1951.

• The people of Canada were awarded the Nansen Medal by the UN for their role in assisting refugees from around the world; this was the 1st time the award was given to an entire nation.

Oct. 10 Defence Minister Perrin Beatty announced that women would be allowed to work as military police, on field ambulances and as air crew aboard military aircraft, but would not be allowed to work in combat units.

Oct. 16 The US Department of Commerce imposed a 15% tariff on all Canadian exports of softwood lumber to the US on the grounds that the Canadian lumber industry was unfairly subsidized. On Nov. 7, the federal govt imposed a heavy import duty on US corn as a retaliatory measure. On Dec. 30, Canadian and US negotiators reached a deal to end the bitter dispute over Canadian softwood lumber exports. Under the agreement, Canada was to impose an export tax of 15% on shipments of softwood lumber, offsetting alleged subsidization of Canadian timber-cutting fees.

Oct. 20 Premier Grant Devine and his Conservatives won the Sask. provincial election. The results gave the Conservatives 38 seats, the NDP 25 and the Liberals 1.

Oct. 22 The Social Credit Party, led by Bill Vander Zalm, won a strong majority in the BC provincial election, taking 47 seats, while the NDP won 22.

Oct. 23 In a unanimous decision, the Supreme Court of Canada declared that the forced sterilization of mentally handicapped persons was unconstitutional. The ruling was made in the case of a PEI mother who sought to have her mentally challenged daughter sterilized.

Oct. 30 Detailed tax information on 16 million Canadians was stolen from a Revenue Canada office in Toronto.

Oct. 31 Treasury Board President Robert de Cotret announced that a consortium led by Bombardier owner Montreal-based Canadair Ltd. would be awarded a billion-dollar maintenance contract for Canada's newly purchased fighter aircraft, the CF–18 Hornet, in spite of a lower bid by Bristol Aerospace Ltd., based in Winnipeg. Que. Premier Bourassa and federal minister of state had met with PM Mulroney Sept. 3 to press the Canadair case. On Nov. 3, Man. premier Howard Pawley led a small delegation, representing Man. business and labour interests, to Ottawa requesting that the PM reconsider the contract. But to no avail: on Dec. 19, Canadair was officially awarded the 1st-phase CF–18 maintenance contract, worth $1.2 billion over 20 years. On Jan. 5, 1988, Defence Department documents obtained by the *Globe and Mail* indicated that the federal cabinet rejected the advice of govt experts when it awarded the CF–18 contract to Canadair Ltd. instead of accepting the cheaper, technically superior proposal of Bristol Aerospace.

Nov. 2 In the biggest foreign takeover in Canadian history to date, Toronto businessman Robert Campeau (b 1923) purchased the New York–based retailer Allied Stores Corp. for $5 billion. In 1985, Allied had $4.1 billion (US) in sales. In another massive move, Campeau acquired Federated Department Stores on Apr. 1, 1988. The Federated flagship store was Bloomingdale's of New York. The deal was worth $6.58 billion. On Jan. 15, 1990, Allied and Federated filed for Chapter 11 bankruptcy protection in a US court. Together, the firms comprised 260 retail outlets; one hundred thousand employees and 300,000 supply workers were affected. The downturn marked the collapse of Robert Campeau's real estate and business empire. The bankruptcy protection had been preceded by

a National Bank of Canada decision (Jan. 4) to seize 13 million shares of Campeau Corp. after it defaulted on a $150 million loan.

Nov. 6 Minister of Consumer and Corporate Affairs Harvie Andre (b 1940) introduced Bill C–22, An Act to Amend the Patent Act, in the House of Commons. The bill would give pharmaceutical manufacturers 10 years' patent protection on new drugs. In return, the pharmaceutical industry promised to invest $14 billion into Canadian drug research. On Apr. 18, 1987, the Senate referred Bill C–22 to the Bonell Committee, which toured the country in late May and early June holding public meetings. Critics argued that increased patent protection would stifle competition and increase the cost of drugs. Multi-national drug companies, though, were adamant that the bill be passed; on July 6, 1987, they declared an investment strike and the suspension of all new research in Canada until the Senate passed it. After much parliamentary wrangling and widespread public opposition, the bill passed Parliament Nov. 19, 1987. Most of the Senate's Liberal majority abstained, thus allowing passage. A Conservative amendment to Bill C–22 — Bill C–91 — which extended patent protection to 20 years was given Assent Feb. 4, 1993. Bill C–91 was retroactive on drugs developed since Dec. 20, 1991. PM Mulroney was forced to use closure to get Bill C–91 through Parliament.

Nov. 8 Thirty-five cm of snow fell on Winnipeg in a 36-hour period. Wind was clocked at 90 km an hour and snowdrifts reached 2.5 m. It was the worst blizzard to hit the Winnipeg area in 20 years.

Nov. 9 Jean Doré (b 1945), leader of the Montreal Citizens' Movement, was elected Mayor of the city, ending 26 years of rule by the Civic Party. Former Civic Party leader Jean Drapeau stepped down June 20, 1986.

Nov. 20 Bata Ltd., one of the world's largest shoemakers, announced in Toronto that it was selling its South African operations, thus joining a growing list of companies pulling out of the apartheid-blighted nation.

Nov. 21 Five Soviet army deserters who had been smuggled out of Afghanistan arrived in Ottawa.

Nov. 22 The Royal Horse Show jumping competition in Toronto was won by a Canadian for the 1st time in 22 years when Ian Millar (b 1947), riding Big Ben, took the event.

Nov. 26 The Bank of BC sold all its assets to the Hong Kong Bank for an undisclosed price.

• Thomson Highway's *The Rez Sisters* was 1st produced by the Act IV Theatre Company and Native Performing Arts company at the Native Canadian Centre of Toronto. The play revolves around 7 sisters from the fictional Wasaychigan Hill Reserve (the rez) on Manitoulin Is., Ont. who plan to change their life fortunes at the "Biggest Bingo in the World" in Toronto. *The Rez Sisters* won the Dora Mavor Moore Award for Best New Play in 1986, and toured cross-Canada to sell-out audiences in 1988.

Nov. 29 American Deborah Brin became the only full-time woman rabbi in Canada, at Toronto's Darchei Noam Reconstructionist Synagogue. Also in 1988, Brin organized the 1st women's prayer service held at the Wailing Wall in Jerusalem.

Nov. 30 Liberal Chief John Turner was endorsed by delegates at a convention in Ottawa as they overwhelmingly turned down a leadership review urged by such prominent Liberals as Marc Lalonde and Senator Keith Davey.

Also in Nov.
• The 1st Honda of Canada plant opened in Alliston, Ont. A 2nd Alliston plant opened Sept. 1998. By 2004, the plants represented a $1.8 billion Honda investment, employed 4,300 and produced 390,000 vehicles a year.

Dec. 2 The Ont. legislature approved an amendment to the Human Rights Code to protect homosexuals from discrimination.

Dec. 10 John Charles Polanyi (b 1929), professor of chemistry at the U. of Toronto, won Canada's 4th Nobel Prize for his work on infrared chemiluminescence (chemical laser technology).

Dec. 16 External Affairs Minister Joe Clark confirmed in the Commons that, as a cost-cutting move, Canada would close embassies in Finland, Ecuador and the United Arab Emirates, and close consulates in Hamburg, Marseilles, Philadelphia and Perth, Australia.

Dec. 22 The CRTC ordered Canadian broadcasters to respect guidelines governing sex-role stereotyping on radio and television as a condition for licence renewals.

Dec. 30 Four players from the Swift Current Broncos junior hockey team (of the Western Hockey League) died in a bus accident while en route from Swift Current to Regina.

• The Duschênes Commission of Inquiry on War Criminals submitted its report to the Governor in Council. After assessing a master list of 774 suspects, and addendums covering a total of 109 others, the commission concluded that 341 suspects never landed in Canada, 21 landed but subsequently left, 86 died in Canada, there was no *prima facie* evidence on 154, and 4 could not be located. Ninety-seven were suspected with no *prima facie* evidence, and 20 positively identified as war criminals. The other cases remained outstanding when the report was issued. The report also recommended 3 alternatives for the prosecution of war criminals in Canada: trying the suspects in Canada under the Criminal Code; extradition for trial elsewhere; or the stripping of citizenship because of the fraud used to get it, followed by deportation. The commission also clarified that the nefarious Nazi doctor Dr. Joseph Mengele never came or applied to come to Canada. In 1987, Parliament passed legislation allowing Canadian courts to try war criminals whose atrocities were committed in foreign countries under foreign laws.

Also in 1986
• The population of Canada was 25,354,064: 17,827,382 (70.4%) lived south of the 49° parallel; 6,898,501 (27.3%) between 49° and 54°; 505,222 (2%) between 54° and 60°; and 78,226 (0.3%) north of 60°. Altogether, 74% of Canadians, or 18,218,596, lived within 150 km of the US border.

• There were 293,090 farms in Canada. The average farm size was 572 ha. Three percent of the total population lived on farms.

• GM Canada and Suzuki Motor Corporation formed a joint venture, establishing the independently incorporated Cami Automotive Inc. to build cars and SUVs in Ingersoll, Ont. The plant cost $500 million; production began Apr. 1989. Cami produced its 500,000th vehicle in Nov. 2003.

• The nation's 1st helicopter factory, the Bell Helicopter Textron Canada Ltd. plant at Mirabel Airport north of Montreal, went into operation. By 2003, the 49,145-m^2 plant produced over 2,700 helicopters (over 50% of the world's commercial turboshaft helicopters) for flight in more than 120 countries.

• The St. Catharines Stompers of the Class A New York–Pennsylvania League was established as an affiliate of the Toronto Blue Jays.

• Cam Fella, the 15.1-hand bay stallion referred to as "The Pacing Machine," was inducted into the Canadian Horse Racing Hall of Fame. Cam Fella was foaled in 1979 and purchased by Norm Faulkner and Norm Clements of Ont. for $140,000. The Standardbred began racing in 1981: and retired in 1983 the richest harness-racer in history, racking up total earnings of $2,041,367. Over that time the horse won 61 of 80 starts (28 consecutively), including the Canadian harness racing Triple Crown, the World Cup, Prix d'Ete, the American-National and the Mohawk Gold Cup. It also set 7 track records and was named Harness Horse of the Year in Canada and the US in 1982 and 1983. At stud, Cam Fella sired 14 million-dollar winners, the most of any Standardbred in history. In May 2000, at 22, Cam Fella was put down following a battle with cancer.

• The covered bridge across Que.'s Saguenay R. at Anse-St.-Jean was destroyed by flood.

• The average male teacher earned $39,000 a year; the average female teacher earned $34,500 ar year.

• The average length of hospital stay in Canada was 11.7 days.

• Architect Eberhard Zeidler (b 1926), Zeidler Roberts Partnership with Musson Caltell Mackey Partnership, and Downs/Archambault and Partners completed Canada Place for Expo '86 in downtown Vancouver. The permanent building is now a trade and convention centre, containing the Pan-Pacific Hotel, Vancouver's World Trade Centre and an IMAX theatre. The exterior of the building is covered by fabric roofs resembling sails, reminiscent of the famous Sydney Opera House in Australia.

• Baker L., NWT (now Nunavut), artist Ruth Annaqtuusi Tulurialik (b 1934) published *Qikaaluktut: Images of Inuit Life*, graphic colour pencil drawings of Inuit life, beliefs and customs, with narrative descriptions by author David F. Pelly.

• Alice Munro's Gov-Gen.'s Award–winning collection of short stories, *The Progress of Love*, was published.

• The children's picture book *Have You Seen Birds* was published, with text by Joanne Oppenheim and illustrations by Barbara Reid (b 1957).

• Yukon-based illustrator Ted Harrison (b 1926) published *The Cremation of Sam Mcgee,* based on the 1907 poem by Robert Service. The Harrison work was a *New York Times* Best Book Selection.

1987

Jan. 5 The BC Supreme Court ruled that the provincial govt had the right to limit the number of physicians billing its medicare system, and also restrict those numbers to specific areas of the province. The practice influenced both the total number of physicians working in BC and also where they worked.

Jan. 8 The Royal Canadian Mint was forced to change the design of its new $1 coin when dies were lost or stolen in transit from Ottawa to Winnipeg on Nov. 3. A design featuring voyageurs was subsequently changed to one bearing an image of the loon. The "loonie," the nation's new $1 coin, was cut by the Mint and placed into circulation later in 1987. The distinctive 11-sided aureate bronze-plated pure nickel coin was designed by wildlife artist Robert-Ralph Carmichael (b 1937). Featured on the "tail's" side was a loon in water, and on the reverse, British monarch Queen Elizabeth II. The loonie replaced the $1 bill to reduce handling costs.

Jan. 17 PM Brian Mulroney fired junior Transport Minister André Bissonette (b 1945) and ordered an RCMP investigation into possible conflict-of-interest violations regarding a suspicious land-flip in Bissonette's riding of St-Jean, Que. On Feb. 23, 1988, Bissonette was acquitted on charges of fraud, breach of trust and conspiracy. Bissonette's campaign manager, however, was found guilty on 1 charge of fraud.

Jan. 18 The popular television drama *Degrassi Junior High* 1st aired on CBC television. (The name changed to *Degrassi High* in 1989 when the fictional characters entered high school.) The urban drama touched on topical youth themes such as relationships, teen pregnancy and drugs. The series came to an end Jan. 1992, but was rekindled through the offshoot *Degrassi: The Next Generation*, which 1st aired in Oct. 2001.

Jan. 27 Colonel Sheila Hellstrom (b 1934) was named brig-gen. of the Canadian Armed Forces, becoming the 1st woman gen. in Canadian history.

Feb. 4 The govts of Canada, the US, New York State and Ont. signed an agreement to reduce pollution from factories, sewage plants and leaking toxic waste dumps that were fouling the Niagara R. The agreement called for a 50% reduction of toxic chemicals flowing into the river by 1996.

Feb. 10 The federal govt pledged $2,745,000 for the Public Lending Right Commission, whereby Canadian authors with books held by Canadian libraries would be paid $40 per title in each sampled library up to a maximum of $4,000 a year. This was the 1st time that Canadian authors earned extra money on books read by borrowers from libraries.

Feb. 11 Teleglobe Canada was purchased for $488 million by Montreal-based telecommunications firm Memotec Data Inc.

Feb. 12 A spokesperson from the Arkansas National Refuge in Texas confirmed that 110 whooping cranes survived the 4,000-km migration from Alb. and Sask. In 1941, there were only 15 of the tall, elegant birds left in the world.

Feb. 15 Vanessa Harwood (b 1948), principal dancer with the National Ballet, appeared with the company for the last time, in a performance of *Coppelia* at the O'Keefe Centre in Toronto. Harwood had been a member of the National Ballet for 22 years.

Feb. 23 Elders IXL, an Australian conglomerate, acquired brewer Carling O'Keefe and its subsidiaries, the Toronto Argonauts football team and the NHL's Que. Nordiques, in a deal worth $392 million.

• From the U. of Toronto's observatory in Chile, astronomer Ian Shelton 1st spotted a spectacular exploding star, a supernova that was the closest seen from Earth since 1604.

Feb. 24 The 1983 agreement giving the US permission to test its ground-hugging cruise missiles in Canada was renewed for another 5 years. The original agreement was to expire at the end of Feb. 1987.

Feb. 28 Novelist Robertson Davies (1914–1995) was presented with the Medal of Honour for Literature by the National Arts Club in New York. He was the 1st Canadian to receive the award.

Mar. 4 External Affairs Minister Joe Clark refused to grant diplomatic status to Gen. Amos Yaron, a former Israeli field commander blamed for negligence in the 1982 massacre of hundreds of Palestinians in Lebanon.

Mar. 9 Chrysler Corp. agreed to purchase American Motors' Canadian operations, including Renault Motor, France's interest in the company. The AMC deal was completed in June. The deal gave Chrysler AMC's assembly plant in Brampton, Ont., which 1st began producing AMC American Ramblers and Rambler Classics in 1962. The plant was refitted to build Jeeps in Apr. 1978. Chrysler also received the massive, supermodern AMC auto plant in Bramelea, Ont.

Mar. 10 A confidential document leaked to the Canadian Press wire service indicated that Canada Post wanted to close 200 post offices over the next year and 1,000 by the time its new business plan was carried out in 1991.

Mar. 11 Lisa Savijarvi (b 1964) of Bracebridge, Ont., a downhill and slalom skier, suffered a shattered right knee and crushed vertebrae in a training accident at Vail, Colorado. She had previously won the World Cup at Furano, Japan, in the super giant slalom. The rising athletic star was forced into retirement after the incident.

Mar. 12 Brian Orser, 7-time Canadian men's figure-skating champion, won the Men's World Title in Cincinnati, Ohio, becoming the 1st Canadian to do so since Donald Jackson in 1962.

Mar. 15 South African Ambassador Glenn Babb visited the Peguis Native reserve in Man. Chief Louis Stevenson explained that conditions suffered by Native Peoples were comparable to those of black people in South Africa. Babb then stated that Canada should not be so critical of South African affairs.

Mar. 18 A Public Service Commission appeal board ruled that a recently employed clerk with Canadian Forces Base (CFB) Chilliwack should not have been hired because her previous 10 years of housework did not qualify as work experience in the wage-labour market.

Mar. 26 Hamilton East Liberal MP Sheila Copps gave birth to a 3.6-kg baby girl — the 1st child born to a working member of Parliament.

Mar. 27 Talks among federal, provincial and Native leaders ended when the representatives failed to agree on a way to entrench Native self-govt in the Constitution.

Apr. 15 PM Mulroney appointed Claire L'Heureux-Dubé (b 1927) to the Supreme Court of Canada. L'Heureux-Dubé became the 2nd woman justice — and the 1st francophone woman — appointed to the Court. Bertha Wilson became the 1st woman Supreme Court justice on Mar. 4, 1982.

Apr. 19 The body of acclaimed filmmaker Claude Jutra (1931–1986) was recovered from the waters of the St. Lawrence R. by provincial police at Quebec City. Jutra, who had been missing since Nov. 5, 1986, was suffering from acute Alzheimer's disease when he disappeared from his Montreal apartment.

Apr. 20 Dr. Louise Galarneau, assistant project director of the Canadian Public Health Association, pledged $35 million on permanent vaccination programs abroad. The association hoped to eradicate several diseases, including polio and tetanus, in underdeveloped countries.

Apr. 30 The Meech Lake Accord, incorporating major constitutional amendments, was agreed to in principle by PM Mulroney and the 10 provincial premiers. Opposition leaders John Turner and Ed Broadbent shook the PM's hand when he arrived from Meech Lake. The accord was based on 5 conditions: recognition of Que. as a distinct society; a greater provincial role in immigration; a provincial role in appointments to the Supreme Court of Canada; limitations on federal spending power; and a veto for Que. on constitutional amendments. Although Que. was legally bound to the 1982 Constitution, Mulroney hoped his new accord would win Que.'s faith in federation. PM Mulroney and the 10 provinces signed Meech Lake during talks on June 2 and 3. Ottawa and the provinces had 3 years to ratify the deal.

May 6 William Potts (1916–1990), better known in the world of Canadian pro wrestling as "Whipper" Billy Watson, was awarded the Order of Ontario for his tireless support of children's charities. Following his death in 1990, Toronto's Bloorview MacMillan Children's Centre established the annual Whipper Billy Watson Graduate Fellowship to support children's rehabilitation research; while Canadian Airlines employees established 2 annual Billy Watson Education Bursaries for disabled students. The wildly popular Whipper was a 2-time world champion whose astounding career stretched 36 years and nearly 7,000 matches. Some of his most memorable bouts came against such national security threats as Hans "The Teuton Terror" Schmidt, The Sheik, and the dreaded Americans Gorgeous George and Wild Bill Longson.

May 22 Rick Hansen (b 1957) completed his 26-month around-the-world "Man in Motion" tour when he rolled his wheelchair into the Oakridge Mall Shopping Centre in Vancouver, BC. Hansen's journey covered 40,073 km, through 34 countries. It began in Vancouver Mar. 21, 1985, and raised tens of millions of dollars for spinal cord research, rehabilitation and wheelchair sports. Hansen had been paralyzed and confined to a wheelchair since a 1973 car accident.

May 27 Former PM Pierre Trudeau attacked the proposed Meech Lake Accord on the Canadian Constitution in a newspaper article published in both Montreal's *La Presse* and the *Toronto Star*. Trudeau warned that the accord would render the federal govt "totally impotent" by shifting powers to the provinces. He also warned that freedoms entrenched in the federal charter would be undermined by the distinct society clause, which gave special status to one group and confused the concept of individual rights.

June 1 One-quarter of the total BC labour force held a 1-day general strike to protest the BC Industrial Relations Act (1987), criticized by labour because it was created without their consultation, and also because it favoured individual, economic interests over collective rights.

June 6 The Atlantic Canada Opportunities Agency, a new regional development program designed to help small- and medium-sized businesses, was created. It had an annual budget of $200 million.

• Clyde Wells (b 1946), a St. John's lawyer, was elected leader of the Nfld. Liberal Party, succeeding Leo Barry, who resigned.

June 16 Twenty thousand members of the Letter Carriers Union began a series of rotating strikes. On June 21, violence erupted on picket lines outside postal facilities in Toronto and Halifax as Canada Post attempted to use part-time workers to move strike-stalled mail. Strikers temporarily returned to work only to begin a nationwide strike Sept. 29. This 2nd strike ended when postal workers were legislated back to the job through the Postal Services Constitutional Act, which was given Assent Oct. 16, 1987.

June 19 Brewers Labatt's and Carling O'Keefe warned they would not be able to compete in the Canadian market against US brewers should the free trade deal be completed; the deal, they argued, would force them to move operations south of the border. On Jan. 19, 1989, 18 days after

the Free Trade Agreement went into effect, Molson and Carling O'Keefe breweries merged into a $1.5 billion firm, with a goal of breaking into the US beer market. The new firm, Molson Brewers, was an equal partnership between Molson and Carling owner Elders IXL of Australia.

June 23 The Que. National Assembly ratified the Meech Lake Accord, the 1st provincial govt to do so. The federal govt ratified the accord in Oct. 25 and gave final approval June 22, 1988, at which time it had been ratified by all provinces but Man., Ont. and NB.

June 25 The Supreme Court of Canada ruled that the CNR actively discriminated against women through its hiring practices. In 1987, women represented 41% of the Canadian labour force but only 0.7% of the CNR's unskilled labour force. The case came to the Supreme Court after Action Travail des Femmes brought the issues to the Human Rights Commission, which ruled that the CNR violated the Canadian Human Rights Act by systematically discriminating against women. The commission ordered the CNR to develop an employment equity program, which it refused to do.

• Drugstore owner Steven Kesler of Calgary was found not guilty in the death of Timothy Smith, a man who robbed his store in Nov. 1986. Kesler was charged with the 2nd degree murder after he shot Smith in the back with a shotgun as Smith fled Kesler's store.

June 30 The federal govt rejected reinstating the death penalty in a free party vote of 148–127. The motion was debated for 8 days, until the govt used closure to force the issue to a vote. Capital punishment was banned in 1967, and the penalty officially removed from the Criminal Code on July 14, 1976.

July 2 The Montreal Alouettes CFL franchise folded. The Winnipeg Blue Bombers were subsequently moved into the Eastern Division to balance the league. The Montreal franchise re-emerged in 1996 when the city took in the orphaned Baltimore Stallions.

July 3 Defence Minister Perrin Beatty declared that women would be moved into combat roles in the air force and could soon be flying CF–18 jet fighter planes. In 1989, Deanne Brasseur and Jane Foster became the 1st 2 Canadian women fighter pilots in the Canadian Armed Forces. Also in 1989, Heather Erxleben (b 1968) of BC became the 1st female combat soldier in the Canadian Armed Forces, joining 3rd Battalion Princess Patricia's Light Infantry based in Victoria, BC. She graduated basic infantry training at CFB Wainwright, Alb. The milestones came after the Canadian Human Rights Commission lifted restrictions on women in the Armed Forces, and ruled that women must be integrated into combat units within 10 years. Submarine service was not covered. By 2001, women represented just over 11% of the forces.

July 9 Hollinger Inc., a holding company owned by financier and publisher Conrad Black, confirmed its purchase of *Saturday Night* magazine. *Saturday Night*'s long-time editor, Robert Fulford, subsequently resigned.

July 13 In the early-morning hours, 174 Asians, mainly Sikhs, landed illegally in Canada aboard a freighter out of the Netherlands. They came ashore at the tiny NS community of Charlesville and were found wandering about the small coastal town in the fog. Residents fed the refugee claimants peanut butter and jam sandwiches with Kool-Aid. Some of the immigrants anxiously requested taxis to Toronto.

July 22 The French research ship *Nadir* challenged Canadian claims to the wreck of the *Titanic* and ignored requests that the ship be left inviolate as a memorial to the more than 1,500 passengers who died when the vessel sank. The *Nadir* salvaged the *Titanic* until Sept. 11, recovering over 1,500 artifacts.

July 23 British Duke (Prince Andrew) and Duchess of York (Sarah Ferguson) officially opened the $10 million Head-Smashed-In Buffalo Jump Interpretative Centre, 49 years after the site was 1st excavated and 6 years after it was designated a UNESCO World Heritage Site. The centre provides descriptions of the Head-Smashed-In Buffalo Jump and the Plains Aboriginal Peoples who used it for 6,000 years. Buffalo gathered near the jump and were driven along marked-off drive lanes and over natural sandstone cliffs measuring up to 10 m in height.

They were then processed at the bottom for food, clothes, tools and other objects.

July 31 The northeast corner of Edmonton was devastated by a tornado, which struck at midafternoon. Many of the 27 fatalities were residents of a mobile-home park. Another 250 people were injured as the tornado reached up to 100 km/h. Four hundred were left homeless.

Aug. 7 Allan Blakeney, having served as leader of the Sask. NDP for 17 years and as premier of the province from 1971–1982, announced his resignation as party leader. He was succeeded by Roy Romanow (b 1939), who was acclaimed leader of the party at a Regina convention on Nov. 7.

Aug. 10 Principal Group, the billion-dollar Edmonton-based financial services company run by Donald Cormie (b 1922), declared bankruptcy. In June, the provincial govt closed First Investors Corp. Ltd. and Associated Investors of Canada Ltd., the company's 2 largest subsidiaries. In July 1989, the report of the Code Inquiry into the collapse of the Principal Group was released, charging Donald Cormie and other Principal officers with fraud and dishonesty and neglect on the part of Alb. Consumer and Corporate Affairs Minister Connie Osterman. And on Jan. 22, 1992, Cormie was fined $500,000 for engaging in misleading advertising and deceptive marketing practices related to an annual chairman's message given to investors in 1985.

Aug. 11 The Supreme Court of Ont. upheld a trust fund created in 1923 to provide scholarships to white Protestant Canadian students. The Court backed its ruling by citing numerous other educational scholarships restricted by race, ethnic origin, sex or creed.

Aug. 30 Toronto sprinter Ben Johnson was crowned the "world's fastest man," smashing a new world record for the 100 m at the World Track and Field Championships in Rome, and outdistancing himself from US arch-rival Carl Lewis. Johnson completed the race in 9.83 seconds — a full tenth of a second faster than the previous record.

Sept. 1–4 The 2nd francophone summit was held in Quebec City as leaders from 41 French-speaking countries from around the world gathered to discuss mutual goals and problems.

Sept. 9 Man. selected the white spruce as its official tree.

Sept. 10 Premier David Peterson led Ont. Liberals to a sweeping election victory, capturing 95 seats out of a possible 130. Bob Rae and the NDP won 19 seats, Larry Grossman and the Conservatives won 16.

• The federal cabinet approved new regulations to ban smoking on all short-haul flights. The ban on in-flight smoking would affect approximately 65% of commercial flights and most flights to and from the US. On Dec. 7, Air Canada became the world's 1st airline to adopt a non-smoking policy.

Sept. 11 Ted Finn resigned as head of CSIS shortly after the agency admitted relying on shaky information to obtain permission for a wiretap that led to criminal charges in the May 1986 shooting of Punjabi cabinet minister Malkiat Singh Sidhu in Vancouver.

Sept. 14 The Toronto Blue Jays walloped the Baltimore Orioles 18–3, smashing 10 home runs and the previous single-game record of 8 homers for a side.

Sept. 15 Team Canada won the 3rd and deciding Canada Cup game in Hamilton, Ont., at Copps Coliseum by a score of 6–5 over the Soviet Union. All 3 final games ended in 6–5 scores, with the first 2 decided in overtime. The legendary goal was scored by Mario Lemieux (b 1965), who took a pass from Wayne Gretzky. With goaltending great Grant Fuhr (b 1962) playing every minute of every game, the 1987 squad boasted perhaps the greatest forward line in the history of hockey: Wayne Gretzky, Mario Lemieux and Mark Messier (b 1961).

Sept. 27 The city of Vancouver honoured one of the nation's most creative and prolific composers by declaring Sept. 27 "Barbara Pentland Day." The New Music Society of Vancouver marked the occasion with a public performance of a chamber work composed by Pentland (1912–2000).

Sept. 30 The Bank of Montreal increased its ownership of Nesbitt, Thomson, a Canadian investment firm, up to 75%.

Oct. 10 Queen Elizabeth II made an official visit to Quebec City, her 1st to the provincial capital since the violent protests of 1964. She opened the Commonwealth Leaders Conference in Vancouver on Sept. 15. The representatives further endorsed sanctions against South Africa.

Oct. 13 Frank McKenna's NB Liberals obliterated Richard Hatfield's 17-year Conservative govt reign, taking all 58 seats in the provincial legislature.

Oct. 16 Paul Holc, born this day at 10:54 a.m., son of Alice and Gordon Holc of Surrey, BC, became the world's youngest heart transplant recipient. The new heart was received at the Loma Linda U. Medical Centre in California.

Oct. 19 The stock market crashed. "Black Monday" brought about the greatest drop in share prices since Oct. 28, 1929. The Toronto Stock Exchange dropped $37 billion; its 360-composite index dropped 11.3% (407.20 points). The New York Stock Exchange fared worse. The Dow Jones dropped 22.62% (508.32 points); stock values dropped by $503 billion.

Oct. 21 The Commons gave final reading to legislation reducing the time to process those claiming refugee status from years to months.

Oct. 25 Curtis Hibbert (b 1966) of Mississauga, Ont., won Canada's 1st-ever World Gymnastics medal at a competition in Rotterdam, Netherlands. Hibbert's near-flawless high-bar routine gave him 2nd place behind world champion Dimitri Bilozertsev of the USSR.

Also in Oct.

• Preston Manning (b 1942), son of former Alb. Premier Ernest Manning, was chosen leader of the newly formed western-based Reform Party at its founding convention in Winnipeg. On Mar. 13, Deborah Grey (b 1952) won a by-election in Beaver R., Alb., and became the 1st Reform member to take a seat in the House of Commons, which she did, to a standing ovation, on Apr. 3, 1989.

• Queen Elizabeth II unveiled Science World, Vancouver's new science centre located within the refurbished 47-m-tall, 1986 Expo Centre geodesic dome. On May 6, 1988, Science World opened its 400-seat IMAX theatre; its 27-m diameter screen was the largest of its type in the world. Science World also boasted 5 permanent and 1 special exhibit gallery covering 4,275 m².

Nov. 2 k.d. lang (b 1961) won the Top Female Vocalist award at the annual Juno Awards ceremony in Toronto. The award had previously been won 7 times by Anne Murray.

Nov. 10 Pierre Marc Johnson resigned as Parti Québécois leader and as member of the National Assembly for the Montreal riding of Anjou, arguing that PQ hard-liners refused to accept a party vote in June to steer a more moderate course on independence. Johnson was replaced by Jacques Parizeau (b 1930) on Mar. 19, 1988.

Nov. 12 Dennis Patterson (b 1949) was elected govt leader in the NWT legislative assembly.

Nov. 17 Toronto Blue Jays left-fielder George Bell (b 1959) was named the American League's Most Valuable Player, edging out Alan Trammell of the Detroit Tigers. The flamboyant and always entertaining athlete from San Pedro de Marcoris, Dominican Republic, hit .308 with 47 home runs and 134 RBI.

• Former Olympians Barbara Ann Scott and Fred Hayward began the cross-Canada Olympic torch relay from atop Signal Hill in St. John's, Nfld. The torch was carried by an estimated 7,342 Canadians in relays, covering 18,000 km. The last torchbearer was 12-year-old Canadian figure-skating hopeful Robyn Perry, who was passed the light during opening ceremonies for the 15th Olympic Winter Games in Calgary on Feb. 13, 1988.

Nov. 26 All 8,500 members of the International Association of Machinists and Aerospace Workers began a series of rotating walkouts against Air Canada. Settlement was reached Dec. 10, after both sides agreed to accept a compromise proposed by federal mediator William Kelly.

Nov. 29 Federal officials halted all shipments of mussels from PEI after several people in Montreal and Moncton were made ill by the Atlantic delicacies.

On Dec. 10, Albert Pomeroy (1916–1987) of Montreal was the 1st victim to die of complications related to consumption of the contaminated mussels. The toxin was domoic acid, which was believed to have originated in a rare seaweed called chondria.

Dec. 9 Hungarian-born Imre Finta (b 1911) of Toronto was charged with transporting more than 8,000 Hungarian Jews to Nazi concentration camps in 1944. He was the 1st in Canada charged on crimes related to the Holocaust. The Supreme Court of Canada acquitted Finta on legal technicalities Mar. 24, 1994.

Also in Dec.

• Canadian actor Tom Jackson and friends performed the 1st Huron Carol in Toronto. The travelling celebration of the spirit of Christmas would become a Canadian institution, raising millions of dollars for food banks across the country.

Also in 1987

• 1,704 Canadians were suffering with AIDS. There would be 10 times this number by 2001.

• There was a record-high 96,200 divorces in Canada.

• A record 26,000 people petitioned to stay in Canada as refugees. El Salvador had the most claimants.

• One hundred and thirty-eight Canadian wildlife species were listed as extinct, endangered or rare by the Committee on the Status of Endangered Wildlife in Canada.

• The Supreme Court of Canada ruled that Justine Blainey had the right to play hockey in a boys' league in Toronto. Prior to arriving at the Supreme Court, Blainey had taken her case to the Ont. Court of Appeal, which found that a clause in the Ontario Human Rights Code permitting sex discrimination in sports was unconstitutional.

• Altar girl Sandra Bernier filed a complaint with the Roman Catholic Church after being denied the right to sit on the altar in a mass given by archbishop Emmett Cardinal Carter (1912–2003) at Sacre-Coeur Church in Toronto.

• The port of Vancouver, the nation's busiest, handled 10,399 vessel arrivals.

• Bruce Peninsula National Park was created on Ont.'s Bruce Peninsula, part of the Niagara Escarpment separating L. Huron and Georgian Bay. The 279-km^2 park is home to a strip of towering dolomite cliffs overlooking the clear, green waters of Georgian Bay. The park protects ancient cedar trees, one of which began life in the year 688, making it over 1,300 years old.

• Fathom Five National Marine Park, Canada's 1st national marine park, was established off the northern tip of Ont.'s Bruce Peninsula. At 112 km^2, the park protects 20 Tobermory islands and 22 historical shipwrecks. The park's clear, deep waters and unique marine features attract scuba divers from around the world.

• About 45 youths were locked up overnight for creating a disturbance following an Alice Cooper concert in Halifax. Most were charged with minor liquor offences after fans poured out of the concert and noisily paraded along downtown streets.

• The Canadian govt, acting in conjunction with the govt of BC, the Nuu-chah-nulth Tribal Council and the Ditidaht First Nations, established Pacific Rim National Park, consisting of Long Beach (a series of beaches on Vancouver Island's west coast), Broken Group Is. (100-plus islands in Barkley Sound) and the West Coast Trail, 72 km of hiking for experienced trekkers. All in all, the park, which had been provisionally signed into existence in 1970, comprises 500 km^2.

• The Prix de Rome was established by the Canada Council for the Arts. The prize recognizes the work of contemporary Canadian architects who show exceptional talent. The recipient receives a grant of $34,000 for living and working costs and has the use of a studio apartment in the Trastevere district of Rome. Recipients of the award have been John Shiner (1987), Jacques Rousseau (1988), Sophia Charlebois (1990), Dereck Revington (1991), John McMinn (1992), Hal Ingberg (1993), Anthony A. Robins (1994), Philip Beesley (1995), Philippe Lupien (1996), Pierre Thibault (1997), Randal Cohen, Anne Cormier, Howard Davis (1998), Peter W. Yeadon

(1999), George Yu, Jason King (2000), Geneviève L'Heureux, Stéphane Pratte, Annie Lebel (2001), Marc Boutin (2002) and Andrew King (2003).

• The Kingston (Ont.) Sheep Dog trials were 1st held. The event would grow to become the largest of its type in Canada.

• Miles Richardson spearheaded a successful campaign to save South Morseby Is. in the Queen Charlottes from logging.

• Toronto wildlife artist Glen Loates (b 1945) completed *Pacific Loon*, pastel on rag paper, now part of the collection of Glen Loates Productions Inc.

• Northrop Frye, one of the most influential thinkers of the 20th century, published *Frye On Shakespeare*, for which he won the Gov-Gen.'s Award. By his death in 1991, the great critic published 24 major works and received 38 honorary degrees worldwide. A Que. native, Frye graduated from the U. of Toronto in 1933, was ordained in the United Church of Canada in 1936 and in 1967 became the 1st university professor at the U. of T. In 1988, U. of T dedicated the Northrop Frye Centre in Victoria U. for the encouragement of humanist scholarship.

• The University of Toronto Press published volume 1 of the *Historical Atlas of Canada*, edited by R. Cole Harris. Subtitled *From the Beginning to 1800*, the project was designed to "report to the Canadian people about the nature of Canada." Cartography and design were by Geoffrey J. Mathews. Volume II, *The Land Transformed, 1800–1900*, was published in 1993, and the last, Volume III, *Addressing the Twentieth Century*, was published in 1990. A distilled edition, *The Concise Historical Atlas of Canada*, was published in 1998.

• Jack Stanley Hodgins published the novel *The Honorary Patron*, set on Vancouver Is.

• Nicole Brossard (b 1943) published the experimental novel *Le Desert Mauve*. It was translated into English in 1990 as *Mauve Desert*.

• *Le Sourd dans la ville (Deaf to the City)*, a film adaptation of the novel by Marie-Claire Blais, directed by Michelle Dansereau, won the Mostra award at the Venice Film Festival.

1988

Jan. 1 Federal Bill C–15 was proclaimed, amending the Criminal Code to include the new offences "sexual interference" and "invitation to sexual touching." The commandments were provided to prohibit adults from engaging in any kind of sexual activity with children under the age of 14.

Jan. 2 PM Brian Mulroney and President Ronald Reagan signed the Free Trade Agreement between Canada and the United States. It included a schedule for the elimination of all trade tariffs between the countries effective Jan. 1, 1989. The PM promised to push the legislation through the Commons as quickly as possible. Within minutes of signing, both Opposition leaders John Turner (Liberal) and Ed Broadbent (NDP) vowed to fight the deal. The free trade legislation was tabled in the House of Commons on May 24. On Aug. 31, after months of acrimony and the last-minute singing of the national anthem in protest, the federal govt passed the Free Trade Bill, 177 votes to 64. Senate approval and Assent came Dec. 30. The agreement was effective Jan. 1, 1989.

Jan. 6 Hydro Que. clinched a deal with New York State to sell $17 billion worth of electricity over 20 years beginning in 1995. This, the largest single export contract in the utility's 25-year history, followed 2 other huge export power sales. In 1987, Que. signed an $8 billion agreement with Vermont and a $15 billion contract with Central Maine Power. The deals proved the feasibility of La Grande Phase I of the James Bay hydroelectricity project (which was completed in 1985), and spurred Hydro Que. toward Phase II, which would be introduced to the public Mar. 1989.

Jan. 9 In his weekly radio address, US President Reagan assured Canadian critics of free trade that his country would not submerge the Canadian identity in a flood of US imports.

Jan. 11 Canada and the US signed an Arctic water pact. The deal stipulated that the US request official Canadian permission to enter Arctic straits and the Northwest Passage. At the same time, the US did not have to recognize Canadian claims over the region. The US contended that Arctic straits and the

Passage were part of international waters; Canada, on the other hand, made claim to the entire Passage.

Jan. 13 PM Brian Mulroney opened a national conference on technology and innovation in Toronto by pledging $1.3 billion in funding for regional science and technology centres on university campuses over the next 5 years.

Jan. 18 After 2 months of debate, PEI residents voted in a plebiscite to accept a federal plan for the private sector to finance and build a fixed link (bridge or tunnel) to NB to replace a long-running ferry service. The voting result showed 60% in favour. Voter turnout was 65%.

Jan. 21 The governing council of the U. of Toronto voted to divest all its interests in South African companies. The move affected $1.26 million worth of holdings.

Jan. 28 In the Dr. Henry Morgentaler decision, the Supreme Court of Canada struck down the nation's abortion law, which provided restricted access to therapeutic abortion. The Court ruled that the law led to unequal access to abortion and thereby violated women's constitutional liberties and "security of the person." The 1st woman justice of the Supreme Court of Canada, Bertha Wilson, wrote the majority judgment.

Feb. 2 Federal Supply and Service Minister Michel Côté was fired for violating conflict-of-interest guidelines after accepting a $250,000 loan from a businessman who received contracts from Côté's ministry.

Feb. 6 The 1st Canadian test-tube quintuplets — 4 boys and 1 girl — were born to Mae and Wayne Collier at Women's College Hospital, Toronto.

Feb. 13–28 The 15th Olympic Winter Games were held in Calgary. More than 60,000 spectators watched the last torchbearer ignite the Olympic flame at McMahon Stadium (it had been carried across Canada some 18,000 km). A record 1,750 athletes from 57 countries participated. Canada won 2 silver medals — Brian Orser, men's single figure skating, and Elizabeth Manley (b 1965), women's single figure skating — and also 3 bronze medals — Tracy Wilson (b 1961) and Robert McCall (1958–1991), dance figure skating, and Karen Percy (b 1966), women's downhill and super giant slalom. Canadian athletes achieved 19 top 8 finishes, almost twice the number achieved in the 1984 Games in Sarajevo. Other Olympic highlights included the highly determined, if not unpolished, British ski jumper Eddie "the Eagle" Edwards, and the equally determined Jamaican bobsledding team. The Calgary Olympics marked the 1st time each day's medals were presented at once in a central location for all to enjoy. The site — Olympic Park — has since become a favourite Calgary destination.

Feb. 29 Svend Robinson (b 1952), NDP MP for the riding of Burnaby, BC, "stepped out" to become the 1st openly gay Canadian member of Parliament.

• Filmmaker Norman Jewison opened the Canadian Centre for Advanced Film Studies (later renamed the Canadian Film Centre). The centre is located in the former residence of industrialist E.P. Taylor, situated on 9 ha in northern Toronto, and provides advanced training to budding Canadian film directors, editors, producers and writers.

Mar. 1 In his 681st game, Edmonton Oiler Wayne Gretzky surpassed Gordie Howe's assist record by notching his 1,050th, 1 more than Howe accomplished in 1,767 games.

Mar. 4 The Medical Research Council set guidelines banning the development of test-tube embryos for research only. It also banned any genetic experiment that could affect human offspring. The council would permit human genetic engineering "only where there is no reason to believe that the genetic alterations will be inherited and only when long-term follow-up was an element of the research proposal."

Mar. 18 The people of Minnesota's Northwest Angle (a small corner of land bordering Man.'s Lake of the Woods) submitted a constitutional amendment in Washington to secede from the Union and join Canada. There was no official Canadian response.

Mar. 21 Ottawa accepted General Agreement on Tariffs and Trade (GATT) rulings demanding

reduced protection of Canadian winemakers and West Coast fish-processing industries.

Mar. 22 Montreal filmmaker Jean Claude Lauzon (1953–1997) won an unprecedented 13 Genie Awards for his film *Un Zoo la nuit* (Night Zoo). The film, which debuted at the Cannes International Film Festival, was Lauzon's 1st feature film. It told the story of an ex-convict on the run from the Montreal police. Lauzon made one more feature film, *Léolo*, in 1992, before dying in a plane crash in northern Que. in 1997 at age 43.

• Filmmaker Norman Jewison received a special achievement award at the Genie Awards. Also in 1988, Jewison won the Best Director award at the Berlin Film Festival for *Moonstruck*, which was also nominated for six Oscars, including Best Picture and Best Director.

Mar. 25 At the World Figure Skating Championships in Budapest, Canada duplicated its showing at the Calgary Olympics, with 2nd-place finishes by Brian Orser and Elizabeth Manley. Kurt Browning (b 1966) of Caroline, Alb., made skating history by successfully completing the 1st quadruple jump in a major competition.

Mar. 29 Bill C-116 received Assent, allowing fathers to collect maternity benefits if their babies' mothers died or became disabled. Provisions of the bill were retroactive to Mar. 1987.

Apr. 12 Deputy PM Don Mazankowski announced that Air Canada, one of the country's largest Crown corporations, would be placed on the trading block. On Sept. 30, the federal govt released 45% of its ownership to the public at $8 per share in the much-anticipated stock offering. On July 6, 1989, the federal govt's balance of shares were sold, completing privatization of the airline.

Apr. 18 The federal govt placed a 12-year halt on oil and gas drilling in the Canadian portion of the rich, but environmentally sensitive, Georges Bank fishing ground off the East Coast, south of NS.

Apr. 26 Gary Filmon and his Man. Tories won 26 seats in the provincial election. The NDP dropped from 29 seats to 12 while the Liberals, led by Sharon

Carstairs, won 20 seats, 19 more than in the previous election. The election was precipitated by a Mar. 8 vote of non-confidence against the former NDP govt led by Gary Doer (b 1948).

Apr. 27 Liberal leader John Turner turned back a serious challenge to his leadership, declaring he intended to stay as leader, despite the fact that 22 members of the caucus had called on him to resign. The revolt dwindled after caucus meetings reaffirmed Turner's leadership.

• Vancouver's Expo '86 site was sold to Hong Kong billionaire Li Ka-shing for $320 million, to be paid over 15 years. Li later presented official blueprints that involved a $3 billion redevelopment of the False Creek area — one of the largest redevelopment projects in North America. The project would involve schools, parks, high-rises, marinas and an extensive seawall. The historic CPR roundhouse would be preserved and used as a community centre. The massive project was slated for completion by 2010.

Apr. 29 George Cohon (b 1937), president of McDonald's Restaurants of Canada, signed a joint Soviet-Canadian agreement in Moscow to develop 20 McDonald's restaurants and a food processing centre in the capital city by the end of 1989. The 1st Soviet-Canadian capital venture marked the beginning of a new USSR policy allowing foreign interests to take as much as 49% of Soviet firms.

May 12 Que. Finance Minister Gérard D. Lévesque (1926–1993) tabled his 1988–1989 budget, with provisions to pay families $500 cash for each of their first 2 babies, and $3,000 for the 3rd and any subsequent children.

May 21 The National Gallery of Canada building, designed by architect Moshe Safdie (b 1938), officially opened in Ottawa. It replaced the Lorne Building site, which had housed the gallery since 1960. The new majestic glass-and-granite landmark contains the Great Hall, a modern tribute to the Library of Parliament. It also houses the Rideau Street Chapel, which formed part of the Convent of Our Lady Sacred Heart. The extraordinary ecclesiastical interior was designed by Georges Bouillon

(1841–1932) in 1887. The convent was demolished in 1972, its chapel dismantled and stored, then reconstructed within the new gallery as a work of art. The National Gallery is home to an exhaustive collection of works of art, including Canadian, Native and Inuit art, American and European prints and drawings, and modern and contemporary art, plus an extensive photograph collection.

May 24 PM Mulroney appointed John Sopinka (b 1933), a practising litigation lawyer and former Montreal Alouette and Toronto Argonaut, to the Supreme Court of Canada, filling the vacancy created by the resignation of Willard (Bud) Estey. Sopinka became the 1st practising lawyer appointed to the court since Yves Pratte in 1977.

May 29 Allison Higson (b 1973) of Toronto set a world record in the women's 200-m breaststroke at the Canadian Olympic trials in Montreal. Her time, 2:27:27 seconds, broke the previous mark of 2:27:40, set by Silke Horner of the German Democratic Republic (East Germany).

June 19–21 Toronto hosted the annual G-7 Economic Summit of leading industrial nations (Canada, the US, Britain, France, West Germany, Japan and Italy). Much of the discussion focused on Soviet liberal reforms. Canada last hosted the summit at Montebello in 1981.

June 20 Progressive Conservative Secretary of State Lucien Bouchard (b 1938), a former Canadian ambassador to France and staunch Que. nationalist who campaigned on the yes side of the 1980 referendum, handily won a by-election in the Que. riding of Lac-St-Jean, his 1st attempt at gaining a federal seat. Bouchard would leave PM Mulroney's Tories to lead the new federal Bloc Québécois in 1990.

June 28 Assent was given to 2 anti-smoking bills: C–51, the Tobacco Products Control Act, which banned many forms of tobacco advertising, and C–204, which gave federally regulated workers smoke-free workplaces. Provisions went into effect in 1990. On Sept. 21, 1995, the Supreme Court of Canada ruled 5–4 to overturn the Tobacco Products Control Act, C–51, on the grounds that the bill violated corporate freedoms of expression.

June 30 Bill C–74, the federal Canadian Environmental Protection Act (CEPA), a set of laws and regulations aimed at protecting Canadians from toxins and pollutants, was proclaimed. The umbrella act brought together the Environmental Contaminants Act, Canadian Water Act, Clean Air Act and the Ocean Dumping Act. The CEPA was updated and replaced by the CEPA (1999), which was proclaimed law Mar. 31, 2000.

Also in June
- Zebra mussels were 1st detected in L. St. Clair. The prolific bivalves, which are known to clog intake valves and compete with native aquatic species, can produce up to 40,000 eggs a year. The mussels quickly spread through the Great Lakes and were transported to inland waters on the hulls of commercial recreation crafts. Their environmental impact is still unknown.

- Dr. Dale Russell of the National Museum of Nature and Dr. Elliot Burden of Memorial U. discovered the leg bones of a duckbill on Bylot Is. in the High Arctic. The remnants of *Hesperornis*, a flightless bird, were the most northerly found dinosaur bones to date.

July 7 The House of Commons approved Bill C–72, an Act Respecting the Status and Use of Official Languages in Canada, which promoted bilingualism and updated the Official Languages Act. The bill guaranteed trials in either official language and provided greater opportunities for civil servants to work in the language of their choice. New Criminal Code provisions giving the accused a right to a hearing in the official language of choice came into effect Jan. 1, 1990.

July 18 An $8.5-billion agreement to develop the Hibernia oil field off Nfld. was signed in St. John's by PM Brian Mulroney, Nfld. premier Brian Peckford and a consortium of 5 oil companies headed by Mobil Oil Inc. of Calgary. After varying investments and pullouts, the Hibernia oil rig platform was pulled out to sea May 23, 1997.

- External Affairs Minister Joe Clark declared that Canada would resume full diplomatic relations with Iran after that country signed a UN truce with warring Iraq. Canadian diplomatic relations with Iraq had been cut in 1980.

July 21 The Emergencies Act received Assent, spelling out the federal govt's constitutional responsibilities and authority in 4 emergency contexts: public welfare emergencies including national disasters and major accidents; public order emergencies constituting threats to national security; international emergencies that threatened Canadian sovereignty and security; and war emergencies involving Canada or its allies. The act replaced provisions in the War Measures Act, 1914.

Aug. 9 Peter Pocklington, owner of the Edmonton Oilers, traded Wayne Gretzky to the Los Angeles Kings for a reported $20 million. The move ushered in bold new efforts to increase revenues and salaries by selling the already overextended sport to whoever was interested: Nashville, Phoenix, Raleigh, San Jose, Florida and Anaheim. Players and owners argued it was "good for hockey;" many got rich. But the fallout for the traditional fan was the loss of small-market Canadian clubs (as the league moved further away from its solid Canadian and northern US fan base) and a diluted player talent pool.

- The Financial Life Assurance Co. stated that everyone applying for its life insurance policy would have to undergo a mandatory AIDS test or be denied coverage.

Aug. 23 Residents of St. Basile Le Grand, Que., were forced to evacuate their homes when a fire at a PCB warehouse threatened the area with toxic smoke.

- The loon was declared the provincial bird of Ont.

Aug. 24 The General Council of the United Church accepted the ordination of practising homosexuals, setting off a fierce debate within the Church.

- Dino Ciccarelli of the Minnesota North Stars was sentenced in a Toronto court to 1 day in jail and fined $1,000 for assaulting Toronto Maple Leafs defenceman Luke Richardson with his stick. The incident occurred in a game the previous Jan.

Aug. 25 Federal Environment Minister Tom McMillan introduced Bill C–156, the Canada Water Preservation Act, in the Commons, which would restrict bulk water exports. The Bill was eventually dropped, but the Free Trade Implementation Act was later accepted, which eliminated all but water in tanks and bottles from the Free Trade Agreement.

Aug. 30 Marathon swimmer Vicki Keith (b 1961) waded into Toronto, marking the crossing of L. Ontario and all 5 Great Lakes in one summer. Her record swim began in L. Erie on July 1. On July 10, 1989, marathon swimmer Vicki Keith became the 1st person to swim the English Channel propelled only by the butterfly stroke. The Kingston, Ont., swimmer was on a 3-continent, 7-swim effort to raise money for disabled children.

Aug. 31 The Moncton French-language daily newspaper *Le Matin* declared bankruptcy, leaving *L'Acadie Nouvelle* of Caraquet the only French-language daily in NB.

Sept. 1 Several new cable television channels came on the air, including Vision Television, YTV and the Family Channel.

Sept. 5 At Pae-Edzo, NWT, PM Brian Mulroney signed a land claims agreement, that gave 15,000 Dene and Métis in the NWT ownership of approximately 10,000 km² of land. The deal also included a share of subsurface mineral rights, as well as special management rights and interests in a total of 180,000 km² of land and $500 million in cash to be paid over 20 years, starting in 1990. Native self-govt was not included in the agreement.

Sept. 6 The Conservatives, led by Premier John Buchanan, won a solid majority in the NS general election. The Tories returned 28 members, the Liberals 21 and the NDP 2.

Sept. 7 Sylvia Fedoruk (b 1927) was appointed the 1st woman lt-gov. of Sask.

Sept. 17–Oct. 2 Canada won 3 gold, 2 silver, and 5 bronze medals at the Seoul Olympics in Korea, the 1st Olympics since 1972 not affected by a major boycott. On Sept. 30, Carolyn Waldo (b 1967) of Edmonton won gold in solo synchronized swimming. On Oct. 1, Waldo captured her 2nd gold along with partner Michelle Cameron (b 1962) in duet

synchronized swimming. And on Oct. 2, Canadian boxer Lennox Lewis (b 1968) of Kitchener, Ont., won gold in the super-heavyweight division. The highlight, and lowlight, of the Games came on Sept. 24 when Ben Johnson won gold in the 100-m dash with a new world record time of 9.79 seconds. On Sept. 27, Johnson was stripped of his medal by the International Olympic Committee (IOC) after testing positive for the use of stanozolol, a banned steroid. Johnson claimed innocence and appealed the decision. The appeal carried no weight, and what was for a few fleeting days one of the greatest achievements in Canadian sports history degraded into a drug controversy that plagued Canadian amateur athletes through much of the 1990s. The Johnson incident led to the Dubin Inquiry into drug use by amateur athletes, which began hearings Jan. 11, 1989.

Sept. 22 PM Mulroney formally apologized on behalf of Canada for the forced internment of 22,000 Japanese-Canadians during WW II. The 13,000 survivors and their families were also given a $291 million settlement package to compensate for both the internment and property confiscated during the war. The settlement was signed by both Mulroney and Art Miki, president of the National Association of Japanese Canadians.

Sept. 23 The Ont. Court of Appeal ruled that the imposition of Christian religious exercises in public schools, as proposed through the Ont. Education Act, was unconstitutional. Four of the 5 judges concluded that the act infringed on the freedoms of conscience and of religion set out in the federal Charter of Rights and Freedoms.

Sept. 26 The Commons approved a $4 billion child-care bill authorizing govt spending to increase the number of daycare spaces from 240,000 to 400,000 over the next 7 years.

Sept. 29 The Nobel Peace Prize was awarded to the UN peacekeeping forces, in which Canadians served an integral part.

Oct. 2 A blockade at the Seaway International Bridge, connecting Ont. at Cornwall with the US, ended. Mohawk had blocked the bridge to protest an Oct. 13 police raid on their Akwesasne reserve in which

7 people were arrested, and cigarettes, drugs and weapons were seized. A similar raid was made in May on the Kahnawake reserve south of Montreal, where Mohawk were arrested for allegedly holding duty-free American cigarettes intended for sale in Canada.

Oct. 17 The Supreme Court of Canada ruled that the disenfranchisement of patients in mental institutions was unconstitutional.

Oct. 22 The Lubicon band near Little Buffalo, Alb., settled a long-standing land claim with Alb., getting 246 km² of additional reserve land with mineral rights to 205 km² of that total. Prior to the deal, on Oct. 15, more than 100 Lubicon, led by Chief Bernard Ominayak, set up a blockade on the disputed land after talks with provincial and federal officials failed.

Oct. 24 The Canadian Track and Field Association suspended sprinter Ben Johnson and his coach, Charlie Francis.

Oct. 26 The UN General Assembly elected Canada to a 2-year term on the UN Security Council.

Nov. 17 Amendments were made to securities regulations, allowing banks, trust companies and credit unions to practise stockbrokering on their premises.

Nov. 19 Toronto's venerable Varsity Stadium held the Vanier Cup men's university football championship for the last time. The U. of Calgary Dinosaurs beat the St. Mary's Huskies 52–23. Varsity Stadium, one of the continent's premier outdoor playing fields was built on U. of Toronto land at Bloor and Devonshire in 1898. Before this time, U. of T. football games were held at King's College Circle, but complaints over crowd rowdiness forced the move to this new location. A 400-seat grandstand was built on the site in 1901 and the permanent wood stadium with 7,200 seats in 1911. A major rennovation in 1950 brought seating capacity to 21,739. The Toronto Argonauts played at Varsity until they moved to CNE Stadium in 1959, and in 1989, the Vanier Cup moved to Toronto's massive concrete and glass SkyDome. Varsity Stadium remains home to the U. of Toronto Blues.

Nov. 21 Led by PM Brian Mulroney, the federal Progressive Conservatives won a 2nd, though smaller, majority in the general election, taking 169 seats. The Liberals under John Turner took 83 seats; the NDP under Ed Broadbent 43. The re-election provided Mulroney with a mandate to conclude the Free Trade Agreement (passed in the Senate and given Assent Dec. 30). The win marked the last time a federal Progressive Conservative govt would ever hold office in Canada. Voter turnout was 75.3%.

Nov. 25 An earthquake measuring 6 on the Richter scale and centred in Baie-St. Paul, Que., shook the eastern half of Canada. There were no casualties and only minor injuries.

Dec. 13 Toronto real estate developer Stephen Mernick bought the assets of the bankrupt PTL ("Praise the Lord") Ministry of Jim Bakker for $65 million US.

Dec. 15 The Supreme Court of Canada struck down Que.'s Bill 101 unilingual sign provisions as contrary to both the federal and Que. charters of rights. On Dec. 21, the Que. National Assembly passed legislation invoking the notwithstanding clause, overriding both the ruling and freedom-of-expression guarantees in the Canadian Charter of Rights and Freedoms. Three anglophone cabinet ministers resigned the day before the notwithstanding legislation was introduced.

Dec. 19 Man. premier Gary Filmon withdrew the Meech Lake Accord resolution from his legislative agenda, stating he wanted to be assured that English-language rights in Que. would be protected. On Dec. 27, Filmon withdrew his support for the accord altogether.

Also in 1988

• Dome Petroleum of Calgary, which was founded in 1950 by Jack Gallagher as Dome Exploration, was purchased by Calgary-based, Chicago-owned Amoco Canada for a record $5.5 billion. The 5th largest US oil company had advanced its multibillion dollar bid on the bankrupt firm in Apr. 1987.

• Drought on the prairies resulted in poor harvests. Combined with low international prices for wheat, western-grain farmers faced one of the worst years since the Depression.

• An Environment Canada study completed this year indicated that 83 of Canada's 122 pulp mills dumped more toxic chemicals into local waters than national standards allowed.

• Ronald J. Dossenbach bicycled from Vancouver to Halifax in 13 days, 15 hours and 4 minutes (approx. 6,000 km), setting a new world record.

• Ethel Blondin-Andrew (b 1951) representing Western Arctic, NWT, was the 1st Aboriginal woman elected to the House of Commons. She was re-elected in 1993, 1997, 2000 and 2004.

• Canada's infant mortality rate was 7.3 deaths per 1,000 babies, the 2nd lowest rate in the world next to Sweden.

• The nation's 307 book publishers produced 7,550 new titles, two-thirds of which were by Canadian authors.

• The Ont. Society for Services to Indo-Caribbean Canadians (OSSICC), established in Toronto in 1986, gave a 6-day conference at York U. to celebrate the 150-year presence of Indo-Caribbeans in Canada.

• Ellesmere Island National Park (37,775 km^2) was established at the northern end of Ellesmere Is. (now Nunavut), only 804 km from the North Pole. It is the world's most northerly park and the 2nd largest national park in Canada after Wood Buffalo. It is also the driest place in the country — a virtual polar desert — receiving only 6 cm of precipitation a year. The park is home to an abundance of wildlife, including muskox, the endangered Perry caribou, lemming, Arctic hare, Arctic wolf and ermine. It is also the summer home to the amazing Arctic tern, whose annual migratory flight to Antarctica is the longest of any bird. The park, which receives less than 200 visitors a year, is also home to L. Hazen, the world's largest Arctic lake. Ellesmere Island National Park was renamed Qittinirpaaq and given full national park status in 2000.

• The Canadian govt declared Gwaii Haanas (Haida for "Islands of Wonder"), consisting of 138 islands (1,470 km^2) within the Queen Charlotte Islands archipelago, a National Park Reserve and a Haida Heritage site. Designated a BC provincial park in 1958 and a UNESCO World Heritage Site in 1981, the Gwaii Haanas preserve includes the 19th-century Haida village site of SGang Gwaay Ilnagaay, on SGang Gwaay (Anthony Is.), which includes remains of totem poles, 10 ruined buildings and 36 mortuary poles, all over 100 years old. Gwaii Haanas also protects the breeding grounds of more than 750,000 seabirds. In 1997, the waters surrounding Gwaii Haanas were selected as a proposed National Marine Conservation area, adding an additional 3,400 km^2 to the protected site.

• Grasslands National Park was established on the Sask.-Montana border. Consisting of 2 land parcels, comprising a total of 907 km^2, the park protects a significant example of mixed-grass prairie and more than 40 grass species. There are also over 3,000 archaeological sites with relics from early settlement by Assiniboine, Cree and Blackfoot First Nations. Major landforms include the Frenchman R. valley and the Killdeer Badlands. Grasslands is home to prairie dogs, prairie plovers, the prong-horn antelope and the swift fox.

• McMaster graduate and research scientist at the Geological Survey of Canada, geologist Paul Hoffman, used the term "the United Plates of America" in a groundbreaking paper that applied a new understanding of plate tectonics to the origins of North America. The paper was entitled "United plates of America, the birth of craton: Early Protozoic assembly and growth of Laurentia."

• Ont. wineries founded the Vintners Quality Alliance, which set quality standards for all wines produced in the province. BC vintners established a similar alliance in 1990.

• The 1st Toyota rolled off the 1st Toyota Canadian auto plant, in Cambridge, Ont. The plant was the 1st outside Japan to produce Lexus vehicles. By 2003, the plant's annual production capacity reached 250,000 vehicles.

• Vancouver writer Daphne Marlatt (b 1942) published her novel *Ana Historic*.

• The Jeff Healey Band, featuring sightless guitarist Jeff Healey, released its debut offering, *See the Light*. The album went platinum in the US and was nominated for a Grammy for Best Instrumental.

• John Kim Bell (b 1952) produced and cocomposed, with Miklos Massey and Daniel Foley (b 1952), the 1st full Native ballet, *In the Land of Spirits*, which premiered at the National Arts Centre (NAC) in Ottawa. Born at the Kahnawake Reserve in Que., Bell was conducting Broadway musicals by the age of 18. He was conductor of the touring International Company for Chorus Line (1979–1980) and apprentice conductor under Andrew Davis of the Toronto Symphony (1980–1981). He also founded the Canadian Native Arts Foundation (CNAF) in 1985 to promote Aboriginal arts through scholarships and other various forms of financial aid. Bell was made an Officer of the Order of Canada in 1997.

• The 1st Yukon International Storytelling Festival was held in Whitehorse. Directed by Yukoners Anne Taylor and Louise Profeit-Leblanc, the story-sharing festival involved a varied selection of performers from 6 countries. The annual event now hosts storytellers from every continent and every province and territory in the country, with a solid representation of local Yukon favourites.

• Charlie Ugyuk (1931–1998) completed his whale-bone sculpture *Harpooned Shaman*. The work is now in the National Gallery of Canada.

1989

Jan. 1 The Canada–US Free Trade Agreement came into effect, initiating a 10-year phase-out of trade barriers between the 2 countries.

• The international Montreal Protocol to protect the ozone layer went into effect, after being ratified by 29 countries and the EEC. The Protocol, signed on Sept. 1987, required member nations to reduce consumption and production of ozone-depleting chlorofluorocarbons (CFCs) to 80% of 1986 levels by 1998. The Protocol was amended in London, England, in 1990, to reduce this number to 50%, and amended in Copenhagen in 1992 to bring CFC production and consumption levels

to zero. Developing countries received qualified grace periods.

Jan. 10 CNCP Telecommunications, established in 1967 when Canadian Pacific Telegraphs and Canadian Pacific Telegraph combined, announced it would close its remaining telegram offices, as telephones, electronic mail and facsimile machines had taken their toll on the telegram business. In May 1990, CNCP was renamed United Communications Inc. and became AT&T Canada in 1996.

Jan. 11 A judicial inquiry into the use of performance-enhancing drugs in amateur sport opened in Toronto. It was headed by Justice Charles Dubin of the Ont. Court of Appeal and known as the Dubin Inquiry. Olympic track coach Charlie Francis (b 1952) completed his testimony at the inquiry on Mar. 10.

Jan. 17 Canada's over 45,000 postal workers voted 51% to make the Canadian Union of Postal Workers (CUPW) their sole bargaining agent. The Letter Carriers Union of Canada (LCUC) lost the battle and its membership and interests were absorbed by CUPW.

Jan. 19 Canadian Airlines International began its purchase of Wardair. The $248 million deal was completed in May. Wardair was Canada's 3rd international passenger airline, established in 1953 by Alb. bush pilot Max Ward. The move left only Canadian and the recently privatized (1988) Air Canada to service the international passenger market.

Jan. 30 The Ont. Court of Appeal ruled that non-union members covered by collective bargaining agreements must continue to pay union dues, and that this tradition called the Rand Formula did not violate the Charter of Rights and Freedoms. The court also ruled that the use of union dues for political purposes was a union matter and not one for the courts.

Jan. 31 Simpson's department store ceased to exist in Montreal when 3 of its stores were converted to Bay outlets, and the remaining 2, including the giant downtown flagship store, were sold. Simpson's had been purchased by the Hudson's Bay Company in 1980.

Feb. 1 Justices Peter Cory of the Ont. Court of Appeal and Charles Gonthier (b 1928) of the Que. Court of Appeal were appointed to the Supreme Court of Canada. BC Supreme Court Chief Justice Beverley McLachlin (b 1943) was the 3rd 1989 Supreme Court justice appointment on Mar. 30.

Feb. 8 Fisheries and Oceans Minister Thomas Siddon reduced the northern cod quota for the Atlantic-coast fishery by 12% due to falling stocks. The move foreshadowed tragedy: a 1992 moratorium on cod followed by the utter collapse of the East Coast industry.

Feb. 13 Former Que. Conservative MP, Michel Gravel (b 1940), was sentenced to a year in prison and fined $50,000. He was found guilty of 15 bribery and fraud charges that included accepting a bribe while standing behind the curtains that surrounded the Commons floor. Charges were connected to govt contracts for construction of the Canadian Museum of Civilization, completed in Hull June 29, 1989.

Feb. 14 The National Film Board (NFB) was awarded an honorary Oscar from the Motion Picture Academy of Arts and Sciences. The award recognized the NFB's 50th anniversary and its commitment to artistic, creative and technological excellence.

Feb. 17 Ottawa temporarily blocked import of Salman Rushdie's novel *The Satanic Verses* after a Muslim group charged that the book blasphemed Islam. The book had already been on sale in Canada for 6 months. On Feb. 19, Customs ruled that the book was not hate literature and removed the ban. National Revenue Minister Otto Jelinek (b 1940) was placed under 24-hour RCMP protection, following the book's release. Canada was the only Western nation to detain the book. On Feb. 21, Canada recalled its chargé d'affaires from Iran to protest Ayatollah Khomeini's *fatwa* calling for the death of Rushdie. The Ayatollah declared the novel an offence to the prophet Mohammed.

Feb. 20 Tony Penikett (b 1946) led the NDP to victory in the Yukon election. His NDP took 9 seats, while the Conservatives captured the remaining 7.

Feb. 22 Country singer k.d. lang received a Grammy for best country music collaboration. lang teamed up with the late Roy Orbison for a rendition of his crooner classic "Crying."

Feb. 27 PM Brian Mulroney and 9 of the 10 provincial premiers met for 4 hours in a futile attempt to resolve differences on the Meech Lake Accord. The PM could not persuade Man. and NB to agree to the accord.

Mar. 1 The federal govt created the Canadian Space Agency "to insure that space science and technology provides social and economic benefit for Canadians." Headquartered in Saint-Hubert, Que., the agency oversees all elements of the Canadian space program.

Mar. 2 For the 1st time a US cruise missile incorporating "stealth" technology was successfully tested over Canada. The missile travelled from the Beaufort Sea down through the Mackenzie R. Valley to the Primrose L. weapons-testing ranges near Cold L., Alb. in just under 5 hours.

Mar. 9 The Supreme Court of Canada, in a 7–0 decision, refused to rule on whether a fetus had constitutional rights under the Charter of Rights and Freedoms until Parliament passed new abortion legislation. The nation's abortion laws had been struck down by the Supreme Court on Jan. 28, 1988. Anti-abortionist Joe Borowski had brought the case before the Supreme Court in an appeal to have the fetus declared a human being with all the protections granted a Canadian citizen. On Nov. 3, compromise abortion legislation, Bill C–43, an amendment to the Criminal Code to prohibit abortion unless a doctor determined that the pregnancy represented a threat to a woman's physical or mental health was introduced in the House of Commons. The House voted on the bill May 29, 1990.

• Stephen Ratkai, born in Canada but raised in Hungary, was sentenced to 9 years in prison by the Nfld. Supreme Court for attempting to obtain classified documents from a US naval base in Argentia, Nfld. Ratkai, who was working on behalf of the Soviets, received the stiffest sentence ever handed out under current espionage laws.

Mar. 10 Track-and-field coach Charlie Francis completed 10 days of testimony at the Dubin Inquiry. He confessed that all his top athletes, including Ben Johnson, had been on performance-enhancing drug regimes without which, he argued, no athlete could successfully compete at the world level. Francis also claimed that national sports officials were aware of widespread drug use among their athletes and agreed to inform the Johnson camp when they planned unannounced tests. Ben Johnson appeared before the Inquiry on June 12.

• An Air Canada plane crashed and burned shortly after takeoff from the airport at Dryden, Ont., killing 24 people. Many of the 45 survivors claimed that the Fokker-28 was not de-iced before takeoff. The airline denied the allegations.

Mar. 16 A unanimous ruling of the Supreme Court of Canada upheld Que.'s right to ban the teaching of English in junior grades of Protestant schools.

Mar. 22 Jeremy Irons won the best actor Genie for his role as twin gynaecologists in David Cronenberg's *Dead Ringers*. Irons became the 1st non-Canadian actor to win a Genie since the Academy of Canadian Cinema changed its rules in 1986 to allow non-Canadians to be nominated.

Mar. 28 Alb. Conservatives won the provincial election but Premier Don Getty lost his Edmonton–Whitemud seat to Liberal candidate Percy Wickman. The Tories won 59 seats, the NDP 16 and the Liberals 8. The NDP and Liberal successes marked the 1st time since 1930 that the legislature had not been filled almost entirely by Social Credit or Conservative members. On May 9, Getty regained his seat in a Stettler by-election.

• Kurt Browning won the Men's World Figure Skating Championship in Paris. Included in Browning's winning program was his signature quadruple jump.

Also in Mar.

• Hydro-Quebec announced that the Great Whale James Bay II hydroelectric project, to complement Phase I, completed in 1985, would be built in the Hudson Bay bioregion. Construction was set to start in 1991 and finish in 1998. Together, Phase I and II would divert and dam waters from 9 rivers. The resultant flood area would cover a region the size of Belgium. The projects would reach an estimated electric-power capacity of 27,000 megawatt (MW) at an estimated total cost of $63 billion. Residual power would be sold to New York, New Hampshire, Maine and Vermont. The controversial Hydro projects were criticized for their potential impact on the environment, especially by local Cree who accepted compensation for construction of Phase I on Nov. 11, 1975. (In May, the Cree of Northern Que. launched the 1st of many lawsuits to block Phase II.) On Mar. 27, 1992 New York pulled out of its $17 billion, 20-year deal to purchase electricity from James Bay. Completion of the $13 billion Great Whale Phase II was subsequently suspended.

Apr. 2 Psychologist Lynda Haverstock was elected leader of the Sask. Liberal Party.

Apr. 7 In Montreal, a lone gunman hijacked a bus carrying 10 passengers and forced it to drive to Parliament Hill. Charles Yacoub, who surrendered peacefully to police, said he was seeking the release of Lebanese prisoners held by Syria and the withdrawal of Syrian troops from Lebanon.

Apr. 10 The Federal Court of Canada temporarily rescinded an environmental licence previously granted to the Rafferty-Alameda dam project in Southern Sask. because authorities had not conformed to the Environmental Assessment Review Process required in the Environmental Assessment Act. The licence was reissued Aug. 31. The Rafferty-Alameda Dam project was a joint US-Canada venture to provide flood control in the Souris R. Basin in North Dakota and Sask. Construction on the Dam was initiated in Feb. 1988 and completed in Dec. 1991; the Alameda section began in 1990 and was completed in 1994. Critics argued that the project would effect water quality, alter river flows and thereby threaten local agriculture and wildlife. On Dec. 21, 1990, the Federal Court of Appeal rejected a bid by 2 Sask. ranchers to stop construction of the dams.

Apr. 19 Federal and provincial environment ministers established a 5-year, $250-million project to clean up abandoned hazardous-waste sites across the country.

1989

Apr. 20 Meech Lake opponent Clyde Wells led the Liberal Party to election victory in Nfld., ending 17 years of Conservative govt rule. The Liberals took 30 of 52 seats, leaving the Conservatives with 22. The NDP lost its 2 seats. Wells, however, lost his Humber East seat in the election. He regained a seat on May 20, when acclaimed in a by-election in the riding of Bay of Islands.

Apr. 21 Tomson Highway's play, *Dry Lips Oughta Move to Kapuskasing*, was 1st performed by the Native Earth Performing Arts Theatre in Toronto. The play received the Dora Mavor Moore Award and Chalmers Awards.

Apr. 26 At an impromptu press conference, Federal Finance Minister Michael Wilson (b 1937) read from his budget, which was released a day ahead of schedule because details of it had been leaked to and broadcast by Global Television Network reporter Doug Small. Small came into possession of a pamphlet called "Budget in Brief" and broadcast details of it a day before the budget was to be tabled. On May 29, Small was charged with possession of stolen property, but avoided prosecution when the charges were thrown out of court. The budget was officially tabled in the House on Apr. 27. Budget highlights included introduction of the new Goods and Services Tax (GST) to replace the federal sales tax Jan. 1, 1991 (a bill for which was voted on in the House Apr. 10, 1990); an increase to the federal surtax on individual incomes; and a tax on family allowance and old age security benefits on those with a net annual income over $50,000.

• A Soviet-Canadian transpolar ski expedition named Operation Polar Bear Bridge reached the North Pole.

May 2 Man. completed public hearings on the Meech Lake Accord in Winnipeg. The govt toured an all-party committee across the province for 1 month, which assessed the opinion of over 300 citizens, only 25% of which accepted Meech Lake as it stood.

• In the largest Canadian corporate buyout since Amoco bought Dome Petroleum in 1988, Toronto-based Imperial Oil acquired Toronto-based Texaco Canada for nearly $5 billion. Texaco Canada was put up for sale in Aug. 1988 after its New York parent, Texaco Inc., lost a $10.5 billion lawsuit and fell into bankruptcy protection.

May 3 John Turner announced in Ottawa he would step down at the next federal Liberal leadership convention. On Oct. 4, the Liberal management committee announced it would delay the Calgary convention to give other candidates time to develop a higher public profile and thereby be able to better compete against top-runner, former Liberal MP Jean Chrétien. The convention was held June 22 to 23, 1990, and Chrétien was selected June 23, 1990, as Liberal leader.

May 4 The federal govt declared Canadians, on a per capita basis, the most wasteful people on earth.

May 5 PM Brian Mulroney ended a 4-day visit to the US, claiming his "business-like and friendly" approach to President George Bush had advanced Canadian interests in Washington.

May 12 Former BC premier Bill Bennett was found not guilty in Vancouver of insider trading related to an estimated $500,000 sell-off of Doman Industry shares. The BC Securities Commission later fined Bennett, his brother Russell and Doman owner Herb Doman, and placed trading bans on the 3 after a lengthy proceeding into the matter.

May 25 Calgary Flames captain Lanny McDonald (b 1953) stood at centre ice in the packed Montreal Forum and raised the Stanley Cup. He had just scored the Cup winner to clinch the series in 6 games and give the Flames their 1st ever Stanley Cup. McDonald's number 9 would later be the 1st number retired by the Flames.

May 30 Premier Joe Ghiz and his Liberal party won a landslide election victory in PEI. The Liberals took 30 of 32 seats, an increase of 9 from the last election.

• NDP justice critic Svend Robinson charged that the Canadian Security Intelligence Service (CSIS) tried to determine, in Dec. 1988, whether Aboriginal protests against NATO defence exercises in Labrador were influenced by foreign interests. Innu had staged sit-ins and occupations at a Labrador air base since the fall of 1988. They demanded an end to low-level NATO training flights, which frightened wildlife and disturbed human activity.

June 2 The Nfld. govt ordered an inquiry into alleged cover-ups of sexual abuse at the Mount Cashel orphanage in St. John's. Its report was released July 18, 1990.

June 3 Toronto's SkyDome opened. The multipurpose facility incorporated a revolutionary retractable roof. It became home to the Toronto Argonauts, Blue Jays and a host of sporting and corporate events. The facility, originally estimated to cost $150 million, was completed for close to $500 million. It opened only 3 years before Baltimore, Maryland's, Camden Yards, which ushered in a continentwide architectural movement toward intimate, old-style ballparks. By the mid-1990s, the massive concrete structure was considered, by many sports fans, an idea whose time had passed.

June 12 External Affairs Minister Joe Clark recalled Canada's ambassador to China over the massacre of pro-democracy protestors at Tiananmen Square in Beijing. Arrangements were made for the evacuation of 550 Canadians from China, and Chinese students studying in Canada were promised sanctuary.

• Ben Johnson appeared before the Dubin Inquiry. He admitted he knowingly took the banned steroids that cost him the Olympic gold in Seoul. Johnson placed much of the blame on his handlers. The Dubin Inquiry concluded Oct. 3, after many leading athletes and coaches testified to the widespread use of anabolic steroids and other banned substances by the country's top Olympic athletes. Dubin recommended that coach Charlie Francis no longer receive federal funding; that athletes and coaches who receive federal funding agree to doping policies, practices and ethical standards; and that the distribution of anabolic steroids come under more stringent controls. Dubin concluded that the use of drugs in sports amounted to a moral crisis. Subsequently, Dr. Jamie Astaphan was reviewed by the College of Physicians and Surgeons of Ont. The review began in 1991, and on June 3, 1991, Astaphan was

suspended from practising medicine for 18 months and fined $5,000 for providing athletes with steroids.

June 18 The Que. Union Nationale party was deregistered as a political party because it could not pay its debts.

June 29 The Canadian Museum of Civilization, designed by Douglas Joseph Cardinal, opened in Hull, Que. on the banks of the Ottawa R. The distinctive, multi-coved exterior is clad with Man. limestone featuring a multitude of fossils, and the interior, a series of copper vaults and domes. The museum's mission is to "preserve and promote the heritage of Canada and all its peoples, to be the repository of the collective memory of Canadians and to play a role in affirming the Canadian Identity."

July 12 PEI became the 2nd province to lose its rail service, as the National Transportation Agency approved a bid by CN Rail to abandon 7 lines on the island as well as a NB line that connected to the PEI ferry.

July 18 Lightning started the worst forest fire in Man.'s history. It burned for 2 months, consumed 2 million ha of boreal forest in northern Man., and was extinguished by rain, 2,600 firefighters, 100 bulldozers, 68 helicopters and 12 water bombers. The fire caused the evacuation of 25 northern communities and an estimated 25,000 people

July 31 Newsworld, the CBC's 24-hour, all-news English-language cable channel, began service. The new channel carried a blend of local, provincial, national and international news, as well as current affairs.

Aug. 2 Federal Consumer and Corporate Affairs Minister Bernard Valcourt resigned from the cabinet after he pleaded guilty in an Edmundston, NB court to an impaired driving charge.

Aug. 8 The Supreme Court of Canada voided a Que. court injunction to prevent Chantal Daigle from ending her pregnancy. The case had been initiated by Daigle's former boyfriend Jean-Guy Tremblay. While the Supreme Court heard the case, it was revealed that Daigle had already obtained the abortion in the US.

Aug. 29 A Que. Superior Court judge lifted an injunction that barred the removal of PCB-contaminated waste from the Baie Comeau dock to a nearby storage site. Earlier in Aug., the PCBs, residue from a fire at a St-Basile-le-Grand warehouse, were turned back from a disposal site in Great Britain. At this time, the only site in Canada licenced to destroy PCBs was located in Swan Hills, Alb.

Also in Aug.

• Art instructors of the Arctic College, Yellowknife, NWT, began offering 15–20 day courses in 17 isolated communities across the North. Instruction was to inspire work in Aboriginal arts and pinpoint people with artistic potential.

Sept. 4 A Canadian Armed Forces Snowbirds aerial display team pilot was killed when his plane collided with another and crashed in L. Ont. during the Canadian National Exhibition (CNE) air show.

Sept. 18 Ont. NDP leader Bob Rae and 15 others were released by police 3 hours after they were arrested for blocking a controversial logging road leading into the old-growth forest region of Temagami, Ont.

Sept. 20 The Amway Corp. agreed to pay Revenue Canada $45 million to settle a 9-year lawsuit in which the govt sought $113 million in unpaid customs, duties and taxes. The out-of-court settlement was the result of federal claims that the Michigan-based firm evaded duties on direct sales into Canada during the 1970s. Amway pleaded guilty to defrauding Customs in a criminal court in 1983, but Revenue Canada had to proceed with civil action to reach this $45 million out-of-court settlement.

Sept. 25 Que. Liberals, under Premier Robert Bourassa, easily won a 4th term in office. They returned 82 members to the National Assembly, while the Parti Québécois won 29 seats. The fledgling Montreal-based English-rights Equality Party took 4 seats.

Sept. 26 The CBC got 2 new bosses: Treasury Board public servant Gérard Veilleux (b 1942) was named president, and veteran broadcaster Patrick Watson (b 1929), chairman.

Sept. 28 Federal Health Minister Perrin Beatty declared that people with AIDS could get the experimental drug DDI (dideoxyinosine) free of charge under an emergency health program. DDI, in its testing, enabled AIDS victims to gain weight and better resist infection.

Oct. 4 Federal Transport Minister Benoit Bouchard (b 1940) ended months of speculation by announcing that half of VIA Rail's trains would be cancelled beginning Jan. 15, 1990, and other services curtailed. In all, 18 of 38 routes would be dropped, and the number of trains running reduced to 191 weekly, down from 405. Furthermore, 2,761 employees would lose their jobs by the new year, 38% of VIA's total workforce of 7,300. On Jan. 15, 1990, Via Rail cut 51% of its train miles, from 12,704 to 6,270. The number of passengers riding Via trains dropped from 6,457 to 3,491, or 46%.

Oct. 6 Former Conservative Justice Minister Ray Hnatyshyn (1934–2002) was named to succeed Jeanne Sauvé as gov-gen. in Jan. 1990.

Oct 16 Stan Waters (1921–1992), a retired air force gen. running for the Reform Party, won Alb.'s — and Canada's — 1st Senate election. Premier Don Getty immediately sent a letter to PM Mulroney listing the names and vote counts of all the candidates in the Senate race, emphasizing that Waters was "the people's choice" and should be appointed without delay. The PM appointed Waters in June 1990. The Alb. govt introduced legislation (the Senatorial Selection Act) providing for the nation's 1st provincial senatorial elections on June 24, 1989. The results, however, were not binding; senators would still have to be appointed by the PM.

Oct. 26 Former PM Pierre Trudeau argued that the premiers should take the Meech Lake Accord back to the negotiating table and redraft what was a "bad deal." Trudeau stated that the agreement would lead to "the demolition of Canada" and accused politicians of being afraid of Que. The comments came at a Montreal launch of his new book *Meech Lake, Trudeau Speaks*.

Oct. 30 Nfld. premier Clyde Wells confirmed that he would introduce a resolution to rescind his province's approval of the Meech Lake Accord.

At the same time, Sask. Premier Grant Devine told a high school audience that the accord was probably already dead. Devine suggested it would be better to start negotiations on a new package of amendments than to amend the existing agreements.

Nov. 6 Employment Minister Barbara McDougall's (b 1937) new unemployment legislation, cutting over $1.3 billion from the unemployment insurance program by making benefits harder to get and harder to keep, passed in the House of Commons. On Feb. 14, 1990, the Senate's Liberal majority sent the legislation back to the Commons, recommending it undergo major structural changes. Senator Jacques Hébert (b 1923) declared the bill a "demolition operation designed to destroy the present unemployment plan."

Nov. 8 An agreement between the city of Montreal, the Que. govt and community groups resulted in Montreal's homeless gaining eligibility for welfare payments for the 1st time.

Nov. 13 Victor Davis (1964–1989), Olympic gold medallist swimmer and former world record holder, died in Montreal from massive injuries sustained after being struck by a car on Nov. 11.

Dec. 2 Audrey McLaughlin (b 1936) became the 1st Canadian woman leader of a national political party. With supporters shouting "Let's make history," McLaughlin won the federal NDP leadership race by a vote of 1,316 to 1,072 on the 4th ballot, beating out former BC premier Dave Barrett at convention in Winnipeg. McLaughlin succeeded Ed Broadbent, who retired after 14 years and 4 federal elections.

Dec. 5 Former Liberal cabinet minister John Munro (1931–2003) and 8 others were charged with dozens of counts of corruption, fraud, breach of trust and other related offences. Munro, who was Indian Affairs minister from 1980–1984, was charged with 34 counts. Rumours circulated that money was diverted from Native Peoples programs into Munro's unsuccessful bid for the Liberal leadership in 1984. The charges were dismissed in 1991. Munro sued Ottawa in 1992 for compensation and received an out-of-court settlement for $1.4 million in 1999, 86% of which went to his lawyers.

Dec. 6 Marc Lépine (1964–1989) opened fire at the École Polytechnique in Montreal, killing 14 women engineering students before turning the gun on himself. The women murdered were: Geneviève Bergeron, Hélène Colgan, Nathalie Croteau, Barbara Daigneault, Anne-Marie Edward, Maud Havernick, Barbara Maria Klueznick, Maryse Laganière, Maryse Leclair, Anne-Marie Lemay, Sonia Pelletier, Michèle Richard, Annie St-Arneault and Annie Turcotte. Lépine also wounded 13 others, 9 women and 4 men. The Montreal Massacre, as it came to be known, provoked discussion throughout the country about violence against women and gun control in Canada.

Dec. 8 The federal govt and 17,000 Inuit of the central and eastern Arctic made a breakthrough toward resolving a long-standing land claim in the NWT. The agreement-in-principle would give the Inuit more than 260,000 km^2 of land, an area almost 4 times the size of NB. It was the largest land claim ever negotiated. The 17,000 Inuit, who were represented by the Tungavik Federation of Nunavut, would also receive $580 million. The final agreement, that led to creation of the new territory Nunavut, was signed May 25, 1993.

Dec. 11 National Sea Products laid off 1,500 East Coast fish plant workers in Canso and Sydney, NS, and St. John's. The move foreshadowed tough times to come.

• Thomson Newspapers purchased the *Financial Times* of Canada from Southam Inc. for an undisclosed sum. The *Financial Times* would be managed by the *Globe and Mail*.

Dec. 15 The Elgin and Winter Garden Theatres re-opened in downtown Toronto after undergoing a $30 million restoration. The theatres had 1st opened in 1913 as Loew's Yonge Street Theatre, part of Marcus Loew's vast theatre chain. The Winter Garden, with its hand-painted botanical scenery, is located 7 stories above the more formal Elgin, with its plaster cherubs, gold filigree and ornate opera boxes.

Dec. 19 Michael Pawlowski (b 1915), a native of Byelorussia, became the 2nd person charged under war crimes legislation. The Renfrew, Ont., resident was charged with 8 counts of murder connected to allegations that he murdered 410 Jews and 80 non-Jewish Poles in Byelorussia in 1942.

• The EEC decided to increase its quotas for cod caught off Nfld. for 1990, despite Canadian objections that countries such as Spain and Portugal were overfishing and depleting stocks.

Dec. 25 A powerful earthquake shook northern Que. and parts of the NWT on Christmas morning. The quake, which measured 6.2 on the Richter scale, struck the Ungava Peninsula of northern Que., Baffin Is., and the eastern part of the NWT. There was no damage or injuries reported, due in part to the sparse population.

Dec. 29 The Winnipeg Crystal Casino, the 1st classic European-styled casino in North America, opened to the public from the 7th floor of the Hotel Fort Garry.

• Between 1989 and 1991, 289,000 Canadian manufacturing jobs were lost, due in part to the ongoing recession, free trade and the lure of lower wages and less expensive start-up and operation costs in Mexico and the United States.

1980–1989 The average unemployment rate for the upcoming decade was 9.3% compared to 6.8% over the 1970s.

Also in 1989

• The Potash Corporation of Saskatchewan, the largest potash producer in the world, was privatized and began a process of acquiring nitrate, phosphate and mill sites worldwide. By 2003, the largest employer in the province had an in-province staff of over 5,100.

• Canada's Corel Corporation released CorelDraw, one of the earliest computer-graphics software packages designed for use by the general public.

• Toronto's Santa Claus parade was 1st broadcast in the Soviet Union.

• The Edmonton Art Gallery presented a retrospective of the works of printmaker John Snow (b 1911). On Nov. 21, 1996, Snow received the Alb. Order of Excellence for service of great distinction for or on behalf of the people of Alb.

• The 1st issue of *Adbusters,* the Vancouver-based "journal of the mental environment," was published under the direction of Kalle Lasn and Bill Schmalz. By 2002, the wildly challenging voice of antiglobalization and anticonsumerism achieved a worldwide circulation of over 100,000.

• Garth Drabinsky and Myron Gottlieb bought the Live Entertainment Inc. (Livent) Production Company division of Cineplex Odeon division, which included Toronto's Pantages Theatre and Andrew Lloyd Weber's *Phantom of the Opera.* Other megaproductions from Livent were: *Joseph and the Amazing Technicolor Dreamcoat, Kiss of the Spider Women, Show Boat* and *Ragtime.*

• Kingston-based rock band the Tragically Hip won their 1st Juno Award for Most Promising Group. Established in 1983 and signed by Universal Musica Canada in 1998, the group of 5 long-time friends — Gord Downie, Gord Sinclair, Paul Langlois, Rob Baker and Johnny Fay — went on to release more than 30 Top 10 songs in Canada, 10 albums by 2003, selling more than 5 million copies collectively, and achieve triple platinum status with their 1989 album *Up To Here.*

• Jazz guitarist Ed Bickert (b 1932) recorded the critically acclaimed *Third Floor Richard,* with bassist Neil Swainson and drummer Terry Clarke.

1990

Jan. 2 Fisheries Minister Tom Siddon (b 1941) cut the Atlantic cod quota to 197,000 tonnes, down from 235,000 in 1989, and 265,000 in 1988. The reduction led to thousands of job losses at Fisheries Products International (FPI) and National Sea Products' plants in Nfld. and NS. Later in Jan., Trade Minister John Crosbie (b 1931) pledged $130 million over 5 years to aid the battered regions. On May 7, the federal govt further offered a $584-million fisheries adjustment package, aimed at assisting laid-off workers, protecting fish stocks and helping communities diversify away from fishing and fish processing.

Jan. 15 An Ont. govt study revealed acid rain had damaged at least 19,000 of the province's 263,000 lakes; 7,250 of which were classified as "dead." Eleven thousand of the acidified lakes were located in the central cottage regions of Haliburton, Muskoka, Parry Sound and North Bay.

Jan. 24 Sports Minister Jean Charest (b 1958) was the 10th minister forced from PM Brian Mulroney's cabinet following revelations that he tried to influence a court decision. Charest allegedly telephoned Que. Superior Court Justice Yvan Macerola to support coach Daniel St. Hilaire, who charged that the Canadian Track and Field Association did not select him to participate in the 1990 Commonwealth Games in Auckland, New Zealand, because it was biased against French Canadians. Justice Macerola eventually ruled that this was, in fact, the case.

Jan. 26 A NS inquiry into the wrongful murder conviction of Donald Marshall Jr., headed by Nfld. Chief Justice Alex Hickman, released its report stating the justice system "failed Donald Marshall Jr. at virtually every turn." The report categorized the justice system as inept and racist in its handling of the case, and censured a 1983 NS Court of Appeal decision which concluded that, although innocent, Marshall was partly the author of his own misfortunes. Marshall, a Mi'kmaq, spent 11 years in prison for the 1971 murder of Sandy Seale. A re-examination of the evidence led to his acquittal May 10, 1983. On Feb. 7, NS Attorney Gen. Tom McInnis officially apologized to Marshall on behalf of the provincial govt,

and promised the govt would schedule provincial court sessions on Native reserves and experiment with an Aboriginal criminal court. In July of the same year the NS govt offered Marshall and his family $700,000 in compensation, over and above the $270,000 given in 1984.

Jan. 29 The Sault Ste. Marie, Ont., city council passed a resolution, 11 votes to 2, declaring "the Soo" a unilingual, English-only municipality. The resolution was created in response to Ont.'s French Language Services Act, passed in 1989 to ensure bilingual municipal services be offered in areas where 10% of the population spoke French. By mid-Feb., some 40 Ont. cities and towns had passed English-only legislation. The tide of antibilingual sentiment led PM Mulroney to introduce a motion in the House on Feb. 15 reaffirming Ottawa's "commitment to support, protect and promote linguistic duality in Canada as reflected in the Constitution Amendment, 1987 (the yet ratified Meech Lake Accord) and the Official Languages Act, 1988."

Also in Jan.
• Funding was established for the Sudbury Neutrino Observatory (SNO), a $61-million observation laboratory built to detect neutrino activity caused by fusion reactions on the sun. Investors included Canada, Ont., the US and Great Britain. Twelve universities were also involved. The SNO, built over 2,000 m underground in Inco's Creighton Mine No. 9, used heavy water provided by Atomic Energy of Canada. SNO began collecting data in 1999.

Feb. 1 The Supreme Court of Canada ruled 7–0 that police must inform all those charged with crimes they had a right to free, legal counsel. The ruling upheld the successful appeal of William Brydges, an Edmonton man charged with the murder of a 79-year-old woman in 1985. Brydges was unable to afford a lawyer and was not informed he could obtain one for free. He therefore felt forced to speak to police without counsel, what the Supreme Court ruled was a violation of his constitutional rights.

Feb. 3 Montreal native Sylvie Fréchette (b 1967) became the 1st synchronized swimmer to receive a perfect score of 10 by all 7 judges at the Commonwealth Games in Auckland, New Zealand.

Feb. 5 Publisher and Holocaust denier Ernst Zundel (b 1939) was sentenced to 9 months in jail in Toronto when the Ont. Court of Appeal upheld 2 lower-court convictions (1985 and 1988) for Zundel's knowingly spreading false information. On Aug. 27, 1992, the Supreme Court of Canada overturned the conviction, stating it ran contrary to freedom-of-expression laws guaranteed in the federal charter.

Feb. 12 Quebecers elected their 1st NDP MP in a by-election in Chambly. Consumer advocate and author of the best-selling *Lemon-Aid* used car guides, Phil Edmonston (b 1944), defeated Clifford Lincoln (b 1928), a former Que. cabinet minister, 26,997 votes to 6,966.

Feb. 12–28 An uncontrollable tire fire raged at Hagersville, Ont.'s, Tyre King Recycling dump, consuming nearly 14 million tires. Black smoke and rivers of toxic sludge spewed from the blaze for 17 days. Several hundred families located within 4 km of the dump were forced to evacuate the area. Cleanup costs were estimated at $50 million. Two young offenders were later charged with mischief in connection to the blaze.

Feb. 20 Finance Minister Michael Wilson tabled the federal budget. Highlights included a personal income tax increase of 9.1%; cuts to health care and education transfer payments totalling $2.5 billion over the next 2 years; and a spending increase of 3.4%, to $147.8 billion, over the next year. The budget was projected to hold the govt's annual deficit to $28.5 billion for the fiscal year ending Mar. 31, 1991.

Feb. 25 The Que. Liberal Party General Council agreed to establish a committee to examine the province's constitutional options should all 10 provinces fail to ratify the Meech Lake Accord by the June 23 deadline. Premier Bourassa (1933– 1996) explained in Quebec City, "We are not announcing the formation of a study group because we want to dismantle the country," but because Quebecers had not given his govt "a mandate to practice federalism on our knees." Bourassa also told his Liberals that Que. would not return to the constitutional bargaining table should Meech collapse.

Mar. 7 Lorne Clarke, chief justice of the NS Court of Appeal, ruled that the province's Mi'kmaqs had a constitutional right to fish for food in all seasons, without licences, although the province's Mi'kmaq would have to abide by federal regulations governing fish-stock preservation. The ruling overturned a 1988 conviction of 3 NS Mi'kmaqs charged with illegal fishing.

Mar. 8 Kurt Browning of Caroline, Alb., won his 2nd straight world figure-skating championship at the Halifax Met Centre. Browning was the 1st Canadian male skater to win consecutive world championships, and the 1st Canadian since Barbara Ann Scott won her 2nd straight in 1948.

Mar. 9 Liberal Premier Clyde Wells threatened to rescind his province's approval of Meech Lake in a speech opening the Nfld. legislature. (Brian Peckford's former Tory govt approved the accord in 1988). Wells objected to the "distinct society" clause, and the exclusion of Senate reform. Federal trade minister and fellow Newfoundlander John Crosbie called Wells's announcement "an act of constitutional vandalism." On Apr. 6, the Nfld. legislature officially rescinded approval. On Mar. 23, Man. Premier Gary Filmon stated he would not ask the Man. legislature to approve Meech until its "flaws" were addressed, specifically the accord's failure to address Senate reform. Although the bulk of federal and provincial politicians denounced these moves, a late Mar. Gallop poll showed that only 23% of Canadians favoured Meech.

Mar. 15 Solicitor Gen. Pierre Cadieux (b 1948) stated in the House of Commons that Sikh RCMP graduates would be allowed to wear turbans and Kirpan ceremonial daggers as part of the traditional RCMP uniform. Baltej Singh Dhillon (b 1966), who began a fight to join the police in 1988, became the 1st Sikh-Canadian RCMP constable following the announcement. Some 200,000 Canadians had previously signed a petition to oppose the accommodation.

Mar. 16 PM Mulroney and Mexican President Carlos Salinas de Gortari signed a bilateral agreement covering such areas as drug enforcement, tourism, cultural exchanges and customs. The agreement included a memorandum of understanding for future negotiations on trade and investment. Total 1989 bilateral trade between Canada and Mexico was $2.2 billion.

Mar. 19 At a Caribbean Commonwealth Conference in Bridgetown, Barbados, PM Mulroney forgave Caribbean country debts to Canada totalling $183 million. Jamaica's debt of $93 million was wiped off the books.

Mar. 21 Premier Frank McKenna introduced a resolution in the NB legislature to ratify Meech Lake if concessions acceptable to all provinces were addressed and later added as parallel legislation. McKenna wanted the accord amended to better secure women's and minority-language rights. He also wanted to get Aboriginal issues back on the table. The next day, PM Mulroney endorsed McKenna's parallel accord proposal. Man. and NB had yet to ratify Meech Lake. Nfld. had rescinded its approval. The deadline for unanimous 10-province approval was June 23. The premiers would meet to hammer out parallel legislation June 3–9.

Mar. 22 Dr. Gerald Bull (1928–1990), Canadian-born ballistics expert and arms consultant to South Africa, Iraq and other countries, was assassinated in Brussels. Bull had been a high-profile guided-missile researcher with the Canadian govt in the 1950s but resigned in 1961 over PM Diefenbaker's 1959 cancellation of the Avro Arrow project.

Mar. 25 Team Canada defeated the US 5–2 in the final of the 1st world women's ice hockey championship in Ottawa. The Canadian team would go on to win the 1st of 6 world championships. Their 1st international defeat came against the US at the 1998 Nagano Olympics.

• Denys Arcand's *Jésus de Montréal* (*Jesus of Montreal*) swept the Genie Awards with 16 nominations and 13 wins. The film, which followed a company of actors staging a dramatization of the Passion of Jesus, won international praise as well, garnering a Prix du Jury at the Cannes International Film Festival, and an Oscar nomination as Best Foreign Film, which it lost to Italy's *Cinema Paradiso*.

Also in Mar.
• Former PM Pierre Trudeau published *Towards a Just Society*, calling Brian Mulroney's free trade deal with the US a "monstrous swindle." During a promotional stop for the book, Trudeau gave his fellow Quebecer another shot, stating that with Meech Lake, Mulroney was "dismantling Canada for the benefit of the provinces."

Apr. 1 NWT Dene-Métis signed an agreement with the federal govt in Yellowknife that gave them title to 181,230 km² of NWT land, including subsurface mineral rights and $500 million over 20 years. On Apr. 9, Yukon Aboriginals settled a land claim dispute with the govt, which gave them title to over 41,000 km² of Yukon land and control over associated resources, plus $232 million.

Apr. 10 The House of Commons passed Bill C–62 to implement and apply the Goods and Services Tax (GST) to the end-use of most goods and services. Finance Minister Michael Wilson had introduced the bill Jan. 24. Alb. Tories David Kilgour (b 1941) and Alex Kindy (b 1930) joined the Liberals and NDP in rejecting the tax. The final vote was 144–114. The 7% GST went into effect Jan. 1, 1991, replacing the federal sales tax (13.5% at the point of elimination), which was 1st introduced in 1924.

Apr. 20 Patricia Starr, former Liberal fundraiser and head of the National Council of Jewish Women, was charged in Toronto with defrauding the Ont. Ministry of Citizenship and Culture. On June 28, 1991, Starr was sentenced to 6 months in jail for misapplication of $33,000 in charitable donations and the fraudulent acceptance of $747,500 in govt grants. She was also fined $3,500 under the Election Finance Act.

Apr. 23 Mohawk Warriors who supported commercial gambling on the 9,000-member Akwesasne Reserve, bordering Ont., Que. and New York State, overran blockades that had been set up by anti-gambling Mohawk opponents Mar. 23. Twenty cars were set on fire. The ensuing violence forced the evacuation of over 500 reserve residents. On May 1 and 2, a 9-hour gun battle left 2 residents dead. About 400 policemen from Que., Ont. and New York State moved into the reserve to restore order. On May 10, during a separate incident, an estimated 100 Ont. Provincial Police (OPP) and RCMP officers swept through the Canadian side of the reserve, seizing weapons and $1 million in illegal drugs. Twenty-one residents were arrested on related criminal charges.

Apr. 22 Canadian Armed Forces pilot Capt. Timothy Kirk was killed in the 3rd CF-18 Hornet crash within 7 days, and the 5th Hornet crash in 4 months. A total of 8 pilots died in 13 crashes from 1982–1990 involving the jet.

May 3 In a landmark ruling, the Supreme Court of Canada made admissible the use of psychiatric evidence in a court of law. The ruling was made in the case of Angelique Lavallée, a Man. woman who killed her abusive common-law husband with a single rifle shot to the back of the head. Lavallée pleaded self-defence before a Man. court jury, and using psychiatric evidence based on the "battered wife syndrome," proved the shooting a desperate act by a chronic-abuse victim who feared for her life. She was acquitted of all charges, but the verdict was overturned by the Man. Court of Appeal, which placed the admissibility of psychiatric evidence before the Supreme Court. The Supreme Court ruling prompted a review begun by Justice Lynn Ratushny in 1995. She studied the cases of 98 women convicts who had killed their partners or guardians but claimed self-defence; by late 1997, two of the woman reviewed received remissions of their sentences, while 2 others were given conditional pardons.

May 19 Federal Conservative Environment Minister Lucien Bouchard, a former Parti Québécois member and long-time friend of PM Mulroney, sent a telegram to the Parti Québécois National Council, offering his congratulations to the PQ, which was preparing to celebrate the 10th anniversary of Que.'s 1st sovereignty referendum (May 20, 1980). Bouchard also noted that Quebecers had an "inalienable right to determine their own destiny." On May 21, Lucien Bouchard resigned his cabinet position and quit the Tory caucus. He then called for Que. independence.

May 24 The Edmonton Oilers won their 5th Stanley Cup in 7 years by defeating the Boston Bruins 4 games to 1. It was their 1st Stanley Cup since

trading Wayne Gretzky to the Los Angeles Kings in 1988. The Oilers defeated the Boston Bruins 4 games to 1.

May 27 RCMP officers seized 35 tonnes of hashish worth an estimated $400 million from an abandoned raft on NS's southern shore. The haul was the biggest hash seizure in North American history. The smugglers escaped into what local fisherman termed a "black" fog. The hashish was destroyed in a NS pulp mill incinerator.

May 29 The House of Commons passed new abortion legislation, Bill C–43, by a vote of 140–131. The bill amended the Criminal Code to prohibit abortion unless a doctor found pregnancy a threat to a woman's health. The legislation was sent to the Senate where it was defeated on Jan. 31, 1991, by a tie vote of 43–43. Justice Minister Kim Campbell (b 1947) stated that the federal govt would not introduce any new abortion legislation. Canada has had no effective abortion law since the Supreme Court ruled Jan. 28, 1988, that existing legislation violated women's constitutional rights.

May 29 Citing lewd and inappropriate behaviour, Toronto police made headlines around the world by threatening to shut down Madonna's *Blonde Ambition* concert at Toronto's SkyDome.

June 3–9 PM Brian Mulroney and the 1st Ministers met in Ottawa to hammer out approval of the Meech Lake Accord. The meeting concluded with all premiers, including those of the 3-holdout provinces (Man., NB and Nfld.), signing an agreement to accept the original Meech Accord but with add-ons. The new amendments included a legal opinion that Que.'s distinct society clause did not override the Canadian Charter of Rights and Freedoms; an agreement on Senate reform to be established within 5 years (otherwise Ont., NS and NB would transfer a total of 10 Senate seats to BC, Alb., Sask., Man. and Nfld.); a pledge to study a "Canada" clause which would entrench gender equality, Aboriginal rights and respect multiculturalism; a provision to give the territories Supreme Court justice appointments; the entrenchment of bilingual laws in NB; and assurances that there would be Aboriginal conferences every 3 years. Nfld.'s Clyde Wells stated his approval was conditional; the ultimate decision would be put before his Nfld. constituency. On June 11, PM Mulroney told the *Globe and Mail* that he deliberately delayed the June 3–9 first ministers meeting until the last minute in order to "roll all the dice," thereby adding pressure on holdout premiers to get Meech ratified by the June 23 deadline. The move cut short public discussion in Man. and made public input in Nfld. impossible.

June 7 Dr. Tom Perry Sr. (d 1991) became the 1st recipient of the Vancouver Citizen's Peace Award. Perry was a prominent social activist and medical researcher who fought against racism and escalating health care costs.

June 15 Premier Frank McKenna and the NB legislature unanimously approved the Meech Lake Accord.

• Man. NDP MLA Elijah Harper (b 1949) refused to consent to the Meech Lake Accord's introduction into the Man. legislature, thereby making impossible the unanimity required for its acceptance. Harper, a Cree, was supported by Man.'s Assembly of Chiefs. He stated that he could not support Meech because it was created over the heads of Native Peoples and failed to adequately address Aboriginal rights. On June 22, Federal Intergovernmental Minister Lowell Murray (b 1936) stated Ottawa was prepared to extend Man.'s deadline, but only if Nfld. approved Meech Lake on that day. Premier Clyde Wells was indignant over the pressure tactic and declined to put the accord to a legislative vote.

June 21 The U. of Northern British Columbia was established when Bill 40, the UNBC Act, was passed in the provincial legislature. UNBC officially opened in Sept 1994 with an estimated 1,500 students enrolled at its main campus in Prince George.

June 22 The Man. and Nfld. legislatures adjourned without voting on the Meech Lake Accord.

• At a Liberal leadership convention in Calgary, Jean Chrétien spoke above the crowd to PM Mulroney: "You gambled with the future of Canada. You brought us to the brink of disaster… Canadians will never, ever forgive you." Man. Liberal leader Sharon Carstairs summarized the Meech affair as "a flawed process, a flawed prime minister, a flawed

accord." Elijah Harper concluded the failure of Meech was proof that Native Peoples must be fully involved in all constitutional dealings.

June 23 The Meech Lake Accord — PM Mulroney's attempt to get Que. to endorse federalism through acceptance of the 1982 Constitution — died without full consent of the provinces.

• Que. Premier Robert Bourassa stated that Que. would not participate in future 1st ministers' conferences.

• Jean Chrétien succeeded John Turner as leader of the federal Liberals at a leadership party convention in Calgary. Chrétien was chosen on the 1st ballot, taking 2,652 votes (57%). Nearest rival Paul Martin Jr. (b 1938) received 1,176 votes (25%); Sheila Copps garnered 499 (11%). Chrétien had been an MP from 1963–1986. He resigned in 1986 to practise law in his hometown of Shawinigan, Que. On Dec. 10, Chrétien regained his seat in the Commons with an election victory in the riding of Beausejour, NB. He vowed, "The government that is destroying the country will be kicked out."

June 26 In the wake of the failed Meech Lake Accord, 4 Que. MPs resigned their party affiliations to become Independents: Progressive Conservatives Louis Plamondon (b 1943), representing Richelieu; Benoît Tremblay (b 1948), representing Tremblay; and Nic Leblanc (b 1941), representing Longueuil. The lone Liberal was Jean Lapierre (b 1956), representing Shefford.

• Justice Minister Kim Campbell introduced Bill C–80 to ban automatic assault weapons and stop the importation of military assault weapons such as the Israeli Uzi and Russian AK–47s. The legislation imposed a maximum of 5 years' imprisonment for the possession of such weapons. The bill died on the order table, but similar restrictions in Bill C–17 were passed and given Assent Dec. 5, 1991. Bill C–17 also placed greater restrictions over the issue of Firearms Acquisition Certificates (FACs) and required new gun owners to pass a gun-safety course.

June 28 Hull, Que., Mayor Michel Leger declared that Queen Elizabeth II's planned tour of Hull on Canada Day was inappropriate in the wake of the failed

Meech Lake Accord. Que. officials cancelled Canada Day celebrations in Quebec City.

• A Gallop poll revealed that PM Mulroney had a popular-approval rating of 17%, the lowest Canadian leadership approval rating in Gallop history.

• Health Minister Perrin Beatty (b 1950) pledged $112 million over the next 3 years to combat the transmission of the HIV virus in Canada, to support the search for a cure and to finance the treatment, care and support of infected persons. The package was part of approximately $168 million already allocated for federal AIDS programs. As of June 12, some 3,824 cases of AIDS had been diagnosed in Canada; 2,282 persons had died of the syndrome.

June 30 Chief Justice of Canada Brian Dickson retired at age 75, the mandatory retirement age for Supreme Court justices. Dickson was succeeded by Antonio Lamer (b 1933) on July 1, who became the 3rd Que. justice on the Supreme Court bench.

July 11–12 One hundred heavily armed Que. police attempted to storm barricades erected by Mohawk members of the Kahnesatake Warrior Society at Oka, Que. A gun battle erupted, resulting in the death of police officer Marcel Lemay (1959–1990). The Oka Mohawk had erected the barricades in Mar. to protest municipal plans to expand a 9-hole golf course on 22 ha of land the Mohawk contended had never been surrendered in treaties. Municipal officials paid $90,000 for the land from a local Realtor. Following the gunplay, a standoff between Mohawk and the Que. police ensued. Military personnel replaced the police on Aug. 20. Tense face-to-face standoffs between Mohawk and soldiers were carried by television stations worldwide. The military was ordered to remove the blockade, and by Sept. 15, the last 50 vigilant protestors had bunkered down with journalists in a Kahnesatake treatment centre. On Sept. 26, the 78-day armed confrontation ended when Mohawk Warriors suddenly emerged from the centre, catching the Armed Forces off guard. Soldiers eventually took about 50 persons into custody.

July 11 Mohawk members of the Kahnawake reserve south of Montreal set up a sympathy roadblock at the Mercier Bridge, the main link between the island of Montreal and South Shore communities. Angry residents of the South Shore city of Chateauguay held nightly anti-blockade demonstrations, some of which involved rock-throwing and anti-Native taunts. Between July 12 and 14, Que. police and RCMP officers used clubs and tear gas on mobs at the bridge. Citizens countered with volleys of bricks, rocks and bottles. Thirty-eight people were injured, including 16 police officers; 25 people were arrested. On Aug. 1, 12,000 irate Chateauguay residents marched on Montreal City Hall demanding that the army be brought in to remove the Mercier Bridge blockade. By late Aug., over 2,600 military personnel with armed vehicles had set up positions near the Kahnawake reserve, and in and around Oka. The Armed Forces threatened it would use whatever force was necessary to dismantle the blockade. A convoy of women, children and elderly Native Peoples subsequently began evacuating the Kahnawake reserve between Aug. 27 and 28. They were attacked by rock-throwing protestors. RCMP and provincial police allegedly made little effort to prevent or halt the assault. Tensions eased at Kahnawake on Aug. 28 when both Mohawk and the military began removing the bridge blockade together. The bridge reopened on Sept. 6.

• Native Peoples constructed road blockades from BC to NB in support of the Oka Mohawk and to raise awareness of unsettled Native land claims.

July 12 BC Attorney Gen. Bud Smith resigned over charges he obstructed justice. Smith had allegedly said in a cellular-phone discussion that he could discredit a lawyer hired by the NDP. The lawyer was in the process of prosecuting former cabinet minister Bill Reid, who had been charged with breach of trust. On Dec. 13, Smith returned to the BC cabinet as minister of regional and economic development under Premier Bill Vander Zalm.

July 25 Lucien Bouchard and 6 other Que. MPs who had broken from Liberal and Conservative ranks announced the formation of a new federal Que. nationalist party, the Bloc Québécois. On Aug. 13, Bloc Québécois candidate Gilles Duceppe (b 1947) won a landslide victory in a by-election in the riding of Laurier–Ste. Marie. Duceppe was the 1st Bloc candidate elected to Parliament.

Also in July

• There were 4,116 personal and business bankruptcies in Canada, the highest monthly total since the 1982 recession.

Aug. 2 Saddam Hussein's Iraqi army overran Kuwait on a spectrum of pretexts including oil prices, Kuwaiti loans to Iraq and territorial claims. On Aug. 6, Canada gave support to UN Security Council measures imposing tight economic sanctions against the country. On Aug. 10, PM Mulroney pledged Canadian military support to a multinational US-led force aimed at forcing an Iraqi withdrawal (the US had sent troops to the region Aug. 7). Two Canadian destroyers and a naval supply ship set sail for the Persian Gulf Aug. 24. They arrived to join the blockade Sept. 27. On Oct. 7, Canadian CF–18 jet fighter planes began arriving for duty in Qatar. Two days later, Canadian fighter pilots began patrols in the Gulf. Each CF–18 was equipped with air-to-air and air-to-ground missiles. The Canadian base in the desert sheikhdom of Qatar was nicknamed "Canada Dry." On Nov. 29, Canada voted with other members of the UN Security Council to authorize the use of force — by "all necessary means" — to drive Iraq from Kuwait if a peaceful withdrawal could not be achieved by Jan. 15, 1991. Only Cuba and Yemen voted against the measure. China abstained. The House of Commons voted 111–82 to approve the UN measure that day.

Aug. 9 The federal govt permitted Ben Johnson to compete for Canada in international track competitions. The govt had imposed a ban on the track star after he tested positive for performance-enhancing drugs at the 1988 Seoul Olympics.

Aug. 12 The youth wing of the Que. Liberal Party presented Premier Robert Bourassa with a document calling for Que.'s "full political autonomy," with some powers delegated to Canada through a "supra-national parliament."

Sept. 6 The people of Ont. handed the NDP its 1st provincial election victory, giving Bob Rae 74 seats and a majority govt. The Liberals under David Peterson won 36 seats, the Conservatives under Mike Harris (b 1945) 20. Liberal leader David Peterson lost his London Centre seat and retired from politics.

Sept. 11 Premier Gary Filmon's Man. Conservatives won a narrow victory in the provincial election. The Tories took 30 seats, the NDP under Gary Doer 20, and the Liberals under Sharon Carstairs 7; there was 1 Independent. The Liberals lost Official Opposition status.

Sept. 12 NS Premier John Buchanan resigned his post to accept an appointment to the Senate. Buchanan was under heat after being accused of funnelling govt contracts to friends and political allies. It was the 1st time a provincial premier resigned his seat for a Senate appointment since Ont. Premier Oliver Mowat in 1896.

• The Canada–Nova Scotia Offshore Petroleum Board gave the green light to commence production at the Cohasset and Panuke oil fields west of Sable Is., NS. The $565-million project, which began production June 3, 1992, became Canada's 1st operating commercial offshore energy project. Production ceased in 1999. The fields, exploited by Lasmo Nova Scotia Ltd., a subsidiary of British Oil, and Nova Scotia Resources Ltd., produced a modest 35 million barrels of oil.

Sept. 18 Toronto lost its bid to host the 1996 Summer Olympics, finishing behind Atlanta, the winner, and Athens, the runner-up.

Sept. 27 With an approval rating hovering in the mid teens, PM Mulroney invoked a previously unused constitutional clause (Section 26) to get an additional 8 new Tory Senators into the Liberal-dominated Upper Chamber. Mulroney had already appointed 13 new Tory senators in 1990. The PM hoped that the subsequent shift in power would kick-start his GST legislation, which had become bogged down in the Senate (it passed the House Apr. 10). The GST effective date was Jan. 1, 1991. Federal Finance Minister Michael Wilson explained on Aug. 30 that any delay would wreak havoc in the business world; Canadian companies had already changed their budgets, schedules and accounting forms to conform to the new tax.

Oct. 4–5 During the ongoing row in the Senate over passage of the GST, Speaker Guy Charbonneau (b 1922) forced a vote on a Liberal procedural motion while the Liberals were out of the room.

The motion was defeated, and the Liberals resorted to a day of blowing horns, pounding on desks and shouting in unison. On Oct. 9, Senate Liberals vowed to filibuster until the Speaker either resigned or was fired. A six-day, 24-hour filibuster ensued, when the Senate suspended its sitting. Meanwhile, the govts of BC and Alb., some private citizens and both federal opposition parties launched legal cases against the GST. Most focused on the constitutional validity of PM Mulroney's move to increase the number of Senate seats to accommodate new Tory appointments. All such efforts were in vain. The GST bill was passed by the Senate and signed into law by Supreme Court Justice John Sopinka on Dec. 17. Liberal members refused to witness the signing ceremony.

Oct. 9 Air Canada announced it would lay off more than 10% of its staff, effective Jan. 31, 1991, and scrap unprofitable routes.

Oct. 18 A 2-week truce was negotiated in the Senate, allowing passage of a long-stalled bill to tax back family allowances and pension benefits from upper-income earners, and another to reform the unemployment insurance system.

• The Supreme Court of Canada ruled 9–0 that an accused must be brought to trial within 8 months of a charge; any delay exceeding this period infringed on the accused's constitutional right to be tried within a reasonable time frame. The ruling was made in the cases of 4 men charged in a Peel Region Ont. court with weapons offences and conspiracy to commit extortion. The plaintiffs had waited 2 years before appearing in court. The Supreme Court stayed the proceedings and censured Peel Region, referring to its court system as the most lax in North America (there were 20,000 individuals awaiting trial in Brampton). By Nov. 8, the Supreme Court's decision had resulted in the dismissal of 1,652 Ont. court cases.

Oct. 25 Employment and Immigration Minister Barbara McDougall (b 1937) initiated a 5-year federal plan to increase immigration to 1.22 million by the end of 1995: 220,000 in 1991, and 250,000 each subsequent year. Preference would be given to those with needed skills. The 1990 immigration quota was 200,000.

Oct. 26 Wayne Gretzky of the Los Angeles Kings scored his 2,000 NHL point. He was the 1st NHLer to reach this pinnacle. The assist gave Gretzky an average of 2.336 points per game. Second to Gretzky in total points was Gordie Howe with 1,850 points (1.047 per game); 3rd was Marcel Dionne with 1,771 points (1.314 per game).

Nov. 15 US President George Bush responded to years of Canadian pressure by signing into law major changes to his country's Clean Air Act. The new legislation cut sulphur dioxide emissions from US power plants by almost 50% by 2000.

• The National Energy Board approved expansion of TransCanada PipeLines. Initial costs were estimated at $546 million; the final cost was $2.6 billion. Expansion included development of the 595-km underground Iroquois Pipeline connecting Iroquois, Ont., to South Commack, Long Island, New York, which officially opened Jan. 28, 1992. The line cost $655 million US and had a daily carrying capacity of 576 million cubic ft. The Iroquois line gave the Alb. oil industry direct access to New York markets through the cross-country TransCanada PipeLine.

• The city council of St. John's voted 6–2 to give Dr. Henry Morgentaler 10 days to close his abortion clinic. Dr. Morgentaler refused to obey the order, arguing that abortion fell under federal, not municipal, law. He threatened to take the city to court. The city did not pursue the matter. Premier Clyde Wells subsequently announced he would not challenge the country's existing abortion legislation.

Nov. 20 Approximately 6,000 workers at Algoma Steel Corp. of Sault Ste. Marie, Ont., voted 91% to end a 112-day strike. The settlement increased wages by $2.89 an hour by 1993, improved pensions and severance pay, and introduced a profit-sharing plan.

Also in Nov.
• The Alberta Métis Settlements Accord land claim settlement was given Assent, providing Alb. Métis 4,856 km² of land and $310 million over 17 years. Although the province retained responsibility for roads and mineral rights over the area, the Métis held veto power over the allotment of mineral

rights, in addition to retaining the right to negotiate with oil and gas developers for royalty overrides.

Dec. 2 PM Mulroney created a 17-member joint Senate-House committee to study ways of making it easier to amend the Constitution. Current law required the unanimous approval of all provinces within 3 years. NDP leader Audrey McLaughlin reacted to PM Mulroney's newest efforts: "Has the prime minister learned anything from the past mistakes? Evidently not." On June 20, 1991, the committee released its report recommending all constitutional changes be approved in a referendum by a majority of citizens in each of the following regional blocks: the West (BC, Alb., Sask. and Man.), Ont., Que. and the Atlantic. However, the committee also stated that referendum results should not be binding, but rather, politicians should determine the ultimate fate of the Constitution.

Dec. 5 CBC president Gérard Veilleux spoke over closed-circuit television to the CBC's 10,733 employees, stating the Crown corporation was slashing $108 million from its $1.15 billion 1991–1992 budget, effective Apr. 1, 1991.

• Five Manitoulin Is., Ont., First Nations bands completed a land claims dispute with the provincial govt. The deal, 1st pursued by Aboriginals in 1862, was the 1st Native land claims settlement completed by the Ont. govt. The First Nations were given title to 2,430 ha of Georgian Bay lands worth an estimated $1.7 million. Also included was a cash settlement of $8.9 million.

Dec. 11 Federal Environment Minster Robert de Cotret (1944–1999) released the Conservative govt's highly anticipated *Green Plan*, a 173-page document pledging $3 billion over 5 years to preserve and clean up the environment. Critics labelled the Green Plan an empty vessel, long on studies, short on concrete procedures or solutions. By 1995, the entire Green Plan was scrapped, with less than one-third of the committed $3 billion spent on the environment.

• The Supreme Court of Canada dismissed the appeal of Donald Andrews and Robert Smith whose convictions on propagating racial hatred were upheld by the Ont. Court of Appeal on July 29, 1988. Smith and Andrews were members of the Nationalist Party of Canada, responsible for publishing the bimonthly *National Reporter*, which was deemed under the Criminal Code to promote hatred against an identifiable group.

Dec. 19 The 1st of 4 plus-800 megawatt (MW) Darlington, Ont., CANDU nuclear reactors went into commercial operation. The 4th went into commercial service on Apr. 17, 1993. Total output exceeded 3,500 MW. By 2003, the Darlington Nuclear Generating Station provided 20% of the province's energy requirements.

Dec. 20 The Alb. govt approved completion of a $1.6 billion pulp mill near Athabasca, which had been halted in Mar. for fear it would pollute the Athabasca R. Production began in 1993. The massive Alberta–Pacific Forest Industries mill was owned by Japanese firms Mitsubishi, Honshu Paper Co., Hokuetsu Paper and Kanzaki Paper Canada, with a 14% Canadian shareholding.

• The Supreme Court of Canada advised Canadian law firms to establish conflict-of-interest guidelines. The announcement was made following a unanimous May 1990, ruling that dismissed a Winnipeg law firm from a case because one of its lawyers had worked on the same case while previously employed by the opposing law firm.

1990–2003 Total annual Canadian university undergraduate enrolment increased by 200,000, with no appreciable increase in the number of full-time faculty.

Also in 1990

• Canada's population was 27,701,000.

• Leaded gasoline was no longer available for use in Canadian automobiles. Lead had been added to gas to increase its octane rating, but its combustion spread a thin layer of toxic lead across the landscape.

• There were over 16.9 million cars registered in Canada.

• Grand Chief of the Grand Council of the Cree in Que. Matthew Coon Come (b 1956) masterminded a canoe trip of Cree elders from James Bay down the Hudson R. to a press conference in New York City, in an attempt to mobilize support against the James Bay II project.

• Federal, provincial, territorial and local governments employed a combined 1,208,355 individuals.

• The Sask. cities of Regina and Saskatoon recorded the highest urban homicide rates in Canada with, 4.72 and 4.32 murders per 100,000 people respectively.

• The Bank of Canada's interest rate was 14.5%.

• There were a record 54,424 bankruptcies in Canada.

• PEI and Ottawa signed the $3.6 million Co-operation Agreement on Cultural Development, which injected $3.6 million into PEI arts and cultural programs.

• There were 86,880 km of railway track in operation in Canada, down from 93,544 in 1986.

• The Canadian tobacco industry produced over 46 billion cigarettes and 191 million cigars.

• Hamilton, Ont., had 28 Air Quality Index "poor" days, the most in the country. Regina came 2nd with 19 and Toronto 3rd with 11. St. John's had 340 "good" days, the most in the country, followed by Vancouver with 326.

• The Prix Gilles-Corbeil Awards were founded to honour French-language writers for an entire body of work. Given every 3 years, the $100,000 prize is the richest literary award in Canada. The 1st recipient was novelist Réjean Ducharme.

• The City of Toronto Archives acquired over 1 million negatives produced by photojournalist and WW II veteran Gilbert Milne (1914–1991). Milne was the 1st to photograph the Allied invasion at Normandy on D-Day.

• The 1st three High River Alb. murals depicting the history of the region were commissioned. The project was spearheaded by the High River District Chamber of Commerce, who invited area artists to select a particular period in history and

gave them permission to use the sides of buildings in the downtown core as their canvases. Fourteen more murals were unveiled over the next four years.

• Austin "Dink" Carroll (1921–1991), sportswriter for the Montreal *Gazette*, and creator of the column "Playing the Field," religiously read by Canadian sports fans for over 15 years, was awarded the Canadian Baseball Hall of Fame and Museum's Jack Graney Award.

• As of 1990, fossils from 49 dinosaur genera had been recorded in Canada, placing the country 4th on dinosaur discovery charts, behind the US (110), China (96) and Mongolia (50).

• $995 million dollars' worth of English-language books, and $257 million dollars' worth of French-language books, were sold in Canada.

• The Toronto-Dominion Bank began sampling the urine of new employees for cocaine, marijuana and opiates, the 1st Canadian bank to do so.

• Journalist Claire Hoy and former Israeli Mossad agent Victor Ostrovsky published *By Way of Deception: A Devastating Insider's Portrait of the Mossad*.

• Ont. native Nino Ricci published his 1st novel, *Lives of the Saints*, 1st of a trilogy drawing on Ricci's own experiences as an Italian-Canadian.

• The *Dictionary of Canadian French*, edited by Sinclair Robinson and Donald Smith, was published.

• George Blondin (b 1923) published *When the World Was New*, a collection of Sahtu Dene legends.

• Oneida Graham Greene (b 1952), born on the Six Nations reserve near Brantford, Ont., was nominated for an Oscar in his supporting role in *Dances With Wolves*. He was the 1st Native American to be nominated for an Academy Award since Chief Dan George was recognized for his supporting role in *Little Big Man* (1970). Greene lost to Joe Pesci for *Goodfellas*.

• Jazz trumpeter Kenny Wheeler recorded the critically acclaimed *Music for Large and Small Ensembles*.

1991

Jan. 1 The 7% federal Goods and Services Tax (GST) came into effect. The new tax yielded an estimated $15 billion by the end of 1995.

• 10,500 Man. nurses in 186 health care facilities went on strike for a 27% pay increase. They returned to work during the 1st week of Feb. after accepting an increase of between 10–13% over 2 years.

Jan. 4 Canada won its 2nd World Junior Hockey medal, beating the Soviets 3–2 before a hometown crowd in Saskatoon. The game was viewed by over 1.44 million people on TSN television.

Jan. 8 The Citizen's Forum on Canada's Future, chaired by Keith Spicer, held its 1st public hearing in Saint John, NB. The 12-member forum was appointed by PM Mulroney in Nov. 1990, to assess public opinion on 14 points, including democracy, leadership, regional identity, language, values, culture, ethnicity, individual rights and social fairness. The forum was televised, and included interchanges between individuals in separate television studios across the country. The Forum's final report was issued June 27.

Jan. 9 Lester & Orpen Dennys suspended operations after Toronto-based parent company Pagurian Corp. declared it would no longer provide financial support to the prestigious fiction house. Five of the company's titles had been nominated for the Gov-Gen.'s Award the previous year.

Jan. 17 Canada officially entered the Gulf War when US-led NATO coalition forces began bombing Iraq forces in Kuwait. Canada contributed over 2,200 military personnel to the effort. The Desert Cats CF–18 fighter squad ran 2,700 missions over Kuwait, the 1st Canadian bombing missions since WW II. Operation Desert Storm concluded with the liberation of Kuwait on Feb. 27. There were no Canadian casualties in the conflict.

Jan. 30 The Que. Liberal Party's Allaire Committee released its constitutional policy report, recommending Que. be given exclusive control over 22 jurisdictions, including communications, energy, the environment, agriculture and regional development. The report also recommended that a referendum on Que. sovereignty be held Dec. 21,

1992, if Ottawa and the provinces were unable to come to agreement on the committee's recommendations. Que. Liberals adopted the Allaire Report Mar. 9, but Premier Bourassa announced he would hold off on a referendum pending the outcome of the Belanger-Campeau Report, to be finalized Mar. 26, 1991.

Also in Jan.
• There were 11.2 million head of cattle in Canada.

Feb. 1 The Hudson's Bay Company declared it would no longer sell furs in any of its stores. Chartered in 1670 to trade for beaver pelts with local Cree along Hudson Bay, HBC soon expanded to control a complex web of outposts and fur trade routes through much of Canada. Company spokespeople reported the sale of fur was no longer profitable in the current economic climate, and that HBC's remaining 20 fur outlets would be closed immediately.

Feb. 4 The Ont. Court of Appeal allowed an anonymous rape victim using the pseudonym Jane Doe to proceed with a $600,000 lawsuit against the Metropolitan Toronto Police Force for neglecting to warn and protect her against a serial sex criminal. She argued that her 1986 rape attack might not have happened had the police acted properly. The actual suit would not be launched until Aug. 1997. In July 1998, Doe won a lengthy court battle against the force. Madame Justice Jean MacFarland ruled the Toronto force had been "utterly negligent," and that Doe's Charter rights had been violated. The Metropolitan Toronto Police Force was ordered to pay Doe $220,000 in damages and $20,000 annually for the next 15 years.

Feb. 5 Trade Minister John Crosbie announced Canada would begin free trade talks with the US and Mexico.

Feb. 11 Yukon Lotteries donated $200,000 to the 50th anniversary celebration of the Alaska Highway. Built in 1942 by the American military, the highway begins in Dawson Creek, BC, runs north through Whitehorse and northwest through the Yukon, and ends in Fairbanks, Alaska.

Feb. 18 An Ont. judge granted Algoma Steel Corp. of Sault Ste. Marie 6 months' bankruptcy protection when the Ont. and federal govts offered the troubled steel firm $15 million in guaranteed loans, and the Royal Bank offered a $60 million line of credit. Five thousand jobs were saved.

Feb. 20 Jazz giant Oscar Peterson won 2 Grammys for his CD, *The Legendary Oscar Peterson Trio Live at the Blue Note*. The famous trio included Herb Ellis on guitar and the great Ray Brown on bass.

Also in Feb.
• The Reichmann family settled a $102 million out-of-court libel suit with *Toronto Life* magazine, in connection with the 1987 article by Elaine Dewar, "The Mysterious Reichmanns — The Untold Story." *Toronto Life* published a 1-page apology to the family as part of the settlement and agreed to pay damages to charities of the Reichmann's choice.

Mar. 7 Milton Born With A Tooth, a member of the Peigan First Nation, was found guilty of weapons charges relating to a Sept. 7, 1990, Native protest of the $350 million Oldman R. Dam under construction upriver from the Peigan reserve, Alb. He was given one and a half years in prison, a ruling upheld on appeal Mar. 14, 1994. In 2001, the federal and Alb. govts concluded a deal with the Peigan providing the 1,300-member Nation with $64.3 million over 8 years as compensation for the dam construction.

Mar. 8 The BC Supreme Court denied the Gitksan-Wet'suwet'en a claim to 569,797 ha of land around Hazelton and Smithers, arguing that the claim expired when the colony joined Confederation in 1871. The case was appealed and eventually ended up in the Supreme Court of Canada, which unanimously ruled Dec. 11, 1997, that First Nations' right to claim ancestral land has never been extinguished.

Mar. 9 Premier Robert Bourassa's Que. Liberal Party adopted lawyer Jean Allaire's Jan. 30 report, calling for a referendum in 1992 pending Canada's willingness to accept the report's power sharing proposals.

Mar. 13 PM Brain Mulroney and US President George Bush signed the Acid Rain Accord, requiring Canada to reduce 50% of its SO_2 and NO_2 emissions by 1994, and the US 50% of its emissions by 2000. The Canadian Coalition on Acid Rain lobbied 9 years for the agreement. Fifty percent of all acid rain that fell on Canada in 1991 was generated in the US. Fourteen thousand Canadian lakes were already deemed dead by the time the agreement was signed.

Mar. 16 The 87-year-old family-run Pascal Hardware chain, based in Montreal, declared bankruptcy, resulting in the closure of 21 stores and the elimination of 1,600 jobs.

Mar. 21 The Supreme Court of Canada ruled that a fetus was not a person and did not have the same rights under the Criminal Code. The ruling was the result of a 6-year legal battle involving 2 Vancouver midwives charged with criminal negligence in a bungled homebirth.

Mar. 25 Two hundred and fifty fishers and fish-plant operatives broke windows and damaged office equipment at the Port-aux-Basques, Nfld., federal fisheries department after it was announced the federal govt planned to cut back on the fishing season. Workers argued that the limited season would not give them the amount of work time needed to qualify for unemployment insurance. Twelve people were arrested.

Mar. 26 The 37-member Bélanger-Campeau Commission, initiated by Premier Robert Bourassa and begun in Quebec City Nov. 6, 1990, finalized its report. The commission recommended that a referendum on Que. sovereignty be held before Oct. 26, 1992, if Ottawa could not agree to a renewed federalism amenable to Que. On June 20, the Que. National Assembly voted 65–29 to hold a 1992 referendum, which was put on hold pending the outcome of further constitutional talks.

Mar. 29 The federal govt allocated $7.9 million in compensation to PEI and NB seed potato farmers whose produce was prohibited in the United States and the rest of Canada when it was found to carry the PVY-n virus, lethal to tobacco, tomato and pepper plants. All affected seed potatoes were destroyed. The ban was lifted in 1993.

Apr. 1 An accord between the federal govt and Que. took effect, giving the province more control over the number and choice of immigrants entering Que., and where they settled. Que. also secured the right to receive up to 30% of all new immigrants to Canada each year.

Apr. 2 Rita Johnston (b 1935) replaced Social Credit Party leader and Premier Bill Vander Zalm to become BC's 1st woman provincial leader. Vander Zalm stepped down amidst conflict-of-interest charges related to the $16-million sale of BC's biblical theme park, Fantasy Gardens. The BC Supreme Court acquitted Vander Zalm of all charges June 25, 1992.

Apr. 4–7 The 56,000-member Reform Party, established in 1987 and led by Preston Manning, held its 4th annual convention in Sask., pledging to become the next major national party.

Apr. 5 Four hundred workers at Curragh Resources Inc.'s Faro Mines, the Yukon's largest private employer, went on strike for increased wages. Seventeen Curragh trucks were vandalized in the strike, which lasted until June 15 and ended in a pay increase of 17.6% over 3 years.

Apr. 9 The Laurentian Bank of Montreal reached out of the Que. market for the 1st time, paying $55 million to acquire the assets and 37 cross-Canada branches of failed Standard Trust of Toronto.

Apr. 12 Canada's longest and most expensive criminal trial to date ended when Toronto businessman Joseph Burnett was acquitted of evading income taxes totalling $2.2 million. Burnett's day in court lasted over 6 1/2 years.

Apr. 15 The Alb. govt tabled its 1st non-deficit budget since 1984, cutting over 600 civil service jobs, increasing health care insurance costs and increasing taxes on liquor.

Apr. 18 Health and Welfare Canada advised 13,500 Meme breast implant recipients to seek medical advice after tests showed they were potentially carcinogenic. The department also banned further use of the Bristol Myers product (the USDA had already removed the implant from the American market). On Jan. 8, 1992, the federal govt placed a temporary ban on all silicon-gel breast implants as

concerns mounted over associated risks. Some 150,000 Canadian women had received implants since the early 1960s. On Jan. 13, 1993, Health and Welfare Minister Benoît Bouchard (b 1940) placed a permanent ban on the sale of all silicone-gel breast implants. Bouchard produced a report showing that 23% of all silicon-implant recipients suffered complications within weeks of surgery.

Apr. 21 Federal Liberal opposition leader Jean Chrétien presented a 9-point unity plan which included Native self-govt, a revised Constitution amending formula, a reformed Senate and a "Declaration of the Nature of Canada" defining and enshrining the 2 official languages. Chrétien called on the govt to hold a referendum on a new Constitution within 10 months.

• New Jersey native Raghib "Rocket" Ismail joined Bruce McNall's Toronto Argonauts with a 4-year contract worth $30.1 million. Ismail became the 2nd highest-paid football player on the continent (to Buffalo Bills QB Jim Kelly) and led the Argonauts to the Grey Cup in his inaugural year.

Apr. 22 A federal report indicated that sewage from the city of Whitehorse was polluting the Yukon R., making the waterway unsafe for drinking and recreation for a distance of 70 km downriver from the city.

• Sask.'s Conservative govt tabled its budget, which cut 600 civil service positions, reduced selected parliamentarians' salaries and placed ceilings on salaries of provincial employees. The province's projected deficit was $265 million.

• Speaking before an audience of 300 at the First Nations Congress of BC, PM Mulroney pledged $300 million to help resolve all 175 land claims disputes by 2000. He promised a Royal Commission to investigate Aboriginal social and economic problems. The audience, long accustomed to such rhetoric, met the PM's comments with silence.

Apr. 24 Alcatel of France purchased Canada's largest producer of cable wire and associated products, the Noranda-owned Canada Wire and Cable Ltd. Canada Wire operated 13 plants in Canada and the US with a staff of 2,200.

• Vice-Admiral Charles Thomas, deputy commander of the Canadian Armed Forces, resigned in protest over upcoming (May 17) cuts to the military, warning that the lives of Canadian soldiers would be put at risk: "If you don't give these kids the tools, some govt, some time, is going to have no choice but to send them somewhere in the world that is ugly. And then they're going to die." Thomas had been with the forces 37 years.

Apr. 29 Ont. treasurer Floyd Laughren tabled his govt's 1st budget, which called for increased spending and a record-setting $9.7 billion deficit.

• Denison Mines Ltd. agreed to close its 35-year-old uranium mines at Elliot L., Ont. They were decommissioned in 1992. The decision was made on the heels of an Ontario Hydro announcement ending its contract to purchase uranium from the company. Denison lost $291.3 million during the 1989 fiscal year. The closure affected 1,500 jobs. Elliot Lake's unemployment rate was 60%.

Also in Apr.

• The PEI govt imposed a moratorium on construction along scenic Cousin's Shore in response to mounting public pressure to halt development of one of Atlantic Canada's most beloved landscapes.

• North Toronto jazz-hip-hop fusion artists The Dream Warriors peaked on British pop charts with singles "My Definition of a Boombastic Jazz Style" and "Wash Your Face in My Sink."

• A Saudi Arabian woman identified as "Nada," claiming refugee status in Canada on the basis of gender-related persecution, had her claim rejected on the grounds she failed to fulfil the description of a victim. The investigating panel: "The claimant would do well, like all her compatriots, to abide by the laws of general application she opposes, and to do this under all circumstances ... in order to study, work or to show consideration for the feelings of her father, who, like everyone else in her large family, was opposed to the liberalism of his daughter." The case spurred the development of the "Guide-lines on Women Refugee Claimants," issued Mar. 9, 1993.

• Que. Justice Louis Tannenbaum ruled that 41 Mohawk charged in the Oka Standoff had the right to be tried in English. The ruling came after Que. Superior Court Justice Benjamin Greenberg overruled requests by Mohawk charged in a parallel case to stand trial in English, stating that the language option guaranteed in the Criminal Code of Canada was "inoperative" in the province of Que.

May 10 Six thousand Sask. nurses from 100 hospitals went on strike for a 2-year, 19% wage increase. The standoff lasted 11 days, and the nurses finally accepted a 9.4–10% increase over 2 years.

May 14 External Affairs Minister Barbara McDougall blamed "errors in judgment" for the fact that Canada granted Mohammed al-Mashat landed immigrant status. The former Iraq ambassador to the US and close adviser to Saddam Hussein was fast-tracked through the Canadian immigration process in 30 days. He arrived in Canada 1 month after the Gulf War ended.

May 17 Defence Minister Marcel Masse (b 1936) announced deep cuts to the military which, eliminated or scaling back operations at CFB bases in Chilliwack, BC, Cornwallis, NS, Shearwater, NS, Goose Bay, Labrador, Shilo, Man., and Baden and Lahr, Germany. Hundreds of millions of dollars in equipment and ammunition purchases were also scrapped, including 1,000 military positions and reductions in the number of new recruits.

June 11 Man. Cree Ovide Mercredi was elected head of the Assembly of First Nations, succeeding George Erasmus at an annual conference held in Winnipeg. The Assembly is Canada's largest Native organization, responsible to 500,000 status Aboriginals.

June 20 A forest fire at Haeckel Hill, Yukon, forced 150 Whitehorse residents to evacuate their homes. The fire covered 150,000 ha and was finally brought under control June 24.

• The federal govt disallowed the sale of Toronto-based De Havilland Aircraft Company to Aerospatiale of France and Alenia of Italy, stating the transfer was unacceptable under the Investment Canada Act. The French-Italian consortium had offered to purchase the manufacturer on condition that Ottawa provide De Havilland with a $500 million cash investment or the equivalent in guaranteed purchase contracts.

June 24 The Pittsburgh Penguins won their 1st Stanley Cup, beating the Minnesota North Stars in 6 games. Pens captain, Montreal native Mario Lemieux scored 44 points in the playoffs, the 2nd highest total since the Oilers' Wayne Gretzky scored 47 points in 1985.

June 27 After hearing over 400,000 participants directly, online, by letter, through live studio telecasts or its 1-800 number, the Citizen's Forum on Canada's Future, chaired by Keith Spicer, issued its final report, which concluded post–Meech Lake Canada was in a crisis of identity, understanding and leadership, and multicultural and bilingual policies were at the root of much national discord. The report suggested that should Que. and Canada be unable to reach agreement over renewed federalism, Quebecers should make a clean break and "pursue their destiny with or without association with what remains of Canada."

July 3 Marcellus Francois, a 24-year-old Haitian immigrant, was shot and killed by police in downtown Montreal. At the time of his killing, Francois was sitting unarmed in his car. The police referred to the incident as a case of "mistaken identity."

July 10 Federal Environment Minister Jean Charest ordered a 2-year, full environmental assessment of Phase I of the $25 billion Great Whale hydroelectric project in Que. Que. Environment Minister Pierre Paradi (b 1950) called the move illegal. Matthew Coon Come, Grand Chief of the Que. Cree, had stated earlier that failure to fully assess the project amounted to "environmental racism," arguing that no such project anywhere in southern Ont. could proceed without an environmental review. On Oct. 2, the Que. govt accepted Charest's order. The Supreme Court of Canada voted unanimously on Feb. 24, 1994, that all future power projects in Que. had to undergo an environmental approval process.

July 11 A Nationair DC–8, leased to Nigeria Airways, crashed shortly after takeoff in Jeddah, Saudi Arabia. All passengers aboard, including 247 Muslim pilgrims returning from Mecca and 14 Canadian crew members, were killed. It was the worst plane crash to date involving a Canadian aircraft.

July 17 Angela Sidney (1902–1991), one of the last fluent speakers of Tagish, an Athapaskan language once common in the Tagish L. region of the Yukon, died. A Tagish elder of the Delsheetaan Nation, she was co-founder of the Yukon International Storytelling Festival. She received the Order of Canada in 1984 for her tireless efforts to preserve Tagish traditions.

July 19 One hundred and fifty people rioted through downtown Halifax after a fight between black and white doormen ignited the city's 200-year-old racial tensions. Fifteen people were injured; 8 were arrested. Community leaders pointed to widespread marginalization of Halifax's 30,000 black residents as root cause.

• U. of Guelph student Gwen Jacob was charged with indecent exposure when she removed her top in public on this hot summer's day. An Ont. court found her guilty on Jan. 27, 1992, and fined her $75. The judge stated that the female breast was "sexually stimulating to men" and should therefore be censored by clothes in public. The Ont. Court of Appeal overturned the ruling on Dec. 10, 1996. Jacob remarked "if we do not want to be perceived as sex objects, we need to control the context in which we present our bodies as sexual." On May 30, 1997, the City of Toronto stipulated that women could go topless in all municipal pools, beaches and buildings.

July 20 BC Premier Rita Johnston retained her leadership position, beating Grace McCarthy (b 1927) at BC's Social Credit leadership convention in Vancouver.

July 21 Pitching great Ferguson "Fergie" Jenkins (b 1942) became the 1st Canadian inducted into baseball's Hall of Fame in Cooperstown, New York. Jenkins pitched a total of 19 Major League seasons with 3 teams: the Philadelphia Phillies, Chicago Cubs and Texas Rangers. The masterful right-hander compiled a record of 284 wins and 226 losses, won 20 or more games in 6 consecutive seasons (seven 20-plus winning seasons in all), and was awarded the Cy Young in 1971. An all-round athlete, Jenkins recorded an incredible 1.00 fielding percentage in 1968, 1976, 1981 and 1983. He also had a few off-season stints with the Harlem Globetrotters in the late 1960s.

July 24 Rev. Douglas Crosby of the Oblate Order of Catholic missionaries apologized to a group of Aboriginals at Lac Ste. Anne, Alb., for abuses the church carried out on First Nations Peoples between 1889 and the 1970s. The priest stated that the Catholic Church had engaged in "cultural, ethnic and religious imperialism."

July 29 The US Coast Guard seized a Canadian fishing vessel in disputed waters between the Queen Charlotte Islands and Alaska Panhandle, claiming the boat was illegally fishing for salmon in American waters. It was the 5th such seizure within 30 days, and hotly disputed by Canadian fisheries.

Aug. 4 A young Canadian baseball squad defeated Taiwan to win Canada's 1st World Youth AAA Baseball Championship, before 5,000 spectators in Westbran Stadium, Brandon, Man.

Aug. 5 Justice Gerald Lang of the Nfld. Supreme Court sentenced former Mount Cashel supervisor Edward English, a Roman Catholic Christian Brother, to 12 years in prison for the sexual and physical assault of boy wards during the 1970s. English received the longest sentence of the 9 Mount Cashel Brothers tried on similar charges. A Royal Commission (1989–1990) verified that wards of Mount Cashel orphanage had suffered physical and sexual abuse at the hands of Christian Brothers in the 1970s. The commission also determined the abuses were ignored by social workers and other public agencies. The Brothers and the Nfld. govt would eventually admit liability in the affair, on May 9, 1995, during a civil suit launched against the institution by a Mount Cashel victim.

Aug. 6 Ont. Premier Bob Rae signed the "Statement of Political Relationship with Ont. First Nations," recognizing the Aboriginal right to self-govt. Ont. became the 1st in Canada to sign such an agreement.

Aug. 7–10 Two thousand five hundred delegates at the Progressive Conservative national policy convention in Toronto voted to recognize Que. as a "distinct society," and Que.'s right to self-determination. Delegates also voted to eliminate the federal multicultural department.

Aug. 12 Parti Québécois candidate Jean Filion, a 52-year-old computer-firm executive representing the riding of Montmorency, won the party's 1st by-election since 1976, taking 13,514 votes. Liberal candidate Claude Desjardin received 8,028 votes.

Aug. 15 The National Gallery purchased 17th-century Italian painter Guido Reni's *Jupiter and Europa* for $3.45 million, the most the gallery paid for any single painting to date.

Aug. 22 The Supreme Court of Canada ruled 7–2 that a rape victim's sexual history was admissible in court, striking down the 1983 "rape shield" Criminal Code provision as a violation of a defendant's right to a fair trial.

Aug. 24 The 45,000-member Canadian Union of Postal Workers (CUPW) began a series of rotating strikes in 8 cities across the country. The dispute concerned job security and job creation. Workers returned to their posts Sept. 6, after Labour Minister Marcel Danis (b 1943) appointed Que. Superior Court Justice Alan Gold to mediate between the CUPW and Canada Post Corp.

Sept. 9 One hundred fifty-five thousand members of the Public Service Alliance of Canada, representing Canada's civil servants, began their 1st nationwide strike following govt proposals to cap wages. The country came to a complete halt. Flights were cancelled and govt agencies were hobbled. It was not until Oct. 3, that civil servants returned to work, after Ottawa introduced back-to-work legislation (Bill C–29), which provided no wage increases in 1991 and a 5% hike in 1992.

Sept. 11 The World Wildlife Foundation (WWF) gave Canada a "C" for its efforts to preserve and protect wilderness areas, stating that only 3.4% of Canadian land and water was set aside for protection. In total, Canadian provinces spent an annual average of 60 cents per person per year on the protection of new wilderness land, and Ottawa 32 cents per person per year.

Sept. 12 Toronto's Amalgamated Transit Union began an 8-day strike over the inclusion and use of part-time workers; 1,700 buses, streetcars and trolleys came to a standstill. The city's 60 km of subway track were deserted; 1.5 million daily public transit users were forced to locate alternative methods of transport.

Sept. 13 A 55-tonne slab of concrete broke from Montreal's beleaguered Olympic Stadium (known locally as "The Big Owe"). No one was injured. The Expos were forced to play 13 home games in other Major League parks.

Sept. 16 Conservative MP William Kempling (b 1921) apologized to Liberal MP Sheila Copps for calling her "a slut" in the House of Commons.

Sept. 23 Frank McKenna's Liberals won another landslide victory in NB, taking all but 12 seats. The Confederation of Regions Party, whose platform included a call to end the province's official bilingualism policies, took 8 seats to become the Official Opposition. NB was Canada's only official bilingual province.

• Mordecai Richler's *New Yorker* article "Inside — Outside" described Quebecers as xenophobic and parochial, angering the province's French-Canadian communities and touching off widespread debate about the relations between Quebecois cultural unity and tribalism. The article was a prelude to Richler's 1992 book release *Oh Canada! Oh Quebec!*

Sept. 24 PM Brian Mulroney presented 28 national unity proposals to the House, including an elected Senate, distinct society recognition for Que., a guaranteed right to hold property and assurances that Aboriginal Peoples would participate in all constitutional deliberations. All proposals were in the form of constitutional amendments.

Sept. 26 The Supreme Court of Canada ruled 4–3 that extradition of a fugitive to the US without a guarantee that the death penalty would not be

imposed (or that, if imposed, would not be carried out) did not violate an individual's Charter rights. The ruling was made in the extradition proceedings of former US marine Charles Ng, charged in the US for a series of 12 torture killings in northern California. Dissenting Justice Peter Cory argued that capital punishment was the "ultimate desecration of human dignity," further stating that "the ceremonial washing of his hands by Pontius Pilate did not relieve him of responsibility for the death sentence imposed by others…"

Oct. 9 Conservative MP Jack Shields (b 1929) apologized to the House of Commons after opposition members accused him of telling African-Canadian NDP member Howard McCurdy (b 1932) to, "Shut up, Sambo."

Oct. 10 The federal govt enacted a farmers' emergency-aid package worth $800 million, to help offset the effects of European and US commodity subsidies.

Oct. 12 Seven hundred workers from 6-grain elevator companies at the port of Thunder Bay, Ont., were legislated back to work after a week-long strike. The federal ruling extended the workers' contract through Jan. 31, 1993. The port, which handled 60% of all prairie wheat shipments, had been closed down during the work stoppage.

Oct. 15 Ont.'s NDP govt allowed the Golden Lake Indian Band to hunt and trap in Algonquin Park.

Oct. 17 The NDP under Mike Harcourt won the BC provincial election, taking 51 of 75 seats. It was the 2nd NDP government in BC history, and the only Socred defeat in 40 years (1972). The Liberals took 17 seats, the Socreds 7.

Oct. 18 Translator, interpreter and teacher Sarah Simon (1901–2001) of Fort McPherson, NWT, was made a member of the Order of Canada for her tireless efforts to preserve the culture and Loucheux language of her Gwich'in 1st Nation. Simon was the 1st to translate the Bible into Loucheux.

Oct. 21 The Sask. NDP under leader Roy Romanow won a resounding victory, taking 53 of the province's

66 seats. Former Premier Grant Devine's PC party took 12 seats (Devine retired to the U. of Sask. in 1992). Romanow immediately appointed 4 women cabinet members, the most in Sask. history.

Oct. 27 One thousand mourners attended the funeral of Native rights activist WW II veteran and Order of Canada recipient Elijah Smith. He died Oct. 1. The Whitehorse funeral was followed by a farewell potlatch at Yukon College, in a building named in Smith's honour.

Oct. 31 Federal Port Moody–Coquitlam MP Ian Waddell (b 1942) was the 1st person since 1913 to be called to the Commons bar and reprimanded by the House Speaker for gross contempt of the House. The rebuke was made in connection to a Nov. 29, incident where Waddell made a lunge for the mace as it was carried from the floor by the sergeant-of-arms.

Also in Oct.
• The National Ballet of Canada announced it would no longer tour Atlantic Canada because the company was unable to sustain the costs of playing before small audiences.

Nov. 3 Allan Legere was convicted of four counts of 1st-degree murder in the torture and beating deaths of three women and a priest in the Miramichi region of NB. After escaping prison guards at a local hospital, Legere, already serving a life sentence for killing a shopkeeper in 1986, was quickly nicknamed the "Monster of Miramichi." Legere's final capture in 1990 ended his reign of terror and concluded one of the largest manhunts in Canadian history.

Nov. 6 Stanislaw Tyminski, a wealthy Canadian businessman and iconoclast, finished 2nd to Lech Walesa in Poland's presidential runoff.

Nov. 18 Bill C–21 took effect, drastically restructuring the ways in which unemployment funds were generated and making it more difficult for people to become eligible, and remain eligible, for unemployment insurance.

Dec. 1–2 The $5 million CBC miniseries *Conspiracy of Silence*, a television drama based on the (Nov. 13,

1971) murder of Man. Cree Helen Betty Osborne and the subsequent cover-up, drew 4.7 million viewers, a record for any Canadian drama to date.

Dec. 23 Ont. Supreme Court Judge Julius Isaac (b 1928), born in Grenada, was appointed chief justice of the Federal Court of Canada, a position he held until Sept. 1999.

Dec. 30 Diana Kilmury of Vancouver became the 1st women to sit on the International Brotherhood of Teamsters' 19-member executive board. The teamsters had a membership of 1.5 million continentwide. Kilmury's rise to vice-presidency and battle with internal corruption was documented in the TV film *Mother Trucker: The Diana Kilmury Story*.

• An Angus Reid poll of 1,505 adults showed Canadians received a failing mean score of 45% when it came to current national events, geography and history. Only 57% of respondents knew John. A Macdonald was Canada's 1st prime minister; 33% knew Wilfrid Laurier was the 1st French Canadian prime minister; and 75% knew there were 10 provinces in Canada.

Dec. 31 An Arctic air mass moved over Vancouver, dumping a record 28–cm of snow on the city in less than 24 hours.

• Eighty inmates at the Yellowknife Correctional Centre went on a 4-hour rampage, destroying most of the male dormitory and causing $200,000 in damages. Forty-five RCMP were called in to quell the riot.

Also in 1991
• Médecins Sans Frontières (Doctors Without Boarders) Canada was founded by Richard Heinzl and Dr. James Orbinski, both of whom had worked extensively in Africa. In its earliest days, MSF Canada was almost entirely a volunteer organization with 60 participants across the country. The 1st MSF Canada field mission was to Cambodia. Over 700 Canadians have been associated with MSF since 1991, in operations ranging from Angola to Bosnia, Liberia to Rwanda, Sir Lanka, Sudan, Afghanistan and Bosnia. In 2003, the international MSF organization was awarded the Nobel Peace Prize.

• Canadian tenor John McDermott released his debut album *Danny Boy*, which went on to sell over 200,000 copies nationwide. Born in Scotland, McDermott's talent for blending traditional Irish and Scottish folk melodies with contemporary styling was discovered while he was working in the circulation department at the *Toronto Star* newspaper. From there McDermott went on to release 9 albums internationally, receive 5 Juno nominations and 3 Canadian platinum records, and establish himself as an international recording superstar.

• Nellie Cournoyea was voted the 1st Aboriginal leader of the NWT. In 1979, she became the 1st Aboriginal woman elected to the NWT legislature.

• The national unemployment rate hovered around 10%. Aboriginal unemployment was 25%.

• The 3 largest religious denominations in Canada were Roman Catholic (45.2% of the population); United Church of Canada (11.5%), and Anglican (8.1%); 12.5% of Canadians held no religious affiliation.

• 16.4% of all dwellings in Ont. were apartments, the nation's highest percentage, compared to PEI at 0.1%, the nation's lowest.

• Over 32 million people flew on Canadian air carriers, compared with just over 2.7 million in 1955.

• Canadian Airlines and parent corporation PWA lost $161.7 million. Air Canada fared worse, losing $218 million.

• PM Brian Mulroney spent $2.95 million on travel abroad.

• 623,704 Canadians were charged with criminal offences.

• 35% of all Canadian homicides were gun-related.

• Yukon govt biologists placed tracking collars on over a thousand moose in a study on the predation habits of wolves: of these moose falling prey to other animals, 27% were killed by wolves; 58% were killed by grizzly bears.

• Legal gambling machines boosted the combined lottery profits of NB, Nfld., NS and PEI to $243 million, up from $170 million in 1990.

• The Doomsday Clock was moved 7 minutes back from Doomsday Midnight as Cold War tensions eased slightly. The clock was maintained by the journal *Bulletin of the Atomic Scientists*; placement of its hands in relation to Midnight — or nuclear annihilation — was determined by the state of world peace.

• Health and Welfare Canada reported 5,647 cases of AIDS in Canada, 3,432 of which ended in death.

• The marriage rate dropped from 9.9% in 1990 to 6.4%, the lowest rate since the Depression.

• The census included its 1st-ever question on common law status.

• Women accounted for 45% of the Canadian labour force.

• 756,095 census respondents claimed to be ethnic Canadians, up from 69,000 in the 1986 census.

• Lauchie Maclean founded Glenora Distillery in Glenora, Cape Breton, Canada's only single-malt distillery. The whisky was crafted from Scottish malt and fresh water from an on-site brook.

• Curragh-owned Sa Dena Hes lead-zinc mine opened in Yukon, 70 km from Watson L. Called the "fastest-built project of its size," the mine employed 160 workers and was to generate 150,000 tonnes of lead and zinc annually. Sa Dena Hes closed 15 months later due to international decreases in the price of metals.

• Throughout Canada, there were 100 fluent speakers of the Haida language: 155 speakers of Kutenai, and 90 speakers of Tlingit. Known as "isolates," these unique Aboriginal languages are considered to have no relation to any other on Earth.

• "The Don't Tax Reading Coalition" failed in its lobbying bid to have the GST removed from printed material.

• Jazz flutist and saxophonist Jane Bunnett (b 1955) recorded *Spirits of Havana*, music infused with the rhythms of Cuba.

• 14% of Canadian immigrants held university degrees compared to 11% of Canadian-born residents.

• Rohinton Mistry (b 1952) published his 1st novel, *Such a Long Journey*, about a man who becomes involved in the politics surrounding the Bangladesh separatist movement in India and Pakistan. It won a host of awards and was shortlisted for the Booker Prize and the Trillium Award.

• U. of Toronto historian Michael Bliss published *A Story of Smallpox in Montreal*, nominated for the Gov-Gen.'s Award for non-fiction. Bliss was nominated again in 1999 for *William Osler: A Life in Medicine*.

• Waterloo, Ont., native David Chilton self-published *The Wealthy Barber: The Common Sense Guide to Successful Financial Planning*, an all-time Canadian best-seller and international success.

• Douglas Coupland (b 1961) published his 1st novel, the influential *Generation X: Tales for an Accelerated culture*. The neologism "Generation X" has since come to define a perceived media-saturated underemployed, overeducated and often original generation born between 1965 and 1980.

1992

Jan. 3 The 45-year-old Miss Canada pageant was cancelled after Baton Broadcasting pulled its sponsorship, calling the annual event "a little dated."

Jan. 6 Toronto Mayor June Rowlands banned the upstart pop group Barenaked Ladies from performing in any city-sponsored event, stating the band's name "objectifies women." The mayor had already banned the group from performing in the city's New Year's Eve celebrations at Nathan Phillips Square on the same grounds. The ensuing publicity hastened the Ladies' rise to international stardom.

Jan. 7 The Ont. NDP govt requested $940 million in

extra federal transfer payments to help shore up its ailing economy.

• MPs Svend Robinson, Geoff Scott (b 1938) and Beryl Gaffney (b 1930) were expelled from China while on a human rights fact-finding mission. They had visited with relatives of dissidents imprisoned after the Tiananmen Square massacre.

Jan. 12 Part 1 of the 3-part CBC television documentary *The Valour and The Horror*, directed by Brian McKenna (b 1945) was aired. The controversial series questioned some of Canada's leadership during WW II and the morality of late-war bombing raids over Germany. On June 25–26, the Senate heard a series of complaints about the series and the CBC. On Mar 7, 1993, the documentary won 3 Geminis: Best Documentary Series; Best Director (Terence McKenna); and Best Writer (Brian McKenna).

Jan. 15 Canada joined 12 European countries in recognizing the new Yugoslavia-breakaway states of Croatia and Slovenia.

• PEI, Que. and Ont. ordered meningitis vaccinations be given to all children after the highly contagious inflammation left 13 dead since Nov. 1991. The vaccination program was the largest in Canada since the Salk polio inoculations of the early 1950s.

Jan. 16 Que. Superior Court Justice Jacques Dufour ruled that "Nancy B.," paraplegic and long-time sufferer of Guillain-Barré syndrome, could legally disconnect from a respirator if she so desired, stating that the discontinuation of medical treatment was not an act of suicide. On Feb. 13, Nancy B. ordered her medical treatment discontinued. She died shortly thereafter in a Montreal hospital.

Jan. 17 The 1st of 5 national Unity Conference discussions on the federal govt's constitutional proposals began in Halifax. The discussions would move to Calgary, Montreal and Toronto, the last talks beginning in Vancouver Feb. 14. The conferences were chaired by Yves Fortier (b 1935) and included discussion sessions with private citizens and interest groups. Concluding recommendations included distinct society recognition for Que., recognition of Aboriginals' inherent right to self-govt and an elected Senate.

Jan. 21 Television Northern Canada, Canada's 1st Northern television network, was launched, broadcasting in 5 time zones to over 100,000 people in 94 communities north of 55° latitude. Programming was scheduled in 10 Aboriginal languages, plus French and English.

Jan. 22 After 19 postponements, Dr. Roberta Bondar of Sault Ste. Marie, became the 1st Canadian woman and the 1st Canadian since Marc Garneau in 1984 to enter outer space. Bondar and 6 other astronauts lifted off from Cape Canaveral on an 8-day mission aboard space shuttle *Discovery*. She carried out 43 life-sciences experiments for 13 countries while in orbit.

• Bombardier Inc. of Montreal purchased controlling interest of troubled Toronto-based De Havilland Aircraft Company for $51 million; the remaining interest was assumed by the Ont. govt. In return, the federal and Ont. govts pledged $589 million in subsidies and investments toward De Havilland.

Jan. 23 The Supreme Court of Canada ruled, in the case of Alb.'s $355 million Oldman R. Dam project, that the federal govt had a right to conduct environmental reviews on any provincial project that might impact on federal jurisdiction. The ruling forced the Alb. govt to seek federal approval to continue with the project.

Jan. 24 The govt of NS placed Sydney Steel Co. (SYSCO) on the trading block. The beleaguered Crown corporation had lost an estimated $3 billion since 1968.

Jan. 27 Thirteen Indian Sikhs who had paid $70,000 each to be smuggled from Germany were found cowering aboard a container vessel in Halifax Harbour. All 13 immediately applied for refugee status.

• Environment Minister Jean Charest pledged $85 million over 6 years to study the greenhouse effect, stating global warming was "one of the biggest long-term threats to the environment."

Jan. 28 Struggling Canadian book publishers received a boost when Communications Minister Perrin Beatty (b 1950) provided $102 million in funding to be distributed over 5 years to firms at least 75% Canadian owned.

Jan.–Apr. 1993 A known total of 22 northern Ont. Native children committed suicide.

Also in Jan.
• York U. began the nation's 1st Ph.D. program in Women's Studies. Initial enrollment consisted of 5 candidates.

• BC rocker Bryan Adams's single "I Do It For You" hit No.1 on the pop charts in 19 countries. The song became Britain's best-selling single.

Feb. 1 PM Brian Mulroney met with Russian President Boris Yeltsin in Ottawa. Mulroney offered Yeltsin reduced tariffs and access to $100 million in credit in return for a secured 5-year market share for Canadian grain.

Feb. 4 Environment Canada warned that further thinning of the ozone layer would significantly increase harmful levels of ultraviolet radiation and increase the likelihood of Canadians contracting skin cancer.

• Calgary-based Gulf Canada Resources pulled out of the $5.2 billion Hibernia oil project, claiming it could no longer afford to participate in the megaproject. On Jan. 4, 1993, the expected replacement for Gulf, New York–based Texaco, withdrew its consideration. On Jan. 15, 1993, the federal govt stepped in to help compensate, taking an 8.5% stake worth $360 million. One billion dollars in federal grants and $1.7 million in federal guaranteed loans had already been invested in the project. On Mar. 25, 1993, Arkansas-based Murphy Oil joined the offshore-development consortium with a 6.5% interest. The Hibernia platform was towed out to sea May 23, 1997.

Feb. 9 Lyn McLeod became the 1st woman to lead the Ont. Liberal Party, defeating Murray Elston, Greg Sorbara, Charles Beer, David Ramsay and Steve Mahoney at the Liberal party leadership convention.

Feb. 10 US Customs ruled that Honda Civics shipped into the US from Alliston, Ont., between 1989–1990, did not meet the 50% Canadian-content requirements set in the Canada-US Free Trade Agreement. Honda was assessed $22 million in back tariffs.

Feb. 11 The GATT ruled against US tariffs on Canadian beer and wine, giving Canadian brewers and winemakers freer access to US markets. On Apr. 25, Canada agreed to remove trade barriers to American beer by Sept. 30, 1993, in compliance with another GATT ruling of Apr. 16.

Feb. 15 Fisheries Products International (FPI) announced it would have to lay off 1,000 Nfld. fishery workers because it could not locate enough cod to complete its quota.

• Six children between the ages of 6 months and 9 years died in a Davis Inlet, Labrador, house fire. The house had no running water, was poorly insulated and was equipped with shoddy wiring, typical of the houses throughout the troubled community of 500.

• Kerrin Lee-Gartner (b 1966) of Calgary won gold in the women's downhill at the Olympic Winter Games in Albertville, France. It was Canada's 1st and only downhill Olympic gold. Canada's other Olympic gold at Albertville came in women's short-track relay. The team consisted of Sylvie Daigle (b 1962), Nathalie Lambert (b 1963), Angela Cutrone and Annie Perreault (b 1971).

Feb. 19 A.J. Casson, the last surviving member of the Group of Seven, died in Toronto. He was 93.

Feb. 21 The federal govt agreed to send 1,200 troops to wartorn Yugoslavia as part of a 31-country UN peacekeeping mission.

Feb. 24 East Coast domestic cod quotas were cut by 35%.

Feb. 25 Conservative Finance Minister Donald Mazankowski tabled the Tory budget. It included cuts in personal income tax, revision of the baby bonus, a provision to allow Canadians to borrow from RRSPs to purchase a 1st home, the merging or closing down of a number of govt agencies and cuts in defence spending, including the elimination of all troops from Europe by 1994.

Feb. 27 The Supreme Court of Canada ruled 9–0 to overturn pornography-distribution charges against Donald Victor Butler. In the process, the Court defined pornography as any sexual material, which includes violence or children, and is degrading or dehumanizing. In 1987, police seized the entire inventory of Butler's Winnipeg video store. He was charged with dozens of counts of possessing and exposing obscene material for distribution and sale. Butler was convicted on 8 charges and acquitted on the rest. In 1989, a Man. Court of Appeal overturned the original decision and convicted Butler on all counts. The Supreme Court rejected the appeal court ruling, based on its new definition of pornography, and ordered a new trial. Butler was subsequently found guilty in 1993 and sentenced to several months in jail.

Feb. 28 The Commons-Senate Committee, comprising Senators and MPs from all 3 federal parties, came to an agreement on proposed constitutional changes, including an elected Senate, distinct society recognition for Que., recognition of Aboriginal Peoples' right to self-govt and the constitutional enshrinement of the nation's social programs. The subsequent report, known as the Dobbie-Beaudoin Report, after co-chairs MP Dorothy Dobbie (b 1945) and Senator Gerald Beaudoin (b 1929), was handed to PM Mulroney Mar. 1.

Also in Feb.

• The inflation rate dropped to 1.6%, the lowest level in nearly 20 years.

• The Grand Council of the Crees of Quebec made a Submission to the United Nations Commission on Human Rights in Geneva entitled *Status and Rights of the James Bay Crees in the Context of Québec's Secession From Canada*. A detailed update called *Sovereign Injustice: Forcible Inclusion of the James Bay Crees and Cree Territory into a Sovereign Québec* was published in 1995. Both pieces pursued the question of Native rights and Aboriginal land in the context of a divided Canada. In 1997, a UN Working Group released a draft Declaration on the Rights of

Indigenous Peoples confirming that indigenous peoples have significant rights under international law, including the right to land, resources and self-determination.

Mar. 1 Ont. courts ruled that, from this time on, all fathers ordered by the court to pay child support would have their wages trimmed (garnisheed) at the source.

Mar. 4 Montreal's 15-month-old Eaton Centre became the city's 3rd major shopping centre to be seized by creditors.

Mar. 6 The federal govt placed a 5-year moratorium on commercial salmon fishing in Nfld. (excluding Labrador) due to an extreme decline in stocks. In late Aug., on the other side of the country, federal Fisheries Minister John Crosbie placed a moratorium on the 1992 Fraser R. salmon season after estimates showed there were 1.2 million less spawning salmon in the river. On Sept. 15, 200 BC fishers on 100 vessels filled Vancouver Harbour to protest the Department of Fisheries and Oceans' management of their industry.

Mar. 9 Alb. Cree Wilson Nepoose was released from prison after the Alb. Court of Appeal overturned his 1986 life sentence for murder.

Mar. 10 The House of Commons unanimously passed a resolution recognizing Métis leader Louis Riel's "unique and historical role as a founder of Man." Riel was hanged in Regina for treason on Nov. 16, 1885, for his leadership of the North-West Rebellion of 1885.

Mar. 11 Ozone warnings were added to Environment Canada weather reports.

Mar. 12 Catherine Anne Fraser, former Edmonton lawyer and Alb. Court of Appeal justice, became the 1st woman appointed chief justice of Alb.

Mar. 17 Bloc Québécois MP Pierrette Venne (b 1945) declared that Mordecai Richler's upcoming book, *Oh Canada! Oh Quebec! Lament for a Divided Nation*, should be banned because prepublication excerpts were inciting hatred against Quebecers.

Mar. 18 Suncor, successor to Great Canadian Oil Sands Ltd., the company that established the 1st commercial oil extraction plan on the Athabascan oil sands on Sept. 30, 1967, became a publicly traded company.

Mar. 19 The House of Commons passed the Canadian Environment Assessment Act, which received Assent June 23, 1992, but was not proclaimed until Jan. 1995. The act, which replaced the 1984 Environment Assessment Review Process, required mandatory environmental reviews on all major projects such as mines, mills and dams that impacted on federal jurisdiction or involved federal funds. Que. hydro-nationalists interpreted the act as one in a long line of bully infringements.

Mar. 25 The federal govt loosened foreign ownership restrictions over Alb.'s oil patch, allowing individual foreign investments of up to $150 million without the necessity of review by Investment Canada.

Mar. 27 A flotilla of 75 men on 4 vessels departed St. John's, Nfld., to draw media attention to overfishing by foreign trawlers off the Grand Banks. Four thousand five hundred Newfoundlanders crowded the docks to support the effort. Foreign vessels continued to fish outside Canada's 200-mile (322-km) limit, despite serious declines in fish stocks. On June 5, a scientific council of the Northwest Atlantic Fisheries Organization (NAFO) determined that north Atlantic cod stocks were at the lowest level ever recorded. The council recommended the Canadian cod quota be reduced from 120,000 tonnes to 25,000 tonnes (the 1988 quota was 266,000 tonnes). Europeans, however, continued to fish off Canadian territorial jurisdiction.

Apr. 1 NHL players, under the direction of association president Bob Goodenow (b 1952), went on strike for the 1st time in the league's 75-year history. Player concerns included licencing fees, free agency and increased revenue sharing. Players returned to the ice Apr. 10.

Apr. 9 Native Peoples were promised the right to self-govt at a 2-day national-unity conference chaired by Constitutional Affairs Minster Joe Clark in Halifax.

Apr. 14 In a public vote, Vancouver residents selected the $125 million Moshe Safdie design for the city's new Library Square (Vancouver Public Library). It would be the most expensive capital project in the city's history to date. The design resembled a massive, 21-storey Roman coliseum.

• The Supreme Court of Canada overturned 39-year-old David Milgaard's 1970 life sentence for the murder of nurse's aide Gail Miller. The ruling was made on the basis of new DNA evidence not available at the time of the original trial. Milgaard was sent to prison at age 16, where he suffered terribly under the hands of older inmates. He twice attempted suicide and was once shot while trying to escape. All told, he spent 22 years in prison for a crime he did not commit. On May 16, 1999, Milgaard was given a $10 million compensation package from the federal and Sask. govts. On Oct. 12, 1999, 47-year-old Larry Fisher was brought to trial in a Yorkton, Sask., courthouse, charged with the 1969 murder. Fisher was found guilty on Nov. 22 and given an automatic life sentence.

Apr. 22 The Gwich'in completed a land claim deal with the federal govt, receiving title to nearly 24,000 km^2 of land in the NWT and northeastern Yukon, along with $75 million to be paid over 15 years.

Apr. 29 Seven hundred prisoners in Montreal's overcrowded, 80-year-old Bordeaux Jail rioted for more than 8 hours, causing $1 million in damages.

Apr. 30 Que. Premier Robert Bourassa declared that the basic elements of the failed Meech Lake Accord — including provincial veto powers, a distinct society clause for Que. and a fixed 1/3 representation on the 9-member Supreme Court — would have to be included in any future constitutional package before Que. would return to the bargaining table. Que. had boycotted all constitutional negotiations since the 1990 failure of Meech Lake.

Also in Apr.
• According to the UN, Canada was the best place in the world to live. The selection was based on such criteria as average education attainment, life expectancy, standard of living and health care.

• Algoma Steel of Sault Ste. Marie emerged from bankruptcy protection with the signing of the Joint Restructuring Process Agreement. Workers invested their pensions into the firm and were given 60% of its voting shares. In return, the Ont. govt provided a $100 million–plus loan guarantee. The deal saved 5,000 jobs.

May 4 One thousand demonstrators, mostly youths, rioted in downtown Toronto. They had gathered to protest the treatment of blacks by Canada's legal system. Hundreds of storefront windows were smashed. There were 30 arrests, and only a few minor injuries. Rioters represented a wide range of cultural backgrounds.

• Residents of the NWT voted to approve the western boundary of the future territory of Nunavut (meaning "our land"), to be established in 1999 (Apr. 1, 1999) from the central and eastern portion of the NWT. The federal govt agreed to give the Inuit ownership and administrative control over the 350,000-km^2 region, including $1.15 billion to be paid over 14 years. On Oct. 30, Inuit, federal and territorial leaders signed an accord to go ahead with creation of the new territory.

May 7 Claude Morin (b 1929), former Parti Québécois cabinet minister, admitted he had been a paid informant for the RCMP during the mid-1970s.

May 9 A gas explosion in a Westray coal mine near Plymouth, NS, claimed the lives of 26 miners. Tremors from the explosion were felt over 1 km away. More than 200 reporters flocked to the scene to cover the 6-day rescue effort to locate workers buried some 350 m below the surface. The search was halted May 15. Only 15 bodies were recovered. The mine was not reopened, and in 1995 it was sealed. On Feb. 1, 1993, the Workers Compensation Board of NS pledged $15 million to families of those killed in the tragedy. Payments included lifetime pensions and $15,000 cash to surviving spouses, child support payments and funeral-cost coverage. On Mar 4, 1993, 18 health-and-safety charges levied against Westray Mines and 4 managers in connection to the 26 deaths were dropped by the Crown so as not to prejudice the outcome of upcoming criminal charges. The move proved disadvantageous. In July, 1993, criminal charges against Curragh Inc. and 2 senior managers of the Westray coal mine were dropped when provincial court Justice Patrick Curran ruled that evidence presented in the case was not solid. A provincial inquiry into the disaster was issued Dec. 1, 1997.

May 15 The Reichmanns' Toronto-based Olympia and York commercial real estate development conglomerate filed for bankruptcy protection in an Ont. court, due in part to debts incurred by its Canary Wharf project in London, England. On Feb. 5, 1993, an Ont. judge signed a court order ending the bankruptcy protection, setting in motion the dissolution of the Reichmann international empire. Olympia Floor and Wall Tile Co., the business that kick-started the Reichmann empire, was virtually the only business left in the hands of brothers Paul, Albert and Ralph.

• Ottawa appealed a US decision to reduce tariffs on Canadian softwood lumber from 14.48% to 6.5%, demanding that all tariffs on Canadian softwood lumber be eliminated immediately. The US-Canada softwood lumber dispute over Canadian subsidies and US punitive tariffs would rage through the 1990s and extend beyond 2003.

May 18 A 3:30 a.m. bomb blast destroyed Dr. Henry Morgentaler's abortion clinic on Harbord St. in central Toronto. There were no injuries and no culprits located.

May 21 The Supreme Court of Canada ruled that the reverse onus on an accused in a case of living off the avails of prostitution was not contrary to the Charter.

May 24 Vancouver native Timothy Stevenson became the 1st openly gay minister ordained by the United Church of Canada.

June 3 The Ont. govt allowed wide-open Sunday shopping, but retained existing regulations forcing retailers to close on all statutory holidays.

June 9 Nine people, including 5 police officers associated with an unlicenced babysitting service in Martensville, Sask., were charged with 170 counts

of physical and sexual abuse. The crimes occurred between 1989–1991, and involved children between the ages of 3 and 12. On Feb. 2, 1994, service operators Ronald and Linda Sterling were found not guilty on all charges. Travis Sterling, their son, was convicted on 8 counts of abuse and given a 5-year sentence. The only other conviction came against a young offender. Charges against the police officers were stayed Feb. 10, 1994.

June 10 An international tribunal ruled that France could control a 10.5-mile wide, 200-mile-long strip of water running south of St-Pierre and Miquelon. The ruling, which involved disputed Nfld. waters, gave France a third of its initial claim.

June 11 At the International Earth Summit in Rio de Janeiro, PM Mulroney was the 1st to sign the UN Convention on Biological Diversity (Rio Convention), an international plan to ensure the preservation of delicate ecosystems and endangered species. Ontario Hydro Chairman Maurice Strong (b 1929) played a pivotal role in organizing the international conference, for which he received the Onassis Delphi Prize later that year. Ten years later (2002), Canada came under attack by the Sierra Legal Defence Fund, which charged that Canada had reneged on its Rio obligations and had failed to adequately protect old-growth forests and endangered species. On Nov. 13, 1995, Montreal was selected as the headquarters of the Secretariat of the Convention, moving into the World Trade Center on Rue St. Jacques the following year.

• Bob White, leader of the Canadian Autoworkers Union, was elected president of the Canadian Labour Congress (CLC). The position came with a $95,000 annual salary. Former national postal workers' (CUPW) president Jean-Claude Parrot was elected vice-president.

June 12 The CRTC extinguished phone company monopolies on long-distance services, allowing Canadians choice among competing service providers.

June 19 Russian President Boris Yeltsin signed an agreement in Ottawa to purchase 1 million tonnes of Canadian wheat for $200 million. The struggling new democracy had already purchased $150 million worth of wheat on credit, which it had yet to pay off. On Aug. 17, the Canadian Wheat Board cancelled 18 wheat shipments to Russia, which was 60 days in arrears of payment.

June 25 The Supreme Court of Canada ruled that the Mulroney govt did have the constitutional, jurisdictional authority to enact the 1991 Goods and Services Tax (GST).

• The Supreme Court of Canada ruled that differing insurance rates for males and females under age 25 was not a matter falling under human rights legislation.

June 30 A petition filed by US steel firms with the US Commerce Department claimed Canada was dumping various steel products into the US at costs ranging from between 8% and 75% below fair market prices. The petition also stated that Canadian steel subsidies caused US unemployment.

• The federal govt agreed to sell India 1 million tonnes of wheat, the 1st sale to the country in 8 years.

Also in June
• Justice Minister Kim Campbell's Bill C–49 was unanimously passed by all 3 parties on second reading. The bill required men to obtain clear, voluntary consent from women, through words or conduct, before engaging in sexual activity (called the "No Means No" law). The bill also restricted use of a rape victim's personal history in court.

July 1 Canada celebrated its 125th birthday.

July 2 Federal Fisheries minister John Crosbie closed Nfld.'s northern cod fishery for 2 years because of dwindling stocks. Cod represented 40% of Nfld.'s entire fishery, or $700 million, in 1991. The closure put 19,000 fishers and plant workers out of work. The moratorium would be extended through the Atlantic Groundfish Management Plan on Dec. 20, 1993, and extend in whole or in part throughout the decade.

July 7 Constitution Affairs Minister Joe Clark and 9 provincial premiers agreed on a series of constitu-

tional proposals in Ottawa. The new unity package formed the basis of a renewed federalism. Que. premier Robert Bourassa abstained from the meeting, consistent with his refusal to attend all constitutional talks since Meech Lake. He did, however, return to the table with all other 1st ministers on Aug. 10 at Harrington L., Que., where all premiers hammered out what would eventually become the Charlottetown Accord (Aug. 28).

July 10 Air Canada announced the layoff of 1,809 employees. On Dec. 14, Canadian Airlines International announced it would cut 15% of its domestic flights.

July 24 The Mulroney govt unveiled plans to purchase 50 EH–101 British-designed military helicopters for $4.8 billion, the 3rd largest defence contract to date. The EH–101s would replace the aging, twin-rotor Labrador fleet. PM Chrétien voided the deal after entering office (Nov. 4, 1993).

July 25 Trade Minister Michael Wilson, together with trade officials from the US and Mexico, met in Mexico City to begin final negotiations of the North American Free Trade Agreement (NAFTA).

July 30 Calgary's Mark Tewksbury (b 1968) beat an Olympic record to take gold in the men's 100-m backstroke at the Summer Olympics in Barcelona, Spain. On Aug. 2, Silken Laumann (b 1964) captured the hearts of millions worldwide, winning the bronze medal in the women's single skulls. Two months earlier, the World Cup champion had been struck by a German boat in a warm-up exercise in Essen, Germany. The crash severed all the muscles, tendons and ligaments between her right shin and ankle. Initial medical reports indicated she would never race again. Other 1992 Summer Olympic highlights included Kathleen Heddle (b 1965) and Marnie McBean (b 1968) taking gold in coxless pairs; Kirsten Barnes, Jessica Monroe, Brenda Taylor and Kay Worthington taking gold in coxless fours; a sweep in coxless eights with both the men's and women's teams taking gold; and Mark McKoy's (b 1961) brilliant sprint for gold in the 110-m hurdles. The most infamous event of the Olympics came on Aug. 6, when synchronized swimmer Sylvie Fréchette was awarded the silver in the solo category. After completion of the 1st portion of her finals, the Brazilian judge mistakenly punched 8.7 instead of 9.7 into an electronic scoring device. Although the judge openly admitted the mistake, Olympic rules dictated that once a score was posted it could not be changed. An immediate appeal to the International Amateur Swimming Federation was flatly rejected. However, Fréchette would finally get her due: in a nationally televised ceremony at the Montreal Forum, Dec. 15, 1993, IOC member in Canada Richard Pound awarded her a 2nd gold after winning a 16-month appeal to the IOC.

• The 1st contingent of 250 Canadian peacekeepers completed its tour of duty in wartorn Sarajevo. There was heavy fighting throughout the day. French, Egyptian and Ukrainian forces replaced the troops.

• After 27 months of testimony, a London, Ont., court sentenced Guy Paul Morin to life in prison for the murder of 9-year-old Christine Jessop, who had been abducted from Queensville, Ont., on Oct. 2, 1984. (Morin had previously been acquitted of the charge, by jury, in 1986.) James Donnelly of the Ont. court denounced the trial as a "travesty," stating he would appeal the verdict. On Feb. 9, 1993, Morin was placed on parole pending an appeal. On Jan. 23, 1995, Morin was exonerated on the basis of DNA testing not previously available at the time of the original conviction. Two years later, in Jan. 1997, Morin received a full apology from Ont. Attorney Gen. Charles Harnick, and was awarded $1.5 million by the Ont. govt to compensate for the wrongful murder sentence.

Aug. 6 The Ont. Court of Appeal ruled that the Canadian Human Rights Act discriminated against gays and lesbians because it did not ensure against discrimination based on sexual orientation.

Aug. 17 Thirty-two-year-old Sgt. Michael Ralph (1960–1992) was killed by an anti-tank mine while serving as a member of the Canadian UN Peacekeeping Forces in Croatia. Over 1,400 troops had been stationed in the former Yugoslavia since Apr. Ralph was the 1st Canadian casualty.

• Rev. Stan McKay, a Man. Cree, became the 1st Native moderator of the United Church of Canada.

Aug. 24 Three Concordia U. engineering faculty members were shot and killed and another fatally wounded by associate professor Valery Fabrikant in a dispute over tenure and plagiarism. On Aug 11, 1993, a Que. Supreme Court found the mechanical-engineering professor guilty of 1st degree murder and sentenced him to 25 years in prison.

Aug. 28 All 1st ministers agreed to a new Constitution package to be put to the people in a national referendum Oct. 26, 1992. The Charlottetown Accord included Senate reform, an increase in the number of House seats to 337, with Que. getting a fixed minimum 25% of seats, the recognition of Que. as a distinct society, the recognition of Aboriginals' inherent right to self-govt and the elimination of trade barriers between provinces.

Sept. 3 The question to be put to Canadians in the Oct. 26 referendum was finalized: "Do you agree that the Constitution of Canada should be renewed on the basis of the agreement reached on Aug. 28, 1992?"

Sept. 5–14 The Stoke Mandeville Paralympic Games took place in Barcelona, Spain. In front of a capacity crowd, the Canadian women's wheelchair-basketball team won the gold medal, beating the US 35–26 in the final round. Canada won 75 medals in total.

Sept. 10 Reform Party leader Preston Manning argued he would vote no in the upcoming Charlottetown Accord referendum, stating, "This thing will lead to chaos."

Sept. 13 Judy Rebick, president of the 3-million-member National Action Committee on the Status of Women, stated her organization supported the "No" side in the upcoming referendum, citing concerns that the accord might transfer too much power to the provinces, and also, the accord failed to address gender inequalities in the Senate.

Sept. 14 Former Liberal cabinet minister, Senate leader and diplomat Paul Martin Sr. died at 89 in Windsor, Ont. Martin spent 33 years in the House and 6 years in the Senate. He retired from politics in 1974. All flags on Parliament Hill were placed at half-mast. His son, Paul Martin Jr., would become PM in 2003.

• The federal govt ended the universality of the Family Allowance system, restricting monthly payments to low-income families with children. The Family Allowance was introduced in 1945 as Canada's 1st universal welfare program, which gave every family with children a monthly cheque to help cover the costs of child rearing.

Sept. 17 South Korea agreed to purchase its 3rd and 4th CANDU nuclear reactors for $1 billion. The reactors went critical in 1998 and 1999. The 1st Korean CANDU reactor went into commercial operation in 1983. By 2003, Canadian-made CANDU reactors would be operational in 5 foreign countries: Argentina, China, India, Romania and South Korea.

Sept. 18 A suspicious explosion at Giant gold mine in Yellowknife, NWT, claimed the lives of 9 miners working 200 m below the surface. Mine workers had been on strike since May 23 (the strike ended Dec. 1, 1993). Six of the 9 who perished were union men who had crossed the picket line. On Oct. 16, 1993, union mine worker Roger Wallace Warren was charged in Yellowknife in connection to the explosion. Following an 11-week trail, Warren was convicted on Jan. 26, 1995 of 2nd degree in the murders, and sentenced to 20 years' imprisonment.

Sept. 21 Former PM Pierre Trudeau openly criticized the Charlottetown Constitutional Accord in an essay published in *Maclean's*. The Montreal lawyer argued that English-speaking Canadians had "not yet realized that the nationalist's thirst will never be satisfied, and that each new ransom paid to stave off the threat of schism will simply encourage the master blackmailers to renew the threat and double the ransom."

• BC Premier Mike Harcourt, PM Mulroney and BC First Nations established the British Columbia Treaty Commission to facilitate and fast-track land claims negotiations. At this time, most of the BC landmass was claimed under Native dispute.

Sept. 22 Calgary Constable Robert Vanderwell was shot and killed during a routine traffic inspection. It was the 1st fatal shooting of a Calgary police officer since 1977.

• PM Mulroney, Premier Roy Romanow and Sask First Nations signed the Sask. Treaty Land Entitlement Act, providing $450 million to help settle existing land debts owed Sask. Native Peoples.

Sept. 23 Goaltender Manon Rhéaume (b 1972) became the 1st woman to play in the NHL, appearing in net for the Tampa Bay Lighting, against the St. Louis Blues in a preseason game.

• Hamilton, Ont.–based Stelco laid off 800 workers in efforts to streamline productivity.

Sept. 24 The Supreme Court of Canada ruled, in the case of U. of Alb. professor Olive Dickason that, in the context of the tenure system, discrimination based on age was reasonable and justifiable. The Native history instructor was told she had to retire at the mandatory age of 65, although she had begun teaching only 10 years earlier.

Sept. 28 In an enthusiastic display in Quebec City, PM Mulroney pretended to rip up the Charlottetown Accord, threatening that a "No" vote in the upcoming referendum would mean the end of Canada. The dollar fell to a four and a half-year low of 79.24 cents US the next day.

Oct. 8 Sixty-one Man. status Indian chiefs came out on the "No" side of the Charlottetown Accord, arguing that it might erode existing treaty rights. The announcement was made despite the efforts of Ovide Mercredi, Grand Chief of the Assembly of First Nations, who campaigned for the "Yes" side.

• The Ottawa Senators defeated the Montreal Canadiens 5–3 before a full house of 10,449 at Ottawa's Civic Centre. It was the new team's 1st NHL game, and the 1st Ottawa NHL franchise in 58 years.

Oct. 12 Montreal-born and McGill-educated California Institute of Technology professor Rudolph Marcus (b 1923) was awarded the Nobel Prize in Chemistry for his work on electron transfer reactions in chemical systems.

Oct. 13 Toronto novelist Michael Ondaatje was named co-winner of the Booker Prize for *The English Patient* a novel set in Italy near the end of WW II. (It would be adapted into a blockbuster Hollywood movie in 1996 and win 9 Oscars, including one for Best Picture.) Ondaatje was the 1st Canadian to win the prestigious international award. His co-recipient was British author Barry Unsworth, for *Sacred Hunger*. Ondaatje was awarded the Gov-Gen.'s literary award for the book on Nov. 30.

Oct. 14 Standard and Poor's of New York reduced Canada's foreign currency debt rating from AAA to AA, due in part, to the ongoing unity crisis.

Oct. 17 Two thousand one hundred workers at the GM–Suzuki Cami Automotive plant in Ingersoll, Ont., ended a month-long strike, accepting an 8.59% wage increase.

Oct. 24 The Toronto Blue Jays beat the Atlanta Braves 4-3 in 11 innings to capture their 1st World Series — the 1st of 2 in a row. The Jays became the 1st Canadian team (and 1st non-American team) to win the series. Manager Cito Gaston became the 1st African-American to lead a team to the coveted title.

Oct. 26 Canadians rejected the Charlottetown Constitutional Accord in a national referendum, despite the support of all 10 provincial leaders and the 3 major political parties: 54.4% voted no; 44.6% voted yes; six of 10 provinces went no, including Que. The referendum voting process cost Canadian taxpayers $103.86 million. Not unlike Meech Lake in 1990, the bulk of federal and provincial representatives had been out of touch with the country, despite the Conservatives' expenditure of $5.2 million on prereferendum opinion polls.

Oct. 27 The Canadian Armed Forces admitted its policies regarding the exclusion of homosexuals violated the Canadian Charter of Rights and Freedoms and, in an out-of-court settlement, awarded former Lt. Michelle Douglas (b 1963), a lesbian who had been forced to resign her commission, $100,000 plus legal costs. A federal judge also demanded that the Forces admit homosexuals, which it agreed to do.

• BC's NDP govt introduced pro-labour legislation banning the use of replacement workers. Bill–84 reintroduced parallel legislation that had been scrapped by the former Socred govt. The Ont. NDP govt followed suit on Nov. 5, also passing legislature banning the use of strike-breakers anywhere in the province.

Oct. 28 More than 6,000 Ont. police officers demonstrated at Queen's Park, Toronto, to protest a new policy requiring officers to file reports every time they drew their pistols. The police had refused to wear full uniforms since Oct. 4 as part of the protest.

Oct. 29 The Supreme Court of Canada loosened statute of limitation restrictions in cases where individuals who had been sexually abused as children decided later in life to sue their assailants.

• PM Mulroney announced he would lead the Conservatives in the next general election.

Oct. 30 A Hercules CC-130 transport plane crashed 20 km from an Alert, NWT, runway, killing 5. Thirteen survivors were stranded for 34 hours in −22°C blizzard conditions.

Nov. 1 CBC television broadcast *In The Key of Oscar*, a 2-hour documentary tracing the life and music of jazz giant and Montreal native Oscar Peterson. Peterson began playing the piano as a youth. He was vaulted into stardom following a "Jazz at the Philharmonic" concert at Carnegie Hall in 1949. He played with the who's who of 20th-century music, including Ella Fitzgerald, Billie Holiday, Dizzy Gillespie, Lester Young, Louis Armstrong and Coleman Hawkins. His legendary trio of Ray Brown and Herb Ellis produced some of the finest recordings in contemporary music.

Nov. 1–Dec. 15 The police collected 20,758 handguns, shotguns and rifles in a national firearms amnesty.

Nov. 2 Petro-Canada cancelled its oil exploration project in Myanmar (formerly Burma) the day Amnesty International published a detailed report showing the troubled Southeast Asian state was riddled with human-rights abuses, including widespread political oppression, torture and murder.

• Canadian astronaut Steve MacLean, aboard the US space shuttle *Columbia*, touched down at Kennedy Space Center after 10 days in outer space.

Maclean was the 3rd and last Canadian to board the shuttle under the National Aeronautic and Space Administration agreement of 1983.

Nov. 5 Sharon Carstairs resigned after 8 years as Man. Liberal Party leader following an exhausting campaign to kill the Charlottetown Constitutional Accord.

• The federal govt released figures revealing ozone levels over Canada had reached record lows.

Nov. 8 Conrad Black's Hollinger Inc. purchased 22.5% of Southam Inc. for $259 million, making Hollinger the biggest shareholder in Canada's largest newspaper chain.

• In efforts to reduce its $16 billion debt, the Sask. NDP govt lifted a 9-year-old moratorium on the expansion of uranium mining in the province.

Nov. 10 RCMP Commissioner Norman Inkster was appointed president of Interpol, the international criminal police agency based in Lyon, France.

Nov. 12 CFL commissioner Larry Smith unveiled plans to expand the league into the US — a CFL 1st. Smith promised Montreal, which dropped out of the league after the 1987 season, another franchise. By the time the Alouettes returned in 1996, CFL franchises in Sacramento, California, Baltimore, Maryland, Shrevesport, Louisiana, Las Vegas, Nevada, Memphis, Tennessee, San Antonio, Texas, and Birmingham, Alabama had come and gone.

Nov. 13 David Irving, a British author who claimed the Nazi concentration camp of Auschwitz was built after WW II as a tourist attraction, lost a deportation hearing and was ordered to leave Canada within 48 hours.

• PM Mulroney appointed Justice John C. Major (b 1931) of the Alb. Court of Appeal to the Supreme Court of Canada, replacing fellow Albertan William Stevenson (b 1934). Major was Mulroney's 4th choice. Prominent female Alb. justices Catherine Fraser, May Hetherington and Ellen Picard each refused the appointment. Major was Mulroney's 9th Supreme Court justice appointment since coming to power in 1984.

Nov. 17 Canadian Airlines International launched a lawsuit against Air Canada, accusing it of fare manipulation and predatory pricing.

Nov. 19 Seven suspected drug smugglers — 4 Canadians and 3 Colombians — were arraigned at La Tuque, Que., after $1 billion of cocaine was seized aboard their plane at an airstrip in Casey, Que. The plane touched down in the northern community after a lengthy pursuit by Canadian jet fighters and helicopters. It was the largest drug bust in Canada to date.

• A Royal Commission on transportation, established in Oct. 1989, tabled its report, recommending the privatization of VIA and the elimination of federal air, rail and highway subsidies over the next 10 years.

Nov. 21 Former Edmonton publisher Mel Hurtig was chosen leader of the new National Party of Canada at a meeting held in Ottawa. The centre-left populist party platform was geared toward the promotion of "integrity, morality, ethics, and openness."

Nov. 23 Federal authorities ordered Netherlands native Jacob Luitjens deported from Canada. Luitjens had been convicted in the Netherlands, *in absentia*, for collaborating with the Nazis during the WW II. He was the 1st war criminal deported from this country.

Nov. 24 Ottawa gave PWA-owned Canadian Airlines a $50 million loan guarantee to keep it afloat during investment negotiations with American Airlines.

• Calgary-based Petro-Canada sold 30.3 million treasury shares worth $250 million to private interests, reducing federal ownership from 80–70%.

• The federal govt passed Bill C–86, amending the Immigration Act so refugee applicants could appeal rulings.

Nov. 25 The federal govt pledged $5 million on make-work projects in Nfld. to help unemployed fisheries workers qualify for unemployment benefits. Sixteen thousand fisheries workers were already receiving $406 a month to compensate for the Mar. 6 closure of the Atlantic cod fisheries.

Nov. 27 Mario Dumont (b 1970), president of the nationalist youth wing of the Que. Liberals, resigned after he was suspended for supporting the "No" side in the Charlottetown Accord campaign. Twenty-two of the wing's 32 executives quit in support.

Nov. 30 Man. MLA Elijah Harper, a central figure in the demise of the Meech Lake Accord, announced his retirement from provincial politics. Harper had represented the riding of Rupertsland since 1981, and was the 1st treaty Aboriginal elected to the Man. legislature.

Also in Nov.
• A joint Canada-US free trade panel ruled that Canadian pork subsidies were legal under existing international trade agreements.

Dec. 1 Canada officially endorsed a UN-sanctioned, US-led coalition to provide military support to aid workers in wartorn Somalia. Over 1,000 Canadian soldiers were sent to the African nation over the month. An estimated 300,000 Somalis had already perished from starvation and war-related disease during the year. On Dec. 15, the crack Canadian Airborne Regiment arrived in Somalia to assume UN peacekeeping support duties. On Dec. 28, Canadian and US troops secured the airfield at Belet Huen in northwestern Somalia.

Dec. 2 Federal Finance Minister Donald Mazankowski announced plans to cut govt spending by almost $7.8 billion over the next 2.5 years. Unemployment services, foreign aid and public service wages were to be hit hardest.

Dec. 5 Former Calgary mayor and PC Environment Minister Ralph Klein won the Alb. Conservative leadership race, beating Nancy Betkowsky (b 1948) to become premier. Klein replaced Premier Don Getty, who retired. Getty had been in politics 25 years, serving 7 years as premier. He had 2 years left in his provincial mandate.

Dec. 17 PM Brian Mulroney signed the North American Free Trade Agreement (NAFTA) in

Ottawa. Mulroney and Presidents George Bush and Carlos Salinas de Gortari, of Mexico, had previously initialled the pact on Oct. 7. Effective Jan. 1, 1994, NAFTA would loosen trade restrictions on the sale and distribution of goods throughout Canada, the US and Mexico and bind a market of over 360 million people. The House of Commons approved the deal on May 7, 1993.

Dec. 18 More than 400 people were evacuated from Oakville, Man., following the derailment of a CN Rail freight train carrying toxic chemicals. Residents returned to their homes Jan. 10, 1993.

Dec. 21 One thousand people were evacuated from downtown St. John's, Nfld., as a fire raged through the city. An entire city block was destroyed, including the 82-year-old Church Lads Brigade Armoury and the Big R restaurant. There were no fatalities.

Also in 1992
• A federal judge ordered the NHL to compensate a number of retired NHL players some $45 million from the $60 million surplus in the league's current pension plan. The NHLers had played in the league between 1947 and 1982, while the pension was active and had sued the NHL over misappropriation of pension funds. Among those involved in the suit were Carl Brewer (1938–2001), Eddie Shack (b 1937), Bobby Hull and Gordie Howe. The Ont. Court of Appeal upheld the decision on Feb. 17, 1994.

• Life expectancy of a Canadian girl born this year passed 80 for the 1st time on record, reaching 80.89 years; it was 79.94 in 1985. Life expectancy for boys was 74.55, 73.30 in 1985.

• Twin Falls Chalet, in the coniferous forest at the base of Twin Falls, in Yoho National Park, BC was declared a National Historic Site. The chalet began as a railway surveyor's shelter in 1908; by 1923 the 14-room spruce chalet became a CPR Rocky Mountain teahouse, one of the many such teahouses that provided simple repast and isolated accommodation to a growing number of hikers and mountain climbers. Twin Falls is accessible only at the end of a 3-hour hike. Other classic Rocky Mountain teahouses still in operation include Lake Agnes (est. 1900), a 90-minute hike from Lake Louise, Banff;

Plain of Six Glaciers (est. 1927), a 6-km hike from Lake Louise; Shadow Lake Lodge (est. 1928) in an isolated alpine meadow between Banff's Ball and Massive mountain ranges; and L. O'Hara (est. 1926) accessible by road in Yoho.

• Canada's average gross domestic product (GDP) per capita was $22,461. The Yukon and NWT had the highest average, at $33,965; Nfld. had the lowest, at $15,890.

• The national unemployment rate peaked at 11.2%, the highest since 1984. The provincial rate was highest in Nfld. at 20.2% and lowest in Sask. at 7.9%.

• The average single or semi-detached house sold for $140,000 in Montreal; $460,000 in Toronto; and $400,000 in Vancouver.

• CN reported a fiscal-year loss of $1 billion.

• Quebec City lawyer Paule Gauthier became the 1st female president of the Canadian Bar Association.

• World-renowned astronomer Helen Hogg was awarded the Commemorative Medal for the 125th anniversary of the Confederation of Canada.

• All 34,000 seats for 2 Grateful Dead shows at Copps Coliseum in Hamilton, Ont., sold out in 56 minutes, a Canadian record. "Deadheads" started lining up a week before tickets went on sale.

• Logging companies harvested 1 million ha of Canadian forest, up from 680,000 in 1975.

• Vancouver artist Ted Dave established the 1st "Buy Nothing Day," a 24-hour moratorium on consumer spending to draw attention to western overconsumption. By 1997, "Buy Nothing Day" would be moved to coincide with the 1st Friday following American Thanksgiving, that nation's busiest shopping day. By 2003, the day of protest would be celebrated in 30 countries worldwide.

• The Canadian govt established Aulavik National Park, 12,274 km² of Western Arctic Lowlands tundra in the NWT. Located largely on Banks Is., Aulavik

(the name means "place where people travel") boasts the 225-km-long Thomson R., one of the most northerly navigable rivers in the world.

• Larry McFarland Architects Ltd. completed the First Nations House of Learning at U. of BC. Its shape and structure were inspired by the longhouses of the Coast Salish, and its gabled roof, supported by cedar logs, was inspired by the cedar houses of the Haida, Kwakwaka'wakw and Nuu-Chan-nulth. The House of Learning provides a meeting place and support facility for Aboriginal students.

• The Supreme Court of Canada ruled to amend the tax status of Aboriginal Peoples based not on "race" as defined by the Indian Act, but by place of residence and location of employer.

• There were 25.2 abortions for every 100 live births, or 100,500 abortions for the year, a record number.

• There was a record 76,139 total bankruptcies.

• Alliance Productions Corporation and Alberta Filmworks Inc. teamed up with CBC, and the TV series *North of 60* was born. Shot in Bragg Creek, Alb., the show (1992–1997) portrayed the daily life and human drama of the small, northern native community of Lynx River. In the series, veteran actor Tom Jackson, as the Band Council Chief of Lynx River, was surrounded by a cast of Native and non-Native actors, including Tina Keeper as the native RCMP Constable Michelle Kenidi, Peter Kelly Gaudreault as RCMP Constable James Harper, Simon Baker as Charlie Muscrat, and Dakota House as the troubled teenager. Guest cameos by actors such as Tantoo Cardinal and Len Cariou were common. When the show was cancelled after 6 very successful seasons the network went on to produce several "made for TV" movies based on the characters of the series.

• The small lead and zinc mining town of Polaris, Cornwallis Is., in the High Arctic, had the highest median income in the nation — $92,800. The national median was $18,600. Other small mining areas also showed exceptional median incomes: Laforge, Que., $54,200; Nanisivik, NWT, $53,300; and Brisay, Que., $51,100.

• *The National/The Journal* hour was moved from 10 p.m. to 9 p.m. Following the death of Barbara Frum, the news package was reformulated into *Prime Time News* and moved back to 10 p.m. It would average 860,000 nightly viewers. The half-hour, 11 p.m. CTV nightly news attracted a nightly viewership of 1.3 million.

• A Statistics Canada study showed that housework represented an unpaid annual labour value of between $211–$319 billion, or 30–40% of the GDP.

• An average of 147,960 Canadians sat in jail on any given day of the year, a third of whom were there for not paying fines.

• Pierre Berton's historical portrait, *Niagara: A History of the Falls,* was published.

1993

Jan. 1 Scheduled federal foreign aid was reduced by 10% over the next 2 years.

• Over 1,800 American-made products, such as furnaces, coffeemakers, diapers and office furniture could now be purchased duty free under an unfolding schedule in the Canada-US Free Trade Agreement.

Jan. 2–3 Seven Montreal-area synagogues were spray-painted with Nazi symbols in random acts of anti-Semitic vandalism. No culprits were found.

Jan. 4 Karhu Canada Inc., the world's largest producer of hockey sticks, was purchased by Finland's Asko Group Holdings for $108 million. Karhu was producer of such popular brands as Koho, Titan, Canadien and Jofa.

• Kim Campbell became the nation's 1st woman defence and veterans affairs minister following a minor federal Conservative cabinet shuffle.

• The Canadian Imperial Bank of Commerce (CIBC) agreed to increase the number of Native Peoples in its Man. employ to 2.1% by 1998. The announcement was made in response to a 1990 Assembly of Man. Chiefs complaint, filed with the Canadian

Human Rights Commission, charging that the bank engaged in discriminatory hiring practices.

Jan. 6 Revenue Canada placed import duties averaging 11.4% on US steel plate following charges made by the Canadian steel industry that US firms were selling products in Canada at below market costs, a trade practice known as "dumping."

• Two hundred and thirty Canadian peacekeepers were deployed in Macedonia as the UN attempted to prevent war from spreading across the boundaries of the former Yugoslav republic of Bosnia-Herzegovina.

Jan. 8 Hydro Quebec gave the James Bay Cree a $50 million compensation package for social and ecological disruptions caused by construction of La Grande James Bay hydroelectric project, which had been completed in 1985. In return, the Cree agreed to drop all current, and refrain from all future, litigation against La Grande — not including demands for environmental reviews.

• Canadian Airlines pilots voted in Calgary to accept a pay cut of 14% in 1993, and 9% in 1994, in a co-operative effort to help keep the struggling airline afloat.

• Fifty fishers, journalists and local politicians from St-Pierre and Miquelon were jailed in St. John's by Canadian maritime authorities for illegally fishing in Canadian waters. The group had left the French territories aboard 2 trawlers Jan. 7. The French fishers had previously been banned from Canadian waters after refusing to abide by Canada's 1992 foreign-catch quotas. On Jan. 15, the French govt paid $1.4 million in bail to free its citizens.

Jan. 11 Montreal-based Henry Birks & Sons Ltd., founded in 1879, filed for bankruptcy protection. With its blue boxes and gold-initial logo and 150 stores nationwide, the venerable jeweller was one of the country's most recognizable and respected retailers. On Feb. 3, Borgosesia SpA of Italy agreed to purchase Birks. The Italian porcelain manufacturer also agreed to preserve the Birks name and 38 of its stores. Jonathan Birks remained president and CEO.

Jan. 14 Canada's oldest brewery, Molson Breweries, established by John Molson in Montreal in 1786, became a foreign-owned company as US-based Miller Brewing Company purchased 20% of the firm for $349 million. Forty percent of the company was already in the hands of Foster's Brewing Company Ltd. of Australia. Molson had been the 2nd most popular imported beer in the US, next to Holland's Heineken.

Jan. 18 A Que. task force report issued under the guidance of Claude Corbo (b 1945), rector of the University of Que. at Montreal, suggested that tensions between Que. police and minorities would ease with increased minority awareness training and the inclusion of more minorities in the police force. The report was issued in the wake of police shooting deaths of 2 Que. black men in 1992.

• Twenty-four Canadian CF–18 jets left CFB Baden-Soellingen, Germany, for Canada, marking the end of this country's 42-year air force presence in Europe. Canadian soldiers stationed in Lahr left for home July 13, ending all permanent Canadian military involvement in Europe. A total of 20,000 Canadian troops had been stationed in Europe since 1954.

Jan. 19 RCMP officers removed gambling machines from 5 Man. Native reserves on the grounds that their use violated provincial law. Native officials responded that the legality of gambling fell under Native, not provincial jurisdiction.

Jan. 21 The Supreme Court of Canada ruled 7–1 that television equipment could be banned from federal and provincial legislatures. The case appeared before the Court after the NS Appeal Court ruled that the CBC had the right to tape proceedings of the NS legislature.

• The Supreme Court of Canada ruled that part of the Income Tax Act giving Revenue Canada the right to enter private homes and offices and seize documents was a violation of the Canadian Charter of Rights and Freedoms.

• Statistics Canada declared that Canada's recession had ended. Over 1 million Canadians had perma-

nently lost their jobs between 1990 and 1992. By year's end, all provinces but Man. experienced positive economic output ranging from 6.3% in Alb. to 0.7% in Nfld. The national average was 2.6%. Man.'s bad 1993 performance (-0.9) was due to weather-damaged wheat crops.

Jan. 22 PM Mulroney appointed Yvon Dumont (b 1951) the 21st lt-gov. of Man. Dumont became the 1st Métis to hold the post, and the 2nd Aboriginal lt-gov. in Canada to date (the 1st was Ralph Steinhauer, who became lt-gov. of Alb. in 1974). At the time of his appointment, Dumont was president of the Métis Federation, which had been engaged in a 10-year land claim dispute with the Crown. He would be replaced as federation president by Gerald Morin (b 1961) on Mar. 4.

Jan. 24 The Art Gallery of Ontario reopened after 7 months' extensive renovations and expansions. The Joey and Toby Tannenbaum Sculpture Atrium was established in honour of the Tannenbaums' $4 million donation to the gallery. In 2000, the Tannenbaums donated approximately $104 million of Asian, Middle Eastern and European art — some 1,800 pieces — to the Royal Ontario Museum, the largest-single private donation to a cultural institution in Canada to date.

Jan. 25 Federal Maritime authorities temporarily detained 8 US scallop draggers for illegally fishing in Canadian waters.

Jan. 26 Over 10,000 farmers gathered in Saskatoon, Sask., demanding govt aid to combat the effects of escalating operating costs and decreasing commodity prices. The average annual Sask. farm net income for the previous year was estimated at $7,000. The previous day (Jan. 25), the federal govt pledged $170 million to help the province's 60,000 farmers. The Wheat Pool argued that farmers required $1.2 billion.

• Constable Simeon Tshakapesh discovered 6 half-frozen Innu children suffering the ravages of gasoline inhalation in an unheated shack in Davis Inlet. By month's end, images of Davis Inlet youth sniffing gasoline and threatening suicide were projected by newscasts worldwide. On Feb. 9, the federal govt promised to provide the necessary money to relocate the community of some 500 by 2002, and in 1996 determined the new townsite would be Natuashish (Little Sango Pond), on the mainland. Relocation was made Dec. 14, 2002. The Nfld. govt had relocated the Innu families to desolate Davis Inlet in 1967. The area was cut off from the mainland a minimum 3 months a year. Homes were shoddily constructed; there was no running water and no sewage-treatment facilities.

• Maj-Gen. Lewis MacKenzie (b 1955), former UN commander of peacekeeping forces in Bosnia-Herzegovina, spoke out against the UN, declaring it weighed down by bureaucracy and riddled with waste and mismanagement.

• Petro-Canada chairman and CEO Wilbert Hopper was fired after leading the Crown corporation to a $9 million profit in 1992. Hopper had been with Petro-Canada since 1976. Petro-Canada would go on to post a $162 million profit in 1993.

Jan. 31 National Sea Products' scallop dragger *Cape Aspy* sank off the southwest coast of NS, 2 days after leaving Lunenburg on a 12-day outing. Three sailors drowned, 11 were rescued.

Also in Jan.
• Mel Hurtig published *A New and Better Canada: Principles and Policies of a New Canadian Political Party*, which set out the platform and goals of the National Party of Canada, established in 1992.

• A total of $18,125 was deducted from the paycheques of 15 senators who had each missed more than 21 days of the current Upper House session.

Feb. 1 The House of Commons approved a constitutional amendment giving the French language equal status in NB. The amendment had initially been part of the failed Charlottetown Accord. Constitutional lawyer Deborah Coyne (b 1955) argued that Parliament could not unilaterally approve and proclaim a constitutional amendment, and filed a challenge with the Federal Court Feb. 15. She maintained her position, but nevertheless dropped the challenge July 5.

• Without announcement, Premium Automotive of Cape Breton closed its doors, packed up and moved it gas-tank-making operations to the US, despite having accepted approximately $2 million in Canadian govt grants over the previous 6 years. On Feb. 5, Premium agreed to pay its former workers a total of $300,000 compensation.

Feb. 3 Ont.'s NDP premier Bob Rae continued his sweeping cost-cutting measures, slashing 8 govt ministries, including the Ministry of Revenue and the Ministry of Colleges and Universities. Five deputy minister positions were also eliminated.

Feb. 7 An estimated 50,000 Quebecers rallied in downtown Montreal against Bill C–105, which would decrease unemployment benefits from 60–57% of insurable earnings, and deny compensation to those who voluntarily quit their jobs. The legislation took effect Apr. 4.

Feb. 9 Edper-Bronfman's Noranda Forest Inc. sold its 49% share in MacMillan Bloedel to a group of investors for $971 million. On Feb. 12, the holdings of Edper-Bronfman's John Labbat Ltd. were sold to an investment group for $993 million.

Feb. 11 Filmmaker Sylvia Hamilton's *Speak It, From The Heart*, documenting the daily lives of black Nova Scotian teenagers, had its inaugural showing at the Ottawa Public Library.

Feb. 12 The minimum age required to purchase tobacco was raised across Canada from 16 to 18.

• Axel Ulrich Contracting Ltd. was fined a record $600,000 on 2 health-and-safety violations connected to the death of Michael White, who fell 42 m while installing glass on the new wing of Toronto's Hospital for Sick Children in July 1991.

• Mill workers at an Abitibi plant in Thunder Bay, Ont., voted 90% to purchase the plant outright for $1. The Ont. govt offered the new owners a $6.5 million loan and a line of credit worth $11.5. Seven hundred jobs were saved. The mill had lost $25 million in 1992.

Feb. 13 The auteur film *Requiem pour un beau sans-coeur* (*Requiem for a Beautiful Heartless Man*) was given the nod as Best Feature Film at Que.'s 11th annual Rendezvous of Quebec Cinema.

Feb. 15 BC's NDP govt initiated plans to close Vancouver's historic Shaugnessy Hospital. The Shaugnessy, built in 1919, was part of a children's-hospital complex renowned for its maternity care.

Feb. 16 Defence Minister Kim Campbell approved the deployment of 1,200 more Canadian troops to the UN peacekeeping operations in Bosnia-Herzegovina. Since Mar. 1992, 1 Canadian peace-keeper had been killed and another 12 seriously wounded in the former wartorn Yugoslavia. The new troops were bound for Sarajevo. By the time peace was signed Dec. 31, 10 Canadian soldiers would have been killed and 50 injured in the conflict.

Feb. 19 BC Liberal leader Gordon Wilson relinquished his duties as opposition leader amidst allegations of marital infidelity and conflicts of interest. He retained the leadership title until the BC Liberal convention slated for summer (Sept. 11).

Feb. 20 Constitutional affairs minister and ex-PM Joe Clark announced he would not seek re-election in the next general election. Clark had spent 21 years in the House. He was Canada's 16th PM, serving from June 4, 1979 to Mar. 2, 1980. He was the nation's 1st western-born PM and, at age 39, the nation's youngest. Clark lost the 1980 general election to Pierre Trudeau and, in 1983, the Conservative leadership to Brian Mulroney. He would return to politics, regaining a seat in the House as leader of the last-gasp Conservatives, on Sept. 10, 2000.

Feb. 21 Keith Henderson was elected leader of Que.'s 4-year-old Equality Party on a platform of eliminating the province's language Bill 101, and its sign law, Bill 178.

Feb. 23 Barbara Frum was posthumously awarded the annual John Drainie Award for outstanding contributions to Canadian broadcasting. The late CBC radio and television broadcaster had died of leukemia on Mar. 26, 1992. Frum began cohosting CBC Radio's *The Way It Is* (later *Weekday*) in 1967. She moved on to host CBC Radio's super-popular *As It Happens* between 1971 and 1982, and then in 1982 became the 1st host of CBC TV's *The Journal* until her death in 1992.

• The BC govt introduced the country's most stringent controls on the use of ozone-depleting chemicals, making mandatory the recycling of many CFCs and placing a moratorium on all CFCs used in motor-vehicle air conditioners, effective Jan. 1, 1997.

Feb. 24 With a national approval rating hovering at 14%, 55-year-old PM Brian Mulroney announced he would not seek re-election and would step down after a replacement was found at the next Tory leadership convention slated for June. The PM's legacy of failed constitutional compromises (Meech Lake and the Charlottetown Accord), controversial free trade agreements (US-Canada and NAFTA) and the unpopular GST had plunged Conservative approval ratings to record lows.

Feb. 25 The Victoria Cross once again became the nation's highest military honour. It had been super-seded in 1972 by the Star of Courage, Cross of Valour and Medal of Bravery, which were awarded to both civilians and military personnel.

• Finance Minister Donald Mazankowski ordered Nfld., PEI, NS, Que., Man. and Sask. to return a total of $609 million in equalization payments, based on an assessment of new Statistics Canada population figures. In turn, the population-equalization adjustment, retroactive to 1991, gave Ont., NB, Alb. and BC a total of $437.5 million, Ont. getting $350 million, or 80%.

Feb. 26 Man. eliminated dental, optical and drug benefits from its social assistance system.

Also in Feb.

• The Supreme Court of Canada, ruling on an appeal by the Nass R. Nisga'a First Nation, unanimously upheld the concept that Aboriginals had title rights to ancestral land, although the Court's decision was split evenly between those judges who believed the Nisga'a still maintained title, and those judges who felt that title had been extinguished as a result of European colonization. The Calder case, as it came to be known (after Nisga'a chief John Calder), demonstrated that English law recognized the concept of Aboriginal title, and paved the way for future land claims negotiations between Canada's federal and provincial govts, and the country's First Nations, Inuit and Métis Peoples. It also paved the way for the Nisga'a land claim settlement signed Apr. 27, 1999.

• Canada imported a record $13.3 billion in foreign goods during the month.

• Vancouver-based Westcoast Energy Inc. sold its subsidiary Westcoast Petroleum to Asian investors for $247 million.

Mar. 1 Montreal's city council was forced to cancel a meeting as 1,000 enraged property owners clamoured through city hall. They were protesting a proposed law that would require property owners to pay the business taxes of nonresidential tenants occupying their properties.

Mar. 2 Supreme Court of Canada proceedings were televised for the 1st time.

Mar. 3 US-based A&A Music declared bankruptcy, leading to the closure of 28 CD and record stores across Canada.

Mar. 4 The Supreme Court of Canada ruled that francophone Manitobans had the right to control French-language education, paving the way for the creation of new French-language school boards.

• Toronto Women's College Hospital signed a $1 million deal with Mead Johnson Canada, makers of Enfalac baby formula. The deal would give the hospital $35,000 annually and supply it with all its baby formula for free.

• Dr. Henry Morgentaler opened a new 5-storey abortion clinic on Bayview Ave., Toronto, to replace the one on Harbord St. bombed May 18, 1992.

Mar. 5 The International Amateur Athletic Federation banned Ben Johnson for life from all amateur competition after the track star tested positive for banned substances at a Montreal track meet on Jan. 17. The move came less than 3 years after the federal govt lifted (Aug. 9, 1990) its lifetime ban on Johnson, which had been imposed after the 1988 Seoul Olympic debacle.

Mar. 9 The Canadian Immigration and Refugee Board (IRB) released the "Guidelines on Women Refugee

Claimants Fearing Gender Related Persecution," making it easier for women refugee claimants to find sanctuary in Canada on the grounds of domestic violence and gender-related persecution.

Mar. 11 Kurt Browning won his 4th world figure skating championship in Prague, Czechoslovakia. Elvis Stojko (b 1972) took the silver. Isabelle Brasseur (b 1970) of St-Jean-sur-Richelieu, Que., and Lloyd Eisler (b 1963) of Seaforth, Ont., won the gold in pairs.

• Health Minister Benoît Bouchard pledged an increase in federal AIDS spending to $42.2 million annually.

Mar. 15 The Ontario Court General Division ruled 2–1 to deny same-sex couples the right to legal, recognized marriages. The ruling was made in the case of Pierre Beaulne and Todd Layland, who were seeking a marriage certificate.

• Thirty-two Hong Kong sailors drowned when the Liberian-registered freighter *Gold Bond Conveyor* went down in heavy seas off the southern coast of NS.

Mar. 18 Two hundred unruly protestors delayed the BC provincial govt's Speech from the Throne for over 2 hours. The group demanded that Clayoquot Sound be protected against logging. On Apr. 13, Premier Michael Harcourt announced that approximately a third of the old-growth forest around Clayoquot Sound would be permanently preserved, and logging companies would be allowed to exploit up to 1,000 ha of the remaining forest every year.

Mar. 20 Dina Bélanger (1897–1929), a sister in the Congregation of Jesus-Marie in Sillery, Que., was beatified by Pope John Paul. Born in St. Roch parish in Quebec City, Bélanger entered the congregation an accomplished concert pianist at age 24 and devoted her life to the teachings of Jesus. The liturgical feast day of Blessed Dina Bélanger is celebrated on Sept. 4 of each year.

Mar. 22 The Hudson's Bay Co. signed a deal estimated at $100 million, transforming 25 BC and Alb. Woodwards stores into Bay and Zellers outlets.

By year's end, the 100-year-old Woodwards would be defunct. Its flagship store on Hastings St. in Vancouver, established in 1903 as the city's 1st department store, was abandoned. It would become a politically charged, illegal home to the city's homeless for over a decade.

• RCMP officers confiscated 100 gambling machines and equipment from the Bear Claw Casino, operated out of an old golf clubhouse on the White Bear Reserve near Carlyle, Sask. The casino opened Feb. 25 in defiance of provincial laws stipulating that all casinos must be jointly operated with the province. On Oct. 11, 1994, Sask. Justice Wallace Goliath cleared the casino operatives of all charges.

Mar. 23 One thousand NS fishery workers and supporters gathered on Halifax Pier to protest the federal govt's handling of the East Coast fisheries and the effects of a 50% reduction in cod quotas in certain Maritime regions.

Mar. 25 Defence Minister Kim Campbell threw her hat into the federal Conservative leadership ring.

• The Supreme Court of Canada ruled 7–0 that, in the dissolution of a common-law marriage, a partner was entitled to a portion of the common estate as compensation for housekeeping and child rearing. The decision was made in the case of William Beblow and Catherine Peter, the latter awarded the former couple's $23,300 home in return for domestic services accrued over a 12-year relationship.

Mar. 27 The Supreme Court of Canada ruled that Elections Act provisions preventing convicts from voting was unconstitutional.

Mar. 29 The PEI Liberal Party, under leader Catherine Callbeck, swept 31 of 32 seats in the provincial election. Callbeck became the 1st woman leader of either a Canadian federal or provincial party to be elected to power. (Callbeck had entered the election as PEI's 1st woman premier because she had replaced the retired Joe Ghiz on Jan. 25.)

Mar. 30 New figures released by Statistics Canada showed that 1.002 million Canadians claimed Aboriginal ancestry, up 41% from the 1986 census.

Apr. 1 Federal Transport Minister Jean Corbeil (1934–2002) grounded all Nationair flights when it was discovered that the airline's National Transport Agency (NTA) licence had been suspended after the firm failed to meet its insurance payments. Four thousand five hundred travellers were stranded worldwide. Nationair, Canada's 3rd largest airline, had filed for bankruptcy protection Mar. 22. The 9-year-old charter airline would go bankrupt May 12, owing $75 million to some 1,350 creditors.

• As Cold War tensions warmed, the federal govt pledged to eliminate 300 CSIS jobs. The spy agency's employment roll would be reduced from 2,760 to 2,465 by year's end.

Apr. 3 PM Mulroney pledged $200 million to help restore Russia's crippled economy. The move pushed total Canadian aid to the former Communist stronghold to $2.6 billion since the Berlin Wall fell in 1989. Russia's inflation rate was rising at a rate of 30% per month.

Apr. 4 Russian President Boris Yeltsin and US President Bill Clinton held a Russia-US summit at Norman MacKenzie House on the U. of BC campus, Vancouver. The presidents discussed arms limitations and civil unrest in the breakoff states of the former USSR. Clinton promised Yeltsin $1.6 billion in aid. Russian newspapers would call Yeltsin Russia's greatest mendicant. On Apr. 15, G-7 nations (Canada, France, Britain, Germany, Italy, Japan, and the US) pledged a total $43.4 billion in Russian aid. This figure included Canada's Apr. 3rd $200 million contribution.

• Canada swept the World Curling Championships in Geneva, Switzerland, when Sandra Peterson (Schmirler, 1963–2000) and her Regina, Sask., rink beat Germany 5–3, and Russ Howard (b 1956) and his Penetanguishene, Ont. rink beat Scotland 8–4. The incredible Schmirler would go on to win the 1994 and 1998 World's, and take her team to gold at the 1998 Nagano Olympics. Shortly after the birth of her daughter, and little over a year after the Olympics, Schmirler was diagnosed with cancer. She died in Mar. 2000.

Apr. 5 Speaking before a Royal Commission, 30 Inuit accused the federal govt of human rights violations when it forced 17 families (87 people) to relocate from Inukjuak, Que., to Grise Fiord and Resolute Bay, NWT, between 1953 and 1955. The Inuit testified that the relocation led to starvations and death.

• The Man. govt tabled the Public Sector Reduced Workweek and Compensation Management Act, cutting up to 15 paid workdays a year (creating 15 long weekdays for some) from approximately 18,000 public service employees. The legislation remained in force throughout 1996.

• Ont. NDP Premier Bob Rae invited 300 officials representing 900,000 public sector workers to Queen's Park to explain why his govt needed to slash 20% from its $27 billion govt payroll.

Apr. 6 The External Affairs Department initiated plans to cut $31 million from its fiscal budget by eliminating embassies in Iraq and Zaire, missions in Vienna, Denver and Melbourne, a high commission in Namibia, and trade offices in Houston, El Segund (California) and Orlando, Florida. Eighty-two Canadian foreign service jobs would be cut in the process.

• The Man. govt introduced its new deficit-busting budget, cutting $100 million in govt spending and increasing the province's reliance on gambling-related revenues.

Apr. 8 Native Peoples from 16 reserves in NB and Que. blocked the Trans-Canada Highway just west of Kingsclear reserve, NB, protesting a NB decision to force status Indians to pay the 11% PST on all purchases made off reserves. Police removed the barricades Apr. 9. On Apr. 10, Premier McKenna stated that the tax would only be applied to goods purchased for use outside NB Native reserves. Aboriginal leaders argued that the provincial govt had no business taxing status Aboriginals.

• A UN human rights committee concluded that Que.'s sign law, Bill–178, passed Dec. 21, 1988, violated freedom-of-expression rights spelled out in the International Covenant on Civil and Political Rights. The committee, however, noted that the law was not egregious as Que. anglophones did not constitute a Canadian minority.

Apr. 15 Statistics Canada reported that the nation's foreign debt was $301 billion, or approximately $11,000 per resident.

Apr. 18 Toronto's Paul Tracy (b 1968) was given the checkered flag at the Grand Prix of Long Beach, California, his 1st Indy Car victory.

Apr. 19 The International Monitory Fund (IMF) warned that the Canadian dollar would spiral and interest rates would climb if the federal and provincial govts did not reduce spending.

Apr. 21 The Parti Québécois set forth its definition of Que. sovereignty as the severance of all political ties with Canada. The PQ further stated that relations between Canada and a sovereign Que. would be governed by separate institutions created specifically for that purpose.

• Que. contractors and manufacturers were banned from competing for NB provincial contracts.

Apr. 23 A 17-year-old West Vancouver high school student orchestrated a rally of over 1,000 demonstrators at the Vancouver Art Gallery to legalize marijuana.

Apr. 26 In the wake of 4 highly publicized deaths of Somali civilians, Defence Minister Kim Campbell ordered an investigation into the conduct of 900 Canadian Airborne Regiment soldiers stationed at Belet Huen in western Somalia. On Feb. 17, soldiers fired into a crowd, killing 1, injuring 3. On Mar. 5, 1 Somali was shot and killed and another wounded while sneaking into the Belet Huen compound. On Mar. 16, Somali teenager Shidane Abukar Arone was found beaten to death by soldiers near the Belet compound. On Mar. 17, soldiers shot and killed a Somali Red Cross representative. The 1st part of the Somalia Inquiry report was issued Aug. 31, stating military authorities knew that the Airborne Regiment unit sent to the conflict had disciplinary problems and "posed a threat to authority." It also noted that the regiment contained white supremacists. Four soldiers were eventually convicted, 2 were imprisoned. On Aug. 25, 1993, it was revealed that the Canadian govt compensated the Arone family $15,000 US for the torture and murder of their son — blood money that released the Canadian govt from any civil lia-bility related to the crime. The Canadian Airborne Regiment, the nation's elite front line paratrooper squad trained not for peacekeeping but for intense front-line spearhead advances through enemy lines, was disbanded in 1995. The final Somalia Commission of Inquiry report was tabled July 2, 1997.

• An Ont. court ruled that Native fishing rights were not restricted to food-for-the-table, but also extended to cover commercial fishing.

Apr. 27 New "stalking" laws were introduced in the House of Commons adding "criminal harassment" to the Criminal Code. The new law was created to protect women and children against continuous and repeated communication, following (stalking) and/or spying. Offenders faced a maximum 5 years' imprisonment. The House passed the legislation in June.

Apr. 28 Air Canada and investment group Air Partners purchased 55% of Houston-based Continental Airlines, creating the 4th largest airline system in North America.

Apr. 29 Federal NDP finance critic Steve Langdon (b 1946) was fired by leader Audrey McLaughlin after criticizing Ont. NDP leader Bob Rae's austere fiscal policies.

• The Federal Court of Appeal ruled in a split decision that homosexual couples were not entitled to old age spousal benefits.

Also in Apr.
• A consortium of 20 doctors led by Dr. Chen Fong opened Calgary's 1st private MRI (Magnetic Resonance Image) clinic, fuelling concerns about health care privatization. The clinic charged $1,000 per scan.

• The unemployment rate rose to 11.4% as 43,000 jobs disappeared across the country over the month.

May 3 Nfld. Liberal Premier Clyde Wells was returned to power in the provincial election on a platform of fiscal restraint and deficit reduction. The Liberals took 34 seats in the 52-seat legislature; the

Conservatives under Len Simms (b 1943) won 17 seats. NDP leader Jack Harris (b 1948) won his party's only seat and was left to lead himself.

May 5 Federal Industry and Trade Minister Michael Wilson received a letter endorsed by 80 environmental groups demanding that the federal govt abandon NAFTA, on grounds that it promoted increased consumption, a root cause of environmental degradation.

• The last vehicle rolled off the production line at Scarborough, Ont.'s, GM van plant. Inside was a black cardboard coffin carrying the inscription "RIP, Scarborough Van Plant, 1952–1993." The plant had produced 1.6 million vans over the previous 19 years. Operations were moved to Flint, Michigan. Three thousand Canadian jobs were lost.

May 6 Alb.'s Conservative govt unveiled its deficit-cutting budget, slashing $127 million in health care and $154 million in family and social services.

• The Que. govt introduced Bill 86, loosening restrictions on the province's French-only sign laws. Signs on business premises were to be in French only; all others could include English only as long as French remained "markedly prominent."

• PM Mulroney left for London, Paris, Bonn and Moscow on a $1 million farewell tour of Europe.

• The CAW and UAW renewed amicable relations after an 8-year jurisdictional conflict, coming together in mutual opposition to NAFTA.

• A bi-national US-Canada panel concluded that US tariffs and duties on Canadian softwood exports were unsupportable under current trade regulations, marking a moral victory for Canada's lumber industry. The softwood dispute, however would continue well into the 21st century.

May 15 Between 60,000 and 100,000 Canadians, including grassroots organizations, environmentalists, unions, the poor, the unemployed and generally disgruntled converged on Parliament Hill in a combination anti-Conservative protest and "Goodbye Brian" celebration. The watershed gathering included calls for more jobs and better job protection, an end to the war in Bosnia, increased environmental protection and an end to free trade. Similar demonstrations were staged in cities throughout the country.

May 16 The UN voted Canada the 2nd-best place in the world to live, based on socioeconomic indicators such as education, life expectancy and gender equality. Japan was rated number 1.

May 18 Police charged Paul Teale (formerly Bernardo) of St. Catharines, Ont., and his estranged wife, Karla Homolka, with the 1st degree murders of teenagers Leslie Mahaffy and Kristen French. Bernardo had been arrested Feb. 17. On July 6, in St. Catharines, Ont., Judge Francis Kovacs sentenced Karla Homolka to 12 years on 2 counts of manslaughter. Homolka had cut a deal with the Crown (referred to in the press as "a deal with the devil") to lessen the charge from 1st degree murder; in return she provided evidence against co-murderer Bernardo. Justice Kovacs banned publication of trial details. On Sept. 1, 1995, following a 4-month trial and the testimony of 86 witnesses, a jury found Bernardo guilty on 2 counts of 1st degree murder; he was given 2 concurrent life sentences. He would be declared a dangerous offender Nov. 3, 1995, and made ineligible for parole. Homolka's release date was July 2005.

May 19 Ont. Finance Minister Floyd Laughren (b 1935) tabled the NDP budget, which increased tax revenues a record $1.6 billion over the next fiscal year. The projected 1993–1994 deficit was $9.2 billion. The next day, Que. Finance Minister Gérard Lévesque (1926–1993) continued the trend, with a Que. tax-grab increase of $1.3 billion over the next fiscal year. The projected Que. 1993–1994 deficit was $4.1 billion.

May 25 PM Brian Mulroney signed the Nunavut Lands Claim Agreement providing Inuit control of a 2.2 million-km² eastern portion of the NWT that would become the new territory of Nunavut on Apr. 1, 1999.

• The NS Liberal Party, under John Savage, beat Don Cameron's Conservatives to win the NS election, taking 40 of 52 seats and ending 15 years of Tory leadership. Wayne Adams, representing the riding of Preston, became NS's 1st African-Canadian MLA.

He would be supply and services minister in the new Liberal cabinet.

May 29 Fourteen Yukon Territory First Nations signed the Umbrella Final Agreement in Whitehorse. The land claims settlement gave the Nations control over 41,400 km² of land — or 8% of the Territory — and $280 million.

May 31 A Que. court imposed a $4 million fine on Tioxide Canada Inc. after finding it guilty on 6 counts of dumping toxins into the St. Lawrence R. It was the largest pollution-related fine in Canada to date.

June 9 The Montreal Canadiens defeated the Los Angeles Kings 4–1 in 5 games to win the Stanley Cup. Post-game celebrations turned ugly with mobs flipping cars and smashing windows in Montreal's downtown core. Damages were estimated at $10 million.

June 13 Kim Campbell defeated Jean Charest 1,817 votes to 1,680 on the 2nd ballot to become federal Conservative party leader and Canada's 1st woman PM. She also became the 1st woman head of state in North America (foreign monarchs excluded). Campbell was sworn into office June 25, replacing Brian Mulroney.

June 15 Alb. Premier Ralph Klein led the Conservatives to a 7th straight majority govt victory, taking 51 of 83 seats in the provincial election. The Liberals under Laurence Decore won 32 seats, taking over Official Opposition status from the NDP who, under Ray Martin, failed to win a seat.

• Canada ended 29 years of peacekeeping operations on the island of Cyprus. Over 30,000 Canadian personnel had kept a tenuous peace between battling Greek and Turkish interests since Canada accepted the 1st UN mission to the hot spot in 1964.

June 17 The Supreme Court of Canada ruled that changes to the Que. Education Act aligning education along linguistic lines (French and English), rather than denominational lines (Catholic and Protestant), were valid under the Constitution. On Dec. 15, 1997, the Senate approved a constitutional amendment to facilitate the change.

June 23 The Senate approved a proposal giving those senators living more than 80 km from Ottawa an extra $6,000 in tax-free travel expenses, over and above the existing tax-free allotment of $10,400. The annual salary of senators was $64,400. On July 12, the Senate bowed to public pressure, rescinding the travel-allowance boost.

• Fisheries Minister John Crosbie and the US agreed to a 1-year deal limiting the US catch of migrating Fraser R. salmon, caught in Washington State waters, to 2.8 million individual fish. In return, Canada would reduce its salmon catch around Vancouver Is. from 3.5 million to 1.7 million fish.

June 29 Statistics Canada reported that 36% of Canadian Aboriginal peoples could fluently converse in an Aboriginal language.

Also in June

• Twenty-four-year-old Cpl. Daniel Gunther of the Royal 22nd Regiment was the 3rd Canadian killed in the former Yugoslavia.

July 10 A monument was unveiled in Pictou, NS, commemorating the No. 2 Construction Battalion. The nation's only all-black military unit was established in 1916 and served in Europe during WW I (1914–1918). In all, 600 African-Canadians served in Europe over the Great War.

July 16 Nineteen were killed when a truck struck a minibus near Lac Bouchette, Que. Only 2 survived what was one of the worst road accidents on Canadian highways to date.

July 21 Northern Telecom (Nortel), the nation's telecommunications giant, reported a 2nd quarter loss of $1 billion. The announcement came with 2,000 Canadian layoffs and another 3,200 globally.

July 22 A Canadian Forces C–130 Hercules crashed 200 km north of Wainwright, AB, while engaged in parachute-assisted equipment drop-offs. Five crew members were killed and 4 injured.

July 23 Twenty-year-old Carlos Costa completed a 52-km swim across L. Ontario, becoming the youngest man — and 1st physically challenged individual — to do so. The double-leg amputee completed the feat in 32 hours.

July 28 The Alb. govt eliminated its prisoner workfare program, which gave prisoners $3 per day for performing menial in-house tasks such as cleaning and yard work.

Aug. 9 Two hundred and fifty anti-logging protestors were arrested along a logging road running into Vancouver Island's Clayoquot Sound, home to some of the oldest and largest trees in the country.

Aug. 11 Dr. Tofy Mussivand, of the U. of Ottawa's Heart Institute, unveiled his new invention, the 1st permanent artificial human heart requiring no exterior attachments. It was called the Electro-hydraulic Ventricular Assist Device, or EVAD.

Aug. 22 A Canadian Bar Association Task Force headed by former Supreme Court Justice Bertha Wilson, reported that 27% of women legal professionals were paid less than their male counterparts, faced fewer chances of upward mobility, and at the same time experienced work-related sexual harassment. The task force concluded that "the dimensions of the problems experienced by women in the legal profession are staggering," and recommended employment programs which traced the progress of women in law. On Feb. 22, 1994, the Canadian Bar Association voted in Jasper to reject such a motion.

Sept. 1 The federal govt imposed strict new health warnings to cover at least 25% of the display surface of all cigarette packages, effective Sept. 1994. The Supreme Court of Canada snuffed out an RJR-Macdonald challenge to the law on Mar. 3, 1994.

Sept. 2 PM Kim Campbell reduced the number of British-built EH–101 military helicopters her govt planned to purchase from 50 to 43, thereby shaving $1 billion from the proposed $4.8 billion contract. The former Conservative govt had announced the original purchase of 50 helicopters on July 24, 1992. They were to replace the aging, twin-rotor Labrador fleet.

• Alb.'s Conservative govt began to privatize its 204 Liquor Control Board outlets.

Sept. 11 Three-term Vancouver Mayor Gordon Campbell was elected new leader of BC's Liberal party on the 1st ballot at the BC party convention. Campbell received 4,141 of 6,540 votes. Former leader Gordon Wilson received 531 votes, or 8% of the total. Wilson would go on to become 1st leader of the new BC Progressive Democratic Alliance Jan. 2, 1994.

Sept. 14 Sixty-year-old Que. Premier Robert Bourassa announced he would resign from politics in 1994. On Dec. 14, Daniel Johnson was proclaimed leader of the Que. Liberals, succeeding Bourassa as Que. premier Jan. 11, 1994. Robert Bourassa's political career spanned 4 tumultuous decades. The Montreal-born lawyer had been educated at both Oxford (on a Rhodes scholarship) and Harvard. He first entered politics as an MNA for Mercier in 1966, and succeeded Jean Lesage as Liberal party leader in 1970. He was a 4-time premier of Que. Bourassa died Oct. 2, 1996 after a lengthy battle with skin cancer.

Sept. 15 Provincial health ministers from 9 provinces and the 2 territories offered a compensation package to individuals and families of those who contracted AIDS after receiving tainted blood between 1979 and 1985 (a period when infected blood was in the Red Cross system, but before contamination testing procedures were in place). The $130 million package gave affected individuals $30,000 a year for life, including up to $80,000 over 4 years to surviving spouses, and $16,000 over 4 years to dependent children. Three hundred and twenty-six of the estimated 954–1,440 who contracted AIDS in the blood scandal died. NS had offered its own compensation package Apr. 14, which the provincial legislature approved May 27. The package gave each victim $30,000 a year for life. Those affected with hepatitis C between 1986 and 1990 would be given compensation Mar. 27, 1998.

Sept. 24 External Affairs Minister Perrin Beatty lifted anti-apartheid sanctions against South Africa. They had been in place since 1986. South African President F.W. de Klerk began chipping away at his state's segregation policies in 1990. Both he and long-time political prisoner, African National Congress president Nelson Mandela shared the 1993 Noble Peace Prize. Mandela would become South Africa's 1st black president in May 1994.

Sept. 30 Sue Rodriguez's last hope for a legal, doctor-assisted suicide was shattered as the Supreme Court of Canada rejected her case 5–4. The 43-year-old mother, suffering the ravages of Lou Gehrig's disease (amyotrophic lateral sclerosis), had been denied the right to medically assisted suicide by both the BC court and BC Court of Appeal. Her case had initiated a private member's bill introduced in the House of Commons Mar. 22; it was rejected 140–25. On Feb. 12, 1994, Rodriguez broke the law — and died peacefully at her home in Saanich, BC.

• The Supreme Court of Canada unanimously ruled in favour of Dr. Henry Morgentaler, striking down 1989 NS legislation banning non–hospital affiliated abortion clinics. The Court ruled that laws governing abortion fell under federal, not provincial, jurisdiction.

Oct. 13 U. of BC biochemist Michael Smith was selected co-winner of the Nobel Prize in chemistry for his contributions to gene technologies. (Co-recipient was Kary Mullis of San Diego.) Smith was the second consecutive Canadian to be awarded the prize in chemistry. (Rudolph Marcus had been awarded the prestigious prize on Oct. 12, 1992.)

Oct. 14 Forty-four environmentalists, including a physician, a grandmother and the leader of the BC Green Party, were each given 45 days in jail and fined between $1,500–3000 for defying a court injunction banning logging protests at roads leading to Clayoquot Sound.

Oct. 16 The federal govt ordered Canadian families and non-governmental staff out of Haiti. It also sent 2 Canadian destroyers and a supply ship to join a US-sanctioned naval blockade aimed at restoring democracy to the impoverished Caribbean island. In 1991, a military coup erupted in Haiti, following the election victory of President Jean-Bertrand Aristide, who was forced to flee. In Sept. 1994, the Canadian govt lifted the ban when military officials agreed to let Aristide return. Canada would also commit over 500 peacekeepers and approximately 100 RCMP to the island between 1994 and 1995 to help restore order and democracy.

Oct. 21 The Supreme Court of Canada overruled a lower-court ruling that prohibited an "access" parent (the non-custodial parent in cases of divorce) from indoctrinating a child in the Jehovah's Witnesses. The Court ruled that religious instruction by the access parent did not violate the federal Charter of Rights and Freedoms.

Oct. 23 Joe Carter hit a 9th-inning home run over the left-field fence in Toronto's SkyDome to beat the Philadelphia Phillies 8–6, and give the Blue Jays their 2nd straight World Series championship. Mitch "Wild Thing" Williams took the loss. Carter's home run was the 1st World Series-ending home run since Bill Mazarowski of the Pittsburgh Pirates silenced the 1960 New York Yankees. Oddly, the full flight of Carter's historic shot was not shown on any telecast. The 1993 Jays sported one of the most powerful offences in MLB history, with 1st baseman John Olerud winning the 1993 American League batting title with a .363 average, followed in order by teammates Paul Molitor (.332) and Roberto Alomar (.326). The last team to field a league's top 3 hitters was the 1893 Philadelphia Phillies, who also lost the championship that year.

Oct. 24 Tracy Latimer, a 12-year-old quadriplegic with a severe form of cerebral palsy who lived in constant, untreatable pain, died from carbon monoxide poisoning, the result of a controversial mercy killing performed by her father, Robert Latimer, a Sask. farmer. On Nov. 4, Robert Latimer was charged and convicted of 2nd degree murder and given a life sentence. The Sask. Court of Appeal ruled 2–1 to uphold the conviction on July 18, 1995. A new trial was subsequently ordered, with the case eventually appearing before the Supreme Court of Canada June 14, 2000. On Jan. 18, 2001, the Supreme Court ruled to uphold the conviction with no parole for 10 years.

Oct. 25 Jean Chrétien's Liberals won a landslide victory in the federal election, taking 178 seats. The venerable Progressive Conservative party was nearly obliterated. Only 2 PCs were elected: Jean Charest (Sherbrooke), the only former Tory cabinet member re-elected; and Elsie Wayne (Saint John). Kim Campbell, who had been PM for 123 days, lost her seat. She was both the 1st woman, and last Progressive Conservative PM in Canadian history.

Lucien Bouchard's Bloc Québécois assumed Official Opposition status, winning 54 seats, 2 more than Preston Manning's Reform Party. The NDP, under leader Audrey McLaughlin, took 9 seats. A record 14 parties ran in the election, despite changes to the Canada Elections Act which required each party to field at least 50 candidates, with a $1,000 deposit on each. The Communist Party, Rhinoceros Party and Social Credit Party failed to field the necessary number of representatives and were denied registration. In all, 2,155 candidates stood for election; of these, 475 were women. Voter turnout was 70.9%.

Also in Oct.

• Ted Magder published *Canada's Hollywood: The Canadian State and Feature Films*, arguing that the Canadian feature-film industry failed to establish a domestic following due to 30 years of retarding cultural policies, connected mostly to the National Film Board and the 1951 Massey Commission. Both the NFB and Massey Commission disapproved of films designed solely to entertain, and neither recommended support of feature-film production.

Nov. 4 Liberal leader Jean Chrétien was sworn in as Canada's 20th prime minister. He immediately cancelled the former Conservative govt's 1992 multibillion-dollar EH–101 military helicopter deal with Britain. Cancellation costs and penalties would cost the Canadian govt upward of $500 million.

• Liberal Sheila Copps became the 1st woman deputy prime minister of Canada. She served in this position until June 10, 1997.

Nov. 15 The 1,275-page report of the Royal Commission on New Reproductive Technologies, appointed in Oct. 1989 and chaired by renowned geneticist Patricia Baird, was tabled in the House of Commons. Titled *Handle with Care*, it recommended that Canada develop new reproductive technology laws to protect citizens against potential dangers related to current and future reproductive and genetic innovations. It also recommended the banning of human cloning and surrogate motherhood, and advised that a national sperm bank be established. Baird further recommended that in-vitro fertilization be covered by provincial health care. The report led to the Human Reproductive and Genetic

Technologies Act, which was tabled in the House of Commons June 14, 1996.

Nov. 16 Finance Minister Paul Martin publicly reported that Canada's deficit was a record $40.5 billion, $5 billion more than the former Conservative govt estimate. It would be approximately $42 billion by the time the budget was tabled Feb. 22, 1994.

Nov. 18–20 PM Jean Chrétien attended the 15-nation Asia-Pacific Economic Co-operation trade summit in Seattle. Total Canadian exports to the 14 other Pacific countries exceeded $133 billion in 1992, while total imports were valued at nearly $188 billion. Chrétien also met US President Bill Clinton on NAFTA, indicating he would not pursue changes to the former Conservative deal.

Nov. 28 The Edmonton Eskimos won their 11th Grey Cup, defeating the Winnipeg Blue Bombers 33–23 at McMahon Stadium in Calgary. Canadian Player of the Game was U. of BC graduate Sean Fleming, who kicked 6 field goals, 2 converts and a single.

Dec. 3 PM Chrétien cancelled the privatization of terminals 1 and 2 at Toronto's Pearson International Airport, citing a report by former finance minister Robert Nixon that referred to the former Tory deal as a product of "political manipulation." The Pearson Development Corp. consortium, which had been transferred control of financing, upgrading and management of the terminals by the former Tories on Aug. 30, would lose an estimated $700 million because of the cancellation.

Dec. 12 The Academy of Canadian Cinema presented its 1st Claude Jutra Award for outstanding achievement by a 1st-time feature-film director. The winner was Vancouver filmmaker John Pozer for *The Grocer's Wife*. The award was named for Que. filmmaker Claude Jutra, one of Canada's finest directors. His feature film, *Mon Oncle Antoine*, was heralded as a Canadian classic.

Dec. 13 Kim Campbell stepped down as leader of the shattered 2-seat federal Progressive Conservative party. Jean Charest became interim leader the next day.

Dec. 14 The Bank of Canada rate was cut to 4.14%, its lowest since Aug. 1963–Nov. 1964 (4.0%).

Dec. 15 Canada and 124 world nations agreed to the establishment of the World Trade Organization (WTO) to oversee and settle disputes related to a new world trade agreement, established under the GATT, reducing tariff barriers between a wide spectrum of goods and services, including textiles, consulting, construction, banking and tourism. Talks on the deal began in Uruguay in 1986. Canadian tariffs would be reduced on such commodities as pulp and paper, farm products, including dairy and poultry. The 26,000-page World Trade Agreement was signed in Apr. 15, 1994, in Marrakesh, and became effective July 1, 1995.

Dec. 16 Human Resources Minister Lloyd Axworthy approved a 7.1% increase in unemployment insurance premiums.

• The Supreme Court of Canada ruled that child-care expenses, in the form of wages paid to a nanny, were not deductible business expenses.

Dec. 20 Federal Fisheries Minister Brian Tobin placed a moratorium on cod fishing covering most of the Atlantic region, effective 1994 (an extension to the 2-year, July 2, 1992, moratorium). Ocean perch quotas were cut in half. The Atlantic Groundfish Management Plan ban would include part of the Gulf of St. Lawrence and would remain in effect, in whole or in part, for the remainder of the decade. On Feb. 17, 1994, the 11-member Northwest Atlantic Fisheries Organization agreed to a 1-year moratorium on cod fishing on the Grand Banks off Canada's 200-mile limit. To aid effected fishers and fisheries workers, the federal govt initiated the Atlantic Groundfish Strategy (TAGS), effective May 15, 1994. The $1.9 billion, 5-year program included early-retirement packages, govt purchases of existing licences, weekly aid to qualified registrants and education-adjustment programs. The program was oversubscribed and by 1996 scaled down to comprise only income support.

Dec. 21 Provincial and territorial leaders met in Ottawa and agreed to a 2-year, $6 billion infrastructure improvement deal. The deal would see Ottawa match infrastructure-improvement investments with the provinces.

Also in Dec.

• The Sask. govt sold its last 579,000 shares of the former Crown corporation Potash Corp. of Sask. Privatization had begun in 1989.

1993–1994 Fifteen thousand Newfoundlanders pulled up roots and moved West.

Also in 1993

• The Roloff Beny estate donated Beny's photographic collection to the National Archives of Canada. The gift consisted of 200,000 images taken in 43 countries.

• NS restricted video-gambling machines to licenced bars only. The machines had been located in such establishments as bowling alleys, laundry marts and corner stores. The move reduced the number of machines from 2,500 to 1,000, shaving $38.6 million from annual govt revenues. The machines had been legalized in the province May 1991, but the govt had since come under pressure by interest groups arguing that they exploited compulsive gamblers.

• Three legal publishers — CCH Canadian Ltd., Carswell Thomson Canada Ltd. and Canada Law Book Inc. — charged in the Federal Court of Canada that the Law Society of Upper Canada violated copyright rules by providing photocopied versions of their publications from the Great Library, Osgoode Hall, and also by giving patrons the means (self-serve photocopy machines) to reproduce the same material. The Supreme Court of Canada overturned the ruling in early 2004, arguing that the photocopying of copyrighted material for the purposes of research did not violate existing copyright laws.

• Five hundred thousand children under age 6 were enrolled in some form of preschool program.

• Each federal party was allowed to spend a maximum $10.5 million on the Oct. 1993 election. The PC spent $10.4 million, the Liberals $9.9, and the NDP $7.4.

• The Canadian rate of inflation was 1.9%.

• The total fish quota (all species) for foreign vessels working Canadian waters was reduced to 50,700 tonnes, down from 55,800 in 1992. The 1991 quota was 96,500 tonnes; in 1990, 215,000 tonnes.

• 628,000 Canadians held more than 1 job.

• Close to 25% of all Canadian jobs were part-time, almost twice the 1975 number.

• Merchandise exports reached a record $181 billion, up from $157 billion in 1992. Merchandise imports also reached a record high $169 billion, up from $148 billion in 1992. The merchandise surplus was $12 billion in 1993, and $9 billion in 1992. It reached a high of $19.8 billion in 1984.

• A Department of Indian Affairs audit showed Aboriginal bands were in debt to the tune of $537.8 million.

• Canada's largest union, the Canadian Union of Public Employees (CUPE), had 412,242 members.

• Ontario Hydro posted a $3.5 billion loss for the year. Budget cuts and increased exports would give it a $846 million profit in 1994. Its debt, however, was $37 billion.

• The Southam Inc. newspaper conglomerate made a $21.6 million profit. It lost $262.9 million in 1992, and $153.2 in 1991.

• 14,101 of 25,549 (55%) of refugee claimants were granted asylum in Canada. The rate was 57% in 1992.

• Air Canada lost $326 million.

• The travel deficit (what Canadian travellers spent outside the country against what foreign travellers spent here) was $7.7 billion, compared to $8.2 billion in 1992.

• BCE Inc. of Montreal ranked 1st among Canadian companies with the highest annual revenue, taking in more than $20.7 billion for the year.

• Mario Lemieux won the NHL's 1992–1993 scoring title despite having missed 23 games for chemotherapy to treat Hodgkin's disease. He scored 160 points, with 69 goals and 91 assists. Lemieux also won the season's Hart Trophy for most valuable player, the Masterton Trophy for player who best exemplified the qualities of perseverance, sportsmanship and dedication to hockey, and the Lou Marsh Award for Best Canadian Athlete of the Year.

• Canadian municipal govts spent a total of $3.2 billion on pollution controls.

• The first 6 pilot episodes of the satirical television series *This Hour Has 22 Minutes* were aired on CBC television. The show became a prime-time hit with a weekly viewership of over 2 million. The cast included Mary Walsh, Rick Mercer, Cathy Jones and Greg Thomey.

• Aboriginal Peoples' Network (APN), a non-political, non-profit social organization, was established in Ottawa to provide a place where Aboriginal and non-Aboriginal people could meet, exchange information and evaluate shared interests.

• The Ottawa Lynx of the Class AAA International League was established as an affiliate of the Montreal Expos.

• The number of smokers in Canada dropped 21% since 1986.

• Universities across the country became centres of protest as students fought tuition increases that had risen between 43% and 160% since the 1985–1986 academic year. For the academic year 1992–1993, undergraduate arts tuition fees ranged from $1,481 at the U. of Ottawa (the nation's lowest) to $2,625 at Acadia, NS, (the nation's highest).

• An estimated 30,000 Canadians were infected with the AIDS virus.

• Alb. architect Douglas Cardinal was chosen to oversee the design of Washington, D.C.'s, $133 million National Museum of the American Indian. His design was incorporated, but Cardinal was fired by the Smithsonian in 1998 over remuneration disputes and deadlines. The museum was slated to open Sept. 21, 2004.

• There were 2,800 registered lobbyists in Ottawa.

• An estimated 300–500 grizzly bears remained in Alb.

• A large landslide in the ancient, geological Champlain Sea "quickclays" at Lemieux, Que., resulted in the abandonment of the township.

• Montreal jazz pianist Oliver Jones recorded the solo album *Just 88*.

• Chelsea Bridge, a Celtic jazz ensemble formed in Ottawa in 1992, won the grand prize at the Montreal Jazz Festival.

• Toronto-based country-rock artists Blue Rodeo recorded, *Five Days in July*, a critically acclaimed CD reminiscent of The Band's *Music from Big Pink* (1968) and Neil Young's *Harvest* (1971).

• The median Canadian charitable contribution as determined from income tax forms was $140, up from $130 in 1992. The highest provincial median was Nfld., at $240.

• Former PM Trudeau published his *Memoirs*.

• The newest of Canada's provincial and territorial legislative buildings, the Legislative Assembly of the Northwest Territories, was completed by a joint venture between Pin-Matthews and Ferguson Simek Clark of Yellowknife, in association with Matsuzaki Wright of Vancouver. The sweeping, open concept building is located on Frame L. in downtown Yellowknife, NWT. The outside walls of the 4,273-m² structure are made of zinc.

• The Canadian International Documentary Film Festival, affectionately known as "Hot Docs," was established in Toronto by the Canadian Independent Film Caucus. It is the largest celebration of documentary films in North America.

• Michael Arvaarluk Kusugak published the picture book *Northern Lights/The Soccer Trails*, illustrated by Vladyana Krykorka.

• Leslie Hamson's (b 1948) play *Land(e)scapes*, focusing on the interaction between four northern women was produced.

• *Scar Tissue*, the 2nd novel by Michael Ignatieff (b 1943), was published and shortlisted for both the Booker Prize and the Whitebread Novel Award.

• Thomas King (b 1947) published *Green Grass, Running Water*, the story of 5 Blackfoot in the town of Closson, Alb. King also published *One Good Story, That One*, a collection of 10 short stories.

• Leonard Cohen published *Stranger Music: Selected Poems and Songs*. Cohen was also one of six 1993 recipients of the Gov-Gen. Performing Arts Awards for lifetime achievement.

• American novelist and part-time Nfld. resident E. Annie Proulx published *The Shipping News*, a novel set in Nfld. The work won the national Book Award in the US, the Pulitzer Prize in 1994, and was made into a feature film in 2001.

1994

Jan. 1 NAFTA (North Amrican Free Trade Agreement) came into effect, creating a trilateral commercial-exchange region between Mexico, the US and Canada, comprising a total of 360 million people.

• Ont. became the 1st province to implement legislation recognizing midwifery as a profession, making Canada the last western nation to do so.

Jan. 4 Residents of Happy Valley and Goose Bay, Labrador, were faced with serious water shortages when many residents left their water running in an attempt to keep residential water pipes from freezing in −30°C temperatures.

Jan. 6 Downhill skiers Ed Podivinsky and Cary Mullen came 1st and 2nd, respectively, at the World Cup event in Saalbach, Austria, the 1st Canadian World Cup 1–2 punch since Crazy Canucks Ken Read and Dave Murray at Chamonix, France, in 1978.

Jan. 14 Arkansas-based retail giant Wal-Mart Stores Inc., founded by Americans Sam and Bud Walton in 1962, purchased 120 of 160 Woolco Canada stores. The remaining 38 Woolcos, owned by New York–based Woolworth Corp., were closed and sold off. The move marked Wal-Mart's first entry into the Canadian market. The sale netted Woolworth an estimated $300 million. Wal-Mart had sales exceeding $55 billion US in 1993.

Jan. 18 The debt-ridden, Toronto-based Canadian Opera Company (COC) appointed conductor

Richard Bradshaw its new artistic director, to replace Brian Dickie who had departed Oct. 1993. Bradshaw would be named general director of the COC in Jan. 1998, the 1st musician to hold the post since Ettore Mazzoleni in the late 1950s. Bradshaw presented a double-billing of Bartok's *Bluebeard's Castle* and Schoenberg's *Erwartung* in his inaugural 1994–1995 event calendar.

Jan. 20–21 Television, radio, telephone and scientific operations were interrupted when communications satellites *Anik E-1* and *Anik E-2* suffered operational problems. *Anik E-1* was back on line within 8 hours. Control of the $300 million *Anik E-2* was regained 5 months later (June 21). In the interim, Canadian broadcasters were forced to rely on US satellite services to maintain regular transmissions.

Jan. 21 Provincial equalization payments increased along a schedule from $7.4 billion in 1994 to a planned $10 billion by 1998–1999. All provinces but BC, Alb. and Ont. received equalization payments.

Jan. 24 Refugee claimants were given the right to work in Canada while they waited the outcome of their claims.

Jan. 27 Markham, Ont., MP Jag Bhaduria resigned from the Liberal caucus to sit as an Independent following allegations he exaggerated his education credentials in campaign literature, and had threatened a former school board employer for not promoting him. Bhaduria had apologized to the House Jan. 24 but came under increasing pressure to resign by MPs and constituents, who gathered a petition signed by 30,000 demanding his removal.

Jan. 31 Newfoundlanders were banned from cod fishing for home consumption ("food-for-the-table") and also from fishing for cod within the tourist industry. Fines were set to a maximum $100,000. The contentious ban was lifted July 21, to allow 10 fish per day per person twice weekly, for both residents and tourists. The commercial moratorium on cod began in 1992 and would extend throughout the decade.

Also in Jan.

• Mario Dumont and Jean Allaire founded the Action Démocratique du Québec (ADQ), a new Que. provincial pro-sovereignty party. Allaire became its 1st leader but was replaced for health reasons by Dumont in Mar. Also in Mar., the ADQ formulated a policy in principle whereby new immigrants to Que. would sign a "social contract" giving them a "moral obligation" to assimilate into Que. society.

Feb. 8 The federal govt reduced cigarette taxes by $5 a carton across Canada after suffering large-scale tax losses to smuggled smokes from the US. The provincial govts of Que., NB, Ont., PEI and NS followed suit. The number of legal cigarettes subsequently sold across the country in Mar. was 4.35 billion, 62.5 million more than in Mar. 1993.

Feb. 8 Atlanta-based Home Depot, the largest home improvement–building supply chain in the US, purchased 75% of the 5-store Aikenhead Home Improvement chain, owned by Molson Companies Ltd. The purchase marked Home Depot's 1st foray into the Canadian market. By 2003, Home Deopt had stores in 7 provinces and employed 18,000 Canadians.

• An 11-day BC longshoreman strike, which had completely crippled West Coast ports, ended with workers getting 65 cents more an hour over each of the next 3 years. Their pre-strike hourly wage was $21.41.

Feb. 11 Seven of 11 Village Foods outlets, NB's only unionized grocery-store chain, were purchased by Atlantic Wholesalers Ltd. The remaining stores were slated for closure; 400 of 900 jobs were placed on the chopping block.

Feb. 12–27 Canada won 13 medals (3 gold, 6 silver, 4 bronze) at the Winter Olympic Games in Lillehammer, Norway, finishing tied in 6th place with the US in the medal standings. Myriam Bédard won 2 gold medals in biathlon (cross-country skiing/shooting) — 1 in the 15-km event, beating her nearest opponent by an incredible 46 seconds, the other in the 7.5-km event. The 3rd gold was awarded to another Que. skier, 1993 World Champion Jean-Luc Brassard, who rose to the top of the freestyle ski moguls event.

Feb. 18 "Jesus Christ" was genericized to read "almighty God" in the 1877 prayer read by Ottawa's

Speaker to open each day's session. Daily reading of the Lord's Prayer was abolished. Reference to Britain's monarch dodged the edit.

Feb. 22 Federal Finance Minister Paul Martin presented the 1st of 10 consecutive Liberal administration budgets. Martin had inherited a deficit of $42 billion for 1993–1994, the largest in Canadian history. Budget highlights included the freezing of 1995–1996 provincial transfer payments for welfare and post-secondary education; and $7 billion cut to the Department of National Defence over 5 years. The venerable military colleges Royal Roads, Victoria, BC, and the College Militaire Royale de Saint Jean, Que. were slated for closure. On July 9, however, the Que. and federal govts agreed to maintain Militaire Royale as a prepatory, non degree-granting college, cutting the cost of Ottawa's involvement from $30 million to $5 million a year. On Dec. 13, Royal Roads was saved from the axe when Ottawa agreed to provide BC with $25 million over 5 years to re-organize it into a civilian school. Royal Roads became a degree-granting affiliate of the U. of Victoria in 1995.

Feb. 24 Veteran civil servant Jocelyne Bourgon was appointed the 1st woman Clerk of the Privy Council.

• Ralph Klein's Alb. govt tabled its budget, which included a $956 million spending reduction for 1994–1995 and the elimination of 1,800 civil servant positions by 1995. The projected deficit was expected to drop from $2.4 billion to $1.5 billion by the end of the 1994–1995 fiscal year.

Feb. 28 The 750,000-member Native Council of Canada became the Congress of Aboriginal Peoples. Jim Sinclair was elected president, defeating Ron George.

Feb.–Mar. The Pikangikum First Nation in northern Ont. suffered a rash of 6 youth suicides, while 12 other youth were airlifted out of the community to solvent-abuse treatment programs in the south. Chief Gordon Peters, who resigned after the tragic events, stated, "Kids in Pikangikum feel a sense of hopelessness and are really isolated."

Also in Feb.

• CBC television aired the final new episodes of its popular night-time drama *Street Legal*, which 1st aired for the 1986–1987 season. The 1-hour drama series revolved around the lives of a group of Toronto lawyers. The cast starred Sonja Smits, Cynthia Dale, and C. David Johnson.

Mar. 1 Brian Mulroney propounded in a speech to business people in Montreal that, had he been leading the Conservatives in the last general election, the Progressive Conservatives might have been re-elected. Mulroney left Kim Campbell with the most unpopular Conservative administration in history; PCs won 2 seats in the 1993 election and would never again find favour amongst Canadians. The party would flounder over the next 10 years, only to fold into the Conservative Party of Canada in 2003.

Mar. 3 A US grand jury indicted Alan Eagleson on 32 counts of fraud, embezzlement and racketeering committed during his tenure as executive director of the NHL Players Association and as a high-profile player agent to the likes of Bobby Orr, Carl Brewer and Andy Bathgate. In Jan. 1998, he was sentenced to 18 months in jail. Eagleson served 6.

Mar. 4 Actor, comedian and former Toronto Argonauts co-owner John Candy died suddenly of a heart attack in Durango, Mexico, while on location for the film *Wagons East*. The comic genius was the creator of such timeless *SCTV* characters as Johnny LaRue, Mr. Messenger, Harry With the Snake on His Face, William B., and Yosh Schmenge. His brilliant parodies included Luciano Pavarotti, Orsen Wells, Darryl Sittler, Red Fisher and Julia Child. Candy was 43.

Mar. 6 The 1st of 2 1994 US cruise missile tests over Canada was conducted over the Beaufort Sea south through the Mackenzie R. delta.

Mar. 11 The Alb. Court of Appeal ruled that the West Edmonton Mall could not retain the name Fantasyland for its amusement park. The ruling ended a 10-year legal squabble with Walt Disney Productions, which claimed exclusive rights over the name used at both Disneyland and Disney World.

Mar. 15 Rogers Communications Inc., the nation's largest cable television company, purchased Maclean-Hunter, which served over 1 million cable subscribers and owned such notable publications as the *Financial Post*, *Maclean's* magazine, and *Chatelaine*. The price, $3.1 billion. On June 18, Rogers sold the US assets of Maclean-Hunter to US-based Comcast Corp. for $1.76 billion.

• The dollar hit 73.30 cents US, the lowest since dipping to 73.20 on Jan. 14, 1987.

Mar. 16 The Canadian Human Rights Commission's 1994 report noted that the nation's treatment of Aboriginal Peoples was Canada's most glaring human-rights issue.

Mar. 18 Finance Minister Paul Martin came under heat in the House by Opposition members who argued that his 100% ownership of Canadian Steamship Lines Inc. (CSL) made it impossible for him to fulfill his role without breaching conflict-of-interest guidelines. Martin had placed CSL, whose ships did not sail under the red maple leaf, in a quasi-blind trust on Feb. 1. He would sell the company to his 3 sons in 2003, before replacing Jean Chrétien as PM.

Mar. 20 Cape Breton's the Rankin Family (Cookie, Heather, Raylene, Jimmy and John Morris) won 4 Juno Awards at celebrations in Toronto, garnering recognition for Canadian Entertainer of the Year, Group of the Year, Best Country Group, and Single of the Year for their hit *Fare Thee Well*.

Mar. 21 The BC legislature voted henceforth to elect, rather than appoint its Speaker.

Mar. 23 Wayne Gretzky of the Los Angeles Kings scored his 802nd goal, passing Gordie Howe as the NHL's all-time leading scorer. It took the Great One 1,117 regular-season games to reach the milestone; Howe scored 801 in 1,767 games. By career's end, Gretzky had 894 regular-season goals and 1,016 total goals (he played in 122 playoff games).

Mar. 23–25 PM Chrétien attended a 3-day NAFTA trade conference in Mexico City, where he registered complaints about Mexican human-rights abuses and recent electoral fraud.

Also in Mar.

• A Canadian Magazine Industry Task Force, established Apr. 1993 and headed by Patrick O'Callaghan and Roger Tasse, urged the federal govt to impose an 80% excise tax on split-run magazines. The task force was created after the 1993 split-run *Sports Illustrated* was produced. Split-runs were foreign (usually US) magazines that included a minimum amount of new content for the Canadian market. Foreign advertising was removed and the space resold for Canadian consumption. The govt feared that advertising dollars would move from Canadian to foreign publications. On Dec. 22, Bill C–103 to create and impose the tax was tabled in the House; it received Assent Dec. 15, 1995. However, on Feb. 21, 1997, an international WTO tribunal ruled that the excise tax on split-run magazines violated international trade regulations. The excise tax was subsequently lifted.

Apr. 7 Statistics Canada reported that the nation's total national, provincial and territorial debt was $661.2 billion, or just over $23,000 per resident. In 1982, the total debt was recorded as $108.9 billion, or $4,339 per resident.

Apr. 14 Sixteen Canadian peacekeepers were held captive in Visoko, Bosnia, by Serbs reacting to the Apr. 10–11 NATO bombing of Gorazde — the 1st ground offensive in NATO history. The peacekeepers were released unharmed Apr. 17. On Nov. 23, Serbs took 400 more peacekeepers hostage, including 55 Canadians. The Canadians were released unharmed Dec. 8 (although another 55 Canadians were temporarily detained by Serbs in May 1995). By the end of Sept. 1994, there were 2,000 Canadian peacekeepers stationed in Bosnia and Croatia, to their peril.

Apr. 15 The federal govt embarked on a $684 million national youth employment project to create summer jobs, internships and school-to-work job creation and training programs over the 1994–1995 fiscal year. Existing student loan programs received $475 million of the total.

Apr. 18 Environment Minister Sheila Copps unveiled a $250 million plan to clean up the Great Lakes and St. Lawrence R. over 6 years. The plan included removal of such wastes as PCBs, elimination of toxic runoffs and spills and zebra mussel control. Two days later, the US Environment Protection Agency reported that only 2% of the total American Great Lakes shoreline water was suitable for drinking or recreation. On Sept. 12, 2001, a *State of the Great Lakes 2001* report issued by the US–Canada International Joint Commission gave the Great Lakes cleanup effort a moderate grade.

Apr. 26 The Supreme Court of Canada ruled that every telephone company in Canada fell within federal jurisdiction. The ruling was made in the case of Que.'s Telephone Gouvernement, which demanded federal, not Que. provincial, regulation.

Apr. 27 MPs voted to make hockey Canada's official winter sport, and lacrosse the official summer sport.

• The Ford Motor Company pledged to invest $400 million into its Oakville, Ont., truck plant, pushing total investment since 1992 to $3 billion.

Apr. 28 The Supreme Court of Canada upheld an Ont. Court of Appeal ruling allowing lawyers to ask potential jurors if they were racist.

Apr. 29 Surly construction workers manhandled NS Premier John Savage in the legislature as Finance Minister Bernie Boudreau attempted to table the provincial budget. The workers were protesting legislation, eventually passed May 9, that allowed non-unionized workers onto the job site. The NS budget, which was not formally presented, included wage cuts affecting 40,000 civil servants, and a $61 million cut to the province's $1.1 billion health department budget.

Also in Apr.

• Canada romped to curling glory as Rick Folk and his Kelowna, BC, rink beat Sweden 3–2 to take the men's World Championship. The Regina, Sask., rink in Oberstdorf, Germany, led by Sandra Schmirler followed suit, beating Scotland 5–3 to take the women's title. In Sofia, Bulgaria, Kim Gelland's Unionville, Ont., rink won the women's World Juniors, while Colin Davidson's Edmonton, Alb., rink took the men's junior World title.

May 5 The Supreme Court of Canada ruled 7–2 that the former Mulroney govt had the right in 1989 to initiate plans to close VIA Rail's 225-km Esquimalt and Nanaimo (E & N) rail service, linking Victoria to Courtenay. The Court ruled that although Ottawa had been obligated to build the E & N as a condition for the colony's entrance into Confederation, Ottawa was not responsible for its upkeep in perpetuity. The railway carried 39,000 passengers in 1993.

May 8 Canada defeated Finland 2–1 in Italy to capture the men's World Hockey Championships, its 1st win since the Trail (BC) Smoke Eaters in 1961.

May 9 The Que. govt cancelled all Kahnewake commercial gasoline licences and all fuel shipments to the region, stating that the sale of gas would not resume until Mohawk retailers paid up on fuel taxes, which had fallen into arrears since 1991. The Mohawk argued that the federal govt had no right to impose the tax.

May 12 Assent was given to Bill C–29 ("Pirate Vessels Bill") to amend the Coastal Fisheries Protection Act, unilaterally giving Canada the right to stop foreign vessels from overfishing outside the 200-mile (322-km) coastal jurisdiction. The internationally contentious bill included fines of up to $500,000 per offending captain, and the right to seize and resell illegal catches.

May 16 Eight thousand one hundred Nfld. teachers began a strike effecting 100,000 students. The educators returned to work June 13, accepting qualified protection against job cuts stemming from the nation's highest provincial outmigration rates.

May 18 The nation's 1st gay rights legislation, Ont.'s Bill 167, passed 1st reading by a vote of 57–52. The NDP bill, which would redefine the definition of spouse, recognize gay marriage and provide same-sex couples equal social and spousal benefits, was defeated at 2nd reading June 9, on a free vote of 68–59.

May 24 Casino Windsor, Ont.'s 1st commercial casino, opened. It generated over $406.8 million in revenue during its 1st 10 months. On Dec. 5, an Ont. Native Council selected the Chippewa Rama Reserve near Orillia, Ont. as the sight for the province's 1st Native-operated casino. Profits would be spread among 131 First Nations groups. Rama, the largest casino in the country, opened July 31, 1996. In July 2000, the Supreme Court of Canada ruled that profits from Rama and other Native-run casinos would be distributed only to registered Ont. Aboriginal bands within the province, and not to Métis or non-Status Peoples.

May 31 Members of the Royal Canadian Legion voted to ban anyone wearing religious headwear from Legion halls. On Aug. 20, 5 Sikh veterans, who had subsequently been denied entry into the Royal halls, joined Queen Elizabeth II for tea at the Commonwealth Games in Victoria, BC.

Also in May

• Atom Egoyan's critical and commercial success *Exotica* won the International Critics' Prize at the Cannes International Film Festival. The dark study of a man's obsession with desire was Egoyan's 6th film. It garnered 13 Genie Award nominations and won 8, including 3 for Egoyan — Best Director, Screenplay and Motion Picture.

June 3 Queen Elizabeth II unveiled her country's 1st war memorial to Canadian soldiers — nearly 50 years after WW II and some 76 years after the Great War. The Green Park Canadian Memorial (in London, England), designed by Pierre Granche, commemorated more than 100,000 Canadians who sacrificed their lives for the freedom of others during the two world wars.

June 6 PM Chrétien attended the 50th anniversary of D-Day at Normandy, where over 1,000 Canadians were killed or wounded along the highly fortified coastal beaches.

June 8 The CRTC approved licences for 8 new specialty services and 2 pay services, effective Jan. 1, 1995. They were Bravo!, Canal D, the Discovery Channel, Life Network, New Country Network, RDI, Showcase, WTN, MoviePix, and MovieMax. The new services joined TSN, MuchMusic, Vision TV and CBC Newsworld as the only specialty stations in the country.

June 13 Senator Daniel Lang chose to retire on his 75th birthday, the mandatory senatorial retirement age. Lester Pearson had appointed Lang to the

Senate in 1964; he was the last senator not affected by the mandatory retirement restrictions implemented in 1965.

June 14 Between 40,000 and 70,000 hockey fans rioted in downtown Vancouver after the Canucks lost game 7 of the Stanley Cup finals to the New York Rangers. Property damage was set at over $1 million. One hundred and six people were charged with related crimes, mostly after the fact, based on videotape evidence.

June 15 Legislation requiring all US fishing vessels to carry a separate, $1,500 licence each time they entered BC waters came into effect.

June 16 The federal govt unveiled its new ethics package, forcing lobbyists to identify their employers, lobbying purpose, goals and methods. The legislation also terminated contingency fees previously given lobbyists who had successfully landed govt contracts. The govt also created the Office of the Ethics Counsellor, with responsibility for the Conflict of Interest and Post-Employment Code for Public Office Holders. Howard Wilson was named the 1st commissioner.

June 24 Over 200 Fête nationale celebrants rioted against police in Quebec City; 23 people were arrested.

June 26 Stephen Leacock's home, at Old Brewery Bay near Orillia, Ont., was declared a National Historic Site by the Historic Sites and Monuments Board of Canada. The home had been purchased by the town of Orillia for $25,000 and opened to the public July 5, 1958.

Also in June

• Staff of the Royal Sask. Museum began excavation in the Frenchman R. Valley, near Eastend, Sask., on "Scotty," a 65-million-year-old Tyrannosaurus rex skeleton.

• An Angus Reid poll showed that 47% of non-Quebecers would rather see Que. secede than make constitutional compromises for the sake of national unity; 44% of the people polled favoured compromise.

July 4 Members of the Saskatchewan Wheat Pool, established in 1924, voted to go public. The Pool had $500 million in assets, 3,000 employees, and represented 60,000 farmers. It netted $28.5 million in 1993. The Sask. Wheat Pool would trade on the Toronto Stock Exchange (TSE) for the 1st time in Apr. 1996.

July 7 Ovide Mercredi was elected to his 3rd term as chief of the Assembly of First Nations, taking 273 votes on the 3rd ballot to defeat Wally McKay. The Assembly represented 533,000 individuals. On Sept. 1, Mercredi told Ottawa it must guarantee the rights of Que. Aboriginals in the event of disunion.

July 8 An international trade commission ruled in favour of the US, recommending that import restraints be placed on Canadian wheat to counteract subsidies determined detrimental to US farmers. On Aug. 2, Canada and the US reached an agreement: a limit was placed on Canadian wheat exports for one year, a joint Commission on Grains was established and a 1-year "peace clause" was implemented to prevent additional restrictions or countermeasures by either country.

July 12 Cape Breton Mi'kmaq and Ottawa agreed to establish Native police forces on 5 of the island's reserves. The forces would combine 15 Mi'kmaq police and incorporate 2 RCMP for 2 years. The 5-year deal would be 52% financed by Ottawa, the remainder by NS.

July 14 All 12 members of the Metropolitan Toronto Housing Authority board were fired following an audit uncovering bribery, fraud and other financial indiscretions. The housing authority was the largest in Canada, with an operating budget of $250 million, 1,000 buildings and approximately 100,000 tenants.

July 16–22 Comet Shoemaker, co-discovered by Canadian astronomer David Levy on Mar. 18, 1993, collided with planet Jupiter.

July 18 Brokerage firm Burns Fry Ltd. was acquired by Bank of Montreal's Nesbitt Thomson for $403 million, making Nesbitt the largest securities firm in the country.

Year

1994

• Provincial premiers signed an interprovincial trade deal in Ottawa reducing trade barriers and standardizing consumer and transportation regulations.

July 20 A fire caused by humans near Penticton, BC, destroyed over 5,500 ha and caused the evacuation of over 3,500 people; 18 homes were destroyed.

July 26 BC Burnaby-Kingsway MP Svend Robinson was sentenced to 14 days in jail for participating in an anti-logging blockade of Clayoquot Sound in 1993.

July 27 BC native Wendy Clay became the 1st woman maj-gen. in the Canadian Armed Forces. The surgeon and pilot was also made surgeon-gen. of the Forces.

July 28 Edmonton-based Shaw Communications purchased Richmond Hill, Ont.–based Classic Communications for $240 million, making Shaw the 2nd largest cable company in Canada next to Rogers.

• Wisconsin Central Transportation Corp. took over the Algoma Central Railway, which ran between Sault Ste. Marie and Hearst, Ont. The Ont. govt gave Wisconsin $7.7 million (a $4.8 million grant and a $2.9 million interest-free loan) and purchased $700,000 in railway shares to facilitate the purchase. The Ont. govt had kept Algoma Central afloat with approximately $40 million in subsidies since 1980.

Aug. 2 A 247-member field hospital unit was deployed to provide humanitarian relief in civil war–torn Rwanda, eastern Africa; a total of 685 Canadian UN peacekeepers would be in the troubled nation by the end of Aug. All were under the general UN command of Maj-Gen. Romeo Dallaire (b 1946), a Canadian in charge of a UN mission that had been deployed to the region in 1993. An estimated 800,000 Rwandans, mainly ethnic Tutsis and politically moderate Hutus, had been slaughtered since Apr. Maj-Gen. Dallaire was replaced in Rwanda by another Canadian, Maj-Gen. Guy Tousignant on Aug. 19. Canadian peacekeepers would begin to come home in the Fall. On Apr. 11, 2000, Dallaire announced his retirement from the Canadian Armed Forces; he would then write the 2003 bestseller *Shake Hands with the Devil:*

The Failure of Humanity in Rwanda, contending that the wholescale slaughter in Rwanda could have been prevented had the UN administration in New York allowed its forces to take a more active role in the conflict.

Aug. 5 Briton Colin Bailey was named chief curator of the National Gallery of Canada. Gallery officials claimed they had searched for a year without locating a Canadian candidate to oversee the federally funded repository of the nation's cultural heritage.

• Husky Oil and the Sask. govt purchased federal and Alb. interests in the Lloydminster heavy-oil upgrader project for an estimated $74 million, giving them a 66% controlling interest in the project. Located along the Alb.-Sask border, the Lloydminster facility transformed heavy oil to refined crude.

Aug. 8 Montreal's storied Civic Party, the party of Jean Drapeau, who held power between 1960 and 1986, folded into the Montrealers' Party.

Aug. 12 The Montreal Expos held the best record in baseball, with 74 wins and 40 losses. The 'Spos were excellently positioned for the Sept. stretch run, standing a full 6 games above the Atlanta Braves in the National League East.

• Major League Baseball players went on strike for the 8th time in big league history. The walkout lasted until Mar. 31, 1995, and cost club owners approximately $1 billion. The 1994 season was cancelled; there were no playoffs and no World Series.

Aug. 15 Federal regulators ordered that the 123-year-old Confederation Life Insurance Co., Canada's 5th largest life insurer, be wound up and its assets liquidated. Confederation, with 230,000 policy holders, lost $29 million in 1993.

• Ont. began enforcing speed limits with photo radar.

Aug. 16 The Canadian Medical Association voted 93–74 to ban member participation in euthanasia and assisted suicide.

Aug. 16-26 Seventy thousand Acadians and Louisiana Cajuns (an American contraction of "Acadian") gathered in NS to celebrate the 1st Acadian International Re-Union and the 1st Acadian World Congress. It was the 1st "formal" get-together since the Acadian Expulsion between 1755 and 1763.

Aug. 18 The XV Commonwealth Games began in Victoria, BC. Canada wrapped up the competition with 41 gold, 42 silver and 46 bronze. A few of the many highlights included gymnast Stella Umeh taking 2 gold and 2 silver; Carole Rouillard winning the women's marathon; and Jeff Adams taking gold in the demonstration 800-m wheelchair race.

Aug. 25 The Algonquin of Golden L., working with the Ont. and federal govts, established a framework to resolve a land claim covering 34,000 km² in the Ottawa Valley between Mattawa and L'Orignal. Negotiations reached into 2004.

Aug. 29 Mel Hurtig, founding member of the 10,000-member National Party, resigned as leader. The party had no MP, and eventually folded Sept. 18, 1994.

Aug. 30 The Ont. govt obtained injunctions ensuring protestors at Toronto, London, Kingston and Bradford abortion clinics remain at least 20 m away from the buildings. Ont. Court Justice George Adams, who granted the injunction, stated that the harassment of pregnant women at these clinics was an "unnecessary humiliation and embarrassment."

Sept. 1 In a case of a Vietnamese man charged with sexual assault, the Supreme Court of Canada ruled that any Canadian charged with a crime must be able to hear the court proceedings — as the case unfolded — in the accused's 1st language, whatever that language might be.

Sept. 2 Members of the Canadian Police Association met in Winnipeg and hammered out a resolution that included a call for life imprisonment without parole for repeat sex offenders, the re-establishment of capital punishment and mandatory 5-year sentences for any gun-related crimes.

Sept. 6 Davis Inlet residents blockaded an airstrip, preventing court officials from re-entering the community. They had driven off a judge and harassed a number of RCMP officers escorting local prisoners to the airstrip on Dec. 16, 1993. In 1995,

three Innu women, including Chief Katie Rich, were convicted of contempt in relation to the incident. This blockade was part of a local demand for an Aboriginal justice and policing system. The RCMP returned Apr. 11, 1995, after an agreement was reached whereby 4 local Innu officers worked alongside RCMP in the community.

Sept. 10 A 13-year-old girl was sent home from her Que. high school for wearing the hijab, a Muslim veil.

Sept. 12 The Parti Québécois, under Jacques Parizeau, who campaigned on a commitment to call another sovereignty referendum, took 77 of 125 legislature seats in the provincial election. (The PQ had won 23 seats in 1985 and 29 seats in 1989.) The Liberals, under Daniel Johnson, won 47 seats. The remaining seat was won by Mario Dumont, leader of the new Parti Action Démocratique.

Sept. 15 Former Man. Liberal leader Sharon Carstairs, MNA Lise Bacon and Landon Pearson, daughter-in-law of the late Lester Pearson, were appointed to the Senate, bringing the number of women senators to a record 18.

Sept. 29 Intergovernmental Affairs Minister Marcel Masse announced the federal govt was obliged to fulfil former PM Mulroney's earlier pledge to Que. — that it would cover costs of implementing the 1992 Charlottetown Accord referendum in the province. Cost: $34 million.

Sept. 30 The Supreme Court of Canada overturned the case against Henri Daviault, who had been convicted of sexually assaulting a woman confined to a wheelchair. The Court ruled that the defendant did not get a fair trial because he was not allowed to use "drunkenness" as a defence. (An upswelling of protest forced the govt to pass Bill C–72 June 22, 1995, ensuring that intoxication could not be used as a defence in cases of sexual assault and battery. By the time this bill was introduced in the House in Feb. 1995, 3 men had already successfully used the "drunken" excuse.) Less than a month later (Oct. 13, 1994), the Supreme Court ordered a new trial for a man who claimed he was not responsible for killing his wife because he had committed the crime while sleepwalking. The man had previously been convicted by 2 lower courts.

• One hundred and twenty employees of the Canadian Auto Workers Union (CAW) ended a 2-week strike against the CAW, coming to terms on an agreement over job security, the use of outside workers and pensions.

Sept.–Dec. The Art Gallery of Ontario hosted the Barnes Exhibit, one of the world's premier collections of impressionist and post-impressionist paintings.

Also in Sept.
• The BC govt declared a state of emergency when some 40 barrels of DDT were discovered at Rainy Hollow, near the Alaska border. The barrels had been buried by the US military in the mid-1970s.

• The Northwest Atlantic Fisheries Organization met in Dartmouth, NS, agreeing to fish-quota reductions outside Canada's 200-mile (322-km) limit and to abide by the moratorium on cod on the tips of the Grand Banks, except on the Flemish Cap, where an 11,000-tonne cod quota was set.

Oct. 1 NHL team owners began a 103-day player lockout.

Oct. 4 Five people linked with the Switzerland-based Order of the Solar Temple were found dead in Morin Heights, Que., victims of an apparent murder-suicide. Forty-eight Solar members were also found dead in 2 areas of Switzerland the same day. Five more Solar members would be found dead in the aftermath of a suspicious house fire in Saint Casimir, Que., on Mar. 23, 1997.

Oct. 5 Federal human resources minister Lloyd Axworthy released an 89-page social policy reform discussion paper, recommending a 2-tiered unemployment system geared toward chronic and occasional users; a permanent reduction in federal post-secondary support; and revisions to federal welfare transfer payments. Combined, the recommendations would reduce federal spending by $38.7 billion over the next year.

Oct. 12 Alb.-born McMaster physics professor Bertram Brockhouse was awarded the Nobel Prize in physics for designing and using the Triple-Axis Neutron Spectroscope in groundbreaking studies on condensed matter. The Nobel marked the 3rd in a row for Canadian scientists: Michael Smith (Oct. 13, 1993) and Rudolph Marcus (Oct. 12, 1992) had both won in the field of chemistry.

• Canadian Western Bank purchased the North West Trust Co., an 11-branch firm founded in 1958, for $92 million. Canadian Western, the only Canadian chartered bank headquartered in western Canada (Edmonton), had 13 branches. The ailing North West had been taken over by the Alb. govt in 1987.

Oct. 14 Marilyn Trenholme was appointed NB's 1st family minister.

Oct. 20 Mary May Simon of Nunuvik, Que., was appointed the country's 1st circumpolar ambassador.

Oct. 24 The 5th and last volume of the *Encyclopedia of Newfoundland* was published. Former premier and Father of Confederation Joey Smallwood initiated the project in 1972.

• The BC govt approved the creation of 17 new parks in the Cariboo-Chilcotin region, part of a widespread re-evaluation of land as recommended by the BC Land Use Commission on Feb. 9. On Mar. 13, 1995, BC Premier Harcourt added plans for another 16 new parks in the Kootenay region, including the Height of the Rockies area between the Palliser and White Rivers. Between 1992 and 1996, the BC govt established 225 new parks and protected regions.

Oct. 30 Pope John-Paul II appointed Montreal archbishop Jean-Claude Turcotte (b 1936) cardinal. Turcotte became Canada's 4th cardinal, joining his peers Carter, Vachon and Gagnon.

Nov. 1 PM Chrétien cut the number of eligible 1995 family-class immigration entrants from 109,000 to 23,000, moving emphasis away from family ties toward skilled workers who could be quickly plugged into the job market.

Nov. 4 Federal Indian Affairs Minister Ron Irwin and NS Mi'kmaq representatives concluded a deal that gave NS Mi'kmaq total control over their own education, including choice of language and curriculum.

Nov. 4–10 PM Chrétien led 9 provincial premiers and 400 private business representatives to China on a 10-day trade mission. The trip cost $1.2 million; over $5 billion in trade deals were signed, including plans to construct a $2.5 billion CANDU reactor. Que. Premier Parizeau refused to participate. China was Canada's 5th largest trading partner.

Nov. 8 Dr. Garson Romalis, a Vancouver gynecologist who performed abortions, was shot and wounded at his home while eating breakfast. Anti-abortion protestors had previously picketed his residence. (Dr. Romalis would again become the victim of anti-abortion violence when he was stabbed by a man in his BC clinic July 11, 2000.) On Nov. 10, 1995, Hamilton, Ont., gynecologist Dr. Hugh Short had his elbow shattered when a bullet ripped through his home. And on Nov. 11, 1997, Winnipeg physician Dr. Jack Fainman was shot and injured in a similar incident. The shootings were allegedly connected to Vermont resident James Charles Kopp, who was captured in France, Mar. 29, 2001, for the 1998 murder of Buffalo, New York, doctor Barnett Slepian. Kopp was sentenced to life imprisonment by a US court in 2003 for the murder of Slepian. A Canadian trial had not been scheduled.

Nov. 15 PM Chrétien and 17 representatives of the other participating Asia-Pacific Economic Co-operation (APEC) countries signed an agreement to implement free trade between them by 2010 (2020 for developing member countries).

• Ont. Auditor Erik Peters issued his annual report, noting that 120 Ont. water-treatment facilities were not meeting health-safety standards; 415 sewage plants were similarly not up to standard.

Nov. 17 Twenty-one-year-old Lisa Neve of Edmonton was labelled a dangerous offender, the only woman so labelled at the time, and therefore considered the most dangerous woman in the country. Justice Alec Murray declared that Neve, who had 22 prior convictions, had a "severe, anti-social personality disorder, which manifests itself in evil, violent and sadistic thoughts." He sentenced her to an indefinite period of incarceration. The Alb. Court of Appeal overturned the ruling on June 29, 1999, noting that the "dangerous offender" label had

been established based on the accused's thoughts not actions.

Nov. 18 Que. Premier Jacques Parizeau shelved the $13 billion James Bay–Great Whale hydroelectric project following unfavourable environmental-review assessments (ordered by the federal govt July 10, 1991.) The future of the project had been in limbo since Mar. 27, 1992, when the New York Power Authority cancelled its $17 billion contract with the planned hydro facility.

Nov. 21 Alb. Premier Ralph Klein travelled to Toronto to receive the 1994 Colin M. Brown Medal for promoting "economic freedom." The recognition was given by the Conservative National Citizen's Coalition.

Nov. 22 Senate Speaker Romeo LeBlanc was appointed the 23rd gov-gen. LeBlanc, who succeeded Ray Hnatyshyn, became the 1st Acadian representative of England's monarch in Canada. He received a salary of $97,400 a year.

Nov. 27 The Baltimore CFLers became the 1st non-Canadian team to reach the Grey Cup finals. They lost to the hometown BC Lions, who won their 3rd Grey Cup.

Nov. 29 Lenna Bradburn became the 1st Canadian woman chief of police outside a Native reserve — in Guelph, Ont.

• Thomson Corp. closed the 123-year-old *Oshawa Times* in the midst of a 3-week strike. The newspaper conglomerate had also closed the BC *Comox District Free Press* during a strike earlier in the year. Thomson would later report a $427 million 1994 loss. The company began a selloff of its Canadian newspaper holdings on July 28, 1995.

Dec. 1 Federal Defence Minister David Collenette tabled a white paper outlining departmental cuts to both civilian and headquarters staff totalling 11,990 jobs, the result of Finance Minister Paul Martin's massive military cutbacks tabled in the Feb. 22 budget.

• Bloc Québécois leader Lucien Bouchard underwent surgery to remove his left leg as a result of an infection known as flesh-eating disease (necrotizing fasciitis). The rare bacterial infection was estimated to affect between 90 and 200 Canadians a year, 20–30% of whom died.

Dec. 7 Que. Premier Jacques Parizeau tabled a draft secession bill in the National Assembly. The bill set out the conditions of Que. sovereignty as a some-what vague yet independent nation-state holding an economic association with the former Canada. The new Que. would use Canadian currency; its inhabitants would retain Canadian citizenship. Also included in the legislation was the question to be put to Quebecers in a sovereignty referendum, the date would later be set as Oct. 30, 1995: "Are you in favour of the act passed by the National Assembly [this draft bill] declaring the sovereignty of Que.?" The referendum question would be changed on Sept. 7, 1995, based on an agreement made between Que. political leaders June 12, 1995.

Dec. 8 Que. Inuit requested that the federal govt protect their interests as Canadians in the event of Que. separation.

Dec. 9–11 PM Chrétien attended the Summit of the Americas in Miami, Florida.

Dec. 14 Statistics Canada released survey results showing that 23% of working women questioned had been sexually harassed at work.

Dec. 16 New York–based Viacom was given federal approval to take over the Canadian assets of Paramount Communications Blockbuster Entertain-ment Corp., which included 110 Famous Player theatres, Prentice Hall Canada publishing, 100 Blockbuster video stores and Canada's Wonderland amusement park in suburban north Toronto. In return, Viacom was required to inject some $418 million into the Canadian film industry over the next 6 years.

Dec. 23 NS Supreme Court Justice Felix Cacchione gave Michael Power and Cheryl Meyers a suspend-ed sentence after the common-law couple pled guilty to the 1991 manslaughter of Meyer's termi-nally ill father, who had requested that they not let him suffer through the agony of brain and lung cancer. Justice Cacchione ruled that the couple had "acted out of compassion, mercy and love."

Dec. 31 An Ont. law banning pharmacies from selling cigarettes came into effect.

1994–1995 It took an average of 136 days for a Canadian convicted of a crime to appear in court. In 2002–2003, it took 197 days.

1994–1997 Bell Canada laid off 12,000 employees in an effort to remain competitive within the deregu-lated telecommunications environment.

Also in 1994
• The average Canadian consumed a record 123.29 kg of fruit, up from 81.15 kg in 1961.

• 69.6% of Canadian households had access to municipal recycling programs; 83.1% of these households used these programs; 22% of Canadian households had their own compost heaps, and 24.4% used their own bags when shopping.

• Canada had a record $219.4 billion in exports and $202.3 billion in imports. The country also showed a $1.3 billion trade surplus with Japan.

• 15,224 refugee claimants were granted sanctuary in Canada; 6,442 were rejected.

• The Atlantic seal quota was set at 50,000 animals.

• There were an estimated 3,000 patronage posi-tions within the federal govt.

• Canada, the US, Australia, Chile, China, Japan, Korea, the Russian Federation and New Zealand formed a Working Group on Criteria and Indicators for the Conservation and Sustainable Management of Temperate and Boreal Forests. The series of crite-ria and indicators used to measure forest manage-ment was called the Montreal Process. In 1995, the 8 countries met in Santiago, Chile, and produced the Santiago Report, and a list of 7 criteria and 67 indicators for sustainable management. Member countries of the Montreal Process were responsible for 90% of the world's boreal and temperate forests.

• A federal fisheries report revealed that an estimat-ed 800,000 sockeye salmon died in the Fraser R. before spawning due to unusually high water temperatures.

• SHL Systemhouse Inc., an Ottawa-based integration giant, sealed a 10-year, $1 billion outsourcing contract with Canada Post Corp. Under terms of the agreement, SHL assumed responsibility for Canada Post's computer and telecommunications operations.

• The Ont. govt sold Toronto's SkyDome for $151 million to a consortium, which included the Ford Motor Company, TSN, Coca-Cola, the *Toronto Sun* and the CIBC. The multipurpose stadium generated approximately $75 million a year.

• Originally planned by Alliance Communications Inc. as a "made for TV" movie, the "Good-Mountie-Tough-Cop" drama, *Due South* went on to become not only a successful Canadian TV series for 3 seasons, but a hit south of the border as well. The show cast Paul Gross as Constable Benton Fraser, a clean-cut Canadian Mountie posted to the Canadian Consulate in Chicago. Together with his "dog," a deaf wolf named Diefenbaker, Constable Fraser was teamed up with the tough, streetwise Chicago policeman, Ray Vecchio, played by actor David Marciano. The show was the 1st Canadian-made series to get a prime-time slot on a US network.

• PepsiCo Inc., through its subsidiary Pizza Hut, acquired worldwide rights to Canadian-based Italian-restaurant concept East Side Mario's. Canadian rights were withheld from the deal. Forty of the 47 units in the chain were based in Canada.

• An estimated 800 Canadian doctors left the country to work elsewhere, mostly in the US. Canadian Medical Association President Bruno L'Heureux noted that the medical "brain drain" represented "a loss of $750 million per year in tax-financed human capital."

• Air Canada posted a profit of $129 million, its 1st showing in the black since 1989.

• The annual Giller Prize for English fiction by a Canadian author, a $25,000 award in memory of former *Toronto Star* assistant book editor Doris Giller (1931–1993), was established. The 1st winner was M.G. Vassanji for the novel *The Book of Secrets*. The Kenya-born writer would win again in 2003 for the novel *The In-Between World of Vikram Lall*, making him the 1st repeat winner in Giller history.

• *Chatelaine* named Peggy Witt, president of Vancouver-based Royal Oak Mines, Woman of the Year.

• International Olympic Committee (IOC) member in Canada, Richard W. Pound, published *Five Rings over Korea: The Secret Negotiations Behind the 1988 Olympic Games In Seoul*.

• Playwright Michel Tremblay was honoured by the govt of France as a Chevalier de l'Ordre des Arts et des Lettres de France.

• Former Conservative PM Joe Clark published *A Nation Too Good to Lose: Renewing the Purpose of Canada*.

• Stevie Cameron (b 1943) published *On the Take: Crime, Corruption and Greed in the Mulroney Years*, charging that Mulroney came to power the old-fashioned way — through back-dealings, kickbacks and favouritism.

• Girl Guides of Canada deleted the traditional pledge of allegiance to the Queen from their induction ceremony.

• Bloc Québécois leader Lucien Bouchard published *On The Record*.

• *Toronto Star's* legendary sports editor Milt Dunnell (b 1905) published a collection of columns, appropriately titled *The Best of Milt Dunnell*. Always outspoken, and well versed in all aspects of his trade, from boxing to horse racing, and hockey to baseball, Dunnell garnered awards and fans wherever he went.

• Sharon Butala (b 1940) published *The Perfection of the Morning: A Woman's Awakening in Nature*, a memoir about a city woman living in rural southwestern Sask.

• Novelist Rudy Wiebe published *A Discovery of Strangers*, a fictional account of the encounter between Native Peoples and the men of Sir John Franklin's Arctic expedition. The book was awarded the Gov-Gen.'s Literary Award for Fiction.

• Poet Al Purdy published his autobiography, *Reaching for the Beaufort Sea*.

• *Thirty-Two Short Films About Glenn Gould*, directed and co-written by François Girard, was released.

• Montreal jazz drummer Franklin Kiermyer (b 1956) recorded *Solomon's Daughter*, which included saxophone master Pharoah Sanders.

• Montreal jazz trumpeter Maynard Ferguson (b 1928) recorded and produced *Live from London*, taken live from the famous Ronnie Scott's Club in London, England.

• Improvisational BC bassist Lisle Ellis (b 1951) recorded the daring *What We Live*, with saxophonist Larry Ochs and drummer Donald Robinson.

• Folk and cowboy-music legend Ian Tyson released the CD *Eighteen Inches of Rain*.

• Singer Susan Aglukark (b 1967) released the CD *Arctic Rose*, 1st issued on an independent label in 1992. Also in 1994, Aglukark became the 1st recipient of the Aboriginal Achievement Award in Arts and Entertainment, was awarded the Canadian Country Music Association's Vista Rising Star Award and received a Juno for Best New Solo Artist.

• Rapper Maestro Fresh-Wes released his 4th CD, *Naah, Dis Kid Can't Be From Canada???!*

• Canada's polka king Walter Ostanek received a Grammy for *Accordionally Yours*. The Slovenian-Cleveland–style polka master would go on to be honoured with 10 Grammy nominations, winning 3, and push his astonishing number of recordings to 50.

• Victoria-born producer and composer David Foster won 4 Grammy Awards for his Hollywood film soundtrack to *The Bodyguard*.

• Novelist Roch Carrier was appointed director of the Canada Council.

1995

Jan. 1 The CBC's all-news French-language television channel Réseau de l'information (RDI) was launched. It would reach a cross-country viewership of over 7 million.

• Miramichi, population 22,000, became NB's 7th city with the amalgamation of Chatham, Newcastle, Loggieville, Nelson, Douglastown and Miramichi.

• CP Rail abandoned its line linking Saint John and Sherbrooke, Que. The move had been approved by the National Transportation Agency Aug. 24, 1993.

Jan. 2 Canada awarded NAFTA partner Mexico $1.5 billion in aid following a 49% devaluation of the peso.

Jan. 11 Dylex Ltd, the country's largest retailer of clothes, filed for bankruptcy protection after falling $230 million into debt. The company had 17,000 employees and 877 stores; its chains included Thrifty's, Tip Top Tailors, BiWay, and Fairweather.

Jan. 12 The loonie dipped to 70.55 cents US, its lowest since it hit 69.20 in 1986.

Jan. 17 An urban study conducted by a Swiss resource group ranked Vancouver second behind Geneva as the best city in the world to live. Vienna was 3rd, followed by Toronto and Luxemburg. Montreal ranked 7th, Calgary 12th.

Jan. 19 Singer-songwriter Gene MacLellan, writer of such hits as *Put Your Hand in the Hand*, and Anne Murray's signature song, *Snowbird*, died, an apparent suicide, at his home in rural PEI.

Jan. 23 BC Premier Mike Harcourt cancelled Alcan's $1.3 billion Kemano II hydroelectric project on the Nechako R. on the grounds it would affect the salmon industry downriver along the Fraser. The town of Kemano, some 70 km southeast of Kitimat, was established between 1949 and 1954 to service the 90-m-tall Kemano dam, completed in 1954. The dam provided electricity to the world's largest aluminum smelter in Kitimat. The remote company town of some 200 would be abandoned in 1999 and burned to the ground by trainee firefighters between 2000 and 2001.

Jan. 31 The David Suzuki Foundation issued its West Coast fisheries report, signalling that coho and chinook salmon populations were at record lows. The reports recommended the BC fishery be cut by 50% to help restore not only salmon stocks, but rockfish, abalone and ling cod. The govt accepted the recommendation, and by Mar. 1997, under the "Mifflin Plan," began cutting the fishery by 50%.

Also in Jan.

• Foreign Affairs Minster André Ouellet opened the Canadian embassy in Beirut, Lebanon. The embassy had been closed since 1985 as a result of Lebanon's 16-year civil war.

Feb. 1 The "Turbot War" began when the Northwest Atlantic Fisheries Organization (NAFO) met in Brussels, to set turbot quotas off Canada's 200-mile (322-km) limit at 27,000 tonnes: Canada received 60% of the total and the European Union (EU) 12%. EU Fisheries commissioner Emma Bonino announced that the splits were unfair, and stated that European nations would not abide by the percentages. Canadian Fisheries Minister Brian Tobin responded in an impassioned speech from Clarenville, Nfld., that he would not stand idly by while Europe destroyed the turbot industry as it did the cod industry. On Mar. 3, Canada charged Portugal with violating turbot quotas and banned its vessels from Nfld. waters; and on Mar. 9, Canada seized and impounded a Spanish trawler, in international waters, on the same grounds. The boat was released Mar. 15 on a $500,000 bond. The turbot war ended Apr. 17 when Canada offered the EU 10,000 tonnes of its allowable catch, on the condition that European boats carry neutral inspectors to assess catches. European NAFO nations officially agreed to the condition on Sept. 15.

Feb. 15 The interim report of the Commission of Inquiry on the Blood System in Canada, headed by Justice Horace Krever, was issued. It concluded that between 1978 and 1985 — at which time HIV-testing mechanisms had been absent — the Canadian blood supply system was contaminated with both HIV and hepatitis C. The report also noted that Canada's blood system was presently as safe as current testing could determine. Justice Krever set out 43 recommendations, including a call for the creation of facilities allowing Canadians to store their own blood; that doctors get consent of patients before blood is used in elective surgery; that doctors warn patients of the potential risks involved with blood use; and that persons who received blood between 1978 and 1985 seek

medical exams. The final Krever report was not issued until Nov. 26, 1997.

Feb. 24 The BC government proclaimed the nation's 1st recall law, whereby any MLA could be removed from office when 40% of all eligible voters in his or her constituency signed a petition for that purpose. The new legislation also included a grassroots initiative law: when 10% of eligible voters in each BC riding gave support to a legislative proposal, it would have to be tabled in the legislature — or put to a referendum.

• Canada and the US signed the Open Skies Treaty in Ottawa during President Bill Clinton's 1st official visit. The treaty provided Canadian and US carriers equal and open access to any flight destination in either country.

Feb. 27 Federal Finance Minister Paul Martin tabled the Liberals' 2nd budget, which included the largest spending cuts in Canadian history. Plans to cut the deficit by $24 billion within 2 years involved a $7 billion reduction in health, welfare and education transfer payments to 1998, the elimination of 45,000 civil service jobs, including deep cuts to National Defence, a $44 million cut to the CBC's operating budget for 1995–1996 and plans to sell off the remaining federal shares in Petro-Canada and privatize CN. Martin also announced the elimination of the Crow's Nest Pass Agreement subsidy, which had been in existence since 1897. The subsidy provided a substantial transport subsidy for the shipment of Canadian grain to Canadian tidewater ports. It was abolished Aug. 1, partly to comply with international trade agreements.

Feb. 28 The House voted 146–79 to pass amendments to the Young Offenders Act, raising maximum sentences for 1st degree murder from 5 years to 10, and from 5 years to 7 for 2nd degree murder.

Mar. 2 Defence Minister David Collenette initiated plans to reduce the number of generals in the Canadian Armed Forces from 93 to 70 over 3 years.

Mar. 9 The Man. govt tabled its 1st surplus budget in 20 years, showing a positive projection of

$48 million. The provincial debt, however, was $14.4 billion.

• One thousand seven hundred federal civil servants received an out-of-court pay-equity settlement worth $62 million, with the federal govt giving them retroactive payment covering 1987–1994, and progressive future raises until pay equity was reached.

Mar. 23 Nfld. Finance Minister Winston Baker tabled his province's 1st balanced budget, with a projected surplus of $1.9 million over the fiscal year ending in 1996.

Mar. 27 Bell Canada cited increased competition and rate regulation as main causes for its plans to lay off 10,000 workers by 1997.

Mar. 28 Parks Ontario was created to manage the province's 265 parks.

Apr. 4 PEI's 1-plane Atlantic Island Airways closed.

Apr. 6 The annual report of NS Auditor Gen. Roy Salmon revealed that $404,000 in goods and cash was lost, including $267,000 in liquor, $24,000 of Justice Department cash and over $20,000 in material from the Halifax Victoria General Hospital.

Apr. 9 A survey of 9 industrial nations, conducted by US-based National Center for Economic Alternatives, listed a dramatic decline in Canada's environmental quality, a drop exceeded only by France. The US, Japan and Germany were also not highly rated.

Apr. 12 The BC govt issued its Forest Practices Code, which set out regulations on clear-cutting practices near streams, slopes, in virgin forests and in scenic places of visual interest. The code became effective June 15.

Apr. 18 US-born Winnipeg resident Carol Shields won the Pulitzer Prize for her novel *The Stone Diaries*. Born in Oak Park, Illinois (as was Ernest Hemingway), Shields moved to Canada in 1957. In 1971, she became a Canadian with dual citizenship.

Apr. 19 The World Wildlife Federation gave Alb. an "F" because of that province's failure to initiate new environmental preservation plans. PEI and BC were given A minuses, the nation's best marks.

Apr. 25 Gary Filmon's Conservative government was re-elected in Man. for a 3rd term. The PC won 31 seats, the NDP under Gary Doer 23, and the Liberals under Paul Edwards 3.

Apr. 26 Toronto-based real-estate giant Bramalea Inc. collapsed after its entire board of directors quit. Board members included former Ont. Premier William Davis, and former Supreme Court Justice Willard Estey. The firm was $3.5 billion in debt.

Apr. 27 The BC govt initiated the Water Protection Act, banning all bulk (non-bottled) water exports from the province. The act was created to protect water against vague or unspecified clauses in Canada's growing list of international treaties.

Apr. 29 Lynn Verge became the 1st woman to head a major Nfld. political party, succeeding the retiring Len Simms as Official Opposition leader of the provincial Progressive Conservatives.

May 5 Bill C–89, *An Act to Provide for the Continuance of the Canadian National Railway Company* [est. 1919] *under the Canada Business Corporations Act and for the Issuance and Sale of Shares of the Company to the Public,* was introduced to the House by Minister of Transport Doug Young; it was approved May 15. The bill allowed for the 100% privatization of the CNR through a public share offering. Ottawa purchased between $400 and $600 million in CN real estate to help offset the Crown corporation's $2.5 billion debt and make it more marketable. CN was privatized Nov. 17.

May 9 Que. Finance Minister Jean Campeau tabled a $3.98 billion deficit budget. He then announced that, if Quebecers did not choose to separate in the upcoming election, he would be forced to raise the PST from 6.5% to 7.5% to compensate for the reductions in federal transfer payment spelled out in the last Paul Martin budget.

May 11 Federal Health Minister Diane Marleau responded to requests from Inuit and First Nations communities, and agreed to establish 6 permanent treatment centres for solvent abuse in Baie-Comeau,

Que., London and Thunder Bay, Ont., Thompson, Man., Prince Albert, Sask., and Williams L., BC.

• Auditor Gen. Denis Desautels tabled a report that included a survey of opinion from civil servants, one-third of whom believed it not a conflict of interest to provide relatives with untendered contracts.

May 12 Seven Que. drugstore chains were given a blanket fine of $2 million by the Que. Superior Court after pleading guilty to price-fixing birth control and other prescription drugs.

May 13 Former Mulroney cabinet minister Bernard Valcourt (b 1952) won the NB Conservative leadership, defeating rivals Scott MacGregor and John Hazen.

May 15 New York–based Dow Corning filed for Chapter 11 bankruptcy protection in a US court. The company faced thousands of lawsuits from women in a number of countries, including Canada, claiming to have suffered complications relating to Dow silicone breast implants. In Apr. 1998, the company reached a $50 million settlement with 10,000 women in Ont. and Que.

May 19 CRTC chairman and former commissioner of official languages, Keith Spicer, tabled a 61-page report calling for increased deregulation of broadcasting and telemedia industries to ensure Canadians were provided better cable and telephone services. The report also recommended increasing regulatory support for Canadian television and video-on-demand content.

May 25 The BC govt introduced the Criminal Records Review Act, making criminal review checks mandatory on all those working with children — including teachers, doctors, chiropractors, nurses and childcare workers. The legislation was adopted in June.

• The Quebec Nordiques, division winners of the previous year, were sold to Comsat Entertainment Group of Denver for $75 million. Little local fuss was made over the deal. The super-talented squad would become the Denver-based Colorado Avalanche powerhouse, and won the Stanley Cup in their 1st season — the 1st team to ever win the

Cup after moving cities. The Nordiques began as a World Hockey League (WHL) franchise in 1972 and entered the NHL in 1979.

• The Supreme Court of Canada ruled 5–4 against Nesbit and Egan, 2 gay men who sued Ottawa for the right to claim a spousal pension under the Old Age Security Act. The Court argued that the spousal pension had been established as compensation for stay-at-home mothers who had forfeited paid labour to raise children. However, the Court did acknowledge for the 1st time that the Charter of Rights and Freedoms protected against discrimination based on sexual orientation.

• The Supreme Court of Canada ruled 5–2 in the case of Susan Thibaudeau that single parents must pay income tax on child-support payments, despite provisions giving non-custodial parents a tax break on the support payments they provided.

• In *Miron v. Trudel*, the Supreme Court of Canada ruled that the exclusion of unmarried partners from accident benefits available to "spouses" under a statutory auto insurance policy violated the Charter of Rights and Freedoms.

May 26 La Fédération des femmes du Québec (FFQ) initiated the Women's March Against Poverty (the Bread and Roses March). More than 800 women marched from various locations in Que. to Quebec City, to demand better job opportunities (bread) and social equality (roses). The women converged to a gathering of over 20,000 in the provincial capital on June 4.

May 28 Jacques Villeneuve, son of legendary Que. Formula 1 driver Gilles Villeneuve, became the 1st Canadian to win the Indianapolis 500. Villeneuve took the lead from Torontonian Scott Goodyear (b 1958) on lap 191 of the 200-lap race to take the $1 million purse.

May 28–July 7 Massive forest fires raged in the northern areas of Sask., Alb., BC, Ont. and NWT, consuming millions of ha of forest. Over $100 million was spent controlling the blazes.

May–June The premier issue of *Sky News, Canadian Magazine of Astronomy and Stargazing* was published by writer, editor, and renowned astronomer Terence Dickinson (b 1943).

June 1 Atlantic Canada's 1st permanent commercial casino opened in the Halifax Sheraton.

June 4 The 1st official plaque commemorating the estimated 1,600 men and women of the Mackenzie-Papineau Battalion, who fought against fascist leader General Francisco Franco of Spain in the Spanish Civil War, 1936–1939, was unveiled at Queen's Park, Toronto. Next to the plaque is a large boulder taken from the battlefield of Gandesa, Spain, in memory of those Canadian "Mac-Paps" who died in battle — nearly half of all the volunteers. Non-interventionist policies made Canadian involvement in the war illegal, despite known fascist atrocities and the 1st whole-scale German bombing of civilian populations.

June 7–9 The South Sask. R. crested its banks, flooding the streets of Medicine Hat, forcing some 5,000 people from their homes.

June 8 Progressive Conservative Mike Harris defeated NDP premier Bob Rae in the Ont. provincial election, becoming the 1st Ont. Conservative leader since 1985. The PCs took 82 seats, Liberals under Lyn McLeod took 30, and Rae's NDP 17. Harris came to power on an extreme right-wing, 1980s Republican-style platform termed the "Common Sense Revolution," which included promises to create boot camps for young offenders, sell off public assets, slash taxes and welfare payments, eliminate hospitals, offload service cost to municipalities and downsize govt. Harris would immediately begin a process of eliminating an unprecedented $8 billion of provincial spending.

• The NB govt agreed to compensate 56 claimants (who had been abused at the Kingsclear Youth Training Centre reform school between 1970 and 1979), $120,000 each. School guard Karl Toft had received a 13-year sentence on Dec. 14, 1992, in relation to the abuses.

June 9 The 131-year-old *Charlottetown Patriot* published its last issue. One of the oldest newspapers in the country, it began publishing in 1864 and covered the Fathers of Confederation meeting in Charlottetown, PEI.

June 12 Jacques Parizeau, leader of the PQ, Lucien Bouchard, leader of the BQ, and Mario Dumont, leader of the ADQ, ratified an agreement setting out the nature of Que. sovereignty which would define the goals and future of Que., should residents decide to separate in the Oct. 30 referendum. The agreement proposed not a clean break but sovereignty bound by a yet-to-be created or agreed-upon "treaty on a new economic and political Partnership" with what would be the remainder of the former Canada.

• The Federal Court of Canada struck down a regulation preventing liquor companies from advertising on TV. The regulation had prevented distillers from showing ads that marketed products containing more than 7% alcohol.

June 13 Bill C–68, an Act Respecting Firearms and Other Weapons, was read for the third time and passed in the House of Commons. It passed the Senate Nov. 22 and was given Assent Dec. 5. The legislation required the registration of all firearms, including rifles and shotguns, over the next 8 years, a firearms licence for the purchase and use of guns, and stiffer sentences for those charged with gun-related crimes. The date for gun registration was Jan. 1, 2003, at which time thousands of gun owners refused registration. Alb., Sask., Man, Ont. and NS also refused to prosecute those who failed to register.

June 15 In the shadow of Que.'s Oct. 30 sovereignty referendum, Moody's Investors Service downgraded the province's long-term debt rating from A1 to A2.

June 17 The G–7 (Japan, Italy, Germany, the US, UK, France and Canada) Summit was held in Halifax. Agreements included an increase to the international monetary emergency fund, the maintenance of the UN presence in Bosnia and the pursuit of a barrier-free global economy.

June 21 The NDP under Premier Roy Romanow was re-elected in Sask., winning 42 of the 58 seats. The Liberals under Lynda Haverstock won 11 seats, the PC under Bill Boyd 5.

June 22 A joint US-Canada commission on the bilateral wheat trade recommended that the Canadian Wheat Board export grain at a fixed price and reveal its methods of determining export prices. The commission also recommended that the US eliminate its export subsidies.

June 28 The RCMP entered into a 5-year licencing agreement with Walt Disney Co. (Canada) Ltd. to manage all marketing of the Canadian Mountie image. The deal expired on Dec. 31, 1999, and was not renewed.

• A religious cross snatched by American colonists during a raid on Louisbourg in 1745 was given to Canada on a permanent-loan basis by Harvard U.

July 5 Premier Mike Harris terminated Ont.'s hated photo radar, a speed-detection system that had been implemented by the former NDP government.

July 17 Local Kahnawake Mohawk police were given municipal-police powers for a 1-year term, during which time RCMP and Que. police would cease patrolling the Que. reserve.

• Christine Silverberg was named Calgary chief of police, the 1st woman police chief of a major Canadian city.

July 20 The Que. govt provided $66 million to the MIL Davie shipyard at Levis, for the construction of 1 ferry and the upgrade of 2 others. The provision came after the struggling shipyard ran out of work and failed to find new work. MIL, Vancouver-based Versatile Pacific, and Saint John Shipbuilding were the last major shipbuilders in the country.

July 21 Ont. Finance Minister Ernie Eves tabled the Harris administration's 1st budget, which included massive ($1.9 billion) spending cuts and plans to eliminate 13,000 public service positions by 1998. The govt's proposed spending cuts would be pushed over $8 billion when a mini-budget totalling an additional $6.2 billion in cuts was tabled Nov. 29. The cuts would be part facilitated through omnibus Bill 26, An Act to Achieve Fiscal Savings, called by critics the "Bully Bill." Passed Jan. 29, 1996, by a vote of 77–47, the over 160 amendments gave the govt sweeping powers to eliminate hospitals, amalgamate municipalities, cap medical-service fees, slash welfare and equity payments,

restructure schools, amend labour legislation, shrink the civil service, sell off public property, and a host of other such powers.

July 26 Investment Canada approved the sale of John Labatt Ltd. to Belgian brewer and holding company Interbrew SA, the 3rd largest brewer in the world. Among the non-brewing assets Interbrew received through the $2.7 billion sale were the Blue Jays, Argonauts and the Toronto SkyDome. Irish immigrant John Kinder Labatt had begun his famous brewery in London, Ont., with the purchase of the Simcoe Street Brewery in 1847.

July 27 Rosemary Kuptana, president of the Inuit Tapirisat, declared that the Inuit in northern Que. would boycott the upcoming (Oct. 30) Que. referendum on sovereignty because the sovereignty question failed to address issues of Native self-government and land claims.

July 28 Alaska fisheries officials refused to cut back the year's Chinook salmon catch from 230,000 to 138,000, despite Canadian demands.

• Conrad Black's Hollinger Inc. bought 19 small Ont. and Sask. newspapers from Thomson Corp. for an estimated $100 million. The deal included the *Prince Albert Herald, Moose Jaw Times Herald, Peterborough Examiner* and the *Orillia Packet*. The sell off continued Apr. 13, 1996, when Hollinger picked up 7 of Thomson's Atlantic dailies, including the *St. John's Evening Telegram*, the *Charlottetown Guardian*, the *Truro Daily News* and the *Bathurst Northern Light*. Black would bring his newspaper holdings to 39 the following week, acquiring 7 more Ont. papers, including the *Sudbury Star, Chatham News* and the *Sarnia Observer*.

July 29 The 1st shipment of PCBs (polychlorinated biphenyls) from federal sites in eastern Canada arrived for incineration at the Swan Hills, Alb., waste-disposal plant. Swan Hills rotary kiln was the only permanent facility in Canada with the capacity to dispose of such hazardous waste.

• Que. police destroyed an estimated $10 million worth of marijuana plants at Kanesatake (Oka), Que.

Aug. 1 Postal rates for 1st class mail in Canada increased from 43 cents to 45 cents. The hike was expected to bring $40 million in extra revenue.

Aug. 2 The 1,000th Tim Hortons franchise opened in Ancaster, Ont. The 1st opened in Hamilton, Ont. in 1964.

• Fisheries Minister Brian Tobin initiated plans to eliminate 36 of Canada's 70 staffed lighthouses over the next 2 years.

Aug. 9 An 11-year-old child was killed in a Montreal bomb blast attributed to a vicious turf war between the Hells Angels and Rock Machine motorcycle organizations. An estimated total of 150 would die in the war by 2001.

Aug. 11 Two Toronto Transit Commission (TTC) subway cars crashed, killing 3 passengers.

Aug. 27 Two RCMP officers were shot at Gustafsen L., BC, during a gun battle with the "Defenders of the Shuswap Nation," who had staked claim to land owned by the James Cattle Co. in June. The Defenders claimed the land as sacred ancestral soil. The standoff ended Sept. 17 with the arrest of 18 Aboriginal men and women. Fifteen were convicted; sentences ranged from 6 months to 8 years, the longest sentence given to "Wolverine" William Ignace, for mischief causing bodily harm.

Sept. 6 Dudley George was shot and killed by OPP officer Kenneth Deane in Ipperwash Provincial Park when more than 40 officers in riot gear moved on approximately 25 unarmed men and women who had occupied the ancestral burial ground since Sept. 3. The group was demanding the return of Chippewa land that had been "temporarily" expropriated for military use in 1942. On Apr. 28, 1997, Kenneth Deane was convicted of criminal negligence causing death; he received a 2-year suspended sentence, was ordered to perform 180 hours of community service and was barred from possessing a firearm for 2 years. On Oct. 2, 2003, the family of Dudley George accepted a $100,000 plus settlement package with the OPP; in return, they dropped a lawsuit against the provincial police.

Sept. 7 Que. Premier Parizeau unveiled a bill giving Que. the right to declare an uncertain form of

independence based on the agreement of June 12, pending the outcome of a successful referendum to be held Oct. 30. The preamble began, "We, the people of Quebec, through the voice of our National Assembly, proclaim: Quebec is a sovereign country." The referendum question, which reflected the clarity of the whole 1995 sovereignty process: "Do you agree that Quebec should become sovereign, after having made a formal offer to Canada for a new economic and political partnership, within the scope of the bill respecting the future of Quebec and of the agreement signed June 12, 1995, Yes or No?" On Sept. 11, Premier Parizeau set the sovereignty referendum for Oct. 30.

• Canadian insurance giants Manulife and Manufacturers Life merged to form a firm with assets exceeding $47 billion. The new firm maintained the Manulife name.

Sept. 8 A Que. Superior Court judge ruled in a challenge presented by Que. lawyer Guy Bertrand that the Que. referendum process was "illegal" and violated the Canadian Charter of Rights and Freedoms. However, the judge did not issue an injunction to halt the referendum, arguing that Quebecers needed to decide their own fate.

Sept. 11 NB Liberals under Premier Frank McKenna won a majority govt in the provincial election, taking 47 of 55 seats and their 3rd consecutive term in power. Tories under Bernard Valcourt won 6 seats; NDP leader Elizabeth Weir won her party's only seat; and the Confederation of Regions (C of R) went from 8 to 0 seats. The election was postponed in one riding due to the ill health of a candidate.

Sept. 13 Ottawa sold 123.9 million shares of Petro-Canada at $14.62 a share, reducing its stake in the firm from 70% to 20%.

Sept. 15 Federal Indian Affairs Minister Ron Irwin and BC Minister John Cashore agreed to a cost-sharing plan between Ottawa and the province to collaboratively settle 44 Native BC land claims, the province to carry the cost of land allotments, and Ottawa coming up with the cash. Cashore estimated that the total cost of settling all current provincial land claims would exceed $10 billion.

Sept. 19 A World Bank study ranked Canada the 2nd richest country in the world next to Australia, according to a new formula based on both economic output and human resources. When ranked by average per capita income, Canada ranked 16th ($20,670 US).

• Aboriginals demonstrated in downtown Calgary to protest their growing alienation from the traditional Canadian health-care system.

Sept. 27 Five thousand protestors marched outside Queen's Park while the Speech from the Throne of the Ont. legislature was presented. Police treated the unruly crowd to pepper spray and compliments from their cudgels.

Oct. 2 Richard Kaligee, chief of the Saugeen First Nations, signed a declaration unilaterally giving the Saugeen control of a 300-km area along the shore of the Bruce Peninsula, southwestern Ont., which included Bruce Peninsula National Park and hundreds of homes and cottages. The document was not recognized by either the Ont. or federal govt.

Oct. 5 Man. emergency-room doctors and pathologists at 5 Winnipeg hospitals ratified a collective agreement to end a month-long strike.

Oct. 10 The Alb. govt sold its last 12% stake of Syncrude to Texas-based Torch Energy for $352.2 million. Syncrude, the largest oil sands producer in the world, produced its one-billionth barrel in Apr. 16, 1998. The 1st barrel was drawn July 30, 1978.

Oct. 11 In an effort to claw back the Atlantic fishery and preserve dwindling stocks, Fisheries Minister Brian Tobin initiated a plan to buy out the licences of 200 East Coast fishers at a cost of $32 million.

Oct. 12–14 Chinese Premier Le Peng visited Canada to discuss international trade issues with PM Chrétien and other Canadian officials.

Oct. 14 Alexa McDonough became national leader of the NDP after the 1st ballot at the party convention in Ottawa. McDonough was actually outvoted by rival candidate Svend Robinson 655–566, but was handed the leadership when it was assumed that the votes given 3rd candidate Lorne Nystrom would fall her way on the 2nd ballot. McDonough

replaced Yukon MP Audrey McLaughlin, who had been interim leader since tendering her resignation as party leader Apr. 18, 1994.

Oct. 16 Residents of the Northwest Territories elected their last members to the legislature before the territory was divided to create Nunavut, the nation's 3rd territory, officially established Apr. 1, 1999.

Oct. 18 In a deal that virtually broke the hearts of tens of thousands of Manitobans, the "small-market" Winnipeg Jets were sold to Americans Richard Burke and Steven Gluckstern for $65 million US. The Jets had begun as a WHL franchise, playing their 1st game Oct. 12, 1972. Their 1st franchise player was the great Bobby Hull, signed from the Chicago Blackhawks for a record $1 million. Hull would be omitted from the 1972 Summit Series because of his WHL affiliation. The Jets entered the NHL in 1979, playing their 1st game Oct. 10 of that year. The team would beat the Los Angeles Kings in their last regular home-season game Apr. 12, 1996, during which star forward Keith Tkachuk scored his 50th goal. The Jets were relocated to the US desert where they began the 1996–1997 season as the Phoenix Coyotes.

Oct. 20 David Tsubouchi, Ont. PC minister of community and social services, presented a Tory "shopping list" for recipients facing welfare cuts of over 20%. The $90-a-month dietary plan included bread but no butter, cereal without sugar, discounted 69-cent dented cans of tuna and lots of beans.

Oct. 26 In the shadow of the upcoming Oct. 30 Que. sovereignty referendum, the Cree and Inuit of the province held their own referendum and voted overwhelmingly against secession.

• Pittsburgh Penguins great Mario Lemieux scored his 500th NHL goal against the New York Rangers. The goal came in his 605th game, making him the second-fastest player to reach the 500 mark (Gretzky scored his 500th in 575 games). Lemieux missed the 1994–1995 season due to fatigue associated with chemotherapy treatment for Hodgkin's disease.

Oct. 27 Tens of thousands of people from across the country descended on Montreal in a massive pro-Canada, vote "Non" rally. Displays included double-sided Canadian and Que. flags, some even carried on hockey sticks.

Oct. 30 Ninety-four percent of eligible Que. voters turned out for Que.'s 2nd sovereignty referendum (1980 was the first): 50.6% voted "Non," 49.4% voted "Oui." 54,288 ballots separated the two sides; 86,473 ballots were rejected. In his concession speech, televised from Montreal's Palais de Congrès, Premier Parizeau exposed the tribal side of Que. nationalism, blaming the defeat on "money and the ethnic vote." He tendered his resignation the next day and was replaced by federal Bloc Québécois leader Lucien Bouchard Jan. 12, 1996. Parizeau said his last to the National Assembly Dec. 15, stating it was the younger generation that voted "Oui," and "It is this generation which, soon, I hope, will have the last word." 74% of Quebecers between 18 and 24 voted "Yes" in the 1995 referendum.

Oct. 31 A Toronto ban on lap dancing was upheld by the Division Court of Ont., which argued, "Close contact dancing is not a constitutionally protected right." Toronto's Cheaters Tavern appealed the ruling, which the Supreme Court denied on Mar. 12, 1997, calling the naked nightclub performance "indecent" and banning it under the Criminal Code.

Also in Oct.
• The remaining 3 Dionne quintuplets, Cécile, Annette and Yvonne, published a biographical account of their childhoods entitled *Family Secrets*, co-written by Jean-Yves Soucy.

• Canada established 3 reserves to protect the Monarch butterfly's habitat during the species' summer sojourn in Canada. These areas, Point Pelee, Long Point, and Prince Edward Point (all in Ont.), were created as part of an agreement reached with Mexico (site of the Monarch's over wintering) to help the species rebreed, thus rebuilding populations decimated by unusually harsh winters and habitat destruction in the south.

Nov. 2 A study by Michael Apps of the Canadian Forestry Service and Werner Kunz of ESSA Technologies in Vancouver reported that northern Canadian forested land had lost approximately one-fifth of its living matter over the last 25 years.

Nov. 3 Canada's 1st NBA teams — and the 1st outside the US — played their 1st regular-season games. The Vancouver Grizzlies upset hometown favourite Portland Trail Blazers 92–80, while the Toronto Raptors dazzled a hometown crowd of 33,306 at SkyDome to beat the New Jersey Nets 94–79.

Nov. 5 Armed with a knife, intruder Andre Dallaire entered 24 Sussex Drive in Ottawa while Jean and Aline Chrétien were in their bedroom. Aline slammed the bedroom door on the man but had to wait between 6–7 minutes for the RCMP to respond. The slow response time was the result of an initial decision by the RCMP to surround, rather than enter, the PM's residence. Four RCMP officers were suspended and 3 supervisors reassigned following the foul-up.

Nov. 9 Canada Post issued a 45-cent stamp commemorating victims of the Nazi Holocaust, 1933–1945.

Nov. 16 Writer, Yukon justice of the peace and syndicated columnist Edith Josie (b 1921) was made a member of the Order of Canada. Josie began her famous "Here Are The News" column in the *Whitehorse Star* in 1963; with wit, wisdom and earthy elegance, Josie offered readers vivid accounts of daily Loucheux life in Old Crow, a village of 200 located on the Procupine R., northern Yukon. The pieces were collected for the book *The Best of Edith Josie, Here Are The News, 1962–1964*, which was published to international acclaim in 1996. In 2000, Josie received the National Aboriginal Achievement Award in the Heritage and Spirituality category.

Nov. 19 The Baltimore Stallions of the CFL became the 1st non-Canadian team to win the Grey Cup, defeating the Calgary Stampeders 37–20. The Stallions would be moved to Montreal as the reincarnated Alouettes the following year.

Also in Nov.
• Less than 1 month after the Que. referendum, war veterans Pierre Roy, Raymond Carrier and Jos Bilocq began flying the Canadian flag each day at Quebec's city hall, in defiance of Quebec City mayor Jean-Paul L'Allier, who had ordered the flag removed shortly after the defeat of Meech Lake in

1990. Roy, Carrier and Bilocq would fly the flag at 5:45 a.m. and then remove it at 9 a.m. before city hall opened. The Maple Leaf would not be officially flown at city hall until Apr. 7, 1998, when the federal govt required all federally funded institutions to fly the national symbol.

• Correctional Services of Canada opened the Edmonton Institution for Women, the 1st of 4 regional prisons and 1 healing lodge to open between 1995 and 1997. The others were: Grand Valley Institution, Kitchener, Ont.; Joliette Institution, Que.; Nova Institution, Truro, NS; and the Okimaw Ohci Healing Lodge, Maple Creek, Sask. The institutions replaced the Prison for Women in Kingston, Ont., which had been until 1995 the only federal prison facility for women in the country. The Kingston prison was officially closed July 6, 2000.

• Canadian peacekeeping troops in Bosnia began their withdrawal following a peace agreement signed between warring ethnic Serbs and Croats. Canadian involvement began after Bosnia-Herzegovina declared independence from Yugoslavia in Feb. 1992. The political schism touched off a three-and-a-half-year ethnic war between Serbs and Croats. Canadian involvement reached 1,200 in 1993. Eleven Canadians died during the peacekeeping missions. Canadian troops, however, would remain in neighbouring Sarajevo where fighting continued.

Dec. 1 Federal Human Resources Minister Lloyd Axworthy unveiled reforms to Unemployment Insurance (UI), which would slash $2 billion from the system by reducing weekly maximum allotments and cutting the entitlement period from 50 to 45 weeks. The reforms would also insure part-time workers.

Dec. 4 Federal Fisheries Minister Brian Tobin and representatives of 24 other countries signed a UN treaty on migratory fish stocks, giving greater control over those migratory fish stocks to countries whose waters the fish traversed. The agreement therefore gave coastal countries such as Canada more control over cod than other countries such as Portugal and Spain, which had to fish for the migratory fish in international waters.

Dec. 6 Over 60% of Alb. farmers voted in a plebiscite to end the Canadian Wheat Board's (CWB) mono-

poly over western grain price-setting and distribution. The CWB had been established on July 5, 1935, to stabilize grain prices during the Depression. From 1943 on, Canadian farmers had been required by law to sell their grain only to the CWB. The results of the Alb. plebiscite had no immediate effect on CWB policy.

Dec. 7 The UN Human Rights Commission rejected claims for compensation from surviving Canadian veterans and widows of veterans who had been imprisoned by the Japanese in Hong Kong during WW II. Claimants, working with the War Amps of Canada, were seeking $20,000 each. Hundreds of Canadians were imprisoned by the Japanese in Hong Kong following its fall in 1941. The POWs were beaten, starved, tortured, brutalized and forced to live on rice and water. Many were sent to Tokyo to work as slave labourers in the shipyards. By the time they were liberated in 1945, most were little more than skin and bones, and many racked with fatal disease.

Dec. 11 Iqaluit was officially chosen as the capital of Nunavut, Canada's newest territory, to be officially established Apr. 1, 1999.

• Thousands of London, Ont., workers walked off the job for a day-long general strike, to protest the Ont. govt's process of slashing $8 billion in public spending.

Dec. 18 Ottawa, the Sask. provincial govt and the Federation of Sask. Indian Nations signed an agreement in Saskatoon to provide justice workshops in 10 communities across the province and work toward incorporating elements of traditional Native justice into the Criminal Code. Eighty percent of persons incarcerated in Sask. were Aboriginals.

Dec. 19 Lt-Gen. Jean Boyle was named chief of the Defence Staff, replacing Alfred de Chasterlain. On Feb. 13, 1996, Boyle declared in an interview that the effectiveness of the nation's military defence had declined to the point where it could not even be sent to war. He resigned Oct. 8, 1996, over a scandal involving document alteration related to the Somalia Inquiry. He was replaced by interim chief Larry Murray, who was succeeded by Gen. Maurice Baril on Sept. 17, 1997.

Dec. 29 Tim Hortons, the doughnut shop founded by popular Maple Leafs star in Hamilton, Ont., in 1964, merged with Wendy's International Inc., the American fast-food hamburger chain, in a deal estimated at $400 million US. By the end of 2003, Tim Hortons, still operating as a separate entity, had 2,343 Canadian and 184 US outlets.

Also in Dec.

• The Parliament of Canada officially recognized Feb. as Black History Month, following a motion introduced by the 1st African-Canadian woman elected to Parliament, Jean Augustine, Liberal MP for the riding of Etobicoke-Lakeshore (Ont.). The 1st-known black person in Canada was linguist, explorer and navigator Matthew Da Costa, who arrived in 1606 and helped build Port Royal. Individual African-Canadian communities began appearing in NS and southern Ont. after the American Revolution in 1776, setting roots in Canada long before the bulk of Canadians made their way to the burgeoning country.

• A survey jointly conducted by *Maclean's* magazine and the CBC indicated that one-third of Canadians believed that a unified Canada would not make it to the 21st century; and 66% wanted no more to do with political-unity discussions.

1995–1996 7,850 students declared personal bankruptcy, up from 4,500 in 1992.

1995–1999 NAFTA's Commission for Environmental Co-Operation reported that the production of hazardous wastes in Canada rose 8%, but decreased by 4% in the US.

Also in 1995

• Asthma rates among children hit 11.2%, up from 2.5% in 1979; the suspected increase was blamed on environmental pollution.

• The average student-loan recipient who graduated from university owed $11,000 in student loans, a 59% increase from 1986.

• 14,076 Canadians were serving time in federal custody, 19,427 in provincial custody.

• Vancouver detective Kim Rossmo completed a computer-assisted method to analyze and assess the spatial elements of serial crime. This geographical profiling system produces a topographic fingerprint that police can use to predict where the serial criminal might live and work, and even where the next crime might occur. Rossmo's often-used geographical profiling method was submitted as a doctoral dissertation to the School of Criminology at Simon Fraser U.

• Vancouver-born Wayson Choy (b 1939) was co-winner of the Trillium Book Award for his best-selling novel *The Jade Peony*. The other co-winner was Margaret Atwood, for *Morning in the Burned House*. The French-language winner was Maurice Henrie for the novel *Le Balcon dan le Ciel*.

• Montreal hockey-equipment manufacturer Camstar Sports Inc., producer of the legendary Bauer skate, was purchased by Oregon-based Nike Inc. for $545 million. By 2004, Nike had moved production out of Canada, leaving only office and warehouse staff.

• Craig Kielburger (b 1982) helped found Free the Children, a non-profit organization mandated to unmask and combat the abuses of child labour around the world. By 2000, Kielburger had travelled to over 30 countries in support of his mission.

• Chapters bookstores, the result of the newly merged W.H. Smith and Coles bookstore chains, opened its inaugural superstores, the 1st in Burlington, Ont., the 2nd in Burnaby, BC. Each could hold up to 100,000 books.

• The Alb. govt established 2 special Minister's Hunt permits, auctioning off to big-game hunters the right to shoot and kill championship game: 1 elk specimen and one bighorn sheep specimen per annum. In 1998 and 1999, Arizonian Sherwin Scott paid a total of $1.1 million US for the privilege of hunting bighorn rams out of season during the rutting period. In 2000, Texan Guinn Crousen paid $200,000 US to bag a bighorn ram with a record-breaking set of antlers.

• The Canadian govt established Vuntut National Park in northern Yukon, the result of a land settlement claim with the Vuntut Gwitch'in First Nations. The 4,345-km² reserve protects large areas of the

Old Crow Flats, recognized by the Ramscar Convention on Wetlands as crucial waterfowl habitat. Vuntut is managed jointly by the Canadian govt and local First Nations.

• Canadians exported $447 million worth of weapons, compared to $506 million in 1994.

• Canadians purchased 87.5 million movie tickets; the average ticket price was $4.99. In 1991, 71.6 million movie tickets were sold at an average price of $5.65.

• Before the Oct. 30 sovereignty referendum, federal Bloc Québécois defence critic Jean-Marc Jacob sent a letter to all Quebecers in the Canadian Armed Forces, requesting they switch their allegiance to the "new country" of Que. in the event of separation.

• For every dollar generated, Canadian distillers paid 83% in taxes, winemakers 65%, and brewers 55%.

• On average, a Canadian woman earned 70 cents for every dollar earned by a man, down from 72 cents in 1993.

• Contralto Maureen Forrester received the 1995 $125,000 Royal Bank Award for "significant contribution to human welfare and the common good." Forrester then gave the companion grant — matching funds provided by the Royal Bank — to the Canadian Foundation for AIDS Research.

• The Canadian trade surplus hit a record $28 billion, up from the previous record of $20 billion in 1984.

• The Canadian government went online at http://canada.gc.ca.

• Master Cape Dorset sculptor Osuitok Ipeelee completed *Bear and Walrus*, stone and ivory, now in the collection of Feheley Fine Arts, Toronto, Ont.

• Sun Company of Philadelphia sold its controlling interest in the publicly traded, Toronto-based Suncor. Suncor then moved its headquarters to Calgary. The province of Ont. had purchased 25% of Sun's interest in Suncor in 1981.

• Aboriginal reserves covered a total of 0.5% of the Canadian landmass.

• There were approximately 2,000 individuals working in call centres in NB.

• Asians accounted for 61.6% of all immigrants to Canada. Europeans were the 2nd-largest group at 18.7% A record-high 227,720 individuals were granted Canadian citizenship.

• Forest fires destroyed 7 million ha of Canadian forest; 50% of these fires were started by lightning, the rest by humans.

• Canada exported 14,310 tonnes of maple syrup and 15,590 tonnes of honey.

• A record 15.8 million hogs were slaughtered in Canada.

• Rohinton Mistry published *A Fine Balance*, which won the Los Angeles Times Book Prize in Fiction, the Giller Prize, the Commonwealth Writers Prize, the Royal Society of Literature's Winfried Holtby Prize and was a Booker Prize finalist. The book was also an Oprah's Book Club selection.

• U. of Toronto professor of forestry John Laird Farrar (1913–1996) published *Trees in Canada*, an identification guide to native and introduced tree species in Canada, organized with photographs according to leaf shape and arrangement.

• Acclaimed Canadian food writer and former food director of *Canadian Living* magazine Elizabeth Baird published *Elizabeth Baird's Classic Canadian Cooking: Menus for the Seasons*.

• Ont.-born actor Jim Carrey (b 1962) became Hollywood's highest-paid actor, earning $20 million for the dark comedy *The Cable Guy* (1996).

1996

Jan. 1 All federally regulated firms were required to up their minimum wage from $4, the federal minimum, to the minimum in the province in which they operated. The provincial minimum-wage spectrum ran from $4.75 in PEI and Nfld., to $7 in BC.

Jan. 4 The Canadian men's national junior hockey team won its 4th consecutive world hockey championship, beating Sweden 4–1 in Boston.

Jan. 5 Federal Justice Howard Wetston voided a law banning prisoners serving a sentence of more than 2 years the right to vote, stating such law violated their Charter rights.

Jan. 9–19 PM Chrétien led a "Team Canada" trade mission to the South Asian countries of India, Pakistan and Indonesia. The delegation, consisting of some 300 businesspeople, signed $2.6 billion in set trade agreements, including plans to build denim and steel plants, develop hospitals and health clinics and sell GM Canada locomotives to Indian Railways.

Jan. 16 The Commission on Systemic Racism in the Ont. Criminal Justice System issued its final report, showing that the incarceration rate of African-Canadians in the province had quadrupled since 1993; that black people were more likely than whites to be incarcerated overnight, be pulled over by police in cars or on the street, and were more likely to be jailed for simple narcotics-possession infractions.

Jan. 17 The Nfld. Liberal Party elected former federal Fisheries Minister Brian Tobin as leader of the party and premier. Tobin, who ran unopposed, succeeded constitutional lawyer and former Meech Lake opponent Clyde Wells, who announced his retirement Dec. 28, 1995. Tobin was sworn in Jan. 26. He called an election 3 days later — for Feb. 22.

Jan. 25 PM Chrétien shuffled his cabinet, adding 2 Que. federalists, neither of whom held seats in the House. The unelected members were Stéphane Dion (b 1955), minister of inter-governmental affairs, and Pierre Pettigrew (b 1951), minister for international co-operation. Both Dion and Pettigrew won seats in Mar. 25 by-elections in Saint-Laurent-Cartierville, and Papineau-Saint-Michel, respectively.

• Leilani Muir was awarded $740,780 by the Alb. court as compensation for being forced to undergo a fallopian-tube sterilization procedure under the Alb. Sexual Sterilization Act. The act, established in 1928, required the forced sterilization of all women classified as "feeble minded." It was voided in 1972. Approximately 3,000 Alb. women had been sterilized under the law.

Jan. 29 Lucien Bouchard, who resigned as leader of the federal Bloc Québécois on Jan. 15, was sworn in as Parti Québécois premier of Que. Bouchard replaced Jacques Parizeau, who resigned the day after the Oct. 30, 1995, Que. sovereignty referendum. Bouchard had announced on Jan. 19 that he would donate his projected $32,000-a-year federal pension to the Que. govt. Bouchard was elected to Que.'s National Assembly on Feb. 19, taking his hometown riding of Jonquière in a by-election.

Feb. 1 The Toronto Stock Exchange (TSE) Index passed the 5,000 mark.

• Calgary's 2nd-longest cold snap in 6 decades finally broke; temperatures had hovered in the minus 20s for 18 days.

• PM Chrétien appointed Liberal MP Shirley Maheu (b 1931) to the Senate, giving the Liberals 51 Senate seats, 1 more than the Conservatives. It was the 1st time the Liberals held the balance of power in the Upper House since 1990.

Feb. 2 The Senate passed the regional constitutional veto bill 48–36, which required unanimous consent of the Atlantic Provinces, Que., Ont., the prairie provinces and BC before any constitutional amendment could proceed.

Feb. 3 Former PM Pierre Trudeau published an essay in the Montreal *Gazette* called, "Lucien Bouchard: Illusionist," charging that Bouchard spiked Que.'s pre–1995 referendum opinion with "fallacies and untruths," "demagogic rhetoric" and unsightly distortions to Canadian history.

Feb. 9 The BC govt implemented a plan to provide one-way bus tickets to applicants who failed to meet the province's welfare residency requirements.

Feb. 10 Lucien Bouchard responded to Trudeau's Feb. 3 comments with a *Gazette* piece of his own headed, "The Problem with Pierre Trudeau."

Bouchard charged that the federalism entrenched in Trudeau's 1982 Constitution was at the root of the current Que.-rest-of-Canada crisis. He also argued that Que. political leaders had been elected to pursue sovereignty, making Trudeau's attacks little more than an assault on Canadian democracy.

Feb. 14 The last episode of CBC's *Mr. Dressup*, starring Ernie Coombs (1927–2001), and Judith Lawrence's beloved puppets Casey and Finnegan, was aired. *Mr. Dresssup* 1st aired in Feb. 1967.

Feb. 15 At a Flag Day rally in Hull, Que., a protestor rushed through the crowd and got in the face of PM Chrétien. The PM casually grabbed the man by the throat and tossed him aside. The incident spawned a new addition to the Canadian lexicon — the "Shawinigan Handshake."

Feb. 17 Michel Gauthier (b 1950) replaced Lucien Bouchard as Bloc Québécois leader and leader of the Official Opposition, taking 104 of 155 delegate votes at the Montreal party convention. Rival MP Francine Lalonde (b 1940) was runner-up.

Feb. 19 The Royal Canadian Mint unveiled the new 2-dollar coin. The design featured an inner aluminum-bronze core — heads, a polar bear on ice floe; tails, the reigning English monarch, Queen Elizabeth II — encircled by a nickel-coloured ring. Initially 60 million coins entered circulation. The tender was known in local parlance as the "toonie."

Feb. 20 The Montreal Airport's Authority ruled to permanently reroute all international and domestic flights from Mirabel, opened in 1975, to Dorval, leaving the massive airport to service only charter and cargo flights. The flights were transferred Sept. 15, 1997.

Feb. 22 NDP MP Glen Clark (b 1957) was sworn in as premier of BC, succeeding Michael Harcourt as party leader. Harcourt had submitted his resignation Nov. 15, 1995, amidst swirling allegations that his party had padded NDP coffers with money generated through charity gaming. The scandal was referred to as "Bingogate." On Sept. 4, 1999, a BC judge placed 77-year-old former NDP finance minister Dave Stupich, the leading culprit in the Bingogate affair, under electronically

monitored house arrest for 2 years less a day for related fraud.

• Brian Tobin's Liberals won a clear majority in the Nfld. provincial election, taking 37 of 48 seats. The Conservatives under Lynn Verge (b 1950) won 9 seats; Verge lost her seat and resigned in Mar. NDP leader Jack Harris (b 1948) won his party's 1st seat, with Yvonne Jones taking the only independent spot.

• Alb. Treasurer Jim Dinning brought down Ralph Klein's 1st formal surplus budget — a projected $23 million in the black. The money was slated for spending on health, education, social services and tax cuts. In Sept. of 1997, 102 Albertans representing a plethora of private and public concerns recommended that any ensuing surplus be reinvested into health and education — and not used to finance further tax cuts.

Feb. 27 Gilbert Parent (b 1935), Speaker of the House of Commons, ruled that the Bloc Québécois would remain the country's Official Opposition party despite intense campaign efforts by the Reform Party to capture the honour. The resignation of Lucien Bouchard on Jan. 15 left each of the 2 parties with 52 seats.

Feb. 29 Calgary-based WestJet, western Canada's low-fare airline, began flight service to Vancouver, Kelowna, Calgary, Edmonton and Winnipeg. The airline had 220 employees and 3 Boeing 737s. The 4 founders included Clive Beddoe, who gathered startup investment capital from local Calgary businesspeople and retailers.

Mar. 6 Federal Finance Minister Paul Martin brought down the Liberal budget. Highlights included no personal or corporate tax increases, a tax reduction for child support recipients, a $13,500 limit on RRSP contributions, the rolling together of Old Age Security and the Guaranteed Income Supplement and $368 million in spending cuts over 1997 and 1998. The target 1996–1997 deficit was $24.3 billion.

Mar. 10 Pop-rock phenom Alanis Morissette (b 1974) took home 5 Juno awards, including Album of the Year for *Jagged Little Pill*, and Best Rock Song for "You Oughta Know."

Mar. 12 Vancouver banned smoking in all city restaurants, becoming the 1st municipality in Canada to enact such a law.

• US President Bill Clinton signed into law the Helms-Burton Act, which would allow Americans to sue foreign companies who had invested in Cuban firms utilizing property confiscated during Castro's 1959 Communist revolution. Under the same law, Canadian executives who ran such businesses could also be denied entrance into the US.

Mar. 14 The EU buckled to pressures from Aboriginal and Canadian trade lobbyists, and delayed a proposed ban on the import of Canadian furs. The Dutch, however, implemented the ban, which had been established in an attempt to force Canadians (and Russians) to end the use of steel-jaw leg-hold traps. The ban was voided July 22, 1997, when Canadian officials agreed to phase out the steel-jaw devices over the subsequent two and a half years.

Mar. 30 Canada Post showed a reduced profit of $28.2 million for the fiscal year ending Mar. It had lost nearly $69 million the previous year.

Also in Mar.

• The Supreme Court of Canada ruled that judges had the right to ban media from courtrooms where media presence could negatively effect the course of justice.

• The 1st issue of *Outpost, Canada's Travel Magazine* was published from Toronto. The popular bi-monthly provides a youthful, unsanitized look at the world, and the world of travel.

Apr. 1 The megacity of Halifax, called the Halifax Regional Municipality, was formed as Halifax, Dartmouth, Bedford, and Halifax County merged. The streamlining of services would save the new city an estimated $20 annually.

• 67,000 Ont. civil servants returned to work after agreeing to a new contract providing improved pensions, seniority-recognition guarantees and limited protection against job loss due to privatization. The Ontario Public Service Employees Union (OPSEU) members had walked off the job Feb. 26. The strike was marred by violence on Mar. 18, when

strikers, attempting to prevent MPPs from entering Queen's Park, clashed with police.

Apr. 3 Alb. introduced bad investments legislation, requiring the govt to get legislative approval before giving any enterprise a guaranteed loan from public coffers.

Apr. 10 The 1st strike in SaskTel's 88-year history began when 3,600 employees walked off the job for better pay and benefits. The strike ended May 1 with workers accepting a 3-year benefit package including wage increases, improved health and RRSP contributions totalling 7% over 3 years.

Apr. 23 MP John Nunziata (b 1955) was removed from the Liberal caucus by PM Chrétien because he had voted against the govt's Apr. 16, budget bill. Nunziata was protesting his party's failure to keep its 1993 election promise to scrap the unpopular Goods and Services Tax (GST). The same day, Finance Minister Paul Martin explained, "It was a mistake in thinking we could bring in a completely different tax without undue economic distortion and within a reasonable timeframe." On May 1, Heritage Minister and Deputy Prime Minister Sheila Copps resigned over the same issue, keeping an Oct. 18, 1993, election-campaign promise to scrap the GST or quit. Copps returned to the House and her cabinet positions June 19, after winning a by-election in Hamilton East, Ont.

• Nfld., NB and NS agreed to fold their respective sales taxes into the GST.

Apr. 24 Man. and the federal govt signed an agreement to establish Wapusk National Park (11,475 km²), stretching south of Churchill, Man., along and east of Hudson Bay. Wapusk (a Cree word for "white bear") is home to the largest polar bear maternity den site in the world. The park also protects hundreds of thousands of nesting sites of such birds as the peregrine falcon, Hudsonian godwit, sandhill crane and gyrfalcon.

Also in Apr.

• The Gov-Gen.'s Caring Canadian Award was created to award Canadians who made extraordinary, unpaid contributions toward individuals, families, communities or humanitarian causes. The 1st recipient was

Mary Fitzpatrick of St. Lawrence, Nfld., who had handcrafted over 1,000 quilts for the needy.

May 1 Solicitor Gen. Herb Gray (b 1931) ordered all medium- and maximum-security inmates of the Edmonton Institution for Women (opened Nov. 1995) removed until security could be increased. There had been 7 escapes and 1 murder at the prison since Feb. 28.

May 2 The Supreme Court of Canada ruled that a custodial parent who makes a major geographical move to a new residence (referred to as a "material change in circumstance") may be subject to a court re-evaluation of the terms of custody.

May 9 In a free vote, the House of Commons passed Bill C–33, 153 to 76, which added "sexual orientation" to the Human Rights Act as a prohibitive ground for discrimination. The other grounds were race, national or ethnic origin, colour, religion, age, sex, marital status, family status, disability and conviction when a pardon was granted. Calgary Southeast MP Jan Brown (b 1947) quit the Reform Party to sit as an Independent the next day, citing that the anti-gay commentary made by Reform Party members during the lead-up to Bill C–33 was inconsistent with her opinions.

May 24 Conrad Black's Hollinger Inc. increased its Canadian newspaper share, taking another 20% stake in Southam Inc. for $294 million. The move pushed Hollinger's share of the newspaper giant to 41%. The purchase also added 20 more papers to Hollinger's 39 Canadian newspaper empire (36 English-language and 3 French-language). The new purchases included the *Vancouver Sun*, *Calgary Herald*, *Ottawa Citizen* and the *Montreal Gazette*. The sale dropped the number of Southam-owned Canadian newspapers to 9, including the *Globe & Mail*. Southam lost $53 million in 1995.

May 28 Glen Clark's NDP govt was re-elected with a majority govt in the BC provincial election, taking 39 of 75 seats. The Liberals under Gordon Campbell (b 1948) won 33 seats, the Reform Party of BC, under Jack Weisgerber, won 2, and the Progressive Democratic Alliance, under former Liberal leader Gordon Wilson, 1.

May 29 After over a decade of wrangling, trade negotiators from Canada and the US finalized an accord in Washington, D.C., setting the total amount of softwood lumber BC, Alb., Ont. and Que. could export to the US at 14.7 billion board feet annually. Penalty taxes would be placed on all lumber over this amount. The agreement extended to Mar. 31, 2001.

May 30 Alb. banned extra billing by its private health clinics. The move came after Ottawa began withholding $420,000 in health transfers per month on the grounds that the over-costs violated the Canada Health Act. The clinics dealt in such areas as abortion, eye care and dentistry.

Also in May
- abebooks.com, the world's largest online marketplace for used, rare and out-of-print books, was founded and launched out of Victoria, BC, by Rick Pura and Keith Waters.

- Prisoners rioted in the Headingley Correctional Institution outside Winnipeg, causing $3.5 million in damages. Forty were injured.

June 5 Que. Auditor Gen. Guy Breton released his annual report showing that the province was owed over $2 billion in 1995 back taxes. He also noted that the province lost an estimated $250 million in revenues each year to the sale and distribution of illegal liquor.

June 13 The Canadian Human Rights Commission ruled that all federal and federally regulated industries must provide same-sex couples with equal employment benefits.

June 14 Bill C–47 (the Human Reproductive and Genetic Technologies Act) was introduced in the House of Commons in an attempt to prohibit genetic recombination that would lead to the creation of animal-human half-breeds. The bill was the outcome of geneticist Patricia Baird's Nov. 15, 1993, Royal Commission report *Handle with Care*. The bill stated, "No person shall knowingly cause the fertilization of a human ovum by sperm of an animal or the fertilization of an animal ovum by human sperm, for the purpose of producing a zygote that is capable of differentiation." The bill, which died in the House before the 1997 election call, also prohibited human cloning, the sale of sperm, and placed a prohibition against sex selection for the purpose of reproduction.

June 15 A cross-Canada Women's March Against Poverty, organized by the National Action Committee on the Status of Women (NAC), concluded at Parliament Hill with an estimated 5,000 calling for an end to child poverty, increased child-care services and better social programs.

June 19–Oct. 27 *Aboriginal Portraits from the National Archives of Canada*, an exhibition of over 140 original photographic portraits, was presented at the National Archives in Ottawa.

June 28 The Ont. Harris govt established a new land-use plan in Northern Ont., giving loggers access to a third of the Temagami old-growth forest. The govt also removed a 24-year moratorium on mining in the region. On Sept. 17, the govt gave prospectors 24 hours to stake claims in the region, sparking a frantic run-through-the-woods by an estimated 600 hopeful prospectors.

July 4 The irreplaceable Stompin' Tom Connors (b 1936) was named to the Order of Canada. Born in Saint John, NB, Connors lived a storied life of good-time rambling, collecting and creating old-time classics from one corner of the country to the other. While other musicians were content to migrate south, Connors stuck to his roots, writing some of the country's best-loved tunes, including "Sudbury Saturday Night," "Tillsonburg," the "Hockey Song," the "Snowmobile Song," "The Old Atlantic Shore" and "Roll On Saskatchewan."

July 8 Discount carrier Greyhound Air began service between Vancouver, Calgary, Edmonton and Toronto. Ticket purchases were on a first-come, first-served basis, and could be obtained at local bus terminals.

July 10 The Yahoo!Canada web site search engine was launched. The search engine allowed users to restrict searches to Canadian sites only.

July 17–21 Severe thunderstorms dropped 277 mm of rain on the Lac-St-Jean–Saguenay region of Que., causing acute flooding of the great Saguenay R. Ten

were killed and over 16,000 evacuated. Main areas hit were La Baie, Jonquière, Chicoutimi and Hébertville. 1,300 homes and 40 businesses suffered severe damage. Related costs pushed beyond $1 billion. On Aug. 21, the Que. Ministry of Environment pointed to Saguenay dam malfunctions as the main factor in the disaster, considered the worst in Canada since Hurricane Hazel in 1954.

July 19-Aug. 4 Canada won 22 medals, including 3 golds, at the Summer Olympics in Atlanta, placing 11th among 78 countries. Donovan Bailey (b 1967) was crowned world's fastest man, winning the 100-m dash in a world-record time of 9.84 seconds. Bailey also anchored the 4 x 100 m relay team, taking gold with Robert Esmie (b 1972), Glenroy Gilbert (b 1968) and Bruny Surin (b 1967). And the amazing team of Kathleen Heddle and Marnie McBean won their third career golds, the most of any Canadians in the 20th century. The duo won in double sculls (they had previously won in pairs and in the eights crew in Barcelona in 1992).

July 30 The *Irving Whale*, an 82.3-m oil barge built in 1966 for J.D. Irving Ltd. of Saint John, NB, was removed from the bottom of the Gulf of St. Lawrence. It sank in 67 m of water Sept. 7, 1970, its belly containing 3,000 tonnes of Bunker C oil and 7.2 tonnes of PCB-infused heating oil. By the time of its recovery, the barge had already leaked an estimated 1,100 tonnes into the gulf. The Canadian Coast Guard charged Irving $42.2 million for the salvage operation. Irving would settle at $5 million in 2000.

July 31 Canada and Israel signed a free trade accord eliminating tariffs on the bulk of agricultural and manufactured goods by Jan. 1, 1997.

Also in July

• Herman Tumurcuoglu created Mamma.com, "The Mother of All Search Engines," as his master thesis at Carleton U., Ottawa. The Internet search engine was one of the 1st to incorporate comprehensive "metasearch" technologies to both search and format results. In 1999, Intasys Corporation of Montreal bought 69% of Mamma for $25 million US.

• Sears Canada laid off 1,200 employees.

• The unemployment rate poked above 10%.

Aug. 6 Catherine Callbeck, Canada's 1st elected woman premier (1993), resigned as premier of PEI following the publication of unfavourable public-opinion polls. Minister of Transportation and Public Works Keith Milligan (b 1950), who won the leadership race in Charlottetown on Oct. 5, replaced Callbeck. Milligan was sworn in as premier Oct. 10.

Aug. 12 US President Bill Clinton killed a proposal by Noranda-owned Crown Butte Resources Ltd. to develop gold and copper exploitation on the outskirts of Yellowstone National Park, established in 1885 as the world's 1st national park.

Aug. 28 Lyse Lemieux was appointed the 1st woman chief justice of the Que. Superior Court.

Sept. 4 The CRTC granted licences to 23 new cable television networks, including the Comedy Network, Teletoon, the History and Entertainment Network and the all-news CTV network.

Sept. 6 Ont.-based Consumers Distributing Inc. went bankrupt. It had filed for bankruptcy protection July 29 after falling $250 million into debt. The firm had 217 outlets and 3,900 employees.

Sept. 9 Workers returned to work at Irving's Oil refinery at Saint John, NB, following a 28-month labour dispute that resulted in 37 severance packages and a lawsuit initiated, then dropped, by picket crossers who took grievance with the Communications, Energy and Paperworkers Union.

Sept. 14 "Lilith Fair, A Celebration of Women in Music," masterminded by singer-songwriter Sarah McLachlan (b 1968), and including such popular performers as Emmylou Harris, Paula Cole and Holly McNarland, debuted at Nat Bailey Stadium in Vancouver, BC. The show was a hit, prompting McLachlan to organize and execute the 1st all-woman touring music festival the next year. Lilith Fair toured for 3 consecutive summers.

Sept. 30 The Yukon NDP, under leader Piers McDonald (b 1955), won 11 of 17 seats in the territorial election. The Yukon Party, led by John Ostashek (b 1936) and the Liberal party, under Ken Taylor, won 3 seats each.

Oct. 2 Twenty-six thousand Canadian Auto Workers (CAW) members went on strike against General Motors Canada. The lack of production caused the Detroit-based parent corporation on Oct. 7 to lay off 1,850 people at 2 different US parts plants. The strike ended Oct. 22, with workers accepting an agreement restricting outsourcing and making overtime voluntary. The strike cost the Canadian economy an estimated $1 billion. GM posted a 3rd quarter 1996 profit of $1.27 billion US.

Oct. 4 David Collenette resigned as minister of national defence over an ethics violation regarding a letter sent by him to the Immigration and Refugee Board to obtain a visa for the husband of a constituent. The move was made during the Somalia Inquiry scandal involving the disappearance of several required defence documents. Collenette was replaced by Doug Young (b 1940). The final Somalia Inquiry report was issued June 2, 1997.

Oct. 7 Heritage Minister Sheila Copps tabled the Banff–Bow Valley environmental study, begun in 1995 and chaired by Robert Page, chairman of the U. of Calgary. The $2 million study included some 500 recommendations, some of which Copps immediately implemented, including the placement of a moratorium on all new commercial development in Banff, the closing of its airstrip, placing quotas on the number of visitors to the national park and putting a resident-population cap of 10,000 on the town.

Oct. 16 An incinerator in the Swan Hills, Alb., PCB waste-disposal site suffered a mechanical breakdown, resulting in the emission of PCBs and other toxins. On Dec. 13, Alb. health officials placed an advisory against eating wild game from anywhere within 30 km of the site.

• The bank rate was 3.75%, its lowest since July 1963.

Oct. 23 The federal government removed the GST on books purchased by libraries, schools, municipalities and charitable organizations.

Oct. 25-26 Toronto workers, social activists and thousands of generally disgruntled Ontarians staged Days of Action, a 2-day protest against Premier

Mike Harris's slash-and-burn fiscal policies. The subway was shut down, hospital services were curtailed and many schools closed. An estimated 75,000 joined the protest on the 26th, lining University Ave. and wending their way toward Queen's Park.

Also in Oct.

• Montreal-born Ont. Justice Louise Arbour (b 1947) was appointed head of the UN War Crimes Prosecution Unit at The Hague, with responsibility for prosecuting crimes against humanity in the former Yugoslavia and trying suspects of genocide in Rwanda. Arbour quickly developed an international reputation for vigilant support of human rights and human dignity. She served on the UN commission until Sept. 1999, when she was appointed to the Supreme Court of Canada where she continued to make important decisions regarding individual and family rights. Arbour stepped down from the Court in 2004 to take a position on the UN High Commission for the Human Rights. She replaced Sergio Vieira de Mello who was killed in a bomb blast in Baghdad, Iraq. Arbour won innumerable awards and distinctions, including the Paris Prix de la Foundation Louise Weiss (1999), Pennsylvania Bar Humanity Award (2000), Franklin and Eleanor Roosevelt Four Freedoms "Freedom from Fear" Medal (2000), National Achievement Award (2001) and the Justice of the World International Prize (2002).

Nov. 6 Ont. Premier Mike Harris launched a Breakfast for Learning program initiative as part of the child-nutrition project. Harris, who had cut welfare by 21.6% since coming to power in 1995, explained the need for the new program: "If you go back 30 or 40 years, where it seemed to be that mom was in the kitchen with a hot breakfast cooking as everyone woke up in the morning, that is not the normal situation now."

Nov. 14 Sask. proclaimed the Public Disclosure Act, giving the police the right to inform residents when a high-risk offender moved into their neighbourhood. High-risk offenders included pedophiles and other sex offenders, robbers, kidnappers and drug traffickers. It was the 1st such law in the country.

• Que. French-Language Minister Louise Beaudoin (b 1945) issued new language policies that included: all govt speeches to business groups be given in French unless otherwise sanctioned; all govt publications distributed to private residences be written in French only; and all federal financial support to firms which did not aide by existing Que. language laws be eliminated.

Nov. 18 Chilean President Eduardo Frei and Canadian PM Chrétien signed the Canadian-Chile Free Trade Agreement, freeing 80% of trade between the two nations. The 1st free trade agreement signed between Chile and a G7 nation went into effect July 4, 1997.

• In the PEI provincial election, the Progressive Conservatives, led by Pat Binns (b 1948), won a majority govt, taking 18 seats; the Liberals under Keith Milligan (b 1950) won 8 seats. The NDP took the remaining seat. The PC win ended 10 years of Liberal rule.

Nov. 21 The Royal Commission on Aboriginal Peoples, headed by George Erasmus, leader of the Assembly of First Nations, and Que. Justice Rene Dussault (b 1939), issued its 3,537-page report, *People to People, Nation to Nation*. The 400-plus recommendations included increasing public spending on Native affairs by $2 billion over 20 years; the establishment of an Aboriginal Parliament, or House of First Peoples to function beside the House of Commons; provide Aboriginals with the necessary land, resources, health and social services training to better ensure the success of Native self-govt, which the Commission also recommended be guaranteed; and the creation of a tribunal to oversee land claims. The report stated, "The main policy direction, pursued for more than 150 years, first by colonial then by Canadian governments, has been wrong… We believe Aboriginal people must be recognized as partners in the complex arrangements that make up Canada…that Aboriginal governments are one of the three orders of government in Canada…" The $58 million Royal Commission was the most costly in Canadian history.

Nov. 28 A bill to privatize Manitoba Telephone passed 3rd reading in the provincial legislature.

The company went up for sale in the Winnipeg, Toronto and Montreal Stock Exchanges Dec. 3.

Dec. 3 Eleanor Norrie, a minister in the cabinet of NS Premier John Savage, announced that the protected designation of a 1,700-ha bog known as Jim Campbell's Barren in northern Cape Breton would be lifted. In early 1997, the Savage govt and Toronto-based Regal Goldfields Ltd., a mineral exploration company whose share tradings had soared before the official announcement was made, came under intense scrutiny from environmentalists, opposition parties and the public as allegations of corruption and insider trading began to circulate. On Oct. 29, 1997, new NS premier Russell MacLellan (b 1940) declared that the bog would be returned to a list of parks and protected areas.

Dec. 16 RCMP and Charlottetown police arrested Roger Charles Bell, a man known as the notorious "PEI Bomber." Bell had set pipe bombs around PEI over a 9-year period, including one at historic Province House in 1995. He had also sent threatening letters to justice officials and the media. Bell was sentenced to 9 years, and later waived his right to appear before the parole board.

Dec. 17 In the worst single attack on Red Cross workers in the organization's 133-year history, 5 female nurses and 1 Dutch architect were murdered in their beds by masked gunmen in the Novye Atagi hospital, near Grozny, Chechnya. Among the dead was Canadian nurse Nancy Malloy (1945–1996).

• Al Leach, Ont. minister of municipal affairs and housing, introduced Bill 103 into the legislature. The bill amalgamated the 6 Toronto-region municipalities (North York, East York, York, Etobicoke, Scarborough and Toronto) into a single "megacity" of approximately 2.3 million. The bill passed on Apr. 21, 1997, despite a 10-day, round-the-clock filibuster by opponents who tabled some 13,000 amendments in efforts to stall passage. The bill took effect Jan. 1, 1998, despite a Mar. 3, 1997, plebiscite showing that an overwhelming majority of Metropolitan Toronto voters opposed megacity.

Dec. 18 In Lima, Peru, Tupac Amaru guerrillas overran a party at Japanese ambassador Morihisa Aoki's residence, taking hundreds of hostages, including nearly every ambassador in the city. Rebel demands included the release of over 400 Tupac prisoners. Included among the hostages was Anthony Vincent (d 1999), Canadian ambassador to Peru. Vincent was later released to serve as a interlocutor between the Peruvian govt and the rebels.

Dec. 23 Ont. Provincial Court Justice Inger Hansen acquitted Brenda Drummond of attempted murder and criminal negligence causing bodily harm. Drummond had tried to end her pregnancy by deliberately shooting herself in the stomach with a pellet gun. Justice Hansen ruled that a fetus was not a person under the law, and the case could therefore not be construed as attempted murder or criminal negligence.

Dec. 28 BC was buffeted with what many observers called "The Snowstorm of the Century." The 2-day assault delivered over 2 feet of snow, which was blown into towering drifts by winds of up to 100 km/h. All was accompanied by record-low temperatures, which included a wind chill peaking at –40C.

Also in Dec.
• Newspaper mogul Conrad Black sold his 24.9% stake in John Fairfax Holdings Ltd., Australia's 2nd-largest newspaper chain, to New Zealand's Brierley Investments Group. Black tried for years to convince Australia to relax its foreign-ownership rules so he could increase his stake. Although he lost that battle, Black's Hollinger International Inc. reaped a $300 million profit on the sale.

• The printing branch of the federal govt, formerly called the Queen's Printer, was sold to Toronto-based St. Joseph's Corp. for $7 million.

Also in 1996
• Historian J.L. Granatstein published *Yankee Go Home: Canadians and Anti-Americanism*, arguing that Canadian anti-American sentiment was generated and used by Canadian business, politicians and cultural groups to support and defend their own interests.

• Toronto Blue Jays pitcher Pat Hentgen won the American League Cy Young Award. He recorded 20 wins, 10 losses, an ERA of 3.22, with 177 strike-outs and 94 walks. It was both the 3rd, and 3rd consecutive, Cy Young in Blue Jays history (Roger Clemens 1997, 1998).

• The Alberta Hail Suppression Project, seeding clouds from planes to reduce the likelihood of menacing hail, was initiated. The project was the 1st of its kind to be funded entirely by the private insurance industry. Between 1988 and 1998, hail destroyed an estimated $1 billion worth of Alb. crops and property.

• Quebecers responding to the 1996 census were two times more likely to consider themselves "ethnic Canadian" than residents living elsewhere. The 1996 census was the 1st to include "Canadian" as an ethnic choice.

• The Ont. provincial park system was named Ontario Parks and given a new stylized lake-and-trees logo. The system was also reorganized along a modern business model, so profits generated by its over 265 parks could be re-invested within the system.

• David Phillips, senior climatologist with Environment Canada, began republishing *The Canadian Weather Trivia Calendar*, an annual collection of illustrations, weather stories, records, history and trivia. It had 1st been published by Environment Canada between 1985–1991

• The average university student carried a debt of $17,000.

• The country's trade surplus with the US was a record $40.7 billion, up from $33.1 billion in 1995.

• The mother tongue of 44% of those attending school in Vancouver was English; Chinese was the 2nd largest grouping at 32%.

• Excluding the 2 official languages, Chinese was the leading language spoken in Canadian homes, followed in rank by Italian, Punjabi, Spanish, Portuguese, Polish and German.

• Statistics Canada showed that there were 3,197,480 visible minorities in Canada, including 860,150 Chinese, 670,585 South Asians and 573,860 of African decent.

• The average Canadian watched 22.8 hours of television each week. Adult men averaged 21.9 hours, adult woman 26.5. Que. had the highest provincial average at 26 hours per week (26.6 hours for French-language television, 22.5 for English-language television). Alb. had the lowest weekly average at 20.3 hours.

• There were 13 commercial casinos in Canada: 2 in NS, 3 in Que., 4 in Ont, 3 in Man., and 1 in Sask. Total gross revenue was $7.5 billion.

• The Royal Bank posted a record profit of $1.43 billion, the highest to date for any Canadian business. Royal profits had been $1.26 billion in 1995.

• The poorest 20% of Canadians experienced an income decline of 3.1%; the incomes of the richest 20% increased by 1.8%.

• The average Canadian consumed 179.43 kg of vegetables, up from 132.83 kg in 1965.

• Eight thousand two hundred eighty-two Canadian farms produced fruit for the market.

• Twenty-three million turkeys were sold in Canada.

• Ministry of Natural Resources scientists noted only 2,000 caribou remained of the great herd once located on Baffin Is. The 1961 population of this breed was 25,000.

• The Canadian govt, acting in agreement with the Inuvialuit, established the 16,340-km² national park of Tuktut Nogait, 170 km north of the Arctic Circle in the Northwest Territories. Bounded on the north by the Beaufort Sea, the park protects the calving grounds of the bluenose caribou.

• Eighteen percent of Vancouver's intravenous-drug users contracted HIV.

• There were 920,640 common law couples in Canada, up from 357,000 in 1981; 40% lived in Que.

• 1996 was the wettest year on record in Canada to date. An estimated $750 million worth of rain-related insurance claims were submitted.

• The Ottawa Rough Riders of the CFL folded. The team, 4-time Grey Cup champions during the 1960s, had spent the last 17 years in pursuit of a winning season, while simultaneously accumulating some $30 million of debt.

• Heritage Canada's Book Development Program was given a $5 million boost by the federal govt, which increased assistance to struggling domestic book publishers by 50%.

• The federal govt blocked attempts by monster US bookstore chains Borders, and Barnes & Noble, to open superstores in Canada. Barnes & Noble would later invest 20% in the Chapters boxstore book chain.

• Ten percent of the total Canadian labour force arrived to work each morning by public transport.

• Department and discount store sales totalled $14.5 billion.

• There was a record 93,860 bankruptcies in Canada — 79,631 personal and 14,229 commercial. The previous record was 78,690 in 1995, which topped the previous record of 76,139 in 1992.

• Statistics Canada reported there were 1,101,960 Aboriginal People living in Canada. Two hundred thirty four thousand Canadians spoke an Aboriginal language. Twenty-seven thousand Canadian Aboriginals were enrolled in post-secondary schools; 800 had been enrolled in 1980.

• The Defence Department reported that the UN owed Canada $60 million for unpaid peacekeeping bills, including costs related to such missions as Cyprus, Rwanda, Haiti and Bosnia.

• One kiloton of ozone-depleting chemicals was produced for use in Canada, down from 24.9 kilotons in 1986.

• Canadian pharmacists filled over 235 million prescriptions.

• 1,578 medical operations in Canada involved the transplant of donated organs.

• US-based Amazon.com, with a 2.5-million-title database, ushered in the era of online bookselling.

Canadian booksellers Indigo and Chapters would begin online operations in 1998.

• York U. professor Robert Bowman received a Grammy for Best Album Notes for his 47,000-word monograph accompanying the 10-CD boxed set *The Complete Stax/Volt Soul Singles, Vol. 3: 1972–1975*, which he co-produced.

• Jazz pianist D.D. Jackson (Robert Cleath Kainier Jackson, b 1967) recorded the explosive *Rhythm-Dance*.

• Sask. jazz pianist Renee Rosnes (b 1962) recorded on Blue Note the critically acclaimed *Ancestors*.

• *Crash*, a much-debated film by David Cronenberg (b 1943) about a group of people obsessed with car crashes and sex, created a stir in Britain where its release was delayed by an "interim ban" that remained in place in at least one borough until 1998. The film won 5 awards at the Genies in Nov. of that year but failed to pick up the Best Motion Picture award, which went to John Greyson's *Lilies*, another controversial film about a Catholic bishop taken hostage in prison and forced to confront his sins.

• Gail Anderson-Dargatz (b 1963) released her 1st novel, *A Cure for Death By Lightning*, which sold over 100,000 books in Canada and won both the BC and VanCity Book Prizes.

• Mi'kmaq poet Rita Joe (b 1932) published her autobiography *Song of Rita Joe*.

• Poet and novelist Anne Michaels published *Fugitive Pieces* for which she won the Trillium Award, the Books in Canada First Novel Award and Britain's Orange Prize.

• Saskatoon author Guy Vanderhaeghe published *The Englishman's Boy*, a view of early Hollywood and the Old West. The novel won the Gov-Gen.'s Literary Award for Fiction.

• Essayist and social philosopher John Ralston Saul (b 1947) published *The Unconscious Civilization*, winning the Gov-Gen.'s Award for Non-Fiction and the Gordon Montador Award for Best Canadian

Non-Fiction Book of Social Issues. Saul was also honoured by the govt of France as a Chevalier de l'Ordre des Arts et des Lettres de France.

• Mavis Gallant published her 900-page epic *Selected Stories* to international acclaim. She was also awarded the Molson Prize for the Arts ($50,000).

• Ann-Marie MacDonald published *Fall On Your Knees*, an Oprah's Book Club selection in 2002.

• Sisters Janet and Greta Podleski, 2 Ottawa natives, published their 1st cookbook, *Loonyspoons*, the fastest book ever to hit the 500,000-copies-sold mark in Canada.

1997

Jan. 2 David Black's Black Press Ltd. purchased 33 western publications — including the *Red Deer Advocate* and 17 other community newspapers — from UK-based Trinity International Publications PLC of England, for $58 million. The purchase brought the western media mogul's number of BC, Alb. and Washington State newspapers to 80, giving Black more English-language papers than anyone else in the country.

• Graham James, long-time major-junior Western Canadian Hockey League coach, was convicted of sexually assaulting young male players under his tutelage, and sentenced to 3 1/2 years in prison. Boston Bruins' winger Sheldon Kennedy, victimized by the coach during the 1984 season, had fingered James. Other NHL and WHL players came forward to support Kennedy and the charges.

Jan. 4 New federal rules governing the application of Employment Insurance (previously Unemployment Insurance) were officially implemented. The new regulations included eligibility requirement determined by hours, not weeks, worked, and a $39,000 ceiling on benefits.

• The Canadian men's junior hockey team beat the US 2–0 in Geneva to win the World Junior Hockey Championship a record 5 times in a row. The championship also marked the nation's 7th in 8 years.

Jan. 6 The legal portion of the "Airbus Scandal" was completed as former PM Brian Mulroney's $50 million libel with the federal govt was settled out of court. Mulroney was given $1.4 million to cover legal fees, $600,000 to cover public relations costs and $15,000 for translation fees. He was also given an apology. Mulroney had sued the govt for libel after the RCMP sent a letter to Swiss authorities on Sept. 29, 1995, suggesting Mulroney, Conservative lobbyist Frank Moores (b 1933) and businessman Karlheinz Schreiber might have received undue financial advantage from the purchase of 34 jets from Airbus Industries in 1988. The RCMP continued to investigate, but on Apr. 22, 2003, officially closed its books on the case. No charges were laid.

Jan. 9 Bombardier secured a deal to provide Atlantic Southeast Airlines of Atlanta, with 30 Canadian regional jets for $825 million, Bombardier's largest deal to date. The company then turned around and bought the Ont. govt's 49% share of De Havilland Inc. for $49 million, giving Bomabardier 100% of the storied Toronto-based plane maker. Bombardier fortunes continued on June 17 when the company nailed a massive deal to provide American Airlines' American Eagle Corp. with 70 CRJ–700 planes — for $1.4 billion.

Jan. 10 Nine hundred Air Ontario, Air Nova, Air BC and Air Alliance pilots — members of the Canadian Air Line Pilots Association (CALPA) — struck to preserve seniority against pilots from parent corporation Air Canada. Pilots returned to work Mar. 12, accepting an increase to wages, with the seniority issue going to arbitration.

Jan. 12 CBC television aired the 1st part of its 4-hour miniseries *The Arrow*, the story of Canada's $400 million Avro Arrow program (scrapped by the Diefenbaker govt in 1959). Shot on location at Winnipeg's International Airport, the production starred Dan Aykroyd, Christopher Plummer, Sara Botsford and Ron White. Keith Leckie wrote the script.

Jan. 14 The federal govt resumed deportation hearings against alleged Nazi war criminals Erich Tobiass, 84, Johann Deuck, 76 and Helmut Oberlander 71, following a Federal Court of Appeal decision that dismissed previous hearings against the men. To quicken the process against the aged defendants, the govt decided to try them not as war criminals, but on the grounds they might have lied about their pasts on immigration papers. Tobiass died in 1997 during court proceedings; Deuck's case was dismissed; Oberlander was still before the courts in 2004. By the end of 1997, approximately 14 alleged war criminals in Canada faced deportation hearings.

Jan. 16 The UN appointed former Ontario Hydro chairman Maurice Strong to help restructure its massive international bureaucracy.

Jan. 20 The sacred 300-year-old, 50-m-tall golden sitka spruce in Port Clements, Graham Is. in the Queen Charlottes, BC, was destroyed by a chainsaw vandal. The tree fell to the ground later in Jan. The Haida Nation believed that the creator formed the *Picea sitchensis* "Aurea" from a boy ancestor; they were to protect the tree, for its death meant the end of the Haida people. Cuttings from the dying sitka were later grafted to saplings in Vancouver Is. Grafts of these were planted in Port Clements' millennium park in 2001, and another at the trunk of the original in 2002.

Jan. 20–22 Foreign Affairs Minister Lloyd Axworthy (b 1939) travelled to Cuba for talks on human rights and social conditions. His action violated the US Helms-Burton Act, signed into law Mar. 12, 1996. There were no repercussions.

Jan. 30 Lise Thibault (b 1939) was sworn in as Que.'s 1st woman lt-gov., succeeding Jean-Louis Roux (b 1923). The place and role of a lt-gov. in late 20th-century Que. was much debated prior to the appointment, with Premier Lucien Bouchard calling the unelected seat "a sequel of a colonial regime."

• The community-based Joint Action Group (JAG), along with federal, provincial, and local officials, pledged $1.67million to search for a solution to Canada's worst toxic waste dump — the Sydney, NS, tar ponds, which seethed with more than 700,000 tonnes of PCB-laced sludge. The site was created over many years as Sydney Steel dumped its coke ovens into the Muggah Creek watershed. The tar ponds remained virtually unaltered by 2004.

Feb. 2 Canadian Catholic priest Rev. Guy Pinard was shot and killed in his rural Rwandan church during a spate of Hutus and Tutsi revenge killings. Approximately 100 Canadian civilians lived and worked in the blighted nation, still reeling from its horrific 1994 civil war.

Feb. 10 The Ontario Labour Relations Board certified an application by the United Steelworkers of America to unionize a Windsor, Ont., Wal-Mart, making it the 1st Wal-Mart in the world to gain union recognition. Workers had voted to unionize the franchise on May 9, 1996. Wal-Mart was 1st established in Rogers, Arkansas, by co-founders Sam and Bud Walton in 1962. It developed into the world's largest retailer.

Feb. 18 Federal Finance Minister Paul Martin tabled the federal budget, setting out a projected deficit of $17 billion for 1997–1998 and $9 billion for 1998–1999. There were no new additions to cuts and no new taxes.

Feb. 24 Residents of Rocky Mountain House in Alb. voted in a referendum, by a margin of 2 to 1, to ban video-lottery terminals from their town.

Feb. 27 Members of the Toronto rock band Rush were appointed Officers of the Order of Canada: singer-bassist Geddy Lee (b 1953) guitarist Alex Lifeson (b 1953), and drummer Neil Pert (b 1952). Rush was the 1st rock band to receive the Order since the national honour was created in 1967.

• Eaton's department store chain filed for protection from its creditors under the Canadian CCA Act after reporting a pre-tax loss of $120 million for 1996. The venerable Canadian department store, 1st opened by Irish immigrant Timothy Eaton in Toronto in 1869, had 85 outlets and over 15,000 employees. Its creditors would approve the chain's $419 million restructuring plan in Sept. In June 1998, the chain issued an Initial Public Offering (IPO) of 11.7 million shares at $15 each. The Eaton family retained 51% of the shares. On Dec. 30, 1999, Sears purchased all common shares of Eaton's and delisted it on the stock market. The move proved unprofitable, and on Feb. 18, 2002, Sears announced its remaining 7 Eaton's stores would either be closed or converted to Sears stores. By year's end, the famous, 133-year-old Eaton's had vanished from the Canadian retail-market scene.

Feb. 28 Allegations were brought forth that employees of Maple Leaf Gardens in Toronto coerced young boys into the hockey shrine with promises of game tickets and autographs and then sexually abused them. Martin Kruze, the primary claimant in the case, committed suicide at the Bloor viaduct in Toronto on Oct. 30, 1997, 3 days after his victimizer, Gord Stuckless, was sentenced to 2 years less a day for his crimes. Kruze 1st made the allegations in 1993, suing Maple Leaf Gardens and settling out of court for $45,000 with the stipulation that he not go public with the story. He did, 4 years later.

Also in Feb.

• Canada Post introduced a new 45-cent stamp in celebration of the Chinese Year of the Ox (which began Feb. 7). Designed by Sheridan College professor Ivy Li, the new stamp featured … a portrait of an ox.

• Unionized construction workers in Cape Breton rioted in Sydney, NS, burning several vehicles and an unfinished apartment building where non-unionized workers had been employed. On Oct. 1, 10 men pled guilty to charges of unlawful assembly or mischief related to the incident.

• Nfld.-based Canadian Blood Bank Corp. was given the nation's 1st federal licence to operate as a private blood bank, providing customers with storage facilities for their own blood.

Mar. 2 Gail Graham (b 1964) of Kelowna, BC, edged out hometown favourite Karrie Webb to take the prestigious Australian Ladies Masters Golf Championship in Gold Coast, Australia. It was Graham's 2nd win since joining the LPGA in 1989. Her first came in 1995 at the Fieldcrest Cannon Classic in North Carolina.

Mar. 3 The Toronto city council implemented a tough new bylaw banning smoking in all 4,500 restaurants and bars in the city. However, it was quickly discovered that bylaw enforcement officers did not have the power to ask a smoker defying the bylaw to produce identification for the purposes of issuing a ticket. Restaurants and patrons began to openly defy the ban.

Mar. 6 The federal govt passed Bill C–71, 139 votes to 37, placing restrictions on cigarette and tobacco advertising at sporting, cultural and other public events, and forcing tobacco companies to place new shock warnings on retail tobacco products, effective Oct. 1, 1998. Many popular events were either cancelled or curtailed due to the subsequent loss of advertising and sponsorship dollars, including the LPGA's 4th Major, the Canadian Open, which folded after the 2000 season.

Mar. 7 VIA Rail implemented a plan to replace its 227 train conductors with computers.

Mar. 9 The 27th annual Juno Awards recognized Alanis Morissette, Céline Dion and Shania Twain with a newly created joint prize for international achievement. Anne Murray presented the award.

Mar. 11 Incumbent premier Ralph Klein and his Conservatives captured 63 of 83 seats in the Alb. provincial election, taking 12 more seats than in 1993. The Liberals under Grant Mitchell won 18 seats, and Pam Barrett's NDP, which had been shut out in the previous election, won 2.

• PM Chrétien appointed Elinor Caplan (b 1944) [Thornhill, Ont.], Judy Sgro (b 1944) [York–South–Weston, Ont.], Sophia Leung (b 1933) [Vancouver–Kingsway] and Judi Longfield (b 1947) [Whitby–Ajax, Ont.] as Liberal candidates for the next general election. The move was part of a liberal plan to raise the number of Liberal woman candidates to 25% of the total.

Mar. 13 Sun Media Corp. began its takeover of the London Free Press, established in 1852 when Josiah Blackburn (1823–1890) purchased the Canadian Free Press for $500. The venerable Ont. paper had a circulation of 105,000.

Mar. 15 Bloc Québécois House leader Gilles Duceppe (b 1947) retained his leadership at the BQ's weekend convention, taking 52.8% of the votes. He became the 1st elected BQ leader. Duceppe took over from outgoing leader Michel Gauthier.

Mar. 19 Oil companies Shell Canada, Chevron, Petro-Canada and Mobil Oil donated their exploration rights to areas off the western coast of South Moresby Is. in BC to the Nature Conservancy of

Canada. The move set in motion plans to convert the island's coastal waters into a national marine park.

Mar. 20 Canadian figure skater Elvis Stojko won gold at the World Figure Skating Championships in Lausanne, Switzerland, despite falling to 4th place after the short program. It was Stojko's 3rd World gold (1994,1995).

Mar. 26 Officials with the Calgary-based mining company Bre-X, suggested there was a possibility that a geologists' Feb. 22, 1995, report showing a massive reserve of gold at Busang, Indonesia, may have been "overstated." On Mar. 19, geologist Michael de Guzman, who would later be partly blamed for "discovering" the fraudulent 70-million-ounce-plus gold deposits, fell mysteriously to his death from a helicopter over Borneo. On Mar. 27, 1997, the Busang mine in Indonesia was indeed found to hold insignificant amounts of gold. Bre-X stocks plunged drastically. On May 4, an independent auditor confirmed the fact. On Nov. 5, 1997 Bre-X Minerals declared bankruptcy.

Mar. 26–May 3 Veteran Canadian stage actor Shirley Douglas ([b 1934] daughter of Tommy Douglas, founder of the NDP) performed in Tennessee Williams's *The Glass Menagerie* with her son, film actor Kiefer Sutherland (b 1966), at the Royal Alexandra Theatre in Toronto.

Mar. 30 Bill C–32, An Act to Amend the Copyright Act, was passed in the House; Assent was given Apr. 25. Provisions included a levy on blank tapes to partially compensate for their use in illegal taping, "parallel importation" protections for exclusive distributors of foreign books in Canada and redefined copyright exemptions for non-profit institutions such as libraries and universities.

Also in Mar.
• The federal govt unveiled the "Mifflin Plan," named after federal fisheries Minister Fred Mifflin (b 1938). The plan aimed to protect dwindling Pacific salmon stocks by eliminating 50% of the West Coast fishery over the next 3–4 years; $180 million was devoted to the buyout of existing licences. Some 1,000 fisheries were paid $6,500 each to sit out the 1998 salmon season.

• Forty-six-year-old Peter Bashucky transported his dead father from Los Angeles to Toronto on ice in the back of his camper. The elder Bashucky, 78, died of a stroke while visiting relatives in California. Bashucky, who said, "Basically, I guess I was in shock," delivered his father's body to a west Toronto funeral home after the 4-day, cross-continent trip. He entered Canada without incident, stating he had nothing to declare.

• In a series of rotating protests, students at McMaster U., the U. of Guelph, York U., Ryerson U., and the U. of Toronto occupied their schools' administration offices, demanding an end to escalating tuition hikes. The average Ont. undergraduate tuition for the upcoming 1997-1998 year was $3,293 (in 1993–1994 it was $2,076). The Canadian average was $2,869 (in 1993–1994 it was $2,023). NS had highest provincial undergraduate average, at $3,892 (for 1993–1994, $2,701); Que. had the lowest, at $1,803 (for 1993–1994, $1,550). (All numbers include both in- and out-of-province fees, but not additional, compulsory fees.)

Apr. 14 Justice Francis Muldoon of the Federal Court ruled that the Canadian Wheat Board's monopoly constituted a reasonable infringement on the wheat trade, as it protected farmers against the vicissitudes of the open market. The case was initiated by the Alb. Barley Commission and the Western Barley Growers Association, who argued that the requirement of all Canadian wheat growers to sell their grain to the board violated constitutional freedoms of association and the right to make a living.

Apr. 19 Sandra Schmirler's Regina rink won the World Curling Championships in Bern, Switzerland, becoming the 1st women's team to win 3 World Championships.

Apr. 22 Emerson, Man., located along the Red R at the US border, was the 1st Man. town evacuated during the "Flood of the Century." Floodwaters had been precipitated by an Apr. 4–7 blizzard, which dumped 50 cm of melting snow into the Red R. watershed. By May 7, the Red at Emerson was an incredible 30 km wide. Floodwaters pushed north, leading to the evacuation of approximately 28,000, including citizens of Morris, Ste. Agathe, St. Jean Baptiste, Rosenort and Ste. Adolphe. On May 1, the Red crested at 7.5 m in Winnipeg, but potential flood-waters were redirected away from the city by the Red R. Floodway. At its peak, the flood covered 2,000 km² of land. On May 5, the waters began to recede. The disaster caused over $300 million in damages, devastated homes, farms and livestock. Over 8,600 Armed Forces personnel, RCMP and Coast Guard vigilantly gave it their all, protecting homes, businesses and cleaning up in the wake.

Apr. 23 The Toronto Stock Exchange (TSE) closed its 145-year-old trading floor and went digital.

Apr. 24 Peter Lerat walked into a Toronto doughnut shop and threatened to kill the Canada goose he had under his arm if customers didn't give him money. Two weeks later, Lerat accosted pedestrians with a racoon — threatening to hit it on the head unless they handed over cash. Charged with extortion in both cases, Lerat appeared in court in early May — completely nude. The charges were later dropped for lack of evidence.

Apr. 26 Assent was given to Criminal Code amendments making participation in a criminal organization illegal. The legislation also included stiffer sentences for possession and use of explosives. The amendments were established in the shadow of a Que. biker turf war between the Hells Angels and Rock Machine, which had resulted in nearly 50 fatalities since 1996. Amendments to further define the term "criminal organization" were tabled in the House Apr. 5, 2001.

May 23 In Bull Arm, Nfld., two pieces of the $5.8 billion Hibernia oil rig platform were joined and towed to a drilling site off the Grand Banks, some 300 km southeast of St. John's, Nfld. The event marked the culmination of a 6-year construction marathon, one of the largest and most expensive offshore oil rig productions in the world. Hibernia created 1,400 new jobs and a renewed form of wealth to a province devastated by dwindling North Atlantic fish stocks. Hibernia was owned by Mobil Oil Canada, Chevron Canada Resources, Petro-Canada, Murphy Oil and Norsk Hydro. The Canada govt, which held an 8.5% share, had pumped over $2.5 billion into Hibernia since oil

was 1st discovered on the offshore site in 1979. The 1st oil was pumped from the new platform Nov. 17; the rig was expected to produce up to 600 million barrels of oil over the next 2 decades.

• Green Gables — recognized around the world as the PEI home of Lucy Maud Montgomery's beloved Anne character — was damaged in a fire. The conflagration came only 7 days before the scheduled opening of Confederation Bridge, linking the island to the mainland. Restoration efforts were swift, and tourists were welcomed back on July 1. Green Gables had attracted 741,000 visitors in 1996.

May 29 Man. First Nations, the Man. govt and Ottawa completed a deal setting aside 445,000 ha of land and $76 million in cash to settle current provincial First Nations' land claims.

• The world's largest pulp-and-paper company, Toronto-based Abitibi-Price Inc., merged with Stone-Consolidated Corp. of Montreal, to form the world's largest newsprint producer. The $4.1 billion merger resulted in Abitibi-Consolidated, with 14 mills in Canada, 3 in the US and 1 in Britain.

May 31 The $1 billion Confederation Bridge (a multi-span concrete box girder type) opened, linking PEI to NB over the Northumberland Strait. The 12.9-km, 2-lane extension of the Trans-Canada Highway was the longest bridge in the world spanning freezing waters. The initial toll for cars was $35. Construction had begun in 1993.

Also in May

• Peter Gzowski taped his last episode of CBC Radio's beloved *Morningside,* in Moosejaw, Sask. Gzowski had done an estimated 27,000 interviews for the show since it 1st aired in 1982. He recalled, "The best interviews were the ones that surprised me. They're not the ones with the prime minister or the great author, but, rather, people like Elly Danica, a victim of sexual abuse, or a scientist whose work gives him pride. Donna Williams, the autistic woman, was very moving. She talked about the streetlights sparkling pink and the colour of each blade of grass."

• The Frederick Horsman Varley Art Gallery opened in historic Unionville, Ont., in honour of the founding member of the Group of Seven. The gallery spanned 13,935 m² and included 100 original Varley pieces, most of which were donated by Unionville resident Kathleen Gormley McKay.

June 1 100-m record holder Donovan Bailey faced American 200- and 400-m specialist Michael Johnson in a 150-m race at the Toronto SkyDome. The result would determine the "Fastest Man in the World," a title traditionally reserved for the 100-m record holder. Johnson was heartily trounced over the 1st half of the race, then pulled up lame to watch Bailey complete the showdown alone.

June 2 Jean Chrétien's Liberals were re-elected in the federal general election, taking 155 seats for a slim 4-seat majority. The Reform Party, under Preston Manning, took 60 seats, ousting the Bloc Québécois and leader Gilles Duceppe as the Official Opposition. The BQ ended the day with 44 seats, the NDP, under Alexa McDonough, 21, and the Progressive Conservatives, under Jean Charest, 20; 1 Independent made the House. Voter turnout was 67%.

June 5 George Kosich, former president of the Hudson's Bay Co., replaced George Eaton as Eaton's chief executive.

June 6 Que.'s "Language Police," the Commission de protection de la langue française, was revived in a National Assembly free vote of 63–24. The enforcement wing of the provincial language charter had been mothballed in 1993.

June 11 For the 4th consecutive year, the UN Development Program voted Canada the best place in the world to live. France was ranked 2nd, Norway 3rd, the US 4th and Iceland 5th.

June 20 Opposition leader Preston Manning announced he would in fact move into Stornoway, the $2 million residence of the Official Opposition leader located at 541 Acacia St. in Rockcliffe Park, Ottawa. Manning had previously stated that the 30-plus-room mansion was too palatial for Opposition needs, but cited public pressures as cause for the change of mind. Stornoway had not been inhabited since 1993. Previous Opposition leader Lucien Bouchard rejected the residential perk and, instead,

lived in the aging mill town of Hull. Stornoway required some $68,000 worth of improvements before Manning moved in.

June 23 As part of year long festivities celebrating the 500th anniversary of John Cabot's arrival in North America, the *Matthew* — a replica of the boat which 1st landed Cabot in North America in 1497 — landed in Bonavista, Nfld. It was met by brass bands, a host of celebrants, both the mayor of Bristol, England (from which the replica had departed), Queen Elizabeth II and Nfld. Premier Brian Tobin.

June 24 More than 100 people were arrested in Quebec City and Montreal for looting and vandalism during raucous St. Jean Baptiste Day celebrations.

June 28 Naomi Bronstein, co-founder of the orphan organization Families for Children, was awarded the $250,000 Royal Bank Award for Canadian Achievement. Bronstein's Healing the Children program, established in 1979, helped bring an estimated 30,000 Guatemalan children to North America for surgery.

Also in June

• The national unemployment rate experienced its biggest monthly surge in 14 years, rising to 10% in June. Statistics Canada reported that Que. accounted for three-quarters of the increase, after losing 41,000 jobs in May.

July 2 Minister of Defence Art Eggleton (b 1943) released the final, scathing report of the Somalia Commission of Inquiry. The 5-volume report was called *Dishonoured Legacy*. It stated the defence system was "rotten to the core," that there was a defence conspiracy to mislead and confuse the inquiry with incorrect and missing text. The deaths of 4 Somalis at the hands of Airborne soldiers in 1993 were blamed on a system of bad management and rudderless soldiers. The report concluded that there be fixed, clear rules for the engagement of Canadian peacekeepers, that the Armed Forces improve its leadership training, and the military justice system be completely revamped. Of the report's 160 recommendations, 132 were either fully or partially implemented.

July 8 Four BC Native groups agreed to demand from environmental groups that they not associate Aboriginal symbols and other imagery with non-Aboriginal politics. A spokesman explained, "We will not allow special-interest environmental groups to hurt us in the same manner they did in their world-wide campaign that successfully banned the seal hunt in Canada and killed the way of life for the Inuit."

July 9 Nfld. native Danielle House (b 1976) was stripped of her Miss Canada title after being convicted of assaulting a woman vying for her ex-boyfriend's affections. Following in the footsteps of fellow Newfoundlander Sharon Tweed, House became a Playboy Playmate, appearing on the cover of the Dec. 1997 edition — in little more than boxing gloves.

July 12 Russell MacLellan (b 1940) won the provincial Liberal leadership in NS, succeeding the retiring Premier John Savage. MacLellan formed his govt July 18. He was later elected to the legislature in a Cape Breton North by-election Nov. 4, 1997.

July 19–22 Three hundred BC fishing boats blockaded an Alaska Ferry Service ferry carrying 300 passengers at the port of Prince Rupert, BC. The move was part of an intense dispute with US fishers over migratory salmon. Alaska sued, but on Jan. 22, 1998, settled for $2.75 million in compensation from the Canadian govt. On Sept. 8, 1997, BC also initiated a lawsuit, for $350 million against US fishers for violating the 1985 Pacific Salmon Treaty. Nothing came of it but the resignation of Robert Wright, Canadian member of the Canada–US Pacific Salmon Treaty Commission, who argued that the lawsuit did little but inflame already worn relations between fishing communities. Wright furthered that the Canadian Department of Fisheries was "full of dinosaurs" and was partially to blame for dwindling West Coast salmon stocks.

July 23 The Quebec City National Capital Commission unveiled a $150,000 bronze statue of former French President Charles de Gaulle on a square near the historic Plains of Abraham. The unveiling came 1 day before the 20th anniversary of de Gaulle's politically charged "Vive le Québec Libre!" speech in Montreal.

July 25 Ralph Klein's Alb. govt placed a $2 user fee on prescription drugs ordered by welfare recipients.

July 27 A 60-m-long memorial to the 516 Canadians killed in the Korean War was unveiled at Meadowvale Cemetery in Brampton, Ont.

July 28 The Commission for Environmental Co-operation ranked Ont. the 3rd worst polluter on the continent, noting that the Harris administration's repeal of environmental legislation had placed the province "on the path to unsustainable development." Texas and Tennessee were ranked 1st and 2nd, respectively.

July 30 Phil Fontaine (b 1944) was elected national chief of the Assembly of First Nations, replacing Ovide Mercredi.

Also in July
• The Health Services Restructuring Commission, an independent body empowered by the Ont. govt to eliminate 4,800 of Ont.'s 24,000 acute-care beds, implemented a series of controversial hospital mergers and closings, including the planned closure of 11 Toronto hospitals. The moves were part of Premier Harris's $1.3 billion cuts to hospitals over 3 years.

Aug. 6 Civic workers, including garbage collectors, went on strike in Vancouver. The strike was settled Sept. 16, with workers taking a 2% raise over 2 years.

Aug. 8 The right-wing Sask. Party was created by 8 dissident Tory and Liberal MLAs (4 of each). On Aug. 21, the party was given Official Opposition status. The Sask. PC party was reduced to only 1 member with the defections — Jack Goohsen, who would in turn leave the party to sit as an Independent. On Nov. 9, the PC party voted to render itself inactive.

Aug. 10 Actress Marie-Soleil Tougas (b 1970) and Québécois film director Jean-Claude Lauzon (b 1953) were killed in a plane crash in northern Que.

Aug. 11 A BC Human Rights Tribunal concluded that breastfeeding was a fundamental human right and as such could be done in public. The case was brought to the tribunal after civil servant Michelle Poirier was prevented from breastfeeding at work following the complaints of several female colleagues.

• Intergovernmental Affairs Minister Stéphane Dion (b 1955) heated up the political climate in Que. when he sent an open letter to Que. Premier Lucien Bouchard, challenging Que.'s right to unilaterally declare its secession from Canada.

Aug. 13 Ontario Hydro announced it would shut down 7 of its 19 operating nuclear reactors following the release of a safety report showing them to be operating at a "minimally acceptable" level. All 4 reactors at Pickering Plant A were mothballed the same year.

Aug. 23–24 Approximately 100 BC fishers staged an illegal salmon-poaching operation to protest Native-only fishing along specified stretches of the Fraser R.

Aug. 28 Ont. Solicitor Gen. Bob Runciman cancelled the grand opening of Ont.'s new Camp Hillsdale "Boot Camp" for young offenders, after 2 youths pummelled a guard and escaped before ceremonies began.

Aug. 29 Marie-Louise Meilleur (1880–1998), of Corbeil, Ont., was recognized by the *Guinness Book of World Records* as the oldest living person. The mother of 12 was 117.

Sept. 2 Seventy-three percent of Nfld. voters supported the creation of secular schools in a second provincial referendum. The change-over from church-run to secular schools, however, required an amendment to the Constitution, which had been denied by the Senate following a similar referendum in 1995.

Sept. 3 A westbound transcontinental VIA train derailed outside Biggar, Sask., killing 1 and injuring 64 others.

Sept. 4 Founder and Chief Executive Heather Reisman opened the 1st Indigo Books & Music Inc. store in Burlington, Ont. The 1,858-m² bookstore

would be the 1st of 2 to open in the year. By 2000, there were 14 Indigos across the country. In Aug, 2001, Indigo merged with Chapters (which had been created in 1995 with the merger of the nation's previous 2 largest bookstore chains, SmithBooks and Coles) to form the nation's largest bookstore chain.

Sept. 10 Toronto police arrested 35 illegal immigrants and laid over 750 charges in connection to an international prostitution ring involving local bawdy houses and the sex trafficking of poor and indebted Asian women from Thailand and Malaysia.

Sept. 14 Nine provincial premiers (Que. was not represented) met in Calgary to hash out the Calgary Declaration, another framework for constitutional reform. This time, the term "distinct society" was thrown out, to be replaced by the "unique character of Que. society."

Sept. 15 Fenfluramine (Ponderal and Pondimin) and dexfenfluramine (Redux), two widely used diet drugs found to cause heart problems, were taken off the market. The drugs had been approved for the Canadian market in 1996 despite warnings from researchers at the Jewish General Hospital in Montreal that they caused high incidences of high blood pressure and associated heart-valve problems.

Sept. 19 The largest lottery prize in Canadian history to this date was won by a student from Richmond Hill, Ont. The take: $21.8 million in the Super 7. The record was beaten Mar. 27, 1998, when a southwestern farming couple won $22.5 million. The record was pushed again in 2003, when a number of Hamilton, Ont., police officers split a $25 million Super 7 jackpot. A record $30 million Super 7 ticket was sold in Brantford, Ont., in 2003 but remained unclaimed until Apr. 2004.

Sept. 23 The First Nations Bank of Canada opened in Saskatoon, Sask. Affiliated with the TD and begun with $2 million of start-up capital provided by the Sask. Indian Equity Foundation (SIEF), the bank included branches in Chisasibi, Que. (opened July 1998) and Walpole Is., southwestern Ont. (opened

Mar. 1999). The bank was created to service individuals and First Nations businesses, and be the institute of choice for land claims money.

Sept. 30 France cancelled plans to issue a postage stamp commemorating former president Charles de Gaulle's 1967 visit to Que., where he buoyed separatist hopes with his Montreal city hall "Vive le Québec Libre!" speech.

Also in Sept.
• The Innocence Project was launched at Osgoode Hall, York U. The innovative student program, formed under the directorship of Professors Dianne Martin and Alan Young, offers DNA testing and other new evidence-gathering legal services on behalf of convicts who claim justice had been denied them.

Oct. 2 Canada recalled its ambassador to Israel when it was discovered that 2 Israeli intelligence men, working under forged Canadian passports, tried unsuccessfully to assassinate a Hamas leader in Jordan. Long-held international respect for the Canadian passport was irreparably damaged. The ambassador returned Oct. 10 following an official apology.

• Ottawa gave the green light to Cardinal River Coals to establish 26 open-pit mines, stretching 23 km by 3.5 km along the border of Jasper National Park, south of Hinton. The decision was upheld on a technicality in a federal court June 12, 1998. In 2000, following widespread international pressure and a drop in coal prices, Cardinal announced it would postpone the project indefinitely.

Oct. 7 NB Premier Frank McKenna, premier since 1987, announced his resignation, effective Oct. 13. He was replaced by interim leader Ray Frenette.

Oct. 9 The Supreme Court of Canada ruled that BC's refusal to provide sign-language interpreters for deaf patients during medical treatments violated equality health care guarantees.

Oct. 13 A sightseeing bus full of senior citizens ran off the road and plunged 20 m into a ravine near Les Eboulements, north of Quebec City; 43 people died and 5 were injured in the Thanksgiving Day tragedy. It was the worst road accident in Canada.

Oct. 14 McMaster graduate and Timmons, Ont., native Myron Scholes (b 1941) won the Nobel Prize in Economics for groundbreaking work in derivative formulas. Scholes was a professor at Stanford U., California.

Oct. 17 Forty thousand protestors from businesses throughout Windsor, Ont., shut down the city for the day to protest Premier Harris's plans to cut $8 billion from the Ont. budget. An estimated $5 billion had already been shaved from provincial spending since Harris came to power in 1995.

Oct. 23 Standard and Poor's upped Alb.'s credit rating from AA to AA-plus, the highest in the country.

Oct. 26 Jacques Villeneuve became the first Canadian to win the overall Formula One championship by finishing 3rd in a race in Jerez, Spain.

Oct. 27 The Toronto Stock Exchange dropped 434.25 points, or 6.17%, its most dramatic decline since Oct. 19, 1987, when it dropped 11.3%.

• The largest teachers' strike in Canada began as 126,000 Ont. primary- and secondary-school teachers walked off the job protesting Tory Bill 160. The bill would centralize education powers within ministry bodies, extend the school year, reduce teacher preparation time, allow non-certified teachers into the classroom and remove principals and vice-principals from teachers' unions; 2.1 million children were effected. The strike ended Nov. 10 with Bill 160 still before the legislature. It passed by a vote of 81–48 on Dec. 12.

Oct. 31 The Supreme Court ruled 7–2 that a pregnant woman cannot be forced to undergo treatment to prevent harm to the fetus, arguing that a fetus was not a person under the law. The ruling was made in the case of a pregnant Winnipeg woman who was ordered by the Man. Court of Queen's Bench to undergo treatment for solvent abuse in Aug. 1996. The woman was already the mother of three, two of whom had brain damage.

Also in Oct.

• Alb.'s 1st private hospital, the Health Resources Group (HRG) hospital, operating out of the old Calgary Grace, began treating patients.

• Shania Twain (b 1965) released her 3rd album, *Come On Over*, which sold over 34 million copies (surpassing even the previous best-selling female country album, *Patsy Cline's Greatest Hits*), making the Timmins, Ont., native the most successful solo female recording artist in history. (Her self-titled 1st album was released Apr. 20, 1993, her ground-breaking 2nd album, *The Woman in Me*, Feb. 7, 1995.) *Come On Over* went platinum an incredible 21 times in Canada, and exceeded platinum sales in 31 other countries. Twain would go on to release another hit album, *UP!*, on Nov. 19, 2002, and take home an entire spectrum of pop and country music awards, including several Junos and Grammys.

Nov. 5 Cap-Rouge near Quebec City was the epicentre of an earthquake measuring 5.2 on the Richter scale. Tremors were felt in NB. Quebec City had last been hit by a Richter 5.9 quake in Nov. 1988.

Nov. 13 Colorado Rockies outfielder Larry Walker (b 1966) of Maple Ridge, BC, was selected MVP of the National League. Walker produced some of the best numbers in the history of baseball: a .366 batting average, 49 home runs, 130 RBI, 409 total bases, including 99 extra base hits, and 143 runs. He also stole an incredible 33 bases. However, Walker lost the 1997 Lionel Conacher Award for top Canadian Male Athlete of the Year to Jacques Villeneuve, who raced his car to Europe's 1997 Formula 1 Championship. The vote was 260–239, the outcome considered by many one of the most baffling in Canadian sports history. In what was generally considered a sheepish concession, Walker was awarded the 1998 Conacher after winning the National League batting crown with a .363 average the following Major League Baseball season.

Nov. 15 The 1st toll section on the Trans-Canada Highway was opened in NS. The 45-km stretch was known as Cobequid Pass.

Nov. 19 Over 45,000 Canada Post workers went on strike over wages, job security and changes to letter-carrier routes. They were legislated back to work on Dec. 3, with a 5.15% wage increase over 3 years.

• Two Toronto GO trains collided at Union Station, downtown Toronto, injuring over 100 passengers.

Nov. 25 Dozens of students were pepper-sprayed and arrested by the RCMP while protesting a motorcade of leaders attending the Asia and Pacific Economic Cooperation (APEC) conference at the U. of BC. The RCMP began its probe into the incident Oct. 2, 1998. Students walked out of the investigation Oct. 15 because they were not given compensation for legal expenses. Solicitor Gen. Andy Scott then resigned as chair Nov. 23 after being accused of making prejudicial comments about the police. He was replaced by Ted Hughes who released the final report Aug. 6, 2001. It indicated that the federal govt did not act to influence the actions of the RCMP nor did it dictate how the RCMP controlled the crowd. Hughes did, however, state that the police "did not meet an acceptable and expected standard of competence and professionalism" that day.

Nov. 26 The Commission of Inquiry on the Blood System in Canada (the Krever Report) issued its final report (an interim report was tabled Feb. 15, 1995). It showed that HIV and hepatitis C infection, caused by contamination of the Canadian blood supply between 1978 and 1985, could have been prevented had the Red Cross warned recipients about the possible health risks. It also stated the Red Cross had been too slow to test for HIV contamination. It recommended the creation of a new blood supply agency using stringent controls and maintaining a database of information on all blood donors and recipients. Earlier, on Oct. 8, 1997, Ont. Court Justice Stephen Borins accused the Red Cross of negligence for not warning recipients about the risks associated with its blood supply. This 1st legal ruling against the Red Cross opened a floodgate of lawsuits, which eventually forced the agency to pursue, and receive, bankruptcy protection July 20, 1998.

Dec. 1 A provincial inquiry into the Westray, NS, mine disaster that resulted in 26 deaths May 9, 1992, was released. Headed by Justice Peter Richard, the report stated that the disaster could have been prevented had govt regulators managed the mine according to code. Blame was pointed at mine managers who ignored safety issues related to roofing supports, and also, the airborne dusts and methane buildups that fuelled the explosion.

Dec. 1–11 One hundred sixty nations from around the world attended the 10-day World Environment Summit in Kyoto, Japan. On the table was the Kyoto Protocol, an international agreement requiring developing countries to strictly curtail greenhouse-gas emissions. Canada signed the Protocol on Mar. 28, 1998, and ratified it Dec. 17, 2002; 120 parties had ratified the agreement by Dec. 2003.

Dec. 3 One hundred twenty countries in Ottawa signed an international treaty banning antipersonnel land mines. Canada was the 1st country to sign and the 1st country to ratify the treaty. The US, Russia, China and India did not commit. Over 100 million land mines were buried worldwide in 1997; an estimated 26,000 people were killed each year because of them. On Dec. 10, Foreign Affairs Minister Lloyd Axworthy was nominated for the Nobel Peace Prize for his involvement in the treaty.

Dec. 11 In a landmark decision (the Delgamuukw decision), the Supreme Court ruled that the Canadian Constitution protected Aboriginal title to land, and that oral histories could be used as a bona fide basis for Native land claims. The case involved the Gitsxan and Wet'suwet'en bands of BC, who argued that their right to land was never extinguished when the British established sovereignty in the 1700s, and they could prove through oral histories that the land they claimed was in fact their ancestral property.

Dec. 12 Indian Affairs Minister Jane Stewart (b 1955) gave the Osoyoo First Nation in southern BC $10 million in compensation for 1,700 ha of Osoyoo land mistakenly sold to Justice J.C. Hayes during the 1870s.

Dec. 13 Montreal boxer Otis Grant (b 1967) won the world middleweight crown, defeating hometown favourite Ryan Rhodes in a unanimous decision in Sheffield, England.

Dec. 14 *The Sweet Hereafter*, a film by Atom Egoyan, won 8 Genies. The work also premiered at the 50th annual Cannes International Film Festival and was honoured with the International Critics' Prize, the Ecumenical Jury Award and the Grand Prix — the highest international award ever won by a Canadian film. Egoyan was also nominated for an Academy Award for Best Director and Adapted Screenplay.

Dec. 22 Dr. Maurice Genereux was the 1st physician in Canada convicted on charges of assisted suicide. Genereux was sentenced in May 1998 to 2 years less a day in prison, plus probation, after admitting he helped 2 HIV-positive patients commit suicide.

Dec. 29 The loonie dipped to 69.46 cents US, its lowest since it reached 69.13 cents on Feb. 4, 1986.

1997–1998 Canada's weather was altered by the most influential of the 12 El Niño patterns to affect Canada in the last 50 years. An El Niño event occurs every 2–7 years and can last from 12–18 months. During an El Niño, winds that normally blow west across the Pacific toward Australia slow down or reverse direction, causing warm water to move east toward South America. The subsequent air-bound moisture and heat can spawn extreme weather as far north as Canada, such as the dry heat that aggravated fires in Alb. in 1998, or the 1998 ice storm in Ont. and Que.

Also in 1997

• Six percent of all Canadian families with young children had stay-at-home dads.

• 87,200 tonnes of fish were "harvested" from Canada's aquaculture industry, worth $388 million.

• Canadian cranberry producers had nearly 2,000 ha under cultivation; 75% of these farms were in BC, 18% in Que. and the remainder in NS, Nfld., Ont., PEI and NB.

• Commercial nuclear power was generated in only 3 provinces: NB, Que. and Ont. Nuclear power represented 21% of the NB power supply, 3% of the Que. supply and 48% of the Ont. supply — or all together, 14% of the total Canadian supply.

• Que. became the 1st province to offer subsidized daycare, for $5 a day. In 2001, BC would activate its program for children between 6 and 12, for $7 a day.

• The nation's 1st direct-to-home satellite networks, ExpressVu Inc. and Star Choice Television Network, went into operation. Custom packages ranged from $7.95 to $45.95 per month.

• The 1997 harp seal quota was raised from 250,000 animals to 275,000; the hooded seal quota was frozen at 8,000. The quota was raised in 2003 to bring the maximum annual harp seal kill to 350,000 animals or a total of 975,000 between 2003–2005 inclusive.

• The BC govt passed legislation creating a protected greenspace called Muskwa Kechika, a 4.4-million ha wilderness reserve in the northern Rockies. In Mar. 2001, the area was expanded to 6.4 million ha. At twice the size of Vancouver Is., Muskwa was the largest protected space in BC.

• The Ont. govt reported that Ontario Hydro lost a record $6.3 billion over the fiscal year.

• Canada Post handled 10.9 billion pieces of mail over the fiscal year.

• Michael Adams, pollster and president of Environics Research Group Ltd., published the best-selling book *Sex in the Snow: Canadian Social Values at the End of the Millennium*.

• Ken Oppel published the children's novel *Silverwing*, a fantasy about bats.

• Author Barry Broadfoot (1926–2003) published the national best-selling oral history *Ten Lost Years: Memories of the Canadians Who Survived the Depression*.

• Biographer Elspeth Cameron (b 1943) published her own biography, *No Previous Experience: A Memoir of Love and Change*.

• Will Ferguson published his humorous book *Why I Hate Canadians*. It was followed with a sequel, *How to Be a Canadian* (2001).

• Singer-songwriter Chantal Kreviazuk (b 1973) released her double-platinum debut album *Under These Rocks and Stones*.

• Calgary's Muttart Art Gallery featured a retrospective of Aboriginal artist and curator Johanne Cardinal-Shubert (b 1942). The exhibit then travelled across the country for another 3 years.

• The base salary for MPs was $64,400, with an accompanying tax-free expense account of $21,300.

• Creditors seized Troy Hurtubise's (b 1963) 66-kg robo-cop-like anti-grizzly bear suit, designed for up-close study of the giant bears without fear of mauling. Hurtubise became an instant celebrity when the NFB produced *Project Grizzly*, a 1996 documentary on the creation and testing of the suit. The film included the bedecked Hurtubise being struck by a moving car and beaten with sledgehammers to determine the suit's effectiveness against potential attacks from the unpredictable omnivore.

• Total profits of Canada's Big Six banks soared to an unprecedented $7.4 billion for the fiscal year, almost 20% higher than in 1996. The Royal Bank — the country's largest — showed the highest corporate profit ever recorded in Canadian history to date — $1.68 billion.

• Approximately 1,000 Czechoslovakian Gypsies applied for refugee status in Canada.

• Celtic singer and composer Lorena McKennitt (b 1957) was awarded *Billboard Magazine's* International Achievement Award. As producer on her own record label, Quinlan Road, she released many internationally acclaimed albums, including *The Book of Secrets* (1997), *A Winter Garden…*(1995), *The Mask & The Mirror* (1994) and *The Visit* (1992).

1998

Jan. 1 Seventy-two Ont. district school boards replaced 129 school boards. In 1967, there had been approximately 1,500 school boards in the province.

Jan. 3–4 Three separate avalanches in the South Columbia Mountains, BC, claimed the lives of 9 skiers and snowmobilers.

Jan. 4 Fifty-seven elected councillors were sworn in at city hall, Toronto, marking the political beginnings of the new megacity. Comprising the former municipalities of North York, Etobicoke, Scarborough, York, East York and Toronto, the new city was the 5th largest in North America with a population exceeding 2.4 million. Colourful former North York Mayor Mel Lastman was elected 1st megacity mayor Nov. 10, 1997. He had been North York's mayor for 25 years. The new city council was the largest in North America.

Jan. 5 Defence Minister Art Eggleton agreed to purchase 15 EH–101 Cormorant helicopters from GKN Westland of Britain and Agusta SpA of Italy for $790 million (the same firm who received a kill fee of $473.5 million when PM Chrétien cancelled the Mulroney deal in 1993). The new Cormorants would replace the 34-year-old search-and-rescue Labrador fleet by the end of 2003.

Jan. 5–10 Record amounts of freezing rain — 85 mm total and 68 mm in 80 hours — coated Eastern Ont., Western Que. and the extreme northeastern US with heavy, wet ice, toppling swaths of trees and knocking out hydro lines over much of the region. Over 1 million households (approximately 4 million people) were without power, some for over 3 weeks. The RCMP, 16,000 regular and reserve military personnel and thousands of civilian volunteers worked to restore power, provide general aid and remove fallen trees crossing roads and piled over cars, homes and fences. During the first few days of the ice storm Health Canada provided 85,088 stretchers, 24,566 beds and 75,900 blankets throughout Ont. and Que.

Jan. 7 Alan Eagleson was sentenced to 18 months in jail by an Ont. Court, General Division, judge for defrauding the NHL players' pension fund. The former founder of the NHL hockey players' union and 1972 Summit Series organizer had been indicted on 30 similar counts of fraud by a US grand jury 4 years earlier. Eagleson was disbarred by the Law Society of Upper Canada on Jan. 22, and subsequently stripped of his Order of Canada honours.

Jan. 8 PM Jean Chrétien appointed Toronto lawyer and constitutional expert Ian Binnie (b 1939) to the Supreme Court of Canada, sparking widespread charges of gender bias. Only 2 women sat on the 9-member Court.

Jan. 22 The BC Supreme Court ruled in favour of 4 U. of BC students who charged that the U. of BC had illegally increased 1996–1997 tuitions through ancillary fees. The ruling forced the university to return over $1 million to 2,500 students.

• The Benevolent and Protective Order of Elks, the nation's largest gender-exclusive fraternity, voted to accept women into the herd. The Order had over 24,000 members and 300 lodges nationwide.

• Louise Frechette (b 1946), deputy minister of national defence and former ambassador to Argentina, was appointed deputy secretary gen. of the UN, the second-highest position in the UN and the 1st Canadian to reach as far.

• Calgary-based energy firms Nova and Trans-Canada PipeLines agreed to a $15.6 billion merger, the largest to date involving any 2 Canadian companies. The deal united $7.02 billion in assets, 6,300 employees and annual revenues exceeding $16.6 billion. The name, TransCanada PipeLines, was retained.

Jan. 23 Jean Chrétien became the 1st Canadian PM to visit Poland. He made the stop while in Europe to pay official respects to those murdered at the Nazi concentration camps of Auschwitz and Birkenau during WW II.

• The Royal Bank and the Bank of Montreal announced plans to merge, bringing together 17 million customers and over $40 billion in stock-related value. On Apr. 16, the Canadian Imperial Bank of Commerce (CIBC) and the Toronto-Dominion Bank announced a merger deal worth $47 billion. In Dec., federal Finance Minister Paul Martin declared the proposed mergers void, arguing that such a concentration of economic power was "not in the best interest of Canadians."

Jan. 26 Over 80 mm of rain caused major flood damage throughout the Maritimes, raising river levels and causing evacuations in Truro, Sydney, Lower Sackville, Fredericton and Saint John.

• Toronto-based Noranda Inc. agreed to sell its 49.5% share of Calgary-based Norcen Energy Resources Ltd., a leading gas and oil exploration company, to Union Pacific Resources Group of Fort Worth, Texas. Union Pacific, the biggest domestic oil driller in the US, paid $3.7 billion for the share — in cash.

Feb. 2 Though he had been a local attraction for close to 15 years, it wasn't until 1998 that a NS groundhog named Shubenacadie Sam scampered onto the North American weather-prediction stage and laid claim to the fact that NS's time zone gave him a 1-hour jump on both Ont.'s Wiarton Willie and Pennsylvania's Punxsutawney Phil.

• The remote community of Fort Chipewyan in northern Alb. was cut off after unseasonably warm (El Niño) weather melted the ice road connecting it and Fort McMurray, 273 km to the south. ("Fort Chip" was connected each mid-Dec. through Mar. with a winter road that included crossings over the frozen Athabasca R.) Since transport trucks could no longer reach the community, supplies had to be flown in and food costs doubled overnight. Stocks of gasoline and propane ran low, and there was concern the town might run out of heating fuel before the road was re-frozen and re-stored.

Feb. 6 Zellers, a Hudson's Bay subsidiary, purchased the beleaguered K-Mart Canada Co. and its 112 outlets for $240 million. K-Mart's competitiveness had eroded since the introduction of Arkansas-based Wal-Mart in 1994.

Feb. 7–Feb. 22 At the Olympic Winter Games in Nagano, Japan, Canada won 4 gold, 5 silver and 4 bronze medals. Highlights included youthful Ross Rebagliati (b 1971), who won the snowboard slalom event but was disqualified after testing positive for marijuana. Rebagliati was later re-instated when it was determined marijuana was not on the list of prohibited performance-enhancing substances. Catriona Le May Doan took gold in 500-m speed skating; Dave MacEachern (b 1967) and Pierre Lueders (b 1970) gold in 2-man bobsleigh; Anne Perreault gold in short-track 500-m speed

skating; and gold for the men's short-track relay speed skating team. And finally, after winning the Canadian and world titles three times during the 1990s, Sandra Schmirler's Sask. team won the 1st ever Olympic gold in women's curling.

Feb. 12 The Toronto Maple Leafs, headed by grocery-store nabob Steve Stavro, purchased the Toronto Raptors of the NBA, Toronto's historic Union Station and the under-construction, 20,000-seat Air Canada Centre for $500 million. The purchase ensured that Leafs and Raptors played under one roof.

• The St. Hubert, Que., McDonald's restaurant was closed after two-thirds of its teenage employees voted to join the local teamsters union. The site would have been the 1st unionized McDonald's in North America.

Feb. 16 On the request of the federal Liberal govt, the Supreme Court of Canada began hearings to determine whether Que. could legally — and unilaterally — secede from the Dominion. Matthew Coon Come, grand chief of the northern Cree, told the Court that it was the duty of the Canadian govt to ensure that Cree land, some 400,000 km^2 in Que., remain in Canada should Quebecers vote to separate. The Bloc Québécois led a demonstration of 1,000 nationalists outside the Court to protest the validity of the hearings. Court conclusions were issued Aug. 19.

Feb. 17 Statistics Canada released data based on answers to controversial 1996 census question No. 19, showing 11.2% of Canadians were "visible minorities." According to the census, a visible minority was classified as someone who was neither "white" nor "Aboriginal." Other statistics released showed that the percentage of visible minorities in Toronto was 32%; Vancouver, 31%; Calgary, 16%; Edmonton, 14%; Ottawa-Hull, 12%; Montreal, 12%; and Winnipeg, 11%.

Feb. 19 The Senate voted unanimously to suspend 73-year-old Senator Andrew Thompson (b 1924), who had attended the Senate a total of 12 times since 1990. The senator's $64,000-a-year salary was also later suspended, as was the standard $10,000-a-year tax-free expense allowance. Thompson, however, remained eligible for a $50,000-a-year pension. The vote to suspend the truant senator was attended by half the Upper Chamber.

Feb. 24 Finance Minister Paul Martin tabled the nation's 1st balanced budget since 1970. Highlights included a $2.5 billion Canada Millennium Scholarship Foundation, providing 100,000 post-secondary scholarships a year, for 10 years, to children of low-income earners.

Feb. 25 Seventy cm of snow fell on southern Man. and Sask.

Feb. 26 The 3 surviving Dionne quintuplets — Annette, Cécile and Yvonne — rejected Ont. Attorney Gen. Charles Harnick's compensation package of $2,000 each a month for life. The quintuplets, born May 28, 1934, were removed from their home by the government and placed on display as a tourist attraction in North Bay, Ont. for nice and a half years. It was estimated that the quintuplets generated over $500 million for the province. The quints lived in Montreal on a combined fixed income of $746 a month and accepted a renewed package from Premier Harris on Mar. 6, worth $4 million, tax free.

Feb. 27 A Halifax judge ruled that there was not enough evidence to convict Dr. Nancy Morisson, a respirologist, of murder in connection to the mercy killing of throat cancer patient, 65-year-old Paul Mills. Morrison had been accused of administering nitroglycerine and potassium chloride to Mills after he had been taken off life support.

Mar. 3 Montreal-based passenger and recreation vehicle manufacturer Bombardier Inc., with 46,000 employees worldwide, landed a $2 billion contract to build passenger trains for Britain. The company used only European shops to build the units. On Oct 1, fortunes were furthered when the firm was awarded a $1 billion contract from Delta Airlines to build thirty 50-seat and twenty 70-seat Canadian Regional Jets (CRJs). On Nov. 20, Bombardier, with Montreal-based Power Corp., was awarded another rail-car contract, this time with China's national railway, worth $550 million.

Mar. 4 Lawyer and educator Mary Ellen Turpel-Lafond (b 1963) became the 1st Aboriginal woman to be appointed a provincial court of Sask. justice.

Mar. 5 Ralph Klein's Alb. caucus agreed to allow Albertans to elect 2 senators-in-waiting in the next provincewide municipal election. Klein proposed that the PM appoint the province's next senator from this list.

Mar. 6 A three-and-half-month-long strike involving 900 workers at a Maple Leaf Foods plant in Burlington, Ont., ended as workers agreed to a $6-an-hour wage cut. The company had threatened to close the plant otherwise.

• BC's 7,500 doctors staged the 1st of three 1-day work stoppages (the others occurred Mar. 13 and 31) to protest a workload estimated to represent 14 unpaid workdays per doctor per year. The walkout was BC's first doctor strike.

Mar. 9 Nfld. Premier Brian Tobin and Que. Premier Lucien Bouchard signed an agreement to begin construction on a $12 billion, 3,500-megawatt (MW) hydro project in the Muskrat Gull Is. region of Churchill R., downriver from the existing Churchill Falls power plant. On Aug. 1, 2002, the two provinces agreed to negotiations in principle, with Innu negotiations still active.

Mar. 10 A combination of rain, melting snow and ice jams caused rivers to overflow throughout south NB, including the Magaguadavic, Nerepis, Saint John, Kennebecasis and Nashwaak Rivers. Roads and driveways were washed out, with rising waters causing mudslides, flooded homes and stranded families. The historic Welsford covered bridge, built in 1921, was also destroyed. Damages exceeded $4 million.

Mar. 12 Waterloo, Ont.-based Mutual Life of Canada purchased Metropolitan Life Insurance of Canada for $1.2 billion. The deal gave Mutual a sales staff of 3,100 and assets exceeding $49.5 billion, making the firm Canada's 2nd largest insurance company next to GreatWest Lifeco Inc.

Mar. 17 Thirty-nine cm of snow fell on Calgary, breaking the city's 100-year-old Mar. snowfall record. The same storm dumped a record 60 cm on Cochrane, Alb., generating 80-cm-high drifts in neighbouring Morley.

Mar. 20 NB fisheries minister ordered the destruction of 1.2 million live aqua-farm-raised salmon, and the relocation of 14 aqua farms from Lime Kiln Bay, Bliss Harbour and Grand Manan's Seal Cove, after some of the stocks were found with infectious salmon anemia. A $2.5 million compensation package was subsequently provided.

Mar. 23 James Cameron's (b 1954) Hollywood blockbuster *Titanic* won 11 Academy Awards.

Mar. 24 Yvonne Attwell became the 1st black woman elected to the NS legislature. The provincial election also included a rare split in the number of seats won, with both the Liberals and NDP taking 19. (Tories took 14 seats). Custom dictated that the incumbent party, in this case the Liberals under Premier Russell MacLellan, remain the governing party.

Mar. 26 Residents of Banff, Alb., voted to increase commercial development by 60,387 m², making way for new malls and the extension of existing commercial sites. Federal Heritage Minister Sheila Copps canned the plans amidst an international outcry to halt further development in the nation's 1st national park. Copps had also stifled an earlier Banff commercial-development proposal in Sept. 1997.

Mar. 27 Federal Health Minister Allan Rock presented a $1.1 billion compensation package to the estimated 20,000 Canadians who contracted hepatitis-C from tainted blood between 1986 and 1990. The package included $800 million from the federal govt and $300 million from the provinces, giving victims a lump sum of between $22,000 and $30,000. In return, recipients agreed not to sue the govts or the Red Cross. An estimated 5,000–7,000 affected before 1986 and after 1990 accepted a $79 million compensation package for the federal govt on Aug. 30, 2000. The compensation ended legal action against the Red Cross. The Ont. and Que. govts agreed later in 1998 to contribute $200 million and $75 million, respectively, to aid those who contracted hepatitis-C before 1986.

Spring Canadian Air Force Sgt. Michael Kipling refused an order to take an anthrax vaccine while on duty during the second Gulf War in Kuwait. Some 400 other Canadian soldiers obeyed military orders and were vaccinated against the deadly biological virus. Kipling believed the vaccine to be unsafe and resigned his commission in an attempt to avoid court martial. In spring 2000, a military court ruled that Kipling was within his Charter rights and acquitted him of all charges.

Apr. 1 A week of severe flooding began in southern Que., as heavy snow melts and ice jams raised water levels in 11 rivers, flooding 113 communities. Two died and more than 4,000 houses were damaged.

Apr. 2 The Supreme Court of Canada handed down its decision in the Delwin Vriend case, ruling that the exclusion of anti-discrimination measures, based on sexual orientation, from the Alberta Individual Rights Protection Act, was a violation of the Canadian Charter of Rights and Freedoms. Vriend, a former lab instructor at King's U. College, was fired Jan. 28, 1991, because he was gay. The high court decision caused waves of anti-gay Alb. protest, including television, newspaper and radio advertisements placed by local church groups.

• The 313-member Royal Newfoundland Constabulary (RNC) was given provincial approval to wear sidearms. Officers had previously kept the weapons in their cruisers. Nfld. officers had been the last in North America to go about their business with little more than their wits.

Apr. 3 Canada and 25 other nations voted at a UN Commission on Human Rights to abolish the death penalty worldwide.

Apr. 7 The Canadian flag was officially flown at Quebec city hall for the first time since the collapse of the Meech Lake Accord in 1990. The flag was raised after the federal govt implemented a rule requiring all federally supported buildings to fly the red maple leaf.

Apr. 17–May 3 Astronaut Dr. Dafydd R. William (b 1954) became the 1st Saskatchewaner in space when he served as Mission Specialist 3 on STS–90 Neurolab for NASA.

Apr. 22 The NB govt ordered Native loggers off all Crown property. The move came after the NB Court of Appeal overturned a Queen's Bench decision to give the province's Native loggers unlimited access to NB Crown land. The order sparked a summer-long dispute, with Natives blockading non-Native access to forests, and provincial govt seizing 11 Native trucks carrying fresh-cut lumber.

Apr. 24 A committee on the status of endangered wildlife in Canada increased its list of jeopardized species to 307. Among those considered vulnerable were the northern cod and five-lined skink; endangered, the northern Leopard frog, hotwater mollusc and sage grouse; and threatened, the hairy prairie clover, black rat snake, 2 varieties of stickleback and the Lake Utopia dwarf smelt. The eastern cougar was removed from the committee's list of jeopardized species.

Apr. 26–28 Jean Chrétien became the 1st PM to visit Cuba since Pierre Elliott Trudeau in 1976.

Apr. 30 Thirty-nine-year-old former federal Progressive Conservative MP Jean Charest (b 1958) became the 1st unchallenged leader of the Que. Liberal Party. He replaced Daniel Johnson, who announced his retirement Mar. 2. Johnson had taken over from Premier Bourassa in 1993 but was defeated 8 months later by Jacques Parizeau and the Parti Québécois.

Also in Apr.
• The BC govt raised the nation's highest provincial minimum wage from $7 to $7.15.

May 8 Calgary's historic 76-year-old Palace Theatre reopened as a 1,200-seat nightclub after an 8-year, $4.1 million renovation. William "Bible Bill" Aberhart made his first broadcast from the Palace in 1925.

May 28 Comedic actor Phil Hartman (b 1948–1998) of Brantford, Ont., was shot and killed by his 3rd wife, in Los Angeles. He was 49. Hartman was a former cast member of *Saturday Night Live* and a regular on the television sitcom *NewsRadio*. He is also remembered as the voice of Troy McClure, an archetypical past-his-prime celebrity featured on the hit cartoon series *The Simpsons.*

May 29 The Supreme Court of Canada ruled 5–3 to void a 1993 federal law banning the publication of political opinion polls within 72 hours of an election.

Also in May
• High winds and dry conditions fanned over 40 fires that raged through Alb.; 2,300 people from Swan Hills were evacuated twice, on May 5 and May 13.

• The Ont. Conservative govt gave permission to Nova Group of Sault Ste. Marie to syphon off 60 million gallons of L. Superior water per year for sale to Asia. The permission was voided following an immediate public outcry.

June 7 Indian Affairs Minister Jane Stewart made a "Statement of Reconciliation" before a gathering of Native leaders in Ottawa, expressing "profound regret for past actions" related to the treatment of Native Peoples at residential schools between 1880 and 1960. The minister also set aside a $350 million healing fund for the victims, and another $250 million to promote Native economic development. The deal was accepted at a conference of the Assembly of First Nations in Mar.

June 9 Three died and 17 were injured after a subcontractor cut into a gas line at a soup kitchen in downtown Montreal. The resulting explosion tore the face off the building. Forty people escaped the building just before the explosion.

June 10 MacMillan Bloedel Ltd., BC's largest logging firm, declared it would phase out all clear cutting and cease cutting in old-growth BC forests.

• Ann Margaret Dickey of Oromocto, NB, held a press conference, stating she had been sexually abused during basic training at a Canadian Forces school in St. Jean, Que., in 1996. The press conference came in the wake of more than 40 accusations of sexual misconduct among members of Canada's military; 6,800 women and 60,500 men made up the Canadian Armed Forces.

June 11 The federal govt agreed to provide $925 million to the Atlantic and BC fisheries to compensate for dwindling catches and reduced quotas. The Atlantic fisheries received $550 million; the BC fisheries $375 million.

June 18 A commuter plane commissioned by General Electric, Propair Flight 420, caught fire soon after takeoff from Dorval Airport, Montreal, and crashed at Montreal's Mirabel Airport. All 11 aboard were killed.

June 19 Gillian Guess was found guilty by a BC court of obstruction of justice and given 18 months in prison. In 1995, Guess had an affair with Peter Gill, who was standing trial for murder. Guess was on the jury of the Gill murder case.

June 22 A 500-page Alb. environment report revealed that only 10% of the province's 350,000 km² boreal forest remained in a wilderness state, the result of oil production, agriculture, mining and logging.

• BC became the 1st province to ensure that its civil service pension benefits covered same-sex couples.

• Palaeontologist Dr. Philip Currie, dinosaur curator at the Royal Tyrrell Museum in Alb., together with Chinese and American colleagues, revealed fossil evidence showing an evolutionary link between dinosaurs and birds. The fossils added weight to a theory suggesting some dinosaurs did not become extinct, but rather, evolved into birds.

June 23 BC Liberal MPP Paul Reitsma resigned after admitting he had written phony letters — under an assumed name — to local newspapers, praising his political acumen and belittling opponents. By resigning, Reitsma avoided the possibility of becoming the 1st Canadian politician to be re-called by his constituents. (BC introduced the nation's 1st recall law Feb. 24, 1995.)

June 25 Peter Frumusa was released from jail by an Ont. General Court justice, who overruled his two 1989 convictions for the 1st degree murders of his in-laws. The 1989 case against Frumusa was made on circumstantial evidence alone, which included a statement by a known jailhouse informant. Frumusa had been in prison 8 years.

• Canada celebrated its homegrown artists, writers, entertainment and sports figures with the official opening of the country's Canadian Walk of Fame in Toronto. In an afternoon ceremony, 14 stars resembling stylized maple leaves were unveiled, embedded in the sidewalk, along a section of King St. in the heart of the city's theatre district. The first

14 Canadians recognized at the inaugural of the Walk were rocker Brian Adams; Pierre Berton; comedians John Candy, Rich Little (b 1938) and Jim Carrey; pianist Glenn Gould; filmmaker Norman Jewison; ballerina Karen Kain; folk artist Gordon Lightfoot; singer Anne Murray; defenceman Bobby Orr; actor Christopher Plummer (b 1929); figure skater Barbara Ann Scott; and race-car driver Jacques Villeneuve.

Also in June

• The Japan Sumo Association staged its 1st Canadian sumo wrestling (sumo basho) tournament at Vancouver's Pacific Coliseum. The event lasted 2 days.

July 20 Conrad Black's Southam Inc. and Sun Media Corp. made a major swap. Southam received $150 million and 80% interest in the *Financial Post*, a paper with a national circulation of over 100,000. In return, Sun Media took over 4 of Southam's Ont. newspapers: the *Hamilton Spectator*, the *Kitchener-Waterloo Record*, *Cambridge Reporter* and the *Guelph Daily Mercury*.

July 22 An Ont. General Court ruling gave the province's Catholic school boards the right to tax Catholics whose children attended their schools. The court ruled that provincial govt taxation violated the Catholic school boards' right to function independently.

July 31 The 75-year-old Alberta Wheat Pool, the 2nd-largest grain handler in the country, merged with the 73-year-old Manitoba Pool Elevator, the country's 5th-largest grain handler, to form Winnipeg-based Agricore. Agricore would be given the green light by the Canadian Competition Bureau to purchase Winnipeg-based United Grain Growers (UGG) in 2001. Under the terms, Agricore divested itself of 7 western grain elevators and another elevator at the Port of Vancouver. The purchase of UGG made Agricore the leading agribusiness in the country.

Aug. 7 The Bank of Canada purchased $500 million in Canadian currency to help prop up the falling Canadian dollar. Within 35 minutes, the dollar rose from 65.15 cents US to 66.17. However, on Aug. 27, the dollar plunged to a record low 63.31 cents US.

Aug. 9 Fire destroyed 24 homes in Salmon Arm, BC, forcing the evacuation of over 7,000 residents. Twelve helicopters, 2 water bombers, 100 pieces of heavy equipment, 50 fire trucks, 100 soldiers and 300 firefighters were required to get the 5,000-ha fire under control. The Salmon Arm fire was only one of 700 that swept through BC during the month, destroying over 55,000 ha of extremely dry forest and grassland. A Silver Creek fire, which started Aug. 2, was so hot that water dumped by bombers vaporized long before it reached the ground. Also during Aug, there were another 100 forest fires in Alb., 60 in Sask., and 44 in Man. Altogether, some 2,625 firefighters and 200 soldiers were battling blazes across the country, as high winds swept embers over tinder-dry forests and grasslands. By year's end, 4.6 million ha of forest were consumed by fire, twice the yearly average.

Aug. 12 Twelve thousand mourners, including 8,000 Canadian, American, and European police decked out in full regalia, attended the funeral of Toronto Det. Constable Bill Hancox, killed in the line of duty Aug. 5. It was the largest police funeral in Canadian history.

• Natural-gas producer Sunoma Energy Corp. of Calgary began its $385 million takeover of Barrington Petroleum Ltd.

Aug. 19 In a referral case initiated by Attorney Gen. and Minister of Justice Allan Rock, the Supreme Court ruled that Que. could not unilaterally secede from Canada, but must first negotiate a constitutional arrangement for the purpose, should a majority of Quebecers vote to separate.

Sept. 1 The Canadian Blood Service bought the beleaguered Canadian Red Cross for $132.9 million.

• The hopeful and the curious converged on a Tim Hortons doughnut shop in Bras d'Or, NS, after reports that an image of Jesus Christ had appeared on an outside wall of the building. The crowd reached 4,000 by day's end.

Sept. 2 Two thousand one hundred Air Canada pilots began a nationwide strike after airline officials and union leaders failed to come to an agreement on a new labour contract. The 13-day work stoppage cost the airline $300 million.

• The Supreme Court of Canada ruled that those with sexually transmittable diseases must first inform their partners before engaging in unprotected sex, or face criminal prosecution. The ruling was made in the case of Henry Cuerriers of Squamish, BC, who failed to inform 2 women, with whom he'd had sex 100 times between 1992–1994, that he was HIV positive.

• Geneva-bound Swissair Flight 111 crashed in the waters off Peggy's Cove, NS, killing all 229 aboard. The pilot reported smoke shortly after takeoff from New York City; contact with ground crews was then lost. Rescue workers and fishers spent a sorrowful two weeks combing the waters for bodies and debris, while Nova Scotians attended to grieving family members who flocked to the scene from Europe.

Sept. 3 The *Globe & Mail* reported that the 15-member executive of Stony Nation reserve north of Calgary paid itself $1.4 million tax-free over the previous fiscal year. The reserve, home to 3,300 people, had an unemployment rate of 90%.

Sept. 8 Two thousand Catholic school board teachers in 72 elementary- and high-school districts across Ont. went on strike to protest increases in instructional time that would see each teacher work an extra period a day. Students returned to class Sept. 29 after the Ont. legislature implemented back-to-work legislation; 210,000 students lost 15 days of class.

Sept. 15 Calgary-based Alberta Energy acquired Calgary-based heavy-oil producer Amber Energy for $750 million. The deal, which was completed Oct. 12, raised Alberta Energy's oil and gas production to 85,000 barrels a day.

Sept. 17 PM Jean Chrétien appointed 4 new senators: Joan Fraser (b 1949), former editor-in-chief of the *Montreal Gazette*; Aurélien Gill (b 1933), former director general of Indian affairs; former Edmonton Tory MP Doug Roche (b 1929); and Vivienne Poy (b 1941), the first senator of Chinese descent. The Roche appointment outraged Albertans, who were to elect 2 senators-in-waiting Oct. 19, from which, Albertans expected, Chrétien would choose their representative. In a strongly worded letter to the

PM, Premier Ralph Klein stated, "You may have seriously set back the cause of national renewal."

Sept. 22 Ten thousand angry gun owners converged on Parliament Hill to protest Bill C–68, requiring all guns to be registered by 2001.

Oct. 2 A Labrador search-and-rescue helicopter that had taken off from CFB Greenwood, NS, crashed in Marsoui, Que., killing 6 crew members. All were in their thirties. The crash left 12-twin rotor Labradors in operation.

Oct. 4 It took only seconds to turn Calgary's General Hospital into a pile of rubble when the abandoned buildings were imploded in a ceremony watched by hundreds on-site and thousands more on television. The hospital, the 4th of the name, was opened in 1953, but had deteriorated to the point where health authorities insisted it could not be renovated to current medical standards. The Calgary Regional Health Authority announced plans to close the facility in July 1994, and the last patient was discharged in June 1997.

Oct. 6 Canada secured a seat at the UN Security Council for the 1st time since 1985, and the 6th time in the council's history.

Oct. 14 Canada's 1st diamond mine, the Ekati Diamond Mine, located in the Lac de Gras region 300 km northeast of Yellowknife, NWT, opened. The mine, owned by BHP of Australia and Dia Met Minerals Ltd. of Kelowna, BC, was to produce 3.5 million carats a year, or 6% of the world's yearly diamond production. On July 19, 2003, the $1.3 billion Diavik diamond mine also opened in the NWT to recover raw diamonds from a geological formation known as kimberlite pipe located under Lac de Gras. British Rio Tinto owned 60% of the mine; Toronto-based Aber Diamond Corp. owned the remaining 40%. Together with Ekati, the two mines were expected to produce 12% of the world's diamonds, ahead of South Africa, which produced 11%. Two other diamond mines in the NWT, Jericho, owned by Tahera Corp., and Snap L., owned by De Beers Canada Corp., were scheduled to open in 2005 and 2006, respectively.

Oct. 20 Telus Corp, the 3rd largest telecommuni-

cations company in Canada, and BC Telecom Inc., the 2nd largest, agreed to merge in efforts to establish a national communications network to compete with the national Bell network.

Oct. 27 The *National Post* appeared in newsstands across the country for the 1st time. Its front-page headline: "Klein backs unite-the-right movement." Canada's 2nd national daily newspaper cost 50¢ a copy, or $12 a month. Its initial subscription was 175,000, which included 120,000 subscriptions carried over from its predecessor, *The Financial Post*. The Southam paper, owned by media mogul Conrad Black, had start-up costs of $25 million. Don Babick was publisher.

Oct. 28 One day after the *National Post* first hit newsstands, Torstar offered $748 million to take over Sun Media. The Sun board unanimously rejected the offer the following day.

• Toronto City Council declared homelessness a state of emergency, giving it the same priority usually assigned floods and other natural disasters. On any given night, only half of the city's homeless could find accommodation in overcrowded emergency shelters, which were chronically 99% full.

• After serving 9 years as a city councillor, Montreal-born Glen Murray (b 1957) won election as mayor of Winnipeg by a margin of more than 10,000 votes.

Oct. 29 The Ont. legislature voted 53–28 to enact the Energy Competition Act, killing Ontario Hydro's 90-year monopoly over the generation and distribution of the province's power.

Oct. 30 Loblaws Co. Ltd., Canada's largest grocery-store chain, bought Que.'s Provigo, for $1.56 billion. The move gave Loblaws total annual sales of $17 billion.

Nov. 2 Empire Co. Ltd., owner of Sobey's, bought Oshawa Group Ltd., which operated IGA stores nationwide. The move made Sobey's the 2nd-largest grocery-store chain in Canada, next to Loblaws.

Nov. 8 Support workers at Pearson International Airport ended a 38-day strike, accepting a deal raising wages 22–47% over the next 6 years. Computer programmers who made $47,876 a year before the deal would make $70,637 by the end of it.

Nov. 10 Jim Antoine became govt leader of the NWT after former leader Don Morin, who faced conflict-of-interest charges, stepped down.

Nov. 12 The Supreme Court of Canada ruled in the case of a Man. divorce, that stepfathers whose marriages break up have the same financial responsibilities toward their stepchildren as natural fathers.

Nov. 13 BC became the 1st province to sue Canadian cigarette companies. The action was taken to recover annual smoking-related health care costs of $400 million. The lawsuit was rejected by a BC court in 2000 on constitutional grounds; it was refiled in Jan. 2001, and again rejected by the BC Supreme Court June 3, 2003, on the grounds that the provincial govt did not have jurisdiction over international tobacco firms.

Nov. 14 Michel Trudeau (1975–1998), youngest son of Margaret and Pierre Trudeau, died while skiing when an avalanche swept him into Kokanee L., BC. His body was not recovered.

• Former PM Joe Clark beat Sask. organic farmer David Orchard to become leader of the federal Tory party. Clark replaced Jean Charest, who had stepped down to head the Que. Liberal Party. Clark had been out of politics 8 years and last led the PC party in 1983. When the Alb. Tory announced his return to politics on June 25, newspaper columnists, who once dubbed him "Joe Who," renamed him, "Joe Why."

• International Co-operation Minister Diane Marleau (b 1943) pledged $100 million over the next 3 years to the Central American countries of Nicaragua and Honduras, which had been ravaged by Hurricane Mitch. The hurricane resulted in an estimated 10,000 deaths.

Nov. 18 Tara Singh Hayer (1936–1998), Sikh publisher of the *Indo-Canadian Times*, was shot and killed in Surrey, BC. The murder capped off a year of Sikh infighting, which began in Jan. when a bloody riot

erupted in a BC temple over the use and placement of tables and chairs.

• Livent Inc., co-founded by Garth Drabinsky and Myron Gottlieb, filed for bankruptcy protection in a Toronto court. Livent, which produced such acclaimed theatrical productions as *Ragtime*, *Showboat* and *Kiss of the Spider Woman*, had been taken over in May by a group of investors that included Hollywood agent Michael Ovitz. Drabinsky and Gottlieb were kept on, but were suspended Aug. 10 amid allegations of fraud and other accounting irregularities.

Nov. 20 Workers at Abitibi-Consolidated Inc. ended a 5-month-long strike, voting to accept annual wage increases of 2% over 5 yrs. The strike shut down 10 mills.

Nov. 23 A Sask. court of appeal ruled that Robert Latimer must serve a 10-year conviction for the "mercy killing" of his 12-year-old disabled daughter. Latimer had been convicted of 2nd degree murder by a Sask. lower court in 1994. On Feb. 6, 1997, the Supreme Court ordered that he be retried. He was convicted again and sentenced to 2 years less a day on Dec. 1, 1997, but sought an appeal, which led to his 10-year conviction.

Nov. 27 White Rose Crafts and Nursery Sales Ltd., of Unionville, Ont., filed for bankruptcy protection in an Ont. court. The firm, which had 42 outlets, was in debt to the tune of $78.5 million.

Nov. 30 Lucien Bouchard and the Parti Québécois won a majority govt with 75 seats. Jean Charest's Liberals took 48 seats, the Action Democratique 1. The Liberals received 43.71% of the popular vote, the PQ 42.7% and the ADQ 11.78%.

• The temperature in Ottawa hit 16.4°C, 15°C above the capital's norm.

Dec. 6 American farmers at Coutts Crossing on the Alb.–Montana border blockaded trucks carrying farm produce into the US. Farmers complained that the Canadian Wheat Board was dumping wheat into their market, causing prices to plummet.

Dec. 7 Two hundred Kingsville District (Ont.) high-school students walked out of class to protest the Dec. 4 strip search of 20 male students suspected in the theft of $90 from a gym locker. The school's vice-principal and a male teacher who supervised the search were subsequently suspended for 10 days without pay.

Dec. 8 NS Labour Minister Russell Mackinnon told the public that his Liberal govt could not provide a compensation package worth $13 million to surviving family members of those killed in the 1992 Westray mining disaster. The announcement came after the NS legislature rejected the minority Liberal govt's compensation proposal Dec. 3.

Dec. 9 Fifty-year-old Liberal MP Shaughnessy Cohen (1948–1998) collapsed at her desk of a brain hemorrhage during Question Period. The Windsor–St. Clair (Ont.) representative died in hospital.

Dec. 10 The Ont. govt gave $278.5 million to 178 hospitals to cover computer costs related to the upcoming Y2K changeover.

Dec. 11 Richard Pound was named chairman of an IOC (International Olympic Committee) investigatory commission to inquire into reports of unacceptable conduct during the bidding process for the 2002 Olympic Winter Games, won by Salt Lake City. Ten IOC members were either expelled or resigned in Mar. 1999, the result of commission findings.

Dec. 16 The BC Supreme Court overruled a 1997 Surrey school board ban of 3 primary-school books (*Asha's Mum*, *Belinda's Bouquet* and *One Dad, Two Dad, Brown Dad, Blue Dad*), which included same-sex couples.

Dec. 18 Former Liberal premier of NS, Gerald Regan, was acquitted of 8 counts of rape, attempted rape and unlawful confinement in charges involving 3 women.

Dec. 21 Torstar purchased 4 southern Ont. newspapers from Sun Media for $350 million: *the Hamilton Spectator*, the *Kitchener-Waterloo Record*, the *Cambridge Reporter*, and the *Guelph Mercury*.

Dec. 22 A Sault Saint Marie court dismissed 1993 charges against two Métis for unlawfully hunting moose, stating that Ont.'s 22,000 Métis held the same hunting and fishing rights as Aboriginals.

Dec. 25 Cynthia Trudell, born in Saint John, NB, was made chair and president of GM's Saturn Corp., the 1st women to head any division of the big 3 US automakers.

Dec. 31 The federal govt relinquished partial control over the directorship of the Canadian Wheat Board (CWB). Where previously all board of directors had been appointed by the Crown, western grain farmers could now elect 10 of 15 members. The other 5, including the president, would still be govt appointees. The CWB, established in 1935, remained the middle agency between farmer and purchaser with power to set all grain prices.

Also in Dec.

• Quebecor bought the Sun Media empire for nearly $1 billion. Sun assets included the Sun newspaper family, the CANOE Internet portal and the Toronto television station Pulse 24.

• Novelist and short-story writer Barry Callaghan (b 1937) was the winner of the 1st W.O. Mitchell Literary Prize. Callaghan, founder of the literary quarterly *Exile* and its publishing arm *Exile Editions*, is the son of Canadian novelist Morley Callaghan (1903–1990).

1998–2000 The Commission for Environmental Cooperation in Montreal found that air pollution produced in Canada rose by 7% but dropped in the US by 8%. Ont.'s Nanticoke coal-fired power station was blamed for 50% of the total Canadian increase.

Also in 1998

• The number of impaired-driving charges in the country exceeded 80,000, down 65% since 1981.

• Average after-tax family income was $49,626.

• Seventeen thousand Canadians sought medical treatment in the US.

• Authority over the London (Ont.) International Airport (YXU) was transferred from Transport Canada to the not-for-profit Greater London International Airport Authority. The airport was the 12th busiest passenger airport in the country.

• Six thousand children lived in homeless shelters in Toronto, an increase from 2,700 in 1988.

• US firms purchased 121 Canadian businesses for $16 billion.

• 4,750,000 Canadians attended pop-music concerts, 719,000 attended the opera.

• Statistics Canada ranked golf as Canada's favourite sport.

• Boston and New York City chefs boycotted NS and Nfld. swordfish in a collective effort to help save dwindling north Atlantic stocks; 92% of the total 1997 Canadian Atlantic swordfish catch, worth $9.2 million, was exported to the US.

• The top 5 greenhouse gas–producing provinces and territories, by total weight in megatonnes, were: Alb., 200; Ont., 197; Que., 89.7; BC, 61.1; and Sask., 59.5. By capita in tonnes, the top five producers were: Alb., 68.8; Sask., 58.1; NB, 27.1; Yukon/NWT, 22.4; and NS, 21.5. The greatest emission increases by region since 1990 were: Yukon/NWT, 28%; Sask., 28%; NB, 27%; BC, 20%; and Alb., 19%.

• Canada hosted the 1st meeting of the 8-country Polar Council, founded to monitor the ecological health of the Arctic. Member countries included the US, Denmark/Greenland, Finland, Iceland, Norway, Sweden, and Russia. Mary Simon, Canada's Ambassador for Circumpolar Affairs, chaired the council from its founding in 1996, through 1998.

• Environment Canada declared 1998 the warmest year on record.

• A $3.3 billion expansion of Terminal 1 at Toronto's Pearson International Airport began, part of a $4.4 billion Pearson improvement plan — the single-largest private construction operation in Canadian history. Terminal 1 improvement included $9 million of new artwork, and was slated for completion in 2004. The massive project would involve no tax dollars.

• The nation's expenditure on NATO was $145 million, down from $181 million in 1993.

• Canadian adults spent a daily average of 3.2 hours watching television, 1.3 hours reading, 8.3 hours at work and 3.6 hours doing housework.

• The sale of Canadian music worldwide totalled $1.44 billion.

• 9.7 million Canadians read a newspaper every day.

• Book revenues for 1998–1999 were $2.2 billion. Sales had grown by 10% over the previous year. The industry in Canada had more than doubled since 1981, when sales were estimated at $932 million. At that time it was estimated that Canadian-owned publishers produced 80% of Canadian-authored titles, although sales of American and British titles accounted for about 75% of total sales revenues.

• El Niño provided Canada with its warmest winter, spring, summer and fall on record.

• Nfld.'s Iceberg Vodka won the gold medal at the 1998 World Spirits Championship in Chicago, garnering 94 points out of a possible perfect score of 100. The company's secret — Ont. sweet corn coupled with water from 12,000-year-old icebergs.

• The Soulpepper Theatre Company was established in Toronto. Founding members included Martha Burns, Susan Coyne, Ted Dykstra, Michael Hanranhan, Stuart Hughes, Diana Leblanc, Diego Metamoros, Nancy Palk, Albert Schultz, William Webster and Joseph Ziegler. Productions included Moliere's *The Misanthrope*, Williams' *A Streetcar Named Desire*, Wilder's *Our Town*, Chekhov's *Platonov*, Beckett's *Endgame* and Ferenc Molnar's *The Play's The Thing*.

• Montreal filmmaker Ezra Soiferman completed the documentary *Tree Weeks*, a humorous look at quick-buck French-Canadian entrepreneurs who flocked to the streets of New York City each Dec. to sell Christmas trees from their vans.

• Bertelsmann, the giant German multimedia conglomerate which began as a religious publisher in 1835, purchased venerable New York–based publisher Random House (the largest English-language trade publisher in the world) and merged it with its 1986 acquisition, Bantam Dell Doubleday. The Canadian assets of both publishing houses would also merge. The Canadian arm of Random House would attract the likes of Yann Martel (b 1963), Carol Shields, Margaret Atwood and Michael Ondaatje.

• Argentine-born Canadian essayist and novellist Alberto Manguel published *Into the Looking Glass Wood*, a collection of reviews, talks and essays.

• The 1st edition of the *Canadian Oxford Dictionary*, edited by Katherine Barber, was published. The nearly 2,000-page reference work sold over 190,000 copies. A 2nd edition was published in 2004.

• Wayne Johnston published his 5th novel, *The Colony of Unrequited Dreams,* about Nfld. and Father of Confederation Joey Smallwood. The novel was shortlisted for a host of awards and won the Thomas Raddall Atlantic Fiction Prize and the Canadian Authors Association Award for Fiction.

• Novelist David Adams Richards (b 1950) published *The Bay of Love and Sorrows*. It was made into a feature film in 2002, also co-scripted by Richards.

• Author Barbara Gowdy published *The White Bone*, a novel following the life story of an African elephant named Mud. The work was nominated for the Gov-Gen.'s Award and the Giller Prize.

• *Imagining Canadian Literature: The Selected Letters of Jack McClelland*, edited by Sam Solecki, was published.

• Alice Munro won the National Book Critics Circle Award for Fiction in the US for *The Love of a Good Woman*.

• Poet Anne Carson (b 1950) published her novel in verse, *Autobiography of Red*.

• Historian J.L. "Jack" Granatstein published *Who Killed Canadian History?,* describing a loss of chronological, political history teaching in the nation's school systems.

1999

Jan. 1 Canada's average household debt was $43,200.

• An avalanche tore through a school in the village of Kangiqsualujjuaq on Ungava Bay in northern Que., where a party of 500 were celebrating the new year; 9 people died, including 5 children; 25 were seriously injured, and airlifted 1,500 km to hospitals in Montreal.

Jan. 2 The 1st of 3 major snowfalls in what was called the "Snowstorm of the Century," dumped 40 cm of snow on Toronto. By Jan. 14, the city would be hit with a total of 120 cm, crippling transportation routes, closing schools, limiting operations at health-care facilities and hampering air traffic at Pearson International Airport. A chinook of laughter spread cross-country as Mayor Mel Lastman called in the army to shovel out the over 5 million residents affected. The military maneuvre cost taxpayers $70 million.

Jan. 7 Twelve thousand Sask. health-care workers, represented by the Canadian Union of Public Employees, went on strike for job parity, resulting in the closure of outpatient clinics, home-care services and the cancellation of elective surgeries across the province.

Jan. 8 Albertan Norbert Reinhart was freed by the Colombian Revolutionary Armed Forces with payment of $170,000 in ransom. Reinhart, owner of Terramundo Drilling Inc., spent 107 days in captivity after switching places with his employee Ed Leonard, who had been kidnapped while taking core samples in the Colombian jungle.

Jan. 14 A 291-page report issued by the Toronto Homeless Action Task Force, formed under Mayor Mel Lastman, recommended that 5,000 new housing units be built over the next 5 years to accommodate the city's increasing number of homeless. Over 3,200 Torontonians, including families with children, sought refuge in homeless shelter on any given night.

Jan. 15 BC Justice Duncan Shaw ruled it legal to possess child pornography under freedoms set forth in the Charter of Rights and Freedoms.

Jan. 27 The Supreme Court of Canada lifted a 100-year-old stipulation exempting railway companies from all liability connected to injury or accident occurring at any railroad crossing in the country. The exemption was voided when the Court ruled in favour of Murray Ryan, who sued Canadian Pacific

Ltd. and Esquimalt and Nanaimo Railway Co. in 1987 after suffering permanent leg injury when his motorcycle tire jammed in a piece of BC track. Railways had been given the special status on the grounds that their contributions to nation building superseded the right of individuals to sue them for negligence.

Jan. 28 Heritage Canada unveiled a plaque in Windsor Station, Montreal, honouring the history and achievements of black railway workers who formed the Order of Sleeping Car Porters in 1918, the 1st Canadian labour union to remove race-based entrance and mobility restrictions within its ranks.

Jan. 29 Albert Britnell Book Shop, once described as "the finest individual bookstore on the American continent," closed its single, family-run store in Toronto. The bookshop was named after its founder, an English immigrant who established the business on Yonge St. in 1893. The closure marked a national trend in a marketplace increasingly dominated by Indigo and Chapters superstores.

Also in Jan.
• Calgary born Todd McFarlane (b 1961), creator of the popular comic *Spawn*, purchased the baseball Mark McGwire used to hit his 70th home run (during the furious 1998 season slug fest between McGwire and Sammy Sosa) for $3 million.

Feb. 1 The Alb. govt enacted its Protection of Children Involved in Prostitution Act, giving police the right to pick up and place teenage prostitutes in treatment centres for up to 72 hours without having to lay charges. Also under the act, johns could be fined a maximum of $25,000 and jailed for up to 2 years. Estimates placed the number of child prostitutes in Calgary at between 150–200.

Feb. 3 Hundreds of curious mourners arrived in Wiarton, Ont. to pay their respects to a stuffed groundhog lying in a small pine coffin. The groundhog was a look-alike stand-in for the town's famous spring-weather forecaster, Wiarton Willie, who had passed away during hibernation. Condolences arrived from around the world and a town spokesperson reported that Willie's Web site was flooded with close to 1 million visitors.

Feb. 4 Ottawa and 9 provincial premiers signed the Social Union Accord, pledging a collective commitment to medicare and ensuring that all Canadians had continued access to adequate, affordable social programs. Que. opted out on jurisdictional considerations.

Feb. 9 The Nfld. Liberals, under the leadership of Brian Tobin, won a majority govt, taking 32 seats. The PC took 14, the NDP 2.

Feb. 14 Sask.'s ban on stripping was lifted when a judge ruled that the liquor control law banning striptease from licenced premises violated freedom-of-expression laws guaranteed under the Charter of Rights and Freedoms.

Feb. 14–15 An ice storm toppled trees and hydro lines, leaving 5,000 Cape Breton homes and offices without electricity.

Feb. 15 Airport maintenance worker Jobie Nutarak (b 1947) was elected Nunavut's first MLA in the soon-to-be territory's first election. Eighteen other members of the legislature were chosen from 71 candidates. Elected officials had no party affiliation. The new govt would commence official duties Apr. 1.

• Royal Oak Mines Inc., incorporated in Canada but based in Kirkland, Washington, sought bankruptcy protection in an Ont. court against creditors, who were owed $5.5 million.

• The CPR donated 1,618 of abandoned track to the 15,000-km Cross Canada Trail.

Feb. 16 Finance Minister Paul Martin tabled the Liberal govt's surplus-driven budget, adding $2.5 billion to transfer payments and $3.5 billion to health-care.

Feb. 25 Senator Eric Bernston (b 1941) became the highest-ranking official from Grant Devine's former Sask. PC party to be convicted in connection to the 1986–1990 swindle of $1 million of taxpayers' money. The former deputy premier was found guilty of using false invoices to defraud taxpayers of $41,000. In all, 21 Tories were charged with various criminal offences in what became known as Saskandal.

• GM Canada Inc. slashed 1,100 jobs from its St. Catharines Ont., workforce in efforts to cut costs and maintain its current market share.

Mar. 5 Minister of State Don Boudria (b 1949) sent a directive to all Crown corporations suggesting they refrain from making any more political contributions. The request was made in the wake of new evidence showing that between 1990 and 1999, Liberals, Conservatives and NDP had all benefited from contributions made by various Crown corporations.

Mar. 8 Viagra, the anti-impotence pill, was given federal approval for use in Canada.

Mar. 9 Canadian composer Harry Somers died. Born in Toronto in 1925, Somers was perhaps best known for *Louis Riel*, the opera he created for Canada's 1967 Centennial. Somers, who had entered the Royal Conservatory of Music at age 16, was a founding member of the Canadian League of Composers and had been named a Companion of the Order of Canada in 1971.

Mar. 15 The U. of Alb. received a record $3.7 million donation to its undergraduate scholarship fund. The money was sent by Victoria, BC, widow, Gladys Young, on behalf of her late husband, Roland Young, who had graduated from the university in 1928. Mr. Young had gone on to become one of the world's leading experts on cobalt.

Mar. 23 Four thousand, five hundred Nfld. nurses went on strike, demanding the govt hire more nurses and provide better wages.

Mar. 24 Four Canadian CF–18s joined a NATO bombing raid on Serbian positions in Prista, Kosovo, and areas north of Belgrade, Yugoslavia. It was the 1st NATO attack on a sovereign nation since the organization was formed in 1949. The attack did not have UN approval. By June, Canada had committed 1,800 troops to the Kosovo conflict.

Mar. 29 A 69-page report issued by Man. Chief Justice Alfred Monnin revealed that leading members of Gary Filmon's Tories had backed independent Aboriginal candidates in at least 3 ridings, in an effort to split NDP votes in the 1995 provincial election. Monnin declared the actions an "unconscionable abasement of the citizen's right to vote." Charges could not be laid due to the statute of limitations.

Apr. 1 Nunavut officially entered Confederation as the country's 3rd territory. Its capital was Iqaluit, its Premier Paul Okalik (b 1964). Inuit represented 82% of the population of over 27,000; the official languages were Inuktitut, English and French. Nunavut has an area of 1.994 million km^2 with a population density of 1.1 per persons per km^2. Its highest point is Mount Barbeau at 2,616 m, its major rivers the Coppermine, Hood, Burnside, Back, Thelon and Kazan.

• The 89-year-old Father Lacombe Centre in Calgary was destroyed by fire. The centre, slated to become the home of St. Mary's College, was the 5th historic site in Calgary destroyed by fire over a 2-year period.

Apr. 13 The Ont. govt sold Highway 407 to Ferrovial of Spain and SN Lavalin of Que. for $3.1 billion, the largest privatization deal in Canada to date. The 67-km toll highway situated north of Toronto was used by 210,000 people a day, resulting in monthly revenues of $9 million. The consortium held rights to the highway for 99 years.

Apr. 14 The Que. govt gave Mohawk First Nations at Kahnawake the right to collect PST-like levies on goods purchased by non-Natives on their reserve.

Apr. 16 Wayne Gretzky played his last NHL game in Canada. His New York Rangers tied the Ottawa Senators 2–2 while the full house chanted, "One more year! One more year!"

Apr. 18 Wayne Gretzky played his last NHL game before a hometown crowd at Madison Square Garden in NYC. The Rangers lost to the Pittsburgh Penguins 2–1 in overtime. "The Great One" was the single-most prolific scorer and playmaker in hockey history. Over a 20-year NHL career that included 4 Stanley Cups and 4 teams — the Edmonton Oilers, Los Angeles Kings, St. Louis Blues and the New York Rangers — No. 99 broke almost every scoring record in the book: most career points (2,857); most career assists (1,963); most career goals (894);

most points in one season (215); most assists in one season (163); most goals in one season (92); most 100-or-more-point seasons (15); most 50-or-more goal seasons (9); most 60-or-more goal seasons (5); and 10 Art Ross Trophies. Later in the year, Gretzky was named Canadian Press–Broadcast News Canadian Male Athlete of the Year.

Apr. 23 The Supreme Court of Canada criticized the country's incarceration rate of 130 per 100,000, second highest among all western nations. It also noted that Canada had the highest young-offender incarceration rate in the western world, and that Aboriginals, although only 3% of the total population, represented 12% of the total prison population.

Apr. 27 BC Premier Glen Clark signed the Nisga'a land claim deal, giving the province's over 5,000 Nisga'a control over 2,000 km² of the Nass Valley, including a restricted form of self-govt, fishing and hunting rights, surface and subsurface mineral rights, and limited policing and judicial authority. The deal, which took over 12 years to finalize, gave the Nisga'a 7% of land initially claimed as their traditional territory and removed the First Nation out from under the Indian Act. The deal was given Assent Apr. 13, 2000, and witnessed by Nisga'a Chief Joe Gosnell and 12 other Nisga'a representatives. The land is located approximately 760 km north of Vancouver.

Also in Apr.
• 97% of all provincially funded libraries offered Internet services.

May 20 The Supreme Court of Canada ruled 8–1 to overturn an Ontario Family Law Act statute defining a spouse as a member of the opposite sex, on the grounds that the statute did not apply to homosexual couples and was therefore unconstitutional.

• The Supreme Court revised the Indian Act, giving Native Peoples who did not live on reserves the right to vote in band elections. The amendment effected 274 bands nationwide.

May 23 Thirty-three-year-old Calgary wrestler Owen Hart (1965–1999), died tragically in the role of Blue Blazer, falling from a cable suspended 12 m above a ring in Kansas City, Missouri.

May 27 A rock band and 9 other Canadians were announced as this year's additions to the Canadian Walk of Fame in Toronto's downtown theatre district. The 1999 inductees to the 2-year-old celebration of Canadian-born talent were the band Rush; vocalist Juliette "Our Pet Juliette" Cavazzi; director David Cronenberg; actors Hume Cronyn (1911–2003); Mary Pickford and Lou Jacobi (b 1913); singers Céline Dion and Buffy Sainte-Marie; Montreal Canadien captain Maurice "The Rocket" Richard; comedians Johnny Wayne and Frank Shuster.

June 1 Canada signed the non-binding Andean Pact with Peru, Colombia, Ecuador, Venezuela and Bolivia, a first step toward the Free Trade Area of the Americas agreement, to be signed in 2005.

June 8 The federal government voted 216 to 55 in favour of preserving the definition of marriage as a union between a woman and a man. The notion was put forward by federal Reform member Eric Lowther.

June 9 Convicted bank robber and one-time novelist Stephen Reid, husband of author Susan Musgrave, was arrested after a wild car chase following a botched bank robbery in downtown Victoria. He was charged with bank robbery and attempted murder and sentenced to 18 years in jail.

June 17 The Extradition Act was amended to ensure Canada would not extradite people to a country where they faced persecution on the basis of race, religion, nationality, ethnic origin, language, colour, political opinion, sex, sexual orientation, age, mental or physical disability or status.

June 28 JDS Uniphase was formed when Uniphase Corp. of San Jose, California, joined Nepean-based JDS FITEL Inc., a cutting-edge fibre-optics firm, in a $9.5 billion merger.

June 30 Tacoma-based forestry giant Weyerhaeuser Co. purchased Vancouver-based MacMillan Bloedel Ltd. for $3.6 billion. MacMillan Bloedel was one of the largest forest products companies in the country, managing over 2 million ha in Canada, including 1.1 million ha in BC. The transaction pushed Weyerhaeuser annual sales to over $20 billion, with an employment roll of 45,000.

July 9 Chuckwagon racer Bill McEwen of Lloyminster, Sask., died of injuries suffered in a wagon race at the Calgary Stampede.

July 12 While countries around the world criticized the criteria and methods used, the UN chose Canada as the best country in the world in which to live. The selection placed Canada ahead of 170 other countries in terms of life expectancy, education and per capita income. In 2nd and 3rd spots, respectively, were Norway and the US.

July 15 Snow fell on the Calgary Stampede. The temperature dipped to 3°C, a record July low. Wind chill was −7°C.

July 20 One hundred and twenty-three Chinese nationals seeking illegal entry into Canada were discovered in the hold of a dilapidated, 55-m ship off the coast of Vancouver Is. The boat had been at sea over 40 days. All aboard claimed refugee status. On Aug. 11, 131 Chinese, including 20 children, were dumped from a ship into the frigid waters of Gilbert Bay in the Queen Charlotte Islands. All made it to shore safely. The RCMP arrested 8 Koreans in the smuggling operation. On Aug. 31, 190 illegal Chinese were hauled aboard the RCMP *Inkster*, the Coast Guard *Tanue* and the HMCS *Algonquin* from a rusted ship that had been at sea 72 days. The majority of those seeking illegal entry were denied refugee status.

Aug. 1 All members of Canada's national roller-hockey team were forced to return their gold medals after goalie Steve Vezina tested positive for banned substances at the 13th Pan-American Games in Winnipeg.

Aug. 9 Two hundered and fifty residents in south Calgary were evacuated after a fire at a Hub Oil recycling plant triggered 40 explosions. It took firefighters ten and a half hours to get the blaze under control.

Aug. 20 Three BC teachers hiking on a glacier in the northern regions of the province discovered the

headless remains of a male Aboriginal hunter who appeared to have died after falling into a crevasse. The remains were flown to Whitehorse, Yukon, for examination, where carbon dating of the man's hat and weapons showed him to be 10,000 years old. The man's head was not recovered.

Sept. 1 Aboriginal Peoples Television Network (APTN), the 1st national Aboriginal television network in the world (evolved from Television Northern Canada [TVNC]) was launched from Winnipeg, Man. For the 1st time in broadcast history, First Nations, Inuit and Métis peoples could broadcast stories of relevance through documentaries, news pieces, dramas, entertainment specials, children's series, cooking shows and educational programs. APTN offered 60% of programming in English, 15% in French and 25% in a variety of Aboriginal languages including: Inuktituk, Cree, Inuinaqtun, Ojibway, Inuvialuktun, Mohawk, Dene, Gwich'in, Mi'kmaq, Slavey, Dogrib, Chipweyan and Tlingit.

Sept. 3 Seven died and 45 were injured in a horrific 82-car pileup along the 401 east of Windsor, Ont. The chain reaction was caused when an isolated, or "freak" fog moved across the highway, restricting driver visibility to only metres.

Sept. 5 Future Master's champion Mike Weir (b 1970), of Bright's Grove, Ont., won his 1st PGA tournament, shooting 64 on Sunday to capture the Air Canada Championship in Surrey, BC. Weir became the 1st Canadian PGA member to win at home since Pat Fletcher (b 1916) won the national championship — the Canadian Open — in 1954.

• French President Jacques Chirac became the first foreign head of state to visit Nunavut.

Sept. 8 PM Jean Chrétien appointed Adrienne Clarkson (b 1939) the nation's 2nd woman gov-gen., or Canada's 26th gov-gen. since Confederation, or the 63rd resident head representative of a foreign monarch since Samuel de Champlain became gov. in 1627. Clarkson, who was born in Hong Kong, was also the first Crown representative not born in either Canada, France or England. A 34-year CBC veteran with two novels to her name, Clarkson replaced Roméo LeBlanc in the $98,000-a-year appointment.

Sept. 12 PM Jean Chrétien committed 600 peace-keepers to an Australian-led mission to end the wholesale slaughter of civilians by pro-Jakarta forces in East Timor. The former Portuguese colony had been under Indonesian rule for 24 years, but voted for independence in an Aug. 30 election.

Sept. 16 The Sask. NDP, under Roy Romanow, won its 3rd straight campaign, but was set back with its first minority govt, taking 29 of 58 seats. The Sask. Party won 26 seats and the Liberals 3.

Sept. 17 The Supreme Court of Canada ruled in favour of Mi'kmaq Donald Marshall Jr., who had been charged by the NS Department of Fisheries and Oceans in Aug. 1993 for fishing out of season. (Marshall had been fishing for eels near Antigonish, NS.) The Court concluded that the Maritime Mi'kmaq had a right to catch fish without restriction, thereby upholding the rights of Aboriginals set out in treaty signed by George II of England in 1760. The ruling divided the Maritime fishing community and sparked conflict between Native and non-Native fishers. On Oct. 3, non-Natives in 150 boats cut Burnt Church Native lobster traps in Mirimachi Bay, NB.

Sept. 21 Gary Doer's NDP won 31 of Man.'s 57 seats, beating 3-time Progressive Conservative incumbent Gary Filmon.

Also in Sept.
• The Rankin Family quit the music business. The popular Celtic band, comprising siblings John Morris, Jimmy, Cookie, Heather and Raylene, produced a popular Cape Breton sound that resulted in the sale of over 2 million records.

Oct. 13 Kingston, Ont., native, Robert Mundell (b 1932) won the Nobel Prize in economics. His groundbreaking studies on global currencies laid the foundation for the Euro dollar. Mundell was professor of economics at New York City's Columbia U.

Oct. 29 John Bitove, former owner of the Toronto Raptors, purchased Scott's Restaurants Inc. for $236.8 million. The move made Bitove the nation's largest fast-food retailer, giving him 338 Kentucky Fried Chicken, Wendy's, Mr. Sub, Nicholby's and Baskin-Robbins outlets.

Oct. 31 *Phantom of the Opera* closed at Pantages Theatre in Toronto. The production had been performed 4,226 times since debuting Sept. 20, 1989, and it was the longest-running Canadian stage musical. The musical swept the Dora Mavor Moore Awards in 1990 taking Best Production, Best Director and Best Actor.

Also in Oct.
• Attorney Gen. Jim Flaherty introduced Bill 5 in the Ont. legislature. It retained the definition of spouse as a member of the opposite sex, but changed all Ont. legislation reading "spouse," to "spouse or same-sex partner," thereby making same-sex couples equal under Ont. law.

Nov. 3 Beverley McLachlin (b 1943), born in Pincher Creek, Alb., was selected Canada's 1st woman Chief Justice of the Supreme Court. McLachlin had been with the court 11 years, and was 1 of 3 women judges on the 9-member Court. She was officially appointed Jan. 7, 2000 and sworn in Jan. 12, 2000.

Nov. 7 A labour conflict involving 2,000 port workers and 71 port companies caused the shutdown of the port of Vancouver, a move which cost the port $90 million a day in lost productivity.

Nov. 9 Richard Pound was named 1st president of the World Anti-Doping Agency, an organization of sport and governmental authorities with a mandate to fight the use of performance-enhancing drugs in sport. The agency was created following a 1998 Tour de France scandal involving cycling teams found in possession of significant quantities of performance dope. In Apr. 2002, the World Anti-Doping Agency formally opened its new headquarters in Montreal, (which was selected as the new site over Lausanne, Switzerland, on Aug. 21, 2001).

Nov. 18 Shoppers Drug Mart and its 825 retail outlets were purchased by Kohlberg Kravis & Roberts Co. of New York City for $2.55 billion in cash.

Nov. 23 Nancy Greene was named Canadian Press–Broadcast News Female Athlete of the Century.

"Tiger" won both the 1967 and 1968 International Ski Federation World Cups. She won gold in giant slalom and silver in slalom at the 1968 Winter Olympics in Grenoble, France. Closest contenders for Female Athlete of the Century were rower Silken Laumann and skater Barbara Ann Scott.

Nov. 29 Forty-one busloads of Canadians left Vancouver, meeting thousands more Canadians in a massive labour-led demonstration at the WTO meetings in Seattle, Washington. The march of over 50,000 turned chaotic as protestors smashed barricades and destroyed property in the downtown core. The city declared a civil emergency. Protestors were pepper-sprayed and clubbed by police. The WTO was an economic organization based in Geneva which fixed trade regulations in 135 countries. Canadian protestors argued that the WTO worked above the heads of citizens and elected officials.

Nov. 30 Major League Baseball owners unanimously approved the $75 million sale of the Montreal Expos to a group led by New York City art dealer Jeffrey Loria, who replaced Claude Brochu as Montreal's president and GM. The Expos drew 773,227 fans in the 1998–1999 season, less than 10,000 per game. In 2003 and 2004, Montreal shared Expos home games with San Juan, Puerto Rico. The storied franchise was moved to Washington, D.C., after the 2004 season.

Also in Nov.

• Ottawa approved the morning-after pill for women. The Preven medication was designed for women who wished to reduce the chance of pregnancy after unprotected sex.

Dec. 8 Air Canada gained control of Canadian Airlines, the 2nd-largest airline in Canada, making Air Canada the 12th-largest commercial carrier in the world.

Dec. 11 Twenty-three-year-old Belgian-bred show-jumping gelding Big Ben was euthanized after suffering a serious colic attack in Perth, Ont. With Ian Millar on board, Big Ben won over 40 Grand Prix victories, including back-to-back World Cups in 1988 and 1989. The horse was retired from competition in 1994.

Dec. 15 The Que. legislature changed the name of the administrative jurisdiction of "Quebec City," to the "region de la capitale nationale."

Dec. 22 San Francisco–based IDG Books of California paid $2.6 million for a 49% share of Canada Publishing Corp., parent company of Macmillan Canada.

Dec. 31 The 1st gas flowed from Tier I of the $3 billion Sable Offshore Energy Project (SOEP), jointly owned by ExxonMobil Canada (50.8%), Shell Canada (31.3%), Imperial Oil (9%), Emea Inc (8.4%) and Moshbacher Operationg Ltd. (0.5%). The project, off the Scotian Shelf near Sable Is., NS, exploits the largest-known remaining gas fields in North America.

Also in Dec.

• Shell Canada Ltd., in partnership with Chevron Canada Resources Ltd. and Western Oil Sands Inc., initiated the $4.1 billion Athabasca Oil Sands Project, with production achieved in 2003. It was the 1st entirely new oil sands project in 25 years, and was expected to supply 10% of Canada's oil requirements. The project consisted of the Muskeg River Mine, north of Fort McMurray, Alb., and the Scotford Upgrader, north of Fort Saskatchewan, Alb.

• An 11-member Ecological Committee appointed by Heritage Minister Sheila Copps concluded that, of the 39 national parks studied, 38 were under severe ecological stress, the result of logging, pollution and local agricultural and industrial activities.

1999–2002 BC spent $21.2 million, Que. $25 million and Ont. $67.4 million on pre-approved health-care performed in the US.

Also in 1999

• 14,400 book titles were published in Canada.

• Canada was the world's 8th most popular tourist destination, with US visitors comprising 78% of the 15.2 million tourists. Ont. and BC were the most visited provinces, hosting 50% and 22% of total visitors respectively.

• Astronaut Julie Payette (b 1963) was selected as a member of mission STS-96, and became the 1st

Canadian to serve on the International Space Station (ISS). The restocking mission lasted 5 days.

• Revenue Canada reported that 78,230 Canadians made $250,000 or more this year, approximately 35% more than in 1997. Revenue Canada also noted that some 600 of these high-income earners collected unemployment insurance at some point during the year.

• Since European contact, an estimated 70% of southern Ont.'s total wetlands disappeared, the result of in-filling or drainage for land development, transportation or agriculture.

• There were 7,252 ha of commercial vineyards in Canada.

• VIA Rail carried 3.8 million passengers and received $170 million in federal funding. It had received $441.5 million in 1990.

• John Sewell (b 1940), author, columnist, urban reformer, former Toronto mayor (1978–1980) and the city's 1st elected (1969) full-time city councillor, completed an advisory role to the city of East London, South Africa, which had begun in 1994 following the election of president Nelson Mandela.

• The Royal Ontario Museum (ROM) returned its largest collection of human remains — over 500 skeletons unearthed by archaeologists in the 1940s — to the Ossossane burial ground near Midland, Ont. Members of the Huron-Wendat Nation came from all over North America to witness the return of their ancestors.

• The federal govt awarded 230,000 former and current public employees, who worked in female-dominated fields, a pay-equity compensation package worth $3.6 billion, to be paid in instalments.

• The Waterfront Regeneration Trust published *The Official Lake Ontario Waterfront Trail Mapbook*. Opened in 1995, the trail includes 450 km of marked trail (with 290 km of undesignated routes), which follows the shores of Lake Ontario from Niagara-on-the-Lake to Brockville, Ont. It passes through 31 communities, 182 parks and nature reserves, 170 boating clubs and marinas and, over

the course of the year, nearly 40 waterfront festivals. The Waterfront Regeneration Trust was founded in 1992; former Toronto mayor (1972–1978) and MP, David Crombie, was the founding chair.

• US interests bought 127 Canadian companies, paying a total of $25 billion.

• Diana Krall's 5th CD, *When I Look In Your Eyes*, went platinum with over 100,000 copies sold nationwide. The CD secured the Nanaimo native's position as one of the world's leading jazz performers.

• Winnipeg became the 1st Canadian city to host the Pan-American Games for the 2nd time. Winnipeg had 1st hosted the Games in 1967 as part of Canada's Centennial celebrations.

• The Montreal Canadiens donated the Maurice "Rocket" Richard Trophy to the NHL, to be awarded annually to the league's top scorer. The 1st recipient was Teemu Selänne of the Anaheim Mighty Ducks (47 goals).

• Film Director David Cronenberg became the first Canadian to sit on the jury at the Cannes Film Festival.

• There were 83,023 total bankruptcies in Canada — 72,997 personal and 10,026 commercial. The total in 1998 was 86,256.

• Canadians spent $17 billion at the gas pump.

• There were 100,314 Canadian books in print, 58,883 in English and 41,431 in French; 643 book publishers were active in the country, up from 322 in 1992.

• Municipalities nationwide issued building permits worth $36 billion, up from $24.6 billion in 1995.

• Supermarket and grocery store sales totalled $54 billion.

• 19.6% of Canadians had a secondary school education; 25.9% had a post secondary-school degree or diploma; and 13.6% had university degrees.

• The World Bank's World Development Indicator (released in 2001) revealed that Canada had 459 cars for every 1,000 Canadians. By comparison, the US had 478, Germany 508, China 3, France 469, India 5, Jordan 49, Israel 220 and New Zealand 481.

• The federal govt finally recognized the efforts and sacrifices of over 12,000 Canadian merchant marine sailors who kept supplies flowing between Canada and Europe during WW II. One in 8 (or 1,629) Canadian merchant mariners died in the effort.

• Kayaker Caroline Brunet (b 1969) was awarded the Lou Marsh Trophy as the nation's top athlete of the year, after taking triple gold at the World Championships in Milan, Italy, in the K-1 200 m, 500 m, and 1,000 m events.

• Environment officials counted only 57 endangered Vancouver Island marmots in the wild. Endemic to Vancouver Island only, the number of these burrow-dwelling brown herbivores was 235 in 1984. Captive breeding programs have offered hope, however: in 2002, a total of 47 marmots were spread among breeding programs at the Calgary Zoo, Toronto Zoo, Mountain View Farm in Langley, BC, and in Washington State.

• Retired Pittsburgh Penguins great, Mario Lemieux, became the new owner and chairman of his old team. The new employer rejoined his teammates on the ice the next year, and in his 1st game back against Toronto (Dec. 27, 2000) scored 1 goal and 2 assists.

• The Canadian Science Centre for Human and Animal Health — 1 of 15 level-4 virology labs in the world capable of dealing with earth's most contagious diseases — went into operation in Winnipeg. The $172 million laboratory was the 1st level-4 lab in the nation and in 2000, received its 1st deadly virus samples: Junin, Lassa, Marburg, and Ebola.

• Some bizarre weather occurrences this year included the driest Feb. in Calgary since 1886, which triggered grassfires in Southern Alb. but had little effect on some of the finest Rocky Mountain skiing conditions to date; an Apr. day in Edmonton that soared to 23°C and led to record spring ice cream sales; and an unseasonably warm spring in Southern Ont. which heightened pine tree pollen levels to the point where waters of the Bay of

Quinte were covered with the golden nutrient, in some places as deep as 15 cm.

• Canada's crime rate hit a 20-year low. Violent crime dipped 2.4%, homicides were down 4.7%, and property crime fell 6.4%. Drug-related crime, however, rose 33%.

• The National Audubon Society declared painter Robert Bateman (b 1930) one of the top 100 environmental proponents of the 20th century.

• David Layton (b 1964), son of poet Irving Layton and godson of Leonard Cohen, published *Motion Sickness*, a memoir of his childhood.

• Poet Ken Babstock (b 1970) published *Mean,* his debut collection. It won the Milton Acorn Award and the Atlantic Poetry Prize.

• Poet Robert Bringhurst published *Story As Sharp As a Knife: The Classical Haida Mythtellers and Their World*, the 1st volume in a trilogy called *Masterworks of the Classical Haida Mythtellers.*

• *For Your Eyes Alone: Robertson Davies' Letters 1976–1995,* selected and edited by Davies's biographer, Judith Skelton Grant, was published.

• Author and newspaper columnist Robert Fulford published *The Triumph of Narrative: Story Telling in the Age of Mass Culture.*

• Poet Tim Lilburn published *To the River*, which was awarded the Saskatchewan Book Awards Book of the Year honours.

• CBC's all-music, commercial-free Galaxie network had 500,000 subscribers. The nation's 1st 24-hour audio pay service 1st aired in 1997. It offered digital sound television channels which could be accessed through cable or satellite. By 2000, Galaxie offered 45 channels covering categories in rock, pop, country, jazz, classical and others.

• Que. composer Luc Plamondon (b 1942) was elected to the Canadian Music Hall of Fame. The prolific artist penned hundreds of songs for a variety of renowned artists including Ginette Reno (b 1946) and Celine Dion. In 1978 Plamondon co-composed with Frenchman Michel Berger the futuristic rock opera *Starmania*. The international hit debuted in Paris in 1979 and has been seen by over 3 million people, with over 5 million albums sold. Plamondon has since produced a number of successful operas, including *La légende de Jimmy* (1990), a musical based on the life of hard luck American actor James Dean, and *Notre Dame de Paris* (1998), based on Victor Hugo's *The Hunchback of Notre Dame*.

2000

Jan. 1 The new millennium arrived without the much-feared — and hyped — Y2K bug (computer foul-ups associated with the time-turnover to 2000). The federal govt had spent $2.5 billion to protect against a millennium switch glitch. Employees at Newfoundland Power, the first major power grid in North America to face the new year and Y2K turnover test, cracked open champagne to celebrate.

Jan. 12 William H. Mercer consultants' global survey ranked Vancouver, together with Zurich, Bern and Vienna, as the best cities in the world to live. Criteria included water, health, crime, political stability and quality of life.

Jan. 13 Federal Agriculture Minister Lyle Vanclief (b 1943) committed $1 billion in aid over 2 years to farmers struggling to compete with soaring production costs, foreign subsidies and low commodity prices. Farmers argued the aid was not enough and staged protests throughout the West.

Jan. 14 The Aboriginal Cultural Property Agreement was signed at the Glenbow Museum, Alb., allowing Blackfoot, Blood, Peigan and Siksika First Nations to retrieve 251 ancestral artifacts from the institution.

Jan. 17 Stephen Kakfwi (b 1948), former leader of the Dene Nation, was chosen premier of the Northwest Territories. He succeeded Jim Antoine, who did not run for re-election.

Jan. 19 A federal internal audit of grants and contributions revealed that $1 billion of taxpayers' money was unaccounted for somewhere in the Human Resources Department. PM Chrétien argued there had been no wrongdoing, only mismanagement. Human Resources Minister Jane Stewart blamed "sloppy administration."

Jan. 21 Industry Minister John Manley (b 1950) quashed a federal plan to provide aid to the nation's 6 NHL franchises, several of which were struggling to compete with relatively small revenues and skyrocketing player salaries (many paid in US dollars). The aid was to have been provided through tax breaks.

Jan. 25 Feature film *Backroads*, written, produced and directed by Cree artisan Shirley Cheechoo (b 1952), premiered at the prestigious independent Sundance Film Festival in Utah. Shot on Manitoulin Is., Ont., in 1998, the work explored the phenomenon of "bear-walking," an Aboriginal belief that stalkers can transform themselves into other beings to track victims.

Jan. 27–30 Reform Party members agreed to merge their 13-year-old party with other, mostly western conservative forces. The new party was named the Canadian Conservative Reform Alliance Party, or CCRAP for short. On Jan. 31, 2000, the unfortunate name was changed to the Canadian Reform Conservative Alliance. On Mar. 25, 92% of Reform members voted to approve the new Alliance. On July 7, former Alb. treasurer Stockwell Day (b 1950) won the Alliance leadership in a runoff, taking 63.3% of the vote to dethrone Preston Manning, the party's founder and 1st leader.

Jan. 31 Federal Finance Minster Paul Martin approved the $8 billion takeover of Canada Trust by Toronto-Dominion Bank. The collaborative, renamed TD Canada Trust brought together $91 billion in personal deposits, 10.2 million Canadian customers, and a 1999 profit of $1.79 billion.

Also in Jan.

• *No Logo: Taking Aim at the Brand Bullies,* authored by Canadian activist-writer Naomi Klein (b 1970), was published in Canada. The book, which became an unofficial text for the anti-globalization movement and an international best-seller, detailed and critiqued the rise of global advertising, corporate-sponsorship branding and the anti-globalization movement.

Feb. 3 The Nfld. govt offered $3,000 to each new nursing graduate to remain in the province for at least 1 year. Half of the 42 Memorial U. nursing graduates of 1999 had already located better-paying jobs outside the province.

• Provincial premiers and territorial leaders met in Quebec City and agreed to call on Ottawa to raise provincial health-care payments to 1994 levels — a $4 billion hike.

Feb. 11 The federal Liberal party introduced Bill C–23, the Modernization of Benefits and Obligations Act, into the House of Commons. The act gave same-sex couples who had lived together for over a year the same tax and social benefits as heterosexual common-law couples. The bill was passed by a vote of 174–72 on Apr. 11, 2000.

Feb. 15 The original Canadian flag, 1st flown on Parliament Hill on Feb. 15, 1965, was removed from PM Chrétien's office and given to the Heritage Department. The late Lester Pearson had given it to the Liberal caucus, which then began a tradition of handing it down along subsequent party ranks.

Feb. 16 Two Aboriginal sisters, Corrine McKeown and Doreen Leclair, were murdered in Winnipeg. They had called 911 five times over eight hours to get help, but to no avail. On Feb. 17, William John Dunlop was arrested after a 5 1/2 hour standoff with police. On Feb. 18, five police officers were suspended and the family given a formal apology for "the failure of the system." Dunlop pleaded guilty to two charges of 1st degree murder and on Apr. 24, 2001, was sentenced to life in prison with no possibility of parole for 17 years.

Feb. 17 Ottawa halted production of the $1,000 bill on the grounds it was used primarily for money laundering. The rare purple bill featured Queen Elizabeth II on the face and the pine grosbeak on the back.

Feb. 21 As many as 400 independent truckers blockaded the Trans-Canada Highway at the NS–NB border, allowing cars and pickup trucks to pass but not commercial vehicles. The workers were protesting the high cost of diesel fuel and tolls. On both Feb. 21 and 22, over 1,500 truckers brought Ont.'s Highway 401 to a grinding halt as they formed a massive slow-moving convoy to protest high fuel costs and low industry wages.

Feb. 24 BC Attorney Gen. Ujjal Dusanjh was sworn in as the country's 1st Indo-Canadian premier. He had won the NDP leadership on the 1st ballot Feb. 20. Dusanjh succeeded NDP premier Glen Clark, who resigned over the Casinogate scandal on Aug. 21, 1999. Clark was charged in the matter Oct. 20, 2000.

Feb. 27 The Canadian men's soccer team beat Colombia 2–0 to take the Football Confederation Gold Cup in Los Angeles, giving Canada its 1st international soccer title. The tournament included 12 teams from North and Central America. Canada was ranked 12th going in.

Feb. 28 Federal Finance Minister Paul Martin tabled his budget in the House of Commons, projecting a balanced budget for this and the next fiscal year.

Also in Feb.

• Over 30 Nfld. politicians were fired for failing to pay their municipal taxes. The terminations came after a (Jan. 1) provincial law came into effect prohibiting all local politicians who owed back taxes from holding office.

Mar. 2 The Alb. govt introduced the Health Care Protection Act, allowing private for-profit clinics to compete on the free market with public hospitals. The clinics would perform surgeries and provide overnight health services. Existing provincial health-care would cover services performed. Bill 11 passed Apr. 12 by a vote of 34–17. Previously, on Jan. 31, Premier Klein, who had increasingly come under pressure from PM Chrétien for supporting private clinics, stated: "The federal govt contributes less than 13 cents of every dollar that Alb. spends on health care. Somebody who pays that small a percentage of the trip cannot demand the right to give directions."

Mar. 7 BC Supreme Court Justice Glen Parrett voided a Nov. 1999 McBride, BC, mayoral election because winning candidate Mike Frazier had distributed fraudulent and condemning literature about his opponent, Maurice Bonneville.

Mar. 14 Alb. Agriculture Minister Ty Lund (b 1938) pledged $4.29 to every Alb. farmer for every acre of working land. The aid package totalled $145 million.

Mar. 15 The House passed the Clarity Bill, C–20, by a vote of 208–55, requiring all referendum questions on Que. secession be clear, and the results embody the will of the people. Bill C-20 passed through the Upper Chamber June 29.

Mar. 16 The Alb. legislature passed the Marriage Amendment Act, Bill 202, by a vote of 32–15. The act banned the issuance of same-sex marriage licences in the province and included provision to invoke the notwithstanding clause should provisions in Bill 202 be deemed in violation of the federal Charter.

• Alb. Treasurer Stockwell Day introduced the country's 1st flat tax, set at 11%. The levy was lowered to 10% in 2001.

Mar. 26 BC began its world curling conquest in Geising, Germany, with Brad Kuhn's Kelowna rink beating Switzerland 8–4 to take gold at the World Junior Curling Championship. The next month, Apr. 8, Kelley Law's Richmond rink beat Switzerland 7–6 to take the Women's World Curling Championship in Glasgow, Scotland. Two days later, Greg McAulay's New Westminster rink beat Sweden 9–4 to take the Men's World Curling Championship.

Mar. 30 Popular Lichtman's News Agency bookstores in Toronto declared bankruptcy, citing an inability to compete with the spread of book boxstores (eg. Chapters). On Mar. 31, Duthie Books of Vancouver filed for bankruptcy protection following recent Vancouver openings of 2 Chapters stores. Duthies had 6 outlets. One Vancouver outlet survived restructuring.

Apr. 1 The Griffin Trust was initiated by Scott Griffin, chairman, with trustees Margaret Atwood, Robert Hass, Michael Ondaatje, Robin Robertson and David Young. The Trust's mandate was to raise public awareness of the crucial role poetry must play in society's cultural life.

Apr. 2 The BC govt legislated striking teachers back to work following a week-long strike that kept 350,000 students out of class.

Apr. 4 A Canadian Centre for Policy Alternatives report was released, showing that 19% of Canadian women (2.2 million) and 14.6% of men (1.6 million) lived in poverty, including 56% of single mothers, and 50% of women over 65.

Apr. 6 Citizenship and Immigration Minster Elinor Caplan tabled a tough new Immigration and Refugee Protection Act (Bill C–31) in the House, which included provisions for quicker deportations of those convicted of serious crimes; life imprisonment and a $1 million fine for those convicted of trafficking in humans; and the denial of immigration sponsorship to welfare recipients, domestic abusers and dead-beat family-support neglecters. The bill died when Parliament dissolved for the federal election. It was reintroduced as Bill C–11 on Feb. 11, 2001, and given Assent Nov. 1, 2001.

Apr. 7 Multimedia giant BCE Inc. successfully acquired CTV for $2.3 billion. On Sept. 15, 2000, BCE Inc. and CTV would begin a $4 billion joint Internet and multimedia venture with Thomson Corp., the *Globe & Mail* and Sympatico.

Apr. 14 The TSE 300 Index dropped 491.90 points, its worst showing since Oct. 19, 1987. Over $1 trillion of stock value was lost in markets across North America, the result of rising US inflation and the devaluation of bloated technology stocks.

Apr. 17 Yukon Liberals took power for the 1st time, taking 10 seats under the leadership of Pat Duncan (b 1960). The NDP won 6 seats, the Yukon Party 1.

• The non-profit social research agency, the Canadian Council on Social Development, ranked Montreal the poorest city in Canada.

• Pat Binns (b 1948) and the PEI Conservatives were returned to power in the provincial election, winning 26 of 27 seats. The lone opposition member was Liberal Ron Mackinley. Both NDP leader Herb Dickieson (b 1954) and Liberal leader Wayne Carew (b 1955) lost their seats.

Apr. 18 The RCMP arrested "Mafiaboy," a 15-year-old Montreal youth charged in connection with the intentional Feb. overloading and jamming of Internet locales CNN, Yahoo!, eBay, Amazon, E*Trade, Excite and associated sites.

Apr. 24 Toronto seamstres, Nguyen Thi Hiep was executed by firing squad in Hanoi after she and her mother had been convicted of drug smuggling in 1997. Canada condemned the action and refused a request by Vietnam to help it join the World Trade Organization (WTO). Canada also refused to participate in 25ᵗʰ anniversary ceremonies marking the end of the Vietnam War. Nguyen Thi Hiep's mother was released Sept. 1 and returned to Canada.

Apr. 26 Weibo Ludwig was sentenced to 28 months in jail in connection to a Suncor oil-well bombing and the destruction of a Norcen well in northern Alb. in 1998. He was released Nov. 14, 2001, after serving 10 months. Richard Boonstra, his co-defendant in the Norcen incident, was given 21 days. Ludwig claimed pollution associated with oil extraction was the cause of health problems and environmental degradation on his Alb. farm. Under provincial law, farmers owned only surface rights to their property and had little control over the development of mineral wells on their own land.

Apr. 28 The 387-member McLeod Lake First Nation of BC completed a land-claim negotiation with the BC and federal govt. The McLeod Lake received $35 million cash and title to 20,000 ha north of Prince George. The claim stemmed from a 1983 lawsuit charging the federal govt with breaking Treaty No. 8 by allowing logging on McLeod L. land.

Also in Apr.

• Canada's annual inflation rate hit a 10-year high of 3.6%. Over the year ending this month, energy prices were up 11.6%, home-heating costs 50%, and fresh fruit and vegetables 17.8%.

May 5 The "I Love You" computer virus hit computers worldwide, causing major clogging problems in networks cross-country. Especially hard hit were the Ont. legislature and federal govt's Parliament Hill systems.

May 6 Montreal's new science centre, the iSci Centre, opened in the historic Old Port area. The site included interactive exhibits, a 3-D Imax theatre and a cinema where the audience could vote to determine how any given plot presented would unfold.

May 15 Premiers from the 4 Atlantic provinces met in Moncton, agreeing to the creation of the Council of Atlantic Premiers, a co-operative political body to support common Atlantic interests.

May 17–21 At least 40 people in Walkerton, Ont., reported to hospital for treatment of E.coli sickness. On May 23, the region's Medical Health Office (MHO) confirmed that Walkerton's water was contaminated. The MHO also discovered that the Ontario Public Utilities Commission (PUC) had discovered E.coli contamination sometime previous to the outbreak but did not notify the public. The result: 7 deaths and more than 2,300 illnesses. A provincial inquiry was launched. On June 29, 2001, Premier Harris became the 1ˢᵗ premier to testify before a judicial inquiry in over 50 years. (A final report from the Ont. Ministry of the Attorney Gen. was tabled May 23, 2002.) On Mar. 27, 2001, the Ont. govt gave the town of Walkerton $15 million to cover costs associated with the E.coli breakout; and in Apr. 2001, Ont. Chief Justice Patrick LeSage ruled in a class action suit that each of Walkerton's 5,000 residents was entitled to $2,000 in compensation. Those directly affected by the outbreak were given the right to apply for further compensation. In 2004, Stan and Frank Koebel, who ran Walkerton's water supply system, stood in court charged with falsifying documents, failing to notify officials of the presence of E.coli and failing to chlorinate water.

May 31 A state funeral was held for Canadian hockey legend Maurice "Rocket" Richard at Notre Dame Basilica in Montreal. Richard died May 27. Number 9 played 18 NHL seasons for the Canadiens, winning 8 Stanley Cups, 5 of them consecutively. He was the 1ˢᵗ 50-goal scorer (1944–1945 season) and the 1ˢᵗ player to score over 500 goals. He won the league's scoring title 5 times.

• A WTO appeal panel upheld an Oct. 13, 1999 WTO decision that concluded the 1965 Canada–US Auto Pact violated fair international trading practices. The Auto Pact allowed US cars to enter the country duty free, but allowed a 6.1% duty on Japanese and European imports. On Oct. 4, Industry Minister John Manley (b 1950) declared the Auto Pact inactive and lifted the 6.1% duty.

Also in May

• Point Pleasant Park, Halifax, was placed under quarantine in an effort to stifle the spread of the brown spruce longhorn beetle. Authorities feared that if left unchecked, spruce longhorn beetles would spread and endanger the provincial lumber trade.

June 3–4 The Jasper-Banff Relay, founded in 1980 by the Chasquis Running Club, was run for the last time. Runners in the 24-hour event covered 285.7 km (177.6 mi) of mountainous terrain alongside the Jasper-Banff Highway. The relay featured 17 stages of varying complexity and terrain, ranging from 14 km to 20.3 km (8.4-12.7 mi). Maximum number of entry teams (each of 17 members, male and female) was capped at 120. Hazards along the route included grizzly bears, mountain goats, cliffs and inclement weather.

June 15 The Ontario Coalition Against Poverty (OCAP) demonstrated against homelessness at Queen's Park. A subsequent clash with police included 18 arrests, 29 injured police officers and the hurling of sundry bric-a-brac and Molotov cocktails. The fray was termed the Queen's Park Riot.

• The Supreme Court of Canada unanimously ruled that the federal govt had the right to make and impose gun legislation, stating, "All guns are capable of killing and maiming… It follows that all guns pose a threat to public safety. As such, their control falls within the criminal law power."

June 19 Stompin' Tom Connors (b 1936) received an honorary doctor of laws degree from the U. of Toronto. In his address to graduates, the writer/singer of such songs as "Bud the Spud," "Sudbury Saturday Night" and "The Hockey Song" said, "I don't know of the hard work that you have put into your studies and all that kind of thing, because the university that I came from is a little one-room school in Skinner's Pond, PEI."

June 23 The 3rd annual celebration of homegrown talent saw 13 new inductees to the Canadian Walk of Fame: contralto Maureen Forrester; actors Donald Sutherland; Michael J. Fox (b 1961) and William Shatner (b 1931); ballet dancer Evelyn Hart; ageless hockey wonder Gordie Howe; Shakespearean actor William Hutt (b 1920); singer-songwriters Joni Mitchell and Neil Young; chanteuse Ginette Reno; painter and sculptor Jean-Paul Riopelle; the

Royal Canadian Air Farce comic team and comedian Martin Short.

June 26 Avie Bennett deeded 75% of the venerable Canadian publishing house McClelland & Stewart to the University of Toronto Press. He sold the remaining 25% to US-owned Random House of Canada for an estimated $5 million.

June 30 *Calgary Herald* journalists ended a strike begun Nov. 8, 1999. Conditions included the choice of returning to work under prestrike conditions, or accepting a severance package.

Also in June
• Armed only with the tools, clothing, seeds and livestock available to 19th-century homesteaders, 2 Canadian couples (along with a Canadian film company) headed into the Man. wilderness to take part in a year-long homesteading adventure that would become the basis of the History Channel's *Pioneer Quest: A Year in the Real West*. For close to 12 months, Tim and Deanna Treadway, and Frank and Alana Logie re-created Canadian pioneer life under the watchful eye of Winnipeg filmmaker Jamie Brown. Over one of the hottest summers and coldest winters on record, the couples built a house, raised livestock, hunted, fished and grew crops. The 9 one-hour episodes became the highest-rated documentary ever to air on a Canadian specialty network, with 624,000 viewers tuning in for the finale.

• PEI fishers were given their first licences to fish shrimp off the coast of Nfld. Their total catch limit was 1,500 tonnes of the total allowable 110,000-tonne quota. The provision enraged Nfld. fishers whose fortunes failed with cod during the 1990s.

• The WTO ranked Canada's health-care system 30th amongst industrialized nations.

July 3 Vanguard, Sask., received more than a year's supply of rain — some 333 mm — over a period of 10 hours, from 4:00 p.m. to midnight. Although the town sustained a severe flash flood, there were no human casualties.

• Calgary implemented "rave" legislation requiring any party attended by more than 250, and held for more than 5 hours, to be licenced and include police and ambulance services. On Aug. 6, Toronto lifted its ban on raves held on public property. The popular youth rave was a techno version of the jazz parties of the 1920s and 30s, the groovefests of the 1970s, or the Grateful Dead shows of the 1980s, with rhythm-driven dancing, hypnotic lighting and ecstasy, the designer narcotic of the new century.

July 11 The city of Halifax voted to phase out the use of lawn pesticides over 4 years.

July 12 Matthew Coon Come (b 1956) was elected the national chief of the Assembly of First Nations, the largest native organization in the country. He succeeded Phil Fontaine.

July 14 A tornado struck Green Acres campground at the Pine L. recreational area, some 45 km southeast of Red Deer, Alb.; 967 people were registered at the popular campground. Ten died, and some 70 RVs were swept into nearby Pine L. The deadly whirlwind, some 1 km wide, generated winds in excess of 300 km/h.

July 20 Over 80 full-masted wooden tall ships from 25 countries arrived in historic Halifax Harbour, all in full sail. They were greeted by welcoming cannon and tens of thousands of sightseers. The majestic wooden throwbacks had left Southampton, England, in Apr. as part of the Tall Ships Race 2000. The Boston-Halifax leg was won by the Russian square-rigger *Mir*. Halifax was the tall ships' only Canadian destination.

• The Ontario Securities Commission imposed a $3 million fine on the Royal Bank Pension Management Division, RT Capital, for "high close" stock manipulation (massive stock selloffs at year end to inflate stock prices and company image). Nine RT officials were banned from trading, and a total of 12 fined by the commission.

July 21 The Ont. Court of Appeal unanimously ruled that employer-enforced drug testing — through mandatory employee urine analysis — violated employee privacy rights, stating, "A urine test is a gratuitous invasion of privacy." The court did, however, allow the use of random Breathalyser tests for employee capability in the performance of essential duties in sensitive jobs.

July 23 The Squamish First Nation voted to accept a $92.5 million out-of-court compensation settlement for prime BC real estate promised them in 1877. The disputed lands included 35 ha at Vancouver's popular Kitsilano Point, 494 ha in the town of Squamish, and 30 ha in North Vancouver.

July 24 Pitney Bowes's 4th annual survey of workplace messaging practices revealed that Canadian office workers sent and received an average of 160 messages a day — as e-mail, voice mail, paper messages, phone calls, faxes and, of course, regular mail.

July 28 Thirteen replicas of 1,000-year-old Viking ships landed at L'Anse aux Meadows, Nfld., marking the 1,000th anniversary of the 1st Vikings' arrival in North America. The replicas, which included the *Snorri*, named after the 1st Viking child born in North America, arrived from Greenland.

July 31 Conrad Black's Hollinger Inc. began its exit from the Canadian publishing arena, selling 149 papers and related Internet portals for $3.5 billion, to Winnipeg-based broadcaster CanWest Global Communications, founded and chaired by Izzy Asper (b 1932). The deal included the 100% sale of 13 major dailies and 50% of the *National Post*.

• The Ont. Court of Appeal ruled that the federal law banning marijuana possession was unconstitutional because it failed to provide for those who possessed it legally for health purposes. The Court ruled that the law would be voided if Ottawa did not amend it within one year.

Aug. 3 A panel of judges at Canada's Federal Court of Appeal overruled a 1998 lower court decision, and allowed Harvard U. Canadian patent rights to a mammal — a genetically modified mouse, the "oncomouse," created for cancer research.

Aug. 4 The new Portland Hotel, designed by acclaimed Canadian architect Arthur Erickson, opened for business on Vancouver's east side. With 60 suites, a library, a doctor's office, a movie theatre, gym, hair salon and private garden, the new Portland was a much-welcome innovation in social housing. Its 1st tenants: 90 "hard-to-house" residents from the neighbourhood.

Aug. 6 After 9 career 2nd place finishes, PEI-born golfer Lori Kane (b 1964) won her first LPGA event, the Michelob Light Classic in St. Louis. She would win 2 more times during the season, and was the runaway winner of the Bobbie Rosenfeld Award as Canada's female Athlete of the Year.

Aug. 10–13 The du Maurier Classic, the LPGA's 4th Major — and Canada's only major golf championship — was played for the last time, as limitations on tobacco advertising forced Imperial tobacco to conclude its sponsorship. American Meg Mallon won the tournament, played at the Royal Ottawa Golf Club in Aylmer, Que.

Aug. 16 PM Chrétien was hit in the face with a pie ("pied") at an agricultural fair in Charlottetown, PEI. The assailant, Evan Brown of the "PEI Bakers Brigade," pulled the stunt to protest the sale of genetically modified foods in Canada. He was charged with assault.

Aug. 21 Telus Corp. of Alb. began its takeover of Clearnet Communications. The $6.6 billion deal created the country's largest wireless communications network, and gave the new firm competitive weight against communications giants Rogers AT&T Wireless Inc., Bell Mobility and Microcell Communications Inc.

Sept. 5 At a ceremony in Nfld. and Labrador, representatives of the Roman Catholic, Anglican, Presbyterian and United Churches apologized to Aboriginal peoples for abuses suffered in church-operated institutions during the 19th and 20th centuries.

Sept. 10 Tiger Woods won the Canadian Open at Glen Abbey, Ont., on what was ranked by viewers of the Golf Station as his greatest shot to date — a 218-yard 6-iron out of a fairway bunker, over a lake and onto the back ledge of the 18th green. The win gave Woods the Canadian title, something that had eluded the great Jack Nicklaus his entire career. It also gave Woods the Triple Crown — the 2000 Canadian, British and US Opens.

• Alliance leader Stockwell Day (b 1950) won a seat in the House after taking the BC riding of Okanagan–Coquihalla in a by-election. He recieved

70% of the popular vote. On Sept. 12, Day showed up for his 1st official press conference on the banks of L. Okanagan wearing a wetsuit and riding a personal, jet-propelled watercraft.

• Former PM and leader of the 5th party Progressive Conservative party, Joe Clark won a by-election in the riding of Kings–Hants, NS, giving him a seat in the House for the 1st time since 1993.

Sept. 11 PM Chrétien and the provincial premiers agreed to a deal providing the provinces with an additional $23.4 billion for health and social programs over the next 5 years.

Sept. 12 Fourteen Burnt Church and Miramichi Bay NS Mi'kmaq lobster fishers were arrested and their boats seized by the RCMP for fishing out of season, despite a Sept. 17, 1999, Supreme Court decision giving Mi'kmaq unrestricted fishing rights in the region. The arrests sparked years of standoffs, hostility and sometimes violence as Native and non-Native fishers, provincial and federal govts, wrestled over how to control, and who controlled, the fishery.

Sept. 13 Montreal-based printer, publisher and broadcaster Quebecor Inc. purchased Groupe Videotron, Que.'s largest cable company, for $5.4 billion.

• *Journal de Montréal* crime reporter Michel Auger was shot 5 times in the back outside his Montreal newspaper office after publishing a 2-page exposé on bikers and organized crime called, "Confusion in the Ranks of the Crime Warlords." Auger survived the attack.

Sept. 30 The body of Pierre Trudeau lay in state on Parliament Hill. Approximately 50,000 Canadians gathered to pay their respects. The former PM had died Sept. 28 of complications related to prostate cancer. On Oct. 3, thousands of mourners and state dignitaries, including Fidel Castro and Jimmy Carter, attended his state funeral at Nôtre Dame Basilica in Montreal.

Also in Sept.
• Canada collected 14 total medals including 3 gold at the Summer Olympics Games in Sydney,

Australia. Simon Whitfield (b 1975) took gold in the men's inaugural triathlon with a furious sprint at the finish; Sebastien Lareau and Daniel Nestor (b 1972) beat the number 1–ranked hometown favourites Mark Woodforde and Todd Woodbridge to win gold in tennis pairs; and perhaps the highlight: the gritty, determined performances of Daniel Igali (b 1974), who took gold in freestyle wrestling. Igali, who emigrated to Canada from Nigeria after the Commonwealth Games in Victoria, was the 1st Canadian to win an Olympic gold in wrestling.

Oct. 1 The Nova Scotia Water Resources Protection Act, banning bulk-water exports over 25 litres, came into effect.

Oct. 6 A Vancouver judge found Boston Bruin defenceman Marty McSorley (b 1963) guilty of assault with a weapon in the Feb. 21 stick-to-the-temple attack on Canucks' tough-guy Donald Brashear (b 1972). McSorley was given an 18-month conditional discharge. The NHL suspended McSorley for 23 games.

Oct. 11 Toronto city counsellors voted 33–21 in favour of shipping the city's garbage to Adams Mine near Kirkland L. Ont. Critics argued the garbage would pollute nearby lakes and contaminate water supplies. The plan was scrapped on Oct. 20 following sustained grassroots protest. Toronto would later contract to have its garbage hauled by truck to dump sites in Michigan, which caused more controversy. On Feb. 7, 2001, London, Ont., Mayor Anne Marie DeCicco and Sarnia Mayor Mike Bradley (b 1955) met with Toronto officials to express concern over the 90 trucks full of Toronto garbage that passed over southern Ont. highways every day en route to Sumpter and Arbor Hills, Michigan. The talks were unsuccessful.

Oct. 20 Former BC premier Glen Clark was charged with fraud and breach of trust related to a casino licencing scandal wherein Clark allegedly provided neighbour Dimitrios Pilarinos with a licence to operate a casino; in turn, Clark was given free home renovations. The RCMP raided Clark's home for evidence in Mar. 1999; the raid was televised, suggesting a police tipoff. The media quickly dubbed the ensuing scandal Casinogate. Clark resigned as premier in Aug. 1999. He was acquitted of the

charges on Aug. 29, 2002. However, on Nov. 19, 2002, Justice H.A.D. Oliver, BC conflict commissioner, ruled that Clark had broken conflict standards in the Pilarinos affair, and suggested Clark contribute $54,000 to cover part of the legal fees associated with the conflict-of-interest inquiry.

Oct. 22 PM Jean Chrétien called an election for Nov. 27 as a Leger Marketing popularity poll gave the Liberals a rating of 48%, Alliance 21%, Bloc Québécois 10%, and the NDP and Progressive Conservative 8% each.

• The CBC began airing *A People's History of Canada*. It ran a total of 16 episodes over 2000 and 2001.

Oct. 24 British author of the Harry Potter series, J.K. Rowling, read for 20,000 young fans and parents at Toronto's SkyDome in what was perhaps the world's largest author reading to date.

Oct. 25 Nortel stocks plunged from $96 to $71, altogether, some $83 billion in market capital, causing the Toronto Stock Exchange (TSE) 300-stock index to drop 840.26 points, its biggest decline since Oct. 19, 1987. Trading overloaded TSE capacity, and by 11:58 a.m., the exchange was forced to close for the day. Eleven million shares had changed hands by that hour. Nortel shares had been as high as $124.50 in July.

Nov. 7 Margaret Atwood won the Booker Prize for her novel, *The Blind Assassin*.

• CBC's satire show *This Hour Has 22 Minutes* posted a petition over the Internet requesting that Stockwell Day's first name be changed to "Doris." More than the proposed requisite of 1 million signed the petition — but to no avail. The CBC show began the petition after it was revealed that the Alliance party would consider holding referendums on any issue if 3% of eligible voters so desired.

Nov. 13 When the Mississauga, Ont., votes were counted, Mayor Hazel McCallion (b 1921) was declared victorious, and returned to the mayor's chair, a position she has held since 1978. The feisty, 5-foot-tall, Gaspé-born McCallion, frequently hailed as "Hurricane Hazel" in area media, appeared confident enough about her re-election to take an early-Nov. trip to China and Japan. "The job of the mayor and councillors carries on whether there's an election or not," she announced.

Nov. 15 The Que. govt introduced Bill 170, amalgamating cities across the province by Jan. 1, 2002. The bill centralized power in Montreal, transforming its 28 municipalities into 26 boroughs, and nearly doubled the city's population to 2 million. Gerald Tremblay (b 1942) was voted new Montreal megacity mayor Nov. 4, 2002, beating out incumbent Pierre Bourque (b 1942), who had held the position since 1994.

Nov. 27 Jean Chrétien's Liberals won a 3rd consecutive majority govt in the federal general election, taking 172 of 301 seats in the House. Stockwell Day's Alliance party assumed Official Opposition status with 66 seats, Gilles Duceppe's Bloc Québécois took 38 seats, Alexa McDonough's NDP took 13, and Joe Clark's Conservatives 12. There were no Independents. Voter turnout was 61.2%, the lowest federal-election turnout to date.

• An inquest blamed mismanagement, surgical error and inexperienced doctors for the deaths of 12 babies at the infant cardiac program of the Winnipeg Health Sciences Centre in 1994. Inquest chair Justice Murray Sinclair concluded that many of cases had been taken on by doctors who did not have the required skills.

Dec. 1 BC became the 1st province to sell the morning-after birth-control pill without a prescription.

Dec. 8 The BC govt began a process of removing or replacing the word "squaw" from the 11 provincial place names that carried the word, such as Squaw Mountain and Squaw L.

Dec. 15 The Supreme Court of Canada ruled 6–3, in the case of Little Sister's Book and Art Emporium of Vancouver, that Customs Canada agents had the right to inspect and seize material they believed was obscene. However, the court ruled it was up to Customs to prove the material was, in fact, obscene under current law, within a maximum 30 days, or release the literature in question. Little Sisters (a store carrying gay and lesbian literature), and Canada Customs, had battled over border book

seizures and obscenity laws since Customs banned the gay magazine *The Advocate* in 1986.

Dec. 29 The National Gallery of Canada posted 110 of its possessions on the Internet. The works of art were believed to have been stolen in Europe during the Nazi occupation. Possible owners could view works on the site and initiate claims.

Dec. 31 *Atanarjuat* ("The Fast Runner") by filmmaker Zacharius Kunuk (b 1957) was produced. Filmed in Igloolik, in the north Baffin region of the Canadian Arctic, *Atanarjuat* was the 1st feature film written, produced, directed and acted by Inuit in the Inuktituk language. It won 6 Genies, a Camera d'Or at the Cannes Film Festival (2001), the Toronto City Award for Best Feature film at the Toronto Film Festival (2001), and the Guardian Award for First Directors at the Edinburgh International Film Festival (2001).

Also in 2000

• Canada's population was 30,770,000.

• The average size of a Canadian family in 2000 was 3.0 people, down from 3.7 people in 1971.

• *Mercy Among the Children*, by David Adams Richards (b 1950) was co-winner of the coveted Giller Prize for fiction with *Anil's Ghost* by Micheal Ondaatje. Richards remains one of the few Canadian writers to win this country's Gov-Gen.'s Award for both fiction and non-fiction, taking the prize for his novel *Nights Below Station Street* in 1988, and for his autobiographical look at growing up in Newcastle, NB, *Lines on the Water: A Fisherman's Life on the Miramichi*.

• Auyuittuq ("the land that never melts") on Baffin Is., Nunavut, was given full national park status (it had operated as a protected site since the 1970s). The 19,707-km² preserve includes the 6,000 km² Penny Ice Cap, the only part of the park not located above the Arctic circle. The park is home to over 38 bird species, including the threatened peregrine falcon and whistling swan.

• 2,307 Canadians were in foreign prisons, 1,500 of which were in the US. Two Canadians sat on death row, both in the US.

• Canadians made 47.2 million trips abroad, spending some $18 billion in foreign countries. Foreign travellers made 48.6 million trips to Canada, spending $15.7 billion in Canada. The 2000 travel deficit ($2.3) had increased from $1.7 billion in 1999.

• Canada exported $361,000 worth of wine to Europe, while importing some $535 million of European wine.

• Sask. Crown corporations posted consolidated earnings of $293 million, up from $216 million in 1999.

• Canada had a record trade surplus of $54.5 billion.

• There were 2,230 certified organic farmers in Canada.

• Sirmilik National Park (22,200 km²) was established at the northern end of Baffin Is., Nunavut. (Sirmilik is an Anlnuit word meaning "place of glaciers.") The park, which includes Bylot Is., is home to the largest colony of snow geese in the world. Its rugged landscape, characterized by towering, snow-capped mountains, deep fjords, glaciers and tundra, is also home to such animals as polar bear, caribou, wolves, black-legged kittiwakes and thick-billed murres.

• There were approximately 2,400 Native reserves across Canada, 1,600 of which were in BC.

• The Big Three auto manufacturers — Ford, GM and Chrysler-Daimler — accounted for 66.3% of the Canadian automobile market, down from 68.1% in 1999.

• Canadians purchased a record 1.552 million automobiles and trucks at dealerships, up from 1.503 million in 1999.

• 227,000 immigrants entered Canada, 2,000 more than scheduled.

• 276,000 Canadian workers joined the private sector, pushing the percent working in private enterprise to 65.5%, the highest rate since 1976.

• Air Canada accounted for 80% of the domestic Canadian airline travel market.

• 3.9 million Canadians worked in the goods sector, while 11.2 million worked in the service sector (including 160,000 in the amusement, gambling and recreation fields — twice the 1990 number).

• The Ont. govt enacted the McMichael Canadian Art Collection Amendment Act (Bill 112), which returned the mandate of the McMichael Gallery to its original vision. In 1965, Robert (1921–2003) and Signe McMichael gave their art collection, home and 14 surrounding acres in Kleinburg to the Ont. govt on the condition that their gallery be continued with a focus on the Group of Seven and contemporary artists. In 1996, they sued the Ont. govt for breach of promise, arguing the gallery's board of directors compromised the founding premise by including modern works.

• Canada Post issued a commemorative 46 cent stamp featuring NS contralto Portia White.

• The total number of Canadian military personnel fell to 56,706, the lowest level since 1950.

• There was a 6% drop (a decrease of 146,000 people) in the number of self-employed Canadians, the first annual decrease since 1986.

• The unemployment rate stood at 6.8%.

• 40% of all Canadian employment was in Ont.

• Alb. employment ranks increased for the 8th consecutive year.

• 1 out of 10 people employed in Sask. worked on a farm, the highest ratio in the country. The province, however, lost 19,000 farm jobs over the year.

• The part-time employment rate for Canadians between the ages of 15–24 was 44%. The 1981 rate was 25.3%.

• Male immigrants to Canada made 40% less than Canadian-born men of similar age and educational background.

• Jazz pianist Oscar Peterson became the 1st Canadian to win the International Music Council UNESCO Prize. The prize is awarded to those "musicians or musical institutions that have contributed to the enrichment and development of music and have served peace, understanding between peoples and international cooperation." Earlier winners included Yehudi Menuhin, Dimitri Shostakovich and Leonard Bernstein.

• Kenn Harper published *Give me my Father's Body*, the true story of Minik, a 6-year-old Eskimo brought to New York from Greenland in 1897, along with his father and 5 compatriots, by Admiral/explorer Robert Peary as living specimens for the American Museum of Natural History.

• Poet and classicist Anne Carson (b 1950) became the 1st woman — and the 1st Canadian — to be awarded the prestigious T.S. Eliot Prize for Poetry for her book *The Beauty of the Husband: A Fictional Essay in 29 Tangos*.

• Poet Al Purdy's last book, *Beyond Remembering: The Collected Poems of Al Purdy*, was published posthumously.

• The 824-page *Encyclopedia of British Columbia*, edited by Daniel Francis, was published.

• Victoria, BC, native Nelly Furtado (b 1978) released her popular debut album, *Whoa Nelly*. It was nominated for 4 Grammys, including Song of the Year, for her hit, "I'm Like a Bird."

2001

Jan. 2 A 2-m long, 60-kg cougar killed a cross-country skier in Banff, the first-known such fatality to occur in Alb. Also in Banff this day another cougar mauled a husky and stalked a woman to the safety of a nearby home. Wildlife authorities explained that the cougars had come down from the mountains to stalk elk wintering in town.

Jan. 4 Health Minister Allan Rock appointed Kevin Keough of Memorial U. the nation's first chief scientist, a position created to promote and enhance health-science research across the country.

• The 1st Ice Hotel in Canada (modelled after an innovative tourist attraction in Stockholm, Sweden) opened in Quebec City. The structure, which cost $500,000 to build, had an interior temperature of

–5°C. Its construction required 4,500 tonnes of snow and 250 tonnes of ice. The novelty inn lured 40,000 guests to the site, each paying $165 CDN a night for resting in a sleeping bag on top of an animal fur which, in turn, covered an ice bed. The Ice Hotel remained in business until Apr. 5, 2001, when the electricity was turned off and the remaining elements of its structure were bulldozed into the St. Lawrence R.

Jan. 9 Conrad Black replaced Don Babick as chairman and publisher of the *National Post*. Babick became president and COO of Southam Publications Inc.

Jan. 11 Que. Parti Québécois Premier Lucien Bouchard announced he would resign from politics when a successor was chosen in Mar. The dollar rose .33 cents US (to 66.91) the same day.

Jan. 14 Same-sex couples Kevin Bourassa and Joe Varnell, and Anne and Elaine Vautour, were married in a double ceremony at the Metropolitan Community Church of Toronto. The couples posted banns in the Christian tradition, which, under an interpretation of provincial law, legally sanctioned the marriages. The provincial govt, however, refused to register the marriages on the grounds that federal law defined marriage as a union between a man and a woman.

Jan. 18 NS Economic Development Minister Gordon Balser announced that the chronically troubled Crown-operated Sydney Steel Corp. (Sysco), established in 1899 as Dominion Iron and Steel, would be liquidated. Doors would be shut by year's end. The announcement was made after a $25 million purchase deal with Duferco Farrell Corp. of Switzerland fell through.

Jan. 27 Lorne Calvert (b 1954) was chosen successor to Roy Romanow as Sask. NDP party leader and provincial premier at the NDP leadership convention in Saskatoon. Calvert took 57.6% of the convention vote; nearest rival Chris Axworthy (b 1947) garnered 42.2%. Calvert was sworn in as premier Feb. 8. Romanow, who had spent 35 years in politics, had announced his resignation Sept. 25, 2000.

• Andrei Knyazev, a Russian diplomat, killed two women in a drunk driving accident in Ottawa.

He escaped Canadian charges by declaring diplomatic immunity, the 3rd time he had done so in Ottawa. (He would later be recalled, and in 2002, found guilty of involuntary manslaughter in the case and sentenced to 4 years in a Moscow labour camp). On Mar. 14, 2001, the federal govt announced that foreign diplomats found drunk behind the wheel would lose their licences; they would be expelled from the country when caught for a second time.

Jan. 31 Chapters Inc. bookstores accepted a $121.5 million hostile takeover bid by Onex CEO Gerald Schwartz and Indigo CEO Heather Reisman. The Competition Bureau approved the deal Apr. 15 on conditions that included the new owners sell 13 superstores and 10 mall stores, cut back on the number of unsold books returned to publishers and provide publishers with quicker payments.

Feb. 2 The federal govt banned the importation of Brazilian beef, claiming the South American country had imported bovine spongiform encephalopathy BSE — mad cow cattle from Europe in the 1990s. Brazil, which had not suffered one case of mad cow disease, claimed the ban a retaliative measure in the ongoing trade dispute over aircraft subsidies (Bombardier, Canada vs Embraer SA, Brazil). Canadian authorities lifted the ban Feb. 23 after Canadian inspectors completed an on-site assessment of the Brazilian beef industry.

Feb. 3 Former Nfld. Health Minister, Roger Grimes (b 1950) won the leadership of the provincial Liberal party, beating John Efford (b 1944) by 14 votes. He was made Nfld. premier Feb. 13, succeeding Brian Tobin, who resigned in Oct. 2000 to become federal industry minister.

Feb. 4 Saudi Arabian authorities arrested William Sampson, a Canadian working for the Saudi govt, in connection to 2 Riyadh car explosions (Nov. 17 and 22, 2000), that killed 2 and injured 3. Sampson confessed to the bombings on television and was convicted and sentenced to death Apr. 2002. Sampson later argued that the confessions were made under torture. He spent 31 months in solitary confinement until King Fahd bin Abdulaziz granted him clemency Aug. 8, 2003.

Feb. 6 Auditor Gen. Denis Desautels (b 1943) issued a scathing report stating the federal govt was not properly managing health-and-safety issues related to the nation's food supply, blood supply, salmon-farming industry and nuclear-power-generation facilities.

Feb. 15 The Supreme Court of Canada unanimously ruled in the case of BC residents Glen Burns and Atif Rafay, both wanted for murder in the state of Washington, that Canada would not extradite wanted criminals to nations that might sentence them to death. Extradition papers were signed for the two on Mar. 28, when American officials pledged that Burns and Rafay, if convicted, would not receive the death penalty.

Feb. 17 Team Canada — a group of provincial premiers, financial representatives and PM Chrétien — returned from a 10-day business tour of China with 294 contracts worth $5.7 billion.

Feb. 19 Federal Environment Minister David Anderson (b 1937) set in motion a 5-year, $120 million plan to cut air pollution by setting car emission controls on new cars for 2004, lowering the level of sulphur in gasoline by 2005, and in diesel by 2006.

Feb. 20 Iraq leader Saddam Hussein placed a general ban on all Canadian exports to retaliate against Canada's support of US military measures in the Middle East. The US Air Force had recently killed 2 and injured 20 in no-fly zone operations over Iraq. Canada shipped some 262,000 tonnes of wheat worth $50 million to Iraq in 2000.

• Falconbridge workers in Sudbury voted to end a strike that began Aug. 1, 2000. The new contract gave each worker a $2,000 signing bonus and a per hour wage increase of $1.07, which included a cost-of-living allowance. The strike cost Falconbridge an estimated $50 million in lost production.

Feb. 22 One thousand four hundred Que. pharmacists were legislated back to work under the province's drug-insurance plan which protected some 3.2 million Quebecers not covered by private or corporate drug insurance policies. The original provincial drug plan, established in 1997, gave pharmacists $6.61 for each prescription filled.

Pharmacists demanded $8.15. New legislation offered $7.47.

Feb. 27 Parti Québécois Finance Minister Bernard Landry (b 1937), who would succeed Lucien Bouchard as Que. premier Mar. 8, began what would become a 7-month-long nationalist crusade, explaining before a crowd in Chicoutimi that Que. was a nation and, as such, it would be "insulting to call Quebec a province" and "absurd" to refer to the region as one would refer to Sask.

• The federal govt located an extra $1.8 billion for transfer payments. Que. would receive the lion's share — $1.5 billion — because it had the slowest rate of economic growth. The rest would be distributed to all provinces except BC, Alb. and Ont.

Feb. 28 Howard Balloch, Canadian ambassador to China and Mongolia, officially included North Korea in his portfolio, thereby becoming the first Canadian ambassador to the Communist state. Balloch would work from the Canadian embassy in Beijing.

Mar. 2 Bernard Landry was proclaimed Parti Québécois leader, replacing Lucien Bouchard, who stepped down from politics. Landry was sworn into office as Que. premier Mar. 8. On Oct. 2, he officially stated the economy, not nationalism, would take priority.

Mar. 6 Federal Industry Minister Brian Tobin pledged $750 million to the newly created Canadian Foundation for Innovation program, to assist teaching hospitals and post-secondary institutions acquire up-to-date research equipment. The move was made to offset the brain drain, the loss of the nation's best and brightest to foreign countries offering better opportunities, wages, fellowships and research facilities.

Mar. 8 NS Judge Patrick Curran dismissed claims that NS Native Peoples had an historic right to log on Crown property, and found 35 NS Native Peoples guilty of illegal logging.

Mar. 12 Ralph Klein began his 3rd consecutive term as Conservative premier of Alb. as his Tories swept to power in a landslide victory. Conservatives won 74 seats, Liberals 7 and the NDP 2. Liberal leader Nancy MacBeth (b 1948) failed to win her riding and retired Mar. 15.

Mar. 13 Canada and the US banned some meat and dairy products (including unpasturized cheese, fresh unprocessed meat, live animals, animal embryos and semen, as well as all farm equipment) from the EU, which had been ravaged by foot-and-mouth disease. Britain had slaughtered 100,000 animals to date in efforts to stifle the contagious animal virus. The voracious foot-and-mouth disease last hit Canada in 1952.

Mar. 14 Farmers in tractors and various other agricultural equipment formed a 5-km-long column in Ottawa to protest sinking commodity prices and soaring production costs. Federal Agriculture Minister Lyle Vanclief (b 1943) was burned in effigy. The federal govt pledged $500 million in farm aid on Mar. 1, but farmers argued the need better approximated $1 billion.

Mar. 15 BC Finance Minister Paul Ramsey tabled his province's new budget, which included $1.85 billion in spending, much of it for new hospitals, schools, daycare and the hiring of new nurses.

• Expansion and refitting of the new Maplehurst Correctional Complex was completed in Milton, Ont. The number of beds increased from 600 to 1,500, making Maplehurst the largest jail in Canada. The new unit also included 6 new self-contained security pods.

Mar. 16 A federal report on minority and female participation in the Armed Forces noted that the military had one of the world's best policys on equality and fair representation but was failing miserably to keep pace with its initiatives. The report revealed that women comprised 11.5% of the Armed Forces, visible minorities 2.5%, and Native Peoples 1.8%.

Mar. 20 Following a lengthy review, NS Justice Minister Michael Baker (b 1957) concluded that NS would maintain its all-season ban on Sunday shopping. Exceptions included tourist outlets, bookstores, corner stores and groceterias. NS was the last province to maintain the full-year ban.

Mar. 31 The five-year Softwood Lumber Agreement between Canada and the US that had been finalized on May 29, 1996, expired. Battles over Canadian lumber subsidies and US duties would rage through 2003, with US duties on Canadian softwood rising to 27.2% in 2002.

Also in Mar.

• The federal govt compensated the Alb. Horse Lake First Nation with a $125 million cash settlement for oil-rich lands surrendered near Fairview in 1928.

• Figure-skating pair Jamie Salé (b 1977), of Red Deer, Alb., and David Pellitier (b 1974), of Sayabec, Que., beat out stiff competition to win the Figure Skating World Championships in Vancouver. The pair, although initially matched in 1996, did not begin to train seriously together until 1998.

Apr. 1 CBC television ran a one-hour special of *This Hour Has 22 Minutes,* featuring comedian Rick Mercer (b 1969) in conversation with Americans about their perceptions of Canada. Among the responses received was that of a Columbia University (New York City) professor who admitted to signing a petition urging Canadians to cease from their habit of setting the country's senior citizens afloat on ice floes to eliminate overpopulation, and an Iowa gov.'s salute to Canada as the country moved from a 20- to a 24-hour time clock.

• Telefilm Canada announced that the overall goal of the Canada Feature Film Fund was to increase Canadian audiences in theatres for Canadian feature films, aiming to capture 5% of the domestic box office by 2006. In May 1984, the govt had announced the National Film and Video Policy to support the promotion and marketing of Canadian feature films. In 1986, a $33-million-a-year feature-film fund was created to invest in high-quality, culturally relevant Canadian theatrical feature films. In Sept. 1988, $11.4 million was added to that. A Distribution Fund was to provide $17 million a year exclusively for distribution and marketing.

Apr. 5 Federal Health Minister Allan Rock (b 1947) created a $480 million federal anti-smoking campaign aimed at reducing by 30% the number of cigarettes sold over the next 10 years. The campaign would include education programs, anti-smoking ads and increased taxes on tobacco products. There was no attempt to ban the sale or distribution of tobacco.

Apr. 11 Ken Fyke, chairman of the $2 million Sask. Commission on Medicare, recommended that the province shut down 50 of its 70 hospitals in an effort to reduce costs and duplication. Premier Lorne Calvert rejected the recommendation Dec. 5.

• Calgary transit workers ended a crippling 7-week strike after coming to terms over a 3-year contract.

Apr. 17 Man. introduced the country's 1st baby bonuses for pregnant women, providing a maximum monthly payment of $81.41 to those with family incomes below $32,000.

Apr. 18 The NB govt struck a deal with the province's doctors, giving each, on average, $50,000 more a year, beginning Mar. 2002. Most NB family doctors earned between $150,000 and $180,000 annually. One thousand NB doctors had staged a 3-day walkout over the issue in Jan.

Apr. 19 Chris Hadfield (b 1959) became the 1st Canadian to freely enter interplanetary space as he stepped into orbit to help fasten the new Canadarm 2 robotic arm to the International Space Station (ISS). Construction of the ISS began in 1998 and it is still under construction. The project is a joint effort of Canada, the US, Japan, Russia and 11 European nations. When completed, the space laboratory will weigh over 1 million pounds and measure 108 m x 88 m.

Apr. 20–22 The third Summit of the Americas was held in Quebec City. Delegates from 34 countries in North, South and Central America, all members of the Organization of American States (OAS), met to discuss the Free Trade Area of the Americas (FTAA), a pan-American free trade agreement to be implemented by 2005. Security for the event was unprecedented — over 6,000 police officers were dispatched to Quebec City and a 3-m-high concrete-and-metal fence was erected around historic Old Town. Approximately 25,000–30,000 anti-globalization activists gathered to protest. The summit cost taxpayers approximately $156 million, 50%

of which went toward security. The first FTAA trade-liberalization pact was signed between Canada and Costa Rica Apr. 23.

Apr. 23 Algoma Steel of Sault Ste. Marie, with debt and liabilities exceeding $1 billion, was given a reprieve against creditors by an Ont. Superior Court. Soaring energy costs and falling world steel prices led to Algoma losses of $76.8 million for the year ending Mar. 31.

Apr. 25 The city of Ottawa approved the nation's toughest and most extensive anti-smoking bylaws, banning smoking in restaurants, bars, private clubs and legions.

Apr. 27 Ont.'s Conservative govt legislated an end to a 4-week strike by school support workers in Toronto and Windsor that had kept 300,000 students out of class.

Also in Apr.
• Budget airline Canada 3000 was given federal approval to purchase rival Royal Aviation of Montreal for $84 million. The firms merged May 1 to form a 40-aircraft fleet serving 21 Canadian cities.

• The BC govt preserved 600,000 ha of virgin coastal valley forest from future logging, including a section of white "spirit" bear habitat near Princess Royal Is.

May 2 PM Chrétien and Heritage Minister Sheila Copps pledged $560 million in support of Canadian art and culture over 3 years, including the development of Internet cultural promotions, the digitization of CBC and NFB archives, money to further bolster CBC productions, and support of art schools.

May 7 US businessman George Gillett closed a deal to purchase 80.1% of the Montreal Canadiens and all of the 21,000-seat Molson Centre from Molson's for $275 million. The NHL approved the deal in June. Although the Canadiens won 24 Stanley Cups, placing them second only to the New York Yankees as North America's most winning professional sporting franchise, no Canadian offers were made on the team.

May 15 Eight Canadian Alliance MPs publicly called for Stockwell Day to resign as party leader, stating they would boycott the Alliance caucus until then. On June 5, senior Alliance MP Deborah Grey stated she did not have confidence in Stockwell Day's ability to lead the party, and on July 3 joined the chorus of other dissidents in calling for Day's resignation. Day did not step down and on July 19, a number of Alliance dissidents, led by Chuck Strahl (b 1957), formed the Democratic Representative Caucus in the House.

May 16 BC Liberals under Gordon Campbell won the BC election, taking 76 of 79 seats. The former NDP government, under Ujjal Dosanjh, was reduced to only 3 seats, and later 2, after losing Victoria to the Liberals in a recount. The Campbell administration was sworn in June 5. The NDP previously held 39 seats, the Liberals 32. NDP leader Ujjal Dosanjh resigned following the election, and was replaced by Joy MacPhail June 16.

May 24 The Supreme Court of Canada ruled 5–2 that Native Peoples must pay duties on goods purchased in the US. The ruling overturned two lower court decisions made on the basis that north-south trade was basic to pre-contact Aboriginal economies and should therefore continue without taxation. The Court ruling was made in the case of Mike Mitchell, Grand Chief of the Akwesasne (his reserve located on the St. Lawrence near Cornwall, Ont.), who refused to pay $142.88 in duties on goods purchased in the US.

May 27 Eric Fairclough (b 1962) became the first Native leader of a major Canadian political party when acclaimed NDP leader for Yukon. Fairclough replaced Piers McDonald who had resigned.

May 28 Nfld. Premier Roger Grimes pledged $50 million over 3 years to clean up the province's drinking-water supplies. Water from 200 of Nfld.'s 607 public drinking-water sources required boiling before consumption.

May 29 The House of Commons passed legislation amending the Young Offenders Act, lowering the age in which youth could receive adult sentences from 16 to 14.

• Houston-based Conoco Inc. purchased Calgary-based Gulf Canada Resources for $6.7 billion in cash. Conoco announced it would pursue development of gas fields in the Mackenzie delta and promote the creation of the Mackenzie Valley Pipeline to stretch from the Beaufort Sea to southern markets.

May 31 Sheila Fraser (b 1950) was appointed auditor-gen., the 1st woman to hold the position. Fraser replaced Denis Desautels, who retired.

Also in May

• The Geological Survey of Canada announced the North Magnetic Pole's position was 81.3 N.E., 110.8 W, noting that the pole moved in a northwesterly direction at approximately 40 km per year. Projected location for 2002 was 81.6 N, 111.6 W.

• Former U. of Windsor professor and renowned short-story writer Alistair MacLeod (b 1936) won the $172,000 IMPAC Dublin Literary Award for his first novel, *No Great Mischief*. The book also received the Trillium Award and the Canadian Booksellers Association Libris Award for Book of the Year. The book tells the story of the MacDonalds, a Scottish family who moved to the New World and slowly dispersed from Cape Breton Is.

• 53% of New Brunswickers voted in a referendum to preserve the province's bar and tavern video-lottery terminals (VLTs). Introduced in 1990, the VLTs generated $110 million annually, $35 million of which was funnelled into provincial coffers.

June 1 Western provincial and territorial leaders finished their annual meeting in Moose Jaw, Sask., agreeing to ban all bulk water exports from their respective jurisdictions.

• Heritage Minister Sheila Copps doled out $28 million to help the Canadian publishing industry, $9.5 million of which was targeted to book publishers suffering widespread instability in the wake of the Chapters bookstore takeover in Jan.

• The Alb. govt offered $93 million to farmers affected by severe drought conditions that had crippled crops and forced ranchers to sell off cattle for lack of feed.

• Stephen Lewis was named UN envoy on AIDS in Africa, to help oversee African AIDS education, prevention and treatment. An estimated 25 million Africans were infected with HIV.

• At Roy Thompson Hall in Toronto, a standing-room-only crowd celebrated the 4th annual inductions to the Canadian Walk of Fame. The new 13 Canadian artists, entertainers, writers and sports figures honoured were: rock icons The Guess Who; artist Kenojuak Ashevak; author Margaret Atwood; Montreal Canadien legend Jean Beliveau (b 1931); figure skater Kurt Browning; Baseball-Hall-of-Famer Ferguson Jenkins; track star Harry Jerome (1940–1982); director Robert Lepage (b 1957); comedian Leslie Nielsen (b 1926); polka king Walter Ostanek; filmmaker Ivan Reitman; opera singer Teresa Stratas (b 1938); and ballerina Veronica Tennant (b 1946).

June 6 Google, regarded by many Internet users as the ultimate search engine, introduced www.google.ca, which allowed users the option of searching the entire web, searching Canada-only references and/or customizing the Google interface to search for either French- or English-language sites. It also provided a tool that translated French-language sites to English, and vice versa.

June 12 A House of Commons motion to confer honorary citizenship on Nelson Mandela was passed following an attempt by Canadian Alliance MP Rob Anders (Calgary West), to block its introduction. South Africa's 1st black president received the honour in Toronto in Nov., joining Swedish diplomat Raoul Wallenberg (Dec. 10, 1985) as the only honorary Canadian citizens.

June 27 NS passed Bill 68, making it illegal for the province's health-care workers to strike. The province's nurses had not received a wage increase in 10 years.

June 28 The Supreme Court of Canada upheld a 1991 Hudson, Que., municipal bylaw banning the use of pesticides on public and private lawns.

June 30 Some 1,000 surviving "Duplessis Orphans" were given compensation package worth an estimated $25–$37 million from the Que. govt. In return, the recipients agreed to drop any further litigation relating to abuses experienced in the province's Catholic Church–run social institutions during the 1940s and 1950s. The deal also absolved the Que. govt of all blame in the matter.

Also in June

• The Art Gallery of Ontario (AGO) opened its "Treasures from the State Hermitage Museum, Russia: Rubens and his Age" exhibit, which ran through Aug. 12. Many of the artworks had never been exhibited in North America.

• Before reluctantly leaving for Mombassa, Kenya, to drum up support for Toronto's 2008 Olympic bid, Toronto Mayor Mel Lastman remarked, "What the hell do I want to go to a place like Mombassa… I just see myself in a pot of boiling water with all these natives dancing around me." He apologized in public 2 weeks later. Toronto lost the Olympic bid to Beijing.

July 1 A 25% across-the-board decrease to BC's income tax took effect.

July 4 Six Aylmer, Ont., siblings between the ages of 6 and 14 were taken into the care of Children's Aid after their parents allegedly spanked them with a paddle. The children were returned on July 26th. The incident led to a Supreme Court challenge on Section 43 of the Criminal Code, established in 1892 to allow spanking for the purposes of "correction" within the bounds of "reasonable force." The Court ruled 6–3 in Jan. 2004, that spanking was acceptable, but only for children between 2 and 12, and without the use of instruments such as belts or rulers.

July 10 The UN released its annual Quality of Life Index, ranking Canada 3rd in the world behind Norway and Australia, respectively. Canada had held the number 1 ranking for the previous 6 years, but fell short following an Organization for Economic Co-operation and Development (OECD) report showing increases in the numbers of Canadians living below the poverty line, and an expanding gap between rich and poor.

July 16 BC Water, Land and Air Protection Minister Joyce Murray (b 1954) overturned a 3-year ban on grizzly bear hunting, which had been imposed by

the former NDP govt. A trophy hunt for the bears began Sept. 1. BC had an estimated 10,000 grizzlies, or 25% of the world's total.

July 20 Nortel reported a Canadian quarterly record loss of $19.4 billion US.

July 31 Conrad Black's Hollinger Inc. continued its exit from the Canadian newspaper business, selling 29 Ont. newspapers, including 16 dailies, to Osprey Media Group Inc. for $220 million. The deal included the *Kingston Whig-Standard*, *Sault Star* and the *Peterborough Examiner*. On Nov. 30, Hollinger sold Osprey the *Chatham Daily News* and the *Sarnia Observer* for $35 million. On Aug. 23, Black sold his remaining 50% interest in the *National Post* to CanWest Global Communications.

Aug. 3–12 The World Championships in Athletics (The Worlds) was held in Edmonton. Over 1,500 athletes attended. The US ranked 1st with 18 medals, Russia 2nd with 19 (but with less points than the US because it won 2 less gold) and Kenya 3rd with 8 medals. Canada was shut out of the medal circle.

Aug. 3 The annual provincial premiers conference convened in Victoria. Premiers agreed to call on Ottawa for an extra $7 billion for health care and the removal of upper caps on provincial equalization payments.

Aug. 7 BC nurses went on strike for increased wages. They returned to work Aug. 9 with a new contract, increasing wages to $32.42 an hour, or a 23.5% increase over three years.

• The BC govt passed legislation ending a 4-month-long public transit strike, which began on issues related to contract labour and part-time work. The back-to-work legislation required worker grievances to be resolved by further negotiation or arbitration.

Aug. 11 A freighter fire in the Welland Canal caused a 2-day shutdown of the only shipping route between L. Ontario and L. Erie.

Aug. 14 Hassan Khosrowshahi sold Future Shop, the nation's largest home-electronics retailer, to US-owned Best Buy Co., for $580 million in cash.

Aug. 18 Regina-born amateur astronomer Vance Petriew (b 1969) discovered the 1st comet found visually from North America since comet Stonehouse in 1998. The Jupiter family comet was discovered with a 20-inch Newtonian reflector on a wooden Dobsonian mount at one of Canada's largest stargazing parties, the Sask. Summer Star Party at Cypress Hills Provincial Park. The comet was designated P/2001 Q2 and named Comet Petriew. Its orbit carries it back to Earth every 5.5 years. Petriew, along with 7 other astronomers, was co-recipient of the 2002 Edgar Wilson Award for amateur comet discoveries.

Aug. 24 Captain Robert Piché glided an Air Transat Airbus A330 over the Atlantic for over 20 minutes before touching it down safely in the Azores. The plane, which was en route from Toronto to Lisbon, had lost the use of both engines due to a fuel leak.

Sept.11 An estimated 6,500 people, including 24 Canadians, were killed after 2 American Airline commuter planes were hijacked and flown into the 2 World Trade Center towers in New York City. A third hijacked plane was flown into the Pentagon in Washington; a fourth crashed outside Pittsburgh killing all aboard. The US Federal Aviation Administration (FAA) then ordered all transatlantic flights rerouted to Canada, followed by an order from Transportation Minister David Collenette (b 1946) to ground all commercial flights leaving Canada. Some 600 Canadian airports were closed. Canadian stock markets were shut down, while all Parliament and govt buildings were put on high-security alert. The attacks were blamed on al-Qaeda leader Osama bin Laden and his al-Qaeda terrorist network, believed to be supported by Afghanistan's ruling Taliban regime.

Sept. 12 Canadian Blood Services opened extra clinics to collect blood for those injured in the World Trade terrorist attacks. Hospitals around Ont. (including Hamilton, London, Kingston, Ottawa and Toronto) made their tertiary-care centres available for emergency cases from New York. The efforts were made in vain as the scope of the tragedy slowly unfolded: emergency workers located virtually no survivors from the collapsed World Trade towers.

• Transportation Minister David Collenette partially resumed flights out of Canada. Several carried RCMP sky marshals to protect against further terrorist activity. Approximately 150 jetliners containing over 21,000 passengers had been stranded in Atlantic Canada where flights had been rerouted and grounded Sept. 11. Gander, St. John's, Stephenville, Moncton, Dartmouth and Halifax each set up massive community efforts to house and feed the stranded in school gymnasiums, town halls, church basements, homes, local inns and hotels.

• A State of the Great Lakes 2001 report issued by the International Joint Commission, a collaboration of US and Canadian environmentalists, gave the Great Lakes cleanup effort a moderate grade.

Sept. 12–13 A number of Ont. Islamic community members reported harassment after the Sept. 11 attacks on New York. The Masjid-an-Noor Mosque in St. Catharines was saved from an arson fire, and an Islamic school in Niagara Falls closed after receiving threatening phone calls. The Canadian Muslim Civil Liberties Association also reported receiving a number of hate e-mails.

Sept. 14 An estimated 100,000 Canadians met on Parliament Hill to mourn those who lost their lives in New York, Pennsylvania and Washington on Sept. 11. A moment of silence was also observed across the country.

Sept. 16 An estimated 50 boats carrying non-Native fishers terrorized Native fishers and cut Native lobster pots on waters off Burnt Church, NB. The incident came after Ottawa issued a food fishery licence Aug. 27, giving Burnt Church Natives unrestricted fishing rights within a specified fishing zone. On Aug. 30, the Fisheries Department confiscated an estimated 86 Native lobster traps, claiming they had been placed outside the designated fishing zone. The Supreme Court ruled Sept. 17, 1999, that Atlantic Mi'kmaq had the right to unrestricted fishing throughout their ancestral land.

Sept. 19 Tropical storm Gabrielle hammered Nfld. More than 100 mm of rain pelted St. John's over a 15-hour period, causing flooding and power outages.

Sept. 26 Struggling Air Canada laid off 5,000 workers, grounded 84 planes and cut 20% of its capacity. On Sept. 30, the carrier reported a $160 million quarterly loss, pointing to the terrorist events in New York on Sept. 11, as a root cause of its current financial crisis. On Oct. 2, the federal govt pledged $160 million in emergency aid to the beleaguered Canadian airline industry; Air Canada received $100 million of it.

Sept. 29 PM Chrétien and the 4 major federal party leaders paid homage at "Ground Zero," the site of World Trade Center disaster.

Also in Sept.
• Canadians watched an average of 21.2 hours of TV per week.

Oct. 1 Canadian Pacific Ltd. dissolved, spinning off all its entities, including Fording Coal, Canadian Pacific Railway, CP Ships, and Fairmont Hotels and Resorts (formerly CP Hotels). The Canadian Pacific Railway was formed Oct. 15, 1872, to build a railway from coast to coast and unify the new Dominion.

Oct. 10 Gen. Louis Joseph, Marquis de Montcalm, was re-united with his troops. Montcalm, shot on the Plains of Abraham Sept. 13, 1759, was carried to Quebec City's Ursuline Convent where he died and his remains entombed. There he remained until several Que. heritage and historical groups lobbied to have him removed and buried at the Quebec Cemetery, alongside the 1,000 French and English troops who died in Canada's most pivotal battle.

• Air Canada launched its new low-fare carrier Tango, to begin flights on Nov. 1, to 8 Canadian cities.

• Foreign Affairs Minister and chair of the new Security Committee John Manley pledged $280 million to help protect Canada against terrorism. A number of national departments and agencies made claims to the funds: Transport Minister David Collenette claimed $91 million to improve airport security; the RCMP $55 million to better finance and equip investigations; Immigration $49 million to better facilitate deportations, investigate security risks and develop landed immigrant identity cards referred to as the "Maple Leaf," effective for re-entry into Canada Jan. 1, 2004. The spy wing of the Defence Department, the Communications Security Establishment, also received an estimated $37 million and the Canadian Security Intelligence Service (CSIS) $10 million.

Oct. 15 The Mackenzie Valley Pipeline deal was signed between the Mackenzie Valley Aboriginal Pipeline Corp., Imperial Oil, Shell Canada, Conoco Inc. and ExxonMobil Canada to establish a 1,300-km pipeline to carry Alaskan gas from the Beaufort Sea, through the Mackenzie Valley, on to an Alb. terminus and then to southern markets. The Aboriginal Pipeline Corp. received a 1/3 share in the proposed project. Production on the $5 billion pipeline was scheduled for 2006; completion was set for 2009. Its initial volume was designed for 0.8 to 1.5 billion cubic feet per day (bcfd).

Oct. 16 Over 2,000 demonstrators took part in a "snake march" through the business and financial district of Toronto to raise attention to global poverty and homelessness.

Oct. 19 In a case brought before it by an Ont. construction firm, members of the Supreme Court of Canada agreed that a Que. law making it mandatory for all construction workers to belong to a union violated the Canadian Charter of Rights and Freedoms. However, the Court ruled 5–4 that the law was acceptable because it provided a degree of stability within the trade.

Oct. 25 A survey issued by the College of Family Physicians of Canada showed that the average family GP worked 73 hours and had, on average, 124 appointments every week. The College concluded that the country immediately required 3,000 new family physicians.

Oct. 30 Sam the Record Man, the Canadian music retail chain opened by Sam Sniderman Sr. in the 1920s, filed for bankruptcy protection. Its 30 outlets could not compete with international giants such as HMV and the increasing free-sharing of copyrighted music over the Internet. The landmark 3 1/2-storey outlet at Yonge and Dundas in Toronto, which held one of the continent's most exhaustive collections of jazz and classical music, was saved through refinancing in 2002.

Oct. 31 Canadian media mogul Conrad Black entered Britain's House of Lords and was dubbed "Lord Black of Crossharbour." Black renounced his Canadian citizenship to receive the distinction, following an Ont. Court of Appeal ruling upholding a long-standing Canadian tradition forbidding Canadian citizens from accepting foreign titles. PM Chrétien made it clear on June 19, 1999, that, as a Canadian, Black could not receive the peerage. Black's subsequent effort to sue Chrétien for use of "arbitrary" power was thrown out of court.

Also in Oct.
• The CIBC laid off 2,000 workers; Alcan laid off 3,600 workers.

Nov. 1 St. John's Anglican Church in Lunenburg, NS, built in 1754, was destroyed by arson.

Nov. 11 Toronto-based Canada 3000, the nation's second-largest airline, filed for bankruptcy protection. The carrier, which had earlier purchased CanJet and Royal Aviation, was victim to the weak loonie, a slumping economy and the loss of travel dollars following the Sept. 11 terrorist attacks on New York. Four thousand eight hundred employees lost their jobs.

Nov. 13 Thomson Corp. sold the *Brandon Sun* and *Winnipeg Free Press* to Canadian Newspapers Inc. for an estimated $150 million in cash. The once-mighty Canadian newspaper giant was left with only 20% of the *Globe & Mail*.

Nov. 14 Industry Minister Brian Tobin and the Canadian Tourism Commission set in motion a $20 million advertising campaign to help invigorate the slumping tourist trade.

Nov. 18 The best meteor shower seen from Canada in 50 years peaked at 3 a.m. PST (6 a.m. EST) with over 1,000 Leonid meteors (sandlike debris from Comet Tempel-Tuttle) streaking across the sky over a 3–4 hour period.

Nov. 23 Atlantic Canada's last colliery coal mine, the Cape Breton Development Corp.'s (DEVCO) Prince mine, was shut; 440 jobs were lost. Its sister mine, Phalen, had closed in 2000. Total job losses exceeded 1,500. Ottawa had invested $1.6 billion into

the beleaguered Crown-owned DEVCO since it was formed in 1967.

Nov. 28 The House of Commons passed Bill C–36 — the country's new anti-terrorism legislation — 190 votes to 47. The bill included provisions for life imprisonment for those who planned terrorist attacks, 14 years for those who engaged in terrorist activity and 10 years for those who supported terrorists. The bill also gave police the right to arrest suspected terrorists without the need of a warrant; the right to maintain a govt–approved list of suspicious organizations; provisions to make it easier for authorities to use wiretaps; and provisions giving authorities the right to seize the assets of those charged with supporting terrorism. The Senate approved Bill C–36 on Dec. 18 by a vote of 45–21.

Also in Nov.
• Roberta Jamieson became the 1st woman to be elected chief of the Six Nations at Brantford, Ont. — the nation's most populous Native reserve.

Dec. 3 The federal govt officially apologized for the execution of 23 Canadian soldiers shot during WW I for cowardice or desertion, stating that the men might have suffered from what is now known as post-traumatic stress syndrome. The names of the executed were then entered in the *Books of Remembrance*, located in the Peace Tower, Parliament Hill, which are opened each day so the name of each fallen Canadian soldier is shown at least once every year.

Dec. 4 Auditor-Gen. Sheila Fraser tabled her 1st report, noting that of the $1.4 billion in federal home-heating refunds issued over the previous fiscal year, only 18% went to low-income earners; the rest was sent to high-income earners, prisoners, the dead and various other non-deserving. Fraser also noted that $800 million in federal revenue was lost to a loophole that allowed Canadian companies to transfer assets to Barbados (where a portion of Finance Minister Paul Martin's Canadian Steamship Lines [CSL] operations were kept).

Dec. 6 The Constitution was amended to alter the name of the province of Newfoundland to Newfoundland and Labrador. The House had approved the name change Oct. 30. Labrador comprised 70%

of the province's total landmass. It had 30,000 inhabitants, compared to Nlfd's 540,000.

Dec. 12 Opposition leader Stockwell Day stepped down, handing over the Alliance leadership to interim leader MP John Reynolds until the party's leadership convention in spring (Mar. 20, 2002).

Dec. 14 Barrick Gold Corp. of Toronto completed a $2.3 billion merger with Homestake Mining Co. of California, making Barrick 2nd only to AngloGold Ltd. of South Africa in total volume of gold produced. It had a capacity of 6.1 million ounces and reserve of 83 million ounces. The acquisition gave Barrick operations worldwide, including mines in Eskay Creek, BC, northern Ont., Nevada, Tanzania and South America.

Dec. 21 Health Canada's 1st commercial crop of medicinal marijuana was readied for distribution to 680 patients. The weed was grown underground, in an abandoned mineshaft in Flin Flon, Man.

Also in 2001

• The population of Canada was 31,021,300; 51% of the total lived in greater Montreal, Ont.'s Golden Horseshoe, the Calgary-Edmonton Corridor and Lower Mainland BC.

• The Canadian Aboriginal population was 1,319,890, or 4% of the total population.

• New census data showed Toronto to be the most ethnically diverse city in North America, with 43.7% of its denizens foreign born. Miami was ranked 2nd with 40.2%, and Vancouver 3rd with 37.5%.

• 49.96% of all new Canadian immigrants moved to Toronto. The second most popular destination was Vancouver, which took in 13.65%.

• 18.4% of all those living in Canada were born abroad, compared to 16.1% in 1991.

• Thirteen million immigrants entered Canada since 1901.

• There were 23,360 commercial fishing vessels registered in Canada.

• 38% of drivers killed in traffic accidents had been drinking, down from 60% in 1982.

• The following shows the nation's 2001 religious affiliations in whole numbers, with percentage changes since 1991 in parenthesis: 12.8 million Roman Catholic (5%); 8.7 million Protestant (–8%); 4.8 million with no religion (43.9%); 780,450 Christian with no affiliation (121%); 579,640 Muslim (129%); 479,620 Christian Orthodox (24%); 329,995 Jewish (3.7%); 300,345 Buddhist (84%); 297,200 Hindu (89%); and 278,415 Sikh (89%).

• Canada exported 18.4% of the world's forest products, including 17.2% of the world's softwood lumber, 21.7% of the world's newsprint and 14.9% of the world's wood pulp.

• Canadian farm animals produced 163.5 billion kg of manure. The top 3 provincial producers were Alb. (55.8 million kg), Ont. (29 million kg) and Sask. (24.8 million kg).

• The Canadian poultry population exceeded 134 million.

• Toronto-born Queen's graduate Shirley Tilghman (b 1946), became the 19th — and 1st woman — president of Princeton U. in New Jersey.

• *Trailer Park Boys* debuted as a series on Showcase television. Originally conceived and shot as a "mockumentary" set in Sunnyvale Trailer Park, the show followed the adventures and misadventures of Julian and Ricky, two boozing, brawling trailer park boys just out of jail. Julian tried to go straight but the tough-talking twosome couldn't stay out of trouble. Created by Mike Clattenberg, John Paul Tremblay and Robb Wells, the series' edgy, off-the-wall humour quickly found a loyal following.

• Somerville House book publishers of Toronto filed for bankruptcy protection.

• Ont. Superior Court Justice Clair Marchand ruled that a realty firm was partly responsible for allowing an intoxicated employee to get behind the wheel after a 1994 staff party. The employee had refused an open invitation to use a cab and instead left the party, and subsequently got into an accident, suffering permanent injury. The ruling required Sutton Group Incentive Realty to pay Linda Hunt $300,000, or 25% of the plaintiff's claim.

• 23% of Canadians smoked, a record low since such statistics were first recorded in the early 1960s. The rates were highest in PEI and Sask., at 28%, and lowest in BC, at 17%.

• The EU exported $18.3 billion of goods to Canada and $351 billion to the US.

• The Ontario Clean Air Alliance issued a report naming the top air polluters in the country: Ontario Power's Nanticoke coal-fired energy plant ranked at the top of the list, followed by Cabot Canada chemicals of Sarnia, Ont., Alb. oil patch producer Syncrude, and Agrium Products of Redwater, Alb.

• Senators and MPs raised their salaries by 20%, the last time federal politicians could vote to increase their own salaries. All future changes, including those for federal judges, would be set on a schedule. In 2001, a senator made $105,840; a backbench MP $131,000; a cabinet minister $194,000; the PM $262,000; and the chief justice of the Supreme Court $262,000.

• In 2001, the number of divorces was 71,144, down from 71,528 in 1981. The number of marriages in 2001 was 147,634, also down from 152,821 in 1981.

• 2,444 Toronto pedestrians were struck by cars; 32 died.

• Canada's six largest banks made a combined profit of $10.6 billion.

• A record 17,945 oil and natural-gas wells were drilled in Canada.

• The *Fitzhenry & Whiteside Canadian Thesaurus* was published. It contained more than 400,000 synonyms, over 70,000 antonyms and more than 13,000 headwords. The project was assembled under the editorial direction of Dr. J.K. Chambers (b 1938), Professor of Linguistics, U. of Toronto.

• Poet George Eliott Clarke's collection, *Execution Poems*, won the Gov-Gen.'s Award for Poetry. The book tells of George and Rufus Hamilton, Clarke's cousins, who murdered a taxi driver in NB and were hanged for the crime in 1949.

• Poet Christian Bök published *Aunoia*, a book using only one vowel for each of its 7 chapters. The book won the Griffin Prize for poetry.

2002

Jan. 14 Postage for domestic mail increased from 47 cents to 48 cents.

• The Confederation Bridge linking PEI and NB was closed twice to tractor-trailers and high-sided transport vehicles as the Maritimes were blasted by what meteorologists labelled a "weather bomb." The storm, with wind gusts of 100 km/h, dumped 36 cm of snow on NB's Acadian Peninsula (disrupting power in Halifax) and battered the Truro, NS, area with winds that reached 165 km/h.

Jan. 15 PM Chrétien shuffled his cabinet following the resignation of Federal Industry Minister Brian Tobin: 30 cabinet ministers and secretaries of state were affected. Included was the removal of Alfonso Gagliano (b 1942) from Public Works over an ethics conflict related to alleged millions of govt sponsorship dollars given to advertising companies linked to the federal Liberal party. Gagliano was made ambassador to Denmark (and fired in 2004 over the same conflict charges). Sheila Copps was made heritage minister. Deputy Prime Minister Herb Gray, who became Canada's first Jewish cabinet minister in 1969, announced his retirement from politics after 40 years in public service. He was replaced by John Manley.

Jan. 18 A splurge of Asian speculation pushed the loonie to a record low 61.75 cents US.

Jan. 19–20 Forty teams from the US and Canada battled for winter glory on frozen Roulston L., NB, for a chance to win the 1st World Pond Hockey Championship. Teams played a 4 on 4 round-robin format on 20 hand-shovelled rinks measuring 150 ft by 75 ft each. The Tobique Puckers beat the Riley Brook Bogan Blazers to win Plaster Rock's inaugural classic.

Jan. 23 North America's 1st floating oil production vessel, the Terra Nova Floating, Production, Storage and Offloading Vessel (FPSO), surpassed a flowrate of 75,000 barrels per day. Owned by various oil companies including Petro-Canada, ExxonMobil Canada, Norsk Hydro Canada Oil & Gas Inc., it is located in the Terra Nova oil field 350 km off the coast of east Nfld. Today the vessel produces, on average, 140,000 barrels of oil daily, to a maximum of 180,000 barrels, and has cost more than $670 million in project development. By year's end, the Terra Nova Development employed 600 people working both onshore and offshore, and contributed $150–$200 million annually to the economy of the province. Petro-Canada discovered the Terra Nova oil field in 1984. Production began in 2002.

Jan. 25 Provincial and territorial leaders completed a health-care summit in Ottawa, vowing to amend the escalating costs of health care alone if Ottawa did not come up with an acceptable solution within 90 days. The federal govt announced it would deal with the matter only after federal health commissioner Roy Romanow tabled his report on the state of health care (Nov. 28).

Jan. 27 The temperature in Toronto reached 10.4ºC — the warmest on city record for this day in 153 years.

Jan. 28 Forty thousand BC public school teachers held a 1-day walkout following new legislation binding them to a 3-year contract. Six hundred thousand students were affected.

Jan. 31 Members of Princess Patricia's Canadian Light Infantry and Lord Strathcona's Horse Light Armoured Regiment of Edmonton began leaving for Afghanistan for combat duty under US command. (The US had begun its campaign against the ruling Taliban regime and its support of the al-Qaeda terrorist network on Oct. 7, 2001. Kandahar was surrendered Dec. 9, 2001, but fierce fighting continued in mountainous terrain.) Canada committed over 2,200 personnel toward the effort. Soldiers would begin filtering home July 28, 2002, after Defence Minister Art Eggleton announced that the country did not have the military resources to sustain a lengthy, overseas operation.

• Reform Party founder Preston Manning resigned his seat in Parliament.

Also in Jan.

• James Bartleman of the Minjikang First Nation, was appointed lt-gov. of Ont. Bartleman, former head of Canada's Mission to the European Union (EU) and 1999 recipient of the National Aboriginal Achievement Award for Public Service, became the first Aboriginal person to hold the position. In 2003, Bartleman spearheaded an initiative to send books donated by people in southern Ont. to remote Northern communities. Donations appeared from across the country, and also Europe; 1.2 million books were delivered by the time the book drive was finished in June 2004.

Feb. 4 Fourteen thousand Alb. teachers began the largest teachers' strike in the province to date, affecting two-thirds of the province's students. Grievances focused on wages and better work conditions. On Feb. 1, the provincial govt declared the action a "public emergency" and legislated the educators back to work.

Feb. 7 The Grand Council of the Cree signed an agreement with the Que. govt and Hydro-Quebec that cleared the way for construction of the 1,200 megawatt (MW) James Bay Hydro project on the Rupert and Eastman Rivers. The Cree received control over natural resources in the region and a minimum $3.5 billion over the next 50 years; in return, they agreed to drop legal action to prevent construction of the hydro project.

Feb. 8–22 Canada won 17 medals at the Olympic Winter Games in Salt Lake City, Utah, its best Winter Olympics showing to date. On Feb. 21, the women's hockey team won gold, defeating the American squad 3–2, despite receiving 11 mostly questionable penalties from the US referee. It was the 1st gold medal awarded to a Canadian hockey team in 50 years. Salt Lake was only the 2nd Olympics to include women's hockey. The Canadian men's hockey team also won gold, its first since 1952. Other highlights included Catriona Le May Doan's gold in 500-m speed skating; and Marc Gagnon's gold in the short-track 500-m event, gold in the 5,000-m relay and bronze in 1,000-m, giving Gagnon a total of 5 Olympic medals and the honour of being the most decorated winter athlete in Canadian Olympic history. The Games were not without controversy. On Feb. 11, Canadian figure skaters Jamie Salé and David Pelletier won silver, largely the result of a French judge who fell to outside pressures and deal making. The scandal was resolved Feb. 15 when the IOC retroactively awarded the gold medal to Salé and Pelletier. The original gold given to the Russians was not rescinded.

Feb. 20 The federal govt set aside a $125 million endowment for the creation of the Trudeau Fellowship, with hopes it would one day rival the prestigious international Rhodes scholarships. The Trudeau Fellowship would support 100 doctoral students and 20 professional scholars each year.

Feb. 25 Paul Kane's oil on canvas, *Scene in the Northwest–Portrait,* sold at auction in Toronto by Sotheby's, in association with Ritchie's, for $5,062,500 — a record for the artist, and the highest price ever paid for a painting in Canada.

Feb. 26 Rising temperatures forced Ottawa's National Capital Commission to close the 7.8-km Rideau Canal to skaters. Those who ventured on the weakening surface were given $100 trespassing fines.

Mar. 1 A Senate committee on national security and defence, chaired by Senator Colin Kenny (b 1943), issued its report, recommending the federal govt spend $4 billion annually and recruit 5,000 more military personnel, including 222 new pilots and 40 aeronautical engineers, to help bolster the nation's flagging military. The total number of personnel in the Armed Forces was 60,000.

Mar. 4 The Canadian Institute for Health Research, a federal agency, issued new federal guidelines allowing research using stem cells collected from human embryos. Stem cells were used in genetic reproduction technologies, experiments on the regeneration of missing or destroyed human tissue, and in the treatment of degenerative diseases such as Parkinson's. The guidelines were issued outside parliamentary consideration. Critics argued on moral grounds that the destruction of the embryo was akin to abortion; others argued that the medical regeneration of human cells would lead

to human cloning. The govt passed legislation on stem cell research Oct. 28, 2003.

Mar. 7 Environment Canada declared that the area stretching from Windsor, Ont., to Quebec City experienced its warmest winter weather on record — at 4.8°C above average seasonal temperatures. It was the region's 19th consecutive winter above seasonal averages.

Mar. 8 The Supreme Court of Canada ruled in a majority decision that residents without Canadian citizenship were not entitled to the same employment opportunities in the civil service afforded Canadian citizens.

Mar. 13 Forty-five thousand Ont. civil service employees belonging to OPSEU went on strike for better wages and increased job security. The strike ended May 5 with the ratification of a new deal giving workers an 8.45% pay increase over three years.

Mar. 17–23 Iqaluit hosted the Arctic Winter Games, the largest international event held in the new Nunavut capital.

Mar. 20 Toronto-born Calgary resident Stephen Harper (b 1959) was elected leader of the Canadian Alliance party, beating out former leader Stockwell Day. Harper received 55% of the party vote, Day 37%. On Apr. 10, 6 former Alliance MPs, who left the fold in 2001 to create the Democratic Representative Caucus, returned to party ranks.

Mar. 21 Air Canada launched its low-fare passenger service Jazz, after merging its regional services Air BC, Air Nova, Air Ontario and Canadian Regional. The budget carrier would serve 80 destinations in Canada and the US and comprise nearly 100 aircraft.

Mar. 23 Ernie Eves was elected to replace Mike Harris as leader of the Ont. Progressive Conservative Party at a leadership convention in Toronto. Eves, a former deputy minister and finance minister, had returned to Ont. politics after a 14-month absence. He was sworn in as Ont.'s 23rd premier Apr. 15. Harris had announced his retirement Oct. 16, 2001, at which time he had a popularity rating of 33%.

Also in Mar.

• British magazine *Restaurant* ranked chef Michael Stadtlander's Eigensinn Farm, located in Singhampton, Ont., the 9th best eating establishment in the world. The restaurant sits 16 and offers 6-course meals, which included herbs, game, poultry and pork raised on site by the proprietor.

Apr. 5 Arson damaged a synagogue in Saskatoon, destroying 3,000 books, including a large collection of irreplaceable religious texts.

• EnCana, an oil and natural-gas exploration and production firm, was formed through the combination of Calgary energy firms PanCanadian Energy Corp. and Alberta Energy Co. Ltd. The merger created the nation's largest petroleum producer with an enterprise value of $27 billion. First quarter profit in May 2003 was $1.25 billion, a record high in the Canadian energy sector.

• Commissioner Robert Laing of the North Battleford Water Inquiry issued a 372-page report into the events that led to the Mar.–Apr. 2001 cryptosporidium parasite contamination of North Battleford's water supply. He placed blame at the feet of the city and the Sask. Environment and Resource Management (SERM) for allowing the city's water-treatment facility to operate without inspection for 10 years. Laing recommended more and rigorous standards, inspections and personnel training for all current and future water-treatment facilities. The cryptosporidium parasite entered the North Battleford water supply on Mar. 20, 2001. It sickened 7,000 and forced residents of the area to boil their water for months afterward.

Apr. 18 Four Canadian soldiers — Sgt. Marc Leger, Cpl Ainsworth Dyer, Pte. Richard Green and Pte. Nathan Smith — were killed, and 8 other soldiers wounded when two American F–16 pilots, Maj. Harry Schmidt and Maj. William Umbach, dropped a 250-kilo laser-guided bomb on a Canadian live-munitions military exercise outside Kandahar, Afghanistan. On Sept. 13, the two US pilots were charged by the US military with involuntary manslaughter and aggravated assault. However, the US military ruled on June 19, that the pilots would not face court martial proceedings in the matter and would instead receive non-judicial penalties.

Both Schmidt and Umbach received military reprimands, with Schmidt a salary forfeiture of $5,672.

Apr. 19 Ont. Justice Arthur Gans stifled the province's efforts to privatize Hydro One, arguing that the govt did not have the legal authority to make a $5.5 billion public offering of the Crown company. The landmark decision was the result of a lawsuit made against the province by 2 unions that represented Hydro One employees, the Canadian Union of Public Employees (CUPE) and the Communications, Energy and Paper Workers Union. Former Premier Mike Harris had announced plans to privatize Hydro One in Dec. 2001.

Apr. 26 The Supreme Court overturned 2 lower-court decisions, ruling 7–0 that US-based satellite television services were illegal in Canada. The decision, made on an appeal brought to the court by Bell ExpressVu, would limit Canadian satellite service subscription choice to Bell ExpressVu and Star Choice Communications Inc.

• Nortel CEO John Roth, who led the telecommunications giant to record stock heights before seeing the company brought to its knees with an overwhelming debt load and overambitious expansion, quit. Nortel shares had plunged on the TSE from over $124 in 2000 to $1.50; capitalization fell over $393 billion since 2001 with the loss of over 60,000 employees. Roth had been guiding the company since 1997. He cashed in stock options worth $54 million in Aug. 2000. On July 25, Nortel shares fell below $1 US for the 1st time in 20 years, to a penny stock of 76 cents on the New York Stock Exchange.

May 3 Moody's Investors Services returned Canada to an AAA credit rating, a status it last held in 1994. Moody's pointed to federal deficit reduction and the diminished threat of Que. sovereignty as reasons for the upgrade.

May 5 Maurice "Mom" Boucher, Montreal leader of the Hells Angels biker gang, was convicted on two counts of 1st degree murder and one count of attempted murder in connection to a call for the execution of three prison guards in 1997. The case came before a jury on appeal following Boucher's 1998 acquittal on the same charges. He was given an automatic life sentence with no chance of parole for 25 years.

May 8 The US Commerce Department imposed protection tariffs on Canadian softwood lumber imports averaging 27.2%, charging that Canada was unfairly subsidizing its lumber industry. On July 26, the World Trade Organization (WTO) ruled in a preliminary judgment that Canada was not unfairly subsidizing its softwood lumber industry and the recent US subsidies were therefore unjustified. The WTO ruling was not binding. The end result: Canada was forced to pay the 27.2% duty on a projected $10 billion of exports, which led to the loss of thousands of industry jobs and the closure of mills throughout BC. The US received an estimated 84% of all Canadian lumber exports.

May 10 Marc Hall, an openly gay 17-year-old student attending a Roman Catholic high school in Oshawa, Ont., won the right at the Ont. Superior Court to take his 21-year-old boyfriend to the prom.

May 21 The loonie hit a 9-month high of 65 cents US.

May 23 Associate Chief Justice Dennis O'Connor issued his final report into Ont.'s drinking water, calling for an immediate provincial investment of $800 million followed by an annual investment of $250 million, to ensure that Ont. residents had continuous access to safe, clean drinking water. Other recommendations included the development of a Safe Drinking Water Act, the creation of a drinking water branch as part of the environment ministry, and a policy to ensure that all drinking water could be traced to source. O'Connor's first report had been issued Jan. 18 and pointed to provincial cutbacks as a cause in the May 2000 Walkerton crisis.

May 28 Skaters Kurt Browning and Catriona Le May Doan hosted the 5th annual celebration of Canadian artists, entertainers, writers and sports figures as 11 new stars were added to the Canadian Walk of Fame in downtown Toronto. The 2002 inductees were comedian Dan Aykroyd; Cirque du Soleil; artist Alex Colville; author Timothy Findley; composer-songwriter David Foster; hockey great Wayne Gretzky; game-show host Monty Hall

(b 1923); director Arthur Hiller (b 1923); bandleader Guy Lombardo (1902–1977); SCTV; and the rock group The Tragically Hip.

Also in May

• British Energy finalized an 18-year lease of the Ont. Bruce nuclear plant, the world's largest, for an estimated $2 billion. The mothballed facility had the potential to fulfill 1/4 of the province's on-line resources when brought to full capacity.

• Statistics Canada reported that St. John's, Nfld., was the most Rubenesque city in the country, with 56.6% of its adult population categorized as overweight. Thunder Bay, Ont. was ranked second at 55.3%, followed by Sudbury, Ont., at 55.2%. Vancouver was the trimmest spot in the country, with an overweight population at 37%, followed by the Que. cities of Chicoutimi, 39%, and Sherbrooke, 39.2%.

June 2 PM Chrétien fired Finance Minister Paul Martin, replacing him with John Manley, who also remained deputy PM and minister of infrastructure and Crown corporations. Martin remained in the House as MP for the Montreal riding of Lassalle-Émard. Chrétien believed Martin had prematurely jockeyed for the PM's position.

June 3 Arthur Andersen Canada wound up public accounting in Canada to merge with Deloitte and Touche LLP, thereby creating the largest accounting firm in Canada. In 2001, Arthur Anderson had 1,400 employees and $230 million in revenue; Deloitte and Touche had 5,600 employees and $895 million in revenue. PriceWaterhouseCoopers, now the second largest firm in the country, had $1.01 billion in revenue in 2001. In 2002, Arthur Anderson, Canada's Chicago-based parent firm, was implicated in the Enron scandal and charged in a US court of obstruction of justice for having shredded its clients — Enron's — documents. The company lost its accounting licence and began selling its foreign assets.

June 5 Federal NDP leader Alexa McDonough announced her resignation. The former NS NDP leader had replaced Audrey McLaughlin as federal NDP leader in 1995. McDonough was replaced by

Jack Layton (b 1950) in Jan. 2003, who became the 1st male federal NDP leader since Ed Broadbent retired in Dec. 1989.

June 7 Bill 84, Que.'s Civil Union Bill, was unanimously passed in the National Assembly, making Que. the first jurisdiction in the world to extend full parental rights to same-sex couples who raise children. The bill also provided same-sex couples equal legal and financial rights and obligations when their relationships ended. The same-sex relationship was termed a "civil union," giving it the same status as a marriage within Quebec's Civil Code.

June 11 A deal was struck between Inco and Nfld. to exploit nickel and copper deposits at Voisey's Bay, Labrador. The mineral project was expected to inject $11 billion into the provincial economy over the next 30 years. Inco had purchased the deposit in 1996 for $4.3 billion. The deal shored up an incomplete Nov. 5, 1997 land-claim deal giving Labrador Aboriginals title to 15,700 km^2 of land in Labrador, and co-control with Nfld. over another 5,600 km^2, including 25% of resource revenue from the region and 3% of revenue from the Voisey's Bay project. Aboriginals were also guaranteed a minimum fixed number of jobs in the project. The massive Voisey's Bay nickel deposit had been discovered in 1993 by prospectors looking for diamonds.

June 12 Canada's newest discount airline, Montreal-based Jetsgo, took to the air with a fleet of 3 aircraft. By 2003, Jetsgo incorporated 14 Boeing MD–83s and 18 Fokker 100s, providing discount flights across Canada, the US, Mexico and the Caribbean.

June 14 The First Nations Governance Act, Bill C–61, to amend the Indian Act, was introduced in the House. The bill required all First Nations without self-governing status to develop codes and methods of accountability regarding reserve elections, financial management and administration. The bill died in the House and was replaced by Bill C–7, which also died in the House in 2003. Matthew Coon Come, Grand Chief of the Assembly of First Nations, remarked of the failed amendment, "This Indian Act was never ours. You do not modernize colonialism, you reject it."

June 16 Russell Mills, who had been publisher of the *Ottawa Citizen* for 16 years (and with the paper a total of 31 years), was fired after printing an editorial calling for the resignation of PM Jean Chrétien. Termination was finalized after Mills met with CanWest chairman Izzy Asper and son David, owners of the *Ottawa Citizen* and known friends of the PM.

June 17 The Action Démocratique du Québec (ADQ) won three provincial by-elections in Que., giving the party 5 of 125 seats in Que.'s National Assembly.

June 26–27 The G8 Summit took place in Kananaskis, Alb. World leaders from Canada, the US, France, Russia, Germany, Italy, Japan, the UK and the European Union met to discuss and coordinate policy on major global concerns, including terrorism, Africa and economic development. The gathering was positioned away from major, concentrated urban areas to limit the number of possible protestors. The 30-hour meeting cost taxpayers an estimated $192 million, the bulk of which covered security costs.

June 26 Over 6,800 outside workers of Toronto's CUPE local 416, including garbage workers, paramedics and park staff, went on strike over job security. Garbage piled up around the city, ferry service was suspended and two major Canada Day events were cancelled. Approximately 15,000 inside workers, including social workers, inspectors, museum and art gallery staff, joined the strike July 3. All were legislated back to work on July 11.

June 27 Canada's newest university, the U. of Ontario Institute of Technology became a legal entity with the passage of Bill 109 by the Legislative Assembly of Ont. Located in Oshawa, Ont., the university opened its doors to its 1st 900 students in Sept. 2003, offering graduate and postgraduate programs and research opportunities.

Also in June

- Jeff Bezos, founder of the on-line bookstore Amazon.com, launched the Canadian counterpart, Amazon.ca from Toronto.

June–July Forest fires ravaged northern Que., forcing mass evacuations. The fires limited access to forests and damaged trees, leading to a temporary layoff of some 6,000 forestry workers.

July 2 The International Ice Hockey Federation (IIHF) officially recognized Montreal's Victoria Skating Rink as the birthplace of ice hockey. The first game was held there on Mar. 3, 1875.

July 3 BC residents voted on 8 points in a referendum to guide the provincial govt in treaty negotiations with Aboriginals. Results showed that most residents wanted Native Peoples to get less control over taxation, land use and self-govt.

• An estimated 2,000 were evacuated from North West R. and Sheshatshiu in central Labrador because of encroaching wildfires. Another fire destroyed over 4,000 ha in the area of Port Hope Simpson, Labrador.

• Eight hundred and sixteen forest fires were ablaze in Alb.; another 686 were reported in Sask.

July 12 The Ont. Superior Court ruled that prohibiting marriages between same-sex couples violated the Canadian Charter of Rights and Freedoms. The ruling was the first in Canada to support the right to same-sex marriages. The court then gave the federal govt two years to expand marriage rights. On July 29, the federal govt announced it would ask leave "to seek further clarity" on the Ont. ruling. On May 1, 2003, the BC Court of Appeal unanimously ruled male-female-only marriages unconstitutional, and gave Ottawa until July 12, 2004, to amend its "union between a man and a women" legislation. Then on June 10, 2003, the Ont. Court of Appeal ruled against the man-woman definition without providing Ottawa time to address the issue. The law was therefore voided in the province, making same-sex marriage legal throughout Ont.

July 18–27 World Youth Day was held in Toronto. Approximately 200,000 Catholic youth from around the world made the pilgrimage. Pope John Paul II held an evening vigil at Downsview Park on July 27, followed by a papal mass on the 28th attended by over 800,000.

July 31 The 1st of over 35 railway shipments of hay, donated by Ont. farmers under the Hay West campaign, left Ont. to help Western ranchers struggling with drought conditions that, in some regions, were the driest in 133 years. Many ranchers had been forced to sell off livestock due to a lack of feed. Alb. and Sask. govts gave drought-affected producers a total of $390 million in aid.

Also in July

• The top 5 prescribed drugs in Canada in the year ending this month were: Synthroid, 6.7 million prescriptions for hyperthyroidism; Lipitor, 6.4 million prescriptions to decrease cholesterol; Premarin, 4.7 million prescriptions as a hormone replacement; Altace, 4.7 million prescriptions to ease hypertension; and Tylenol No. 3, 4.6 million prescriptions as an analgesic.

Aug. 1 The Toronto City Council passed a resolution stating it discriminatory to limit the legal definition of "marriage" to a union between a man and a woman.

Aug. 6 Joe Clark announced he would resign as federal leader of the Progressive Conservatives before the May 2003 Tory leadership convention. The announcement was made prior to the Tory leadership review scheduled for late Aug.

• The City Council of Moncton approved legislation ensuring all municipal literature designed for the public would be issued in both official languages.

Aug. 7 Justice Marie Deschamps (b 1952) of the Que. Court of Appeal was appointed to the Supreme Court of Canada, (replacing Claire L'Heureux-Dubé [b 1927]). Deschamps became the 3rd woman justice sitting on the Court. The others were Louise Arbour, appointed Sept. 15, 1999, and Louise LeBel (b 1939), appointed Jan. 7, 2000.

Aug. 18 Ninety four members of the federal Liberal party agreed to a loyalty pledge confirming their support for PM Chrétien through the completion of his term in office, Feb. 2004. On Aug. 21, amidst months of questioning about his future as PM, Chrétien formally announced he would not run for political office again.

Aug. 27 The Alb. Heritage Savings Trust Fund posted a $582 million loss, its worst quarterly loss to date. The Fund stood at $11.8 billion.

Aug. 28 Montrealer Éric Gagné (b 1976), relief pitcher for the National League Los Angeles Dodgers, saved a game against the Arizona Diamondbacks to preserve a 1–0 lead. He would go on to save every single game at every single opportunity until July 5, 2004, amassing a Major League record of 84 consecutive saves, and beating the previous record set by Tom Gordon by an incredible 30 saves. Gagné was awarded the National League Cy Young Award Nov. 13, 2003.

Also in Aug.

• GM closed its Pontiac Firebird and Chevrolet Camaro assembly plant in Broisbriand, Que., after phasing out the long-popular muscle cars; 1,200 jobs were lost.

Sept. 4 A Senate Committee on Illegal Drugs issued its 600-page report, recommending the legalization of marijuana for those over 16. A bill to reform Canadian marijuana laws was then introduced in the House May 27, 2003.

Sept. 9 Several hundred protestors forced the cancellation of a scheduled speech by former Israeli Prime Minister Benjamin Netanyahu at Concordia U. in Montreal. Riot police were called in to quell the unrest. Netanyahu had spoken in Winnipeg Sept. 8; Concordia was the second on his four-city lecture tour of Canada.

Sept. 17 Health officials announced that West Nile virus was the cause of death for a 70-year-old man from Mississauga, Ont. It was the country's first-known West Nile–related fatality. The West Nile virus was first located in Uganda in 1937; the first North American outbreak occurred in New York City in 1999. By 2000, the virus had spread to the border along New York, Que. and Ont. By the end of 2002, the virus was located in NS, Que., Ont., Man. and Sask.

Sept. 24 Toronto police and other security personnel forcibly removed an estimated 125 people from a downtown shantytown known as Tent City, a ramshackle affair on a vacant lot, which served as a base to the homeless and the transient, some of which had lived on the land for as long as two years. The land was owned by Home Depot, which initiated the mass ejection.

Sept. 26 Jeff Adams (b 1971) climbed the 1,776 stairs to the top of Toronto's CN Tower in a wheelchair. The 31-year-old Torontonian, a 6-time world champion wheelchair athlete, said his 6-hour effort was meant to symbolize the need for disabled persons to overcome accessibility barriers "one step at a time."

Sept. 27 With 280 of what had once been a 1,500-employee workforce on hand as witnesses, the last truck rolled off the line at Western Star Trucks in Kelowna, BC. Originally founded in 1967, the truck maker had been sold to two Calgary-based resource companies, Nova and Bow Valley, in 1981. Beset by financial difficulties in 1991, the company was sold to Australian Terry Peabody, who in turn sold it in 2000 to Daimler-Chrysler. Western Star trucks still exist but are manufactured by Daimler-Chrysler's Freightliner plant in Portland, Oregon.

Sept. 30 The CBC announced that sportscaster Ron McLean would not be returning as co-host of *Hockey Night in Canada*. Don Cherry's (b 1934) foil wanted to up his salary beyond the estimated $500,000 a year given national news anchor Peter Mansbridge (b 1948). Public pressure forced McLean's return in Oct. — for an estimated renumeration of between $450,000 to $500,000 a year.

Also in Sept.

• BCE Inc. sold its Yellow Pages directory division to the Ontario Teachers' Pension Plan and US buyout specialists Kohlberg Kravis Roberts (KKR) for $3 billion to help finance its 20% re-acquisition of Bell Canada.

Oct. 1 Nfld.'s 930 doctors went on strike to achieve parity with their Maritime colleagues and to force a solution to the acute lack of physicians in the province. The doctors returned to work Oct. 18 when the province placed $50 million on the arbitration table.

Oct. 4 Queen Elizabeth II, and her husband Prince Philip, Duke of Edinburgh, touched down in Iqaluit, the first stop on an 11-day Golden Jubilee tour of Canada. At the same time, Deputy PM John Manley expressed to reporters in Montreal, "I don't think it necessary to continue with the monarchy."

Oct. 13 International Forest Products (Interfor) announced it would cease all logging in BC that impacted habitat of the endangered spotted owl. Of the estimated 25 pairs of owls left in BC, the province's Ministry of Water, Land, and Air Protection could only locate 2 breeding pairs by this date.

Oct. 16 The CAW and Daimler-Chrysler came to an agreement for the construction of a new $1 billion Windsor auto plant to be completed by 2005. The new agreement ensured that non-unionized workers in the plant would be covered by union-approved wage schedules.

Oct. 17 Navistar International Corp. announced it would close its Chatham, Ont., heavy truck plant and move operations to Mexico. A company statement explained that the move was a "necessary step to address competitive market conditions." An estimated 2,200 jobs would be lost. In Sept. 2003, the Ont. govt pledged $32 million and the federal govt $33 million to keep the plant in Ont. At that date, 1,300 Chatham Navistar workers were laid off.

Oct. 30 Talisman, a leading Alb. oil company, sold its 25% stake in the Greater Nile Petroleum Operating Co. in Sudan for $1.2 billion, to Oil and Natural Gas Corp. of India. The sale followed 3 years of intense pressure brought by 23 international groups, including Oxfam, World Vision and the Canadian Labour Congress, who charged that Talisman and its CEO, Jim Buckee, provided Sudan's Khartoum-based govt with millions in revenues, which it then used to violently displace thousands of Sudanese to clear the way for oil exploration.

Also in Oct.
• Environmental Defence Canada published, "It's Hitting the Fan: The Unchecked Growth of Factory Farms in Canada," which called for a moratorium on all intensive livestock operations (ILOs) until a number of recommendations were met, including: the creation of federal standards on manure application and storage and separation of ILOs from water

bodies and human habitation; the elimination of all non-medicinal veterinary drugs; ILOs report pollution outputs to the National Pollutant Release Inventory; and that the govt update its cruelty to animal legislation.

Nov. 11 George Bowering (b 1935) was named the Parliament's 1st poet laureate.

Nov. 12 A suspected audiotape of al-Qaeda leader Osama Bin Laden was broadcast on Al-Jazeera television, warning several western countries, including Canada, of impending terrorist attacks because the countries had allied with the "iniquitous American government" in the overthrow of Afghanistan's Taliban regime.

Nov. 19 Publishing mogul Ken Thompson donated $70 million in cash and $300 million in art (an estimated 2,000 works) to the Art Gallery of Ontario (AGO). Thompson also contributed another $50 million toward gallery renovations.

Nov. 28 Federal health-care commissioner Roy Romanow tabled his report on the state of Canadian health care, recommending a federal infusion of $15 billion into the health-care system over the next 2 years, followed by an annual federal investment of $6.5 billion. Romanow also recommended that a drug plan be implemented to cover excessive prescription costs; full medical coverage for the chronically ill, mentally ill, terminally ill, and temporary coverage for those recently discharged from hospitals. Other recommendations included more money be spent on the purchase of MRI and CAT scanners, and ensurances from the provinces that all federal health-care funds go toward health-care provisions. The report had been 18 months in the making.

• Short-story writer Mavis Gallant was the recipient of the 2002 Blue Metropolis International Literary Grand Prix, a $10,000 award recognizing a lifetime of literary achievement.

Also in Nov.
• Construction began on the Ontario College of Art & Design's newest building, the Sharp Centre for Design. This space-saving 8,361 m² building sits 26 m above street level atop the college's main

facilities at 100 McCaul St., and is supported by 14 colourful "legs." A joint venture between British Young & Wright Architects, the centre is named after its lead benefactors, Rosalie and Isadore Sharp, and is part of the college's $42.5 million expansion program, scheduled for completion in Aug. 2004.

Dec. 1 Paul Kane's 1851 oil painting, *Portrait of Maungwudaus,* was sold by Levis Art Auctions and Appraisals in Calgary, Alb., to an unidentified American buyer for $2.4 million, fetching the most for any canvas ever sold to date in western Canada.

Dec. 14 Five hundred and fifty Mashuau Inuit, residents of Davis Inlet, Labrador, relocated to a new townsite, Natuashish (Little Sango Pond), on the mainland. The new community, which cost over $152 million to build, was funded largely by the Department of Indian and Northern Affairs (DIAND), but all decisions regarding its construction and services were the responsibility of the Inuit. Natuashish consists of 133 houses, a nursing station, school, store, fire hall, community wharf, airstrip, reservoir, sewage-treatment plant, recreation facilities and a community police station.

Also in Dec.

• Ottawa sold 83,399 ounces of gold — approximately 1/8 of its total reserve — to take advantage of rising prices, leaving approximately 599,000 ounces in reserve. In 1980, the govt's gold reserves totalled 21 million ounces.

• A *Toronto Star* survey found that over 20% of all annual Canadian retail jewelry purchases were made in Dec.; over 19% of the country's annual retail music purchases occurred during the same month. Other annual Dec. retail-spending percentages included 17% on toys, hobbies and souvenirs, almost 16% on books, 8.9% for food and groceries, plus 13% each on sporting goods: household furniture/appliances; and clothing. Liquor, beer and wine accounted for almost 13%, and general merchandise for 13.6%.

• 2002–2003 The BC Ministry of Water, Land and Air Protection authorized the extermination of 6 protected Golden Eagles as a way to protect the last 21 surviving Vancouver Is. marmots. Four birds

were shot in 2002, 2 were shot in 2003 — all lured with deer carcasses to a site near Nanaimo.

• A record 61,000 females were registered in hockey leagues across the country.

• Automobile insurance rates soared in most provinces as insurance firms tried to recover from record losses in the wake of the Sept. 11 terrorist attacks on New York City. Rates increased by 58% in PEI; 71% in NB; 66% in NS; 64% in Labrador and Nfld.; 37% in Que.; 30% in Ont.; and 59% in Alb.

Also in 2002

• Thirty-two of the world's 438 nuclear reactors were Canadian-designed CANDU (Canada Deuterium Uranium) reactors.

• Over the 10-year span, from 1992 to 2002, some 8,035 bird-aircraft collisions were reported in Canada.

• Some 46,000 Canadians were awarded Queen's Jubilee Medals in celebration of Queen Elizabeth II's golden jubilee. Recipients were selected on the basis of their service to community, to their fellow Canadians or to the country as a whole.

• The general minimum wage per hour by province and territory was: Nunavut, $8.50; BC, $8.00; Que., $7.30; Yukon, $7.20; Ont., $6.85; Man., $6.75; Sask., $6.65; NWT, $6.50; PEI, $6.25; NB, $6.00; Nfld., $6.00; NS, $6.00; and Alb., $5.90.

• 82% of Canadian exports were sent to US markets; 19% of American exports entered Canada. In 2003, the World Trade Organization (WTO) suggested Canada was too reliant on the US and recommended it seek to diversify its export trade beyond its southern border.

• Some 18,000 migrant farm workers laboured in Canadian farms at one time during the year. Most worked for low pay, were not protected under collective bargaining rights and were forced to pay unemployment premiums for benefits they could not receive. The majority of migrant workers were from Mexico and the Caribbean. In 1996, the number of migrant farm workers in Canada was approximately 1,000.

• Ford Motor Co. of Canada employed 12,920 Ont. workers in its 7 plants in Oakville, St. Thomas and Windsor. Daimler-Chrysler had 12,763 workers at 5 plants in Windsor and Brampton, Ont. And General Motors of Canada employed 18,674 workers at 6 plants in Oshawa, Windsor, St. Catharines and London.

• 99% of Canadian homes had at least 1 colour television, 92% had a videocassette recorder, 36% a DVD player, 64% a computer and 52% a cell phone.

• Canadian publishing experienced one of its worst years ever with the bankruptcy of General Publishing and General Distribution Services. Creditors claimed an estimated $45.7 million against the firms. The federal govt subsequently announced $2.5 million in relief for those Canadian publishers whose titles had been distributed by General. The 79-year-old company included Stoddart Publishing, a major Canadian imprint with such authors as Arthur Black, David Suzuki, Maude Barlow and David Foot.

• Carol Welsman was voted Vocalist of the Year at the 2002 National Jazz Awards in Toronto.

• Yann Martel (b 1963) won the Man Booker Prize winner for his novel, *Life of Pi*. Martel created controversy and headlines when he announced that he got the idea for the novel 12 years earlier from a book review of *Max and His Cats* by Brazilian writer Moacyr Scliar.

• Steven Kimber's *Sailors, Stackers and Blind Pigs*, a history of Halifax during the WW II, was published.

• *The Canoe, A Living Tradition*, edited by John Jennings, was published.

• Rohinton Mistry published *Family Matters*, the story of a family in Bombay who battle societal pressures to gain true love. It won a host of awards and was nominated for the Man Booker Prize and shortlisted for the International IMPAC Dublin Literary Award.

• *Better to Have Loved: The Life of Judith Merrill*, co-written by science fiction writer Judith Merrill (1923–1997) and her granddaughter Emily Pohl-Weary, was published posthumously. It won a

Hugo Award and was a finalist for the Toronto Book Awards.

• The romantic curling comedy, *Men With Brooms*, directed by and starring Paul Gross, opened in 207 Canadian theatres across Canada and boasted box office earnings of $1,040,000 on its 1st weekend. It was Gross's debut as a director.

• Christine Cushing, host of Food Network Canada's *Christine Cushing Live,* published *Fearless in the Kitchen: Innovative Recipes for the Uninhibited Cook.*

• Napanee, Ont.–born rock-child Avril Lavigne (b 1984) had a hit single with "Complicated," from her debut album *Let Go*. The album garnered 8 Grammy nominations and, by 2004, had sales in excess of 14 million copies.

• Barbados–born Austin Clarke (b 1934) was awarded the Giller Prize for his 9th novel, *The Polished Hoe*.

• West Coast master artist Freda Diesing won a National Aboriginal Achievement Award for her contribution to Northwest Coast art and culture. Her unique carving style, found throughout her totem-pole collection, helped awaken the nation's interest and appreciation of Northwest Coast Indian art. One of the first female carvers on the Northwest Coast, Diesing left a legacy in her more than 15 students who continue to earn their living following her innovative style.

• The National Archives purchased the Winkworth Collection of Early Canadian Art from collector Peter Winkworth (b 1929). The collection, consisting of over 700 watercolours and drawings, 3,300 plus prints, and 9 paintings, is one of the most significant historical acquisitions in National Archives' history.

• The total number of women in the labour force reached 60.7%, a record high.

• Women held 14% of all corporate officer positions within those Canadian companies listed on the Fortune 500, up from 12% in 1999.

• Average high-school grades required to get into science programs at the following universities, with 1998 requirements in parenthesis: U. of BC,

85% (82%); U. of Alb., 70% (70%); U. of Toronto, 84% (76%).

• The Caisse de dépôt et placement du Québec, the nation's largest pension-fund manager, lost $8.55 billion in investments, most of it coming in the telecommunications, technology and media arenas. It was the largest loss since the Caisse was founded in 1966. The Ontario Teachers Pension Plan, Canada's 2nd-largest pension-fund manager, also experienced investment losses — $3.3 billion — thereby reducing its portfolio to $66.2 billion.

• Fish producers FPI of St. John's reported a profit of $13.8 million; Highliner of Lunenburg, NS, $10.2 million; and Clearwater of Bedford, NS, a July–Dec. profit of $30.4 million. The companies had profited from increased shellfish prices, and the processing of fish caught in regions near China, Vietnam, Ecuador and Chile.

• The nation's 5 highest-paid executives, taking into account salary, bonuses, stock option gains, etc., were: Frank Stronach, chairman, Magna International Inc., $58,137,289; Richard Currie, former president, George Weston Ltd., $48,058,056; Galen Weston, chairman, George Weston Ltd., $31,996,185; Pierre Lessard, CEO, Metro Inc., $28,310,200; and Robert Burton, CEO, Moore Corp. Ltd., $20,932,279.

• *Forbes* magazine published its annual list of the world's richest people, placing publishing giant Kenneth Thomson and family 13th in the world; with $14.9 billion in assets, they were the only Canadians listed in the top 25. American Bill Gates of Microsoft led the pack with $52.8 billion in assets. Rounding off the top 5 Canadians on the list, with world rankings and business type in parenthesis, were: Galen Weston and family, $4.2 billion (82nd, retail); James, Arthur and John Irving, $4.1 billion (84th, oil); Charles Bronfman, $2.5 billion (157th, Vivendi); Bernard Sherman, $2.5 billion (157th, pharmaceuticals); and Jeffrey Skoll, $2.2 billion (191st, eBay).

• The salary of leading Ontario Power Generation executives was: Chairman William Farlinger, $250,000, plus benefits; CEO Ron Osborne, $850,000, plus $100,000 in compensation; and COO Graham Brown, $750,000, plus over $800,000 in bonuses.

• There were 7,600 Canadians with over $10 million of invested wealth, compared to 2,520 in 1993.

• The average annual income of the top 10% of earners in Canada was $185,070, up from $161,460 in 1990. The average annual income of the lowest 10% of income earners was $10,341, an increase of $81 since 1990.

• A College of Family Physicians of Canada poll showed that 4.5 million Canadians (15%) did not have a family physician.

• Canadians charged a total of $135.7 billion to their Visa and MasterCards, and withdrew a further $18.9 billion in credit-card cash advances. The total number of credit cards in circulation in Canada was 76.2 million, half of which were active.

• The national crime rate dropped 2% from 2001. Que. and Ont. had the lowest crime rates in the country, respectively; Sask., followed by Man., had the highest.

• There were 583 homicides in Canada, up from 553 in 2001.

• There were 1.2 million property crimes nation-wide, the lowest in 30 years.

• The number of robberies involving guns dropped 62% since 1992.

• The B'nai Brith of Canada reported 459 incidents of anti-Semitism across the country, the most since it began documenting such incidents in the early 1980s. Three hundred and twenty-four of the cases were reported in Toronto and surrounding area.

• Average governmental agricultural subsidies per farm in US dollars, with subsidies per ha of farm-land in parenthesis, by selected country: Canada, $11,000 ($62 ha); US $16,000 ($94 ha); EU $17,000 ($730 ha); Japan $27,000 ($9,028 ha); Mexico $1,000 ($75 ha).

2003

Jan. 1 Provisions in Bill C–68 (1995) requiring the registration of all firearms took effect; 200 protestors marched on Parliament Hill, 2 of which were charged with illegally carrying a firearm. An esti-mated 2 million guns remained unregistered across the country.

• Health Canada published new regulations requir-ing food labels on most packaged foods to list content values for calories, total fat, saturated fat, transfat, cholesterol, sodium, carbohydrates, fibre, sugar, protein, vitamins A and C, calcium and iron.

• NB's Official Language Act came into effect, requiring all municipal council meeting minutes and municipal literature, including notices, bylaws, and building and street signage to be in both French and English.

Jan. 2 Ont. Court Judge Douglas Phillips ruled in a simple marijuana possession case that the federal law against possession was invalid. The judge delayed the ruling 1 year to give the federal govt time to amend the Criminal Code. Further Ont. court cases (Jan. 10 and May 16) supported the previous ruling. However, on Dec. 23, the Supreme Court of Canada ruled 6–3 that the Ont. possession rulings related only to those who required marijua-na for health purposes, arguing that pot smoking for recreation was not guaranteed under the Constitution. Therefore, possession for recreational purposes remained a criminal offence under the Criminal Code.

Jan. 9 NHL's Ottawa Senators filed for bankruptcy protection after reporting debts of $165 million. They would restructure through a sale to Eugene Melnyk (b 1959), chairman and CEO of Biovail phar-maceutical company. Melnyk assumed the role of Senators chairman and gov. Aug. 26. The Buffalo Sabres would be the second team to file this year, on Jan. 14, after showing debts of $200 million (US).

Jan. 11 Hayley Wickenheiser (b 1978) became the 1st woman non-goalie to play men's professional hockey, scoring an assist with Kirkkonummi Sala-mat of Finland and helping the team to a 7–3 victory.

Jan. 13 Preliminary hearings began in Port Coquitlam, BC, marking the beginning of criminal prosecution against Robert Pickton, charged with 15 counts of 1st degree murder in connection with

the disappearance of over 60 women from Vancouver's east side since 1978. Pickton was arrested Feb. 22, 2002, based on DNA evidence taken from his Port Coquitlam pig farm. Pickton faced 22 1st degree murder charges by Dec. 2003 with the total count still incomplete.

Jan. 15 Ont. university applications swelled 47% by this day's deadline for the 2003–2004 academic season, the result of a "double cohort" graduating class of Ont. Grade 12s and last Grade 13 class. Altogether across Canada, 50,000 more undergrad-uates enrolled in Canadian universities for the 2003–2004 year, the largest increase ever.

• Popular Canadian fashion retailer Cotton Ginny, together with its Tabi subsidiary, was given bank-ruptcy protection after reaching a debt of $47.5 million. The firm had 205 stores nationwide and 2,800 employees. On Mar. 1, Toronto real estate out-fit Continental Saxon Group agreed to pick up the bulk of Cotton Ginny outlets for $1.5 million, including the debt.

Jan. 20 An avalanche at Durrand Glacier, near Revelstoke, BC, killed 7 backcountry skiers and snowboarders, including 4-time world snowboard-ing champion, American, Craig Kelly.

Jan. 27 CanWest sold 30 of its southern Ont. newspa-pers to Markham, Ont.–based Osprey Media Group for $193.5 million. The deal included the St. Catharines *Standard*, Brantford *Expositor*, Niagara Falls *Review* and the Welland *Tribune*.

Also in Jan.

• The *Financial Times* ranking of the world's best business schools placed the U. of Toronto's Rotman School of Management 21st best in the world and tops in Canada. Western's Ivey School of Business was ranked 22nd in the world, 2nd in Canada, followed by York's Schulich School of Business at 26th overall, and 3rd best in the country. In May, the *Financial Times* ranked Queen's U. School of Business as having the number 1 execu-tive education program outside the US.

• A study published in *Nature* suggested that by 2100, Canada's average seasonal temperatures would be 11 degrees warmer than currently, transforming wetlands, forests and disrupting all dependent insect and animal life.

• The national inflation rate, fuelled by rising oil prices, hit 4.5%, a 12-year high.

• Melissa Crawford, born Dec. 27, 1983, with permanent brain damage due to oxygen deprivation associated with her delivery, and her family of Smiths Falls, Ont., were awarded a cash settlement of $9.5 million in a malpractice suit against 2 doctors. The payment was the largest lump-sum malpractice settlement in Canada.

• Statistics Canada began using its new official yardstick to measure poverty, the market-basket measure. Based on a family of 4, the measure set disposable income (total income less taxes and payroll deductions, support payments, child care, out-of-pocket medical expenses) against a "basket" of basic goods and services (including food, clothing, footwear, shelter, transportation, telephone costs, postage, etc). If the basket exceeded disposable income, then the family was placed below the official poverty line. Elements within the basket were based on local prices, allowing Statistics Canada to factor in geographical price disparities — and effects — for the first time.

Feb. 12 The federal govt announced it would send a total of 3,000 troops to police wartorn, post-Taliban Afghanistan, starting with a rotation of 1,500 soldiers in the summer (July 13). The troops formed part of the International Security Assistance Force (ISAF), which came under NATO command Aug. 11. Critics called the move a political manoeuvre ensuring Canada would not have the military resources available to support a US-planned invasion of Iraq.

Feb. 17 Thousands of Canadians in towns and cities across the nation gathered to protest US plans to invade Saddam Hussein's Iraq. The rallies were part of a worldwide protest that ran from Feb. 17–18. An estimated 10 million people worldwide were involved. Canada's largest protest was held in Montreal on the 17th, with an estimated 150,000 participants. The outcries were made as Republican president George W. Bush lobbied the international community to join a "coalition of the willing" to fight the "axis of evil," a rhetoric-powered scheme based on erroneous evidence suggesting Iraq was stockpiling "weapons of mass destruction," or "WMDs." The UN, however, refused to sanction the invasion because its weapons inspectors could not locate any WMDs. On Mar. 17, despite American threats of economic censure for those that did not participate, PM Chrétien officially refused support without UN approval, stating the next day, "We think it is better not to have war as the first instance but as the last instance."

• A state of emergency was declared in Badger, Nfld., as the Badger, Exploits and Red Indian Rivers simultaneously rose and flooded the town. One thousand people were evacuated. Temperatures then dropped to –20ºC, transforming floodwaters into a diversity of rock-solid ice floes.

Feb. 18 Federal Finance Minister John Manley presented the Liberal administration's 10th consecutive budget, increasing federal spending by $25 billion over 3 years. Dubbed Jean Chrétien's "retirement budget," highlights included increases in annual child-support payments, $2 billion to meet requirements spelled out in the Kyoto Protocol (much of it later pledged to promote the hydrogen fuel-cell industry and make Canadian homes more energy efficient), an 8% increase in foreign aid totalling $1.4 billion over 3 years, $935 million to day care programs over 5 years, $10 million set aside to restore Canadian heritage buildings, and over $30 million for the establishment and maintenance of a new crime unit to fight corporate fraud and various other white-collar indiscretions.

• As conflict in Iraq loomed, the average national price of regular gasoline hit a record 82 cents per litre. On Mar. 11, the price soared to 84.2 cents, at which time the average price in Vancouver was 91.4 cents; Calgary 77.1 cents; Toronto 83.9 cents; Montreal 85.4 cents; and Halifax 85.8 cents.

Feb. 20 The U. of Toronto announced it had lost $400 million in investments only 3 years after hiring US investment manager Donald Lindsey to oversee its Asset Management Corp., a separate branch of the university designed to oversee endowment funds.

Feb. 21 The Ont. govt gave the green light to 4 private firms to operate MRI and CAT scan services in the province. It also pledged to provide the firms with $4.6 million annually.

Feb. 23 Jazz vocalist and pianist Diana Krall was awarded a Grammy for her internationally acclaimed album *Live in Paris*.

Feb. 28 Eight tobacco executives, including Canadian executives Pierre Brunelle, former president and CEO of RJR-Macdonald, and Stanley Smith, former vice-president of sales, were charged by the RCMP for defrauding the govt of $1.2 billion in taxes. The charges were made in connection to an alleged smuggling scheme said to have been executed between 1991–1996, whereby Canadian– and Puerto Rican–made cigarettes were smuggled from the US into Canada, tax free, and sold on the black market. A $1 billion smuggling-taxation lawsuit initiated by Ottawa against RJR-Macdonald had been thrown out of a New York court on jurisdictional grounds in July 2000.

• Fording Inc., the former coal-mining branch of Canadian Pacific, concluded a $1.8 billion compromise merger with Teck Cominco Ltd. of Vancouver and Sherritt Int. Corp. of Toronto. The deal gave Fording a near monopoly on coal in western Canada. The new entity was named Fording Canadian Coal Trust. Teck Corp. and Cominco Ltd. had merged in a $1.5 billion deal to form Teck Cominco on Apr. 30, 2001.

Also in Feb.
• The inflation rate hit 4.6%, a 12-year high.

• A study published in the *Archives of Internal Medicine* concluded that the common cold reduced Canadian productivity by as much as $6 billion a year.

• GlaxoSmithKline pharmaceuticals announced it would not supply drugs to Canadian firms that provided Internet drug services to US markets, following widespread complaints by US pharmacies that on-line sales of inexpensive, price-regulated Canadian drugs were flooding US markets and undercutting local sales. In Apr., AstraZeneca announced it would not sell drugs to Canadian

pharmacies that exceeded traditional, pre-Internet purchase levels.

Mar. 4 The US placed a 3.94% duty on Canadian durum (used primarily in pasta) and hard spring wheat (baking), charging that the commodities were unfairly subsidized. By Aug. 29, the duties on durum and spring would hit 13.55% and 14.16%, respectively.

Mar. 6 In the case of Joe Markevich, the Supreme Court of Canada ruled that Revenue Canada must first request back taxes within 6 years, and cannot initiate proceedings to get those taxes back after this period. Mr. Markevich owed close to $1 million in back taxes. The ruling eliminated an estimated $1.26 billion from Revenue Canada ledgers.

• In a class action suit involving 600,000 people, the Ont. Court of Appeal ruled that credit agencies can be held liable when they circulate false information that negatively impacts on a person's credit rating.

• The Canada-NS Petroleum Board granted qualified approval for Hunt Oil Ltd. of Dallas, Texas, and Corridor Resources Inc. of Halifax, to begin seismic explorations for oil off Cape Breton Is. in 2004. Fishers and environmentalists argued the seismic soundings would disrupt spawning activity and damage shellfish beds.

Mar. 7 The CIBC initiated plans to reduce its occupancy costs by eliminating 150 branches over 3 years. The bank, which had a total of 1,139 branches, had already cut 147 branches since 1999. CIBC profit for the year ending Nov. was $1.9 billion.

Mar. 12 The federal govt pledged an additional $750 million over 5 years to its existing annual allotment of $570 million to bilingual programs nationwide, with a stated goal of ensuring 50% of all high-school graduates could speak both official languages by 2013.

Mar. 14 Toronto health officials established a telephone hotline for anyone who had recently travelled to China and was thought to have contracted a mysterious pneumonia-like ailment sweeping through Asia. On Mar. 5, Sui-chu Kwan of Toronto was the first-known Canadian resident to die from what became known as severe acute respiratory syndrome, or SARS. Her son, Chi Kwai Tse, would also succumb to SARS on Mar. 13. On Mar. 25, Scarborough Grace Hospital was closed to all new patients and visitors in an effort to stifle the outbreak. On Mar. 26, Ont. health officials called for a 10-day quarantine for anyone who had been in the hospital after Mar. 16. Premier Ernie Eves declared SARS a provincial emergency on Mar. 26. On Mar. 27, the World Health Organization (WHO) requested Canadian officials screen all passengers for SARS who boarded Canadian planes. Health officials also closed all Toronto and Simcoe County hospitals to newcomers and required all hospital staff to wear protective clothing and masks. By the end of Mar., all 215 Ont. hospitals were curtailing all non-urgent surgery; most outpatient clinics had been closed. There would be over 300 SARS cases and 43 related deaths in the Toronto region over the remainder of the year.

Mar. 18 Thirty-one Canadian international-law professors from 15 universities signed an open letter expressing that a US-led attack on Iraq "would be a fundamental breach of international law and would severely threaten the integrity of the international legal order that has been in place since the end of the Second World War."

Mar. 20 The US, with Australia, Spain, Jordan, Turkey, Bulgaria, Kuwait, Czech Republic and Slovakia, invaded Iraq at dawn. Saddam Hussein's 24-year reign over Iraq officially ended Apr. 9 with the toppling of his likeness in downtown Baghdad.

Mar. 21 Following the US-led invasion of Iraq on Mar. 20, Alb. Premier Ralph Klein sent a letter to US ambassador Paul Cellucci praising his country's "leadership role in ridding the world of terrorism." PM Chrétien quickly responded it was the PM, not provincial premiers, who spoke for Canada on matters of foreign policy.

Mar. 31–Apr. 1 Floods ravaged Atlantic Canada following a 100-mm downpour over 24 hours. Two people were killed, roads and bridges were washed out and 55,000 in Saint John, NB, were left without electrical power. A mudslide in Corner Brook, Nfld., took out part of the Trans-Canada Highway. NS was hardest hit, with damages in excess of $7 million.

Also in Mar.

• According to the international Inter-Parliamentary Union, Canada placed 36th among 182 countries when it came to women's participation in federal politics: 20.6% (62 of 301) of House of Commons seats were held by women.

• A study backed by the Que. Ministry of Health showed 25% of 16-year-old Que. boys and 13% of 16-year-old Que. girls had higher than healthy blood pressure levels because they were overweight. Among 13-year-olds, 19% of boys and 14% of girls showed the same signs.

Apr. 1 Air Canada, the world's 11th-largest airline, filed for bankruptcy protection in an Ont. Superior Court. Rising labour and fuel costs, increased domestic competition, the costly acquisition of Canadian Airlines in 2000, widespread concerns about flight safety in the wake of Sept. 11, and through the lead-up to the invasion of Iraq, the preliminary effects of SARS — all cut into profits and forced the carrier into the courts.

Apr. 3 Calgary-based Suncor Energy approved a $3 billion plan to expand operations in the Alb. oil patch. The move would increase Suncor production by 50%, or 330,000 barrels a day, by 2007.

Apr. 5 Twenty-nine-year-old Robert Ghiz, son of former PEI Liberal leader Joe Ghiz, won the PEI Liberal leadership on the first ballot, beating rival Alan Buchanan by 161 votes.

Apr. 10 The dollar hit 68.79 US, a three-year high.

• Four hundred and fifty Black Diamond–cheese makers in Belleville, Ont., won a 16% wage increase to Feb. 28, 2007, following a contracted labour dispute.

Apr. 13 Mike Weir of Bright's Grove, Ont., accepted the coveted Green Jacket from 2002 winner Tiger Woods, joining the ranks of Jack Nicklaus, Arnold Palmer, Ben Hogan, Jimmy Demaret, Sam Snead and Byron Nelson as winner of golf's most prestigious championship, the Masters. Weir scored 70, 68, 75, 68, on Augusta, Georgia's, historic 7,290-yard, par 72 layout, beating Len Mattiace in the 1st hole of sudden death. Weir's dramatic

Sunday finish marked the first golf Major won by a Canadian.

Apr. 14 Former federal Conservative MP Jean Charest led the Que. Liberal Party to a majority win in the provincial election, taking 76 seats. The Parti Québécois won 45 seats, the ADQ 4. Charest was sworn into office Apr. 29.

Apr. 23 The World Health Organization (WHO) issued an international travel advisory, warning that SARS-plagued Toronto should be avoided by all those not on essential business. The US Center for Disease Control dismissed the all-out warning, and instead advised American visitors to avoid hospitals only. The World Health Organization removed Toronto from its list May 14.

• The Ont. Provincial Police (OPP) laid 12 breach-of-trust and public-endangerment charges against brothers Stan and Frank Koebel in connection to the Walkerton, Ont., E.coli breakout, which resulted in 7 deaths and 2,300 illnesses. The Koebels were in charge of the Walkerton public water system.

Apr. 28 Following a 17 1/2-year RCMP probe, trial began in a BC Supreme Court, in Vancouver, against Vancouver businessman Ripudaman Singh Malik and Kamloops labourer Ajaib Singh Bagri, both charged in the murder of the 329 who died aboard Air India Flight 182 which exploded midflight off the coast of Ireland June 23, 1985. Malik and Bagri were arrested and charged with Canada's worst mass murder on Oct. 27, 2000. Both had been denied bail in Jan. 2001. The case against the men was bolstered by evidence given by mechanic Inderjit Singh Reyat, in return for a 5-year, plea-bargain sentence for manslaughter. Reyat had confessed to supplying material for the bomb that caused the tragedy. The case continued into 2004.

Also in Apr.
• Highliner (formerly called National Sea Products) of Lunenburg, NS, sold all its fish quotas and last 9 deep-sea trawlers to Clearwater Seafoods Ltd. of Halifax. The move removed Highliner entirely from the waters. Instead, the company would focus on the processing and marketing of fish products.

May 2 The Committee on the Status of Endangered Wildlife in Canada (COSEWIC) officially designated the northern cod an endangered species. COSEWIC estimated that 99% of the cod population had disappeared over the last 40 years as a result of overfishing, governmental mismanagement in Canada and abroad, and a blind "dumb luck" faith in the limitlessness of the sea. Canadian northern cod quotas over the last 20 years reflected the dramatic decline: set between 220–230,000 tonnes a year in the 1980s, followed by a moratorium on the fishery in 1992, the fishery was reopened and the quota set at 9,000 tonnes in 1999, 7,000 tonnes in 2000, 5,600 tonnes in 2001, and 5,600 tonnes in 2002 — of which most Atlantic fishers could not complete. In Apr. 2003, the northeastern Nfld. and Gulf of St. Lawrence cod fishery was completely shut, leaving only limited cod fishing off Nfld.'s southeast coast.

May 3 An estimated 250 enraged NB fishers and supporters set fire to 3 Department of Fisheries and Oceans boats, another owned by Big Cove Aboriginals, and a Department of Fisheries building at Shippagan Wharf. The destruction followed a late-Friday-afternoon federal fisheries announcement that the Gulf of St. Lawrence crab quota was reduced from 22,000 tonnes to 17,000, a 20% cut to crabber incomes

May 9 Gulf Islands National Park Reserve was established in BC's Straight of Georgia lowlands, covering 33 km^2, including 16 islands. The reserve is a popular spot for whale watching, its waters home to an abundance of porpoise, dolphin, seals, sea lions and seabirds.

May 11 Canada won the World Hockey Championship in Helsinki, Finland, as Anson Carter (b 1974) scored in overtime to beat the Swedish national squad 3–2. It took referees nearly 10 minutes to review the goal from replays to determine whether the puck, which slid under netminder Mikael Tellqvist, actually entered the crease. The win marked Canada's first at the World's since 1977.

May 19 The Canadian Hockey Association (CHA) increased the legal body-checking age for boys from Atom (9- and 10-year-olds) to Pee-Wee (11- and 12-year-olds). The age had been reduced to Atom based on controversial statistics gathered in a Lakehead U. study. It was reversed to Pee-Wee following a chilling critique of the study by CBC television's *Disclosure*.

May 20 The US, and a host of other countries including Mexico, Japan and South Korea, placed a ban on Canadian beef imports following the discovery of a single case of mad cow disease (bovine spongiform encephalopathy) which originated from a herd of 150 cattle on a Wanham farm in northern Alb. The cow had been sent to a slaughterhouse on Jan. 31 and couldn't walk. It was rejected, slaughtered and sent for inspection; the samples sat unaddressed until the National Centre for Animal Health in Winnipeg confirmed the disease mid-May. There were 13.7 million head of cattle in Canada in 2002, 42% of which were in Alb. The US accounted for some $700 million worth of beef imports, or 1 million live cattle per year, most under 30 months old. The ban on live cattle remained through 2003; however, the US began accepting qualified cuts of beef on Aug. 8; and Mexico on Oct. 2.

May 21 Denys Arcand's *The Barbarian Invasions* (*Les Invasions Barbares*) drew an 8-minute standing ovation at its premiere at the Cannes International Film Festival in May 2003, but lost the coveted Palme d'Or to Gus van Sants' *Elephant*. In Feb. 2004, the work garnered an Oscar for Best Foreign Film at the Academy Awards, the first Canadian film to win in that category. Only three Canadian films had ever been nominated for Best Foreign Film — all by Arcand (*Jesus of Montreal* [1990] and *The Decline of the American Empire* [1986]).

May 22 In the wake of SARS and the May 20 US ban on beef, the Canadian dollar dropped 1.33 US cents to 72.69 US, the sharpest decline since the dollar dropped 1.84 US to 97.09 US Nov. 29, 1976, the month René Lévesque and the Parti Québécois beat Robert Bourassa's Liberals in the Que. provincial election.

May 26 PM Chrétien offered a $60 million aid package to suffering African countries, including $30 million for agricultural improvements, $24 million to fight the ravages of AIDS and $6 million for children affected by war.

May 27 The federal Liberal party introduced Bill

C–38, the "Cannabis Reform Bill," which would decriminalize simple marijuana and hashish possession, replacing jail sentence options with fines. The bill set out that those under 18 found with 15 g or less of marijuana would be liable to a $100 fine; adults a $150 fine. For those under 18 found with 1 g or less of hashish, a $200 fine; for adults, a $300 fine. The existing Criminal Code provided up to a $1,000 fine and a maximum sentence of 6 months for minor-possession violations. C–38 died on the Order Paper when Parliament prorogued in Nov.

• The WTO (World Trade Organization)ruled on the long-standing softwood lumber dispute that the US countervailing duty of 18.79% on softwood, which pushed average US softwood duties to 27%, was not justified as there was no clear indication that Canadian provinces were unfairly subsiding the lumber industry. Canada had made the WTO challenge May 3, 2002.

May 29 The 5-ha Distillery District in southeastern downtown Toronto opened on the site of the old Gooderham and Worts distillery, established in 1832. The city's newest tourist destination incorporated cobblestone walkways, 44 refurbished redbrick and limestone heritage buildings, with restaurants and oyster bars, art galleries and performance venues.

May 30 Douglas Lake Ranch, located at Douglas L., south of Kamloops, BC, was sold to businessman Stanley Kroenke, owner of the NBA Denver Nuggets and NHL Colorado Rockies. The price tag: $68.5 million. Former WorldCom Inc. CEO Bernard Ebbers previously owned the site. Douglas Lake is the nation's largest private ranch, with 58,000 ha and more than 20,000 head of cattle. John Douglas Sr. founded the business in 1872 on 130 ha.

• "Tom Thomson," a major exhibition of the artist's oil sketchings, paintings and works on paper, opened at the AGO, Toronto, running until Sept. 7.

May 31 Peter MacKay won the leadership of the Progressive Conservative party in a runoff with Calgary lawyer Jim Prentice. MacKay replaced Joe Clark, who stepped down prior to the race. MacKay won with support of rival candidate David Orchard, who offered the backing when MacKay agreed not to pursue a merger with the Canadian Alliance party. On Oct. 16, MacKay agreed to merge his party with the Alliance. David Orchard returned to farming in Borden, Sask.

June 3 The Man. NDP, under the leadership of Gary Doer, was re-elected with a majority govt on a platform to increase spending on health care and education. The NDP took 35 seats, Conservatives 20, and the Liberals 2. The provincial election marked the worst Man. voter turnout — 55% — in over 50 years.

• The Ont. govt legislated an end to a Toronto Catholic elementary-school teachers' lockout, which had kept 69,000 children out of class since May 16.

June 6 Ottawa software giant Corel Corp., known for its WordPerfect and CorelDRAW programs, accepted a $97.6 million (US) purchase offer from venture capital firm Vector Capital Corp. of San Francisco.

June 9 The NB Progressive Conservative Party, under Premier Bernard Lord, was returned to power with a reduced majority. PC seats dropped from 47 to 28. Liberals, under Shawn Graham (b 1968), won 26 seats, and NDP leader Elizabeth Weir (b 1948) won the only NDP seat in the province.

• Approximately 2.5 million viewers tuned in to the hunt for a Canadian singing sensation as CTV kicked off *Canadian Idol* — an impressive audience given that CTV launched the reality show in direct competition to game 7 of the Stanley Cup finals and without an audience in NB where the network was obliged to provide provincial election-night coverage. By Sept. 16, when 23-year-old crooner Ryan Malcolm of Kingston, Ont., emerged as the winner after an 8-city, 11-week, coast-to-coast tour, the show had set records as the most-watched Canadian television show of all time.

June 10 The Ont. Court of Appeal ruled that the province could not deny same-sex couples the right to legally binding marriages, thereby making same-sex marriages legal throughout the province. Chief Justice Roy McMurtry noted that any "purpose that demeans the dignity of same-sex couples is contrary to the values of a free and dem-

ocratic society…" The same day, Ont. residents Michael Leshner and Michael Stark became the 1st same-sex couple in Canada to be issued a marriage licence. They were named *Time* magazine's Canadian Newsmakers of the Year.

June 11 Legislation to amend the Canada Elections Act was passed in the House of Commons by a vote of 172 to 62. It banned large private and corporate contributions to political parties, substituting instead a total $22 million a year in public funds.

June 17 Ottawa pledged $190 million to farmers affected by the mad-cow fallout. Part of a federal-provincial compensation package, the aid would reach $315 million with full provincial participation.

June 23 Long-time Liberal adviser and privacy commissioner (since 2000) George Radwanski resigned following disclosure of what critics charged were excessive entertainment expenses. On Oct. 1, Auditor-Gen. Sheila Fraser issued a report noting Radwanski had misled Parliament by falsifying documents to fudge his spending, which included a $400 lunch and $800 limousine rides. MPs voted Nov. 6 to find Radwanski in contempt of Parliament for the fiduciary obfuscation, the 1st such decision since R.C. Miller in 1913 for refusing to answer parliamentary questions on public finances.

• *The Report* magazine (previously known as *Alberta Report* and *Western Report*) ceased publication after a 30-year run.

June 25 Championship rider Jim Elder (b 1934) became the 1st equestrian to be hounoured in the Canadian Walk of Fame. The 10 other inductees whose stars were unveiled that year were: NHL coach Scotty Bowman (b 1933); figure skater Toller Cranston; supermodel Linda Evangelista (b 1965); cartoonist Lynn Johnson; *Saturday Night Live* creator/producer Lorne Michaels; comedian Mike Myers; author Luc Plamondon (b 1942); singer-songwriter Robbie Robertson; director David Steinberg (b 1942); and singer Shania Twain.

June 30 The Canadian Space Agency's smallest space telescope, MOST (Microvariability and Oscillations of Stars Telescope), was launched from

Siberia to provide information on stars beyond our solar system. It circled Earth every 100 minutes at 27,000 km/h and became operational in early Aug.

Also in June

• Montreal's Pointe-à-Callière archaeology museum in Old Montreal held the "Pieces of the Dead Sea Scrolls" exhibit, which included three, 2,000-year-old sections of the scrolls, which had been found in a cave near the Dead Sea in 1947. The 3 sections were the first to be exhibited anywhere in the world, including Israel.

• The Alberta Energy and Utilities Board ordered 938 gas wells around the oilsands closed ("shut in") to insure they did not negatively affect subsurface pressures required to extract bitumen from the oilsands. Many well owners successfully applied for exemptions. Affected gas firms were compensated through provincial royalty breaks.

Summer Filming began in Rouleau, Sask., on *Corner Gas*, the 1st network-television series to be filmed entirely in Sask., and CTV's 1st-ever "original narrative comedy series." Created by comedian Brent Butt (b 1966), a native of Tisdale, Sask., the series portrayed life in the fictional town of Dog River where Butt's character, Brent LeRoy, owns the local gas station. The 1st show aired in Jan. 2004 to 1.2 million viewers and continued to be watched by more than a million a week.

July 1 The Nature Conservancy of Canada, founded in 1962 as a non-profit organization dedicated to the purchase and protection of rare and ecologically sensitive land, announced this Canada Day it had created 10 new conservation areas, one in each province, covering a total of 6,200 ha. The new areas pushed total Conservancy acquisitions in Canada to over 692,000 ha.

July 2 Vancouver and bid partner Whistler, BC, were selected by the International Olympic Organization (IOC) to host the 2010 Winter Olympic Games, beating out nearest rival Pyeongchang, South Korea, by a vote of 56–53. (The Vancouver bid budget was $34 million.) The provincial and federal govts were expected to provide $620 million in capital investments to cover construction of a speed-skating oval at Simon Fraser U., a winter sport centre and

upgrade the highway between Vancouver and Whistler.

• A Nfld. Royal Commission on Reviewing and Strengthening Our Place in Canada completed the 14-month study that assessed public opinion across the province. The report concluded that despite experiencing the nation's highest unemployment rate, the lowest per capita income and the highest provincial outmigration rates, Newfoundlanders wanted to remain within Confederation.

July 6 A grouping of low-rent homes known as Guindonville, located in a wooded area of Val-David north of Montreal, was demolished to make way for a parking lot and ecotourist information centre. Protests led to 8 arrests.

July 11 Montreal photojournalist Zahra Kazemi, who held both Canadian and Iranian citizenship, was arrested in Tehran on spying charges. She subsequently died of a fractured skull and brain hemorrhage after an Iranian inquest determined she had been severely beaten while in custody. Iranian authorities ignored pleas from her son, Stephan Hachemi, and demands from Ottawa that her body be returned home to Montreal, and instead buried her in Iran on July 23. In 2004, Iranian intelligence agent Mohammed Reza Aghdam Ahmadi was charged in Kazemi's death but acquitted by an Iranian court on July 24, 2004, on the grounds that the death was an accident. The next day, Hachemi rejected $12,000 from the Iranian govt, which was offered as compensation for his mother's death.

July 13 The Canadian flag was raised at the International Security Assistance Force (ISAF) headquarters in Kabul, Afghanistan, marking Canada's official involvement in the restructuring and policing of wartorn Afghanistan. Policing of the city's southern and western sections would begin Aug. 15. The patrol area was home to 800,000 of the city's 3.5 million residents.

July 16 Phil Fontaine defeated Matthew Coon Come to become National Grand Chief of the Assembly of First Nations. Fontaine, who had previously served as Grand Chief between 1997–2000, pledged the

Assembly would assume a more aggressive approach toward Native rights: "To the govts of Canada, I say to you, sometimes we will be at each other's throats, sometimes we will be pulling in the same directions, but we will always be there."

• Émilie Heymans (b 1981) of St. Lambert, Que., won Canada's first World Aquatic Championship gold in tower diving after being awarded 2 perfect 10s on her last 10-m dive in Barcelona, Spain.

July 26 Former Montreal Expos' catcher Gary Carter became the first player to enter baseball's Hall of Fame at Cooperstown, New York, in a Canadian team uniform. "The Kid" played for the Expos from 1974–1984, and also in 1992. His record with the team included 1,503 games, 1,427 hits, a .270 average, 220 home runs, and 823 RBI. He also appeared in 7 All-Star games as an Expo. Despite expressing an interest in entering the Hall of Fame as a New York Met, a team with which he played 600 games and won a World Series, it was the Hall that decided Carter should go in as an Expo.

July 27 An agreement in principle was signed between Indian Affairs Minister Robert Nault (b 1955), BC Premier Gordon Campbell and Tsawwassen First Nations Chief Barry Seymour, increasing Tsawwassen reserve land, located between Vancouver and the US border, from 290 ha to 717 ha, plus a non-contiguous strip of 62 ha. The first post-Confederation Aboriginal treaty to include Greater Vancouver Regional District lands would also provide the First Nations band with $10.1 million cash, commercial fishing rights and the right to seek reassessment of reserve lands falling under the region's agriculture-only Agricultural Land Reserve policy.

July 28 BC Court Justice William Kitchen ruled that the federal govt's 1992 decision to provide Native Peoples exclusive commercial fishing rights along stretches of the Fraser R. was a racial policy that violated the Canadian Charter of Rights and Freedoms. The ruling made way for non-inclusive access to the Fraser fishery, against the protests of Native Peoples, who argued that the federal govt's 1992 decision was based not on race but historical right.

• Two hundred were arrested for participating in an illegal demonstration following a massive protest of WTO meetings in downtown Montreal. Local outlets of large corporations, such as the Bank of Montreal, Burger King and the Gap, were vandalized. Protestors argued that the WTO was an undemocratic institution whose binding decisions did not reflect the interests of the world's poor.

July 30 The Rolling Stones and 13 other bands, including the Guess Who, Blue Rodeo and Rush played at an 11-hour SARS benefit on the former Downsview Air Force Base in Toronto to show the world, in the words of Mick Jagger, that "Toronto's back and it's booming." To accommodate the estimated 490,000 in attendance, the TTC (Toronto Transit Commission) placed an extra 25 subway cars and 270 buses on its lines. Volunteers distributed over 450,000 bottles of water to concert-goers who kept the site's 3,500-plus portable toilets in constant use. The Rolling Stones had begun an intimate relationship with the city, with 2 legendary shows at the El Mocambo in 1977.

• PM Chrétien appointed Justice Morris Fish (b 1938) of the Que. Court of Appeal to the Supreme Court of Canada, the first Que. anglophone to hold a seat on the Court since Douglas Abbott (1899–1987) on July 1, 1954. Fish was Chrétien's 6th and last Supreme Court appointment.

Also in July

• Canada slipped to 8th among 175 countries on the UN's Quality of Life index, following Norway, Sweden, Iceland, Australia, the Netherlands, Belgium and the US, respectively. Canada was listed 1st through the 1990s, 2nd behind Norway in 2001, and 3rd behind Norway and Sweden in 2002.

• George Weston Ltd., headed by Galen Weston, purchased the prestigious British department store Selfridges for $1 billion US. George Weston Ltd. was ranked as Canada's top revenue-generating private business in 2002.

Aug. 1 Sixty homes near Barriere, BC, were destroyed by wildfire; 2,500 residents were evacuated. Premier Gordon Campbell declared a state of emergency as windy conditions, coupled with a record dry spell to create some of the most severe forest-fire conditions in Canadian history. By Aug. 3, 10,000 people in Barriere, McLure and vicinity were forced to flee. The next day, BC appealed to Ottawa for disaster relief, its $56 million annual firefighting budget near exhausted. The Barriere-McClure fire began July 30, from a cigarette discarded by a volunteer firefighter. By Aug. 10, residents started to return home to an estimated $8.2 million in damages. By mid-Aug., 4 major forest fires had yet to be contained within the BC interior, forcing still more evacuations and uncertainty: a fire located southwest of Ashcroft; a fire northeast of Kamloops; a fire southwest of Chase; and a fire southwest of Kelowna. Fires were also reported in Yoho (BC), Kootenay (BC) and Banff (Alb.) National Parks. Also, an Alb. stretch between Crow's Nest Pass and Waterton Lakes National Park was threatened; a state of emergency was declared, and by Aug. 3, 16,000 ha in the region were ablaze and over 1,000 evacuated in the areas near Hillcrest and Blairmore.

Aug. 5 The NS Progressive Conservative govt, under the leadership of Premier Dr. John Hamm (b 1938), was returned to power with a minority govt, dropping from 31 to 25 seats. The NDP, under Darrell Dexter, won 15 seats; the Liberals, under Danny Graham, 12.

• 140 mm of rain fell in less than 3 hours in the southern section of Que. between Montreal and the provincial capital. Victoriaville was hit by flash floods that knocked out bridges and washed out roads, homes and cottages. At least 3 residents had to be airlifted to safety by helicopter.

Aug. 12 A massive hailstorm caused an incredible $50 million damage to crops in northern Alb.

Aug. 14 Electrical surges along power lines near Cleveland, Ohio, caused a 30-plus-hour blackout throughout Ont., and Michigan, Ohio, New York, New Jersey, Connecticut and Massachusetts. Some 50 million people were affected. Airline service was delayed, trains stalled, subways and streetcars stopped, factory production and assembly lines came to a standstill. Domestic and commercial foodstuffs in refrigerators and freezers spoiled. Premier Ernie Eves requested all non-essential govt service workers to stay home the following week as

utilities struggled to get back on-line. Rolling blackouts caused the CNE (Canadian National Exhibition) to open 4 days later than scheduled. 19 million work hours were lost. The national GDP dropped 0.7% in Aug, mostly due to the blackout (Ont. represented 42% of the total Canadian GNP). The cause of the blackout was traced to an unplanned FirstEnergy Corp. of Ohio plant shutdown, which caused a disasterous ripple effect throughout the northeast gridline.

Aug. 15 NS Premier John Hamm appointed Barry Barnet (b 1961), a Lucasville MPP and caucasian, the province's first minister of African Nova Scotian affairs.

Aug. 20 Alb. Learning Minister Dr. Lyle Oberg called for compulsory physical education in all Alb. elementary and secondary schools. His plan would require all able students to perform 20–30 minutes of daily exercise to reduce growing rates of obesity. On Nov. 5, Resorts of the Canadian Rockies Inc. offered every Grade 2 student in Alb. free ski passes to L. Louis, Nakiska and Fortress Mountain, in an effort to quell rising child-obesity rates. Statistics Canada reported that 37% of Canadian children between 2 and 11 were overweight, and up to half of these obese.

• Canadian Aid workers Gillian Clark and Christopher Klein-Beekham were killed and 5 other Canadians injured when a suicide bomber driving a truck detonated an explosive outside UN headquarters in US-occupied Iraq. No one claimed responsibility.

Aug. 21 Residents in 1,000 homes south of Kelowna, BC, were evacuated as a spectacular fire, caused by a lightning strike Aug. 16, raged out of control along the slopes of Okanagan Mountain, completely destroying Okanagan Provincial Park. On Aug. 22, the fire reached Lakeshore Dr. in southern Kelowna, forcing the evacuation of 7,000. By Aug. 24, 6,000 of those evacuated were allowed back; 244 homes had been destroyed, along with homes in the outlying areas of Naramata. At least $200 million in insurance claims were made by early Sept. Fires would again threaten the region in early Sept., causing more mass evacuations.

Aug. 23 Ukkusiksalik National Park was established in Nunavut. Covering 20,000 km^2, the park includes Wager Bay — a massive inland sea located off the northwest coast of Hudson Bay — and a host of wildlife, including polar bears, beluga whales, ringed and bearded seals.

Aug. 26 The Royal Bank of Canada (RBC) reported a record quarterly profit of $783 million.

• Bombardier concluded a wild year, selling its prestigious recreational-products division, which made the famous Ski-Doo and Sea-Doo. The Bombardier family, led by Bombardier chairman Laurent Beaudoin (b 1938), took 35%; US-based equity firm Bain Capital LLC, took 50%; and the Caisse de Dépôt et placement du Québec assumed the remaining 15%. The move followed a company decision to focus on the production of jets, rail cars and equity through its Bombardier Capital division. Earlier in the year (Apr. 3), Bombardier posted a $1 billion loss over the previous quarter. Four days later (Apr. 7), Bombardier signed a $7.8 billion deal to supply subway cars and related products to upgrade London, England's, historic Underground. Then on May 12, Bombardier Aerospace of Montreal was awarded a split deal with rival Embraer SA of Brazil to supply 85 of 170 planes to US Airlines for $3.3 billion. Bombardier would later (Sept. 15) secure a $1.2 billion contract with Sky West Airlines of Utah to supply 30 regional jets.

Aug. 27 Perdita Felicien (b 1980) of Pickering, Ont., became the 1st Canadian woman to win a gold in track and field, taking the 100-m hurdles at the Stade de France, St-Denis, France, in a Canadian record time of 12.53. Felicien would go on to win the 2003 Bobbie Rosenfeld Canadian Press Female Athlete of the Year award.

Also in Aug.
• The Okanagan-Kelowna fires destroyed 14 of 18 Kettle Valley Railway trestles in the Myra Canyon. Mostly constructed of creosote-soaked Douglas fir, these beautifully webbed timber structures towered over valley floors, some by as much as 50 m. They were constructed for the Kootenay-to-Pacific Kettle Valley Railway, completed July 13, 1916. Estimated cost to replace the trestles to original specifications was $15 million.

Sept. 1 The province of Ont. deeded 8,000 km^2 of lake beds and 56 km^2 of islands to connect existing, yet discontinuous, protected areas, thereby creating the world's largest freshwater preserve — an area covering some 24,000 km^2. The deeded area included contiguous waters running from Wabakimi Provincial Park south and along L. Nipigon, south to L. Superior, connecting to Sleeping Giant Provincial Park on Black Bay, and eastward to Terrace Bay.

Sept. 4 Petro-Canada announced it would close 100 of its 1,500 gas stations by 2005. Existing, high-traffic locations would expand to include groceries and fast-food services.

Sept. 10 The BC govt spent $545 million from its annual budget to fight wildfires. Over the previous 10 years, BC lost an annual average of 23,800 ha of land to wildfire, less than 1/10 of the 250,000 ha already decimated in 2003.

Sept. 11 Canadian Golfer Marlene Stewart Streit (b 1934) won the US Senior Women's Amateur title at Austin, Texas's, Barton Creek Resort, after playing 47 holes of match play golf. Just shy of her 70th birthday, Streit beat out much younger players to win her sixth straight national championship in 6 decades.

Sept. 12 The Asian beetle, a wood-boring insect with a destructive penchant for hardwood trees, was first discovered in Canada after a windstorm toppled trees in Woodbridge, Ont., exposing the large creatures to startled residents. Provincial authorities proposed the beetles were accidentally imported in packaging material. The beetles had already been found in New York City and Chicago, forcing officials there to destroy all infected trees.

Sept. 16 A Canadian Alliance motion to maintain the legal definition of marriage as that between a man and a woman was defeated in the House of Commons by a vote of 137–132.

Sept. 19 The Supreme Court of Canada unanimously ruled in the case of Métis Steve Powley and son, of Sault Ste. Marie, whose guns and moose had been confiscated Oct. 22, 1993, because they had been hunting without a licence. The Court concluded

Métis were a distinct Aboriginal group with the same legal status as other Canadian Aboriginals. The ruling, upheld an Ont. Court of Appeal decision of Feb. 23, 2001, which recognized that as Métis individuals, Powley and his son had a constitutional right to hunt for food, and therefore, required no licences or permits to do so.

Sept. 21 Former Liberal Finance Minister Paul Martin was made unofficial PM designate after receiving the necessary 2,902 Liberal delegate votes for the upcoming leadership convention Nov. 14 (after which he became the official PM-in-waiting). Heritage Minister Sheila Copps came second with 364 votes. Martin had lost the Liberal leadership race to Jean Chrétien June 23, 1990. He was made federal finance minister in Nov. 1993, holding the position until he was fired and replaced June 2, 2002, by John Manley. Martin would be sworn in as PM on Dec. 12.

Sept. 23 US President George Bush appealed to the UN in New York for help in bringing the increasingly volatile Iraq under control. He did not get it. Prior to the invasion, Bush declared that the UN would condemn itself to irrelevancy if its members did not join the "coalition of the willing." By early 2004, estimates showed that the invasion killed between 5,000–10,000 Iraq civilians, with an untold number of casualties. Over 650 coalition lives were also lost, including 555 Americans. The US also suffered 3,164 casualties.

Sept. 24 Ground was broken in Oakville, Ont., for the $5 million Mississauga-Oakville Emergency Veterinary Clinic, the largest private veterinary hospital in Canada. The 1,950-m^2 animal-treatment facility, due to open in 2004, is scheduled to include a cancer-treatment unit, an orthopaedic-surgery unit, MRI and CAT scanners, 3 operating rooms, 3 wards, 16 individual kennels and 6 examination rooms.

Sept. 25 Toronto-based Maple Leaf Foods Inc. purchased processed-meat producer Schneider Corp. for $413 million from Smithfield Foods Inc, which had purchased Schneider in 1998.

• CBC aired filmmaker Harry Rasky's (b 1928) documentary *Nobody Swings On Sunday*, a portrait of Jewish life in Toronto during the 1930s. The title referred to the fact that playground swings were padlocked on Sundays in Ont. The documentary also chronicled the quota system at U. of Toronto's School of Medicine, and the fact that no Jews were allowed at Trintiy or St. Michael's Colleges.

Sept. 28 Toronto-based Manulife Financial Corp, established in 1887, purchased Boston-based John Hancock Financial Services Inc., established in 1776, for $15 billion. Manulife had 13,000 employees, John Hancock 7,962. The purchase made Manulife the second-largest publicly traded company in the country after the RBC.

• Hurricane Juan warnings were issued for mainland NS and Cape Breton.

Sept. 29 Hurricane Jaun lashed the Maritimes, striking hardest in Halifax with winds gusting to 185 km/h, the highest on record for the region. Three hundred thousand people were without electricity as 4,500 km of service wire in the Halifax region was mostly wiped out. Over 14,000 were still without electricity by Oct. 4. Winds also destroyed old residential and park oaks, maples and elms, whipping branches and roots into homes and crushing cars. Wharves were damaged and boats tossed like corks. Damage estimates reached into the tens of millions.

Also in Sept.
• Alcan of Montreal completed its $4.8 billion purchase of European aluminum giant Pechiney SA of France, making it the world's largest aluminum producer. (Alcoa of Pittsburgh was 2nd.)

Oct. 1 Amr Moussa, the 1st Arab League leader to visit Canada, met with both Foreign Affairs Minister Bill Graham (b 1939) and PM Chrétien. Graham added his condemnation to Israel's construction of a 3.5-m-high, 700-km-long wall between Palestinian communities, including the West Bank and Israel, stating its construction was detrimental to the peace process. In certain areas, the wall would be 8 m high, paralleled on the Palestinian side by a 2-m-deep ditch, a 3-m-high electrified fence and rolls of 2-m-high barbed wire.

Oct. 2 Dalton McGuinty (b 1955) and the Ont. Liberal Party won 72 of 103 seats to end 8 years of Tory rule. Ernie Eves' Tories won 24 seats, the NDP under Howard Hampton (b 1952) won 7 seats, and lost Official Opposition status. Voter turnout was 52%. The Liberals quickly discovered that the Tories had left them with a $5.6 billion deficit, not a balanced budget, as claimed by Eves throughout the election campaign.

• There were 425,681 civil servants in Ont. When the Conservatives obtained power in 1995, there were 431,864.

Oct. 3 Two Canadian soldiers — Cpl. Robie Beeren-fenger and Sgt. Robert Short — were killed on patrol in Kabul, Afghanistan, when their lightly armoured standard-issue Iltis jeeps ran over a land mine. Two thousand Canadian soldiers were stationed in Kabul, serving under NATO.

Oct. 6 Syrian-born Canadian Maher Arar (b 1970) was released from a Syrian jail where he had been held 12 months. He had been deported to Syria from JFK Airport, New York, on unsubstantiated charges that he was linked to the al-Qaeda terrorist network. On Nov. 4, Arar spoke publicly, explaining he had been tortured; he also called for a Royal Commission into the reasons why — and how — his rights had been violated. Allegations would later surface that the RCMP provided US authorities with information on Arar prior to his deportation.

Oct. 12 The main section of the 89-year-old timber-frame Minaki Lodge, north of Kenora, Ont., burned to the ground. The structure had been built in 1914 by the Grand Trunk Pacific Railway, and rebuilt after a June 11, 1925, fire. Calgary developer Phil Archer purchased Minaki for $2 million in 1984. The building, estimated value of over $40 million, was not insured.

Oct. 15 BC Forestry Minister Mike de Jong and representatives of the 640-member Gitga'at First Nation signed BC's 1st revenue-sharing agreement, which gave the Aboriginal group $1.57 million over 5 years, and licence application rights to harvest up to 290,000 cubic m of primal forest south of Prince Rupert.

Oct. 15–22 Southern BC was inundated with record-smashing torrential rains, which caused widespread

damage. Lillooet R. flooding caused over 800 evacuations from Pemberton and Squamish and places in between along Highway 99, including Mount Currie and Whistler. At one point, the area received 20 cm in 24 hours, which caused bridge and road washouts and an estimated $20 million in damages. Altogether, the Squamish area received an incredible 45.4 cm over 5 days, and the Elaho Valley a near-incomprehensible 60 cm in 4 days, breaking records reaching back to 1881. The storm was linked to weather generated in the Hawaiian Islands.

Oct. 16 The 63-seat federal Canadian Alliance Party (leader, Stephen Harper), and the 15-seat Progressive Conservative party (leader, Peter MacKay) agreed to "Unite the Right" by forming the new Conservative Party of Canada. The agreement was ratified in Dec. by 96% of the Alliance membership and 90% of the PC membership. A leadership convention was slated for Spring 2004, with Harper, Tony Clement and former CEO of Magna International, Belinda Stronach, vying for the honour. The party had no logo or platform.

Oct. 20 Kirk Jones of Michigan was the 1st to go over the Canadian side of Niagara Falls with nothing on but his clothes — and witness another day. Onlookers claimed the man climbed over the wrought-iron fence, waded into the Niagara R. and slid over the precipice on his backside. He then swam to safety from the base of the falls and waved to the gathering crowd. Jones was charged with mischief and illegal performance of a stunt.

Oct. 21 The Nfld. Conservative Party, under the leadership of Rhodes scholar and multimillionaire Danny Williams, ended 15 years of Liberal power, taking 34 seats in the provincial election. Liberals, under Roger Grimes, took 12 seats, and the NDP under Jack Harris (b 1948) 2. Voter turnout was 72%. Williams made $230 million when he sold Atlantic Cable to Rogers Communications Inc in 2000.

• A private member's bill was passed in the House to commemorate the annual Day of the Holocaust, Yom Ha'Shoah. The date varied each year in connection to the Jewish calendar.

Oct. 22 The Chinese govt awarded the Bank of Nova Scotia, Guangzhou Branch, established in 1982, a licence to deal in Chinese currency — the renminbi. It was the 1st Canadian bank to be given the right.

Oct. 24 PM Chrétien pledged over $692 million to VIA Rail to help it upgrade services, and also, critics claimed, as a parting shot to his successor, Paul Martin, who would be left to pick up the tab. Martin immediately told VIA officials not to cash the cheque.

Oct. 28 The House passed Bill C–13, the Assisted Human Reproduction Act, by a vote of 149–109. The bill established a govt agency to provide approval for the medical use of embryos in stem cell research. The legislation also banned human cloning, animal-human hybrid production, the commercial use of a woman's womb and the sale of sperm and ova. C–13 was the offshoot of the Nov. 15, 1993, Royal Commission on New Reproductive Technologies report tabled by geneticist Patricia Baird. C–13 died as Parliament prorogued in Dec. The bill was re-introduced in the new year as Bill C-6 and given Assent Mar. 29, 2004.

Oct. 29 The World Economic Forum ranked Canada 16th on global economic competitiveness, cast between the UK at 15th and Australia at 17th. Finland was ranked number 1, the US 2 and Sweden 3. Canada had been ranked number 3 in 2001 and 9th in 2002.

Oct. 31 The Supreme Court of Canada ruled that it was not unconstitutional to take DNA samples from crime suspects.

Also in Oct.

• The Canadian Institute for Health Information published the Women's Health Surveillance Report, the nation's 1st comprehensive report on the state of Canadian women's health. Conclusions included: 42% of women between 15 and 24 reported having been abused by their partners; 81% of single mothers lived below the poverty line; 40% of those between 15 and 17 did not use contraceptives on a regular basis; and the mortality rate of rural women 15–19 was 2.5 times higher than the city rate for the same age group.

• Twenty-two-year-old Halifax native Erik Demaine (b 1981) received the $500,000 (US) MacArthur

Foundation grant for his work in computational origami (the science of folding and unfolding). Demaine entered Dalhousie at age 12 and began his doctoral thesis at the U. of Waterloo at age 14. He became an assistant professor at the Massachusetts Institute of Technology (MIT) at age 20.

• The Canadian Auto Workers Union (CAW) won a successful campaign to force Terra Footwear, a leading manufacturer of safety boots, to take down its billboards showing booted women "workers" in sexually suggestive poses.

• A Vancouver Board of Trade report was issued, showing that Vancouver's property crime resulted in a loss of $128 million a year, tops in Canada and 2nd in North America only to Miami. It also noted that 8.7% of all Vancouver property crimes were solved.

Nov. 5 The Sask. NDP, under Lorne Calvert, returned to power with 30 seats and a narrow majority. The Sask. Party under Elwin Hermanson (b 1952) won 28 seats; no Liberals were elected.

Nov. 6 The Supreme Court of Canada ruled 5–4 that it had a right to enforce and oversee the implementation of its rulings to ensure that legislators acted on SCC rulings in a timely manner.

• The federal Liberals tabled an incomplete bill in the House to provide AIDS-riddled African nations with inexpensive drugs, by allowing generic-drug manufactures to bypass existing patent laws (for that purpose only). Canada was the first to table such a bill. All parties agreed to pass the completed legislation when re-introduced in 2004. The parliamentary move followed a Sept call by a UN Special Envoy to Africa asking all industrial nations to rejig their drug-patent legislation so Africa could access inexpensive, life-preserving medicines.

• After 40 years in govt, PM Chrétien took his seat in the House for the last time.

Nov. 7 Harold Radford, NS's last WW I veteran, passed away, followed on Nov. 19, by Rev. Cyril Martins, Alb.'s last WW I veteran. The deaths left the country with less than 10 known surviving Canadian veterans of the War to End All Wars.

Nov. 9 The Canadian men's national baseball team qualified for the 2004 Olympic Games in Athens by beating Mexico 11–1. It was the 1st Canadian baseball team to qualify for the Olympics.

Nov. 10 David Miller won 44% of the vote and 22 of 44 wards to win the Toronto mayoral race, beating nearest rivals John Tory 38% and Barbara Hall 9%. Miller succeeded Mel Lastman, who retired. Forty-four candidates ran for mayor; voter turnout was 39%. Miller was sworn in Dec. 1. On Dec. 3, he fulfilled a campaign promise to eliminate former city council approval of a proposed $22 million bridge to the Toronto Islands Airport.

Nov. 11 Toronto Blue Jays pitcher Roy Halladay won the American League Cy Young Award, the fourth award in team history (Pat Hentgen, 1996; Roger Clemens, 1997 and 1998). The Denver, Colorado native finished the year with a 22–7 record and a 3.25 ERA. He took 26 of 28 1st-place votes.

Nov. 13 Montrealer Éric Gagné, stellar relief pitcher for the National League Los Angeles Dodgers, became the 1st Canadian to win the Cy Young Award since the great Fergie Jenkins in 1971. His 2003 numbers pushed into the ridiculous: he saved 55 games in 55 opportunities (he hadn't blown a save since Aug. of the 2002 season); he finished the year with a 1.27 ERA; had 137 strikeouts over 82 1/3 innings; was the 1st pitcher to ever record 100 more strikeouts than hits; and was the 1st to have 2 consecutive 50-plus save seasons.

• Halifax Mayor Peter Kelly broke ground on the Halifax Harbour sewage-collection system, designed to reroute an estimated 180 million litres of raw sewage dumped into the picturesque harbour each day to 3 new water-treatment plants. Raw, untreated sewage had been dumped into the harbour ever since Edward Cornwallis founded Halifax in 1749.

Nov. 17 Conrad Black, Lord of Crossharbour, was invited to retire as CEO of Chicago-based Hollinger International Inc. following charges related to $32 million worth of unauthorized payments given to company executives. Black acquiesced, tendering his resignation, effective Nov. 21.

Nov. 18 The federal govt agreed to provide Ont. with a $330 million SARS aid package.

• *Effet de Neige*, a 1906 oil by J.W. Morrice, sold for $1.5 million at Sotheby's in Toronto, a record price for a work by the late great Que. artist.

Nov. 19 Alvin Curling (b 1939), Ont. MPP for Scarborough-Rouge, was appointed Speaker of the Ont. legislature. Curling became the 1st African Canadian to hold the position.

Nov. 22 The Edmonton Oilers faced off against the Montreal Canadiens for the NHL's 1st outdoor game at Commonwealth Stadium in Edmonton. A record 57,167 hardy fans braced -19ºC temperatures to watch the hometown team squeak by the Habs 4–3. A record regular-season audience of 2.747 million watched on CBC's *Hockey Night in Canada*. The game was preceded by a "Heritage Classic," featuring retired greats from the Oilers and Canadiens led by Wayne Gretzky and Guy Lafleur. Former Oiler and active New York Ranger, Mark Messier, received special permission to join his long-retired colleagues for the Classic.

Nov. 23 Métis Carole James became leader of the BC NDP at a party convention in Vancouver. James beat out Leonard Krog (b 1953) to become the 1st Aboriginal to lead a major Canadian political party.

Nov. 25 Indebted BC Rail was sold to CN for an estimated $1 billion.

• The RBC posted a year-end profit of over $3 billion, a Canadian bank record. It made $2.76 billion in 2002. The Bank of Montreal also posted a $1.82 billion profit, up from $1.42 billion in 2002. On Nov. 26, the TD posted a profit of $989 million, up from a red figure of $160 million in 2002. CIBC posted a profit of $1.9 billion, up from $492 million in 2002.

Dec. 8 Man. and Ottawa signed a $240 million deal to upgrade the Red R. Floodway.

Dec. 10 BC Ferries was shut down for the 1st time in 25 years as striking workers defied back-to-work legislation. BC Ferries carried an average 60,000 people and 22,000 vehicles a day. Strikers, who walked out over proposed wage cuts, hours and outsourcing, returned to work Dec. 12. Grievances were put to mediation.

Dec. 12 Paul Martin was sworn in at Rideau Hall as the nation's 21st prime minister. His new 39-member cabinet included 11 women.

Dec. 16 Newly crowned Masters champ Mike Weir was awarded the annual Lou Marsh Award for Oustanding Canadian Athlete, beating out Cy Young winner Éric Gagné by 1 vote. Weir won 3 of 21 tournaments entered, finishing 5th on the money list with $4.92 million US. On Dec. 30, Weir again beat out Gagné for the Lionel Conacher CP Male Athlete of the Year award. Both he and Gagné received the same number of 1st-place votes, but the golfer had 2 more 2nd-place votes.

Dec. 17 Canadian businessman Michael DeGroote, founder of Laidlaw Transport, donated a record $105 million to McMaster University's medical school, to be renamed in his honour.

Dec. 18 The Court of Arbitration for Sport awarded cross-country skier Beckie Scott a gold medal from the 2002 Salt Lake City Winter Olympics; the 2 Russian skiers who finished 1st and 2nd had failed their drug tests.

• The Canada-Newfoundland Offshore Petroleum Board awarded ChevronTexaco Corp, Exxon Mobil Corp and Imperial Oil collective oil exploration rights in the 2,000–3,000-m-deep Orphan Basin, north of Hibernia. The rights cost the firms $672.7 million in total.

Dec. 23 The US Department of Agriculture (USDA) announced that samples taken from a Washington State dairy cow showed signs of mad cow disease (bovine spongiform encephalopathy). Canada immediately placed a qualified ban on both live and processed US meats. The cow was later linked to an Alb. farm.

Dec. 24 The PEI Employment Standards Act was amended to provide islanders with up to 8 weeks of unpaid leave to care for terminally ill family members.

• International dairy-products producer Parmalat Finanziaria SpA of Italy went into bankruptcy in the midst of a multibillion-dollar fraud scandal. Its Canadian units included Black Diamond cheeses, Balderson Cheese, Lactantia, Astro Yogurt, Beatrice and Parkay.

Dec. 28 Oakville, Ont., native Mike Vanderjagt, of the Indianapolis Colts, kicked his 43rd consecutive field goal to beat the Houston Texans 20–17. He finished the season with 37 consecutive field goals and, stretching from the previous season, beat the previous NFL record of 41 in a row.

Dec. 30 The loonie reached a 10-year high: 77.26 cents US.

Also in Dec.

• TransAlta, through its subsidiary Vision Quest began construction on 38 giant wind turbines near Pincher Creek, Alb., to produce a total of 68 megawatts. By summer 2004, Vision Quest operated nearly 100 wind turbines in fields near Pincher Creek and Fort MacLeod.

Also in 2003

• Over 3,800 military members of the Canadian Armed Forces were deployed in various missions overseas, including Afghanistan, the Balkans, Haiti, Golan Heights, Democratic Republic of the Congo and Sierra Leone.

• Approximately one-third of all oil produced in Canada came from the Alb. oilsands. The oilsands comprise three regions in Alb. — Athabasca, Cold L. and Peace R. In total the Alb. oilsands cover 141,000 km^2. As of Jan. 1, 2003, 25 firms involved in 59 projects were paying royalties under Alb.'s oilsands royalty laws.

• The $6.5 million Luminous Veil, a suicide-prevention barrier making it nearly impossible to leap from the 490-m-long, 40-m-high Bloor St. Viaduct, was completed. Designed by U. of Waterloo architect Professor Derek Revington, the barrier, which won the 1999 Canadian Architect Award of Excellence, is constructed of more than 9,000 steel rods, each 5 m tall and spaced 13 cm apart along both sides of the bridge across the Don R. Originally approved by Toronto City Council in

1998, construction was delayed by funding problems and concerns. Because of the delay, critics said, the viaduct was the site of an estimated 94 suicides.

• A living eastern white cedar (*Thuja occidentalis*), located on the Niagara Escarpment in Ont., was determined by members of the Cliff Ecology Research Group of the U. of Guelph to be 1,316 years old, placing the year of its germination at 688 CE. A dead escarpment cedar was estimated at 1,890 years old. The Niagara Escarpment is home to 8 livings cedars that are each over 1,000 years old, and also, 110 of the oldest trees in the province.

• Four new *Hinterland Who's Who* public service wildlife vignettes were filmed from $100,000 bequeathed to the Canadian Wildlife Service by late Quebecer Alexander Lakos. The once-ubiquitous television interludes, with the distinctive theme music and request to "contact the Canadian Wildlife Service in Ottawa," were first aired in the early 1960s. The new shows focused on the polar bear, loon, leatherback turtle and monarch butterfly.

• New Statistics Canada data showed that Canada was the most educated industrialized nation with 41% of those gainfully employed holding post-secondary degrees or diplomas. The US ranked second at 37% and Ireland 3rd at 36%.

• Medical school tuition fees for the 2003–2004 year, by selected institution: U. of T, $16,207; McMaster, $14,445; Dalhousie, $10,460; U. of BC, $10,272; U. of Calgary, $9,932; U. of Sask. $9,774; U. of Man. $7,595; Memorial, $6,250; McGill, $3,559; and U. de Montréal $2,224.

• Canada had 4.7 MRI (magnetic resonance imaging) machines per million persons; Austria 11.6; Finland 11.7; the US 17.4; and Japan 23.2. Canada had 10.3 CAT (computed axial tomography) scanners per million; Switzerland 18.5; Italy 19.6; Austria 26.3; South Korea 27.3; and Japan 84.4.

• Not a good year for Lloydminster, Sask., police, who cleared only 5% of their crime cases — the worst record in the country. (A crime was "cleared" when a criminal charge was laid or a suspect identified.)

• A Canadian Institute for Health Information report ranked Canada 4th among industrialized nations on health-care spending, with a total public and private investment of $121.3 billion in 2003, or 10% of its GDP. The US ranked 1st, followed by Switzerland and Germany, respectively.

• The average weekday sale of the *Globe & Mail* was 316,644 copies; the *National Post*, 247,576 copies. The average Saturday *Globe* sold 393,474 copies and the *Post* 274,321.

• Ont. was the 3rd leading regional producer of environmental pollution in North America, behind Texas and Ohio, respectively.

• The Toronto Public Library system had more books in circulation than any other public system in the world.

• Canada's wood bison population was estimated to be 3,536 animals.

• World Vision's winter catalogue included photographs of Canadian children (in the Innu community of Natuashish, Nfld.), with the slogan, "Help Children in Canada."

• A car was stolen in Canada every 3 minutes.

• The average annual cost of auto insurance ranged from $787 in Man. to $2,504 in Ont. The 4 lowest rates were in provinces with public systems: Man., Que. ($903), Sask. ($904) and BC ($1,105).

• One of Canada's premier nonfiction houses, Macfarlane Walter and Ross, publishers of such best-sellers as David Foot and Daniel Stoffman's *Boom Bust and Echo* (300,000 copies sold), and Stevie Cameron's *On the Take,* ceased operations. The company, founded by John Macfarlane, Jan Walter and Gary Ross as a branch of General Publishing in the late 1980s, had published the 2002 Gov-Gen.'s award-winning *Saboteurs: Wiebo Ludwig's War Against Big Oil.*

• Artist Chester Brown (b 1960) published the graphic novel and national best-seller *Louis Riel: A Comic Strip Biography.*

• Former media mogul Conrad Black published *Franklin Delano Roosevelt: Champion of Freedom*.

• Internationally acclaimed poet Margaret Avison was awarded the Griffin Poetry Prize, at $40,000 the world's richest prize in poetry, for her work, *Concrete and Wild Carrot*.

• Casting was held for the Radio-Canada sitcom *Les Bougon*. The French-language comedy series, which debuted in Jan. 2004, starred Que. actor Rémy Girard as Paul Bougon, the head of a family of con artists who worked extremely hard finding ways not to work.

• Michael Ignatieff published *Empire Lite: Nation-building in Bosnia, Kosovo and Afghanistan*. The 134-page paperback was priced at $25.00.

• Richard Van Camp (b 1971) published his picture book *What's the Most Beautiful Thing you Know about Horses*, illustrated by George Littlechild (b 1958).

• Canadian science fiction novelist Robert J. Sawyer won the Hugo Award for his novel *Hominids*, the first in his Neanderthal Parallax trilogy. The award, sponsored by the World Science Fiction Society, is sometimes referred to as the People's Choice Award because winners must receive a majority vote from the 5,000 members of that society. Sawyer was presented with the honour at the World Science Fiction Society Convention (Torcon) in Toronto.

• Mark Abley's *Spoken Here*, a compelling portrait of the world's endangered languages, was published.

• There were 3,500 hockey rinks in Canada, and 500,000 Canadians had registered for minor hockey.

Books

Abbott, Elizabeth, ed. *Chronicle of Canada*. Montreal: Chronicle Publications, 1990.

Abonyi, Arpad, ed. *1990 Canada Facts: An International Business Comparison*. Ottawa: Prospectus Publications, 1989.

Alexander, Bryan and Cherry Alexander. *The Vanishing Arctic*. New York: Facts on File, 1997.

Allen, Robert S. *The British Indian Department and the Frontier in North America, 1755-1830*. Canadian Historic Sites: Occasional Papers in Archaeology and History, No. 14. Ottawa: Indian and Northern Affairs, 1975.

Anderson, Charles W. *Grain: The Entrepreneurs*. Winnipeg: Watson & Dwyer Publishing, 1991.

Anderson, Ellen. *Judging Bertha Wilson: Law as Large as Life*. Toronto: University of Toronto Press, 2001.

Anderson, Gary. *Atlantic Salmon Fact & Fantasy*. Montreal: Salar Publishing, 1990.

Andrew, J.V. *Enough! Wake-up English-Speaking Canada! Enough of this Absurdity*. Kitchener, Ont.: Andrew Books, 1988.

Andrews, Allen. *Brave Soldiers, Proud Regiments: Canada's Military Heritage*. Vancouver: Ronsdale Press, 1997.

Angus, James T. *A Respectable Ditch: A History of the Trent-Severn Waterway 1833–1920*. Montreal: McGill–Queen's University Press, 1988.

Archer, John H. and Charles B. Koester. *Footprints in Time: A Sourcebook in the History of Saskatchewan*. House of Grant (Canada), 1965.

Axelrod, Alan and Charles L. Phillips. *Encyclopedia of Historical Treaties and Alliances*. Vols. I & II. New York: Facts on File, 2001.

Backhouse, Constance. *Colour-Coded: A Legal History of Racism in Canada, 1900–1950*. Toronto: University of Toronto Press (for The Osgoode Society for Canadian Legal History), 1999.

Baird, David M.
- *Lighthouses of Atlantic Canada*. Calgary: Red Deer Press, 2003.
- *Northern Lights: Lighthouses of Canada*. Toronto: Lynx Images, 1999.

Bairstow, Frances, ed. *The Dynamics of Change: Labour Relations on the Montreal Waterfront*. Montreal: McGill University Industrial Relations Centre, 1970.

Baker, Carlos. *Ernest Hemmingway: A Life Story*. New York: Colliers, 1969.

Baker, G. Blaine and Jim Phillips, eds. *Essays in the History of Canadian Law in Honour of R.C.B. Risk*. Toronto: University of Toronto Press (for The Osgoode Society for Canadian Legal History), 1999.

Bakvis, Herman, ed. *Canadian Political Parties: Leaders, Candidates and Organization*. Vol. 13. Toronto: Dundurn Press (for the Royal Commission on Electoral Reform and Party Financing and Canada Communication Group), 1991.

Ball, Norman et al. *Building Canada: A History of Public Works*. Toronto: University of Toronto Press, 1988.

Barmash, Isadore, ed. *Great Business Disasters: Swindlers, Bunglers and Frauds in American Industry*. Rev. ed. New York: Ballantine Books, 1973.

Barnett, Donald C. *Poundmaker*. Don Mills, Ont.: Fitzhenry & Whiteside, 1976.

Barnsley, Roland and John H. Pierce. *The Public Gardens and Parks of Niagara*. St. Catharines, Ont.: Vanwell Publishing, 1989.

Barris, Ted and Alex Barris. *Days of Victory: Canadians Remember: 1939–1945*. Toronto: Macmillan of Canada, 1996.

Bartlett, Gillian and Janice Galivan. *Canada: History in the Making*. Toronto: John Wiley & Sons (Canada), 1986.

Bassett, John M.
- *Samuel Cunard*. Don Mills, Ont.: Fitzhenry & Whiteside, 1976.
- *Timothy Eaton*. Don Mills, Ont.: Fitzhenry & Whiteside, 1980.

Bibliography

Bassett, John M. and A. Roy Petrie.
>   • *Laura Secord*. Rev ed. Markham, Ont.: Fitzhenry & Whiteside, 2003.
>   • *William Hamilton Merritt*. Don Mills, Ont.: Fitzhenry & Whiteside, 1974.

Basque, Garnet, ed. *Frontier Days in British Columbia*. Surrey, BC: Heritage House, 2000.

Batten, Jack.
>   • *In Court*. Toronto: Macmillan of Canada, 1982.
>   • *Judges*. Toronto: Penguin Books, 1987.

Bayer, Fern. *The Ontario Collection*. Markham, Ont.: Fitzhenry & Whiteside (for the Ontario Heritage Foundation), 1984.

Beals, C. S., ed. *Science, History and Hudson Bay*. Vols. One & Two. Ottawa: Department of Energy, Mines and Resources, 1968.

Bearden, Jim and Linda Jean Butler. *Shadd: The Life and Times of Mary Shadd Cary*. Toronto: NC Press, 1977.

Beddoes, Dick. *Pal Hal: The Uninhibited No-Holds Barred Account of the Life and Times of Harold Ballard*. Toronto: MacMillian, 1989.

Beecroft, Margaret S. *Windings: A History of the Lower Maitland River*. Maitland Valley Conservation Authority, 1984.

Benham, Mary Lile.
>   • *Nellie McClung*. Rev. ed. Markham, Ont.: Fitzhenry & Whiteside, 2000.
>   • *Paul Kane*. Don Mills, Ont.: Fitzhenry & Whiteside, 1977.

Bennett, Paul W., Cornelius J. Jaenen et al. *Emerging Identities: Selected Problems and Interpretations in Canadian History*. Scarborough, Ont.: Prentice–Hall Canada, 1986.

Benson, Nathaniel A. *None of it Came Easy: The Story of James Garfield Gardiner*. Toronto: Burns & MacEachern, 1955.

Bercuson, David J. *Maple Leaf Against the Axis: Canada's Second World War*. Toronto: Stoddart, 1995.

Bercuson, David and J.L. Granatstein. *The Collins Dictionary of Canadian History: 1867 to the Present*. Toronto: Collins, 1988.

Berton, Pierre.
>   • *The Arctic Grail: The Quest for the North West Passage and the North Pole, 1818–1909*. Toronto: Doubleday Canada, 2001.
>   • *Dionne Years*. Toronto: Penguin Canada, 1991.
>   • *Flames Across the Border: 1813–1814*. Toronto: Doubleday Canada, 2001.
>   • *The Great Depression, 1929–1939*. Toronto: Doubleday Canada, 2001.
>   • *The Great Lakes*. Toronto: Stoddart, 1996.
>   • *Hollywood's Canada: The Americanization of Our National Image*. Toronto: McClelland & Stewart, 1975.
>   • *The Invasion of Canada*. Toronto: Doubleday Canada, 2001.
>   • *Klondike: The Last Great Gold Rush, 1896–1899*. Toronto: Doubleday Canada, 2001.
>   • *The Last Spike: The Great Railway, 1881–1885*. Toronto: Doubleday Canada, 2001.
>   • *Marching as to War: Canada's Turbulent Years*. Toronto: Doubleday Canada, 2001.
>   • *My Country: The Remarkable Past*. Toronto: Anchor Canada, 2002.
>   • *The Mysterious North: Encounters with the Canadian Frontier*. Toronto: McClelland & Stewart, 1991.
>   • *My Time: Living with History*. Toronto: Doubleday Canada, 1998.
>   • *The National Dream: The Great Railway, 1871–1881*. Toronto: Doubleday Canada, 2001.
>   • *Niagara: A History of the Falls*. Toronto: Anchor Canada, 2002.
>   • *Pierre Berton's Canada*. Toronto: Stoddart, 1999.
>   • *Pierre Berton's Seacoasts of Canada*. Toronto: Stoddart, 1998.
>   • *The Promised Land: Settling the West, 1896–1914*. Toronto: Anchor Canada, 2002.
>   • *Vimy*. Toronto: Doubleday Canada, 2001.
>   • *Welcome to the 21st Century*. Toronto: Doubleday Canada, 2000.

Berton, Pierre, ed. *Great Canadians: A Century of Achievement*. Toronto: The Canadian Centennial Publishing Company, 1965.

Best, Dave. *Canada: Our Century in Sport*. Markham, Ont.: Fitzhenry & Whiteside, 2002.

Bierman, John. *Dark Safari: The Life Behind the Legend of Henry Morton Stanley*. New York: Knopf, 1990.

Bileski, Kasimir et al. *Unitrade Specialized Catalogue of Canadian Stamps*. Toronto: The Unitrade Press, 1994.

Birney, Earle. *Ice Cod Bell or Stone.* Toronto: McClelland & Stewart, 1962.

Bissell, Claude. *Halfway up Parnassus: A Personal Account of the University of Toronto 1932–1971.* Toronto: University of Toronto Press, 1974.

Black, Conrad.
> • *Duplessis.* Toronto: McClelland & Stewart, 1977.
> • *A Life in Progress.* Toronto: Key Porter, 1993.

Blaise, Clark. *Time Lord: The Remarkable Canadian Who Missed His Train and Changed the World.* Toronto: Vintage Canada, 2001.

Blakeley, Phyllis Ruth. *Nova Scotia: A Brief History.* Toronto: J. M. Dent & Sons, 1955.

Blanchard, James J. *Behind the Embassy Door: Canada, Clinton and Quebec.* Toronto: McClelland & Stewart, 1998.

Bliss, J.M. *Canadian History in Documents: 1763–1966.* Toronto: The Ryerson Press, 1966.

Bliss, Michael. *Right Honourable Men: The Descent of Canadian Politics from Macdonald to Mulroney.*
> Toronto: HarperPerennial, 1995.

Blodgett, Jean et al. *The McMichael Canadian Art Collection.* Toronto: McGraw–Hill Ryerson, 1989.

Blumenson, John. *Ontario Architecture: A Guide to Styles and Building Terms, 1874 to the Present.* Markham, Ont.: Fitzhenry & Whiteside, 1990.

Bogle, Don et al. *Continuity and Change: Canada: A History of Our Country from 1900 to the Present.* Markham, Ont.: Fitzhenry & Whiteside, 2000.

Boiteau, Denise. *Early Peoples: Origins: A History of Canada.* Markham, Ont.: Fitzhenry & Whiteside, 1988.

Bombardier Annual Report: Year Ended January 31, 2002. Montreal: Bombardier, Inc.

Borins, Sandford F. *The Language of the Skies: The Bilingual Air Traffic Control Conflict in Canada.*
> Kingston, Ont.: McGill Queen's University Press, 1983.

Bothwell, Robert et al.
> • *Canada 1900–1945.* Toronto: University of Toronto Press, 1990.
> • *Canada since 1945: Power, Politics and Provincialism.* Toronto: University of Toronto Press, 1993.

Bourniot, J.G. *The Story of Canada.* Toronto: The Copp, Clark Company, 1901.

Bowen, Lynne. *Muddling Through: The Remarkable Story of the Barr Colonists.* Vancouver: Douglas & McIntyre, 1992.

Boyer, Elizabeth. *Marguerite de la Roque: A Story of Survival.* Toronto: Popular Library, 1977.

Bradford, Robert D. *Historic Forts of Ontario.* Belleville, Ont.: Mika Publishing Company, 1988.

Bradley, A. G.
> • *Sir Guy Carleton (Lord Dorchester).* Toronto: University of Toronto Press, 1966.
> • *Wolfe.* London: Macmillan and Company, 1923.

Bredin, Thomas F. *Confederation 1867: Selected Sources – from Durham's Report to the British North America Act.*
> Toronto: McClelland and Stewart, 1968.

Brennan, Brian.
> • *Alberta Originals: Stories of Albertans Who Made a Difference.* Calgary: Fifth House, 2001.
> • *Building a Province: 60 Alberta Lives.* Calgary: Fifth House, 2000.
> • *Scoundrels and Scallywags: Characters from Alberta's Past.* Calgary: Fifth House, 2002.

Brisebois, Michel. *Impressions: 250 Years of Printing in the Lives of Canadians.* Markham, Ont.: Fitzhenry & Whiteside, 1999.

Broadfoot, Barry.
> • *Ten Lost Years 1929–1939: Memories of Canadians Who Survived the Depression.* Don Mills, Ont.: PaperJacks, 1973.
> • *Years of Sorrow, Years of Shame: The Story of the Japanese Canadians in World War II.* Toronto: Doubleday Canada, 1977.

Bibliography

Brode, Patrick. *Casual Slaughters and Accidental Judgments: Canadian War Crimes Prosecutions, 1944–1948.*
    Toronto: University of Toronto Press (for The Osgoode Society for Canadian Legal History), 1997.

Brodie, Janine. *The Political Economy of Canadian Regionalism.* Toronto: Harcourt Brace Jovanovich (Canada), 1990.

Brosseau, Mathilde. *Gothic Revival in Canadian Architecture.* Canadian Historic Sites: Occasional Papers in Archaeology and History, No. 25.
    Ottawa: Parks Canada, 1980.

Brown, Craig, ed. *The Illustrated History of Canada.* Toronto: Lester & Orpen Dennys, 1987.

Brown, Desmond H. *The Birth of a Criminal Code: The Evolution of Canada's Justice System.* Toronto: University of Toronto Press, 1995.

Brown, George W. *Building the Canadian Nation.* Toronto: J. M. Dent & Sons, 1958.

Brown, Lorraine. *200 years of Tradition: The Story of Canadian Whisky.* Markham, Ont.: Fitzhenry & Whiteside, 1994.

Brown, Ron.
        • *Ghost Towns of Ontario: Volume 2.* Toronto: Cannonbooks, 1983.
        • *The Train Doesn't Stop Here Anymore: An Illustrated History of Railway Stations in Canada.* Toronto: Lynx Images, 1998.

Bruce, Harry. *The Pig That Flew: The Battle to Privatize Canadian National.* Vancouver: Douglas & McIntyre, 1997.

Bruce, Jean. *After the War.* Don Mills, Ont.: Fitzhenry & Whiteside (for the Minister of Supply and Services), 1982.

Buck, George H. *From Summit to Sea: An Illustrated History of Railroads in British Columbia and Alberta.* Calgary: Fifth House, 1997.

Buckingham, William and Geo. W. Ross. *The Hon. Alexander Mackenzie: His Life and Times.* Toronto: Rose Publishing Company, 1892.

Bumsted, J.M. *The Winnipeg General Strike of 1919: An Illustrated History.* Winnipeg: Watson Dwyer Publishing, 1994.

Bushnell, Ian. *The Federal Court of Canada: A History, 1875–1992.* Toronto: University of Toronto Press
    (for The Osgoode Society for Canadian Legal History), 1997.

Cahill, Barry. *The Thousandth Man: A Biography of James McGregor Stewart.* Toronto: University of Toronto Press
    (for The Osgoode Society for Canadian Legal History), 2000.

Calef, George. *Caribou and the Barren-Lands.* Willowdale, Ont: Firefly Books, 1995.

Callbeck, Lorne C. *The Cradle of Confederation: A brief history of Prince Edward Island from its discovery in 1534 to the present time.*
    Fredericton: Brunswick Press, 1964.

Cameron, Alex A. *Canada's Heritage.* Toronto: J.M. Dent & Sons, 1955.

Cameron, Christina and Janet Wright. *Second Empire Style in Canadian Architecture.* Canadian Historic Sites: Occasional Papers in
    Archaeology and History, No. 24. Ottawa: Parks Canada, 1980.

Cameron, Stevie. *Ottawa Inside Out.* Toronto: Key Porter, 1979.

Campagna, Palmiro. *Storms of Controversy: The Secret Avro Files Revealed.* Toronto: Stoddart, 1992.

Campbell, H.C., ed. *How to Find Out About Canada.* London: Pergamon Press, 1967.

Campbell, Marjorie Wilkins.
        • *McGillivray: Lord of the Northwest.* Toronto: Clarke, Irwin and Company, 1962.
        • *The North West Company.* Toronto: The Macmillan Company of Canada, 1957.
        • *The Silent Song: A Daughter's Tribute to a Reluctant Pioneer.* Calgary: Fifth House, 1999.

Canada: The Growth of a Great Nation. Switzerland: Auge International. July 1976.

The Canadian Encyclopedia. Vols. I, II, III, and IV. Edmonton: Hurtig Publishers, 1988.

Canadian Global Almanac. Annual. Toronto: John Wiley & Sons.

Canadian Journal of Native Studies. (Bi-annual). Brandon, MB: Society for the Advancement of Native Studies.

Canadian News Facts: The Indexed Digest of Canadian Current Events. Annual. Toronto: Marpet Publishings.

Canadian Recreational and Home Almanac: 1969. Toronto: Star Reader Service and Compton Associates, 1969.

Canadian World Almanac and Book of Facts. Annual. Toronto: Global Press.

Careless, J.M.S.
　　　• *Canada: A Story of Challenge*. Rev. ed. Toronto: Macmillan of Canada, 1963.
　　　• *The Canadians: George Brown*. Don Mills, Ont.: Fitzhenry & Whiteside, 1979.

Carter, Margaret. *Early Canadian Court Houses*. Studies in Archaeology, Architecture and History. Ottawa: Parks Canada, 1983.

Carter, Velma and Levero (Lee) Carter. *The Black Canadians: Their History and Contributions*. Rev. ed. Edmonton: Reidmore Books, 1993.

Cartwright, Richard J. *Reminiscences*. Toronto: William Briggs, 1912.

Casselman, Bill. *Casselman's Canadian Words*. Toronto: Copp Clark Ltd., 1995.

Cauz, Louis E. *The Plate: A Royal Tradition*. Toronto: Deneau Publishers & Company, 1984.

Cawker, Ruth and William Bernstein. *Contemporary Canadian Architecture: The Mainstream and Beyond*.
　　　Markham, Ont.: Fitzhenry & Whiteside, 1988.

Cekota, Anthony. *Entrepreneur Extraordinary: The Biography of Thomas Bata*. Rome:
　　　University Press of the International University of Social Studies, 1968.

Chambers, Lori. *Married Women and Property Law in Victorian Ontario*. Toronto: University of Toronto Press
　　　(for The Osgoode Society for Canadian Legal History), 1997.

Chapman, Vernon. *"Who's in the Goose Tonight?": An Anecdotal History of Canadian Theatre*. Toronto: ECW Press, 2001.

Chaput, Marcel. *Pourquoi je suis Séparatiste*. 4th ed. Montreal: Les Èditions du jour, 1961.

Charlebois, Dr. Peter. *The Life of Louis Riel*. Toronto: NC Press, 1978.

Chartrand, Paul L.A.H. *Manitoba's Métis Settlement Scheme of 1870*. Saskatoon: University of Saskatchewan Native Law Centre, 1991.

Chevrier, Lionel. *The St. Lawrence Seaway*. Toronto: Macmillan of Canada, 1959.

Chisholm, Anne and Michael Davie. *Beaverbrook: A Life*. London: Pimlico, 1992.

Chisholm, Barbara and Andrea Gutsche. *Superior: Under The Shadow of the Gods*. Toronto: Lynx Images, 1998.

Chrétien, Jean. *Straight from the Heart*. Toronto: Key Porter, 1985.

Cinq-Mars, J. and Richard E. Morla, *Blue Fish caves and Old Crow basin: A new Rapport, in Ice Age Peoples of North America*, ed. Bonnichsen and
　　　Turnmire, Corvallis: Oregon State University Press, 1999:212-220.

Clark, Andrew. *A Keen Soldier: The Execution of Second World War Private Harold Pringle*. Toronto: Knopf Canada, 2002.

Clark, Bruce W. and John K. Wallace. *Canada: Land of Diversity*. 3rd ed. Scarborough, Ont.: Prentice Hall Ginn Canada, 1996.

Clark, Joe. *A Nation Too Good to Lose*. Toronto: Key Porter, 1994.

Clemence, Verne. *David M. Baltzan: Prairie Doctor*. Markham, Ont.: Fitzhenry & Whiteside, 1995.

Coates, Ken and Fred McGuinness. *Manitoba: The Province and The People*. Edmonton: Hurting Publishers, 1987.

Cochrane, Jean. *The One Room School In Canada*. Calgary: Fifth House, 2001.

Colby, C.W. *Canadian Types of the Old Règime 1608–1698*. New York: Henry Holt, 1908.

Bibliography

Collard, Edgar A.
  • *Canadian Yesterdays*. Toronto: Longmans, Green and Co., 1955.
  • *Oldest McGill*. Toronto: The Macmillan Company, 1946.
  • ed. *The McGill You Knew: An Anthology of Memories 1920–1960*. Don Mills, Ont.: Longman Canada, 1975.

Collins, Gilbert. *Guidebook to the Historic Sites of the War of 1812*. Toronto: Dundurn Press, 1998.

Collins, Paul. *Hart Massey*. Don Mills, Ont.: Fitzhenry & Whiteside, 1977.

Colombo, John Robert.
  • *Colombo's 101 Canadian Places*. Willowdale, Ont.: Hounslow Press, 1983.
  • *Colombo's Canadian References*. Toronto: Oxford University Press, 1976.
  • *Colombo 's Canadian Quotations*. Edmonton: Hurtig, 1974

Conway, J.F. *The West: The History of a Region in Confederation*. 2nd ed. Toronto: James Lorimer & Company, 1994.

Cook, Peter. *Massey at the Brink: The Story of Canada's Greatest Multinational and Its Struggle to Survive*. Toronto: Collins, 1981.

Cook, Ramsay et al. *Dictionary of Canadian Biography*. Vols XIV. Toronto: University of Toronto Press, 1998.

Cosentino, Frank and Don Morrow. *The Canadians: Lionel Conacher*. Don Mills, Ont.: Fitzhenry & Whiteside, 1981.

Cotè, Langevin. *Heritage of Power: The Churchill Falls Development from Concept to Reality*. Labrador: Churchill Falls Corp., 1972.

Cotè, Marcel and David Johnston. *If Québec Goes ...The Real Cost of Separation*. Toronto: Stoddart, 1995.

Cowan, John. *Canada's Governors–General: 1867–1952*. Toronto: York Publishing Company, 1952.

Craig, Gerald M., ed. *Lord Durham's Report*. Toronto: McClelland & Stewart, 1964.

Cramm, Frank and Garfield Fizzard.
  • *The Atlantic Edge: Living in Newfoundland and Labrador*. St. John's: Breakwater; Markham, Ont.: Fitzhenry & Whiteside, 1986.
  • *Our Province: Newfoundland and Labrador*. St. John's: Breakwater; Markham, Ont.: Fitzhenry & Whiteside, 1983.

Cramond, Mike. *Of Bears and Man*. Markham, Ont.: Fitzhenry & Whiteside, 1986.

Creighton, Donald.
  • *Canada's First Century 1867–1967*. Toronto: Macmillan of Canada, 1970.
  • *The Forked Road: Canada 1939-1957*. Toronto: McClelland & Stewart, 1976.
  • *John A. Macdonald: The Old Chieftain*. Toronto: Macmillan of Canada, 1952.
  • *John A. Macdonald: The Young Politician*. Toronto: Macmillan of Canada, 1952.

Creighton, Douglas. *Sunburned: Memoirs of a Newspaperman*. Toronto: Little, Brown and Company (Canada), 1993.

Crosbie, John C. *No Holds Barred: My Life in Politics*. Toronto: McClelland & Stewart, 1997.

Crowe, Keith J. *A History of the Original Peoples of Northern Canada*. Montreal: McGill–Queen's University Press
  (for the Arctic Institute of North America), 1974.

Cruise, David and Alison Griffiths. *Lords of the Line: The Men Who Built the CPR*. Markham, Ont.: Penguin (Canada), 1989.

Cruxton, J. Bradley and W. Douglas Wilson. *Spotlight Canada*. 4th ed. Toronto: Oxford University Press, 2000.

Curry, Ralph L. *The Leacock Medal Treasury: 4 Decades of the Best Canadian Humour*. Toronto: Lester & Orpen Dennys, 1984.

Cybulski, J. W. et al. "An Early Human Skeleton from South-Central British Columbia :Dating and Bioarchaeological Inference,"
  Canadian Journal of Archaeology, 1981(5):49-59.

Dafoe, John W. *Clifford Sifton in Relation to His Times*. Toronto: Macmillan Canada, 1931.

Damania, Laura. *Egerton Ryerson*. Don Mills, Ont.: Fitzhenry & Whiteside, 1975.

Dancocks, Daniel G. *Welcome to Flanders Fields*. Toronto: McCelland & Stewart, 1988.

Davey, Frank. *From There to Here: A Guide to English–Canadian Literature Since 1960*. (Our Nature–Our Voices, Vol. II). Erin, Ont.: Press Porcepic, 1974.

Davis, Mary B., ed. *Native America in the Twentieth Century: An Encyclopedia*. New York: Garland, 1996.

Dawson, Joan. *The Mapmaker's Eye: Nova Scotia through Early Maps*. Halifax: Nimbus Publishing and The Nova Scotia Museum, 1988.

De Brou, Dave and Bill Waiser. *Documenting Canada: A History of Modern Canada in Documents*. Saskatoon: Fifth House, 1992.

Dechene, Louise. *Habitats and Merchants in Seventeenth Century Montreal*. Montreal: McGill–Queen's University Press, 1992.

Deener, David R., ed. *Canada–United States Treaty Relations*. Durham, NC: Duke University Press, 1963.

Dempsey, Hugh A.
  • *A Blackfoot Winter Count*. Occasional Paper No. 1. Calgary: Glenbow Museum, 1965.
  • *Charcoal's World: The True Story of a Canadian Indian's Last Stand*. Calgary: Fifth House, 1998.
  • *Firewater: The Impact of the Whisky Trade on the Blackfoot Nation*. Calgary: Fifth House, 2002.
  • *The Golden Age of the Canadian Cowboy: An Illustrated History*. Saskatoon: Fifth House, 1995.
  • *Red Crow: Warrior Chief*. Calgary: Fifth House, 1995.
  • ed. *William Parker: Mounted Policeman*. Edmonton: Hurtig Publishers, 1973.
  • *Calgary: Spirit of the West*. Saskatoon: Fifth House, 1994.

Dendy, William. *Lost Toronto: Images of the City's Past*. Rev. ed. Toronto: McClelland & Stewart, 1993.

Denhez, Marc. *The Canadian Home: From Cave to Electronic Cocoon*. Toronto: Dundurn Press, 1994.

Dewar, Elaine. *Bones: Discovering the First Americans*. Toronto: Random House Canada, 2001

Dewdney, Selwyn and Franklin Arbuckle. *They Shared to Survive: The Native Peoples of Canada*. Toronto: Macmillan of Canada, 1975.

Diefenbaker, John G. *One Canada: The Crusading Years 1895–1956*. Toronto: Macmillan of Canada, 1975.

Dillehay, Tom D. *The Settlement of the Americas: A New Prehistory*. New York: Basic Books, 2000

Djwa, Sandra. *The Politics of the Imagination: A Life of F.R. Scott*. Vancouver: Douglas & McIntyre, 1987.

Djwa, Sandra. and R. St J. Macdonald, eds. *On F. R. Scott*. Montreal: McGill–Queen's University Press, 1983.

Doherty, Brian. *Not Bloody Likely: The Shaw Festival: 1962–1973*. Toronto: J.M. Dent & Sons (Canada), 1974.

Dominion Bureau of Statistics.
  • *Canada: One Hundred: 1867–1967*. Ottawa, 1967.
  • *Canada 1964: The Official Handbook of Present Conditions and Recent Progress*. Ottawa, 1964.

Donaldson, Gordon. *Eighteen Men: The Prime Ministers of Canada*. Toronto: Doubleday Canada, 1985.

Doran, Charles F. *Forgotten Partnership: U.S.–Canada Relations Today*. Markham, Ont.: Fitzhenry & Whiteside, 1984.

Dotto, Lydia. *Canada in Space*. Toronto: Irwin Publishing, 1987.

Douglas, Ann. *The Complete Idiot's Guide to Canadian History*. Scarborough, Ont.: Prentice Hall Canada, 1997.

Dowling, Phil. *The Mountaineers: Famous Climbers in Canada*. Canmore, AB: Coyote Books, 1995.

Downie, Mary Alice and Mary Hamilton. *'and some brought flowers': Plants in a new world*. Markham, Ont.: Fitzhenry & Whiteside Ltd., 2002.

Duff, J. Clarence and Sarah Yates. *Toronto Then & Now*. Markham, Ont.: Fitzhenry & Whiteside, 1984.

Duggan, James. *Paul-Emile Léger*. Don Mills, Ont.: Fitzhenry & Whiteside, 1981.

Duivenvoorden Mitic, Trudy. *People in Transition: Reflections on Becoming Canadian*. Markham, Ont.: Fitzhenry & Whiteside, 2001.

Dunan, Marcel, ed. *Larousse Encyclopedia of Modern History from 1500 to the Present Day*. New York: Harper & Row, 1964.

Bibliography

Dunn, John M. *The Relocation of the North American Indian*. San Diego, CA: Lucent Books, 1995.

Easterbrook, W.T. and Hugh G. J. Aitken. *Canadian Economic History*. Toronto: University of Toronto Press, 1988.

Eaton, Diane and Garfield Newman. *Canada: A Nation Unfolding*. Toronto: McGraw–Hill Ryerson, 1994.

Eber, Dorothy Harley. *When the Whalers Were Up North: Inuit Memories from the Eastern Arctic*. Montreal: McGill–Queens University Press, 1989.

Eccles, W. J. *The French in North America 1500–1783*. Markham, Ont.: Fitzhenry & Whiteside, 1998.

Ellis, Chris J. and Neal Ferris. 1990 *The Archaeology of Southern Ontario to A.D. 1650*. Occasional Publication of the London Chapter, OAS No. 5. London.

English, John. and Norman Hillmer, eds. *Making a Difference? Canada's Foreign Policy in a Changing World Order*. Toronto: Lester Publishing, 1992.

Erasmus, Peter (as told to Henry Thompson). *Buffalo Days and Nights*. Calgary: Fifth House, 1999.

Evans, Allan S. and I.L. Martinello. *Canada's Century*. Toronto: McGraw-Hill Ryerson, 1978.

Ewing, Sherm. *The Ranch: A Modern History of the North American Cattle Industry*. Missoula, Montana: Mountain Press Publishing Company, 1995.

Eyles, Nick. *Ontario Rocks: Three Billion Years of Environmental Changes*. Markham, Ont.: Fitzhenry & Whiteside, 2002.

Faries, Dr. Emily and Sarah Pashagumskum. *A History of Quebec and Canada*. Chisasibi, Que.: Cree School Board/ Instructional Services, 2002.

Ferguson, Bob. *Who's Who in Canadian Sport*. Self-published, 1999.

Ferns, Henry and Bernard Ostry. *The Age of Mackenzie King*. Toronto: James Lorimer & Company, 1976.

Filey, Mike. *I Remember Sunnyside: The Rise & Fall of a Magical Era*. Rev. ed. Toronto: The Dundurn Group, 1996.

Fillmore, Stanley and R.W. Sandilands. *The Chartmakers: The History of Nautical Surveying in Canada*. Toronto: NC Press Ltd., 1983.

Fischler, Stan and Shirley Fischler. *Fischlers' Hockey Encyclopedia*. Markham, Ont.: Fitzhenry & Whiteside 1975.

Fladmark, Knut R. 1986 British Columbia Prehistory, Archaeological Survey of Canada, National Museum of Man, Ottawa.

Flanagan, Thomas. *Louis 'David' Riel: Prophet of the New World*. Toronto: University of Toronto Press, 1979.

Fleming, Patricia & Thomas Carpenter. *Traditions in Wood: A History of Wildfowl Decoys in Canada*. Camden East, Ont.: Camden House Publishing, 1987.

Flint, David. *Henry Pellatt*. Markham, Ont.: Fitzhenry & Whiteside, 1992.

Ford, Robert A.D. *Our Man in Moscow: A Diplomat's Reflections on the Soviet Union*. Toronto: University of Toronto Press, 1989.

Foster, Peter. *Other People's Money: The Banks, the Government and Dome*. Toronto: Totem Books, 1984.

Fram, Mark and John Weiler et al. *Continuity with Change: Planning for the Conservation of Ontario's Man-Made Heritage*. Toronto: Ontario Ministry of Culture and Recreation, Historical Planning and Research Branch, 1981.

Fram, Mark. *Ontario Hydro, Ontario Heritage: A study of strategies for the conservation of the heritage of Ontario Hydro*. Toronto: Ontario Ministry of Culture and Recreation, 1980.

Fraser, Graham. *René Lévësque and the Parti Québécois in Power*. 2nd ed. Montreal: McGill–Queen's University Press, 2001.

Fréchette, Sylvie with Lilianne Lacroix. *Gold at Last*. Toronto: Stoddart, 1993.

Freeman, Bill and Richard Nielsen. *Far From Home: Canadians in the First World War*. Toronto: McGraw–Hill Ryerson, 1999.

Friesen, Gerald. *The Canadian Prairies: A History*. Toronto: University of Toronto Press, 1993.

Frison-Roche, Roger. *Hunters of the Arctic*. (Trans. Len Ortzen). Toronto: J.M. Dent & Sons (Canada), 1974.

Frith, Royce. *Hoods on the Hill: How Mulroney and his gang rammed the GST past Parliament and down our throats*. Toronto: Coach House Press, 1991.

Frost, Stanley Brice.
  • *James McGill of Montreal*. Montreal: McGill–Queen's University Press, 1995.
  • *The Man in the Ivory Tower: F. Cyril James of McGill*. Montreal: McGill–Queen's University Press, 1991.
  • *McGill University For the Advancement of Learning*. 2 vols. Montreal: McGill–Queen's University Press, 1984.

Frost, Sydney. *Once a Patricia (Memoirs of a Junior Infantry Officer in World War II)*. St. Catharines, Ont.: Vanwell Publishing, 1988.

Fullerton, Douglas H. *Graham Towers and his Times*. Toronto: McClelland & Stewart, 1986.

Gadd, Ben. *Handbook of the Canadian Rockies*. Jasper, AB: Corax Press, 1986.

The Gallery/Stratford. *Coasts, the Sea, and Canadian Art: July 28 to October 1, 1978*. Stratford, 1978.

Gardner, Alison F. *James Douglas*. Don Mills, Ont.: Fitzhenry & Whiteside, 1976.

Garrod, Stan.
  • *Sam Steele*. Don Mills, Ont.: Fitzhenry & Whiteside, 1979.
  • *Samuel de Champlain*. Don Mills, Ont.: Fitzhenry & Whiteside, 1981.

Geddes, Gary and Phyllis Bruce. *15 Canadian Poets*. Toronto: Oxford University Press, 1970.

Geist, Valerius. *Buffalo Nation: History and Legend of the North American Bison*. Saskatoon: Fifth House, 1996.

Gibson, Dale. *Attorney for the Frontier: Enos Stutsman*. Winnipeg: The University of Manitoba Press, 1983.

Gibson, William C. *No Time to Slow Down*. Vancouver: UBC Alumni Association, 1996.

Gillen, Mollie.
  • *Lucy Maud Montgomery*. Rev. ed. Markham, Ont.: Fitzhenry & Whiteside, 1999.
  • *The Masseys: Founding Family*. Toronto: The Ryerson Press, 1965.
  • *The Wheel of Things: A Biography of L. M. Montgomery*. Markham, Ont.: Fitzhenry & Whiteside, 1997.

Glazebrook, G.P. deT. *A History of Transportation in Canada*. Vols. I and II. Toronto: McClelland & Stewart Limited, 1967.

Godfrey, Charles. *John Rolph: Rebel with Causes*. Madoc, Ont.: Codam Publishing, 1993.

Gordon, John. *The Great Golf Courses of Canada*. Revised and Updated. Toronto: Warwick Publishing Inc., 1993.

Gordon, Walter. *A Political Memoir*. Toronto: McClelland & Stewart, 1977,

Gould, Allan.
  • *The New Entrepreneurs: 75 Canadian Success Stories*. Toronto: Seal Books, 1990.
  • *Scarborough: An Economic Celebration*. Windsor Publications, 1988.

Gould, Ed. *Oil: The History of Canada's Oil & Gas Industry*. Hancock House, 1976.

Government of Canada. *Indian Treaties and Surrenders*. 3 Vols. Reprinted form the 1912 Original. Saskatoon: Fifth House, 1993.

Graham, Ron. *One-Eyed Kings: Promise and Illusion in Canadian Politics*. Don Mills, Ont.: Totem Books, 1987.

Granatstein, J.L.
  • *W.L. Mackenzie King*. Rev. ed. Markham, Ont.: Fitzhenry & Whiteside, 2002.
  • *The Generals: The Canadian Army's Senior Commanders in the Second World War*. Toronto: Stoddart, 1993.
  • *Ottawa Men: The Civil Service Mandarins 1935–1957*. Toronto: Oxford University Press, 1982.
  • *Who Killed Canadian History?*. Toronto: HarperCollins, 1998.
  • *Yankee Go Home? Canadians and Anti-Americanism*. Toronto: HarperCollins, 1996.

Bibliography

Granatstein, J.L. and Norman Hillmer.
- *For Better or for Worse: Canada and the United States to the 1990s*. Toronto: Copp Clark Pitman, 1991.
- *Prime Ministers: Ranking Canada's Leaders*. Toronto: HarperCollins, 1999.

Granatstein, J.L. and Peter Neary.
- *The Good Fight: Canadians and World War II*. Toronto: Copp Clark, 1995.

Grand Council of the Crees. *Sovereign Injustice: Forcible Inclusion of the James Bay Crees and Cree Territory into a Sovereign Québec*. Nemaska, QC, 1995.

Graves, Donald E. *Red Coats & Grey Jackets: The Battle of Chippawa 5 July 1814*. Toronto: Dundurn Press, 1994.

Gray, Charlotte. *Canada: A Portrait in Letters 1800-2000*. Toronto: Doubleday Canada, 2003.

Gray, James H.
- *Booze: When Whisky Ruled the West*. Calgary: Fifth House, 1995.
- *The Boy from Winnipeg*. Calgary: Fifth House, 1996.
- *Men Against the Desert*. Calgary: Fifth House, 1996.
- *R.B. Bennett: The Calgary Years*. Toronto: University of Toronto Press, 1991.
- *Red Lights on the Prairies*. Calgary: Fifth House, 1995.
- *The Roar of the Twenties*. Toronto: Macmillan of Canada, 1975.

Green, Lorne Edmond. *Sandford Fleming*. Don Mills, Ont.: Fitzhenry & Whiteside, 1980.

Greenwood, Barbara. *A Pioneer Story: The Daily Life of a Canadian Family in 1840*. Toronto: Kids Can Press, 1994.

Greenwood, F. Murray and Beverley Boissery. *Uncertain Justice: Canadian Women and Capital Punishment 1754–1953*. Toronto: Dundurn Press (for The Osgoode Society for Canadian Legal History), 2000.

Greenwood, F. Murray and Barry Wright. *Canadian State Trials: Law, Politics, and Security Measures, 1608-1837*. Vol. 1. Toronto: University of Toronto Press (for The Osgoode Society for Canadian Legal History) 1996.

Grosvenor, Edwin S. and Morgan Wesson. *Alexander Graham Bell: The Life and Times of the Man Who Invented the Telephone*. New York: Harry N. Abrams, 1997.

Guillet, Edwin C. and Jessie E. McEwen. *Finding New Homes in Canada*. Toronto: Thomas Nelson & Sons, 1938.

Guthrie, Ann. *Don Valley Legacy: A Pioneer History*. Erin, Ont.: The Boston Mills Press, 1986.

Gutkin, Harry, and Mildred Gutkin. *The Worst of Times, The Best of Times: Growing Up in Winnipeg's North End*. Markham, Ont.: Fitzhenry & Whiteside, 1978.

Gwyn, Richard.
- *The Northern Magus: Pierre Trudeau and Canadians*. Markham, Ont.: PaperJacks, 1986.
- *The Shape of Scandal: A Study of Government in Crisis*. Toronto: Clarke, Irwin & Co., 1965.

Gwynne-Timothy, J.R.W. *Western's First Century*. London: University of Western Ontario, 1978.

Hacker, Carlotta. *Crowfoot*. Rev. ed. Markham, Ont.: Fitzhenry & Whiteside, 1999.

Haggart, Ron and Aubrey E.Golden. *Rumours of War*. Toronto: New Press, 1971.

Haines, Francis. *The Buffalo: The story of American bison and their hunters from prehistoric times to the present*. New York: Thomas Y. Crowell, 1975.

Hall, D. J. *Clifford Sifton*. Don Mills, Ont.: Fitzhenry & Whiteside, 1976.

Hallett, Mary and Marilyn Davis. *Firing the Heather: The Life and Times of Nellie McClung*. Saskatoon: Fifth House, 1993.

Hamilton, William B. *Local History in Atlantic Canada*. Toronto: Macmillan of Canada, 1974.

Hancock, Lyn with Marion Dowler. *Tell Me, Grandmother*. Toronto: McClelland & Stewart, 1985.

Hannon, Leslie F. *Canada At War: The Record of a Fighting People*. Toronto: McClelland and Stewart, 1968.

Harbron, John D. *C.D. Howe*. Don Mills, Ont.: Fitzhenry & Whiteside, 1980.

Hardy, W. G., ed. *The Alberta Golden Jubilee Anthology: 1905–1955*. Toronto: McClelland and Stewart, 1955.
    • *Alberta: A Natural History*. Edmonton: MisMat Corporation, 1967.

Harring, Sidney L. *White Man's Law: Native People in Nineteenth-Century Canadian Jurisprudence*. Toronto: University of Toronto Press (for The Osgoode Society for Canadian Legal History), 1998.

Harris, C.J. et al. *The Canadian Pocket Encyclopedia: Quick Canadian Facts*. Surry, BC: Canex Enterprises, 1985.

Harris, Jane E. *Glassware Excavated at Beaubassin, Nova Scotia*. Canadian Historic Sites: Occasional Papers in Archaeology and History, No. 13. Ottawa: Indian and Northern Affairs, 1975.

Harris, Michael.
    • *Lament for an Ocean: The Collapse of the Atlantic Cod Fishery: A True Crime Story*. Toronto: McClelland & Stewart, 1998.
    • *Rare Ambition: The Crosbies of Newfoundland*. Toronto: Penguin Books, 1993.

Harris, Reginald V. *The Oak Island Mystery*. Toronto: McGraw-Hill Ryerson, 1958.

Harrison, Pamela. *The First Original Authentic Unexpurgated Great Canadian Quiz Book*. Toronto: John Wiley & Sons (Canada), 1977.

Harrison, W.E.C. *Canada in World Affairs 1949 to 1950*. Toronto: Oxford University Press, 1967.

Harvison, C.W. *The Horsemen*. Toronto: McClelland & Stewart, 1967.

Havighurst, Walter. *Three Flags at the Straits: The Forts of Mackinac*. Englewood Cliffs, NJ: Prentice–Hall, 1966.

Haxby, James A. *The Royal Canadian Mint and Canadian Coinage Striking Impressions*. Ottawa: The Royal Canadian Mint, 1986.

Haxby, J.A. and R.C. Willey. *Coins of Canada*. Toronto: The Unitrade Press, 1995.

Hayes, William A. *Beaverbrook*. Don Mills, Ont.: Fitzhenry & Whiteside, 1979.

Head, Ivan L. and Pierre Elliott Trudeau. *The Canadian Way: Shaping Canada's Foreign Policy, 1968–1984*. Toronto: McClelland & Stewart, 1995.

Heaps, Leo, ed. *Our Canada: The Story of the New Democratic Party Yesterday, Today and Tomorrow*. Toronto: James Lorimer & Company, 1991.

Heath, Frances M. *Sault Ste. Marie: City by the Rapids: An Illustrated History*. Burlington, Ont.: Windsor Publications, 1988.

Henighan, Tom. *Ideas of North: A Guide to Canadian Arts and Culture*. Vancouver: Raincoast Books, 1997.

Heron, Craig. *Booze: A Distilled History*. Toronto: Between the Lines, 2003.

Hiemstra, Mary. *Gully Farm: A Story of Homesteading on the Canadian Prairies*. Calgary: Fifth House, 1997.

Hill, Robert. *Voice of the Vanishing Minority: Robert Sellar and the Huntingdon Gleaner, 1863–1919*. Montreal: McGill–Queen's University Press, 1999.

Hilliker, John and Donald Barry. *Canada's Department of External Affairs Coming of Age, 1946–1968*. Vol. II. Montreal: McGill–Queen's University Press, 1995.

Hillis, Doris. *Voices & Visions: Interviews with Saskatchewan Writers*. Moose Jaw: Coteau Books, 1985.

Hillmer, Norman, ed. *Pearson: The Unlikely Gladiator*. Montreal: McGill–Queen's University Press, 1999.

Hillmer, Norman et al, eds. *A Country of Limitations: Canada and the World in 1939*. Ottawa: Canadian Committee for the History of the Second World War, 1996.

Hillmer, Norman and J.L. Granatstein. *Empire to Umpire: Canada and the World to the 1990s*. Toronto: Copp Clark Longman, 1994.

Hitsman, J. Mackay *The Incredible War of 1812, a Military History*. Toronto: University of Toronto Press, 1965.

Bibliography

Hodgson, Lynn–Philip. *Inside–Camp X*. Port Perry, Ont.: Blake Book Distribution, 1999.

Holtje, Steve and Nancy Ann Lee. *Music Hound Jazz: The Essential Album Guide*. Detroit: Visible Ink Press, 1998.

Hood, George N. *Against the Flow: Rafferty-Alameda and the Politics of the Environment*. Saskatoon: Fifth House, 1994.

Hooks, Gwen. *The Keystone Legacy: Recollections of a Black Settler*. Edmonton: Brightest Pebble Publishing, 1997.

Horwood, Harold and Ed Butts.
> • *Bandits & Privateers: Canada in the Age of Gunpowder*. Toronto: Doubleday (Canada), 1987.
> • *Joey: The Life and Political Times of Joey Smallwood*. Toronto: Stoddart, 1989.

Houston, William. *Documents Illustrative of the Canadian Constitution*. Toronto: Carswell & Co., 1891.

Howard, Oswald. *The Montreal Diocesan Theological College: A History from 1873 to 1963*. Montreal: McGill University Press, 1963.

Huck, Barbara and Doug Whiteway. *In Search of Ancient Alberta*. Winnipeg: Heartland Publications, 1998.

Hudson, John C. *Across this land: A Regional Geography of the United States and Canada*. Baltimore: Johns Hopkins, 2002.

Hume, Mark. *The Run of the River*. Vancouver: New Star Books, 1992.

Hursey, Roberta. *Heritage Hunter's Guide to Alberta Museums*. Edmonton, Alb.: Brightest Publishing Co. Ltd., 1996.

Hutchison, Bruce.
> • *The Fraser (The Great Rivers of Canada)*. Toronto: Clarke Irwin & Company, 1965.
> • *The Incredible Canadian: A Candid Portrait of Mackenzie King: His Works, His Times, and His Nation*. Toronto: Longmans, Green and Company, 1952.
> • *Mr. Prime Minister 1867- 1964*. Don Mills, Ont.: Longmans Canada, 1964.
> • *The Struggle for the Border*. Don Mills, Ont.: Longmans, Greene and Company, 1955.

Hyde, Susan and Michael Bird. *Hallowed Timbers: The Wooden Churches of Cape Breton*. Erin, Ont.: Boston Mills, 1995.

Indian and Northern Affairs Canada.
> • *Canadian Inuit Sculpture*. Ottawa, 1988.
> • *First Nations in Canada*. Ottawa, 1997.

Indian Treaties and Surrenders (Canada) from No. 281 to No. 483. Vol. 3. Saskatoon: Fifth House, 1993.

Industry Canada. *Canada: A Portrait*. Ottawa, 1999.

Jackson, James A. *The Centennial History of Manitoba*. Toronto: Manitoba Historical Society in association with McClelland and Stewart, 1970.

James, Donna. *Emily Murphy*. Rev. Ed. Markham, Ont.: Fitzhenry & Whiteside, 2000.

Jenkins, Phil. *River Song: Sailing the History of the St. Lawrence*. Toronto: Penguin/Viking, 2001.

Joe, Rita and Lesley Choyce, eds. *The Mi'kmaq Anthology*. Lawrencetown, NS: Pottersfield Press, 1997.

Johnson, Brian D. *Brave Films, Wild Nights: 25 Years of Festival Fever*. Toronto: Random House (Canada), 2000.

Johnson, Patricia M. *Canada Since 1876: Selected Historical Sources*. McClelland and Stewart, 1968.

Johnston, David, Deborah Johnston and Sunny Handa. *Getting Canada Online: Understanding the Information Highway*. Toronto: Stoddart, 1996.

Johnston, Donald. *Up the Hill*. Montreal: Optimum Publishing Int'l., 1986.

Johnston, Gordon. *More "It Happened in Canada"*. Richmond Hill, Ont.: Scholastic-TAB Publications, 1976.

Jones, David. *Flin Flon: A Northern Community*. Toronto: Holt, Rinehart and Winston of Canada, 1968.

Jones, David Laurence. *Tales of the CPR*. Calgary: Fifth House, 2002.

Kalman, Harold. *A History of Canadian Architecture.* Vols. 1 & 2. Toronto: Oxford University Press, 1994.

Kaplan, William.
- *Bad Judgment: The Case of Mr. Justice Leo A. Landreville.* Toronto: University of Toronto Press (for The Osgoode Society for Canadian Legal History), 1996.
- *Presumed Guilty: Brian Mulroney, the Airbus Affair, and the Government of Canada.* Toronto: McClelland & Stewart, 1998.

Karpeles, Maud, ed. *Folk Songs from Newfoundland.* Hamden, CT: Archon Books, 1970.

Kelly, Graham. *The Grey Cup.* Red Deer, Alb.: Johnson Gorman Publishers, 1999.

Kelly, William H. and Nora Hickson Kelly. *The Musical Ride of the Royal Canadian Mounted Police.* Austin, TX: Equimedia, 1998.

Kidd, Bruce. *Tom Longboat.* Markham, Ont.: Fitzhenry & Whiteside, 1992.

Kidd, Martha Ann. *Peterborough's Architectural Heritage.* Peterborough Architectural Conservation Advisory Committee, 1978.

Kierans, Eric, with Walter Stewart. *Remembering.* Toronto: Stoddart, 2001.

Kilbourn, William. *PipeLine: TransCanada and the Great Debate: A History of Business and Politics.* Toronto: Clarke, Irwin & Company, 1970.

King, M. Christine. *E.W.R. Steacie and Science in Canada.* Toronto: University of Toronto Press, 1980.

Kingsmill, A.B. *Dr. Alan Brown: Portrait of a Tyrant.* Markham, Ont.: Fitzhenry & Whiteside, 1995.

Kingwell, Mark and Christopher Moore. *Canada Our Century: 100 Voices – 500 Visions.* Toronto: Doubleday, 1999.

Kinietz, W. Vernon. *The Indians of the Western Great Lakes: 1615–1760.* Michigan: University of Michigan Press, 1965.

Klassen, Henry C. *A Business History of Alberta.* Calgary: University of Calgary Press, 1999.

Knelman, Martin. *Home Movies: Tales from the Canadian Film World.* Toronto: Key Porter, 1987.

Koch, W. John. *Martin Nordegg: The Uncommon Immigrant.* Edmonton: Brightest Pebble Publishing, 1997.

Konstam, Angus. *Historical Atlas of Exploration.* New York: Checkmark Books, 2000.

Kroetsch, Robert. *Alberta.* Toronto: Macmillan of Canada, 1968.

Krueger, Ralph, Ray Corder and John Koegler. *This Land of Ours: A New Geography of Canada.* Toronto: Harcourt Brace Jovanovich (Canada), 1991.

Kurlansky, Mark. *Cod: A Biography of the Fish that Changed the World.* Toronto: Alfred A. Knopf (Canada), 1997.

Labrèche-Larouche, Michelle. *Emma Albani.* Montreal: XYZ Publishing, 1994.

Lambert, Richard S. *The Adventure of Canadian Painting.* Toronto: McClelland & Stewart, 1947.

LaPierre, Laurier. *Sir Wilfrid Laurier and the Romance of Canada.* Toronto: Stoddart, 1996.

Lavallée, Omer. *Van Horne's Road: An illustrated account of the construction and first years of operation of the Canadian Pacific transcontinental railway.* Don Mills, Ont.: Railfare, 1977.

Lévesque, René. *My Québec.* Toronto: Methuen, 1979.

Layton, Irving. *Waiting for the Messiah: A Memoir.* Toronto: McClelland & Stewart, 1985.

LeBourdais, D.M. *Metals and Men: The Story of Canadian Mining.* Toronto: McClelland & Stewart, 1957.

Le Bourdais, Isabel. *The Trial of Steven Truscott.* Toronto: McClelland & Stewart, 1966.

Leacock, Stephen.
- *Montreal: Seaport and City.* Toronto: McClelland & Stewart, 1948.
- *The Unsolved Riddle of Social Justice.* Toronto: S.B. Gundy, 1920.

Leavitt, Robert M.
- *Maliseet & Micmac: First Nations of the Maritimes*. Fredericton: New Ireland Press, 1995.
- *Mi'kmaq of the East Coast*. Markham, Ont.: Fitzhenry & Whiteside Ltd., 2000.

Lecker, Robert and Jack David, eds. *The Annotated Bibliography of Canada's Major Authors*. Vol. 5. Downsview, Ont.: ECW Press, 1984.

Legget, Robert F.
- *Canals of Canada*. Vancouver: Douglas, David & Charles, 1976.
- *Railways of Canada*. Vancouver: Douglas and MacIntyre, 1987.

Lemieux, Carlotta. *E. Cora Hind*. Rev. ed. Markham, Ont.: Fitzhenry & Whiteside, 2003.

Lemieux, L.J. *The Governors–General of Canada 1608–1931*. London: Lake & Bell Ltd., 1931.

Lerman, Norman and Betty Keller. *Legends of the River People*. Vancouver: November House, 1976.

Leslie, Rosella. *Sunshine Coast: A Place to Be*. Surrey, BC: Heritage House, 2001.

Lévesque, René. *Memoirs*. (trans. Philip Stratford). Montreal: McClelland & Stewart, 1986.

Lewington, Peter. *Canada's Holsteins*. Markham, Ont.: Fitzhenry & Whiteside, 1983.

Lewis, Jefferson. *Something Hidden: A Biography of Wilder Penfield*. Toronto: Doubleday Canada, 1981.

Lightbody, Mark and Tom Smallman. *Canada: A Travel Survival Kit*. 4th ed. Hawthorn, Australia: Lonely Planet Publications, 1992.

Lindsay, John. *Palaces of the Night: Canada's Grand Theatres*. Toronto: Lynx Images. 1999.

Lippy, Charles H., Robert Choquette and Stafford Poole. *Christianity Comes to the Americas: 1492–1776*. New York: Paragon House, 1992.

Lisée, Jean–FranÁois. *In the Eye of the Eagle*. Toronto: Harper Collins, 1990.

Liss, Nancy and Ted Liss. *Curious Canadians*. Markham, Ont.: Fitzhenry & Whiteside, 2002.

Livesey, Robert and A.G. Smith. *Discovering Canada: The Fur Traders*. Toronto: Stoddart, 1989.

Looker, Janet. *Disaster Canada*. Toronto: Lynx Images, 2000.

Lord, Barry. *The History of Painting in Canada: Toward a People's Art*. Toronto: NC Press, 1974.

Luxton, Meg. *More Than a Labour of Love: Three Generations of Women's Work in the Home*. Toronto: Women's Press, 1980.

Lyons, J.B. *William Henry Drummond: Poet in Patois*. Markham, Ont.: Fitzhenry & Whiteside, 1994.

MacBeth, R.G. *The Romance of the Canadian Pacific Railway*. Toronto: The Ryerson Press, 1924.

MacDonald, Joan. *The Stanstead College Story*. Sherbrooke, QC: The Board of Trustees of Stanstead College, 1977.

MacDonald, L. Ian. *From Bourassa to Bourassa: Wilderness to Restoration*. 2nd ed. Montreal: McGill–Queen's University Press, 2002.

MacEwan, Grant.
- *...and Mighty Women too: Stories of Notable Western Canadian Women*. Saskatoon: Western Producer Prairie Books, 1975.
- *Fifty Mighty Men*. Saskatoon: Western Producer Prairie Books, 1985.
- *John Ware's Cow Country*. Saskatoon: Western Producer Prairie Books, 1973.
- *Memory Meadows: Horse Stories from Canada's Past*. Vancouver: Greystone Books, 1976.
- *Métis Makers of History*. Saskatoon: Western Producer Prairie Books, 1981.

Macintosh, Donald and David Whitson. *The Game Planners: Transforming Canada's Sport System*. Montreal: McGill–Queen's University Press, 1994.

Macintosh, Donald and Michael Hawes. *Sport and Canadian Diplomacy*. Montreal: McGill–Queen's University Press, 1994.

Macintosh, Donald et al. *Sport and Politics in Canada: Federal Government Involvement since 1961*. Kingston, Ont.: McGill–Queen's University Press, 1987.

MacDonald, George F. and Richard I. Inglis. *1976 The Dig: An Archaeological Reconstruction of a West Coast Village*, National Museum of Man.

MacKay, Donald.
> • *The Lumberjacks*. Toronto: Natural Heritage/ Natural History Inc., 1998.
> • *The People's Railway: A History of Canadian National*. Toronto: Douglas & McIntyre, 1992.

MacKirdy, K.A., J.S. Moir and Y.F. Zoltvany. *Changing Perspectives in Canadian History: Selected Problems*. Rev. ed.
> Toronto: J.M. Dent & Sons (Canada), 1971.

MacLean, Doug. *Canadian Geographic Quiz Book*. Markham, Ont.: Fitzhenry & Whiteside, 1999.

MacLennan, Hugh. *Seven Rivers of Canada*. Toronto: Macmillan of Canada, 1961.

Macmillan, Cyrus. *McGill and its Story: 1921–1921*. Toronto: Oxford University Press (Canada), 1921.

Macpherson, Ken. *The River Class Destroyers of the Royal Canadian Navy*. Toronto: Charles J. Musson, 1985.

MacRae, Marion and Anthony Adamson. *The Ancestral Roof: Domestic Architecture of Upper Canada*.
> Toronto: Clarke, Irwin & Company, 1963.

MacSkimming, Roy. *The Perilous Trade: Publishing Canada's Writers*. Toronto: McCelland & Stewart, 2003.

Magder, Ted. *Canada's Hollywood: The Canadian State and Feature Films*. Toronto: University of Toronto Press, 1993.

Maitland, Leslie. *Neoclassical Architecture in Canada*. Studies in Archaeology, Architecture and History. Ottawa: Parks Canada, 1984.

Malcolm, Andrew H. *The Canadians*. Markham, Ont.: Fitzhenry & Whiteside Ltd., 1985.

Malkus, Alida. *Blue-Water Boundary: Epic Highway of the Great Lakes and the St. Lawrence*. New York: Hasting House, Publishers, 1960.

Mallory, J. R. *The Structure of Canadian Government*. Toronto: Macmillan of Canada, 1971.

Marchak, M. Patricia. *The Integrated Circus: The New Right and the Restructuring of Global Markets*. Montreal: McGill-Queens UP, 1991.

Marshall, Ingeborg. *The Red Ochre People*. Toronto: Douglas & McIntyre Ltd., 1977.

Marshall. S.L.A. *Crimsoned Prairie: The wars between the United States and the Plains Indians during the winning of the west*.
> New York: Charles Scribner's Sons, 1972.

Martinello, I.L. *Call Us Canadians*. Toronto: McGraw-Hill Ryerson, 1976.

Masson, Jack K. and James D. Anderson. *Emerging Party Politics in Urban Canada*. Toronto: McClelland and Stewart, 1972.

Masters, Donald C. *A Short History of Canada*. Toronto: D. Van Nostrand, 1958.

Mathieson, W.D. *Billy Bishop*. Markham, Ont.: Fitzhenry & Whiteside, 1989.

Mayer, Roy.
> • *Inventing Canada: One Hundred Years of Innovation*. Vancouver: Raincoast Books, 1997.
> • *Scientific Canadian: Invention and Innovations from Canada's National Research Council*.
> > Vancouver: Raincoast Books, 1999.

Mayles, Stephen. *William Van Horne*. Don Mills, Ont.: Fitzhenry & Whiteside, 1976.

McCabe, Kevin and Alexandra Heilbron. *The Lucy Maud Montgomery Album*. Markham, Ont.: Fitzhenry & Whiteside, 1999.

McCall-Newman, Christina. *Grits: An Intimate Portrait of The Liberal Party*. Toronto: Macmillan of Canada, 1982.

McCart, Joyce and Peter McCart. *On the Road with David Thompson*. Calgary: Fifth House, 2000.

McClane, A.J., ed. *McClane's New Standard Fishing Encyclopedia: An International Angling Guide*. New York: Henry Holt, 1974.

McClement, Fred. *The Flaming Forests*. Toronto: McCelland & Stewart, 1969.

Bibliography

McClung, Nellie. *Clearing in the West: My Own Story*. Toronto: Thomas Allen & Son, 1976.

McCormick, Peter. *Canada's Courts*. Toronto: James Lorimer & Co., 1994.

McDonald, Kenneth. *Red Maple: How Canada Became the People's Republic of Canada in 1981*. Richmond Hill, Ont.: BMG Publishing, 1977.

McDonald, Marci. *Yankee Doodle Dandy: Brian Mulroney and the American Agenda*. Toronto: Stoddart, 1995.

McDougal, Bruce.
> • *Charles Mair*. Don Mills, Ont.: Fitzhenry & Whiteside, 1978.
> • *John Wilson Murray*. Don Mills, Ont.: Fitzhenry & Whiteside, 1980.

McDougall, J.L. *Canadian Pacific: A Brief History*. Montreal: McGill University Press, 1968.

McFadden, Fred.
> • *Origins: A History of Canada*. Markham, Ont.: Fitzhenry & Whiteside, 1989.
> • et al. *Canada: The Twentieth Century*. Markham, Ont.: Fitzhenry & Whiteside, 1993.

McFarlane, Brian. *Proud Past, Bright Future: One Hundred Years of Canadian Women's Hockey*. Toronto: Stoddart, 1994.

McGhee, Robert. 1976. *The Burial at L'Anse-Amour*, Archaeological Survey of Canada, National Museum of Man, Ottawa.

McGill, Jean. *The Joy of Effort: A Biography of R. Tait McKenzie*. Oshawa, Ont.: The Alger Press, 1980.

McIlwraith, Thomas F. *Looking for Old Ontario: Two Centuries of Landscape Change*. Toronto: University of Toronto Press, 1998.

McInnis, Edgar. *The North American Nations*. Toronto: J.M. Dent & Sons (Canada), 1963.

McKelvey, Margaret and Merilyn McKelvey. *Toronto: Carved in Stone*. Markham, Ont.: Fitzhenry & Whiteside, 1984.

McKenna, Brian and Susan Purcell. *Drapeau*. Toronto: Clarke, Irwin & Company, 1980.

McKillop, A.B. *The Spinster & The Prophet: Florence Deeks, H.G. Wells and the Mystery of the Purloined Past*. Toronto: Macfarlane Walter & Ross (for The Osgoode Society for Canadian Legal History), 2000.

McLean, Don.
> • *Fifty Historical Vignettes: Views of the Common People*. Regina: Gabriel Dumont Institute, 1987.
> • *Home From the Hill: A History of the Metis in Western Canada*. Regina: Gabriel Dumont Institute, 1987.

McLeod, Jack, ed. *The Oxford Book of Canadian Political Anecdotes*. Toronto: Oxford University Press, 1988.

McMillan, Alan D. *Native Peoples and Cultures of Canada*. Vancouver: Douglas & McIntyre, 1988.

McNaught, Kenneth.
> • *J.S. Woodsworth*. Don Mills, Ont.: Fitzhenry & Whiteside, 1980.
> • *The Pelican History of Canada*. Penguin Books, 1976.

McPherson, M. A. *Silk, Spices, and Glory: In Search of the Northwest Passage*. Calgary: Fifth House, 2001.

McRoberts, Kenneth. *Quebec: Social Change and Political Crisis*. Toronto: McClelland and Stewart, 1988.

Mednick, Robin and Wendy Thomas, eds. *Heroes in our Midst*. Toronto: McClelland & Stewart, 2001.

Melhuish, Martin. *Oh What a Feeling: A Vital History of Canadian Music*. Kingston, Ont.: Quarry Press, 1996.

Mellen, Peter. *Landmarks of Canadian Art*. Toronto: McClelland and Stewart, 1978.

Melnyk, George, ed. *Riel to Reform: A History of Protest in Western Canada*. Saskatoon: Fifth House, 1992.

Merritt, Allen S. and George W. Brown. *Canadians and Their Government*. Rev. ed. Toronto: J. M. Dent & Sons (Canada), 1971.

Milani, Lois Darroch. *Robert Gourlay, Gadfly: Forerunner of the Rebellion in Upper Canada, 1837*. Thornhill, Ont.: Ampersand Press, 1971.

Millar, Nancy. *Once Upon a Tomb: Stories from Canadian Graveyards*. Calgary: Fifth House, 1997.

Miller, J.R. *Skyscrapers Hide the Heavens: A History of Indian–White Relations in Canada*. Toronto: University of Toronto Press, 1989.

Miller-Barstow, D.H. *Beattie of the C.P.R.: The Story of Sir Edward Beattie*. Toronto: McClelland & Stewart, 1951.

Mills, G.E. and D.W. Holdsworth. *The B.C. Mills Prefabricated System: The emergence of ready-made buildings in western Canada*. Canadian Historic Sites: Occasional Papers in Archaeology and History, No. 14. Ottawa: Indian and Northern Affairs, 1975.

Milner, Marc. *Canada's Navy: The First Century*. Toronto: University of Toronto Press, 1999.

Miquelon, Dale. *Dugard of Rouen: French Trade to Canada and the West Indies, 1729–1770*. Montreal: McGill–Queen's University Press, 1978.

Mirvish, Ed. *Honest Ed Mirvish: How to build an empire on an orange crate or 121 lessons I never learned in school*. Toronto: Key Porter, 1993.

Mitchell, David J. *W.A.C. Bennett and the Rise of British Columbia*. Vancouver: Douglas & McIntyre, 1983.

Moir, John S. and Robert E. Saunders. *Northern Destiny: A History of Canada*. Toronto: J. M. Dent & Sons (Canada), 1970.

Molloy, Tom. *The World is Our Witness: The Historic Journey of the Nisga'a into Canada*. Calgary: Fifth House, 2000.

Monet, Jean. *The Cassock and the Crown: Canada's Most Controversial Murder Trial*. Montreal: McGill–Queen's University Press, 1996.

Moogk, Peter.
   • *Building a House in New France*. Markham, Ont.: Fitzhenry & Whiteside, 2002.
   • *La Nouvelle France: The Making of French Canada – A Cultural History*. East Lansing, MI: Michigan State University Press, 2000.

Moore, Tom. *Wilfred Grenfell*. Don Mills, Ont.: Fitzhenry & Whiteside, 1980.

Morchain, Janet and Mason Wade. *Search for a Nation: Canada's Crises in French–English Relations 1759–1980*. Markham, Ont.: Fitzhenry & Whiteside, 1984.

Morf, Gustave. *Terror in Quebec: Case Studies of the FLQ*. Toronto: Clarke Irwin & Company, 1970.

Morgan, Murray. *One Man's Gold Rush: A Klondike Album*. Seattle, WA: University of Washington Press, 1995.

Moriarty, Dick et al, eds. *Canadian/American Sport, Fitness and the Law*. Toronto: Canadian Scholars' Press, 1993.

Moritz, Albert and Theresa Moritz.
   • *The Oxford Illustrated Literary Guide to Canada*. Toronto: Oxford University Press, 1987.
   • *Stephen Leacock: His Remarkable Life*. Don Mills, Stoddart, 2000 .

Morris, Alexander. *The Treaties of Canada with the Indians of Manitoba and the North-West Territories, including the negotiations on which they were based*. Calgary: Fifth House, 1991.

Morris, John A. H. *Morrises' History of Prescott 1800–2000*. Prescott, Ont.: St. Lawrence Printing Company, 2001.

Morrison, R. Bruce and C. Roderick Wilson, eds. *Native Peoples: The Canadian Experience*. Toronto: McClelland & Stewart, 1986.

Morritt, Hope. *Rivers of Oil: The Founding of North America's Petroleum Industry*. Kingston, Ont.: Quarry Press, 1993.

Morse, Eric W. *Fur Trade Canoe Routes of Canada/Then and Now*. Ottawa: Department of Indian Affairs and Northern Development, 1971.

Morton, Desmond.
   • *A Military History of Canada from Champlain to the Gulf War*. Toronto: McClelland & Stewart, 1992.
   • *Wheels: The Car in Canada*. Toronto: Umbrella Press, 1998.

Morton, Desmond. and J.L. Granatstein.
   • *Victory 1945: Canadians from War to Peace*. Toronto: HarperCollins, 1995.
   • *A Short History of Canada*. Edmonton: Hurtig, 1983.

Morton, W.L. *The Kingdom of Canada: A General History from the Earliest Times*. 2nd ed. Toronto: McClelland & Stewart, 1970.

Mountain Horse, Mike. *My People the Bloods*. Calgary: Glenbow Museum and Blood Tribal Council, 1989.

Bibliography

Muhlstein, Anka. *La Salle: Explorer of the North American Frontier*. (Trans. Willard Wood). New York: Arcade Publishing, 1994.

Multiculturalism Directorate, Department of the Secretary of State. *The Canadian Family Tree: Canada's Peoples*. Don Mills, Ont.: Corpus, 1979.

Munro, William Bennett. *American Influences on Canadian Government*. Toronto: Macmillan of Canada, 1929.

Murphy, Larry. *Thomas Keefer*. Don Mills, Ont.: Fitzhenry & Whiteside, 1977.

Murray, Jock, O.C., and Janet Murray. *Sir Charles Tupper: Fighting Doctor to Father of Confederation*. Markham, Ont.: Fitzhenry & Whiteside, 1999.

Myers, Jay. *The Fitzhenry & Whiteside Book of Canadian Facts and Dates*. 2nd Edition. Markham, Ont.: Fitzhenry & Whiteside, 1986.

Nader, Ralph, Nadia Milleron and Duff Conacher. *Canada Firsts*. Washington, DC: Center for Study of Responsive Law, 1993.

Nash, Knowlton. *Kennedy & Diefenbaker: The Feud that Helped Topple a Government*. Toronto: McClelland & Stewart, 1991.

Neale, Gladys E., ed. *Voices 3: Canadians Who Made a Difference*. Saint John, NB: Laubach Literacy of Canada, 1993.

Neering, Rosemary.
• *Emily Carr*. Rev. ed. Markham, Ont.: Fitzhenry & Whiteside, 2000.
• *Louis Riel*. Rev. ed. Markham, Ont.: Fitzhenry & Whiteside, 1999.

Nevitte, Neil. *The Decline of Deference: Canadian value change in cross-national perspective*. Peterborough, Ont.: Broadview Press, 1996.

Newby, M. Dalyce. *Anderson Ruffin Abbott: First Afro-Canadian Doctor*. Markham, Ont.: Fitzhenry & Whiteside, 1998.

Newman, Peter C.
• *The Canadian Establishment: Volume One*. Toronto: Seal Books, McClelland & Stewart–Bantam Ltd., 1979.
• *The Canadian Revolution From Deference to Defiance*. Toronto: Penguin Books, 1996.
• *The Distemper of Our Times: Canadian Politics in Transition: 1963–1968*. Toronto: McClelland and Stewart, 1968.
• *Portrait of a Promised Land: Canada–1892*. Toronto: Penguin (Canada) and McClelland & Stewart, 1992.

Nicholson, Byron. *In Old Quebec and Other Sketches*. Quebec: Commercial Printing Company, 1908.

Nicol, John D. *Jack Haney*. Markham, Ont.: Fitzhenry & Whiteside, 1989.

Nolin-Raynault, Michelle. *The Bank of Montreal Building on Place d'Armes 1845-1901*. Montreal: Varia Press, 1999.

Nostbakken, Janis and Jack Humphrey. *The Canadian Inventions Book: Innovations, Discoveries and Firsts*. Toronto: Greey de Pencier, 1976.

Nova Scotia: The Doers and Dreamers Complete Guide to the Festival Province of Canada. Nova Scotia Department of Tourism and Culture, 1990.

Nowell, Iris. *Women Who Give Away Millions: Portraits of Canadian Philanthropists*. Toronto: Hounslow Press, 1996.

Nowlan, Alden. *Campobello: The Outer Island*. Toronto: Clarke Irwin & Company, 1975.

O'Connor, D'Arcy. *The Money Pit: The story of Oak Island and the world's greatest treasure hunt*. New York: Coward, McCann & Geoghegan, 1978.

Oliver, Michael. *The Passionate Debate: The Social and Political Ideas of Quebec Nationalism 1920–1945*. Montreal: Véhicule Press, 1991.

Oliver, Peter. *Terror to Evil-Doers: Prisons and Punishments in Nineteenth-Century Ontario*. Toronto: University of Toronto Press (for The Osgoode Society for Canadian Legal History), 1998.

Ontario Association of Agricultural Societies. *A History of Agricultural Societies and Fairs in Ontario: 1792–1992*. Peterborough, Ont., 1992.

Ormsby, Margaret A. *British Columbia: a History*. Toronto: Macmillan of Canada, 1958.

Overbury, Stephen. *Finding Canadian Facts Fast*. Toronto: Methuen, 1985.

Palardy, Jean. *The Early Furniture of French Canada*. (Trans. Eric McLean). Toronto: Macmillan of Canada, 1963.

Parker, Elyse. *A Guide to Heritage Structure Investigations*. Ontario: Ministry of Culture and Recreation, 1979.

Passfield, Robert W. *Building the Rideau Canal: A Pictorial History*. Markham, Ont.: Fitzhenry & Whiteside (in association with Parks Canada), 1982.

Patterson, R.M. *Dangerous River*. Toronto: Stoddart, 1989.

Patterson, Tom and Allan Gould. *First Stage: The Making of the Stratford Festival*. Toronto: McClelland & Stewart, 1987.

Percival, Walter Pilling. *Across the Years: A Century of Education in the Province of Quebec*. Montreal: Gazette Printing Company, 1946.

Percy, H.R.
- *Joseph Howe*. Don Mills, Ont.: Fitzhenry & Whiteside, 1976.
- *Thomas Chandler Haliburton*. Don Mills, Ont.: Fitzhenry & Whiteside, 1980.

Perkins, Mary Ellen. *A Guide to Provincial Plaques in Ontario*. Toronto: Natural Heritage/Natural History
    (for the Ontario Heritage Foundation), 1989.

Petrie, A. Roy.
- *Alexander Graham Bell*. Rev. ed. Markham, Ont.: Fitzhenry & Whiteside, 1999.
- *Henri Bourassa*. Don Mills, Ont.: Fitzhenry & Whiteside, 1980.
- *Joseph Brant*. Rev. ed. Markham, Ont.: Fitzhenry & Whiteside, 2003.
- *Sam McLaughlin*. Don Mills, Ont.: Fitzhenry & Whiteside, 1982.

Phillips, Charles L. and Alan Axelrod. *Encyclopedia of Historical Treaties and Alliances form the 1920s to the Present*.
    New York: Facts on File, 2001.

Phillips, David.
- *The Day Niagara Falls Ran Dry! Canadian Weather Facts and Trivia*. Toronto: Key Porter, 1993.
- *The Canadian Weather Trivia Calendar*. Annual. Calgary: Fifth House.

Pickersgill, J.W.
- *Louis St. Laurent*. Rev. ed. Markham, Ont.: Fitzhenry & Whiteside, 2001.
- *My Years with Louis St. Laurent: A Political Memoir*. Toronto: University of Toronto Press, 1975.
- *Seeing Canada Whole: A Memoir*. Markham, Ont.: Fitzhenry & Whiteside, 1994.

Porter, Gordon L. and Diane Richler, eds. *Changing Canadian Schools: Perspectives on Disability and Inclusion*.
    North York, Ont.: The Roeher Institute, 1991.

Porter, John. *The Vertical Mosaic: An analysis of social class and power in Canada*. Toronto: University of Toronto Press (paperback), 1967.

Pound, Richard W.
- *Chief Justice W.R. Jackett: By the Law of the Land*. Montreal: McGill–Queen's University Press, 1999.
- *Stikeman Elliott: The First Fifty Years*. Montreal: McGill–Queen's University Press, 2002.

Pratt, E.J. *The Collected Poems of E.J. Pratt*. 2nd ed. Toronto: Macmillan of Canada, 1962.

Precious, Carole.
- *Thomas Carbide Willson*. Don Mills, Ont.: Fitzhenry & Whiteside, 1980.
- *J.-Armand Bombardier*. Markham, Ont.: Fitzhenry & Whiteside, 1984.

Priamo, Carol.
- *Mills of Canada*. Toronto: McGraw–Hill Ryerson, 1976.
- *Sault Industry*. (pamphlet). Ontario: Ministry of Citizenship and Culture; Ministry of Northern Affairs.

Price, Richard, ed. *The Spirit of the Alberta Indian Treaties*. Edmonton: Pica Pica Press, 1987.

Proctor, Steven, ed. *Canada Gold: Canadian Men & Women Hockey Champions*. Etobicoke, Ont.: Winding Stair Press, 2002.

Provencher, Jean. *René Lévësque: Portrait of a Québécois*. (Trans. David Ellis). Montreal: Gage Publishing Ltd., 1975.

Province of British Columbia. *Frontier to Freeway: A Short Illustrated History of the Roads in British Columbia*.
    Ministry of Transportation and Highways, 1986.

Prudhomme History Committee. *Life as It Was: Prud'homme, Saskatchewan 1897–1981*. Prudhomme, SK, 1981.

Pullen, Charles. *The Life and Times of Arthur Maloney, The Last of the Tribunes*: Toronto: Dundurn Press
(for The Osgoode Society for Canadian Legal History), 1994.

Putnam, Donald F., ed. *Canadian Regions: A Geography of Canada*. Toronto: J. M. Dent & Sons (Canada), 1952.

Putnam, Donald F. and Robert G. Putnam. *Canada: A Regional Analysis*. Toronto: J. M. Dent & Sons (Canada), 1970.

Quinn, David B. *North America from Earliest Discovery to First Settlements: The Norse Voyages to 1612*. New York: Harper Row Books, 1975.

Quinn, Herbert E. *The Union Nationale: Quebec Nationalism from Duplessis to Lévesque*. 2nd ed. Toronto: University of Toronto Press, 1979.

Quirin, William L. *The Story of the Lesley Cup Matches*. Virginia Beach: The Donning Company Publishers, 1997.

Raddall, Thomas H. *The Path of Destiny: Canada from the British Conquest to Home Rule: 1763–1850*. Toronto: Doubleday Canada, 1957.

Rajasekharan, P.T. *Nobel Laureates All (1901 to 1990)*. Bangalore, India: Panther Publishers, 1991.

Ramsay, Bruce. *Rain People: The Story of Ocean Falls*. Vancouver: Ocean Falls Centennial '71 Committee, 1971.

Rankin, Lisa K. Schurr et al. 1990. "Amerindian mitochondrial DNAs have rare Asian mutations at high frequencies, suggesting they derived from four primary maternal lineages." *American Journal of Human Genetics* 46:613-623.

Rawlinson, H. Graham and J.L. Granatstein. *The Canadian 100: The 100 Most Influential Canadians of the 20th Century*. Toronto: Little, Brown and Company (Canada), 1997.

Ray, Arthur J. *Indians in the Fur Trade: their role as hunters, trappers and middlemen in the lands southwest of Hudson Bay, 1660–1870*. Toronto: University of Toronto Press, 1974.

Ray, Janet. *Emily Stowe*. Rev. ed. Markham, Ont.: Fitzhenry & Whiteside, 2002.

Reader's Digest. *True North Strange and Free*. Montreal: Reader's Digest Books and Home Entertainment, 2002.

Redekop, Magdalene. *Ernest Thompson Seton*. Don Mills, Ont.: Fitzhenry & Whiteside, 1979.

Reid, Jamie. *Diana Krall: The Language of Love*. Markham, Ont.: Quarry Press, 2002.

Reid, Raymond, ed. *The Canadian Style: Today and Yesterday in Love, Work, Play and Politics*. Don Mills, Ont.: Fitzhenry & Whiteside, 1973.

Rhodes, Richard. *A First Book of Canadian Art*. Toronto: Owl Books, 2001.

Richardson, A.H. *Conservation by the People: The History of the Conservation Movement in Ontario to 1970*. Toronto: University of Toronto Press (for the Conservation Authorities of Ontario), 1974.

Richardson, Ronald E, George H. McNevin and Walter G. Rooke, eds. *Building for People: Freeway and Downtown – New Frameworks for Modern Needs*. Toronto: The Ryerson Press and Maclean–Hunter, 1970.

Riegler, Natalie. *Jean I. Gunn: Nursing Leader*. Markham, Ont.: Fitzhenry & Whiteside, 1997.

Riendeau, Roger. *A Brief History of Canada*. Markham, Ont.: Fitzhenry & Whiteside, 2000.

Rinfret, J. Edouard. *Histoire du Barreau de Montréal*. Cowansville, QC: Les Èditions Yvon Blais, 1989.

Roberts, Leslie.
   • *The Chief: A Political Biography of Maurice Duplessis*. Toronto: Clarke, Irwin & Company, 1963.
   • *The Life and Times of Clarence Decatur Howe*. Toronto: Clarke, Irwin & Company, 1957.
   • *Noranda*. Toronto: Clarke, Irwin & Company, 1956.

Robins, John D., ed. *A Pocketful of Canada*. Toronto: Wm. Collins Sons (Canada), 1948.

Robinson, Clayton L.N. *J.C. Boileau Grant: Anatomist Extraordinary*. Markham, Ont.: Fitzhenry & Whiteside, 1993.

Roland, Charles G.
   • *Clarence Hincks: Mental Health Crusader*. Toronto: Dundurn Press, 1989.
   • *Harold Nathan Segall: Cardiologist and Historian*. Markham, Ont.: Fitzhenry & Whiteside, 1995.

Romney, Paul. *Mr. Attorney: The Attorney General for Ontario in Court, Cabinet, and Legislature 1791–1899*. Toronto: University of Toronto Press (for The Osgoode Society for Canadian Legal History), 1986.

Ross, Don. *Discovering the Thousand Islands*. Kingston, Ont.: Quarry Press, 2001.

Ross, Eric.
- *Beyond the River and the Bay: Some observations on the state of the Canadian northwest in 1811*. Toronto: University of Toronto Press, 1970.
- *The Canadas in 1841: Full of Hope and Promise*. Montreal: McGill–Queen's University Press, 1991.

Rothney, Gordon O. *Canada In One Nation*. House of Grant (Canada), 1966.

Rotstein, Abraham, ed. *Power Corrupted: The October Crisis and The Repression of Quebec*. Toronto: New Press, 1971.

Royal Canadian Mounted Police: 1873–1973. Regina: Regina Chamber of Commerce, 1972.

Royal Commission on Aboriginal People. *People to People, Nation to Nation: Highlights from the Report of the Royal Commission on Aboriginal People*. Ottawa, 1996.

Rudd, W.V. *Peace River Project: Review of Construction, September 1961 to March 1969*. Vancouver: British Columbia Hydro and Power Authority, 1969.

Russell, Hilary. *All that Glitters: A memorial to Ottawa's Capitol Theatre and its predecessors*. Canadian Historic Sites: Occasional Papers in Archaeology and History, No. 13. Ottawa: Indian and Northern Affairs, 1975.

Russell, Peter H., ed. *Leading Constitutional Decisions*. Toronto: McClelland & Stewart, 1965.

Ryan, Judith Hoegg. *Growth of a Nation Series: The Mine*. Don Mills, Ont.: Fitzhenry & Whiteside, 1984.

Saunders, Kathleen. *Robert Borden*. Don Mills, Ont.: Fitzhenry & Whiteside, 1978.

Saunders, Robert. *R.B. Bennett*. Don Mills, Ont.: Fitzhenry & Whiteside, 1979.

Schull, Joseph.
- *Battle for the Rock: The Story of Wolfe and Montcalm*. Toronto: Macmillan of Canada, 1960.
- *Laurier*. Toronto: Macmillan of Canada, 1965.

Schwartz, Georges and Gérard A. Montifroy. *Sports et Géopolitique: les dangers du marché américain*. Montreal: Editions Sciences et Culture, 2001.

Scott, Chic. *Pushing the Limits: The Story of Canadian Mountaineering*. Calgary: Rocky Mountain Books, 2002.

Scott, F.R. *Selected Poems*. Toronto: Oxford University Press, 1966.

Scott, Irene G. *Canadian Vignettes: The Trek of the Overlanders*. Burns and MacEachern, 1968.

Sealey, D. Bruce. *Jerry Potts*. Don Mills, Ont.: Fitzhenry & Whiteside, 1980.

Sharp, Mitchell. *Which Reminds Me ... A Memoir*. Toronto: University of Toronto Press, 1994.

Sharpe, Robert J. *The Last Day, the Last Hour: The Currie Libel Trial*. Toronto: The Osgoode Society, 1988.

Sharpe, Robert J. and Kent Roach. *Brian Dickson: A Judge's Journey.* Toronto: University of Toronto Press, 2003.

Sheffe, Norman.
- *Casimir Gzowski*. Don Mills, Ont.: Fitzhenry & Whiteside, 1975.
- *Goldwin Smith*. Don Mills, Ont.: Fitzhenry & Whiteside, 1976.

Shewchuk, Murphy.
- *The Craigmont Story*. Surry, BC: Hancock House Publishers, 1983.
- *Okanagan Country: An Outdoor Recreation Guide*. Merritt, BC: Sonotek Publishing, 1992.

Bibliography

Siggins, Maggie.
- *Bassett: John Bassett's forty years in politics, publishing, business and sports*. Toronto: James Lorimer & Company, 1979.
- *Revenge of the Land: A century of greed, tragedy, and murder on a Saskatchewan farm*. Toronto: McClelland & Stewart, 1992.
- *Riel: A Life of Revolution*. Toronto: HarperPerennial, 1995.

Silversides, Brock V.
- *The Face Pullers: Photographing Native Canadians: 1871–1939*. Saskatoon: Fifth House, 1994.
- *Looking West: Photographing the Canadian Prairies, 1858–1957*. Calgary: Fifth House, 1999.

Simpson, Patricia. *Marguerite Bourgeoys and Montreal: 1640-1665*. Montreal: McGill–Queen's University Press, 1997.

Sisler, Rebecca. *Art for Enlightenment: A History of Art in Toronto Schools*. Markham, Ont.: Fitzhenry & Whiteside and LEARNXS Foundation, 1993.

Skelton, Oscar Douglas.
- *General Economic History of the Dominion 1867-1912*. Toronto: The Publishers' Association of Canada Limited, 1913.
- *Life and Letters of Sir Wilfrid Laurier*. 2 vols. New York: The Century Co., 1922.

Smart, Stephen B. and Michael Coyle, eds. *Aboriginal Issues Today: A Legal and Business Guide*. North Vancouver, BC: Self-Counsel Press, 1997.

Smith, Arthur Britton. *Legend of the Lake: The 22-Gun Brig Sloop Ontario 1780*. Kingston, Ont.: Quarry Press, 1997.

Smith, Denis. *Rogue Tory: The Life and Legend of John G. Diefenbaker*. Toronto: Macfarlane Walter & Ross, 1995.

Smith, I. Norman. *The Unbelievable Land: 29 Experts Bring Us Closer to the Arctic*. Ottawa: Information Canada, 1971.

Smith, James K.
- *Alexander Mackenzie*. Don Mills, Ont.: Fitzhenry & Whiteside, 1976.
- *David Thompson*. Rev. ed. Markham, Ont.: Fitzhenry & Whiteside, 2003.

Smith, P.J. *Population and Production: An Introduction to Some Problems in Economic Geography*. Toronto: J.M. Dent & Sons (Canada), 1971.

Snell, John Ferguson. *Macdonald College of McGill University: A History from 1904–1955*, Montreal: McGill University Press, 1963.

Spalding, David. *Into the Dinosaurs' Graveyard: Canadian Digs and Discoveries*. Toronto: Doubleday Canada, 1999.

Spigelman, Martin. *Wilfrid Laurier*. Rev. ed. Markham, Ont.: Fitzhenry & Whiteside, 2000.

Spry, Irene M. *The Palliser Expedition: The dramatic story of western Canadian exploration 1857–1860*. Calgary: Fifth House, 1995.

Stacey, C. P. *Quebec, 1759: The Siege and the Battle*. Toronto: Macmillan of Canada, 1959.

Stanley, George F.G. *Canada Invaded: 1775–1776*. Toronto: Hakkert, 1973.

Stark, Peter. *Ring of Ice: True Tales of Adventure, Exploration, and Arctic Life*. New York: The Lyons Press, 2000.

Statistics Canada.
- *Canada Year Book 1974*. Ottawa: Minister of Industry, Trade and Commerce, 1974.
- *Canada Year Book 1988*. Ottawa: Minister of Supply and Services, 1987.
- *Canada Year Book 1990*. Ottawa: Minister of Supply and Services, 1989.

Stephenson, Marylee. *A Visitor's Guide: Canada's National Parks*. Scarborough: Prentice Hall, 1997.

Stewart, Gordon, Brian Antonson et al. *Canadian Frontier: Exciting Stories from Canada's History*. No. 3. Antonson Publishing, 1978.

Stewart, Roderick.
- *Norman Bethune*. Rev. ed. Markham, Ont.: Fitzhenry & Whiteside, 2002.
- *The Mind of Norman Bethune*. Rev ed. Markham, Ont.: Fitzhenry & Whiteside, 2002.

Stewart, Walter. *As They See Us*. Toronto: McClelland and Stewart, 1977.

Stewart, W. Brian. *A Life on the Line: Commander Pierre Etienne Fortin and his Times*. Ottawa: Carleton University Press, 1997.

Stock, Leo Francis, ed.
- *Proceedings and Debates of the British Parliaments respecting North America.* Vol. IV, 1728-1739. Baltimore: Carnegie Institution of Washington, 1937.
- *Proceedings and Debates of the British Parliaments respecting North America.* Vol. V, 1739-1754. Baltimore: Carnegie Institution of Washington, 1941.

Sturgis, James. *Adam Beck.* Rev. ed. Markham, Ont.: Fitzhenry & Whiteside, 2003.

Stursberg, Peter. *Lester Pearson and the American Dilemma.* Toronto: Doubleday Canada, 1980.

Such, Peter. *Vanished Peoples: The Archaic Dorset & Beothuk People of Newfoundland.* Toronto: NC Press, 1978.

Sufrin, Eileen. *The Eaton Drive: The campaign to organize Canada's largest department store: 1948 to 1952.* Don Mills, Ont.: Fitzhenry & Whiteside, 1982.

Surtees, Lawrence. *Pa Bell: A. Jean de Grandpré & the Meteoric Rise of Bell Canada Enterprises.* Toronto: Random House, 1992.

Suthern, Victor. *To Go Upon Discovery.* Toronto: Dundurn Press, 2000.

Sutton-Smith, Peter and Barbara Sutton-Smith. *Canadian Handbook of Pressed Glass Tableware.* Rev. ed. Markham, Ont.: Fitzhenry & Whiteside Ltd., 2000.

Swainson, Donald. *Sir John A. Macdonald: The Man and the Politician.* Kingston, Ont.: Quarry Press, 1989.

Swanson, W.W. with P.C. Armstrong. *Wheat.* Toronto: Macmillan of Canada, 1930.

Swatridge, Leonard A., Ian A. Wright et al. *Canada: Exploring New Directions.* Markham, Ont.: Fitzhenry & Whiteside, 2000.

Symons, R.D.
- *Many Patrols: Reminiscences of a Game Officer.* Regina: Coteau Books, 1994.
- *Where the Wagon Led.* Calgary: Fifth House, 1997.

Tammemagi, Hans and David Jackson. *Unlocking the Atom: The Canadian Book on Nuclear Technology.* Hamilton, Ont.: McMaster UP, 2002.

Tammemagi, Hans. *Exploring the Hill: A Guide to Canada's Parliament Past and Present.* Markham, Ont.: Fitzhenry & Whiteside, 2002.

Taylor, William W. and C. Paola Ferreri, eds. *Great Lakes Fisheries Policy and Management: A Binational Perspective.* East Lansing, MI: Michigan State University Press, 1999.

The Book Trade in Canada: Your Complete Guide to the Canadian Publishing Marketplace. Toronto: Quill & Quire, 2003.

The Milepost: All-The-North Travel Guide. Annual. Augusta, Georgia: Morris Communications, 2004.

Thirkell, Fred and Bob Scullion. *Frank Gowen's Vancouver, 1914-1931.* Surrey, BC: Heritage House, 2001.

Thomas, Bettye Colliere and V.P. Franklin. *My Soul is a Witness: A Chronology of the Civil Rights Era, 1954-1965.* New York: Henry Holt, 1999.

Thomas, Lewis G. et al, eds. *The Prairie West to 1905: A Canadian Sourcebook.* Toronto: Oxford University Press, 1975.

Thompson, John Herd. *Forging the Prairie West: The Illustrated History of Canada.* Toronto: Oxford University Press, 1998.

Thomson, Colin A. *Blacks in Deep Snow: Black Pioneers in Canada.* Don Mills, Ont.: J.M. Dent & Sons (Canada), 1979.

Thomson, Dale C. *Jean Lesage & The Quiet Revolution.* Toronto: Macmillan of Canada, 1984.

Tindall, George Brown. *America: A Narrative History.* 2nd ed. New York: W.W. Norton & Company, 1988.

Topalovich, Maria. *And the Genie Goes To ...Celebrating 50 Years of the Canadian Film Awards.* Toronto: Stoddart, 2000.

Tozer, Ron and Dan Strickland. *A Pictorial History of Algonquin Provincial Park.* Whitney. Ont.: Friends of Algonquin Park/ Ontario Ministry of Natural Resources, 1986.

Trigger, Bruce G. *Natives and Newcomers: Canada's "Heroic Age" Reconsidered.* Montreal: McGill-Queen's University Press, 1986.

Trofimenkoff, Susan Mann. *The Dream of Nation: A Social and Intellectual History of Quebec*. Toronto: Gage Publishing, 1983.

Trudeau, Pierre Elliott. *Federalism and the French Canadians*. Toronto: Macmillan of Canada, 1968.

Tuck, James A.
• *Newfoundland and Labrador Prehistory,* National Museum of Man, Ottawa, 1976.
• *Maritime Provinces Prehistory,* National Museums of Canada, Ottawa, 1984.

Tucker, Albert. *Steam Into Wilderness: Ontario Northland Railway 1902–1962*. Don Mills, Ont.: Fitzhenry & Whiteside, 1978.

Turnbull, Christopher J. The Augustine Site: A Mound from the Maritimes, *Archaeology of Eastern North America* 4 (Winter) 1976: 50-62.

Turner, John Peter. *The North–West Mounted Police 1873–1893*. (2 vols.). Ottawa, 1950.

Unitt, Doris and Peter Unitt. *Treasury of Canadian Glass*. Peterborough, Ont.: Clock House Publications, 1969.

Vallance, J.D. *Untrodden Ways*. Victoria, B.C., 1957.

Vallières, Pierre. *White Niggers of America*. (trans. John Pinkham). Toronto: McClelland & Stewart, 1971.

Vancouver Public Library. *Great Canadian Books of the Century*. Vancouver: Douglas & McIntyre, 1999.

Vanek, David. *Fulfilment: Memoirs of a Criminal Court Judge*. Toronto: Dundurn Press, 1999.

van Steensel, Maja, ed. *People of Light and Dark*. Ottawa: Department of Indian Affairs and Northern Development, 1966.

Varley, Peter. *Canada* (Introduction by Kildare Dobbs). Toronto: Macmillan of Canada, 1969.

Verchere, David R. *A Progression of Judges: A History of the Supreme Court of British Columbia*. Vancouver: University of British Columbia Press, 1988.

von Baeyer, Edwinna. *Rhetoric and Roses: A History of Canadian Gardening 1900– 1930*. Markham, Ont.: Fitzhenry & Whiteside, 1984.

Wade, Mason. *The French Canadians 1760–1967*. Vols. 1 & 2. Rev. ed. Toronto: Macmillan of Canada, 1968.

Waiser, Bill. *All Hell Can't Stop Us: The On-to-Ottawa Trek and Regina Riot*. Calgary: Fifth House, 2003.

Waite, Peter B. *John A. Macdonald*. Rev. ed. Markham, Ont.: Fitzhenry & Whiteside, 1999.

Waldman, Carl.
• *Atlas of the North American Indian*. Rev. ed. New York: Facts on File, 1985.
• *Encyclopedia of Native American Tribes*. Rev. ed. New York: Facts on File, 1999.

Walker, Franklin A. *Catholic Education & Politics in Upper Canada*. Toronto: J.M. Dent & Sons (Canada), 1955.

Walker, James W. St. G. *"Race," Rights and the Law in the Supreme Court of Canada Historical Case Studies*.
The Osgoode Society for Canadian Legal History and Wilfrid Laurier University Press, 1997.

Wallace, Robert. *Producing Marginality: Theatre and Criticism in Canada*. Saskatoon: Fifth House, 1990.

Wardle, Bill. *The Mounted Squad: An Illustrated History of The Toronto Mounted Police: 1886–2000*. Markham, Ont.: Fitzhenry & Whiteside, 2002.

Warkentin, John, ed. *Canada: A Geographical Interpretation*. Toronto: Methuen, 1968.

Watson, Patty Jo and Mary Kennedy. 11991 The Development of Horticulture in the Eastern Woodlands of North America: Women's Role.
In *Engendering Archaeology,* ed. Gero, Joan and Margaret Conkey. Oxford: Basil Blackwell, pp. 255-275.

Weber, Bob. *Saskatchewan History Along the Highway*. Red Deer: Red Deer College Press, 1998.

Weintraub, William.
• *City Unique: Montreal Days and Nights in the 1940s and '50s*. Toronto: McClelland & Stewart, 1996.
• *Getting Started: A Memoir of the 1950s*. Toronto: McClelland & Stewart, 2001.

Wente, Margaret. *I Never Say Anything Provocative: Witticisms, anecdotes and reflections by Canada's most outspoken politician,*
John G. Diefenbaker. Toronto: Peter Martin Associates, 1975.

Wershler, Terri and Judi Lees. *The Ultimate Guide: Vancouver*. Vancouver: Greystone Books, 1996.

Weston, Greg. *Reign of Terror: The inside story of John Turner's troubled leadership*. Toronto: McGraw–Hill Ryerson, 1988.

Whitaker, W. Denis and Shelagh Whitaker.
    • *Rhineland: The Battle to End the War*. Toronto: Stoddart, 1989.
    • *Tug of War: The Canadian Victory that Opened Antwerp*. Toronto: Stoddart, 1984.

Whitehead, Ruth Holmes. *Elitekey: Micmac Material Culture from 1600 A.D. to the Present*. Halifax: The Nova Scotia Museum, 1980.

Whitfield, Carol. *Sir Sam Hughes (1853–1921)*. Canadian Historic Sites: Occasional Papers in Archaeology and History, No. 13. Ottawa: Indian and Northern Affairs, 1975.

Williams, David Ricardo.
    • *Matthew Baillie Begbie*. Don Mills, Ont.: Fitzhenry & Whiteside, 1980.
    • *Duff: A Life in the Law*. Vancouver: University of British Columbia Press, 1984.
    • *Just Lawyers: Seven Portraits*. Toronto: The Osgoode Society for Canadian Legal History, 1995.

Williams, Jack. *The Story of Unions in Canada*. Toronto: J.M. Dent & Sons (Canada), 1975.

Wilson, Edmund. *O Canada: An American's Notes on Canadian Culture*. New York: The Noonday Press, 1966.

Wilson, Garrett and Kevin Wilson. *Diefenbaker for the Defence*. Toronto: James Lorimer & Company, 1988.

Wilson, Lawrence M. *This Was Montreal in 1814, 1815, 1816 and 1817*. Montreal: Chateau de Ramezay, 1960.

Wilson, Mary Carol. *Marion Hilliard*. Don Mills, Ont.: Fitzhenry & Whiteside, 1977.

Wilton, Carol, ed. *Inside the Law: Canadian Law Firms in Historical Perspective*. Toronto: The Osgoode Society for Canadian Legal History, 1996.

Wittke, Carl. *A History of Canada*. Toronto: McClelland & Stewart, 1941.

Woodcock, George.
    • *100 Great Canadians*. Edmonton: Hurtig Publishers, 1980.
    • *The Canadians*. London: The Athlone Press, 1980.
    • *Gabriel Dumont*. Rev. ed. Markham, Ont.: Fitzhenry & Whiteside, 2003.
    • *Faces from History: Canadian Profiles & Portraits*. Edmonton: Hurtig Publishers, 1978.

Woods, Shirley E. *The Molson Saga 1786–1986*. Toronto: Doubleday Canada, 1986.

Worrall, James. *My Olympic Journey: Sixty years with Canadian sport and the Olympic Games*. Toronto: Canadian Olympic Assoc., 2000.

Wright, James V.
    • *Ontario Prehistory: An Eleven-thousand-year Archaeological Outline,* National Museum of Man, Ottawa, 1972.
    • *Six Chapters of Canada's Prehistory,* National Museum of Man, Ottawa, Van Nostrand Reinhold Ltd. Toronto, 1976.
    • *Quebec Prehistory,* National Museum of Man, Van Nostrand Reinhold Ltd, Toronto, 1979.
    • *A History of the Native People of Canada, Volume 1 (10,000-1,000 B.C.),* Mercury Series, Archaeological Survey of Canada, No. 152. Canadian Museum of Civilization, Ottawa, 1995   .
    • *A History of the Native People of Canada, Volume 2 (1,000 B.C. –A.D. 500),* Mercury Series, Archaeological Survey of Canada, No. 152. Canadian Museum of Civilization, Ottawa, 1999   .

Yee, Paul. *Struggle and Hope: The Story of Chinese Canadians*. Toronto: Umbrella Press, 1996.

Young, Brian. *The Politics of Codification: The Lower Canadian Civil Code of 1866*. Montreal: McGill–Queen's University Press and The Osgoode Society for Canadian Legal History, 1994.

Young, Scott and Margaret Hogan. *The Best Talk in Town*. Toronto: Clarke, Irwin & Co., 1979.

Ziff, Bruce. *Unforeseen Legacies: Reuben Wells Leonard and the Leonard Foundation Trust*. Toronto: University of Toronto Press (for The Osgoode Society for Canadian Legal History) 2000.

Zuuring, Peter. *The Arrow Scrapbook: Rebuilding a Dream and a Nation*. Dalkeith, Ont.: Arrow Alliance Press, 1999.

Bibliography

NEWSPAPERS

Calgary Herald

Charlottetown Guardian

Daily Courier (Kelowna)

Daily Gleaner (Fredericton)

Edmonton Journal

Financial Post (Toronto)

Globe and Mail (Toronto)

Halifax Chronicle-Herald

Hamilton Spectator

Hill Times (Ottawa)

Kingston This Week

Kingston Whig-Standard

La Presse (Montreal)

Leader Post (Regina)

Le Devoir (Montreal)

Le Droit (Ottawa)

Le Soleil (Montreal)

Le Soleil (Quebec City)

L'Evangéline (Moncton)

London Free Press

Montreal Gazette

Montreal Star

National Post (Toronto)

Ottawa Citizen

Ottawa Journal

Peterborough Examiner

Red Deer Advocate

Regina Leader Post

Star Phoenix (Saskatoon)

Sudbury Star

Telegraph Journal (Saint John)

The Province (Vancouver)

The Record (Kitchener-Waterloo)

The Telegram (St. John's)

Thunder Bay Chronicle-Journal

Times & Transcript (Moncton)

Toronto Star

Toronto Sun

Toronto Telegraph

Vancouver Sun

Victoria Times Colonist

Whitehorse Star

Windsor Star

Winnipeg Free Press

Winnipeg Tribune

Yellowknifer

MAGAZINES

Adbusters, Journal of the Mental Environment

Canadian Business

Canadian Geographic

Chatelaine

Cité libre

Elm Street, Canada's Magazine of Substance and Style

Geist, Canadian Ideas Canadian Culture

History Magazine

L'Actualité

Maclean's, Canada's Weekly Newsmagazine

National Post Business

Outpost Magazine

R.O.B. Report on Business Magazine

Saturday Night, Canada's Magazine

The Beaver, Canada's History Magazine

The Financial Post Magazine

The Globe & Mail Report on Business Magazine

The Hockey News

THIS Magazine

INDEX

Index

Index

Index

Index

Index

Index

Index

Index

Index

Index

Index

Index

Index

Index

Index

Index

Index

Index

Index

Index

Index

Index

Index

Tekakwitha, Kateri, 436, 627

Telefilm Canada, 650, 822

Teleglobe Canada, 673

telegraph, 210, 211, 221, 223, 225, 250, 269, 281, 284, 313, 330
  air-to-ground, 355
  CNCP Telecommunications, 510, 687
  CPR telegraph, 280, 299, 312, 324
  Fessenden Wireless Telegraph Company of Canada, 346
  Marconi Wireless Telegraph Company, 379
  Montreal Telegraph Company, 213
  New Brunswick Electric Telegraph, 215
  New York, Newfoundland and London Telegraph Company, 228, 232
  Newfoundland Electric Telegraph, 222
  Pacific Cable Act, 329–30
  transatlantic, 233, 235, 241, 253
  Western Union Telegraph Company, 255, 280

telephone, 277, 281, 285, 348, 547, 581,745
  Bell Telephone Company of Canada, 289, 586, 756
  communications satellites, 550
  dial phones, 349, 350
  directories, 287, 294
  employees strike, 347
  Hamilton District Telegraph Company, 285
  long-distance service, 719
  microwave relay system, 498, 510
  Saskatchewan Government Telephones (SaskTel), 448, 768
  transatlantic, 399, 473
  Trans-Canada Microwave Radio Relay Network, 480

Telesat Canada, 577, 658

television, 460–61, 463, 464, 466, 468, 469, 475, 528, 571, 585, 598, 599, 619, 628, 644, 652, 712, 774, 798, 827
  Les beaux dimanches, 539
  Aboriginal Peoples Television Network (APTN), 741, 803
  Al-Jazeera, 838
  cable TV, 628, 644, 684, 691, 744, 748, 771
  Canadian content, 492, 498, 559, 644
  Canadian Idol, 848
  Canadian Television Network (CTV), 495, 653, 655, 727
  Corner Gas, 849
  Due South, 753
  Gemini Awards, 506, 521, 579, 659, 714
  Global Television, 587
  Hinterland Who's Who, 858
  Inuit Broadcasting Corporation, 638
  music videos, 652
  Ontario Educational Communications Authority (TV Ontario), 564
  pay-TV, 647, 746
  Pioneer Quest, 813
  political debates, 542, 652
  Radio-Québec, 540
  satellite networks, 787, 833
  SCTV, 604–05, 834
  specialty channels, 746
  Supreme Court proceedings, 731
  Television Northern Canada, 715
  Trailer Park Boys, 829
  see also Canadian Broadcasting Corporation (CBC)

Telgmann, Oscar F., 312

Telus Corp., 795, 815

Temagami (Ont.), 692, 770

temperance movement, 50, 178, 179, 216, 225, 278
  Canada Temperance Act, 248, 293

temperance movement (cont.), prohibition, 225, 230, 231, 316, 319, 320, 321, 322, 323, 329, 372, 390, 400
  Temperance Colonization Company, 294
  Women's Christian Temperance Union, 278

Temple Emanuel synagogue, 246

Temple, Thomas, 52, 53, 61, 62

Le Temps (Mtl.), 296

Le Temps (Ottawa), 296

Tennant, Veronica, 824

Terra Footwear, 855

Terra Nova, 23, 24

Terra Nova National Park, 477

Terror (ship), 187, 189

terrorism, 550, 657, 773, 799, 826, 827, 828, 831, 838, 845, 854

Tessier, Dr. Xavier, 174

Testo, John, 564

Tett, Johnny, 490

Tewksbury, Mark, 720

textile industry, 290, 295, 342, 356, 420, 447, 634

thalidomide, 492

Thames River (Ont.), 291

Thanadelthur, 84, 85

Thanksgiving, 29, 475

Thatcher, Colin, 653–54

Thatcher, Margaret, 630, 661

Thatcher, Wilbert Ross, 509, 529, 536, 552, 567

Le Théâtre de Neptune, 34, 505

Theatre of Action Collective, 413

Theatre Royal (Halifax), 210

Theller, Edward Alexander, 192, 193, 194, 197

Thériault, Yves, 441, 482

Therien, Fr. Joseph Adeodat, 324

Theyanoguin, 100

Thibaudeau, Susan, 757

Thibault, Jean-Baptiste, 202, 262, 264

Thibault, Lise, 777

Thibault, Pierre, 679

Index

Index

Index

Index

Index

Index